A POLICE BIBLIOGRAPHY

AMS Studies in Criminal Justice. No. 3

ISSN: 0273-2991

Other titles in this series:

1. Peterson, J. *Forensic Science. Scientific Investigation in Criminal Justice.* 1975
2. Bouza, A. V. *Police Intelligence: The Operations of an Investigative Unit.* 1976.

A POLICE BIBLIOGRAPHY

Published and Unpublished Sources through 1976, With an Addendum

Jack E. Whitehouse

With a Foreword by

John P. Kenney

AMS PRESS, INC.
NEW YORK, N.Y.

Library of Congress Cataloging in Publication Data

Whitehouse, Jack E.
A police bibliography.

Includes index.
1. Police—Bibliography. I. Title.
Z7164.P76W45 [HV7921] 016.3632 77-15909
ISBN 0-404-16040-9

MANUFACTURED IN THE UNITED STATES OF AMERICA

For Ruth,

Without whom . . . and all that jazz.

FOREWORD

Recognizing the need for a single source of reference to the literature of law enforcement, Dr. Whitehouse has set about to fill a long-deplored information gap. In the past two decades the proliferation of books, monographs, articles, reports, and documents relating to the administration of police functions has been phenomenal. Yet it has been virtually impossible to discover from any one resource center what is available in the field; thus both the scholar and practitioner have been severely hampered in their research efforts. This bibliography contains the most important contributions in recent decades to all areas of law enforcement. In addition it includes classics that are essential reading for scholar and practitioner alike.

Dr. Whitehouse is eminently qualified for this important undertaking. He has not only been a police practitioner but has devoted most of his professional life to research in law enforcement. His personal library has to be the envy of most public institutions that house police and criminal justice literature. Furthermore, he has personally examined most of the references cited in the bibliography.

This bibliography is a most important contribution to the literature of police work and will be welcomed by all whose professional concerns require the published resources of law enforcement and criminal justice.

John P. Kenney, Ph.D
Professor of Criminal Justice
California State University
Long Beach, California

INTRODUCTION

I have eaten your bread and salt.
I have drunk your water and wine.
The deaths ye died I have watched beside
And the lives ye led were mine.
— Rudyard Kipling

I know many books which have bored their readers, but I know of none which has done real evil.
— Voltaire

Books are good enough in their own way, but they are a mighty bloodless substitute for life.
— Robert Louis Stevenson

Any serious study of the criminal justice system must begin with the police who are central to the entire enforcement/adjudication structure. The policeman is the representative of the criminal justice system one observes daily. We see him driving his patrol car, or on the television news; we hear his siren, and the noise from his helicopter. He is the man we call when we have a prowler, lose our children, have our car stolen, and even when we fight with our wives. The policeman is always there. Judges, prison guards, and parole officers are relatively obscure functionaries with which the average citizen rarely has contact. Everything in the criminal justice system begins and ends with the police officer. He determines who will become involved in the other criminal justice sub-systems — courts, parole, probation, and prisons. How well these later agencies perform will determine who will once again become a police problem.

In researching material for this book, one cannot help but be impressed with the extraordinary volume of material available about the police. The days of the apple stealing beat cop are hopefully over. The contemporary police function encompasses an incredible variety of specialized knowledge, technical expertise, complicated equipment, and people skills, that seem overwhelming. We live in an age of "information explosion." It is not important that a police officer be knowledgeable of every aspect of law enforcement. However, it is essential that sources be available for him to locate and competently research any area he may be interested in.

The purpose then, of this bibliography, is to bring together a significant portion of the literature involved with the police enterprise. An attempt has been made to present a broad interdisciplinary approach to the material. Obviously one must review and include traditional works. On the other hand, it is equally important to include information from non-police sources. The police are too insular as it is. Restricting references solely to police literature would only reinforce this insularity. This bibliography includes a wide range of reference material that will be of value to those involved in law enforcement and others in the various fields of the social sciences. It is hoped that this work will help bring some understanding to those studying police problems and functions. Sincere effort was made to present the negative aspects of law enforcement as well as the positive. Constructive criticisms can only enhance the police function. Some of this material is emotional, politically oriented and unfounded. On the other hand, most criticisms should warrant careful attention since they are well considered and offer opportunities for improvement and reform.

The police do not operate in a vacuum within the community. Not only are they a major component of the criminal justice system, but are also a principal unit in society. Consequently, several sections covering social problems have been included in this bibliography. Also, the part on community relations included references to minority groups, racism, slavery, police operations in ghettos, and the like. Relations with the community are too important to be left to the skills of public relations "experts."

There is a lengthy section covering the police of the world. The American police can certainly learn from the practices of democratic police agencies in foreign countries. Comparative police studies are increasingly recognized as an important area for study and research. Terrorism is reviewed at some length, including anti-terrorist methods. I fear we live in the age of the barbarian and the police wil be in the forefront in the fight to combat this frightening menace to the free world.

The remaining sections cover everything from abandoned vehicles to a description of the police of Zaire, and almost everything in between. There are 18 parts, 48 chapters, 17,400 entries, and almost 1,100 subheadings. Emphasis has been placed on police field operations and support services for that purpose. Other material is included solely because of its importance to the principal police functions.

Please bear in mind that this bibliography has been compiled by a book collector, not a professional bibliographer. Undoubtedly, a professional would have organized this work differently and followed rules which have been ignored by an amateur. I have simply tried to combine common sense with my perceptions of the needs of the police service. What these parts, chapters, and sub-sections represent is at least a starting point for the user. Some sections are far more complete than others. Even those headings with only a few entries represent a beginning for the researcher.

This is not a perfect bibliography by far, and I doubt if such a thing exists. No doubt criticisms will be leveled for omitting a book or an article or some information deemed important by the user. These criticisms will probably be valid. The literature of law enforcement is so vast that no one man can be aware of every important work, certainly not I.

It would be nice to say that this has been a labor of love. It has been something less than that. Only when the manuscript was completed did I feel anything akin to affection for this project. It has been a lot of plain hard work. The reader must decide if these efforts have been worthwhile.

METHODOLOGY

The methods used to compile this bibilography were simple rather than complex. The principal national police journals were reviewed as a starting point. These included: *The FBI Law Enforcement Bulletin, Journal of Criminal Law, Criminology and Police Science, Journal of Police Science and Administration, Law and Order, Police, Police Chief,* and because of its national availability and quality, *The Journal of California Law Enforcement.*

File cards were made on articles deemed important enough for inclusion. Book review sections, footnotes, and the brief bibliographies found in journals were also reviewed and bibliography cards made on appropriate entries. Several volumes listing books in print were consulted and law enforcement works were extrapolated. Several university libraries with law enforcement collections were visited and their material was reviewed. Listings from my own modest personal library were also included.

While most of the material found in this bibliography comes from primary sources, including various other bibliographies, some of which were in mimeographed form, several accession lists were consulted, including those from police libraries around the world.

Extremely important sources were the subject and author guides from the National Criminal Justice Reference Service. The books offer rather complete entries, are generally annotated, and are current as well as accurate. A number of entries were included from these sources along with their annotations.

Many bibliographies were obtained from the staff at the Learning Resource Center, FBI National Academy, Quantico, Virginia. These bibliographies were excellent and directly related to the police enterprise.

CLASSIFICATION AND ORGANIZATION

The classification system used here is detailed and, hopefully, logical. In order to make a book-length bibliography useful it must be broken down into as many logical headings and subheadings as possible.

The parts, chapters, and subheadings were selected and classified according to the needs of the working police officer rather than the academician. Few academic types are interested in areas such as police counter-terrorist activities, dangerous police situations, and organized crime control, but these are areas of vital concern to the real world situations our policemen face daily.

Logical segments of material are grouped together according to function. For example, all field operations are together. Next, investigation is separated from this broad category. Investigative functions are grouped together in three consecutive chapters. Narrowing this down even further, one will find investigative techniques listed in one of these three chapters.

It is, of course, impossible to list everything together. For instance, the user will find information about homicide described under the chapters on Investigation, Scientific Criminal Investigation, Specific Crimes, and other subheadings which are listed in the Index.

The section of Comparative Police Administration requires some additional explanation. Each country was listed that had at least some information available about it. When there was a wealth of material the entries were listed under five broad subheadings: General, Crime, Criminal Law, Police History, and Police.

Great Britain was listed in a chapter of its own for several reasons. First of all, this country's police history and its contemporary police problems closely parallel our own. Our police heritage is found in Great Britain and it is extremely important for American policemen to understand where they've been in order that they may determine where they are and where they are going. Secondly, the mass of material which is available about Great Britain does not lend itself to a brief list of subheadings.

The subheadings in police history posed something of a problem. Where does 'police history' begin? After receiving a lot of conflicting advice I arbitrarily chose World War II as the dividing line. For good or evil, World War II changed almost everything in the world, including the police. Therefore, references published prior to this event were listed under the histories of the various countries, including the United States.

SELECTION OF ENTRIES

The criteria used to include an entry was based on the answer to two questions; does it pertain to the police enterprise and, if so, does it have a known source?

An effort has been made to be inclusive rather than selective. It is acknowledged that some, perhaps, much, of the material listed is of little value. Value, on the other hand, is a relative term and even though a book or article may be totally negative it may illustrate to the researcher that certain approaches, concepts, or ideas are not helpful to his particular study.

Some subjects are covered in great detail; others are disappointingly brief. Every effort has been made to present material covering both sides of an issue. No attempt has been made to include only the positive aspects of law enforcement and ignore the negative. Criticisms of the police are included along with praise.

Materials from obviously biased sources were not included. Pro-police journals such as the John Birch Society's

American Opinion were avoided. On the other hand, a number of books, reports, and pamphlets published by the American Civil Liberties Union were included. The policeman can expect little comfort from most ACLU publications. These works were included because of the statistical, analytical, and comparative value.

In selecting entries, emphasis was placed on books and articles published since 1960. This was a general guideline. A great number of published works with earlier publication dates were also included.

Some books and articles published in foreign countries are listed, too. The vast majority of these are from Great Britain. Much of this material was published in book form simultaneously in the United States. Our better libraries have periodicals that were published abroad. In any event, these works were too important to ignore.

ENTRY FORMAT

In reviewing formats used by others one finds a variety to choose from. The one used in this work is a modified form of several of the most widely used guides being circulated today. Also, unnecessary words have been deleted from book entries. For example, a volume published by Charles C. Thomas Publishing Company will simply be listed as C. C. Thomas. It seemed like a great waste of time, energy, and space to keep repeating words such as 'Press Inc., Books, Inc., Publishing Corporation,' etc.

Information pertaining to journals varies in completeness. In most cases the reader will find the volume and number of the issue, the date, and the inclusive page numbers. Unfortunately, some entries contain less information than is desirable. However, in all cases there is enough data to identify and locate the journal in question.

LIMITATIONS

It is sometimes easier to state what a book is *not* about than what it *is* about. This may be the case here. This bibliography is not a reference which covers the whole criminal justice field. This book is about the police alone, and the few criminal justice subject areas which are covered are included solely because of their importance and/or interest to the police service.

CROSS-REFERENCES

Some books and articles were regarded as important enough to list them in several places. These were kept to a minimum and only about 300 are cross-referenced.

ANNOTATIONS

Annotations are included on material where the title does not convey adequate information to the researcher. It should be noted that the classification system reduces the need to annotate each and every article or book. By and large, those annotations that are included are descriptive rather than critical. In some cases I have taken the liberty of adding a praiseworthy word such as "excellent," or the like, on material that I am familiar with. Very few entries have negative comments.

ERRORS

This bibliography is as accurate as strong human effort permits. Each entry has been checked for accuracy several times by different people. However, there is no doubt in my mind that some mistakes and errors have occurred. As indicated elsewhere, some information was obtained from secondary sources where there was no way to determine the accuracy of the entry. There is much room for error in the copying process — from journal entry to file card to typist to printer. Most certainly these errors are my own and I would be most pleased to have any of these pointed out to me by the user.

HOW TO USE THIS BOOK

1. Consult the Table of Contents for an overview of the material contained in this bibliography.

2. Look through the Index for subject headings in which you are interested. This index is cross-referenced and highly detailed.

3. Always check the 'General' headings in the areas of your interest. For example, if you are interested in Burglary Investigation, the references listed under INVESTIGATION—GENERAL should also be reviewed since some of these undoubtedly contain information relating to your subject.

ACKNOWLEDGEMENTS

One of the nicest parts in authoring a book is the opportunity to publicly thank the people who have assisted in making a volume like this possible.

Special thanks must go to my friend and mentor, Dr. John P. Kenney, whose wise counsel, advice, and support contributed greatly to completion of this work. Thanks must also go to Linda Bresnan, Carolyne McGowan, Dorothyan Young, Susan Ponder, Oliver E. Clark, and Norman L. Whitehouse whose interest went from *Boys Life* to *Playboy* while helping Dad with the project.

I am extremely grateful to Professor Samuel G. Chapman for sending me his card file on police dog use. The completeness on attitude surveys is due in large measure to the bibliography received from Dr. Harold D. VanAlstyne.

My warmest gratitude goes to Roberta Colicott for the outstanding job she did in typing the manuscript.

Last, but not least, I must express heartfelt appreciation to my family for suffering through two years of hard research. Everyone became weary from filling out 5 × 8 file cards, filing, organizing, and in the end, beating the 'beast' as the project became known to us.

TABLE OF CONTENTS

SUMMARY

COMPLETE LISTING

PART III. FIELD OPERATIONS—SPECIALIZED FUNCTIONS

PART IV. FIELD OPERATIONS—POLICE TACTICS

PART V. FIELD OPERATIONS—NON-CRIMINAL POLICE ACTIVITIES

PART VI. STAFF AND AUXILIARY SERVICES

PART VII. MANAGEMENT, ADMINISTRATION AND SUPERVISION

PART VIII. POLICE PERSONNEL MANAGEMENT

PART IX. POLICE EDUCATION AND TRAINING

PART X. POLICE-COMMUNITY RELATIONS

PART XI. POLICE EQUIPMENT

PART XII. LAW ENFORCEMENT—ISSUES AND PROBLEMS

PART XIII. COMPARATIVE POLICE ADMINISTRATION

PART XIV. THE BARBARIANS—TERRORISM AND VIOLENCE

PART XV. THE CRIME PROBLEM

PART XVI. ISSUES AND PROBLEMS IN CRIMINAL JUSTICE

PART XVII. SOCIAL PROBLEMS

PART XVIII. MISCELLANEOUS

ABBREVIATIONS

ABA	American Bar Association
AMA	American Management Association
Annals	*Annals of the American Academy of Political and Social Science*
BNDD	Bureau of Narcotics and Dangerous Drugs
ed.	Editor or edition
FAA	Federal Aviation Administration
FBI	Federal Bureau of Investigation
GPO	Government Printing Office
IACP	International Association of Chiefs of Police
LAPD	Los Angeles Police Department
LEAA	Law Enforcement Assistance Administration
NCJRS	National Criminal Justice Reference Service
n.d.	No date
NILECJ	National Institute of Law Enforcement and Criminal Justice
n.n.	No name (i.e., publisher)
n.p.	No place
NTIS	National Technical Information Service
Unpub.	Unpublished
vol.	volume

PART I
LAW ENFORCEMENT AGENCIES

LAW ENFORCEMENT AGENCIES

POLICE AGENCIES—GENERAL

Boston. Governors Commission on Law Enforcement and Administration of Justice. *The Police in Massachusetts.* Boston: December 21, 1967.

Chen, Teh-Show. "Police Systems in California." Unpub. M.A. thesis. University of California at Berkeley, 1948.

Congressional Quarterly, Inc. *Crime and the Law—The Fight by Federal Forces to Control Public Problem One in America.* Washington, DC: Congressional Quarterly Inc., 1971.
A compilation covering criminal justice agencies and all types of crimes.

Granfield, John P. "Publicly Funded Law Enforcement Agencies in the U.S." *Police Chief,* XLII:7 (July 1975), 24-26.

Gregory, Ronald. *Law Enforcement in the United States of America.* Devon-Cornwall Constabulary [Eng.]:1968.
Report of a study tour of Eastern Seaboard American Police Departments April 1, 1968 to June 30, 1968.

Hickey, Edward J. "Trends in Rural Police Protection." *Annals,* 291 (January, 1954), 22-30.

Kapsch, Stefan J. *Minnesota Police Organization and Community Resource Allocation.* Saint Paul: Minnesota State Planning Agency, 1970.

Kenney, John P. *The California Police.* Springfield, IL: C.C. Thomas, 1964.
Discusses factors which have made California Police Agencies unique.

"Law Enforcement in Kentucky." *Kentucky Law Journal,* 52:1 (1963-1964, entire issue).

Millspaugh, Arthur Chester. *Crime Control by the National Government.* NY: Da Capo. [1937] 1972.
Presents the historical background, organization, and functioning of the Federal Government in crime control.

National Advisory Commission on Criminal Justice. "Standards and Goals." *Police.* Washington, DC: GPO (January 23, 1973).

National Institute of Mental Health. *Role of Federal Agencies in the Crime and Delinquency Field (A Compilation of Federal Support Programs).* Washington, DC: GPO, 1970.
Federal Assistance programs under which projects have been or could be funded are listed by department and agency.

Nelson, Dalmas H. *Administrative Agencies in the U.S.A.: Their Decisions and Authority.* Detroit: Wayne State University Press, 1963.

Ohio Commission on Local Government Services. *Local Law Enforcement Services in Ohio.* Washington, DC: NCJRS (Microfiche), 1973.

Ottenberg, Miriam. *The Federal Investigators.* NY: Pocket Books, 1962.
Popular account of activities of 17 federal investigative agencies. Contains list of additional agencies.

Packman, Martin. "Federal Police Activity." *Editorial Research Reports* (January 12, 1954), 23-35.

President's Commission on Law Enforcement and Administration of Justice Task Force Report. *The Police.* Washington, DC: GPO, 1967.

Silver, I. *Crime Control Establishment.* Englewood Cliffs, N.J.: Prentice-Hall, 1974.
Articles critically examining federal and non-federal agencies and their roles in defining and pursuing 'crime' and 'criminals'.

Smith, Bruce. *Police Systems in the United States.* 2nd ed. rev. NY: Harper & Row, 1960.

Texas Commission on Law Enforcement Officer Standards and Education. *Law Enforcement Agencies of Texas—A Survey.* Washington, DC: NCJRS (Microfiche), 1973.

U.S. Congress Joint Economic Committee. *Federal Criminal Justice System, Hearings.* Washington, DC: GPO, 1970.

U.S. Justice Department. *Federal Law Enforcement and Criminal Justice Activities—Attorney General's Annual Report, 1971.* Washington, DC: NCJRS, 1972.
Attorney general's report contains an official analysis of the law enforcement functions of the various federal agencies and organization.

Williams, Harrison Grant. *The Peace Officer in California: Concept and Development.* Unpub. Master Crim. Thesis. University of California at Berkeley, 1964.

FEDERAL AGENCIES

Agency for International Development

"The Agency for International Development Helps Brazilians Fight War on Crime." *Police,* 10:4 (March-April, 1966), 85-86.

Engle, Byron. "A I D Assistance to Civil Security." *Police Chief,* XXXIX (May, 1972), 24-28.
Development, mission and accomplishments of A I D's Training Division and the International Police Academy.

Pell, Robert. "Former California Policeman Plies His Trade in Vietnam." *Police,* 10:3 (January-February, 1966), 49-51.

Bureau of Narcotics and Dangerous Drugs

Anslinger, Harry J. *The Protectors.* NY: Farrar, Straus, 1964.

Anslinger, Harry J. and William F. Tompkins. *The Traffic in Narcotics.* NY: Funk & Wagnalls, 1953.

Buse, Renee. *The Deadly Science.* Garden City, NY: Doubleday, 1965.

Ingersoll, John E. "BNDD." *Police Chief,* XXVII:1 (January, 1970), 26-28.
Describes the reorganization, functions and services of U.S. Justice Departments Bureau of Narcotics and Dangerous Drugs.

U.S. Bureau of Narcotics. *Report of a Study of the Mission, Organization and Management of the U.S. Bureau of Narcotics.* Washington, DC: U.S. Bureau of Narcotics, 1968.

Border Patrol

The Border Patrol: Its Origin and Work. Washington, DC: GPO, 1967.

Crawford, William. *The United States Border Patrol.* NY: Putnam, 1965.

Moore, Herman. "Functions and Duties of the U.S. Border Patrol. *FBI Law Enforcement Bulletin* (February, 1971).

Myers, John. *The Border Wardens.* Englewood Cliffs, NJ: Prentice-Hall, 1971.

Rak, Mary. *Border Patrol.* San Francisco, CA: R and E Research Assoc. [1938] 1971.

Whitehead, Don. *Border Guard.* NY: Avon, 1963.

Coast Guard

Dionisio, Riccardo R. "Department of Transportation: U.S. Coast Guard Intelligence." *Police Chief,* XLII:7 (July, 1975), 52-53.

Ellis, Ridsdale. *Coast Guard Law Enforcement.* Cambridge, MD: Cornell Maritime, 1943.

Gurney, Gene. *United States Coast Guard.* NY: Crown, 1973.

Huntoon, Emery. *Intercept and Boards.* Portland, OR: Binford, 1975.

"Recreational Boating Laws and Safety Regulations." *FBI Law Enforcement Bulletin,* 36:6 (June, 1967), 14-20.

Customs Service

Acree, Vernon D. "U.S. Customs Assistance Programs." *Police Chief,* XLII:7 (July, 1975), 36-37.

Acree, Vernon D. "U.S. Customs Fights Organized Crime." *Police Chief,* XLII:2 (February, 1975), 32-33.

Ambrose, Myles J. "How U.S. Customs Fights the Drug Traffic." *Police Chief,* 38:1 (January, 1971), 60-63.

Coon, Thomas F. and Nicholas S. Sabatino. "U.S. Customs—Performing at the World's Busiest Port." *Police,* 8:2 (November-December, 1963), 19-24.

Roark, Garland. *The Coin of Contraband, the True Story of United States Customs Investigator Al Scharff.* Garden City, NY: Doubleday, 1964.

Settel, Arthur. *A Pictorial History of the United States Customs Service.* NY: Crown, 1976.

Federal Aviation Administration

Burkhardt, Robert. *The Federal Aviation Administration.* NY: Praeger, 1967.

Conarroe, Milford T. "Law Enforcement Essential to Air Safety." *Police Chief,* XLI:2 (February, 1974), 22-24.

Messer, R. A. "Anti-hijacking Program." *Law Officer,* 6:4 (1973).
Describes activities of FAA Air Transportation security field offices.

Whitenah, Donald R. *Safer Skyways: Federal Control of Aviation 1926-66.* Ames, IA: Iowa State University Press, 1966.

Federal Bureau of Investigation

Cochran, Louis. *FBI Man: A Personal History.* NY: Duell, Sloan & Pierce, 1966.

Coulter, Prevost A. "The FBI and Its Future." *FBI Law Enforcement Bulletin,* 39:8 (August, 1970), 13-15.

Demaris, Ovid. *The Director.* NY: Harper & Row, 1976.

DeToledano, Ralph. *J. Edgar Hoover: The Man in His Time.* New Rochelle, NY: Arlington House, 1973.

Doig, Jameson W. "A Symposium—The Police in a Democratic Society." *Public Administration Review,* 28 (1968).

"Four Decades of Service." *FBI Law Enforcement Bulletin,* 41:9 (September, 1972), 3-7, 29-30.

Jeffers, H.P. *Wanted by the FBI.* NY: Hawthorne, 1972.
Concise history of the Ten Most Wanted Fugitives Program.

Kelley, Clarence M. "United States Department of Justice: FBI Assistance to the Law Enforcement Community." *Police Chief,* XLII:7 (July, 1975), 40-43.

Lowenthal, Max *Federal Bureau of Investigation.* Westport, CT: Greenwood [1950], 1971.

Millen, William A. *Crime, FBI's Hoover and You.* NY: Exposition Press, 1970.

Murdy, Ralph G. "A Follow-Up Study of FBI Service." *Police,* (January-February, 1963), 50-52.

Nash, Jay R. *Citizen Hoover: A Critical Study of the Life and Times of J. Edgar Hoover and His FBI.* Chicago: Nelson Hall, 1972.

Nelson, Jack and Ronald Ostrow. *FBI and the Berrigans: The Making of a Conspiracy.* NY: Coward, 1972.

Overstreet, Harry and Bonaro Overstreet. *The FBI in Our Open Society.* NY: W.W. Horton, 1969.

Turner, William W. *Hoover's FBI, The Man and the Myth.* Los Angeles: Sherbourne, 1970.

Ungar, Sanford J. *FBI.* Boston: Atlantic Little Brown, 1976.

Watters, Pat. *Investigating the FBI.* Garden City, NY: Doubleday, 1973.

Whitehead, Don. *Attack on Terror: The FBI Against the Ku Klux Klan in Mississippi.* NY: Funk & Wagnalls, 1970.

Whitehead, D.F. *The FBI Story: A Report to the People.* NY: Random House, 1956.

Forest Service

Barney, Daniel R. *The Last Stand: The Nader Study Group Report on the U.S. Forest Service.* Washington, DC: Study of Responsive Law, 1972.

Bell, Frank C., et al. *Size of Ranger District Study.* Washington, DC: GPO, 1968.

Comrey, A.L., J.M. Pfiffner and H.P. Breem. *Studies in Organizational Effectiveness: The U.S. Forest Survey.* Los Angeles: Office of Naval Research, University of Southern California, 1951.

DeVall, William B. and Steve Metcalf. *The Forest Service and Its Clients: A Study in Conflict Resolution.* Paper presented at the American Sociological Convention, New Orleans, 1972.

Frome, Michael. *The Forest Service.* NY: Praeger, 1971.

Hendee, John Clare. *Organization and Management in the Forest Service.* Washington, DC: GPO, February, 1962.

Kaufman, Herbert. *Forest Ranger: A Study in Administrative Behavior.* Baltimore: Johns Hopkins University Press, 1967.

Immigration Naturalization Service

Coon, Thomas F. "The Immigration and Naturalizations Under Foreign Law (England)." *Journal of Criminal Law, Criminology and Police Science,* 52:1 (May-June, 1951).

Coon, Thomas F. "The Immigration and Naturalization Service." *Police* (July-August, 1964).

Greene, James F. "The United States Immigration and Naturalization Service vs Foreign-Born Law Violators." *Police Chief,* XLII:2 (February, 1975), 28-29.

Internal Revenue Service

Aubry, Arthur S., Jr. "Inspection in the Internal Revenue Service." *Police,* 15:6 (July-August, 1971), 5-12.

Aubry, Arthur S., Jr. "The Internal Revenue Service Intelligence Division." *Police,* 13:4 (March-April, 1969), 35-41.

Bacon, Donald. "How the IRS Enforces the Tax Laws." *FBI Law Enforcement Bulletin* (March, 1971).

Chommie, John C. *The Internal Revenue Service.* NY: Praeger, 1970.

Green, Lou. *The Racketeers.* NY: Vantage Press, 1970.

Irey, Elmer Lincoln. *The Tax Dodgers.* NY: Greenberg, 1948.

IRS Intelligence Division "The 'Watchdogs' of Internal Revenue." *Journal of California Law Enforcement* (July, 1969), 8-12.

Messick, Hank. *Secret File.* NY: Putnum, 1969.

Justice, Department of

Eliff, J.T. *Crime, Dissent, and the Attorney General—The Justice Department in the 1960's.* Beverly Hills, CA: Sage, 1971.
Description of the social, political, and philosophic forces which shaped policy-making in the Justice Department from 1960 through 1969.

Houston, Luther A. *The Department of Justice.* NY: Praeger, 1967.

Houston, Luther A. et al. *Roles of the Attorney General of the United States.* Washington, DC: AEI, 1968.

Kennedy, Robert F. *The Pursuit of Justice.* NY: Harper & Rowe, 1964.

Navasky, Victor S. *Kennedy Justice.* NY: Atheneum, 1971.

Marshals

Hoffman, Paul. "How Cops Hide Mafia Informers." *Argosy,* 28:5 (May, 1975), 38-41.
Program of the U.S. Marshall's Office.

Lunney, Thomas F. "Organization, Mission and Function of the Office of United States Marshal." *Police,* 9:4 (March-April, 1965), 88-89.

Military Law Enforcement

Bailey, Charles H. "USAF Police-Community Relations." *Police,* 13:6 (July-August, 1969), 49-53.

Batson, Thomas E. "Air Force Security Police Operations." *Police Chief,* XXXVI:1 (January, 1969), 32-34.

Carlyle, T. "They Tell It to the Army." *Nations Business,* 32:86 (April, 1944).
Discusses training of military police in the army.

Daxe, Arnold. "Military Policemen—A Modern Perspective." *Military Police Journal* (April, 1972), 6-8.

Dieckmann, Edward A., Sr. "Trained Seals in A Squirrel Cage." *Police,* 5:5 (May-June, 1961), 12-14.

Evans, Clarence H. "Military Police as Shot Gun Riders." *Law and Order,* 19:7 (July, 1971), 91.
Military police as third officer in communities near military installations.

Everett, Robinson O. "Criminal Investigation Under Military Law." *Journal of Criminal Law, Criminology and Police Science,* 46:5 (January-February, 1956), 707-721; 46:6 (March-April, 1956), 892-904.

Glasgow, M. "Germany's Griffins: Swift, Strong, Vigilant." *Military Police Journal,* 22:11 (1973), 18-23.
Duties and organizations of the U.S. 15th MP Brigade stationed in West Germany.

Moody, William T. "Guardian For Peace." *FBI Law Enforcement Bulletin* (January, 1975), 16-19.
Describes the activities of the 91st Security Police Group, Minot Air Force Base, Minot, North Dakota.

Newham, T.J. and T.A. Fleek. "The Air Force Approach to Professional Police." *Police Chief* (May, 1967).

Security Police Handbook. Washington: GPO, 1971.
Manual providing instructions, procedures and techniques to improve Air Force Security Police effectiveness in mission accomplishment.

Postal Inspection Service

Aubry, Arthur S., Jr. "The United States Postal Inspection Service." *Police,* 13:2 (November-December, 1968), 29-35.

Denniston, Elinore. *America's Silent Investigators: The Story of the Postal Inspectors Who Protect the United States Mail.* NY: Dodd Mead, 1964.

Kahn, E.J., Jr. *Fraud—The United States Postal Inspection Service Service and Some of the Fools and Knaves it Has Known*. NY: Harper & Row, 1973.

Makris, John N. *The Silent Investigators: The Great Untold Story of the United States Postal Inspection Service*. NY: Dutton, 1959.

Secret Service

Anderson, Jack and Fred Blumenthal. "The Secret Service: It Keeps Our Presidents Alive." *Parade* (September 26, 1954).

Ansley, Norman. "The United States Secret Service." *Journal of Criminal Law, Criminology and Police Science,* 47:1 (May-June, 1956), 93-109.

Bargeron, C. "Men Who Guard The President." *Nations Business,* 34 (June, 1946), 101-104.

Baughman, Urbanis E. and L. Robinson, *Secret Service Chief*. NY: Harper & Row, 1962.

Bowen, Walter S. and Harry E. Neil. *United States Secret Service*. Philadelphia: Chilton, 1960.

Crump, Irving. *Our United States Secret Service*. NY: Simon & Schuster, 1947.

Dorman, Michael. *Secret Service Story*. NY: Delacorte, 1967.

"Duties and Dangers of Presidential Guardians." *Literary Digest,* 99 (October, 1928), 34-40.

Ferguson, Henry N. "America's Secret Service." *California Highway Patrolman,* 35 (May, 1971), 14-15, 43-45.

Knight, H. Stuart. "The United States Secret Service: Ten Years Since." *Police Chief,* XLII:7 (July, 1975), 32-35.

Leiro, A. "Mission Sans End; Presidential Vigil." *New York Times Magazine* (January 4, 1953).

Neal, Harry Edward. *The Story of the Secret Service*. NY: Grosset & Dunlap, 1971.
History of secret service 1965-1971. Covers contemporary duties and functions protecting the president, suppressing counterfeiting, protecting visiting heads of state.

Reilly, Michael F. "I Guarded FDR." *Saturday Evening Post* (in five parts: September 7, 14, 21, 28, and October 5, 1946).

Reilly, Michael F. *Reilly of the White House*. NY: Simon & Schuster, 1947.

Rowley, James. "The Executive Protective Service." *FBI Law Enforcement Bulletin* (April, 1971).

Rowley, James J. "The United States Secret Service." *FBI Law Enforcement Bulletin,* 19:6 (June, 1970), 2-6, 27-29.

"Secret Services Latest Job—Protecting Nixon's Rivals." *U.S. News and World Report* (April 3, 1972), 30-31.

Sugrue, Thomas. *Starling of the White House*. NY: Simon & Schuster, 1946.

"The Secret Service: It Keeps Our Presidents Alive." *Parade* (September 26, 1954).

"They Always Guard Their Man." *Scholastic,* 49 (October 7, 1946).

"Tighter Guard Over Ike." *Newsweek,* 44 (August, 1954), 26.

Treasury

Aubry, Arthur S., Jr. "The Alcohol and Tobacco Tax Division." *Police* (January-February, 1968).

Irey, Elmer L. and William Slocum. *The Tax Dodgers: The Inside Story of the T Men's War With America's Political and Underworld Hoodlums*. NY: Greenberg, 1948.

MacDonald, David R. "Treasury Department: Assistance Programs to State and Local Law Enforcement." *Police Chief,* XLII:7 (July, 1975), 28-30.

Neal, Harry E. *Six Against Crime: Treasury Agencies in Action*. NY: Messner, 1959.

Phillips, Max D. "A Study of the Office of Law Enforcement Coordination U.S. Treasury Department." *Journal of Criminal Law, Criminology and Police Science,* 54:3 (September, 1963), 369-377.

Tully, Andrew. *Treasury Agent: The Inside Story*. NY: Simon & Schuster, 1966.

Miscellaneous Federal Agencies

Aubry, Arthur S., Jr. "Civil Aeronautics Board: Enforcement Division." *Police,* 13:5 (May-June, 1969), 65-71.

Aubry, Arthur S., Jr. "The Investigation Program of The United States Civil Service Commission." *Police,* 13:3 (January-February, 1969), 6-13.

Bautels, John R., Jr. "1975: A Year of Crisis." *Police Chief,* XLII:2 (February, 1975), 60-62.

Black, J.W. "American Police and Tourists from Abroad." *Police Chief,* XXXV:2 (February, 1968), 18-20.
Activities of U.S. Travel Service, U.S. Department of Commerce.

Finlator, John. "Drug Abuse Control." *FBI Law Enforcement Bulletin,* 36:6 (June, 1967), 6-10.

Graziano, John V. "Department of Agriculture: Third Largest Criminal Investigative Force in Federal Government." *Police Chief,* XLII:7 (July, 1975), 54-55.

Shepard, George H. "Youth Service Systems—An Innovative Concept in Prevention." *Police Chief,* XL:2 (February, 1973), 48-53.

Smalley, Wayne L. "The AEC Radiological Assistance Program." *FBI Law Enforcement Bulletin,* 43:10 (October, 1974), 3-9.

Stewart, Harold F. "U.S. Park Police." *Law and Order,* 8:9 (1960).

Velde, Richard W. "Law Enforcement Assistance Administration: Programs to Aid State and Local Agencies." *Police Chief,* XLII:7 (July, 1975), 44-51.

STATE AGENCIES

Alletto, William C. "Legislative and Organizational Proposals for the Creation of a State Department of Justice and Public Safety for the State of Illinois." *Police,* 10:2 (November-December, 1965), 61-67.

Alletto, William C. "The State—The Administration of Justice and Law Enforcement." *Police,* 8:4 (March-April, 1964), 75-80.

Bishop, John L. "Police Duties and Operations on Ohio Turnpike." *FBI Law Enforcement Bulletin,* 27:2 (February, 1958), 3-8.
Activities of Ohio State Highway Patrol.

Blair, Robert. "Role of a State Investigative Agency." *FBI Law Enforcement Bulletin,* (June, 1968).

Boomer, John R. "Collective Violence and the California Highway Patrol." *Law and Order* (May, 1972).

Brandt, A.P. "Rural Police Problems in Alaska." *The Police Yearbook.* Washington, DC: IACP, 1959.

Brandt, August P. "Territorial Police Department Serves Citizens of Alaska." *FBI Law Enforcement Bulletin,* 26:5 (May, 1957), 3-6.

California Crime Technological Research Foundation. *Design of a Model State Identification Bureau.* Sacramento: Search Group Inc., 1973.

California State Police. *California—State Police—Model Emergency Plan for State Facilities.* Washington, DC: NCJRS (Microfiche) n/d.
An open-ended plan for state facilities that can be tailored to each facilities needs in meeting a variety of emergency situations.

Coakley, Leo J. *Jersey Troopers.* New Brunswick, NJ: Rutgers University Press, 1971.

Comparative Data Report—Division of State and Provincial Police. Gaithersburg, MD: IACP, 1969.
Comparisons are made on state to state basis within the fields of administration, operations, services and information services.

Cramer, James. "Police Forces of the World: California Highway Patrol." *Police Review* [Eng.], 67 (November, 1959).

"The DPS Story." *Texas Peace Officer,* 3 (May, 1965), 4-21.
Activities of Texas Department of Public Safety including Texas Rangers.

Ellis, James H. "The Connecticut Resident State Police System." *Police,* 5:1 (September-October, 1960), 69-72.

Gladstone, Edward A. and Thomas W. Cooper. "State Highway Patrols: Their Functioning and Finance." *Police Chief,* 35:5 (May, 1966), 31-36.

Guernsey, Elwood W. *State Trooper: Study of an Occupational Self.* Unpub. Ph.D. Dissertation, Florida State University, 1965.

Hallstead, William F. "Patroling for Safety." *Law and Order,* 12:9 (September, 1964), 90-91.
Activities of Maryland State Police.

Hickey, Edward J. "Trends in Rural Police Protection." *Annals of the American Academy of Political and Social Science,* 291 (January, 1954), 22-30.
Growth of state police agencies and decline of the Sheriff and Constable.

"The Illinois Bureau of Investigation—An Innovation in Law Enforcement." *Police,* 15:2 (November-December, 1970), 71-72.

Kelly, David B. "New Jersey State Police." *Law and Order* (February, 1972), 76-78.

Kelly, John C. "Connecticut's Resident State Police System." *The Police Yearbook.* Washington, DC: IACP, 1958.

Kirkman, H.M. "Development of the Florida Highway Patrol." *FBI Law Enforcement Bulletin,* 28:3 (March, 1959), 3-6, 13.

Kirwin, William E. "New York State Police." *Virginia Trooper,* 18 (October, 1970), 2-5.

Monroe, David G. *State and Provincial Police: A Study of Police Functioning in the United States and Canada.* Evanston, IL: IACP and The Northwestern University Traffic Institute, 1941.

Myers, John J. "Alaska State Troopers Get Enforcement Help in Bush Area." *Law and Order,* 20:1 (January, 1972), 56-59.

O'Brien, Daniel. "Half-century Mark for Illinois State Police." *Police Chief* (June, 1972).
A 50 year history of the Illinois State Police.

Project Search—Design of a Model State Identification Bureau. Sacramento: California Crime Technological Research Foundation, 1973.
Survey and analysis of State Identification Bureau operations with particular attention to activities in New York, Virginia, South Carolina and Oregon.

Quill, Mary Vincent and David Kennamer. "A Birthday with Nostalgia." *Law and Order,* 21:9 (September, 1973), 28-29.
Article on Kentucky State Police.

Scott, Ralph D. "The Arkansas State Police Traffic Program." *Law and Order* (June, 1970).

Shaw, Eleanor F. "Our Friends The Maryland State Police." *Police* (March-April, 1967).

Torres, Donald. "The Colorado Bureau of Investigation." *Police Chief,* XXXIX:3 (March, 1972).

Torres, Donald. "The Kansas Bureau of Investigation: A State Investigative Agency." *Police Chief,* 39:2 (February, 1972), 36-39.

Torres, Donald. "The Minnesota Bureau of Criminal Apprehension: A State Investigative Agency." *Police Chief,* 39:1 (January, 1972), 42-45.

Torres, Donald. "The Oklahoma Bureau of Investigation." *Police Chief,* XXXIX:4 (April, 1972), 80-82.

Vollmer, A. and A. Parker. *Crime and the State Police.* Berkeley: University of California Press, 1935.

Watson, Richard A. *Law Enforcement in Missouri: State Highway Patrol.* Columbia, MO: Bureau of Gov't Research, University of Missouri, December, 1960.

Webb, Walter Prescott. *The Texas Rangers: A Century of Frontier Defense.* Austin: University of Texas Press, 1965.

Wechter, Harry L. "The Resident State Policeman in Connecticut." *Law and Order,* 13:9 (September, 1965), 60-65.

Wechter, Harry L. "What Is a State Policeman." *Law and Order,* 15:2 (February, 1967), 72-73.

Woo, Tao Fu. *State Police and State Highway Patrols.* Unpub. M.S. thesis, University of Colorado, 1949.

COUNTY AGENCIES

Alletto, William C. "Guidelines in Organization for Sheriff's Departments of Large (Metropolitan) Counties." *Police* (March-April, 1963).

Alletto, William C. "The Sheriff's Role in Law Enforcement." *Police* (July-August, 1961).

Arend, Russell A. "Independent County Police Agencies." *American County Government* (May, 1967), 38-40.

Brammer, Dana B. and James E. Hurley. *Study of the Office of Sheriff in the United States—Southern Region, 1967.* Washington, DC: NCJRS, 1968.
The development of a broad knowledge base of southern sheriff's operation, responsibilities, needs, and potentialities.

Brown, Lee P. "The Changing Role of the County Sheriff." *Police Chief,* XLII:3 (March, 1976), 50-52.

Bynum, Lindley and Idwal Jones. *Biscailuz, Sheriff of the New West.* NY: Morrow, 1950.

Coon, Thomas F. "The New Jersey Sheriff—Restoration of an Old Image." *Police,* 7:4 (March-April, 1963), 37-39.

Esselstyn, T.C. *Crime and its Control in the Hinterland.* Unpub. Doctorate dissertation, NY University, 1952.

Gladwin, Irene. *Sheriff: The Man and His Office.* London: Gollanez, 1974.

Hollister, Charles A. *The Organization and Administration of the Sheriff's Office in Arizona.* Unpub. M.A. thesis, University of Arizona, 1946.

Horan, Michael J., John M. Baines and S.G. Hajjar. "The Sheriff's Role in Law Enforcement." *Police* (September, 1971).

Kennard, John P. "An English Policeman in the United States." *FBI Law Enforcement Bulletin,* 36:10 (October, 1967), 12-15.

Lane, Jean R. "Maui County Police Department." *Police* (July-August, 1960).

Lawder, Lee E. "Suffolk County (NY) Revisited." *Law and Order,* 14:11 (November, 1966), 56-69, 81.

Lohman, Joseph D. "The Sheriff in Enforcement and Correction." *Journal of Criminal Law, Criminology and Police Science,* 46:1 (January-February, 1955), 588-589.

Misner, Gordon E. "The St. Louis County Department of Police." *Journal of Criminal Law, Criminology and Police Science,* 48:6 (March-April, 1958), 652-659.

Police Services in St. Louis County, A Plan of Improvement. Chicago: Public Administration Service, 1967.

MUNICIPAL AGENCIES

Anderson, Clinton H. *Beverly Hills is My Beat.* Englewood Cliffs, NJ: Prentice Hall, 1960.

Anderson, Lynn F. and Windell M. Bedichek. *Municipal Police Administration in Texas: A Survey.* Austin, TX: Austin Institute of Public Affairs, 1957.

Barnes, Frank C. "A Unique Approach to Law Enforcement, Delinquency, and Community Relations." *Police Chief,* XL:2 (February, 1973), 58-63.

Berkley, George E. *The Democratic Policeman.* Boston: Beacon, 1969.

Braun, B.G. *The Milwaukee Police Department.* Ann Arbor: Bureau of Government Institute of Public Administration, University of Michigan, 1955.

Bruno, Hal. "Chicago's Scholarly Cop." *The Reporter,* 34 (March 24, 1966).
Describes the Chicago Police Department since Orlando W. Wilson took command. Chicago has fewer policemen than six years ago, but a double civilian staff.

Brooks, Thomas R. "New York's Finest." *Commentary,* 40 (August, 1965), 29-30.

Buckley, John L. "Law Enforcement in the Space Age." *Law and Order,* 13:4 (April, 1965), 50-51.
Problems relating to Cape Kennedy and surrounding municipal police agencies.

Caddell, Walter A. "For Police Efficiency." *The American City,* 72:105 (December, 1957).
A report on inadequacy of police departments in Westchester County, NY and a suggested method for improvement through an organization called Community Protective Association Inc.

Callahan, John J. "Viability of the Small Police Force." *Police Chief,* XL:3 (March, 1973), 56-59.

Cramer, James. "Police Forces of the World: Honolulu." *Police Review (GB),* 67 (March 13, 1959).

"Crime, Part II: What a City Should Expect from Police." *Life* (September 16, 1957).

Criminal Justice System in Polk County, Iowa, V 2, Law Enforcement—Description and Analysis—An Interim Report. Springfield, VA: NTIS, 1972.

Daley, Robert. *Target Blue.* NY: Delacorte, 1973.

Dallas Police Department. *Dallas—Police Department—Innovations and Programs, 1971.* Washington, DC: NCJRS (Microfiche) 1971.

"Dayton's Mod Cops." *Newsweek* (November 9, 1970), 51.

Deutsch, A. "Is Your Police Force Obsolete?" *Colliers,* 134 (October 1, 1954).

"Disorganization of Metropolitan Law Enforcement and Some Proposed Solutions—The Illinois Cook County Situations." *Journal of Criminal Law, Criminology and Police Science,* 43:1 (May-June, 1952), 63-78.

Donovan, L.O. *Municipal Police—A Rural and Urban Comparison.* Ann Arbor, MI: University Microfilms, 1971.
Identification of community and police department characteristics which are related to the policeman's background characteristics, behavior and attitudes.

Eastman, George D. "The Bureau of Police of the City of New Rochelle, New York." *City Manager* (November 15, 1957).

Ercul, J.P. "Complete Reorganization Evident in Pueblo Police Department." *Colorado Policeman,* 11:1 (1974), 2-5.

Folley, Vern L. "Your Police Department—Bigger or Better." *Pennsylvanian* (May, 1968).

Force, Frank. "Running a Small Police Force." *The American City,* 76:112 (July, 1961).

Frank, S. "World's Busiest Police Beat." *Saturday Evening Post,* 227 (June 25, 1955), 26-27.

Geis, Gilbert. *Municipal Law Enforcement in Oklahoma.* Oklahoma City, OK: Crime Study Commission, 1955.

Glazer, Nathan. *Cities in Trouble.* Chicago: Quadrangle Books, 1970.

Gleason, J.M. "Policing the Small Cities." *The Annals of the American Academy of Political and Social Science,* 291 (January, 1954), 21-39.

Governmental Research Institute. *St. Louis Police Department: A Resurvey.* St. Louis: Governmental Research Institute, 1948.

Hahn, Harlan. *Police in Urban Society.* Beverly Hills, CA: Sage, 1971.

Hahn, H. "A Profile of Urban Police." *Law and Contemporary Problems,* 36:4 (Autumn, 1971), 449-466.

Hewitt, William H. "Parma Police Department: One of Ohio's Most Progressive." *Police,* 10:2 (November-December, 1965), 18-26.

Institute of Public Administration. *The New York Police Survey.* NY: Institute of Public Administration, 1952.

The International Association of Chiefs of Police. *An Organizational Study of the Police Department, New York City, NY.* Washington, DC: IACP. 1967.

Jenkins, Herbert T. *Keeping the Peace.* NY: Harper & Rowe, 1970.

Jenkins, H.T. "Police Challenges and Changes in Atlanta." *Police Chief,* XXXIV:11 (November, 1967), 28-34.

Klein, Herb. *The New York Police: Damned if They Do, Damned if They Don't.* NY: Crown Publishers, 1968.

Lane, P.B. "The Los Angeles Police Department." *Outpost,* 42 (February, 1964), 4-7.

Larsen, Christian L. "Maryland's Local Police Systems." *The American City,* 65:125 (December, 1950).
A comparison of police departments of 60 Maryland Muncipalities.

Leonard, Donald S. *A Survey of the Police Department.* San Antonio, TX: San Antonio Police Department, 1957.

Linkon, Gordon Ed. "Disorganization of Metropolitan Law Enforcement and Some Proposed Solutions." *Journal of Criminal Law, Criminology and Police Science,* 43 (May-June, 1952), 63-78.

Liu, Daniel S.C. "A Cosmopolitan Metropolis Policed by Honolulu's Finest." *Police,* 11:1 (September-October, 1957), 29-33.

Longstretch, John K. and Bruce T. Olson. *A Study of the Benton Harbor, Michigan Police Department.* East Lansing: Institute for Community Development, Michigan State University, 1967.

"Los Angeles: The Hard-Liner." *Newsweek,* 77 (March 15, 1971).

MacNamara, Donal E.J. *New Jersey Municipal Police Survey.* Trenton: New Jersey Law Enforcement Council, 1958.

MacNamara, Donal E.J. *Report of a Survey: Madison, New Jersey Police Department.* NY: New York Institute of Criminology, September, 1961.

MacNamara, Donal E.J. *A Survey of the Princeton, New Jersey Police Department.* NY: New York Institute of Criminology, December, 1958.

MacNamara, Donal E.J. and Michael J. DeLusa. *Report of a Survey: Police Department, Township of Woodbridge, Middlesex, New Jersey.* NY: New York Institute of Criminology, May, 1962.

MacNamara, Donal E.J. and Michael J. DeLusa. *Report of a Survey: Verona, New Jersey Police Department.* NY: Institute of Criminology, January, 1962.

MacNamara, Donal E.J. and Robert A. Smith. *Bristol's Police Problems.* NY: Institute of Criminology, 1965.

MacNamara, Donal E.J. and Paul B. Wesson. *The Millburn, New Jersey Police Department Survey.* NY: New York Institute of Criminology, 1959.

McAllister, Robert and Floyd Miller. *The Kind of Guy I Am.* NY: McGraw-Hill, 1957.

McDowell, C.O. *Police in the Community.* Cincinnati: Anderson, 1975.

McIntyre, Donald M., Jr. *Law Enforcement in the Metropolis.* Chicago: American Bar Foundation, 1967.

Misner, Gordon E. "Recent Development in Metropolital Law Enforcement." *Journal of Criminal Law and Criminology,* 50 (January-February), 1960 497-508.

Misner, Gordon E. "The Urban Police Mission." *Issues in Criminology,* 3:1 (1967), 35-46.

Murphey, Arthur. "Police Departments in Georgia." *Georgia Local Government Journal,* 7 (December, 1957), 11-12.
Compares the number of police employees in selected cities in terms of population, rank, etc.

"New York City Police Department." *SDC,* 8 (October, 1965), 25-27.

Niederhaffer, Arthur. *Behind the Shield: The Police in Urban Society.* Garden City, NY: Doubleday, 1967.

Oh, John C.H. "Police in a Midwestern Community." *Police* (January-February, 1970).

Ostrom, E. and W.H. Baugh. *Community Organization and the Provision of Police Services.* Beverly Hills, CA: Sage Publications Inc., 1973.
Police services in the Indianapolis Metropolitan area are examined to compare larger scale, centralized police departments with small, community-controlled departments.

Ostrom, E. and R.B. Parks. *Suburban Police Departments—Too Many and Too Small.* Beverly Hills, CA: Sage, 1973.

Parker, Alfred E. *The Berkeley Police Story.* Springfield, IL: C.C. Thomas, 1972.

Parker, William H. "Policing Los Angeles." *The Jonathan* (June, 1951).

Perry, D.C. *Police in the Metropolis.* Columbus, OH: Charles E. Merrill, 1975.

"Police: The Thin Blue Line." *Time* (July 19, 1968).

President's Commission on Law Enforcement and Administration of Justice. *Task Force Report: The Police.* Washington: GPO, 1967.

Redding, Stan. "KKD 490 Houston." *Texas Peace Officer,* 2 (March, 1964), 5-27.

Reynolds, Quintin. *Headquarters.* NY: Harper & Row, 1955.

Rice, Robert. "A Normal Week for Crime in Chicago." *New York Times Magazine* (June 18, 1967).

Rubinstein, Jonathan. *City Police.* NY: Farrar Straus & Giroux, 1973.

Excellent account of patrolman activities in Philadelphia. Reviews formal and informal codes of conduct.

"A Saturday with the Police in Stockton, California." *The Police Chief* (June, 1968).

"Self Portrait N.Y. 1968." *Spring 3100* (November, 1968) (Entire issue).

Senate Committee on the District of Columbia. *Crime and Law Enforcement in the District of Columbia: Hearings and Report.* NY: Arno, [1952] 1971.

Skolnick, Jerome M. *Justice Without Trial: Law Enforcement in Democratic Society.* NY: Wiley, 1966.

Snibbe, John R. and Homa M. Snibbe. *Urban Policeman in Transition: A Psychological and Sociological Review.* Springfield, IL: C.C. Thomas, 1973.

Sommers, William A. "The Birth of a Police Department." *Police.* 5:2 (November-December, 1960), 64-67.

Stern, Chester. "Policing New York." *Job* (August 8, 1975), 5.

St. Petersburg Public Safety Agency. *Public Safety—St. Petersburg Style.* Washington, DC: NCJRS, 1973.

"Strong Arm of the Law." *Time* (July 7, 1958), 14-17.

Thomas, Edward. "Comments From Small Departments." *Law and Order,* 16:7 (July, 1968), 48-49.

Vandervelde, Marjorie. "Chief of Police on the Last Frontier." *Law and Order,* (July, 1973).

Discusses activities and organizations of Juneau, Alaska Police Department.

Webb, Jack. *The Badge.* Englewood Cliffs, NJ: Prentice Hall, 1958.

Wildhorn, Sorrell. *Research on New York Cities Police Problems.* NY: Rand, November, 1968.

Wilson, James Q. *Varieties of Police Behavior.* Cambridge, MA: Harvard University Press, 1968.

CAMPUS POLICE

Abranson, Stephen A. "A Survey of Campus Police Departments: Screening and Selection Practices." *Police Chief,* XLI:7 (July, 1974), 54-56.

Adams, Michael F. "Seton Crime Patrol." *Law and Order,* 17:6 (June, 1969), 104-107.

Armistead, Timothy W. "Police on Campus." *Issues in Criminology* (Fall, 1969), 171-184.

Bagley, Gerald L. "Collimation of the Campus Cop." *Industrial Security,* XIV (April, 1971).

Barber, John C. "University Police—A Role in Education." *Journal of California Law Enforcement* (April, 1975), 159-162.

Bartram, John L. and Larry E. Smith. "A Survey of Campus Police Forces." *Journal of the College and University Personnel Association,* XXI (November, 1969).

Becker, Ralph. "Contract Security's New Answer to Old Problems." *American School and University,* XL (July, 1968), 37-38.

Bretnor, Reginald. "When Constabulary Duty's To Be Done." *California Monthly,* LXXVIII (April-May, 1968).

Brinkley, Gary M. "The University Police: Changes Which Must Be Made." *Police* (August, 1972), 46-49.

Cahill, Thomas J. "Law and Order on the Campus." *FBI Law Enforcement Bulletin,* 39:3 (March, 1970), 18-20.

Calder, James D. "Policing and Securing the Campus: The Need for Complementary Organizations." *Police Chief,* XLI:11 (November, 1974), 60-64.

"Campus Security Needs Professionals with Emphasis on People Problems: Here are Four Aspects of Challenge." *College University Business,* 48 (April, 1970), 94-99.

Carlson, George W.H. "Campus Security." *FBI Law Enforcement Bulletin,* 39:10 (October, 1970), 16-22.

Chandler, C. Lee and John W. Shainline. "Campus Police Emphasis Is Shifting from Security to Enforcement, Parking Problems to Problem People." *College and University Business,* XLVI (March, 1969).

Couper, David C. "The Need for Excellence in Campus Policing." *The Police Chief,* 38:1 (January, 1971), 58-59.

Etheridge, Robert F. *A Study of Campus Protective and Enforcement Agencies at Selected Universities.* Unpub. Ph.D. dissertation, Michigan State University, 1958.

Fitzpatrick, P.J. "Contract Guard Service." *American School and University,* 37 (July, 1965).

Gardner, I.C. "How to Prepare for a Bomb Scare." *American School and University,* 42 (Fall, 1970).

Gelber, Seymour. *The Role of Campus Security in the College Setting.* Washington, DC: GPO, 1972.

Gorda, B.L. *Cops or Guards—Campus Dilemma.* Washington, DC: NCJRS. (Microfiche) n/d.

Examination and discussion of the police versus security dilemma experienced by academic institutions when faced with determining the composition, objectives, and authority of campus protection organization.

Holloman, Frank C. "The New Breed: College and University Police." *Police Chief,* 39:2 (February, 1972), 41-45.

Innarelli, Alfred V. *The Campus Police.* Hayward, CA: Precision Photo—Form Co., 1968.

International Association of College and University Security Directors. *Security Service Analysis.* Macomb, IL: Western Illinois University, 1970.

Jones, Elroy J. "The New Image for the Campus Security Officer." *Security World,* 7 (May, 1970), 25-26.

Kenney, John P. *University and College Campus Policing: Some Considerations.* Long Beach, CA: Institute for Police Studies, California State College at Long Beach, 1969.

Kennon, Leslie B. "The Student Police on the Campus." *Law and Order,* 8:7 (July, 1960), 6-7.

Kleberg, John. "Selection Process of Police Officers in First Line of Campus Defense." *College and University Business,* XLVIII (April, 1970).

"Lady Guards Strengthen This University's Security." *American School and University.* 40 (July, 1968), 37-38.

"Lowering the Toll of Vandalism." *American School and University,* 38 (August, 1966), 26-27.

Mann, F.H. "A New Image for Campus Police." *FBI Law Enforcement Bulletin,* 42:2 (1973), 13-17, 30.

McDaniel, William E. "Safety and Security on the Campus." *The Police Chief* (April, 1970), 68-70.

Milborrow, E.A. "Security on the Campus." *Security Gazette,* 16:8 (1974), 296-298.

Nielsen, Swen C. *General Observation of Organizational and Administrative Concepts of University Police.* Unpub. Master's thesis, Brigham Young University, 1970.

Nielson, S.C. *General Organizational and Administrative Concepts for University Police.* Springfield, IL: C.C. Thomas, 1971.

Nielsen, Swen C. "Policing Policies." *College Management,* V (July, 1970).

"Police Cadets on a College Campus." *FBI Law Enforcement Bulletin,* 39:9 (September, 1970).

Powell, John. "Campus Security Needs Professional with Emphasis on People Problems: Here Are Four Aspects." *College and University Business,* XLVII (April, 1970), 94-99.

Powell, John W. "The History and Proper Role of Campus Security." *Security World,* 8 (March, 1971), 18, 20-22; and (April, 1971), 19-25.

Powell, John. "Professionalizing Campus Security." *Security World,* IV (May, 1967), 23-27, 38.

Powell, John. "Security Today." *College Management,* IV (October, 1969).

Powell, J.W. "Ten Important Questions Colleges Are Asking about Security Today." *College Management,* 4 (October, 1969), 35-38.

Richert, John R. and Lewis Leitner. "A Model for Recruiting and Testing Campus Security Officers." *Police Chief,* XLI:7 (July, 1974), 76-78.

Robinson, W.S. "University Confrontation." *Police Chief,* 38:1 (January, 1971), 26-33.

Scott, Erick J. *College and University Police Agencies.* Bloomington: Indiana University, Department of Political Science, 1976.

"Security Radios Also Serves Other Functions on This Campus." *American School and University,* 40 (July, 1968), 41-42.

"Security System for Maximum Protection." *American School and University,* 38 (August, 1966), 23-25.

Shanahan, Michael G. "A Criminal Justice Venture: The University of Washington Police Department." *Police Chief,* XLI:7 (July, 1974), 72-75.

"Student Rebels Versus School Defenders: A Partisan Account." *Urban Review,* 4 (October, 1969), 9-17.

Symposium. "Should Campus Security Police Be Armed?" *College Management,* 4 (October, 1969), 44-46.

"Upgrade UCLA Police Over Three-Year-Period." *UCLA Weekly* (May 10, 1971).

Webb, Joseph C., Jr. "The Well-Trained, Professional University Police Officer Fact or Fiction?" *FBI Law Enforcement Bulletin* (April, 1975), 26-31.

"What Can A Security Check-Up Do for You?" *College Management,* 4 (October, 1969), 40-43.

Willis, John. "Improving Communications in Patrols and Emergencies." *American School and University,* XIL (July, 1969).

INDIAN POLICE

Benge, William B. "Law and Order on Indian Reservations." *Federal Bar Journal,* XX:3 (Summer, 1960), 223-229.

Bobo, D. *Law and Order on the Mississippi Choctaw Reservation.* Springfield, VA: NTIS, 1970.
Study of the special problems of law enforcement in an American Indian tribal community with a proposed code of criminal procedure and recommended remedial actions.

Clum, John T. "The San Carlos Apache Police." *New Mexico Historical Review,* 4 (1929), 203-219; 5 (1930), 67-92.

Families of Certain Indian Policemen. Serial #3028, Washington: Bureau of Indian Affairs, 1896.

Foreman, Carolyn Thomas. "The Light-Horse in the Indian Territory." *Chronicles of Oklahoma.* XXXIV:1 (Spring, 1956), 17-43.

Gruler, George H. *Definition and Jurisdiction of Indian Reservations and Indian Country.* Roswell, NM: Indian Police Academy, n/d.

Hagan, William. *Indian Police and Judges: Experiments in Acculturation and Control.* New Haven, CT: Yale University Press, 1966.

Hamm, Carl W. and Richard W. Kobetz. "Contemporary Problems in Law Enforcement on American Indian Reservations." *Police Chief* (July, 1976), 58.
A review of historical and contemporary developments in the criminal justice system for American Indians and some of the steps now being taken to overcome the unique problems presented.

"Indian Police Academy Promotes Professional Proficiency." *Police Chief,* 39:10 (October, 1972), 64-66.

Describes activities at U.S. Indian Police Academy at Roswell, New Mexico. Academy provides centralized training location for Indian Police officers.

Jones, Oakah L., Jr. "The Origins of the Navajo Indian Police, 1872-1873." *Arizona and the West,* VIII:3 (Autumn, 1966), 225-238.

Kobetz, Richard W. and Carl W. Hamm. "Contemporary Problems in Law Enforcement on American Indian Reservations." *Police Chief,* XXXVII:7 (July, 1970), 58-61.

Llewellyn, Karl N. and E.A. Hoebel. *The Cheyenne Way: Conflict and Case Law in Primitive Jurisprudence.* Norman: University of Oklahoma Press, 1941.

Lloyd, Bob. "The Navajo Police Department." *Law and Order,* 8:6 (1960), 6-14.

MacLeod, William Christie. "Police and Punishment Among Native Americans of the Plains." *Journal of Criminal Law and Criminology,* XXVIII:2 (May-June, 1937), 181-201.

McNeil, Irving. "Indian Justice." *New Mexico Historical Review,* XIX:4 (October, 1944), 261-70.

Metarelis, George S. "Lawmen for the Reservation," *FBI Law Enforcement Bulletin* (July, 1971).

Myers, John J. "Alaska State Troopers Get Enforcement Help in Bush Area." *Law and Order,* 20:1 (January, 1972), 56-59.

Describes the training of Eskimos as police aids in bush areas.

Police for Indian Reservations. Serial #1935, Washington, DC: Bureau of Indian Affairs, 1880.

Prassel, Frank R. *Western Peace Officer: A Legacy of Law and Order.* Norman: University of Oklahoma Press, 1972.

Has excellent chapter and other references about Indian Police.

Taylor, T.W. *States and Their Indian Citizens.* Washington, DC: GPO, 1972.

History of the development and the current relationships between tribal, state and Federal Government activities.

Thompson, William P. "Courts of the Cherokee Nation." *The Chronicles of Oklahoma,* 11:1 (March, 1923).

Tidwell, Dean. "The Indian Career Officer." *Police Chief* (November, 1969), 30-31.

Police academy established in New Mexico in March 1969, trans tribal and bureau law of officers in program geared specifically to them.

U.S. Department of the Interior—Bureau of Indian Affairs. *Combined Tribal and Bureau Law Enforcement Services—Annual Report 1972.* Washington, DC: NCJRS, (Microfiche) 1972.

Crime information for nationwide Indian Country based on reservation police statistics contributed by local tribal and bureau law enforcement agencies.

U.S. Department of the Interior—Bureau of Indian Affairs. *Indian Criminal Justice Program Display, July 1974.* Washington, DC: NCJRS, (Microfiche) 1974.

PORT SECURITY

Cooley, William J. "Port Security—A Systems Survey." *Port of London* (February, 1972), 48-52.

Coon, Thomas F. "Waterfront Commission Investigator." *Police,* 7:1 (September-October, 1962), 42-47.

Deutschman, Louis H. "Policing the Waterfront." *FBI Law Enforcement Bulletin,* 41:10 (October, 1972), 18-21, 28-30.

Fair, Marvin L. *Port Administration in the United States.* Cambridge, MD: Cornell Maritime, 1954.

Jones, Thomas F. "Port Security." *Police Chief,* XXXIV (November, 1967), 35-37.

Activities of Waterfront Commission Police of NY Harbor.

Kaitz, Joseph. "The Bulwark Against Organized Crime on the Waterfront." *Police Chief,* XLII:2 (February, 1975), 38-39.

Law Enforcement Activities of the Waterfront Commission of N.Y. Harbor.

WILDLIFE ENFORCEMENT

Bavin, Clark R. and Allen T. Studholme. "Wildlife Law Enforcement at the Federal Level." *Police,* 9:1 (September-October, 1964), 26-30.

McLean, Herbert. "Alaska's Creek Robber War." *Law and Order,* 14:4 (April, 1966), 30-35, 91.

Alaska's Fish and Game Department investigating commercial fisherman illegally fishing inland streams.

Peay, Golden B. "Enforcement of Fish and Game Laws." *FBI Law Enforcement Bulletin,* 36:2 (February, 1967), 9-13.

Phillips, Jerry. "Wilderness Law Enforcement." *Criminologist* (Summer, 1974), 24-29.

Sherman, Gene H. "Aircraft in Fish and Game Enforcement." *FBI Law Enforcement Bulletin* (October, 1973), 26.

Sigler, William F. *Wild Life Law Enforcement 2nd Ed.* Dubuque, IA: William C. Brown, 1972.

MISCELLANEOUS SPECIAL POLICE AGENCIES

Anderson, Thomas H. "The Police of Guam." *Police Chief,* XXXVII (January, 1970), 46-47.

Caputo, Rudolph R. "The New York State Harness Racing Commission." *Police,* 10:1 (September-October, 1965), 36-39.

DeLong, Hal. "Policing the Nation's Largest Public Island Park." *Police* (July-August, 1968), 69.

DeMarco, Joseph E. "Policing a Famous Landmark." *FBI Law Enforcement Bulletin* (September, 1974), 16-21.

Activities of Niagara Frontier State Park.

Meyer, C. William. "Policing A Man-Made Wonder of the World." *FBI Law Enforcement Bulletin,* 38:6 (June, 1969), 3-5, 20.

Activities of the Chesapeake Bay Bridge Tunnel District Police.

O'Rourke, Thomas J. "Organization and Role of a Transit Police Deparment." *FBI Law Enforcement Bulletin,* 28:4 (April, 1959), 3-10.

Schatz, Donald. "The New York City Housing Authority Police." *FBI Law Enforcement Bulletin* (November, 1966).

Taylor, L.B. "The Story of Cape Canaveral's Security Police Department: Space Age Police Force." *Law and Order,* 8 (May, 1960), 6-11.

Wren, Christopher S. "Rivalry in Blue: Housing Police vs. the City Police." *The New York Times* (February 15, 1973).

PART II
FIELD OPERATIONS—PATROL, INVESTIGATION AND TRAFFIC

PATROL OPERATIONS

PATROL—GENERAL

Adams, Thomas F. *Police Patrol: Tactics and Techniques.* Englewood Cliffs, N.J.: Prentice Hall, 1971.

Bahn, Charles. "Reassurance Factor in Police Patrol." *Criminology* 12:3 (November, 1974), 338-345.

Betlash, Roy A. "A System of Patroling in Suburban Areas." *FBI Law Enforcement Bulletin.* 26:2 (February, 1957), 13-16.

Blum R. and E. Comber. *President's Commission on Law Enforcement and Administration of Justice—Police Field Procedures Report.* Washington: NCJRS, n/d.
Relevant supporting activities, standard practices, new and novel procedures, and general problems are discussed and evaluated.

Brostron, Curtis. "Concepts of Police Patrol and The Strategy and Tactics of Line Operations." *Police.* 6:5 (May-June, 1962), 42-45.

Brown, Charles E. "Discussion: Evaluative Research in Policing—The Kansas City Experience." *Police Chief.* XLII:6 (June, 1975), 40-45.

Chapman, Samuel G. *Police Patrol Readings 2nd Ed.* Springfield, IL.: C.C. Thomas, 1972.

Clark, Donald E. "Patrol Function." *Law and Order.* 13:3 (March, 1965), 68-69.

Clift, Raymond E. "The Objectives of Police Patrol." *Police.* 3:3 (January-February, 1959), 35-36.

Crawford, James H. "Combined Selective Patrol." *Police Chief.* 38:8 (August, 1971), 32-34.
Combines foot and motor control.

Darragh, Charles. "Beat Patrol." *Police.* 3:4 (March-April, 1959), 30-32.

Davis, Edward M. and Lyle Knowles. "A Critique of the Report: An Evaluation of the Kansas City Preventive Patrol Experiment." *Police Chief.* XLII:6 (June, 1975), 22-27.

Elliott, J.F. "Random Patrol." *Police.* 13:2 (November-December, 1968), 51-58.

Farmer, D.J. "Strengthening Patrol Operations." *National Sheriff.* 27:1 (1975), 8-9, 25-29.

Felkenes, G. and P. Whisenand. *Police Patrol Operations—Purpose, Plans, Programs, and Technology.* Berkeley, CA.: McCutchan, 1972.

Folley, Vern. "Examining The Patrol Function Thru 'Practical Police Problems'." *Law and Order* (January, 1976).

Folley, Vern L. *Police Patrol Techniques and Tactics.* Springfield, IL.: C.C. Thomas, 1973.

Gourley, G.D. and A.P. Bristow. *Patrol Administration.* Springfield, IL.: C.C. Thomas, 1970.
Administrative techniques to supplement patrolman manpower including utilization of police women, police dogs, integrated police-fire personnel and police cadets.

Grayson, H.V. "Bakersfield Police Used Motorcycles as Patrol Units on Day Shifts." *Western City.* 35 (September, 1959).

"IACP Position Paper on the Kansas City Preventive Patrol Experiments." *Police Chief.* XLII:9 (September, 1975), 16-20, 64.

Iannone, Nathan F. *Principles of Police Patrol.* N.Y.: McGraw-Hill, 1975.

International Association of Chiefs of Police. *Patrol Operation, 2nd Ed.* Gaithersburg, MD.: IACP, 1970.

Kelling, George L. *Kansas City Preventive Patrol Experiment: A Summary Report.* Washington: Police Foundation, 1974.

Kelling, G.L. et al. *Kansas City (MO) Preventive Patrol Experiment: A Technical Report.* Washington: Police Foundation, 1974.

Kelling, George L. and Tony Pate. "Response to: The Davis-Knowles Critique of the Kansas City Preventive Patrol Experiment." *Police Chief.* XLII:6 (June, 1975).

Kelling, George L. and Tony Pate. "Response to IACP Position Paper." *Police Chief.* XLII:12 (December, 1975), 36-37.

McCreedy, Kenneth R. *Theory and Methods of Police Patrol.* Albany, N.Y.: Delmar, 1974.

McNamara, Joseph D. "A Statement: The Kansas City Preventive Patrol Experiment." *Police Chief.* XLII:6 (June, 1975).

Murphy, Patrick V. "A Commentary: The Davis-Knowles Observations of the Kansas City Preventive Patrol Experiment: A Summary Report." *Police Chief.* XLII:6 (June, 1975).

O'Neill, Joseph F. "Operation Find." *FBI Law Enforcement Bulletin.* 40:11 (November, 1971), 3-6, 29.
Patrol vehicles are dispatched to predesignated locations after robberies and other major crimes.

O'Rourke, Thomas J. "High Visibility Patrol: Cherry Hill, New Jersey, Experiments." *Police Chief.* XLII:6 (June, 1975), 46-47.

Payton, George T. *Patrol Procedure.* 4th Ed. Los Angeles: Legal Book, 1971.

Pittman, Loran M. "It's the Little Things That Count." *FBI Law Enforcement Bulletin.* 38:7 (July, 1969), 11, 22-23.

Police Foundation. *The Kansas City Prevention Patrol Experiment: A Technical Report.* Washington: Pairo & Pairo, 1974.

"Riding a Beat with a Police Pro." *National Observer* (July 4, 1966).

Schell, Theodore H. et al. *Traditional Preventive Patrol.* Washington: LEAA (June, 1976).

Sconfitto, Carl J. and Paul H. O'Grady. "Rochester Police Department Tries a Preventive Patrol Pilot Program." *Law and Order.* 21:11 (November, 1973), 34-36, 38, 40-41.

Shanaham, D.T. *Patrol Administration—Management by Objectives.* Boston: Holbrook, 1975.

Skinner, L.E. *Patrol Techniques.* Washington: NCJRS, 1968.

Skousen, W. Cleon. "Latest Report on Selective Patrol Techniques." *Law and Order.* 13:8 (August, 1965), 14-16, 18.

Skousen, W. Cleon. "Will the Aberdeen Patrol Plan Work in America?" *Law and Order.* 13:9 (September, 1965), 12-16, 34.

Sweeney, Thomas T. and William Ellingsworth. *Issues in Police Patrol: A Book of Readings.* Washington: The Police Foundation, 1973.

"A Synopsis: Introduction to Discussion of the Kansas City Preventive Patrol Experiment." *Police Chief.* XLII:6 (June, 1975), 20-21.

Tytell, Harold. "Citizens Patrol Commanders and the Kansas City Preventive Patrol Experiment." *Police Chief.* XLII:11 (November, 1975), 42-43.

Voelker, Charles. "From Marked to Unmarked in 3 to 5 Minutes." *Law and Order.* 21:11 (November, 1973), 28.

Wayne State University. *Model of and Problems Encountered in a Metropolitan Police Department—Final Report.* Springfield, VA.: NTIS, 1971.

Whisenand, Paul M. *Patrol Operations.* Englewood Cliffs, N.J.: Prentice Hall, 1971.

Wilson, J.V. *Increase of Patrol Effectiveness by Purchase of Additional Vehicles and Provision of More Conspicuous Marking and Color Configuration for all Vehicles.* Baltimore: Williams & Wilkins, n/d.

BASIC CAR PLAN

Davis, Edward M. "Basic Radio Car Plan." *IACP Yearbook.* Gaithersburg, MD.: IACP, 1971, pp. 38-43.

Davis, Edward M. "Neighborhood Team Policing: Implementing the Territorial Imperative." *Crime Prevention Review* (October, 1973).

Lehr, Donald J. and Patrick Quinn. "Community Oriented Policing." *Law and Order* (March, 1976), 78-81.

Los Angeles Police Department. *Basic Car Plan.* Los Angeles: LAPD, 1971.

Los Angeles Police Department, *Basic Car Plan Handbook.* Los Angeles: LAPD, 1971.

Los Angeles Police Department. *Basic Car Plan Newsletter.* Los Angeles: LAPD, 1971.

BICYCLE PATROL

Lee, Edward L. "Back to Bikes for Baltimore." *Police Chief.* XXXIX (May 5, 1972).

Mooney, William J. "Operation of a Bicycle Patrol." *FBI Law Enforcement Bulletin* (November, 1968), 12-15.

"Sheriff Indicates Bicycle Patrol in Marina Del Ray." *Sheriff Star News.* 32 (June, 1970).

Tobias, Jerry J. "Bloomfield Township Police Test Bicycle Patrols." *Michigan Police Journal.* 39:5 (November-December, 1971).

DEPLOYMENT

Bennett, W. and J. Dubois. *Use of Probability Theory in the Assignment of Police Patrol Areas.* Springfield, VA.: NTIS, 1970.

Bloch, Peter B. *Equality of Distribution of Police Services: A Case Study of Washington, D.C.* Washington: Urban Institute, 1974.

Brown, W. "Patrol Deployment: An Analysis." *Canadian Police Chief.* 62:3 (1973), 17-20, 37-38.

Byrne, Edward C. "Deploying Police Personnel." *Law and Order.* 22:5 (May, 1974), 44-46, 48, 50, 52, 54.

Caldwell, Robert. *Optimal Distribution Policy for Mobile Police Patrols.* Unpub. Ph.D. dissertation, Durham University, 1971.

Campbell, G.L. *Spatially Distributed Queuing Model for Police Patrol Sector Design.* Springfield, VA.: NTIS, 1972.
An analytic tool for studying deployment and dispatching of police patrol forces at the district and precinct levels.

Carlin, Jerry L. and Colin L. Moodie. "An Evaluation of Some Patrol Allocation Methods." *Police.* 16:1 (September, 1971), 56-60.

Chaiken, Jan M. and Richard C. Larson. *Methods for Allocating Urban Emergency Units.* N.Y.: Rand (May, 1971).

Chaiken, Jan M. *Number of Emergency Units Busy at Alarms Which Require Multiple Services.* Springfield, VA.: NTIS, 1971.
Mathematical formula for the deployment of urban emergency vehicles.

Chelst, K. *Interactive Approach to Police Sector Design—Working Paper.* Washington: NCJRS (Microfiche), 1974.

Elliott, J.F. "The Concept of an Offensively Deployed Police Force." *Police.* 13:1 (September-October, 1968), 65-71.

Elliott, J.F. *Interception Patrol—An Examination of the Theory of Random Patrol as a Municipal Police Tactic.* Springfield, IL.: C.C. Thomas, 1973.
Examination of the theory of random search and its application to crime prevention and criminal apprehension through the design of interception patrols.

EBM Data Processing Division. *LEMRAS—Law Enforcement Manpower Resource Allocation System.* Washington: NCJRS, (Microfiche), 1969.

Fischer, C.J. and R.L. Smith. "Tampa Selective Deployment." *Police Chief.* XXXVI:6 (June, 1969) 52-57.

Gaunt, Robert B. *Field Deployment of Police Patrol Forces and the Use of Electronic Data Processing Equipment.* Unpub. Master's thesis, Los Angeles: University of Southern California, 1965.

Giertz, J.F. *Economic Analysis of the Distribution of Police Patrol Forces.* Springfield, VA.: NTIS, 1970.

Gregory, J.L. "Patrol Distribution: The Need for Research." *Police.* 16:5 (1972), 35-39.

Kessler, Francis R. "Don't Ride a Dead Horse." *FBI Law Enforcement Bulletin.* 34:11 (November, 1965), 14-16.

Kinble, J.P. "Utilizing Field Personnel More Effectively." *Police Chief.* XXXV:3 (March, 1968), 12-15.

Kolesar, Peter and Warren E. Walker. *Simulation Model of Police Patrol Operations Executive Summary.* Santa Monica, CA.: Rand, 1975.

Kreutzer, W.F. "A Simplified Method of Patrol Distribution." *Police Chief.* XXXV:7 (July, 1968), 32-41.

Larson, R.C. *Illustrative Police Sector Redesign in District 4 in Boston.* Washington: NCJRS, (Microfiche), 1974.

Larsen, R.C. *Urban Police Patrol Analysis.* Cambridge, MA.: MIT University Press, 1969.

Lipsett, F.R. and J.G. Arnold. "Computer Simulation of Patrol Operations of a Semi-Rural Police Force." *Journal of Police Science and Administration.* 2:2 (June, 1974), 190-207.

Los Angeles Police Department. *Distribution of Personnel Within a Geographical Division.* Los Angeles: LAPD, 1965.

Meacham, Craig L. "Manpower Deployment Treaties for Cities in the 50,000 to 100,000 Classification." *Police.* 13:3 (January-February, 1969), 48-51.

McGuire, James T. "Put the Troopers Where the Action Is." *FBI Law Enforcement Bulletin.* 39:8 (August, 1970), 2-5, 26.

McHugh, William C. "Flexibility in Deployment of Police Patrols." *FBI Law Enforcement Bulletin.* 38:8 (August, 1969), 17-22.

Mitchell, P.S. "Optimal Selections of Police Patrol Boats." *Journal of Criminal Law, Criminology and Police Science.* 63:4 (1972), 577-584.

Morrison, G.I. "A Fluid Patrol Force Concept." *Law and Order.* 12:10 (October, 1964), 98-101.

Piggins, Edward S. "The Assignment and Distribution of Police Personnel for Most Effective Coverage." *IACP Yearbook.* Washington: IACP, 1956.

Police Beat Survey. Oakland, CA.: Statistical Bureau Oakland Police Department (August, 1955).

Skousen, W. Cleon. "Take Patrol Where the Action Is." *Law and Order.* 21:2 (February, 1973), 8-13.

St. Louis Metropolitan Police Department. *Allocation of Patrol Manpower Resources in St. Louis Police Department.* Vol. I and II: St. Louis Police Department (January, 1968).

St. Louis Metropolitan Police Department. *Use of an Incident Seriousness Index in the Deployment of Police Patrol Manpower. Methods and Conclusions.* Vol. I and II: Springfield, VA.: NTIS, 1972.
Study of the feasibility of using the Sellin-Wolfgang index of crime seriousness in order to distribute police patrols more effectively.

Walton, Frank E. "Selective Distribution of Police Patrol Force. *Journal of Criminal Law, Criminology and Police Science.* 49:2 (July-August, 1958), 165-171.

Walton, Frank E. "Selective Distribution of Police Patrol Force. History, Current Practices, Recommendations." *Journal of Criminal Law, Criminology and Police Science.* 49:4 (November-December, 1958), 379-390.

Wilson, O.W. *Distribution of Police Patrol Force.* Chicago: Public Administration Service, 1941.

FOOT PATROL

Bannon, James D. "Foot Patrol: The Litany of Law Enforcement." *Police Chief.* XXXIX:4 (April, 1972), 44-45.

Bryne, Edward C. "Mobile Patrol Supplemented By Use of Foot Patrols." *Law and Order.* 22:11 (November, 1974), 34, 36, 38, 40, 41.

Dynet, Robert. "A Case For the Foot Patrolman." *Law and Order.* 8:7 (July, 1960), 20, 22.

"Importance of Foot Patrol in the Large Cities." *The American City.* 65:17 (May, 1950).
Statistics on use of foot patrolmen.

Kinn, Richard M. "The Foot Patrolman Prevents Crimes." *The American City.* 75:95 (December, 1959).

Pendland, Melvin B. and Wayne G. Gay. "Foot Patrols: The Fort Worth Experience." *Police Chief.* XXXIX:4 (April, 1972), 46-48.

Perone, Ralph. "Basic Steps for the Man on Foot." *Law and Order.* 13:7 (July, 1965), 18-19.

MOTOR SCOOTER PATROL

Mende, Arnold L. "Motor Scooter Patrol." *Law and Order.* 14:6 (June, 1966), 26-28.

Mishkin, B.D. "Police Patrols in New York City." *International Criminal Police Review.* 28:265 (1973), 36-44.

Morche, J. and J. Colling. "Detroit's New 'Community Oriented Patrol." *Police.* 13:2 (November-December, 1968), 93-94.

"Scooter Patrol." *Spring 3100.* 41 (January, 1970), 9-15.

Spreen, Johannes F. "The Motor Scooter—An Answer to a Police Problem." *Journal of Criminal Law, Criminology and Police Science.* 57:2 (September, 1966), 349-353.

Wilson, J.V. *Experimental Use of Motor Scooters in Patrol and Tactical Operations—Final Narrative Report.* Baltimore, MD.: Williams & Wilkins, n/d.

ONE MAN CARS

Brannon, Bernard C. "A Report on One Man Police Patrol Cars in Kansas City." *Journal of Criminal Law, Criminology and Police Science.* 47:2 (July-August, 1956), 238-252.

Clowers, Norman L. "One and One-Half Man Cars?" *Police.* 4:4 (March-April, 1960), 78-79.

Day, Frank D. "The Issue of One Man vs. Two Man Police Patrol Cars." *Journal of Criminal Law, Criminology and Police Science.* 46:5 (January-February, 1956), 698-706.

Kirkwood, Robert H. "Effect of Single and Multiple Patrols on Police Fatalities." *Police.* 2:3 (January-February), 13-18.

"One Officer and a Suspicious Car." *Spring 3100.* 26:10 (November, 1955), 4-6.

Runyan, Richard T. and Samuel Ostertag. "The One Man Patrol Car." *Police.* 2:6 (July-August, 1958), 7-8; (September-October, 1958), 15-17; (November-December, 1958), 9-11.

Runyan, Richard T. and F. Samuel Ostertag. "The One Man Patrol Car—Approaching a Stopped Automobile." *Police.* 3:3 (January-February, 1959), 15-17.

Runyan, Richard T. and F. Samuel Ostertag. "The One Man Patrol Car—Overtaking and Stopping Felony Suspects." *Police.* 3:4 (March-April, 1959), 26-27.

Runyan, Richard T. and F. Samuel Ostertag. "The One Man Patrol Car—Patrol Procedure When a Crime is in Progress." *Police.* 4:3 (January-February, 1960), 60-61.

Runyan, Richard T. and F. Samuel Ostertag. "The One Man Patrol Car—The Role of the Dispatcher." *Police.* 4:2 (November-December, 1959), 6-7.

Runyan, Richard T. and F. Samuel Ostertag. "The One Man Patrol Car—Routine Operations Under Normal Conditions." *Police.* 4:4 (March-April, 1960), 17-18.

Runyan, Richard T. and F. Samuel Ostertag. "The One Man Patrol Car—Searching and Arresting Felons." *Police.* 3:5 (May-June, 1959), 6-8.

Spartenburg Police Department. *One Man Patrol Car.* Washington: NCJRS.
Series of training bulletins designed to facilitate the shift from a two-man system of automobile patrol to a one-man system.

Wilson, O.W. "One Man vs. Two Men in Patrol Cars." *Public Management* (April, 1940), 111-112.

RESPONSE TIME

Bammi, D. *Allocation of Police Beats to Patrol Units to Minimize Response Time to Calls for Service.* Washington: NCJRS, (Microfiche), n/d.

Bammi, D. and S.B. Smith. *Design of Police Patrol Beats to Minimize Response time to Calls for Service.* Washington: NCJRS, (Microfiche), n/d.

Bennett, W. and J. Dubois. *Use of Probability Theory in the Assignment of Police Patrol Areas.* Springfield, VA.: NTIS, 1970.
Program developed a system of random patrol that reduces the time required for an officer to respond to a call.

Goetzke, R.E. "Reduction of Variables in Police Response Time Measurement." *Law and Order.* 22:11 (November, 1974), 84-85.

Nerenstone, M.A. *Patrol Tactics to Minimize Response Time.* Washington: NCJRS, (Microfiche), 1970.

Pate, Tony et al. *Police Response Time—Its Determinants and Effects.* Washington: Police Foundation, 1976.

TACTICAL PATROL

Andersen, R.R. "Strike Force Against Street Crime." *FBI Law Enforcement Bulletin.* 41:5 (May, 1972), 3-5, 30.

Donald, Howard C. "Use of the 'H Units' by San Jose Police." *Police.* 8:2 (November-December, 1963), 35-36.

Eastman, George D. "The Flexible Unit—A Unique Striking Force." *Police.* 4:6 (July-August, 1960), 14-17.

Elliott, James. "An Experiment in Enforcement: The Crime Control Team." *Law and Order.* 17:12 (December, 1969), 98-102, 108.

Elliott, James Franklin and Thomas J. Sardino. *Crime Control Team, An Experiment in Municipal Police Department Management and Operations.* Springfield, IL: C.C. Thomas, 1971.

Forbus, Lloyd V. "Implementation of a Tactical Unit." *Law and Order.* 18:5 (May, 1970), 44-51.

Halper, Andrew and Richard Ku. *New York City Police Department Street Crime Unit.* Washington: LEAA, 1975.

Kelly, David B. "State Police Tactical Patrol—A Very Logical Conclusion. *Police Chief.* XL:5 (May, 1973), 66-69.

Mooney, William R. "The Special Operations Group." *FBI Law Enforcement Bulletin* (April, 1972), 11-14, 32.

Pileggi, Nicholas. "Gestapo or 'Elite'?—The Tactical Patrol Force." *The New York Times Magazine* (July 21, 1968).

Pitts, Connie H. "A Tactical Operations Unit." *FBI Law Enforcement Bulletin* (January, 1975), 10-13.

Wayne State University. *Model of and Problems Encountered in a Metropolitan Police Department—Final Report.* Springfield, VA.: NTIS, 1971.
The tactical operations system is defined as consisting of the operational systems of patrol and communications.

TAKE HOME VEHICLE PROGRAMS

Churchill, Winston L. "Twenty-four Hour Patrol Power." *FBI Law Enforcement Bulletin* (November, 1970), 2-5, 25.

Mullins, K.B. et al. *Preliminary Twelve Month Study of the Lexington (KY) Metropolitan Police Department's Home Fleet Plan*. Washington: NCJRS, 1974.

Prince George's County Police Department. *Personal Patrol Car Program' Evaluation Report*. Washington: NCJRS, 1973.

St. Paul Police Department—Take Home Vehicles—Progress Report. Washington: NCJRS, 1971.

Sweitzer, R.B. and G. San Felice. "The Personal Patrol Car Program. *FBI Law Enforcement Bulletin*. 42:9 (1973), 16-20.

Sweitzer, Roland B. and Glacamo San Felice. "The Personal Car Program for Police Officers." *Law and Order*. 21:11 (November, 1973), 50-55, 58.

Vanderbosch, Charles G. "Twenty-Four Hour Patrol Power." *Power Chief*. XXXVII:9 (September, 1970), 34.

TEAM POLICING

Angell, J. et al. *Evaluation Report on the Model Cities Team Policing Unit of the Holyoke (MA) Police Department*. Washington: NCJRS (Microfiche), 1972.

Bayer, William J. "Police Team Operations Guide." *Law and Order*. 23:6 (June, 1975), 60-64.

Bloch, Peter B. and David Specht. *Neighborhood Team Policing*. Washington: LEAA, 1973.

Bloch, Peter B. and Cyrus Ulberg. "The Beat Commander Concept." *Police Chief*. XXXIX:9 (September, 1972), 55-63.

Cordrey, John and Gary Pence. "An Analysis of Team Policing in Dayton." *Police Chief*. XXXIX:8 (August, 1972), 44-49.

Elliott, J.F., John F. O'Connor, Thomas J. Sardino. "Experimental Evaluation of the Crime Control Team Organization Concept." *Police*. 13:5 (May-June, 1970), 44-53.

Goodin, Carl V. "Effective Personalized Patrol." *Police Chief*. XXXIX:11 (November, 1972), 18-19, 66.

Holyoke Police Department. *Holyoke (MA) Team Police Experiment-Supplemental Reports and Appendices*. Washington: NCJRS, (Microfiche), 1973.

Kenny, John P. "Team Policing Organization. A Theoretical Model." *Police* (August, 1972).

Koverman, Robert B. "Team Policing: An Alternative to Traditional Law Enforcement Techniques." *Journal of Police Science and Administration*. 2:1 (March, 1974), 15-19.

McArdle, E.C. and W.N. Betjemann. "A Return To Neighborhood Police." *FBI Law Enforcement Bulletin*. 41:7 (1972), 8-11, 29.

Mitchell, Howard E. *Unit-Beat Policing in Great Britain*. A Technical Report to the Ford Foundation, Philadelphia: University of Pennsylvania, October, 1967.

Murphy, Patrick V. and Peter B. Bloch. "The Beat Commander." *Police Chief*. XXXVII:5 (May, 1970), 16-19.

O'Brien, John T. "The Neighborhood Task Force in New Brunswick, New Jersey." *Police Chief*. XLII:6 (June, 1975), 48-49.

O'Malley, H.C. *Holyoke (MA) Team Policing Experiment—Evaluation Report*. Washington: NCJRS (Microfiche), 1973.

Phelps, Lourn. "Richmond Police Department Revises Patrol System." *Journal of California Law Enforcement* (April, 1969), 185-190.

Phelps, Lourn G. and Lorne Harmon. "Team Policing—Four Years Later." *FBI Law Enforcement Bulletin*. 41:12 (December, 1972), 2-5, 28.

Phelps, L. and R. Murphy. "Team Patrol System in Richmond, CA." *Police Chief*. XXXVI:6 (June, 1969), 48-51.

Rand, Mark. "Unit Beat Policing: Time for a Fresh Approach." *Criminologist* (November, 1970).

Sepe, John. *Cop Team*. N.Y.: Pinnacle, 1975.

Sherman, Lawrence W. et al. *Team Policing: Seven Case Studies*. Washington: Police Foundation, 1973.

Skolnick, Jerome H. "The Berkeley Scheme: Neighborhood Police." *The Nation* (March 22, 1971), 372-373.

Smith, Lyle E. and Jack W. Greene. "The Tacoma Police Team." *Police Chief* (April, 1974), 42-45.

Tortoriello, Thomas R. and Stephen J. Blatt. "Client Service: Implications for Organizational Change." *Police Chief*. XLI:11 (November, 1974), 34-38.

Tortoriello, Thomas R. and Stephen J. Blatt. *Community Centered Team Policing: A Second Year Evaluation*. Dayton, OH.: Dayton Montgomery County Criminal Justice Center, 1973.

Wright State University. *Dayton—Police Department—Evaluation of the Community Centered Team Policing Program 1971*. Washington: NCJRS, (Microfiche), 1971.

INVESTIGATIVE METHODS AND TECHNIQUES

IDENTIFICATION OF PROPERTY

Bradley, Van Allen. *The Book Collectors Handbook of Values 1976-1977.* N.Y.: G.P. Putnam, 1975.
Details prices on first editions.

" 'Fingerprinting' Fine Arts." *Police.* 16:9 (May, 1972), 58, 63.
Description of the Chapman-Gerrard Coding Method for positive identification for works of art.

Gibson, John P. " 'Fingerprinting' Works of Art." *Police Chief.* 39:10 (October, 1972), 290-292.
Method for identifying paintings and other art objects. Also discusses the International Art Registry.

"How the New Diamond Fingerprinting System Works." *International Criminal Police Review.* 28:28 (1974), 222-223.
Eight tests are used to identify each diamond. 1-cut, 2-weight, 3-color, 4-clarity, 5-colorprint, 6-crystal print, 7-goniometer contour print, 8-grades of polishing.

Howell, David H. "Gem-Stone and Jewelry Identification." *National Police Officer.* 7 (April, 1938), 4-6.

Kovel, Ralph and Terry. *The Kovel's Complete Antiques Price Lists.* N.Y.: Crown, 1975.

Kovel, Ralph and Terry. *The Kovel's Collectors Guide to Limited Editions.* N.Y.: Crown, 1975.

Kovel, Ralph and Terry. *The Kovel's Official Bottle Price Lists.* N.Y.: Crown, 1975.

Liddicoat, Richard T., Jr. *Handbook of Gem Stone Identification.* 9th ed, LA: Gemological, 1972.

Policeman's Primer on Jewelry. N.Y.: Jeweler's Security Alliance of the United States, 1958.

Webster, Robert. "Fingerprinting Jewelry, 1975." *Criminologist.* 35:36 (1975), 15-20.

Webster, R. "The Role of Gemmology." *Medical Science Law.* 12P1 (1972), 31-42.

IDENTIFICATION OF PERSONS

Eye Witness Identification

Johnson, W.B. *Eyewitness Identification of Offenders—State-of-the-Art Survey and Research Recommendations.* Washington: NCJRS (Microfiche), 1973.

Sobel, Nathan. *Eye-Witness Identification: Legal and Practical Problems.* N.Y.: Boardman, 1972.

Wall, P.M. *Eye-Witness Identification in Criminal Cases.* Springfield, IL.: Charles C. Thomas, 1971.

Line-Ups

Doob, Anthony N. and Hershill Kirshenbaum. "Bias in Police Line-Ups—Partial Remembering." *Journal of Police Science and Administration.* 1:3 (September, 1973), 287-293.

Hicks, W. Lloyd. "Video Recording in Police Identification." *The Journal of Criminal Law, Criminology and Police Science.* 59:2 (June, 1968), 295-297.

"The Line-Up." *Spring 3100.* 23 (January, 1952), 6-9.

Milos, Charles. "Projecting Color Slides Replaces Old Police Line-Up." *Law and Order.* 17:4 (April, 1969), 22-26.

Pitts, Mahlon E. "How Sound is Your Police Line-Up." *FBI Law Enforcement Bulletin.* 40:12 (December, 1971), 2-6, 25.

Ringel, William E. *Identification and Police Line-Ups.* Binghamton, N.Y.: Gould, 1968.

Steele, W.W., Jr. "Kirby vs. Illinois: Counsel at Line-Ups." *Criminal Law Bulletin.* 9:1 (1973), 49-58.

Travelstead, C.E. "Legal Aspects of the Line-Up as an Identification Procedure." *Illinois Police Association Official Journal.* 27:1 (1974), 33-35.

Zeichner, Irving B. "Line-Up Identification Rules." *Law and Order.* 16:1 (January, 1968), 72.

Identification Kit

Cohen, Akiba A. "Number of Features, and Alternative Per Feature in Reconstructing Faces with the IdentiKit." *Journal of Police Science and Administration.* 1:3 (September, 1973), 349-354.

Kube, Nicholas J. "To the 'Pen' with Pencil." *Police.* 1:2 (November-December, 1956), 7-12.

Lombard, William. "Increase and Efficiency at Less Cost." *Law and Order.* 12:8 (August, 1964), 6-7.

MacAloon, Frank. "Building Faces for Suspect Identification." *Law and Order.* 21:2 (February, 1973), 76-77.

"A New Police Investigative Tool." *Police.* 4:3 (January-February, 1960), 16-17.

Owens, Courtney. "Identi-Kit Enters Its 2nd Decade—Ever Growing at Home and Abroad." *Fingerprint and Identification.* 52 (November, 1970).

Penry, J. "Photo-Fit." *Criminologist.* 9:31 (1974), 19-28.
Describes facial identification system for males and females.

Identification by Documents

Bell, Aaron. "Phony Driver's License Racket." *The California Highway Patrolman.* October, 1969.

Bennett, Ralph K. "Paper People: The Hidden Plague." *Readers Digest* (June, 1976), 99-102.

Drivers License Guide. Redwood City, CA.: Drivers License Guide, 1975.

Lex. "Case for Identity Cards." *Solicitors Journal.* (February 28, 1975). 142-144.

Yonamine, Ernest T. "Hawaii's Civil Identification Program." *FBI Law Enforcement Bulletin.* 43:12 (December, 1974), 12-13.

Physical Identification

Allen, A.L. *Personal Descriptions.* London: Butterworth & Co., 1950.

Allison, H.C. *Personal Identification.* Boston: Holbrook, 1973.
Methods used to identify suspects and victims.

Anderson, C.W.B. *The Facial Index System, An Aid to the Tracing of Persons "Wanted" by the Police.* Rangoon: British Burma Press, 1911.

Anghelescu, Ion. "Identification of Persons by Voice and Phonation in Rumania." *International Criminal Police Review.* 28:274 (January, 1974), 2-9.

Bachofner, Will. "Washington State Patrol's New Identification Section." *Law and Order.* 22:5 (May, 1974), 64-67.

Feldman, Sandor S. *Mannerisms of Speech and Gestures in Everyday Life.* N.Y.: International University Press, 1959.

Fisher, Edward C. "Identification Procedures and Constitutional Rights." *Traffic Digest and Review* (September and October, 1967).

Frappoli, Carlo L. "Nationwide Fingerprinting for Disaster Victim Identification." *Law and Order.* 11:5 (May, 1963), 26.

Frykholm, K.O. et al. "Marking of Dentures in Sweden." *International Police Review* (November, 1970).

Glanvill, Michael E. "Mistaken Identity." *Criminologist* (Summer, 1974), 70-72.

"Identification in Perspective." *FBI Law Enforcement Bulletin.* 39:3 (March, 1970), 8-10.
The legal aspects of identification.

Ronchese, Francesco. *Occupational Marks and Other Physical Signs, A Guide to Personal Identification.* N.Y.: Grune and Stratton, 1948.
Description of deformities and occupational diseases and characteristics.

Rouse, Allison M. "Pre-Trial Photo Identification." *Journal of California Law Enforcement* (July, 1973), 1-8.

Rudov, M.H. and E.S. Okonski. *Computer Aiding in the Human Identification of Criminal Suspects.* Springfield, VA.: NTIS, 1968.
Several esixting data systems were studied and used as a basis for the proposed appads (automatic processing of personal appearance data system).

Schildecker, Charles B. "Miami Police Inaugurate Video Identification." *FBI Law Enforcement Bulletin.* 36:11 (November, 1967), 14-18.
Miami Police Department program which video tapes each prisoner except traffic violators and drunks.

Sharp, Harold S. *Handbook of Pseudonyms and Personal Nicknames.* Metuchen, N.J.: Scarecrow, 1972.

Sully, Clifford. *Mistaken Identity.* N.Y.: Longmans, Green, 1925.

U.S. Immigration and Naturalization Service. *Foreign Versions of English Names.* Washington: U.S. Immigration and Naturalization Service, 1962.

Yin, R.K. *Face Recognition—A Special Process.* N.Y.: Rand, 1970.

Yonemura, G.T. *Image Quality Criterion for the Identification of Faces—Law Enforcement STARDS Program.* Washington: GPO, 1974.

Zavala, Albert and James J. Paley. *Personal Appearance Identification.* Springfield, IL.: C.C. Thomas, 1972.

INFORMATION SOURCES

Bouman, R. *Sources of Information and Their Use—An Outline.* Salem: Oregon Board on Police Standards and Training, 1968.

Carroll, John M. *Confidential Information Sources: Public and Private.* Los Angeles: Security World, 1975.

Foster, R.K. *World Post Marks.* N.Y.: Hippocrene, 1975.

International Telephone Directory. 19th ed., N.Y.: International Publications Service, 1975.

Liebers, Arthur and Carl Vollmer. *The Investigators Handbook.* N.Y.: Arco, 1954.

Murphy, Harry J. *Where's What.* N.Y.: Quadrangle, 1976.
Excellent document prepared by CIA for Security Investigations. Lists numerous sources of information.

Patterson, D. *World List of Forensic Science Laboratories.* London: The Forensic Science Society, n/d.

Price, Carroll S. "Sources of Information." *Police.* 4:3 (January-February, 1960), 30-35; 4:4 (March-April, 1960), 47-51.

Regency International Directory of Inquiry Agents, Private Detectives, Debt Collecting Agencies. 10th ed. N.Y.: International Publications Service, 1976.

Tannrath, A.M. *How to Locate Skips and Collect.* Chicago: John A. Patton, 1948.

Whatmore, Godfrey. *News Information. The Organization of Press Cuttings in the Libraries of Newspaper and Broadcasting Services.* London: Archon, 1965.

TRANSLATING SERVICES

American Translators Association. P.O. Box 129, Croton-on-Hudson, NY, 10520.
Has over 900 members and will answer inquiries.

Finley, Ian F. *Language Services in Industry.* Brooklyn Heights, N.Y.: Beekman, 1973.

Into English Translations. 124-128 North 4th Street, Camden, N.J.
Information Services: provides translation, consulting and literature-searching, duplication, and abstracting indexing cards for a fee.

INFORMANTS

Bennett, Wayne. "Contacting and Paying Informants." *Law and Order.* 21:4 (April, 1973), 28-31.

Cochran, Murray. "Should Police Departments or Individual Officers Make Deals." *Police Chief* (March, 1972).

DeGarmo, James W., Jr. "Confidential Informants, Whose?" *Law and Order.* 20:4 (April, 1972), 80-83.

Fisher, Edward C. "Police Use of Informers." *Traffic Digest and Review* (June, 1967).

Gutterman, Melvin. "The Informer Privilege." *The Journal of Criminal Law, Criminology and Police Science.* 58:2 (March, 1967), 32-64.

Harney, Malachi L. and John C. Cross. *The Informer in Law Enforcement.* 2nd ed., Springfield, IL.: C.C. Thomas, 1968.

"The Informers Privilege Versus The Constitution: A Doctrinal Dilemma." *Journal of Criminal Law, Criminology and Police Science.* 50 (1960).

"The Informer Privilege: What's In A Name?" *The Journal of Criminal Law and Criminology.* 46 (1973).

"The Informer's Privilege: Should It Be Recognized in Grand Jury Proceedings: Should It Be Extended to Civic Anti-Crime Organizations?" *Journal of Criminal Law, Criminology and Police Science.* 46 (1956).

Katsampes, Paul L. "Informants: Motivations and Inducements." *Police.* 16:4 (December, 1971), 52-53.

Lewes, Milton. "Portrait of an Informer." *This Week* (March 22, 1964).

Lunday, Joseph R. "The Invisible Police." *Nation.* 209 (December 8, 1969), 629-632.

McCollum, T.P. "Sketching the Parameters of the Informer Privileges." *American Criminal Law Review.* 13:1 (1975), 117-137.

Marx, Gary T. "Thoughts on a neglected category of social movement participants: The agent provocateur and the informant." *American Journal of Sociology.* 80:2 (1974), 402-442.

North, Steven E. ". . .The Whole Truth—Protecting Your Informant." *Law and Order.* 22:6 (June, 1974), 80-81.

Rissler, Larry E. "The Informer's Identity at Trial." *FBI Law Enforcement Bulletin* (February, 1975), 21-25.

Robertson, Geoffrey. *Reluctant Judas: The Life and Death of the Special Branch Informer Kenneth Lennon.* London: Temple Smith, 1976.

Seibert, J.L. and G.T. Gitchoff. "The Strategy of Narcotics Law Enforcement: Its Implication and Effects." *Journal of Drug Issues.* 2:4 (1972), 29-36.

Tyler, Roy A. "Police Use of Informants in the Preparation of Search Warrants." *Police Chief.* XXXVII:11 (November, 1971), 24-25.

Walsh, J.L. "Research Note: Cops and 'Stool Pigeons'—Professional Striving and Discretionary Justice in European Police World." *Law Society Review.* 7:2 (1972), 229-306.

MEMORY AND OBSERVATION

Basinger, Louis F. *The Techniques of Observation and Learning Retention.* Springfield, IL.: C.C. Thomas, 1973.

Cole, J.H. "Motion Pictures Provide Memory for Investigators." *Law and Order.* 14:2 (February, 1966), 26, 28-31.

Hogan, John C. and Mortimer D. Schwartz. "The Manly Art of Observation and Deduction." *Journal of Criminal Law, Criminology and Police Science.* 55:1 (March, 1964), 157-164.

Lawder, Lee E. "The Detectives' Most Important Tool: Memory and Observation." *Law and Order.* 18:12 (December, 1970), 96-98.

Penry, J. *Looking at Faces and Remembering Them. A Guide to Facial Identification.* London: Elek, 1971.

MODUS OPERANDI

McArthur, Jack. "Modus Operandi: Traditional Police Tool with Some Modern Innovations." *Police.* 10:4 (March-April, 1966), 15-21.

Modus Operandi and Crime Reporting. Sacramento: Bureau of Criminal Identification and Investigation, 1961.

Monroe, Keith. "The Detective Who Never Sleeps." *The Saturday Evening Post.* CCXXVI (October 15, 1953).

SURVEILLANCE

Brindy, James. "Simplified Memory Jogger." *Law and Order.* 16:5 (May, 1968), 106.
Use of a simple form to check off vehicle details. Useful in surveillance.

Cox, D.P. *Equipment Systems Limitations in Surveillance Operations—Equipment Systems Improvement Program Report.* Washington: NCJRS, 1973.

DeGarmo, James W., Jr. "The Nature of Physical Surveillances." *The Police Chief.* XLII:2 (February, 1975), 57-58.

Feaker, Fred E. "Patrol—Surveillance Carl." *Law and Order.* 21:11 (November, 1973), 74-77.

King, Douglas W. "Surveillance Made Easier." *Law and Order.* 13:1 (January, 1965), 18-21.

Nugent, Howard W. "Surveillance in the Investigation of Arson and Other Felonies." *Police.* 9:4 (March-April, 1965), 39-41.

Piersante, Vincent W. "Surveillance Techniques." *Police.* 10:1 (September-October, 1965), 72-78.

Shaw, William. "Miniature Tracking Transmitters." *Law and Order* (January, 1973), 24.

Shaw, William. "The Legal Aspects of Radio Beacon Tracking Transmitters." *Law and Order* (September, 1973), 32.

Siljander, Raymond P. *Applied Surveillance Photography.* Springfield, IL.: C.C. Thomas, 1975.

UNDERCOVER

Agnew, Derek. *Undercover—Agent Narcotics: The Dramatic Story of a World Secret War Against Drug Racketeers.* London: Souvenir, 1959.

Barefoot, J. Kirk. *Undercover Investigations.* Springfield, IL.: C.C. Thomas, 1976.

Barefoot, J. Kirk. *Undercover Operations.* Springfield, IL.: C.C. Thomas, 1975.

Berdin, R., R. Seaver and J. Seaver. *Code Name Richard.* N.Y.: E.P. Dutton, 1974.
An Autobiography of the 'control man' who broke the French Connection with his testimony.

"CBS or Cops? Police Disguised as Newsmen." *Newsweek* (September 23, 1968), 90.

Divale, William Tulio. *I Lived Inside the Campus Revolution:* N.Y.: Cowles, 1970.

Dix, G.E. "Undercover Investigations and Police Rulemaking." *Texas Law Review.* 53:1 (1975), 203-294.
Lengthy article which examines legal and other aspects of police under cover operations.

Green, James J. "Plainclothed Police Personnel: An Identification Problem." *FBI Law Enforcement Bulletin* (April, 1975), 16-21.

Hicks, Randolph D. *Undercover Operations and Persuasion.* Springfield, IL: C.C. Thomas, 1973.

Mohr, R. "Quite Legal, Quite Ethical: Espionage at Kent State." *Nation* (January 29, 1973).

Motto, C.J. *Undercover.* Springfield, IL.: C.C. Thomas, 1971.

"Police Infiltration of Dissident Groups." *Journal of Criminal Law, Criminology and Police Science.* 61:2 (June, 1970), 181-194.

Sellas, Precy. "Surveillance in a Go-Go Club." *Law and Order.* 15:2 (February, 1967), 26-32.
Use of movie camera by undercover officers.

Thompson, Ron. "How to Shoot Undercover Pictures That Get Convictions." *Law and Order* (April, 1974), 36.

Trendle, N.B. "Undercover Operator." *Australian Police Journal* (October, 1975), 281-287.

U.S. Department of the Army. *Techniques of Surveillance and Undercover Investigations.* Washington: Department of the Army, November 2, 1965.

Whited, Charles. *Chiodo Undercover Cop.* Chicago: Playboy, 1974.

CRIMINAL INVESTIGATION

INVESTIGATION—GENERAL

Andrews, Allen. *Intensive Inquiries.* N.Y.: St. Martin's, 1973.

Berg, Stanton O. "Sherlock Holmes: Father of Scientific Crime Detection." *Criminologist.* 6 (Winter, 1971), 19-32.

Block, Eugene. *The Vindicators.* N.Y.: Pocket Books, 1965.
Popular account of cases where police have investigated to prove innocence of suspected and convicted persons.

Bowden, K.J. "Criminal Investigation and the Methodology of the Science." *The Australian Police Journal* (July, 1958).

Brett, Dennis T. *Crime Detection.* Cambridge, England: National Book League, 1959.

Brierley, J. "Series Incident Squad." *Police World* (British Section), 17 (1972), 10-14.
Each crew consists of an investigator, a scientific aids office and a vehicle examiner.

Buckden, J. "A Special Police Inquiry Team Could Share That Nationwide Inquiry Load." *Police Review.* 83:4313 (1975), 1144-1145.
Suggests temporary teams be organized to meet special needs.

Chapman, S.G. and D.E. Clark. "The Investigative Priority Index Concept." *International Criminal Police Review.* 27:261 (1972), 221-229.

Clark, Thurston and John J. Tigue, Jr. *Dirty Money.* Simon & Schuster, 1975.
Discusses white collar crime. Swiss and tax haven banks. Money washing and other financial crimes.

Cochran, Murray O. "Should Police Departments or Individual Officers Make Deals." *Police Chief* (March, 1972).

Deeley, Peter. *The Manhunters.* London: Hodder & Stoughton, 1970.

"Detective Division." *Spring 3100.* 22 (July-August, 1951), 9-17.

Department of Defense. *Investigative Legal Principles.* Washington: GPO, n/d.

Dienstein, William. *Techniques for the Crime Investigator.* Springfield, IL.: C.C. Thomas, 1974.

Ellison, Katherine and John M. Burney. "Dealing With The Victim During Investigation." *FBI Law Enforcement Bulletin* (April, 1975), 13-15.

Fischer, Jacob. *The Art of Detection.* New Brunswick, N.J.: Rutgers University Press, 1948.

Fitzgerald, M.J. and P.B. Weston. *Handbook of Criminal Investigation.* N.Y.: Arco, 1951.

Fricke, Charles W. *Criminal Investigation and the Law.* LA.: Legal Book Corp., 1975.

Gerber, Samuel R. and Oliver Schroeder, Jr. *Criminal Investigation and Interrogation.* 1972 rev. ed. with 1972

Appendix of Supplemental Material. Cincinnati: W.H. Anderson, 1972.
Series of edited lectures dealing with scientific aids to investigation, surveillance, observation and description, interrogation, and investigation of specific crimes.

Gleason, Everett. "Detective Bureau Plays Vital Part in Police Work." *FBI Law Enforcement Bulletin*. 26:11 (November, 1957), 11-14.

Greenberg, B. and J.L. Fenton. *Enhancement of the Investigative Function, V. 3—Investigative Procedures—Selected Task Evaluation—Final Report—Phase 2*. Springfield, VA.: NTIS, 1973.

Greenberg, B. and O.S. Yu. *Enhancement of the Investigative Function, V. 1—Analysis and Conclusions—Final Report—Phase 1*. Springfield, VA.: NTIS, 1972.

Gross, H. and R.L. Jackson. *Criminal Investigation—A Practical Textbook for Magistrates, Police Officers and Lawyers*. 5th ed. London: Sweet & Maxwell, 1962.

Guven, E. "The Importance of Time and Place in Crime Investigation." *International Criminal Police Review* (April, 1967), 118-120.

Horgah, John J. *Criminal Investigation*. NY: McGraw-Hill, 1974.
Text encompassing guidelines and requisites for all phases of investigative operations and examining specific offenses and related investigative techniques.

Houghton, Robert A. "Los Angeles Police Department Experiments with Investigator Unification." *Journal of California Law Enforcement* (April, 1969), 209-212.

Inbau, Fred E. "The Social and Ethical Requirements of Criminal Investigation and Prosecution." *Criminal Law Quarterly*. 3 (1960).

Kauffman, R. "Changing Role of the County Sheriff, Part 5 Team Policing—The Generalist Investigation Role." *Police Chief*. 43:8 (August, 1976), 79-83.

Kelley, Clarence M. "Major Case Squad for Metropolitan Areas." *FBI Law Enforcement Bulletin* (May, 1973), 23-25.

Kirk, Paul L. *Crime Investigation*. 2nd ed. N.Y.: Wiley, 1974.

Leonard, V.A. *Criminal Investigation and Identificaion*. Springfield, IL.: C.C. Thomas, 1971.

Leonard, V.A. *The Police Detective Function*. Springfield, IL.: C.C. Thomas, 1970.

Liebers, Arthur and Carl Vollmer. *Investigators Handbook*. 3rd ed., N.Y.: Arco, 1972.

Luisi, Gerhard and Charles Samuels. *How To Catch 5,000 Thieves*. N.Y.: Macmillan, 1962.

Markle, Arnold. *Criminal Investigation and Presentation of Evidence*. St. Paul, MN.: West, 1976.

Muller, Howard W. "The Training and Practice of the Criminal Investigator." *Law and Order*. 19:2 (February, 1971), 42-44, 46, 48, 55.

O'Hara, Charles E. *Fundamentals of Criminal Investigation*. 3rd ed. Springfield, IL.: C.C. Thomas, 1973.

Ostler, R.D. "Criminal Investigation—Criminals Incorporated." *Police Journal*. 38:4 (April, 1965), 161-174.

Prestbo, John A. *Sleuthing*. Homewood, IL.: Dow Jones, 1976.

Randall, Richard W. "Contact Lenses." *Law and Order*. 16:4 (April, 1968), 30.

Samen, Charles S. "Questions and Answers." *Law and Order*. 20:9 (September, 1972), 58-59.

Small, Edward. "The Detective Function." *Police*. 13:4 (March-April, 1969), 68-73.

Soderman, Harry and John J. O'Connell. *Modern Criminal Investigation*. 5th ed. N.Y.: Funk & Wagnalls, 1962.

Souryal, Safwat S. "The SCART of Criminal Investigation." *Journal of Police Science and Administration*. 2:4 (December, 1974), 444-457.

Southwestern Law Enforcement Institute. *Institute of Criminal Investigation*. Springfield, IL.: C.C. Thomas, 1962.

Svensson, Arne and Otto Wendel. *Crime Detection*. N.Y.: Eisevier Press, 1955.

U.S. Department of the Army. *Military Police Investigations (FM 19-20)*. Washington: GPO, 1967.

Vanderbosch, Charles G. *Criminal Investigation*. 2nd ed., Gaithersburg, MD.: IACP, 1971.

Ward, Richard H. *Introduction to Criminal Investigation*. Reading, MD.: Addison-Wesley, 1975.

Weston, Paul B. and Kenneth M. Wells. *Criminal Investigation for Police*. Englewood Cliffs, N.J.: Prentice-Hall, 1976.

Williamson, F.F. "The Investigation Officer." *Journal of The Forensic Science Society* (October, 1968).

Willmer, M.A. *Crime and Information Theory*. Chicago: Aldine, 1970.
The struggle between the police and criminal is represented in a theoretical game situation as a battle over information.

Younger, Evelle J. "Practical Tips of Potential Value in Conducting Investigations." *Journal of California Law Enforcement* (July, 1967), 41-43.

AIRCRAFT ACCIDENTS

Aircraft Fire Investigators Manual. Boston: National Fire Protection, 1972.

Great Britain Department of Trade. *Memorandum of the Investigation of Civil Air Accidents*. rev. ed., Washington: NCJRS, (Microfiche), 1974.

Harper, Charles R. "Aircraft Accident Investigation." *Police Chief* (November, 1963).

ANONYMOUS LETTERS

Mendelsohn, Oscar. *Liars and Letters Anonymous*. Melbourne, Aust: Lansdowne Press, 1961.

Russell, Robert B. "The Anonymous Letter Writer." *Law and Order*. 13:10 (October, 1965), 8-9.

Shulenberger, W.A. "Anonymous Letters." *Identification News*. 13:6 (June, 1963), 4-6.

ARSON

Adams, J.Q. "Incendiary Devices and Methods." *The Fire and Arson Investigator.* 13:1 (July-September, 1962), 39-51.

Adams, John Q. "Searching the Fire Scene." *Police.* 9:1 (September-October, 1964), 15-19.

Aletto, William C. "Organizing An Arson Squad in Fire Departments of Large Cities." *Police* (March-April, 1968).

Ashcroft, J.W. *Investigation of Fires, Issued for the Guidance of Police Officers and Others.* London: HMSO, 1949.

"Automobile Fire Investigation." *Police.* 3:2 (November-December, 1958), 16-18; 3:3 (January-February, 1959), 6-10; 3:4 (March-April, 1959), 7-11.

Barlay, S. *Fire. An International Report.* London: Hamish Hamilton, 1972.
Review of thousands of case histories of fires in Europe, the U.S. and Australia. Topics cover all aspects of fire including fire investigation, arson and pyromania.

Barracato, John. *Arson!* N.Y.: Norton, 1976.

Battle, Brendon P. and Paul B. Weston. *Arson: A Handbook of Detection and Investigation.* N.Y.: Greenberg, 1954.

Bennett, Glenn D. "The Arson Investigator and Technical Aids." *Journal of Criminal Law, Criminology and Police Science.* 49:2 (July-August, 1958), 172-177.

Bennett, Glenn D. "The Detroit Arson Squad." *Police.* 4:4 (March-April, 1960), 38-42.

Berdan, George W. "Investigation of Wildland Fires." *Police.* 7:6 (July-August, 1963), 45-52.

Best, L. Morris. "Some Practical Factors in Arson Investigations." *FBI Law Enforcement Bulletin* (January, 1958), 11-13.

Cobb, S.S., Jr. "At the Fire Scene." *Police.* 5:4 (March-April, 1961), 28-31.

Connor, J.A. "Arson Investigation." *Military Police Law Enforcement Journal.* 1:5 (1975), 50-51.

Davis, Joseph H. "Suicide By Fire." *Journal of Forensic Sciences.* 8:4 (October, 1962), 393-397.

DeArmond, H.T. "Automobile Arson Investigation." *Fire Arson Investigation.* 25:3 (1975), 16-18.

Doud, Donald. "Investigation of Charred Documents." *Police.* 8:5 (May-June, 1964), 17-21.

Econ, Dan. "Physical Evidence in Arson Investigations." *Police.* 5:5 (May-June, 1961), 57-62.

Feeheley, Thomas J. "Arson Evidence." *Police.* 10:3 (January-February, 1966), 31-38.

Feeheley, Thomas J. "Suggestions for Improving Arson Investigations." *Journal of Criminal Law, Criminology and Police Science.* 47:3 (September-October, 1956), 357-367.

Fire Fighters Responsibility in Arson Detection. rev. ed., Boston: National Fire Protection, 1971.

"Fire Investigation Into Cause and Criminal Investigations of Arson." *Utah Peace Officer* (September, 1970), 24-27.

Fitch, Richard D. and Edward A. Porter. *Accidental or Incendiary.* Springfield, IL.: C.C. Thomas, 1968.

Fox, Vernon. "The Behavioral Criminologist in Arson Investigation." *Police.* 7:3 (January-February, 1963), 68-70.

Glassman, Mitchell. "The Applicability of the Mail Fraud Statute to Arson Cases." *Police.* 8:4 (March-April, 1964), 17-19.

Gold, Louis H. "Psychiatric Profile of the Firesetter." *Journal of Forensic Sciences.* 7:4 (October, 1962), 404-417.

Hendrickson, Dar. "Determining the Origin and Cause of Fire." *Police.* 8:3 (January-February, 1964), 32-36.

Hill, C.P. "Cleaning, Overhauling and Securing the Fire Scene." *Fire and Arson Investigator.* 16:4 (April-June, 1966), 43-51.

Hopper, William H. "Arson's Corpus Delicti." *Journal of Criminal Law, Criminology and Police Science.* 47:1 (May-June, 1956), 118-119.

Hopper, William H. "Burning Time—Candles." *Police.* 8:6 (July-August, 1964), 14-16.

Hopper, William H. "Circumstantial Aspects of Arson." *Journal of Criminal Law, Criminology and Police Science.* 46:1 (May-June, 1955), 129-134.

Hopper, William H. "Elements Necessary for an Arson Conviction." *Police.* 1:1 (September-October, 1956), 14-19.

Huron, Benjamin S. and Donald M. O'Brien. *Elements of Arson Investigation.* N.Y.: Reuben M. Donnelly, 1963.

Hurtean, William K. "Arson Investigation and the Collecting of Evidence." *Security World.* 11:3 (March, 1974), 18-19.

Johnson, Allen. "Fingerprints of Fire." *Police.* 6:5 (May-June, 1962), 55-60.

Joling, Robert J. "Legal Commentaries on Suicide by Fire." *Journal of Forensic Sciences.* 7:4 (October, 1962), 397-403.

Keller, E. John. "Fire Investigation—An Act of Coordination and Cooperation." *Law and Order.* 21:9 (September, 1973), 97, 103.

Kelly, R.A. "How Fire Detectives Track Down Arson." *Popular Science* (November, 1961).

Kennedy, John. "Investigation Arson Incentives." *Journal of Criminal Law, Criminology and Police Science.* 47:6 (March-April, 1957), 709-716.

Kettering, Paul T. "Magnesium Bombs in Arson." *Law and Order.* 12:6 (June, 1964), 76-77.

Key, D.N. "Techniques of Automobile Fire Investigation." *International Association of Arson Investigation News Letter.* 11 (1952).

Krik, Paul L. *Fire Investigation.* N.Y.: Wiley, 1969.

Lawder, Lee. "Robbery with a Match." *Law and Order.* 8:1 (January, 1960), 8-10, 12.

Leahy, D.L. "With an Eye Towards Arson." *Fire Arson Investigator.* 25:1 (1974), 34-41.

Lying, John R.X. "Arson Motives." *Law and Order.* 17:11 (November, 1969), 96-114.

Lockwood, Joseph E. "Arson and Sabotage." *Journal of Criminal Law, Criminology and Police Science.* 45:3 (September-October, 1954), 340-348.

Macdonald, John M. "Many Motivations Are Behind Acts of the Arsonist." *FBI Law Enforcement Bulletin* (July, 1960).

May, Robert E. "Arson: The Most Neglected Crime on Earth." *The Police Chief* (July, 1974).

Nicol, Joseph D. and Lee Overley. "Combustibility of Automobiles: Results of Total Burning." *Journal of Criminal Law, Criminology and Police Science.* 54:3 (September, 1963), 366-368.

Priar, L.L. "Clues and Leads in Arson Investigation." *Police.* 5:1 (September-October, 1960), 52-58, 64.

"Problems of Arson Investigation Arising under State Fire Marshal Acts." *Journal of Criminal Law, Criminology and Police Science.* 47:4 (November-December, 1956), 457-467.

Reineri, Louis, Jr. "Physical Evidence in Auto Arson Investigation." *Police.* 4:2 (November-December, 1959), 25-28.

Ross, I. "Fraud Fires Flare Up: Arson for Profit." *Reader's Digest* (May, 1965).

Rossiter, William D. "Investigation of Fires Resulting in Death." *Police.* 4:5 (May-June, 1960), 39-42; (July-August, 1960), 31-33.

Rossiter, William D. "Techniques in Handling Arson Investigations." *FBI Law Enforcement Bulletin.* 26:4 (April, 1957), 4-7.

Salzenstein, Marvin A. "Spontaneous Combustion." *Police.* 6:5 (May-June, 1962), 52-54.

Savage, John J. "Arson Case Preparation." *Police.* 10:1 (September-October, 1965), 26-29.

Savage, John J. "Investigative Techniques Applied to Arson Investigation." *Journal of Criminal Law, Criminology and Police Science.* 48:2 (July-August, 1957), 213-218.

Schmideberg, Melitta. "Pathological Firesetters." *Journal of Criminal Law, Criminology and Police Science.* 44 (1954), 54.

Schuck, J.P. "Rural Investigation of Arson." *Police.* 5:6 (July-August, 1961), 28-33.

Shifflett, Glen A. "Investigating Automobile Fire Causes." *Journal of Criminal Law, Criminology and Police Science.* 49:3 (September-October, 1958), 276-279.

Smith, Miles B. "The Investigator Arrives at the Fire Scene." *Police.* 7:4 (March-April, 1963), 59-65.

Smith, W.O. "Debt-Ridden Autos Big Business." *International Association of Arson Investigation News Letter.* 11:1 (July-September, 1960), 16-19.

Steinmetz, Richard C. "Investigation of Incendiary and Sabotage Fires." *Police Journal (NY)* 27 (November-December, 1941), 3, 22-24.

Stevens, S.L. "Physical Evidence in Arson Investigation." *Police.* 6:1 (September-October, 1961), 52-55.

Stewart, William D., Jr. "Arson Device? The Case of an Electromechanical Hookah." *Journal of Police Science and Administration.* 2:2 (June, 1974), 208-209.

Straeter, Raymond L. "Insurance Motive Fires." *Journal of Criminal Law, Criminology and Police Science.* 46:2 (July-August, 1955), 277-280.

Sutton, B. "Pyromania and Psychopathic Firesetters." *Fire Arson Investigator.* 25:2 (1974), 23-36.

"Teamwork in Fire Scene and Arson Investigations." *Fire Arson Investigator.* 25:3 (1975), 22-26.

Tuttle, Harris B. "Photography Plays Major Role in Arson Investigation." *Police.* 8:2 (November-December, 1963), 40-43.

Wakefield, E.A. "Arson." *Royal Canadian Mounted Police Gazette* (October, 1949).

Wakefield, E.A. "Rural Arson Problems." *Journal of Criminal Law, Criminology and Police Science.* 46:1 (January-February, 1955), 613-620.

Walker, Glenroy M. "Recognition, Collection and Preservation of Evidence in Arson Cases." *Police.* 5:2 (November-December, 1960), 61-63; 5:3 (January-February, 1961), 60-61.

Watson, A.S. "Arson Investigation." *Security Gazette.* 13:10 (1971).

Wetherington, W.R. "Establishing the Point of Origin and Determining the Cause." *Fire and Arson Investigator.* 16:4 (April-June, 1966), 2-7.

ART CRIME

Adams, Laurie. *Art Cop.* NY: Dodd Mead, 1974.

Arnold, David O. *Sculptures.* Berkeley, CA.: Glendessary, 1970.

Baynes-Cope, A.D. "Frauds and Forgeries in Libraries and Museums." *Journal of Forensic Science Society.* 13:3 (1973), 169-174.

Baynes-Cope, A.D. "Museum Frauds and Forgeries—Intentional and Unintentional." *Medical-Legal Journal.* 43:1 (1975), 25-34.

Bossard, A. "Theft of Cultural Property." *International Criminal Police Review.* 28:276 (1974), 58-74.

"Chemical Standards May Authenticate Art Work." *Science News Letter* (November 6, 1965).

Clamen, Michel. "Museums and the Theft of Works of Art." *International Criminal Police Review* (February, 1975), 51-58.

Cole, Sonia M. *Counterfeit.* N.Y.: Abelard-Schuman, 1957.
Forgery of works of art.

DeWaal, H. Van. T. Wurtenberger and W. Froentjes. *Aspects of Art Forgery.* The Hague, Netherlands: Martinus Nijhoff, 1962.

Esterow, Milton. *The Art Stealers.* NY: Macmillan, 1966.

Fleming, Stuart J. *Authenticity in Art: The Scientific Detection of Forgery.* Bristol, GB: Institute of Physics, 1975.

Forbes, J.S. "Fakes and Forgeries of British Antique Silverware." *The Criminologist* (February, 1969).

Jeppson, Lawrence. *The Fabulous Fraud: Fascinating Tales of Great Art Forgeries.* N.Y.: Weybright & Talley, 1970.

Leitch, David. *The Discriminating Thief.* N.Y.: Holt, Rhinehart & Winston, 1969.
Story of Xavier Richier, Master Art Thief in France in the 1960s.

Mendax, Fritz. *Art Fakes and Forgeries.* N.Y.: Philosophical Library, 1956.

Middlemas, Keith. *Double Market: Art Theft and Art Thieves.* Farnborough: Heath, 1975.

Moat, Edward. *Memoirs of an Art Thief.* London: Arlington Books, 1976.

Pollock, George. "Scotland Yard Masters the Art Thieves." *Reader's Digest* (February, 1974), 65, 67, 69.

Savage, Gordon. "Crooks Cash in on Antiques Trade." *Antiques Trade Gazette* (July 3, 1976), 1.

Schuller, Sepp. *Forgers, Dealers, Experts. A Strange Chapter in the History of Art.* N.Y.: Putnams, 1960.

"Still Life with Pasta; Forging of Modern Italian Masters." *Newsweek* (June 28, 1965).

Tegel, Heinrich F. "New Problems for the Police Within the European Art Business." *Journal of Criminal Law, Criminology and Police Science.* 53 (1962).

Thompson-Noel, Michael. "Art Thefts: The White Collar Crime Wave." *Financial Times.* 19 (January, 1974), 15.

United Nations Social Defense Research Institute. *Protection of the Artistic and Archaeological Heritage: A View from Italy and India.* Rome: UN Social Defense Research Institute, 1976.

Whitehead, John. *This Solemn Mockery: The Art of Literary Forgery.* New Rochelle, N.Y.: Arlington, 1973.

AUTO THEFTS

"Auto Theft." *FBI Law Enforcement Bulletin.* April, 1957.

"Auto Theft Ring Broken by Joint Investigation." *FBI Law Enforcement Bulletin.* August, 1953.

"Auto Theft Rings." *FBI Law Enforcement Bulletin* August, 1971.

"Auto Thefts—Causes and Prevention." *FBI Law Enforcement Bulletin* (July, 1963).

"Automobile Theft." *FBI Law Enforcement Bulletin* (January, 1975).

Brickell, David. *Vehicle Theft Investigation.* Santa Cruz, CA.: Davis, 1975.

Chilimidos, R.S. *Auto Theft Investigation.* LA: Legal Book Corporation, 1971.

Connelie, William G. "New York St. Auto Theft Unit Investigates Auto Crash Parts Business." *Police Chief* (December, 1976).

Davis, William J. "Resume of National Automobile Theft Bureau Services." *FBI Law Enforcement Bulletin* (December, 1953).

Deaken, Donna. "Automobile Body Primers: Their Application in Vehicle Identification." *Journal of Forensic Science* (April, 1975).

"Fake Automobile Titles." *FBI Law Enforcement Bulletin* (February, 1952).

Glab, Jim. "Is That Car Running Hot?" *Law and Order* (June, 1976).

Gothard, J.A. "Evaluation of Automobile Paint Flakes as Evidence." *Journal of Forensic Science* (July, 1976).

Hansson, Paul F. and John Daniel. "Organization of a Modern Auto Theft Bureau." *FBI Law Enforcement Bulletin* (November, 1955).

"Keys to Thefts: Master-Key Mail Order Houses Make Car Thievery Easy." *Newsweek* (August 9, 1965).

"Systems Used in Professional Car Theft Operations." *FBI Law Enforcement Bulletin* (January, 1952).

Themes, Leonard. "Auto-Theft Investigation Kit." *FBI Law Enforcement Bulletin* (November, 1964).

"Tools of Auto Theft Trade." *FBI Law Enforcement Bulletin* (July, 1953).

"Use of Junk Titles for Stolen Automobiles." *FBI Law Enforcement Bulletin* (April, 1952).

"Vehicle Engine Identification Numbers." *The Police Chief* (May, 1972).

Vehicle Identification Guide. N.Y.: Motor Vehicle Identification Guide, 1975.

Vehicle Theft Investigation Manual. Gaithersburg, MD: IACP, 1972.

Williams. Thomas A. "Auto Theft: The Problem and the Challenge." *FBI Law Enforcement Bulletin* (December, 1968).

BOMB INCIDENTS

Bomb Incidents—Investigation

"As Bombing in the U.S. Soar; Who's to Blame, The Motives." *U.S. News and World Report* (May 17, 1971), 25.

"Bomb Scene Investigations and the FBI Laboratory." *FBI Law Enforcement Bulletin* (March, 1972).

"Bombing: A Way to Protest and Death; Bombs Exploding at the Manhattan Headquarters of Mobil Oil, IBM and General Telephone and Electronics." *Time* (March 23, 1970), 8.

"Bombing the Banks." *Time* (January 17, 1972), 18.

Brodle, Thomas G. *Bombs and Bombings—A Handbook to Detection, Disposal and Investigation for Police and Fire Departments.* Springfield, IL.: C.C. Thomas, 1972.

Durfee, Richard A. *Bombs, Explosives and Incendiary Devices.* Cocoa Beach, FL: Police Science Press, 1961.

Fagerstrom, Dorothy. "Danger Bosquad at Work." *Law and Order* (November, 1962).

Gjerde, John. "The Mystery of 'The Wednesday Grenade Man'." *FBI Law Enfocement Bulletin.* 37:1 (January, 1968), 17-20.

Lamb, Ralph J. "Clark County Explosive Ordinance Detail." *FBI Law Enforcement Bulletin.* 38:11 (November, 1969), 3-6, 19.

"Law Enforcement and the Handling of Bombing Cases." *FBI Law Enforcement Bulletin* (September, 1959, October, 1959).

Lenz, Robert R. "The Bomb Squad." *Police.* 16:3 (November, 1971), 39-43.

Ley, Willy. *Bombs and Bombing.* N.Y.: Modern Age, 1941.

"A Manual For Bomb Attacks." *Security World.* 5 (May, 1968), 14-16, 46.

"National Bomb Data Center." *FBI Law Enforcement Bulletin.* 42:12 (1973), 13-15.
Describes function and objectives of the NBDC.

Newhouser, C.F. *Bomb Scene Procedures: The Protective Response. . .* Washington: IACP, National Bomb Data Center.

Pierce, G. McGuire. *Destruction by Demolition, Incendiaries and Sabotage.* Boulder, CO: Paladin, 1974.

Ronayne, John A. "Investigating Crimes Involving Explosions." *Police.* 4:2 (January-February) 64-67, 4:4; (March-April, 1960), 11-16.

Ronayne, John A. "Package Bombs and Their Investigation." *Police.* 4:1 (September-October, 1959), 6-12.

"Scare City: Planting of Bombs in New York City." *National Review* (December 2, 1969).

Stoffel, Joseph F. "Basement Bombers: A Fire-Police Responsibility." *Police.* 10:2 (November-December, 1965), 6-10.

Stoffel, Joseph F. "Determining the Cause of an Explosion." *Police.* 7:3 (January-February, 1963), 64-66.

Stoffel, J.F. *Explosives and Homemade Bombs.* Springfield, IL: C.C. Thomas, 1970.
Prepares law enforcement officers for investigating, handling, and disposing of explosives during their normal police work.

Stoffel, Joseph F. "Explosives and the Police Officer." *The Criminologist* (August, 1969).

Stoffel, Joseph F. "Explosives and the Police Officer." *Police.* 7:1 (September-October, 1962), 6-10.

Styles, S.G. "Car Bombs." *Journal of Forensic Science Society.* 15 (1975), 93-87.

U.S. Department of the Army. *Special Forces Demolition Techniques.* Bolder,CO.: Panther, 1970.

Worsham, Robert. "Bomb and Explosives Investigations." *Identification News.* 20 (May, 1970).

Wylie, E.M. "They Deal With the Mad Bombers: New York City's Bomb Squad." *Reader's Digest* (August, 1961).

Yallop, H.J. "Investigations of the Causes of Explosions." *Journal of Forensic Science Society.* 5:1 (January, 1965), 6-10.

Zmuda, Charles W. "Bombing Incidents." *Police.* 15:3 (January-February, 1971), 6-10.

Bomb Handling and Disposal

Applegate, Rex. "Bomb Handling System." *Law and Order.* 18:10 (October, 1970), 60-61, 64-66.

Behrndsen, Darrel J. *Guidelines to the Handling of Hazardous Materials.* Denver, CO.: Source of Safety, 1973.

Brodie, T.G. *Bombs and Bombing: A Handbook to Detection, Disposal and Investigation.* Springfield, IL.: C.C. Thomas, 1972.

Hanson, R.W. "The Use of Shotgun Shells for Minimizing Risks Involved in moving of Bomb Packages." *Police.* 16:4 (December, 1971), 62-63.

Lenz, Robert R. "Backyard Explosives." *Police.* 9:2. (November-December, 1964), 36-39.
Characteristics of homemade bombs.

Lenz, Robert R. *Explosives and Bomb Disposal Guide.* Springfield, IL.: C.C. Thomas, 1965.

Newhouser, C.R. and Charles S. Stevenson. *Transportation, Storage and Destruction of Bomb Materials.* Gaithersburg, MD.: IACP, National Bomb Data Center, 1972.

Pike, E.A. *Protection Against Bombs and Incendiaries for Business, Industrial and Educational Institutions.* Springfield, IL.: C.C. Thomas, 1972.
Illustrated guidebook for the handling of homemade bombs and incendiary devices.

"Proper Handling of Explosives in Law Enforcement." *FBI Law Enforcement Bulletin* (April, 1953).

Rogers, B.T. and R.W. Taylor. "Total Confinement of Clandestine Device Explosions." *FBI Law Enforcement Bulletin.* 42:8 (1973), 2-7, 31.

"Safety Precautions for the Handling of Homemade Bombs." *FBI Law Enforcement Bulletin.* 26:9 (September, 1957), 16-18.

Styles, S.G. "Bombs and Bomb Beaters." *International Defense Review* (October, 1976), 817-819.

Talmadge, Ralph W., Jr. "Explosives Disposal Assistance from the U.S. Army." *FBI Law Enforcement Bulletin.* 37:1 (January, 1968), 9-11.

"Trickiest Bomb." *Security World* (February, 1973).

Explosives

Breece, Dan. "Explosives." *Informant.* 2 (May, 1970), 4-6.

Cook, Melvin Alonzo. *The Science of High Explosives.* N.Y.: Reinhold, 1958.

Ellern, Herbert. *Military and Civilian Pyrotechnics.* N.Y.: Chemical Pub. Co., 1968.

"Explosives—Some Technical Aspects and Suggestions." *FBI Law Enforcement Bulletin* (August, 1955).

Fordham, S. *High Explosives and Propellants.* N.Y.: Pergamon, 1969.

Gregory, C.E. *Explosives for Engineers.* 2nd ed., Brisbane: University of Queensland Press, 1966.

Meidi, James H. *Explosive and Toxic Hazardous Materials.* Beverly Hills, CA: Glencoe, 1970.

Stoffel, Joseph F. "Dynamite and Blasting Caps." *Police.* 8:1 (September-October, 1963), 23-25.

U.S. Department of the Army. *Explosives and Demolitions* (FM 5-25). Washington: GPO, 1959.

Bomb Threats and Search Techniques

Barret, James R. "Bomb Scares and Vandalism." *The Police Yearbook.* Washington: IACP, 1957.

"Bomb Threats and Bomb Search Techniques." *Security World.* 9:10 (November, 1972), 20-21, 23-31, 60-61.

Bomb Threats and Bomb Techniques. Washington: Alcohol, Tobacco and Firearms Division, U.S. Treasury Department, 1971.

Carroll, Leslie A. "Bomb Scare: A Medical Centers Program." *Security World.* 7 (December, 1970), 29-32.

Chamberlin, Charles S. "A Bomb Is Set to Go Off at 3:00 P.M." *Police Chief.* XLI:5 (May, 1974), 60-61.

Chase, L.J. *Bomb Threats, Bombing and Civil Disturbances—A Guide for Facility Protection.* Corvallis, OR: Continuing Education Publications, 1971.

Freimuth, Kenneth C. "Bomb Threats!!!" *Military Police Journal* (May, 1972), 21-24.

Gupta, Om P. "Short-Notice Bomb-Scare Warning System." *Police.* 16:2 (October, 1971), 14-15.

Jupiter, Robert M. "Bomb Threats and Bomb Blasts." *Police Chief.* XXXVII:6 (June, 1970), 14-17.

Levy, A.D. "Bombs and Bombing Threats." *Skyscraper Management* (September, 1970).

"Limiting Useless Bomb Searches." *Office* (September, 1971).

"Living with Bomb Threats." *Chemical Engineering* (February, 22, 1971).

McCollum, David, Jr. "Some Points on Bombs and Bomb Threats." *FBI Law Enforcement Bulletin* (April, 1971).

National Association of Manufacturers. *Bomb Threats—Suggested Action to Protect Employees and Property.* Washington: National Association of Manufacturers, n/d.
Detailed procedures to be followed prior to, during, and after bomb threat incidents are listed.

Nett, B. "Case History of A Bomb Hoax." *Airline Management and Marketing* (November, 1970).

Wachenhut, G.R. "Business is the Target of Bombings and Bomb Hoaxes." *Office* (September, 1971).

Walsh, C.V. "Command Decision: When to Evacuate Your Building." *Security World.* 10:3 (1973), 37-38, 40-43.

"What to Do About a Bomb Scare." *American Druggist* (July 26, 1971).

Prevention of Bomb Attacks

"Bombings Spark Tighter Security." *Industry Week* (December 28, 1970).

Crockett, Thompson S. and George B. Goering. *Bomb Security Guidelines: The Preventive Response.* Gaithersburg: IACP, National Bomb Data Center, 1972.

Goering, George B. "Basics for Bomb Emergency Planning." *Security World.* 7 (June, 1970).

"How to Defuse Plant Bombings." *Factory* (May, 1971).

"Is Your Business a Bomb Target." *Industry Week* (June 27, 1970).

Kenton, L. "Industry Goes to Bomb Classes." *Industrial Management* (May, 1974).

Kleinschrod, W.A. "There Is a Bomb Planted in Your Office." *Administrative Management* (August, 1970).

Knowles, Graham. *Bomb Security Guide.* Culver City, CA.: Security World, 1976.

Love, C. Robert. "Planning for Bomb Incidents." *Law and Order* (April, 1960).

McGuire, E.P. "When Bombing Threatens." *Conference Board Record* (September, 1971).

"Protection Against Letter Bombs and Explosive Devices." *Security Gazette.* 14:12 (December, 1972), 478-479.

BURGLARY

Black, Susan. "A Reporter at Large: Burglary." *New Yorker.* 39 (December 7, 1963), 63-64.
A comprehensive discussion of legal definitions, burglars, MOs, characteristics, habits, motives, ways of life.

Black, Susan. "A Reporter at Large: Burglary." *New Yorker.* 39 (December 14, 1963), 89-91.
Discussion of police handling of burglary cases, techniques of pursuing burglars, relationship between detectives and burglars, sketches of two cases, phony burglaries, unreported burglaries.

Bowers, John. "Big City Thieves." *Harper's Magazine.* 234 (February, 1967), 30-54.
Describes various MO's of burglars. Interviews with two burglars and a Locksmith.

"Burglar Keys." *RCMP Gazette.* 25:3 (March, 1953).

"Burglars Prey on Small Banks." *FBI Law Enforcement Bulletin* (October, 1965).

"Burglary—Its Drain on the Public." *FBI Law Enforcement Bulletin.* 35:1 (January, 1966), 16-21.

"The 'Burning Bar' Reviewed." *Security World* (March, 1969).

Cochran, Murray O. "Police Science Traps Lone Wolf Burglar." *Law and Order.* 12:7 (July, 1964), 12-13.

Cole, Richard B. "The Burning Bar." *Police.* 15:6 (July-August, 1971), 52-53.
The Thermal Lance, aka The Burning Bar can penitrate the most substantial vault construction. Has noise and smoke drawbacks.

Conner, Lawrence. "When Mourners Go to Services, Robbers Break in Some Homes." *National Observer* (January 4, 1971), 12.
Indianapolis experienced a rash of burglaries in homes temporarily empty because occupants were attending funerals. The burglars presumably got addresses and funeral information from newspapers.

Dussia, Joseph. "Investigation of Safe Burglaries." *FBI Law Enforcement Bulletin.* 36:11 (November, 1967), 7-13.

Dussia, Joseph. "Safe Burglary Investigation." *Security World* (September, 1968).

Einreinhof, Emery. "A Palm Print and a Belt Buckle." *Law and Order*. 14:7 (July, 1966), 16-21.

Franssen, F. "An Ingenious Case of Safe-Breaking." *International Criminal Police Review* (May, 1958).

Friedman, Albert B. "The Scatological Rites of Burglars." *Western Folklore*. 27 (July, 1968), 171-179.
Depositing a pile of feces has been considered by some thieves as a protective good luck measure.

Henrick, James P., Jr. "Big Business for Burglars." *FBI Law Enforcement Bulletin* (October, 1968), 2-6, 22-23.
Investigation of coin telephone burglaries.

Powers, Thomas. "Secrets Of A Safecracker." *The Observer Review* (March 17, 1968).

Remsberg, Charles and Bonnie Remsberg. "Aristocrats of Crime Jewel Thieves." *New York Times Magazine* (December 27, 1964).
Discusses various types of jewel thieves, a growing number of whom display a viciousness and predilection for violence that the old pros deplore.

Scarr, Harry A. *Patterns of Burglary*. 2nd rev. ed. Washington: LEAA, 1973.

Stonehouse, R.J. and J. Dumbauld. *Safe Burglaries in California—An Analysis of Selected Offenses*. Sacramento: California Department of Justice Division of Law Enforcement, 1970.
Analysis of such related factors as place and time of occurrence, report and arrest, premise and safe entry methods, tools, detection, and property type and value.

"The Thermal Burning Bar." *FBI Law Enforcement Bulletin*. 37:2 (February, 1968), 10-11.

"Use of 'Primacord' as an Explosive Agent on Safes." *RCMP Gazette*. 24:9 (September, 1962).

Webb, Donald G. *Investigation of Safe and Money Chest Burglary*. Springfield, IL.: C.C. Thomas, 1975.

CATTLE RUSTLING

Cheney, William G. "Cattle Rustling." *FBI Law Enforcement Bulletin*. 36:2 (February, 1967), 17-22.

Plott, Larry B. "Ways to Halt Cattle Rustling." *FBI Law Enforcement Bulletin* (September, 1975), 14-15.

COUNTERFEITING

Glasser, Lynn. *Counterfeiting in America: The History of an American Way to Wealth*. N.Y.: Potter, 1968.

Gustafson, P. "They Trap Counterfeiters Everywhere." *Popular Science*. 163 (July, 1953), 49-53.

"International Currency Counterfeiting." *International Criminal Police Review* (December, 1966), 296-301.

McCabe, R.J. "Counterfeit Currency." *Australian Police Journal* (July, 1975), 203-213.

Mathyer, Jacques. "Problem of Banknote Security in 1975." *International Criminal Police Review* (July, 1976), 146-152.

Singn, D.M. "Counterfeit Coins." *Indian Police Journal* (July, 1972), 55-60.

Smith, Donald. "A Case of Counterfeiting." *Police Journal (GB)*, (November, 1964), 525-534.

"A Typical Counterfeiting Organization." *International Criminal Police Review* (April, 1963), 123-124.

DEFENSE INVESTIGATION.

Bliss, Edward N., Jr. "Defense Detective." *Journal of Criminal Law, Criminology and Police Science*. 47:2 (July-August, 1956), 264-265.

Bliss, Edward N., Jr. *Defense Investigation*. Springfield, IL.: C.C. Thomas, 1956.

Wels, Kirk. "Investigation for Defense As Well As Prosecution." *Police*. 6:5 (May-June, 1962).

EMBEZZLEMENT

Arleo, Dominick L. and James C. Hughes. "The Auditor's Role After Detecting a Larceny or Embezzlement." *U.S. Army Audit Agency Bulletin* (Fall, 1971).

Cardwell, Harvey. *The Principals of Audit Surveillance*. Princeton, N.J.: Van Nostrand, 1960.

Davidson, B. "Nemesis of the Bank Embezzlers." *Coronet* (January, 1960).

"Embezzlement-Motives, Methods and Precautions." *FBI Law Enforcement Bulletin* (August, 1958).

"The Forty Thieves." *FBI Law Enforcement Bulletin*. 39:8 (August, 1970), 21-25, 29-30.

"Insurance Investigators Trace Embezzlers." *Journal* (May-June, 1974).

Pennington, W.J. "Methods of the Embezzler." *Financial Executive* (June, 1964).

Riemer, Svend H. "Embezzlement: Pathological Basis." *Journal of Criminal Law, Criminology and Police Science* 32 (1941-42).

St. John, E.A. "Accountant vs. Embezzler." *Journal of Accountancy* (June, 1924).

"Various Forms of Embezzlement: Case of F.D. Reese." *Time* (July 16, 1965).

EXTORTION

"Fifteen-Year Extortion Plot Solved." *FBI Law Enforcement Bulletin*. 26:5 (May, 1957), 20-22.

Hepworth, Mike. *Blackmail: Publicity and Secrecy in Everyday Life*. London: Routledge & K. Paul, 1975.

"Techniques and Aspects of Extortion Problem." *FBI Law Enforcement Bulletin*. 26:12 (December, 1957), 16-20; 27:1 (January, 1958), 18-21.

FORGERY

Baker, J. Newton. *Law of Disputed and Forged Documents*. Charlottesville, VA.: Michie, 1955.

Berry, J.R. "How Document Detectives Catch Crooks." *Popular Science* (April, 1964).

Black, David A. "Forgery Above a Genuine Signature." *Journal of Criminal Law, Criminology and Police Science.* 53 (1962).

Black, David A. "Forged Signatures More Skillfully Written than the True Signature." *Journal of Criminal Law, Criminology and Police Science.* 53 (1962).

Black, David A. "Fraudulent Check Notations." *Journal of Criminal Law, Criminology and Police Science.* 54 (1963).

Britt, Steuart Henderson and Ivan N. Mensh. "The Identification of One's Own Handwriting." *Journal of Criminal Law, Criminology and Police Science.* 34 (1943-44).

Bradley, Julio. "Sequence of Pencil Strokes." *Journal of Criminal Law, Criminology and Police Science.* 54 (1963).

"Case of a Master Check Passer." *FBI Law Enforcement Bulletin* (June, 1955).

Clark, P.F. "Handwriting Examinations." *The Austrailian Police Journal.* 11:3 (July, 1957), 215-221.

Cole, Alwyn. "The Examinations of Forgeries." *Identification News.* 19:1 (January, 1959), 3-4.

"Combating the Bad Check Artist." *FBI Law Enforcement Bulletin.* 28:3 (March, 1959), 12-13.

Conway, James V.P. "The Identification of Handwriting." *Journal of Criminal Law, Criminology and Police Science.* 45 (1954-55).

Dowdall, Edward. "Catching Check Passers." *FBI Law Enforcement Bulletin* (October, 1954), 8-9.

"Easy to Forge: Stock and Bond Certificates." *Forbes* (April 1, 1973).

Fricke, Charles W. "The Successful Trial of Forgery Cases." *Police.* 2:4 (March-April, 1958), 48-50.

Godown, Linton. "Sequence of Writings." *Journal of Criminal Law, Criminology and Police Science.* 54 (1963).

Harris, John J. "Disguised Handwriting." *Journal of Criminal Law, Criminology and Police Science.* 43 (1952-53).

Harris, John J. "How Much Do People Write Alike: A Study of Signatures." *Journal of Criminal Law, Criminology and Police Science.* 48 (1957-58).

Harrison, Wilson R. *Forgery Detection. A Practical Guide.* NY: Praeger, 1964.

Hilton, Ordway. "Can the Forger Be Identified From His Own Handwriting." *Journal of Criminal Law, Criminology and Police Science.* 43 (1952-53).

Hilton, Ordway. "Contrasting Defects of Forged and Genuine Signatures." *Fingerprint and Identification.* 46:4 (October, 1964), 3-6, 11-14.

Kelly, James H. and Susan E. Morton. "How Many Forgers." *Journal of Police Science and Administration.* 2:2 (June, 1974), 164-168.

Keyes, Robert. "Camera Lucida—An Instrument for Forgery." *Fingerprint and Identification.* 48:5 (November, 1966), 3-5, 23.

Keyes, Robert. "Forgery by Tracing." *Fingerprint and Investigation.* 48:2 (August, 1966), 3-7, 27.

Lacy, George J. "Handwriting and Forgery Under Hypnosis." *Journal of Criminal Law, Criminology and Police Science.* 34 (1943-44).

Lawder, Lee E. "Notes on The Paperhanger." *Law and Order.* 20:20 (October, 1972), 68, 70, 72.

Lemert, Edwin M. "The Behavior of The Systematic Check Forger." *Social Problems.* 6 (1958), 141-149.

Livingston, Orville B. "Bogus Check File Classified By Trademarks." *Journal of Criminal Law, Criminology and Police Science.* 39 (1948-49).

Mathyer, Jacques. "The Expert Examination of Signatures." *Journal of Criminal Law, Criminology and Police Science.* 52 (1961).

Mathyer, Jacques. "The Influence of Writing Instruments on Handwriting and Signatures." *Journal of Criminal Law, Criminology and Police Science.* 60 (1969).

McGuire, Edward Patrick. *The Forgers.* Bernardsville, NJ: Padric, 1969.

Morland, N. "Solving Crimes on Paper." *Science Digest* (March, 1963).

Olson, K. *The Ball-Point Rip-Off: A Forgery Investigator's Handbook.* Santa Cruz, CA: Davis, 1975.

O'Neil, P. "Tracking Down the Forger." *Life* (September 15, 1972).

Puri, D.K.S. "A 'Model' Forgery." *International Criminal Police Review.* 185 (February, 1965), 52-54.

Puri, D.K.S. "Forgery by Physical Transfer." *Journal of Criminal Law, Criminology and Police Science.* 59:2 (March, 1968), 144-147.

Purtell, David J. "The Identification of Checkwriters." *Journal of Criminal Law, Criminology and Police Science.* 45:2 (July-August, 1954), 229-235.

Regan, Joseph L. and Phillip J. McLaughlin. "Specialized Police Investigation For Fraudulent Checks." *FBI Law Enforcement Bulletin.* 26:2 (February, 1957), 7-9.

Reinhardt, James M. "Psychographology in Handwriting Identification." *Police.* 2:5 (May-June), 7-14.

Rhodes, Henry Taylor Fowkes. *The Craft of Forgery.* London: J. Murray, 1934.

Schulenberger, W.A. "The Taking of Handwriting and Handprinting Specimens in the Field." *Identification News.* 22:12 (December, 1972), 7-9.

"Some Crooks Sign Their Names on the Evidence." *FBI Law Enforcement Bulletin.* 37:4 (April, 1968), 20-22.

Sternitzky, Julius L. *Forgery and Fictitious Checks.* Springfield, IL.: C.C. Thomas, 1955.

Sternitzky, Julius L. "Suggestions to Officers on Forgery Investigation." *Police.* 1:6 (July-August, 1957), 31-35; 2:3 (January-February, 1958), 10-12.

"Stolen, Forged and Counterfeit Traveler's Checks." *FBI Law Enforcement Bulletin* (February, 1960).

FRAUD

Fraud Investigation

"Airline Ticket Frauds." *Royal Canadian Mounted Police Gazette* (December, 1964).

Armstrong, Frank. *Gypsy Fortune Teller and the Sucker.* Los Angeles, CA.: Crescent, 1975.

Balter, Harry G. *Tax Fraud and Evasion.* 4th ed. Boston: Warren, 1975.

Barmash, Isadore. *Great Business Disasters: Swindles, Bungles, and Frauds in American Industry.* Chicago: Playboy Press, 1972.

Boughourian, Gay F. and Jose A. Alcantara. "Gypsy Fortune-Tellers and Your Community." *Police Chief.* XLII:6 (June, 1975), 71-74.

Cadmus, Bradford and Arthur J.E. Child. *Internal Control Against Fraud and Waste.* Hemel Hampstead: Prentice-Hall, 1974.

Carey, Mary and George Sherman. *A Compendium of Bunk or How to Spot a Con-Artist: A Handbook for Fraud Investigators, Bankers, and Other Custodians of the Public Trust.* Springfield, IL.: C.C. Thomas, 1976.

Crowley, William F. "A New Weapon Against Confidence Games." *Journal of Criminal Law, Criminology and Police Science.* 50:3 (September-October, 1959), 233-236.

Del Castilio, Guillermo. "An Unforeseen Aspect of Fraud." *International Criminal Police Review* (January, 1965), 27-28.

Ferguson, R.A. "In Canada: International Fraud." *Police Chief.* XLII:2 (February, 1975), 34, 36.

Freeman, Roger A. *Tax Loopholes: the Legend and the Reality.* Plano, TX: American Enterprise, 1973.

Glick, Rush G. and Robert S. Newsom. *Fraud Investigation: Fundamentals for Police.* Springfield, IL.: C.C. Thomas, 1974.

Haldane, R.A. *With Intent to Deceive: Frauds Famous and Infamous.* NY: British Book Center, n/d.

Keller, E. John. "Corporate Fraud." *Law and Order.* 21:12 (December, 1973), 56-57; 22:2 (February, 1974), 37.

Kelson, Charles. "Insurance Fraud Investigations." *Police Chief.* XLII:5 (May, 1975), 60-61.

Kossack, N.E. "Economic Crime: The Crippler." *FBI Law Enforcement Bulletin.* 44:3 (1975), 3-6.

Loertscher, W. "Forgery and Counterfeiting of Swiss Watches." *International Criminal Police Review.* 28:278 (1974), 114-119.

MacDonald, J.M. and C.D. Brannan. "False Reports of Armed Robbery." *FBI Law Enforcement Bulletin.* 42:3 (1973) 24-29.

Review of the motives for false reports—insurance gain, to explain loss of money, gunshot wounds, revenge to avoid arrest and others.

Miller, James D. "The Old Beer in the Coke Can Trick." *Law and Order.* 18:1 (January, 1970), 8.

Murray, J.G.E. "Some Aspects of Fraud, Control and Investigation." *Journal of Criminal Law, Criminology and Police Science.* 49:1 (May-June, 1958), 78-88.

National College of District Attorneys. *National College of District Attorneys: Summary of the Welfare Fraud Seminar.* Washington: NCJRS (Microfiche), 1974.

O'Neal, W.G. "Insurance Fraud—A Crime." *FBI Law Enforcement Bulletin.* 39:7 (July, 1970); 39:8, 11 31.

Pratt, Lester A. *Bank Frauds: Their Detection and Prevention.* 2nd ed., N.Y.: Ronald, 1965.

U.S. Internal Revenue Service. *Confidential Official IRS Tax Audit Guide.* N.Y.: Arco, 1975.

"White-Collar Crime Strikes Home: FHA-Related Frauds." *FBI Law Enforcement Bulletin* (December, 1975), 12-15.

Woods, N. Morgan. "Fraudulent Automobile Insurance Claims." *Police.* 6:1 (September-October, 1961), 15-17.

Confidence Games and Swindles

Blum, R.H. *Deceivers and Deceived—Observations on Confidence Men and Their Victims, Informants and Their Quarry, Political and Industrial Spies and Ordinary Citizens.* Springfield, IL.: C.C. Thomas, 1971.

Deeson, A.F.L. *Great Swindlers.* N.Y.: Drake, 1972.

Franklin, Charles. *They Walked a Crooked Mile: An Account of the Greatest Scandals, Swindlers, and Outrages of All Times.* N.Y.: Hart, 1969.

Gasser, Robert Louis. "The Confidence Game." *Federal Probation.* 27 (1963), 47-54.

Gibson, Walter B. *The Bunco Book.* Holyoke, MA.: Radner, 1946.

Hancock, Ralph and Henry Chafetz. *The Compleat Swindler.* N.Y.: MacMillan, 1968.

Harpending, Asbury. *Great Diamond Hoax and Other Stirring Incidents in the Life of Asbury Harpending.* Norman: University of Oklahoma Press, 1958.

Hyman, Alan. *The Rise and Fall of Horatio Bottomley: The Biography of a Swindler.* London: Cassell, 1972.

Klein, Alexander. *The Double Dealers. Adventures in Grand Deception.* Philadelphia: Lippencott, 1958.

Lepera, Patsy Anthony and Walter Goodman. *Memoirs of a Scam Man.* NY: Ferrar, Straus & Giroux, 1974.

MacDonald, John C.R. *Crime is a Business: Buncos, Rackets, Confidence Games.* Stanford, CA.: Stanford University Press, 1939.

Maurer, David W. *The American Confidence Man.* Springfield, IL.: C.C. Thomas, 1974.

Maurer, David W. *The Big Con.* Indianapolis: Bobbs Merrill, 1940.

Morrison, R. "Confidence Tricksters." *Police Journal* (1931), 543-552.

Moore, Maurice C. *Frauds and Swindles.* London: Gee, 1947.

Nash, Jay Robert. *Hustlers and Con-Men.* N.Y.: Evans, 1976.

Oughton, F. *Fraud and White Collar Crime.* London: Elek, 1971.

Schur, Edwin M. "Sociological Analysis of Confidence Swindling." *Journal of Criminal Law, Criminology and Police Science.* 48 (1957), 296-304.

Smith, Percy J. *Con-Man: The Personal Reminiscences of an Ex-Detective, Inspector Percy J. Smith.* London: Herbert Jenkins, 1938.

Sparrow, Gerald. *Con-Man.* London: Arthur Barker, 1975.

Swindled: Classic Business Frauds of the Seventies. Homewood, IL: Dow Jones, 1976.

Washburn, W. and E.S. De Long. *High and Low Financiers: Some Notorious Swindlers and Their Abuse of Our Modern Stock-Selling System.* Indianapolis: Bobbs-Merrill, 1932.

Weil, Yellow Kid. *The Con Game and the "Yellow Kid" Weil.* NY: Dover, 1974.

Consumer Fraud

Berton, Pierre. *The Big Sell: An Introduction to the Black Arts of Door to Door Salesmanship and Other Techniques.* N.Y.: Knopf, 1963.

Crowther, Sam and Irvin Winehouse. *Highway Robbery.* N.Y.: Stein, 1966.

Gentry, Curt. *The Vulnerable Americans.* Garden City, N.Y.: Doubleday, 1966.

Margolius, Sidney. *The Innocent Consumer VS The Exploiters.* N.Y.: Trident, 1967.

Morris, Eileen. "Crimes Committed by Contractors Against Their Clients and the Public: Bribes, Frauds, Kickbacks, and Price Fixing." *Canadian Police Chief* (July, 1976), 8-9.

Reeves, Herman. *Consumer Protection in the States.* Lexington, KY.: Council of State Governments, 1970.

Roper, William L. "Car Repair Rackets Add to Accident Toll." *California Highway Patrolman.* 35 (June, 1971).

Rosefsky, Robert. *Frauds, Swindles and Rackets: A Red Alert for Consumers.* Chicago: Follett, 1973.

Springer, John L. *Consumer Swindles and How to Avoid Them.* Chicago: Regnery, 1970.

Trump, Fred. *Buyer Beware!* NY: Abingdon, 1965.

U.S. Post Office Department. *Mail Fraud Law Protecting Consumers, Investors, Businessmen, Medical Patients, Students.* Washington: GPO, 1969.

Vollmuth, E. "Fraudulent Business Practices." *International Criminal Police Review.* 30:289 (1975), 158-165.

Zeichner, Irving B. "False Pretenses: Auto Repairs." *Law and Order* (December, 1971), 40-41.

Credit Card Fraud

Association of Credit Card Investigators. *National Credit Card Security Conference 1972—Transcript of Proceedings.* Washington: NCJRS, (Microfiche), 1972.

Illinois Legislative Investigating Commission. *Credit Card Fraud in Illinois.* Chicago: Illinois Legislative Investigating Commission, 1972.
Study of fraudulent practices and their effects on consumers, businessmen, and the credit card industry.

Lipson, Milton. "Crime and the Credit Card." *FBI Law Enforcement Bulletin.* 39:6 (June, 1970), 12-15, 30; 39:7 (July, 1970), 20-24.

Lipson, Milton. "Law Enforcement and the Credit Card." *Journal of California Law Enforcement* (July, 1970), 8-12.

Maynard, Michael M. "Computers Combat Credit Card Fraud." *Police* (July-August, 1970).

Scully, Robert J. "Credit Card: An Investigative Tool." *Police Chief.* XXXIX (May 5, 1972), 61-67.

Weishe, Gerald V. "Credit Card Fraud." *Security World* (December, 1967).

Fraudulent Securities

"Fraudulent Securities." *FBI Law Enforcement Bulletin.* 27:2 (February, 1958).

Illicit Traffic in Stolen Securities—A Report to the Illinois General Assembly. Chicago: Illinois Legislative Investigating Commission, 1973.

U.S. Congress House Select Committee on Crime. *Organized Crime: Techniques for Converting Worthless Securities into Cash.* Washington: GPO, 1972.

U.S. Congress Senate Committee on Government Operations. *Organized Crime Securities: Thefts and Frauds.* Washington: U.S. Government Printing Office, 1972.

Yeager, M.G. "Gangster As White Collar Criminal—Organized and Stolen Securities." *Issues in Criminology.* 8:1 (Spring, 1973), 49-73.

HOMICIDE

Adams, Brian C. *Medical Implications of Karate Blows.* S. Brunswick, N.J.: A.S. Barnes, 1969.

Adams, Nathan M. "Case No. HO 74-2092, Homicide." *Reader's Digest* (December, 1976), 109-117.

Adams, Thomas F. "Dead Bodies." *Police.* 9:3 (January-February, 1965), 94-95.

Adelson, Lester, Robert W. Huntington III and Donald T. Reay. "A Prisoner Is Dead." *Police.* 13:1 (September-October, 1968), 49-58.

Alfaro, Vince. "Homicide." *Police.* 15:5 (May-June, 1971), 17-21.

Andrews, A. *Intensive Inquiries—Seven Chief Constables Open CID Files on Their Most Remarkable Murder Investigations.* N.Y.: St. Martin, 1973.

Bailey, F.L. and H.B. Rothblatt. *Crimes of Violence—Homicide and Assault.* Rochester, N.Y.: Lawyers Cooperative, 1973.
Guidelines for attorneys in the tactical and substantive issues in the defense of crimes of violence.

Barnes, Margaret. *Murder in Coweta County.* N.Y.: Reader's Digest Press, 1976.

Beddoe, Harold L. "Deaths From Cutting and Stabbing." *Police*. 3:2 (November-December), 1958 24-28.

Bornstein, Frederick P. "Homicide by Electrocution." *Journal of Forensic Sciences*. 7:4 (October, 1962), 516-519.

Boudouris, James. "Methods of Homicide." *Police*. 16:2 (October, 1971), 5-8.

Buckmaster, Thomas F. "Unusual Developments in Homicide Investigations." *FBI Law Enforcement Bulletin*. 37:7 (July, 1963), 17-19.

Bugliosi, Vincent and Curt Gentry. *Helter Skelter*. N.Y.: Bantam, 1975.

Cawley, Donald F. "Homicide Investigation." *Police Chief* (April, 1974).

"Cooperative Police Work." *FBI Law Enforcement Bulletin*. 26:3 (March, 1957), 25-27.

Crossley, Richard P. "A System for Determination of the Time of Death: The Crossley Checklist." *Police Chief*. XLI:3 (March, 1974), 65-58, 85.

Dieckmann, Edward A. *Practical Homicide Investigation*. Springfield, IL.: C.C. Thomas, 1961.

Ford, Richard and A. Moseley. "Motor Vehicular Suicide." *Journal of Criminal Law, Criminology and Police Science*. 54:3 (September, 1963), 357-359.

Nickels, E.M. "Fundamentals of Homicide Investigation." *Police Law Quarterly*. 4:2 (975) 11-18.

Gelb, Barbara. *On the Tracks of Murder: Behind the Scenes With a Homicide Command Squad*. Caldwell, N.J.: Morrow, 1975.

Gibbens, T.C.N. "Sane and Insane Homicide." *Journal of Criminal Law, Criminology and Police Science*. 49:2 (July-August, 1958), 110-115.

Hackl, F. "Bullet Wounds." *International Criminal Police Review*. 27:257 (1972), 106-107.

Harris, Raymond I. *Outline of Death Investigation*. Springfield, IL.: C.C. Thomas, 1962.

Henry, Russell C. "Death Investigations." *FBI Law Enforcement Bulletin*. 34:12 (December, 1965), 7-11, 19-21.

"Homicide Investigation." *Journal of Criminal Law and Criminal Law and Criminology*. 36:6 (March-April, 1946) (entire issue).

Homicide Investigation: Practical Information for Coroners, Police Officers and Other Investigators. 2nd Ed., Springfield, IL.: C.C. Thomas, 1967.

Houghton, Robert A. *Special Unit Senator: The Investigation of the Assassination of Senator Robert F. Kennedy*. N.Y.: Random House, 1970.

Hughes, Daniel J. *Homicide Investigative Techniques*. Springfield, IL.: C.C. Thomas, 1974.

Kessler, William Frederic. *The Detection of Murder*. NY: Greenberg, 1953.

Kimball, Leonard N. "The Old Golf Bag." *Law and Order*. 18:7 (July, 1970), 86-87.

Kimball, Leonard. "The Talking Matchbook." *Law and Order*. 20:3 (March, 1972), 60-62.

Kuhn, E.A. "The Shell Lake Murders." *The Criminologist* (February, 1969).

Los Angeles Police Department. *Homicide Investigation Guidelines*. Los Angeles: LAPD, 1970.

Luke, James L. "Asphyxial Deaths by Hanging in New York City, 1964-1965." *Journal of Forensic Science*. 12:3 (July, 1967), 359-369.

Lushbaugh, C.C., Jesse Rose and Dean Wilson. "A Practical Means for Routine Approximation of the Time of Recent Death." *Police*. 5:1 (September-October, 1960), 10-13.

MacDonald, J.M. *Homicidal Threats*. Springfield, IL.: C.C. Thomas, 1968.
A five to six year follow-up study of 100 patients who made homicidal threats.

McBay, Arthur J. "Problems of the New Drugs in Poisoning Cases." *Police*. 7:3 (January-February, 1963), 26-29.

Merkeley, Donald Karl. *The Investigation of Death*. Springfield, IL.: C.C. Thomas, 1957.

Myre, Daniel C. *Death Investigation*. Gaithersburg, MD.: IACP, 1974.

Oughton, Frederick. *Murder Investigation*. London: Elek, 1971.

Patel, N.S. "Suicide, Place, Position and Clothing." *Criminologist*. 7:25 (1972), 51-54.

Pitchess, Peter J. "Proof of Murder by Insulin—A Medico-Legal First." *FBI Law Enforcement Bulletin* (January, 1969), 16-19.

Ramu, M. "Death Due to a Tear Gas Shell: Report of a Case." *Journal of Forensic Sciences*. 12:3 (July, 1967), 383-385.

Reinhardt, James M. "The 'Gentle' Sex Murderer." *Police* (March-April, 1957), 12-14.

Reinhardt, James M. "The Sex Killer. A Special Problem of Investigation." *Police*. 5:3 (January-February, 1961), 10-13.

Richardson, Leo. "The Investigation of the Natural Death." *Law and Order*. 21:7 (July, 1973), 46-52.

Rizer, Conrad K. "A Person Falls From a Window." *Journal of Criminal Law, Criminology and Police Science*. 56:3 (September, 1965), 366-371.

Scott, P.D. "Fatal Battered Baby Cases." *Medicine, Science and the Law*. 13:3 (July, 1973), 197-206.

Snyder, Lemoyne. *Homicide Investigation*. Springfield, IL.: C.C. Thomas, 1967.

Southwestern Law Enforcement Institute. *Institute on Homicide Investigation Techniques, 1961*. Springfield, IL.: C.C. Thomas, 1961.

Sullivan, Francis C. "Dying Declarations." *Police*. 4:3 (January-February, 1960), 46-47.

Tannahill, Reay. *Flesh and Blood: A History of the Cannibal Complex*. London: Hamilton, 1975.

Van Meter, C.W. *Case Study in Police Administration and Criminal Investigation (Based on Law Enforcement Procedures in Dallas, Texas, November 1963).* Carthage, IL.: Journal Printing Company, 1974.
Description and discussion of the law enforcement activities before, during, and after the assassination of President John F. Kennedy in November 1963.

Williams, Emlyn. *Beyond Belief: A Chronicle of Murder and its Detection.* London: Hamilton, 1967.

Wolfgang, Marvin E. "Suicide by Means of Victim-Precipitated Homicide." *Journal of Clinical and Experimental Psychopathology.* 20:4 (December, 1959), 335-349.

ILLEGAL LIQUOR

Davis, Rex D. "The Traffic in Illicit Liquor." *Police.* 8:4 (March-April, 1964), 6-9.

Grayson, Lonnie. "Teamwork, Ingenuity and Science Smash Bootleg Operations." *Law and Order.* 16:7 (July, 1968), 68-71.

Licensed Beverage Industry. *A Survey of Illegal Distilling in the U.S. Today: A Special Story.* N.Y.: Licensed Beverage Industry, 1950.

Maurer, David W. *Kentucky Moonshine.* Lexington: University Press of Kentucky, 1974.

Starr, John. *The Purveyor: The Shocking Story of Today's Illicit Liquor Empire.* N.Y.: Holt, Rinehart and Winston, 1961.

KIDNAPPING

"Catching the Kidnappers: Case of Eugene Paul Getty II." *Time* (January 28, 1974), 50.

Denis, Guy. "The Kidnapping of Young Eric Peugeot—A Rare Crime in France." *International Criminal Police Review* (March, 1963), 66-75; (April, 1963), 109-116.

"Getty Affair: A Report from the Italian Police." *International Criminal Police Review* (June-July, 1975), 166-170.

Suzuki, Sadatoshi. "Computer Catches Kidnapper." *FBI Law Enforcement Bulletin* (June, 1975).

NARCOTICS

Adams, Nathan. "Night of the Big Drug Bust." *Reader's Digest* (January, 1974), 112-116.

American Pharmaceutical Association. *Handbook of Non-Prescription Drugs.* Washington: APA, 1971.

Ansley, Norman. "International Efforts to Control Narcotics." *Journal of Criminal Law, Criminology and Police Science.* 50:2 (July-August, 1959), 105-113.

Blum, Richard H. *Drug Dealers—Taking Action.* San Francisco: Jossey Bass, 1973.

Bretnall, G.C., Jr. "Non-Chemical Field Test for Marijuana." *Law and Order.* 18:1 (January, 1970), 54.

Brock, Herb. "Kentucky State Police Battles The Drug Problem." *Law and Order.* 23:7 (July, 1975), 56-58.

Bruun, Kettil. et al. *Gentlemen's Club: International Control of Drugs and Alcohol.* Chicago: University of Chicago Press, 1975.

Clark, Evert and Nicholas Horrock. *Contrabandista.* NY: Praeger, 1973.

Conneley, Bob. "Narcotics—Useage, Control, Measures, and Enforcement." *Law Officer.* 2 (Winter, 1969), 14-17.

Cooper, Herston. *Investigators Manual on Drugs and Narcotics.* N. Miami, FL.: National Law Enforcement Academy, 1970.

Drug Enforcement Administration. *Guidelines for Narcotic and Dangerous Drug Evidence Handling and Security Procedures.* Washington: U.S. Department of Justice, 1975.

Earp, W. *Clark County (NV)—Narcotics Enforcement Task Force—Yearly Report, July 1, 1973 Thru October 31, 1974.* Washington: NCJRS (Microfiche), 1974.

Eszterhas, Joe. *Nark!* San Francisco: Straight Arrow Books, 1974.

Finlator, J. *Drugged Nation—A "NARC'S' Story."* N.Y.: Simon & Schuster, 1973.

Freeman, B. *Narcotics Cases—Prosecution and Defense.* N.Y.: Practicing Law Institute, 1970.
Collection of articles detailing the statutory and medical considerations as well as the legal limitations on prosecution of drug abuse.

Garza, Manuel R. *Multi-Agency Narcotic Units: Prescriptive Package.* Washington: NCJRS, 1975.

Glaser, D. and V. O'Leary. *Control and Treatment of Narcotic Use.* Washington: GPO, 1968.
Physiological effects of narcotics, modern social changes in drug use, personality traits of narcotic users, and the suppression of narcotics.

Goodrich, Leland M. *New Trends in Narcotics Control.* N.Y.: Carnegie, 1960.

Gottreich, J.I. "Dealing with Drug Abusers." *Police Law Quarterly.* 2:3 (1973), 28-34.

Grizzle, G.A. *Law Enforcement Policies Directed Toward Controlling Possession and Sale of Illegal Drugs.* Springfield, VA.: NTIS, 1973.

Hanks, Melvin L. *Narc: The Adventures of a Federal Agent.* N.Y.: Hastings House, 1973.

Harney, Malachi L. "The 'New Look' at Narcotics is Just the Same Old Sack." *Police.* 3:4 (March-April, 1959), 28-29; 3:5 (May-June, 1959), 31-33; 3:6 (July-August, 1959), 53-55.

Harney, Malachi L. and John C. Cross. "The Narcotics Undercover Man." *Police* (September-October, 1966).

Helbrant, Maurice. *Narcotic Agent 319.* N.Y.: Vanguard, 1941.

Hildebrand, James A. "The Undercover Narcotics Officer—Practice and Techniques." *Police* (January, 1972).

Jackson, Bruce. "Police on the Junkie Beat." *Atlantic* (January, 1967).

Katz, H.A. "The Law Enforcement Response to the Drug Abuse." *Police Law Quarterly.* 2:2 (1973), 9-12.

King, William. "Spoon Cases: A Quick Method of Identifying Heroin." *Police.* 5:1 (September-October, 1960), 73.

Kobetz, Richard W. "Drug Abuse Prevention: A Challenge of the Present." *Police Chief.* XXXIX:4 (April, 1972), 18-24.
Efforts by Interpol and BNDD to curb the manufacture and distribution of illegal drugs.

Krotoszynski, B.K., J.M. Mullaly, and A. Dravnieks. "Olfactronic Detection of Narcotics and Other Controlled Drugs." *Police.* 13:3 (January-February, 1969), 20-25.

Kuest, R.D. "Consolidating Efforts to Control Drug Abuse." *FBI Law Enforcement Bulletin.* 41:1 (1972), 10-13.

Lidz, Charles W. "The Cop-Addict Game: A Model of Police-Suspect Interaction." *Journal of Police Science and Administration.* 2:1 (March, 1974), 2-10.

McCloud, Douglas G. "Drug Abuse: Whose Problem?" *Law and Order.* 18:12 (December, 1970), 24-26.

Macivor, J.C. *Evaluation of the Idaho Bureau of Narcotic and Drug Enforcement.* Washington: NCJRS (Microfiche), 1974.

Mitchell, R.K. "South Dakota Policeman Infiltrates Narcotics Ring." *Law and Order.* 17:8 (August, 1969), 23-25.

Moore, Robin. *French Connection: The World's Most Crucial Narcotics Investigation.* Waltham, MA.: Little, 1969.

"The Narcotic Evil." *Spring 3100.* 22 (December, 1951), 5-11.

New York State Temporary Commission of Investigation. *Narcotics Law Enforcement in New York City—A Report by the New York State Commission of Investigation.* Washington: NCJRS (Microfiche), 1972.

Pace, D.F. and J.C. Styles, *Handbook of Narcotics Control.* Englewood Cliffs, N.J.: Prentice-Hall, 1972.
Overview of basic problem drugs, their classification, use, regulation, and detection.

Schiand, A. and A. Burton. *Solo: Self-Portrait of an Undercover Cop.* N.Y.: Dodd Mead, 1973.
Narrative of the experiences of an undercover narcotics officer of the New York City Police Department.

Siragusa, Charles. *The Trail of the Poppy: Behind the Mask of the Mafia.* Englewood Cliffs, N.J.: Prentice Hall, 1966.

Skousen, W. Cleon. "How to Beat the Narcotics Racket." *Law and Order.* 12:4 (April, 1964), 18-23.

Sosa, J.B. "Drug Trafficking Takes to the Air." *FBI Law Enforcement Bulletin.* 43:2 (February, 1974), 2-5.

Standards for the Staffing and Organization of Municipal Narcotics and Dangerous Drugs Enforcement Units. Washington: IACP, 1970.

Superson, Edward T. *Investigation of Narcotics.* Sacramento, CA.: Citadel, 1975.

U.N. Division of Narcotic Drugs. *Recognition of Narcotic Drugs, Psychotropic Substances and Drug Abusers: A Guide for Law Officers.* Geneva: Division of Narcotic Drugs, 1973.

Unlisted Drugs Index—Guide. Chatam, N.J.: Unlisted Drugs, 1969.

U.S. Treasury Department, Bureau of Narcotics. *Traffic in Opium and Other Dangerous Drugs.* Washington: GPO, 1966.

Voety, Harold L., Jr. "Which Drug Policy is Least Cost: Addict Control or Control of Supply." *Journal of California Law Enforcement.* 10:4 (April, 1976), 148-153.

Ware, Mitchell. *Operational Handbook for Narcotic Law Enforcement Officers.* Springfield, IL.: C.C. Thomas, 1975.

Williams, Kater W. "Drug Undercover Operations." *FBI Law Enforcement Bulletin.* 43:11 (November, 1974), 29-32.

Wilson, Charles O. and T.E. Jones. *American Drug Index 1975.* rev. ed. Philadelphia: Lippincott, 1975.

OBSCENE AND ABUSIVE PHONE CALLS

Allen, Franklin C. "Abusive Phone Calls as a Federal Offense." *Valor.* 9 (January-April, 1970).

Handloser, James A. "Abusive Telephone Calls." *FBI Law Enforcement Bulletin* (November, 1968), 6-10.

"The Hoax—An Expensive Joke." *Security Gazette.* 15:11 (1973), 4-8.
How the law handles telephone hoaxes in Great Britain. Description of court cases.

Spargo, John S. "Obnoxious Anonymous Telephone Caller." *Law and Order.* 14:1 (January, 1966), 21, 50.

Tait, Lee C. "The Call Nobody Wants." *Police Chief.* XXXLV:3 (March, 1967), 48-49.

PICK POCKETS

Campion, Daniel J. *Crooks Are Human Too.* Englewood Cliffs, NJ: Prentice Hall, 1957.

Maurer, David W. *Whiz Mob. A Correlation of the Technical Argot of Pick Pockets With Their Behavior Patterns.* University: University of Alabama Press, 1955.

POACHING

O'Meara, David C. "The Maine Way to Deer Poacher Sleuthing." *FBI Law Enforcement Bulletin.* 43:11 (November, 1974), 26-28.

Watson, John. *Poachers and Poaching.* N.Y.: British Book Center, 1974.

Worrall, Geoff R., ed. *Confessions of a Poacher.* Rhyl: Tideline, 1972.

RAPE

Amir, M. *Patterns in Forcible Rape.* Chicago: Chicago University Press, 1971.

Amir, Menachem. "Victim Precipitated Forcible Rape." *Journal of Criminal Law, Criminology and Police Science.* 58:4 (December, 1967), 493-502.

Bailey, F.L. and H.B. Rothblatt. *Crimes of Violence—Rape and Other Sex Crimes.* Rochester, N.Y.: Lawyers Cooperative Publishing Company, 1973.

Guide for the criminal defense attorney representing a defendant charged with, a sex crime, including information on pre-trial procedures, trial tactics, defenses, and specific aspects of the law.

Barber, R. "An Investigation into Rape and Attempted Rape Cases in Queensland." *Australian and New Zealand Journal of Criminology.* 6:4 (1973), 214-230.

Bard, Morton. "Crisis Intervention and Investigation of Forcible Rape." *Police Chief.* XLI:5 (May, 1974), 68-74.

Boyle, Jack G. "Rape—Mental Capacity to Consent." *Journal of Criminal Law, Criminology and Police Science.* 22 (1931-32).

Enos, W.F., J.C. Bryce and G. Mann. "The Medical Examination of Cases of Rape." *Forensic Sciences.* 17:1 (January, 1972), 50-56.

Fairly, Kenneth W. "The M.C. Parker Rape Case." *Police.* 8:2 (November-December, 1963), 78-82.

Graves, L.R., Jr. "Medicolegal Aspects of Rape." *Medical Aspects of Human Sexuality* (April, 1973), 109-117.

Lichenstein, G. "Rape Squad: Manhattan Sex Crimes Squad." *NY Times Magazine* (March 3, 1974).

MacDonald, John. *Rape: Offenders and Their Victims.* Springfield, IL.: C.C. Thomas, 1971.

MacDonald, John M. "Rape." *Police.* 13:4 (March-April, 1969), 42-46.

Nissen, Clyde. "Age of Consent Statute—Reversible Error." *Journal of Criminal Law, Criminology and Police Science.* 25 (1934-35).

Perr, Irwin N. "Statutory Rape of an Insane Person." *Journal of Forensic Sciences* (October, 1968).

"Rape Wave: Creation of Rape Investigation and Analysis Unit." *Newsweek* (January 29, 1973).

Shook, Howard C. "Revitalized Methods Needed for Investigation of Rape Complaints." *Police Chief.* XL:12 (December, 1973), 14-15.

Smithson, D. et al. "Rape: Is the Criminal Investigation Enough." *Law and Order.* 23:3 (March, 1975), 50, 53.

Stratton, John. "Rape and the Victim." *FBI Law Enforcement Bulletin* (November, 1975).

Sutherland, Sandra Fox and Donald J. Scherl. "Patterns of Response Among Rape Victims." *American Journal of Orthopsychiatrics.* 40 (1970), 503-511.

Vitulio, Louis R. "Physical Evidence in Rape Cases." *Journal of Police Science and Administration.* 2:2 (June, 1974), 160-163.

Wernle, Robert Frederick. "Habeas Corpus—Uncorroborated Testimony in Prosecution for Rape of an Insane Female." *Journal of Criminal Law, Criminology and Police Science.* 29 (1938-39).

Zeichner, Irving. "According to Law: Recommendations for the Rape Squad." *Law and Order* (July, 1974), 64, 75.

ROBBERY

Cochran, Murray O. "The Bank Robbing Brothers." *Law and Order.* 14:7 (July, 1966), 48-50.

Conklin, J.E. *Robbery and the Criminal Justice System.* Philadelphia: Lippincott, 1972.

"Criminal Law: Armed Robbery—Use of A Dangerous Weapon Subsequent to the Taking (People vs Pond)." 337 2nd 877, *Iowa Law Review.* 46:151 (Fall, 1960).

Feder, Sid. *The Great Brinks Hold Up.* Garden City, N.Y.: Doubleday, 1961.

"For the 'Want' of a Horse—A Bank Robber Is Caught." *FBI Law Enforcement Bulletin.* 35:5 (May, 1966), 12-18.

"The 'Loan' Bank Robber." *FBI Law Enforcement Bulletin* (November, 1970), 21-24.

MacDonald, John M. and Don Brannan. "The Investigation of Robbery." *Police Chief.* XLI:1 (January, 1974), 68-75.

MacDonald, John M. and Don Brannan. "The Investigation of Robbery." *Texas Police Journal.* 22:1 (1974), 4-7, 19-21; 22:2 (1974), 9-10, 21.

Ottenburg, M. "Robberies—Anatomy of Bank Robbery." *Look.* 29 (October 19, 1965), 124-127.

Ozenne, Tim. "Economics of Bank Robbery." *Journal of Legal Studies* (January, 1974), 19-51.

"Profile of a Bank Robber." *FBI Law Enforcement Bulletin.* 34:11 (November, 1965), 2-7, 20-22.

Ward, Richard H. et al. *Police Robbery Control Manual.* Washington: LEAA, 1975.

SECURITY INVESTIGATIONS

American Society for Industrial Security. *Guide to Security Investigations.* Washington: American Society for Industrial Security, 1970.

Buckley, John L. "Central Index File—Europe." *Law and Order.* 12:2 (February, 1964), 50-55.

Security clearance unit for overseas companies dealing with NATO.

Coon, Thomas F. "Government Security and Investigations." *Police.* 8:4 (March-April, 1964), 69-72.

Moore, Harry W., Jr. "Federal Personnel Loyalty—Security Programs." *Police.* 8:4 (March-April, 1964), 20-23.

SEX CRIMES

Brown, William P. "Police-Victim Relationships in Sex Crimes Investigations." *Police Chief.* XXXVII:1 (January, 1970), 20-24.

Ellis, Albert and Ralph Brancale. "The Psychology of Sex Offenders." Springfield, IL.: C.C. Thomas, 1956.

Gigeroff, Alex K. *Sexual Deviations in the Criminal Law.* Toronto, Canada: University of Toronto Press, 1968.

Kyler, Clare W. "Camera Surveillance of Sex Deviates." *Law and Order.* 11:1 (November, 1963), 16-18, 20.

McKee, William F. "Evidentiary Problems: Camera Surveillance of Sex Deviates." *Law and Order.* 12:8 (August, 1964), 72-74.

Mozes, Eugene B. *Crime and Passion: A Sexual Side of Crime in Contemporary Life.* Derby, CT.: Monarch, 1960.

Reinhardt, James Melvin. *Sex Perversions and Sex Crimes.* Springfield, IL.: C.C. Thomas, 1957.

Still, A. "Police Inquiries in Sexual Offenses." *Journal of Forensic Science Society.* 15:3 (1975), 183-188.

SHOPLIFTING

Cameron, M.O. *Booster and the Snitch—Department Store Shoplifting.* N.Y.: Free Press, 1964.

Edwards, Loren E. *Shoplifting and Shrinkage Protection for Stores.* Springfield, IL.: C.C. Thomas, 1958.

Griffin, R.K. "Modern Shopping Centers: The Shoplifter in Paradise." *Police Chief.* 38:9 (September, 1971), 66-67.

Griffin, Roger K. "Shoplifting in Supermarkets." *Police Chief* (July, 1964).

Hale, Hebert R. "Shoplifters: Their Methods and How to Apprehend Them." *FBI Law Enforcement Bulletin* (November, 1953).

Keller, E. John. "The High Cost of Crimes Against Business." *Law and Order.* 20:7 (July, 1972), 64-65.

"Shoplifting—A Growing Occupation." *Law and Order.* 12:7 (July, 1964), 45.

THEFT

Brereton, George. "Car Clouting." *California Peace Officer.* 68 (July-August, 1955).

"Let's Trap the Trappers." *FBI Law Enforcement Bulletin.* 41:1 (January, 1972), 25-27.
Thefts from night depositories at banks. Techniques is to install a trap device which can be recovered by the thief.

Maltby, G.W. "Attempted Thefts From Banks Day-Night Deposit Box." *International Criminal Police Review* (October, 1968), 230-231.

Nelson, Alfred T. and Howard E. Smith. *Car Clouting.* Springfield, IL.: C.C. Thomas, 1958.
Thefts from motor vehicles.

Nelson, Alfred T. and Howard E. Smith. "A Major Police Problem" *Police.* 2:6 (July-August, 1958), 19-24.

Nelson, Alfred T. and Howard E. Smith. "A Major Police Problem—Theft From Vehicle." *Police.* 3:1 (September-October, 1958), 7-14.

"Trailers are Tempting Targets for Thieves." *FBI Law Enforcement Bulletin.* 41:8 (August, 1972), 10-13, 28-30.
Theft of travel trailers and mobil homes.

Venning. Colin. "Road Freight Thefts." *International Criminal Police Review* (May, 1965).

Willrich, N. and T.B. Taylor. *Nuclear Theft—Risks and Safeguards—A Report to the Energy Policy Project of the Ford Foundation.* Cambridge, MA.: Ballinger, 1974.
Analysis of the possibility that nuclear materials may be stolen from the fast-growing U.S. nuclear power industry and used to make weapons.

VICE

Vice Enforcement

Craven, Joseph Donald. "Law Enforcement and Public Opinion." *Journal of Criminal Law, Criminology and Police Science.* 49:4 (November-December, 1958), 377-378.

Devlin, Patrick. *Enforcement of Morals.* N.Y.: Oxford University Press, 1970.

Egen, Frederick W. *Plainclothesman: Handbook of Vice and Gambling Investigation.* N.Y.: Arco, 1959.

Pace. D.F. *Handbook of Vice Control.* Englewood Cliffs, N.J.: Prentice Hall, 1971.
Textbook for policemen outlining the problems of vice enforcement detailing an organization for vice control, and offering guidelines for enforcement.

Rogers, Charles H. "Police Control of Obscene Literature." *Journal of Criminal Law.* 57 (December, 1966), 430-482.

Skolnick, J.H. "Coercion to Virtue—The Enforcement of Morals." *Southern California Law Review.* 41:3 (1968).

Skolnick, Jerome H. and J. Richard Woodworth. "Bureaucracy Information and Social Control: A Study of a Moral Detail." In David J. Bordua, ed. *The Police: Six Sociological Essays.* N.Y.: Wiley, 1967.

Skousen, W. Cleon. "The Chief's Responsibility for Vice Control." *Law and Order.* 16:9 (September, 1968).
In five parts, ends January 1969.

Skousen, W. Cleon. "The Chief's Responsibility for Vice Control." *Law and Order.* 21:11 (November, 1973), 8, 10, 12, 14-15; 21:12 (December, 1973), 8-9, 11-13.

Skousen, W. Cleon. "The Chief Takes a Look at the Vice Squad." *Law and Order.* 11 (August, 1963). 14-19.

Skousen, W. Cleon. "Professional Policies for a Vice Squad." *Law and Order.* 10 (September, 1963), 14-16, 18, 23.

Smith, Edgar A. *Advance Techniques of Vice Control.* Beverly Hills, CA.: Institute of Criminal Justice, 1971.

Thompson, Jim. "Common Law Crimes Against Public Morals." *Journal of Criminal Law, Criminology and Police Science* (November-December, 1958), 350-357.

Williams, John B. *Vice Control in California.* Beverly Hills, CA.: Glencoe, 1964.

Gambling Investigation

Buck, Frederick S. *Horse Race Betting: A Complete Account of Par-Mutual and Bookmaking.* NY: Greenburg, 1946.

Bullen, George M., Jr. "Local Investigation of Illegal Gambling Operations." *FBI Law Enforcement Bulletin* (March, 1971), 11-15.
Techniques and guidelines used by Delaware State Police in gambling cases.

Cole, K.C. "Learning the Odds in Las Vegas: Gambling School at the Hotel Mint." *Saturday Review* (January, 1973).

Coon, Thomas F. "Gambling Investigations." *Police.* 6:5 (May-June, 1962), 16-17.

Culin, Stewart. *Gambling Games of the Chinese in America.* Las Vegas, NE.: Gamblers, 1965.

Drzazga, John. *Wheels of Fortune.* Springfield, IL.: C.C. Thomas, 1963.
An extensive study of gambling in all its phases. Also, gambling and gambling equipment along with methods and apparatus for cheating are explored at length.

Elliott, J.F. "Some Thoughts on the Control of Organized Gaming." *Police* (January-February, 1969), 35-40.
Strategy designed to eliminate organized gambling by making it unprofitable to operate a gambling activity.

"Gambling Investigations." *FBI Law Enforcement Bulletin.* 38:7 (July, 1969), 17-19.
Discusses some of the problems inherent in gambling investigations.

Garcia, Frank. *Marked Cards and Loaded Dice.* Englewood Cliffs, N.J.: Prentice Hall, 1962.

Goren, Charles. *Go With the Odds.* London: Macmillan, 1969.
Well known bridge expert discusses all types of gambling with emphasis on the odds. It is basic and simplified reading.

Havemann, E. "How to Beat the Dogs." *Sports Illustrated* (August 27, 1973), 70-71.

Hindelag, Michael J. "Bookies and Bookmaking: A Descriptive Analysis." *Crime and Deliquency.* 17:3 (July, 1971), 245-255.

Jacoby, Oswald. *How to Figure the Odds.* Garden City, N.Y.: Doubleday, 1947.
Well known bridge expert discusses all forms of gambling with emphasis on the odds. Similar to the Goren book.

King, Rufus. *Gambling and Organized Crime.* Washington: Public Affairs Press, 1969.

King, Rufus. "The Pinball Problem in Illinois—An Over Due Solution." *Journal of Criminal Law, Criminology and Police Science.* 57:1 (March, 1966), 17-26.

King, Rufus. "The Rise and Decline of Coin-Machine Gambling." *Journal of Criminal Law, Criminology and Police Science.* 55:2 (June, 1964), 199-207.

Levinson, Horace C. *Chance, Luck and Statistics.* N.Y.: Dover, 1963.
Both the theory of chance or probability and the science of statistics are presented in easy to understand language.

Livingston, A. *Dealing With Cheats.* Philadelphia: Lippincott, 1973.

Mayer, Gary. *Bookie: My Life in Disorganized Crime.* N.Y.: Hawthorn Books, 1974.

Moss, Michael S. "Horse Doping: Laboratory and Forensic Aspects." *Criminologist.* 8:28 (Spring, 1973), 39-49.

Newman, David. *Esquire's Book on Gambling.* N.Y.: Harper, 1962.

"Raw Deal; Cheating in Nevada Gambling." *Newsweek* (September 17, 19u3), 82-83.

"Razzle Dazzle and Related Gambling Games." *FBI Law Enforcement Bulletin.* 38:2 (February, 1969), 12-16.
The purpose of this article is to acquaint law enforcement officers with carnival-type games which involve "fast count" techniques and overwhelming odds against the player.

Radner, Sidney H. *How to Spot Card Sharps and Their Methods.* N.Y.: Wehman, 1957.

Roebuck, Julian B. "The Negro Numbers Man as a Criminal Type: The Construction and Application of a Typology." *Journal of Criminal Law, Criminology and Police Science.* 54:1 (March, 1963), 48-60.

Scarne, John. *Scarne on Cards.* N.Y.: Crown, 1973.
Detailed study of major gambling card games. Methods of cheating at cards, including false shuffles and deals and the marking or altering of cards.

Scarne, John. *Scarne on Dice.* Harrisburg, PA.: Stockpole, 1962.
Detailed study of various dice games, particularly craps. Odds developed for various possibilities in dice games. A study of various methods of manipulating dice and/or altering dice.

Scarne, John. *Scarne's Encyclopedia of Games.* N.Y.: Harper and Row, 1973.
The latest book by the foremost gambling author. Book mainly emphasizes rules and strategy in various card games.

Scarne, John. *Scarne's New Complete Guide to Gambling.* NY: Simon & Schuster, 1974.

Silver, Edward S. "Organized Gambling and Law Enforcement." *Journal of Criminal Law, Criminology and Police Science.* 50:4 (1959-1960).

Skousen, W. Cleon. "Challenging the Gambling Syndicate." *Law and Order.* 11:11 (November, 1963), 10-15.

Skousen, W. Cleon. "Gambling: A Special Challenge to the New Chief." *Law and Order.* 22:2 (February, 1974), 8-13.

Sullivan, George. *The History of Lotteries.* N.Y.: Dodd Mead, 1972.

Turner, Wallace. *Gamblers' Money.* Boston: Houghton Mifflin, 1965.

Ullocking, J.H. "Cock Fighting." *Police College Magazine* (Autumn, 1965), 105-113.

U.S. Congress House Select Committee on Crime. *Organized Criminal Influence in Horseracing.* Washington: GPO, 1973.

Williams, Frances E. *Lotteries, Laws and Morals.* N.Y.: Vantage, 1958.

Gambling—General

Allen, David D. *The Nature of Gambling.* N.Y.: Coward McCann, 1952.

Asbury, Herbert. *Sucker's Progress.* N.Y.: Mead, 1938.
An informal history of gambling in America from the colonies to Canfield.

Bergler, Edmund. *The Psychology of Gambling.* N.Y.: Hill & Wang, 1957.

Blanche, Ernest E. *You Can't Win: Facts and Fallacies About Gambling.* Washington: Public Affairs Press, 1949.

Bloch, Herbert A. "The Sociology of Gambling." *American Journal of Sociology* (November, 1951).

Buck, Frederick Silas. *Horse Race Betting.* N.Y.: Arco, 1971.

Davidson, Joseph B. *Inside Horseracing.* N.Y.: Arco, 1973.

Dubins, Lester E. and Leonard J. Savage. *How to Gamble if You Must.* N.Y.: McGraw-Hill, 1965.

Flanagan, Tom. *Beat the Races.* N.Y.: Arco, 1973.

Fraikin, Glenn L. *Inside Nevada Gambling: Adventures of a Winning System Player.* N.Y.: Exposition, 1965.

Gamblers Anonymous. 3rd ed., Los Angeles: Gamblers Anonymous, 1973.

Herman, Robert D. *Gambling.* N.Y. Harper & Row, 1967.

Jacoby, Oswald. *Jacoby on Gambling.* N.Y.: Hart, 1963.

Jones, J. Phillip. *Gambling Yesterday and Today: A Complete History.* North Pomfret, VT: David & Charles, 1973.

Livingston, J. *Compulsive Gamblers.* Springfield, VA.: NTIS, 1971.
Investigation into the nature of compulsive gamblers and compulsive gambling.

Ludovici, Laurence J. *The Itch for Play.* London: Jarrolds, 1962.

McQuaid, Clement. *Gambler's Digest.* Northfield, IL.: Follett, 1971.
In the author's own words, this book provides the reader with everything you need to know to win.

Marchant, Larry. *The National Football Lottery.* N.Y.: Holt, Rinehart & Winston, 1973.

Maskelyne, John Nevil. *Sharps and Flats.* Los Angeles: Los Angeles Gamblers Book Club, 1971.

Smith, Harold S. *I Want to Quit Winners.* Englewood Cliffs, N.J.: Prentice Hall, 1961.

Thorpe, Edward O. *Beat the Dealer.* N.Y.: Random House, 1962.
Well known mathematician gives detailed methods of winning in blackjack.

Wilson, Alan N. *The Casino Gamblers Guide.* N.Y.: Harper & Row, 1965.

Wykes, Alan. *The Complete Illustrated Guide to Gambling.* Garden City, NY: Doubleday, 1964.
A worldwide survey of the art of gambling which concentrates on the way to beat and win.

Loan Sharking

Illinois Crime Investigating Commission. *Report on Criminal Usury in the Chicago Area.* Chicago: Illinois Crime Investigating Commission, 1970.

International Research and Technology Corporation. *Loansharking Indicators—Development and Use.* Washington: NILECJ, 1972.

New York State Commission of Investigation. *An Investigation of the Loan Shark Racket.* Albany, N.Y.: State Commission of Investigation, 1965.

Seidl, John Michael. *Upon the Hip: A Study of the Criminal Loan Shark Industry.* Unpub. Ph.D. dissertation, Harvard University, 1969.

Sherrid, Samuel D. "The Mathematics of Loan Sharking." *Police Chief.* XLII:2 (February, 1975), 59.

Procuring

Hall, Susan. *Gentleman of Leisure: A Year in the Life of a Pimp.* NY: New American Library, 1973.

Powis, D. "Catching Ponces." *Police Review.* [ENG.] 82:4271 (1974), 1505-1508; 82:4272 (1974), 1534-1537.

Prostitution

Acton, William. *Prostitution.* N.Y.: Praeger, 1969.

Bilek, Arthur J. and Alan S. Ganz. "The B-Girl Problem: A Proposal Ordinance." *Journal of Criminal Law, Criminology and Police Science.* 56:1 (March, 1965), 39-44.

Fry, Monroe. *Sex, Vice, and Business.* N.Y.: Ballantine, 1959.

George, B.J., Jr. "Legal, Medical and Psychiatric Considerations in the Control of Prostitution." *Michigan Law Review.* 60 (1962).

Greenwald, Harold. *The Elegant Prostitute.* N.Y.: Ballantine, 1970.

Harris, Sara. *They Sell Sex: The Call Girl and Big Business.* Greenwich, CT.: Fawcett, 1960.

Hinojosa, Antonio V. "Cases of International Proxenetism in Spain." *International Criminal Police Review* (June-July, 1965).
White slave activities.

Keiser, R. *The Vice Lords.* N.Y.: Holt, Rinehart & Winston, 1969.

"Prostitutes: The New Breed." *Newsweek.* 78 (July 12, 1971).

Sheehy, Gail. *Hustling.* N.Y.: Delacorte, 1973.

Skousen, W. Cleon. "How to Beat The Call Girl Racket." *Law and Order.* 12:1 (January, 1964), 14-15, 19.

Skousen, W. Cleon. "Sex Racketeers." *Law and Order.* 11:12 (December, 1963), 12, 14, 16-17.

Techniques of Law Enforcement Against Prostitution. Washington: GPO, 1943.

Thornton, Robert Y. "Organized Crime in the Field of Prostitution." *Journal of Criminal Law, Criminology and Police Science.* 46 (March-April, 1956).

Velarde, A.J. and M. Warlick. "Massage Parlors: The Sensuality Business." *Society.* 11:1 (1974), 63-74.

Winick, Charles and Paul M. McKinsie. *The Lively Commerce.* Chicago: Quadrangle, 1971.

MISCELLANEOUS INVESTIGATIONS

California Department of Alcoholic Beverage Control. *ABC Enforcement Manual: A Manual Prepared to Assist Peace Officers in the Conduct of Investigations of Violations of the Alcoholic Beverage Act.* Sacramento: Department of Alcoholic Beverage Control, n/d.

Constable, John. " 'Illegal' Immigration: Policy and Law." *Race* (January, 1974), 361-369.

Illinois Legislative Investigating Commission. *Fireworks: Plant Explosions and Bootleg Traffic in Illinois—A Report to the Illinois General Assembly.* Washington: NCJRS (Microfiche), 1974.

International Association of Chiefs of Police. *Boating Accident Investigation Manual.* Gaithersburg, MD.: IACP, 1975.

"A Look at Selective Service Violations." *FBI Law Enforcement Bulletin.* 35:11 (November, 1966), 22-23.

Rios, Omar G. "The Chronic Mexican-Alien Immigration Offender." *Federal Probation.* 34 (September, 1970), 57-60.

SCIENTIFIC CRIMINAL INVESTIGATION

FORENSIC ASPECTS OF INVESTIGATION—GENERAL

Arthur, Richard O. *The Scientific Investigator.* Springfield, IL.: C.C. Thomas, 1965.

Ayers, K.M. and C.J. Stahl, "Experimental Injuries of the Eye Caused by a Tear Gas Pen Gun Loaded with Orthochlorobenzalmalononitrile." *Journal of Forensic Science.* 17:4 (1972), 547-554.

Berg, Stanton O. "Sherlock Holmes: Father of Scientific Crime Detection." *Journal of Criminal Law, Criminology and Police Science.* 61:3 (September, 1970), 446-452.

Beveridge, William. *The Art of Scientific Investigation.* Melbourne: Heinemann, 1950.

Bradford, Lowell W. "Criminalistics Looks Forward. *Journal of Criminal Law, Criminology and Police Science.* 60:1 (March, 1969), 127-130.

Bradford, Lowell W. "General Criminalistics in the Courtroom." *Journal of Forensic Sciences.* 11:3 (July, 1966), 358-472.

Brunelle, Richard L. "The Role of Forensic Science in the Bureau of Alcohol, Tobacco, and Firearms." *Identification News.* 22:11 (November, 1973), 3-9.

Camps, Francis E. "Tar Oil Immersion." *The Criminologist* (February, 1969).

Ceccaldi, P.F. "From Crime to Evidence. An Essay in Criminalistic Philosophy." *International Criminal Police Review.* 28:264 (1973), 2-8.

Cederbaums, Juris G. and Selma Arnold. *Scientific and Expert Evidence in Criminal Advocacy.* N.Y.: Practicing Law Institute, 1975.

Clark, L.G. "The Instruments of the Chemist." *Australian Police Journal.* 26:3 (1972), 199-215.

Clark, P.D.B. "Forensic Type Examinations—An Analysis." *Journal Forensic Science Society.* 12:4 (1972), 559-566.

Courville, Cyril B. *Forensic Neuropathology.* Mundelein, IL.: Callaghan, 1964.

Curry, A.S. *Methods of Forensic Science.* N.Y.: Wiley, 1964.

Cuthbert, C.R.M. *Science and the Detection of Crime.* N.Y.: Philosophical Library, 1958.

Cuttenplan, Henry L. "Scientific Services in a Law Enforcement Agency." *Bulletin Society Professional Investigators* (October, 1966), 27-31.

Davies, Geoffrey. *Forensic Science.* Washington: American Chemical Society, 1975.

Devonport, Graham. "The Use of Fluorescent Powders in Police Work." *Police Journal.* 42:3 (March, 1969), 131-133.

Dragel, D.T. "Science vs. the Law." *Analytical Chemistry.* 37:3 (March, 1965), 27A-32A.

Howard, L.R.C. "Investigations of Torture Allegations by the Forensic Psychologist." *Journal of Forensic Science Society* (1974), 299-309.

Hormachea, Carroll. *Source Book in Criminalistics.* Reston, VA.: Reston Publishing, 1974.

Inbau, Fred E., Andre A. Moenssens and Louis R. Vitullo. *Scientific Police Investigation.* Philadelphia: Chilton, 1972.

Johnson, Marlin W. "Science and Law Enforcement Partners in Progress." *Journal of Forensic Sciences.* 10:2 (April, 1965), 113-120.

Kind, S. and M. Overman. *Science Against Crime.* Garden City, N.Y.: Doubleday, 1972.

Kirwan, W.E. and D. Hardy. "Laundry and Dry Cleaners Marks." *NY State Bureau of Criminal Investigation Bulletin.* 21:2 (1956), 3-8.

Lloyd J.B.F. "Luminescence of Tire Marks and Other Rubber Contact Traces." *Journal of Forensic Science Society.* 16:1 (1976), 5-19.

Lucas, N. *Laboratory Detectives—How Science Traps the Criminal.* N.Y.: Taplinger, 1971.

Lundquist, F. *Methods of Forensic Science.* V. 1. N.Y.: Wiley, 1972.

Lundquist, F. *Methods of Forensic Science.* V. 2. N.Y.: Wiley, 1973.

Magans, Orville R. "Watch Mark File Is Useful Aid to the Investigation." *FBI Law Enforcement Bulletin.* 28:7 (July, 1959).

Moenssens, Andre A., Ray Edward Moses and Fred E. Inbau. *Scientific Evidence in Criminal Cases.* Mineola, N.Y.: Foundation, 1974.

Morland, Nigel. *An Outline of Scientific Criminology.* N.Y.: St. Martin's, 1972.

Muir, A.A. "The Use of Scientific Aids in Crime Detection." *Journal of Forensic Science Society.* 4:3 (March, 1964), 119-123.

Nadeau, Tom. "A Device to Locate Decomposing Bodies." *Law and Order.* 22:7 (July, 1974), 45.

National Institute of Law Enforcement and Criminal Justice. *Trace Metal Detection Technique in Law Enforcement.* Washington: GPO, 1970.
A trace metal detection technique (TMDT) has been developed to determine whether a suspect or nonmetallic material has been in contact with metal objects.

O'Brien, Kevin and Robert C. Sullivan. *Criminalistics: Theory and Practice.* Boston: Holbrook, 1973.

O'Hara, C.E. and J.W. Osterburg. *Introduction to Criminalistics—The Application of the Physical Sciences to the Detection of Crime.* Bloomington, IN.: Indiana University Press, 1972.

Ormrod, R. "The Medico-Legal Aspects of Sex Determination." *Medical Legal Journal.* 40:3 (1972), 78-88.

Osterburg, James. "Significant Concepts in Scientific Criminal Investigation." *Law and Order.* 12:7 (July, 1964), 26-29.

Osterburg, James W. "What Problems Must Criminalistics Solve." *Journal of Criminal Law, Criminology and Police Science.* 59:1 (September, 1968), 427-483.

Peterson, J.L. *Utilization of Criminalistics Services by the Police: An Analysis of the Physical Evidence Recovery Process.* Washington: NCJRS, 1972.
Recommendations for criminalistics organizations and resource management, improved training provisions, and research to attack fundamental investigative problems.

Richardson, James R. *Scientific Evidence for Police Officers.* Cincinnati: Anderson, 1963.

Shaw, William. "An Introduction to Forensic Chemistry." *Law and Order.* 19:11 (November, 1971), 16-18, 20-21, 27; 19:12 (1971), 22, 26, 28-31.

Shaw, William. "An Introduction to Ultraviolet: Black Light and Its Application to Police Work." *Law and Order.* 16:7 (July, 1968), 24-32.

Sullivan, Robert C. and Kevin O'Brien. "For All The Work That Is To Be Done." *Police Chief.* XXXVII:5 (May, 1970), 40-45.

Sullivan, Robert C. and Kevin P. O'Brien. "The Need for a Convergence of Effort in Modern Forensic Science." *Police.* 13:5 (May-June, 1969), 11-12.

Thurston, Gavin. *Coronership.* London: Barry Rose, 1976.

Turner, William W. *Criminalistics.* Rochester: Aqueduct, 1965.

Turner, William W. *Invisible Witness: The Use and Abuse of the New Technology of Crime Investigation.* N.Y.: Bobbs Merrill, 1968.

Tuteur, Werner and Ulrich Venzlaff. "Forensic Psychiatry in the United States and West Germany." *Journal of Forensic Science.* 14:1 (January, 1969), 69-98.

Ullyett, Kenneth. *Criminology: The Science of Crime Detection.* London: Franklin Watts, 1972.

Walls, H.J. *Forensic Science: An Introduction to the Science of Crime Detection.* N.Y.: Praeger, 1968.

Wilber, Charles Grady. *Forensic Biology for the Law Enforcement Officer.* Springfield, IL.: C.C. Thomas, 1974.

BITE MARKS

"Bite Marks Identification." *Canadian Society of Forensic Science Journal.* 5:4 (December, 1972), 142.

Furness, J. "Bite Marks in Non-Accidental Injuries of Children." *Police Surgeon.* 6 (1974), 75-85.

Furness, John. "Teeth Marks and Their Significance in Cases of Homicide." *Journal of Forensic Science Society.* 9:3 & 4 (December, 1969), 169-175.

Layton, J.J. "Identification from a Bite Mark in Cheese." *Journal of the Forensic Science Society.* 6:2 (April, 1966), 76-80.

Marshall, W., J. Potter and W. Harvey. "Bite Marks in Apples—Forensic Aspects." *Criminologist.* 9:32 (1974), 21-34.

Osborne, H. Butler. "The Value of Bite Mark Evidence." *International Journal of Dentistry.* 1:2 (October, 1973), 13-15.

Simon, A., H. Jordan and K. Pforte. "Successful Identification of a Bite Mark Sandwich." *International Journal of Forensic Dentistry.* 2:3 (1974), 17-21.

Yano, Masaharu. "Experimental Studies on Bite Marks." *International Journal of Forensic Dentistry.* 1:2 (October, 1973), 13-15.

BLOOD

Cayzer, I. and P.H. Whitehead. "The Use of Sensitized Latex in the Identification of Human Blood Stains." *Journal of Forensic Science Society.* 13:3 (1973), 179-181.

Chastain, J.D. "Blood and Blood Stains in Criminal Investigation." *Police.* 3:1 (September-October, 1958), 37-38.

Culliford, B.J. *Examination and Typing of Blood Stains in the Crime Laboratory.* Washington: GPO, 1971.

"Examination of Biological Fluids." *FBI Law Enforcement Bulletin.* 41:6 (1972), 12-15, 30.

Hayward, J.W. and A.L. Bosworth. "Esterase D Typexnin

Human Blood Stains." *Journal of Forensic Science Society.* 15:4 (1975), 289-292.

Jay, B.W.H. "Haptoglobin Polymorphism—Another System to Differentiate Blood Groups." *Canadian Society Forensic Science Journal.* 8:1 (1975), 21-26.

King, L.A. "The Value of Biochemical Profiling for the Discrimination of Blood Stains." *Journal Forensic Science Society.* 14:4 (1974), 323-327.

Khalap, S., M. Pereira and S. Rand. "Gm and Inv Grouping of Blood Stains." *Medical Science Law.* 16:1 (1976), 40-43.

MacDonell, H.L. *Flight Characteristics and Stain Patterns of Human Blood.* Washington: GPO, 1972.

MacDonell, H.L. "Institute on the Physical Significance of Blood Stain Evidence." *Law and Order.* 21:7 (1973), 32-37, 71.

Melville, W. "Blood Group Determination: The Starch Gel Electrophoresis Techniques Applied." *Police Journal.* 44:4 (1971), 302-305.

Nuorteva, P. "Age Determination of a blood Stain on a Decaying Shirt by Entromological Means." *Forensic Science.* 3:1 (1974), 89-94.

Sivaram, S. "Differentiation Between Stains of Human Blood and Blood of Monkey." *Forensic Science.* 6:3 (1975), 145-152.

CHROMATOGRAPHY

Baitsholdt, A.D. "Coming—'Routine' Chromatography of Evidence." *Law and Order.* 14:11 (November, 1966), 60-63.

Barker, A.M.L. and P.O.B. Clarke. "Examination of Small Quantities of Lipstick." *Journal of Forensic Science Society.* 12:3 (1972), 449-451.

Brackett, James W. and Lowell W. Bradford. "Comparison of Ink Writing on Documents by Means of Paper Chromatography." *Journal of Criminal Law, Criminology and Police Science.* 43 (1952-53).

Kempe, Carl R. "Gas Chromatograph." *Law and Order.* 12:12 (December, 1965), 62-63.

Rice, D.D. and J.M. Trowell. "Determination of Vobtiles in Solids and High Boiling Liquids by Gas Chromatography." *Analytical Chemistry.* 39:2 (February, 1967), 157-162.

CRIME LABORATORIES

Anthony, Robert J. "Philadelphia Police Lab Aided by Analytic Instruments." *Law and Order.* 20:7 (July, 1972), 22-24, 26, 53.

Arthur, R.O. *Scientific Investigation.* Springfield, IL.: C.C. Thomas, 1970.

The text offers suggestions on selected subjects in the effective operation of a crime laboratory.

Ayoob, Massad F. "The ATFB'S Atomic Crime Lab." *Law and Order.* 21:7 (July, 1973), 58-61.

Bonamarte, M.F. and A.H. Principe. "Regional Crime Lab for Northern Illinois." *Police Chief.* XXXVI:5 (May, 1969), 18-21.

Crime Laboratories—Three Study Reports. Springfield, VA.: NTIS, 1969.

National survey and state study on consolidation of police services providing information for improvement of state and local laboratory system.

"Crime Laboratories Symposium." *FBI Law Enforcement Bulletin.* 43:2 (February, 1974), 10.

Dragnich, Alix. "The Police Lab." *Law and Order.* 20:7 (July, 1972), 30-31, 34-36.

Effron, Harlod. "The U.S. Army's Crime Lab in Japan." *Law and Order.* 16:7 (July, 1968), 57-62.

Gunn, John W., Jr. and Richard S. Frank. "Planning a Forensic Science Lab." *Police Chief.* 39:1 (January, 1972), 36-41.

Guttenplan, Henry L. *Role of the Police Laboratory in a Law Enforcement Agency: A Comparative Organizational Study.* Unpub. Ph.D. dissertation, New York University, 1965.

Hall, Jay Cameron. *Inside the Crime Lab.* Englewood Cliffs, N.J.: Prentice Hall, 1974.

Kempe, Carl R. "The Scientist and the Laboratory." *Police.* 9:3 (January-February, 1965), 27-29.

Kirk, P.L. *Crime Investigation—Physical Evidence and the Police Laboratory.* N.Y.: Wiley, 1953.

Introductory and reference volume for the police investigator and practicing criminalist, covering a broad spectrum of evidence and its analysis.

Kirk, Paul L. and Lowell W. Bradford. *The Crime Laboratory: Organization and Operation.* Springfield, IL.: C.C. Thomas, 1965.

Krendel, E.S. and R.M. Dummer. *Management Planning for Forensic Science Laboratories.* Springfield, VA.: NTIS, 1971.

Lawder, Lee E. "State Forensic Laboratory Aids Law Enforcement." *Law and Order.* 22:3 (March, 1974), 28-29.

Loth, David. *Crime Lab.* N.Y.: Simon & Schuster, 1964.

Luppmann, Walter. "How to Work with Your Crime Laboratory." *Law and Order.* 17:10 (October, 1969), 107-108.

McDaniel, Frederick R. "Labops: A System Analysis of Laboratory Operations." *Journal of Police Science and Administration.* 1:4 (December, 1973), 454-458.

Osterburg, James W. *The Crime Laboratory.* Bloomington: Indiana University Press, 1967.

Osterburg, James W. "The Police Crime Laboratory as an Investigative Aid." *Law and Order.* 13:10 (October, 1965), 64-67.

Paholke, Arthur R. "Safe Recognition." *Law and Order.* 21:7 (July, 1973), 62-63.

Rehling, C.J. and C.L. Rabren. *Alabama's Master Plan for a Crime Laboratory Delivery System.* Washington: GPO, 1973.

Steindler, R.A. "The Crime Lab—What It Can Do For You." *Law and Order.* 21:7 (July, 1973), 22, 25-27, 71.

"A Team Against Crime—Law Enforcement and The Laboratory." *FBI Law Enforcement Bulletin.* 36:11 (November, 1967), 3-6.

Wichmann, Robert. "Drug Overload." *Law and Order.* 19:12 (December, 1971), 65.
Utilizations of private laboratories in identifying and reporting suspect drugs.

CRIME SCENE INVESTIGATION

Aubry, Arthur S., Jr. "The Collection of Evidence." *Police.* 7:4 (March-April, 1963), 40-43.

Crowley, W.D. "Initial Action at the Scene of a Crime." *Australian Police Journal.* 17:2 (April, 1963), 105-111.

Cunningham, D.K. "Police Duties at the Scene of the Crime." *Police.* 6:2 (November-December, 1961), 77-78.

Curtis, E.K. "Forensic Science Scenes of Crime Officers." *Australian Police Journal.* 22:1 (January, 1968), 29-45.

Fox, R.H. and C.L. Cunningham. *Crime Scene Search and Physical Evidence Handbook.* Washington: GPO, 1973.
Detailed guidelines for the criminal investigator in the protection and reporting of the crime scene and the collection and preservation of various types of evidence.

Grant, D. "Fingerprints in Unexpected Places." *Police Journal.* 45:1 (1972), 66-68.

Harris, Raymond I. "Accessory After the Fact—The Officer on the Scene(?)" *Police.* 7:6 (July-August, 1963), 6-13.

Inbau, F.E. and A.A. Moenssens. *Scientific Police Investigation.* Radnor, PA.: Chilton, 1972.
Guide for the working patrolman on possibilities for scientific criminal investigation, with measures for preserving and collecting evidence at the crime scene.

Jones, James H. and Joseph L. Peterson. *Evidence Technician Program Manual—Optimizing Crime Scene Search Operations.* N.Y.: Criminal Justice Center, John Jay College of Criminal Justice, 1976.

Kind, S.S. "The Scene of the Crime." *Police.* 15:2 (November-December, 1970), 55-65.

McArthur, Jack. "Crime Scene Sketching." *Police.* 8:5 (May-June 1964), 39-42.

MacDonell, H.L. *Flight Characteristics and Stain Patterns of Human Blood.* Washington: NCJRS, 1971.

Muller, Howard W. "Inspection of Localities." *Law and Order.* 20:3 (March, 1972), 42-43, 62-63.

Samen, Charles C. "The Evidence Collection Unit—A New Approach to Scientific Crime Detection." *Law and Order.* 19:7 (July, 1971), 68-71, 78.

Samen, Charles C. "Major Crime Scene Investigation—Part III: Sketching the Scene." *Law and Order.* 19:10 (October, 1971), 72-74, 76-79.

Samen, Charles C. "Major Crime Scene Investigation—Part IV: Search Patterns." *Law and Order.* 19:11 (November, 1971), 76-80.

Samen, Charles C. "Major Crime Scene Investigation—Part V: Developing Invisible Evidence." *Law and Order.* 19:12 (December, 1971), 50-56.

Samen, Charles C. "Major Crime Scene Investigation—Part VII: Casting (Shoe and Tire Impressions)." *Law and Order.* 20:3 (March, 1972), 52-57.

Samen, Charles C. "Major Crime Scene Investigation—Part VIII: Blood Stain Evidence." *Law and Order.* 20:4 (April, 1972), 84-86, 88, 90.

Schernhorst, John N. "The Scene Plan." *Police.* 13:5 (May-June, 1969), 42-51.

Schernhorst, John N. "Forensic Photogrammetry." *Police.* 9:2 (November-December, 1964), 6-10.
Photogrammetry is the art of taking exact measurements from photographs. Used in mapping accident and crime scenes.

Shulman, Alan R. "On-The-Spot Fingerprint Photo." *Law and Order.* 16:7 (July, 1968), 17-23.
Use of Poloroid C.U.-5 Close Up. Camera for crime scene recording including fingerprints.

Svensson, Aren and Otto Wendel. *Techniques of Crime Scene Investigation.* N.Y.: Elsevier, 1965.

Whittaker, Edward. "Crime Scene Search and the Preservation of Evidence." *Identification News.* 20 (May, 1970).

Wisconsin Department of Justice. *Criminal Investigation and Physical Evidence Handbook.* 2nd ed. Madison, WS.: Wisconsin Department of Administration, 1973.
Basic procedural guidelines outlining necessary and efficient methods for the recognition, collection and preservation of evidentiary materials.

Wood, A.C. "Scientific Examination at the Scene." *Law and Order.* 6:3 (March, 1958), 12.

DRUGS

"Abstract: Multiple Testing of Suspect Drugs." *Law and Order.* 23:4 (April, 1975), 85.

Angiolelli, Rocco J. "False Results Produced by Drug Field Test Kits." *Law and Order.* 20:8 (August, 1972), 50-51, 98.

DeAngelis, G.G. "Drug Testing—Techniques and Issues." *Drug Forum.* 3:3 (1974), 199-213.

Duquenois, P. "Chemical and Physiological Identification of Indian Hemp." *UN Bulletin on Narcotics.* 2:3 (July, 1950), 30-33.

Duquenois, P. and H. Negm. "Identification and Assay of Cannabis Indica." *Journal Egypt Medical Association.* 21 (1938), 224-227.

Gearine, James E. and Bernard F. Grabowski. *Methods of Drug Analysis.* Philadelphia: Lea & Febiger, 1969.

Hider, Cecil L. "Preparation of Evidence in Illicit Anphetamines Manufacturing Prosecutions." *Forensic Science Society Journal.* 9 (July, 1969), 75-79.

Mausolf, Norman, et al. "Pitfalls in the Use of Drug Field-Testing Kits." *Police Chief.* XL:3 (March, 1973), 46-47.

Thornton, John I. and Duayne J. Dillon. "Identification of the Opium Poppy." *Journal of Forensic Science Society.* 5:4 (October, 1965), 199-200.

Thornton, John I. and G.R. Nakamura. "The Identification

of Marijuana." *Journal of the Forensic Science Society*. 12:3 (July, 1972), 461-519.

Tobias, Jerry J. and Robert Taylor. "Suburban Narcotics Mini-Laboratory." *Law and Order*. 18:2 (February, 1970), 48-51.

EAR IDENTIFICATION

Hirschi, Fritz. "International Burglars Convicted on Unusual Evidence." *International Criminal Police Review*. 25:239 (June-July, 1970), 184-193; 25:240 (August-September, 1970), 219-222.

Iannarelli, Alfred V. "Ear Identification." *International Criminal Police Review*. 221 (October, 1968), 226-229.

Iannarelli, Alfred V. "Ear Identification—A Positive Means of Identification." *Valor*. 9 (May-August, 1970).

Iannarelli, Alfred V. *The Iannarelli System of Ear Identification*. Brooklyn Foundation Press, 1964.

Scaillet, M. "An Unusual Identification." *International Criminal Police Review*. 26 (February, 1971), 41-43.

EXHUMATION

Camps, Francis E. "Exhumation." *Criminologist* (Winter, 1972), 73-76.

Craig, D.G. "Exhumation." *Police Surgeon* (October, 1974), 98-103.

EXPLOSIONS AND FIRES

Adams, Donald L. "The Extraction and Identification of Small Amounts of Accelerants from Arson Evidence." *Journal of Criminal Law, Criminology and Police Science*. 47 (1956-57).

Burd, David Q. "Arson and Fire Investigation: The Function of the Criminalist." *Journal of Forensic Sciences*. 7:4 (October, 1962), 417-430.

Byall, E.B. and C.M. Hoffman. "Identification of Explosive Residues in Bomb Scene Investigations." *Journal of Forensic Sciences* (January, 1974).

Forestier, H. "Characterization of Explosives Traces After an Explosion." *International Criminal Police Review*. 28:277 (1974), 99-106.

Handy, A.E.A. "The Role of the Criminal Laboratory in an Arson Case." *International Criminal Police Review* 185 (February, 1965), 34-41.

Hoffman, C.M. and E.B. Byall. "Identification of Explosive Residues in Bomb Scene Investigations." *Journal of Forensic Sciences*. 19:1 (January, 1974), 54-63.

Lucas, C.M. "What the Laboratory Can Do For the Arson Investigator." *Fire Arson Investigator*. 24:2 (1973), 58-64.

Pinnick, R.W. "Preservation of Physical Evidence in Fire Cases." *Fire Arson Investigator*. 25:3 (1975), 55-57.

Reneri, L., Jr. "Physical Evidence in Auto Fires." *Fire Arson Investigator*. 25:3 (1975), 18-21.

"Safe Insulation and its Value in Crime Detection." *FBI Law Enforcement Bulletin*. 43:11 (1974), 23-25.

Yallop, H.J. "Breaking Offences with Explosives—The Techniques of the Criminal and the Scientist." *Journal Forensic Science Society*. 14:2 (1974), 99-102.

FINGERPRINTS

Fingerprints—General

"An Analysis of Standards in Fingerprint Identification." *FBI Law Enforcement Bulletin* (June, 1972).

Block, Eugene B. *Fingerprinting: Magic Weapon Against Crime*. N.Y.: David McKay, 1969.

Bridges, Burtis C. *Practical Fingerprinting*. N.Y.: Funk & Wagnalls, 1963.

Browne, Douglas G. *Fingerprints*. N.Y.: Dutton, 1954.

Browne, Douglas Gordon. *Fingerprints: Fifty Years of Scientific Crime Detection*. London: G.G. Harrap, 1953.

Califana, Anthony L. "Enlarging a Fingerprint on Glass 34 Years Old." *Law and Order*. 20:7 (July, 1972), 62-63.

Califana, Anthony L. "Fingerprinting the Deceased." *Law and Order*. 17:12 (December, 1969), 46-47.

Califana, Anthony L. "How to Take Legible Fingerprints." *Law and Order*. 18:10 (October, 1970), 78-80, 82, 84, 104.

Califana, Anthony L. "Latent Fingerprints on the Human Body and Secretions." *Law and Order*. 23:7 (July, 1975), 23.

Califana, Anthony L. "Unusual Fingerprint Identification." *Law and Order*. 20:4 (April, 1972), 72-74.

"Chemical Development of Latent Impressions." *FBI Law Enforcement Bulletin* (August, 1970).

Cherrill, Fred. *Fingerprints Never Lie*. N.Y.: Macmillan, 1954.

Cummins, Harold. "Ancient Finger Prints in Clay." *Journal of Criminal Law, Criminology and Police Science*. 32 (1941-42).

"Fingerprint Mutilation." *FBI Law Enforcement Bulletin* (June, 1957).

Field, Annita Tolivar. *Fingerprint Handbook*. Springfield, IL.: C.C. Thomas, 1959.

"Fingerprinting: A Story of Science vs Crime." *FBI Law Enforcement Bulletin* (July, 1971).

"Fingerprint Work in Major Public Disasters." *FBI Law Enforcement Bulletin* (September, 1958).

"Fingerprints by Wire: Chicago." *American City* (October 28, 1966).

Galton, Sir Francis. *Finger Prints*. N.Y.: Macmillan, 1892.

Ghorbani, Mustafa. "Transmission of Fingerprints—New Suggestion in the Field of Fingerprinting." *International Criminal Police Review*. 161 (October, 1962), 255-258.

Haiker, W.R. "Foolproof Fingerprinting." *Law and Order*. 18:7. (July, 1970).

Hammond, Bertie James. "Finger Prints and the Ruxton Murders." *Journal of Criminal Law, Criminology and Police Science.* 43 (1952-53), 805.

"IAI Adopts Resolution on Number of Friction Ridge Characteristics for Positive Identification. *Police Chief.* XLI:2 (February, 1974), 50.

Keating, Robert E. "Half of Family Has No Fingerprints." *Law and Order.* 18:7 (July, 1970), 22-23, 26-27.

Kingston, C.R. and P.L. Kirk. "Historical Development and Evaluation of the '12 Point Rule' in Fingerprint Identification." *International Criminal Police Review.* 186 (March, 1965), 62-69.

Lail, Harold A. "Fingerprint Recover With Electronography." *Police Chief.* XLII:10 (October, 1975), 34, 39-40.

Lawder, Lee E. "No Tubes, No Glass, No Roller or Mess." *Law and Order.* 11:8 (August, 1963), 20, 49.

Liebenberg, I.J. "Obtaining a Print from a Mummified Finger." *Journal of Criminal Law, Criminology and Police Science.* 41 (1950-51).

Moenssens, Andre A. *Fingerprints and the Law.* Philadelphia: Chilton, 1969.

Moenssens, Andre A. *Fingerprint Techniques.* Philadelphia: Chilton, 1971.

New York State Identification and Intelligence System. *Fingerprinting Techniques.* Albany, N.Y.: New York State Identification and Intelligence System, n/d.

Puri, Dewan K.S. "Is It Possible to Determine to Which Hand a Thumb Print Belongs." *International Criminal Police Review.* 195 (February, 1966), 49-53.

Science of Fingerprints—Classification and Uses. Washington: GPO, 1973.

Smith, Bruce C. "Fingerprints." *Law and Order.* 22:7 (July, 1974), 36-38.

Taelour, Francis D. and Robert Brush. "Fingerprint Records for the Small Department." *FBI Law Enforcement Bulletin.* 36:9 (September, 1967), 9-12.

Taylor, L.B. "Infallible Fingerprints." *Law and Order.* 17:10 (October, 1969), 74-82, 118.

Vandiver, James J. "Fingerprint Procedure." *Law and Order.* 22:10 (October, 1974), 70-74.

Wilton, George W. *Fingerprints: History, Law and Romance.* Detroit, MI.: Gryphon Books, 1971 [repr. of 1938 ed.].

Wilton, George W. *Fingerprints—Scotland Yard and Henry Faulds.* Toronto: W. Green & Son, Edinburgh: Carswell.

Automated Fingerprint Processing

"Automated Fingerprint Processing—A Step Forward." *FBI Law Enforcement Bulletin* (October, 1971).

"Automated Fingerprint Records for Royal Canadian Mounted Police." *Police Chief* (October, 1971).

"Automated Print System Could Have Wide Impact." *Electronics* (May 10, 1971).

Banner, Conrad S. and Robert M. Stock. "The FBI's Approach to Automatic Fingerprint Identification." *FBI Law Enforcement Bulletin* (January, 1977), 2-9, 24; (February, 1975), 26-31.

Bradley, Gerald O. "Automatic Fingerprint Search Techniques Employing the Videofile System." *Police.* 13:3 (January-February, 1969), 52-57.

"Computer Encoding of Fingerprints." *Science News* (May 25, 1968).

"Computer Reads Fingerprints with only Minor Trouble." *Machine Design* (May 29, 1969).

"FBI to Automate Fingerprint System." *Electronics* (September 13, 1973).

Metropolitan Atlanta Council of Local Governments. *Automated Identification of Latent Fingerprints.* Springfield, VA.: NTIS, 1970.

Explanation of the background, development, operation and maintenance of an automated fingerprint identification system used by the Atlanta Police.

Tou, J.T. *Pictorial Pattern Recognition—Automatic Interpretation and Classification of Fingerprints.* Springfield, VA.: NTIS, 1970.

An approach for automatic interpretation and classification of pictorial patterns which can be adequately characterized by their intensity boundaries.

Wegstein, J.M. *Automated Fingerprint Identification.* Washington: GPO, 1970.

Procedure for determining if two impressions were made by the same finger by using the X and Y coordinates and the individual directions of the minutiae.

Fingerprint Classification

Califana, Anthony. "Simplified Version of the NCIC Technique for Coding Fingerprints." *Law and Order.* 22:3 (March, 1974), 46-48, 50; 22:4 (April, 1974), 20-22.

Chamberlain, Charles. "Identifying Latent Impressions Through the Five Finger File System." *Law and Order.* 23:7 (July, 1975), 26-27, 36.

"Classification of Deformed and Mutilated Fingers." *FBI Law Enforcement Bulletin.* 9 (February, 1940), 3-11.

"Classification of the Scarred Fingerprint." *FBI Law Enforcement Bulletin* (April, 1955).

Engert, Gerald J. "International Corner." *Identification News.* 14 (May, 1964), 8-10.

The Japanese Fingerprint System.

"Establishment of a Local Fingerprint Identification Bureau." *FBI Law Enforcement Bulletin* (December, 1958).

"FBI International Fingerprint Exchange Program." *FBI Law Enforcement Bulletin* (February, 1965).

Weiner, Fred. "Fingerprint Projector Helps Classify Over 100,000 Cards." *Law and Order* (November, 1975), 76-77.

Footprints

"Classification of Foot Prints." *FBI Law Enforcement Bulletin.* 40:10 (October, 1971), 23-27.

Edberg, Sanford, Arthur Mandella and Charles H. Hochman. "The Use of Footprints for Identification in Infanticide: Report of a Case." *Journal of Forensic Sciences.* 10:2 (April, 1965), 225-231.

"Footprinting of Infants." *FBI Law Enforcement Bulletin.* 35:10 (October, 1966), 8-11.

Forgery of Fingerprints

Gupta, Sia Rani. "Forgeries in Fingerprints." *International Criminal Police Review.* 208 (May, 1967), 133-139.

Keyes, R. "Forgery of Fingerprints." *Fingerprint and Identification Magazine.* 48:8 (February, 1967), 3-7, 13-17.

Lip Prints

Suzuki, Kazuo. "Personal Identification by Means of Lip Prints." *Journal of Forensic Medicine.* 17 (April-June, 1970), 52-57.

Palm Prints

Alexander, H.L.V. *Classifying Palmprints—A Complete System of Coding Filing and Searching Palmprints.* Springfield, IL.: C.C. Thomas, 1973.
Description and essential technical data for a system of palm classification and identification.

Califana, Anthony. "A Simple Method for Taking Palm Prints." *Law and Order.* 18:7 (July, 1970), 34-35.

Prinslow, R.J. "Palm Printing." *Law and Order.* 18:4 (April, 1970), 32-33.

U.S. Department of the Treasury. *Guide to Taking Palm Prints.* Washington: GPO, n/d.

Vargas, Gonzalo Gil. "The Filing of Palm Prints—An Experiment Undertaken in Colombia." *International Police Review.* 164 (January, 1963), 2-5.

FIREARMS

Ballistics

Burrard. Gerald. *The Identification of Firearms and Forensic Ballistics.* 3rd ed., N.Y.: Barnes, 1962.

Churchman, J.A. "Bullet Recovery." *International Criminal Police Review.* 87 (April, 1955), 109-119.

Drake, Victor. "Shotgun Ballistics." *Journal of Forensic Science Society* (September, 1962).

Jauhari, M., S.M. Chatterjee and P.K. Ghosh. "Remaining Velocity of Bullets Fired Through Glass Plates." *Journal of,Forensic Science Society.* 14:1 (1974), 3-7.

Katsimaglis, James. "Ballistics Problems: Ricochet and Stray Bullets." *International Criminal Police Review.* 196 (March, 1966), 76-83.

Kijewski, H. "Problems in the Interpretation of Gunshots Through Glass." *Journal Legal Medicine.* 74:3 (1974), 167-175.

Newquist, A.M. "Test Bullet Recovery System." *Association of Firearm Tool Mark Examiners Journal.* 5:1 (1973), 9.

Petty, Charles S. and John E. Hauser. "Rifled Shotgun Slugs." *Journal of Forensic Sciences.* 13:1 (January, 1968), 114-123.

Sinha, J.K., V.K. Mettrotra and L.A. Kamar. "Bullet Identification by Nonstriated Lane and Groove Marks of Abnormally Undersized Barrels." *Forensic Science.* 4:1 (1974), 43-45.

Thomas, R. "Contribution to the Identification of Smooth Bore Firearms." *International Criminal Police Review.* 28:280, 190-193.

Skolrood, R.W. "Comparison of Bullets Fired From Consecutively Rifled Cooey .22 Calibre Barrels." *Canadian Society Forensic Science Journal.* 8:2 (1975), 49-52.

White, Henry P. and Munhall D. Burton. *Cartridge Headstamp Guide.* Belair, MD.: H.P. White Laboratory, 1963.

Firearms Identification

Berg, S.O. ".22 Firing Pin Impression File." *Identification News.* 14:9 (September, 1964), 4.

Dillan, Duayne and John Thornton. "Identification Notes on the Gyrojet Weapons System." *Journal of the Forensic Science Society.* 7:3 (July, 1967), 146-150.

Gyngell, Dudley Stuart Hawtrey. *Armourers Marks.* London: Thorsons, 1959.

Hatcher, J.S. *Textbook of Firearms Investigation.* Marines, N.C.: Small Arms Technical Publishing, 1935.

King, Daniel P. "Legal Aspects of Firearms Evidence." *Police.* 6:6 (July-August, 1962), 45-46.

Kirwan, W.E. and A.B. Hart. "Firearms Identification Problems. *Bulletin of the Bureau of Criminal Investigation.* 1956.

Krenia, V. "Submachine Gun Identification Notes." *Journal of Forensic Sciences.* 9:1 (January, 1964), 148-152.

Logan, H.C. "Grip Marks on American Handguns." *American Rifleman.* 110:10 (October, 1962), 55-56.

Matthews, J.H. *Firearms Identification.* Madison: University of Wisconsin Press, 1962.

Matthews, J. Howard. *Firearms Identification: The Laboratory Examination of Small Arms, Rifling Characteristics in Handguns and Notes on Automatic Pistols—Vol 1.* Springfield, IL.: C.C. Thomas, [1962] 1973.

Matthews, J. Howard. *Fire Arms Identification: Original Photographs and Other Illustrations of Handguns—Vol 2.* Springfield, IL.: C.C. Thomas [1962] 1973.

Matthews, J. Howard. *Firearms Identification: Original Photographs and Other Illustrations of Hand Guns, Data on Rifling Characteristics of Handguns and Rifles—Vol 3.* Springfield, IL.: C.C. Thomas, 1973.

Millard, J.T. *Handbook in the Primary Identification of Revolvers and Semi-Automatic Pistols.* Springfield, IL.: C.C. Thomas, 1974.

Nichol, R.C. and V. Krema. "Identification Notes on Firearms Rifled Eight Right." *Journal of Forensic Sciences.* 10:2 (April, 1965), 148-157.

Schiml, N.P.G. "Miniature Pistol Identification." *RCMP Gazette.* 25:12 (December, 1963), 15-16.

Treasury Department. *Firearms Identification for Law Enforcement Officers.* Washington: GPO, 1970.
Visual aid and description of weapons classified in firearms under the National Firearms Act of 1968.

Gun Shot Residue

Bosen, S.F. and D.R. Scheuing. "A Rapid Microtechnique

for the Detection of Trace Metals From Gunshot Residues." *Forensic Science.* 21:1 (1976), 163-170.

Hudson, G.D. and S.J. Butcher. "The Detectin and Determination of Metal Trace on Hands." *Journal of Forensic Science Society.* 14:1 (1974), 9-18.

Midkiff, C.R., Jr. "Detection of Gunshot Residues: Modern Solutions for an Old Problem." *Journal of Police Science Administration.* 3:1 (1975), 77-83.

Nag, N.K. and M. Mazundar. "Detection of Firearm Discharge Residues in Bloodstained Articles by Fluorescence." *Forensic Science.* 5:1 (1975), 69-71.

Pillay, K.K.S., W.A. Jester and H.A. Fox. "Gunshot Residue Collection Using Film-Life Techniques." *Forensic Science.* 4:2 (1974), 145-153.

Pillay, K.K.S. and J. Sagans. "Gunshot Residue Collection Using Film-Life Techniques for Neutron Activation Analysis." *Journal Police Science Administration.* 2:4 (1974), 388-394.

Price, George. "Firearms Discharge Residues on Hands." *Journal of Forensic Science Society.* 5:4 (October, 1965), 199-200.

FOOTWEAR EVIDENCE

Abbott, John Reginald. *Footwear Evidence.* Springfield, IL.: C.C. Thomas, 1964.

Mansfield, E.R. "Footwear Impressions at Scenes of Crime." *Police Journal.* 43:2 (February, 1970), 93-96.

Joling, Robert J. "Shoeprints: Quantum of Proof." *Journal of Forensic Sciences.* 13:2 (April, 1968), 223-236.

Lucock, L.J. "Identifying the Wearer of Worn Footwear." *Journal of the Forensic Science Society* (April, 1967).

Ostler, R.D. "Shoe Impressions in Snow." *Police Journal.* 36:11 (November, 1963), 532-535.

Petty, Charles S-, Roger A. Smith and Thomas A. Hutson. "The Value of Shoe Sole Imprints in Automobile Crash Investigations." *Journal of Police Science and Administration.* 1:1 (March, 1973), 1-10.

Puri, Dewan K.S. "Footprints." *International Criminal Police Review* (April, 1965), 106-111.

"Ripple Soles Misleading Evidence." *Police Chief.* 30:3 (March, 1963), 45.

FORENSIC ASPECTS OF DEATH INVESTIGATION

Death Investigation—General

Adelson, Lester. "Role of the Pathologist in Arson Investigation." *Journal of Criminal Law, Criminology and Police Science.* 45:6 (March-April, 1955), 760-768.

Beddoe, Harold L. "Methods of Investigation in the Identification of Human Remains." *Journal of Forensic Sciences* (July, 1956).

Beddoe, Harold L. "Problems of Identifying a Body." *Police.* 3:3 (January-February, 1959), 11-14.

Breazeale, Edward L. and Eugene F. Suarez. "Estimating the Time of Death." *Police.* 6:2 (November-December, 1961), 49-51.

Califana, Anthony L. "Identification of Deceased." *Law and Order.* 21:11 (November, 1973), 18-19.

Camps, F.E. "Symposium on Identification of Human Remains." *Journal of Forensic Medicine.* 7:6 (1960).

Cooper, P. *Medical Detectives.* N.Y.: David McKay, 1973.

Davis, Joseph H. "Pathological Techniques in Fire Investigation." *Police.* 8:5 (May-June, 1964), 81-82.

DeSaram, G.S.W. "Estimation of the Time of Death by Medical Criteria." *Journal Forensic Medicine.* 4:47 (1958).

DiMaio, V.J.M. and W.U. Spitz. "Variations in Wounding Due to Unusual Firearms and Recently Available Ammunition." *Journal Forensic Science.* 17:3 (1972), 377-386.

Dutra, Frank R. "Medicolegal Examination of Bodies Recovered from Burned Buildings." *American Journal of Clinical Pathology.* 19 (1949), 599-607.

Fatteh, A. *Handbook of Forensic Pathology.* Philadelphia: Lippincott, 1973.

Fatteh, A. "Homicidal Gunshot Wound of Mouth." *Forensic Science Society Journal.* 12:2 (April, 1972), 347-349.

Fisher, Russell S. et al. "Techniques of Identification Applied to 81 Extremely Fragmented Aircraft Fatalities." *Journal of Forensic Sciences.* 10:2 (April, 1965), 121-135.

Gold, Louis H. "Invitation to Homicide." *Journal of Forensic Sciences.* 10:4 (October, 1965), 415-421.

Gonzales, Thomas A. et al. *Legal Medicine, Pathology, and Toxicology.* N.Y.: Appleton Century Crofts, 1954.

Gordon, I., R. Turner and T.W. Price. *Medical Jurisprudence.* 3rd ed. Baltimore: Williams & Wilkins, 1953.

Gradwohl, R.B.H. *Legal Medicine.* St. Louis, MO.: C.V. Mosby, 1954.

Havard, J.D.J. *The Detection of Secret Homicide: A Study of the Medicolegal System of Investigation of Sudden and Unexplained Deaths.* N.Y.: St. Martin's Press, 1960.

Huelke, Donald F. and Paul W. Gikas. "Investigations of Fatal Automobile Accidents from the Forensic Point of View. *Journal of Forensic Sciences.* 11:4 (October, 1966), 474-484.

Ilan, E. "Identifying Skeletal Remains." *International Criminal Police Review* (February, 1964), 42-45.

Jaaskelainen, A.J. "A Method for the Estimation of Age in the Identification of Mass Casualties." *Journal of Forensic Sciences.* (October, 1968).

Jackson, Robert. *The Crime Doctors.* London: Muller, 1966.

Kempe, Carl R. "The Chloride Test as a Technique in the Investigation of Suspected Drownings." *Police.* 46 (July-August, 1960), 6-9.

Knight, B.H. "The Dating of Human Bones." *Criminologist.* 16 (Winter, 1971), 38-40.

Knight, B. "The Dynamics of Stab Wounds." *Forensic Science.* 6:3 (1975), 249-255.

Lyle, H.P. and F.B. Cleveland. "Determination of the Time of Death by Body Heat Loss." *Journal of Forensic Science.* 1:4 (1956), 11.

Lyle, Herbert P., Klaus L. Stemmer and Frank B. Cleveland. "Determination of the Time of Death. A Consideration of Post-Mortem Physical Changes." *Journal of Forensic Science Society.* 4:2 (April, 1959), 167-175.

Mant, A.K. *Modern Trends in Forensic Medicine—V. 3.* London: Butterworth, 1973.

Mattoo, B.N. and A.K. Wani. "Casualty Criteria for Wounds from Firearms with Special Reference to Shot Penetration." *Journal of Forensic Sciences.* 14:1 (January, 1969), 120-128.

Naeve, W. "Forensic Maritime Medicine." *Journal Legal Medicine.* 73:4 (1973), 321-324.

Peters, Larry G. "Coe-Flex Method of Identification." *Police Chief.* XLII:5 (May, 1975), 66.
Fingerprinting technique of cadavers.

Petty, Charles S. "Multiple Causes of Death. The Viewpoint of a Forensic Pathologist." *Journal of Forensic Sciences.* 10:2 (April, 1965), 167-178.

Picton, Bernard. *Murder, Suicide or Accident: The Forensic Pathologist at Work.* N.Y.: St. Martin's, 1971.

Polson, C.J. *Essentials of Forensic Medicine.* 2nd ed. Springfield. IL.: C.C. Thomas, 1965.

Race, George J. and William M. Nickey, Jr. "Identification of Bodies Including Skeletal Remains and Determination of the Time of Death." *Police.* 6:6 (July-August, 1962), 6-10.

Rentoul, E. and H. Smith. *Glaster's Medical Jurisprudence and Toxicology.* 13th ed. Edinburgh: Churchill Livingstone, 1973.

Siegel, Henry, Milton Helpern and Theodore Ehrenreich. "The Diagnosis of Death from Intravenous Narcotism." *Journal of Forensic Sciences.* 11:1 (January, 1966), 1-16.

Simpson, Keith. *Modern Trends in Forensic Medicine.* 2nd series, N.Y.: Appleton Century Crofts, 1967.

Simpson, Keith. *Taylor's Principles and Practice of Medical Jurisprudence.* Boston: Little Brown.

Smith, Sydney. *Mostly Murder.* N.Y.: David McKay, 1959.

Sopher, Irvin M. "The Role of the Forensic Pathologist in Arson and Related Investigations." *FBI Law Enforcement Bulletin.* 41:9 (September, 1972), 8-12, 30-31.

Sopher, Irvin M. and William C. Masemore. "The Police Officer and the Medical Examiner System." *Police.* 16:3 (November, 1971), 23-26.

Spitz, Werner U. and Russell S. Fisher. *Medicolegal Investigation of Death: Guidelines for the Application of Pathology to Crime Investigation.* Springfield, IL.: C.C. Thomas, 1973.

Spitz, Werner U. & Russell M. Wilhelm. "Stud Gun Injuries." *Journal Forensic Medicine.* 17:1 (January-March, 1970), 5-11.

Stevens, P.J. "Medical Aspects of Fatal Aircraft Accident Investigation." *Police College Magazine* (Spring, 1968), 11-17.

Stewart, T.D. "What the Bones Tell-Today." *FBI Law Enforcement Bulletin.* 41:2 (February, 1972), 16-20, 30-31.

Thorwald, Jurgen. *Crime and Science: The New Frontier in Criminology.* N.Y.: Harcourt Brace Jovanovich, 1969.

U.S. Army Intelligence. *Forensic Medicine.* Springfield, VA.: NTIS, 1954.
Includes life reactions, necrosis and necrotic phenomena, causes of death and violent deaths, mechanical injuries, poisoning, mechanical suffocation and burns.

Van Hecke, Thomas W. "The Medicolegal Diagnosis of Death by Drowning. *Journal of Forensic Sciences* (January, 1963).

Waaler, E. "The Identification of the Victims of the Fire at the Stalheim Hotel in June 1959." *International Criminal Police Review.* 161 (October, 1962), 242-254.

Watanabe, T. *Atlas of Legal Medicine.* 2nd ed. Philadelphia: Lippincott, 1972.
This volume, illustrated with photographs, many in color, presents the effects and evidence of death from suicide, murder, and accidental and natural causes.

Wecht, Cyril H. "The Medical Evidence in the Assassination of President John F. Kennedy." *Forensic Science Gazette.* 4:4 (September, 1973), 9-19.

Woodruff, Richard S. "The Forensic Pathologist in Medicolegal Investigation." *FBI Law Enforcement Bulletin.* 37:2 (February, 1968), 7-9, 21-22.

Wroblewski, B.M. "Estimation of Time of Death by Eye Change." *Forensic Science* (May, 1973), 201-205.

Crib Death

Andrews, P.S. "Cot Deaths and Malnutrition: The Role of Dehydration." *Medical Science Law.* 15:1 (1975), 47-50.

Asch, Stuart S. "Crib Deaths: Their Possible Relationship to Post Partum Depression and Infanticide." *Journal of the Mount Sinai Hospital.* 35 (1968), 214-220.

Bergman, Abraham J. and Bruce Beckwith. *Sudden Infant Death Syndrome.* Seattle: University of Washington Press, 1970.

Bergman, Abraham et al. *Sudden Unexpected Deaths in Infants.* N.Y.: MSS Information Corp. 1974.

Camps. Frances M. and R.C. Carpenter. *Sudden and Unexpected Death in Infancy.* Baltimore: Williams & Wilkins, 1972.

Geertinger, Prebon. *Sudden Death in Infancy* Springfield, IL.: C.C. Thomas, 1968.

"Risk of Cot Deaths." *British Medical Journal.* 3:5985 (1975), 664.

"Sudden Infant Deaths." *Police Review.* 82:4263 (1974), 1259.

FORENSIC ASPECTS OF SEX CRIME

Brackett, J.W. "The Acid Phosphatase Test for Seminal Stains: The Importance of Proper Control Tests." *Journal of Criminal Law, Criminology and Police Science.* 47 (1956-57).

Cameron, J.M. "The Pathologist and Sexual Crime." *Criminologist.* 9:31 (1974), 29-36.

Eckert, W.G. "Forensic Aspects of Sex Crimes and Problems." *Inform.* 3:4 (1971), 3-7.

Greene, Roger S. and David Q. Bind. "Seminal Stain Examination: A Reagent for Destruction of Supporting Fabric." *Journal of Criminal Law, Criminology and Police Science.* 37 (1946-47).

Hazen, Claude B. "Measurement of Acid Phosphatase Activity to Identify Seminal Stains." *Journal of Criminal Law, Criminology and Police Science.* 46 (1955-56).

Kaye, Sidney. "The Acid Phosphatase Test for Seminal Stains: A Study of Reliability of Aged Stains." *Journal of Criminal Law, Criminology and Police Science.* 41 (1950-51).

Kaye, Sidney. "Identification of Seminal Stains." *Journal of Criminal Law, Criminology and Police Science.* 38 (1947-48).

Kempe, Carl L. "Possible Interference in the Acid Phosphatase Tests for Seminal Fluid Stains." *Journal of Criminal Law, Criminology and Police Science.* 49 (1956-59).

Kind, Stuart S. "The Use of the Acid Phosphatase Test in Searching for Seminal Stains." *Journal of Criminal Law, Criminology and Police Science.* 47 (1956-57).

Kind, S.S. and C.G. Broster. "Case Note: Contraceptive Sheath Lubricant." *Journal of Forensic Sciences.* 5:2 (April, 1965), 115.

Nakamura, G.R. et al. "The Use of Recording Spectrophotometer for the Detection of Acid Phosphatases in Seminal Stains." *Journal of Criminal Law, Criminology and Police Science.* 49 (1958-59).

Paul, D.M. "The Medical Examination in Sexual Offences." *Medical Science Law.* 15:3 (1975), 154-162.

Raju, P.S. and N.K. Iyengar. "Acid Phosphatase As a Specific Test for the Identification of Seminal Stains." *Journal of Criminal Law, Criminology and Police Science.* 55 (1964).

Rife, David W. "Scientific Evidence in Rape Cases." *Journal of Criminal Law, Criminology and Police Science.* 31 (1940-41).

Rupp, J.C. "Sperm Survival and Prostatic Acid Phosphatase Activity in Victim." *Forensic Sciences.* 24:2 (1969), 177-183.

Shupe, Lloyd M. "A Rapid Method for Detection of Seminal Stains." *Police.* 6:2 (November-December, 1961), 70-72.

Swann, G.C. "The Wayne Boden Murders." *International Journal Forensic Dentistry.* 2:4 (1974), 34-42.

Willot, G.M. "The Role of the Forensic Biologist in Cases of Sexual Assault." *Journal of Forensic Science Society.* 15:4 (1975), 269-276.

FORENSIC ODONTOLOGY

Berry, D.C. and A.C. Hunt. "Identification by Dental Characteristics." *Medicine, Science and Law.* 7:2 (April, 1967), 67-69.

Cameron, J.M. "Forensic Dentistry." *International Journal Forensic Dentistry.* 2:5 (1974), 54.

Fernhead, R.W. "Dental Aspects of the Identification of Young Persons." *Journal Forensic Medicine.* 7 (1960), 11-13.

Furness, J. "Forensic Dentistry." *International Journal Forensic Dentistry.* 1:2 (1973), 2-3.

Haines, Daniel H. "Identification in Mass Disasters From Dental Prosthesis." *International Microform Journal of Legal Medicine.* 8:3 (July-September, 1973).

Harvey, W. "Teeth and Forensic Science." *Criminologist.* 8:28 (1973), 3-20.

Knott, N.J. "Identification by Teeth." *Police Journal.* 40:5 (May, 1967), 209-213.

Levine, Lowell J. "Forensic Odontology Today—A 'New Forensic Science." *FBI Law Enforcement Bulletin.* 41:8 (August, 1972), 6-9, 26-28.

Luntz, Lester L. and Phyllis Luntz. *Handbook for Dental Identification.* Philadelphia: Lippincott, 1974.

GLASS

Butterworth, A. et al. "A Report on the Investigation into the Trace Elements Present in Vehicle Headlamp and Auxiliary Lamp Glasses." *Journal of Forensic Science Society.* 14:1 (1974), 41-45.

Dabbs, M.D.G. and E.F. Pearson. "Some Physical Properties of a Large Number of Window Glass Specimens." *Journal Forensic Science.* 17:1 (1972), 70-78.

McCrone, W.C. "Collaborative Study of the Microscopical Characterization of Glass Fragments." *Journal of Association of Official Analytical Chemist.* 56:5 (1973), 1223-1226.

McJungkins, P. and J.I. Thornton. "Glass Fracture Analysis." *Forensic Science.* 2:1 (1973), 1-27.

Smalldon, K.W. and C. Brown. "The Discriminating Power of Density and Refractive Index for Window Glass." *Journal of Forensic Science Society.* 13:4 (1973), 307-309.

HAIR AND FIBER

Appleyard, H.M. *Guide to the Identification of Animal Fiber.* Leeds, England: Wool Industries Research, 1960.

DeForest, P.R. and P.L. Kirk. "Forensic Individualization of Hair." *Criminologist.* 8:27 (1973), 35-45.

"Don't Miss a Hair." *FBI Law Enforcement Bulletin* (May, 1976), 9-15.

Obrusnik, I. et al. "The Variation of Trace Elements Concentrations in Single Human Head Hairs." *Forensic Science*. 17:3 (1972), 426-439.

Prasad, A.N. "Susceptibility of Hair to the Influence of Bacteria." *International Criminal Police Review*. 30:286 (1975), 86-89.

Schneider, V. "The Investigation of Hair with the Aid of the Scanning Electron Microscope." *Journal Legal Medicine*. 71:2 (1972), 94-103.

MICROSCOPY

Becker, Heinrich. "The Infra-Red Microscope as an Aid to Police Investigations." *International Criminal Police Review* (March, 1963), 84-88.

Brown, J.L. and J.W. Johnson. "Electron Microscopy and X-ray Microanalysis in Forensic Science." *Journal of Association of Official Analytical Chemistry*. 56:4 (1973), 930-943.

Dreger, A.A. "A Comparison Microscope for Document Examination." *Canadian Society of Forensic Science Journal*. 6:4 (1973), 175-183.

"Microscope and Crime." *Nature*. 236:5348 (1972), 427-428.

Papauskas, L. "The Scanning Electron Microscope: A New Way to Examine Holes in Fabrics." *Journal Police Science Administration*. 1:3 (1973), 362-365.

Shaw, William. "Forensic Science Gets a Valuable Tool: The Scanning Electron Microscope." *Law and Order*. 19:4 (April, 1971), 15-18, 20-21.

Speeter, D. and J. Ohnsorge. "Determination of Shot Direction from Bones with Scanning Electron Microscopy." *Journal Legal Medicine*. 73:2 (1973), 137-143.

Taylor, M.E. "Scanning Electron Microscopy in Forensic Science." *Journal of Forensic Science Society*. 13:4 (1973), 269-280.

PAINT

Crown, David A. *Forensic Examination of Paints and Pigments*. Springfield, IL.: C.C. Thomas, 1968.

Leete, C.G. and R. M. Mills. *Reference Collection of Automotive Paint Colors*. Washington: National Bureau of Standards, U.S. Department of Commerce, 1975.

Manura, J.J. and R. Saferstein. "Examination of Automobile Paints by Laser Beam Emission Spectroscopy." *Journal of Association of Official Analytical Chemists*. 56:5 (1973), 1227-1233.

"Paint Examination Techniques Utilized in FBI Laboratory." *FBI Law Enforcement Bulletin*. 42:4 (1973), 3-9.

Tweed, F.T. et al. "The Forensic Microanalysis of Paints, Plastics and Other Materials by an Infrared Diamond Cell Technique." *Forensic Science*. 4:3 (1974), 211-218.

Wheals, B.B. and W. Noble. "The Pyrolysis Gas Chromatographic Examination of Car Paint Flakes As an Aid to Vehicle Characterization." *Journal of Forensic Science Society*. 14:1 (1974), 23-32.

PHOTOGRAPHY

Photography—General

Adams, Charles A., Jr. "Mug Shots for a Small Department." *Law and Order*. 23:4 (April, 1975), 26.

Brexler, Otto. "Training Parodies." *Law and Order*. 17:4. (April, 1969).

Burnosky, F.J. "In Color—Canton Converts to Color Photo Files." *Police Chief*. 33:5 (May, 1966), 24-26.

Califana, Anthony. "Elementary Photography." *Law and Order*. 18:4 (April, 1970), 71, 73-74.

Campbell, Russell. *Practical Motion Picture Photography*. Cranbury, N.J.: A.S. Barnes, 1971.

Carter, W.E. "Photography at New Scotland Yard." *Forensic Photographer*. 3:9 (1974), 7-9.

Caufield, James M. "Legal Photography." *Professional Photographer*. 81 (December, 1954), 54-55.

Cleveland, Robert C. *Architectural Photography of Houses*. N.Y.: F.W. Dodge, 1953.

Conrad, Edwin. "Color Photography: An Instrumentality of Proof." *Journal of Criminal Law, Criminology and Police Science*. 48:3 (September-October, 1957), 321-323.

Crime Scene Photography—A Professional Procedures Program. Arlington, VA.: Police Science Services, 1974.

Criminal Detection Devices Employing Photography. Rochester, N.Y.: Eastman Kodak.

Crumb, Owen. "Photography—The Investigator's Tool." *Law and Order*. 12:4 (April, 1964), 6-8, 10-11.

Daidone, Peter. "Color Pictures for Better Identification." *Law and Order*. 13:2 (May, 1965), 6-7, 75.

Davis, Phil. *Photography*. Dubuque, IA.: Brown, 1972.

Dey, Luther M. "Kodak Law Enforcement Seminars Show Photography Roles in Crime Control." *Law and Order*. 19:4 (April, 1971), 38-42, 44, 54.

Dey, Luther M. "Night Crime—Scene Photography Needs Special Techniques, Equipment." *Law and Order*. 21:4 (April, 1973), 38-40.

Dey, Luther M. "Photography and the Riot." *Kodak Law Enforcement Photography Bulletin*. 1:4.

Dey, Luther M. "Photographing Traffic Accidents." *Law and Order*. 16:4 (April, 1968), 22-26, 84.

Dobbs, Horace. *How to Use Your Camera Under Water: A Practical Guide to Underwater Photography*. 2nd ed. Garden City, N.Y.: Amphoto, 1973.

"Do's and Don'ts of Photography During a Snowstorm." *Law and Order*. 12:4 (April, 1964), 12.

Ehrilch, S.G. and Leland B. Jones. *Photographic Evidence: The Preparation and Use of Photographs in Criminal and Civil Cases*. London: MacLaren, 1967.

Fagerstrom, Dorothy. "The Power of Photography—A Survey." *Law and Order.* 14:4 (April, 1966), 37-40.

Glidwell, Charles R. "Police Photography in the Small Department." *Law and Order.* 18:4 (April, 1970), 90-92.

Goldman, Paul. "Light and Police Photography." *Law and Order.* 21:4 (April, 1973), 54, 56, 58, 60.

Heathcote, A.E. "If You Can See It, You Can Photograph It." *Police Journal.* 36:4 (April, 1963), 171.

Heyert, Murray. "Take Pictures in the Dark with a Night Vision Scope Lens System." *Law and Order.* 18:9 (September, 1970), 38-39, 95-96, 98, 100, 102.

Hoag, George S. "Police Photography at Work." *Law and Order.* 20:4 (April, 1972), 26-32.

Holmes, S. "Photography and Jaywalking." *Law and Order.* 6:4 (April, 1958), 6.

Horak, Charles J. "Color Photography in Police Work." *Law and Order.* 11:12 (December, 1963), 48-52.

"How to Photograph an Accident." *Kodak Law Enforcement Photography Bulletin.* 2:4 (1967), 1-3.

James, Ed. "A Police Photograph Shoots for One of the World's Most Critical Audiences." *Law and Order.* 22:4 (April, 1974), 44, 46.

Johnson, Leo M. "Public Relations Photography." *Law and Order.* 23:4 (April, 1975), 34-36.

Johnson, Leo M. "36 mm Surveillance Still Photography." *Law and Order.* 21:5 (May, 1973), 52-54, 56, 58, 60-61.

Kaplun, Harry G. "Life Size Color Projections Speed Identifications in Nassau County N.Y." *Law and Order.* 14:4 (April, 1966), 22, 24-25, 78.
Instead of mug books, slides are utilized.

Kennedy, John. "Photography in Arson Investigations." *Journal of Criminal Law, Criminology and Police Science.* 46:5 (January-February, 1956), 726-736.

Kerr, Harold. "Photography Foils Felons." *Law and Order.* 19:4 (April, 1971), 46-48, 54.

Konkle, Robert K. "The Trooper and the Camera." *Law and Order.* 17:4 (April, 1969), 53-55.

Little, J.P. "Scene of Crime Photography." *Forensic Science Society Journal.* 4:2 (December, 1963), 57-59.

Lydle, Chris. "The Photography of Small Objects." *Law and Order.* 15:1 (January, 1967), 66-74.

Lydle, Chris. "Telephotography: The Long Eye of the Law." *Law and Order.* 16:2 (February, 1968) (in four parts, ends with May 1968 issue).

McDonald, James A. "Filters Make More Accurate Representations in Physical Evidence Photography." *Law and Order.* 20:4 (April, 1972), 34-36.

MacDonnell, Herbert L. "A Single Exposure Test Strip Method for Photomicrography, Photomicrography and Poloraid Photography." *Law and Order.* 12:4 (April, 1964), 14, 16.

Mauk, Arthur A. "Have Your Tried Automatic?" *Police Chief.* 33:5 (May, 1966), 20, 22.

Merit, Roger. "Filters—An Important Tool of Law Enforcement Photographers." *Law and Order.* 22:4 (April, 1974), 23-28.

Murphy, Burt. *Police and Crime Photography.* N.Y.: Verland, 1960.

"New Developments in Instant Photography." *International Criminal Police Review* (October, 1964).

Nicks, D.L. "The Camera Looks at Arson." *Police.* 4:3 (January-February, 1960), 75-77.

O'Hara, Charles E. *Photography in Law Enforcement.* Rochester, N.Y.: Eastman Kodak, 1959.

Palmer, J. "A Picture Record Kit—New Tool for Police." *Law and Order.* 22:7 (1974), 46-48, 53.

"The Photo Unit." *Spring 3100.* 34 (December, 1963), 11-16, 44.

Ploscowe, Arthur W. "Every Policeman a Photographer." *Law and Order.* 16:4 (April, 1968), 16-21.

Pountney, Harold. *Police Photography.* London: Elsevier, 1971.

Richards, Gerald B. "Establishing an Internal Photographic Unit." *FBI Law Enforcement Bulletin* (August, 1975).

Samen, Charles S. "Major Crime Scene Investigation—Part II—Basic Photography." *Law and Order.* 19:9 (September, 1971), 16-20.

Sansone, Sam J. "An Efficient Photography Operation." *Law and Order.* 14:9 (September, 1966), 84-87.

Scott, Charles C. *Photographic Evidence: Preparation and Presentation.* 3 vols., St. Paul, MN.: West, 1967.

Sellas, Percy R. "Photography: Shortest Distance Between Two Points—Crime Scene to Prison." *Law and Order.* 13:12 (December, 1965), 50-52.

Siljander, Raymond P. *Applied Surveillance Photography.* Springfield, IL.: C.C. Thomas, 1975.

Spira, S.F. "Close-Up Photography." *Law and Order.* 13:4 (April, 1965), 18-19.

Thompson, Dana L. "On the Spot Photographs Solve Small Department's Evidence Problem." *Law and Order.* 17:4 (April, 1969), 29-32.

Thompson, Ron. "How to Shoot Undercover Pictures that Get Convictions." *Law and Order.* 22:4 (April, 1974), 36-38, 40, 42.

Tobias, Marc Weber. "A Total Photographic System Concept." *Law and Order.* 21:4 (April, 1973), 84-85.

Tuttle, Harris. "Color Photography in Law Enforcement." *The Police Yearbook.* Washington: IACP, 1958.

Tuttle, Harris B. "Color Photography in Police Science." *Law and Order.* 8 (April, 1960).

Tuttle, Harris B. "Criminal Detection Devices Employing Photography." *Police.* 1:3 (January-February, 1957), 7-11.

Tuttle, Harris B. "Photography's Place in Law Enforcement Today." *Police.* 1:1 (September-October, 1956), 9-13.

Von Bremen, Uif. "Systematic Application of Specialized Photographic Techniques." *Journal of Criminal Law, Criminology and Police Science.* 58:3 (September, 1967), 410-413.

Walpole, Don. "Photography in Arson Investigation." *Photomethods* (August, 1975).

Wesson, Jerry. "Police Photography in Pittsburg." *Law and Order.* 13:4 (April, 1965), 10-12, 14, 72.

Aerial Photography

Bird, J. Brian and A. Morrison. "Space Photography and its Georgraphical Applications." *Geographical Review.* 54 (October, 1964), 463-486.

Kondo, I. Kenneth and Peter C. Unsinger. "A System of Using Aerial Photographs in Police Patrol Work." *Law and Order.* 20:11 (November, 1972), 82-85.

Moreland, J.D. and M.M. Miller. "Photographic Mapping of Accident Sites." *Police Journal* (February, 1963).

Smith, Coustance B. *Evidence in the Camera: The Story of Photographic Intelligence in World War II.* North Pomfret, VT.: David & Charles, [1957] 1974.

Wolf, Alfred L. "Aerial Photography as a Legal Tool." *American Bar Association Journal.* 52 (June, 1966), 543-547.

Dark Room

Byrnes, Frank K. "How to Do It: From Color Slide to Picture in Less Than Ten Minutes." *Police Chief.* XLII:7 (July, 1975), 64.

D'Anglo, James S. "Your Darkroom Operation: More Efficient, More Versatile." *Law and Order.* 20:4 (April, 1972), 46-48, 50.

Holtz, David D. "Metropolitan Police, Washington D.C.: New Mechanized Photo Lab Cuts Turnaround From Weeks to Hours." *Police Chief.* XLII:10 (October, 1975), 41-43.

Schulmar, Alan R. "Color Photo I D Card Prepared in Two Minutes." *Law and Order.* 19:4 (April, 1971), 28-33.

Shaw, William. "Simplified Developing and Printing." *Law and Order.* 20:9 (September, 1972), 18, 20, 22, 24, 26.

Watkins, Derek. *Practical Photographic Enlarging.* Englewood Cliffs, N.J.: Prentice Hall, 1974.

Video Tapes

Brunkow, Paul A. "Instant Replay and DWI Suspects." *Police.* 15:3 (January-February, 1971), 79-81.
Use of video tape recordings to record the drunk driver sobriety test.

D'Angelo, James S. and Joseph Missonellie. "Using Video Equipment for Police Work." *Law and Order.* 22:4 (April, 1974), 62, 64-65, 80-82.

Gebhardt, R.H. "Video Tape in Criminal Cases." *FBI Law Enforcement Bulletin.* 44:5 (1975), 6-10.
Outlines use of video tape for confessions, statements, admissions, re-enactments, line-ups, crime scene investigations, etc.

Hanson, Herbert E. "Mobile Video Recorder for Law Enforcement." *Law and Order.* 14:3 (March, 1966), 48-50, 52-53.

Jennings, Ken. "Napa (CA.) Uses Color TV to Reduce DWI." *Law and Order* (February, 1976), 52-53, 61.
Use of video tape to film drunk drivers taking sobriety test. The chief reports that of 1,200 arrests only 17 have gone to trial, 15 were found guilty, one found not guilty and one resulted in a hung jury.

Perry, Greg. "Guilty Drunks Stay Guilty with TV Instant Replay." *Law and Order.* 17:4 (April, 1969), 16-17.

Rifas, R.A. *Legal Aspects of Video Tape and Motion Pictures in Law Enforcement.* Evanston, IL.: Traffic Institute Northwestern University, 1972.

Shaw, William. "Economical Video Tape Recorders—Have They Come of Age?" *Law and Order.* 14:2 (February, 1966), 34, 36, 38-39.

Smith, L.D. "Video Tape Recordings and the Drunk Driver. 19:6 (June, 1971), 37.
Describes the use of a portable audio-video recorder and the type of light needed for nightime photography.

Stroh, Thomas F. *The Uses of Video Tape in Training and Development.* N.Y.: AMA, 1968.

Tuttle, Harris B. "Drunken Driver Movies Save Taxpayers $100,000." *Law and Order.* 12:5 (May, 1964), 58-60.
Field use of 16 mm sound movie cameras for use in filming sobriety tests. Author indicates voice test extremely revealing and that very few filmed tests go to court.

"Videotape Recordings New Liaison Between Police and Courts." *Police.* 12:1 (September-October, 1967), 6-9.

Zippel, Robert. "Plead Guilty—They Have Moving Pictures." *Law and Order.* 14:4 (April, 1966), 8-10, 48.
Use of sound film in sobriety tests. In Anaheim CA. drunk driving conviction rate increased from 50% to 94%. Court time dropped to almost 0.

PHOTOGRAPHY—LABORATORY ASPECTS

Califana, Anthony L. "Photographing Latent Fingerprints on Glass." *Law and Order.* 21:7 (July, 1973), 16-21.

Carlson, C.E. "The Camera and the Scratch Mark." *Law and Order.* 16:4 (April, 1968).
Photographing jewelers identification marks.

Cameron, J.M., R. Ruddick and J.H. Grant. "Ultra-Violet Photography in Forensic Medicine." *Forensic Photography.* 2:3 (1973), 9-12.

Eastman Kodak Company. *Infra-Red and Ultra-Violet Photography.* Rochester, N.Y.: Eastman Kodak, 1961.

Edmunds, Rodney B. "Crime Lab Camera Systems." *Law and Order.* 19:12 (December, 1971), 124-126.

"Laboratory Examinations of Photo-related Evidence." *FBI Law Enforcement Bulletin.* 41:5 (1972), 10-15.

Missonelli, Joseph and James S. D'Angelo. "Preparing Fingerprint Visuals." *Law and Order.* 21:4 (April, 1973), 34-35, 82.

Stevens, G.W.W. *Microphotography, Photography at Extreme Resolution.* N.Y.: Wiley, 1957.

PHYSICAL EVIDENCE

Brunelle, R.L. "Novel Techniques for the Examination of Physical Evidence—Their Admissibility as Evidence." *Journal of the Association of Official Analytical Chemists.* 56:6 (1973), 1391-1400.

Cochran, Murray O. "Physical Evidence—A Potent Weapon for Conviction." *Law and Order.* 13:10 (October, 1965), 32-33.

King, William. "The Packaging of Narcotics in Evidence." *Police.* 4:3 (January-February, 1960), 20-22.

Neimeyer, M.K. "Evidence Preservation." *Law and Order.* 20:7 (July, 1972), 28-29.

Parker, B. and J. Peterson. *Physical Evidence Utilization in the Administration of Criminal Justice.* Springfield, VA.: NTIS, 1972.
Study conducted at the Berkeley Police Department on the use of science and technology in providing proof for physical links between a criminal and his crime.

Shupe, Lloyd M. "Preservation of Physical Evidence in Criminal Cases." *Police.* 10:1 (September-October, 1965), 81-83.

Steindler, R.A. "How to Handle Evidence." *Law and Order.* 19:12 (December, 1971), 90-92, 94, 96-97.

Steindler, R.A. "What You Should Know About Evidence." *Law and Order.* 19:7 (July, 1971), 64-66, 76, 78.

Vandiver, James V. "Evidence That Can Be Physically Matched." *Law and Order.* 22:7 (July, 1974), 16-19.

QUESTIONED DOCUMENTS

Document Examination—General

Bates, B.P. *I.S.Q.D.—Identification System for Questioned Documents.* Springfield, IL.: C.C. Thomas, 1970.
A method of handwriting analysis is discussed in its relationship to the identification of questioned documents.

Black, David A. "Decipherment of Charred Documents." *Journal of Criminal Law, Criminology and Police Science.* 28 (1947-48).

Black, David A. "The Microscope in Documents Examination." *Journal of Criminal Law, Criminology and Police Science.* 42 (1951-52).

Clark, Paul F. "The Examination of Questioned Documents by The New South Wales Police." *International Criminal Police Review* (April, 1966), 117-122.

"Document Examination from a Photocopy." *FBI Law Enforcement Bulletin.* 36:2 (February, 1967), 23-24.

Doud, Donald. "Witness or Advocate—Questioned Document Examiner." *Illinois Bar Journal* (August, 1954).

Doulder, Howard C. "Examination of a Document Case." *Journal of Forensic Sciences.* 10:4 (October, 1965), 433-440.

Harrison, Wilson R. *Suspect Documents, Their Scientific Examination.* N.Y.: Praeger, 1958.

Hilton, Ordway. "Pencil Erasures—Detection and Decipherment." *Journal of Criminal Law, Criminology and Police Science.* 54 (1963).

Hilton, Ordway. "Photographic Methods for Deciphering Erased Pencil Writing." *International Criminal Police Review* (February, 1955).

Hilton, Ordway. "Proof of an unaltered Document." *Journal of Criminal Law, Criminology and Police Science.* 50 (1959-60).

Hilton, Ordway. *Scientific Examination of Documents.* Chicago: Callaghan, 1956.

Longhetti, Anthony and P.L. Kirk. "Restoration and Decipherment of Erasures and Obliterated or Indented Writing." *Journal of Criminal Law and Criminology.* 41 (1951), 519-522.

Osborn, Albert. *Questioned Documents.* N.Y.: Boyd, 1940.

Osborn, Paul A. "The Trial of a Document Case." *Journal of Forensic Sciences.* 10:4 (October, 1965), 422-432.

Quirke, Arthur Joseph. *Forged, Anonymous and Suspect Documents.* London: Routledge, 1930.

Swett, George G. "The Importance of Copies in Document Inquiries." *Journal of Forensic Sciences.* 11:4 (October, 1965), 485-495.

Tholl, Joseph. "Competence and Questioned Documents." *Police.* 19:3 (January-February, 1965), 50-52.

Walker, Joseph T. and Parker A. Glass. "Visualization of Writing on Charred Paper." *Journal of Criminal Law, Criminology and Police Science.* 42 (1951-52).

Handwriting

Beacon, Mary S. "Handwriting By the Blind." *Journal of Forensic Sciences.* 12:1 (January, 1967), 37-59.

Holt, Arthur G. *Handwriting in Psychological Interpretations.* Springfield, IL.: C.C. Thomas, 1965.

Ruenes, Rafael Fernandez. "Perception and Handwriting Identification." *Journal of Forensic Sciences.* 12:1 (January, 1967), 102-111.

Stangohr, Gordon R. "Opposite Hand Writings." *Journal of Forensic Sciences* (July, 1968).

Ink

Crown, David A., James V.P. Conway and Paul L. Kirk. "Differentiation of Blue Ballpoint Pen Inks." *Journal of Criminal Law, Criminology and Police Science.* 52 (1963).

Fryd, C.F.M. "The Examination of Inks on Documents." *Medical Science Law.* 14:2 (1974), 87-92.

Godown, Linton. "New Nondestructive Document Testing Methods." *Journal of Criminal Law, Criminology and Police Science.* 55 (1964).

Hammon, Bette L. "Analyzing Ballpoint Inks." *Law and Order.* 16:7 (July, 1968), 35-39, 98.

Kelly, J.H. "Spectrofluorometric Analysis of Ballpoint Ink." *Journal of Police Science and Administration.* 1:2 (1973), 175-181.

Kevern, R.M. "Infrared Luminescence from Thin Layer Chromatogranis of Ink." *Journal of Forensic Science Society.* 13:1 (1973), 25-28.

Lehner, Sigmund. *Ink Manufacture.* London: Scott Greenwood, 1926.

Mitchell, C. Ainsworth. *Inks: Their Composition and Manufacture.* London: Griffin, 1937.

Paper

Grant, J. "The Role of Paper in Questioned Document Work." *Journal of Forensic Science Society.* 13:2 (1973), 91-95.

Jahans, Gordon A. *Paper Testing and Chemistry for Printers.* London: Pitman, 1931.

Leicester, Sheldon. *Practical Studies for Paper Manufacture.* London: Griffin, 1933.

Vasistha, S.K. and S.C. Vasistha. "Three Chemical Tests for Comparing the Age of Paper." *Journal of Criminal Law, Criminology and Police Science.* 53 (1962).

Pens

Black, David A. "Fiber Tipped Pens." *Journal of Criminal Law, Criminology and Police Science.* 57 (1966).

Black, David A. "Identifying Ball Pens by the Burr Striations." *Journal of Criminal Law, Criminology and Police Science.* 61 (1970).

Hilton, Ordway. "Characteristics of the Ball Pen and Its Influence on Handwriting Identification." *Journal of Criminal Law, Criminology and Police Science.* 47 (1956-1957).

RADIOLOGY

Graham, D. *The Use of X-Ray Techniques in Forensic Investigations.* Edinburgh: Churchill Livingstone, 1975.

Kerr. F.M. "The Place for Penetrating Radiations and Particles in Forensic Laboratories." *Canadian Society Forensic Science Journal.* 7:3 (1974), 177-187.

Nag, N.K. and N. Basak. "Radiology and Crime Detection." *Indian Police Journal.* 19:4 (1973), 50-53.

Nag, N.K., N. Basak and T. Mazumder. "The Role of Radiology in the Identification of Forged Notes." *Journal Police Science Administration.* 2:3 (1974), 250-254.

Neiss, A. "X-Rays and Police Science." *International Criminal Police Review* (August-September, 1962), 202-205.

SOIL

Jones, Leland V. "The Role of Dust, Dirt and Debris in Criminal Investigation." *Police.* 5:2 (November-December, 1960), 14-16.

Murray, R.C. and J.C. Tedrow. *Forensic Geology: Earth Science and Criminal Investigation.* New Brunswick, N.J.: Rutgers University Press, 1975.

TOOL MARKS

Brooks, Andrew J., Jr. and Richard A. Meyers. "The Recognition of Burglary Tools." *Law and Order.* 20:7 (July, 1972), 14, 16-18.

Davis, John E. *An Introduction to Tool Marks, Firearms and the Striagraph.* Springfield, IL.: C.C. Thomas, 1958.

Grodsky, Morris. "Tool Marks in Investigation." *International Police Academy Review.* 4 (January, 1970), 14-18.

TOXICOLOGY

Arena, Jay M. *Poisoning: Toxicology. Symptoms and Treatment.* 3rd ed. Springfield, IL.: C.C. Thomas, 1974.

Bagchi, K.N. "Poisons and Poisoning: Arsenic." *Indian Police Journal.* 18:4 (1972), 67-79.

Bodin, F. and C.F. Cheinisse. *Poisons.* N.Y.: McGraw Hill.

Bour, H. and I.M. Ledingham. *Carbon Monoxide Poisoning.* N.Y.: Elseview, 1967.

Bradwell, D. "Reconstruction of an Arsenic Poisoning." *Journal of Forensic Sciences.* 8:2 (April, 1963), 295-302.

Brookes, Vincent J. and Morris B. Jacobs. *Poisons.* Huntington, N.Y.: Krieger, [1958] 1975.

Buchanan, William D. *Toxicity of Arsenic Compounds.* N.Y.: Elsevier, 1962.

Chao, T.C. and C.Y. Yap. "A Case of Mercury Poisoning." *Journal of Forensic Sciences.* 12:1 (January, 1967), 68-76.

Chastain, J.D. "Laboratory Toxicology and the Investigator." *Police.* 3:3 (January-February, 1959), 32-34.

Cholak, J. "Analysis of Evidence with Special Emphasis on the Detection of Poisons." *Journal of Criminal Law, Criminology and Police Science.* 47:4 (November-December, 1956), 482-489.

Cooper, Peter. *Poisoning by Drugs and Chemicals.* 3rd ed. (Yr. Bk.) Newark, N.J.: MEDS, 1974.

Creekmore, Hubert. *Daffodils are Dangerous: The Poisonous Plants in Your Garden.* N.Y.: Walker, 1966.

Gee, D.J. "Autopsy and the Detection of Fatal Poisoning." *Criminologist* (August, 1973), 3-12.

Haard, Karen and Richard Haard. *Poisonous and Hallucigenic Mushrooms.* Berkeley, CA.: Cloudburst, 1975.

Kingsbury, John M. *Poisonous Plants of the United States and Canada.* 3rd ed. Englewood Cliffs, N.J.: Prentice Hall, 1964.

Muenscher, W.C. *Poisonous Plants of the United States.* rev. ed. N.Y.: Macmillan, 1951.

Polson, C.J. and R.N. Tattersall. *Clinical Toxicology.* London: English Universities Press, 1969.

Timperman, J. and R. Maes. "Suicidal Poisoning by Sodium Chlorate." *Journal of Forensic Medicine.* 13:4 (October-December, 1966), 123-129.

Turner, William W. *Drugs and Poisons.* Rochester, N.Y.: Aquaduct, 1965.

TYPEWRITERS

Brown, Charlotte and Paul L. Kirk. "Identification of Typewriter Ribbons." *Journal of Criminal Law, Criminology and Police Science.* 46 (1955-1956).

Casey, M.A. and D.J. Purtell. "IBM Correcting Selectric Typewriters: An Analysis of the Use of the Correctable Film Ribbon in Altering Typewritten Documents." *Forensic Science.* 21:1 (1976), 208-212.

Cromwell, D. "A Method of Indicating the Manufacturer of Courier Style-Type Fonts." *Journal Police Science Administration.* 1:3 (1973), 303-310.

Crown, David A. "Class Characteristics of Foreign Typewriters and Typefaces." *Journal of Criminal Law, Criminology and Police Science.* 59 (1968).

Fryd, G.F.M. "The Forensic Examination of Typewriting Today." *Medical Science Law.* 14:4 (1974), 237-242.

Gayet, Jean. "Efforts at Disguise in Typewritten Documents." *Journal of Criminal Law, Criminology and Police Science.* 46 (1955-1956).

Gupta, S.R., T.R. Nehra and H.L. Bami. "An Assessment of the Interpol Typewriter Classification System." *Journal of Police Science and Administration.* 1:4 (December, 1973), 409-413.

Hilton, Ordway. "The Influence of Variation on Typewriting Identification." *Journal of Criminal Law, Criminology and Police Science.* 50 (1959-1960).

Hilton, Ordway. "Some Practical Suggestions for Examining Writing from the Electric Typewriter." *Journal of Police Science Administration.* 3:1 (1975), 59-65.

Kessell, T.R. "Mechanical Addressing Methods." *Forensic Science.* 21:2 (1976), 422-426.

Swett, George G. "The Dating of Typewriting." *Journal of Criminal Law, Criminology and Police Science.* 50 (1959-1960).

VOICE PRINTS

Baker, Donald L. "Voice Identification Through Sound Spectography." *Journal of California Law Enforcement* (October, 1973), 95-97.

Becker, R.W. *Semiautomatic Speaker Recognition System.* Washington: NCJRS, 1972.

Block, Euguene B. *Voiceprinting: How the Law Can Read the Voice of Crime.* N.Y.: David McKay, 1975.

Burke, John P. and Ralph O. Coleman. "Speaker Identification." *Criminologists* (Autumn, 1973), 46-52.

Cederbaums, Juris. "Voiceprint Identification: A Scientific and Legal Dilemma." *Criminal Law Bulletin* (July-August, 1969).

Corey, G.C. and R.R. Kangas. "Voiceprints: An Investigative Aid." *Military Police Journal.* 22:3 (1972), 4-9.

Hecker, M.H.L. *Speaker Recognition: An Interpretive Survey of the Literature.* Washington: American Speech and Hearing Association, 1971.

Hennessy, J.J. and C.H.A. Romig. "A Review of the Experiments Involving Voiceprint Identification." *Journal of Forensic Science.* 16:2 (1971), 183-198.

Jones, W.R. "Danger: Voiceprints Ahead." *American Criminal Law Review.* 11:3 (1973), 549-573.

Kersta, L.G. "Voiceprint Identification and Application." *Fingerprint and Identification.* 51:11 (May, 1970), 3-8.

Kersta, L.G. "Voiceprint Identification." *Fingerprint and Identification.* 45:1 (July, 1963), 3-7.

Kersta, L.G. and E.W. Nash. "Voice Identification." *International Criminal Police Review.* 28:264 (January, 1973), 9-18.

McDaed, Thomas. "The Voiceprint." *Criminologist* (February, 1968).

Michigan State Police. *Voice Identification Research.* Washington: GPO, 1972.

Nash, E.W. "Voice Identification with the Aid of Spectographic Analysis." *Journal of Official Analytical Chemists.* 56:4 (1973), 944-946.

Nash, E.W. and Oscar I. Tosi. "Identification of Suspects by the Voiceprint Technique." *Police Chief.* 38:12 (December, 1971), 49-52.

Papcun, G. et al. *Equipment Systems Improvement Program: Development Voiceprint Applications Manual.* Washington: NCJRS, 1973.

Romig, C.H.A. and James J. Hennessy. "The Legal Dilemma of Voiceprint Identification." *Police Chief.* XXXVII:6 (June, 1971), 44-48.

Romig, Clarence H.A. and James Hennessy. "Voiceprint Identification as a Law Enforcement Tool." *Law and Order.* 19:7 (July, 1971), 36-38, 40, 42, 44.

Tosi, O. and E. Nash. "Voiceprint Identification: Rules for Evidence." *Trial.* 9:1 (1973), 44-48.

Voice Print Identification Research. Washington: GPO, 1972.

Describes the present state of research and offers guidelines for use of voiceprint techniques and application of voice identification methods in criminal investigation.

"Voice Spectrograms." *International Criminal Police Review* (June-July, 1973), 45, 47.

Welch, E.J., Jr. "Voiceprint Identification: A Reliable Index?" *Trial.* 9:1 (1973), 45, 47.

Ziechner, Irving B. "Voiceprints." *Law and Order* (March, 1975), 68-69.

TRAFFIC

ABANDONED VEHICLES

"The Abandoned Car." *Traffic Digest and Review.* 19 (February, 1971) entire issue.

Abrams, Leonard I. "Abandoned Car Crisis." *Minnesota Municipalities.* 55 (February, 1970), 42-43.

Abrams, Leonard I. "Abandoned Cars and the Environmental Crisis." *Phoenix Quarterly* (Fall, 1969).

Berks County Planning Commission. *Scenic Roads and Auto Graveyards: Beauty Versus Blight.* Information Bulletin #13, Reading, PA (August, 1965).

Carr, D.E. "Only the Giant Car-Eater Can Save Us: 40 Million Junked Autos." *New York Times Magazine* (May 4, 1969).

Central Iowa Regional Planning Commission. *Suggested Program for Control of Junked Cars and Other Large Metal Scrap.* Des Moines, IA.: 1966.

Cornell University Center for Environmental Quality Management. *The Recycle of Auto Hulks: An Assessment.* Ithaca, N.Y.: 1970.

"Death in the Streets: Problem of Disposing of Abandoned Cars." *Time* (June 17, 1966).

Garland, Thomas N. *Practices, Problems and Proposals of Automobile Disposal.* Denver: Inter-County Regional Planning Commission, 1966.

General Motors Corporation. *How to Harvest Abandoned Cars.* Detroit: General Motors Corporation, 1971.

Harkin, D.A. and W.K. Porter. *Methods for Junk Car Removal in Wisconsin.* Madison: University of Wisconsin (October, 1970).

Harloff, Eileen Martin. "The Problem of Abandoned Vehicles." *Local Government Throughout the World* (March-May, 1966).

Lindsay, John V. "Abandoned Autos: One City's Experience." *Phoenix Quarterly* (April, 1969).

Lloyd, G. Stephan. "Chicago's War Against Abandoned Automobiles." *Traffic Digest and Review* (September, 1964).

McDonough, James J. "Chicago's Abandoned Car Towing Program." *Traffic Digest and Review* (February, 1971).

Management Information Service. *Removal of Abandoned Automobiles.* Report #258, Washington: International City Management Association, 1965.

Massachusetts League of Cities and Towns. *Abandoned Motor Vehicle Procedures in Various Cities and in Boston.* Boston: Massachusetts League of Cities and Towns, 1966.

New York Citizens Budget Commission. *How Stolen Cars Die: The New York City Experience.* N.Y.: New York's Citizens Budget Commission (January, 1972).

New York Citizens Budget Commission. *New York's Growth Industry: Abandoned Cars.* N.Y.: New York's Citizens Budget Commission, 1969.

Northern Virginia Regional Planning Commission. *Legal Aspects of Junk Auto Disposal.* Falls Church, VA.: 1967.

Northwestern Traffic Institute. "The Abandoned Car." *Traffic Digest and Review.* 19 (Fall, 11971) entire issue.

Redden, John L. "National Guard Helps Round-Up Abandoned Autos in Newark." *Traffic Digest and Review* (February, 1971).

"Removal of Junked Vehicles from Private Property: A Suggested Ordinance." *Kansas Government Journal* (November, 1970).

Removing Vehicles from the Roadway. Evanston, IL.: Northwestern University Traffic Institute, 1971.
General provisions regarding towing and impounding cars including the legal aspects and the techniques of towing.

Storm, Bill. "The Piggy Back Truck." *Law and Order.* 14:4 (April, 1966) 18-21.
Truck can pickup as many as 3 abandoned vehicles at one time.

"Super Street Litter Needs a Special Hauler: Junked Cars." *American City* (October, 1967).

Traffic Institute, Northwestern University. *Removing Vehicles from the Roadway.* Evanston, IL.: Northwestern University Traffic Institute, 1971.

Truett, John T. "The Abandoned Car Nuisance." *Law and Order.* 15:12 (December, 1967) 110-112.

Vanderjagt, Guy. "A Serious Environmental Problem: Abandoned Vehicles." *Traffic Digest and Review* (February, 1971).

Wohl, Martin. *The Junk Vehicle Problem: Some Initial Thoughts.* Washington: Urban Institute, June, 1970.

ACCIDENTS

"Auto Accidents: Top Killer of U.S. Youths." *U.S. News and World Report* (September 13, 1971).

Baker, J. Stannard. "Single Vehicle Accidents on Route 66." *Journal of Criminal Law, Criminology and Police Science.* 58:2 (December, 1967) 583-595.

Baker, J.S. and L.R. Horn. *Inventory of Factors Suggested as Contributing to Traffic Accidents.* Washington: NCJRS (Michrofiche), n/d.

Baker, J.S. and H.L. Ross. *Concepts and Classification of Traffic Accident Causes.* Washington: NCJRS (Microfiche), 1960.
The object of this study was to provide a plan for analyzing a specific accident to discover the contributing factors and their relationship.

Baker, Susan P. and Werner U. Spitz. "Fatally Injured

Drivers: Clues from Medical Examiners, Police and DMV." *Police.* 15:6 (July-August, 1971), 67-72.

Collins, James C. and Joe L. Morris. *Highway Collision Analysis.* Springfield, IL.: C.C. Thomas, 1974.

DeSilva, Harry Reginald. *Why We Have Automobile Accidents.* N.Y.: Wiley, 1942.

Gikas, Paul W. *The Prevention of Highway Injury.* Ann Arbor: University of Michigan Press, 1967.

Graham, J. Wallace. "Fatal Motorcycle Accidents." *Journal of Forensic Sciences.* 14:1 (January, 1969), 79-86.

Haddon, William. *Accident Research: Methods and Approaches.* N.Y.: Harper & Row, 1964.

Huelke, Donald F. and Paul W. Gikas. "Causes of Deaths in Automobile Accidents." *Police.* 13:2 (November-December, 1968), 81-89.

Hutcheson, F.F. "Car-Train Collisions: Goliath Always Wins." *Law and Order.* 18:6 (June, 1970), 20-21, 24-25, 28-29.

Kearney, Paul William. *Highway Homicide.* N.Y.: Crowell, 1966.

Konkie, Robert K. "Analogue 1000." *FBI Law Enforcement Bulletin.* 38:8 (August, 1969), 12-16, 22.
Analysis of 1000 traffic accidents with fatalities.

Lykes, Norman Roberts. *A Psychological Approach to Accidents.* N.Y.: Vantage, 1954.

"Motor Vehicle Accident Costs Washington Metropolitan Area Report in Brief." *Police* (September-October, 1967), 89-93.

Nahum, A.M. "Physician: Police Collision Injury Investigation." *Police Chief.* XXXVI:11 (November, 1968), 60.
MD program to study for results of traffic accidents.

National Safety Council. *Accident Facts.* Chicago: National Safety Council Annual.

Robert, H.J. *The Causes, Ecology and Prevention of Traffic Accidents.* Springfield, IL.: C.C. Thomas, 1971.

Rudge, Tom. "Murder on Our Highways." *Law and Order.* 18:6 (June, 1970), 14-16, 18.

Schutz, Dan F. "Traffic Accidents." *FBI Law Enforcement Bulletin.* 38:5 (May, 1969), 10-11, 22.

Sevitt, Simon. "Death After Road Traffic Accidents." *Medicine, Science and the Law* (October, 1968).

"Sleepy Driver Guilty of Reckless Homicide." *Police.* 1:2 (November-December, 1956),34.
Description of a New Jersey Court decision.

Tocchio, O.J. "Traffic Accidents, Not Crime, Nation's Greatest Killer!" *Police.* 7:6 (July-August, 1963), 23-26.

Yoss, Robert E. and David D. Daly. "The Sleepy Driver." *Police.* 13:4 (March-April, 1969), 6-10.

Classification of Accidents

Shirk, Blair. "Maryland Takes A New Look at Highway Accident Reporting." *Police Chief.* XXXIX:8 (August, 1972), 28-29.

Traffic Accident Data Project Steering Committee. *Manual on Classification of Motor Vehicle Traffic Accidents.* (2nd ed.) Chicago: National Safety Council, 1970.

CITATIONS

Isaacson, Norman. "The Traffic Summons as Persuasive Communications." *Law and Order.* 21:11 (November, 1973), 70-73, 77.

Taylor, John R. "Traffic Citation Quotas: Fact or Fiction?" *Police Chief* (February, 1973).
Problem neither black nor white but a shade of gray. When traffic citations are increased the number of accidents decreases correspondingly. Informal "norms" are expected in most police departments. Discusses informal organization which redefines formal rules.

Traffic Institute. Northwestern University. *Citations in Traffic Law Enforcement.* Evanston, IL.: Northwestern University Traffic Institute, 1966.

DRIVERS

Parry, Meyer H. *Aggression on the Road.* N.Y.: Barnes & Noble, 1968.

"The Senior Driver." *Traffic Digest and Review.* 13 (March, 1965)
Entire issue devoted to senior citizens and driving.

Sheehe, Gordon H. "Factors Influencing Driver Attitudes, Skills and Performance." *Police* (November-December, 1964).

Weiers, Ronald M. *License to Kill: The Incompetent American Motorist and How He Got That Way.* Philadelphia: Chilton, 1968.

Willet, T.C. *Criminal on the Road: A Study of Serious Motoring Offenses and Those Who Commit Them.* London: Tavistock, 1964.

DRIVERS LICENSE

Aaron, Thomas J. "Foreign Licensed Drivers and Their Vehicles." *Law and Order.* 14:6 (June, 1966), 30-35, 74.

Exotech Systems Inc. *Improving the Enforcement of Driver License Denials, Suspensions and Revocations, Part 1, Preliminary Guidelines.* Springfield, VA.: NTIS, 1970.

Exotech Systems Inc. *Improving the Enforcement of Driver License Denials, Suspensions and Revocations, Part 2, Technical Report.* Springfield, VA.: NTIS, 1970.

Fisher, Edward C. *Driver Licensing and the Law.* Evanston, IL.: Northwestern University Traffic Institute, 1967.

Hricko, Andrew R. "Driver License Suspension: A Paper Tiger." *Police Chief.* XXXVII:2 (February, 1970), 20-23.

Kennamer, David. "License Examiners Must Expect the Unexpected." *Law and Order.* 21:11 (November, 1973), 42-44.

Lee, E.I. "The American Driving Permit: Vehicle of Deceit."

Journal of California Law Enforcement. 9:1 (1974), 15-19.

United States Driver License Guide—USA and Canada. Redwood City, CA.: Drivers License Guide Company, Annual.

Illustrations of drivers' licenses, license tags, credit cards, plus relevant coding and regulatory data for these documents.

DRIVING UNDER THE INFLUENCE

Addams, Stanton. "Driving Under the Influence." *Police.* 7:6 (July-August, 1963), 27-30.

American Medical Association. *Alcohol and the Impaired Driver.* Chicago: American Medical Association, 1970.

Anderson, Eugene D. and James B. Greer. "DWI Re-education: An Experimental Approach." *Police Chief.* XLI:11 (November, 1974), 22-23.

Arthur Young and Company. *Factors Influencing Alcohol Safety Action Project Police Officer's DWI (Driving While Intoxicated) Arrests—Final Report.* Washington: NCJRS (Microfiche 1974).

Bacon, Selden D. "Traffic Accidents Involving Alcohol in the U.S.A.: Second-Stage Aspects of a Social Problem." *Quarterly Journal of Studies on Alcohol* (May, 1968), 21-22.

Barber, William E. "Drunk Drivers: What Michigan Is Doing About Them." *Police Chief.* XXXVII:9 (September, 1970), 42-46.

Borkenstein, Robert F. "A Panoramic View of Alcohol, Drugs and Traffic Safety." *Police.* 16:11 (July, 1972), 6-15.

Borkenstein, R.F. et al. *The Role of the Drinking Driver in Traffic Accidents.* 1964. Bloomington, IN.: Department of Police Administration Indiana University, 1964.

Bowden, K.M. "Driving Under the Influence of Alcohol." *Journal of Forensic Medicine.* 13:2 (April-June, 1966), 44-67.

Bridge, Carl J. *Alcoholism and Driving.* Springfield, IL.: C.C. Thomas, 1972.

Bridge, Carl J. "Drunk Driving Arrests and Alcoholism." *Police.* 15:2 (November-December, 1970), 29-31.

Campbell, H.E. "The Role of Alcoholism Fatal Traffic Accidents." *Traffic Digest.* 65:3 (March, 1965), 24-26, 36-37.

Cook, T. and D. Gath. *Drunkenness Offense.* Elmsford, N.Y.: Pergamon, 1969.

Craig, Glen. "The Drinking Driver—Prime Target for Major Legislation." *Journal of California Law Enforcement* (October, 1969), 49-52.

Cramton, Roger C. "The Problem of the Drinking Driver." *American Bar Association Journal.* 54:10 (October, 1968), 995-999.

Crancer, Alfred Jr. "Driving Records of Illegal Drug Users." *Police Chief.* XXXVI:2 (February, 1969), 41-43.

"Drinking and Driving." *FBI Law Enforcement Bulletin.* 37:12 (December, 1968), 12-14.

"The Drinking Driver." *Traffic Digest and Review* (May, 1964 and June, 1964).

Entire issues devoted to DWI.

Erwin, R.E. *Defense of Drunk Driving Cases, Criminal/Civil.* rev. ed., N.Y.: Matthew Bender, 1967.

Fagerstrom, Dorothy. "The Drinking Driver: A National Problem." *Law and Order* (June, 1971 and September, 1961).

Filkins, L.D. *Alcohol Abuse and Traffic Safety—A Study of Fatalities DWI Offenders, Alcoholics, and Court-Related Treatment Approaches.* Springfield, VA.: NTIS, 1970.

The methodology and conclusions of the Highway Safety Research Institute (HSRI) on the abusive use of alcohol and traffic safety.

Forney, R.B. and F.W. Hughes. *Combined Effects of Alcohol and Other Drugs.* Springfield, IL.: C.C. Thomas, 1968.

Freeman, B. *Drunk Driving Cases: Prosecution and Defense.* N.Y.: Practicing Law Institute, 1970.

Collection of articles detailing the background, elements, trial and dispositions of criminal prosecutions for driving under the influence of alcohol.

Garner, Gerald W. "The Police Role in Alcohol-Related Traffic Offenses." *FBI Law Enforcement Bulletin.* 41:2 (February, 1972), 9-11.

Hansman, F.S. "Driving Under the Influence." *The Australian Police Journal.* 13:2 (1959), 116-137.

Harte, Richard A. "The Search for Harry Wilson—Problem Drinker: Problem Driver." *Law and Order.* 19:12 (December, 1971), 44, 46-48.

Hudson, Page, A.J. McBay and R.F. Turk. "Drug Involvement in Automobile Driver and Pedestrian Fatalities." *Journal of Forensic Sciences* (January, 1974), 90.

Human, M.M. "The Social Characteristics of Persons Apprehended for Driving While Intoxicated." *Quarterly Journal of Studies on Alcohol* (1968), 168-170.

Kirwan, William E. "A Long Look at Alcohol." *Law and Order.* 19:6 (June, 1971), 38-40, 42, 44, 48, 5r.

LeBlanc, Arthur G. and Mark E. Brennan. "The Drinking Driver: Use of Videotape and Personality Testing in Detection and Study." *Police Chief.* XL:12 (December, 1973), 58-67.

Lipmann, Walter. "Alcohol and the Driver." *Law and Order.* 17:6 (June, 1969), 97-102, 112.

Little, Joseph W. *Administration of Justice in Drunk Driving Cases.* Gainesville, FL.: University Presses, 1975.

Little, Joseph W. "Who Is the Deadly Drinking Driver." *Journal of Criminal Law, Criminology and Police Science.* 59:4 (December, 1968), 619-623.

Miller, Seward E. "The Effects of Alcohol on Driving." *Police.* 5:5 (May-June, 1961), 22-24.

Oates, J.F. Jr. *Factors Influencing Arrests for Alcohol-Related Traffic Violations Final Report.* Washington: NCJRS (Microfiche), 1974.

Pitchess, Peter J. "Sheriff Focuses on Drunk Drivers." *Police Chief.* XLI:11 (November, 1974), 16-17.

"Police Launch Campaign Against the Drinking Driver." *Law and Order.* 17:6 (June, 1969), 48-56.

Pollack, S. *Drinking Driver and Traffic Safety Project.* Springfield, VA.: NTIS, 1970.

Rhling, C.J. "The Drug Impaired Driver Furnishes a Hazard on the Highways." *Journal of California Law Enforcement* (January, 1967), 156-159.

Rivo, Julian D. "The Problem of the Drinking Driver." *Police Chief.* XXXII:11 (November, 1965), 14-16.

Ross, H.L. "Britain's Drinking-Driving Experience." *Traffic Safety.* 74:7 (1974), 8-11, 35-36.

Ross, H.L. "The Scandinavian Myth: The Effectiveness of Drinking-and-Driving Legislation in Sweden and Norway." *Journal of Legal Studies.* 4:2 (1975), 285-310.

Schenck, W.J. "The Drinking Driver: Citations Instead of Jail?" *Police Chief.* XXXIX:7 (July, 1972), 38-40.

Schmidt, Wolfgang. "The Role of Alcoholism in Motor Vehicle Accidents." *Traffic Safety.* 61:6 (December, 1962), 21-27.

Selzer, M.L. "The Alcoholic Driver: Myth or Menace?" *Psychiatric Opinion.* 6 (1969), 11-15.

Selzer, M.L. et al. "Alcoholism, Mental Illness and the 'Drunk Driver'." *American Journal of Psychiatry.* 120 (1963), 326-331.

Smart, R.G. "Marijuana and Driving Risk Among College Students." *Journal of Safety Research.* 6:4 (1974), 155-158.

Smith, F.D. "Too Little—But It's Not Too Late." *Law and Order.* 19:12 (December, 1971), 66-68, 70, 72, 74.

Sullivan, H.W. "A Study: Roles of Alcohol, Drugs and Organic Factors in Fatal Single Vehicle Accidents." *Police Chief.* XXXV:3 (March, 1968), 16-22.

Traffic Institute, Northwestern University. *Driving Under the Influence of Alcohol or Drugs.* Evanston, IL.: Northwestern University Traffic Institute, 1966.

U.S. Department of Transportation, National Highway Traffic Safety Administration. *Manual for a Selective Traffic Enforcement Program for Alcohol-Related Motor Vehicle Crashes.* Washington: GPO, 1972.

Wilson, Bill. "How Georgia Combats the Drinking Driver." *Law and Order.* 21:7 (July, 1973), 72-76.

Zylman, Richard. "Are Drunk Driving Laws Being Enforced?" *Police Chief.* XXXVII:9 (September, 1970), 48-53.

Zylman, Richard. "Drinking and Driving: After It's Legal to Drink at 18." *Police Chief.* XLI:11 (November, 1974), 18, 20-21.

Zylman, Richard. "When It Became Legal to Drink at 18 in Massachusetts and Maine: What Happened?" *Police Chief.* XLIII:1 (January, 1976), 56-59.

Zylman, Richard and Selden D. Bacon. "Police Records and Accidents Involving Alcohol." *Quarterly Journal of Studies on Alcohol* (May, 1968).

EMERGENCY CALL BOXES

Guest, William. "Los Angeles Emergency Call System." *Law and Order.* 19:12 (December, 1971), 98, 100, 102.

Hansen, E.L. "Emergency Signalinaling System." *Law and Order.* 22:2 (February, 1974), 67.

Kulikowsky, Ronald N. "Free Emergency Telephones for Superhighways." *FBI Law Enforcement Bulletin* (January, 1967), 2-5, 20.

Sullivan, Harold W. "Emergency Call Boxes on Freeway." *Western City.* 5 (May, 1965), 36-37.

ENFORCEMENT

Enforcement—General

Allen, Edward J. "Acquiescence to Manslaughter." *Police.* 4:3 (January-February 1960), 23-25.

Anderson, John P. "Take the Stress Out of Traffic Stops." *Law and Order.* 23:6 (June, 1975), 36, 38, 45-46.

Bell, K.C. "The Case for a Separate Road Traffic Corps." *Police College Magazine.* 13:2 (1974), 8-13.

Brandt, Warren H. "Speed Limits—Theory and Practice." *FBI Law Enforcement Bulletin.* 35:3 (March, 1966), 2-6.

Broad, Thomas. "Stabilizing Traffic Control by Ordinance." *Law and Order.* 14:6 (June, 1966), 77-78.

Byrne, Edward C. "Preventive and Selective Enforcement of Traffic Laws." *Law and Order.* 23:6 (June, 1975), 18, 20-22.

Cable, Keneth M. "Warning: Speed Checked By Radar." *Law and Order.* 18:9 (September, 1973), 108-110.

Chiaramonte, Robert M. "Tactical Traffic Squads Do the Job." *Law and Order.* 15:1 (January, 1967), 44-45.

Crowell, Harry W. "Rigid Traffic Law Enforcement Cuts Accident Rate." *FBI Law Enforcement Bulletin.* 26:12 (December, 1957), 7-9, 20.

Fehrle, W.R. "Town Traffic." *Law and Order.* 14:6 (June, 1966), 16-23.

Gardiner, John A. "Police Enforcement of Traffic Laws: A Comparative Analysis." in James Q. Wilson, ed. *City Politics and Public Policy.* N.Y.: Wiley, 1968.

Goetzke, Richard E. "Enforcement Effort." *Law and Order.* 22:6 (June, 1974), 36, 38, 40, 42.

Hrunek, Jack. "Bicycle Riders Get Tickets Too." *Law and Order.* 13:5 (May, 1965), 62, 64, 87.

Huddleston, Burt. "Operation Saturation." *Law and Order.* 16:6 (June, 1968), 86-91.

Khanne, T.S. *Administration of Traffic Enforcement.* N.Y.: Publication Service International, 1960.

Kramer, Richard P. "A Traffic Engineer Takes a Hard Look at Traffic Enforcement." *Law and Order.* 17:8 (August, 1969), 110-114.

Latchaw, James A. "Does Traffic Law Enforcement Carry Its Weight?" *Law and Order.* 15:9 (September, 1967), 55-56.

Lauer, Alvin Ray. *The Psychology of Driving: Factors of Traffic Enforcement.* Springfield, IL.: C.C. Thomas, 1960.

Leonard, V.A. *Police Traffic Control.* Springfield, IL.: C.C. Thomas, 1971.
Combined manual and text describes the requirements and programs for effective traffic control in a small or medium sized community.

Liswood, Steve. "Operation It's 55." *Police Chief.* XLII:7 (July, 1975), 65-63.
California Highway Patrol method of escorting groups of cars on the freeway with a poster on the back of their car stating "It's 55".

Long, W.A. (Bill). "Eliminate the Negative Approach to a Traffic Problem." *Law and Order.* 12:10 (October, 1964), 60.

Milardo, Donald T. "43.7% Accident Reduction." *Law and Order.* 22:6 (June, 1974), 14, 16-20.

"Police Courtesy vs. Laxity." *The American City.* 65:19 (August, 1950).

Reuben, Don H. "Reckless Driving: Is It A Distinguishable Offense?" *Journal of Criminal Law, Criminology and Police Science.* 41 (1950-1951).

Richman, J. "Police Auxiliaries: Traffic Wardens—Some Sociological Aspects." *Police Journal.* 46:2 (1973), 125-149.

Rutherford, J.W. "Reducing Traffic Accidents Through Selective Enforcement." *Police Chief.* XXXVIII:5 (May, 1971), 8, 75.

Schultz, Donald O. *Police Traffic Enforcement.* Dubuque, IA.: W.C. Brown, 1975.

Scott, Ralph D. "The Arkansas State Police Traffic Program." *Law and Order.* 18:6 (June, 1970), 82-87, 90.

Shumate, R.P. *Effect of Increased Patrol on Accidents, Diversion and Speed.* Evanston, IL.: Northwestern University Traffic Institute, 1958.

Slavin, James M. *The Role of Traffic Law Enforcement in Traffic Accident Prevention.* Saugatuck, CT.: Eno Foundation for Transportation, 1967.

Smith, J.L. "Solving the Campus Traffic Problem." *Law and Order.* 24:6 (June, 1976), 16-18.

Smith, R. Dean. *Police Traffic Responsibilities.* Gaithersburg, MD.: IACP, 1969.

Smith, R.D. and B. Keenan. *Police Traffic Responsibilities.* Springfield, VA.: NTIS, 1969.
Analysis of police traffic systems in nine political jurisdictions is synthesized into manpower allocation models.

Southwestern Lawn Enforcement Institute. *Traffic Law Enforcement—A Guide for Patrolmen.* Springfield, IL.: C.C. Thomas, 1963.

Sullivan, Harold W. "Automobile Safety: Highway Safety Acts Affect Law Enforcement." *Journal of California Law Enforcement* (July, 1967), 35-40.

Techniques for Radar Speed Detection. IL.: Northwewestern University Traffic Institute, 1967.
Selection of a site for speed measurement, preparation of the radar instrument for operation, and proper use to meet court requirements.

Thompson, John T. *City Traffic Law Enforcement in Texas.* Austin, TX: Austin Institute of Public Affairs, n/d.

Thompson, Robert Baird. "Traffic Officers: Soldiers of Safety." *Law and Order.* 19:3 (March, 1971), 56, 58-63.

Traffic Institute, Northwestern University. *Officer-Violator Relationships.* Northwestern University Traffic Institute, Evanston, IL.: 1969.

Traffic Institute, Northwestern University. *Reckless Driving and Homicide.* Evanston, IL.: Traffic Institute Northwestern University, 1970.

Traffic Institute, Northwestern University. *Traffic Patrol for Law Enforcement.* Northwestern University Traffic Institute, Evanston, IL.: 1961.

U.S. Department of Transportation. *Highway Safety Program Manual. Vol. 15, Police Traffic Services.* Washington: GPO, 1969.

Weston, P.B. *Police Traffic Control Function.* 2nd ed. Springfield, IL: C.C. Thomas, 1972.

Wilson, P.R. and D. Chappell. "The Effects of Police Withdrawal from Traffic Control: A Comparative Study." *Journal of Criminal Law, Criminology and Police Science.* 61:4 (1970), 567-572.

Witheford, David K. *Speed Enforcement Policies and Practice.* Saugatuck, CT.: Eno Foundation for Transportation, 1970.

Wright, Edward L. "From Alabama: A Program for Hit-and-Run Violations." *FBI Law Enforcement Bulletin* (September, 1972).

Motorcycle Units

Banton, Gene, et al. "The Motorcycle Officer: His Image in the Community." *Police Chief.* XXXIX:6 (June, 1972), 77-78.

Bennet, J.A. "Police Motorcycle Busy in Riverside, CA." *American City.* 71:25 (January, 1956).

Brown, R.A. "Effective Police Motorcycle Enforcement in Alton, IL." *American City.* 72:156 (February, 1957).

Crawford, William. "The Motorcycle Patrolman." *Law and Order.* 15:11 (November, 1967), 48-55.

Goldman, Sam. "The Motorcycle in Police Work." *Law and Order.* 16:11 (November, 1968), 50-53, 82.

Haye, James E. "One Motorcycle Is Worth Six Cars in Traffic Control." *The American City.* 66:135 (August, 1951).

Koenig, Walter R. "The Motorcycle Squad." *Law and Order.* 17:9 (September, 1969), 22-26.

"Motorcycle Officers, Los Angeles." *The American City.* 59:105 (May, 1944).

"Police Prove Popular With Cycle Fans." *Law and Order.* 22:11 (November, 1974), 100, 106.
Describes police motorcycle competitions.

Robinson, Ivan A. and F.B. Childers. "How We Attacked

the Motorcycle Safety Problem." *Police Chief.* XXXV:3 (March, 1968), 44-46.

Skousen, W. Cleon. "Motorcycle Corps Developed into Year-Round Unit." *FBI Law Enforcement Bulletin.* 26:11 (November, 1957), 17-19.

Skousen, W. Cleon. "The Chief Takes A Look At The Solo Motorcycle." *Law and Order.* 21:8 (August, 1973), 8, 10, 12, 14, 16.

Skousen, W. Cleon. "The Chief Takes A Look at the Solo Motorcycle." *Law and Order.* 16:2 (February, 1968), 30-34.

Sullivan, Harold W. "The Motorcycle in Police Work: An Evaluation." *California Peace Officer.* 12:5 (November-December, 1961), 34-35.

Young, Clement J. "Motorcycles in Patrol Work." *Public Management.* 36:61 (March, 1954).

INSPECTION OF VEHICLES

Beck, E.W. "Motor Vehicle Inspection: II. California's Random Program." *Police Chief.* XXXIV:9 (September, 1967), 30-39.

Beck, Eugene W. "Studies Fail to Show Effect of Vehicle Inspections on Accidents." *Journal of California Law Enforcement* (July, 1967), 23-31.

Buxbaum, Robert C. and Theodore Colton. "Relationship of Motor Vehicle Inspection to Accident Mortality." *Journal of the American Medical Association* (July 4, 1966), 101-106.

Meyer, Albert J. and Thomas F. Hoult. *Motor Vehicle Inspection. A Report on Current Information, Measurement, and Research.* Detroit: Institute for Regional and Urban Studies, Wayne State University, 1963.

Overton, M.B. "Motor Vehicle Inspection in Louisiana." *Police Chief* (February, 1968), 48-49.

Terry, R.M. "Motor Vehicle Inspection: Virginia's Mandatory Program." *Police Chief.* XXXIV:9 (September, 1967), 25-28.

"The Case for Compulsory Motor Vehicle Inspection." *Law and Order.* 14:4 (April, 1966), 82, 84.

INTOXICATION TESTING

American Medical Association. *Alcohol and the Impaired Driver: A Manual on the Medicolegal Aspects of Chemical Tests for Intoxication.* Chicago: American Medical Association, 1968.

Argeriou, M. "Refusal to Take Breathalyzer Test: Rebuting Adverse Presumption." *Criminal Law Bulletin.* 11:3 (1975), 350-355.

Donigan, R.L. *Chemical Tests and the Law.* Evanston, IL: Traffic Institute Northwestern University, 1966.

Glendening, Blaine L. "Kansas Pioneers: New Detection of Drunken Drivers." *Law and Order.* 19:11 (November, 1971), 68-71.
Describes the Alco-Analyzer.

Insurance Institute for Highway Safety. "Breath Testers." *Police Chief.* 38:8 (August, 1971), 30.

Kretschumer, John D. "Why Have Pre-Arrest Breath Testing." *Law and Order.* 23:7 (July, 1975), 28, 30.

Prouty, R.W. and B. O'Neil. *An Evaluation of Some Qualitative Breath Screening Tests for Alcohol.* Washington: Insurance Institute for Highway Safety (May, 1971).

Sego, P. "The Breathalyzer Reblown." *Criminal Law Review* (March, 1973), 153-163.

Smith, William C. "Breathalyzer Experience Under Operational Conditions Recommended by the California Association of Criminalists." *Journal of Forensic Science Society.* 9 (July, 1969), 58-64.

Stinson, Palmer. "Simple Field Test Helps Detect Oakland DWI's." *Traffic Safety.* 63 (December, 1963), 20-21, 36.

Turner, R.F. "Chemical Tests for Intoxication-Prosecution Viewpoint." *Trauma.* 1 (1959), 19-46.

Watts, L.P. "Some Observations on Police Administered Tests for Intoxication." *North Carolina Law Review.* 45:1 (December, 1966), 35-118.

INVESTIGATION

Investigation—General

Baker, J.S. *Problems of Determining Causes of Specific Accidents.* Evanston, IL.: Traffic Institute Northwestern University (July, 1963).

Baker, J.S. *Traffic Accident Investigation Manual.* Evanston, IL.: Traffic Institute Northwestern University, 1975.

Beddoe, Harold L. "Hit-Run Murders: Examination of the Body." *Journal of Criminal Law, Criminology and Police Science.* 49:3 (September-October, x958), 280-284.

Benner, L. Jr. "Accident Investigations: Multilinear Events Sequencing Methods." *Journal of Safety Research.* 7:2 (1975), 67-73.

Byrne, Edward C. "Improving Investigations of Hit and Run Traffic Accidents." *Law and Order.* 19:6 (June, 1971), 56-60.

Chrastil, Warren L. "Hit and Run." *Law and Order.* 16:7 (July, 1968), 64.

Cooke, Joseph D. Jr. "Traffic Accident Investigation Checklist." *Military Police Journal.* 19 (January, 1970), 17-20.

Davis, Charles A. "Notes on Physical Evidence in Pedestrian Hit and Run Accident." *Journal of Criminal Law, Criminology and Police Science.* 50:3 (September-October, 1959), 302-306.

Ford, Richard and A.L. Moseley. "Motor Vehicular Suicide." *Journal of Criminal Law, Criminology and Police Science.* 54 (1963).

Greenwald, Robert. "Scientific Evidence in Traffic Cases." *Journal of Criminal Law, Criminology and Police Science.* 59:1 (March, 1968), 57-73.

Gunn, Herman M. "Suicide in a Moving Automobile on a Highly Traveled Highway." *Journal of Criminal Law, Criminology and Police Science.* 43 (1952-1953).

Hand, Bruce A. *Traffic Investigation and Control.* Columbus, OH.: Merrill, 1976.

Hatch, John P. "Accident Location." *Law and Order.* 19:6 (June, 1971), 24, 26, 28, 30.
Article examines the mathematics involved in accident investigation.

Hirsh, Paul. *The Nighttime Accident Problem.* N.Y.: Pageant, 1957.

Hitchcock, Claude R. "The Policeman at the Scene of the Accident." *Police.* 13:3 (January-February, 1969), 16-19.

Hoag, Gene. "Hit and Run? Maybe Not." *Law and Order.* 18:7 (July, 1970), 88, 98-99.

"Investigation of Fatal Road Accidents." *Journal of the Forensic Science Society.* 1:1 (September, 1960), 12-28.

Johnson, R.G. "Accident Investigations. The Logic Tree: An Aid to the M.P." *Military Police Law Enforcement Journal.* 1:5 (1975), 31-34.

Jones, H. "Accident Investigation." *Law and Order.* 20:6 (June, 1972).

Lacy, G.W. *Scientific Automobile Accident Reconstruction.* NY: Matthew Bender, 1968.

MacDonald, John M. "Deliberate Death on the Highway." *Police.* 9:4 (March-April, 1965), 30-31.

Perrone, Ralph A. "Accident Investigations (Not As A Matter of Routine)." *Law and Order.* 12:6 (June, 1964), 8-10.

Peterson, Bonita J. and Charles S. Petta. "Sudden Natural Death Among Automobile Drivers." *Journal of Forensic Sciences.* 7:3 (July, 1962), 274-285.

Reilly, Joseph P. "Accident Investigation: The Human Factor." *Law and Order.* 24:6 (June, 1976), 44-48, 71.

Rizer, Conrad K. "Estimating the Speed of a Motor Vehicle in a Collision." *Journal of Criminal Law, Criminology and Police Science.* 58 (1967).

Romig, C.H.A. and T.J. McGrevy. "Investigation of Hit and Run Accidents." *Military Police Journal.* 21:10 (1972), 9-11.

Slavin, James M. "Weakness in Traffic Accident Investigation." *FBI Law Enforcement Bulletin.* 37:2 (February, 1968), 2-6, 17-20.

Smith, H. Ward. "Physical Evidence in the Investigation of Traffic Accidents." *Journal of Criminal Law, Criminology and Police Science.* 48:1 (May-June, 1957), 93-102.

Spring, Eugene. "Accident Investigation Team." *Law and Order.* 24:6 (June, 1976), 72-74.

Truett, John. "Investigating the Accident." *Law and Order.* 13:1 (January, 1965), 72, 74.

Turner, William W. *Traffic Investigation.* 2 vols., Rochester, N.Y.: Aquaduct, 1965.

Williams, John F. "Physical Evidence in Hit and Run Traffic Deaths." *Criminal Law, Criminology and Police Science.* 50:1 (May-June, 1959), 80-85.

Wright, Edward L. "A Program for Hit and Run Violations." *FBI Law Enforcement Bulletin.* 41:9 (September, 1972), 16-21, 31-32.

Skid Marks

Auten, James H. "A Programmed Instruction Approach to Speed Estimates Based Upon Skidmark Evidence." *Police.* 16:3 (November, 1971), 27-31.

Rifas, R.A. *Legal Aspects of Skidmarks in Traffic Cases.* Evanston, IL.: Northwestern University Traffic Institute, 1970.

Rifas, Richard A. "Legal Aspects of Skid Marks in Traffic Cases." *Traffic Digest and Review.* 18 (June-July, 1970, August, 1970, September, 1970).

MEDICALLY RESTRICTED DRIVERS

Crancer, Alfred Jr. and Lucille McMurray. "Accident and Violation Rates of Washington's Medically Restricted Drivers." *Police.* 13:3 (January-February, 1969), 90-94.

Mears, M. "Diabetes and Driving." *Law Society's Gazette.* 72:11 (1975), 310.

Waller, Julian A. *Medical Impairment to Driving.* Springfield, IL.: C.C. Thomas, 1974.

PARKING

Firth, Victor G. "Pittsburg (Kansas) Unique Parking Summons Force." *Police.* 13:5 (May-June, 1969), 91-93.

Peet, Creighton. "A Solution to a Parking Problem." *Law and Order.* 12:6 (June, 1964), 40-41, 68.
Purchase of several lots and installation of parking meters.

VanBuren, W.C. "Parking Ticket with Built-In Collector." *Law and Order.* 16:6 (June, 1968), 56-57.

PEDESTRIANS

Baran, Stephen. "Protecting the Fellow on Foot." *Law and Order.* 13:6 (June, 1965), 6.

Haddon, W. et al. "A Controlled Investigation of the Characteristics of Adult Pedestrians Fatally Injured by Motor Vehicles in Manhattan." *Traffic Safety.* 62:6 (June, 1963), 5-18.

Traffic Institute, Northwestern University. *Pedestrian Offenses.* Evanston, IL.: Traffic Institute Northwestern University, 1972.

Traffic Institute, Northwestern University. *Pedestrian Violations.* Evanston, IL.: Traffic Institute Northwestern University, 1961.

Williams, Don. "The Pedestrian Program in Rochester, New York." *Law and Order.* 13:6 (June, 1965), 8-12, 66.

TRAFFIC CONTROL

Baudek, John. "Streets, Highway and Railroad: A Triangular Traffic Problem." *Law and Order.* 24:6 (June, 1976), 20-21.

Drew, Donald. *Traffic Flow Theory and Control.* N.Y.: McGraw-Hill, 1968.

Sandler, Craig D. "Mini Computer Controls Traffic Problems." *Law and Order.* 23:6 (June, 1975), 48, 50.

Squibb, George and Alix Dragnich. "Traffic Control." *Law and Order.* 20:6 (June, 1972), 50-54, 56, 58.
Describes the many facets of traffic control ie accidents, pedestrian, barricades and other equipment.

TRAFFIC CONTROL DEVICES

Graves, Fred. "Computerized Traffic in Metro Toronto." *Law and Order.* 18:12 (December, 1970), 82-83.

Manny, Thomas. "Computerized Signal System to Control Vehicle Traffic." *Law and Order.* 18:6 (June, 1970), 78-81.

Shaw, William. "Automated Traffic Systems Will Be A Big City Necessity." *Law and Order.* 14:4 (April, 1966), 42-44, 46.

U.S. Department of Transportation. *Manual on Uniform Traffic Control Devices for Streets and Highways.* Washington: GPO, 1971.
National standards and specifications for signs, markings, signals, islands, controls for construction and maintenance operations, and for school traffic control.

TRAFFIC ENGINEERING

Baerwald, J.E., ed. *Traffic Engineering Handbook.* 3rd ed., Washington: Institute of Traffic Engineers, 1965.

Rodgers, Lionel. "How to Make Traffic Counts." *Law and Order.* 18:12 (December, 1970), 74-79.

Teasley, Harvey D. "Shreveport Corrects Mystic Maze." *Law and Order.* 13:4 (April, 1965), 60-61.

Teasley, Harvey D. "Traffic Engineering Reduces Accidents." *Law and Order.* 12:6 (June, 1964), 16-17.

Truett, John T. "Accident Records and Traffic Engineering." *Law and Order.* 14:12 (December, 1966), 80-81.

TRAFFIC LAW

Fisher, E.C. *Legal Aspects of Speed Measurement Devices.* Evanston, IL.: Traffic Institute Northwestern University, 1967.

Fisher, Edward C. *Right of Way in Traffic Law Enforcement.* St. Louis: Thomas Law Co. 1956.

Joscelyn, K.B. and R.K. Jones. *Systems Analysis of the Traffic Law System.* 3 vols., Springfield, VA.: NTIS, 1971 and 1972.

Kearney, Edward F. "Are Your Traffic Laws Modern and Uniform?" *Police Chief* (September, 1973).

TRAFFIC SAFETY

Baker, Robert Fulton. *The Highway Risk Problem: Policy Issues in Highway Safety.* N.Y.: Wiley, 1971.

Franey, W.M. *Maryland's Highway Safety Needs in Police Traffic Services.* Springfield, VA.: NTIS, 1969.

Freeman, Theodore F. "Recruiting for Traffic Safety." *Law and Order.* 24:6 (June, 1976), 24.

Gibbens, Murray E. "Prevention of Automobile Casualties." *Police.* 3:6 (July-August, 1959), 12-16.

Gurdjian, Elisha S. et al. *Impact Injury and Crash Protection.* Springfield, IL.: C.C. Thomas, 1970.

Harper, William W. "Prevention and Reduction of Injuries in Traffic Collisons." *Journal of Criminal Law, Criminology and Police Science.* 43:4 (1952-1953), 515-529.

Hausman, Robert. "Dead Men Tell No Tales, But Chemists Make Them Talk." *Police.* 3:5 (May-June, 1959), 69-72.

Heimstra, Norman W. *Injury Control in Traffic Safety.* Springfield, IL.: C.C. Thomas, 1970.

International Association of Chiefs of Police. *Highway Safety Policies for Police Executives.* Gaithersburg, MD.: IACP, 1969.

Koltnow, Peter G. "The '3 × 80' Safety Campaign: Community Help for Traffic Law Enforcement." *Police Chief.* XLII:8 (August, 1975), 57-59.

Lauer, A.R. "Basic Factors of Safe Automobile Driving." *Police.* 4:3 (January-February, 1960), 57-59 (March-April, 1960), 60-61.

Miller, H.B. "Calling All Police." *Police.* 2:6 (July-August, 1958), 28-30.

Nader, Ralph. *Unsafe at Any Speed.* N.Y.: Pocket Books, 1966.

National Highway Safety Bureau. *Highway Safety Program Standards.* Washington: GPO, 1969.

Pyle, Howard. "The Traffic Safety Job Is Not Being Done." *Police.* 14:3 (January-February, 1970), 27-29.

Rosenow, John H. and Robert W. Watkins. "Physician's Role in Highway Safety." *Police.* In five parts, 13:5 (May-June, 1969), through 14:3 (January-February, 1970).

Schoenphoester, Lloyd. "Public Relations Via Radio Aids in Accident Prevention." *Law and Order.* 12:7 (July, 1964), 60-61.
Traffic safety via public radio.

Slater, Stephen L. "Motorcycle Safety Program." *Law and Order.* 19:6 (June, 1971), 99.

Sullivan, Harold W. "Promoting Traffic Safety on Highways is a Challenge." *Journal of California Law Enforcement* (April, 1968), 213-217.

"The Question of Motor Vehicle Safety Seat Belts. *Police.* 1:2 (November-December 1956), 30-33.

Waters, Howard. "Implements of Husbandry." *Law and Order.* 18:8 (August, 1970), 86-88.
Solution to slow moving farm vehicles on public roads.

Zylman, Richard. "Overemphasis on Alcohol May Be Costing Lives." *Police Chief.* XLI:1 (January, 1974), 64-67.

PART III
FIELD OPERATIONS—SPECIALIZED FUNCTIONS

SPECIALIZED POLICE FUNCTIONS

AVIATION OPERATIONS

Aviation—General

"Air Age." *FBI Law Enforcement Bulletin.* (December, 1948).

"Air Patrol Commissioned." *National Sheriff.* 13 (January-February, 1961).

"Airplanes Spot 90 mph Drivers." *Colorado Sheriff and Peace Officer.* 10 (December, 1969), (January, 1970).

"Beat of Wings; New York's Air Police." *New York Times Magazine* (May 21, 1950), 50-51.

Burdette, F.H. "The Case for a Police Air Arm." *Police Journal (GB).* 20 (January-March, 1947), 77-78.

Cook, LeRoy. "Missouri Highway Patrol Evaluates New Aircraft." *Law and Order.* 20:5 (May, 1972), 86-88, 94.

"Cops in the Blue." *Spring 3100.* 40 (October, 1969), 9-21.

Crawford, William. "Border Patrol Aviation." *Law and Order.* 16:2 (February, 1968), 43-46, 81.

Crawford, William. "Policemen With Wings." *Law and Order.* 14:8 (August, 1966), 23-25, 58.

Danaher, Tom A. "Surveillance From the Sky." *Law and Order.* 16:12 (December, 1968), 60-63.

Dument, Robert. "Superhighway Patrolled From Air." *Law and Order.* 16:5 (May, 1968), 86-88.

"El Paso Sheriff Department Adds 19 Man Sky Patrol." *Sheriff's Association of Texas.* 15 (January, 1947).

"El Paso Sheriff Skyway Patrol." *Sheriff's Association of Texas.* 15 (February, 1947).

Felkenes, George T. "Some Legal Aspects of Aircraft Usage as an Aid to Law Enforcement." *Journal of California Law Enforcement* (January, 1968), 128-140.

"Fixed Wings Complement Police Copters." *Rotor and Wing* (October, 1972).

"Flying Highway Patrol; Nevada Police." *Flying.* 69:21 (July, 1961).

"Flying Policemen Move Traffic: Philadelphia." *The American City.* 74:114 (December, 1962).

"Forty Years of Police Aviation." *Spring 3100.* 40 (October, 1969), 10-21.

Gibbons, Harry J. "Airborne Policemen Work to Advantage in Law Enforcement" *FBI Law Enforcement Bulletin* (November, 1952), 6.

Gilmouthe, Rupert L. "The Use of Small Aircraft in Police Work." *FBI Law Enforcement Bulletin.* 28:3 (March, 1959), 9-12.

Green, Barney. "How to Fly Safely in the Mountains." *Rotor and Wing* (March-April, 1973), 8, 32-33.

Guthrie, C. Robert. "Helicopter vs Fixed Wing: A Comparison." *Journal of California Law Enforcement.* 8:3 (January, 1974), 131-139.

Harris, Jess C. "Airplanes Increase Police Coverage in Nevada." *FBI Law Enforcement Bulletin.* 26:6 (June, 1957), 15-16.

Hegarty, James J. "AMES: Air Medical Evacuation Systems." *Police Chief* (June, 1970), 22, 26, 28.

Jones, B. "Why No Aircraft?" *Police College Magazine* (Autumn, 1966), 29, 33.

Kimball, Leonard N. "Kentucky's Flying Cops." *Law and Order.* 22:7 (July, 1974), 42-44.

Latchaw, A.J. *Aircraft: Another Enforcement Tool for Police.* Evanston, IL.: Traffic Institute Northwestern University, 1964.

"Lawmen on Sky Duty." *FBI Law Enforcement Bulletin.* 35:10 (October,1966), 12-13.

Los Angeles County Sheriff's Department. *Manual of Aerial Patrol: Development, Implementation and Operations.* Washington: NCJRS, 1968.

McDonald, William B. "Military Aircraft for Law Enforcement." *Law and Order.* 21:11 (November, 1973), 20-21, 44.

McGuire, James T. "Speed Check from the Air by Illinois State Police." *Police.* 16:1 (September, 1971), 5-8.

Maltz, Michael D. "Evaluation of Police Air Mobility Programs." *Police Chief.* 38:4 (April, 1971), 34-36, 38-39.

Morris, William H. and J. L. Jones. "State Police Aircraft Scores Again." *Police.* 6:4 (March-April, 1962), 12-15.

"Napa County Sheriff Squadron Has Jet." *California Peace Officer.* 8 (July-August, 1958).

Nichols, J.B. *Equipment Systems Improvement Program: Development—Evaluation of Aerial Vehicles for Law Enforcement Application.* Washington: NCJRS, 1973.

Raffensberger, R. and H. Koffenberger. "Identification: A Key to Successful Helicopter Patrols." *Police Digest.* 2:1 (1973), 27-31.
Program for marking patrol vehicles and roof tops.

Reisch, Martin C. "The Flying Policemen of Dade County, Florida." *Law and Order.* 16:5 (May, 1968), 62-63.

"Sheriff's Aero Squadron: Stanislaus County." *California Peace Officer.* 9 (November-December, 1958).

Smith, Leo M. "Air to Ground Operation on Minnesota Highway." *Police Chief.* 28 (April, 1961), 22-24.

Smith, Paul M. "Kentucky State Police Spread Their Wings." *FBI Law Enforcement Bulletin* (September, 1970), 2-6.

"Somebody Up There." *Newsweek.* 59:28 (January, 1962).

Helicopters

Adwill, James. *Helicopters in Action.* N.Y.: Meridith, 1969.

American Society of Planning Officials. *Helicopters.* Chicago: American Society of Planning Officials, 1965.

Arthur Young and Company. *Evaluation of OCJP (Office of Criminal Justice Planning) Funded Helicopter Patrol Projects—Final Report.* Washington: NCJRS (Microfiche) 1974.

Arthur Young and Company. *Helicopter Patrol Project—Cluster Evaluation: Phase 1 Report.* Washington: NCJRS (Microfiche) 1974.

Arthur Young and Company. *Helicopter Patrol Project—Cluster Evaluation: Status Report.* Washington: NCJRS (Microfiche) 1973.

Ayoob, Massad F. "Small Helicopter Wings Can Be Effective for Cops." *Law and Order.* 22:11 (November, 1974), 76-78, 80.

Bartlett, Hale C. "Helicopter Ambulances: An Evaluation of their Operational and Economic Feasibility." *Traffic Digest and Review.* 19 (July, 1971), 1-7.

Beall, J.R. and R.E. Downing. *Helicopter Utilization in Municipal Law Enforcement—Administrative Considerations.* Springfield, IL.: C.C. Thomas, 1972.

Becker, Bob. "New Jersey State Police Launch Helicopter Bureau." *Law and Order.* 17:11 (November, 1969), 44-46, 62.

Becker, Harold K. "Do Police Helicopters Justify Their Cost?" *American City.* 84 (November, 1969), 70-71.

Bennett, P.H.. "Helicopter in Police Work." *Australian Police Journal* (October, 1973), 245-253.

"Big New Whirl in Helicopters." *Fortune* 73: (April, 1966), 124-131.

Blevins, Gary. "Kern County Copter Keeps Thieves on Run." *Law and Order.* 22:2 (February, 1974), 78-79.

Brown, Donald J. "The Whirlybird and the Safety Campaign." *Law and Order.* 14:6 (June, 1966), 24-25.

Burden, Earl. "Helicopter Patrol Services." *Law and Order.* 21:11 (November, 1973), 66-69.

"Chicago Fire Department's Air Rescue Unit." *Rotor and Wing* (March-April, 1973), 10, 32.

"Chicago's Flying Firemen." *FAA Aviation News* (March, 1973), 6.

Coburn, R.F. "Police Units Expand Helicopters Operations." *Aviation Week and Space Technology* (January 13, 1969).

Coleman, R.R. *Pennsylvania—Helicopter Ambulance Study—Final Report.* Washington: NCJRS (Microfiche) 1969).

Coon, Thomas F. "Law Enforcement Technology Welcomes the Chopper 'Copper'." *Police.* 13:5 (May-June, 1969), 6-8.

"County Sheriff Uses Helicopter." *American City.* 73:13 (November, 1958).

Datnow, Frank. "How Los Angeles Cares for It's Copters." *Rotor and Wing* (March-April, 1973), 17-19.

Davis, E.M. "ASTRO: Los Angeles Police Department Helicopter Program." *Police Chief.* XXXVIII:11 (November, 1971), 10, 66-67.

Deutsch, Patricia. "Sky Knight, The Heavenly Prowl Car." *Readers Digest* (April, 1968).

Diltz, Douglas. "Helicopters—Regular Police Patrol Vehicles." *Law and Order.* 13:11 (November, 1965), 6-8, 10.

District of Columbia Metropolitan Police Department. *Crime Reduction Through Aerial Patrol.* Springfield, VA.: NTIS.

Assessment of the effectiveness of helicopters for aerial patrol in a more densely populated community with more severe weather conditions than the Los Angeles area.

Dix, Bruce. "Helicopters and the Police Service." *Police College Magazine* (March, 1954), 171-176.

Driscoll, Tom. "Helicopters: The Key to Crime Control." *Rotor and Wing* (December, 1971).

Fisher, B.E. "Emergency Helicopter Rescue Scheme for Highrise Buildings." *Police Journal (GB)*, (April-June, 1975), 113-121.

Fisher, B.E. *London (England)—Police: Helicopters Rescue Scheme for Highrise Buildings.* Washington: NCJRS (Microfiche) 1974.

Greene, Barney. "Piston Copters Are Not Obsolete. . .Yet." *Rotor and Wing* (July-August, 1973), 18-21.

Hagan, Peter F. "Helicopter: The Latest Police Tool Used by the Traffic Division of the Los Angeles Police Department." *American City.* 75 (April, 1960), 124-125.

Harris, Carl L. "Helicopter Works for Memphis P. D." *Law and Order.* 18:2 (February, 1970), 84-86.

Hegarty, J.J. "AMES: Air (Helicopter) Medical Evaluation Systems." *Police Chief.* XXXVII:6 (June, 1970), 22-28.

"Helicopters, the Latest Police Tool." *American City.* 75:123 (April, 1960).

"Helicopter Capabilities Sparking Strong Market in Western Europe." *Aviation Week and Space Technology* (May 28, 1973), 181-185.

"Helicopter Patrols Combat Crime." *Law Enforcement Journal* (Winter, 1974).

"Helicopter Used to Locate Stolen Car." *FBI Law Enforcement Bulletin* (February, 1970), 22.

"Hovering Helicops: New York Aerial Police." *New York Times Magazine* (April 19, 1964), 102-104.

Jet Propulsion Laboratory. *Effectiveness Analysis of Helicopter Patrols*. Pasadena, CA.: Jet Propulsion Laboratory, 1972.

Klotzback, Walter E. "The Helicopter: New York Police on Patrol." *Journal of Criminal Law, Criminology and Police Science*. 48:5 (January-February, 1958), 547-550.

Lateef, A. Barbi. "Helicopter Patrol in Law Enforcement: An Evaluation." *Journal of Police Science and Administration*. 2:1 (March, 1974), 62-65.

Law Enforcement Assistance Administration. *Utilization of Helicopters for Police Air Mobility*. Washington: NCJRS, 1971.

Los Angeles County Sheriff's Department. *Manual of Aerial Patrol: Development, Implementation and Operations*. Washington: NCJRS, 1968.

Lynn, Norman. "Patrol Helicopter Mobility Effective in Crime Control." *Law and Order*. 21:11 (November, 1973), 82-85.

McMahon, H.D. "Helicopter Adds Versatility to Police Work." *American City* (October, 1969).

Milgang, H. "Beat of Wings, New York Air Police." *New York Times* (May 20, 1950), 50-51.

Nell, Steven M. "Alternative Identification in Decision-Making: Implementating A Helicopter Patrol." *Police Chief*. XXXVI:7 (July, 1969), 18-28.

Page, Ralph. "Well Equipped Chopper Gets Results." *Law and Order*. 18:2 (February, 1970), 92-94.

Project Sky Knight: A Demonstration in Aerial Surveillance and Crime Control. U.S. Department of Justice, LEAA (May, 1968).

"Project Sky Knight: Helicopters Join War Against Crime." *Utah Peace Officer* (June-August, 1968), 32-35.

Purko, Joe. "Los Angeles Builds Separate Helicopter Facility." *American City* (June, 1971).

Reynolds, William F. "Airborne Assistance for Railroad Crime." *FBI Law Enforcement Bulletin*. 43:8 (August, 1974), 17-21.

Ropelewski, R.R. "Los Angeles Police Find Helicopters Effective." *Aviation Week and Space Technology* (July 17, 1972).

"Sheriffs Use Bell 47's for Patrol Work—Los Angeles County Sheriff's Department." *Aviation Week*. 71:95-6 (December 14, 1959).

Simonsen, Clifford E. "Helicopter Patrol." *Police Chief*. XLII:10 (October, 1975), 30, 32-33.

Skagen, R. "Seattle's New 'Air One' Helicopter Program Proves Valuable Addition to Special Operations Division." *Washington Law Enforcement Journal*. 2:1 (1972), 12-13, 15.

Spangler, Bob. "Cameraman in a Helicopter." *Law and Order*. 13:8 (August, 1965), 8-9.

Stambler, Irwin. "Turbing Helicopters in San Bernadino (Cal)." *Law and Order*. 22:11 (November, 1974), 92-96.

St. Louis Helicopter Project: A Cooperative Effort Among Fourteen Railroad Departments. Washington: U.S. Department of Transportation Office of Transportation Security (November, 1973).

U.S. Department of Transportation National Highway Traffic Safety Administration. *Helicopters in Emergency Medical Service: NHTSA (National Highway Traffic Safety Administration) Experience to Date, December 1972*. Washington: NCJRS (Microfiche) 1973.

Utilization of Helicopters for Police Air Mobility. Washington: NCJRS, 1971.

Law Enforcement Agencies which use helicopters were surveyed to ascertain the types of activities for which helicopters are used.

Wasserman, Lauren M. "Lakewood's Airborn Police Augment Ground Patrol." *Western City*. 43 (February, 1967), 21-22, 33.

Whisenand, Paul. "The Use of Helicopters By Police: Administration and Applications." *Police Chief*. XXXVI:2 (February, 1969), 32-40.

Wolfum, C.E. "Police Helicopter Operations, Los Angeles, California." *Traffic Digest Report*. 5 (September, 1957), 1-3.

STOL

Cornell Aeronautical Laboratory Inc. *Police Air Mobility: STOL Evaluation Phase I*. Buffalo, N.Y.: Cornell University, 1970.

Dade County Public Safety Department. *Dade County Public Safety Department—STOL*. Springfield, VA.: NTIS, 1971.

INTELLIGENCE OPERATIONS

Police Intelligence Operations

Alletto, William C. "The Arson Squad and Intelligence Operations." *Police*. 16:4 (December, 1971), 38-40.

Baker, Bruce R. "Police and Procedures for the Portland Police Intelligence Division." *Police Chief*. XLII:3 (March, 1976), 58-61.

Baker, E. Jo and C. Michael York. "Communication or Confrontation." *Law and Order*. 20:10 (October, 1972), 86-89.

Activities of civil disorder technical assistance unit within Georgia Department of Public Safety.

Bartels, John R. Jr. "Drug Enforcement Administration's Unique Concept: Unified Intelligence." *Police Chief*. XLII:7 (July, 1975), 38-39.

Bishop, Wayne H. "Intelligence Systems: LEIU (Law Enforcement Intelligence Unit): An Early System." *Police Chief*. 38:9 (September, 1977), 30, 32.

"BNDD Says New Intelligence System Identifies Worldwide Drug Nets." *Crime Control Digest* (October 16, 1970).

Bouza, Anthony V. *Police Intelligence: The Operations of an Investigative Unit*. N.Y.: AMS, 1976.

Boydston, H. E. "The Santa Clara Valley Intelligence Unit." *Texas Police Journal*. 22:1 (1974), 16-19, 22:2 (1974), 12-15.

Callahan, W.T. *Prevention and Control of Collective Violence, Vol. 3: Guidelines for Intelligence Personnel.* Washington: GPO, 1972.

Coon, Thomas F. "The Court Says New Jersey Police May Keep Intelligence Files." *Police.* 15:2 (November-December, 1970), 69-70.

Coon, Thomas F. "Intelligence Files." *Police.* 6:4 (March-April, 1962), 26-27.

Davidson, Bill. "The Mafia Can't Crack Los Angeles." *Saturday Evening Post.* 238 (July 31, 1965), 23-27.

Davis, Edward M. "Police Intelligence and The Right to Privacy." *Journal of California Law Enforcement* (January, 1976), 93-95.

Dionisio, Riccardo R. "Department of Transportation: U.S. Coast Guard Intelligence." *Police Chief.* XLII:7 (July, 1975), 52-53.

Dreifus, Claudia. "New York's Red Squad BOSS is Watching." *The Nation* (January 25, 1971), 102-108.

Dvornik, Francis. *Origins of Intelligent Services.* New Brunswick, N.J.: Rutgers University Press, 1973.
Contains many examples of secret police operations, methods of communication and internal control.

Ehlke, R. "Political Surveillance and Police Intelligence Gathering: Rights, Wrongs and Remedies." *Wisconsin Law Review* (1972), 175-199.

Garmire, Bernard L. "A New Methodology for the Miami Police to Combat Organized Crime." *Police Chief.* 38:9 (September, 1971),26-29.
The combining of vice, narcotics and Intelligence units into the Special Investigation Section. Special sub-units assigned to operate against organized crime.

Gates, Daryl. "The Law Enforcement Intelligence Unit." *California Peace Officer.* 15 (January-February, 1965).

Godfrey, E. Drexel Jr. and Don R. Harris. *Basic Elements of Intelligence.* Washington: Department of Justice—LEAA, 1971.

Gourley, D.D.. "A Final Solution to the Problem of Organized Crime." *Police Chief.* 39:2 (February, 1972).
Author advocates the formation of an economic Intelligence Unit and strengthening IRS Laws especially those relating to disclosure of information.

Gourley, Dudley D. "In Brief: Some Management Problems—The Role of Police Intelligence." *Police Chief.* XL:2 (February, 1973).

Gutman, R. M. "Chicago's Red Squad." *Progressive* (September, 1975).

Hamilton, James. "LEIU—It's Objectives and Operations." *Police Year Book.* Washington: IACP, 1961.

Hamilton, James E. "Police Intelligence Units Recommended to Cope with Organized Crime." *Police Chief* (December, 1955).

Hosford, J. Sr. *Police Intelligence Operations.* North Miami, FL.: American Federation of Police, 1973.

IBM Data Processing Division. *Law Enforcement Information System: East Valley (CA.) Information System—Organized Crime Intelligence Unit.* Washington: NCJRS (Microfiche) 1974.

Kelly, David B. "The Name of the Game." *Police Chief.* XXXIX:9 (September, 1972), 28-30.

Koh Kong Song. "The Need for an Intelligence Unit in the Criminal Investigation Department." *Singapore Police Journal* (January, 1972), 29-42.

Lo Schiavo, Nino John. "Law Enforcement Intelligence Unit." *Police Chief* (February, 1975), 46.

McGreevy, Thomas J. "Police Intelligence Operations." *Police.* 8:4 (March-April, 1964), 46-52.

Metzdorff, H.A. "The Module Concept of Intelligence Gathering." *Police Chief.* 42:2 (February, 1975), 52-58.
Advocates the use of an analysis to control and direct investigators within the team.

Michigan Department of Attorney General, Organized Crime Division. *Criminal Intelligence Service Manual.* Lansing, MI.: Department of Attorney General, 1969 (Unpub.).

Minto, Michael F. "The Criminal Intelligence Squad." *Police Chief.* XLII:2 (February, 1975), 40-44.

National Association of Attorneys Generals. *Organized Crime Control Units.* Washington: LEAA, 1972.

New England State Police Administrator's Conference. *New England Regional Criminal Intelligence Information System.* Montpelier, VT.: New England State Police Administrators Conference, 1968.

New York City Police Department. *New York City—Police Department: Public Security Activities of the Intelligence Division—Procedures.* Washington: NCJRS (Microfiche).

New York Division of Criminal Justice Services. *New York—Division of Criminal Justice Services: Annual Report, 1st September 1, 1972-December 31, 1973.* Washington: NCJRS (Microfiche) 1974.
This Division is responsible for the New York State Identification and Intelligence System.

New York State Identification and Intelligence System. *A New Concept in Criminal Justice and Information Sharing.* Albany, N.Y.: NYSIIS, 1967.

New York State Identification and Intelligence System. *New York State Identification and Intelligence System—Annual Report, 1971: A System in Motion.* Washington: NCJRS (Microfiche) 1971).

"New York State Identification and Intelligence System." *SDC.* 8 (October, 1965), 22-25.

New York State Identification and Intelligence System. *Security System for Organized Crime Intelligence Capability.* Washington: LEAA, n/d.

Owens, Robert L. "Intelligence: The Police Dimension." *Military Police Journal.* 16 (September, 1966), 7-9 (October, 1966), 18-21.

Perkus, Cathy, ed. *COINTELPRO.* N.Y.: Monaro, 1976.

Pfaelzer, Mariana R. and Allan D. Bersin. "The Police and Public Disorder Intelligence: The Los Angeles Experience." *Crime Prevention Review.* 2:4 (July, 1975), 1-8.

Phillips, G.W. et al. *Evaluation of the Michigan Intelligence Network Team.* Washington: NCJRS (Microfiche) 1974.

Raynor, William C. "Police Intelligence." *Police Chief.* XLII:2 (February, 1975), 18.

Rochford, James M. "Police Intelligence and Organized Crime Enforcement." *Police Chief.* XLII:2 (February, 1975), 47-49.

Schiavo, N.J.L. "Law Enforcement Intelligence Unit." *Police Chief.* 42:2 (1975), 46-82.

Schultz, Donald O. and Loran A. Norton. *Police Operational Intelligence.* Springfield, IL.: C.C. Thomas, 1968.

Schwein, Edwin Eugene. *Combat Intelligence: Its Acquisition and Transmission.* Washington: Infantry Journal, 1936.

Scott, S. K. "Police Operational Intelligence: The Key to Survival." *Enforcement Journal.* 10:4 (1971), 20-21.

Skousen, W. Cleon. "The Intelligence Unit." *Law and Order.* 14:6 (June, 1966), 68-73.

Skousen, W. Cleon. "The National Network of Police Intelligence Units." *Law and Order.* 14:7 (July, 1966), 10-14.

Technology Management Inc. *New England Organized Crime Intelligence System—Evaluation Concepts and Plan.* Washington: NCJRS (Microfiche) 1971.

Ulmer, R.G. and R.J. Eckenrode. *Evaluation of the New England Organized Crime Intelligence System (NEOCIS) Final Report.* Springfield, VA.: NTIS, 1972.

U.S. Department of the Army. *Combat Intelligence.* Washington: Department Headquarters, 1967.

U.S. Department of the Army. *Stability Operations Intelligence.* Washington: Department Headquarters, 1970.

U.S. Treasury Department, Internal Revenue Service, Intelligence Division. *Digest of Wagering Operations.* Washington: GPO, 1963.

Vandiver, James V. "Acquisition and Disposition of Police Front Line Information." *Journal of Police Science and Administration.* 2:3 (September, 1974), 288-296.
Use of tactical intelligence and information by Police Organizations.

Virginia: Organized Crime Detection Task Force—Report. Richmond: Virginia State Crime Commission, 1971.

Weinberg, M. California: *Evaluation of Organized Crime and Criminal Intelligence Branch's Integrated Program to Combat Organized Crime—Final Report.* Washington: NCJRS (Microfiche) 1972.
Evaluates planning, intelligence data collection, processing, analysis and dissemination, together with personnel administration, training and new program needs.

Willes, E. W. "Criminal Intelligence Service Canada." *Police Chief.* 38:9 (September, 1971), 18-19.

Wolf, John B. "Police Intelligence: Focus for Counter-Terrorist Operations." *Police Journal (GB).* (January-March, 1976), 19-27.

Yates, D.M. and W. Russell. "On Line Data Retrieval for a Local Police Intelligence Unit." *Police Research Bulletin* (November-October, 1970), 5-12.

Zunno, Frank A. "Let's Put Intelligence in Perspective." *Police Chief.* 38:9 (September, 1971), 46-47.

Zunno, Frank A. "NYSIIS and NEOCIS." *Police Chief.* 38:9 (September, 1971), 31-32.

Internal Security and Counter Intelligence

Altenburg, Arthur J. "Notes on Building Security." *Police Chief.* 37:11 (November, 1970), 38, 40-41.
General principles regarding designing security into a facility.

Arthur, Richard O. "The Subversive in the Police Department." *Law and Order.* 12:7 (July, 1964), 64-65.
Description of subversive infiltration of police agencies and counter intelligence activities.

Hansen, David A. "Some Observations on Police Station Security.: *FBI Law Enforcement Bulletin.* 41:4 (April, 1972), 2-4, 28-29.

Kentile, Omer N. "Lock Tightens Station House Security." *Law and Order.* 20:8 (August, 1972), 100-101.

Pattern, Eugene P. "Counter-subversive Activities." *Valor* (July-August, 1965).

Peel, J.D. "Establishing a Security Bureau in Your Department." *Police.* 16:2 (1971), 42-47.

Stephens, Gary W. "Are We Really Security Conscious?" *Police Chief.* XL:12 (December, 1973).

Thorsen, Roger. "Button, Button, Who's Got the Button?" *Police.* 4:2 (November-December, 1959), 29-30.
The handling of classified documents and records.

U.S. Department of the Army. *Counter Intelligence Operations (FM 30-17).* Washington: GPO, 1968.

Codes and Ciphers

Baker, Wayne G. *Cryptanalysis of the Single Columnar Transposition Cipher.* Rutland, VT.: C.E. Tuttle, 1961.

"Codes: Policy Collectors Discover that Codes are Fragile." *Spring 3100.* 23:4 (April, 1952), 10-13.

"Codes and Secret Inks in War." *Fingerprint and Identification.* 22:12 (June, 1941), 3-6, 18-20.

"Crime and Cryptology." *FBI Law Enforcement Bulletin* (April, 1970), 13-14.

Cuelenaere, Alphonse. "Cryptophotography." *International Criminal Police Review* (November, 1956), 284-290.

D'Agapyeff, Alexander. *Codes and Ciphers.* rev. ed. London: Oxford University Press, 1949.

Friedman, William F. and Elizabeth Friedman. *The Shakespearean Ciphers Examined.* N.Y.: Cambridge University Press, 1957.

Gaines, Helen F. *Cryptanalysis: A Study of Ciphers and Their Solution.* N.Y.: Dover, 1956.

Geffe, Philip R. "How to Protect Data with Ciphers that are Really Hard to Break." *Electronics* (January 4, 1973), 99-101.

Hooker, C.W.R. "The Desciphering of Crytograms." *Police Journal* (GB) 1 (October, 1928), 621-633.

Kahn, David. *Code Breakers.* N.Y.: Macmillan, 1967.

Kooken, Don L. "Cryptography in Criminal Investigation." *Journal of Criminal Law and Criminology.* 26 (March-April, 1936), 903-919; 27 (May-June, 1936), 75-96.

Laffin, John. *Codes and Ciphers: Secret Writing Through the Ages.* N.Y.: Abelard-Schuman, 1964.

Lamb, Geoffrey. *Secret Writing Tricks.* Nashville, TN.: Nelson, 1975.

Langen, Henry E. "Fingerprint Ciphers." *Fingerprint and Identification.* 32 (1951), 15-19, 31.

Levine, Jack. "Variable Matrix Substitution in Algebraic Cryptography." *AMR, Mathematical Monthly* (March, 1958), 170-179.

Levine, Jack. *Word List of Words Containing no Repeated Letters.* Raleigh, NC.: North Carolina State College of Agricultural and Engineering Department of Math, 1958.

Locard, Edmond. "Cryptography in Criminal Matters." *International Criminal Police Review.* 1:2 (October-November, 1946), 17.

"A Look at Codes and Ciphers." *FBI Law Enforcement Bulletin.* 36:1 (January, 1967), 17-20.

Lysing, Henry. *Secret Writing: An Introduction to Cryptograms Ciphers and Codes.* N.Y.: David Kemp, 1936.

Norman, Bruce. *Secret Warfare: The Battle of Codes and Ciphers.* Washington: Acropolis, 1974.

Shulman, David. "Ciphers and Their Solutions." *Police Journal (GB).* 25 (July-August, 1939).

Turner, Ralph. "The Development of Invisible Writing with Sulphocyanic Acid." *Journal of Criminal Law and Criminology.* 32 (1941-1942), 257-258.

Williams, Eugenia. *An Invitation to Cryptograms.* N.Y.: Simon & Schuster, 1959.

International Intelligence Activities

Agee, P. "Why I Quit the CIA and Spilled the Beans." *Esquire* (June, 1975).

Alsop, S. "Soviet Spymasters: Soviet Espionage Apparatus in the U.S." *Saturday Evening Post* (May 22, 1965).

Altavilla, Enrico. *The Art of Spying.* Englewood Cliffs, N.Y.: Prentice Hall, 1967.

Bailey, G. "Cultural Exchange as the Soviets Use It." *Reporter* (April 7, 1966).

Berndorff, Hans Rudolf. *Espionage.* N.Y.: Appleton, 1930.

Blackstock, Paul W. *Agents of Deceit: Frauds, Forgeries and Political Intrigue Among Nations.* Chicago: Quadrangle, 1966.

Blackstock, P.W. "Agents of Deceit: Fraud, Forgeries and Political Intrigue Among Nations." *Saturday Review* (September 10, 1966), 300.

Brown, Anthony K. *Body Guard of Lies.* N.Y.: Harper & Row, 1975.

Carpozi, George. *Red Spies in Washington.* N.Y.: Trident, 1968.

Carroll, John Millar. *Secrets of Electronic Espionage.* N.Y.: Dutton, 1966.

"CIA Scandal—and the Backlash." *U.S. News and World Report* (January 13, 1975).

"Cloak and Dagger Behind the Scenes." *Saturday Evening Post* (March 3, 1962).

Copeland, Miles. *Without Cloak or Dagger.* N.Y.: Simon & Schuster, 1974.

Coulson, Thomas. *Mata Hari: Courtesan & Spy.* N.Y.: Harper & Brothers, 1930.

Dallin, David J. *Soviet Espionage.* New Haven, CT.: Yale University Press, 1955.

Dasch, George John. *Eight Spies Against America.* N.Y.: McBridge, 1959.

Deacon, Richard. *A History of the British Secret Service.* N.Y.: Taplinger, 1970.

DeToledano, Ralph. *Spies, Dupes and Diplomats.* N.Y.: Duell, Sloan & Pearce, 1952.

Donovan, James Britt. *Strangers on a Bridge: The Case of Colonel Abel.* N.Y.: Atheneum, 1964.

Downes, Donald C. *The Scarlet Thread: Adventures in War Time Espionage.* London: D. Verschoyle, 1953.

Dulles, Allen Weish. *The Craft of Intelligence.* N.Y.: Harper & Row, 1963.

Dulles, Allen Welsh. *Great True Spy Stories.* N.Y.: Harper & Row, 1968.

"Espionage: How the Deadly Game is Played." *Newsweek* (December 11, 1961).

Farago, Ladislas. *War of Wits: The Anatomy of Espionage and Intelligence.* N.Y.: Funk & Wagnall's, 1954.

Firmin, Stanley. *They Came to Spy.* N.Y.: Hutchinson, 1946.

Foote, Alexander. *Handbook for Spies.* London: Museum Press, 1949.

Gollomb, Joseph. *Spies.* N.Y.: Macmillan, 1928.

Gramont, Sanche de. *The Secret War.* N.Y.: Putnam, 1962.

Granovsky, Anatoli. *I Was an NKVD Agent: A Top Soviet Spy Tells His Story.* N.Y.: Devin-Adiar, 1962.

Greenberg, D. S. "Security Practices: Nonmilitary Agencies Still Hold to Vestiges of Procedures Developed in the 1950's." *Science* (May 7, 1965).

Hamilton, P. *Espionage and Subversion in an Industrial Society: An Examination and Philosophy of Defense for Management.* London: Hutchinson, 1967.
Survey of the British experience with espionage and subversion undertaken to obtain industrial information for economic or political advantage.

Heilbrun, Otto. *The Soviet Secret Services.* London: Allen & Unwin, 1956.

Huminik, John. *Double Agent.* N.Y.: New American Library, 1967.

Hunt, E. Howard. *Undercover: Memoirs of an American Secret Agent.* N.Y.: Berkley, 1974.

Huss, Pierre John. *Red Spies in the U.N.* N.Y.: Coward-McCann, 1962.

Hutton, J. *School for Spies: The ABC's of How Russia's Secret Service Operates.* N.Y.: Coward-McCann, 1962.

Hyde, H.M. "Composite Portrait of the Soviet Spy." *New York Times Magazine* (February 16, 1964).

Irwin, William Henry. *What You Should Know About Spies and Saboteurs.* N.Y.: Norton, 1943.

Jefferson, M. "Master of Spies: Memoirs of General Frantesik Moravec." *Newsweek* (June 2, 1975).

Joesten, Joachin. *They Call It Intelligence.* N.Y.: Abelard-Schuman, 1963.

Jones, John Price. *The German Secret Service in America.* Boston: Small, Maynard, 1918.

Kaznacheev, Alexander. *Inside a Soviet Embassy: Experiences of a Russian Diplomat in Burma.* Philadelphia: Lippincott, 1962.

Kent, Sherman. *Strategic Intelligence.* Princeton, N.J.: Princeton University Press, 1966.

Kirkpatrick, Lyman B. *The U.S. Intelligence Community: Foreign Policy and Domestic Activities.* N.Y.: Hill & Wang, 1973.

Landau, Henry. *The Enemy Within: The Inside Story of German Sabotage in America.* N.Y.: Putnam, 1937.

"Mafia Spies in Cuba." *Time* (June 9, 1975).

Newman, Bernard. *German Secret Service at Work.* N.Y.: McBride, 1940.

Newman, Bernard. *Spy.* N.Y.: Appleton-Century, 1935.

Newman, Joseph. *Famous Soviet Spies: The Kremlin's Secret Weapon.* Washington, D.C.: News and World Report, 1973.

Orlov, Alexander. *Handbook of Intelligence & Guerrilla Warfare.* Ann Arbor: University of Michigan Press, 1963.

Penkovskiy, Oleg. *The Penkovskiy Papers.* Garden City, N.Y.: Doubleday, 1965.

Philby, Kim. *My Silent War: The Soviet Master Spy's Own Story.* N.Y.: Grove, 1968.

Pilat, Oliver Ramsay. *The Atom Spies.* NY: Putnam, 1952.

Platt, Washington. *Strategic Intelligence Production.* N.Y.: Praeger, 1965.

Ransom, Harry H. *Intelligence Establishment.* Cambridge, MA.: Harvard University Press, 1970.

"Rattling Skeletons in the CIA Closet." *Time* (January 6, 1975).

Reber, Jan R. "The Essence of Espionage." *Assets Protection* (Spring, 1975) 7.

Reinhardt, Guenther. *Crime Without Punishment: The Secret Soviet Terror Against America.* N.Y.: Hermitage House, 1952.

Reiss, Curt. *Total Espionage.* N.Y.: Putnam, 1941.

"School for Spies: Institute for Industrial Protection, Japan." *Time* (December 14, 1962).

Seth, Ronald. *Encyclopedia of Espionage.* Garden City, N.Y.: Doubleday, 1974.

Seth, Ronald. *Secret Servants: A History of Japanese Espionage.* N.Y.: Farrar, Straus & Cudahy, 1957.

Seth, Ronald. *Unmasked: The Story of Soviet Espionage.* N.Y.: Hawthorne, 1965.

"Spies and Circuses: A Spy Hunt in Arab States." *Newsweek* (January 6, 1968).

"Spies Symposium." *Esquire* (May, 1966).

"Spies We Caught and What They Were After." *U.S. News and World Report* (July 15, 1963).

Spiro, Edward. *Shadow of a Spy: The Complete Dossier on George Blake.* London: Frewin, 1967.

Tietjen, Arthur. *Soviet Spy Ring.* N.Y.: Coward-McCann, 1961.

Tulley, Andrew. *CIA: The Inside Story.* N.Y.: Morrow, 1962.

Tulley, Andrew. *The Super Spies: More Secret, More Powerful Than the CIA.* N.Y.: Morrow 1969.

"Under the Table: British Security Procedures." *Time* (May 21, 1965).

U.S. Committee on Un-American Activities. *Conduct of Espionage Within the United States by Agents of Foreign Communist Governments: Hearings Before 90th Congress, 1st Session.* Washington: GPO, 1971.

U.S. Congress Senate. Committee on the Judiciary. *Subcommittee to Investigate Administration of the Internal Security Act and Other Internal Security Laws.* Washington D.C.: GPO, 1970.

Voska, Emmanual Victor. *Spy & Counterspy.* N.Y.: Doubleday Doran, 1940.

Walker, W.S. "Spying: The Second Oldest Profession." *Saturday Review* (May 25, 1963).

"What Soviet Spies Are up to in the U.S." *U.S. News and World Report* (June 17, 1963).

Wighton, Charles. *Hitler's Spies and Saboteurs: Based on the German Secret Service War Diary of General Lahousen.* N.Y.: Holt, 1958.

Wise, David. *The Espionage Establishment.* N.Y.: Random House, 1967.

Wynne, G. and O. Penkovsky. "Spies in Moscow: More Than Meets the Eye." *Newsweek* (May 20, 1963).

"You Were Expecting Maybe James Bond? Israeli-Egyptian Espionage." *Time* (June 5, 1964).

Zahn, G.C. "007's of Real Life: The Non-Fiction List." *Commonwealth* (December 8, 1972).

JUVENILE CONTROL

Juvenile Enforcement

Adams, F.W.H. "New York Police Tackle Delinquency." *American City.* 70:5 (September, 1955).

Adams, G.B. et al. *Juvenile Justice Management.* Springfield, IL.: C.C. Thomas, 1973.

Adams, Thomas F. "Establishing a Juvenile Division for a Police Department Serving a City of 100,000." *Police* (January-February, 1963), 46-49.

Alexander, S. "Protecting the Children of Life-Threatening Parents." *Journal of Clinical Child Psychology.* 3:2 (1974), 53-54.

American Humane Association. *Sexual Abuse of Children: Implications for Case-Work.* Denver: American Humane Association, 1967.

Berkowitz, Bernard. "The Juvenile Officer." *Police.* 11:1 (September-October, 1957), 37-38.

Brennan, James J. "Police and Delinquent Youth." *Journal of Criminal Law, Criminology and Police Science.* 46:6 (March-April, 1956), 886-891.

Brennan, James J. "Public Relations in Police Work with Delinquents." *Police.* 9:4 (March-April, 1965), 14-16.

California Bureau of Criminal Identification and Investigation. *Enforcement Officers Manual and Guide to Absent Parent Problems.* San Francisco: Bureau of Criminal Identification and Investigation, 1960.

Carter, Robert M. and C. Thomas Gitchoff. "An Alternative to Youthful Mass Disorder." *Police Chief.* XXXVII:7 (July, 1970), 52-56.
Creation of youth commissions with guidelines.

Chwast, Jacob. "Police Methods for Handling Delinquent Youth." *Journal of Criminal Law, Criminology and Police Science.* 46:2 (July-August, 1955), 255-258.

Connecticut Department of Children and Youth Services. *Institute on Police Relations With Troubled Juveniles, 1st—Conference Proceedings: University of Bridgeport, Connecticut, May 22-23, 1973.* Washington: NCJRS (Microfiche) 1973.

Cornelius, John J. "How to Establish a Youth Division." *Law and Order* (December, 1974), 26-30.

Costa, Rudy. "Police—Youth Program Begins Fourth Year at Norwalk (CT)." *Law and Order.* 20:12 (December, 1972), 28-29.

Damos, James Peter. "Four Program Models in Delinquency." *FBI Law Enforcement Bulletin.* 43:1 (January, 1974).

DeSmet, J. *Youth Squads—NCJRS Translation.* (Washington: NCJRS, 1975.
Police Juvenile work in Antwerp.

Dienstein, William. "Delinquency Control Techniques as Influences by Beliefs and Attitudes of Police Personnel." *Police.* 5:1 (September-October, 1960), 23-26.

Drake, Francis M. "A Juvenile Officer at Work." *Law and Order.* 12:8 (August, 1964), 12, 14.

Eldefonso, Edward. *Youth Problems and Law Enforcement.* Englewood Cliffs, N.J.: Prentice Hall, 1972.

Ellingston, John R. "New Police Methods with Children." *American City.* 64 (January, 1949).
The duties of a Juvenile Bureau and its connection with agencies, courts, and schools.

Flammang, C.J. *The Police and the Unprotected Child.* Springfield, IL.: C.C. Thomas, 1970.

Gitchoff, G.T. "Police Response to Juvenile Hostility in Suburbia." *Police Chief.* 38:1 (January, 1971), 52-57.

Heller, Dorothy K. "Child Molesters and Their Victims." *Law and Order.* 14:5 (May, 1966), 22-24, 64.

Hicks, Harry C. "Juvenile Delinquency and One Vehicle for Its Control." *Police Chief.* 39:10 (October, 1972), 278-283.

Holman, Mary. *The Police Officer and the Child.* Springfield, IL.: C.C. Thomas, 1962.

Jameson, Samuel H. "The Policeman's Non-Official Role in Combating Gangs and Vandalism." *Police.* 1:5 (May-June, 1957), 45-49.

Keller, E. John. "School Security: The Role of the Police." *Law and Order.* 20:12 (December, 1972), 50-52.

Kenney, John Paul and Dan G. Pursuit. *Police Work With Juveniles and the Administration of Juvenile Justice.* 5th ed., Springfield, IL.: C.C. Thomas, 1975.

Kobetz, R.Q. and B.B. Bosarge. *Juvenile Justice Administration.* Gaithersburg, MD.: IACP, 1973.

McEachern, A.W. and R. Bauzer. "Factors related to Disposition in Juvenile Police Contacts." In M. W. Klein, ed. *Juvenile Gangs in Context: Theory, Research, and Action.* Englewood Cliffs, N.J.: Prentice Hall, 1967.

McLennan, Robert M. "California's Antiquated Juvenile Justice System—A Program for Reform." *Journal of California Law Enforcement* (April, 1975), 145-155.

Melchionne, Theresa M. "Delinquency Control Programs." *Law and Order* (April, 1964; May, 1964; June, 1964).

Neaman, Thomas J. Jr. "Professional Police Approach to the Juvenile Offender." *Law and Order* (December, 1974), 34-36.

O'Hara, Gerald P. "Why Detain Juveniles?" *Police.* 8:5 (May-June, 1964), 76-68.

Parsons, Malcom B. "The Administration of Police Juvenile Services in the Metropolitan Regions of the United States." *Journal of Criminal Law, Criminology and Police Science.* 54:1 (March, 1963), 114-117.

Patterson, J.R. "The Structure and Function of a Police Juvenile Bureau." *Canadian Police Chief.* 62:2 (1973), 15-17.

Piliavin, Irving and Scott Briar. "Police Encounters with Juveniles." *American Journal of Sociology* (September, 1964), 206-214.

Pizzuto, C.S. *Police Juvenile Unit—A Study in Role Consensus.* Ann Arbor, MI.: University Microfilms, 1968.
Analysis of the role, the functions, and the operations of specialized juvenile police units.

Pursuit, Dan G. et al. *Police Programs for Preventing Crime and Delinquency.* Springfield, IL.: C.C. Thomas, 1972.

Rinck, Jane E. "Supervising the Juvenile Delinquent." *Annals of the American Academy of Political and Social Science.* 291 (January, 1954), 78-86.

Rosenthal, E. and M. Sevy. *Gang Problem in Philadelphia: Proposals for Improving the Programs of Gang-Control Agencies.* Washington: NCJRS (Microfiche) 1974.

Savord, George H. "Responsibilities of Police in Dealing with Non-Students on Campus." *Journal of California Law Enforcement* (October, 1968), 98-102.

Shimota, Kenneth L. "A Study of Police Services to Children in a Rural Wisconsin County." *Journal of Criminal Law, Criminology, and Police Science.* 56:2 (June, 1965), 257-259.

Skousen, W. Cleon. "Should the Small Department Have a Juvenile Officer." *Law and Order.* 23:6 (June, 1975), 10-12, 14-16.

Sorensen, Christine B. "Every Officer a Youth Specialist?" *Law and Order.* 17:11 (November, 1969), 66-71, 72.

Stallings, Harold L. *Juvenile Officer*. NY: Crowell, 1954.

Sundeen, R. A. Jr. "A Four-Dimensional Perspective on Police Typologies." *Criminology*. 12:3 (1974), 328-337.

Terry, Robert M. "The Screening of Juvenile Offenders." *Journal of Criminal Law, Criminology and Police Science*. 58:2 (June, 1967), 173-181.

Tobias, Jerry J. "The Guidance Oriented Youth Bureau Revisited in 1972." *Law and Order*. 21:12 (December, 1973), 34-36, 38.

Tobias, Jerry J. "Guidelines for Disposition of Juvenile Cases." *Police Chief*. 39:10 (October, 1972), 40-43.

Tobias, Jerry J. "Today's Youth Officer as I See Him/Her." *Police Chief*. XL:6 (June, 1973), 55-57.

Tobias, Jerry J. and Charles Lacy. "A Guidance Oriented Police Youth Bureau." *Law and Order*. 18:8 (August, 1970), 30-43, 34-35, 45.

Voigt, Lloyd L. "Need for a Community Program for Troubled or Maladjusted Children." *Police*. 4:4 (March-April, 1960), 65-67.

Wattenberg, William W. and Noel Buf. "The Effectiveness of Police Youth Bureau Officers." *Journal of Criminal Law, Criminology and Police Science*. 54:4 (December, 1963), 470-475.

Webster, C. Edward. "Youth Bureau for a Small Department." *Law and Order*. 15:5 (May, 1967), 36-40, 44.

Weiner, N.L. and C.V. Willie. "Decisions by Juvenile Officers." *American Journal of Sociology*. 77 (September, 1971), 199-210.

Wells, Richard A. "Subsidizing Police Juvenile Services." *Law and Order*. 18:5 (May, 1970), 96, 106-109.

Wheeler, S. *Controlling Delinquents*. N.Y.: Wiley, 1968.

William and Mary College. *Police Juvenile Handbook*. Springfield, VA.: NTIS, n/d.

Handbook designed to aid the police officers of Norfolk, Cheasapeake, Portsmouth, and Virginia Beach, Virginia in encounters with juveniles.

Winters, J.E. "The Role of the Police in Prevention and Control of Delinquency." *Federal Probation* (June, 1957), 3-6.

Runaways

Ambrosino, Lillian. *Runaways*. Boston: Beacon, 1971.

Ambrosino, Lillian. "Youth Trouble: Runaways." *Today's Education*. 60:9, 26-28.

Bock, Richard D. and Abigail English. *Got Me on the Run: A Story of Runaways*. Boston: Beacon, 1973.

Chapman, Christine. *America's Runaways*. N.Y.: Morrow, 1976.

David, L. "Are You Runaway—Prone? Teenage Girl Runaways." *Seventeen*. 10 (July, 1973), 22-24.

English, C.J. "Leaving Home: A Typology of Runaways." *Society*. 10 (July, 1973), 22-24.

Hildebrand, J.A. "Reasons for Runaways." *Crime and Delinquency*. 14:1 (1968), 42-48.

Hildebrand, J.A. "Why Runaways Leave Home." *Journal of Criminal Law, Criminology and Police Science*. 54:2 (1963), 211-216.

MacLeod, C. "Street Girls of the 70's." *Nation*. 218 (April 20, 1974), 486-488.

"More Kids on the Road—Now It's the Throw-Aways." *U.S. News and World Report*. 76:19 (May 12, 1975), 49-50.

Peters, W. "Riddle of Runaway Teenagers." *Good Housekeeping*. 166 (June, 1968), 88-89.

Raphael, Maryanne and Jenifer Wolf. *Runaways: America's Lost Youth*. N.Y.: Drake, 1974.

"Runaway Kids." *Life*. 63 (November 3, 1967), 18-29.

"Runaways: A National Problem." *Time*. 102 (August 27, 1973).

"Runaways: A Non-Judicial Approach." *New York University Law Review*. 49:1 (1974), 110-130.

"Runaways: Rising U.S. Worry." *U.S. News & World Report*. 75 (September 3, 1973), 34.

Weiss, Walter F. *America's Wandering Youth: A Sociological Study of Young Hitchhikers in the United States*. Hicksville N.Y.: Exposition, 1974.

Welch, Mary Scott. "The New Runaways." *McCalls* (November, 1974), 51.

School Liaison

Alcorn, Wesley F. "The School Resource Officer in Saginaw, Michigan." *Police Chief*. XLII:6 (June, 1975), 56-58.

Becker, Harold K. "The Student and the Law." *Police Chief*. XXXIX:3 (March, 1972), 75-77.

Bouma, D.H. and D.G. Williams. *Evaluation of a Police School Liaison Program*. Springfield, VA.: NTIS, 1970.

Bouma, Donald H. and Donald G. Williams. "Police in the Schools." *Police Chief*. XXXIX:9 (September, 1972), 50-52.

Cain, M. and M. Dearden. "Initial Reactions to a New Juvenile Liaison Scheme." *British Journal of Criminology*. 6:421 (1966), 428.

Clinton, John. "Working with Youth." *Law and Order*. 21:12 (December, 1973), 58-60, 71.

Costa, Rudy. "Police School Program, Norwalk, Connecticut. A Community Relations Effort." *Law and Order*. 21:3 (March, 1973), 44-49.

Davids, Frederick E. "Michigan State Police 'Goes' Juvenile." *Police Chief*. 37 (October, 1970), 46, 48, 50, 52.

Emerine, Steve. "Police in the Schools." *Law and Order*. 15:8 (August, 1967), 8-11, 18.

Feaker, Fred E. "Can We Help You Focus on Youth?" *Law and Order*. 21:12 (December, 1973), 28-30, 32.

Hartford, William S. "Officer Bill: Color Him Friendly." *Law and Order*. 18:5 (May, 1970), 90-92, 94-95.

Hoobler, Raymond L. "San Diego: Secondary Schools' Task Force." *Police Chief*. XL:6 (June, 1973), 28-30.

Isom, James Edward. "Law Enforcement in Public Schools: A Case Study." *Journal of California Law Enforcement*. 8:3 (January, 1974), 140-145.

Jenkins, Harry P. "Police Become High School Class Instructors." *Law and Order*. 21:3 (March, 1973), 34-36.

Johnson, Ron A. "The School Resource Officer Program." *Law and Order* (December, 1975), 28-34.

LaDucer, D. and J. Krans. "Post Implementation Review of the Orange County (CA.) Sheriff's Department Student and the Law Programs." *Law and Order*. 21:12 (December, 1972), 35-36, 38, 40, 42, 44.

Law in American Society Foundation. *Law in American Society Foundation—Illinois Project: Exemplary Project Nomination Package*. Washington: NCJRS (Microfiche) 1973.

Mackenzie, A.M. "Police Involvement in the Education of Children and Young Persons." *Police College Magazine*. 12:4 (1973), 5-7.
Author states police instructors are more effective than normal teachers.

Mack, J.A. *Police Juvenile Liaison—Practice and Evaluation*. Glasgow: School of Social Study University of Glasgow, 1968.

Milwaukee Public Schools. *Justice and You Course—A Pilot Program in Law for High School Students in the Milwaukee Public Schools—Interim Report*. Washington: NCJRS (Microfiche) 1974.

Minneapolis Police Department. *Minneapolis: Police-School Liaison Program (Cooperative Program of Minneapolis Police Department and the Minneapolis Public Schools)—Final Report September 1966-August 1968*. Washington: NCJRS, 1968.

Minnesota Governor's Commission on Crime Prevention and Control. *Minnesota—Police-School Liaison Projects: An Evaluation*. Washington: NCJRS (Microfiche) 1973.

Morrison, June. "The Controversial Police-School Liaison Programs." *Police*. 13:2 (November-December, 1968), 60-64.

Parker, Peter. "The Subject is Crime." *Police Chief*. XXXVII:5 (May, 1970).

Pitchess, Peter J. "Student and the Law: The Challenge of Our Time." *Journal of California Law Enforcement*. 4:3 (January, 1970), 110-114.

Riccardi, Anthony. "Tell It Like It is." *Law and Order*. 17:6 (June, 1969), 108-109.

Robinson, Donald W. "Police in the Schools." *Phi Delta Kappa*. 48 (February, 1967), 278-280.

Shephard, George H. and Jesse James. "Police: Do They Belong in the Schools?" *American Education* (September, 1967).

Spain, Norman M. "Criminal Justice: A Relevant Course for High School." *Police Chief*. XLI:6 (June, 1974).

Volpe, A. Anthony. "Operation Civic Awareness." *Law and Order*. 19:1 (January, 1971), 28-29, 70.

Volpe, Al. "Project Understanding." *Law and Order*. 23:4 (April, 1975), 72-73.

Wright, Harold A. "The Youth and the Criminal Justice System." *Law and Order*. 20:6 (June, 1972), 62-65.

Youth Service Bureau

Canlis, Michael N. "Now Is Time to Establish Neighborhood Youth Services Agencies." *Journal of California Law Enforcement* (April, 1968), 203-207.

Norman, S. *Youth Service Bureau: A Key to Delinquency Prevention*. Hackensack, N.J.: National Council on Crime and Delinquency, 1972.
Basic principles and guidelines for establishing and operating youth service bureau's.

Seymour, J.A. "Youth Services Bureaus." *Law Society Review*. 712 (1972), 247-272.

Tobias, Jerry. "A Program for the 70's—The Suburban Youth Bureau." *Police Chief* (November, 1969), 26-29.

U.S. Department of Health, Education and Welfare Youth Development and Delinquency Prevention Administration. *Challenge of Youth Service Bureau's*. Washington: GPO, 1973.
Summary of a national survey to identify organizational principles, target areas, funding, staff, and program content of youth service bureau's.

Youth Development and Delinquency Prevention Administration. *Youth Service Bureau's and Delinquency Prevention*. Washington: GPO.
Overview of the organization and functions of neighborhood youth service agencies.

MARINE POLICE

Surface Operations

Anderson, Vernon A. "Awareness Is the Key to Successful Water Patrol." *FBI Law Enforcement Bulletin* (April, 1970), 2-4, 27.

Anderson, Vernon A. "Awareness Keeps Hennepin County Sheriff's Water Patrol Successful." *Law and Order*. 18:6 (June, 1970), 44-45, 95.

Boyd, Ellsworth. "Watchdogs of the Chesapeake." *Law and Order* (September, 1966).

Cato, B.G. "Rescue via Radar." *Law and Order*. 13:5 (May, 1965), 12-14.

Cox, Dick. "River Patrols in California." *Law and Order*. 13:5 (May, 1965), 16-18, 20, 22.

Draznin, Yaffa. "Watching the Waterways of the Windy City." *Law and Order*. 13:5 (May, 1965), 8-9.

Garden, A. Newell. "Marine-Patrol to the Rescue." *Law and Order*. 12:5 (May, 1964), 6-9.

Hughes, Carroll J. "Year-Round Police Marine Division." *Law and Order*. 17:8 (August, 1969), 34-36.

Matt, A. Robert. "Law Enforcement Officers of the Sea." *Law and Order*. 8:2 (1960), 5-10.

Newman, B.W.E. "Inshore Rescue Boats." *Police College Magazine* (Autumn, 1966), 26-28.

"Police Patrol Boats Cut Crime, Save Lives." *American City*. 86 (July, 1971).

Richmond, Harry. "The Davy Jones Boat." *Law and Order*. 7 (July, 1959).

Steeber, Robert A. "Seen and Heard on Waterways." *Law and Order.* 12:5 (May, 1964), 14, 16.

Underwater Operations

Ashley, George W. "New York State's Trooper Divers." *Police Chief* (May, 1960).

Burling, Howard L. "Skin Diving in Police Work." *Law and Order* (August, 1960).

Charles, William F. "Underwater Patrolman." *Law and Order.* 7 (January, 1959).

Childs, Joseph A. "Michigan State Police Organize Diving Squad." *FBI Law Enforcement Bulletin* (June, 1958).

Eccleston, Oran H. "A Diving Unit for Handling Underwater Jobs." *FBI Law Enforcement Bulletin* (June, 1954).

Jacobs, Will. "Life Saving Techniques with Scuba Equipment." *Law and Order.* 12:5 (May, 1964), 10-11.

Hagger, R.B. "Per Mare Ad Jetsam." *Police World.* 3 (August-September, 1958), 25-29.

Hockin, H.J. "Underwater Search Units." *Police College Magazine* (Autumn, 1966), 35-40.

Nelson, Arthur E. "Underwater Investigation." *FBI Law Enforcement Bulletin.* 35:2 (February, 1966), 2-5.

"New York City's Underwater Recovery Team." *Spring 3100* (November, 1974), 13.

Porter, J.D. "Seattle's Underwater Police." *Police.* 2:4 (March-April, 1958), 13-16.

"Recovery of Bodies in Drowning Accidents." *FBI Law Enforcement Bulletin* (November, 1950), 17.

"Skin Diving' Techniques by a Small Department." *FBI Law Enforcement Bulletin* (November, 1958).

Taylor, Gertrude M. "The Underwater Recovery Service of the New Jersey State Police." *Law and Order.* 19:7 (July, 1971), 92-94.

Tutuska, B. John. "Diving for Community Service—Diving Deputies." *Police.* 7:2 (November-December, 1962), 25-27.

"Underwater Investigators." *L A Police Beat.* 12 (June, 1958), 7-8.

Wood, Alan C. "Police Frogmen." *Law and Order.* 6 (October, 1958), 6-11.

MOUNTED (HORSE)

Baggallay, E. P. Burrell. "Metropolitan Mounted Police." *Police Journal* (*GB*), (1930), 185-200.

Benjamin, Philip. "The 'Finest' on Horseback." *Police.* 1:6 (July-August, 1957), 12-14.

Campbell, Judith. *Police Horses.* Cranbury, N.J.: A. S. Barnes, 1968.

Cella, Philip. "A Mounted Unit for Effective Park Patrol." *FBI Law Enforcement Bulletin* (March, 1971).

Coon, Thomas F. "The Police Man and Mount in This Atomic Age." *Police.* 10:3 (January-February, 1966), 86-89.

Job, Glen T. "Sheriff's Mounted Posse Increases Police Strength." *FBI Law Enforcement Bulletin* (February, 1958).

Luglauer, E. "Reporter at Large: New York Mounted Police." *New Yorker.* 38:168 (November 24, 1962).

"Mounted Methods Still Effective." *Baltimore Police Department Newsletter.* 5 (June 30, 1971), 1-2.

Sassone, Rich. "New York's Mounted Police." *Law and Order.* 20:11 (November, 1972), 38-44.

"Shield on the Saddle: About Horses—How They Are Trained for Police Work." *Spring 3100.* 21 (May, 1950), 20-23.

Suchy, Emil. "Symkhana—Updated." *Law and Order.* 17:9 (September, 1969), 56-62.

"Use of Horses in Law Enforcement." *Police Chief* (March, 1970).

Way, Gail R. "American River Parkway: A Law Enforcement Problem." *Journal of California Law Enforcement* (January, 1975), 111-113.

POLICE DOG USE

Police Dogs—General

Albino, J. "Scout Dogs: Four Footed Radar in Viet Nam." *Popular Mechanics* (September, 1967).

Allardice, C. "Selecting a Police Dog." *Kenya Police Review* (September, 1973), 24-31.

Archer, Caleb. "An Historical Review of Military Dogs." *Military Police Journal.* 15 (May, 1966), 4-6.

"Baltimore Canine Corps Proves Affective." *Policeman's Association News.* 5 (June, 1959).

Begley, Frank and Les Kennon. "St. Louis Police Dogs." *Law and Order.* 7 (May, 1959), 62-63.

Breazeale, Frank V. "Man's Best Friend Fights Crime." *FBI Law Enforcement Bulletin.* 35:8 (August, 1966), 2-5.

"Businessman's Best Friend." *Journal of American Insurance.* 46 (May-June, 1970), 27-29.

"A Canine Corps for Chicago Police." *Police Chief* (March, 1961).

"Career Handler Cares for Dogs at Log Center." *Military Police Journal* (August, 1964).

Chapman, Samuel G. "The Dog in Law Enforcement: A Brief Resume." *Police.* 4:5 (May-June, 1960), 52-56.

Chapman, Samuel G. *Dogs in Police Work: A Summary of Experience in Great Britain and the United States.* Chicago: Public Administration Service, 1960.

Chapman, Samuel G. "Whether to Use Police Dogs." *Police.* 6:1 (September-October, 1961), 62-67.

Conway, Walter. "The National Champion K-9 Unit." *Law and Order.* 23:5 (May, 1975), 62-64.

Cox, Brian F. and P.F.S. Fife. "The Dog as a Police Officer." *Australian Police Journal.* X (July, 1956), 200-207.

"Criminal Beware, Police Dogs Here!" *Police Journal (St. Louis),* 11 (September-October, 1958), 4-5.
Police dogs in London.

Darwish, Abdel Karim. "Dogs and Police Service." *Law and Order.* 7 (September, 1959), 6-7, 14-15.
Use of police dogs in Egypt.

"Dearborn Police Start Canine Division." *American City.* 70 (March, 1955).

Department of the Air Force. *USAF Military Working Dog Program Utilization and Proficiency Evaluation.* Washington: GPO, 1972.
Manual contains guidance for the deployment of dog teams, training, and administration and proficiency inspection.

DeVilliers, I.P. "Dogs as Detectives in South Africa." *Police Journal (GB),* (1929), 188-192.

"Dog Limitations." *National Sheriff.* 13 (January-February, 1961).

"Dogs and Police Work." *Police Journal (GB),* 45 (February, 1961).

"Dogs in Police Work in India." *Indian Police Journal* (July, 1969, October, 1969).

"Dogs of the RCMP." *Royal Canadian Mounted Police Quarterly* (January, 1951).

"Dogs Patrol the Subways: Policeman Dog Teams in Philadelphia." *American City* (July, 1966).

Dorn, Walter H. "Man-Dog Teams Serve St. Louis Most Effectively." *FBI Law Enforcement Bulletin* (March, 1961).

Edwards, Loren E. *Shoplifts and Shrinkage Protection for Stores.* Springfield, IL.: C.C. Thomas, 1958,
Use of watch dogs. pp. 171-175.

Elam, F. Leland. "Four-Footed Police." *Iowa Sheriff* (August, 1942).

"England to Import Police Dogs." *Police Chief* (September, 1959).

Ferguson, W.N. III "Psychological Deterrent Value of the Patrol Dog." *Military Police Law Enforcement Journal.* 1:5 (1975), 52-53.

Fishler, Barry. "Development of a Superdog." *Law and Order.* 19:12 (December, 1971), 75, 77-78, 80-81.

Floyd, P. B. "His Master's Voice by Radio." *American City* (February, 1964).

Fuid, Leonard Felix. "The Use of Police Dogs: A Summary." *Journal of Criminal Law and Criminology.* 3 (1912).

Garten, O. D. "Police Dog Corps Proves Successful in Richmond VA." *FBI Law Enforcement Bulletin* (May, 1959).

Gebriel, Kassa Wolds. "Watch-Dogs Drugged with Cannabis." *International Criminal Police Review* (January, 1974).

Gifford, C.D. "Police Dogs in Saarland." *Police Journal.* 45:2 (April-June, 1972), 164-171.

Greening, J.A. "Using Dogs in Police Work." *Public Management.* 22 (March, 1940), 75-77.

Hadlock, Walter J. "Sentry Dogs and Motor Pool Security." *Military Police Journal* (June, 1969).

Handel, Leo A. *A Dog Named Duke: True Stories of German Shepherds at Work With the Law.* Philadelphia: Lippincott, 1966.

Hattinger, Anton. "A Police Dog Proves His Worth in Austria." *International Criminal Police Review.* XV (June-July, 1960), 184-186.

Hepborn, T.M. "Baltimore's Police Dogs." *American City.* 72 (October, 1957).

Herbert, John F. "Delaware State Police Use Dogs." *Police Chief* (May, 1959).

Hershner, W.B. "Dog Policeman: Lancaster, PA." *American City.* 77 (May, 1962), 37-38.

Holman, Arthur. *My Dog Rex: The Story of Police Dog Rex III, Told by His Handler.* NY: Funk, 1957.

"Houston's Canine Corps." *Police Chief* (January, 1961), 26.

"The K-9 Corps of Korea." *Military Police Journal.* 9 (August, 1959), 20-21.

Kelley, Leo T. "Baltimore Police Dogs Report." *American City.* 74:35 (November, 1959).

Kelley, Leo T. "The Canine Corps in Baltimore." *Police Chief.* 26 (July, 1959), 4-5, 27.

Kelley, Leo T. "The Canine (K-9) Corps of the Baltimore Police Department." *Police.* 4:2 (November-December, 1959), 19-24.

Kelley, Leo T. "The K-9 Corps of the Baltimore Police Department." *American City.* 74:122 (October, 1959).

Kjellquist, Robert L. "The Small Department and the K-9 Corps." *Law and Order.* 12:2 (February, 1964), 8-9.

Kraft, Henry B. "Uncle Sam's Watch Dogs." *Police Chief.* 25 (October, 1958), 31-33.

Krush, John C. "Use of Police Dogs in Catastrophe Situations." *FBI Law Enforcement Bulletin* (November, 1975), 24-27.

Leonard, M.L. "K-9 Transport: New Orleans." *American City.* 77:31 (March, 1962).

Long, Charles J. and William E. Routt. "A Review of Police Dog Programs in the United States." *Police.* 16:9 (May, 1972), 64-67.

Lo Bello, Nino. "The Greatest Detective in Dogdom: Dox of Italy." *Readers Digest.* 77 (August, 1960), 57-68.

McCain, E.G. "Police Dogs on Three Wheels." *Police Chief* (August, 1961).

Maloney, J.A. "Dogs: What is their Place in Security." *Security and Protection* (February, 1976), 18, 20.

"Man's Best Friend Fights Crime." *FBI Law Enforcement Bulletin.* 35:2 (August, 1966).

Marders, Irvin E. *How to Use Dogs Effectively in Modern Police Work.* Cocoa Beach, FL: Police Science Press, 1960.

"Miami Adds a K-9 Corps." *Police Chief* (January, 1961).

The Minstrel. "Keeping Dogs in their Places. Some uses and Limitations of Guard Dogs." *Security Gazette.* 16:4 (1974), 151-152.

"Mobile Patrol Dogs." *Law and Order* (November, 1961).

"Muggers Beware: This Baby Bites." *Life*. 72 (June 2, 1972), 86-87.

Mundis, Jerrold J. *The Guard Dogs*. N.Y.: McKay, 1970.

Newlan, Clarke. *Police Dogs in Action*. NY: Dodd Mead, 1974.

"New Zealand Police Dogs." *Police World*. 3 (October-November, 1958), 20-21.

Nott-Bower, John. "Development and Use of Police Dogs in London." *FBI Law Enforcement Bulletin* (September, 1955), 6-27.

Osborn, Don. "Dogs in Red Coats." *Shoulder Strap*. XXV (1952), 11.

Penven, Donald S. "A K-9 Unit for the Small Community." *Law and Order*. 21:10 (October, 1973), 60-62.

"The Police Dog in Kenya." *Police Life* (August, 1959), 6-7.

"Police Dogs." *Law and Order* (September, 1967), 23.

"Police Dogs Help Solve Manpower Problem at Scotland Yard." *California Peace Officer*. 9 (January-February, 1959), 12-13, 41.

"Police Service Dogs: Interesting Cases." *Royal Canadian Mounted Police Gazette* (December, 1972).

Pugliese, Nicholas R. "The Sentry Dog." *Virginia Trooper* (August, 1961).

"R C M P Service Dog Section." *Royal Canadian Mounted Police Gazette* (November, 1973).

Revering, Andrew C. "Are Police Dogs Reasonable Force?" *Police Chief* (September, 1974).

"Rex, A Police Dog." *International Criminal Police Review*. XII (May, 1957),151-153.

Roehrick, Edward W. "Chicago Police Department Canine Patrol Unit." *Police*. 5:6 (July-August, 1961), 6-9.

Russell, Donald. "Fort Meyer Dogs Assume New Role." *Military Police Journal* (September, 1963).

"Salt Lake Police K-9 Corps." *Utah Peace Officer* (October, 1959), 36, 39.

Salt, Valerie and Colin Salt. *Born to Obey*. London: Collins, 1972.
The story of trained Alsations in the New Zealand Police Force.

Sandrock, Tom. "1500 Dogs with a Nose for Crime." *SARP* (October, 1975), 18-19.

"The Sentry Dog of the 24th." *Military Police Journal* (September, 1967).

"Sentry Dog Operations." *Military Police Journal* (August, 1967).

"Sentry Dog Program in Action." *Military Police Journal* (March, 1972).

"Sentry Dogs: Big Help in Vietnam War." *U.S. News & World Report* (November 9, 1965).

Shaw, Eleanor F. "Dogs—On Guard." *Police*. 10:3 (January-February, 1966), 19-24.

Shaw, Eleanor. "Why Not More Police Dogs?" *Police Chief*. XXXV:7 (July, 1968), 56-58.

Shepherd, Cyril. "Dogs in the Police Service." *Police Journal (GB)*. XXV (July-September, 1952), 218-222.

Shepherd, Cyril. "Police Dogs." *New Zealand Police Journal*. XVIII (August-September, 1954), 231.

"Sheriff Uses Canines." *Utah Peace Officer* (October, 1959), 39.

Skousen, W. Cleon. "Do's and Don'ts for a K-9 Corps." *Law and Order* (August, 1960).

Skousen, W. Cleon. "Do's and Don'ts for a K-9 Corps, Part XVI." *Law and Order*. 21:5 (May, 1973), 82-89.

Skousen, W. Cleon. "When Does A Police-Dog Program Pay Off?" *Law and Order* (May, 1973).

Sloane, Charles F. "Dogs in War, Police Work and on Patrol." *Journal of Criminal Law, Criminology and Police Science*. 46:3 (September-October, 1955), 385-395.

Stowe, Leland. "How K-9s Catch Crooks." *Reader's Digest* (November, 1974).

Tarrant, Bill. "Canine First Aid." *Field and Stream* (August, 1974; September, 1974).

"Top Dog on Sheriff's Staff." *California Peace Officer*. 8 (November-December, 1957).

"Trained Doberman Pinschers of the Berkley CA. Police Department." *Pacific Coast International* (September-October, 1940).

"Transportation Provided for K-9 Corps Members." *FBI Law Enforcement Bulletin* (April, 1962).

"United Kingdom, Police Dogs in England." *International Criminal Police Review*. XIV (November, 1959), 285-286.

U.S. Department of the Air Force. *U.S.A.F. Sentry Dog Program*. Washington: GPO, 1967.

U.S. Department of the Air Force. *U.S.A.F. Working Dog Program*. Washington: GPO (April, 1971).

U.S. Department of Transportation. U.S. Coast Guard. *Dog Parachute*. Washington: GPO (July, 1973).

"Use of Police Dogs a Fad?" *Police Chief* (December, 1959).

"Virginia State Police Activate a Canine Corps." *Police Chief* (October, 1961).

"Virginia State Police Field Uniform for Canine Corps." *Police Chief* (October, 1962).

Vitt, V.R. "End of an Era" *R C M P Quarterly*. 35 (October-December, 1969), 26-36.

Walsh, David E. "Police Dogs." *Law and Order*. 15:9 (September, 1967), 22-26.

Weekenstoo, H.J. "Dogs in the Service of the Dutch State Police." *International Criminal Police Review*. VI (October, 1951- November, 1951).

Weil, Frederick. "Canine Corps of the U.S. Air Force." *Police Chief* (January, 1961).

"When, Where and If—To Use Police Dogs." *Police Chief* (May, 1960).

"Zama Builds Dog Patrol Vehicle." *Military Police Journal* (September, 1964).

Bloodhounds

"Bloodhounds Trail Arsonist." *FBI Law Enforcement Bulletin* (August, 1955).

Castle, Leo J. "Bloodhounds: A Tool in Law Enforcement." *FBI Law Enforcement Bulletin* (May, 1972) 26-30.

Donahue, Vincent J. "Hound Dog Man." *Police.* 6:4 (March-April, 1962), 16-25.

Fairly, Kenneth W. "The Tale of the One-armed Trusty and 'His' Hound Dogs." *Police.* 8:5 (May-June, 1964), 68-69.

"Sheriff's Office Uses Bloodhounds With Good Results." *FBI Law Enforcement Bulletin* (March, 1963).

Spencer, Hollis. "Arkansas Police Use Bloodhounds with Good Results." *FBI Law Enforcement Bulletin* (July, 1960).

Williams, Mason. "The Bloodhound for Police Work." *Law and Order.* 19:9 (September, 1971), 68, 70, 72, 74.

Detector Dogs: Narcotics, Bombs and Bodies

Blanchard, D. and H.R. Bradley. "Canine Detectors in Narcotics Control." *Police Chief.* XXXVI:6 (June, 1969), 20-30.

Bradley, Holley D. "Dogging Drugs: Narcotics Detector Dogs." *FBI Law Enforcement Bulletin* (September, 1972); 26-29 (October, 1972), 8-11, 28.

Bradley, Holley D. "Narcotics Detector Dogs." *Military Police Journal* (March, 1973).

Bradley, Holley D. "'Nose' for the Job: Narcotic Detector Dogs." *Military Police Journal* (March, 1973), 5-10.

"Brandy and Sally Find Sweet Smell of Success with Bomb Squad." *Spring 3100* (May, 1972).

Cahill, T. Patrick. "Canine Detectors." *FBI Law Enforcement Bulletin.* 42:7 (July, 1973), 16-22.

Harney, Malachi L. and John C. Cross. *The Narcotic Officers Notebook.* Springfield, IL.: C.C. Thomas, 1961, 236-240.
Use of dogs as narcotic detectors.

Payne, C.D. and R.W. Walker. "The Use of Trained Police Dogs for Corpse Detection." *Police Research Bulletin* (Spring, 1973).

Romba, J.J. *Training Dogs for Heroin Detection, Interim Report.* Springfield, VA.: NTIS, 1971.
Exploratory work in odor discrimination and behavior control techniques performed with dogs to enable them to search for heroin.

Ryan, James E. "Canine Supersnoots Foil JFK Bomb Plant." *Spring 3100* (May, 1972).

Thompson, Timothy. "Airport Police Get Bomb Dogs." *Minnesota Police Journal* (December, 1974).

Walker, R.W. and C.D. Payne. "The Use of Trained Police Dogs for Corpse Detection." *Police Research Bulletin.* 21 (1973), 37-47.

Dog Training

Arundel, R. "Police Dogs and Their Training." *Royal Canadian Mounted Police Quarterly* (April, 1936).

Cecil-Gurney, P. L. "Police Dog Training: German Practice." *Police Journal.* (GB) III (October, 1930), 526-534.

Kessopulos, Gust. *Dog Obedience Training.* Cranbury, N.J.: A.S. Barnes, 1975.

Olnas, K.I. "Super Dogs are Made, Not Born." *Popular Mechanics* (November, 1972).

"Park Force Begins Training Dogs for Policing." *Policeman's Association News.* 51 (July, 1959).

Pearsall, Milo and Charles G. Lerdham. *Dog Obedience Training.* N.Y.: Scribner, 1958.

Police Dogs—Training and Care. 2nd ed., London: Her Majesty's Stationery Office, 1973.

Saunders, Blanche. *The Complete Book of Dog Obedience: A Guide for Trainers.* N.Y.: Howell, 1972.

Saunders, Blanche. *Training You to Train Your Dog.* Garden City, N.Y.: Lippman, 1965.

Scott, Tom. *Obedience and Security Training For Dogs.* N.Y.: Arco, 1969.

Stumm, Johannes. "How German Police Train Their Dogs." *Illinois Policeman and Police Journal* (September-October, 1951).

"Training Sentry Dog Teams for Vietnam." *Military Police Journal* (January, 1968).

Watson, Sam D. *Dogs for Police Service, Programming and Training.* Springfield, IL.: C.C. Thomas, 1963.

Woodhouse, Barbara. *Dog Training My Way.* N.Y.: Stein & Day, 1972.

German Shephards

All About the German Sherherd. N.Y.: British Book Center, 1974.

Bennett, Jane G. et al. *Complete German Shepherd Dog.* 4th ed. N.Y.: Howell, 1970.

McKenney, G. M. "The Noblest of Them All, the German Shepherd." *Royal Canadian Mounted Police Gazette.* XXI:12 (1959), 18.

Rath, Hugh J. "Small Community Takes Pride in Its German Shepherds." *FBI Law Enforcement Bulletin* (March, 1962).

Schalk, E. Mansfield. *German Shepherds.* rev. ed. Neptune, NJ: TFH, 1974.

Strickland, Winifred G. and James A. Moses. *The German Shepherd Today.* N.Y.: Macmillan, 1974.

Legal Aspects of Dog Use

Kingham, T. Barry. "Marijuana Detection Dogs As An Instrument of Search: The Real Question." *Army Lawyer* (May, 1973).

Lederer, F. and C.M. Lederer. "Admissibility of Evidence found by Marijuana Detection Dogs." *Military Police Journal.* 22:9 (1973), 22-25.

Lederer, Frederic I. and Calvin M. Lederer. "Marijuana Dog Searchers After United States vs. Unrue." *Military Police Law Enforcement Journal* (Summer Quarter, 1974).

Revering, A.C. "Are Police Dogs Reasonable Force?" *Texas Police Journal.* 22:10 (1974), 7-10, 18-19.

York, Leon J. "The Dog as a Legal Witness." *National Police Journal* (Autumn, 1973).

Zeichner, Irving B. "Tracking By Dog: According to Law." *Law and Order* (November, 1968).

Search and Rescue

Morris, C. "Large Scale Searches with Police Dogs." *Police Journal* (July, 1970).

Reid, G.E. "Search and Rescue Dogs." *Police* (September, 1974).

"USAMPS Tracker Dogs Provide Key to Tennessee Mountain Search Mystery." *Military Police Journal* (April, 1970).

SWAT

Ayoob, Massad F. "Special Weapons and Tactics." *Law and Order* (October, 1975), 56-60.

Beck, G.N. "SWAT: The Los Angeles Police Special Weapons and Tactics Team." *FBI Law Enforcement Bulletin.* 41:4 (April, 1972), 8-10, 30.

Law Enforcement Journal. "SWAT: (Special Weapons and Tactics Force)." *Police (GB).* (November, 1975), 16-17.

Lunsford, L. G. "Tactical Teams for Smaller Departments." *Law and Order.* 23:4 (April, 1975), 66-67, 70-71.

Pitts, C.H. "A Tactical Operations Unit." *FBI Law Enforcement Bulletin.* 44:1 (January, 1975), 10-13.
Tactical operations unit augments regular patrol and line units are trained to handle riots, barricaded criminals, snipers, bomb disposal etc.

Tafoya, William L. "Special Weapons and Tactics." *Police Chief.* XLII:7 (July, 1975), 70-74.
Describes purpose organization, training, equipment, planning, logistics, personnel, selection and duties.

PART IV
FIELD OPERATIONS—POLICE TACTICS

POLICE TACTICS—GENERAL

TACTICS—GENERAL

"General Police Operations." *Police Chief.* XXLV:5 (May, 1967), 14-24.

Kenney, John P. and John B. Williams. *Police Operations: Policies and Procedures.* 2nd ed., Springfield, IL.: C.C. Thomas, 1973.

Kinsella, Joseph W. "Volunteers—Our Men of Action." *Law and Order* (March, 1976), 33-36.
Police officers who volunteer for special frequently dangerous assignments.

MacDonnell, Herbert L. "Using Dyes and Powders or Tracing." *Law and Order.* 14:8 (August, 1966), 69-73.

Mooney, W.R. "Special Operations Group—Chicago's Answer to Unusual Demands for Police Service." *FBI Law Enforcement Bulletin.* 41:4 (April, 1972), 11-14, 32.

Murphy, Glen R. and Roy E. Hollady. "The Hundred System." *Police.* 5:3 (January-February, 1961), 26-30.
Technique for rapidly surrounding and saturating an area around a major incident.

Nelder, Alfred J. "Aggressive Police Activity Reduces Crime." *Police Chief.* 38:1 (January, 1971).

Skousen,W. Cleon. "Car Seven, May Day! May Day!" *Law and Order.* 12:9 (September, 1964), 12-15.

Shaw, William. "Miniature Tracking Transmitters." *Law and Order.* 21:1 (January, 1973), 24, 26-30.

Snibbe, Richard H. "Manpower and the Residential Community." *Police.* 13:2 (November-December, 1968), 58-59.

Tiffany, Lawrence P. et al. *Detection of Crime-Stopping and Questioning, Search and Seizure, Encouragement and Entrapment.* Waltham, MA.: Little Brown, 1967.

ARREST

Boutwell, J. Paul. "Warrantless Entry to Arrest." *FBI Law Enforcement Bulletin.* 42:12 (December, 1973); 43:1 (January, 1974).

Fichter, Joseph H. *Police Handling of Arrestees: New Orleans Experience.* Loyola University of the South, 1964.

Fisher, E.C. and R.L. Donigan. *Laws of Arrest (With 1973 supplement).* Evanston, IL.: Traffic Institute Northwestern University, 1967.

Foote, Caleb. "Law and Police Practice: Safeguards in the Law of Arrest." *Northwestern University Law Review.* LII: 1957.
A questioning look at dubious Police arrest practices

Gardner, T.J. and V. Manian. *Principles and Cases of the Law of Arrest, Search and Seizure.* N.Y.: McGraw-Hill, 1974.

Greenwood, Peter W. *An Analysis of the Apprehension Activities of the New York City Police Department.* N.Y.: Rand (September, 1970).

Holmgren, R. Bruce. "What Are Reasonable Grounds for Arrest?" *Chicago—Kent Law Review.* 42 (Fall, 1965), 101-142.

Markle, Arnold. *The Law of Arrest and Search and Seizure: A State's Attorney's Guide for the Prosecution and/or the Law Enforcement Officer.* Springfield, IL.: C.C. Thomas, 1974.

O'Connell, John D. and C. Dean Larsen. "Detention, Arrest and Salt Lake City Police Practices." *Utah Law Review.* 9 (Summer, 1965), 593-625.

"Requisites of a Valid Arrest." *Criminal Law Review* (January, 1954), 6-20.

"Safeguards in the Law of Arrest." *Northwestern University Law Review.* 52 (March-April, 1957).

Sullivan, John J. "A New Law of Arrest in New York." *Police Chief.* 39:1 (January, 1972), 22-23.

Waddington, Lawrence C. *Arrest, Search and Seizure.* Beverly Hills: Glencoe, 1974.

CHEMICAL AGENTS

Applegate, Rex. "The Chemical Mace." *Law and Order.* 14:6 (June, 1966), 48-56, 76.

Applegate, Rex. "The Ferret Barricade Round." *Law and Order.* 18:8 (August, 1970), 112-115.

Applegate, Rex. "Mace Revisted." *Law and Order.* 16:10 (October, 1968), 48-54.

Applegate, Rex. "The New Multi-Purpose Riot Control Grenade." *Law and Order.* 13:3 (March, 1965), 53-58, 60.

Applegate, Rex. "Tear Gas—CN and CS." *Law and Order.* 12:7 (July, 1964), 41-45.

Coon, Thomas F. "A Maze of Confusion over Amazing Mace." *Police.* 13:2 (November-December, 1968), 45-47.

Crockett, Thompson S. "Aerosol Irritant Projectors." *Police Chief.* XXXVII:1 (January, 1970), 42-45.

Crockett, T.S. "Agents—Tactical Use of Riot Agents." *Police Chief.* XXXVI:5 (May, 1969), 60-72.

Crockett, Thompson S. *Police Chemical Agents Manual. . .* Washington: IACP, Professional Standards Division, 1968.

Crockett, Thompson S. "Riot Control Agents: Field Evaluation of Chemical Agent Grenades." *Police Chief.* XXXVI:7 (July, 1969), 53-61.

Crockett, T.S. "Riot Control Agents: Riot Agent Delivery Systems." *Police Chief.* XXXVI:4 (April, 1969), 56-64.

Crockett, Thompson S. "Riot Control Agents: Standard Aerosol Irritant Projector." *Police Chief* (February, 1969).

"Gentle Persuasion: Aerosol Bomb." *Time* (September 1, 1967).

Hatchew, Don. "The Chemical Mace—Does It Really Work." *Minnesota Police Journal.* 40 (December, 1968), 18-19.

International Association of Chiefs of Police. *Field Evaluation of Chemical Agent Grenades.* Gaithersburg, MD.: IACP, 1969.

International Association of Chiefs of Police. *Riot Control Agent Information Series.* Gaithersburg, MD.: IACP, 1969.

Factors which influence the effectiveness of chemical agents employed by the tactical objectives for which such agents are appropriate.

Jones, Eugene S. *Law Enforcement Chemical Agents and Related Equipment.* Santa Cruz, CA.: Davis, 1970.

Manual of Tear Gas Information Written Expressly for the Tear Gas Officer. Saltsburg, PA.: Federal Laboratories, 1967.

MacLeod, Ian F. "Chemical Mace: Ocular Effects in Rabbits and Monkeys." *Journal of Forensic Sciences.* 14:1 (January, 1969), 34-47.

Rose, Steven, ed. *CBW: Chemical and Biological Warfare.* Boston: Beacon, 1969.

Swearengen, Thomas F. "The Gas Gun in Riot Control." *Law and Order* (May, 1972), 38-40, 42-44.

Swearengen, T. F. *Tear Gas Munitions: An Analysis of Commercial Riot Gas Guns, Tear Gas Projectiles, Grenades, Small Arms.* Springfield, IL.: C.C. Thomas, 1966.

Past and all present tear gases and nauseating agents are described with irritant agents in the form of solids, liquids and dust.

U.S. Department of Justice. Bureau of Prisons. *Use of Tear Gas and Smoke.* Washington: GPO (November, 1949).

Weinert, C.R. "The Proper Use of Tear Gas as a Police Weapon." *Police Chief* (January, 1961).

CIVIL RIGHTS ENFORCEMENT

Caldwell, Arthur B. "Cooperation Between State and Federal Law Enforcement Officials in Civil Rights." *Police.* 8:6 (July-August, 1964), 70-73.

Turner, James P. and K. William O'Connor. "Enforcing Criminals Civil Rights Statutes." *Police Chief.* 38:9 (September, 1971), 56, 58-59.

U.S. Commission on Civil Rights. *The Federal Civil Rights Enforcement Effort: One Year Later November 1971.* Washington: GPO, 1971.

U.S. Commission on Civil Rights. *The Federal Civil Rights Enforcement Report: A Reassessment.* Washington: GPO, 1973.

U.S. Commission on Civil Rights. *The Federal Civil Rights Enforcement Effort—1974. Vol. 1: To Regulate in the Public Interest.* Washington: GPO, 1974.

"Violence Trap: Arranged Bombing to Catch Terrorists in Mississippi." *Nation* (March 9, 1970).

Whitehead, Don. *Attack on Terror: The FBI Against the Ku Klux Klan in Mississippi.* Funk & Wagnalls, 1970.

COURTROOM TESTIMONY

Anderson, Raymond G. "The Arson Investigator in Court." *Police.* 9:3 (January-February, 1965), 53-57.

Brown, Lee and E. Gardner. "A Judge's Views on Law Enforcement and Training." *FBI Law Enforcement Bulletin.* 42:9 (September, 1973), 8-11.

Burke, John J. "Testifying in Court." *FBI Law Enforcement Bulletin* (September, 1975), 8-13.

Cato, B.H. "The Presentation of Scientific Evidence in the Courts: Improving Its Effectiveness." *Journal of Forensic's Science Society.* 14:2 (1974), 93-98.

Cerny, Joe H. "Tips to Police Witnesses." *Police.* 3:4 (March-April, 1959), 39-42.

Clark, J. "The Police Officer as a Witness." *FBI Law Enforcement Bulletin.* 42:3 (1973), 16-17.

Degen, William A. H. "The Status of the Handwriting Expert and His Experiences in Court." *International Criminal Police Review* (June-July, 1968), 152-158.

Erisman, Fred. "How a Defense Lawyer Hopes to Profit from the Testimony of an Officer." *Police.* 4:2 (November-December, 1959), 54-57.

Evans, W. V. "Expert Witness." *Industrial and Engineering Chemistry.* 46:25A, 26A, 28A (August, 1954).

Gordon, F. A. "Giving Evidence." *Police Journal.* (GB) (October, 1954), 481-484.

Grant, Julius. "The Problems of the Defense Expert." *Journal of Forensic Science Society* (December, 1969), 191-198.

Harris, John J. "Preparation for Trial from a Document Examiner's Viewpoint." *Journal of Forensic Sciences.* 7:3 (July, 1962), 351-356.

Heffron, Floyd N. *The Officer in the Courtroom.* Springfield, IL.: C.C. Thomas, 1955.

Hill, Donald J. "Who's On Trial." *Law and Order.* 12:10 (October, 1964).

Livingston, Hazel. *Officer on the Witness Stand.* Los Angeles: Legal Book, 1967.

Moenssens, Andre A. "The Fingerprint Witness in Court." *Fingerprint and Identification.* 54:10 (April, 1973).

Morris, Donald W. "Preparation of a Case for Court." *Police.* 7:2 (November-December, 1962), 46-50.

North, Steven E. ". . .The Whole Truth—Watch Your Tongue." *Law and Order.* 21:2 (February, 1973), 54-55, 75.

North, Steven E. ". . .The Whole Truth—Your Day in Court." *Law and Order.* 22:11 (November, 1974).

Oblinger, Walter L. "The Police Officer as a Witness." *Police.* 1:4 (March-April, 1957), 15-19.

Pantaleoni, C. A. *Handbook of Courtroom Demeanor and Testimony.* Englewood Cliffs, N.J.: Prentice Hall, 1971.

Pepper, Darrell L. "Some Factors Influencing Testimony." *Police.* 3:5 (May-June, 1959), 65-68.

Perone, Ralph. "The Police Officer in Court." *Law and Order.* 13:3 (March, 1965), 72-82.

Petersen, David. *The Police Officer in Court.* Springfield, IL.: C.C. Thomas, 1975.

Pettine, Raymond S. "The Police Witness." *FBI Law Enforcement Bulletin.* 39:2 (February, 1969), 5-7, 22.

"The Police Officer as a Witness." *FBI Law Enforcement Bulletin.* 42:3 (March, 1973), 16-17.

Riggs, Clinton E. "The Police Officer Witness." *Police.* 5:5 (May-June, 1961), 64-68.

Rubin, Charles J. "The Peace Officer's Role as Testifying Witness in a Criminal Case." *Journal of California Law Enforcement* (October, 1968), 93-97.

Schafer, William J. III. "Pointers for Witnesses." *Police.* 16:3 (November, 1971), 66-67.

Sellers, Clark. "Preparing to Testify." *Journal of Criminal Law, Criminology and Police Science.* 56:2 (June, 1965), 235-240.

Shaw, William. "Exploring the Role of the Expert Witness." *Law and Order* (October, 1975), 44-50.

Spies, Frank. "Testimony in a Driving Under the Influence Case." *Law and Order.* 17:5 (May, 1969), 102-105.

Spies, Frank. "Traffic Offense Trial Checklist." *Law and Order.* 17:11 (November, 1969).

Tierney, Kevin. *Courtroom Testimony: A Policeman's Guide.* N.Y.: Funk & Wagnalls, 1970.

Traffic Institute Northwestern University. *Traffic Officer in Court.* Evanston, IL.: Traffic Institute Northwestern University, 1965.

Tuchler, M. "Credibility of a Witness." *Journal of Forensic Sciences.* 8:3 (July, 1963), 325-338.

Tuter, Werner. "Murder and Attempted Murder—Practical Hints for Psychiatric Testimony." *Journal of Forensic Sciences* (October, 1964).

Tuttle, Harris B. "The Police Photographer in Court." *Law and Order.* 13:4 (April, 1965), 8-9, 16, 78.

Walker, C.M. "On the Witness Stand." *Police Chief.* XXXVI:9 (September, 1969), 21-26.

Woodall, Benjamin. "Testimony and Witness Errors in Major Trials." *Police.* 4:6 (July-August, 1960), 34-36.

Wright, Edward T. "Fifteen Easy Ways for a Police Officer to Lose his Case in Court." *Law and Order.* 13:10 (October, 1965), 10-11.

FALSE ALARMS

Brennan, John S. "False Fire Alarms—A Program for Prevention." *FBI Law Enforcement Bulletin.* 43:12 (December, 1974), 16-21.

Greene, Jerry W. *A Comprehensive Review of the False Alarm Problem.* Oakland, CA.: Greene Associates, 1976.

REPORT WRITING

Administration Office of the United States Courts. *Presentence Investigation Report.* Washington: GPO, 1965.

Guidelines and format for presentence reports detailing essential and optional data which the probation officer should obtain.

Coon, Thomas F. "The Shield, The Gun, the Detective—and Semantics." *Police.* 12:1 (September-October, 1967), 73-74.

Chambers, James. "Report Writing." *FBI Law Enforcement Bulletin.* 35:1 (1966), 13-15.

Cunningham, D. *Reading Approach to Professional Police Writing.* Springfield, IL.: C.C. Thomas, 1972.

Textbook for improvement in writing skill in the fields of corrections, criminology, law enforcement and police administration.

Cunningham, D. and Fred J. Graves. "Simplified Report Writing." *Police.* 6:4 (March-April, 1962), 72-73.

Dienstein, William. *How to Write a Narrative Investigation Report.* Springfield, IL.: C.C. Thomas, 1969.

Ellis, James H. "Police Report Writing." *Law and Order.* 7:10 (October, 1959).

Flesch, Rudolf. *How to Be Brief.* N.Y.: Harper & Row, 1962.

Gabard, E. Caroline and John P. Kenney. *Police Writing.* Springfield, IL.: C. C. Thomas, 1957.

The authors take a look at the various demands of police writing. How one goes about researching and organizing material for the police type article or report is discussed.

Gallagher, W. Graydon. "Ideas on Report Writing." *Journal of Forensic Sciences.* 10:4 (October, 1965), 446-464.

Gallagher, William J. *Report Writing for Management.* Reading, M: Addison-Wesley, 1969.

Gammage, A.Z. *Basic Police Report Writing.* Springfield, IL.: C.C. Thomas, 1960.

Gammage, Allen Z. *Study Guide for Basic Police Report Writing.* Springfield, IL.: C.C. Thomas, 1975.

Gaum, Carl G., Harold F. Graves and Lynee S.S. Hoffman. *Report Writing.* N.Y.: Prentice Hall, 1950.

Griffin, John I. "Better Charts for Police Reports." *Police.* 5:1 (September-October, 1960), 38-40.

Hartfor, Bruce D. "The Names of Colors in Police Report Writing." *Law and Order.* 17:4 (April, 1969), 78-81.
Lists a number of different colors and their terms. Useful in interviews and report writing.

Hazelet, John C. *Police Report Writing.* Springfield, IL.: C.C. Thomas, 1960.

Kuhn, Charles L. *The Police Officer's Memorandum Book.* Springfield, IL.: C.C. Thomas, 1964.

Linton, Calvin D. *How to Write Reports.* N.Y.: Harper, 1954.

McLaughlin, John B. "The Narcotics Report." *Law and Order.* 18:12 (December, 1970), 36, 38.

Nelson, John G. *Preliminary Investigation and Police Reporting: A Complete Guide to Police Written Communication.* Beverly Hills, CA.: Glencoe, 1970.

North, Steven E. ". . .The Whole Truth—Reading and Writing." *Law and Order.* 23:9 (September, 1975).

Parham, Sidney F. Jr. *Fundamentals of Legal Writing.* Charlottesville, VA.: Michie, 1967.

Patterson, Frank M. "The Language of Police Reports." *Police Chief.* XLI:7 (July, 1974).

Patterson, Frank M. and Patrick D. Smith. *A Manual of Police Writing.* Springfield, IL.: C.C. Thomas, 1969.

Pearsal, Thomas E. *Audience Analysis for Technical Writing.* N.Y.: Glencoe, 1969.

Romig, Clarence. "Improving the Traffic Accident Report." *Military Police Journal* (January, 1973).

Rubin, Charles J. "Probable Cause on the Police Report." *Journal of California Law Enforcement* (January, 1970), 138-142.
Indicates factors necessary to show probable cause in police reports.

Santmyers, Selby S. *Practical Report Writing.* Scranton, PA: International Textbook, 1950.

Shaw, William. "Write the Way You Speak." *Law and Order.* 23:3 (March, 1975), 21-24.

Shaw, William. "Writing Isn't Easy. . .But Who Sez You Have to Be an English Professor." *Law and Order.* 20:12 (December, 1972), 18, 20-21.

Sigband, Norman B. *Effective Report Writing.* N.Y.: Harper & Row, 1960.

Skousen, W. Cleon. "Report Writing Under the Gun." *Law and Order.* 12:8 (August, 1964), 22-24.

Squires, Harry A. *Guide to Police Report Writing.* Springfield, IL.: C.C. Thomas, 1965.

Tobias, Jerry J. and Phillip Denomme. "Working Toward a More Sophisticated Follow-Up Procedure." *Law and Order.* 19:9 (September, 1971), 46-50.

U.S. Office of Education. *Preparing Evaluation Reports: A Guide for Authors.* Washington: GPO, 1970.

Wild, Lionel D. *Preparing Effective Reports.* Indianapolis, IN.: Odyssey, 1967.

"Writing Better Reports." *Royal Canadian Mounted Police Gazette* (July-August, 1971).

SECURITY CHECKS

Baus, Robert H. "Business Security Checks." *Law and Order.* 17:8 (August, 1969), 116-117.

Campbell, James R. "Vacation House Check Utilizes Police Cadets." *Police Chief.* XLI:6 (June, 1974).

Murphy, Jack E. "Vacation Patrol." *Law and Order.* 15:5 (May, 1967).
Police check homes where residents are on vacation.

STOP AND FRISK

Arizona State University. *Model Rules—Stop and Frisk—Approved Draft.* Washington: NCJRS (Microfiche) 1973.

Colodner, Warren H. "Probable Cause Held Not Requisite for Stop and Frisk." *Police.* 10:1 (September-October, 1965), 30-32.

Guminski, Arnold T. "Stop and Frisk and Arrest, Search and Seizure, the California View." *Journal of California Law Enforcement* (April, 1970), 191-200.

Inbau, Fred E. and James R. Thompson. "Stop and Frisk: The Power and the Obligation of the Police." *Journal of Criminal Law, Criminology and Police Science.* 59:3 (September, 1968), 333-334.

Kuh, Richard H. "New York's 'Stop and Frisk' Law." *Law and Order.* 12:10 (October, 1964), 34-36.

Kuh, Richard H. "Reflections on New York's 'Stop and Frisk' Law and Its Claimed Unconstitutionality." *Journal of Criminal Law, Criminology and Police Science.* 56:1 (March, 1965), 32-38.

Schwartz, Herman. "Stop and Frisk (A Case Study in Judicial Control of the Police)." *Journal of Criminal Law, Criminology and Police Science.* 58:4 (December, 1967), 433-464.

Sindell, S.L. "Stop and Frisk: Police Protection or Police State." *Intramural Law Review—New York University School of Law.* 21 (1966), 180-190.

Souris, Theodore. "Stop and Frisk or Arrest and Search—The Use and Misuse of Euphemisms." *Journal of Criminal Law, Criminology and Police Science.* 57:3 (September, 1966), 251-264.

Stern, Loren G. "Stop and Frisk: An Historical Answer to a Modern Day Problem." *Journal of Criminal Law, Criminology and Police Science.* 58:2 (December, 1967), 532-542.

Younger, Evelle J. "Stop and Frisk. Tell It Like It Is." *Journal of Criminal Law, Criminology and Police Science.* 58:3 (September, 1967), 293-302.

TRANSPORTING PRISONERS BY AIR

Federal Aviation Administration. "Rules for Escorting Prisoners via Air Transportation." *Law Officer.* 6:4 (1973), 49-50.

King, Glen D. "Guidelines Issued by FCC for Air Security." *Police Chief.* XXXVII:5 (May, 1971), 20-26.
Regulations by FCC defines procedures for armed police officers on aircraft.

Mathews, Robert O. "Use of Charter Airlines in Extradition Cases." *FBI Law Enforcement Bulletin* (January, 1976), 9-11.

UFO'S

Fry, D.W. *The White Sands Incident.* Chicago: Best, 1967.

Hynek, J. Allen. *UFO Experience: A Scientific Inquiry.* Chicago: Regnery, 1972.

Hynek, J. Allen. "The UFO Mystery." *FBI Law Enforcement Bulletin* (February, 1975), 16-20.
Activities of center for UFO studies Northfield, IL. Author describes how police officers have been involved in UFO sightings. The center has a Toll Free Hot Line for Law Enforcement Agencies.

Jacobs, David M. *The UFO Controversy in America.* Bloomington: Indiana University Press, 1975.

Klass, P.J. *UFO's Explained.* N.Y.: Random, 1975.

Stemman, Roy, ed. *Visitors from Outer Space.* Garden City, N.Y.: Doubleday, 1976.

VANDALISM

"How to . . . Coping with Halloween Pranksters." *Police Chief.* 33:6 (June, 1966).

Solomon, Ben. "Vandalism—What Can We Do About It?" *Police.* 7:1 (September-October, 1962), 71-74.

Tsampikou, John M. "The Graffiti Problem: How Philadelphia Is Coping with It." *Police Chief.* XXXIX:7 (July, 1972), 23-30.

"War Declared on Pranksters." *FBI Law Enforcement Bulletin.* 35:5 (May, 1966).
Ohio State Highway Patrol program to eliminate the throwing of objects from highway overheads at or into moving vehicles.

WARRANTS

Higgins, George V. "Warrants Upon Warrants: The Pen Register and Probable Cause Under Omnibus Crime Control." *Journal of Criminal Law, Criminology and Police Science.* 60:4 (December, 1969), 455-463.

Mintz, John A. "Changing Concepts in Warrant Objectives." *FBI Law Enforcement Bulletin.* 41:1 (January, 1972), 21-24.

Mintz, John A. "Formal Considerations in Search Warrant Applications." *FBI Law Enforcement Bulletin.* 40:11 (November, 1971), 21-23.

INTERROGATION

INTERROGATION—GENERAL

Adams, Thomas F. "Interviews and Interrogation." *Police.* 8:1 (September-October, 1963), 50-53.

Almand, Benjamin F. IV "Methods of Interrogation." *Police.* 15:4 (March-April, 1971), 65-72.

Arthur, Richard O. and Rudolph R. Caputo. "Interrogation for Investigators." *Law and Order* (January-March, 1959).

Aubry, Arthur S. and Rudolph R. Caputo. *Criminal Interrogation.* Springfield, IL.: C.C. Thomas, 1975.

Biderman, Albert D. and Herbert Zimmer. *The Manipulation of Human Behavior.* N.Y.: Wiley, 1961.

Brady, John. *Interviewing Techniques.* Cincinnati, OH.: Writers Digest, 1975.

Bristow, Allen P. "Atmosphere in the Interrogation Room." *Police.* 7:2 (November-December, 1962), 59-62.

Brown, Lawrence. "Police Interrogation Dilemma." *Police.* 8:3 (January-February, 1964), 75-77.

Buglio, J. "Documents and Interrogation." *Military Police Journal* (March, 1972).

Chapple, Norman L. "Police Interrogation in Britain and the United States." *Police.* 16:2 (October, 1971), 18-24.

Crowley, W.D. "Interrogation of Suspects." *International Criminal Police Review.* 28:269 (August, 1973), 203-210.

Crowley, W.D. "Interviewing." *Australian Police Journal.* 18:3 (July, 1964), 181-185.

Cunningham, C. "Interrogation." *Medical Legal Journal.* 41:2 (1973), 49-62.

Curtis, S.J. "Stress vs. Empathy Interview Techniques." *Police.* 3:1 (September-October, 1958), 51-53; (November-December, 1958), 55-57.

Daloia, Robert J. "The Truth and the Investigator." *Law and Order.* 12:9 (September, 1964), 18-21, 40.

Deb, R. "The Interrogation of Suspects." *International Criminal Police Review* (October, 1958), 239-248.

Dexter, Lewis Anthony. *Elite and Specialized Interviewing.* Evanston, IL.: Northwestern University Press, 1970.

Dienstein, William. "The Importance of Words in Questioning Techniques." *Police.* 1:4 (March-April, 1957), 47-51.

Ellis, Albert. "Interrogation of Sex Offenders." *Journal of Criminal Law, Criminology and Police Science.* 45:1 (May-June, 1954), 41-47.

Finkelmeier, L. "Objective Interrogation Through the Psychology of Questioning." *Fire Arson Investigator.* 23:4 (1973), 23-33.

Goodsall, J.E. "The Professional Interviewer." *Police Review.* 82:4241 (1974).

Gordon, F.A. "Interrogation." *Police.* 10:1 (September-October, 1965), 11-14.

Grassburger, R. "Women as Defendents or Witnesses." *International Criminal Police Review* (November, 1951), 306-311.

Griffin, Roger K. "Why People Confess: Reflecting on 1000 Interrogations." *Security World.* 7 (May, 1970), 20-22.

Groisser, Phillip L. *How to Use the Fine Art of Questioning.* N.Y.: Lieber-Atherton, 1964.

Hatherill, G.H. "The Means of Interrogation." *Medico-Legal Journal.* 32:4 (1964), 164-175.

Hornaday, William Temple II. "The Effects of Authority Factors in Interrogation." *Journal of Criminal Law, Criminology and Police Science.* 55:3 (September, 1964).

Inbau, F.E. "A Legal Impediment to the Interrogation of Suspected Employees." *Security World.* 12:9 (1975).

Inbau, Fred E. "Police Interrogator—A Practical Necessity." *Journal of Criminal Law, Criminology and Police Science.* 52 (1961).

"Interrogation Efficiency and Protection of the Suspect Through the Model Code of Pre-arraignment Procedure: A Step Beyond Miranda." *Iowa Law Review.* 60:2 (1974), 395-412.

"Interrogation of Criminal Suspects." *Northwestern University Law Review.* 59 (1964).

"Interrogation Techniques." *Idaho State Bar.* 30 (1956).

Johnson, Madeline L. "Interviewing the Youthful Arson Suspect." *Law and Order* (February, 1962).

Johnson, Madeline. "Interviewing Youth." *Law and Order* (July, 1959).

Kahn, Robert Louis and Charles F. Cannell. *The Dynamics of Interviewing: Theory, Technique and Cases.* N.Y.: Wiley, 1957.

Kidd, Worth R. *Police Interrogation.* N.Y.: R.V. Basuino, 1940.

Lawder, Lee F. "Notes on: Questioning Children." *Law and Order.* 20:7 (July, 1972), 50, 52-53.

Loftus, E. "Incredible Eye Witness." *Psychology Today.* 8:7 (1974), 116-119.

Lyng, John Francis X. "Interrogation." *Law and Order.* 12:9 (September, 1964), 77-80.

McDonald, Hugh C. *The Practical Psychology of Police Interrogation.* Santa Ana, CA.: Townsend, 1963.

McKee, W.R. "Introduction to the Profession of Interviewing and Interrogation." *Police.* 1:3 (January-February, 1957), 46-49.

Merton, Robert King. *The Focused Interview: A Manual of Problems and Procedures.* Glencoe, IL.: Free Press, 1956.

Mulbar, Harold. *Interrogation.* Springfield, IL.: C.C. Thomas, 1951.

National District Attorneys Association. *Confessions and Interrogation After Miranda—A Comprehensive Guideline of the Law (Revised December 1972) Including Addendum.* Chicago, IL.: National District Attorneys Association 1972).
Relevant issues in Miranda situations with a compilation of facts, policies and case law.

O'Neal, Wyatt G. "Interrogation in Arson Investigations." *Police.* 6:2 (November-December, 1961), 35-38.

Palumbo, Paul A. "Effective Interviewing." *Law and Order.* 23:9 (September, 1975), 18, 20-23.

Payne, Stanley L. *The Art of Asking Questions.* Princeton, N.J.: Princeton University Press, 1951.

"Police Interrogation Privileges and Limitations: An International Symposium." *Journal of Criminal Law.* 52 (1961).

"Police Interrogation: The Right to Counsel and to Prompt Arraignment." *Brooklyn Law Review.* 27 (1960).

Pray, Ed. "Criminal Interrogation and Confessions: The Ethical Imperative." *Wisconsin Law Review.* 1 (1968), 173-183.

Price, Carroll S. "Interviews, Interrogations and Use of the Polygraph." *Police.* 4:4 (March-April, 1960), 52-55; (May-June, 1960), 32-35; (July-August, 1960), 50-53; (September-October, 1960), 47-49; (November-December, 1960), 48-50.

"Psychology and Techniques of Interrogation." *Law and Order.* 21:9 (September, 1973), 24-27, 82.

Reinhardt, James Melvin. "The Wish to Confess." *Police.* 14:1 (September-October, 1969), 50-52.

Scaparone, M. "Police Interrogation in Italy." *Criminal Law Review* (October, 1974), 581-588.

Schultz, Leroy G. "Interviewing the Sex Offender's Victim." *Journal of Criminal Law, Criminology, and Police Science.* 50:5 (January-February, 1960), 448-452.

Specter, Arlen and Marvin Katz. *Police Guide to Search and Seizure, Interrogation and Confession.* Philadelphia: Chilton, 1967.

"Supreme Court and Restrictions on Police Interrogations." *Ohio State Law Journal.* 25 (Fall, 1964).

U.S. Department of the Army. *Intelligence Interrogation.* Washington: Department Headquarters U.S. Department of the Army, 1973.

Van de Kamp, John K. "Search and Seizure: Interrogation and the Admissibility of Confessions." *Security World* (February, 1968).

Van Meter, C.H. *Principles of Police Interrogation.* Springfield, IL.: C.C. Thomas, 1973.

Wicks, R.J. *Applied Psychology for Law Enforcement and Correction Officers.* N.Y.: McGraw-Hill, 1974.

Wicks, R. and E. Joseph. *Techniques in Interviewing for Law Enforcement and Corrections Personnel.* Springfield, IL.: C.C. Thomas, 1972.
Chapters cover the conduct of initial interviews, skills for

establishing a sound relationship with the interviewee and nonverbal communication.

Witt, J.W. "Non-coercive Interrogation and the Administration of Criminal Justice: The Impact of Miranda on Police Effectuality." *Journal of Criminal Law, Criminology and Police Science.* 64:3 (1973), 320-332.

Zeitz, Leonard, Richard J. Medalie and Paul Alexander. "Anomie Powerlessness and Police Interrogation." *Journal of Criminal Law, Criminology and Police Science.* 60:3 (September, 1969), 314-322.

CONFESSIONS

"Admissibility of Involuntary Confessions Confirmed by Subsequent Facts." *De Paul Law Review.* 6 (Spring-Summer, 1957).

"Confessions and Improperly Obtained Evidence." *Australian Law Journal.* 30 (June, 1965).

"Confirmation by Subsequent Facts." *Law Quarterly Review.* 72 (April, 1956).

"Confessions: A Warning Light." *New Zealand Law Journal.* 28 (January 22, 1952), 12-13.

"Confessions in Criminal Cases." *Trial Lawyers Guide* (February, 1957).

Hirtle, Stanley. "Inadmissable Confessions and their Fruits: A Comment on Harrison vs. United States." *Journal of Criminal Law, Criminology and Police Science.* 60:1 (March, 1969), 58-64.

Horowitz, Milton W. "The Psychology of Confession." *Journal of Criminal Law, Criminology and Police Science.* 47:2 (July-August, 1956), 197-204.

"Interrogation by the Police: Admissibility of Statements by Accused." *Irish Law Times.* 83 (July 2, 1949), 169-170.

Kennedy, John K. "Some Practical Suggestions for the Taking of Criminal Confessions." *Journal of Criminal Law, Criminology and Police Science.* 48:6 (March-April, 1958).

Maslach, C. *Truth About False Confessions.* Springfield, VA.: NTIS, 1970.
Manner in which confessions are obtained and conditions under which subjects believe their false confessions are true.

Neubauer, D.W. "Confessions in Prairie City: Some Causes and Effects." *Journal of Criminal Law and Criminology.* 65:1 (1974), 102-112.

North, Steven E. ". . .The Whole Truth—Confessions—Useful or Not?" *Law and Order.* 21:9 (September, 1973), 96-103.

"Psychology of Confession." *Journal of Criminal Law, Criminology and Police Science.* 47 (July-August, 1956).

Reik, Theodor. *The Compulsion to Confess: On the Psychoanalysis of Crime and Punishment.* N.Y.: Farrar, 1959.

Rogge, Oteje J. *Why Men Confess: From the Inquisition to Brainwashing.* N.Y.: Nelson, 1959.

Schafer, William J. *Confessions and Statements.* Springfield, IL.: C.C. Thomas, 1968.

Singer, Leonard. "Admissibility of Confession of Codefendant." *Journal of Criminal Law, Criminology and Police Science* (June, 1969), 195-203.

"Voluntary Confessions: Prior Unrelated Crimes—Admissibility." *University of Cincinnati Law Review.* 23 (1954), 106-108.

"Voluntary False Confessions—A Neglected Area in Criminal Justice." *Indiana Law Journal.* 28 (Spring, 1953), 374-392.

Walsh, M.P. "Taking a Voluntary Confession." *Police Law Quarterly.* 4:2 (1975), 5-10.

FIELD INTERROGATION

Adams, Thomas F. "Field Interrogations." *Police.* 7:4 (March-April, 1963), 26-29.

Bristow, Allen P. *Field Interrogation.* Springfield, IL.: C.C. Thomas, 1964.

Crawford, William. "Field Interrogation." *Law and Order.* 13:5 (May, 1965).

Hotis, John B. "The Miranda Warning During a Street Encounter." *FBI Law Enforcement Bulletin.* 41:2 (February, 1972), 12-14.

Pitcher, Wayland D. "The Law and Practice of Field Interrogation." *Journal of Criminal Law, Criminology and Police Science.* 58:4 (December, 1967), 465-492.

Runyan, Richard T. and F. Samuel Ostertag. "Field Interrogation of Pedestrians." *Police.* 3:6 (July-August, 1959), 51-53.

Runyan, Richard T. and F. Samuel Ostertag. "The One-Man Patrol Car—Field Interrogation of Pedestrians." *Police.* 3:6 (July-August, 1959), 51-52.

Remington, Frank J. "The Law Relating to 'on the street' Detention, Questioning, and Frisking." *Journal of Criminal Law, Criminology and Police Science.* 51 (December, 1960), 386-394.

Reich, Charles A. "Police Questioning of Law Abiding Citizens." *Yale Law Journal.* 75 (1966), 1161-1172.

Seay, Howard W. "Certain Factors Relevant in Sanctioning Field Inquiries." *Law and Order.* 20:11 (November, 1972), 49-50, 52, 54-58, 80.

Stahl, Warren. "Juvenile Card Referral System." *Law and Order.* 12:6 (June, 1964), 45-46, 66.
Field officer fills out field interrogation card on juveniles involved in minor offenses and then parents are informed by mail of activity.

Thompson, Jim. "Police Controls over Citizen Use of the Public Streets." *Journal of Criminal Law, Criminology and Police Science.* 49 (1959), 562-569.

Tiffany, Lawrence P. "The Fourth Amendment and Police-Citizen Confrontations." *Journal of Criminal Law, Criminology and Police Science* (December, 1969).

Waddington, Larry. "Stopping and Questioning by Police Officers on Public Streets." *Journal of California Law Enforcement* (October, 1966).

HYPNOSIS

Arons, Harry, "Areas of Application, Contradictions, Legal and Ethical Considerations in Hypnosis." *Police.* 9:2 (November-December, 1964), 11-15.

Arons, Harry. "Hypnosis Clears Two Murder Suspects." *Police.* 6:6 (July-August, 1962), 19-22.

Arons, Harry. *Hypnosis in Criminal Investigation.* Springfield, IL.: C.C. Thomas, 1967.

Arons, Harry. "Hypnosis: A New Tool in Police Work." *Police.* 6:1 (September-October, 1961), 68-71.

Derrick, Charles C. "Interrogation by Hypnosis." *Police Chief.* 26 (March, 1959), 26-29.

Edmunds, Simeon. "Hypnosis and Crime." *Police.* 7:1 (September-October, 1962), 11-16.

Hammerschlag, Heinz E. *Hypnotism and Crime.* Hollywood, CA.: Wilshire, 1957.

Levendula, Deszo. "The Possible Role of Hypnosis in Criminal Investigation." *Criminal Investigation and Interrogation.* Cincinnati: Anderson, 1962, pp.339-340.

Levy, Sheldon S. "Hypnosis and the Legal Immutability." *Journal of Criminal Law, Criminology and Police Science.* 46:3 (September-October, 1955), 333-346.

McCawley, Joe B. "Police Hypnosis En Masse." *Police Chief.* XL:2 (February, 1973).

Moenssens, Andre A. "Lie Detection Under Hypnosis and the Law." *Police.* 8:3 (January-February, 1964), 67-69.

Schenck, Jerome M. *Studies in Scientific Hypnosis.* Baltimore: Williams & Wilkins, 1956.

Tocchio, O.J. "Lie Detection Under Hypnosis." *Police.* 8:1 (September-October, 1963), 9-11.

NARCOANALYSIS

Gall, J.C. "Case Against Narcointerrogation." *Journal of Forensic Sciences* (January, 1962).

Geis, Gilbert. "In Scopolamine Veritas: The Early History of Drug Induced Statements." *Journal of Criminal Law, Criminology and Police Science.* 50:4 (November-December, 1959), 347-357.

Geis, Gilbert. "The Status of Interrogation Drugs in the United States." *Journal of Forensic Medicine.* 8:1 (January-March, 1961), 29-33.

Gelber, Seymour. "Removing Inhibitions Through Narcoanalysis in Criminal Investigation." *Police* (January-February, 1967).

Gerson, M.J. and V.M. Victoroff. "Experimental Investigation into validity of Confessions obtained under Sodium Amytal Narcosis." *Journal Clinical Psychopathology.* 9 (July, 1948).

Hanscom, C.B. "NARCO Interrogation." *Police.* 11:2 (November-December, 1957), 44-50.

MacDonald, John M. "Narcoanalysis and Criminal Law." *American Journal of Psychiatry.* 111 (October, 1954).

MacDonald, John M. "Truth Serum." *Journal of Criminal Law, Criminology and Police Science.* 46:2 (July-August, 1955), 259-263.

Matthews, James H. "Narco-Analysis for Criminal Interrogation." *Lancet.* LXX:8 (August, 1950), 283-289.

Moenssens, Andre A. "Narcoanalysis in Law Enforcement." *Journal of Criminal Law* (November-December, 1961).

Muehlberger, C.W. "Interrogation under Drug Influence." *Journal of Criminal Law, Criminology and Police Science.* 42 (1951).

Rolin, Jean. *Police Drugs.* N.Y.: Philosophical Library, 1956.

Sheedy, Charles E. "Narcointerrogation of a Criminal Suspect." *Journal of Criminal Law, Criminology and Police Science.* 50 (1959-60).

NON-VERBAL COMMUNICATIONS

Body Talk: A Handbook on Non-Verbal Behavior. Mt. Vernon, N.Y.: Peter Pauper, 1975.

Eisenberg, Abne and Ralph Smith. *Nonverbal Communication.* Indianapolis: Bobbs-Merrill, 1971.

Fast, Julius. *Body Language.* Philadelphia: Evans, 1970.

Frames, Lester, ed. *Nonverbal Communications.* N.Y.: Plenum, 1964.

Hinde, R.A. ed. *Nonverbal Communication.* New Rochelle, N.Y.: Cambridge University Press, 1972.

Knapp, M. *Nonverbal Communication.* N.Y.: Holt Rhinehart & Winston. 1972.

McCardle, Ellen S. *Nonverbal Communications.* N.Y.: Dekker, 1974.

Mehrabian, Albert. *Nonverbal Communications.* Chicago: Adline, 1972.

Morrison, G.I. "Practical Aspects of Non-Verbal Communication for Law Enforcement Situations." *Law and Order.* 22:5 (May, 1974), 34, 36-38.

Plimer, Patricia et al. eds. *Nonverbal Communication of Aggression.* N.Y.: Plenum, 1975.

Ruesch, Jurgen and Weldon Kees. *Nonverbal Communication: Notes on the Visual Perception of Human Relations.* Berkeley: University of California Press, 1956.

POLYGRAPH

Polygraph—General

Adams, Thomas F. "Field Preparation for the Polygraph." *Police.* 9:4 (March-April, 1965), 17-19.

Arnold, Edwin W. "Polygraph Tests Using an Interpreter." *Police.* 5:4 (March-April, 1961), 53-55.

Arthur, Richard O. "New Advances in Polygraph." *Law and Order.* 14:8 (August, 1966), 88-89.

Arthur, Richard O. and James C. Young. "Should A Law Enforcement Polygraphist Examine His Fellow

Officer? Yes!—No!? *Law and Order*. 22:11 (November, 1974), 104-106.

Barefoot, J.K. "On the Side of Truth. APA Discusses the Polygraph. History and Techniques." *Security World*. 9:6 (1972), 20-29; 9:7 (1972), 50-60.

Blum, Richard H. and William Osterloh. "The Polygraph Examination as a Means for Detecting Truth and Falsehood in Stories presented by Police Informants." *Journal of Criminal Law, Criminology and Police Science*. 59:1 (March, 1968), 133-137.

Burack, Benjamin. "A Critical Analysis of the Theory, Method, and Limitations of the 'Lie Detector.'" *Journal of Criminal Law, Criminology and Police Science*. 46:3 (September-October, 1955), 414-426.

Burdick, A.H. "Use of an Interpreter During a Polygraph Examination." *Polygraph*. 2:4 (1973), 309-325.

Burkey, Lee M. "The Case Against the Polygraph." *American Bar Association Journal*. 51:9 (September, 1965), 855-857.

Byrne, William. "Some Functional Aspects of the Polygraph." *Law and Order*. 19:7 (July, 1971), 24-27, 44, 75.

Clark, J.P. and L.L. Tifft. "Polygraph and Interview Validation of Self Reported Deviant Behavior." *American Sociological Review*. 31 (August, 1966), 516-523.

Cohen, J. Arnold. "The Integrated Control-Question Technique." *Police*. 6:1 (September-October, 1961), 56-58.

Dienstein, William. "Morality and Lie Detection." *Police*. 8:5 (May-June, 1964), 35-38.

Edel, E.C. and J. Jacoby. "Examiner Reliability in Polygraph Chart Analysis: Identification of Physiological Responses." *Journal of Applied Psychology*. 60:5 (1975), 632-634.

Faulk, J. Frank Jr. "South Carolina Polygraph Solves Four Murders." *Police*. 2:4 (March-April, 1958).

Ferguson, R.J. *Scientific Informer*. Springfield, IL.: C.C. Thomas, 1971.
Polygraphy is one of the most effective scientific techniques devised for protection of the innocent in law enforcement, private industry and government thus far.

Ferguson, R.J. Jr. and A.L. Miller. *Polygraph for the Defense*. Springfield, IL.: C.C. Thomas, 1974.

Goodman, W. "Lie Detectors Don't Lie." *New York Times Magazine* (January 24, 1965).

Gwynne, Jeffery L. "The Specific Concern Test for the Detection of Deception." *Journal of Police Science and Administration*. 2:1 (March, 1974), 38-39.

Horvath, Frank S. "Verbal and Nonverbal Clues to Truth and Deception During Polygraph Examinations." *Journal of Police Science and Administration*. 1:2 (June, 1973), 138-152.

Horvath, Frank S. and John E. Reid. "The Reliability of Polygraph Examiner Diagnosis of Truth and Deception." *Journal of Criminal Law, Criminology and Police Science*. 62:2 (June, 1971), 276-281.

Keller, E. John. "Polygraph: A Primary or Secondary Tool." *Law and Order*. 21:11 (November, 1973), 64-65.

Kubis, J.F. *Quantitative Analysis of Polygraphic Data*. Springfield, VA.: NTIS, 1965.
Evaluation of factors which affect the interpretation of lie-detector data.

Leonard, V.A. *Academy Lectures on Lie Detection*. Springfield, IL.: C.C. Thomas, 1968.

Lucas, J.A. "The Polygraph and the Innocent." *Polygraph*. 3:2 (1974), 189-204.

Lykken, D.T. "The Right Way to Use a Lie Detector." *Psychology Today*. 8:10 (1975), 56-60.

More, Harry W. Jr. "Polygraph Research and the University." *Law and Order*. 14:3 (March, 1966), 73-75, 78.

More, Harry W. Jr. "The Use of Standard Deviation in Polygraph Chart Interpretations." *Law and Order*. 15:9 (September, 1967), 62-64.

Musser, B.H. "What to Look for in a Polygraph Examiner." *American Polygraph Association Newsletter*. 6:1 (1974), 4-5.

Myatt, M.W. 'Doc'. "Polygraph Clears Victim of Mistaken Identify." *Police*. 1:5 (May-June, 1957), 40-41.

Myatt, M.W. 'Doc'. "The Polygraph in Homicide Investigation." *Police*. 3:1 (September-October, 1958), 46-50.

Pearl, Dori J. "Why a Female Polygraphist." *Law and Order*. 23:7 (July, 1975), 32-34, 36.

Pfaff, Roger A. "The Polygraph: An Invaluable Judicial Aid." *American Bar Association Journal*. 50 (December, 1964), 1130-1133.

Pigott, L. "Polygraph: The Big Question!" *Law Officer*. 5:3 (1972), 37-38.

"The Polygraph as a Truth Detector." *Officer*. 72 (August, 1970), 39-41.

Rainey, R.P. Jr. "Scientific Interrogation in Criminal Cases." *Police*. 3:6 (July-August, 1959), 35-38.

Steel, Robert D. "Who Is a Fit Polygraph Subject." *Police*. 3:6 (July-August, 1959), 32-34.

Use of Polygraphs and Similar Devices by the Federal Government. Washington: GPO, 1974.

Yeschke, Charles L. "Ethics and the Polygraph Examiner." *Journal of Criminal Law, Criminology and Police Science*. 56:1 (March, 1965), 109-112.

Young, J.C. "Should a Law Enforcer Polygraphist Examine His Fellow Officers? Yes!" *Journal Polygraph Science*. 9:3 (1974), 1-2.

Legal Aspects of Use of Polygraph

Adams, Thomas F. "Legal Aspects of the Polygraph." *Police*. 6:2 (November-December, 1961), 52-58.

Altarescu, H.S. "Problems Remaining for the 'Generally Accepted' Polygraph." *Boston University Law Review*. 53:2 (1972), 375-405.

Ansley, N., ed. *Legal Admissibility of the Polygraph*. Springfield, IL.: C.C. Thomas, 1975.

Dabrowski, Albert S. "The Polygraph Revisited: An Argument for Admissibility." *Criminal Law Bulletin.* 6:2 (March, 1970), 63-80.

Durand, P.P. "The Polygraph and the Criminal Law: An Overview." *Polygraph.* 3:4 (1974), 395-400.

Ferguson, R.J. and A.L. Miller. *Polygraph in Court.* Springfield, IL.: C.C. Thomas, 1973.
Arguments concerning the use of lie detectors as a means of truth verification and the accuracy of the results.

McKee, Roger A. "The Polygraph and the Police." *Police Chief.* 38:2 (February, 1971), 52-54.
Discusses the legal aspects of the polygraph when used in police personnel investigation.

Romig, C.H. "The Dilemma of the Admissibility of Polygraph Evidence." *Polygraph.* 1:3 (1972), 125-133.

Romig, Clarence H.A. "The Status of Polygraph Legislation of the Fifty States." *Police.* 16:1 (September, 1971), 35-41.

Pre-Employment Screening with Polygraph

Arthur, Richard O. "How Many Robbers, Burglars, Sex Criminals Is Your Department Hiring This Year?" *Law and Order* (June, 1972), 84, 86, 88, 90.

Arthur, Richard O. "Polygraph Picks Potential Policemen." *Journal of Polygraph Studies* (September-October, 1967).

Barton, M.F. "Polygraph as a Police Pre-employment Selection Tool." *Polygraph.* 3:4 (1974), 401-411.

Blum, Richard H. "The Polygraph Examination in Law Enforcement Personnel Selection." *Police.* 12:2 (1967), 60-75.

Elam, Gerald. "Polygraph: An Aid in Recruiting." *Law and Order.* 8:7 (July, 1960), 24, 26-27.

Fox, D.A. "Screening Police Applicants." *Polygraph.* 1:2 (1972), 80-83.

Gugas, Chris. "A Scientifically Accurate Method of Personnel Screening." *Police.* 6:2 (November-December), 19-24.

Horvath, Frank. "The Police Candidate Polygraph Examination: Considerations for the Police Administrator." *Police.* 16:10 (June, 1972), 33-39.

Riley, Paul T. "Use of the Polygraph for Pre-employment Testing of Police Recruits." *Police.* 5:6 (July-August, 1961), 42-43.

Romig, C.H. "Improving Police Selection with the Polygraph Technique." *Polygraph.* 1:4 (1972), 207-220.

Swank, Calvin J. and Keith N. Haley. "The Objections to Polygraph Screening of Police Applicants." *Police Chief.* XXXIX:6 (June, 1972), 73-76.

Territo, Leonard. "The Use of the Polygraph in the Pre-Employment Screening Process." *Police Chief.* XLI:7 (July, 1974), 51-53.

"Truth or Consequences: Use in Employment Interviewing." *Time* (March 19, 1973).

Washnis, George J. "Polygraph Test for City Employees." *Public Personnel Review.* 23 (July, 1962), 192-198.

Wheeler, D.E. "Pre-Employment use of Polygraph." *Texas Police Journal.* 10 (August, 1962).

Voice Stress Evaluation

"Big Brother Is Listening: Psychological Stress Indicator." *Time* (June 19, 1972).

Kubis, J.F. "Comparison of Voice Analysis and Polygraph as Lie Detection Procedures." 3:1 (1974), 1-47.

"New Trap for Liars: Psychological Stress Evaluator." *Newsweek* (June 19, 1972).

"Stress Test, Who's Lying? Psychological Stress Evaluator at the Watergate Hearings." *Newsweek* (July 23, 1973).

Tobias, M.W. "The Use of the Psychological Stress Evaluator in Arson Investigations." *Fire Arson Investigator.* 25:2 (1974), 4-12.
Describes the use of psychological stress evaluator machine.

U.S. Department of the Army. U.S. Army Land Warfare Laboratory. *Detection of Emotional Stress by Voice Analysis: Final Report.* Washington: NCJRS (Microfiche) 1972).

ORGANIZED CRIME CONTROL

Adams, Thomas F. "Organized Crime in America." *Police.* 6:5 (May-June, 1962), 6-7.

Anderson, Annelise. *Organized Crime: The Need for Research.* Washington: LEAA, (December, 1970).

"Appalachin Aftermath." *Police Chief* (March, 1961).

"Appalachin's Mob Is in and Its Secret Is Out." *Life* (January 25, 1960), 24-25.

Aspen, Marvin E. "Legal Methods for the Suppression of Organized Crime. Investigative Function of the Prosecuting Attorney." *Journal of Criminal Law, Criminology and Police Science.* 48:5 (January-February, 1958), 526-531.

Bachelder, W.K. "The Suppression of Bookie Gambling by a Denial of Telephone and Telegraph Facilities." *Journal of Criminal Law and Criminology* (July, 1949).

Baker, Russell. "Equitable Remedy to Combat Gambling in Illinois." *Chicago—Kent Law Review* (September, 1950).

Bilek, Arthur J. and Alan S. Ganz. "The Pinball Problem: Alternative Solutions." *Journal of Criminal Law, Criminology and Police Science.* 56:4 (December, 1965), 432-445.

Blakey, G. Robert. *Aspect of the Evidence Gathering Process in Organized Crime Cases.* Appendix C of President's Commission Task Report Organized Crime. Washington: GPO, 1967.

Butler, Arthur and Marvin E. Aspen. "Legal Methods for Suppression of Organized Crime." *Journal of Criminal Law and Criminology.* 48 (November-December, 1959), 414-430.

Carnahan and International Crime Countermeasures Conference. Lexington, KT.: University of Kentucky, 1974.

Carnahan Conference on Crime Countermeasures. Lexington, KT.: University of Kentucky, 1975.

Chamber of Commerce of the United States. *Deskbooks on Organized Crime.* Washington: Chamber of Commerce, 1969.

"Combating Organized Crime." *American Academy of Political and Social Science.* 347 (May, 1963).

Commission of Enquiry Into the Administration of Justice on Criminal and Penal Matters in Quebec. *Crime, Justice and Society, Vol. 3: Crime in Quebec, Tome 3—Organized Crime.* Washington: NCJRS (Microfiche).
Includes an analysis of the functioning of organized crime and recommendations for legislative, criminal justice and social reform designed to undermine the necessity for organized crime operations.

Davidson, Bill. "The Mafia Can't Crack Los Angeles." *Saturday Evening Post* (July 31, 1965).

Denison, George. "The Legal Weapon the Mafia Fears Most." *Readers Digest* (June, 1970), 81-85.

DeMattei, Kenneth. "The Use of Taxation to Control Organized Crime." *California Law Review* (June, 1951).

Dewey, Thomas E. *Twenty Against the Underworld.* Garden City, N.Y.: Doubleday, 1974.

Dosi, Giusepe. "M.M.M. War in Sicily: How Mussolini, Mori and the Italian Police Smashed the Mafia: Part 1—The Island of Fire; Part 2—The Strategy of Victory." *Police Journal (GB).* (1932), 184-202; 356-377.

Eastman, George. "Further Consideration on Organized Crime." *Police.* 10:1 (September-October, 1965), 47-49.

"Equitable Devices for Controlling Organized Vice." *Journal of Criminal Law, Criminology and Police Science.* 48:6 (March-April, 1958), 623-633.
Use of Civil law action to help curb organized crime.

"Federal Regulation of Gambling." *Yale Law Journal* (December, 1951).

Final Report of the American Bar Association Commission on Organized Crime to the American Bar Association. N.Y.: Groslay, September 2, 1952.

Flittie, William J. "Civil Restraints: Another Weapon for the Battle with Organized Crime." *Police Chief.* XLII:2 (February, 1975), 66-70.

Garrett, E. *Police and Organized Crime, Organized Crime and Law Enforcement.* N.Y.: Grisby, 1952.

Gartner, Michael. *Crime and Business: What You Should Know About the Infiltration of Crime into Business—And of Business into Crime.* Princeton, N.J.: Dow Jones, 1971.

Gaynor, Malcolm M. "Indirect Control of Organized Crime Through Liquor License Procedure." *Journal of Criminal Law, Criminology and Police Science.* 49:1 (May-June, 1958), 65-68.

Giannoules, Kenneth S. "Interpol—Your APB to the World." *Police Chief* (November, 1973), 16-19.

Hewitt, William H. "Politics and Organized Crime in America." *Police.* 10:1 (September-October, 1965), 40-46.

Hill, Albert Fay. *The North Avenue Irregulars: A Suburb Battles the Mafia.* N.Y.: Cowles, 1968.

Hundley, William G. "The Nature of Interstate Organized Crime and Problems in Law Enforcement." *Notre Dame Lawyer.* 38:6 (1963), 627-637.

"Interchange of Information Battles Organized Crime." *FBI Law Enforcement Bulletin* (January, 1962).

Johnson, Earl Jr. "Organized Crime: Challenge to the American Legal System." *Journal of Criminal Law, Criminology and Police Science.* 53 (December, 1962-March, 1963).

Kaitz, Joseph. "The Bulwark Against Organized Crime on the Waterfront." *Police Chief.* XLII:2 (February, 1975).

Keating, Kenneth B. "Organized Crime: What Can Congress Do about It?" *Journal of Criminal Law, Criminology and Police Science.* 51 (November-December, 1962).

Kelley, Clarence M. "Mutual Cooperation in the Fight Against Organized Crime." *Police Chief.* XLII:2 (February, 1975), 24-26.

Kennedy, Robert F. *The Enemy Within.* N.Y.: Harper, 1960.

Kennedy, Robert F. "The Program of the Department of Justice on Organized Crime." *Notre Dame Lawyer.* 38:6 (1963), 637-640.

King, Rufus G. "The Control of Organized Crime in America." *Stanford Law Review* (December, 1951).

Kleindienst, Richard G. "The Proper Function of the United States Government in the Fight Against Organized Crime." *Police Chief.* 38:9 (September, 1971), 12-15.

Kucharski, R. *Organized Crime Control Legislation, January, 1975.* Washington: NCJRS (Microfiche) 1975.

Lavine, Emanual H. *Cheese It—The Cops Account of an Effect to Stamp Out Organized Crime in Denver.* N.Y.: Vanguard, 1936.

Law Enforcement Assistance Administration. *Police Guide on Organized Crime.* Washington: GPO, 1972.
Brief introduction for the police officer concerning his contacts with organized crime.

"Legal Methods for the Suppression of Organized Crime (A Symposium)." *Journal of Criminal Law, Criminology and Police Science.* 48:4 (November-December, 1957; January-February, 1958).

Lumbard, Eliot H. "Local and State Action Against Organized Crime." *Annals of the American Academy of Political and Social Science* (May, 1963).

Lynch, William S. "The Police Function and Organized Crime." *Police Chief.* XLII:2 (February, 1975), 30-31.

Maas, Peter. *The Valachi Papers.* N.Y.: Putnam, 1968.

Martin, Raymond V. *Revolt in the Mafia.* N.Y.: Duell, Sloan, & Pearce, 1963.

Methvin, Eugene H. "Progress in the War Against the Mafia." *Readers Digest* (June, 1972), 137-141.

Mollenhoff, Clark R. *Strike Force: Organized Crime and the Government.* Englewood Cliffs, N.J.: Prentice Hall, 1972.

National Association of Attorneys General. *Organized Crime Control Legislation.* Washington: NCJRS (Microfiche) 1974.

National Association of Attorneys General. *Organized Crime Control Units.* Washington: NCJRS (Microfiche) 1974.

National Council on Crime and Delinquency. *Search Warrants and Organized Crime: A Policy Statement.* N.Y.: National Council on Crime and Delinquency, 1966.

Nepote, J. "Interpol and Organized Crime." *International Criminal Police Review.* 28:282 (1974), 230-236.

Nepote, Jean. "Interpol and Organized Crime." *Australian Police Journal* (October, 1975), 253-266.

"Organized Crime and Law Enforcement: A Problem for the People." *American Bar Association Journal.* 38 (January, 1952), 26-29.

"Organized Crime Committee." *Police Chief.* XLII:2 (February, 1975), 71-72.
Committee of IACP offered proposals to curb organized crime.

"Organized Crime." *Police Chief.* XXXII:12 (December, 1965), 44-48.

"Outlaw of Pinball Machines Is Sought by Attorney General." *Look* (March 28, 1961).

Pace, Denny F. and Jimmy C. Styles. *Organized Crime: Concepts and Control.* Englewood Cliffs, N.J.: Prentice Hall, 1975.

Paulsen, Monrad G. "Civil Liberties and the Proposals to Curb Organized Crime." *Notre Dame Lawyer.* 38:6 (1963), 699-711.

Peterson, Virgil W. "Obstacles to Enforcement of Gambling Laws." *Annals* (May, 1920).

Ploscowe, Morris. "New Approaches to the Control of Organized Crime." *Annals of the American Academy of Political and Social Science.* 347:75 (May, 1963).

Proceedings of the Attorney General's Conference on Organized Crime. Washington: Department of Justice, 1950.

President's Commission on Law Enforcement and Administration of Justice. *President's Commission on Law Enforcement and Administration of Justice: Task Force Report—Organized Crime.* Washington: GPO, 1967.
Determination of why organized crime has been expanding despite efforts to control it and recommendations for improving control strategy.

"Problem of Categorizing and Controlling Organized Crime." *Albany Law Review.* 36:2 (Winter, 1972), 330-368.

"The Problem of the Department of Justice on Organized Crime." *Notre Dame Lawyer.* 38:6 (1963), 637-640.

Rector, Milton G. "Association Action Against Organized Crime." *Association Management* (September, 1969).

"Robert Kennedy Speaks Out on Organized Crime." *U.S. News and World Report* (January 9, 1961).

Sagalyn, Arnold. "The Pursuit of International Criminals Through Interpol." *Journal of Criminal Law, Criminology and Police Science.* 57:2 (1966), 193-196.

Salerno, Ralph F. "Organized Crime: An Unmet Challenge to Criminal Justice." *Crime and Delinquency* (July, 1969).

Salerno, Ralph F. and Dwight C. Smith. "The Use of Strategies in Organized Crime Control." *Journal of Criminal Law, Criminology and Police Science.* 61:1 (1970), 101-111.

Silver, Edward S. "Organized Gambling and Law Enforcement." *Journal of Criminal Law, Criminology and Police Science.* 50 (November-December, 1959).

Siragusa, Charles. *The Trail of the Poppy: Behind the Mask of the Mafia.* Englewood Cliffs, N.J.: Prentice Hall, 1966.

Skousen, W. Cleon. "Challenging the National Gambling Syndicate." *Law and Order.* 22:3 (March, 1974), 52-56.

Smith, Dwight C. Jr. "Cooperative Action in Organized Crime Control." *Journal of Criminal Law, Criminology and Police Science.* 59:4 (December, 1968), 491-498.

Smith, Dwight C. Jr. et al "The Use of Strategies in Organized Crime Control." *Journal of Criminal Law, Criminology and Police Science.* 61:1 (March, 1970), 101-111.

Sondern, Frederic Jr. "They Busted the Rackets in Youngstown." *National Municipal Review* (October, 1950).

Sowle, Claude R. "Organized Crime in Chicago: The Untapped Forces of Change." *Journal of Criminal Law, Criminology and Police Science.* 55:1 (March, 1964), 111-113.

Suggested State Legislation Program for 1953. Chicago: Council of State Governments. November, 1952 pp. 117-119.
Devoted to legislation concerning law enforcement and the control of organized crime.

Sunderland, Louis. "Illinois Circumventing the Corrupt Prosecutor." *Journal of Criminal Law, Criminology and Police Science.* 48:5 (January-February, 1958), 531-543.

"Two Approaches to the Problem of Preventing the Use of Interstate Communications Facilities to Aid Illegal Gambling Interests." *Georgetown Law Journal* (November, 1951).

U.S. Committee on Government Operations. *Federal Effort Against Organized Crime: Report of Agency Operations.* Washington: GPO, 1968.

U.S. Committee on Government Operations. *Federal Effort Against Organized Crime: Role of the Private Sector.* Washington: GPO, 1971.

Van Cise, Philip S. *Fighting the Underworld.* N.Y.: Houghton Mifflin, 1936.

Wessel, Milton R. "The Conspiracy Charge as a Weapon Against Organized Crime." *Notre Dame Lawyer.* 38:6 (1963), 689-699.

Zumbrun, Alvin J.T. "Organized Crime, Gambling and Law Enforcement." *Police.* 8 (March-April, 1964), 58-63.

ANTI-TERRORISM

ANTI-TERRORISM—GENERAL

"Aids to the Detection of Explosives—A Brief Review of Equipment for Searching out Letter Bombs and other Explosive Devices." *Security Gazette.* 17:2 (February, 1975), 48, 49, 61.

Allbach, D.M. "Countering Special-Threat Situations." *Military Police Law Enforcement Journal.* 2:2 (Summer, 1975), 34-40.

"Anti-Terrorists." *Economist* (September 16, 1972).

Arias, M. "Bolivia: Guevara Adventure Ends." *Christian Century* (April 3, 1968).

Atwater, J. and B. Crozier. "Time to Get Tough with Terrorists." *Readers Digest* (April, 1973).

Azar, E.E. "Towards the Development of an Early Warning Model of International Violence." in J.D. Ben-Dak, ed. *The Future of Collective Violence—Societal and International Perspectives.* Lund Sweden Student Literature, 1974, 145-164.

Barsilay, David. *British Army in Ulster.* Belfast: Century Services, 1973.

Bassinouni, M.C. "Methodological Options for International Legal Control of Terrorism." in M.C. Bassinouni. *International Terrorism and Political Crimes.* Springfield, IL.: C.C. Thomas, 1975, 485-292.

Bassinouni, M.C. "Political Offense Exception in Extradition Law and Practice." in M.C. Bassinouni. *International Terrorism and Political Crimes.* Springfield, IL.: C.C. Thomas, 1975, 398-447.

"Brazil: Death of a Guerrilla." *Economist* (September 25, 1971).

Burton, Anthony. "Urban Guerrilla Warfare: The Technological Response." *Battle.* 5 (1974), 31-36.

"Business Digs in Against Terrorists: American Companies in Brazil and Argentina." *Business Week* (November 29, 1969).

"Calling 'Robbie.'" *Police Review.* 81:4197 (1973).
Describes anti-terrorists telephone called Robbie in Northern Ireland. Frightened witnesses are encouraged to talk to authorities through this medium. Method also useful to fight ordinary crime.

Chamber of Commerce of the United States. *Violence Against Society*. Washington: Chamber of Commerce of the U.S., 1971.
Transcript of a conference of businessmen and experts in the police field on the subject of bombings in the U.S. and what the businessmen can do to help prevent them.

Cherico, P. "Security Requirements and Standards for Nuclear Power Plants." *Security Management*. 18:6 (January, 1975), 22-24.

"Che's Diary." *Time* (July 12, 1968).

"Che Slain." *Senior Scholastic* (October 26, 1967).

Clarke, W.A. "Frustrate the Bomber by Using the Fluoroscope Letterbomb Detector." *Police Review (GB)*. January 3, 1975), 4-5.

Clutterbuck, Richard. "Police and Urban Terrorism." *Police Journal (GB)*. (July-September, 1975), 204-214.

"Convincing the Cynics: Campaign to Flush out Communist Guerrillas." *Newsweek* (April 24, 1967).

Copeland, M. "Unmentionable Uses of a CIA: Counter-Terrorist Activity." *National Review* (September 14, 1973).

Deschutter, B. "Problems of Jurisdiction in the International Control and Repression of Terrorism." in M.C. Bassinouni. *International Terrorism and Political crimes*. Springfield, IL.: C.C. Thomas, 377-390.

Dixon, J. "Britain May Need Special Weapons and Tactics Teams to Fight Urban Guerrillas." *Police Review (GB)*. (May 21, 1976), 644-646, 648.

"Drive to Halt Terror Bombings." *U.S. News and World Report* (March 15, 1971).

Elmes, F. "Wages of Sin." *Police Review*. 82:4235 (1974).
Critical of poor governmental resolve in handling terrorists. Recommends International Policy against conceding anything to terrorists.

Epstein, David G. "Combating Campus Terrorism." *Police Chief*. 38:1 (January, 1971), 46-47, 49.

"Fight Terror with Terror? Classroom Game." *Senior Scholastic* (April 23, 1973).

"Flight of Dog: And Other Terrorism and Anti-Terrorism Tactics." *Newsweek* (August 20, 1973).

Fooner, Michael. "The Vulnerable Society: Crisis in Technology, Terror and Victimization." *Police Chief*. XLI:2 (February, 1974), 26-27.

"Greece Takes Tougher Stand Following Airport Terrorism." *Aviation Week and Space Technology* (August 13, 1973).

Green, L.C. *Nature and Control of International Terrorism*. Alberta, Canada: University of Alberta, 1974.

Griffith, John. "Arrest Under Prevention of Terrorism Act." *Justice of the Peace* (January 4, 1975), 2-3.

"Guerrillas on the Run." *Time* (August 2, 1971).

"Guerrillas on Trial." *Time* (December 9, 1974).

Hillard, J.Z. "Countersubversive Operations in Urban Areas." *Military Review*. 46:6 (1966), 12-19; 47:9 (1967), 27-35.

"Historical Introduction to International Legal Control of Terrorism." in M.C. Bassinouni *International Terrorism and Political Crimes*. Springfield, IL.: C.C. Thomas, 1975, pp. 467-473.

Hoffacker, L. "U.S. Government Response to Terrorism—A Global Approach." in M.C. Bassinouni *International Terrorism and Political Crimes*. Springfield, IL.: C.C. Thomas, 1975, pp. 537-545.

Hubbard, D. "Extortion Threats: The Possibility of Analysis." *Assets Protection*. 1:2 (Summer, 1975), 17-19.

"Israel's Fierce Reprisals for Munich." *Newsweek* (September 25, 1972).

Jenkins, R. *England—Prevention of Terrorism (Temporary Provisions) A Bill*. London: Her Majesty's Stationery Office, 1974 (Microfiche).

Jenkins, B.M. *Soldiers Versus Gunmen: The Challenge of Urban Warfare*. Santa Monica, CA.: Rand, 1974 (Microfiche).

Jenkins, B.M. *Terrorism Works Sometimes*. Santa Monica, CA.: Rand, 1974.

Jones, S.V. "Invention of the Month: Atomic Detector for Suitcase Bombs." *Science Digest* (December, 1964).

Kasurak, Peter. "Coping with Urban Guerrilla: Democracy's Dilemma." *Canadian Defense Quarterly* (1974), 41-46.

Knorr, K. "Unconventional Warfare: Strategy and Tactics in International Political Strife." *Annals of the American Academy of Political and Social Science* (1962).

Lador-Lederer, J.J. "A Legal Approach to International Terrorism." *Israel Law Review*. 9:2 (1974).

Legum, C. "How to Curb International Terrorism." *Current* (January, 1973).

Littlejohn, R.F. "Eliminating the Urban Guerrilla." *Military Police Journal*. 22:3 (1972), 20-23.
Describes tactics and precautionary measures.

McCrary, E. "Coping with Terrorism in Argentina." *Business Week* (March 9, 1974).

Mahoney, H.T. "After a Terrorist Attack: Business as Usual." *Security Management*. 19:1 (March, 1975), 16, 18, 19.

Mallison, W.T. and S.V. Mallison. *The Concept of Public Purpose Terror in International Law: Doctorines and Sanctions to Reduce the Destruction of Human and Material Values*. House of Representatives: Subcommittee on International Organizations and Movements, 93rd Congress, 2nd Session, pp. 63-79.

Miraval, Anthony J. "High Rise Security." *Security Management* (May, 1973).

Moss, R. *Counter Terrorism*. London: Economist Brief, 1972.

"No More Tribute for Terror." *Time* (March 22, 1971).

O'Farrell, Patrick. "British Army in Northern Ireland." *Pacific Defense Reports* (December-January, 1975), 13-16.

Ofer, Yehuda. *Operation Thunder: The Entebbe Raid—The Israelis' Own Story*. Harmonsworth: Penguin, 1976.

OSS Sabotage and Demolition Manual. Boulder, CO.: Paladin, n/d.

Pamplin, Richard H. "What Should We Do to the Terrorists?" *Police (GB).* (February, 1975).

"Perils of Peron: Crackdown on Terrorist Groups." *Time* (February 4, 1974).

"Precautions Against Letter Bombs." *Security Gazette* (January, 1974), 10-12.

Price, D.L. "Ulster—Concensus and Coercion, Part 2: Security Force Attrition Tactics." *Conflicts Studies.* 50 (October, 1974), 7-24.

Private Security Advisory Council. *Prevention of Terroristic Crimes—Security Guidelines for Business Industry and Other Organizations.* Washington: NCJRS, 1976.

Report of the Commission to Consider Legal Procedures to Deal with Terrorist Activities in Northern Ireland. London: Her Majesty's Stationary Office, 1972 (Microfiche).

Shaw, P.D. "Extortion Threats—Analytic Techniques and Resources." *Assets Protection.* 1:2 (Summer, 1975), 5-16.

Street, Harry. "Prevention of Terrorism (Temporary Provisions) Act 1974." *Criminal Law Review* (April, 1975), 192-199.

Tinnin, David B. *The Hit Team.* Boston: Little Brown, 1976.
Israelis assassination team organized to hunt down the leaders of Black September, after the Munich Olympics murders.

"Trap for a Terrorist: Capture of Racial and Anti-Semitic Criminal." *Newsweek* (July 15, 1968).

Truby, David. *Silencers, Snipers and Assassins.* Boulder, CO.: Paladin, 1972.

United Kingdom. *Report of the Committee of Privy Counselors Appointed to Consider Authorized Procedures for the Interrogation of Persons Suspected of Terrorism.* London: Her Majesty's Stationary Office, 1972 (Microfiche).

United States Department of State. *Role of International Law in Combating Terrorism.* Bureau of Public Affairs Office of Media Services, 1973.

Venter, A.J. *The Terror Fighters: A Profile of Guerrillas Warfare in Southern Africa.* Capetown: Purnell, 1969.

"Violence Trap: Arranged Bombing to Catch Terrorists in Mississippi." *Nation* (March 9, 1970).

Wilkinson, Paul. "Pros and Cons of Hanging Terrorists." *Police.* (GB) (February, 1976), 24-25.

Williamson, Tony. *Counterstrike Entebbe.* London: Collins, 1976.

Wolf, J.B. "Terrorist Manipulation of the Democratic Process." *Police.* 48:2 (1975), 102-112.
Author points out that democratic police systems lack the resources and training to control terrorism. In America it is unlikely that the police will use their intelligence system nor will the courts suspend civil liberties long enough to uncover terrorists.

Zlataric, B. "History of International Terrorism and its Legal Control." in M.C. Bassinouni *International Terrorism and Political Crimes.* Springfield, IL.: C.C. Thomas, 1975, pp. 474-484.

AIRPORT SECURITY

"Airlines Need New Pirate Detectors." *Business Week* (March 11, 1972).

"Airports Seek to Shift Security Burden." *Aviation Week and Space Technology* (January 27, 1973).

"Anti-Hijacking System Being Used by TWA." *Aviation Week and Space Technology* (December 22, 1969).

Boltwood, C.E. et al. "Skyjacking, Airline Security, and Passenger Reactions toward a Complex Model for Prediction." *American Psychologist.* 27 (June, 1972), 539-545.

Buckley, W.F. "Frisking: the Social Dividends. Searching Airline Passengers." *National Review* (December 22, 1972).

Cooke, W.C. "Airport Security Searches: A Rationale." *American Journal of Criminal Law.* 2:2 (1973), 128-145.

"Constitutionality of Airport Searches." *Michigan Law Review.* 72:1 (1973), 128-157.

Donahue, Paul G. "Search of Persons for Weapons at Airports." *FBI Law Enforcement Bulletin.* 43:3 (March, 1974).

"FAA to Initiate Passenger Search." *Aviation Week and Space Technology* (March 3, 1969).

"FAA Requires Hijack Screening." *Aviation Week and Space Technology* (February 7, 1972).

"Halt! Who Flies There? Preventing Further Fedayeen Terrorism at European Airports." *Time* (January 21, 1974).

Hubbard, David G. "Skyjacker and Security: A Disconcerting Profile." *Security World.* 16:28 (1973), 16-28.

Kahrl, R.C. "Search and Seizure: Stop and Frisk—Reasonableness of a Personal Search in an Airport Setting: *United States vs. Moreno.*" *Ohio State Law Journal.* 34:4 (1973), 896-906.

Keller, E. John. "Airport Security—Management's Responsibility." *Law and Order.* 20:10 (October, 1972), 57-58.

Keller, E. John. "Coordinate of Perish-Airport Security Cooperation." *Law and Order.* 20:9 (September, 1972).

Keller, E. John. "Law Enforcement in Airport Security." *Law and Order.* 20:11 (November, 1972), 46-47.

Keller, John E. "Security Briefs." *Law and Order* (September, 1972), 64; (October, 1972), 57-58; (November, 1972), 46-47.
Describes various aspects of airport security.

Landry, J.E. "Airport Security: Excerpts from an Address." *Aviation Week and Space Technology* (May 14, 1973).

McCann, Robert S. "Sky Harbor Security Program." *FBI Law Enforcement Bulletin.* 42:1 (January, 1973), 16-19, 32.

McCollum, J.R. "Warrantless Searches Under Anti-Hijacking Program." *Baylor Law Review.* 26:4 (1974), 604-615.

Marrett, John. "Civil Aviation Security." *Security Management* (November, 1973).

"Missile Alert: Preventing Arab Attacks at Airports all across Western Europe." *Newsweek* (January, 1974).

Moore, Kenneth C. *Airport, Aircraft and Airline Security.* Culver City, CA.: Security World, 1976.

Potter, A.N. Jr. "Security Training: The Airport Operator's Responsibility." *FBI Law Enforcement Bulletin.* 43:8 (1974), 13-15.

Potter, Anthony N. "Towards Improved Airport Security." *Security World.* 11:7 (July-August, 1974), 145-146.

"Searching for Weapons." *Science News* (September 26, 1970).

Teteris, Jeannie Y. "Airport Anti-hijack Searches After *Schneckloth:* A Question of Consent or Coercion." *Ohio State Law Journal.* 34:4 (1973), 879-895.

Wegner, Werner. "Dogs, Drugs and the Customs: Airport Searches." *International Criminal Police Review* (February, 1976), 39-45.

"Why Not Frisk?" *Nation* (June, 1970).

Wright, J.K. "Hijacking Risks and Airport Frisks: Reconciling Airline Security with the Fourth Amendment." *Criminal Law Bulletin.* 9:6 (1973), 491-517.

ANTI-SKYJACKING

"Air Guards to Ride Shotgun." *Senior Scholastic* (September, 28, 1970).

"Airlines Demand Stiffer Hijack Penalties." *Aviation Week and Space Technology* (July 6, 1970).

"Airlines, Government Accelerate Efforts at Hijacking Prevention." *Aviation Week and Space Technology* (January 27, 1969).

"Anti-Hijacking Efforts Advance." *Aviation Week and Space Technology* (February 19, 1973).

"Anti-Hijacking Moves Accelerate in Wake of Pilots Work Stoppage." *Aviation Week and Space Technology* (July 3, 1972).

"Anti-Hijacking Plans Augmented." *Aviation Week and Space Technology* (November 9, 1970).

"Armed Courier Thwarts TWA Hijack Attempt." *Aviation Week and Space Technology* (September 21, 1970).

"As Armed Guards Move into Airport." *U.S. News and World Report* (February 19, 1973).

Conarroe, Milford T. "Law Enforcement Essential to Air Safety." *Police Chief* (February, 1974), 22-24.

Coleman, H.S. "Britains Weigh Boycott of Arab Airlines." *Aviation Week and Space Technology* (November 6, 1972).

Coleman, H.S. "Hijack Policy Reflects Conservative View." *Aviation Week and Space Technology* (April 13, 1970).

Coleman, H.S. "IFALPA pushing to Thrust Hijack Issue Before U.N." *Aviation Week and Space Technology* (September 15, 1969).

Davis, B.O. "Outlook: A Sharp Decline in Hijackings." *U.S. News and World Report* (December 28, 1970).

Davis, B. "Tougher Tactics in the War Against Plane Hijackers." *U.S. News and World Report* (July 17, 1972).

"Death to Hijackers: Ethiopian Gambit." *Newsweek* (December 27, 1969).

Doty, L. "Anti-Hijacking Drive Gains Added Impetus." *Aviation Week and Space Technology* (October 19, 1970).

Doty, L. "Anti-Hijacking Proposals Proliferate." *Aviation Week and Space Technology* (September 21, 1970).

"Europe Tightens Mideast Flight Security." *Aviation Week and Space Technology* (June 12, 1972).

Evans, A.E. "Aircraft Hijacking—What Is Being Done." in M.C. Bassinouni, *International Terrorism and Political Crimes.* Springfield, IL.: C.C. Thomas, 1975, 219-247.

"Halting Hijackers: How One System Is Working Out." *U.S. News and World Report* (November 17, 1969).

"Homing in on Curbs Against Skyjacking." *Business Week* (November 25, 1972).

"How Airlines Make Skyjacking Harder." *Business Week* (July 29, 1972).

"How to Foil a Hijacking: Israelis Defeat Arabs at Lydda Airport." *Newsweek* (May 22, 1972).

Hubbard, David G. "The Skyjacker and Security: A Disconcerting Profile." *Security World* (July-August, 1973).

Lee, A. "International Suppression of Hijacking." in M.C. Bassinouni, *International Terrorism and Political Crimes.* Springfield, IL.: C.C. Thomas, 1975, 248-256.

Mason, B.J. "Grounding the Skyjacker: B.O. Davis and the Sky Marshal Plan." *Ebony* (November, 1972).

Meyers, R. "Stopping the Hijacker: International Association of Airline Security Officers." *Saturday Review* (October 21,1972).

"Perilous War on the Skyjacker: With Psychiatrist D.G. Hubbards Proposals." *Life* (August 11, 1972).

Schultz, M. "How the Airlines Hope to Stop the Hijackers." *Popular Mechanics* (May, 1970).

"Shoot-Out in the Sky: Ethiopian Airlines Boeing 720B." *Newsweek* (December 18, 1972).

"Shoot-Outs Thwart Attempted Hijackings." *Aviation Week and Space Technology* (July 10, 1972).

"Sky Marshal Program Graduates First Class." *Aviation Week and Space Technology* (January 4, 1971).

"U.S. Cities Munich Terrorist Acts in Asking Tough Hijacking Pact." *Aviation Week and Space Technology* (September 11, 1972).

U.S. Senate. *Aircraft Hijacking Convention.* Washington: GPO, August 5, 1971.

Warren, G.I. "Assessing Progress in Developing Systems to Curb Aerial Hijackings." *International Perspectives* (January-February, 1974), 37-39.

Watkins, H.D. "Anti-Hijacking Steps, Penalties Stiffer." *Aviation Week and Space Technology* (July 17, 1972).

"When Armed Guards Ride Your Plane." *U.S. News and World Report* (September 28, 1970).

COUNTERINSURGENCY

Agency for International Development. *Program Guide to Participant Training in Public Safety.* Washington: Department of State, Agency for International Development, 1964.

Barber, Noel. *War of the Running Dogs: How Malaya Defeated the Communist Guerrillas, 1948-1960,* London: Collins, 1971.

Furniss, Edgar S. Jr. *Counterinsurgency: Some Problems and Implications.* N.Y.: Council on Religion and International Affairs, 1966.

Galula, David. *Counterinsurgency Warfare: Theory and Practice.* N.Y.: Praeger, 1964.

Green, Thomas N. ed. *The Guerrilla and How to Fight Him.* N.Y.: Praeger, 1962.

Holman, Dennis. *Mau Mau Manhunt.* N.Y.: Pyramid, 1964.
Outstanding account of police intelligence, undercover and counterinsurgency efforts during the Mau Mau uprising in Kenya.

Hosmer, S.T. *Counterinsurgency: A Symposium, April 16-20, 1962.* N.Y.: Rand, 1963.

Kee, Robert J. "Algiers—1957: An Approach to Urban Counterinsurgency." *Military Review* (April, 1974), 73-84.

Kitson, F. *Low Intensity Operations: Subversion, Insurgency, Peace-Keeping.* Hamden, CT.: Shoe String, 1971.

"Law Enforcement Faces the Revolutionary Guerrilla Criminal." *FBI Law Enforcement Bulletin.* 39:12 (December, 1970), 20-22, 28.

Miller, Roger J. and James A. Cochran. "Counterinsurgency in Perspective." *Air University Review.* XIV:4 (September-October, 1963), 64-74.

Newman, T.J. "The Role of the Police in Counterinsurgency." *Police Chief.* XXXIII:2 (February, 1966-March, 1966).

O'Ballance, Edgar. *Malaya: The Communist Insurgent War, 1948-1960.* Hamden, CT.: Shoe String, 1966.

Orlov, Alexander. *Handbook of Intelligence and Guerrilla Warfare.* Ann Arbor, MI.: University of Michigan Press, 1963.

Osanka, Franklin M. *Modern Guerrilla Warfare: Fighting Communist Guerrilla Movements 1941-1961.* N.Y.: Free Press of Glenco, 1962.

Pustay, John S. *Counterinsurgency Warfare.* N.Y.: Free Press, 1965.

Rusziak, Nicholas D. "Police-Military Relations in a Revolutionary Environment." *Police Chief.* XXXIII:9 (September, 1966), 29-33.

Short, Anthony. *Communist Insurrection in Malaya 1948-1960.* N.Y.: Crane Russek, 1974.

Thompson, Robert. *Defeating Communist Insurgency: The Lessons of Malaya and Vietnam.* N.Y.: Prager, 1966.

"Trends in Urban Guerrilla Tactics." *FBI Law Enforcement Bulletin.* 42:7 (July, 1973), 3-7.

Trinquier, Roger. *Modern Warfare: A French View of Counterinsurgency.* N.Y.: Prager, 1964.

U.S. Department of the Army. *Counter Guerrilla Operations (FM31-16).* Washington: GPO, 1967.

Valeriano, Napoleon D. and Charles T.R. Bohannon. *Counter Guerrilla Operations: The Philippine Experience.* N.Y.: Praeger, 1962.

HOSTAGE SITUATIONS

"Blood Hostages: Texas State Penitentiary Breakout Attempts.: *Time* (August 12, 1974).

Cawley, Donald F. "The Williamsburg Incident: Anatomy of a Siege." *Police Chief.* XLI:1 (January, 1974), 30-34.

Culley, John A. "Hostage Negotiations." *FBI Law Enforcement Bulletin* (October, 1974).

Culley, J.A. *Hostage Negotiations.* Washington: NCJRS (Microfiche) 1974.

Hassel, Conrad V. "The Hostage Situation: Exploring the Motivation and the Cause." *Police Chief.* XLII:9 (September, 1974), 55-58.
Excellent paper covering various aspects of hostage situations.

"Hostage Incidents: Part I." *Spring 3100* (January-February, 1974, March 1974).

"Hostage Squad: New York City's Detective Bureau Hostages Negotiating Team." *Newsweek* (June 24, 1974).

James,T. "Rescuing Hostages: To Deal or Not to Deal." *Time* (September 18, 1972).

"Kidnap, Extortion and Hostage Situations." *Law Enforcement Bulletin* (July-August, 1974).

Kobetz, Richard W. "Hostage Incidents: The New Police Priority." *Police Chief.* XLII:5 (May, 1975), 32-35.

Kuper, Martin W. "Police Handling of Kidnapping Cases, the Taking of Hostages and Extortion." *Criminalistics* (December, 1973).

Middendorff. *New Developments in the Taking of Hostages and Kidnapping: A Summary—NCJRS Translation.* Washington: NCJRS, 1975.
Describes kidnapper types and personalities. Favors a tougher approach by police.

Souchon, Henri. "Hostage Taking: It's Evolution and Significance." *International Criminal Police Review* (July, 1976), 168-173.

PROTECTING DIGNITARIES AND EXECUTIVES

Adkins, Elmer H. "Protection of American Industrial Dignitaries and Facilities Overseas." *Security Management* (July, 1974).

Bloomfield, L.M. and G.F. Fitzgerald. *Crimes Against International Protected Persons—Prevention and*

Punishment: An Analysis of the U.N. Convention. N.Y.: Praeger, 1975.

Diamond, Harry, ed. "Operation Security." *Police.* 7:2 (November-December, 1962), 51-54.
Security operations by N.Y.P.D. concerned with protecting 26 foreign heads of state.

Fawcett, J.E.S. "Kidnappings versus Government Protection." *World Today.* 26:9 (1970), 359-362.

Grodsky, M. "Protection of Dignitaries." *International Police Academy Review.* 6:4 (October, 1972), 1-6.

Herzberg, E. "Executives Learn to Live with Danger." *International Management* (September, 1973).

Keller, E. John. "Executive Protection." *Law and Order.* 22:6 (June, 1974), 76-77.

More, Harry W. Jr. "Why Assassinations? . . .Principles of Protective Security for Dignitaries." *Military Police Journal.* 15 (July, 1966), 10-13.

Murphy, J. "Role of International Law in the Prevention of Terrorist Kidnapping of Diplomatic Personnel." in M.C. Bassinouni, *International Terrorism and Political Crimes.* Springfield, IL.: C.C. Thomas, 1975, pp. 285-313.

Najmuddin, Dilshad. "The Kidnapping of Diplomatic Personnel." *Police Chief.* XL:2 (February, 1973), 18-23.

Rayne, F. "Executive Protection and Terrorism." *Top Security.* 1:6 (October, 1975), 220-225.

United States Congress House Committee on Internal Security. *Political Kidnapping, 1968-73,* Washington: GPO, 1973.
Description of major attempted or successful kidnapping, terrorist groups responsible, and security measures and international efforts to combat the problem.

U.S. Congress Senate Commission on the Judiciary. *Terroristic Activity Hostage Defense Measures—Part 5.* Washington: GPO (July 25, 1974) (Microfiche).

CONTROL OF CIVIL DISORDER

RIOT AND CROWD CONTROL TACTICS

Adams, Michael F. "Campus Unrest: Police Coping Response." *Law and Order.* 19:5 (May, 1971), 28-32, 44-46.

Adams, Thomas F. "Crowd and Riot Control." *Police.* 8:4 (March-April, 1964), 54-57.

Adelson, Marvin. *Observations on Emergency Operations in a Civil Disorder.* Santa Monica: Systems Development Corporation, 1966.

Ailes, James C. "Riot Squad for a Small Department." *Law and Order.* 14:12 (December, 1966).

Applegate, Rex. "Bubbles and Banana Peels." *Law and Order.* 13:9 (September, 1965), 22-25.

Applegate, Rex. *Crowd and Riot Control.* 6th ed., Harrisburg, PA.: Stackpole, 1964.
Book discusses in great detail, hand to hand fighting, crowd and riot control, close combat techniques for both the police officer and military personnel. Development of training programs described.

Applegate, Rex. "The Organization and Tactics of Professional Riot Forces." *Indian Police Journal* (July, 1970).

Applegate, Rex. "Super-Sonic Sound: New Police Weapon." *Law and Order.* 16:5 (May, 1968), 28-34.
High output public speaker units for use during riots.

Applegate, Rex. *Riot Control—Material and Techniques.* Harrisburg, PA.: Stackpole, 1969.
Review of the most effective personnel deployment tactics, chemical agents, and special equipment.

Applegate, Rex. "When Riot Duty Calls." *Law and Order.* 12:2 (February, 1964), 22-24.

Birtles, William. "Common Law Power of the Police to Control Public Meetings." *Modern Law Review.* 36:6 (1973), 587-599.

Callahan, W.T. *Prevention of Control of Collective Violence, V 1—Guidelines for the Chief of Police.* Washington: GPO, 1972.

"Civil Disturbances, Mass Processing and Misdemeanants: Rights, Remedies and Realities." *Journal of Criminal Law, Criminology and Police Science.* 61:1 (March, 1970), 39-50.

Coates, J.F. "Wit and Humor: A Neglected Aid on Crowd and Mob Control." *Crime and Delinquency.* 18:2 (1972), 184-191.

Coleman, James S. *Community Conflict.* Glencoe, IL.: Free Press, 1957.

Cox, Jerry. "Portable, Lightweight Chemical Agent Generator." *Law and Order.* 19:5 (May, 1971), 52, 54.

"Creative Restraint: Riot Control Tactics of Hong Kong Police." *Newsweek* (May 18, 1970).

Cutting, Ron C. "Crowd Control For a Small Community." *FBI Law Enforcement Bulletin.* 39:6 (June, 1970), 16-20.

Darr, Lawrence A. "The Holding Quad." *Law and Order.* 21:7 (July, 1973), 18, 20-21.

Deane-Drummond, A.J. *Riot Control.* N.Y.: Crane Russak, 1975.

Demma, Joe. "Slipping Through the Confrontation." *Law and Order.* 17:10 (October, 1969) 34-36.

Diamond, Harry, ed. "Crowd Control and Riot Prevention." *Police.* 9:4 (March-April, 1965), 52-59; 10:1 (September-October, 1965), 92-96.

Dimmitt, Lawrence M. "The Police Officer and the Hostile Crowd." *Law and Order.* 21:3 (March, 1973), 37-39.

Donovan, Bob. "Anatomy of a Demonstration." *Security World* (July-August, 1966).

Emergency Mobilization Manual. Philadelphia: Police Department, 1968.

Farmer, David J. *Civil Disorder Control: A Planning Program of Municipal Coordination and Cooperation.* Chicago: Public Administration Service, 1968.

Fletcher, C.D. St. Q. "Riot Control in Hong Kong." *FBI Law Enforcement Bulletin* (December, 1969).

Gates, Daryl. "Control of Civil Disorders." *Police Chief.* XXXV:5 (May, 1968), 32-34.

Grimshaw, Allen D. "Actions of Police and the Military in American Race Riots." *Phylon.* 24 (Fall, 1963), 271-289.

Grimshaw, Allen D. "Police Agencies and the Prevention of Racial Violence." *Journal of Criminal Law, Criminology and Police Science.* 54:1 (March, 1963), 110-113.

Herramann, William W. "Riot Prevention and Control: Operations Research Response." *Journal of California Law Enforcement* (October, 1969), 65-72.

International Association of Chiefs of Police. *Civil Disorders: After Action Reports—A Report to the Attorney General of the United States Reviewing the Experiences of Eight American Cities During the Civil Disorders of March-April, 1968.* Washington: NCJRS (Microfiche).
Examines the effectiveness of command and control procedures, mobilization, field operations, fire service, and a variety of support services.

Janowitz, Morris. *Social Control of Escalated Riots.* Chicago: University of Chicago Press, 1968.

Kimble, Joseph. "Patience and Planning—The Key to Controlling Demonstrations." *Law and Order.* 13:9 (September, 1965), 71-78.

Kimble, Joseph. "Planning for Civil Disorders." *Police Chief.* XXXV:5 (May, 1968), 29-31.

Knowlton, Harold E. "Controlling Motorcycle Crowds." *FBI Law Enforcement Bulletin.* 38:12 (December, 1969), 7-10.

Lane, Marvin G. "Police Planning and Operations for Riot Control." *FBI Law Enforcement Bulletin.* 27:8 (August, 1958), 20-22.

Leary, Howard R. "Role of Police in Riotous Demonstrations, Symposium." *Notre Dame Law Journal.* 40:5 (1965), 499-507.

Looney, Francis B. "The Human Factor in Crowd Control." *Law and Order.* 18:5 (May, 1970), 34-35, 82.

Louis, Lee. "Shotguns: A Psychological Deterrent." *Law and Order.* 13:8 (August, 1965), 66-68.

Meharg, W. "Police Problems in Times of Civil Disturbances." *Police Surgeon* (April, 1975), 102-108.

Methevin, Eugene H. *The Riot Makers: The Technology of Social Demolition.* New Rochelle, N.Y.: Arlington, 1970.

Milander, H.M. "Campus Apprehensions of College Students." *Police Chief.* XXXIX:11 (November, 1972), 70-71.

Momboisse, Raymond E. *Confrontations Riots, Urban Warfare.* Sacramento: MSM Enterprises, 1969.

Momboisse, Raymond E. *Control of Student Disorder.* Sacramento: MSM Enterprises, 1968.

Momboisse, Raymond E. "Manpower and Command in Riots." *Police.* 12:1 (September-October, 1967), 34-40.

Momboisse, R.E. *Riots, Revolts and Insurrections.* Springfield, IL.: C.C. Thomas, 1970.
Treatment of the problem of crowd control demonstrations, civil disobedience, riots and counter insurrections.

Morgan, James P. and John Dankel. "Community Action Unit." *Police Chief.* XL:3 (March, 1973), 36-37.
Police work directly with demonstrators to head off violence.

Morgan, J.P. Jr. "Confrontation Management." *Police Chief.* 38:1 (January, 1971), 20-22, 24.
Intensity reduction rather than total suppression is a concept to reduce the danger of violent confrontations.

Mulkeen, William J. "Civil Rights Demonstrations." *Law and Order.* 12:5 (May, 1964), 37-43.

Newman, T.J. *Conflict Management Manual.* Springfield, VA.: NTIS, 1973.
Training and procedural document prepared for Louisiana police troopers acting as members of troop tactical units in response to civil disturbance emergencies.

Pegg, Charges F. "Comments on Riots and Mobs." *Law and Order.* 16:5 (May, 1968), 48-49, 104.

Peterson, Philip L. "Psychological Factors in Mobs and Riots." *Police.* 6:5 (May-June, 1962), 18-20.

Peterson, Philip L. "Psychology and Riot Prevention." *Police.* 6:6 (July-August, 1962), 42-44.

Platt, Anthony and Sharon Dunkle. *The Administration of Justice in Crisis: Chicago April 1968.* Chicago: University of Chicago Press, 1968.

Sagalyn, Arnold. "Danger of Police Over-reaction." *Journal of Criminal Law, Criminology and Police Science.* 60:4 (December, 1969), 517-519.

Samuels, D.W. and D.O. Egner. *Riot Control—Analysis and Catalog—Final Report.* Springfield, VA.: NTIS, 1969.
Provides a systematic analysis of some types of civil disturbances and a survey of related developmental material.

Sealy, Lloyd. "Prevention of Civil Disorders." *Police Chief.* XXXV:5 (May, 1968).

Shaw, William. "Technology and Riot Control." *Law and Order.* 19:5 (May, 1971), 18, 20-25.

Smith, R. Dean and Richard W. Kobetz. *Guidelines for Civil Disorder and Mobilization Planning.* Gaithersburg, MD.: IACP, Professional Standards Division, 1968.

Stevenson, Jan A. "The Pepper Fog Happens." *Law and Order.* 17:6 (June, 1969), 59-70.
Portable tear gas generator.

Stiles, Gerald C. "New Hampshire State Police Riot Control Tactics Successful." *Law and Order.* 14:10 (October, 1966), 72-74.

Strom, Bill. "The Civil Disobedience Unit." *Law and Order.* 15:3 (March, 1967), 74-77.

Taylor, W.S. *Handbook on Basic Crowd Control Techniques.* Washington: NCJRS, 1968.

Thomas, Herman J. "One Departments Confrontation Strategy." *FBI Law Enforcement Bulletin.* 42:1 (January, 1973), 2-8.

Towler, Judy E. "By the Book: Police Role in Racial Conflicts." *Newsweek* (March 1, 1965).
A critical examination of "the Police Role in Racial Conflicts".

U.S. Congress Senate Subcommittee on Administrative Practice. *Federal Handling of Demonstrations, Hearing—Part 1.* Washington: GPO, 1970.

Weaver, Bill W. "The Geography of a Riot." *Police Chief.* XXXLV:4 (April, 1967), 24-25.

Wagner, D. "The Reluctant Army: The Functioning of Police Departments During Civil Disturbances." *American Behavioral Science.* 16:3 (1973), 326-342.

"Where Even Police Are Not Safe." *U.S. News and World Report.* 51 (October 9, 1961), 106-111.
Reports from New York, Los Angeles, Philadelphia, Chicago and Washington about the mob outbreaks and riots.

Whittaker, Charles C. "The Causes and Effect Upon Public Order of Planned Mass Violations of Our Laws." *Police Chief.* XXXLV:4 (April, 1967), 12-22.

Younger, Evelle J. "Authority of County, City Law Enforcement Agencies on Campuses." *Journal of California Law Enforcement* (April, 1968), 218-219.

RUMOR CONTROL

Allport, Gordon W. and Leo Postman. *The Psychology of Rumor.* N.Y.: Holt, 1947.

Allport, Gordon W. and Leo Postman. *The Psychology of Rumor.* N.Y.: Russell & Russell, 1965.

Chaplain, James P. *Rumor Fear and the Madness of Crowds.* N.Y.: Ballentine, 1959.

Fitzgerald, Edward T. "Rumor Process and Its Effect on Civil Disorder." *Police Chief.* 38:4 (April, 1971), 16-32.

Jacobson, David J. *The Affairs of Dame Rumor.* Cedar Knolls, N.J.: Colonial, 1948.

James, Ed. "Rumor Control." *Law and Order.* 18:7 (July, 1970), 54, 98.

Knopf, Terry A. "Police and Rumors." *Police Chief.* XLI:3 (March, 1974), 80-84.

Knopf, T.A. *Rumors, Race and Riots.* New Brunswick, N.J.: Rutgers University Press, 1975.

McLaughlin, John B. "Rumor and the Police Department." *Law and Order.* 16:5 (May, 1968), 64-65.

Norris, W.N. "Shelby County Organizes Rumor Control Squad." *Police Chief.* XXXVI:5 (May, 1969).

Sinha, Durganand. "Behavior in a Catastrophic Situation: A Psychological Study of Reports and Rumors." *British Journal of Psychology.* 43 (1952), 200-229.

Taylor, Herbert S. "The Rumor Clinic." *FBI Law Enforcement Bulletin.* 38:7 (July, 1969), 7-10.

Williams, Larry and Gerald Erchak. "Rumor Control Centers in Civil Disorders." *Police Chief.* XXXVI:5 (May, 1969), 26-32.

THE MILITARY IN RIOT CONTROL

Aaron, Thomas J. "A Military Force in My Community." *Law and Order* (December, 1965), 18-19, 96-97.
Use of military forces during riots, laws and functions.

Glick, Edward Bernard. *Peaceful Conflict: The Non-Military Use of the Military.* Harrisburg, PA.: Stackpole, 1967.

Grimshaw, Allen D. "Actions of Police and the Military in American Race Riots." *Phylon* (Fall, 1963), 271-289.

"The Guard vs. Disorder." *The National Guardsman.* XXIV (June, 1970), 2-7, 9-13, 40.

Higham, Robin D. *Bayonets in the Streets: The Use of Troops in Civil Disturbances.* Lawrence, Kansas: University Press, 1969.

Laturno, Gary M. "Military Participation in Civilian Law Enforcement." *FBI Law Enforcement Bulletin* (April, 1975), 22-25.
Describes the legalities of military involvement in civilian law enforcement in non-riot situations. Details restrictions.

National Association of Attorneys General. Committee on the Office of Attorney General. *Legal Issues Concerning the Role of the National Guard in Civil Disorders.* Raleigh, N.C.: National Association of Attorneys General, 1973.

Swisher, Paul B. *Military Civil Action.* Palo Alto, CA.: American Institutes for Research, June, 1972.

Turner, Carl C. "Military Assistance During Civil Disturbances." *FBI Law Enforcement Bulletin.* 35:3 (March, 1966), 12-15.

Turner, Carl C. "Use of the National Guard to Cope with Civil Disturbances." *Police Chief.* XXIV:12 (December, 1967), 52-55.

Wilson, Frederick. *Federal Aid and Domestic Disturbances 1787-1903.* N.Y.: Arno. (Repr. of 1903 ed.)

CIVIL DISORDER

Civil Disorder—General

Archer, Jules. *Riot! A History of Mob Action in U.S.* N.Y.: Hawthorn, 1974.

Armstrong, Gregory. *Protest: How it Runs, Where it is Going.* N.Y.: Harper Row, 1968.

Armstrong, Gregory. *Protest: Man Against Society.* N.Y.: Bantam, 1969.

Boehme, Lillian R. *Carte Blanche for Chaos.* New Rochelle, N.J.: Arlington, 1970.

Cape, William H. "Menace of Riot Proneness in a Community." *Law and Order.* 13:4 (April, 1965), 68-70, 72.

Cape, William H. "Policemen, Dissenters, and Law-Abiding Citizens." *Police Chief.* XXXVIII:11 (November, 1971), 45-50.

Chappell, Bill. "Some Call It Dissent." *Police.* 15:1. (September-October, 1970) 77-79.

Chicago Corporation Counsel. *The Strategy of Confrontation: Chicago and the Democratic National Convention.* Chicago: Chicago Corporation Counsel, 1968.

Chicago Riot Study Committee. *Report of the Chicago Riot Study Committee to the Honorary Richard J. Daley on April 1968 Riots.* Chicago: Riot Study Committee, 1968.

Chicago University Law School. *Criminal Justice in Extremes: Administration of Justice During the April 1968 Chicago Disorder.* Chicago: Foundation Press, 1969.

Functioning of the Cook County, Illinois Criminal Justice System in response to the mass arrests made during the April 4, 1968 riot.

Conant, Ralph W. *The Prospects for Revolution: A Study of Riots, Civil Disobedience, and Insurrection in Contemporary America.* N.Y.: Harper & Row, 1971.

Corsi, J.R. and R.G. Lewis. *Confrontation or Accommodation: The American Legion and the Peoples Army Jamboree in Portland.* Springfield, VA.: NTIS, 1972.

Report on the response of Government agencies to a threatened confrontation.

Cromwell, Paul F. Jr. and Robert L. Lewis Jr. "Crowds, Mobs, and Riots: A Sociological Analysis." *Police.* 16:1 (September, 1971), 30-32.

Davis, Arthur M. "Vietnam Moratorium Day Syracuse." *Law and Order.* 18:8 (August, 1970), 36-38, 40, 42, 44-45.

Davies, J.C. *When Men Revolt and Why.* N.Y.: Free Press, 1971.

Dynes, R. and E. Quantarelli. "Organization as Victim in Mass Civil Disturbances." *Issues in Criminology.* 5 (1970), 181-193.

Earl, Bill. "Secret Sabatoge War Raging Across America." *Saga* (January, 1969).

Eisenhower, Milton S. *The Rule of Law: An Alternative to Violence—A Report to the National Commission on the Causes and Prevention of Violence.* North Nashville, TN.: Aurora, 1970.

Hughes, Helen M., ed. *Crowd and Mass Behavior.* Rockleigh, N.J.: Holbrook, 1972.

Kerner, Otto. "Report of National Advisory Commission on Civil Disorders." *Journal of California Law Enforcement* (July, 1968), 28-36.

Kogan, Bernard R., ed. *The Chicago Haymarket Riot: Anarchy on Trial.* Boston: Heath, 1959.

Lane, Mark. *Chicago Eyewitness.* N.Y.: Alsor-Honor, 1968.

Lohman, Joseph D. "Violence in the Streets." *Notre Dame Lawyer* (1965), 517-526.

McEvoy, James and Abraham Miller. *Black Power and Student Rebellion.* Belmont, CA.: Wadsworth, 1969.

Mailer, Norman. *Armies of the Night.* N.Y.: World, 1968.

Methvin, Eugene H. *The Riot Makers.* New Rochelle, N.Y.: Arlington, 1970.

Miami Study Team. *Miami Report—The Report of the Miami Study Team on Civil Disturbances in Miami, Florida During the Week of August 5, 1968.* Washington: GPO,1969.

Momboisse, Raymond M. "A Crossroad in History." *Law and Order.* 14:9 (September, 1966), 32-40.

National Commission on Causes and Prevention of Violence. *To Establish Justice, To Insure Domestic Tranquility.* Washington: GPO, 1969.

Report of the National Commission on the causes and prevention of violence, created to determine the causes of violence in the United States and find methods of prevention.

Rankin, R.S. *When Civil Law Fails: Martial Law and its Legal Basis in the U.S.* Durham, N.C.: Duke University Press, 1939.

Rude, George F. *Crowd in History, 1730-1884.* N.Y.: Wiley, 1964.

Russell, Eric F. *The Rabble Rousers.* Evanston, IL.: Regency, 1963.

Sahid, Joseph R. *Rights in Concord: The Response to the Counter-Innaugural Protest Activities in Washington, January 18-20, 1969, A Staff Report of the National Commission on the Causes and Prevention of Violence.* Washington: GPO, 1969.

Short, J.F. and M.E. Wolfgang. *Collective Violence.* Chicago, IL.: Aldine, 1972.

Readings in theory and research on violence as a group phenomenon, with analysis of the forms, sources and meanings of riot and rebellion.

Skolnick, Jerome. *The Politics of Protest, Violent Aspects of Protest and Confrontation.* Washington: GPO, 1969.

Stark, M.J.A. et al. "Some Empirical Patterns in a Riot Process." *American Sociological Review.* 39:6 (1974), 865-876.

Stein, David Lewis. *Living the Revolution: The Yippies in Chicago.* Indianapolis, IN.: Bobbs-Merrill, 1969.

"Strategy of Confrontation—Chicago and the Democratic National Convention 1968." *Law and Order.* 16:12 (December, 1968), 72-105.

Walker, Daniel. *Rights in Conflict: Chicago's 7 Brutal Days.* N.Y.: Grosset, 1968.

Wilson, O.W. "Civil Disturbances and the Rule of Law." *Journal of Criminal Law, Criminology and Police Science.* 58:2 (June, 1967), 155-159.

Campus Disruptions

American Bar Association. *Report of the Commission on Campus Government and Student Dissent.* Chicago: American Bar Association, 1970.

Astin, Alexander W. and Alan E. Bayer. *Campus Disruption During 1968-1969.* Washington: American Council on Education, 1969.

Avorn, Jerry L. et al. *Up Against the Ivy Wall.* N.Y.: Atheneum, 1969.

Baker, Michael A. et al. *Police on Campus: The Mass Police at Columbia University*. (Spring, 1968) N.Y.: New York Civil Liberties Union, 1969.

Becker, Howard S. *Campus Power Struggle*. Chicago: Aldine, 1970.

Bell, Daniel and Irving Kristol. *Confrontation: The Student Rebellions and the Universities*. N.Y.: Basic, 1969.

Buchman, James M. and Nicos E. Devletoglou. *Academy in Anarchy: An Economic Diagnosis*. N.Y.: Basic, 1970.

Burck, Charles. "Student Activists—Free Form Revolutionaries." *Fortune* (January, 1969).

Califano, Joseph A. *The Student Revolution: A Global Confrontation*. N.Y.: W.W. Norton, 1969.

Carling, Francis. *Move Over: Students, Politics, Religion*. N.Y.: Sheed Ward, 1968.

Coyne, J.R. "Kunstler Constituency: Rioting by Columbia Students." *National Review* (May 5, 1970).

Dennan, George. *Democracy and the Student Left: Angry Students vs The Establishment—The Dialogue that Turned to Violence*. Boston: Little Brown, 1968.

Douglas, Bruce. *Reflections on Protest: Student Presence in Political Conflict*. Atlanta, GA.: Knox, 1967.

Draper, Hal. *Berkeley: The New Student Revolt*. N.Y.: Grove, 1965.

Ehrenreich, Barbara and John Long March. *Short Spring: The Student Uprising at Home and Abroad*. N.Y.: Monthly Review, 1969.

Erikson, Eric. *Identify: Youth and Crisis*. N.Y.: Norton, 1968.

Feuer, Louis S. *The Conflict of Generations: The Character and Significance of Student Movements*. N.Y.: Basic, 1968.

Foster, Julian and Durward Long, eds. *Protest: Student Activism in America*. N.Y.: Morrow, 1969.

Frankel, Charles. *Education and the Barricades*. N.Y.: Norton, 1968.

Gerzon, Mark. *The Whole World Is Watching: A Young Man Looks at Youth's Dissent*. N.Y.: Viking, 1969.

Glazer, Nathan. "The Jewish Role in Student Activism." *Fortune* (January, 1969).

Jencks, Christopher and David Reisman. *The Academic Revolution*. Garden City, N.Y.: Doubleday, 1968.

Kelman, Steven. *Push Comes to Shove: The Escalation of Student Protest*. Boston, (Houghton Mifflin, 1970).

Kunen, James Simon. *The Strawberry Statement: Notes of a College Revolutionary*. N.Y.: Random House, 1969.

Lankes, George A. "Campus Violence and the Law." *Police Chief* (March, 1970), 38-42.

Lee, Calvin B.T. *The Campus Scene: 1900-1970*. N.Y.: McKay, 1970.

"Liberating the Campus from 'Liberators'." *Life* (February 28, 1969).

Long, Priscilla, ed. *The New Left: A Collection of Essays*. Boston: Sargent, 1969.

Luce, Phillip Abbott. *Road to Revolution*. San Diego, CA.: Viewpoint, 1969.

McEvoy, James and Abraham Miller. "On Strike, Shut It Down: The Crisis at San Francisco State College." *Trans-Action* (March, 1969), 18-23.

Mallery, David. *Ferment on the Campus: An Encounter With the New College Generation*. N.Y.: Harper Row, 1966.

Methvin, Eugene R. *Riots*. New Rochelle, N.Y.: Arlington, 1970.

Miller, Michael V. and Susan Gilmore, eds. *Revolution at Berkeley the Crisis in American Education*. N.Y.: Dial, 1965.

Orrick, William H. Jr. *Shut It Down: A College in Crisis. San Francisco State College, October 1968—April 1969*. Staff Report on the National Commission on the Causes and Prevention of Violence, Washington: GPO, 1969.

Rappopart, Roger and Lawrence J. Kirshbaun. *Is the Library Burning? A Report on American Students, Student Unrest and Student Power*. N.Y.: Random, 1969.

Ragan, Donald L. *Campus Apocalypse: The Student Search Today*. N.Y.: Seabury, 1969.

Schlesinger, Arthur Jr. "Joe College Is Dead." *Saturday Evening Post* (September 21, 1968).

Teodori, Massimo, ed. *The New Left: A Documentary History*. Indianapolis, IN.: Bobbs Merrill, 1970.

Tussman, Joseph. *Experiment at Berkeley*. London: Oxford University Press, 1969.

Van Hoffman, Nicholas. *Two, Three, Many More*. Chicago: Quandrangle, 1969.

Wallerstein, Immanual. *Universities in Turmoil: The Politics of Change*. Patterson, N.J.: Antheneum McClalland, 1969.

Warsaw, Steven. *The Trouble at Berkeley*. Berkeley, CA.: Diablo, 1965.

Ways, Max. "The Facility Is the Heart of the Trouble." *Fortune* (January, 1969).

Willhelmsen, Frederick. *Seeds of Anarchy: A Study of Campus Revolution*. Dallas: Argus Academic, 1969.

Civil Disobedience

Ball, T. *Civil Disobedience and Civil Deviance*. Beverly Hills, CA.: Sage, 1973.
A look at the sources of the ideas of civil disobedience and civil deviance, tracing development through time.

Bassett, James E. "Public Order Is the First Order of Government." *Law and Order*. 16:6 (June, 1968), 92-94.

Crawford, Curtis, ed. *Civil Disobedience: A Case Book*. N.Y.: Crowell, 1973.

Coffin, William Sloan and Morris I. Liebman. *Civil Disobedience: Aid or Hindrance to Justice*. Washington: American Enterprise Institute for Public Policy Research, 1972.

Gould, Jay. "Civil Disobedience—Prelude to Anarchy." *Law and Order* (April, 1966), 86-89.

Grange, Joseph. "Dissent and Society." *Police Chief.* XXXVIII:11 (November, 1971), 38-44.

Johnson, Elmer H. "A Sociological Interpretation of Police Reaction and Responsibility to Civil Disobedience." *Journal of Criminal Law, Criminology and Police Science.* 58:3 (September, 1967), 405-409.

LeGrande, J.L. "Nonviolent Civil Disobedience and Police Enforcement Policy." *Journal of Criminal Law, Criminology and Police Science.* 58:3 (September, 1967), 393-404.

Morris, Earl F. "American Society and the Rebirth of Civil Disobedience." *American Bar Journal.* 54 (1968).

Smith, Bill. "The Clergy and Civil Disobedience." *Police Chief.* XXV:12 (December, 1968), 44-48.

Velvel, Lawrence R. *Undeclared War and Civil Disobedience: The American System in Crisis.* N.Y.: Dunellen, 1970.

Racial Conflicts

ACLU of Southern California. *Day of Protest, Night of Violence: The Century City Peace March.* Los Angeles: Sawyer, July, 1967.
ACLU analysis of war protest demonstration. Numerous alegations to police misconduct.

Allen, R.F. and C.H. Adair, eds. *Violence and Riots in Urban America.* Worthington, OH.: Jones, 1969.

Barbour, Floyd. *The Black Power Revolt.* Boston: Porter Sargent, 1968.

Berson, Lenora E. *Case Study of a Riot: The Philadelphia Story.* N.Y.: Institutes of Human Relations Press,1966.

Besag, Frank P. *Anatomy of a Riot: Buffalo—1967.* Buffalo: State University of N.Y. Press, 1967.

Blavner, Robert. "Whitewash over Watts." *Trans-Action.* 3:3 (1966).

Boskin, Joseph. *Urban Racial Violence in the Twentieth Century.* N.Y.: Glencoe, 1969.

Brown, Earl. *Why Race Riots? Lessons from Detroit.* Washington: Public Affairs Institute, 1944.

Clor, Harry M., ed. *Civil Disorder and Violence.* Chicago: Rand, 1972.

Cohen, Nathan. *The Los Angeles Riots: A Socio-Psychological Study.* N.Y.: Praeger, 1970.

Connery, Robert. *Urban Riots: Violence and Social Change.* N.Y.: Random, 1969.

Conot, Robert. *Rivers of Blood, Years of Darkness.* N.Y.: Morrow, 1967.

Department of the Army. *Task Force Washington—After Action Report.* Springfield, VA.: NTIS, 1968.
A summary of army operations involving civil disorders in Washington, D.C. which developed from the assassination of Dr. Martin Luther King.

Fogelson, Robert M. "From Resentment to Confrontation: The Police, the Negroes, and the Outbreak of the Nineteen Sixties Riots." *Political Science Quarterly.* 83 (June, 1968), 217-247.

Fogelson, Robert M. *Violence as Protest: A Study of Riots and Ghettos.* Garden City, N.J.: Doubleday, 1971.

Fogelson, Robert M. and Richard Rubenstein, eds. *Mass Violence in America: The Los Angeles Riots.* N.Y.: Arno, 1969.

Gilbert, B.W. *Ten Blocks from the White House—Anatomy of the Washington Riots of 1968.* N.Y.: Praeger, 1969.

Gomez, David F. "Chicanos Besieged: The Bloody Fiesta." *Nation.* 212 (March 15, 1971), 326-328.

Heaps, Willard. *Riots, U.S.A.* N.Y.: Seabury, 1966.

Hersey, John. *The Algiers Motel Incident.* N.Y.: Knopf, 1968.

Jacobs, Paul. *Prelude to Riot.* N.Y.: Random, 1966.

Kapsis, R. and B. Saunders. *Reconstruction of A Riot—A Case Study of Community Tensions and Civil Disorder.* Waltham, MA.: Brandeis University, 1970.
Study of a 4 day civil disturbance in 1968 in the city of Richmond, CA.

Lincoln, James H. *The Anatomy of a Riot: A Detroit Judge's Report.* N.Y.: McGraw-Hill, 1968.

Locke, Hubert G. *The Detroit Riot of 1967.* Detroit, MI.: Wayne State University Press, 1969.

McCague, James. *The Second Rebellion: The Story of the New York City Draft Riots of 1863.* N.Y.: Dial, 1968.

Marx, Gary T. "Civil Disorder and the Agents of Social Control." *Journal of Social Issues.* 26:1 (Winter, 1970), 19-57.

Masotti, L.H. and D.R. Bowen. *Riots and Rebellions—Civil Violence in the Urban Community.* Beverly Hills, CA.: Sage, 1968.

Mitchell, J. Paul. *Race Riots in Black and White.* Englewood Cliffs, N.J.: Prentice-Hall, 1970.

Morgan, W.R. and T.N. Clark. "The Cause of Racial Disorders: A Grievance Level Explanation.: *American Sociological Review.* 38:5 (1973), 611-624.

National Advisory Commission on Civil Disorders. *Report of the National Advisory Commission on Civil Disorders.* N.Y.: Bantam, 1968.

Oberschall, Anthony. "The Los Angeles Riot." *Social Problems.* XV (Winter, 1968), 297-310.

Post, Argie White. *Rape of Detroit: An Eyewitness Report of a City's Devastation.* N.Y.: Exposition, 1975.

"Race Troubles: Record of 109 Cities." *U.S. News and World Report* (August 14, 1967), 28-30.

Rosst, P.H. *Ghetto Revolts.* Chicago: Aldine, 1970.
A comparison of the revolts of the 60's and early riots of the 20th century, representative of collective defiance of established property relationships.

Rudwick, Elliot M. *Race Riot at East St. Louis—July 2, 1917.* Carbondale: Southern Illinois University Press, 1964.

Sanburg, Carl. *The Chicago Race Riots, July, 1919.* N.Y.: Harcourt, 1969.

Schuler, Edgar A. "The Houston Race Riot 1917." *Journal of Negro History.* XXIX (July, 1944).

Sears, David O. and John B. McConahay. *Politics of Violence: The New Urban Blacks and the Watts Riot.* Boston: Houghton Mifflin, 1973.

Shapiro, Fred C. and James W. Sullivan. *Race Riots: New York 1964.* N.Y.: Crowell, 1964.

Shogan, Robert and Thomas Craig. *The Detroit Race Riot: A Study in Violence.* Philadelphia: Clinton, 1964.

"Seven Days in August—The Watts Riots." *Police Chief.* XXXLV:4 (April, 1967), 26-32.

Tuttle, W.M. *Race Riot—Chicago in the Red Summer of 1919—Studies in American Negro Life.* N.Y.: Atheneum, 1970.

Chicago race riot of 1919 is analysed and chronicled as to its causes in terms of individuals as well as of groups.

U.S. Committee on Un-American Activities. *Subversive Influences in Riots, Looting, and Burning: Hearing Before 90th Congress 1st Session 1968.* Washington: GPO, 1968.

Werstein, Irving. *July 1863: The Incredible Story of the Bloody New York City Draft Riots.* N.Y.: Messner, 1957.

White, Walter. "Behind the Harlem Riots." *New Republic* (August 16, 1943).

Williams, Lee Sr. and Lee Williams Jr. *Anatomy of Four Race Riots: Racial Conflict in Knoxville. Elaine (Arkansas) Tulsa and Chicago 1919-1921,* Jackson, MI.: University Press of Mississippi, 1972.

DANGEROUS SITUATIONS

DANGER—GENERAL

Blanks, W. Winfield. "Officer Needs Help!" *Police Chief* (February, 1971).

"Detailed Analysis of Police Killings Shows Job Hazards. "*FBI Law Enforcement Bulletin* (January, 1963).

A 20-month study conducted by the FBI showed that police patrol response to disturbance calls takes the greatest toll of lives. . .The Danger in these situations is usually from the emotionally enraged or mentally disturbed person.

Fox, Harry G. "Is It Worth All This?" *Law and Order.* 16:12 (December, 1968), 44-49.

Lease, Richard J. "Police Combat Skills and Related Skills as Living Assurance." *Police* (July-August, 1964).

Levine, Howard. "Officer in Peril. "*Police Chief* (September, 1970).

Scott, Edgar E. "Alertness in Handling Suspects is Urged. "*Police* (July-August, 1959).

Strait, Edward M. "Victims of Routine: Three Patrolmen Disarmed." *Law and Order.* 21:11 (November, 1973), 56-58.

Tauber, Ronald K. "Danger and the Police: A Theoretical Analysis." *Issues in Criminology.* 3:1 (Summer, 1967), 69-81.

U.S. Army. *Guide to Viet Cong Boobytraps and Explosive Devices.* Washington U.S. Army, 1966.

Whitman, Howard. "Who Would Want to Be a Cop?" *Readers Digest* (September, 1971).

AMBUSHES

Ayoob, Massad F. "Ambush." *Law and Order.* 22:10 (October, 1974), 62-68.

International Association of Chiefs of Police. *Ambush Attacks—A Risk Reduction Manual for Police.* Gaithersburg, MD.: IACP, 1974.

Tamm, Quinn. "Some Solutions to an Intolerable Situation." *Police Chief.* 37:12 (December, 1970), 44-46.

Counter measures to sniper attacks, ambushings, bombings and unprovoked assaults on police officers.

ASSAULTS ON POLICE

Anable, David. "British Police Peril Stirs Arms Debate." *Christian Science Monitor* (August 17, 1966).

Arenberg, Gerald S. "A Study of Police Officers Line of Duty Deaths in the U.S." *Law and Order.* 8:12 (December, 1960).

Arm, Walter. "Cop Fighting—What Are Its Implications." *Police Chief* (April, 1962).

"Assualting or Killing Federal Officers." *FBI Law Enforcement Bulletin.* 26:7 (July, 1957).

Bennett, Richard O. "The Traffic Hot-Head." *Police Chief.* XXXII:II (November, 1965), 20-26.

"Boulder Cop Killers Hitting More Often." *U.S. News and World Report* (September 14, 1970).

Bristow, Allen P. "Police Officer Shootings—A Tactical Evaluation." *Journal of Criminal Law, Criminology and Police Science.* 54 (1963), 93-95.

Bristow, Allen P. "Preliminary Report, Police Officer Shooting Study." *Journal of Criminal Law, Criminology and Police Science.* 52 (1961), 472-474.

Brooks, Pierce R. *Officer Down—Code Three.* Schiller Park, IL: Motorola Teleprograms, 1975.

Cardarelli, Albert P. "An Analysis of Police Killed by Criminal Action: 1961-1963." *Journal of Criminal Law, Criminology and Police Science.* 59:3 (September, 1968), 447-453.

Chapman, Samuel G., ed. *Perspectives on Police Assaults in the South Central United States.* 3 vols., Washington LEAA (June, 1974).

Cobb, Belton. *Murdered on Duty*. London: W.H. Allen, 1961.
A chronicle of English Policemen murdered on duty starting in the 1800's.

"Comments on the Traffic Hot-Head." *Police Chief.* XXXII:II (November, 1965), 26-30.

Cook, Louise. "Tempo Quickening in Assaults Against Policemen in U.S." *Pacific Stars and Stripes* (September 21, 1970).

Creamer, J. Shane and Gerald D. Robin. "Assaults on Police." *Police* (March-April, 1968).

Culver, Dorothy C. *Death Rates for Policemen and Firemen.* Berkeley: University of California Bureau of Public Administration (February 12, 1937) (typed).

Dettleff, John S. "A Tribute to Officer Forrest Allen Hall." *Law and Order.* 18:1 (January, 1970).

Fagerstrom, Dorothy. "Public Brutality to Police Officers." *Law and Order.* 16:5 (May, 1968), 23-26.
Survey examining deaths and assaults on police.

"Farwell to Bill Sikes." *Time.* 98 (September 6, 1971).

Federal Bureau of Investigation. *Law Enforcement Officers Killed—Summary 1973.* Washington: NCJRS (Microfiche), 1974.

Horstman, Preston L. "Assaults on Police Officers: How Safe Are You?" *Police Chief.* XL:12 (December, 1973), 44-53.

Keller, John. "Lock the Barn Door Now." *Law and Order.* 12:9 (September, 1964), 8-10.

"Killing Cops: The New Terror Tactics." *U.S. News and World Report* (August 31, 1970).

"Killing Cops: Signs of a Nationwide Plot." *U.S. News and World Report* (October 19, 1970).

"Kill the Cops! Teenagers Riot During Labor Day Weekend." *Newsweek* (September 21, 1964).

Los Angeles Police Department. *Attacks on Los Angeles Police Officers.* Los Angeles: LAPD, 1971.

McDermott, Thomas F. "It Makes a Difference Who is Killed." *Police.* 15:4 (March-April, 1971), 3-4.

McGhee, Gary L. and Raymond L. Walters. "The Martial Arts vs. The Police." *Law and Order* (February, 1976), 58-61.
Describes the use of Marshal Arts being used against Police. Also examination of police counter measures.

Okonkwo, C.O. "Assaulting a Police Officer in the Execution of his Duty." *Nigerian Law Journal.* 7 (1973), 1-12.

Paradis, Victor J. "Circumstances Surrounding Deaths of On Duty California Peace Officers." *Journal of California Law Enforcement* (October, 1968), 61-68.

"Police Killings in 1973—A Record Year." *FBI Law Enforcement Bulletin.* 43:4 (1974), 13-15.

"The Police Officer: Primary Target of the Urban Guerrilla." *FBI Law Enforcement Bulletin.* 41:2 (February, 1972), 21-23.

"Police Officers Killed in the Line of Duty." *FBI Law Enforcement Bulletin.* 35:4 (April, 1966), 25-28.

Police Weapon Center. *Annual Law Enforcement Casualty Summary.* Washington: IACP Annual.

Portland Police Bureau. *Analysis of Assaulted and Non-Assaulted Officers by Height, Weight, Tenure and Assignment.* Portland OR: Portland Police Bureau, (February, 1973).

Reichert, Irving F. "Shoot-Out in Kensington High Street: The British Response to a London Bank Robbery." *California State Bar Journal* (1973), 144-150.

Rodgers, P.G. "Pressurized Cans as Flame Throwers." *RCMP Gazette.* 31:1 (January-1969), 12-13.

Russell, Ken. "Seven Years—Seven Hundred U.S. Policemen Killed." *Police* (July, 1974), 16-17.

Shook, Howard C. et al. "Police Casualty Analysis." *Police Yearbook.* (Gaithersburg MD.: IACP, 1974), 53-61.

Stobart, R.M. "Assaults on Police." *Police (GB)*, (January, 1972), 22-23.

Stobart, R.M. "Serious Assaults on Police." *Police.* 45:2 (1972), 108-126.
Study of incidents in the Metropolitan Police, the Liverpool and Bootle Constabulary and the South Wales Constabulary. Factors examined were the hour, the day, the rank, women police, number of assailants, number of police officers, weapons and other factors.

Tamm, Quinn. "Editorial." *Police Chief.* XXXVII:5 (May, 1970).

Tamm, Quinn. "Report From Quinn Tamm." *Law Enforcement.* 25 (November-December, 1970).

"They Were Killed, Maimed, Injured to Preserve Law and Order." *Law Officer* 3 (Winter, 1971), 3-9.

Thomas, J.E. "Killed on Duty: An Analysis of Murders of English Prison Service Staff Since 1850" *Prison Service Journal* (July, 1972), 9-10.

Tullett, Tom. *No Answer From Fox Trot II* London: Michael Joseph's, 1967.
Describes the murder of three British Policemen.

U.S. Department of Justice. "Killing of Officers Is Problem Facing Police and Public." *FBI Law Enforcement Bulletin.* XXX (November, 1961), 21-22.

"War Against the Police—Officer Tell Their Stories." *U.S. News and World Report* (October 26, 1970).

"Where Even Police Are Not Safe: 48 Killed, 9,261 Hurt in U.S. Cities." *U.S. News and World Report* (October 9, 1961).

Wilson, Jerry V. "Deadly Force." *Police Chief* (December, 1972).

Wisconsin Department of Justice. *Wisconsin—Assaults on Law Enforcement Officers,* 11 (January, 1974). Washington: NCJRS, 1974.

DECOY OPERATIONS

ABT Associates, Inc. *New York City Anti-Crime Patrol—Exemplary Project Validation Report.* Washington: NCJRS (Microfiche), 1974.

Cromwell, Paul F. Jr. and Nancy Saunders. "Task Force: An Innovation in Crime Control." *Police Chief.* 39:10 (October, 1972), 50-52.
Activities of the San Antonio Police Department Crime Task Force.

Fox, Harry G. "Grannies with Badges." *Law and Order.* 18:8 (August, 1970), 82-84.
Activities of the stake-out unit in Philadelphia. Policemen dress like old women in high crime areas.

Harper, Edward S. and Bruce M.W. Shaw. "Crime Prevention with the Operative Deployment System." *Police.* 6:3 (January-February, 1962), 10-13.
Undercover, decoy operations of St Louis Police Department.

"Special Bronx Unit Strikes Back at Muggers of the Elderly." *Spring 3100* (January-February, 1976), 6-7.

Whited, Charles. *Decoy Man—The Extraordinary Adventures of an Undercover Cop.* Chicago: Playboy, 1973.

FUGITIVE SEARCHES

"Enlisting Public Assistance in Fugitive Hunts." *FBI Law Enforcement Bulletin.* 26:5 (May, 1957) 9-12.

Federal Bureau of Investigation. *Detection of Humans in Concealed Prepared Positions, Final Report.* Springfield, VA.: NTIS, 1963.

Luekenga, Raymond. "Teamwork Brings Quick Apprehension of Prison Escapees." *FBI Law Enforcement Bulletin* (April, 1953).

Rytten, Jack Edward. "The Delaware Valley Fugitive Search Plan." *Law and Order* (February, 1958).

"Search for a Killer: In Assistance to the FBI and the Bureau of Identification." *Police Reporter* (November, 1966).

"Techniques in Pursuit of the Fleeing Felon." *FBI Law Enforcement Bulletin* (July, 1957), 7-10.

GRAND THEFT AUTO

Achord, B. "Detection and Identification of Stolen Vehicles." *Texas Police Journal.* 22:9 (1974), 1-5, 19-21.

Fagerstrom, Dorothy. "Operation Corral." *Law and Order.* 14:6 (June, 1966), 12-15.
Method to apprehend stolen vehicles by observers in radio contact with a computer.

Glab, S.I. Jim. "Is That Car Running Hot?" *Law and Order.* 24:6 (June, 1976), 68-71.

Griswold, W.J. "How Cops Spot Stolen Cars." *Popular Science* (March, 1965).

Lewis, David Ed. *Motor Vehicle Identification Guide—1975.* N.Y.: Motor, 1975.

National Automobile Theft Bureau. *Passenger Vehicle Identification Manual, 1974.* MA: Palmer, 1974.
Pocket sized booklet contains locations and explanations of vehicle ID and engine numbers.

Northwestern University Traffic Institute. *Locating and Identifying Wanted Vehicles.* Evanston, IL.: Traffic Institute Northwestern University, 1972.

Rowe, Wayne F. "The Stolen Car and the Traffic Officer." *Police.* 4:4 (March-April, 1960), 68-73.

GUN FIGHTS

Ayoob, Massad F. "Vehicular Aspects of Police Gunfight Situations." *Law and Order.* 20:10 (October, 1972), 34-40, 43.

Chalkley, Mason T. "Why Fast Draw?" *Law and Order.* 12:4 (April, 1964), 34-36, 40.

Cherry, William A. Bill. "Counter Measures Against the Barricaded Gunner." *Law and Order.* 22:10 (October, 1974), 12-14.

Greenwood, Colin. "Confronting the Armed Criminal." *Police (GB).* (August, 1976), 18–19; (September-October, 1976), 26, 28–29.

Martin, T.F. and L.L. Priar. "Police Techniques in Gun Fights." *Journal of Criminal Law, Criminology and Police Science.* 46:3 (September-October, 1965), 396-403.

Masotti, L.M. and J.R. Corsi. *Shoot-Out in Cleveland, Black Militants and the Police.* Washington: GPO, 1969.
The 1968 gun battle between Cleveland police and black snipers, the rioting and arson which followed, and the methods which were used to restore order.

Oboz, Paul. "Hits and Misses: A Survey on Firearms Effectiveness by Police Officers." *Law and Order.* 16:4 (April, 1968), 32-34.
Survey involving police shootings—excellent.

Praiar, L.L. and T.F. Martin. "Police Techniques in Gun Fights." *Journal of Criminal Law, Criminology and Police Science.* 46:3 (September-October, 1955), 396-403.

Rychetnik, Joe. "Holdout for Your Life." *Law and Order.* 11:11 (November, 1963), 54-56, 58.

Williams, Mason. "The Heene Report—Part III: Fire Fights." *Law and Order.* 18:12 (December, 1970), 84, 86, 88, 98.
Criticism of 38 ammunition, examples of fire fights.

POLICING SPECIAL EVENTS

Bednarz, Edward. "Policing the New York World's Fair." *Law and Order.* 12:8 (August, 1964), 8-11.

Byrd, James W. "Cheyenne Frontier Days." *FBI Law Enforcement Bulletin.* 40:10 (October, 1971), 2-5, 30.

Dunkerley, L.S. "Causes and Control of Soccer Hooliganism." *Police College Magazine* (Spring, 1970), 34-38.

Gelber, Seymour. "Security of the 1968 Republican National Convention." *Police.* 13:5 (May-June, 1969), 72-76.

Hand, L. Clark. "Security at Scouting Jamborees." *FBI Law Enforcement Bulletin.* 39:3 (March, 1970), 12-17.

Johnston, Robert W. "Holiday Weekend Disturbances." *FBI Law Enforcement Bulletin.* 36:9 (September, 1967), 14-19.
Policing Fort Lauderdale FL over the Easter Holidays.

Kay, Barbara A., N. Jeane Hartman, and Clyde B. Vedder.

"The Bikini Patrol." *Police*. 7:6 (July-August, 1963), 31-34.
Fort Lauderdale FL Police Department beach patrol during holiday season.

McCaffery, H. "Sheriff Uses Two-Way Radio and Good Planning to Police Fair Ground Crowds." *Law and Order*. 21:1 (January, 1973), 40-41.

O'Brien, G.M. "Victoria Police Face Challenge of Olympic Games." *FBI Law Enforcement Bulletin* (November, 1956), 3-10.

Summers, Roger. "Planning and Policing a Rock Festival." *Law and Order*. 18:10 (October, 1970), 68-69.

Tyler, Roy A. "Rock. . .Festival or Fiasco?" *Police Chief* XL:3 (March, 1973), 34-37.

PROWLERS

Harsch, John. "Handling the Prowler Call." *Law and Order*. 14:12 (December, 1966), 26-29.

Lawder, Lee E. "Notes on the Prowler Call." *Law and Order*. 20:7 (July, 1972), 54-56, 58.

"The Prowler—A Community Menace." *FBI Law Enforcement Bulletin*. 33:4 (April, 1964), 3-6, 21-23.

PURSUIT DRIVING

Byrne, Edward. "Safety Consideration in Traffic Police Work." *Law and Order*. 22:6 (June, 1974), 44-46,
Discusses Code 3 runs and other factors.

Dougherty, E.E. "Pursuit Driving." *Alumni News, Southern Police Institute*. 3:2 (1959), 3, 4, 7-11.

Dougherty, Edward E. "Pursuit Driving." *Police*. 4:5 (May-June, 1960), 19-22; (July-August, 1960), 37-39.

Duncan, Bill. "Pursuing Safer Pursuits." *Law and Order*. 13:11 (November, 1965), 12-15, 53-54.

Elliott, J.F. and Thomas J. Sardino. "Assessment of the Risk of Using Emergency Driving Procedures for Responding Police Units." *Police*. 16:10 (June, 1972), 18-19.

Engel, Lyle K. *Handbook of High Performance Driving*. N.Y.: Dodd, 1975.

Fennessy, E.F. and T. Hamilton. *Study of the Problem of Hot Pursuit by the Police*. Springfield, VA.: NTIS, 1970.

Frazier, Dick. "High Speed Pursuit." *Police Chief* (May, 1961).

Jones, E.W. *Police Pursuit Driving*. Raleigh, N.C.: Department of Motor Vehicles, 1967.

"Manual for Police Pursuit Driving Tactics." *Police Chief* (August, 1959).

Roberts, J.T. Jr. "High Speed Chase—Calculated Risk or Reckless Driving?" *Military Police Journal*. 22:11 (1973), 6-7.

Runyan, Richard T. and F. Samuel Ostertag. "The One Man Patrol Car—High Speed Pursuit." *Police* 4:1 (September-October, 1959), 29-30.

Saul, John R. "High-Beam Wig Wag." *Law and Order*. 16:5 (June, 1968), 24-28.
Headlights wig wag when using siren and red lights.

Scheidt, E. "The Case for Police Pursuit." *RCMP Gazette*. 26:4 (April, 1964), 1-4.

Traffic Institute Northwestern University. *Pursuit in Traffic Law Enforcement*. Evanston, IL.: Traffic Institute, Northwestern University, 1967.

U.S. Internal Revenue Service. *Pursuit Driving: A Handbook for Law Enforcement Officers*. Washington: GPO, 1957.

Wahlem, Howard. "The Fleeing Motorist." *Law and Order*. 17:10 (October, 1969), 117-118.

RADIATION

Abbatt, John D. et al. *Protection Against Radiation: A Practical Handbook*. Springfield, IL: C.C. Thomas, 1961.

Curtis, Richard and Elizabeth Hogan. *Perils of the Peaceful Atom: The Myth of Safe Nuclear Power Plants*. Garden City, N.J.: Doubleday, 1969.

De Matteo, Alfred and Robert C. Ritter. "Rescue Involving Radiation Exposure." *Law and Order* (November, 1975), 22-25, 29.

Oberhofer, Martin. *Safe Handling of Radiation Sources*. N.Y.: International Publications Service, 1975.

Safe Handling of Plutonium. N.Y. Unipub., 1974.

Safe Handling of Radionnuclides. N.Y.: Unipub., 1973.

Safe Operation of Nuclear Power Plants. N.Y.: Unipub., 1969.

Safety Considerations in the use of Ports and Approaches by Nuclear Merchant Ships. N.Y.: Unipub., 1968.

Safe Use of Radioactive Tracers in Industrial Processes. N.Y.: Unipub., 1974.

"Some Suggestions Concerning Atomic Radiation Hazards." *FBI Law Enforcement Bulletin*. 27:7 (July, 1958), 16-19.

"Training Regarding Hazards of Nuclear Industry." *FBI Law Enforcement Bulletin*. 26:11 (November, 1957).

ROAD BLOCKS

Clark, Robert J., C.W. Young and T.R. Berrum. "Western Nevada Has Cooperative Roadblock Plan." *FBI Law Enforcement Bulletin* (March, 1958).

Hamilton, A.M. and R.R. Lester. "Planning and Aerial Survey Strength Roadblock System." *FBI Law Enforcement Bulletin* (November, 1957), 22-26.

Jansen. A.E. "San Diego's Road-Block System." *FBI Law Enforcement Bulletin* (April, 1949).

Kebach, Rolland. "Roadblock Net Traps Longtime Grain Thief." *FBI Law Enforcement Bulletin* (November, 1958).

Lester, Robert R. "Okalahoma Officers Use Double Circle Roadblock System." *FBI Law Enforcement Bulletin* (June, 1952).

"Michigan Lawmen Devise Effective Blockage System" *FBI Law Enforcement Bulletin* (April, 1961).

O'Leary Jeremiah. "A Portable Road Block." *FBI Law Enforcement Bulletin,* 38:11 (November 1969), 9-11, 20.

Schwartz, John *Police Roadblock Operations.* Springfield, IL.: C.C. Thomas, 1962.

Schwartz, John "Roadblock Plan Organized for Lehigh Valley." *FBI Law Enforcement Bulletin.* 26:7 (July, 1957), 3-6, 24.

"Spikeblock." *FBI Law Enforcement Bulletin.* 41:2 (February, 1972), 24-25.
Description of steel alloy spikes for use in roadblock operations.

ROBBERY

Hammond, Robert E. "A Letter From Torrance, CA." *Law and Order.* 16:1 (January, 1968), 64.

Kelley, Clarence M. "Response to Silent Bank Alarms." *FBI Law Enforcement Bulletin.* 28:8 (August, 1969), 3-6.

Robbery Events: A Risk Reduction Manual for Police. Gaithersburg, MD.: IACP, 1975.

Roche, Joseph. "The Police and the Silent Alarm." 18:1. *Law and Order* (January, 1970), 72-78.

SEARCH OF BUILDINGS

Fea, Allan. *Secret Chambers and Hiding Places.* rev. 3rd ed. Detroit, MI: Singing Tree, [1901] 1971.

Powis, David. "How to Succeed in Searching Premises." *Police Review* (August 15, 1975), 108-120, 131.

Squires, Granville. *Secret Hiding Places: The Origins Histories and Discriptions of English Secret Hiding Places Used by Priests, Cavaliers, Jacobites and Smugglers.* Detroit: Gale, [1934] 1971.

Walsh, Jude T. "Search of Buildings." *Law and Order.* 20:4 (April, 1972), 20-22, 24, 20:5; (May, 1972), 90, 92, 94, 20:6; (June, 1972), 30, 32, 34-37.

SEARCHING SUSPECTS

McIntyre, Donald M. and Nicholas D. Chabraja. "The Intensive Search of a Suspect's Body and Clothing." *Journal of Criminal Law, Criminology and Police Science.* 58:1 (March, 1967), 18-26.

Olson, O.D. *Techniques and Mechanics of Arrest.* Washington: NCJRS, 1968.
Arrest techniques are listed under categories of approach, commands, frisk, and search, automobile stops, routine shakedown, and known felony suspects.

Priar, L.L. and T.F. Martin. "Searching and Disarming Criminals." *Journal of Criminal Law, Criminology and Police Science.* 45:4 (November-December, 1954), 481-485.

SELF DEFENSE

Self Defense—General

Callum, Myles. *Body Building and Self Defense.* N.Y.: Barnes & Noble, 1963.

Fairbairn, W.E. *Get Tough.* Boulder, CO.: Paladin, 1974.

Goodbody, John. *The Japanese Fighting Arts.* Cranbury, N.J.: Barnes, 1969.

Gruzanski, Charles V. "Self Defense for Police Officers." *Police.* 7:3 (January-February, 1963), 6-9; 7:4 (March-April, 1963), 30-32; 7:5 (May-June, 1963); 7:6 (July-August, 1963), 53-57; 8:1 (September-October, 1963); 8:2 (November, December, 1963).

Gruzanski, Charles V. "Self Defense for Police Officers." *Police* 8:5 (May-June, 1964), 6-12.

Harris, Malcolm. *Effective Unarmed Combat.* N.Y.: Acro, 1974.

Harris, Malcolm. *Unarmed Close Combat: A Manual of Self-Defense.* London: Pelham, 1972.

Koga, R.K. and J.G. Nelson. *Koga Method: Police Weaponless Control and Defense Techniques.* Beverly Hills, CA.: Glencoe, 1967.
System of weaponless defense combining elements of the martial arts, practical physiology and elementary psychology applied to the law enforcement situation.

McEvoy, Harry K. "It's Fun to Throw a Knife." *Police.* 9:3 (January-February, 1965), 69-72.

McGhee, Gary L. and Raymond L. Walters. "The Issues Now: Martial Arts vs. Traditional Police Training." *Police Chief.* XLII:3 (March, 1976).

Makiyanna, Thomas H. *The Techniques of Aikido: A Science of Physical Self Defense.* Honolulu: Old Island Books, 1960.

Martone, John. *Handbook of Self Defense for Law Enforcement Officers: Law Enforcement Officers Manual of Offensive and Defensive Techniques.* N.Y.: Arco, 1974.

Pines, D.A. "Defensive Methods That Work." *Law and Order.* 18:6 (June, 1970), 34-35, 38-42.

Sylvain, George. *Defense and Control Tactics.* Englewood Cliffs, N.J.: Prentice Hall, 1971.

Tegner, Bruce. *Defense Tactics for Law Enforcement Vet, Weaponless Defense and Control.* Ventura, CA.: Thor, 1972.

Tegner, Bruce. *Savate: French Foot Fighting, Self Defense Sport.* Ventura, CA.: Thor, 1960.

Judo

Bartlett, Eric G. *Judo and Self Defense.* NY: Arco, 1971.

Dominy, Eric. *Judo: Basic Principles.* NY: Sterling, 1975.

Geesink, Anton. *Go-Kyo Principles of Judo.* N.Y.: Arco, 1968.

Harrison, Ernest J. *Judo: Art of Ju-Jitsu.* Hackensack, N.J.: Wehaman, 1960.

Kim, Daeshik. *Judo* Dubuque, IA.: William C. Brown, 1969.

Lebell, Gene and L.C. Coughran. *Handbook of Judo* N.Y.:Cornerstone, 1975.

Moynahan, James McCauslin. *Police Ju-Jitsu.* Springfield, IL.: C.C. Thomas, 1962.

Porter, Phillip S. *Judo from the Beginning.* San Francisco, CA.: Japan Publications, 1974.

Karate

Kim, Daeshik and Tom Leland. *Karate and Personal Defense.* Dubuque, IA.: William C. Brown, 1971.

Kozuki, Russell. *Competing in Karate: Free Style Fighting Techniques.* N.Y.: Sterling, 1974.

Moynahan, James M. Jr. "Karate—The Art of Self-Defense." *Police.* 7:2 (November-December, 1962), 36-38.

Stick Fighting and Night Sticks

American Federation of Police. *Police Nightstick—Use: Techniques—Handbook for Lawmen.* North Miami, FL.: American Federation of Police, n/d.

Barrett, D. "The Police Baton." *Law and Order.* 20:10 (October, 1972), 44-45, 58.

Clark, Erland Fenn. *Truncheons: Their Romance and Reality. . . With a Short Sketch of Bow Street Runners, Townsend and the Origin of the Police.* London: Herbert Jenkins, 1934.

Folley, Vern L. "The Prosecutor: The New Concept Police Baton." *Law and Order.* 20:9 (September, 1972), 46-50.

Hatsumi, M. and Q. Chambers. *Stick by Me.* Cedar Knolls, N.J.: Wehman.

Hatsumi, Massaki and Quentin Chambers. *Stick Fighting: Techniques of Self Defense.* Scranton, PA.: Kodansha, 1971.

Koga, R.K. and J.G. Nelson. *Koga Method: Police Baton Techniques.* Beverly Hills, CA: Glencoe, 1968.
Illustrated text, designed for individual study and class instruction, covers philosophy, principles and techniques of police baton use.

Lawder, Lee E. "The Unfriendly Persuaders." *Law and Order.* 16:5 (May, 1968), 42-45.

Moynahan, James. *The Yawara Stick and Police Baton.* Springfield, C.C. Thomas, 1963.

"Technique and Use of the Police Baton." *FBI Law Enforcement Bulletin.* 37:7 (July, 1963), 12-16; 22, 37:8 (August, 1968), 18-22; (September, 1968), 16-20.

Tegner, Bruce. *Stick Fighting for Self Defense: Yawara Police Club, Aikado, Kane, Quarter-Staff.* Hollywood, CA.: Thor, 1961.

Tegner, Bruce. *Stick Fighting: Self Defense.* Ventura, CA.: Thor, 1972.

Tegner, Bruce. *Stick Fighting Sport Forms: Stick Fencing, Sword Stick, Staff Sport Fighting.* Ventura, CA.: Thor, 1973.

Waller, Stanley. "How the Policeman Got His Truncheon." *Police Journal (GB).* 38 (November, 1965), 517-524.

Wrestling

Camaione, David N. and Kennith G. Tillman. *Wrestling Methods.* N.Y.: Ronald, 1968.

Clayton, Thompson. *Wrestling for Fun.* Cranbury, NJ: Barnes 1973.

Maertz, Richard C. *Wrestling Techniques: Take Downs,* Cranbury, NJ: Barnes 1970.

Sasahara, Shozo. *Fundamentals Of Scientific Wrestling.* Washington, DC: International Publications Service, 1968.

SNIPERS

"The Age of Snipers" *Police Chief.* XXXIV: 7 (July 1967).

Bailey, M. "Aerial Anti-Sniper Tactical Program" *National Sheriff.* 27:1 (1975), 10-28.
Author advocates the use of radio controlled model planes equipped with gas or explosive devices to combat the sniper lodged in high places.

Bailey, Melvin. "The Sniper—A Law Enforcement Problem." *FBI Law Enforcement Bulletin.* 38:10 (October, 1969), 7-9.

Counter Sniper Guide. Fort Benning, GA.: U.S. Army Markmanship Training Unit, n/d.

Fitzgibbon, Henry A. "Police Procedure Against the Sniper Menace. *Law Enforcement Executive.* 2 (November, 1967), 1-8.

Fitzgibbon, H.A. "Procedures for Handling the Sniper Menace." *Police Chief.* XXXIV:11 (November, 1967), 40-42.

Fitzgibbon, Henry A. "Sniper Menace." *Police Chief* (November, 1967).

Knopf, Terry Ann. "Sniping Incidents." *Law and Order.* 17:5 (May, 1969), 28-36.

Knopf, Terry Ann. "Sniping—A New Pattern of Violence?" *Transaction.* 6:9 (July-August, 1969).

Oregon Board on Police Standards and Training. *Sniper Suppression and Building Clearance.* Washington: NCJRS, 1968.

"Snipers on Ambush: Police Under the Gun." *Time* (September 14, 1970), 13-15.

Steele, David E. "A New Countersniper System." *Law and Order* (October, 1971).

Shore, C. *With British Snipers to the Reich.* Georgetown, S.C.: Small Arms Technical, 1948.

U.S. Department of the Army. *Counter Sniper Guide.* Washington: GPO.

Wolff, F.L. and J.F. Pearson. "What It Takes to Build and Fly a Radio-Controlled Model Copter." *Popular Mechanics* (April, 1973).

STAKE OUTS

Bell, Edward J. "Stake-Out Teams." *FBI Law Enforcement Bulletin* (April, 1967).

Flanigan, John C. "Silent Radio Communication During Stake Out." *FBI Law Enforcement Bulletin.* 38:12 (December, 1969), 11-13.

Gary, J.K. "Macon (GA) Holds Down Crime Rate." *Law and Order* (February, 1976), 56-57, 66.
Anti-crime techniques used by police—anti-armed robbery squad of crack marksmen.

STOPPING VEHICLES

Gardner, Harold J. "Traffic Contacts in Law Enforcement." *Police*. 2:6 (July-August, 1958), 46-48.

Langford, Beryl et al. *Stopping Vehicles and Occupant Control*. Springfield, IL.: C.C. Thomas, 1960.

Soccorsy, William A. "Protect Yourself on Traffic Stops." *Law and Order*. 22:6 (June, 1974), 52, 54-55.

Williams, Mason. "So You Want to Stop a Car." *Law and Order*. 23:9 (September, 1975), 64, 66, 68.
Describes the use of various weapons. Author suggests that barricade penetrating tear gas projectile is best—when available.

STRIKES

Clegg, H.A. "Strikes." *Political Quarterly*. 27 (July-September, 1956).

Dacus, Joseph A. *Annals of The Great Strikes in the United States*. N.Y.: Arno, [1877] 1969.

Dayal, I. et al. *Anatomy of a Strike: A Systems Application to Understanding Events in an Organization*. Mystic, CT: Verry, 1973.

Kidner, R. "Picketing in Perspective." *Criminal Law Review* (May, 1975), 256-270.
Outlines the law's weakness in the area of picketing in Great Britain; praises the police handling of Miners Strikes.

Trice, J.E. "Picketing in Perspective." *Criminal Law Review* (May, 1975), 271-282.
Police tactics at Miners Strikes in Great Britian.

Vessey, S.C. "Understanding Workers on Strike." *Police Journal*. 46:4 (1973), 321-337.

Walsh, Timothy J. "Law Enforcement Controls in Labor Disturbances." *Police*. 8:6 (July-August, 1964), 25-31.

CRIME PREVENTION

CRIME PREVENTION—GENERAL

Adams, Gary. "Crime Prevention: An Evolutionary Analysis." *Police Chief*. 38:12 (December, 1971), 52-57.

Aerospace Corporation. *Equipment Systems Improvement Program: Development System Analysis—Recording System for Illegal Telephone Calls*. Washington: NCJRS (Microfiche) 1973.

Akers, R.L. and E. Sagarin. *Crime Prevention and Social Control*. N.Y.: Praeger, 1974.

Ambassador College Press. *Crime Can Be Stopped . . . Here's How*. Pasadena, CA.: Ambassador College Press, 1970.

American Enterprise Institute for Public Policy Research. *Special Analysis: Combatting Crime*. Washington: American Enterprise Institute for Public Policy Research, 1967.

Army Engineer R & D Laboratory. *Railroad Sabotage Detection Research, 18 June 1964—15 October 1965, Final Technical Report*. Springfield, VA.: NTIS, 1965.
A method of detection by monitoring acoustic or vibration signals introduced into the rail.

Atlanta Regional Commission. *Atlanta: Police Department—Anti-Robbery/Burglary Semi-Annual Evaluation Report, March-September 1973*. Washington: NCJRS (Microfiche) 1973.
An appraisal based on robbery and burglary rates, on-site apprehension rates, and arrest clearance rates.

Australian Institute of Criminology. *Australian Crime Prevention and Treatment—Research Resources and Needs—An Exercise in Co-Ordination—Proceedings of the First Residential Conference of the Australian Institute of Criminology. Vol. 2*. Washington: NCJRS (Microfiche) 1974.

Australian Institute of Criminology. *Crime Prevention and the Community: Whose Responsibility?* Canberra: Australian Institute of Criminology, 1974.

Bagot, Michael H. "Civil Recourse in Fire Losses." *Journal of Criminal Law Criminology and Police Science*. 45:4 (November-December, 1954), 491–498.

Barry, John L. "What the Police Can Do About 'Saturday Night Specials.'" *Police Chief*. XL:5 (May, 1973), 22-23.

Bennett, Charles L. "Mobilizing Community Support." *Police*. 6:3 (January-February, 1962), 62-64.

Birkenstock, J.L. "The Police and the Job Corps." *Police Chief*. XXXIV:9 (September, 1967), 52-53.
Describes the crime prevention aspects of the Job Corps and other job Corps activities.

Blandow, W.F. "Protecting Private Homes, Business Premises Shops and Factories Against Burglaries and Theft." International Criminal Police Review. 30:286 (1975), 66-79 and 30:287 (1975), 98-107.

Blount, Winston M. "Let's Put the Smut Merchants Out of Business." FBI Law Enforcement Bulletin. 40:12 (December, 1971), 7-10.

Boggs, Sarah L. "Formal and Informal Crime Control: An Exploratory Study of Urban, Suburban and Rural Orientations." *Sociological Quarterly*. 12 (Summer 1971), 319-327.

Brenner, Rod. *National Neighborhood Watch Program.* Washington: NCJRS, 1974.

Cabe, J.G. *States and Criminal Justice.* Lexington, KY.: Council of State Governments, 1971.
Review of the crime problem and state crime control activities.

Campbell, James R. "Vacation House Check Utilizes Police Cadets." *Police Chief* (June, 1974).

Cannell, R. and R. Howell. *Catalog of Projects to Reduce Crime—Western LEAA Region 9.* Springfield, VA.: NTIS, 1971.

Carol, A. *City Crime.* N.Y.: Council on Municipal Performance, 1973.
A determination and discussion of the crime cause factors in the thirty largest metropolitan areas in the United States and suggestions to facilitate the reduction of crime.

Chaiken, J.M. and M.W. Lawless. *Impact of Police Activity on Subway Crime.* Santa Monica, CA.: Rand, 1974.

Church, Orin. "Crime Prevention: A Stitch in Time." *Police Chief* (March, 1970), 52-54.
Discusses the operation of the Security Unit of the Seattle Police Department which advises and encourages businesses regarding security devices such as locks alarms, and burglar proof glass.

Clark, Lewis J. "Crime Prevention Program Succeeds in a Small Town." *FBI Law Enforcement Bulletin.* 27:7 (July, 1958), 10-13.

Coates, Joseph. "Structural Factors Influencing the Future of Crime and Crime Control." *Police Chief.* XLI:11 (November, 1974), 43-46.

Combating Felonious Crimes by Citizen Involvement—Evaluation: Final Report. Springfield, VA.: NTIS, 1972.
Evaluation of a 1971 San Jose Project to reduce the incidence of burglary, robbery, auto theft, and rape and to involve citizens in preventing and reporting crimes.

Committee for Economic Development. *Reducing Crime and Assuring Justice.* N.Y.:: Committee for Economic Development, June, 1972.

Cook, J. Bernard. "Security Problems. Safety and Security: Bank Building." *Building Research* (March-April, 1967), 19-27.

Cudmore, S.C. et al. *Great Britian: Police Research and Planning Branch-Progress Report on the Study of Methods of Combating Crime.* Washington: NCJRS (Microfiche) 1965.

D'Alfonso, John. *The Crime Game.* San Diego, C.A.: Viewpoint, 1969.

Despard, A.W. "How You Can Prevent Employee Embezzlement." *Management Review* (February, 1970).

DiGennaro, Arthur F. "Crime Prevention—The Media and the Police." *Law and Order.* 21:3 (March, 1973), 50-53.

Dutoit, P.J. "The Role of the Police as a Crime Preventive Force." *Crime Punishment Corrections.* 3:2 (1974), 12-13.

Elliott, J.F. "Some Thoughts on the Control of Organized Gaming." *Police.* 13:3 (January-February, 1969), 35-40.

Etzioni, A. et al. *Community Crime Control—An Exploratory Study.* Washington: NCJRS (Microfiche) 1973.

Ferguson, R. Fred. "Policemen: Agents of Change—A Crime Prevention Report." *Crime Prevention Review.* 2:3 (April, 1975), 1-13.

Fillis, D.J. and D.D. Detton. "The Need for Crime Prevention in Contemporary Society: A Challenge to Law Enforcement." *Police Chief.* XXXVI:6 (June, 1969), 58-62.

Franke, D. *America's 50 Safest Cities.* New Rochelle, N.Y.: Arlington, 1974.
Profiles of the 50 communities of 50,000 or more with the lowest crime rates as determined by computer analysis of FBI statistics for 1970 and 1971.

Gluck, Sheldon S. and Eleanor T. Gluck, eds. *Preventing Crime: A Symposium.* Millwood, N.Y.: Kraus, 1936.

Gold, Robert. "Urban Violence and Contemporary Defensive Action." *Journal of the American Institute of Planners* (May, 1970).

Goldsmith, Jack. "Community Crime Prevention and the Elderly: A Segmental Approach." *Crime Prevention Review.* 2:4 (July, 1975), 18-19.

Gray, B.M. *Crime Specific Planning—An Overview.* Springfield, VA.: NTIS, 1973.
Techniques are given for planning programs aimed at reducing specific crimes rather than improving the criminal justice system.

Grenough, John L. "Crime Prevention: A New Approach—Environmental Psychology and Criminal Behavior." *Journal of Police Science and Administration.* 2:3 (September, 1974), 339-343.

Griffiths, H.P. "Crime Prevention—The New Approach." *Australian Police Journal* (January, 1958).

Haggard, John V. "No-Fund Budget—New Weapon for Old Crimes." *Law and Order.* 17:12 (December, 1969), 120-124.

"Help Stop Crime!" *Police Chief.* XL:6 (June, 1973), 24-25.
Florida's Police Public Education Program on Crime prevention.

Henke, S. *Alternative to Fear—A Citizen's Manual for Crime Prevention Through Neighborhood Involvement.* Walnut Creek, CA: Lex Cal, Tex, 1975.
Citizen's Handbook which explans the concepts which provide the framework and context for community crime prevention programs and outlines the steps for starting such programs.

Higgins, Louis Lundell and Elwin H. Fitzpatrick. *Criminology and Crime Prevention.* N.Y.: Bruce, 1958.

Horwitz, Herbert R. "British Crime Prevention." *American Scholar.* 40 (Autumn, 1971), 677-685.

Kaufman, Ulrich. *How to Avoid Burglary, Housebreaking and Other Crimes.* N.Y.: Crown, 1967.

Kelling, G.L. et al. *The Kansas City Preventive Patrol Experiment: A Technical Report.* Washington: Police Foundation, 1974.

Kirkpatrick, R. and R.C. Stevens. *Comprehensive Research Program in Crime Prevention.* Springfield, V.A.: NTIS, 1969.
Determination of major crime problems in metropolitan

Washington and definition of research projects that address major elements of preventive activity.

Klein, Gordon D. "A Score of Progress." *FBI Law Enforcement Bulletin*. 35:11 (November, 1966), 3-7.
Activities of crime prevention week.

Komara, Donald F. "Concerned Citizen's Action Hotline." *Police Chief*. XLI:6 (June, 1974), 18-19.

Leonard, V.A. *Police Crime Prevention*. Springfield, IL: C.C. Thomas, 1972.

Lewin, Stephen ed. *Crime and Its Prevention*. N.Y.: Wilson, 1968.

Liu, Daniel S.C. "Crime Prevention." *Police*. 2:5 (May-June, 1958), 15-19.

Louviere, V. "How to Counter the Counterfeiter." *Nations Business* (May, 1973).

Lux, Henry E. "One Crime Free Day." *Police Chief*. XXXVII:5 (May, 1970).

Lyle, Sydney. "Exploring Crime Prevention." *Law and Order*. 23:3 (March, 1975), 60-62.

McLean, Robert Joe. *Education for Crime Prevention and Control*. Springfield, IL: C.C. Thomas, 1975.

Mandell, M. *Being Safe*. NY: Saturday Review Press, 1972.
Description of the many and varied deterrents to crimes against propertv.

Marshall, Peter. "England's Police Crime Prevention Service." *Security World* (October, 1971), 48-52.

Maryland University, Institute of Criminal Justice and Criminology. *Research on Street Crime Control*. Washington: NCJRS, 1972.

Mayall, K.L. *California—Office of Criminal Justice Planning: Region M—Project Number 1686—Executive Summary*. Washington D.C.: NCJRS (Microfiche) 1974.
Evaluation of the designs, techniques, and effectiveness of anti-crime programs in 3 jurisdictions, together with a recommended evaluation strategy.

Miller, Andrew J. "Arsenal Against Crime." *Law and Order*. 14:10 (October, 1966), 38-43, 94.
The role of the Salvation Army in jails and corrections.

Miller, Herbert F. "Reversing the Crime Trend in Washington." *Police Chief*. XXXVIII:7 (July, 1971), 48-50.

Murphy, Michael J. "Law Enforcement and 'Operation Security.'" *Law and Order*. 12:10 (October, 1964), 70, 72, 74.

National Advisory Commission on Criminal Justice Standards and Goals. *Call for Citizen Action—Crime Prevention and the Citizen*. Washington: NCJRS 1974.
A general overview, of the need for citizen involvement in the prevention of crime, and an appendix listing several already existing citizen action programs.

National Advisory Commission on Criminal Justice Standards and Goals. *Community Crime Prevention—Report of the National Advisory Commission on Criminal Justice Standards and Goals*. Washington: GPO, 1973.
Community support and involvement in the reduction of criminal opportunity, the delivery of public services, and government integrity.

National Advisory Commission on Criminal Justice Standards and Goals. *National Strategy to Reduce Crime*. Washington: GPO, 1973.

National Council on Crime and Delinquency. *Citizen Action to Control Crime and Delinquency—Fifty Projects, Rev. Ed.* Hackensack, NJ: National Council on Crime and Delinquency, 1969.
This catalogue lists citizen action projects for crime prevention, police, courts, and corrections, which may be undertaken in response to specific crime-related or crime-causing problems.

National Institute of Law Enforcement and Criminal Justice. *Planning Guidelines and Programs to Reduce Crime*. Springfield, VA: NTIS, 1972.
Planning guidelines and programs to reduce stranger-to-stranger crime and burglary.

"National Neighborhood Watch Program." *FBI Law Enforcement Bulletin*. 43:1 (January, 1974).

National Retired Teachers Association. *American Association of Retired Teachers Association—Crime Prevention Program*. Washington: NCJRS (Microfiche) n/d.
Instruction for private groups on how to present a crime prevention program.

Palmer, S. *Prevention of Crime*. N.Y.: Behavioral Publications, 1973.
Overview of the nature and extent of crime in the United States, its social causes and proposed means of deterrence.

Parker, J.A. and A.C. Brownfeld. *What the Negro Can Do About Crime*. New Rochell N.Y.: Arlington, 1974.

"Paroles are Painful." *Law and Order*. 15:2 (February, 1967), 76-77.

Patridge W.R. *Albuquerque Bernalillo County—LEAA Pilot Cities Program—First Phase, Final Report*. Springfield, VA: NTIS, 1972.
Goals, Methods, Findings and Conclusions of the initial phase of five year criminal justice research project to improve the system for reducing crime and delinquency.

Peterson, Bill. "Crime Prevention at the Primary Level." *Journal of California Law Enforcement* (January, 1970), 143-148.

Pettit, Ronald E. "Public Relations—Crime Prevention Program." *Law and Order*. 16:10 (October, 1968), 96-103.

"Prevention Is the Only Way to Go." *Police Chief*. XXXLV:6 (June, 1967), 38-43.

"Profiles in Crime." *FBI Law Enforcement Bulletin*. 35:7 (July, 1966), 2-5.
The FBI's ten most wanted fugitive program.

Protect Your Business Against Small Crime: A Guide for the Small Businessman. N.Y.: Drake, 1974.

Pursuit, Dan G. et al. *Police Programs for Preventing Crime and Delinquency*. Springfield, IL.: C.C. Thomas, 1972.

Quinney, Richard. *Critique of Legal Order: Crime Control in Capitalist Society*. Boston: Little Brown, 1973.

Rardin, Ronald L. and Paul Gray. "Analysis of Crime Control Strategies." *Journal of Criminal Justice* (1973), 339-346.

Reddin, Thomas. "Police Weapons for the Space Age." *Police Chief.* XXXIII:11 (November, 1966), 10-17.

Rogers, Keith M. and W.G. Whitham. *Detection and Prevention of Business Losses.* N.Y.: Arco, 1962.

Rosberg, Robert. "Anti-Crime Clinics." *Police Chief.* XLII:3 (March, 1976), 56-57.

Rothery, Frank. "The Bank Protection Act of 1968 and the Law Enforcement." *Law and Order.* 17:10 (October, 1969), 84-97.

Sagalyn, Arnold. "The Problem of Crime." *Police Chief.* XXXIII:9 (September, 1966), 26-28.
Crime prevention by use of science, technology and architecture.

Seares, R.S. "Operation House Watch." *Police.* 1:6 (July-August, 1957), 54-56.

"Security Glass Has Role in Crime Deterrence." *Police.* 14:3 (January-February, 1970), 79-81.

"Show and Tell." *FBI Law Enforcement Bulletin.* 35:11 (November, 1966), 8-11.
Winston-Salem Police Department mobile crime prevention activities including a mobile crime prevention exhibit in a 10 x 50′ trailer.

Silvestri, Samuel. "Public Relations Equates with Public Opinion." *Police Chief.* XLII:3 (March, 1976), 26-28.

Sisney, Vernon V. "What to Do if You Are Kidnapped." *Police.* 6:1 (September-October, 1961).

Smith, R. Dean. "U.N. Non-Governmental Organizations Alliance for Social Defense." *Police Chief.* XLII:5 (May, 1975), 20-24.
U.N. crime prevention organizations and their activities.

Snibbe, Richard H. "A Concept for Police in Crime Prevention." *Police.* 13:6 (July-August, 1969), 29-32.

Sperling, Robert E. "Quick Apprehension at Small Cost." *Law and Order.* 13:10 (October, 1965), 82-83.
Hotline to Police Department from businesses to prevent forgeries, robberies etc.

Strategies for Combatting the Criminal Receiver of Stolen Goods—An Anti-Fencing Manual for Law Enforcement Agencies. Washington: GPO, 1976.

Tokyo: One City Where Crime Doesn't Pay. Philadelphia: Citizens Crime Commission of Philadelphia, 1975.

Trojanowicz, R.C., J.M. Trojanowicz and F.M. Moss. *Community Based Crime Prevention.* Pacific Palisades, CA.: Goodyear, 1975.
Social parameters of crime prevention, a description of major realities in which crime prevention is forced to operate, and several alternatives to the current direction of criminal justice.

United Nations. *Crime Prevention and Control—Note by the Secretary General (United Nations).* Washington: NCJRS (Microfiche) 1972.
Examines the problem of crime, strategies for crime prevention; priority areas for action; and the role of the United Nations.

United States Congress. House Select Committee on Crime. *Street Crime: Reduction Through Positive Criminal Justice Responses, Report.* Washington: GPO 1973.
Police approaches, juvenile and adult correctional programs, and judicial reform as implemented in various cities.

U.S. Department of Health Education and Welfare. National Institute of Mental Health. *Juniper Gardens Project: A Study in Community Crime Control.* Washington: NCJRS (Microfiche) 1974.

U.S. Department of Housing and Urban Development. *Federal Crime Insurance Program—Questions and Answers.* Washington: NCJRS (Microfiche) 1973.

U.S. Law Enforcement Assistance Administration. *Planning Guidelines and Programs to Reduce Crime.* Washington: U.S. Department of Justice, 1972.

Veza, Daniel T. "Indianapolis Crime Alert." *FBI Law Enforcement Bulletin.* 36:12 (December, 1967), 8-11.

"Wall Street's Own Watchdogs." *Business Week* (July 29, 1967).

Weller, Bruce C. "The Police Role in Prevention." *Police Chief.* 33:7 (July, 1966), 51-54.

"What the Police Can—And Cannot—Do About Crime." *Time* (July 13, 1970).

Williams, Robert T. "On Crime Prevention: After the Fact—Before the Fact." *Police Chief.* XL:6 (June, 1973), 20-22, 77.

Woods, Arthur. *Crime Prevention.* N.Y.: AMS, [1918] 1975.

ALARM SYSTEMS

Asper, Ellis. "An Alarming Problem." *Law and Order.* 22:6 (June, 1974), 70-75.

"Automotive Burglar Alarms." *Locksmith Ledger.* 31 (October, 1970), 19-20.

Brann, D.R. *How to Install Protective Alarm Devices.* N.Y.: Directions Simplified, 1972.

Caffrey, J.J. "Protection by Electronic Watchmen." *Law and Order.* 11:12 (December, 1963), 8-9, 11.

Chleboun, T.P. and K.M. Duvall. *Evaluation of Small Business and Residential Alarm Systems.* 2 Vols. Springfield, VA.: NTIS, 1972.

Cole, R. *Protect Your Property—The Application of Burglar Alarm Hardware.* Springfield, IL.: C.C. Thomas, 1971.
Description and evaluation of various available burglar alarm systems.

Cunningham, John E. *Security Electronics.* Indianapolis, IN.: H.W. Sams, 1970.

Cedar Rapids Police Department. *Evaluation of the Effect of a Large Scale Burglar Alarm System.* Springfield, VA.: NTIS, 1970.

Cedar Rapids Police Department. *Installation, Test and Evaluation of a Large Scale Burglar Alarm System for a Municipal Police Department, Interim Report.* Springfield, VA.: NTIS, 1972.

Cedar Rapids Police Department. *Installation, Test and Evaluation of a Large Scale Burglar Alarm System for a Municipal Police Department—Report of the Second Year of Operation.* Springfield, VA.: NTIS, 1972.

Forbat, J.E. "Anti-intruder Protection of Office Buildings

and Property Using Inertia Sensors." *Security Gazette.* 17:1 (1975).

Gray, Donald A. "Burglar Alarms—Pros and Cons." *Law and Order.* 22:2 (February, 1974), 62, 64-66.

Hudson, Phillip R. "In Madeira, Ohio: Patrol Car Monitored Alarm System." *Police Chief.* XLII:10 (October, 1975).

Lenay, T.W. "Alarm Sensors and Systems." *Security World.* 8 (March, 1971), 28-30, 32; (April, 1971), 29-34.

McCain, E.G. "Streamlined Alarm Panel Board." *Law and Order.* 17:5 (May, 1969).

Maddock, G.D.S. *Methods of Intruder Alarm Control—A Study of the Methods Used to Control the Number of False Alarm Calls Reaching the Police in Germany, Denmark and Sweden.* Washington: NCJRS (Microfiche) 1974.

North, M.R. "Personal Attack Alarms: How Effective are they as a Protection Against Armed Assaults?" *Security Gazette.* 17:9 (1975), 306-307.

O'Neill, J.F. "Intercepting Crime: Tac II—The Electronic Stakeout." *FBI Law Enforcement Bulletin.* 43:6 (1974), 2-6.
Wireless alarm system with receiver at Police Station.

Reiss, M.H. "Selecting Intrusion Devices for Your School—Some Basic Understanding of Audio, Microwave, and Ultrasonic Intrusion Detection Systems." *Security World.* 11:2 (1974), 24-25, 57.

"Report: Alarm Systems." *Police Chief.* XXXIX:11 (November, 1972), 52-53.

Shaw, William. "The Leased Telephone Line and Radio as Applied to Alarm Systems." *Law and Order.* 12:4 (April, 1964), 26-28, 63.

Shaw, William. "A Mini-Computer Based Alarm System for Small Towns." *Law and Order* 21:8 (August, 1973), 72-76.

Shaw, William. "A Wrist Alarm for Every Citizen." *Law and Order.* 23:8 (August, 1975), 8-13.

University of Kentucky. *International Electronic Crime Countermeasures Conference, 1st—Proceedings, July 18-20, 1973, Edinburgh Scotland.* Springfield, VA.: NTIS, 1973.

Weber, T.L. *Alarm Systems and Theft Prevention.* Los Angeles: Security World, 1973.

Weber, Thad L. *Think Like a Thief: Alarm Systems ana Theft Prevention.* Los Angeles: Security World, 1973.

Wilkie, Francis E. "Police Monitoring of Hold-Up and Burglary Alarms." *Police Chief* (April, 1974), 65-66, 82.

ARCHITECTURAL AND NEIGHBORHOOD DESIGN

Angel, Shlomo. *Discouraging Crime Through City Planning.* Berkeley: Institute of Urban and Regional Development, University of California, February, 1968.

Fairley, W. and M. Liechenstein. *Improving Public Safety in Urban Apartment Dwellings-Security Concepts and Experimental Design for New York City Housing Authority Buildings.* N.Y.: Rand, 1971.

Fabrri, J. "Crime Prevention—Before or After the Fact." *FBI Law Enforcement Bulletin.* 42:1 (1973), 20-24.
Advocates police involvement in urban planning and new construction.

H.U.D. Residential Security. Washington: GPO, 1973.
Collection of articles covering areas such as increased security through architectural design, security planning methodology and the Federal Crime Insurance program.

Healy, R.J. *Design for Security.* N.Y.: Wiley, 1968.
Definition of the nonbusiness losses which face industrial or organizations, with recommendations for deterrence through physical layout and security devices.

Jeffrey, C. Ray. *Crime Prevention Through Environmental Design.* Beverly Hills, CA.: Sage, 1971.

Luedtke, G. and E. Lystad. *Crime and the Physical City—A Pilot Study Prepared for the NILECJ.* Springfield, VA.: NTIS, n/d.
This study is based on premise that physical design of urban neighborhoods may be used to reduce crime.

Mann, Lawrence and George Hagevik. "The 'New' Environmentalism: Behaviorism and Design." *Journal of the American Institute of Planners* (September, 1971).

Newman, Oscar. *Architectural Design for Crime Prevention.* Washington: NCJRS, 1973.

Newman, Oscar. *Defensible Space: Crime Prevention Through Urban Design.* N.Y.: Macmillan, 1972.

Newman, Oscar and Berry Hersh. *Immediate Measures for Improving Security in Existing Residential Areas.* N.Y.: Center for Residential Security Designs, 1972.

Panhandle Regional Planning Commission. *Study of Building Codes as Related to Crime Prevention.* Springfield, VA.: NTIS, 1972.
Analysis of crime trends nationwide and in Texas, study of prior research on construction standards and crime, and conclusions based on this analysis.

Urban Design, Security and Crime: Proceedings of a National Institute of Law Enforcement and Criminal Justice Law Enforcement Assistance Administration Seminar on April 12 and 13, 1972. Washington: NCJRS, 1973.
Security measures for preventing burglary and stranger-to-stranger crimes that occur in and around residences and businesses in the urban community.

AUTO THEFT PREVENTION

"Auto Theft Program." *FBI Law Enforcement Bulletin* (September, 1975).

Beasley, R. "You and the Car Thief." *Locksmith Ledger.* 34:3 (1973), 47-49.
Precautionary measures for car owners and brief description of how thieves and joy riders operate.

Caggiano, A.C. "Build a Pair of Simple Alarms." *Popular Mechanics.* (January, 1973).

California Highway Patrol. *California—Highway Patrol—Theft Control Project: Program Guidelines.* Washington: NCJRS (Microfiche) 1974.

Dielsi, F.J. "Vehicle Alarm System." *Popular Electronics* (June, 1972).

Feraud, H. "Suggested Measures for the Prevention of Motor Vehicle Theft." *International Criminal Police Review* (April, 1964).

Frye, J.T. "Electronics and Car Thievery." *Popular Electronics* (October, 1972).

Gannon, R. "Protect Your Car from the Steal—and—Strippers." *Popular Science* (September, 1966).

Green, S. "To Stop a Thief." *Hot Rod* (May, 1972).

Jessup, Frank A. "The Auto Theft Problem and the State Police." *FBI Law Enforcement Bulletin* (January, 1956).

Johnston, D. "Don't Help a Good Boy Go Bad." *N.Y. Times Magazine* (October 6, 1968).

Kearney, P.W. "To Keep You Car From Being Stolen." *Readers Digest* (November, 1965).

"Law Enforcement's Answer to the Auto Theft Problem." *FBI Law Enforcement Bulletin* (July, 1953).

McMullen, T. "Stop, Thief!" *Hot Rod* (March, 1965).

McCluggage, D. "How to Make your Car Thief—Resistant." *American Home* (October, 1972).

Reddin, Thomas. "Operation Grass Roots." *Police Chief.* XXV:6 (June, 1968), 34-40.

Ribicoff, A. "Car Stealing Made Simple." *Popular Mechanics* (July, 1966).

Scott, Ralph D. "Keep the Pressure on Car Thieves." *FBI Law Enforcement Bulletin.* 39:9 (September, 1970), 16-20, 31.

Schmieg, Anthony L. "Auto Theft—Every Minute." *Police Chief.* XXXIII:11 (November, 1966), 26-32.

Scott, Ralph D. "Keep the Pressure on Car Thieves." *FBI Law Enforcement Bulletin* (September, 1970).

Seifert, Alan L. "Should Young Auto Thieves Go Unprosecuted." *Police Chief* (April, 1974).

Schlueter, F.W. "17 Ways to Thiefproof Your Car." *Popular Mechanics* (July, 1972).

Sherman, William F. "Engineering Work Directed to Auto Theft Prevention." *FBI Law Enforcement Bulletin* (July, 1956).

Turner, R.A. "Automobile Insurance and Law Enforcement." *Texas Police Journal.* 21:12 (1974), 1-4, 21.
Twenty insurance companies have formed a special unit known as the Anti-Car Theft Committee to promote anti-car theft.

Terrill, William H. "Program Against Car Thefts Call for Cooperation." *FBI Law Enforcement Bulletin.* 28:3 (March, 1959), 21-23.

VanRaalte, Ronald C. "Checking Auto Thefts." *Law and Order* (February, 1974).

Wharton, D. "New Gadgets to Stop Auto Theft." *Readers Digest* (February, 1968).

Williams, Thomas A. "Auto Theft: The Problem and the Challenge." *FBI Law Enforcement Bulletin.* 37:12 (December, 1968), 15-17.

BICYCLE THEFT PREVENTION

Carsten, Victor. "The Case for Bicycle Licensing." *Law and Order.* 21:12 (December, 1973), 20-22, 24.

Kirk, R. "Bicycle Security." *Locksmith Ledger.* 34:3 (1973), 77, 79-80.

BURGLARY PREVENTION

American Justice Institute. *Burglary in San Jose—Technical Report: February 1972.* Springfield, VA.: NTIS, 1972.

Brighton, Arthur F. "Reducing Burglary Through Management by Objective." *Law and Order.* 24:6 (June, 1976), 42-55.

"Burglary Prevention and the Police." *Security Gazette.* 17:6 (1975), 213-214.

Cousins, Margaret. "How to Foil the Burglar." *House Beautiful* (February, 1969), 72-73.
Recommendations for the householder.

Crooks, R.A. and W.K. Ratcliff. *Oceanside CA.: Crime Specific Burglary—Final Report and Evaluation, 1st Year.* Washington: NCJRS (Microfiche) 1974.

Davis, John Richelieu. "Burglary Prevention." *Police.* 5:4 (March-April, 1961), 64-68.

Dragnich, Alix. "Operation Watch Dog." *Law and Order.* 22:11 (November, 1974), 70, 72, 74.
Burglary prevention program in Greenwich Connecticut.

Efraimsson, O. "Burglary Protection in Sweden: Police and Insurance Insistence is Bringing Improved Security Provision." *Security Gazette.* 14:1 (1972), 14-15.

Galub, Jack. "Burglars Will Get You If You Don't Watch Out." *American Home* (September, 1970).

Holcomb, Richard L. *Protection Against Burglary.* Iowa City: University of Iowa, 1953.

Hanna, Jim. "Crime-Specific Burglary Handbook." *Journal of California Law Enforcement.* 9:1 (July, 1974), 24–30.

Hendren, W.A. *King County (WA)—Department of Public Safety: Residential Burglary Prevention Program—Final Report.* Washington: NCJRS (Microfiche) 1973.

"How to Foil the Industrial Burglar." *Supervisory Management.* 14 (October, 1969), 39-41.

Joyce, R.P. *Developing and Implementing a Burglary Prevention Program—Summary Report.* Washington: NCJRS (Microfiche) 1973.

Kearns, John G. "Oakland: 'Inviting' Burglars Is Illegal." *Security World* (December, 1966).

McDonald, T.D. *Fargo (ND)—Police Department: Crime Prevention Unit—An Evaluation of 'Operation*

Identification.' Washington: NCJRS (Microfiche) 1974.

Moolman, Val. *Practical Ways to Prevent Burglary and Illegal Entry.* N.Y.: Cornerstone Library, 1970.

Murphy, Robert B. and Stanley Horton. "Focus on Burglary: A Management Approach to Prevention of Crimes." *Police Chief.* XLII:11 (November, 1975), 30-34.

Riley, James W. "Stockton's Program is Working." *Journal of California Law Enforcement* (January, 1975), 93-95.

Rockwell, Joanne W. "Crime Specific. . .An Answer." *Police Chief.* XXXIX:9 (September, 1972), 38-43.

Ross, John E. "In Kalamazoo, Michigan: A New Wrinkle in Crime Prevention." *Police Chief.* XLII:9 (September, 1975), 46-47.
Burglary prevention program utilizing a large semi-trailer.

Security Planning Corp. *Residential Security.* Washington: GPO, 1973.
Assessment of security measures, focusing on deterrents to burglary, discussing cost effectiveness, physical security and design, group action and public policy.

"Salt Lake City Anti-Burglary Campaign." *Police Chief.* XLI:5 (May, 1974), 57-58.

Vanacour, Martin. "Operation Security." *Police Chief.* XLII:13 (March, 1976), 32-34.

Worsnop, Richard L. "Burglary Prevention." *Editorial Research Reports* (January 17, 1968), 43-60.
Presents an overall discussion of burglary in addition to recommending precautionary measures.

White, Thomas W. et al. *Police Burglary Prevention Programs.* Washington: NCJRS, 1975.

CHILD MOLESTATION PREVENTION

Arnstein, Helen S. "What to Tell Your Child About Sex Molesters and Other Community Dangers." *Family Circle.* 62 (January, 1963).

Boecherer, Carl A. "Accent on Protecting Children." *Law and Order.* 13:3 (March, 1965), 22-23.
Programs warning against child molesters.

Booth, Willis D. Jr. "Pat and Gabby Help Protect Florida Youth." *Law and Order.* 13:7 (July, 1965), 36-41.

"Color for Safety." *FBI Law Enforcement Bulletin.* 39:5 (May, 1970).

Engel, Karl. "Working Together." *Law and Order.* 16:5 (May, 1968), 91-93.

Jalaty, Al. "Block Parent Program." *Police Chief.* XXXIV:11 (November, 1967), 44-45.

CITIZEN CRIME COMMISSIONS

Atlanta Commission on Crime and Juvenile Delinquency. *Opportunity for Urban Excellence—Report of the Atlanta Commission on Crime and Juvenile Delinquency.* Washington: NCJRS (Microfiche) 1966.

Chamber of Commerce of United States. *Marshaling Citizen Power Against Crime.* Washington: Chamber of Commerce, 1970.

Cleveland, Herbert H. "Drug Abuse Councils." *FBI Law Enforcement Bulletin* (November, 1970), 9-12, 29.

Law Enforcement Assistance Administration. *Role of State Organized Crime Prevention Councils.* Springfield, VA.: NTIS, n/d.
Relationship of the council concept to the Safe Streets Act and establishment of guidelines for the organization and functions of such councils.

National Association of Attorneys General. *Organized Crime Prevention Councils.* Washington: NCJRS (Microfiche) 1973.

Peck, Leo G. "Developing a Precinct or District Committee." *Police Chief.* 32:3 (March, 1965), 24-27.

Peterson, Virgil W. "How to Form a Citizen's Crime Commission." *Journal of Criminal Law, Criminology and Police Science.* 46:4 (November-December, 1955), 485-499.

Schilder, L. Clark. "The Organization and Functions of Citizens Crime Commissions." *Police.* 3:6 (July-August, 1959), 71-73.

Zumbrun, Alvin J.T. "Problems and Rewards in Organizing and Directing a Citizen Crime Committee." *Police.* 6:5 (May-June, 1962), 39-41.

COMMUNITY PATROL

Alex, W.N. *Bromley Heath (MA) Community Patrol—1st Year End Report.* Washington: NCJRS (Microfiche) n/d.

Calame, Byron E. "Community Patrol." *Wall Street Journal* (August 2, 1967).

Knoph, Terry Ann. *Youth Patrols: An Experiment in Community Participation.* Waltham, MA.: Lenberg Center for the Study of Violence, Brandeis University, 1969.
Analysis of programs involving young people who work in their own communities to help maintain security.

Marx, G.T. and D. Archer. *Community Police Patrols—An Exploratory Inquiry.* Springfield, VA.: NTIS, 1972.
Empirical research and collection of data on citizen mobilization around issues of crime, order and law enforcement.

New York Police Department. *The Civilian Patrol Program.* N.Y.: NYPD, June, 1972 (Mimeo).

FORGERY PREVENTION

Boze, Carroll W. "Retail Red Alert." *FBI Law Enforcement Bulletin.* 40:10 (October, 1971), 6-8, 30.

"How to Prevent Check Forgeries." *Good Housekeeping* (November, 1971).

Kolodny, L. *Outwitting Bad Check-Passers.* Washington: NCJRS (Microfiche) 1969.

McDonald, John R. Jr. "The Little Black Box." *Police Chief.* 39:10 (October, 1972).
Forgery prevention by the use of fingerprint identification on checks. Device used is called the Indicator.

"Thumbs Down: Thumbprint Deterrent to Bad Check Passers." *Time* (July 24, 1972).

Train, R. "Beating The Forger." *Security Gazette.* 15:10 (1973), 367-368.
Describes police and airline security efforts to combat ticket forgeries and bank note counterfeiting in Great Britian.

HIJACKING PREVENTION

Keller, E. John. "Truck Hijacking." *Law and Order.* 22:4 (April, 1974), 48-49.

U.S. Department of Transportation. *Truck Top Markings for Visual Identification.* Washington: GPO, 1973.
Project to determine the most useful sizes, shapes, location and colors for markings which facilitate recovery of hijacked trucks.

"Truckers' Alert." *Police Chief.* XXXIV:11 (November, 1967).

JUVENILE DELINQUENCY PREVENTION

Adams, Gary B. "The Juvenile Officer and Prevention." *Police Chief.* XL:2 (February, 1973), 54-57.

Broad, Thomas. "Two-Part Juvenile Program." *Law and Order.* 14:12 (December, 1966).

Brown, Roscoe C. and Dan W. Dodson. "The Effectiveness of a Boy's Club in Reducing Juvenile Delinquency." Annals. 322 (1959).

Butler, J.R. *Albuquerque Bernalillo County Youth—Related Property Crime Reduction Program: Evaluation Design.* Springfield, VA.: NTIS, 1973.

Cape, William H. "Combatting Juvenile Delinquency." *Police.* 13:3 (January-February, 1969), 60-64.

Carter, G.W. *Analysis of Student Achievement Through a Volunteer Program—An Evaluation Research Report of the Visa Project.* Washington: NCJRS (Microfiche) 1974.

Chiavamonte, Robert M. "War on Pranksters." *Law and Order.* 14:3 (March, 1966).
Ohio State Highway Patrol Program to reduce the throwing of objects from highway overheads to vehicles on highway.

"Final Report of the Ad Hoc Committee on the Prevention and Management of Conflict and Crime in the Schools." *Crime Prevention Review.* 2:4 (July, 1975), 38-43.

Goode, John E. "A Juvenile Delinquency Demonstration Project." *Law and Order. 19:5* (May, 1971), 92-93.
Jacksonville FL. Police Department has hired college graduates to act as Police Youth Specialists. These specialists are assigned to local schools to assist with juvenile problems.

Kreins, Edward S. "A Community Resource Program for Youth." *Police Chief.* XXXIX:3 (March, 1972), 36-41.

Kimble, Joseph P. "Four-Letter Words for Teen-agers." *Police.* 10:2 (November-December, 1965), 88-90.

Kolstad, C.K. "Microwaves Stop School Vandals." *Security World.* 11:2 (1974), 20-21, 54.

Leonard, R.F. *Anthology on Procedural Due Process in School Disciplinary Cases.* Chicago: National District Attorneys Association, 1974.
Four articles on the subject of explusion, suspension, and student due process.

Maciver, R.M. *Prevention and Control of Delinquency.* Chicago: Aldine, 1968.

Olson, M.C. and J.B. Carpenter. *Survey of Techniques Used to Reduce Vandalism and Delinquency in Schools.* Washington: NCJRS, 1971.
Presents a profile of the school vandalism problem and provides a compilation of opinions and suggestions of school administrations to lessen the problem.

O'Keefe, J.A. "A Police Program for Youth." *Youth Authority Quarterly.* 22:1 (1969).

Project Map Inc. *Community Action Agency—Youth Development Program Manual: A Technical Assistance Pamphlet.* Washington: NCJRS (Microfiche) 1972.

Runyon, Howard L. "A Place to Go." *Law and Order.* 18:9 (September, 1970), 86-88, 90, 92, 94, 96, 98, 100, 102.
The building of a youth center in a small community.

Reckless, W.C. and S. Dinitz. *Prevention of Juvenile Delinquency—An Experiment.* Columbus: Ohio State University Press, 1972.
Results of a project which focused on the build-up of good self-concept of preadolescent inner-city youth who are showing signs of gravitating toward delinquency.

Rojanowicz, Robert C. "Factors that Affect the Functioning of Delinquency Prevention Programs." *Police Chief* (February, 1971), 42-47.

Reitman, A. and J. Follman. *Corporal Punishment in the Public Schools—The Use of Force in Controlling Student Behavior.* N.Y.: ACLU, 1972.
A review and criticism of the practice of allowing teachers the right to use force in maintaining classroom discipline.

Robin, Gerald D. "Anti-Poverty Programs and Delinquency." *Journal of Criminal Law, Criminology and Police Science.* 60:3 (September, 1969), 323-331.
Studies in Cincinnati and Detroit show that participation in Anti-Poverty Programs is unrelated to delinquency prevention or reduction.

Rubin, Ted. *Law as an Agent of Delinquency Prevention.* Washington: U.S. Youth Development and Delinquency Prevention Administration, 1971.

Stoutt, Tony. "Rhymes Against Crime." *Police Chief.* XLII:3 (March, 1976), 54-55.
Crime prevention program in elementary schools.

Schnabolk, Charles. "Safeguarding the School Against Vandalism and Violence." *Nation's Schools.* 94:2 (August, 1974).

Stratton, J.R. and R.M. Terry. *Prevention of Delinquency—Problems and Programs.* N.Y.: MacMillan, 1968.
This text of readings is designed to provide an overview and illustrate issues common to the control and prevention of delinquency.

Sedlar, Tom. "Dance Club for Teens." *Law and Order.* 15:3 (March, 1967), 40-46.
Police sponsored program for teenagers. Program guidelines included.

Tait, C. Downing Jr. and Emory F. Hodges Jr. "Delinquency Prevention: A Review and Proposal." *Police.* 8:4 (March-April, 1964), 36-39.

Trajanowicz, Robert C. "Factors That Affect the Functioning of Delinquency Prevention Programs." *Police Chief.* 38:2 (February, 1971), 42-43, 44-47.

Willard, Boyd T. "Methods to Combat Juvenile Crime." *Police Chief.* XXXVIII:11 (November, 1971), 54-56.

LOCKS

Freimuth, K.C. *Lock Security.* Santa Cruz, CA.: Davis, n/d.

Freimuth, Kenneth C. "Understanding Lock Security." *Military Police Journal* (February, 1973), 7-12.

Hogg, Garry. *Safe Bind, Safe Find: The Story of Locks, Bolts and Bars.* London: Phoenix, 1961.

Johnson, Donald. "Legal Safe Crackers Work with Police." *Vox-Cop.* 10:2 (January-February, 1954).

Kotch, Leon. "Security Demands Public Education." *Police.* 13:4 (March-April, 1969), 84-87.

Locksmith Ledger. *Clever Clues for Locksmiths.* Wood-Ridge, N.J.: Locksmith Ledger, n/d.

Locksmith Ledger. *How to Open Locks Without Keys or Picks.* Wood-Ridge, N.J.: Locksmith Ledger, n/d.

The Locksmith's Official Safe and Vault Manual. Detroit, MI.: Jaf, 1948.

Latham, Sid. "Secrets of Security." *Police.* 1:4 (March-April, 1957), 20-21 24-26.

Marchand, Henry. "The Master Key System." *FBI Law Enforcement Bulletin* (October, 1974).

Paholke, Arthur R. "Safe Recognition." *Security World.* 7 (September, 1970), 83-84.

Peyronnet, Jacques. "Safe Locks." *International Criminal Police Review* (May, 1975), 138-143.

Roper, C.A. *Complete Handbook of Locks and Locksmithing.* Blue Ridge Summit, PA.: Tab, 1976.

Shaw, William. "Coming—A New Breed of Locks." *Law and Order.* 17:1 (January, 1969), 32-39, 78.

MARKING PROPERTY

Crawford, James H. "Number Thieves Avoid." *Police Chief.* XLI:6 (June, 1974).

Flanigan, John C. "Thefts Reduced by Program of Hubcap Marking." *FBI Law Enforcement Bulletin.* 26:10 (October, 1957), 21-23.

Gavin, Joseph. "Operation Identification Goes Nationwide." *Law and Order.* 21:5 (May, 1973), 66-69.
Anti-burglary program involving marking of potential loot.

Lee, E.L. "Operation Identification: A Step in the Right Direction." *Police Chief.* XXXIX (August, 1972), 50-52.

National Exchange Club. *Operation Identification—Action Kit.* Washington: NCJRS (Microfiche) n/d.

NARCOTICS PREVENTION

Elia, Michael V. "Narcotic Addict Control and Crime Reduction Program." *Journal of California Law Enforcement.* 10:4 (April, 1976), 144-147.
Police program which showed a drastic reduction in crime as addicts were arrested and taken off the streets.

Konkle, Robert A. "A Program to Deter Marijuana Sales." *Law and Order.* 17:8 (August, 1969).
Those arrested for marijuana sales are referred to IRS for tax assessments.

Lieberman, F., P. Garoff and M. Gottesfeld. *Before Addiction: How to Help Youth.* N.Y." Behavioral, 1973.

Lowes, Peter D. *The Genesis of International Narcotics Control.* Geneva: Libraire Droz, n/d.

National Council on Crime and Delinquency. *Alternatives to Drug Abuse Conference—Second Proceedings—Part 1.* Springfield, VA.: NTIS, 1973.
Part one of proceedings of 1973 conference directed toward correcting community problems which encourage drug abuse.

National Council on Crime and Delinquency. *Alternatives to Drug Abuse Conference—Proceedings—Part 2.* Springfield, VA.: NTIS, 1972.
The conference covered alternatives attempting to encourage the drug abuser to develop a new, drug free life style.

Pilot, Joan. "The Two-Edged Sword: Education and Enforcement." *Law and Order.* 16:11 (November, 1968), 55-57.
Police Drug Abuse Prevention Program.

POLICE AND CITIZEN COOPERATION

Casper, Joseph J. "Mutual Responsibility—Police and Citizens." *Law and Order.* (September, 1968), 25-30, 91.

Clark, Ben. "Law Enforcement Needs Citizen Cooperation in Combating Community Problems." *Police.* 10:3 (January-February, 1966), 82-85.

Dawson, William S. "Smokey in a Blue Wrapper with a Camera at Milepost 50." *Police Chief.* XLII:7 (July, 1975), 58-61.
Expanded use of CB radios has resulted in greater assistance from citizens in reporting crime and emergencies.

Drekhan, Fred F. "Developing Citizen Involvement." *Law and Order.* 17:8 (August, 1969).

Eisenberg, Terry et al. *Police Community Action: A Program for Change in Police Community Behavior Patterns.* N.Y.: Praeger, 1973.

Evans, Courtney A. "Policeman-Citizen Teamwork." *Law and Order.* 14:9 (September, 1966), 12-46.

Higgins, Larry D. "Petaluma Reports on Crime Check." *Police Chief.* XXXVII:6 (June, 1970).

Holladay, Everett F. "People's Anti-Crime Effort: PACE." *Police Chief.* XXXIV:11 (November, 1967), 48-49.

Lawder, Lee E. "Operation Crime Stop." *Law and Order.* 14:4 (April, 1966), 26-28, 94.

Mihanovich, Clements. "Programming for Citizen Participation in Police Action Programs." *Police Chief.* 32:3 (March, 1965).

Parkinson, John P. "Who Is Responsible for Stopping Crime?" *Police Chief.* XL:4 (April, 1973).

"People and Police: Community Radio Watch." *Police Chief.* XXIV:11 (November, 1967).
Program enlists the users of dispatcher controled two-way radio equipped vehicles to act as observers for the police.

Tracy, Richard J. "Crime Check Delivers." *Police Chief.* XXXVII:6 (June, 1970), 44-46.

University of Rochester. *PAC-TAC—Police and Citizens: Together Against Crime—Experimental Action Program.* Springfield, VA.: NTIS, 1973.
Experimental program where civilians and police officers work as two man teams, patrolling fixed beat areas.

Wand, Hal. "Extra Eyes and Ears for a Police Department." *Police* 13:4 (March-April, 1969) 96-98.
Community radio watch program; participants are private or public companies who own radio dispatched vehicles. Drivers report emergencies and crimes.

RAPE PREVENTION

"Defending Yourself Against Rape." *Ladies Home Journal* (July, 1973).

Gilpatric, Diane. "Rape Prevention: Everybody's Business." *Military Police Law Enforcement Journal.* 11:2 (Summer, 1975).

Griffin, Deborah. "Be Safe From Rape." *FBI Law Enforcement Bulletin* (December, 1974), 9-11.

Keefe, Mary L. and Henry T. O'Reilly. "Developing a Pertinent Rape Prevention Program." *Law and Order* (March, 1976), 64-67.

ROBBERY PREVENTION

Chaiken, Jan M., Michael W. Lawless and Keith A. Stevenson. *Impact of Police Activity on Crime: Robberies on the New York City Subway System.* N.Y.: Rand, 1974.

District of Columbia Metropolitan Area Transit Commission. *Scrip System of the D.C. Transit System, Washington D.C.—Final Report.* Springfield, VA.: NTIS, 1970.
Analyzes effects and feasibility of issuing scrip or redemption coupons as change in lieu of cash, in order to eliminate robberies of bus driver.

Feeney, Floyd and Adrianne Weir. "Prevention and Control of Robbery." *Criminology* (May, 1975), 102-105.

Gunn, L.G. *Commercial Robbery in a Medium-Sized City—Columbus, Georgia—Equipment systems Improvement Program Report.* Washington: NCJRS, 1973.
Study of armed robbery of business establishments using the series of events surrounding the crime and the action and reaction of the participants.

Haefner, E. *Chicago—Systems Analysis of Effectiveness of Tactics in Preventing CTA Bus Robberies.* Evanston, IL.: Traffic Institute Northwestern University, 1971.
Criminal intent and enforcement countermeasures presented through game and utility models in a cost-effectiveness framework.

"How to Minimize the Bank Robbers Loot." *FBI Law Enforcement Bulletin.* 39:5 (May, 1970), 26-29.

Lamson, P.A. "A Concentrated Robbery Reduction Program." *FBI Law Enforcement Bulletin.* 40:12 (1971), 16-20, 26.

Lee, J.F. "Reward Program Pays off." *FBI Law Enforcement Bulletin.* 42:4 (1973), 18-21.

Lorenz, Robert W. "Armed Robbery Prevention." *Security World.* 7 (January, 1970), 12-13, 15.

McLaughlin, A.J. and P. Doherty. *Miami (FL.)—Police Department-Robbery Control Project—Final Report, October 1, 1971—December 31, 1973.* Washington: NCJRS (Microfiche) 1975.

Mason, J.R. "The Robbery Alert." *Law and Order.* 18:5 (May, 1970), 84-85.

Meltzer, Robert J. "Optimum Utilization of Bank Protection and Surveillance Cameras." *Police.* 16:9 (May, 1972), 6-10.

Nicholas, John F. and James D. Bannon. "Stress—Zero Visibility Policing." *Police Chief.* XXXIX:6 (June, 1972), 32-36.

O'Neill, William P. "Security Camera In A Crime Prevention Program." *Law and Order.* 23:4 (April, 1975), 46, 48-49.
Use of cameras in high robbery risk stores. Camera takes one frame every 1.25 seconds.

Robbery Events—A Risk Reduction Manual for Police. Gaithersburg, MD.: IACP, 1975.

Stanford Research Institute. *Reduction of Robberies and Assaults of Bus Drivers. Vol. 3: Technological and Operational Methods.* Springfield, VA.: NTIS, 1970.
Causes, prevention, and results including scope of the problem, use of protective devices for doors, identification of suspects and surveillance.

"The Silent Witness." *FBI Law Enforcement Bulletin.* 36:7 (July, 1967), 17-19.
Hidden cameras in banks.

Ward, R.H. and T.J. Ward. *Manual for Robbery Control Projects.* Washington: NCJRS, 1975.

SELF PROTECTION

Barnes, Robert Earl & Ronald Sarro. *Are You Safe From Burglars?* Garden City, N.Y.: Doubleday, 1971.

"Booming Industry—Home Safeguards." *U.S. News and World Report.* (October 26, 1970).
Discussion of various electronic devices to protect homeowners and apartment dwellers from burglars.

Bunting, James. *Protection of Property Against Crime.* Folkestone (GB): Bailey Bros. & Swinfen, n/d.

Clifford, Martin. *Security! How to Protect Yourself, Your Home, Your Office and Your Car.* N.Y.: Drake, 1974.

Griffin, Al. *Home and Apartment Security.* Chicago: Regnery, 1975.

Hair, Robert and Sara Baker. *How to Protect Yourself Today*. N.Y.: Pocket, 1971.

Hunter, George. *How to Defend Yourself, Your Family and Your Home*. N.Y.: McKay, 1967.

Kaufmann, Ulrich. *How to Avoid Burglary, House-Breaking and Other Crimes*. N.Y.: Crown, 1967.

Moolman, Val. *Practical Ways to Prevent Burglary and Illegal Entry*. N.Y.: Cornerstone, 1970.

Wainwright, John. *Guard Your Castle: A Plain Man's Guide to the Protection of His Home*. London: Gentry, 1973.

White, Lionel. *Protection: Yourself, Your Family and Your Property in an Unsafe World*. Chatsworth, CA.: Books for Better Living, 1974.

STREET LIGHTING

Siemon, Joyce M. and Larry Vardell. "A Bright Answer to the Crime and Energy Question." *Police Chief*. XLI:6 (June, 1974), 53-55.

Wright, R. et al. *Impact of Street Lighting on Crime*. Washington: NCJRS (Microfiche) 1974.

THEFT PREVENTION

Deeley, Patrick J. "Suggestions for the Prevention of Jewel Thefts." *FBI Law Enforcement Bulletin*. 27:8 (August, 1958), 12-14.

Hata, Bill. "Demonstration Halts Employee In-Plant Stealing." *Law and Order*. 12:10 (October, 1964).

"How to Foil Stock Thieves." *Business Week* (June 21, 1969).

Keller, E. John. "Cargo Security—The Neglected Child." *Law and Order*. 21:8 (August, 1973).

Keller, E. John. "Police Community Relations—Theft Prevention Program." *Law and Order*. 22:9 (September, 1974), 68, 70.

Loss, Prevention Institute. *Anti-Shoplifting Guide for Retailers*. Washington: NCJRS (Microfiche) 1971.
This guide is in the form of a checklist for store security personnel and management which enumerates some of the options available to curtail shoplifting.

Leachman, Robert B. and Philip Althoff. *Preventing Nuclear Theft: Guidelines for Industry and Government*. N.Y.: Praeger, 1972.

Murphy, Robert M. "A Secure Facility for High Value Aircargo." *FBI Law Enforcement Bulletin*. 41:12 (December, 1972), 6-11.
Airport buildings specifically designed for items of extraordinary value at JFK International Airport in NYC.

Meyer, Schuyler M. III. "A Crusade Against Shoplifting." *Police Chief*. XLI:6 (June, 1974), 34-36.

Meisner, Dwayne. "Weapons in the War on Office Thefts." *Administrative Management*. (July, 1974).

U.S. Department of Transportation Office of Transportation Security. *Cooperative Approach to Cargo Security in the Trucking Industry*. Washington: GPO, 1973.
Study of cost-effective security improvements made on the cargo terminals of seven interstate motor carriers which corrected major problems and reduced cargo claims.

TIPSTER PROGRAMS

Abramson, M. "Box 100, New York's Address for Informers' Tips." *New York Times Magazine* (September 15, 1963).

Hagan, Lawrence C. "The Tipster Program: A Community Program to Increase Apprehensions." *Police Chief*. XLII:9 (September, 1975).
System where information is obtained from citizens on a confidential basis.

"TIP: Turn in a Pusher: Phone Tampa 229-6445—The Pushers Pushed." *Newsweek* (August 9, 1971).

PART V
FIELD OPERATIONS—
NON-CRIMINAL POLICE ACTIVITIES

NON-CRIMINAL POLICE OPERATIONS

NON-CRIMINAL—GENERAL

Croake, J.W. and D.R. Farcus. "The Policeman as a Quasi Marriage Counselor." *Marriage Family Counselors Quarterly*. 8:2 (1973), 11-13.
Authors advocate training in marriage and family counseling techniques for police officers.

Cybil, Peter. "Shoeshine Boys." *Law and Order*. 13:11 (November, 1965), 60, 62.
Control of shoeshine boys by licensing.

Estes, Kenneth H. "Career Day Program." *Law and Order*. 18:7 (July, 1970), 48.
Police involvement in High School career day program.

Feaker, Fred. "Two Functional Programs." *Law and Order*. 18:8 (August, 1970), 15-16, 18.
Chaplains on call by rotation for emergencies. Also program where elderly and shut-ins are contacted by telephone to insure their welfare.

Gardner, Martin A. Sr. "Overcoming the Language Barrier in Police Work." *Law and Order*. 15:8 (August, 1967), 66-67.
Author proposes a simple translation manual for police officers with words strictly relating to crime.

Gompert, Frank. "By Any Other Name." *Law and Order*. 17:5 (May, 1969), 57.
Describes the importance of properly serving subpoenas.

"Handling Hazardous Highway Cargoes." *Police Chief* (February, 1966).

Howard, John P. "Acting as Host for a Police Show." *Law and Order* (March, 1966), 76-77.

"How Effective Is Litter Law Enforcement." *Police Chief*. XXXIX:4 (April, 1972), 78-79.

Knapp, Sherman R. "Hot Wires—The Hows and Whys; the Do's and Don'ts." *FBI Law Enforcement Bulletin*. 38:5 (May, 1969), 2-6.
Excellent article on the handling of downed electric power lines.

LeVan, Raymond E. "Parade Planning and Security." *FBI Law Enforcement Bulletin*. 34:9 (September, 1965), 12-17.

Mazuran, Joseph. "Police Department Sponsors Youth Job Program." *FBI Law Enforcement Bulletin*. 27:4 (April, 1958), 20-22.

Moody, L.A. "Landlords and Tenants—Oakland's Landlord/Tenant Intervention Unit." *Police Chief*. 39:3 (March, 1972), 32-34.

Morgenbesser, M. "The Role of a Police Officer in a Drug Treatment Program." *Contemporary Drug Problems*. 3:2 (1974).

Reiter, Wilma H. "Fire." *Police*. 9:3 (January-February, 1965), 88-91.
Fire prevention in institutions.

Rocco, Therese L. "Service with Compassion." *FBI Law Enforcement Bulletin* (January, 1969), 12-15, 24.
Missing Persons Bureau, Pittsburg, PA. Police Department.

Shaw, Diane. "Police Response to a Stable Fire." *Law and Order*. 21:2 (February, 1973), 42, 44, 46, 48, 50, 52.

Surratt, James E. and William G. Katzenmeyer. "Police Services for Public Schools." *Police Chief*. XLII:6 (June, 1975), 59-60.
Police duties at schools include traffic control, spectator control, protection against vandalism, patrol on and off campus and instruction.

ALCOHOLISM AND THE POLICE

Alcoholism—General

Aaron, James E. and Albert J. Shafter, eds. *The Police Officer and Alcoholism*. Springfield, IL.: C.C. Thomas, 1963.

Bacon, Margaret and May B. Jones. *Teenage Drinking*. N.Y.: Crowell, 1968.

Bacon, Seldon. "Alcohol, Alcoholism and Crime." *Crime and Delinquency*. 9 (1963), 1-15.
In the amateur thief as the amount of alcohol is increased, any poorly controlled anti-social tendencies are allowed greater freedom.

Block, Marvin A. *Alcoholism: Its Facets and Phases*. N.Y.: Day, 1965.

Blum, E.M. *Alcoholism*. Washington: Joint Venture, 1967.
Overview of the current methods for the psychological and social treatment of alcoholism.

Burgess, Louise Bailey. *Alcohol and Your Health*. Los Angeles: Charles, 1973.

Chafetz, Morris E. and Harold W. Demone Jr. *Alcoholism and Society*. N.Y.: Oxford University Press, 1962.

Chafetz, Morris. et al., eds. *Frontiers of Alcoholism*. N.Y.: Science House, 1970.

Cook, T. et al. *The Drunkeness Offense*. N.Y.: Pergamon, 1969.

Erskin, H. *Alcohol and the Criminal Justice System—Challenge and Response*. Washington: NCJRS, 1972.
Treatment and education on alcohol programs are shown as leading to a decrease in alcohol related crime.

Fagerstrom, Dorothy. "The ABC's of Alcoholism." *Law and Order*. 16:9 (September, 1968), 42-44, 95.

Forney, Robert B. and Francis W. Hughes. *Combined Effects of Alcohol and Other Drugs.* Springfield, IL.: C.C. Thomas, 1968.

Goodwin, D.W. "Alcohol in Suicide and Homicide." *Quarterly Journal of Studies on Alcohol.* (March, 1973).

Grad, F.P. *Alcoholism and the Law.* Dobbs Ferry N.Y.: Oceana, 1971.

A study of present legal approaches to public intoxication and treatment of alcoholism and the extent of the alcoholics' criminal responsibility, with the inclusion of a model treatment act.

Grigsby, Shaw Earl. "The Raiford Study: Alcohol and Crime." *Journal of Criminal Law and Police Science.* 54:3 (September, 1963), 296-306.

Jackson, Joan K. "The Seattle Police Department Rehabilitation Project for Chronic Alcoholics." *Federal Probation.* 24 (1958), 36.

Jacobson, George. *Alcoholism: Diagnosis and Assessment.* N.Y.: Behavioral, 1976.

Jones, Howard. *Alcoholic Addiction: A Psycho-Social Approach to Abnormal Drinking.* London: Tavistoc, 1963.

Karpman, B. *The Alcoholic Woman—Case Studies in the Psychodynamics of Alcoholism.* Washington: Linacre, 1948.

Kinsey, Barry A. *The Female Alcoholic: A Social Psychological Study.* Springfield, IL.: C.C. Thomas, 1966.

Kullner, Robert and Albert B. Lorinez. "Alcoholism and Addiction in Urbanized Sioux Indians." *Mental Hygiene.* 51 (October, 1967), 530-542.

Leven, Rals and Vincent Vandre. "A California Study of Relationships Between Drinking and Crime." *Police.* 6:1 (September-October, 1961), 18-21.

Lovald, Keith and Holger R. Stub. "The Revolving Door: Reactions of Chronic Drunkenness Offenders to Court Sanctions." *Journal of Criminal Law, Criminology and Police Science.* 59:4 (December, 1968), 525-530.

McGeorge, John. "Alcohol and Crime." *Medical Science and the Law.* 3:2 (January, 1963), 27-48.

Maddox, George L. and B.C. McCall. *Drinking Among Teenagers: A Sociological Interpretation of Alcohol Use by High School Students.* New Brunswick, N.J.: Rutgers Center of Alcohol Studies, 1964.

Manos, S.S. "Anatomy of a Revolution: Law, Change and the Public Inebriate." *Journal of Drug Issues.* 5:3 (1975), 207-219.

Miller, Gary J. "Alcoholism, Police, Courts: A Changing Phenomena." *Police.* 12:6 (1968), 84-86.

Miller, Gary J. "The Future Role of the Police in the Treatment of Alcoholism." *Police,* 13:3 (January-February, 1969), 58-59.

Nimmer, Raymond T. *Two Million Unnecessary Arrests, Removing a Social Service Concern from the Criminal Justice System.* Chicago: American Bar Foundation, 1971.

Peters, Bettye. "San Diego's Anti-Alcohol Classes." *Law and Order.* 15:1 (January, 1967), 54-62.

Pittman, David J., ed. *Alcoholism.* N.Y.: Harper & Row, 1967.

Pittman, D.J. and C.W. Gordon. *Revolving Door: A Study of the Chronic Police Case Inebriate.* Glencoe, IL.: Free Press, 1958.

President's Commission on Law Enforcement and Administration of Justice. *Drunkenness: Task Force Report.* Washington: GPO, 1967.

Roderick, Carmon S. "Expectations and Socializations Experiences Related to Drinking Among U.S. Servicemen." *Quarterly Journal of Studies on Alcohol* (1971), 1040-1047.

Schuckit, M.A. and D. Cahalan. *Evaluation of Alcohol Treatment Programs.* Washington: NCJRS (Microfiche) 1974.

Strachan, J.C. *Alcoholism: Treatable Illness.* N.Y.: Heinman, 1968.

Trice, Harrison. *Alcoholism in America.* N.Y.: McGraw Hill, 1967.

U.S. Department of Health Education and Welfare. National Institute of Mental Health. *Alcohol Abuse and Alcoholism: Proceedings of the Joint Conference Sponsored by the Departments of Health, Education and Welfare, Justice and Transportation University of Maryland, February 21-23, 1972.* Washington, DC: NCJRS (Microfiche), 1972.

Williams, Roger J. "Identifying and Treating Potential Alcoholics." *Journal of Criminal Law, Criminology and Police Science.* 49:3 (September-October, 1958), 218-221.

Detoxification Centers

ABT Associates Inc. *Boston Alcohol Detoxification Project—Exemplary Project Validation Report.* Washington: NCJRS (Microfiche) 1974.

Summary of operations and assessment of goal achievement, replicability, measurability, efficiency, and accessibility along with a review of project strengths and weaknesses.

Brostron, Curtis. "The Detoxification Center." *FBI Law Enforcement Bulletin* (December, 1967), 6-8.

Kendis, J.B. and J.M. Weber. *St. Louis Detoxification and Diagnostic Evaluation Center—Project Summary, Final Project Summary and Final Evaluation Report.* Washington: NCJRS, 1970.

Need, development and operation of a 30 bed detoxification center with medical and social services.

Stegel, H.H. *Alcohol Detoxification Programs—Treatment Instead of Jail.* Springfield, IL.: C.C. Thomas, 1973.

Suggestions for establishing a community-supported detoxification program.

Siegel, Harvey. "P-CR Detoxification Centers." *Police Chief.* 38:3 (March, 1971), 58-59.

Younger, Eric E. "The Inebriate." *Police Chief.* XXXIX:5 (May, 1972), 30-32.

ANIMAL CONTROL

Beck, Alan M. *The Ecology of Stray Dogs: A Study of Freeranging Urban Animals.* Baltimore: York, 1973.

Clark, Charles R. "Barking Dog Complaints." *Police Chief.* XL:3 (March, 1973), 40-41.

Committee on Animal Health. *Control of Rabies.* Washington: National Academic Science, 1973.

Godlovich, Stanley and Rosaland Godlovich, eds. *Animals, Men and Morals: An Inquiry into the Mal-Treatment of Non-Humans.* N.Y.: Taplinger 1972.

Nellius, Andrea. "Animal Control Unit." *Law and Order.* 18:10 (October, 1970), 50-52.

The Public Safety Animal Control Unit of the Dade County, Florida, Public Safety Department.

Slayton, John E. "When Man's Best Friend Becomes a Problem." *Law and Order.* 12:1.

Dog catcher employed by Vancouver WA. Police Department describes methods for handling loose dogs.

CIVIL DEFENSE

Buckley, John L. "Recent Changes in the Civil Defense Program." *Law and Order.* 11:5 (May, 1963), 12-15, 66.

Erlich, Ken. "Davenport Civil Defense Network Fights Flood with 'Guts' and Radio." *Police.* 10:3 (January-February, 1966), 90-91.

Page, Richard A. "Full-Time Dispatch Service for CD Operations." *Law and Order.* 11:5 (May, 1963), 8-10.

Pittman, Stewart L. "Accent on Civil Defense." *Law and Order.* 11:5 (May, 1963).

Weaver, Leon. "The Role of Law Enforcement in Civil Defense." *Police.* 5:5 (May-June, 1961), 55-56.

FIRST AID

First Aid—General

Aaron, James E. et al. *First Aid and Emergency Care: Prevention and Protection of Injuries.* N.Y.: Macmilan, 1972.

Adams, Brian C. *Medical Implications of Karate Blows.* Cranbury, N.J.: A.S. Barnes, 1969.

Adams, Michael F. "The Bloodless Emergency." *Law and Order.* 19:6 (June, 1971), 72, 74.

Adams, Michael F. "The Industrial Emergency." *Law and Order.* 16:10 (October, 1968), 92-94.

"Drowning Accidents." *Police Review.* 82:4233 (1974).

Reviews methods of preventing drowning accidents by police with a number of recommendations.

"Emergency Medical Identification." *FBI Law Enforcement Bulletin.* 35:3 (March, 1966), 14-15.

Use of wristlet, anklet, medallion emergency identification.

"Emergency Obstetrics and Police Officers." *FBI Law Enforcement Bulletin.* 26:2 (February, 1957), 10-11.

Empleton, Bernard E., ed. *First Aid for Skin and Scuba Divers.* N.Y.: Association Press, 1976.

Erven, L.W. and H.N. Gruber. *First Aid and Emergency Rescue.* Beverly Hills, NA.: Glencoe, 1970.

Fairfield, Letitia. *Epilepsy, Grand Mal, Petit Mal, Convulsions.* N.Y.: Philosophical Library, 1957.

Feldman, Stanley and Harry Ellis. *Principles of Resuscitation.* Philadelphia: Davis, 1967.

Findeiss, J. Clifford. *Emergency Medical Care, Vol 1.* N.Y.: Stratton, 1974.

Gardner, Alvin. *Paramedical Pathology: Fundamentals of Pathology for the Allied Medical Occupations.* Springfield, IL.: C.C. Thomas, 1972.

Goudy, T.G. "Accident Call." *Law and Order.* 16:5 (May, 1968), 54.

Gustavson, George A. "Closed Chest Heart Massage." *Law and Order.* 17:5 (May, 1969), 96-99.

Hamilton, Andrew. "Firemen Paramedics." *Science Digest.* (August, 1971).

Hampton, Oscar P. "Emergency Medical Services and Police Officers." *Police Chief.* XXXVII:9 (September, 1970), 38-41.

Hartley, Joel. *First Aid Without Panic.* N.Y.: Hart, 1975.

Hartley, Joel. *New Ways in First Aid.* N.Y.: Hart, 1971.

Huszar, Robert J. *Emergency Cardiac Care.* Bowie, MD.: Brady, 1974.

Jones, Jeremy. "The Matter of Life or Death: Medic Alert." *Law Officer.* 4 (June, 1971), 74-75.

Jones, Ronald C. "Bites and Stings." *Police.* (May-June, 1968).

Levin, I.A. and A.B. Longacre. "Antibacterial Therapy in Infections Resulting from Human Bites." *Journal of the American Medical Association* (1951).

McCord, Hallack. "Unconscious Persons Can Hear." *Police.* 9:3 (January-February, 1965), 96.

Advises against making statements within hearing of unconscious persons which may be damaging to the victim.

Moore, Mary. *Medical Emergency Manual: Emergency Medicine.* Baltimore: William & Wilkins 1972.

O'Brien, G.R., J.L. Costecki and H. Colbert. "The Human Bite." *New York Journal of Medicine* (1955).

Phillips, Peter J. "Disaster First Aid." *Police.* 13:1 (September-October, 1968), 82-89.

Roddy, W. Lee. "Medic Alert—An Aid to Officers in an Emergency." *Police.* 9:4 (March-April, 1965), 28-29.

Rowe, Ed B. "The Importance and Limitations of Immediate Care." *Police.* 12:2 (November-December, 1968), 24-26.

Rush, Allen and Richard A. Brose. "10-48: A Call for a New Kind of Assistance." *Police Chief.* 37:7 (July, 1971), 40-43.

Safar, Peter and Martin C. McMahon. "New Method of Artificial Respiration Gains Recognition." *Police.* 3:6 (July-August, 1959), 6-11.

Stephenson, Hugh E. *Immediate Care of the Acutely Ill and Injured.* St. Louis, MO.: Mosby, 1974.

Stringer, Llewellyn. *Emergency Treatment of Acute Respiratory Disease: A Manual for Ambulance and Emergency Room Personnel.* (Rev. ed). Bowie, MD.: Brady, 1972.

White, Gregory J. *Emergency Childbirth. A Manual.* Franklin Park, IL.: Police Training Foundation, 1958.

Waisbren, Burton A. *Emergency Care Handbook.* N.Y.: Drake, 1975.

Waters, John. "The Law Officer and First Aid on the Highway." *Law and Order.* 16:6 (June, 1968), 18-22, 106.

Young, Carl B. Jr. "Acute Heart Emergencies." *Police.* 11:2 (November-December, 1957), 12-14.

Young, Carl B. Jr. *First Aid and Resuscitation.* Springfield, IL.: C.C. Thomas, 1954.

Young, Carl B. Jr. *First Aid for Emergency Crews: A Manual on Emergency First Aid Procedures for Ambulance Crews, Law Enforcement Officers, Fire Service Personnel, Wrecker Drivers, Hospital Staffs, Industry Nurses.* Springfield, IL.: C.C. Thomas, 1970.

Young, Carl B. Jr. "Resuscitation." *Police.* 1:6 (July-August, 1957), 7-8.

Young, Carl B. Jr. "Traffic Accidents, First Aid and the Police Officers." *Police.* 1:3 (January-February, 1957), 33-37.

Poisons

Brooks, V.J. *Poisons.* Huntington, N.Y.: Krieger, 1975.
Contains information on most types of poisons. Also describes emergency techniques including radiation hazards.

Dreisbach, Robert H. *Handbook of Poisoning: Diagnosis and Treatment.* 8th ed. Los Altos, CA.: Lange, 1974.

Kaye, Sidney. "Death Due to Poisoning." *Police.* 3:1 (September-October, 1958), 39-41.

Kaye, Sidney. *Handbook of Emergency Toxicology.* Springfield, IL.: C.C. Thomas, 1954.

Naimark, George M. "Killer on the Loose in Your Town." *Police.* 8:4 (March-April, 1964), 73.

Poisonous Animals

Banner, Albert H. "Poisonous Marine Animals, A Synopsis." *Journal of Forensic Sciences.* 12:2 (April, 1967), 180-192.

Benson, Jerome. "Tetraodon (Blowfish) Poisoning." *Journal of Sciences* (October, 1956).

Halstead, Bruce W. *Poisonous and Venomous Making Animals of the World.* (Rev. ed.) Princeton, N.J.: Darwin, 1976.

Parris, Henry M. "Snake Venom Poisoning." *Medical Times.* 89:6 (1961), 595-602. Russell, Findlay E.

Russell, Findlay E. *Poisonous Making Animals.* Neptune, N.J.: TFH, 1972.

Smith, Hobart M. and Floyd Boys. "Determination of Snakebite as Dangerous or Harmless." *Police.* 7:4 (March-April, 1963), 6-13.

Smith, Hobart M. and Floyd Boys. "What Law Enforcement Officers Should Know About Snakes and Their Kin." *Police.* 2:6 (July-August, 1958), 31-39.
Excellent article with many photographs of poisonous reptiles.

Stejneger, Leonhard. *Poisonous Snakes of North America.* Seattle: Shorey, 1893.

Ambulance Services

Curry, George J., ed. *Immediate Care and Transport of the Injured.* Springfield, IL.: C.C. Thomas, 1965.

Dunlap and Associates Inc. *The Economics of Highway Emergency Ambulance Services.* Washington: Department of Transportation, 1969.

Farrington, J.D. "Emergency Medicine Today: The Registry of Ambulance Attendants." *Police Chief.* XXXIX:7 (July, 1972), 74-75.

Freeman, G.L. "Police Emergency Ambulance." *Colorado Policeman.* 10 (1973), 92, 94.

Littleton, J.T. "Transportation of the Acutely Injured—A Neglected 'Disease' with a 'Cure'." *Police.* 9:2 (November-December, 1964), 16-21.

Marlow, Ben M. "The Emergency Transport System." *Law and Order.* 18:9 (September, 1970), 62-63, 66, 68.
Utah Highway Patrol system for handling emergency transportation problems. System uses aircraft and vehicles. Highway patrolmen, not only transport people but also blood, medication, medical equipment etc.

Owen, J.K. "Community Emergency Ambulance Services." *Police Chief.* 34:1 (January, 1967), 28-30.

"Police Ambulance Service Proves Value After Operation Test in San Diego." *Western City.* 39 (October, 1963), 48.

Stevenson, K.A. *Operational Aspects of Emergency Ambulance Services.* Washington: NCJRS (Microfiche) 1971.

Young, Carl B. *Transportation of the Injured.* Springfield, IL.: C.C. Thomas, 1958.

POLICE DISASTER OPERATIONS

Police Disaster Operations—General

Bristow, Allen P. *Police Disaster Operations.* Springfield, IL.: C.C. Thomas, 1972.

Caro, D. "Major Disasters." *Lancet.* 2:7892 (1975), 1309-1310.

Cotter, Cornelius P. *Jet Tanker Crash: Urban Response to Military Disaster.* Lawrence: University Press of Kansas, 1968.

Crowe, Bazel E. "Disaster Government in Marathon, Florida After Hurricane 'Donna'." *Police.* 6:3 (January-February, 1962), 22-24.

Cushman, C. "Ten Thirty-three Traffic—Plane Crash. Police Procedures for Aircraft Accidents" *Texas Police Journal.* 22:5 (1974), 4-6.

Diamond, Harry, ed. "Police Duties and Responsibilities at the Scene of an Emergency or Disaster." *Police.* 8:1 (September-October, 1963, May-June, 1964).

Eastman, George D. "Disaster Planning." *FBI Law Enforcement Bulletin* (April, 1949).

Enrlich, Ken. "A City vs. the River." *Law and Order.* 13:8 (August, 1964), 26-30.

Fisher, B. *Major Disasters—A Study Report on the Swiss Planning and Organization Structure for Dealing with Catastrophe, and Current Police Planning and Equipment for Use in Major Disasters in England and Wales.* Washington: NCJRS (Microfiche) 1971.

Fisher, Brian. "Moorgate: The Disaster That No One Expected." *Outpost* (October, 1975), 8-13.

Foley, R.J. Jr. "Disaster Without Warning." *Law and Order.* 14:9 (September, 1966), 30-31.

Garb, Solomon and Evelyn Eng. *Disaster Handbook.* N.Y.: Springer, 1969.

Garner, Gerald W. "The Police Role In the Severe Weather Alert Plan." *FBI Law Enforcement Bulletin.* 43:4 (April, 1974).

Hannon, James F. "Power Failure and the Police." *FBI Law Enforcement Bulletin* (November, 1975), 16-23.

Hobbs, Howard L. "Police Operations During A Natural Disaster." *FBI Law Enforcement Bulletin* (June, 1971).

Hool, Leonard E. "A Disaster Plan for a Small Community." *Law and Order.* 14:3 (March, 1966), 28-32, 34.

Hubbard, N.L. "The Earthquake and the Highway Patrol." *California Highway Patrol.* 35 (1971), 32-33, 36-37, 40-42.

Johnstone, Carlisle. "Disaster Plan Is Placed in Effect During Hurricane." *FBI Law Enforcement Bulletin* (June, 1961).

Kane, Walter C. "And the Crowds Came. . ." *Police Chief.* 33:7 (July, 1966), 14, 16.
Describes tornado in Loveland, Colorado. Advice on crowd control.

Kennedy, W.C. *Police Department in Natural Disaster Operations.* Springfield, VA.: NTIS, 1969.

Kennedy, Will C. "Police Departments: Organization and Tasks in Disaster." *American Behavioral Scientist.* XIII (January-February, 1970).

King, Richard A. "Police Response to Disasters." *FBI Law Enforcement Bulletin.* 43:5 (May, 1974), 26-37.

Leonard, V.A. *Police Pre-Disaster Preparation.* Springfield, IL.: C.C. Thomas, 1973.

London Police. *London—Police—Major Incidents: Background Information, Notes on the Emergency Services, Local Authorities, Public Utilities, etc. and Their Intervention at Major Incidents.* Washington: NCJRS (Microfiche) 1974.

Los Angeles County Sheriff's Department. *Region 1 (Disaster) Law Enforcement Services.* Los Angeles: Los Angeles County Sheriff's Department, 1963.

Magruder, John T. Sr. "Emergency Operations Center." *FBI Law Enforcement Bulletin* (April, 1970) 4-9, 29-31.

Minnich, J.T. "The FBI's Disaster Squad." *Australian Police Journal.* 23:2 (April, 1969).

O'Neal, Robert A. "Death Out of Darkness." *FBI Law Enforcement Bulletin.* 34:4 (April, 1966), 2-5, 14-16.

Philips, Robert V. "Emergency Operations for Earthquake Victims." *Western City.* 47 (June, 1971).

Stiver, Phil R. "Intensive Light." *Police Chief.* 38:2 (February, 1971), 24.
Plans for lights at disaster scenes.

Surgey, Eric. T. "Guidelines for Officers in Case of a Major Disaster." *Police Review (GB).* (January 2, 1976), 14-15.

Tamm, Quinn. "Handling Disaster Problems is Law Enforcement Task." *FBI Law Enforcement Bulletin.* 26:3 (March, 1957), 13-19.

Unsworth, Susan. "Disaster Unit in the Ministry of Overseas Development." *Journal of Administration Overseas* (April, 1976), 85-91.

U.S. Department of the Interior. *Emergency Preparedness Progress in the Electric Utility Industry.* Washington: GPO, 1973.
Illustration and explanation of emergency plans of a number of electric utilities, and demonstration of the interest of the electric power industry in the program.

Watson, Ben M. and Joseph N. Baker. "Burbank Prepares for Disaster Emergency Operations." *Western City Magazine.* 42 (October, 1966), 33-34.

Way, A.G.P. "The Po Valley Floods, 1951." *Police Journal (GB).* (October, 1964), 471-480.

Whelan, Janet. *Aftermath: The Tasman Bridge Collapse—Criminological and Sociological Observations.* Canberra, Australia: Institute of Criminology, 1976.

Whisenand, Paul M. "Municipal Police Services in a Disaster Preparedness Program: A Role Analysis." *Police.* 13:3 (January-February, 1969), 65-73.

Disasters—General

Adams, David. *The Minneapolis Tornadoes, May 6, 1975: Notes on the Warning Process.* Columbus, OH.: Disaster Research Center, Ohio State University, 1965.

Alley, Rewi. *Man Against Flood: A Story of the 1954 Flood on the Yangtse and of the Reconstruction That Followed It.* Peking: New World Press, 1956.

Anderson, William A. *Disaster and Organizational Change: A Study of the Long-Term Consequences in Anchorage of the 1964 Alaska Earthquake.* Columbus, OH.: Disaster Research Center, Ohio State University, 1969.

Anderson, William A. "Military Organizations in Natural Disaster: Established and Emergent Norms." *American Behavioral Scientist.* 13 (January-February, 1970), 415-422.

Backes, Nancy. *Great Fires of America.* Waukesha, WI.: Country Beautiful, 1973.

Bailey, Maria. "Communication Planning for Disasters." *Security World.* 8 (June, 1971), 20-23.

Brouillette, John R. "The Department of Public Works: Adaptation to Disaster Demands." *American Behavioral Scientist.* 13 (January-February, 1970), 369-379.

Brouillette, John R. and James Ross. *Organizational*

Response to the Great Chicago Snow Storm of 1967. Columbus: Disaster Research Center, Ohio State University, 1967.

Benzaquin, Paul. *Fire in Boston's Coconut Grove.* Chatsworth, CA.: Brandon, 1969.

Baird, D.M. "Montreal High-Rise Fire." *Quarterly Journal of the National Fire Protection Association.* 157:2 (October, 1963).

Bixby, William. *Havoc: The Story of National Disaster.* N.Y.: Longmans Green, 1961.

Baker, G.W. and D.W. Chapman. *Man and Society in Disaster.* N.Y.: Basic, 1962.

Cooper, Charles F. "Ecology of Fire." *Scientific American.* 204 (1961), 150-160.

Clifford, R.A. *The Rio Grande Flood: A Comparative Study of Border Communities in Disaster.* Washington: National Research Council, National Academy of Sciences, 1956.

Drabek, Thomas E. "Methodology of Studying Disasters." *American Behavioral Scientist.* 13 (January-February, 1970), 331-343.

Douglas, William O. *The Three Hundred Year War: A Chronicle of Ecological Disaster.* N.Y.: Random, 1972.

Demerath, Nicholas J. and Anthony Wallace. "Human Adaptation to Disaster." *Human Organization.* 16 (1957), 1-40.

Dynes, Russell R., E.L. Quarantelli and Gary Kreps. *A Perspective on Disaster Planning.* Columbus: Disaster Research Center, Ohio State University, 1972.

Form, William H. and Sigmund Nosow. *Community in Disaster.* N.Y.: Harper, 1958.

Fritz, Charles E. "Disaster Compared in Six American Communities." *Human Organization.* 16 (Summer, 1957), 6-9.

Fletcher, Robert D. "The Donora Smog Disaster: A Problem in Atmospheric Pollution." *Weatherwise.* 2:3 (June, 1949), 56-60.

Form, William Humbert. *Community in Disaster.* N.Y.: Harper, 1958.

Grieve, Hilda. *Great Tide: The Story of the 1953 Flood Disaster in Essex.* Chelmsford, England: County Council of Essex, 1959.

Galbreath, M. *Fire in High Buildings.* Ottawa: National Research Council of Canada, 1968.

Haas, J. Eugene and Robert S. Ayre. *The Western Sicily Earthquake of 1968.* Washington: National Academy of Sciences, 1969.

Healy, Richard J. *Emergency and Disaster Planning.* N.Y.: Wiley, 1969.

Hoehling, A.A. *Disaster: Major American Catastrophies.* N.Y.: Hawthorne, 1973.

Kogan, Herman and Robert Cromie. *Great Fire Chicago, 1871.* N.Y.: Putnam, 1971.

Kotschnic, W.M. "Natural Disasters: Agenda for Action." *Department of State Bulletin.* 59 (November 25, 1968), 549-553.

Leonard, V.A. *Police Pre-Disaster Preparation.* Springfield, IL.: C.C. Thomas, 1973.

Linehan, Urban J. *Tornado Deaths in the United States.* Washington: Weather Bureau of U.S. Department of Commerce, 1956.

Moore, Harry Estill. *Tornadoes Over Texas: A Study of Waco and San Angelo in Disaster.* Austin: University of Texas Press, 1958.

Malloy, M.T. "Firetraps in the Sky." *National Observer* (October 21, 1972).

Mills, E.D. "Emergency Aid." *Architectural Review.* 141 (June, 1967), 409-412.

National Fire Protection Association. *Manual of Hazardous Chemical Reactions.* Boston: National Fire Protection Association, 1968.

Robinson, Donald B. *The Face of Disaster.* Garden City, N.Y.: Doubleday, 1959.

Steinbrugge, Karl U. *Earthquake Hazard in the San Francisco Bay Area: A Continuing Problem in Public Policy.* Berkeley: Institute of Governmental Studies, University of California, 1968.

Sims, John and Duane Baumann. "The Tornado Threat: Coping Styles of the North and South." *Sciences.* 176:4042 (June 30, 1972), 136-1392.

Sheehan, Leslie and Kenneth Hewitt. *A Pilot Survey of Global Natural Disasters in the Past Twenty Years.* Toronto: University of Toronto, 1969.

Slette, A.L. III. "System Wide Disaster Plan." *Safety Education.* 41 (April, 1962), 15-16.

Schneider, David. "Typhoons on Yap." *Human Organization.* 16 (Summer, 1957), 10-15.

Steinhart, Carole and John S. Steinhart. *Blowout: A Case Study of the Santa Barbara Oil Spill.* Belmont, CA.: Duxbury, 1972.

Shorter, G.W. *Fire in Tall Buildings.* Ottawa: National Research Council of Canada, 1967.

Siporin, M. "Experience of Aiding the Victims of Hurricane Betsy." *Social Service Review.* 40 (December, 1966), 378-389.

Smith, Dewitt, ed. *Disaster and Disaster Relief.* Philadelphia: American Academy of Political and Social Science, 1957.

Shaskolsky, Leon. *Volunteerism in Disaster Situations.* Columbus: Disaster Research Center, Ohio State University, 1967.

Taubman, Bryna. "What Are Your Chances of Surviving a High-Rise Fire?"*New York.* 7:21 (May 27, 1974), 65-69.

Tripp, S.R. "Cooperation on Disaster Emergency Relief." *Department of State Bulletin.* 53 (September 6, 1965), 419-423.

Taylor, James B. *Tornado: A Community Responds to Disaster*. Seattle: University of Washington Press, 1970.

U.S. Department of the Interior Bureau of Reclamation. *Catalog of Dam Disasters, Failures and Accidents*. Washington: GPO, 1970.

Casualties

Cornell University Medical College. *The Treatment of Mass Civilian Casualties in a National Emergency*. Ithaca, N.Y.: Cornell University Press, 1968.

Rutherford, W.H. "Casualty Screening at a Major Disaster." *Police Surgeon* (April, 1975), 81-85.

Stefens, P.J. and S.W. Tarlton. "Identification of Mass Casualties: Experience in Four Civil Air Disasters." *Medicine, Science and the Law* (April, 1963).

Human Behavior in Disasters

American Psychiatric Association. *First Aid for Psychological Reactions in Disasters*. Washington: American Psychiatric Association, 1964.

Baker, G.W. and D.W. Chapman, eds. *Man and Society in Disaster*. N.Y.: Basic, 1962.

Barton, Allen H. *Communities in Disaster: A Sociological Analysis of Collective Stress Situations*. Garden City, N.Y.: Doubleday, 1969.

Barton, Allen H. *Social Organization Under Stress: A Sociological Review of Disaster Studies*. Washington: National Research Council, National Academy of Sciences, 1963.

Barton, Allen H., George W. Baker and Dwight W. Chapman, eds. "The Emergency Social System." *Man and Society in Disaster*. N.Y.: Basic, 1962.

Bates, F.L. et al. *The Social and Psychological Consequences of a Natural Disaster: A Longitudinal Study of Hurricane Audrey*. Washington: National Research Council, National Academy of Sciences, 1963.

Baumann, Duane D. and C. Russell. *Urban Snow Hazard: Economic and Social Implications*. Urbana, IL.: University of Illinois, Water Resources Center, 1971.

Bettelheim, Bruno. "Individual and Mass Behavior in Extreme Situations." *Journal of Abnormal and Social Psychology*. XXXVIII (1943), 417-452.

Blum, Richard H. and Bertrand Klass. *A Study of Public Response to Disaster Warnings*. Menlo Park, CA.: Stanford Research Institute, 1956.

Carroll, John J. and Salvador Parco. *Social Organization in a Crisis Situation: The Taal Disaster*. Manila: Phillippine Sociological Society, 1966.

Danzig, Elliott R., Paul W. Thayer and Lila R. Galanter. *The Effects of a Threatening Rumor on a Disaster Striken Community*. Washington: National Research Council, National Academy of Sciences, 1958.

Disaster Research Group. *Field Studies of Disaster Behavior: An Inventory*. Washington: National Research Council, National Academy of Sciences, 1961.

Dynes, Russell R. *Organized Behavior in Disaster*. Lexington, MA.: Lexington, 1970.

Fogleman, C.W. and V.J. Parenton. "Disaster and Aftermath: Selected Aspects of Individual and Group Behavior in Critical Situations." *Social Forces*. 3 (1959), 129-135.

Form, William H. and Charles P. Loomis. "The Persistence and Emergence of Social and Cultural Systems in Disasters." *American Sociological Review*. 21 (1956), 180-185.

Fritz, Charles E. and J.H. Mathewson. *Convergence Behavior in Disasters: A Problem in Social Control*. Washington: National Research Council, National Academy of Sciences, 1957.

Gillespie, D.K. "Psychological First Aid." *Journal of School Health*. 33 (1963), 391-395.

Grosser, George H., Henry Wechsler and Milton Greenblatt, eds. *The Threat of Impending Disaster: The Contributions to the Psychology of Stress*. Cambridge, MA.: MIT Press, 1964.

Hass, J. Eugene. "Lesson for Coping with Disasters in the Committee on the Alaska Earthquake." *The Great Alaska Earthquake of 1964: Human Ecology*. Washington: National Research Council, 1970, pp. 39-51.

Ikle, Fred C. *Social Aspects of War Time Evacuation of American Cities*. Washington: National Academy of Sciences, National Research Council Disaster, Research Group Publications, 1956.

Ikle, Fred C. *The Social Impact of Bomb Destruction*. Norman: University of Oklahoma Press, 1958.

Islam, M. Aminul. *Human Adjustment to Cyclone Hazards: A Case Study of Char Jabbar*. Toronto: University of Toronto, 1971.

James, W. "On Some Mental Effects of the Earthquake: Excerpt from 'Memories and Studies." In A.J. Carr and W.R. Steinhoff, eds. *Points of Departure*. N.Y.: Harper, 1960, pp. 35-42.

Killian, Lewis M. "The Significance of Multiple Group Membership in Disaster." *American Journal of Sociology*. 62 (January, 1952), 309-314.

Kilpatrick, F.P. "Problems of Perception in Extreme Situations." *Human Organization*. 16 (Summer, 1957), 20-22.

Lachman, Roy and William J. Bonk. "Behavior and Beliefs During the Recent Volcanic Eruption at Kapocho Hawaii." *Science*. 131 (1961), 1095-1096.

Lomnitz, Cinna. "Casualties and Behavior of Populations During Earthquakes." *Bulletin of the Seismological Society of America*. 60 (August, 1970), 1309-1313.

Loomis, C.P. "Social System Under Stress Disasters and Disruption." *Social Systems*. Princeton, N.J.: Van Nostrand, 1960.

Minnis, Mhyra S. *The Voice of the People in Disaster and After: A Study in Residential Integration*. Lubbock, TX.: Technical University, 1971.

"Organization and Group Behavior in Disasters." *American Behavioral Scientist.* 13:3 (January-February, 1970) (entire issue).

Perry, S.E. *The Child and His Family in Disaster.* Washington: National Research Council, National Academy of Sciences, 1956.

Walace, A.F.C. *Human Behavior in Extreme Situations.* Washington: National Academy of Sciences, National Research Council, Disaster Research Group Publications, 1956.

Wolfenstein, Martha. *Disaster: A Psychological Essay.* Glencoe, IL.: Free Press, 1957.

POLICE SOCIAL SERVICES

Crisis Intervention

Auten, James. "The Domestic Disturbance: A Policeman's Dilemma." *Police Chief.* 39:10 (October, 1972), 16-17, 20, 22.

Bard, Morton. "Alternatives to Traditional Law Enforcement." *Police* (November-December, 1970), 20.

Bard, M. *Family Crisis Intervention—From Concept to Implementation.* Washington: NCJRS, 1974.

Bard, Morton. "Iatrogenic Violence." *Police Chief.* 38:1 (January, 1971), 16-17.
Discusses intra-familial violence and a training of police to handle family crisis situations.

Bard, M. and J. Zacker. "Assaultiveness and Alcohol Use in Family Disputes—Police Perceptions." *Criminology.* 12:3 (1974), 281-292.

Bard, M. and J. Zacker. *Police Family Crisis Intervention and Conflict Management—An Action Research Analysis.* Springfield VA.: NTIS, 1972.
Study of two methods of resolving personal and family disputes by police in low income housing projects and by precinct crises intervention units.

Barocas, H.A. "Crisis Intervention and Iatrogenic Reactions." *Group Analysis.* 6:1 (1973), 36-37.
Criticism of police intervention in family crisis situations. Author assumes all police officers possess authoritarian personalities.

Barocas, H.A. "Urban Policeman: Crisis Mediators or Crisis Creators?" *American Journal of Orthopyschiatry.* 43:4 (1973), 632-639.

Berrey, Thomas G. "Police in Domestic Action." *Police Chief.* XLII:9 (September, 1975), 30-32.

Coffey, Alan R. *Police Intervention into Family Crisis.* Santa Cruz, CA.: Davis, 1975.

Columbus City Attorney. *Citizen Dispute Settlement—The Night Prosecutor Program of Columbus Ohio: An Exemplary Project.* Washington: NCJRS, 1974.
Nature and results of a diversion program dealing with family, neighborhood, and personal animosities as well as other minor complaints brought to the attention of the police.

Donovan, Edwin J. and John F. Sullivan. "Police Response to Family Disputes." *FBI Law Enforcement Bulletin.* 43:9 (September, 1974), 3-6.

Flint, Robert T. "Crisis Intervention Training." *FBI Law Enforcement Bulletin* (August, 1974), 6-9, 21.

Johnson, B.J. *Hotline for Youth.* Washington: GPO, 1968.
Use of teen hotlines as a crisis intervention resource to provide listening and communications for youth.

Kobetz, R.W., ed. *Crisis Intervention and the Police—Selected Readings.* Gaithersburg, MD.: IACP, 1974.

Lester, D. and G.W. Brockopp. *Crisis Intervention and Counseling by Telephone.* Springfield, IL.: C.C. Thomas, 1973.

London (Ontario) Police Force. *London (Ontario) Police Force—Family Consultant Services: Annual Report 1974.* Washington: NCJRS (Microfiche) 1974.

Lundman, Richard J. "Domestic Police Citizen Encounters." *Journal of Police Science and Administration.* 2:1 (March, 1974), 22-27.

Lundman, R.J. *Domestic Police Citizen Encounters.* Washington: NCJRS (Microfiche) n/d.

McGree, R.K. *Crisis Intervention in the Community.* Baltimore: University Park, 1974.

McGee, T.F. "Some Basic Considerations in Crisis Intervention." *Community Mental Health Journal.* 4 (1968).

Meyer, John C. Jr. "Social Aspects of Peace Keeping: Handling Personal Crisis Situations." *Police.* 16:11 (July, 1972), 41-45.

Mills, P. *Crisis Intervention Resource Manual.* Vermillion, S.D.: University of South Dakota, 1973.

National Institute of Law Enforcement and Criminal Justice. *Citizen Dispute Settlement: The Night Prosecutor Program of Columbus Ohio.* Washington: LEAA, 1974.

Newman, Charles L. "The Constructive Use of Police Authority with Youth and Family in Crisis." *Police* (May-June, 1968), 18-23.

Newman, Charles L. "Police and Families: Factors Affecting Police Intervention." *Police Chief.* XXXIX:3 (March, 1972), 24-30.

Parad, Howard J., ed. *Crisis Intervention: Selected Readings.* N.Y.: Family Service Association of America, 1965.

Parnas, Raymond I. "The Police Response to the Domestic Disturbance." *Wisconsin Law Review* (1967), 914-960.

Parnas, Raymond I. "The Response of Some Relevant Community Resources to Intra-Family Violence." *Indiana Law Journal.* XLIV:44 (1969).

Phelps, Lourn G., Jeffrey A. Schwarz and D.A. Liebman. "Training an Entire Division in Domestic Crisis Intervention." *Police Chief* (July, 1971).

Randolph, C.C. *Practical Theology for Crisis Intervention.* Nashville, TN.: Contact Teleministry, 1970.
Description of the establishment of a telephone answering service for emergency psychological assistance to the community.

Reiser, Martin. "Survey of Family Disturbance Calls and Mentally Ill Calls 1968." *Los Angeles Police Department.* 1968 (Mimeo).

Schwartz, A.J. "Crisis-communication and the Police Officer." *Police.* 16:6. 1972, 11-13.

Specter, G. and W. Claiborn. *Crisis Intervention.* N.Y.: Behavioral, 1973.

Walton, R.E. *Interpersonal Peacemaking Confrontations and Third Party Consultation.* Reading, MA.: Addison Wesley, 1969.

Handicapped

Collins, K.J. "The Deaf and the Police." *FBI Law Enforcement Bulletin.* 42:12 (1973), 2-6.
Describes NYPD system of emergency telephone and teletypewriter system which enables the deaf to contact police.

The Commission on Peace Officer Standards and Training. *Police/Public Contacts Involving Hearing, Speech and Language Disorders.* Sacramento: California Officer of Procurement, Publication Section, 1975.

Hewitt, S.E.K. "Police Should Be More Aware of the Problems of the Mentally Retarded." *Police Review (GB).* 83:4314 (1974), 1187-1195.

Langston, Paul. "Alarm Systems for the Elderly and Handicapped." *Social Work Today.* 18 (March, 1974), 44-45.

Pitchess, Peter J. "Communications Systems for the Deaf." *Police Chief.* XXXIX:4 (April, 1972), 56.
Describes emergency teletypewriter system which enables the deaf to communicate with police.

Stone, Bob. "He Speaks with His Hands." *Law and Order.* 14:3 (March, 1966), 18, 22-24, 65.
Chicago Police Officer trains the deaf in traffic safety. Officer uses sign language to communicate.

Mental Illness

Aubry, Arthur J. Jr. "The Criminal Psychopath in Law Enforcement." *Police.* 8:1 (September-October, 1963), 18-22.

Bard, Morton. "Extending Psychology's Impact Through Existing Community Institutions." *American Psychologist.* 24:6 (June, 1969), 610-612.

Bard, Morton. "Family Intervention Police Teams as a Community Mental Health Resource." *Journal of Criminal Law, Criminology and Police Science.* 60:2 (June, 1969), 247-250.

Bittner, Egon. "Police Discretion in Emergency Apprehension of Mentally Ill Persons." *Social Problems.* 14 (1967).

Brown, I.A. "Managing the Unruly Patient." *Police* (November-December, 1966).

Ephross, P.H. and P. French. "Social Service and the Police." *Hospital and Community Psychiatry.* 23 (1972), 61-63.

Fowler, Herbert B. "Police Handling of Emotionally Disturbed People." *FBI Law Enforcement Bulletin* (January, 1971), 16-20, 31.

Friedman, Merton H. "Community Mental Health Education with Police." *Mental Hygiene* (April, 1965).

Harris, Forrest D. "Psychiatric Emergencies: Handling of the Mental Ill." *Police* (March-April, 1968) 28-29.

Hewitt,S.E.K. "Police Should Be More Aware of the Problems of the Mentally Retarded." *Police Review (GB).* 19: (September, 1975) 1187-1195.

Hartley, Cope. "Specialized Police Work in Handling Mental Patients." *FBI Law Enforcement Bulletin.* 26:8 (August, 1957), 8-12.

Lantham, David. "Arresting the Insane." *Criminal Law Review* (September, 1974), 515-528.

Lauer, Robert, Charles Fosterling and Edward Colbach. "Police Are Mental Caregivers." *Police Chief* (November, 1973), 49-51.

McConahy, Malcolm W. "The Role of the Police in Mental Health." *Police.* 6:3 (January-February, 1962), 16, 78.

Mathews, R.A. and L.W. Rowland. *How to Recognize and Handle Abnormal People.* N.Y.: National Association for Mental Health, 1964.
Considerations for identifying the mentally ill and for handling violent and depressed persons and those suffering from physical illness or amnesia.

Moushigian, Charles and Everett Haley. "Mental Health Services in a Law Enforcement Setting." *Journal of California Law Enforcement.* 8:4 (April, 1974), 184-190.
Referral Service, Inter-Agency Program.

Parlour, Richard R. and Richard A. Ibaney. "Psychiatric Contributions to the Processes of the Law." *Police* (September-October, 1963).

Notifications

Craig, Y. "Police and Bereavement Communication." *Police Journal (GB).* 47:3 (1974), 246-250.

Kalaidjian, William G. "Notification." *Law and Order* (March, 1976), 69-71.

Kutscher, Austin H. *Death and Bereavement.* Springfield, IL.: C.C. Thomas, 1974.

Lawder, Lee E. "Breaking the 'Bad News' Call." *Law and Order.* 20:5 (May, 1972), 20-22.

Lindemann, E. "Symtomatology and Management of Acute Grief." *American Journal of Psychiatry.* 25 (1944).

Richardson, L. "Notification of Death." *FBI Law Enforcement Bulletin.* 44:5 (1974), 14-15.
Author suggests that officer have some advance of prior knowledge of person(s) to be notified and never make notification alone.

Rape Counseling

Amir, Menachim. *Patterns in Forcible Rape.* Chicago, IL.: University of Chicago Press, 1971.

Burgess, Ann Wolbert, and Lynda Lytle Holmstrom. *Rape: Victims of Crises.* Bowie, MD.: Brady, 1974.

Burgess, Ann Wolbert, and Lynda Lytle Holmstrom. "The Rape Victim in the Emergency Ward." *American Journal of Nursing.* 73:10. (October, 1973).

"Code R for Rape." *Newsweek* (November 13, 1972) 75.

Holstrom, Lynda L. and Ann W. Burgess. "Rape: The Victim and the Criminal Justice System." *International Journal of Criminology and Penology* (March, 1975), 101-110.

MacDonald, J.M. *Rape: Offenders and Their Victims.* Springfield, IL.: C.C. Thomas, 1971.
Authoritative analysis of rape which looks at the crime from the viewpoint of the offender, his victim, the physician, the psychiatrist, the police and the lawyer.

Massey, Joe B., Celso-Ramon Garcia and John P. Emich. "Management of Sexually Assaulted Females." *Obstetrics and Gynecology.* 38 (1971), 29-36.

Meyer, Mary. "Rape: The Victim's Point of View." *Police Law Quarterly.* 3:3 (1974), 38, 44.

Rowan, C.T. and D.M. Mazie. "The Terrible Trauma of Rape." *Readers Digest* (March, 1974), 198.

Stratton, John. "Law Enforcement's Participation in Crisis Counseling for Rape Victims." *Police Chief.* XLII:3 (March, 1976), 46-49.

Stratton, John. "Rape and the Victim: A New Role for Law Enforcement." *FBI Law Enforcement Bulletin* (November, 1975), 3-6.

Schultz, Leroy, ed. *Rape Victimology.* Springfield, IL.: C.C. Thomas, 1975.

Social Services

Chisholm, Dennis C. "Mobile Family Services Unit." *Police Chief.* XLI:12 (December, 1974), 16.

Cumming, Elaine, Ian M. Cumming and Laura Edell. "Policeman as Philosopher, Guide and Friend." *Social Problems.* 12:3 (Winter, 1965), 276-286.

Graham, Harold H. "Community Services." *FBI Law Enforcement Bulletin* (October, 1975), 24-26.

Harrison, Dorothy E. "New Dimensions in Community Development." *Law and Order.* 19:4 (April, 1971), 70-71.

Jenkins, Herbert T. "Utilizing Community Resources—A Report from Atlanta." *Police Chief.* XXXI (September, 1964), 25.

King, Glen D. "P-CR: Storefront Centers." *Police Chief.* 38:3 (March, 1971), 30-32.

Kopmeyer, M.R. "A Policeman's Job Is to . . . Help!" *Police* (July-August, 1970).

Mathis, Michel. "Priority Puzzle: What Are Police Policing?" *Christian Science Moniter* (January 12, 1968), 12.

Minnesota Governor's Commission on Crime Prevention and Control. *Minnesota—Police Referral Project: An Evaluation.* Washington: NCJRS (Microfiche) 1973.
Referral of non-criminal calls to appropriate social service agency.

O'Connell, Gerald and Harold Johnson. "The Blue Beret: A New Police Image." *Police Chief.* XLI:6 (June, 1974), 58-60.

O'Neill, Michael E. and Carlton J. Bloom. "The Field Officer: Is He Really Fighting Crime?" *Police Chief* (February, 1972).

"Police Chief Cites Assistance From Family Service." *Police.* 13:5 (May-June, 1969), 89-90.

Pomrenke, Norman E., C.E. Cherry and H. Burton. "A New Approach to Crime Prevention—Community Services." *Police Chief.* XXXLV:4 (April, 1967), 33-41.

Punch, Maurice and Trevor Naylor. "Police: A Social Service." *New Society.* 24:554 (May 17, 1973), 358-361.
Survey in Essex, Great Britain indicated 59% of all calls were of a service nature the remaining 41% related to law enforcement.

Stroh, Jay R. "Police Community Service Program Successful in Inglewood, CA." *Police Chief.* XLI:6 (June, 1974), 20.

Vollmer, August. "The Policeman As A Social Worker." *Policemen's News* (June, 1919).

Whitehouse, Jack E. "Compiling a Police Social Service Referral Directory." *Law and Order.* 20:3 (March, 1972), 48-51, 58-59.

Whitehouse, Jack E. "Historical Perspectives on the Police Community Service Function." *Journal of Police Science and Administration.* 1:1 (March, 1973), 87-92.

Whitehouse, Jack E. "Law Enforcement and Community Programs." *Journal of California Law Enforcement.* 8:1 (July, 1973), 28, 33-39.
Slightly revised version of "Compiling a Police Social Service Referral Directory" cited above. Lists sample table of contents and advice on how to compile a pocket sized referral directory for field officers.

Young, Frank M. *Social Welfare Functions of the Police in a Changing Society.* Dundee, Scotland: City of Dundee Police, 1974.

Social Work in Police Agencies

Burns, Jeremy. "Distinguishing the Rules and Responsibilities of Police and Social Workers." *Social Work Today* (February 19, 1976), 709.

Chwast, Jack. "Casework Treatment in a Police Setting." *Federal Probation.* 18 (1954).

Colbach, Edward M. and Charles D. Fosterling. *Police Social Work.* Springfield, IL.: C.C. Thomas, 1976.

Cowger, C.D. and C.R. Atherton. "Social Control: A Rationale for Social Welfare." *Social Work.* 19:4 (1974), 456-462.
Authors advocate deeper social worker involvement in social control.

Euler, James et al. "The Police Social Worker: A Community Broker." *Police Chief.* XLI:6 (June, 1974), 28-32.

Michaels, Rhoda A. and Harvey Treger. "Social Work in Police Departments." *Social Work.* 18:5 (1973), 67-75.

Richan, Willard C. and Allen R. Mendelsohn. *Social Work: The Unloved Profession.* N.Y.: New Viewpoints, 1973.

Treger, Harvey. "The Police-Social Work Team: A New Model for Community Service." *Law and Order.* 21:3 (March, 1973), 40–41, 64.

Treger, Harvey. *The Police-Social Work Team: A New Model for Interprofessional Cooperation—A University*

Demonstration Project in Manpower Training and Development. Springfield, IL.: C.C. Thomas, 1975.

Treger, Harvey et al. "Police-Social Work Team Model: Some Preliminary Findings and Implications for System Change." *Crime and Delinquency*. 20:3 (July, 1974), 281-290.

Trojanwicz, Robert C. "The Contrasting Behavioral Styles of Policemen and Social Workers." *Public Personnel Review*. 32 (October, 1971), 246-251.

Yeow Shang Yang. "Role of Police in Social Work." *Singapore Police Journal* (January, 1972), 90-114.

SEARCH AND RESCUE

Rescue Techniques

Adams, James and Lee Brenner. "Police Officer: Emergency Medical Technicians." *Law and Order* (November, 1975), 66-68.

Aircraft Rescue and Fire Fighting Vehicles. Boston: National Fire Protection, 1970.

"Air Rescue Flights Begin in Fairbanks." *Aviation Week and Space Technology*. (August 21, 1967).

Best, Donald R. "Car-over Rescue." *Police*. 10:4 (March-April, 1966), 44-46.

Brosnan, Thomas J. *Emergency Rescue Techniques*. Santa Cruz, CA.: Davis, 1970.

Buchanan, James V. "Pittsburgh's Special Service Patrol." *Law and Order*. 13:11 (November, 1965), 67.

"Chicago Fire Departments' Air Rescue Unit." *Rotor and Wing* (March-April, 1973).

City of London Constabulary. *Emergency Helicopter Rescue Scheme for Highrise Buildings*. London: City of London Constabulary, 1974.

Egan, Cy. *Some Very Special Men: The Emergency Service to the Rescue*. N.Y.: Harper & Row, 1974.

"The Emergency Service Division—Operation Rescue!" *Spring 3100* (April, 1950), 20-23.

Fagerstrom, Dorothy. "Emergency—Get Me the Police." *Law and Order*. 16:1 (January, 1968), 40.

Fisher, E. "Emergency Helicopter Rescue Scheme for High-Rise Buildings." *Police Journal*. 48:2 (1975), 113-120.

"Flathead County Rescue and Life Saving Association." *Law Enforcement Bulletin* (November, 1949).

Gillmouthe, Rupert L. "Hood River County Rescue Groups." *FBI Law Enforcement Bulletin* (November, 1973).

Gilpin, Henry. "Search and Rescue Team." *FBI Law Enforcement Bulletin* (September, 1975), 16-21.

Glass, Albert J. "The Psychological Aspects of Emergency Situations." *Police* (July-August, 1970).

Grant, Harvey D. "Vehicle Rescue: A System of Operations." *Law and Order* (December, 1975), 46.

Henderson, Harry. "Call for Mr. Emergency." *Readers Digest*. 69 (October, 1956), 187-194.

Jones, Emmet L. "Police Fire Emergency Rescue." *Police Chief* (January, 1965).

Kenny, Raymond J. "Ice Rescue Techniques." *FBI Law Enforcement Bulletin*. 37:1 (January, 1968), 2-7.

Lobsenz, Norman M. *Emergency*. N.Y.: McKay, 1958.
Popular account of the Emergency Service Division of the NYPD.

Ludwig, Donald J. and William T. Brennan. "Appraising the Police Emergency Rescue Program." *Police* 8:4 (March-April, 1964), 28-30.

MacInnes, Hamish. *Call Out*. London: Hodder & Stoughton, 1973.

McAlpin, Niall. "Mountain Beat." *Police (GB)*. (January, 1974), 16-18.
Royal Ulster Constabulary Mountain Rescue Team.

McGuire, James J. and Matthew L. Byrne. "History and Function of the Emergency Service District of the New York City Police Department." *Police*. 13:6 (July-August, 1969), 54-59.

Marshall, Lewis A. and John A. Murphy. "Benefits of Rescue Squad Service in Providence, R.I." *FBI Law Enforcement Bulletin* (July, 1958).

Nalley, Gann L. "Operations of a Rescue Squad in Little Rock." *FBI Law Enforcement Bulletin*. 26:3 (March, 1957), 23-25.

Schwartz, Stephen H. *Police Emergency Squad*. N.Y.: Grosset & Dunlap, 1975.

Search Techniques

Bastrup, Harold A. "The Missing Child." *Law and Order*. 17:4 (April, 1969), 92-93, 111.

Bland, Frank. "Planned Program of Search and Rescue Work." *FBI Law Enforcement Bulletin* (June, 1959), 3-22.

Burnstad, T.R. "An All Purpose Posse." *FBI Law Enforcement Bulletin* (October, 1954), 26-28.

Clemmons, Bryan. "An Air Patrol Expedites the Sheriff's Work." *FBI Law Enforcement Bulletin* (October, 1954), 23-25.

Clifford, Alice E. "A Child Is Missing." *Police Chief* (March, 1959), 22.

Department of the Army. *National Search and Rescue Manual*. Washington: GPO (July, 1973).

Flake, James. "Search and Rescue Team." *Law and Order*. 14:8 (August, 1966), 32-34.

Gilmouthe, Rupert L. "The Use of Small Aircraft in Police Work." *FBI Law Enforcement Bulletin* (March, 1959), 9-12.

Hipskind, V.K. "How to Search for a Missing Child." *FBI Law Enforcement Bulletin* (August, 1954), 19-21.

Jensen, T.G. "The Aeroplane and Search and Rescue." *Australian Police Journal*. 27:2 (1973), 107-124.

McDougall, C.A. "Mountainous Area Search and Rescue Can Be Dangerous." *FBI Law Enforcement Bulletin* (April, 1962), 5-8.

McGrath, Richard T. "Rescue of Persons Lost in Black Hills." *FBI Law Enforcement Bulletin* (October, 1958), 21-23.

McKenzie, Arthur R. "Specialized Unit Answers Calls of Search and Rescue." *FBI Law Enforcement Bulletin* (August, 1960), 15-17.

McLean, Ken. "The R.U.C. Mountain Rescue Team." *Constabulary Gazette* (December, 1973), 15.

Nimmo, George M. "Organization of Search Parties for Lost Persons." *FBI Law Enforcement Bulletin*. 26:1 (January, 1957), 6-8.

Parmenter, Russell E. "Search and Rescue . . .Challenge of Alaska." *Military Police Journal* (February, 1964), 5-7.

Richardson, Cecil. "Hunting for Lost Persons." *FBI Law Enforcement Bulletin* (August, 1954), 22.

"Terrain Search by Helicopter." *FBI Law Enforcement Bulletin* (May, 1954), Inside back cover.

Trafton, William W. "Hunters in Alaska File Travel Plans for Added Safety." *FBI Law Enforcement Bulletin* (February, 1960).

Tracking

Ayala, Henry V. "Tracking Prison Escapees Is an Art." *FBI Law Enforcement Bulletin* (February, 1964), 3-22.

Hicks, Sam. "Tracking—A Vanishing Heritage." *Police*. 4:5 (May-June, 1960), 43-46.

Patton, Fred O. "Art of Tracking Wanted, Lost and Missing Persons." *FBI Law Enforcement Bulletin* (January, 1956), 3-23.

Sardone, L.T. "Australia's Uncanny Black Trackers." *Law and Order* (September, 1956).

"Techniques in Pursuit of the Fleeing Felon." *FBI Law Enforcement Bulletin*. 26:7 (July, 1957), 7-10.
Discusses tracking, road blocks and use of dogs, airplanes and surveillance.

SNOW MOBILING

Coricoran, Edward W. "Snow Mobiling within the Law." *FBI Law Enforcement Bulletin*. 43:3 (March, 1974).

Redmond, Richard C. "Are You Having a Problem with Snowmobiling?" *Law and Order*. 18:1 (January, 1970), 24, 52.

Vaupel, Carl F. Jr. "A Modern Recreation and Transportation Concern for Police—Snowmobiles." *Police*. 15:4 (March-April, 1971), 24-26.

PART VI
STAFF AND AUXILIARY SERVICES

STAFF AND AUXILIARY SERVICES

STAFF SERVICES—GENERAL

Dale, Ernest and Lyndale F. Urwick. *Staff in Organizations*. N.Y.: McGraw, 1960.

Friedman, Lucy N., Samuel S. Herrup and Hans Zeisel. "Saving Police Man Power Through Court Appearance Control." *Journal of Police Science and Administration*. 1:2 (June, 1973), 131-137.

Grant, Jack E. "Tell the Boss—Don't Ask." *Public Personnel Review*. 19 (April, 1958).

Hanley, David M. "Staff Study." *Law and Order*. 23:5 (May, 1975), 66-67.
Outlines proper format for police staff studies.

Peel, John Donald. "Establishing a Security Bureau in Your Department." *Police*. 16:2 (October, 1971), 42-47.
Guidelines for licensing and training of private security agencies.

Taussig, John N. *Expense Account Control*. N.Y.: AMA, 1967.

CHAPLAINS

Asmuth, Robert. *Creature with a Billy Club: The Story of Police Beat Chaplain*. Plainfield, N.J.: Logos, 1971.

Carter, Charles R. "The Police Chaplain." *FBI Law Enforcement Bulletin*. 38:9 (September, 1969), 2-5.

Dooley, R. Joseph. "My Uniformed Parish." *FBI Law Enforcement Bulletin*. 41:10 (October, 1972), 3-7, 28.

Fox, Harry G. "Preachers with Badges—Police-Community Clergy." *Police Chief*. XLI:11 (December, 1974), 57-59.
Activities of police-community clergy unit in Philadelphia.

Kalaidjiam, William G. "The Police Chaplain." *Law and Order*. 13:9 (September, 1965), 36-39.

Massey, Charles E. "Chaplaincy for the Police Force." *R.C.M.P. Quarterly* (July, 1975), 30-33.

Powers, Richard C. "When the Chapel Meets the Street." *Police Chief*. 16:5 (May, 1974), 58-59.

Ryan, Gerald J. "The Role and Contribution of a Chaplain to a Community Police Department." *Law and Order*. 19:9 (September, 1971), 86, 88-89, 91.

Sylle, Edward. "A Chaplaincy Program for Better Police-Community Relations." *Police Chief*. XLI:2 (February, 1974), 18-19.

Wentink, William R. "The Evaluation of a Chaplain's Department." *Law and Order*. 24:6 (June, 1976), 56-64.

DEBRIEFING

Blain, Terry. "The After Action Report." *Military Police Journal*. 17 (January, 1968).

Gordon, F.A. "De-Brief." *International Criminal Police Review*. 27:257 (1972), 114-116.
De-briefing teaches what has been learned, what mistakes have been made and how to improve future situations. Planning of future actions is aided by the lessons of the past.

EDUCATION CO-ORDINATION

Kelley, Clarence M. "The College Co-ordinator: A New Police Post." *Police Chief*. XXXVII:4 (April, 1970), 48-50.
Police position Kansas City Police Department advises personnel on college courses, seminars, special short courses and other programs.

Hancock, Donald. "The Police Administrator's Role in Correlating Academic Resources." *Police Chief*. XXXIX:4 (April, 1972), 53-55.

INTERNAL AFFAIRS

Internal Affairs—General

Beigel, Herbert. "Criminal Law: The Investigation and Prosecution of Police Corruption." *Journal of Criminal Law and Criminology*. 65:2 (1974), 135-136.

Benford, M.D. "Disciplinary Review Officer." *Law and Order*. 20:6 (June, 1972), 28-29, 58.
Inspector reviews cases which carry a penalty of less than 30 days; others go to department trial board.

Blanks, William W. "Guardians of Integrity." *Law and Order*. 20:3 (March, 1972) 12-15.

Brown, Lee P. "Handling Complaints Against the Police." *Police* (May-June, 1968).

Caulfield, B.A. *Chicago—Police Department: Access to Information, Personnel Practices and Internal Control—A Review of Major Reports*. Washington: NCJRS (Microfiche).
This review deals with sections of reports by LEAA, the IACP and two reports by the Chicago Commission on human relations concerned with the problem of information access, personnel practices and internal affairs.

Cohen, Bernard. *The Police Internal Administration of Justice in New York City*. N.Y.: Rand, 1970.

Crane, Richard A. and Gregory J. Schlesinger. *Citizen Complaints of Police Misconduct and the Internal Affairs Division of the Chicago Police Department*.

Chicago: Chicago Police Department, May 15, 1971. (Mimeo).

Dempsey, Robert R. "Police Disciplinary Systems." *Police Chief* (May, 1972).
The results of a survey of disciplinary procedures in forty-six police departments.

Forbus, Lloyd V. "Internal Investigations." *Law and Order.* 19:5 (May, 1971), 88-91.

"Grievance Response Mechanisms for Police Misconduct." *Virginia Law Review.* 55 (June, 1969), 909-951.

Harding, R.W. "Police Disciplinary Procedures in England and Western Australia." *University of Western Australia Law Review.* 10 (June, 1972), 195-222.

Haywood, A. "The Handling of Complaints Investigations." *Police Review.* 80:4156 (1972); 80:4157 (1972), 80:4159 (1972).
Articles which closely examine the investigations against police officers in Great Britain.

Hillgren, James S. and L.W. Spradlin. "A Positive Disciplinary System for the Dallas Police." *Police Chief.* XLII:7 (July, 1975), 65-67.

New York City Police Department. *New York Police Department: Corruption Control Manual.* Washington: NCJRS (Microfiche) n/d.
Detailed procedure manual for investigating complaints against police.

Zavislak, H.C. "The Citizen Complaint Process—More Than a Necessary Evil." *Police Chief.* XLII:3 (March, 1976), 65.

Trial Boards

Iannone, Marvin D. *The Discriptive Study of the Disciplinary Program of the Los Angeles Police Department.* Unpub. Masters thesis, California State College at Los Angeles, 1967.

Los Angeles Police Department. *Board of Rights Manual: Rules and Procedures Governing the Conduct of Board of Rights Hearings.* Los Angeles: LAPD, 1953.

Los Angeles Police Department. *Board of Rights Manual.* Los Angeles: LAPD, 1971.

Citizen Complaints Against the Police

American Civil Liberties Union. *The Matter of Redress.* Los Angeles: ACLU, 1969.
Account and statistics from ACLU sponsored neighborhood police complaint center.

Barnabas, A. *Citizen's Grievances and Administration.* N.Y.: International Publications Service, 1969.

Chevigny, P.G. *Police Complaints—A Handbook.* N.Y.: American Civil Liberties Union, 1971.
A guidebook for lawyers for handling cases in which their client is alleging police abuse of authority or police misconduct.

"Complaints Against the Police." *Criminal Law Review.* (April, 1973).

Gellhorn, Walter. *When Americans Complain: Governmental Grievance Procedures.* Cambridge, MA.: Harvard University Press, 1966.

Hudson, James R. "Police-Citizen Encounters That Lead to Citizen Complaints." *Social Problems.* 18 (Fall, 1970), 179-193.

Khan, A.N. "Complaints Against Police in Australia." *Police Review (GB),* (October 15, 1976).

Naegele, Timothy D. "Civilian Complaints Against the Police in Los Angeles." *Issues in Criminology.* 3:1 (Summer, 1967), 7-34.

Parker, J.L. "Complaints Against Police—Could We Accept the Ombudsman." *Police College Magazine* (Autumn, 1969), 44-46, 57.

"Police Act 1976: Part 1— Complaints Against the Police." *Police Review (GB),* (August 20, 1976), 1047-1055.

Russell, K. "Police Complaints." *New Society.* 23:541 (1973), 360-361.

Schwartz, Lois B. "Complaints Against the Police." *University of Pennsylvania Law Review.* 118 (June, 1970), 1023-1035.

Whitehouse, Jack E. "Citizen Complaints and Commendations." *Law and Order.* 15:12 (December, 1967), 82-85.
Best evidence shows that police receive eight commendations for each complaint.

JAIL ADMINISTRATION

Jail Administration—General

Alexander, Myrl E. *Jail Administration.* Springfield, IL.: C.C. Thomas, 1957.

Burns, H. *Origin and Development of Jails in America.* Carbondale, IL.: Southern Illinois University, n/d.
Brief historical essay on the origin and development of jails in America with a second section on jail conditions of the present.

Cushman, R.C. *Memorandum on the 'Jail Problem'—Advice to the County Executive and Advice to the Sheriff.* Springfield, VA.: NTIS, 1973.

Goldfarb, Ronald. *Jails: The Ultimate Ghetto of the Criminal Justice System.* N.Y.: Anchor, 1975.

Murphy, J.E. "The Planning of Jail Facilities." *Police Chief.* 37:11 (November, 1970), 42-48.

Olsen, Adolph S. "Clay County Regional Juvenile Detention Center." *FBI Law Enforcement Bulletin.* 42:1 (January, 1973), 14-15, 29-31.

Pappas, Nick. *The Jail—Its Operation and Management.* Washington: U.S. Bureau of Prisons, 1971.

Plautz, Michael. "A New Look in Jails." *Law and Order* (January, 1976).

Powledge, F. *Seeds of Anguish—An ACLU Study of the D.C. Jail.* Washington: American Civil Liberties Union, 1972.
American Civil Liberties Union investigation of intake procedures, living conditions, and disciplinary practices in the District of Columbia Jail.

Shulman, Harry Manuel. "What Is Wrong with American Prisons and Jails." *Journal of Criminal Law, Criminology and Police Science.* 45:6(March-April, 1955), 662–667.

Skousen, W. Cleon. "Suggestions for a Jail Manual." *Law and Order*. 23:4 (April, 1975), 8, 10, 12, 14, 16.

"Specialized Searches for Prison Security." *FBI Law Enforcement Bulletin*. 35:12 (December, 1966), 13-14.

U.S. Bureau of Prisons. *New Roles for Jails: Guidelines for Planning*. Washington: U.S. Bureau of Prisons, 1969.

Escapes

Canada Solicitor General. *Canada—Commission of Inquiry on Penitentiary Security Within the Quebec Region—Preliminary Report on the Escape of Five Inmates, on May 13, 1973 from the Correctional Development Center in the City of Laval*. Washington: NCJRS (Microfiche) 1973.

Finds that deficiencies in performance by personnel were the major factor exploited in the escape, with weaknesses in physical facilities and management being involved to a lesser degree.

Holt, N. *Escape from Custody*. Washington: NCJRS (Microfiche) 1974.

Luszki, Walter A. "Beating the Underground Molers." *Journal of Criminal Law, Criminology and Police Science*. 48:1 (May-June, 1957), 103-105.

Morrow, William R. "Escapes of Psychiatric Offenders." *Journal of Criminal Law, Criminology and Police Science*. 60:4 (December, 1969), 464-478.

LEGAL ADVISORS

Burpo, John H. "Advancing the Police Legal Advisor Concept." *Police Chief*. XXXVI:9 (September, 1969), 29-30.

Caplan, Gerald M. "The Police Legal Advisor." *Journal of Criminal Law, Criminology and Police Science*. 58:3 (September, 1967), 303-309.

Dallas Police Department. *Dallas—Police Department: Legal Aids for Police—Interim Evaluation Report, July 1, 1973 to December 31, 1973*. Washington: NCJRS (Microfiche) 1974.

English, Robert E. "Lawyers in the Station House?" *Journal of Criminal Law, Criminology and Police Science*. 57:3 (September, 1966), 283-290.

Heath, Edwin D. Jr. "The Police Legal Unit." *FBI Law Enforcement Bulletin*. 41:8 (August, 1972), 22-25.

Inbau, Fred. "The Police Legal Advisor—Is He Needed in Your Department?" *FBI Law Enforcement Bulletin*. 26 (March-April, 1971), 17-18.

Inbau, F.E. "Police Legal Advisors: Their Role." *Police Yearbook*. Washington: IACP, 1971.

Landenslager, Samuel. "Proving Legal Assistance to Small and Rural Law Enforcement Agencies: The Regional Legal Advisor." *Police Chief*. 16:8 (August, 1974), 53-58.

Palmer, John W. "The Police Para-Professional: An Alternative to the Police Legal Advisor." *Police Chief*. XL:12 (December, 1973), 56-57.

Schmidt, W.W. *Guidelines for a Police Legal Unit*. Gaithersburg, MD.: IACP, 1972.

Wise, H. Lake. *Dallas Police Legal Liaison—An Exemplary Project*. Washington: NCJRS, 1976.

Wise, H. Lake. *Legal Liaison Division of the Dallas Police Department*. Washington: LEAA (March, 1976).

LIBRARY SERVICES

Baril, L.J. and F.S. Horvath. *Law Enforcement Libraries—Final Report*. Washington: NCJRS (Microfiche) 1971.

Baril, L.J. and F.S. Horvath. *Law Enforcement Libraries—Final Report: Extract Bibliography*. Washington: NCJRS (Microfiche).

A listing of about 900 books and other material recommended for inclusion in a police library.

"Books for Your Library." *Police Review (GB)*, 82:4243 (1974), 585-586.

Suggestions for books and periodicals to be selected for a police library.

Boughourian, Gay F. "The Professional Law Enforcement Library: A Checklist and Guide for Planning." *Police Chief*. XLI:1 (January, 1974), 53-56.

Brett, D.T. "The Police College Library." *Police Journal (GB)*, 39 (January, 1966), 26-31.

Coffield, C.H. "Criminology Reference Library." *Police*. 6:2 (November-December, 1961), 32-34.

Crooke, William M. "An Information Center." *Police*. 6:4 (March-April, 1962), 39-40.

Dolan, Margaret M. "A New Image for the Police Officer." *Law and Order*. 12:4 (April, 1964), 68-69.

Describes the use of law libraries.

"Growing Library Is Aid to Policeman." *Police Journal (St. Louis)*, 17 (April, 1964), 6-7.

Hasler, Terry. "It's a Library for Everyone: Commissioner's Reference Library." *Job* (January 9, 1976), 4.

Horvath, Frank and William Horn. "A System for Establishing Law Enforcement Libraries." *Police Chief*. XXXIX:6 (June, 1972), 58-61.

Leonard, V.A. "The Police Library." *Police*. 2:6 (July-August, 1958), 39.

McMurray, Wallace. "Salvaging an Important Training Aid from File 13." *Law and Order*. 12:2 (February, 1964), 60-61.

Suggest cataloging of police journals for police academies.

Martello, Francis L. "Building a Bibliotheke." *Police*. 5:5 (May-June, 1961), 69-70.

Osborne, Andrew. *Serial Publications: Their Place and Treatment in Libraries*. Chicago: Chicago American Library Association, 1955.

Shaw, William. "The Kodak Technical Library." *Law and Order*. 20:4 (April, 1972), 38, 40, 42, 44, 50.

"Training Division Room 108." *Chicago Police Star*. 8 (February, 1967).

Vandiver, James V. "Bound Police Periodicals: Priceless References." *Law and Order*. 18:12 (December, 1970), 42, 50.

PAPER WORK

James, Edward. "Don't Cut Down on Paperwork Reporting—Eliminate It!" *Law and Order.* 19:12 (December, 1971), 34-35.

James, Edward. "How to Put 'Immediacy' into Report Handling." *Law and Order.* 23:5 (May, 1975), 42, 50.

Lucas, Ed. "Eliminating Paperwork for the Police Officer." *Law and Order.* 14:2 (February, 1966), 62-64, 76.

Rieder, Robert J. "Police Paperwork Problem." *Law and Order.* 18:10 (October, 1970), 96-97, 99-104.

Weber, Warren C. and Edwin F. Duran. "Montclair Streamlines Its Police Reporting Procedures." *Police Chief.* XLI:7 (July, 1974), 38-39.

Wikoff, J.M. "Trimming Paper Work Puts More Men on Street." *Law and Order.* 15:12 (December, 1967), 30-31.

PSYCHOLOGISTS

Mann, Philip A. *Psychological Consultation with a Police Department: A Demonstration of Cooperative Training in Mental Health.* Springfield, IL.: C.C. Thomas, 1973.

Megerson, John S. "The Police Counselor Concept." *Law and Order.* 18:9 (September, 1970), 123-124.
The use of counselors in solving the emotional problems of police officers.

Rankin, James H. "Preventive Psychiatry in the Los Angeles Police Department." *Police.* 1:6 (July-August, 1957), 24-29.

Reisner, Martin. "The Police Department Psychologist." *Police.* 14 (1970).

Reisner, Martin. "The Police Psychologist: A New Role." *Professional Psychology* (May, 1973), 119-120.

Reisner, Martin. "The Police Psychologist as Consultant." *Police* (January-February, 1971).

Reisner, Martin. "Psychological Research in an Urban Police Department." *Police* (November, 1971).

Reisner, Martin. "A Psychologist's View of the Badge." *Police Chief* (September, 1970).

Schlossberg, Harvey and Lucy Freeman. *Psychologist with a Gun.* N.Y.: Coward, McCann & Georghegan, 1975.

Wagner, Marcia. "Action and Reaction: The Establishment of a Counseling Service in the Chicago Police Department." *Police Chief.* XLIII:1 (1976), 20-23.

PROPERTY STORAGE

Crooke, William M. "Property Control." *Police.* 8:3 (January-February, 1964), 46-49.
The handling of the property of others by police for use as evidence or safe keeping or distruction as contraband.

Garza, D. and James J. Worsham. "Police Property Storage." *Police Chief.* XLI:1 (January, 1974) 51-52.

"Lakewood Department Institutes 'Identifical' for Property and Evidence Control." *Colorado Policeman.* 10:3 (1973).

PUBLIC INFORMATION

Blucher, P.R. "Ontario Provincial Police Public Information Program." *Canadian Police Chief.* 63:3 (1974), 9-11, 32.

DiGennaro, Arthur F. "Public Information Branch—May We Help You?" *Police Chief.* XL:3 (March, 1973), 30-33.

Eike, D.R. "Needed: Police Information—Police Understanding." *Police Chief.* XXXV:2 (February, 1968), 36-37.

Gray, B.M. *Police Reports to the Public.* Springfield, VA.: NTIS, 1973.
Outline of the minimum basic data elements which should be utilized in the preparation of police reports to city officials and to the general public.

Hayward, Frank P. "Developing the Public Information Function." *FBI Law Enforcement Bulletin* (February, 1975), 13-15.

Mitchell, M. Carter. *Public Information and Law Enforcement.* Santa Cruz, CA.: Davis, 1975.

Page, Ralph. "Police Public Information—Who—What—When—Why—How." *Police Chief.* 37:9 (October, 1970), 28, 256.

Sills, Arthur J. "The Police Blotter and the Public's Right to Know." *FBI Law Enforcement Bulletin* (June, 1969), 6-8.

PURCHASING

Aerospace Corporation. *Equipment Systems Improvement Program—Law Enforcement Development Group Annual Operating Plan. Fiscal Year 1974.* Washington: NCJRS (Microfiche) 1973.

Aerospace Corporation. *Equipment Systems Improvement Program—Law Enforcement Development Group Annual Operating Plan Fiscal Year 1974.* Washington: NCJRS (Microfiche) 1973.

Aljian, George W. *Purchasing Handbook.* 3rd ed. N.Y.: McGraw Hill, 1973.

Ammer, Dean S. *Purchasing and Materials Management.* Lexington, MA.: Lexington, 1974.

Ayoob, Massad F. "Product Evaluations." *Law and Order.* 121:4 (April, 1973), 111.

Buckley, John L. "Selecting Security Equipment Systems." *Law and Order.* 12:4 (April, 1964), 30-33, 70.

Busch, Ted. "Competitive Bidding: Boon or Boondoggle." *Law and Order.* 16:2 (February, 1968), 72-76.

Callahan, Leo F. et al. "The Performance Guarantee: A Reasonable Alternative for Law Enforcement Hardware Systems Acquisition." *Police Chief.* XLI:11 (November, 1974), 24-25.

England, Wilbur B. *Purchasing and Materials Management: Principals and Cases.* Homewood, IL.: Irwin, 1975.

Heinritz, Stuart F. and Paul V. Farrell. *Purchasing: Principals and Applications.* 5th ed. Englewood Cliffs, N.J. Prentice Hall, 1971.

Kudrna, Dennis A. *Purchasing Managers Decision Handbook.* Boston: Cahners, 1975.

Ku, R. and E. Bunten. *LEAA Police Equipment Survey of 1972 V1—The Need for Standards Priorities for Police Equipment: Law Enforcement Standards Program.* Washington: NCJRS (Microfiche) 1974.

"The Police: Victims of Product Profiteers." *Police Chief.* 39:2 (February, 1972).

Deplores shady businessmen moving into police equipment fields.

Shaw, William. "User Oriented Product Evaluation." *Law and Order.* 21:4 (April, 1973), 62-66.

"Timely Tips on Uniform Purchasing and Maintenance." *Police Chief.* XLII:10 (October, 1975).

RECORDS

Records—General

Bradley, Robert E. "Power Files Relieve Record Burden." *Law and Order.* 13:3 (March, 1965), 48, 70.

Cole, Jim. "Record Keeping." *Law and Order.* 21:9 (September, 1973), 104-105, 107.

Coon, Thomas F. "Miscellaneous Files." *Police.* 7:6 (July-August, 1963), 42-44.

Cross, Harold L. *The People's Right to Know: Legal Access to Public Records and Proceedings.* N.Y.: Columbia University Press, 1954.

David, Edward M. "An Automated Field Interview System." *FBI Law Enforcement Bulletin.* 42:9 (September, 1973), 24-28.

Fagerstrom, Dorothy. "Simplicity and Flexibility in Records." *Law and Order.* 23:9 (September, 1975), 90-92.

Hanna, D.G. and J.R. Kleberg. *Police Records System for the Small Department.* Springfield, IL.: C.C. Thomas, 1969.

A guide to establish a workable police records function for the small law enforcement agency.

Hewitt, William H. *Police Records Administration.* N.Y.: Aqueduct, 1968.

Hipskind, V.K. "Police Personnel Accident Reports and Records." *Police.* 9:4 (March-April, 1965), 74-76.

Hunter, T.P. "Records Systems in Small Police Departments." *Police.* 6:3 (January-February, 1962), 52-56.

Institute of Public Administration. *Crime Records in Police Management.* N.Y.: Institute of Public Administration, 1952.

International Association of Chiefs of Police. *National Crime Information Center—Article File: Report on Legislation Relating to Serially Numbered Property.* Washington: NCJRS (Microfiche) Program.

Article file is a computerized storage system for recording stolen property.

McGhee, A. Lee. *Police Records Manual.* Athens, GA.: Institute of Government, University of Georgia, 1970.

MacKay, Neil. "Eliminating Bulky Filing." *Law and Order.* 14:9 (September, 1966), 90-93.

"National Bomb Data Center." *FBI Law Enforcement Bulletin.* (December, 1973).

National Commission on Urban Transportation. *Maintaining Accident Records.* Chicago: Public Administration Service, 1958.

Northwestern University Traffic Institute. *Improvement of the Present System of Traffic Accident Records.* Evanston, IL.: Northwestern University Traffic Institute, 1963.

"R.C.M.P. Canadian Bomb Data Centre." *Royal Canadian Mounted Police Gazette* (November, 1973).

"Reporting and Researching Traffic Accidents." *Police Chief.* XXXIX:4 (April, 1972), 58-60.

Shaw, William. "Updating Previous Reports." *Law and Order.* 22:9 (September, 1974), 52, 54-56, 60, 62-63.

Simonis, Francis J. "New York State's Reference Marker System." *Police.* 16:11 (July, 1972), 36-37.

Traffic records system designed to reduce accidents and provide accurate location identification for highway hazards.

Traffic Institute Northwestern University. *Improvement of the Present System of Traffic Accident Records.* Evanston, IL.: Traffic Institute, Northwestern University, 1963.

"Transport and Repair of Records." *FBI Law Enforcement Bulletin.* 34:10 (October, 1965), 16-17.

United States Department of Justice. *Manual of Police Records.* Washington: GPO, July, 1966.

Vandiver, James V. "Juvenile Records are Justifiable." *Police.* 15:2 (November-December, 1970), 41-42.

Williston, Robert M. "Collection and Correlation of Accident Reports." *Traffic Digest* (August, 1966).

Witte, William M. "Records System Improvement Reduces Crime Rate in Las Vegas." *Police.* 13:5 (May-June, 1969), 77-79.

Expunction of Criminal Records

Blunt, Robert C. "Developments in the Law: Expunction of Arrest Record Entries." *FBI Law Enforcement Bulletin* (May, 1976), 28-31.

Damaska, Mirjan R. "Adverse Legal Consequences of Conviction and Their Removal: A Comparative Study." *Journal of Criminal Law, Criminology and Police Science.* 59:4 (December, 1968), 542-568.

Kogon, Bernard and Donald L. Loughery Jr. "Sealing and Expungement of Criminal Records—The Big Lie." *Journal of Criminal Law, Criminology and Police Science.* 61:3 (September, 1970), 378-392.

"Police Records of Arrest: A Brief for the Right to Remove them from Police Files." *St. Louis University Law Journal* (Winter, 1972).

"Privacy at your Fingertips—The Right of an Acquitted to Retrieve Fingerprints and Photograph Records." *Southwestern Law Journal* (August, 1972).

Shappley, W.L. Jr. "Branded: Arrest Records of the

Unconvicted." *Mississippi Law Journal*. 44:5 (1973), 928-946.

Microfilm

Avedon, Donald. *Computer Output Microfilm*. Silver Springs, MD.: National Microfilm Association, 1971.

Dobrovolny, Fred. "Microfilming Identification Records." *FBI Law Enforcement Bulletin*. 38:2 (February, 1969), 2-4, 20.

Finkel, William P. "Project Datum." *Law and Order*. 21:9 (September, 1973), 16-17, 20-22, 108.

McLuen, W.D. "The Instant Information Team—Microfilm and Computer." *Law and Order*. 20:8 (August, 1972), 24-26.

Mack, Frank. "Microfilm Use Reduces Local Crime and Identifies Suspects." *Law and Order*. 23:9 (September, 1975), 26, 28, 30.

"Microfilm System Codes and Retrieves Vital Records." *Law and Order*. 20:6 (June, 1972), 104.

Rome Air Development Center, New York. *Summary of the State-of-the-Art in Microfilm Document Storage and Retrieval Systems*. Springfield, VA.: NTIS, 1969.
Summary of the state-of-the-art information storage and retrieval systems specifically on microfilm based systems.

Spiva, Wayne E. "Microfilm Fingerprints: Automated System for Latent Fingerprint Files." *Police Chief*. 37:2 (February, 1971), 34-36.

West, Joy. "Microfilm Solves Paperwork Dilemma." *Law and Order*. 17:5 (May, 1969), 106-110.

Zweifel, Stanley, Andrew J. Sotak, and John Di Donato. "Microfilm Retrieval System Reveals Crime, Traffic, Accident Patterns." *Law and Order*. 21:4 (April, 1973), 76-83.

Privacy Issues

Bushkin, Arthur A. and Samuel I. Schaen. *Privacy Act of 1974—A Reference Manual for Compliance*. McLean, VA.: System Development Corporation, 1976.

Metz, Douglas W. "Privacy Considerations in Criminal Justice Information Systems." *Police Chief*. XLII:10 (October, 1975), 265-267.

U.S. Comptroller General. *How Criminal Justice Agencies Use Criminal History Information—Report to the Senate Subcommittee on Constitutional Rights*. Washington: NCJRS (Microfiche) 1974.

Zimmerman, Michael A., Donald F. King and Michael E. O'Neill. *How to Implement Privacy and Security—Department of Justice Regulations Title 28 and Beyond*. San Jose, CA.: THEOREM, 1976.

REPORT DISTRIBUTION

Houston, Sam. "Information Flow: A Key Factor in Law Enforcement." *Law and Order*. 18:7 (July, 1970), 28-30.

Hammons, Bill and Hal Heavener. "Breaking the Information Bottleneck." *Law and Order*. 16:10 (October, 1968), 78-80.
Use of copying machines for report distribution.

"Copying and Distributing Reports in a Police Department." *Police*. 16:1 (September, 1971), 63-65.

REPORT FORMS

Webster, Edward C. "The Consolidated Crime Report." *Law and Order*. 17:10 (October, 1969), 44-51.

Webster, Edward C. "Crime Investigative Reports." *Law and Order*. 13:8 (August, 1965), 64-65.

REPORT WRITING SYSTEMS

Bartlett, Joseph P. "New Reporting System Reduces Paperwork and Increases Effectiveness for New Haven Police." *Law and Order*. 19:3 (March, 1971), 48-51.

Brown, Donald J. "A Small Department Increases Report Efficiency." *Law and Order* (March, 1965), 80, 82.

Calvert, M.M. "Word Processing Frees Officers From Clerical Work." *Law and Order*. 19:7 (1971), 56, 58-60.

Davis, E. Cal. "Systems Improvements by Vancouver (Washington) Police Department." *Law and Order*. 19:4 (April, 1971), 88-91, 97-98.
Use of dictaphone for report writing. System can be utilized from outside telephones.

Edwards, James. "Call-In and Record System." *Law and Order*. 17:5 (May, 1969), 100-101.
Field officers telephone reports to station which are recorded and later typed.

Edwards, James. "Montclair Gains Thousands of Man Hours." *Police Chief*. XLII:10 (October, 1975).
Use of dictaphone system via telephone for report writing.

Gould, J.S. "Louisville 'Writes' Reports in Record Time." *Police Chief*. XXXVI:2 (February, 1969).

Kiser, Tom. "Word Processing Cuts Reporting Chores." *Law and Order*. 23:6 (June, 1975).
Use of dictaphones operated in the field for report writing.

"Los Angeles and Long Beach Police Streamline Report Processing." *Police*. 8:5 (May-June, 1964), 72-74.
Field reports are handprinted by officers and mechanically duplicated instead of using typed carbons.

One Write—A System for Efficient Report Writing: Police Management Procedures. Sacramento: California Office of Procurement, 1972.

Skousen, W. Cleon. "How to Get Patrol Reports from the Field in Minutes." *Law and Order*. 21:1 (January, 1973), 8-15.

Skousen, W. Cleon. "Police Reports in Less than One Hour." *Law and Order*. 8 (September, 1960), 50-52.

Sweeney, Earl M. "An Incident Report System for a Small Department." *Law and Order*. 20:8 (August, 1972), 36-38, 40.

Van Burren, W.C. "Santa Cruz Police Department—One-Write Form System." *Law and Order*. 18:12 (December, 1970), 28-30.

SAFETY PROGRAMS

Banton, Gene. "Preventing Police Vehicle Accidents in Memphis." *Police Chief* (July, 1973).

Boye, Robert F. "The Role of Safety in a Police Department." *Police.* 14:1 (September-October, 1969), 29-33.

Bushnell, Veto A. "Police Safety Precautions During Accident Investigations." *Law and Order* (March, 1961).

Firenze, R.J. *Guide to Occupational Safety and Health Management.* Dubuque, IL.: Kendall Hunt, 1973.

Florio, A.E. and George T. Stafford. *Safety Education.* N.Y.: MacGraw Hill, 1969.

Hipskind, V.K. "The Departmental Safety Officer." *Police.* 7:1 (September-October, 1962), 66-70.

Hipskind, Verne K. *Personnel Safety for Public Employees.* Springfield, IL.: C.C. Thomas, 1965.

Kramer, Milton D. *Safety Supervision in Motor Vehicle Fleets.* N.Y.: National Conservation Bureau, 1947.

Lindstrom, Charles L. "Reducing Police Vehicle Accidents." *Law and Order.* 20:6 (June, 1972), 20-23.

National Safety Council. *Guidelines for Developing an Injury and Damage Reduction Program in Municipal Police Departments—A Manual of Recommended Methods for Managing and Operating an Injury and Damage Reduction Program.* Washington: NCJRS, 1973.
Methods, procedures, and programs for planning organization, managing and operating an injury and damage reduction function in a municipal police department.

Peterson, Dan. *Safety Management: A Human Approach.* Englewood Cliffs, N.J.: Aloray, 1975.

Planek, T.W. and R.C. Fowler. *Development of an Injury and Damage Reduction Function for Municipal Police—Final Report.* Springfield, VA.: NTIS, 1971.
Definition of vehicular and non-vehicular accident, injury and damage problems among municipal police and recommended programs and methods to reduce them.

Public Employee Safety Manual: Police Department. Chicago: National Safety Council, 1974.

Robinson, Ivan A. and F.B. Childers. "How We Attacked the Motorcycle Safety Problem." *The Police Chief* (March, 1968).

Schenkelbach, Leon. *Safety Management Primer.* Homewood, IL.: Dow Jones Irwin, 1975.

Shaw, L. and H.S. Sichel. *Accident Proneness.* Elmsford, N.Y.: Pergamon, 1971.

Simonds, Robin H. and John V. Grimaldi. *Safety Management Accident Cost and Control.* rev. ed. Homewood, IL.: Dow Jones Irwin, 1963.

Thygerson, Alton L. *Safety: Principles, Instruction and Readings.* Englewood Cliffs, N.J.: Prentice Hall, 1973.

Weston, Paul B. "Firearms Safety for Police Officers—A Discussion." *Police.* 5:6 (July-August, 1961), 61-64.

VEHICLE FLEET MANAGEMENT

Arkin, Joseph. "The Economics of Leasing Police Cars." *Police Times.* 7 (May, 1970).

"Motor Transport Maintenance Division." *Spring 3100.* 22 (July-August, 1951).

Public Technology Inc. *Vehicle Replacement Package.* Washington: NCJRS, n/d.

Pudinski, Walter. "How the Highway Patrol Keeps Rolling." *Law and Order.* 21:12 (December, 1973), 48-50.
Operation of the fleet of 2,025 vehicles used by the California Highway Patrol. Article discusses purchase, maintenance and resale.

Wynne, G. Ray. *Police Transportation Management.* San Marcos, CA.: Auto Books, 1965.

SCHEDULING

Scheduling—General

Brunner, D. George. "Law Enforcement Work Schedules: Officers, Reactions." *Police Chief.* XLII:1 (January, 1976), 30-31.

Catalog of Computer Programs, Materials, Training and Technical Assistance for Designing Work Schedules. St. Louis, MO.: Institute for Public Program Analysis, 1975.

Drossman, Melvyn M. "Design of a Duty Schedule." *Police Chief.* XLI:7 (July, 1974).

Heller, N.B. and J.T. McEwen. *Computerized Scheduling of Police Manpower—V 1—Methods and Conclusions.* Springfield, VA.: NTIS, 1973.
Methods and conclusions of a project to develop computerized techniques for constructing work schedules for police officers.

Heller, N.B. and J.T. McEwen. *Computerized Scheduling of Police Manpower—V 2—Evaluation and Program User's Manual.* Washington: NCJRS, 1973.
Appendices to a report on a project to develop computerized techniques for constructing police work schedules.

McGinnis, William H. "Small Department Work Schedule." *Police Chief.* XLI:7 (July, 1974), 61-63.

Pelitt, Ronald E. "Manpower Scheduling." *Law and Order.* 16:7 (July, 1968).

U.S. Department of Justice. *What Law Enforcement Can Gain from Computer Designed Work Schedules.* Washington: GPO, 1974.

Four Ten

Allenspach, Heine. *Flexible Working Hours.* Washington: International Labor Office, 1975.

Allen, William A. "Four-Day Work Week: Another Approach." *Police Chief.* XL:1 (January, 1973), 48-49.

Baum, S.J. and W. McEwan Young. *Flexible Working Hours: A Practical Guide.* Park Ridge, N.J.: Noyes, 1974.

Bolton, J. Harvey. *Flexible Working Hours.* Washington: International Publishing Service, 1971.

Brown, Paul. "Cycle Scheduling for Eight and Ten Hour Days." *Police Chief* (April, 1974), 38-41.

Cann, William. "Our 4/40 Basic Team Concept." *Police Chief*. XXXIX:12 (December, 1972), 56-64.

Cann, William. "4/40 Basic Team Concept." *Law and Order*. 21:5 (May, 1973), 16-22, 51.

Cypress Police Department. *PAR (Pooling All Resources) Policing—Final Report May 10, 1972 Through June 30, 1973*. Washington: NCJRS (Microfiche) 1973.

"Europe Likes Flexi-Time Work." *Business Week* (October 7, 1972), 80-92.

"Experiments and Progress on 4-Day 40-Hour Work Week." *UCLA Weekly* (March 6, 1972).

"The Four Day Work Week. . .And What to Do About It." *Mechanics Illustrated*. 67 (July, 1971), 50–51.

"The Four-Day Workweek—Fad or Future in Law Enforcement." *Florida Police Chiefs Association Bulletin*. 8 (January-February, 1972).

Gates, Bradley L. "The Four Day–Forty Hour Work Week." *Journal of California Law Enforcement* (October, 1971).

Hand, F.D., R.T. Burgess and J.S. Wilson. "A Four–Ten Plan for Moderate and Large Police Patrol Operations." *Law and Order* (November, 1975), 8-12, 65.

Lilley, Aaron L. "The Four-Day Work Week." *Perspectives in Defense Management* (Spring, 1973).

McEwen, J.T. *Four–Ten Plan: Police Explore Potential of 4-Day Work Week*. Washington: NCJRS, 1972.

Mang, Norbert V. "Evolution of Labor Utilization." *Journal of California Law Enforcement* (July, 1974), 12-14.
Describes pros and cons of 4 day work week.

Poor, Riva, ed. *4 Days, 40 Hours: Reporting a Revolution in Work and Leisure*. Cambridge, MA.: Bursk & Poor, 1970.

Poor, Riva. *Reporting a Revolution in Work and Leisure: 27 4-Day Firms*. Cambridge, MA.: Bursk & Poor, 1970.

Robitaille, Earle W. "Manpower When You Need It." *FBI Law Enforcement Bulletin*. 39:10 (October, 1970), 23-25.

Robitaille, Earle W. "Ten Hour Shift Study—'Ten Plan.' " *Journal of California Law Enforcement* (July, 1970), 13-17.

Robitaille, Earle W. "Ten Plan." *Police Chief*. XXXVII:9 (September, 1970), 16-20.

Wade, Michael. *Flexible Working Hours in Practice*. N.Y.: Halstead, 1974.

Wheeler, Kenneth E. *The Four Day Week*. N.Y.: AMA, 1972.

Wheeler, Kenneth E. "Small Business Eyes the Four-Day Work Week." *Harvard Business Review* (May-June, 1970).

Whisenand, P.M. "The Four Day Work Week in Law Enforcement." *Management Information Service*. 3 (September, 1971), 1-4.

COMMUNICATIONS

COMMUNICATIONS—GENERAL

Amedick, P.F. "Cherry Hill NJPD Installs Dual-Purpose Portable Communications Systems." *Law and Order*. (February, 1970).

Anderson, Ralph E. "The Function of a Police Communications Unit." *Police* (September-October, 1969).

Anselmi, William J. "CLEAN: A Military Approach to Communications by the Pennsylvania State Police." *Police Chief*. XXXIX:11 (November, 1972), 46-50.

APCO Project—A National Training Manual and Procedural Guide for Police and Public Safety Radio Communications Personnel. Springfield, VA.: NTIS, 1967.
A basic guide for all forms of public safety communications.

Atlantic Research Corporation. *Florida County and Municipal Law Enforcement Communications Plan*. Washington: NCJRS (Microfiche) 1973.

Bevan, D. "The Eyes and Ears of the Future." *Police Review (GB)*, 19 (July 30, 1971), 965-969, 978.

Bolas, Stanley M. et al. "Erie County Benefits From Central Police Services." *Law and Order*. 122:2 (February, 1974), 52, 54-55.

Campbell, Frank D. "The Indianapolis Police Communication System." *Police*. 3:6 (July-August, 1959), 24-25.

Carlson, A. Bruce. *Communication Systems: An Introduction to Signals and Noise in Electrical Communication*. N.Y.: McGraw Hill, 1968.

Casselberry, Robert L. "Digital Communications Systems." *Law and Order*. 16:1 (January, 1968), 36-39.

"Chicago Installs New Communication's Equipment." *Traffic Digest and Review* (January, 1965), 15-16.

"Consolidated Computerized Communications." *Public Safety Systems* (September-October, 1968), 10-12.

Costigan, Daniel M. *FAX: The Principles and Practices of*

Facsimile Communication. Philadelphia, PA.: Chilton, 1971.

Cox, James D. "New Pennsylvania State Police Communications System Now Operational." *Law and Order*. 23:2 (February, 1975), 24-25.

Crittenden, Bradford. "Communications and Computer Combat Auto Thefts." *Law and Order*. 14:1 (January, 1966), 14-17, 49.

Dyba, Jerome E. "Integrating Police Dispatching, Incident Reporting, Records Retrieval, Manpower Reporting." *Police Chief*. XXXVI:1 (January, 1969), 30-31.

"Electronic System Improves Police Communications." *Law and Order*. 18:7 (July, 1970), 80, 82.

Foley, R.J. Jr. "Solid State Communications Equipment." *Law and Order* (January, 1966).

Frederick, Steve. "The Command Terminal." *Law and Order*. 19:6 (May, 1971), 68-70, 76-78.

Hughes Aircraft Co. *Design Study and Master Plan for an Improved Command Control Communications System Serving the Emergency Service Departments of the City of Los Angeles*. Springfield, VA.: NTIS, 1971.
Systems analysis of communications need and development of design and master implementation plan for the recommended system.

Huskisson, Harry C. "An Electronic Wonderland." *FBI Law Enforcement Bulletin*. 39:7 (July, 1970), 12-15, 27-28.

Interdepartment Radio Advisory. *Communications in Support of Emergency Medical Services*. Washington: NCJRS (Microfiche) 1973.
An emergency medical services communications system plan adaptable to both urban and rural areas.

King, John J. "Communications Update for Rural Communities." *Law and Order* (February, 1976), 32-37.

Lamb, William F. "Police Communications, A Pragmatic Concept." *Law and Order* (February, 1976), 42-47, 51.

Leon, George and Leo G. Sands. *DIAL 911: Modern Emergency Communications Network*. Rochelle Park, N.J.: Hayden, 1975.

Leonard, V.A. *The Police Communications System*. Springfield, IL.: C.C. Thomas, 1970.

Lombard, W.M. *Rochester (N.Y.) Police Bureau—Final Report Phase 2—Applicability of the Rochester Tactical Communications System Concept to Other Medium Sized Cities*. Springfield, VA.: NTIS, 1969.
Determination of the applicability of a study to other communities by means of questionnaires and interviews.

Lombard, W.M. *Rochester (N.Y.) Police Bureau—Final Report Phase 1—Study of the Tactical Communications System*. Springfield, VA.: NTIS,
Systems study approach determining operational requirements and system constraints.

Maas, R. "Inter Agency Communication Coordination." *Law and Order*. 22:2 (February, 1974), 20-21.

MacAloon, Frank G. "New Mexico State Police Communications System." *Law and Order*. 21:1 (January, 1973), 46-48.

Malone, Harry N. "Iowa Builds a Better Communications System." *Police Chief*. XLII:10 (October, 1975), 50-51.

Marin, Glenn A. "Police Communications in Transition." *Police Chief*. XXXVII:7 (July, 1971), 61-64.

Mason, Robert A. "A Brief History of Police Communications." *Police*. 3:4 (March-April, 1959), 50-52.

Meehan, James B. "Modernized Computerized Communications: An Aid in Crime Prevention." *Police*. 15:5 (May-June, 1971), 39-43.

Nailen, R.N. "High Speed Information Network." *Law and Order*. 16:1 (January, 1968), 6-21, 66.

"New Communications Will Improve Law Enforcement." *FBI Law Enforcement Bulletin*. 36:1 (January, 1967), 6-10.

Page, Richard A. "Expansion Causes Problems." *Law and Order* (October, 1975), 52-55.

Page, R.A. "How 21 Police Agencies Cooperate With Total Communications." *Law and Order*. 23:2 (February, 1975), 33, 36, 38, 40-41.

Page, Dick. "New Communications Concept Serves New Police Department." *Law and Order*. 21:1 (January, 1973), 56-59.

Painter, W.C. "Digital Communications for Public Safety Promises Solutions to Basic Problems." *Law and Order*. 21:1 (January, 1973), 50-52, 54-55.

Read, David R. "Handsfree Helicopter Communications." *Law and Order*. 17:6 (June, 1969), 47.

Reinke, R.W. "Design and Operation of Police Communications Systems." *Police Chief* (June, 1965; July, 1965; September, 1965).

Remsberg, Charles. "What Happens When You Call the Cops." *Popular Science*. 180 (April, 1962), 100-103.

Rhoades, Otto. "Illinois State Police Emergency Network." *FBI Law Enforcement Bulletin*. 36:10 (October, 1967), 7-9.

Rieder, Robert J. "Emergency Communications for Police and Fire Departments." *Police*. 15:4 (March-April, 1971), 49-53.

Rieder, Robert J. "A Systems Approach to Command and Control for Law Enforcement." *Police Chief*. XXXVII:7 (July, 1970), 24-29.

Robitaille, Earl W. "A Command and Control System." *Law and Order*. 22:5 (May, 1974), 22-23, 26, 28, 30.

Schmieg, A.L. "Total Communications." *Police Chief* (November, 1964), 46-47.

Shaw, William. "Are Law Enforcement Communications Breaking Down." *Law and Order*. 15:8 (August, 1967), 63-64.

Shaw, William. "An Introduction to Law Enforcement Electronics and Communications." *Law and Order*. 13:3 (March, 1965) [in 3 parts, ending with (March, 1966) 14:3].

Shaw, William. "Effective Communication (It's More Complicated Than You Think)." *Law and Order*. 22:2 (February, 1974), 14-16, 18, 22-23.

Shaw, William. "Federal Technical Assistance Agency Needs

Your Help." *Law and Order.* 15:3 (March, 1967), 54-58.

Shaw, William. "We Cannot Tolerate a Communications Breakdown." *Law and Order.* 18:1 (January, 1970), 34, 36, 39-40, 42, 45.

Shaw, William. "What You Should Know About Microelectronics." *Law and Order.* 14:10 (October, 1966), 64-70, 74.

Soderholm, Craig. "Modern Communications in Michigan City, Indiana." *Law and Order.* 13:1 (January, 1965), 44-47.

Taylor, Louis L. "Integrated Communication, Command and Control for Law Enforcement." *Police.* 15:1 (September-October, 1970), 80-81.

Thompson, Ted. "Campbell County (VA.) Sheriff's Communications Network." *Law and Order.* 21:1 (January, 1973), 38-39.

Tobias, Marc W. *Police Communications.* Springfield, IL.: C.C. Thomas, 1974.

Wight, Ralph W. "Communications Control Center." *Law and Order.* 13:1 (January 1965), 8-12.

William B. Carr and Associates Inc. *Fort Worth (TX.)—Police Department—Survey of Present Police Department Communications System.* Washington: NCJRS (Microfiche) 1972.

Wise, Leon M. "Police Communications Survey of Large Cities." *Law and Order.* 16:6 (June, 1968), 80-82.

Wise, Leon W. "Police Communications Survey of Small Cities." *Law and Order.* 17:1 (January, 1969), 16-22, 80.

Yefsky, S. Arthur and John D. Hodges. "Field Communications for Command and Control." *Police Chief.* XXXVII:7 (July, 1970), 34-42.

ALLOCATING EMERGENCY VEHICLES

Chaiken, J.M. and R.C. Larson. *Methods for Allocating Urban Emergency Units.* Springfield, VA.: NTIS, 1971.

Hauser, N. and G.R. Gordon. *Computer Simulation of a Police Emergency Response System.* Springfield, VA.: NTIS, 1969.
Structure, implementation and results of several computer simulation models of the New York City police department.

Larson, R.C. *Approximating the Performance of Urban Emergency Service Systems.* Washington: NCJRS (Microfiche) n/d.
This highly technical monograph presents an approximate procedure for computing selected performance characteristics of an urban emergency service system.

Larson, R.C. *Response of Emergency Units—The Effects of Barriers, Discreet Streets, and One-Way Streets.* Springfield, VA.: NTIS, 1971.

Walker, W.E. *Approach to Solving Municipal Emergency Service Deployment Problems.* Washington: NCJRS (Microfiche) 1974.
Report on the work done by the New York City Rand Institute in developing testing, documenting and disseminating new methods and approaches to the deployment of emergency service vehicles.

COMMUNICATIONS LOGGING—RECORDING

Dodge, Bud. "Communications Logging Equipment." *Law and Order* (June, 1968), 74-75.
Recording equipment used to tape radio calls and incoming telephone complaints.

Dorsey, Milton. "Audio Communications Recorded." *Law and Order.* 13:1 (January, 1965), 32-33.

Lauder, Jack. "All Messages Recorded." *Law and Order.* 14:12 (December, 1966), 32.
Use of tape recorders on police switchboard. All radio traffic is recorded also.

Mochan, Bruce W. "Telephone Monitors Have Multiple Functions." *Law and Order* (October, 1975), 16-17.
Tape recording of incoming calls on police switchboards.

Perry, Gregg. "Recording for Efficiency." *Law and Order.* 13:6 (June, 1965), 64-65.
Communications logging systems of all radio transmissions.

COMMAND POST

Becker, William J. "SPRINT: New York City's Computer-Oriented Emergency Command System." *Police Chief.* XXXVII:7 (July, 1970), 30-33.

Carson, Dale G. and Millard P. Richardson. "Mobile Emergency Command Center." *FBI Law Enforcement Bulletin* (December, 1973), 16-21.

Chiaramonte, Robert M. "A Mobile Command Post." *Police Chief* (November, 1969), 22-23, 39.

Kohn, Judith. "Command Post." *Law and Order* (December, 1974), 46-49.

McVey, W.C. "Emergency Communications Van." *Police Chief.* XL:2 (February, 1973), 44-47.

O'Mara, Michael W. "From a Used Bus to Mobile Command Post." *FBI Law Enforcement Bulletin.* 38:12 (December, 1969), 17-19.

O'Reilly, Robert E. "The Communications Van." *Law and Order.* 13:10 (October, 1965).

Page, R.A. "Voices from the Van." *Law and Order.* 18:1 (January, 1970), 30-32.
Communications Center used by Ohio Highway Patrol. Mobile command post is a large semi-trailer and tractor.

Rinta, Arthur A. "Disaster Preparedness." *Law and Order.* 14:12 (December, 1966), 18-24.
Use of converted bus for mobile command post.

DISPATCHING

ABT Associates Inc. *Muskegon County (MI.)—Central Police Dispatch—Exemplary Project Validation Report.* Washington: NCJRS (Microfiche) 1975.

Carroll, A.B. et al. *Computer Aided Dispatching for Law Enforcement Agencies.* Washington: NCJRS (Microfiche) n/d.
This report describes the system, operation, functions, and editing capabilities of the automated interactive dispatch (AID) System.

Hoobler, Raymond L. and Ken Fortier. "For the San Diego Police Department: A Computer Aided Dispatch System." *Police Chief.* XLII:10 (October, 1975), 22-24.

McDonnell, John J. *Central Police Dispatch.* Washington: LEAA, n/d.

Pitchess, Peter J. "New Computer-Based Dispatching System Cuts Response Time." *Police Chief.* 38:2 (February, 1971), 8, 61.

Rieder, Robert J. "Dispatching Loads in a Communications Center: A Case Study of the Tulsa Police Department." *Police.* 14:5 (May-June, 1970), 22-27.

Smith, I.K. "Syracuse's Ambition: Instant Dispatch." *Law and Order.* 14:1 (January, 1966), 58-62.

Stevenson, K.A. *Analyzing the Process of Screening Calls for Emergency Service: Technical Report.* Washington: NCJRS (Microfiche) 1974.

The authors provide a methodology for characterizing the quality of a screening program and for establishing the conditions under which the introduction of screening can improve service.

Wight, Ralph W. *Radio Dispatch Center Operating Procedure Handbook.* Los Angeles: Ralph W. Wight Associates, 1975.

MOBILE COMPUTERS—TELEPRINTERS

Bennett, William J. "Two-Way Verbal Transmission Vs the MCT's." *Police Chief.* XXXIX:11 (November, 1972), 54-59.

Describes mobile digital communications system in Palm Beach County Sheriff Office.

Carlson, R.L., J.M. Tellez and W.L. Schreiber. "Mobile Teleprinters." *Police Chief.* 38:12 (December, 1971), 58-60.

Crutcher, H. "So You Want to Use Mobileprinters!" *APCO Bulletin* (December, 1968).

Elliot, M. "Mobile Teleprinters for Public Safety Communications." *APCO Bulletin* (December, 1968).

"In-Car Computers Cut Vital Time for Police Messages." *American City* (April, 1973).

Kelley, T. and J. Ward. *Investigation of Digital Mobile Radio Communication.* Washington: LEAA, October, 1973.

Kirk, John F. "Getting the Message: Telecommunications in the Patrol Car." *FBI Law Enforcement Bulletin* (July, 1975).

McGahan, Chuck. "Mobile Teleprinters in Use by Gates (N.Y.) Police Department." *Law and Order.* 21:1 (January, 1973), 42.

"Mobile Computers to Give Patrolmen More Data Faster—Atlantic City, N.J." *American City* (May, 1973).

Oss, G.K. "ARCOM: An Alternate Approach to Mobile Digital Communications." *Law and Order.* 22:2 (February, 1974), 56, 59-60.

"Police Communications" *FBI Law Enforcement Bulletin.* 43:1 (January, 1972)

Use of teleprinters in patrol vehicles.

Shaw, William. "Direct Computer Access from Police Mobiles Is Now a Reality." *Law and Order.* 23:2 (February, 1975), 12, 14, 16, 18, 20.

Stiver, Phil. "Communications Confidentiality." *Law and Order.* 20:11 (November, 1972), 86-87, 90.

Teleprinters in patrol vehicles.

Spiegel, Marshall. "The New 'Black Box' in Vegas." *Law and Order* (February, 1976), 18-21, 51.

Visual screen response in patrol cars.

Wilson, Eugene W. "Minneapolis Police Department Dispatches Via Mobile Printer." *Law and Order.* 20:1 (January, 1972), 14-16, 18, 20, 43.

NINE-ELEVEN (9-11)

Burke, Martin. "Omaha Provides Regional 911 Service." *Law and Order.* 19:3 (March, 1971), 24-26.

Corbin, William E. "A 'Universal' Police Telephone Number." *APCO Bulletin* (November, 1967).

Felperin, K.D. and S.C. Ivy. *Nine-One-One in Florida—System Concept—Final Report.* Washington: NCJRS (Microfiche) 1974.

George, Praul Associates. *Allentown (PA.)—Emergency Communications Systems: Final Evaluation Report.* Washington: NCJRS (Microfiche) 1974.

An evaluation of the Allentown, PA. Nine-One-One emergency telephone communications system.

Leon, George and Leo G. Sands. *DIAL 911: Modern Emergency Communications Network.* Rochelle Park, N.J.: Hayden, 1975.

O'Malley, J.J. Jr. "911: What It's All About." *Law Officer.* 7:1 (1974), 35-37.

"Public Safety: 911 Goes Regional." *American City.* 86 (April, 1971).

Reinke, Roger W. "911 Grows Up: Four Years Old and Acting It." *Police Chief.* XXXVIII:11 (November, 1971), 16-22.

Roush, J. Edward. "911—A Hot Line for Emergencies." *Readers Digest* (December, 1968).

Yung, T.J. et al. *Nine-One-One in Florida: A Preliminary Report.* Washington: NCJRS (Microfiche) 1974

PORTABLE RADIOS

Cooper, M. "Personal Police Communications." *Communications* (August, 1968), 45-48.

Dobson, R.E. "Pocket Radio Equipment." *Traffic Digest and Review* (February, 1965), 17-19.

Hilliard, Andrew. "Portable Radios Replace Mobiles in South Pasadena." *Law and Order.* 23:2 (February, 1975), 48-49.

Key, W. "The Personal Transceiver: A Report from the National Institute." *Police Chief* (November, 1969), 14-15.

Law Enforcement Standards Laboratory. *Mobile EM Receivers—Law Enforcement Standards Program.* Washington: NCJRS, 1975.

Lamke, Ken. "Portable Radios Aid Police Operations." *Law and Order.* 12:1 (January, 1964), 8-9.

Lees, D.E. "The PREP—Personal Radio Equipped Police System in Detroit." *Law and Order* (January, 1967), 30-32.

Mitchell, Dan. "Portable Radios Save $60,000 for New Jersey Police." *Police.* 10:1 (September-October, 1965), 90-91.

Page, Dick. "Police Personal Portables—Putting Radio Where It Belongs." *Communications* (August, 1971), 33-34.

Potthoff, E.H. and W.A. Yule. "Radios for Beat Patrolmen New Police Communication System." *Michigan Municipal Review* (December, 1963).

Shaw, William. "Needed: A Good Small Personal Radio Transceiver." *Law and Order.* 16:4 (April, 1968), 62-68, 72.

Sheehan, John H. "Portable 2-Way Radios Improve Efficiency of Watertown Police." *Law and Order.* 18:5 (May, 1970), 86-89.

RADIO

Allen, Arthur E. "Do It Yourself: A Method of Field Radio Communication While Wearing a Gas Mask." *Police Chief.* XXV:11 (November, 1968), 53-54.

Anderson, Harold. "Four Frequency Operation Improves Efficiency." *Law and Order.* 14:1 (January, 1966), 24-26, 28-29.

Associated Public-Safety Communications Officers, Inc. *Illinois Police Communications Study—Phase 1.* Springfield, IL.: Illinois State Police, 1968.

Associated Public Safety Communications Officers. *Public Safety Communications—Standard Frequency Coordinator's Manual.* New Smyrna Beach, FL.: Associated Public Safety Communications Officers, 1971.
Guide to selecting and recommending to the applicant and Federal Communications System, a radio frequency which will cause the least amount of interference.

Bergeron, F.J. "Municipal Departments Share Radio Communications System." *Public Works* (April, 1969), 102-103.

Brose, Aldred G. "Radio Communications Department Services Law Enforcement in North Dakota." *FBI Law Enforcement Bulletin* (April, 1972), 25-28.

Chino Police Department. *Automated Status Reporting for Police Communications. Final Report.* Springfield, VA.: NTIS, 1971.
Eliminating congested radio traffic that delayed or interfered with communications of field officers and the dispatcher in the Chino Police Department was studied.

Cross, Claude. "Oregon Develops Radio Cooperation." *Law and Order* (September, 1971), 58-59.

DeLadurantey, Joseph C. and Daniel R. Sullivan. "X-Emergency Command Control Communications System Is Coming." *Police Chief.* 16:5 (May, 1974), 48-50.

Drake, George M. "U H F Police Communications Goes Hollywood." *Law and Order.* 20:7 (July, 1972), 60-61, 63.

Dudley, E.J. "Camden (N.J.) Police Lease Two-Way Radio System." *Law and Order.* 18:1 (January, 1970), 22-23.

Eckert, R.P. and P.M. Kelly. "Public Safety, the Radio Spectrum and the President's Task Force in Communications Policy." *IEEE Spectrum.* 6 (January, 1969), 37-46.

Ehrlich, Ken. "A Radio System Designed to Fill a Need." *Law and Order.* 14:1 (January, 1966), 10, 12, 48.

Foley, R. "A 'Showcase' Radio System." *Law and Order.* 13:1 (January, 1965), 64-65, 69.

Foley, R. "A Two-Way Radio System Is Only as Good as Its Base Station." *Law and Order.* 16:1 (January, 1968), 24-25.

Gabriel, Charles F. "Onondaga County Police Agencies Make Mobile Radio District Idea Work." *Law and Order.* 23:2, 42-47, 51.

IIT Research Institute. *Illinois Police Communications Study, Phase 2, V 1—Allocation of Spectrum to the Police Radio Service.* Springfield, VA.: NTIS, 1969.

IIT Research Institute. *Illinois Police Communications Study, Phase 2, V2—Initial Development of Implementation Plans.* Springfield, VA.: NTIS, 1969.

IIT Research Institute. *Illinois Police Communications Study, Phase 2, Summary.* Springfield, VA.: NTIS, 1969.

Leef, Bob. "How to 'Program' Police Radio Communications for Public Listening." *Law and Order* (February, 1976), 39.

Lees, Daniel E. "The PREP System in Detroit MI." *Law and Order.* 15:1 (January, 1967), 30-32.

McEwen, Harlin R. "Vehicular Radio Repeaters." *Law and Order.* 23:9 (September, 1975), 46, 48, 50, 52.

Mooney, Lawrence F. "Police Radio Network Services 11 Cities." *Law and Order.* 20 (January, 1972), 22-24, 26.

National Institute of Law Enforcement and Criminal Justice. *Fixed and Base Station FM Transmitters—Law Enforcement Standards Program.* Washington: NCJRS (Microfiche) 1974.

New York City Transit Authority. *Two-Way Radio Communication Mass Transportation Demonstration Project—Final Report.* Springfield, VA.: NTIS, 1968.
Description and evaluation of a communication system for New York City's subway system, designed to maintain on-time service and effective police coverage.

"North Carolina Counties Improve Radio Comunications." *Journal* (May-June, 1974).

Page, Richard A. "Philadelphia System Stresses Fast Response." *Law and Order.* 15:1 (January, 1967), 22-27.

Page, R.A. "New Hampshire State Police Radio Repeater Improves Mobile Coverage." *Law and Order.* 17:1 (January, 1969), 27-30, 80.

Page, Richard A. "Philadelphia System Stresses Fast

Response." *Law and Order.* 15:1 (January, 1967), 22-27.

Page, Richard A. "Radio Has Come a Long Way." *Law and Order.* 21:10 (October, 1973), 66-67, 80.

Page, R.A. "Texas Police Convert Radio Systems." *Law and Order.* 22:2 (February, 1974), 74-77.

"Police Radio Simplifies Enforcement." *American City.* 68 (May, 1953).

"Public Safety Helmets Increase Communication Convenience." *Police.* 15:2 (November-December, 1970), 11.
Communications equipment installed in police helmet.

Reinke, Roger W. "Police Radio—Public Entertainment or Law Enforcement Tool?" *Police Chief* (November, 1969). 16-17, 34-35.

Rhoades, I.O. "Illinois State Police Emergency Radio Network." *FBI Law Enforcement Bulletin* (October, 1967), 7-9.

Rotta, Frank. "Miniature Radios Help St Louis Police Capture Thugs." *Police.* 8:1 (September-October, 1963), 82-84.

Scheober, W.A. and C.W. Allen. "How Two-Way Radio Helps Guard Small Towns." *American City* (October, 1957).

Schultz, Vern. "Elkhart Police Department Increases Use of Two-Way Radio." *Law and Order.* 18:1 (January, 1970), 26-28.

Shaw, William. "The Introduction of Radio Telephony to Police Communications." *Law and Order* (January, 1972), 34, 36-38.

Shaw, William. "Transmission and Reception on the Same Channel—Simultaneously." *Law and Order.* 19:1 (January, 1971), 30-34.

"Simultaneous Monitoring Radio System." *Law and Order.* (January, 1963), 12-14.

Smith, Dollie L. "The Red Mike." *Law and Order.* 19:2 (February, 1971), 64-66.
Describes the use of Statewide emergency radio network in Illinois. Officers can communicate car to car no matter what department they are from.

Taggert, H.E. et al. *Mobile EM Transmitters-Law Enforcement Standards Program.* Washington: NCJRS, 1974.

Tulloch, Donald P. "The Barnstable County Police Radio System services Community Needs." *FBI Law Enforcement Bulletin.* 40:11 (November, 1971), 10-14, 30.

"Twenty-four Hour Radio Service for Small Departments." *FBI Law Enforcement Bulletin.* 26 (January, 1957).

Wand, Hal. "Single Radio Center Unites Monterey County." *Law and Order.* 22:2 (February, 1974), 42-46.

Wand, Hal. "Two-Way FM Radio Aids Customs Port Investigators." *Law and Order.* 17:1 (January, 1969), 24.

Zmuda, Charles W. "Developing a Data Radio Channel." *Police Chief* (November, 1969), 18-19.

Radio Codes

Brooks, Pierce, R., ed. *Ten Code Versus Speech Communication.* Sacramento, CA.: California Office of Procurement, 1975.

Fieler, Kenneth E. "Car 54 What are You." *Law and Order* (November, 1975), 46-50.
An introduction to coded car numbers and coded systems.

Rosemeier, F.W. *Handbook of Spoken Radio Communication Used by Public Safety Organizations.* Cologne, West Germany: Carl Heymanns Verlag, 1971.

Radio Procedure

Adams, T.F. "Police Radio Procedure." *Police* (May-June, 1963), 35-38.

Garner, Gerald W. "Improving Police Radio Procedures." *Police Chief.* XXXIX:7 (July, 1972), 71.

SCRAMBLER SYSTEMS

Baker, H.C. "Voice Privacy Transmission." *Techniques Communication News* (June, 1972), 38-41.

Carlson, R.L., J.M. Tellez and W.L. Schreiber. "Privacy of Voice Communication." *Security World.* (May, 1972), 49-53.

Hauler, Paul D. "Scramblers and Law Enforcement Radio Communications Security." *Law and Order.* 22:4 (April, 1974), 77-79, 82.

McCalmont, A.M. and W.J. Eramo Jr. "Communications Privacy." *Telecommunications.* (October, 1970).

Miller, C.K. "Voice Scramblers in Two-Way Systems." *Communications News* (August, 1972), 32-33.

Shannon, Claude E. "Communication Theory of Secrecy Systems." *Bell System Technical Journal.* 28:4 (October, 1949), 656-715.

Shaw, William. "A Non-Technical Explanation of Voice Scramble System." *Law and Order.* 22:7 (July, 1974), 20, 22, 24, 26.

Shaw, William. "A Scrambler System for Two-Way Radio Network." *Law and Order.* 14:5 (May, 1966), 34-42.

Sugar, George R. *Voice Privacy Equipment for Law Enforcement Communications Systems—Law Enforcement Standards Program.* Washington: NCJRS, 1974.

Vouga, Claude A. "Speech Scrambling in Police Radio Communications." *Law and Order.* 22:2 (February, 1974), 26, 28-30.

TELECOMMUNICATIONS

Burton. A. *Police Telecommunications.* Springfield, IL.: C.C. Thomas, 1973.
System description, covering telephones, radios or teletypewriters allowing centralized control of police personnel dispersed over an area of operation.

California Department of California Highway Patrol. *Patrols: Telecommunications Systems Manual.* Sacramento: Department of Highway Patrol, 1968.

"CLETS: California Law Enforcement Telecommunications System." *Police.* (November-December, 1970).

IIT Research Institute. *Police Telecommunication Systems.* Washington: GPO, 1971.

Listen, Jack N. "A Modern Telecommunications Center for Effective Law Enforcement." *FBI Law Enforcement Bulletin.* 39:9 (September, 1970), 12-14.

Ray, John. "Tele-Communications Net Keeps Tabs on Criminals." *Law and Order.* 19:9 (September, 1971), 34-35.

Shaw, William. "Law Enforcement Telecommunications Systems." *Law and Order.* 21:5 (May, 1973), 8, 11-14.

Sohn, Robert L. *Innovations in Law Enforcement Telecommunications.* Springfield, VA.: NTIS, n/d.

TELEPHONES

Corbin, William E. "Emergency Telephones Provide Link Between Police and the Community." *Police.* 13:1 (September-October, 1968) 87-98.

Emergency Telephone Communications Workshop—Summary of Proceedings. Springfield, VA.: NTIS, 1970.

Field, Jeffrey. "What To Do In A Telephone Blackout." *Law and Order.* 13:8 (August, 1965), 10-12, 24.
Fire, which destroyed telephone switching center. Describes police—fire emergency procedures.

TELETYPE

Haukedahl, S.P. "State Teletype Network Links Midwest Law Enforcement Agencies." *Law and Order* (January, 1962), 10-11.

McKinley, Dick. "Teletypewriter and Computer Combine to Speed Apprehensions." *Law and Order.* 17:1 (January, 1969), 52-55.

"New Police Teletypewriter Network." *Police Chief* (March, 1966), 23.

Shaw, William. "Law Enforcement Teletypewriter Service." *Law and Order.* 11:12 (December, 1963), 28-29, 31-32, 34.

Telcom Inc. *Milwaukee Police Teleprinter Study, Final Report.* Washington: NCJRS, 1969.

VEHICLE LOCATING SYSTEMS

Beebe, R.M. "Vehicle Location System." *Law and Order.* 19:11 (November, 1971), 30, 37-38.

Brown, F.R. and R.M. Jekel. *Automatic Vehicle Monitoring System—Final Report.* Springfield, VA.: NTIS, 1973.
Design and testing by one of four corporations for a real time automatic vehicle monitoring system (AVM) using a phase multilateration comparison technique.

Buck, R. Salwen H. *Channel Measurements for Automatic Vehicle Monitoring Systems Final Report.* Springfield, VA.: NTIS, 1974.
Co-Channel and adjacent channel electromagnetic interference measurements were conducted on the Sierra Research Corporation and the Chicago Transit Authority Automatic Vehicle Monitoring (AVM) Systems.

Camp, Eugene J. "St Louis Flair System: Fleet Location and Information Reporting." *Police Chief.* XLII:10 (October, 1975), 8-9.

Carlson, Robert L., J.M. Tellez and W.L. Schreiber. "Automatic Vehicle Locator Systems." *Police Chief.* 38:11 (November, 1971), 51-53.

Doering, R.D. *Application of Automatic Vehicle Locator Systems in Police Operations—Proceedings of Symposium—Orlando, Florida, September 10-11, 1974.* Washington: NCJRS (Microfiche) 1974.

Fey, R.L. *Automatic Vehicle Location Techniques for Law Enforcement Use.* Washington: NCJRS, 1974.

Hallett, J.N. "Automatic Vehicle Location Systems." *Intercom.* 4 (1973), 2-5.

Institute of Public Adminstration. *Urban Vehicle Monitoring: Technology, Economics and Public Policy, V 1, Summary Report.* Springfield, VA.: NTIS, 1972.
Nature of automatic vehicle monitoring (AVM) systems, possible applications, potential user demands, pricing policy, financing and demonstration projects.

Institute of Public Administration. *Urban Vehicle Monitoring: Technology, Economics and Public Policy—Economic and Institutional Analysis and Appendices, Final Report.* Springfield,VA.: NTIS, 1972.
Benefits of various automatic vehicle monitoring (AVM) functions when applied to the operations of specific user groups.

Lukes, M. and R. Shea. *Monitor-CTA (Chicago Transit Authority)—Final Report: An Urban Mass Transportation Demonstration Project Study of Automatic Vehicle Monitoring.* Springfield, VA.: NTIS, 1973.

Murray, W.S. and W.C. Scales. *Overview of Automatic Vehicle Monitoring Systems.* Springfield, VA.: NTIS, 1973.

Rieder, Robert J. "Police Car Location System." *Law and Order.* 19:6 (June, 1971), 62-64, 66, 68, 70.

Roth, S.H. *Automatic Vehicle Monitoring Technology Review.* Springfield, VA.: NTIS, 1971.
Overview of the state-of-the art on automatic vehicle monitoring (AVM) technology and the advantages and disadvantages of various system techniques.

Scales, W. *Urban Field Tests of Four Vehicle Location Techniques.* Springfield, VA.: NTIS, 1973.
Review of four electronic techniques tested in Philadelphia covering test site selection, route design, testing procedure, and performance results.

Shaw, William. "Automatic Location of Radio Transmitters." *Law and Order* (February, 1964), 34-36.

Sierra Research Corporation. *Automatic Vehicle Monitoring System—Final Report.* Springfield, VA.: NTIS, 1971.
Design by one of four corporations for a real-time automatic vehicle monitoring (AVM) system which locates vehicles by phase multilateration is described.

Teledyne Systems Company. *Loran (Long-Range Radio Navigation) Automatic Vehicle Monitoring Systems. V 1—Study Results.* Springfield, VA.: NTIS, 1972.

Teknekron, Inc. *Urban Vehicle Monitoring—Technology, Economics and Public Policy V 2—Technical Analysis and Appendices, Final Report*. Springfield, VA.: NTIS, 1970.
Technical evaluation of different types of automatic vehicle monitoring (AVM) systems and the experiments forming the basis of these evaluations.

INFORMATION SYSTEMS

INFORMATION SYSTEMS—GENERAL

Adams, Ronald T. "Helping Police Communicate—Data with Voice." *Communications Magazine* (August, 1971), 12-14.

"Alabama Prison System is 'Road Block' Against Escapes." *Police*. 13:6 (July-August, 1969), 14-17.

"ALERT: Automated Law Enforcement Response in Kansas City, MO." *Police Chief*. XXXV:11 (September, 1968), 69.

Bagdikian, Ben. *The Information Machines: Their Impact on Men and the Media*. N.Y.: Harper & Row, 1971.

Blum, E.H. *Community Information Utility and Municipal Services*. N.Y.: Rand, 1972.
Description of the design and purposes of a municipal services information systems, a community information utility (CIU).

Boring, James. "Computer Controlled Traffic." *Law and Order*. 14:6 (June, 1966), 64.

Brostron, Curtis. "Computer-Assisted Resource Allocation Expanded in St Louis." *Police Chief* (November, 1968).

Buckley, John L. "Computers, Automation and Security." *Law and Order*. 13:3 (March, 1965), 58, 60.

Buckley, John L. "The Future of Computers in Security and Law Enforcement." *Law and Order*. 13:8 (August, 1965), 36-38; 13:9 (September, 1965), 48-52.

"Cincinnati's Regional Advanced Law Enforcement System Revised for Use on Smaller Computer." *Police Chief*. 38:9 (September, 1971), 60-62.

Chambelain,G.M. "Turn Congested Streets into Green Wave Arterials." *American City and County* (February, 1976).

Cohn, S.I., ed. *Law Enforcement Science and Technology. II*. Washington: Thompson, 1969.

Cohn, S.I. and W.B. McMahon, eds. *Law Enforcement Science and Technology III*. Washington: Thompson, 1970.

Colton, K.W. *Computers and the Police Revisited: A Second Look at the Experience of Police Departments in Implementing New Information Technology.*. Washington: NCJRS (Microfiche) 1974.
The results of a survey of police departments across the country to assess the impact of computers and computer related techniques on police operations.

Colton, K.W. *Use of Computers by Police—Patterns of Success and Failure*. Washington: International City Management Association, 1972.
Some of the benefits and costs, and variables that influence the effective use of computers by police.

Columbus, E.G. *Automatic Data Processing: A Practical Police Tool*. N.Y.: IBM, 1967.

Columbus, E.G. "Automatic Data Processing: A Practical Police Tool." *Police Chief*. XXXLV:5 (May, 1967); (September, 1967).

Columbus, E.G. "Basic Computer Concepts." *Police Chief* (September, 1968), 14.

Columbus, E.G. "A Practical Data Processing System." *Law and Order*. 13:7 (July, 1965), 9-14, 64.

Comber, Edward V. "Criminal Justice Study Officers Aids in Information Management." *Journal of California Law Enforcement* (January, 1967), 185-188.

"Computer Catches a Traffic Violator." *American City* (March, 1966).

"Computerized Crime Fighting." *Police* (March-April, 1967).

"Computerized Police Communications." *American City*. 86 (May, 1971), 32-33.

"Computers for Cops." *Newsweek* (June 5, 1972).

"Computer Network Protects 207,000 Boston Suburbanites: Suburban Police Automated Information System." *American City* (March, 1973).

"Computers Play Cops and Robbers." *Business Week* (January 15, 1966).

"Computers—Sherlock Holmes Style." *Police* (July-August, 1967).

Conroy, George E. "Los Angeles Automates Its Want/Warrant System." *Police Chief* (April, 1971).

Coogan, Timothy. "Minicomputers in Small-Medium Departments." *Law and Order*. 24:6 (June, 1976), 58-60, 86.

Cooper, G. *Project Search—International Symposium on Criminal Justice Information and Statistics System—Proceedings 1972*. Sacramento: California Crime Technological Research Fund, 1972.

Progress and developing trends in the field of advanced information and statistics systems, emphasizing system design, application and evaluation.

Couger, J. Daniel and Fred R. McFadden. *Introduction to Computer Based Information Systems.* N.Y.: Wiley, 1975.

Davies, Donald Watts. *Communication Networks for Computers.* N.Y.: Wiley, 1973.

DeWeese, J.T. "Giving the Computer a Conscience: FBI's National Crime Information Center." *Harper's* (November, 1973).

Dial, O.E. *Municipal Information Systems—The State of the Art in 1970.* Springfield, VA.: NTIS, 1971.
Survey of 79 cities across the U.S. to determine the extent of usage of computer technology in municipal affairs.

Edwards, David M. and James V. Ryan. "A Comprehensive and Integrated Police Information System." *Police Chief.* XLII:10 (October, 1975), 10-12, 70.

"Electronic Pinch: Computer Oriented Retrieval of Auto Larcenists." *Science Digest* (1965).

Evans, G.R. *Literature Survey of Information Storage and Retrieval Systems (Manual and Automated) for Law Libraries.* Springfield, VA.: NTIS, 1968.

Farell, J. *Textir (Test Indexing and Retrieval)—A Natural Information Retrieval System.* Springfield, VA.: NTIS, 169.
An experimental study on computer retrieval of crime data in the natural English language.

Farr, M.A.L., B. Chadwick and K.K. Wong. *Security for Computer Systems.* Rochelle Park, N.J.: Hayden, 1972.

"FBI's Computer Center Deters Crime." *Law Officer.* 3 (Spring, 1970).

Gallati, Robert R.J. "Criminal Justice: Computers Related Technology and the Scientific Method." *Police.* 13 (September-October, 1968).

Gallati, Robert R.J. "The Role of the Courts in a State-Wide Criminal Justice Information System." *Police.* 16:9 (May, 1972), 18-23.

Gerbner, George. et al. *The Analysis of Communication Content.* N.Y.: Wiley, 1969.

Greenwood, P.W. *Potential Uses of the Computer in Criminal Courts.* N.Y.: Rand, 1971.
Some examples of information systems for court use are presented which illustrate various levels of interaction between man and computer in the decision making process.

Grindley, Kit and John Humble. *The Effective Computer.* N.Y.: AMA, 1974.

Hathaway, Gregory O. "Modern Data Processing." *FBI Law Enforcement Bulletin.* 35:4 (April, 1966), 6-9, 20-21.

Hegarty, James J. "Arizona's Instant Information System." *Law and Order.* 16:7 (July, 1968), 81-82, 100.

Hemphill, C.F. Jr. and J.M. Hemphill. *Security Procedures for Computer Systems.* Homewood IL.: Dow Jones Irwin, 1973
Measures to guard against both natural and man-made threats against installation and data security.

Hoobler, Raymond L. "San Diego Command and Control." *Police Chief.* XXXIX:5 (May, 1972), 70-71.

IBM. *Urban Management Information System. V 12*—Police Department. Springfield, VA.: NTIS, 1969.
Discussion of objectives and responsibilities of the New Haven Police Department and proposals for the use of information systems to handle problem areas.

"Instant Police Check: Law Enforcement Automated Data System." *Science Digest* (March, 1968).

James, I.T. "The Computer and the Police." *Police Review (GB),* 80:4141 (1972), 656-657, 676.

James, Ed. "New York State Speeds Summary Criminal Histories with Facsimile Transmission." *Law and Order.* 20:10 (October, 1972), 65.

Katzenback. N.B. et al. "Crime Data Centers: The Use of Computers in Crime Detection and Prevention." *Columbia Human Rights Law Review* (Winter, 1972).

Kavanagh, H.I. "CARD Saves Lives in Maryland." *Police Chief.* 37:5 (May, 1966), 27-30.

Kelley, Dale A. "Data Processing in the Small Police Department: What to Do Until the Computer Arrives." *Journal of California Law Enforcement* (January, 1975), 96-98.

Kelne, Nathan. "A New Computer Program to Predict and Deter Crime. Law and Order. 15:1 (January, 1967), 8, 21.

Kenney, John P. "The California Integrated Law Enforcement Information System" *Police.* 12:1 (September-October, 1967), 10-15.

King, Donald and H.L. Kurkjian. "WALES: Washington D.C.: Area Law Enforcement System." *Police Chief.* XXXV:11 (November, 1968), 31, 35.

Kinsey, Duane. "Ohio's State-Wide Police Information Network." *Law and Order.* 16:1 (January, 1968), 74-75.

Kochen, Manfred. *Principles of Information Retrieval.* N.Y.: Wiley, 1974.

Kubis, J.F. *Studies in Lie Detection, Computer Feasibility Considerations.* Springfield, VA.: NTIS.
The experiments which form the basis of this research have special reference to feasibility considerations, namely the possible use of a computer in lie detection.

Lamb, Ralph. "From Posse to Computer." *Police.* 15:1 (September-October, 1970), 34-39.

Lance, Jerome. "USAC and the Long Beach Public Safety Information System." *Police Chief.* XXXIX:6 (June, 1972), 79-81.

Louviere, V. "Computerizing Call for Police." *Nations Business* (February, 1974).

Lucas, Henry C. *Computer Based Information Systems in Organizations.* Chicago, IL.: Science Research, 1973.

Luethje, David J. "Auto-Statis: The Birth of a System." *Police Chief.* XXVI:1 (January, 1969), 24-29.
Input is also obtained from all surrounding states and the National Automobile Theft Bureau.

Lundell, E. *Computer Use: An Executive's Guide.* Boston: Allyn & Bacon, 1973.

McDonell, R.E. "Computers in Law Enforcement." *Police.* 13:2 (November-December, 1968), 76-80.

McDowell, William D. "A County-Wide Information Network that Preserves the Local Police Force." *Law and Order.* 20:6 (June, 1972), 76-78, 80, 82.

McFarlan, F.w. and Richard L. Nolan. *Information Systems Handbook.* Homewood, IL.: Dow, Jones, Irwin, 1975.

Mansell, John R. "Information System Integrates Police, Fire and Emergency Data." *Law and Order.* 21:4 (April, 1973), 42, 44, 46, 48, 50, 106.

Maynard, Michael M. "Computerized Information System is Major Ally for Nashville Metropolitan Area Police." *Law and Order.* 20:4 (April, 1972), 64-66, 68.

Maynard, Michael. "The Instant Information Network in Ohio." *Law and Order.* 24:6 (June, 1976), 32-36.

Maynard, Michael. "Instant Information Via Computer." *Law and Order.* 17:12 (December, 1969), 38-45.

Meadow, Charles T. *Man-Machine Communication.* N.Y.: Wiley, 1970.

Mendozzi, Edwin J. "Automated Allocation of Traffic Enforcement Services." *Law and Order.* 17:6 (June, 1969), 84-86, 90.

Murphy, John J. "The Computer and Official Retrieval of Fugitives." *Police Chief.* XLII:12 (December, 1975), 56-63.

"National Bomb Data Center." *FBI Law Enforcement Bulletin* (December, 1973), 13-15.

"The National Crime Information Center." *FBI Law Enforcement Bulletin.* 43:1 (January, 1974).

National Crime Information Center. *National Crime Information Center—Agency Identifiers.* Washington, D.C.: NCJRS (Microfiche) 1973.

"NCIC—A Tribute to Cooperative Spirit." *FBI Law Enforcement Bulletin.* 41:2 (February, 1972), 2-5, 26-28.

North Carolina Department of Justice. *North Carolina—Police Information Network.* Washington: NCJRS (Microfiche) n/d.

Philips, Harry. "KCPD Patrolmen Increase 'Hits' with Computer." *Law and Order.* 17:3 (March, 1969), 50-59.

Phoenix, Arizona. *LEADS (Law Enforcement Assistance Development System) Project. Police Records and Data System Study—Final Report V 1: Project Description.* Washington: NCJRS, 1968.

Phoenix, Arizona. *LEADS (Law Enforcement Assistance Development System) Project. Police Records and Data System Study—Final Report V 2: System Description and Implementation.* Washington: NCJRS, 1968.

Plants, J.R. "Statewide Computer Based Law Enforcement Information Systems." *Law Enforcement Science and Technology* (1967).

Postley, John A. *Computers and People.* N.Y.: McGraw Hill, 1960.

Reinler, G. Hobard and Robert M. Ingleburger. "Information Technology." *Police Chief.* XXXVII:5 (May, 1970), 28-31.

Rieder, Robert J. *Law Enforcement Information Systems.* SprinFIELD, IL.: C.C. Thomas, 1972.

Rose, Michael. *Computers, Managers and Society.* Hammondsworth: Penguin, 1969.

Sanders, Donald H. *Computers and Management.* N.Y.: McGraw Hill, 1970.

Sargent, Francis. "The National Crime Information Center and Massachusetts." *Computers and Automation* (December, 1973).

Shaw, John Clark. *Managing Computer System Projects.* N.Y.: McGraw Hill, 1970.

Shaw, William. "The Computerized Society—Required Reading." *Law and Order.* 19:7 (July, 1971), 80-84.

Shaw, William. "Some Basic Notes on Electronic Data Processing. *Law and Order.* 20:8 (August, 1972), 16-19, 26.

Shryock, J.R. and G.L. Smith. "Small-Scale Computer Serves Suburban Police Department." *Law and Order.* 17:11 (November, 1969), 80-84.

"Success of NCIC Systems." *FBI Law Enforcement Bulletin* (October, 1968), 7-11, 23.

"Texas Crime Information Center." *Texas Lawman.* 39 (November, 1970), 28-29.

Tynan, J. "Computers Catch Suspended Licenses: Connecticut." *American City* (January, 1968).

Tynan, John J. "Computers Help Connecticut Down Auto Violations." *Law and Order.* 13:6 (June, 1965), 40-44.

"Univac for Louisiana State Police." *Law and Order.* 14:8 (August, 1966), 66-68.

U.S. Federal Bureau of Investigation. *National Crime Information Center Operating Manual—FBI.* Washington: 1970 (loose-leaf).

U.S. Housing and Urban Development Department. *Urban and Regional Information Systems: Support for Planning in Metropolitan Areas.* Washington: GPO, 1969.

Vickery, Bryan. *Information Systems.* Hamden, CT.: Shoestring, 1973.

Videtti, Joseph A. Jr. "Application of Computers in Law Enforcement." *Police.* 13:6 (July-August, 1969), 33-39.

Vierra, J, "Computers and the Law." *Police.* 13:3 (1969), 95-98.

Vogeler, John. "A New Information Retrieval System." *Law and Order.* 13:3 (March, 1965), 32.

Wand, Hal. "Computer Controlled Two-Way Radio Network." *Law and Order.* 21:4 (April, 1973), 68-70, 72, 74.

Wasserman, Joseph J. "Plugging the Leaks in Computer Security." *Harvard Business Review* (September-October, 1969).

Waters, S.J. *Introduction to Computer Systems Design.* N.Y.: International Publications Service, 1974.

Weiss, Eric A. *Computer Usage: Application.* N.Y.: McGraw Hill, 1970.

Whisenand, Paul M. "A Data Processing System for Law

Enforcement." *Police.* 10:2 (November-December, 1965), 11-14.

Whisenand, Paul M. and Kenneth L. Draemer. "Police Automatic Data Processing In Orange, Los Angeles Counties." *Journal of California Law Enforcement* (October, 1966), 92-97.

Wilkins, R. "Threat of Law Enforcement Technology." *Current* (April, 1972).

Williams. D.L. "Real-Time Computer Systems for the Police Department." *Law and Order.* 12:7 (July, 1964), 8-10, 15.

Yefsky, S.A., ed. *Law Enforcement Science and Technology.* Washington: Thompson, 1967.

Zane, Thomas L. "An Automated Police Information System." *Military Police Journal* (January, 1967).

COMPUTER LANGUAGES

General

Automated Education Center. *A User's Guide to the Adam System.* St. Clair Shores, MI.: Management Information Service, n/d.

Elson, Mark. *Concepts of Programming Languages.* Chicago: Science Research, 1973.

Heaps, H.S. *Introduction to Computer Languages.* Englewood Cliffs, N.J.: Prentice Hall, 1972.

Pratt, Terance. *Programming Languages: Design and Implementation.* Englewood Cliffs, N.J.: Prentice Hall, 1975.

Rosen, Saul, ed. *Programming Systems and Languages.* N.Y.: McGraw Hill, 1967.

Basic

Albrecht, R. et al. *Basic.* N.Y.: Wiley, 1973.

DeRossi, C.J. *Learning Basic Fast.* Englewood Cliffs, N.J.: Reston, 1974.

Maratek, Samuel. *Basic.* N.Y.: Academy Press, 1975.

Sass, C.J. *Basic Programming and Applications.* Rockleigh, N.J.: Allyn, 1976.

Scott, Peter F. *Programming in Basic.* Mystic, CT.: Verry, 1975.

Cobol

Armstrong, Russell M. *Modular Programming in Cobol.* N.Y.: Wiley, 1973.

Berk, M. *Programmers Cobol.* N.Y.: McGraw Hill, 1970.

Bernard, S.M. *System 3-60 Cobol.* Englewood Cliffs, N.J.: Prentice Hall, 1968.

Davis, G. and C. Litecky. *Elementary Cobol Programming.* N.Y.: McGraw Hill, 1971.

DeRossi, C. *Learning Cobol Fast: A Structured Approach.* Englewood Cliffs, N.J.: Reston, 1976.

Feingold, Carl. *Fundamentals of Cobol Programming.* 2nd ed. Dubuque, IA.: William C. Brown, 1973.

Lysegard, Anna. *Introduction to Cobol.* N.Y.: Oxford University Press, 1968.

Sprowls, R.C. *Computing with Cobol.* Scranton, PA.: Canfield, 1974.

Fortran

Engelshon, H.S. *Conversational Fortran.* N.Y.: Macmillan, 1975.

Boguslavsky, B. *Elementary Computer Programming in Fortran IV.* Englewood Cliffs, N.J.: Reston, 1974.

Day, A.C. *Fortran Techniques.* N.Y.: Cambridge University Press, 1972.

DeTar, D.F. *Principles of Fortran Programming.* Reading, MA.: W.A. Benjamin, 1972.

Dimitry, D.L. and T.H. Mott, Jr. *Introduction to Fortran IV Programming.* N.Y.: Holt, Rinehart & Winston, 1966.

Kallin, Sten. *Introduction to Fortran.* N.Y.: Petrocelli, 1972.

Nickerson, R. *Fundamentals of Fortran Programming.* Englewood Cliffs, N.J.: Winthrop, 1975.

Stuart, F. *Fortran Programming.* rev. ed. N.Y.: Wiley, 1970.

Vickers, F.D. *Fortran Four: A Modern Approach.* N.Y.: Holt, Rinehart & Winston, 1970.

COMPUTER SECURITY

California Intergovernmental Board of Electronic Data Processing. *Guidelines Establishing Requirements for Security and Confidentiality of Information Systems.* Washington: NCJRS (Microfiche) 1974.

Carnahan Conference on Electronic Crime Counter-Measure: 1972 Proceedings. Lexington: Kentucky University, 1972.

Considerations of Data Security in a Computer Environment. N.Y.: IBM, 1970.
Protection of data from accidental or intentional disclosure to unauthorized persons and from unauthorized modification.

Gallati, Robert R.J. "SEARCH—Security and Privacy Considerations." *Police.* 16:3 (November, 1971), 32-38.

Katzan, H. Jr. *Computer Data Security.* N.Y.: Van Nostrand Reinhold, 1973.
A discussion of the theoretical and practical aspects of computer data security in modern computer and information systems.

Keller, E. John. "The Indiscreet Computer—A Computer Security Program." *Law and Order.* 22:8 (August, 1974), 91-92.

Renninger, C.R. and D.K. Branstand. *Government Looks at Privacy and Security in Computer Systems—Summary of a Conference Held at the National Bureau of Standards, Gaithersburg, Maryland, November 19-20, 1973.* Washington: GPO, 1974.

Schiedermayer, P.L. "The Many Aspects of Computer Security." *Police Chief.* XXXVII:7 (July, 1970), 20-21, 64-67.

"So You Think You Want a Theft-Proof Computer?" *Security World* (October, 1972), 38.

Thorsen, June E., ed. *Computer Security. Equipment, Personnel, and Data.* Los Angeles: Security World, 1974.

Turn, R. and H.E. Peterson. *Security of Computerized Information Systems.* Springfield, VA.: NTIS, 1970.
Vulnerabilities of computerized information systems to electronic crime are surveyed and remedial measures suggested.

U.S. Department of Commerce. *International Electronic Crime Counter-Measures Conference.* Springfield, VA.: NTIS, 1973.

Van Tassel, Dennis. *Computer Security Management.* Englewood Cliffs, N.J.: Prentice Hall, 1972.

Van Tassel, Dennis. "Information Security in a Computer Environment." *Computers and Automation* (July, 1969).

PLANNING AND RESEARCH

COST BENEFIT ANALYSIS

Layard, Richard, ed. *Cost Benefit Analysis.* Baltimore: Penguin, 1975.

Mishan, E.J. *Cost Benefit Analysis: An Informal Introduction.* N.Y.: Praeger, 1971.

Newton, Trevor. *Cost Benefit Analysis in Administration.* Mystic, CT.: Verry, 1974.

Page, Louis O. and David L. Belson. "A System to Account for Costs and Effectiveness." *Police Chief.* XLII:9 (September, 1975), 42-43.

Peters, G.H. *Cost-Benefit Analysis and Public Expenditure.* Levittown, N.Y.: Transatlantic, n/d.

Slott, I. and W.M. Sprecher. *Cost Effectiveness and Criminal Justice.* N.Y.: American Society of Mechanical Engineers, 1972.

CRIME ANALYSIS

Arthur D. Little Inc. *Futuristic Community Development—Crime Impact: East Central Florida, 1974-1984.* Cambridge, MA.: Arthur D. Little, Inc. 1973.

Beattie, Ronald H. "Problems of Criminal Statistics in the United States." *Journal of Criminal Law, Criminology and Police Science.* 46:3 (July-August, 1955), 178-186.

Biderman, Albert D. "Surveys of Population Samples for Estimated Crime Incidence." *Annals* (November, 1967).

Black, D.J. "Production of Crime Rates." *American Sociological Review.* 35 (August, 1970), 733-748.

Bonger, W. *Criminality and Economic Conditions.* Bloomington: Indiana University Press, 1969.

Brown, Donna. "The UCR Program: Development of Standardized Audit." *Police Chief.* XLI:12 (December, 1974), 34-38.

Budnick, F.S. *Crime-Correlated Area Model: An Application in Evaluating Intensive Police Patrol Activities.* Washington: NCJRS, 1972.
Development and potential uses of a statistical model for estimating crime levels in one section of a city form the levels in other statistically similar areas of that city.

California Department of Justice Bureau of Criminal Statistics. *Crime and Delinquency in California, 1973—Law Enforcement Component Program Report (Crimes and Arrests).* Washington: NCJRS (Microfiche) 1974.
Provides statistical information about crimes, arrests dispositions, jail population and personnel engaged in law enforcement activities.

Chambliss, W.J. and R.H. Nagasawa. "On the Validity of Official Statistics: A Comparative Study of White, Black and Japanese High-School Boys." *Journal of Research in Crime and Delinquency.* 16 (January, 1969).

Colston, M.A. "A Measure of Crime Seriousness." *Australian Police Journal.* 27:3. 1973, 198-204.

Crime in Eight American Cities—National Crime Panel Survey of Atlanta, Baltimore, Cleveland, Dallas, Denver, Newark, Portland and St Louis: Advance Report. Washington: NCJRS, 1974.

Davis, George F. "A Study of Adult Probation Violation Rates by Means of the Cohort Approach." *Journal of Criminal Law, Criminology and Police Science.* 55:1 (March, 1964), 70-85.

Doleschal, E. *Criminal Statistics.* Rockville, MD.: National Institute of Mental Health, 1972.

Falk, Gerhard J. "The Influence of Season on the Crime Rate." *Journal of Criminal Law, Criminology and Police Science.* 43 (1953), 199-213.
Analyses number of index offenses reported by the police in eight American cities according to month and time of day.

Federal Bureau of Investigation. *Uniform Crime Reports.* Washington: FBI Annual.

Ferracuti, Franco, Rosita Perez Hernandez and Marvin E. Wolfgang. "A Study of Police Errors in Crime Classification." *Journal of Criminal Law, Criminology and Police Science.* 53 (March, 1962), 113-119.
Study of 86 police officers charged with classification of crimes in Puerto Rico. Results of a classification test revealed a large proportion of errors.

Gansenier, Duane G. and Lyle Knowles. "The Relationship Between Part I Crimes and Economic Indicators." *Journal of Police Science and Administration.* 2:4 (December, 1974), 395-398.

Griffin, John I. "New Perspectives in Police Statistics." *Journal of Criminal Law, Criminology and Police Science.* 46-6 (March-April, 1956), 879-881.

Griffin, J.I. *Statistics Essential for Police Efficiency.* Springfield, IL.: C.C. Thomas, 1972.
Introductory textbook for use in police science curricula, emphasizing practical application of statistical techniques in police work.

Harries, K.D. *The Geography of Crime and Justice.* N.Y.: McGraw Hill, 1974.
Author shows that crime and justice differ greatly from place to place.

Harries, Keith D. "The Geography of Crimes: A Case for the Police Chief as Interpreter." *Police Chief.* XLII:10 (October, 1975), 262-264.

Heller, N.B. and J.T. McEwen. "Applications of Crime Seriousness Information in Police Departments." *Journal of Criminal Justice.* 1:3 (1973), 241-253.

Hindelang, M.J. "The Uniform Crime Reports Revisited." *Journal of Criminal Justice.* 2:1 (1974), 1-17.

Hindelang, M. and C.S. Dunn. *Source Book of Criminal Justice Statistics. 1973.* Washington: NCJRS, 1973.
Compilation of criminal justice and related statistics which are currently available from the publications of a variety of governmental and private organizations.

Home Office. *Criminal Statistics, England and Wales. 1974.* London: Home Office, 1975.

Hoover, J. Edgar. "A Look at Bank Robbery Statistics." *FBI Law Enforcement Bulletin.* 36:4 (April, 1967), 11-13, 26.

International Criminal Police Organization. *International Crime Statistics.* Paris: Interpol Annual.

Iskrant, Albert P. and Paul V. Joliet. *Accidents and Homicide.* Washington: Vital and Health Statistics Monographs, American Public Health Association, issued periodically.

Kennedy, Daniel B. "The Relationship Between Pre-Riot Crime and Riot Activity." *Police Chief.* XXXVIII:7 (July, 1971), 58-60.

Kinzer, John G. "An Unresolved Issue: Crime Displacement." *Police Chief.* 16:8 (August, 1974), 66-67.

Kyllonen, R.L. "Crime Rate versus Population Density in United States Cities: A Model." *General Systems.* 12 (1967), 137-145.

Lunden, Walter A. "The Saturation Point in Crime." *Police.* 10:4 (March-April, 1966), 57-59.

Metropolitan Washington Council of Governments. *Interjurisdictional Crime in the Washington Metropolitan Area: A Preliminary Report on the Maryland Suburban Jurisdictions.* Washington: NCJRS (Microfiche) 1973.

Meyer, J.C. Jr. and W.E. Taylor. "Analyzing the Nature of Police Involvements: A Research Note Concerning the Effects of Forms of Police Mobilization." *Journal of Criminal Justice.* 31:2 (1975), 141-146.
Analysis of police field activities, police initiate a larger percentage of activities than was supposed.

Norris, Fred F. "Accepting Crime Statistics." *Police.* 6:6 (July-August, 1963), 40-41.

O'Neill, Michael E. "Crime Analysis: A Neglected and Ill-Defined Process." *Journal of California Law Enforcement* (October, 1973), 107-110.

O'Neill, Michael E. and Carlton J. Bloom. "The Field Officer: Is He Really Fighting Crime?" *Police Chief.* 39:2 (February, 1972), 30-32.
Analysis of field activities for Long Beach CA. Police Department.

Ohlin, Lloyd E. "The Effect of Social Change on Crime and Law Enforcement." *Notre Dame Lawyer.* 43 (1968), 834-846.

Pedersen, Paul A. Jr. "Prima County Sheriff's Grid Reporting System." *Police Chief.* XLII:5 (May, 1975), 70-71.
Use of grid system to analyze crime and other police problems.

Police Crime Analysis Unit Handbook. Washington: LEAA, 1973.

Price, J.E. "A Test of the Accuracy of Criminal Statistics." *Social Problems.* 14 (Fall, 1966), 214-222.

Rizek, Conrad. *Police Mathematics.* Springfield, IL.: C.C. Thomas, 1955.

Robinson, S.M. *Can Delinquency Be Measured?* Montclair, N.J.: Paterson Smith, 1972.
Research on the measurement of juvenile delinquent behavior, the use of definitions, and a study of delinquents in New York.

Ruchelman, Leonard. *Police Statistics: A Comparative Study of Three Cities.* Cambridge, MA.: Ballinger, 1974.

Sagi, Phillip C. and Charles F. Wellford. "Age, Composition and Patterns of Change in Criminal Statistics." *Journal of Criminal Law, Criminology and Police Science.* 59 (1968), 29-36.

Schmit, S. Marilyn. "Factors Related to Low Crime Rates in Urban Areas—Milwaukee." *Police.* 16:10 (June, 1972), 54, 58.

Schwartz, E.P. *National Symposium on Methods, Procedures and Techniques for Crime Analysis, Prevention and Planning-St Louis, Missouri, October 10-12, 1974—Proceedings and Recommendations.* Washington: NCJRS (Microfiche) 1974.

Skogan, W.G. "Measurement Problems in Official and Survey Crime Rates." *Journal of Criminal Justice.* 3:1 (1975), 17-32.

Strahan, Bruce L. et al. "Geographic Base Files: A Tool for Effective Agency Operations." *Police Chief.* XLII:12 (December, 1975), 46-49.
Computer operated geographic base file used in dispatching, crime analysis, manpower allocation etc.

"Substantial Amounts of Crime Go Unreported." *Journal* (May-June, 1974), 68-69.

Sutherland, Edwin H. *On Analyzing Crime.* Chicago: University of Chicago Press, 1973.

U.S. Bureau of the Census. *Report on the National Needs for Criminal Justice Statistics.* Washington: GPO, 1968.

U.S. Department of Justice. *Computer Mapping: A New Technique in Crime Analysis.* Washington: LEAA, 1967.

U.S. Federal Bureau of Investigation. *Uniform Crime Reporting Handbook: How to Prepare Uniform Crime Reports.* Washington: FBI, July, 1966.

Walker, N. *Crimes, Courts and Figures: An Introduction to Criminal Statistics.* Harmondsworth: Penguin, 1971.

Wallerstein, James S. and Clement J. Wyle. "Our Law-Abiding Law-Breakers." *Probation.* 25 (April, 1947), 107-112.
Study of 1,698 New York citizens of whom 17% of the males and 4% of the females admitted to burglaries.

Weis, Kurt and Michael E. Milakovich. "Political Misuses of Crime Rates." *Society* (July-August, 1974), 27-33.

Wheeler, Stanton. "Criminal Statistics: A Reformulation of the Problems." *Journal of Criminal Law, Criminology and Police Science.* 48:3 (September, 1967), 317-324.

Wilkins. Leslie T. "New Thinking in Criminal Statistics." *Journal of Criminal Law, Criminology and Police Science.* 56:3 (September, 1965), 277-284.

Willoughby, E.L. and James A. Inciardi. "Estimating the Incidence of Crime." *Police Chief.* XLII:8 (August, 1975), 69-70.

Cost of Crime

Baker, James A. and Travis E. Reed. *Cost of Crimes Against Business.* Rev. ed. Washington: U.S. Department of Commerce, 1976.

Becker, G.S. "Crime and Punishment: An Economic Approach." *Journal of Political Economy* (March-April, 1968).

Cloninger, Dale Owen. *The Economics of Crime and Law Enforcement.* Sarasota, FL.: Ommi-Print, 1975.

Flesisher, Belton M. *The Economics of Delinquency.* Chicago: Quadrangle, 1966.

Fowler, N. *Cost of Crime.* Washington: NCJRS (Microfiche) 1973.
An estimate of the monetary cost of crime is derived from the cost of crime services (police, prisons and probation) the direct cost of monetary crimes, as well as the costs of insurance and security.

Friedman, Lee S. *Economics of Crime and Justice.* Morristown, N.J.: General Learning, 1976.

Henry, Jack. *What Price Crime?* London: Hutchinson, 1945.

"The High Cost of Civil Disorder." *Security World.* 7 (July-August, 1970).

Kaplan, Lawrence J. and Dennis Kessler. *An Economic Analysis of Crime: Selected Readings.* Springfield, IL.: C.C. Thomas, 1976.

Law Enforcement Assistance Administration. *Analysis of 2994 Victims of Crime: Act of 1972.* Springfield, VA.: NTIS, 1972.
An analysis to provide estimates and information relevant to the annual costs of a nationwide victims of crime program.

Miller, Gary J. "What Are the Economic Aspects of Public Intoxication Arrests?" *Police.* 13:5 (May-June, 1969), 96-99.

National Institute of Law Enforcement and Criminal Justice. *Expenditure and Employment Data for the Criminal Justice System, 1969-1970.* Washington: GPO, 1972.

National Criminal Justice Information and Statistics Service. *Expenditure and Employment Data for the Criminal Justice System, 1970-1971.* Washington: GPO, 1973.

National Criminal Justice Information and Statistics Service. *Trends in Expenditure and Employment Data for the Criminal Justice System, 1971-1975.* Washington: NCJRS, 1977.

Newman, Charles L. "The War on Crime." *Federal Probation.*:4 (1966), 35-38.
The author says that no matter what estimate of the cost of crime is given in the United States, it cannot hope to include the costs in terms of loss in productive manpower and the social costs which cannot be measured in dollars.

Patterson, P.L. and E.Q. Unwin. *California Criminal Justice Cost Study, V I: A Cost Reporting System and Final Technical Report.* Washington: NCJRS (microfiche) 1972.
A method of reporting the true costs of criminal justice operations.

Rogers, A.J. *Economics of Crime.* Hinsdale, IL.: Dryden, 1973.

Rottenberg, Simon. *The Economics of Crime and Punishment.* Washington: American Enterprise Institute for Public Policy Research, 1973.

Swimmer, G. "The Relationship of Police and Crime—Some Methodological and Empirical Results." *Criminology.* 12:3 (1974), 293-314.

Cost of Police Services

Emerson, R.D. *Economic Analysis of the Provision of Police Services.* Ann Arbor, MI.: University Microfilms, 1970.

Giertz, J.E. *Economic Approach to the Allocation of Police Resources.* Ann Arbor, MI.: University Microfilms, 1970.

Gladstone, Edward A. and Thomas W. Cooper. "State Highway Patrols: Their Functioning and Finance." *Police Chief* (May, 1966), 31-36.

Gourley, Dudley D. "New Methods for Financing the Police Function." *Police Chief.* XLII:11 (November, 1975), 20-21.
Author suggests the purchase of bonds and investments; special taxes on industries or businesses with high crime rates; the criminal should be made to work to pay for the police costs involved; all young people who are mentally and physically fit could be drafted into the police force for a 2-year period at minimum salary; the earnings of organized crime should be confiscated to support the police function.

Gylys, Julius A. "Empirical Analysis: The Future of Central City Police Expenditures." *Police.* 15:4 (March-April, 1971), 21-23.

Horwitz, L.K. and E.B. Croft. *Local Criminal Justice Appropriations in Monroe County New York: Information Paper #1.* Springfield, VA.: NTIS, 1973.

International City Manager's Association. *Municipal Yearbook.* Washington: ICMA Annual.
Contains statistical data on municipal police agencies.

Jones, E. Terrence. "Impact of Crime Rate Changes on Police Protection Expenditures in American Cities." *Criminology* (February, 1974), 516-524.

Lunden, Walter A. "Major Crimes, Spending for Police Protection and Police Efficiency in the United States 1960-1969." *Police.* 15:5 (May-June, 1971), 10-12.

Olsen, Bruce T. *Police Expenditures.* Washington: President's Commission on Law Enforcement and Administration of Justice, 1967.

Walzer, N.C. *Economics of Scale and Municipal Police Services.* Ann Arbor, MI.: University Microfilms, 1970.

DEMOGRAPHY

Bahl, Roy W. and Sara Mills Mazie, eds. "Metropolitan Fiscal Structures and the Distribution of Population within Metropolitan Areas." *Population Distribution and Policy: The U.S. Commission on Population Growth and the American Future Research Reports, V 5.* Washington: GPO, 1972.

Barclay, George W. *Techniques of Population Analysis.* N.Y.: Wiley, 1958.

Benjamin, Bernard. *Demographic Analysis.* N.Y.: Praeger, 1969.

Bogue, Donald J. *Principles of Demography.* N.Y.: Wiley, 1969.

Gibbs, Jack P. and Leo F. Schnore. "Metropolitan Growth: An International Study." *American Journal of Sociology.* 66 (September, 1960), 160-170.

Kammeyer, Kenneth C.W., ed. *Population Studies: Selected Essays and Research.* Chicago: Rand McNally, 1969.

Kynell, Kermit S. "The Police and Population: A Critical Analysis." *Police.* 5:4 (March-April, 1961), 19-22; 5:5 (May-June, 1961), 18-21.
Relationship of population to police problems.

Pielou, E.C. *Population and Community Ecology: Principles and Methods.* New ed. Alhambra, CA.: Borden, 1975.

Population. 25 vols. Totowa, N.J.: Irish Academy Press, 1971.

EVALUATION

Agency for International Development. *Evaluation Handbook.* Washington: Agency for International Development, 1971.

Alberts, D.S. *Plan for Measuring the Performance of Social Programs: The Application of Operations Research Methodology.* N.Y.: Praeger, 1970.
A methodology to measure the performance or effectiveness of a social action is developed by applying the techniques of operational research.

Albright, Ellen. *Evaluator's Manual for Anti-Crime Impact Projects.* Washington: U.S. Department of Justice, January, 1973.

Anderson, S.B. *Encyclopedia of Educational Evaluation—Concepts and Techniques for Evaluating Education and Training Programs.* San Francisco: Jossey Bass, 1975.

Bloch, Peter B. and David Specht. *Evaluation of New York City's Rapidly Expanding Neighborhood Team Policing Program.* Washington: Urban Institute, 1973.

Cain, G.G. and R.G. Hollister. *Methodology of Evaluating Social Action Programs.* Washington: NCJRS (Microfiche) 1969.

Carter, Robert M. "The Evaluation of Police Programs." *Police Chief.* XXXVII:11 (November, 1971), 57-60.

Council of Europe Library Berger-Levrault. *Methods of Evaluation and Planning in the Field of Crime: 1st Criminological Colloquium—Strasbourg. November 28-30, 1973.* Washington: NCJRS, 1974.

Drake, A.W. *Analysis of Public Systems.* Cambridge, MA.: MIT Press, 1972.
Recent studies on the use of quantitative formal models as aids to decision makers for improved delivery of public services.

Dubois, Philip. *Research Strategies for Evaluating Training.* Chicago: Rand McNally, 1970.

Galvin, Raymond T. "Law Enforcement: A Comparative View." *Police Chief.* 38:8 (August, 1971), 64-71.
Advocates increased studies of a comparative nature.

Germann, Clark. "Evaluation of State Information and Education Programs." *Law and Order.* 23:6 (June, 1975).

Hatry, Harry P. et al. *Practical Program Evaluation for State and Local Governments.* Washington: Urban Institute, 1973.

Hennessy, James J. "The Evaluation of Program Impact." *Police Chief.* XLI:5 (May, 1974), 36-37.

International City Management Association. *Measuring the Effectiveness of Basic Municipal Services—Initial Report.* Washington: NCJRS (Microfiche) 1974.
Identifies and measures the effectiveness of various services. Provides suggestions for data collection procedures.

Kinzer, J.G. *Evaluation in Criminal Justice Programs: Guidelines and Examples.* Washington: GPO, 1973.

Knowles, Lyle. "Evaluating Training and Educational Programs in Criminal Justice." *Journal of Police Science and Administration.* 1:3 (September, 1973), 336-344.

Knowles, Lyle and John Timko. "Evaluating Educational Programs in Criminal Justice: A Technique for Obtaining Responses from Participants." *Journal of Police Science and Administration.* 2:1 (March, 1974), 107-114.

Lewis, J.H. *Evaluation of Experiments in Policing: How Do You Begin (Four Cases).* Washington: NCJRS, 1972.

Lindberg, Roy A. and Theodore Cohn. *Operations Auditing.* N.Y.: AMA, 1972.

Lipton, Douglas. *Effectiveness of Correctional Treatment: A Survey of Treatment Evaluation Studies.* N.Y.: Praeger, 1975.

Luksus, Edmund G. "The Analytical Method." *Journal of California Law Enforcement* (July, 1973), 9-15.

Maltz, M.D. *Evaluation of Crime Control Programs.* Washington: GPO, 1972.

Marx, G.T. *Alternative Measures of Police Performance—Working Paper.* Washington: NCJRS (Microfiche) 1974.
A categorization of currently used measures, measures of individual performance, the quality of emergency service, use

of unobtrusive measures, the citizen survey and measures for contrasting cities and departments.

Murry, Charles A. and Robert E. Krug. *National Evaluation of the Pilot Cities Program: Executive Summary.* Washington: NCJRS, 1975.

National Institute of Law Enforcement and Criminal Justice. *Performance Measurement and the Criminal Justice System: Four Conceptual Approaches.* Springfield, VA.: NTIS, 1976.

Northwestern University Traffic Institute. *Evaluation and the Police Supervisor.* Evanston, IL.: Traffic Institute Northwestern University, 1973.

Owens, R.G. and A.D. Hamaan. "Evaluating the Training Program." *Police Chief.* XXXIII:2 (February, 1966), 22-24.

Police Technical Assistance: An Evaluation of Training of Foreign Police Official in the United States. Washington: International Cooperation Administration, 1957.

Rochford, James. "Determining Police Effectiveness." *FBI Law Enforcement Bulletin.* 43:10 (October, 1974).

Rose, Homer C. "Plan for Training Evaluation." *Training and Development Journal.* 22:5 (May, 1968).

Schwab, G. *Evaluation Handbook.* 2nd ed. Washington: NCJRS (Microfiche) 1974.

St Petersburg Police Department. *Evaluation Manual: A Guide for Police Agencies.* Washington: NCJRS (Microfiche) 1974.

Suchman, Edward A. *Evaluative Research Principles and Practices in Public Service and Social Action Programs.* N.Y.: Sage, 1967.

Sutherland, Jon H. and Michael S. Werthman. *Comparative Concepts of Law and Order.* Glenview, IL.: Scott Foresman, 1971.

Tyler, W.L. *Measurement of Partial and Total Crime Solution in a Criminal Justice System.* Ann Arbor, MI.: University Microfilms, 1973.

Webb, Kenneth and Harry P. Hatry. *Obtaining Citizen Feedback: The Application of Citizen Surveys to Local Governments.* Washington: Urban Institute, 1973.

Weidman, Donald R. et al. *Intensive Evaluation for Criminal Justice Planning Agencies.* Washington: NCJRS, 1975.

Weiss, C.H. *Evaluation Research: Methods for Assessing Program Effectiveness.* Englewood Cliffs, N.J.: Prentice Hall, 1972.

Wilson, Gerald R. *Administrative Assessment Program.* Danville IL.: Interstate, 1972.

Wholey, Joseph S. et al. *Federal Evaluation Policy.* Washington: Urban Institute, 1970.

Willmer, M.A.P. *On the Application of Decision Tree Theory to Criminal Investigation.* Washington: NCJRS (Microfiche).

FLOWCHARTING

Lenher, John. *Flowcharting: An Introductory Text and Workbook.* Princeton, N.J.: Auerbach, 1972.

Spear, Mary E. *Practical Charting Techniques.* N.Y.: McGraw Hill, 1969.

GRANTS

Coster, Clarence M. "Grantsmanship...Is a Science." *Police Chief.* 37:12 (December, 1970), 15-17.

Grantsmanship: Money and How to Get It. Rev. ed. Chicago: Marquis, 1973.

Murphy, Lawrence E. "Grant Development: The Functions and Personnel." *Police Chief.* XXXIX:4 (April, 1972), 40-43.

Noe, Lee, ed. *The Foundation Grants Index.* N.Y.: Columbia University Press, 1975.

Pitt, Paul J. "Grantsmanship is a Professional Responsibility." *Police Chief.* XXXVII:5 (May, 1971), 29, 71.

Rush, James R. "Grantsmanship Is Plan Implementation." *Police Chief.* XXXVII:5 (May, 1971), 28, 72.

Taylor, Edward M. "A Celery Stalk for Police: Seeking Funds From Outside Sources." *Police Chief.* XXXIX:4 (April, 1972), 34-39.

Turner, Roland, ed. *The Grants Register, 1977-1979.* N.Y.: St. Martin's, 1976.

Watson, Nelson A. "Grantsmanship. . .Is An Art." *Police Chief.* 37:12 (December, 1970), 14, 16.

GRAPHIC PRESENTATION

Shaw, William. "Skillful Slide Preparation Can Enhance Your Presentation." *Law and Order.* 23:4 (April, 1975), 20, 22-24, 44.

Smart, L. Edwin and Sam Arnold. *Practical Rules for Graphic Presentation of Business Statistics.* Columbus: Ohio State University, Administration Science, 1965.

Schmid, Calvin F. *Handbook of Graphic Presentation.* N.Y.: Ronald, 1954.

Spear, Mary Eleanor. *Charting Statistics.* N.Y.: McGraw Hill, 1952.

Griffin, John I. "Effective Statistical Presentation for Police Administrators." *Journal of Criminal Law, Criminology and Police Science.* 48:4 (November-December, 1957), 462-467.

Lutz, R.R. *Graphic Presentation Simplified.* N.Y.: Funk & Wagnalls, 1949.

Rogers, Anna C. *Graphic Charts Handbook.* Washington: Public Affairs, 1961.

PLANNING

Ayres, Robert U. *Technological Forecasting and Long-Range Planning:* N.Y.: McGraw Hill, 1969.

Bolan, Richard S. "Community Decision Behavior: The Culture of Planning." *Journal of the American Institute of Planners* (September, 1969), 301-310.

Boyce, Ronald. *Regional Development and the Wabash*

Basin. Montgomery: University of Alabama Press, 1964.

Authors present the many facets of regional planning and how it affects local government and organizations; contains some insights on political questions. Shows how community organizations become involved in and attempt to deal with regional planning.

Branch, Melville C. *Planning: Aspects and Applications*. N.Y.: Wiley, 1966.

Brown, Robert M. "Urban Planning for Environmental Health." *Public Health Reports*. 79:3 (March, 1964), 201-204.

Cape, William H. "Holiday Law Enforcement Preparedness." *Law and Order*. 13:12 (December, 1965), 8-10, 31-33.

Carbone, William H. "Commitment to Planning: A Regional Approach." *Police Chief*. XLII:7 (July, 1975), 68-70.

Chaiken, J. et al. *Criminal Justice Models—An Overview*. Washington: NCJRS, 1975.

Clavel, Pierre. "Planners and Citizens' Boards: Some Applications of Social Theory to the Problem of Plan Implementation." *Journal of the American Institute of Planners*. 34:3 (1968), 130-139.

Cronkhite, C.L. "Participative Planning at Work in the Criminal Justice Community." *FBI Law Enforcement Bulletin*. 44:2 (February, 1965), 8-12.

Stresses the importance of involving "working level" personnel in the planning process.

Diggles, W.J. *Police Planning and Analysis Office*. Springfield, VA.: NTIS, 1973.

Structure, functions and resource requirements of a planning and analysis unit for a local police department.

Erikson, M. James. "The Criminal Justice Planner and You." *Police Chief*. XLIII:1 (January, 1976), 60-61.

Ewing' David W. *The Human Side of Planning: Tool or Tyrant?* N.Y.: Macmillan, 1969.

Faludi, Andreas. *A Reader in Planning Theory*. Elmsford, N.Y.: Pergamon, 1973.

Felkenes, G.T. "Police Planning: A Stimulus for Needed Organizational Change." *Police*. 16:10 (June, 1972), 24-27.

Fisk, J.G. *California—Office of Criminal Justice Planning: Strategic Evaluation Plan*. 2 vols. Washington: NCJRS (Microfich) 1974.

Friedmann, John and William Alonso. *Regional Development and Planning*. Cambridge, MA.: MIT Press, 1964.

Gill, D.R. *Micklenburg Criminal Justice Pilot Project: Interim Report*. Springfield, VA.: NTIS, 1971.

Gilliam, Harold. "The Fallacy of Single-Purpose Planning." *Daedalus*. 96:4 (Fall, 1967), 1142-1157.

Griffin, Gerald R. "Goal Setting for Police Organizations." *Police Chief*. 16:5 (May, 1974), 32, 34, 74.

Hendricks, James F. "Creative Thinking." *Law and Order*. 17:6 (June, 1969), 110-111.

Hipskind, V.K. "Developing Procedures Through Analysis." *Police*. 10:4 (March-April, 1966), 82-84.

Hoffman, M. *Criminal Justice Planning*. Chicago: American Society of Planning Officials. 1972.

Report addresses the entire network of direct services available for dealing with the problems of crime and the criminal.

Holleb, Doris B. *Social and Economic Information for Urban Planning*. Chicago: University of Chicago Press, 1969.

Howard, M.K. *Regional Criminal Justice Planning—How Are Funding Priorities Established*. Springfield, VA.: NTIS, 1973.

Methods used by criminal justice regional planning units (PRU's) in ranking project proposals, and use of these methods in Santa Clara County, CA.

Hyman, Herbert H. "Planning with Citizens: Two Styles." *Journal of the American Institute of Planners* (March, 1969).

Kastens, Merritt L. *Long Range Planning for Your Business: An Operating Manual*. N.Y.: AMA, 1976.

Kenney, John P. *Police Management Planning*. Rev. ed. Springfield, IL.: C.C. Thomas, 1959.

Key, Charles R. and Miles R. Warren. "Kansas City: Long Range Planning." *Police Chief*. XXXIX:5 (May, 1972), 72-75.

Lee, Colin. *Models in Planning*. Elmsford, N.Y.: Pergamon, 1973.

McLean, Mary. *Local Planning Administration*. 3rd ed. Chicago: International City Managers Association, 1959.

Marion County Criminal Justice Coordinating Council. *Marion County (IN.)—Criminal Justice Coordinating Council: Comprehensive Plan for the City and the County of Indianapolis*. Washington: NCJRS (Microfiche) 1974.

Meier, Richard L. *Development Planning*. N.Y.: McGraw Hill, 1965.

Minneapolis Police Department. *Minneapolis Police Department: Long Range Plan*. Washington: NCJRS (Microfiche) 1974.

National Association of Counties Research Foundation. *Regional Criminal Justice Planning: Manual for Local Officials, Part 2—Developing a Regional Criminal Justice Plan*. Washington: NCJRS, 1971.

Part 2 is a guide to acquaint local elected officials of general purpose governments with the steps involved in preparing a regional criminal justice plan.

New, Colin. *Requirements Planning*. N.Y.: Halsted, 1974.

Oberlender, Len, ed. *Quantitative Tools for Criminal Justice Planning*. Washington: GPO, 1975.

Peat, Marwick, Mitchell and Company. *Program Planning Techniques*. Springfield, VA.: NTIS, 1972.

Planning: New Tools and Perspectives. N.Y.: AMA, 1974.

Pomeroy, Wesley A. "New Trends in Police Planning." *Police Chief*. 38:2 (February, 1971), 16, 18, 21.

Powell, M.D. and D. Murray. *Regional Criminal Justice Planning—Manual for Local Officials, Part 1: Regional Criminal Justice Planning and Local Officials*. Washington: NCJRS, 1971.

This manual assists county and local governing units in developing regional criminal justice planning programs.

Rolett, V. *Mecklenburg Criminal Justice Pilot Project—Annotated List of Publications.* rev. ed. Springfield, VA.: NTIS, 1974.

Good example of material generated by a large research project.

Rosen, Stephen. *Long Range Planning: A Presidential Perspective.* N.Y.: AMA, 1973.

Rothschild, William E. *Putting it All Together: A Guide to Strategic Thinking.* N.Y.: AMA, 1976.

Selznick, Philip. *TVA and the Grass Roots.* Berkeley: University of California Press, 1949.

A thorough, although not very empirical, contribution to the study of complex organizations; contains valuable insights into the politics of regional planning. Deals with the problem encountered when complex organizations become involved in regional planning.

Simmons, W.W. *1974-1975 Exploratory Planning Briefs.* N.Y.: AMA, 1975.

Threshold of Planning Information Systems. Chicago: American Society of Planning Officials, 1967.

Collection of papers on planning urban and regional information systems including geographic implications of urban systems and data processing for planning.

Turner, J. *Extent of Planning Activity in Selected Law Enforcement Agencies.* Washington: NCJRS (Microfiche) 1973.

Uppal, J.C. *Criminal Justice Planning in the States.* Washington: NCJRS (Microfiche) 1974.

PLANNING AND RESEARCH

California Highway Patrol Research and Development Section. "Research Projects." *Police.* 5:3 (January-February, 1961), 72.

Cincinnati Police Department. "Planning and Research Projects." *Police.* 5:2 (November-December, 1960), 60.

Davis, Orval. "A Look at Technical Research and Development for Police Departments." *FBI Law Enforcement Bulletin.* 38:4 (April, 1969), 15-20.

Ehlers, E.C., T. Schuler and R.H. Webb Jr. "Planning and Research Organizations—A Status Report." *Journal of California Law Enforcement.* 7:3 (1973), 109-116.

Hollady, Roy E. "Police Planning and Research." *Police.* 5:4 (March-April, 1961), 72-73.

Law Enforcement Assistance Administration. *Introductory Reading Materials on Planning and Research Units in Police Departments (Selected Readings).* N.Y.: McGraw Hill, 1967.

Oakland Police Department. "Police Planning and Research." *Police.* 4:6 (July-August, 1960), 72-74; 5:1 (September-October, 1960), 74.

Olson, Bruce. "A Center for Police Planning and Research: A Proposal." *Journal of Criminal Law, Criminology and Police Science.* 50:3 (September-October, 1959), 296-301.

Simon, Richard. "The Planning and Research Division of the Los Angeles Police Department." *Journal of Criminal Law and Criminology.* 44 (September-October, 1953), 365-373.

RESEARCH

Blalock, Hubert. *An Introduction to Social Research.* Englewood Cliffs, N.J.: Prentice Hall, 1970.

Blalock, Hubert, and Ann Blalock. *Methodology in Social Research.* N.Y.: McGraw Hill, 1968.

Bottoms, Albert M. and Ernest K. Nilsson. "Operations Research." *Police Chief.* XXXVII:5 (May, 1970), 22-26.

Caplan, Gerald M. "Concern and Choice: The Selection of Program Priorities in Criminal Justice Research." *Journal of Criminal Justice* (1973), 289-298.

Clark, Robert S. "The Police Administrator in a World of Research." *Police Chief.* XLII (December, 1975), 50-52.

Forcese, D. and S. Richter. *Social Research Methods.* Englewood Cliffs, N.J.: Prentice Hall, 1973.

Fox, J.C. and R.J. Lundman. "Problems and Strategies in Gaining Research Access in Police Organizations." *Criminology.* 12:1 (1974), 52-69.

Krausz, E. and S.H. Miller. *Social Research Design.* N.Y.: Longman, 1974.

Lee, F. *Manual for the Law Enforcement Questionnaire.* Brookport, IL.: Psychometric Affiliates, 1970.

National Institute of Law Enforcement and Criminal Justice. *National Institute of Law Enforcement and Criminal Justice—Criminal Justice Research 1974.* Washington: NCJRS, 1974.

Description of the National Institute of Law Enforcement and Criminal Justice, its subdivisions and some of its research and program activity.

Twain, D. and E. Harlow. *Research and Human Services—A Guide to Collaboration for Program Development* Washington: GPO, 1970.

Report based on a series of conferences which considered issues basic to the optimal use of research in agency program development.

Viano, Emilio C., ed. *Criminal Justice Research.* Lexington, MA.: Lexington, 1975.

Wright, M. ed. *Use of Criminology Literature: Information Sources for Research and Development.* London: Butterworths, 1974.

STATISTICAL ANALYSIS

Calley, Truman L. *Fundamentals of Statistics.* Cambridge, MA.: Harvard University Press, 1947.

Clark, V.A. and M.E. Tartar. *Preparation for Basic Statistics.* N.Y.: McGraw, 1968.

Cohen, Lillian. *Statistical Methods for Social Scientist.* Englewood Cliffs, N.J.: Prentice Hall, 1954.

Croxton, Frederick E. and Dudley J. Cowden. *Applied General Statistics.* 2nd ed. Englewood Cliffs, N.J.: Prentice Hall, 1955.

Edwards, Bernard. *Sources of Social Statistics.* N.Y.: Heinemann, 1974.

How to Use Statistics. Boston, MA.: National Fire Protection, 1974.

Huff, Darrell. *How to Lie With Statistics.* N.Y.: W.W. Norton, 1954.

Kingston, C.R. and P.L. Kirk. "The Use of Statistics in Criminalistics." *Journal of Criminal Law, Criminology and Police Science.* 55:4 (December, 1964), 514-521.

Mulholland, H. and C.R. Jones. *Fundamentals of Statistics.* N.Y.: Plenum, 1969.

Wallis, W. Allen and Harry V. Roberts. *Statistics: A New Approach.* Glencoe, IL.: Free Press, 1956.

POLICE-PRESS RELATIONS

POLICE-PRESS RELATIONS

Bantey, Bill. "The Press and the Police." *Police Yearbook.* Washington: IACP, 1962.

Barber, Carter. "A Magna Carta for Media-Police Relations." *Police Chief.* XXXVII:9 (September, 1970), 28-31.

Barber, C. "Model Police-Press Pact Works Smoothly in Pasadena." *Editor and Publisher* (August 15, 1970).

Burke, Martin. "Beaumont Police: Hot Line Speeds Tips to News Media." *Law and Order.* 18:7 (July, 1970), 64-67.

Blake, H.S. "The Peace Officer and the Press." *Police Chief.* XXIII:4 (April, 1956).

Caaells, Andy. "Blueprint for Cooperation." *Police Chief.* XXXVI:3 (March, 1969), 18-20.

Capreol, E. "Police Hotline Speeds Tips to All News Media." *Editor and Publisher* (August 26, 1967).

Carlman, Leonard M. "A Police Press Manual." *Police Chief.* XXXIX:3 (March, 1972), 64-66.

Carley, Jack. "Law Enforcement and Relationship with Free Press." *FBI Law Enforcement Bulletin.* 31:10 (October, 1962); 31:11 (November, 1962).

Carter, R.M. "The Media and the Law Enforcement Image." *Military Police Journal.* 21:8 (1972), 5-9.

"Chief Takes Handcuffs Off Crime Reporting." *Editor and Publisher* (February 28, 1970.)

"Civic Inquiry Eases Tiff Between Press and Police." *Editor and Publisher* (June 5, 1971.)

Clift, Raymond E. "Police, Press and Public Relations." *Journal of Criminal Law, Criminology and Police Science.* 39:5 (January, 1949.)

Copp, William C. "Big Story vs Caution." *Law and Order.* 11:12 (December, 1963), 5, 59.
At times police must operate without press interference.

Creese, Mary. "We Can Help You If You'll Let Us." *FBI Law Enforcement Bulletin.* 39:10 (October, 1970), 7-10, 28-29.

Daley, Robert. "NYPD Improves Its Image." *Police Chief.* XXXIX:7 (July, 1972), 32-33.

Davis, E.M. "A Press Relations Guide for Peace Officers." *Police Chief.* XXXIX:3 (March, 1972), 67-71.

Earle, Howard H. "More on Police Rapport with the Press and Public." *Police.* 7:4 (March-April, 1963), 47-49.

Earle, Howard H. "The Supervisor and the Press." *Police.* 6:3 (January-February, 1962), 6-9.

Ellingsworth, Bill. "KCPD Teletype System Informs News Media and Public." *Law And Order.* 17:12 (November, 1969), 74-76.
Police news disseminated to 10 news agencies in the Kansas City area by teletype.

Elliott, George F. "The Printed Word as a Tool." *Law and Order.* 8:10 (October, 1960).

Elmes, F. "Kiss and Tell." *Police Review.* (G), 81:4195 (1973).

Feaker, Fred. "Informing the Public." *Law and Order.* 21:9 (September, 1973), 60, 62, 64-65.

Friedman, R. "Press: Police Problems—How to Solve Them." *Editor and Publisher* (December 28, 1968).

Filbright, N.H. "Police Reporter Jots Down Some Guideposts." *Editor and Publisher* (April 11, 1970).

Goodman, J.C. "Police-Press Relations." *Police.* 9:5 (May-June, 1965).

Gordon, Robert D. "Does Your Department Have a Media Relations Program? Why Not?" *FBI Law Enforcement Bulletin* (August, 1973), 18-23.

Harpster, Jack. "Winning An Important Ally." *Law and Order.* 18:12 (December, 1970), 52-53, 66.

Hughes, Edward. "The Case for the Press." *Police Chief.* XXVIII:4 (April, 1961).

Kelly, W.H. "Criminal Investigations and Release of News for Publication." *Canadian Society of Forensic Science.* 6:3 (1973), 115-132.

Keogh, J.E. *Law Enforcement and Fire Department Manual on News Media and Public Relations.* North Miami, FL.: American Federation of Police, 1973.

King, C.R. "Kidnap News Blackouts Aid Law Officers." *Editor and Publisher* (November 16, 1974).

Klein, Herbert G. "A Matter of Mutual Respect." *FBI Law Enforcement Bulletin.* 35:7 (July, 1966), 6-7.

Klyman, Fred. "Optimizing the Criminal Justice Agency-News Media Relationship." *Police.* 16:10 (June, 1972), 41-45.

LaCouture, Ron. "The Police, the Press and Public Relations." *Police.* 5:5 (May-June, 1961); 5:6 (July-August, 1961); 6:1 (September-October, 1961).

Livingston, Michael K. "The News Media and the Police." *Texas Police Journal.* 23:9 (October, 1975).

McKnight, Felix R. "Cooperation Between Chiefs and Editors." *Police Yearbook.* Washington: IACP, 1957.

Maley, D. "Photographers Train Police Rookies in Newsmen's Methods." *Editor and Publisher* (August 23, 1969).

Mehler, M. "Cops Air Groups, Seek Answers at Police Press Seminar." *Editor and Publisher* (September 1, 1973).

Mertz, Lewis J. "No Comment!" *Police Chief.* XXXIX:3 (March, 1972), 62-33.

Milemore, George R. "Our Press Relations Officer." *Police Chief.* XXIII:9 (September, 1965).

Mitchell, M. Carter. "Police-Media Relations." *Law and Order.* 22:3 (March, 1974), 20-21, 26, 69.

"News Media Code for Covering Civil Disorders." *Police Chief.* XXXLV:3 (March, 1967), 58.

Pittman, Loren M. "Put Your Best Words Forward." *Police.* 16:2 (October, 1971), 26-28.

"Police-Press Relations Strained." *Security World* (December, 1974).

"Police Laud Newshouse Paper for Withholding Kidnap News." *Editor and Publisher* (November 30, 1974).

"Police and the Press Learn Together." *Police Chief.* XXV:2 (February, 1959).

"Police Recruits are Briefed on Relations with Reporters." *Editor and Publisher* (March 14, 1970).

Prenter, F. "Drafting Police Statements to the Press." *International Criminal Police Review* (April, 1969).

Robertson, Phil. "Teamwork Between Press and Law Enforcement is Mutually Beneficial." *Journal of California Law Enforcement* (January, 1969), 151-153.

Scott, J. "Trading Jobs Improves Police-Press Relations." *Editor and Publisher* (March 9, 1974).

Skousen, W. Cleon. "The Police and the Press." *Law and Order.* 10:3 (March, 1962).

Skousen, W. Cleon. "The Police and the Press." *Law and Order.* 21:4 (April, 1973), 8, 10-12, 14.

"Suggested Day-to-Day Press Releases." *Police Chief.* XXXLV:3 (March, 1967), 33-40.

Tackett, J. "Hotline Phones Help Police and Reporters." *Editor and Publisher* (November 18, 1967).

"Teletype System Used by Kansas City Police Keeps News Media Better Informed." *Police Chief.* XXXVII:1 (January, 1970), 38-40.

Thomas, J.L. "The Police and the Press." *Canadian Police Bulletin* (June, 1949), 8.

Tobias, Richard M. "Police-Press Relations." *Law and Order.* 17:11 (November, 1969), 6.

Van Cleave, Guy F. "Police-Press Relations." *Colorado Sheriff and Peace Officer.* 10 (February-March, 1970), 57-58.

Williams, Gerald O. "Crime News and Its Relation to Police-Press Policies." *Police.* 8:4 (March-April, 1964); 8:5 (May-June, 1964); 8:6 (July-August, 1964); 9:1 (September-October, 1964).

Wilson, Jerry V. and Paul Q. Fuqua. *The Police and the Media.* Boston: Educational Associates, 1975.

NEWS MEDIA

Bagdikian, Ben H. *The Information Machines: Their Impact on Men and the Media.* N.Y.: Harper & Row, 1971.

Barron, Jerome A. *Freedom of the Press for Whom? The Right of Access to Mass Media.* Bloomington: Indiana University Press, 1973.

Bretz, Rudy. *A Taxonomy of Communication Media.* Englewood Cliffs, N.J.: Prentice Hall, 1971.

Burke, John Gordon. *Print, Image and Sound.* Chicago: American Library Association, 1972.

Bush, Chilton R. *Newspaper Reporting of Public Affairs.* N.Y.: Appleton Century Crofts, 1951.

Caldwell, Morris G. "Sensational News in the Modern Metropolitan Newspapers." *Journal of Criminal Law and Criminology.* XXXIII:2 (July-August, 1932).

Casselman, Chet. "Responsibility in Radio-TV News Coverage." *FBI Law Enforcement Bulletin.* 36:6 (June, 1967), 12-13.

Chafee, Zechariah Jr. *Government and Mass Communications on Freedom of the Press.* 2 vols. Chicago: Chicago University Press, 1947.

Chase, Stuart. *Power of Words.* N.Y.: Harcourt Brace, 1953.

Cirino, Robert. *Don't Blame the People: How the News Media Uses Bias, Distortion and Censorship to Manipulate Public Opinion.* N.Y.: Random, 1972.

Colegrove, Albert M. "Attitudes Towards Crime News—A Newspaperman's View Point." *National Parole and Probation Association Journal.* 4:4 (October, 1958).

Commission on Freedom of the Press. *A Free and Responsible Press: A General Report on Mass Communication—Newspapers, Radio, Motion Pictures, Magazines and Books.* Chicago: Chicago University Press, 1947.

Cooper, Kent. *The Right to Know: An Exposition of the Evils of News Suppression and Propaganda.* N.Y.: Farrar, 1956.

"Crime of Crime Reporting." *Crime and Delinquency.* 7 (1961).

Dawson, William. *Guide to the Press of the World.* Folkstone: Dawson, 1974.

Deland, Paul S. "Crime News Encourages Delinquency and Crime." *Federal Probation.* 11:2 (April-June, 1947).

Derby, Stafford. "Crime News Writing and Its Role as a Crime Stimulant." *National Parole and Probation Association Journal.* 4:5 (October, 1958).

"Does Crime Sell Newspapers?" *Police.* 3:6 (July-August, 1959).

Efron, Edith and Clytia Chambers. *How CBS Tried to Kill a Book.* N.Y.: Manor, 1973.

Evans, Harold. *Freedom of the Press.* St. Albins: Hart Davis MacGibbon, 1974.

Gerald, J. Edward. *Social Responsibility of the Press.* Minneapolis: University of Minnesota Press, 1963.

Hohenberg, John. *Free Press—Free People: The Best Cause.* N.Y.: Columbia University Press, 1971.

Hudon, Edward G. "Freedom of Speech and Press in America." *Georgetown Law Journal.* 32 (1963).

Hudon, Edward G. *Freedom of Speech and Press in America.* Washington: Public Affairs Press, 1963.

Jones, Marjorie. *Justice and Journalism.* London: Chchester, 1974.

Kerby, William F. *Role of the Press in Today's Society.* Ann Arbor: University of Michigan Business Res., 1972.

Knightley, Phillip. *First Casualty: The War Correspondant as Hero, Propagandist, and Myth Maker.* N.Y.: Harcourt Brace Jovanovich, 1975.

Konvitz, Milton R. *First Amendment Freedoms.* Ithaca: Cornell University Press, 1963.

Lange, D.C. and R.K. Baker. *Mass Media and Violence.* Washington: GPO, 1969.

Larsen, Otto N. *Violence and the Mass Media.* N.Y.: Harper & Row, 1968.

McLuhan, Herbert Marshall. *Understanding Media.* NY.: McGraw Hill, 1964.

Martin, Kingsley. *The Press and Public Wants.* London: Hogarth, 1974.

Pfuhl, Erwin H. *Relationship of Mass Media to Reported Delinquency Behavior.* Unpub. Ph. D. Dissertation, Washington State University, 1960.

Pickerell, A.G. and M. Lipman. *Courts and the News Media.* Berkeley, CA.: Project Benchmark, 1974.

"The Police, the Media and Ethics." *Police Chief.* XLII:3 (March, 1976), 8.

Rissover, Frederic and David Birch. *Mass Media and the Popular Arts.* N.Y.: McGraw Hill, 1971.

Roscoe Pound American Trial Lawyers Foundation. *First Amendment and the News Media—Final Report: Annual Chief Justice Earl Warren Conference on Advocacy in the United States, June 8-9, 1973.* Cambridge, MA.: Roscoe Pound American Trial Lawyers Foundation, 1973.

Rourke, F.E. *Secrecy and Publicity: The Dilemmas of Democracy.* Baltimore: John Hopkins University Press, 1961.

Rucker, Bryce. *The First Freedom.* Carbondale: Southern Illinois University Press, 1968.

Rudwick, Elliott M. "Negro Crime and the Negro Press." *Police.* 5:3 (January-February, 1961), 66-68.

Saulsbury, Don D. "Which Photo Do You Believe." *Police Chief.* XXXVII:5 (May, 1971), 10.

Schroeder, Theodore. *Free Press Anthology.* N.Y.: Free Speech League, 1909.

Sprague, Charles A. "The People's Right to Know." *Public Management.* XXVIII:12 (December, 1956).

Steigleman, Walter A. *Newspaperman and the Law.* Dubuque, IA.: W.C. Brown, 1950

FAIR TRIAL—FREE PRESS ISSUE

American Bar Association. *Rights of Fair Trial and Free Press.* Chicago: Illinois American Bar Association, 1969.
Standards of conduct for lawyers, law enforcement officers and judical proceedings in order to limit pre-trial prejudicial publicity.

Basta, Donald K. "Free Press—Fair Trial: How may a Defendant's Rights to a Fair Criminal Trial be Protected from Prejudicial Newspaper Publicity." *Journal of Criminal Law, Criminology and Police Science.* 50:4 (November-December, 1959), 374-384.

Brannan, Richard G. "Freedom of the Press vs Pretrial News Release: A View from the Arena." *Police Chief.* XL:12 (December, 1973), 68-72.

Buckley, F.W. *Judicial Interpretation of Powers and Responsibilities to Deal with Excessive Publicity in American Criminal Cases.* Ann Arbor, MI.: University Microfilms, 1966.

Bush, Chilton R., ed. *Free Press and a Fair Trial: Some Dimensions of the Problem.* Athens. GA.: University of Georgia Press, 1971.

"Case Against Trial by Newspaper: Analysis and Proposal." *Northwestern University Law Review.* 57 (1962).

"Constitutional Law: A Changing View Toward Trial by Newspaper." *Oklahoma Law Review.* 16 (1963).

"Criminal Law-Handling Publicity in the Trial of a Sensational Criminal Case." *Lawyer's Guide.* 6 (1962).

Duncan, Bill. "Free Press—Fair Trial." *Law and Order.* 15:5 (May, 1967), 8-11, 76.

Felsher, Howard and Michael Rosen. *The Press in the Jury Box.* N.Y.: Macmillan, 1966.

Forer, Lois G. "A Free Press and a Fair Trial." *American Bar Association Journal.* 39 (September, 1953).

"Free Press—Fair Trial Guidelines." *Police Chief.* XLI:3 (March, 1974).

Friendly, Alfred and Ronald L. Goldfarb. *Crime and Publicity.* N.Y.: Twentieth Century Fund, 1967.
All aspects of the news media's impact on trials is dealt with in this book. Many famous cases are discussed in an effort to describe the effects of publicity. All the legal ramifications of both the British and American system regarding this problem are also discussed.

Gerald, J. Edward. *The Press and the Constitution, 1931-1947.* Minneapolis: Minnesota University Press, 1948.

Gillmor, Donald M. *Free Press and Fair Trial.* Washington: Public Affairs Press, 1966.

Gillmor, D.M. and J.A. Barron. "Free Press vs Fair Trial: A Continuing Dialogue." *North Dakota Law Review.* 41 (1965), 156-184.

Goggin, T.P. and G.M. Hanover. "Fair Trial vs Free Press: The Psychological Effect of Pretrial Publicity on the Juror's Ability to be Impartial: A Plea for Reform." *Southern California Law Review*. 38 (1965), 672-688.

Griswold, E.N. "When Newsmen Become Newsmakers: Problem of Publicity Before and During a Trial." *Saturday Review* (October 24, 1964).

Haines, Rush T. II. "The Aftermath of Sheppard: Some Proposed Solutions to the Free Press—Fair Trial Controversy." *Journal of Criminal Law, Criminology and Police Science*. 59:2 (June, 1968), 234-247.

Holmes, Joseph I. "Crime and the Press." *Journal of Criminal Law and Criminology*. XX:1 (May, 1929), XX:2 (August, 1929).

Inbau, Fred E. *Free Press—Fair Trial*. Evanston, IL.: Northwestern University School of Law, 1964.

Isaacs, Norman E. "The Crime of Crime Reporting." *Crime and Delinquency* (October, 1961), 312-320.

Jaffe, Carolyn. "The Press and the Oppressed—A Study of Preducidial News Reporting in Criminal Cases.', *Journal of Criminal Law, Criminology and Police Science*. 56:1 (March, 1965), 1-17; 56:2 (June, 1965), 158-173.

King, Daniel P. "Freedom of Press vs Fair Trial: A Case Study." *Police*. 9:3 (January-February, 1965), 84-86.

Leavitt, Jack. "Splendid Ignornace: The Mainspring of a Fair Trial *Crime and Delinquency*. 14:3 (1968), 207-215.

Lewis, A. "Case of Trial by Press." *New York Times Magazine* (October 18, 1964).

Lofton, John. *Justice and the Press*. Boston: Beacon, 1966.

Marine, Gene. "The Jury Said Death." *Nation*. 183:14 (May 19, 1956).

Meyer, Bernard S. "The Trial Judge's Guide to News Reporting and Fair Trial." *Journal of Criminal Law, Criminology and Police Science*. 60:3 (September, 1969), 287-298.

Mueller, G.O.W. "Problems Posed by Publicity to Crime and Criminal Proceedings." *University of Pennsylvania Law Review*. 110 (1961).

Murthy, N.V.K. "Freedom of the Press and Fair Trial in the U.S.A." *Journalism Quarterly*. 36:3 (Summer, 1959).

Newman, Thomas R. "Free Press: Fair Trial—Rights in Collision." *New York University Law Review*. 34:7 (November, 1959).

Osterburg, James W. "Freedom of the Press vs the Right to a Fair Trial." *Law and Order*. 12:9 (September, 1964), 42-44.

Pangborn, Arden J. "Can Self-Regulation Preserve a Free Press and a Fair Trial." *Quill*. XLII:2 (March, 1954).

Reardon, Paul C. "The Fair Trial-Free Press Standards." *American Bar Association Journal* (April, 1968).

Reynolds, J.H. "The Gag Order, Exclusion and the Press's Right to Information." *Albany Law Review*. 39:2 (1975), 317-335.

Sagri, Sidney. *Free Press, Fair Trial*. Chicago: Hauberg, 1966.

Sisk, Larry. "Maintaining a Free Press, Fair Trial and Effective Law Enforcement." *Journal of California Law Enforcement* (July, 1966), 30-34.

Stanton, Frank. "Fair Trial and Free Press." *Police Chief*. 33:12 (December, 1966).

Straight, Michael. *Trial by Television*. Boston: Beacon, 1954.

Sullivan, Harold Wadsworth. *Trial by Newspaper*. Hyannis, MA.: Patriot, 1961.

Taure, Joseph G. "Fair Trial, Free Press Revisited." *American Bar Association Journal* (May, 1969).

Treuhaft, Decca M. "Trial by Headline." *Nation* (October 26, 1957).

"Trial by Newspaper." *Fordham Law Review*. 28:61 (1964).

"Two Forums of Criminal Trial: The Courtroom and the Press." *Syracuse Law Review*. 14 (1963).

Waller, George. *Kidnap: The Story of the Lindbergh Case*. N.Y.: Dial, 1961.

Wright, J. Skelly. "A Judge's View: The News Media and Criminal Justice." *American Bar Association Journal*. 50 (1964).

PART VII
MANAGEMENT, ADMINISTRATION AND SUPERVISION

MANAGEMENT AND ADMINISTRATION

ADMINISTRATION

Angell, John E. "Responsiveness: An Obligation and a Technique of the Police Administrator." *Police Chief.* XXXVI:3 (March, 1969), 22-26.

Baker, R.J. *Administrative Theory in Public Administration.* Atlantic Highlands, N.J.: Humanities, 1972.

Bassi, L.R. "Administrative Courage." *Police.* (July-August, 1970).

Becker, Harold K. *Issues in Police Administration.* Metuchen, N.J.: Scarecrow, 1970.

Bernstein, Marver H. *The Job of the Federal Executive.* Washington: Brookings Institution, 1958.

Bopp, William J. *Patrol Administration: Selected Readings.* Boston, MA.: Holbrook Press, 1975.

Buechner, John C. *Public Administration.* Belmont, CA.: Dickenson, 1968.

Caldwell, Arthur B. "Efficient Police Administration of Law Enforcement as a Foundation of American Life Under the Rule of Law." *Police.* 7:3 (January-February, 1963), 79-82.

Costello, Timothy W. *Psychology in Administration.* Englewood Cliffs, N.J.: Prentice Hall, 1963.

Dimock, Marshall E. and Gladys Orgen Dimock. *Public Administration.* 4th ed. N.Y.: Holt Rinehart & Winston, 1969.

Dubin, Robert. *Human Relations in Administration.* Englewood Cliffs, N.J.: Prentice Hall, 1968.

Dvorin, Eugene P. and Robert H. Simons. *From a Moral to Human Beaurocracy: The Coming Journey of Public Administrations.* San Francisco, CA.: Canfield, 1972.

Eastman, G.D. and E.H. Eastman. *Municipal Police Administration.* 7th ed., Washington: International City Management Association, 1971.

Evans, Courtney A. "The Future of Law Enforcement Administration." *Police Chief.* XXV:12 (December, 1968), 32-35.

Fox, Vernon. "Sociological and Political Aspects of Police Administration." *Sociological Social Research* (October, 1966).

Gladden, E.N. *A History of Public Administration.* 2 vols. London: Frank Cass, 1972.

Hills, William G. et al. *Conducting the Peoples Business: The Framework and Functions of Public Administration.* Norman: University of Oklahoma Press, 1973.

Kenney, John P. *Police Administration.* rev. ed. Springfield, IL.: C.C. Thomas, 1975.

Kenney, John P. "Police Administration: A Multi-Dimensional View." *Journal of California Law Enforcement* (July, 1970), 27-30.

Koch, Harry W. *Administration and Supervision.* San Francisco: Ken Books, 1972.

McCloskey, Charles C. "Police Administration Services." *FBI Law Enforcement Bulletin.* 38:9 (September, 1969), 9-11.

MacNamara, D.E.J. "American Police Administration at Mid-Century." *Public Administration.* 10 (Summer, 1950), 181-190.

Moore, Harry W. Jr. *Effective Police Administration: A Behavioral Approach.* San Jose, CA.: Justice Systems Development, 1975.

Parker, William H. *Parker on Police.* Springfield, IL.: C.C. Thomas, 1957.

Perry, David C. and Paula Sornoff. *Politics at the Street Level: The Select Case of Police Administration and the Community.* Beverly Hills, CA.: Sage, 1973.

Pfiffner, John M. and Robert Presthus. *Public Administration.* N.Y.: Ronald, 1967.

Phelan, Joseph G. "Police Administration—Which Approach, Democratic, Authoritarian, or. . .?" *Police.* 9:4 (March-April, 1965), 32-34.

Phillips, Jewell Cass. *Municipal Government and Administration in America.* N.Y.: Macmillan, 1958.

"The Police in a Democratic Society: A Symposium." *Public Administration Review.* 28:5 (September-October, 1968), 393-430.

Pollis, Harry J. "Police Administration: A Fresh Approach." *Police Chief.* XLII:3 (March, 1976), 14, 82.

Ready, R.K. *Administrator's Job: Issues and Dilemma's.* N.Y.: McGraw Hill, 1967.

Remington, F. et al. *Criminal Justice Administration.* N.Y.: Bobbs Merrill, 1969.

Shanahan, Donald T. *Patrol Administration: Management by Objectives.* Boston: Holbrook, 1975.

Tead, Ordway. *Administration: Its Purpose and Performance.* Hamden, CT.: Shoe String [1959] 1968.

Unsinger, Peter C. and Jack L. Kuykendall. *Community Police Administration*. Chicago: Nelson Hall, 1975.

Waldo, Dwight. *The Administrative State: A Study of the Political Theory of American Public Administration*. N.Y.: Ronald, 1948.

Wilson, J.Q. "Emerging Patterns in American Police Administration." *Police Journal*. 46:2 (1973), 155-166.

Wilson, James Q. "Dilemmas of Police Administration." *Public Administration Review*. 28:5 (September-October, 1968), 407-417.

Wilson, O.W. and Roy C. McLaren. *Police Administration*. 3rd ed. N.Y.: McGraw Hill, 1972.

BUREAUCRACY

Blau, Peter M. *Bureaucracy in Modern Society*. N.Y.: Random, 1956.

Blau, Peter M. *Dynamics of Bureaucracy*. rev. ed. Chicago: University of Chicago Press, 1973.

Bordua, David J. and Albert J. Reiss Jr. "Command, Control and Charisma: Reflections on Police Bureaucracy." *American Journal of Sociology*. 72 (July, 1966), 68-76.

Boyer, William. *Bureaucracy on Trial: Policy Making by Government Agencies*. Indianapolis, IN.: Bobbs, 1964.

Crozier, Michael. *Bureaucratic Phenomenon*. Chicago: University of Chicago Press, 1964.

Dyer, Frederick C. and John M. Dyer. *Bureaucracy vs Creativity*. Coral Gables, FL.: University of Miami Press, 1965.

Fox, Douglas M. *Politics of City and State Bureaucracy*. Pacific Palisades, CA.: Goodyear, 1973.

Hyneman, Charles. *Bureaucracy in a Democracy*. N.Y.: AMS, [1950] 1976.

Jacopy, Henry. *Bureaucratization of the World*. Berkeley: University of California Press, 1975.

Jaques, Elliott. *A General Theory of Bureaucracy*. N.Y.: Heinemann, 1976.

Katz, Elihu and Brenda Danet. *Bureaucracy and the Public*. N.Y.: Basic, 1972.

Manzer, Lewis E. *Political Bureaucracy: The American Public Service*. Glenview, IL.: Scott Foresman, 1973.

Meyer, Marshall. *Bureaucratic Structure and Authority*. N.Y.: Harper & Row, 1972.

Niskanen, William A. Jr. *Bureaucracy and Representative Government*. Chicago: Aldine, 1971.

Schott, Richard. *Bureaucratic State: Evolution and Scope*. Morristown, N.J.: General Learning Press, 1974.

Shapiro, H.R. *The Bureaucratic State*. N.Y.: Samizad, 1975.

MANAGEMENT

Abegglen, James C. *Management and the Worker: The Japanese Solution*. Cranton, PA.: Kodansha, 1973.

Albers, Henry H. *Management: The Basic Concepts*. N.Y.: Wiley, 1972.

Albers, Henry H. *Principles of Management: A Modern Approach*. 4th ed. N.Y.: Wiley, 1974.

American Management Editorial Staff. *The Chief Executive Office and Its Responsibilities*. N.Y.: AMA, 1975

Appley, Lawrence A. *Management in Action*. N.Y.: AMA, 1956.

Barnard, Chester Irving. *The Functions of the Executive*. Cambridge, MA.: Harvard University Press, 1968.

Batten, J.D. *Tough-Minded Management*. N.Y.: AMA, 1969.

Beer, Stafford. *Cybernetics and Management*. N.Y.: Wiley, 1959.

Bellows, Roger, Thomas Gilson and George Odiorne. *Executive Skills: Their Dynamics and Development*. Englewood Cliffs, N.J.: Prentice Hall, 1962.

Bloch, Peter B. and Donald R. Weidman. *Managing Criminal Investigations*. Washington: LEAA June, 1975.

Browder, Lesley Jr. *Emerging Patterns of Administrative Accountability*. Berkeley, CA.: McCutchan, 1971.

Byrd, Richard E. *Guide to Personal Risk Taking*. N.Y.: AMA, 1974.

Campbell, John P. *Managerial Behavior: Performance and Effectiveness*. N.Y.: McGraw-Hill, 1970.

Carlisle, Howard M. *Situational Management*. N.Y.: AMA, 1973.

Chapman, S.G. *Falls City (NB.)—Police Department: Organization and Management Study—Police Technical Assistance Report*. Washington: NCJRS, 1975.

"Chief Executive Job Gets More Difficult." *Business Week* (January 6, 1973).

Clapp, D.E. et al. "Engineering Management Methodology Applied to Police Department Operations." *Police*. 16:10 (June, 1972), 6-17.

Columbus, Eugene G. "Management By Systems." *Police Chief*. XXXVII:7 (July, 1970), 14-16.

Cornbusch, S.M. and W.R. Scott. *Evaluation and the Exercise of Authority*. San Francisco, CA.: Jossey Bass, 1975.
Results of a 10 year research program on authority systems in formal organizations.

Crabtree, Charles T. *Investigation Control and Management System*. Springfield, VA.: NTIS, 1973.

Dale, Ernest. *Management: Theory and Practice*. 3rd ed. N.Y.: McGraw Hill, 1973.

Davis, Richard M. "Police Management Techniques for the Medium-Size Department." *Police Chief*. XXXVII:7 (July, 1970), 44-50.

Drucker, Peter F. *Effective Executive*. N.Y.: Harper & Row, 1967.

Drucker, Peter Ferdinand. *Management: Tasks, Responsibilities, Practices*. N.Y.: Harper & Row, 1974.

Drucker, Peter F. *Practice of Management*. N.Y.: Harper & Row, 1964.

Fandel, Samuel. "Operational Problems of a Local Police Precinct." *Police*. 13:3 (January-February, 1969), 74-80.

Feinberg, Mortimer R. *Effective Psychology for Managers*. Englewood Cliffs, N.J.: Prentice Hall, 1965.

Golde, Roger A. *Muddling Through: The Art of Properly Unbusiness Like Management*. N.Y.: AMA, 1976.

Gourley, G. Douglas. "Encouraging Compliance with Policies." *Police*. 5:1 (September-October, 1960), 61-64.

Gourley, G. Douglas. "What Is Police Management?" *Police*. 3:5 (May-June, 1959), 34-37, 3:6 (July-August, 1959), 60-62.

Grosman, Brian A. *Police Command: Decisions and Discretion*. Toronto: Macmillan, 1975.

Gross, Bertram M. *Managing of Organizations*. 2 vols. N.Y.: Free Press, 1964.

Guseman, John L. "Law Enforcement as a Business." *FBI Law Enforcement Bulletin* (January, 1969), 9-11, 22.

Haiman, Theo and William G. Scott. *Management in the Modern Organization*. Boston: Houghton Mifflin, 1970.

Hanna, D.G. and W.D. Gentel. *Guide to Primary Police Management Concepts*. Springfield, IL.: C.C. Thomas, 1971.

Nature of the police administrator's role and functions which must be carried out by the managers of today's increasingly complex law enforcement agencies.

Harman, Douglas and Cole Hendrix. "The Challenge of Managing Law Enforcement." *Public Management* (April, 1973), 2-6.

Hodgetts, Richard M. *Management: Theory, Process and Practice*. Philadelphia: Saunders, 1975.

Howells, George William. *Human Aspects of Management*. London: Henemann, 1969.

Hunt, N.C. and W. Duncan Reekie, eds. *Management in the Social and Safety Services*. N.Y.: Barnes & Noble, 1974.

Jun, Jong S. and William B. Storm. *Tomorrow's Organizations: Challenges and Strategies*. Glenview, IL.: Scott Foresman, 1973.

Kaufman, C.N. "The Danger from Within: Organization Stagnation." *FBI Law Enforcement Bulletin*. 42:2 (1973), 3-6, 27-28.

Discusses symptoms of stagnation applicable to all police agencies.

Kazmier, Leonard J. *Principles of Management: A Program for Self-Instruction*. N.Y.: McGraw Hill, 1969.

Keller, E. John. "Management by Priority, A Useful Tool in Security Administration." *Law and Order*. 21:10 (October, 1973).

Kempner, Thomas, ed. *Handbook of Management*. N.Y.: Crane Russak, 1971.

Kenney, John P. *Police Management Planning*. Springfield, IL.: C.C. Thomas, 1959.

Koontz, Harold and Cyril O'Donnell. *Principles of Management*. N.Y.: McGraw Hill, 1972.

Leavitt, Harold J. *Managerial Psychology*. Chicago: University of Chicago Press, 1964.

Leonard, V.A. and H.W. More, Jr. *Police Organization and Management*. 3rd ed. Mineola, N.Y.: Foundation Press, 1971.

Comprehensive inventory of principles and procedures for the administration of the police enterprise.

Levinson, Harry. *The Great Jackass Fallacy*. Boston: Division of Research, Harvard Business School, 1973.

Likert, Renis. *New Patterns of Management*. N.Y.: McGraw Hill, 1961.

Lock, D.L., ed. *Guide to Management Techniques*. 2nd ed. N.Y.: Halsted, 1973.

Loen, Raymond O. *Manage More by Doing Less*. N.Y.: McGraw Hill, 1971.

Lundstedt, Steven. "Social Psychological Contributions to the Management of Law Enforcement Agencies." *Journal of Criminal Law, Criminology and Police Science*. 56:3 (1965).

Lynch, Ronald G. *The Police Manager*. Boston: Holbrook, 1975.

McFarland, D.E. *Management: Principles and Practices*. 4th ed. N.Y.: Macmillan, 1974.

McGregor, Douglas. *The Human Side of Enterprise*. N.Y.: McGraw Hill, 1960.

McGregor, Douglas. *The Professional Manager*. N.Y.: McGraw Hill, 1967.

McMurry, Robert N. *The Maverick Executive*. N.Y.: AMA, 1974.

"Managing the Patrol Function." *Police Chief*. XLI:8 (August, 1974).

Martin, Charles C. *Project Management: How to Make It Work*. N.Y.: AMA, 1976.

Merrill, Harwood, ed. *Classics in Management*. rev. ed. N.Y.: AMA, 1970.

More, H.W., Jr. *Critical Issues in Law Enforcement*. Cincinnati, OH.: Anderson, 1972.

Articles organized topically around the role of the police in relation to the aims and activities of society.

More, Harry W., Jr. "Principles of Organization and Management as Applied to Law Enforcement Agencies." *Police*. 10:2 (November-December, 1965), 50-54.

Morgan, J.P., Jr. "Confrontation Management." *Police Chief* (January, 1971).

Morgan, John S. *Managing the Young Adults*. N.Y.: AMA, 1967.

Newman. T.J. and T.A. Fleek. "The Air Force Approach to Professional Police Management." *Police Chief*. XXXLV:5 (May, 1967), 31-43.

Newman, William H. and Charles E. Summer, Jr. *The*

Process of Management. Englewood Cliffs, N.J.: Prentice Hall, 1961.

Nichols, J.F. "The Seven Delinquent Children of Management." *Police Chief*. XXXLV:5 (May, 1967), 56-61.

Philips, Victor S., Jr. and Richard F. Shomper. *Management in Bureaucracy*. N.Y.: AMA, 1974.

Plippo, Edwin B. and Gary M. Munsinger. *Management*. 3rd ed. Rockleigh, N.J.: Allyn, 1975.

"Police Management: Operations in Prevention and Investigation." *Police Chief*. XXXLV:5 (May, 1967), 10-11.

Police Management System. Gaithersburg, MD.: IACP, 1967.
Basic operations of a police department administrator, and the planning staffing, directing, controlling and decision-making involved in accomplishing his objectives.

Pollard, H.R. *Development of Management Thought*. N.Y.: Crane Russak, 1974.

Pudinski, Walter. "Management By Results in the California Highway Patrol." *Journal of California Law Enforcement*. 8:4 (April, 1974), 194-198.

Pudinski, Walter. "Managing for Results." *Police Chief*. XL:1 (January, 1973), 38-41.

Reddin, W.J. *Managerial Effectiveness*. N.Y. McGraw Hill, 1970.

Reed, Thomas Harrison. *Municipal Management*. N.Y.: McGraw Hill, 1941.

Reeves, Elton T. *Practicing Effective Management*. N.Y.: AMA, 1975.

Reeves, Elton T. *So You Want to Be a Executive!* N.Y.: AMA, 1975.

Reeves, Elton T. *So You Want to Be a Manager!* N.Y.: AMA, 1971.

Rhodes, W.R. "A Behavioral Science Application to Police Management." *Police Chief*. XXXVII:5 (May, 1970), 46-50.

Skousen, W. Cleon. "Notes for a New Chief." *Law and Order*. 14:12 (December, 1966), 11-16; (January, 1967), 10-16; (February, 1967), 80-84.

Skousen, W. Cleon. "Running a Chief's Office." *Law and Order*. 15:5 (May, 1967), 70-76.

Skousen, W. Cleon. "Suggestions for a Chief's New Office." *Law and Order*. 15:3 (March, 1967), 22-28.

Skousen, W. Cleon. "Spotlight on a Bogged Down Detective Division. *Law and Order*. 16:4 (April, 1968), 10-15.

Southwestern Law Enforcement Institute. *Police Management*. Springfield, IL.: C.C. Thomas, 1964.

Strentz, Thomas. "Transactional Analysis and the Police." *Police Chief*. XLII:10 (October, 1975), 248-250.

Terry, George R. *Principles of Management*. Homewood, IL.: Irwin, 1972.

Valentine, Raymond F. *Initiative and Managerial Power*. N.Y.: AMA, 1973.

Van Fleet, James. *Guide to Managing People*. Englewood Cliffs, N.J.: Prentice Hall, 1968.

Wagner, Harvey M. *Principles of Management Science*. 2nd ed. Englewood Cliffs, N.J.: Prentice Hall, 1975.

Weber, Ross A. *Management: Basic Elements of Managing Organizations*. Homewood, IL.: Irwin, 1975.

Whisenand, Paul M. and Fred Ferguson. *The Managing of Police Organizations*. Englewood Cliffs, N.J.: Prentice Hall, 1973.

Whiteside, Lynn W. *Effective Management Techniques for Getting Things Done*. Englewood Cliffs, N.J.: Prentice Hall, 1968.

Williamson, Charles Donovan. *An Executive Operations Technique*. Englewood Cliffs, N.J.: Prentice Hall, 1963.

Yoshino, M.Y. *Japans Managerial System: Tradition and Innovation*. Cambridge, MA.: MIT Press, 1969.

Zaffarano, Joan. "The I'm OK—You're OK Management Approach." *Administrative Management* (September-October, 1973).

MANAGEMENT BY OBJECTIVES

Batten, J.D. *Beyond Management by Objectives*. N.Y.: AMA, 1966.

Carroll, Stephen J., Jr. and Henry L. Tosi, Jr. *Management by Objectives: Applications and Research*. N.Y.: Macmillan, 1973.

Hetland, Richard R. "MBO: Let's Set Managing Objectives." *Supervisory Management*. 18:2 (February, 1973), 2-10.

Humble, John W. *How to Manage by Objectives*. N.Y.: AMA, 1973.

Jamieson, Bruce D. "Behavioral Problems with Management by Objectives." *Academy of Management Journal*. 16:3. (September, 1973) 496-505.

Leek, C.C. "Management by Objectives." *Police Journal*. 44 (July, 1971), 213-223.

Levinson, Harry. "Management by Whose Objective." *Harvard Business Review*. 48 (July-August, 1970), 125-134.

McConkey, Dale D. "Management by Objectives: How to Measure Results." *Business Horizons*. 7 (Fall, 1964), 47-54.

McConkey, Dale D. *MBO for Nonprofit Organizations*. N.Y.: AMA, 1975.

McConkey, Dale D. "MBO—Twenty Years Later: Where Do We Stand?" *Business Horizons*. 16:4 (August, 1973), 25-36.

MBO: What's in It for You. N.Y.: AMA, 1975.

Murray, Richard K. "Behavioral Management Objectives." *Personnel Journal*. 52:4 (April, 1973), 304-306.

Olsson, David E. *Management by Objectives*. Palo Alto, CA.: Pacific, 1968.

Peart, Leo E. "Management by Objectives." *Police Chief*. 38:4 (April, 1971), 54-56.

Peart, Leo E. "A Management by Objective Plan." *Police Chief*. XXXVII:6 (June, 1971), 34-40.

Raia, Anthony P. *Managing by Objectives*. Glenview, IL.: Scott Foresman, 1974.

Reddin, William J. *Effective Management by Objectives: The 3-D Method of MBO*. N.Y.: McGraw Hill, 1971.

Reif, William E. and Gerald Bassford. "What MBO Really Is." *Business Horizons*. 16:3 (June, 1973), 23-30.

Shanahan, Donald T. *Patrol Administration: Management by Objectives*. Boston: Holbrook, 1975.

Stone, David M. "Management by Objectives." *Law and Order*. 19:10 (October, 1971), 34-37, 71.

Varney, Glenn H. *Management by Objectives*. Chicago: Cartnell, 1971.

Explains the MBO concept and presents guidelines for designing and implementing an MBO program. Includes section on planning and reviewing performance.

MANAGEMENT INFORMATION SYSTEMS

Brightman, Richard. *Information Systems for Modern Management*. N.Y.: Macmillan, 1971.

"Computer Aids Police Management." *American City*. (February, 1972).

Conover, Robert N. "Management Information: Law Enforcement's Forgotten Need." *FBI Law Enforcement Bulletin*. 43:11 (November, 1974), 3-9.

Garland Division. *Dallas Police Department: Command and Control Study—Final Report. (Issued in Two Unnumbered Volumes)*. Washington: NCJRS (Microfiche) 1973.

Garland Division. *Dallas Police Department: Command and Control Study—System Modeling Report*. Washington: NCJRS (Microfiche) 1972.

Huntington Beach Police Department. *Huntington Beach CA.—Police Department: Police Command and Control—Phase 2*. Washington: NCJRS (Microfiche).

ORGANIZATION

Organization—General

Alletto, William C. "Guidelines in Organization for Sheriff's Departments of Large (Metropolitan) Counties." *Police*. 7:4 (March-April, 1963), 73-76.

Alletto, William C. "Public Safety in State Government: A Procedural Guide to Organization." *Police*. 14:5 (May-June, 1970); (July-August, 1970); and (September-October, 1970).

Angell, J.E. "Toward an Alternative to the Classic Police Organizational Arrangements: A Democratic Model." *Criminology*. 9:2-3 (1971), 185-206.

Advocates basic model composed of 3 sections: (1) General services, (2) Coordination and information, (3) Specialized services. Would not be hierarchial.

Blau, Peter Michael and W. Richard Scott. *Formal Organizations: A Comparative Approach*. San Francisco: Chandler, 1962.

Cavanaugh, William. "Unitization Really Works." *Police Chief*. XLI:7 (July, 1974), 64-66.

Cizanckas, Victor I. "Uniform Experiment and Organization Development." *Police*. 16:1 (September, 1971), 45-49.

Committee Report on District Reorganization. Cincinnati, OH.: Cincinnati Police Department, June, 1954.

Committee Report on District Reorganization. Cincinnati, OH.: Cincinnati Police Department. September, 1957.

Dale, Ernest. *Organization*. N.Y.: AMA, 1967.

Davis, Edward M. "Pencil Pushers or Street Cops." *Police Chief*. XLII:5 (May, 1975), 18-19, 82.

Elliott, J.B. "The Crime Control Team." *Police*. 13:5 (May-June, 1969), 35-41.

Etzioni, Amitai. *Complex Organizations: A Sociological Reader*. N.Y.: Holt, Rinehart and Winston, 1961.

Famularo, Joseph J. *Organization Planning Manual*. N.Y.: AMA, 1971.

Gebhardt, Robert E. "Environment and Organization Design." *Journal of Criminal Law and Administration*. 10:4 (April, 1976), 158-162.

Gourley, Gerald Douglas. *Effective Municipal Police Organization*. Beverly Hills, CA.: Glencoe, 1970.

Hutchinson, John G. *Organizations: Theory and Classical Concepts*. N.Y.: Holt, Rinehart and Winston, 1967.

Jayewardene, C.H.S. *Organizing the Police for Modern Times*. Ottawa: Department of Criminology, University of Ottawa, 1974.

Kassoff, N.C. *Organizational Concepts*. Gaithersburg, MD.: IACP, 1967.

Formal organization and informal organization, the viable social matrix existing within the formal organization are outlined and discussed.

Kenny, John P. "A Master Plan for Reorganization of the Police Department, City and County of Denver." *Police*. 7:4 (March-April, 1963), 66-69.

Leavitt, Harold J., William R. Dill and Henry B. Eyring. *The Organizational World*. N.Y.: Harcourt Brace Jovanovich, 1973.

Leonard, V.A. *Police Enterprise: Its Organization and Management*. Springfield, IL.: C.C. Thomas, 1969.

Principles of organization are reviewed particularly for the smaller police departments of 50 to 75 officers.

Levinson, Harry, Janice Molinari and Andrew G. Spohn. *Organizational Diagnosis*. Cambridge, MA.: Harvard University Press, 1972.

Levitt, Theodore. *The Third Sector: New Tactics for a Responsive Society*. N.Y.: AMA, 1973.

Likert, Rensis. *The Human Organization: Its Management and Value*. N.Y.: McGraw Hill, 1967.

March, James G. *Handbook of Organizations*. Chicago: Rand McNally, 1965.

Mott, See Paul. *The Characteristics of Effective Organization*. N.Y.: Harper & Row, 1972.

Murphy, Patrick V. and David S. Brown. *The Police Leader Looks at the Changing Nature of Police Organization*. Washington: Leadership Resources, 1973.

Pfiffner, John M. and Frank P. Sherwood. *Administrative*

Organization. Englewood Cliffs, N.J.: Prentice Hall, 1960.

Pursley, Robert D. "Traditional Police Organization: A Portent of Failure?" *Police*. 16:2 (October, 1971), 29-30.

Sandler, Georgette Bennett and Ellen Mintz. "Police Organizations: Their Changing Internal and External Relationships." *Journal of Police Science and Administration*. 2:4 (December, 1974), 458-463.

Skousen, W. Cleon. "Reorganizing a Run Down Patrol Division." *Law and Order*. 15:8 (August, 1967), 22-26, 94.

Skousen, W. Cleon. "Reorganizing a Run Down Patrol Division." *Law and Order*. 20:10 (October, 1972), 8-13.

Smith, R.D. *Organization: Police Functions*. Gaithersburg, MD.: IACP, n/d.

Principles to be followed when establishing a police departmental structure with emphasis on the need for defining and grouping similar tasks and functions.

Steiner, Gary A., ed. *Creative Organization*. Chicago: University of Chicago Press, 1965.

Weisbord, Marvin R. et al. *Improving Police Department Management Through Problem Solving Task Forces: A Case Study in Organization Development*. Reading, MA.: Addison Wesley, 1974.

Organizational Behavior

Argyris, Chris. *Understanding Organizational Behavior*. Homewood, IL.: Dorsey, 1960.

Berkeley, George E. *Administrative Revolution: Notes on the Passing of Organization Man*. Englewood Cliffs, N.J.: Prentice Hall, 1971.

Blau, Peter M. *Dynamics of Bureaucracy: A Study of Interpersonal Relationships in Two Government Agencies*. Chicago: University of Chicago Press, 1963.

Brown, J. Douglas. *The Human Nature of Organizations*. N.Y.: AMA, 1973.

Cain, M.E. *Society and the Policeman's Role*. London: Routledge and Kegan Paul, 1973.

Sociological study of police organization and behavior in England, explaining police behavior in terms of role pressures and definitions.

Cancilla, Robert C. "Individual and Organizational Needs." *Police* (April, 1972).

DuBrin, Andrew J. *Fundamentals of Organizational Behavior and Applied Prospectives*. Elmsford, N.Y.: Pergamon, 1974.

Haney, William V. *Communication and Organizational Behavior Text and Cases*. Rev. ed. Homewood, IL.: Irwin, 1967.

Hare, A. Paul. *Small Groups*. N.Y.: Knopf, 1955.

Hersey, Paul. *Management of Organizational Behavior: Utilizing Human Resources*. Englewood Cliffs, N.J.: Prentice Hall, 1962.

Kidner, John. *Kidner Report: How to Operate in Bureaucracy at One Half Horsepower*. Washington: Acropolis, 1975.

Lawrence, Paul R. *Organizational Behavior and Administration: Cases, Concepts and Research Findings*. Homewood, FL.: Irwin, 1965.

Mailick, Sidney. *Concepts and Issues in Administrative Behavior*. Englewood Cliffs, N.J.: Prentice Hall, 1962.

Munro, Jim L. *Administrative Behavior and Police Organization*. Cincinnati, OH.: W.H. Anderson, 1974.

Sayles, Leonard and G. Strauss. *Human Behavior and Organizations*. Englewood Cliffs, N.J.: Prentice Hall, 1966.

Schein, Edgar H. "Organizational Psychology: Problems and Prospects for the Future." *Training and Development Journal* (March, 1973).

Smith, Peter B. *Groups Within Organizations*. N.Y.: Harper & Row, 1973.

"Structural Determinants of Individual Behavior in Organizations." *Administrative Science Quarterly* (March, 1973).

Trantanella, Charles. "Group Dynamics." *Management Accounting* (November, 1972).

Wicker, Allan and Claudia E. Kauma. "Effects of a Merger of a Small and a Large Organization on Member's Behavior and Experiences." *Journal of Applied Psychology* (February, 1974).

Whyte, William H., Jr. *The Organization Man*. Garden City, N.Y.: Doubleday, 1957.

Organizational Development

Burke, W. Warner. *Current Issue in Organizational Development*. N.Y.: Behavioral, 1976.

McGill, Michael E. *Organization Development for Operating Managers*. N.Y.: AMA, 1976.

Margulies, Newton and Anthony P. Raia. *Organizational Development*. N.Y.: McGraw Hill, 1972.

Organizational Development: A Closer Look. N.Y.: AMA, 1974.

Robinson, Revis O. II. "Organization Development: An Action Plan for the Ontario Police Department." *Journal of California Law Enforcement*. 8:4 (April, 1974), 177-183.

Weisbord, Marvin R., Howard Lamb and Alan Drexler. *Improving Police Department Management Through Problem Solving Task Forces: A Case Study in Organizational Development*. Reading, MA.: Addison Wesley, 1974.

SUPERVISION

Anderson, John P. "Sewing on the Stripes." *Law and Order.* 23:5 (May, 1975), 16, 18-19.

Benton, Louis. *Supervision and Management.* N.Y.: McGraw Hill, 1972.

Bittel, Lester R. *What Every Supervisor Should Know.* N.Y.: McGraw Hill, 1959.

Boettinger, Henry M. *Moving Mountains or the Art and Craft of Letting Others See Things Your Way.* N.Y.: Macmillan, 1969.

Brannan, Richard G. "The New Police Supervisor." *Law and Order.* 14:8 (August, 1966), 28-30.

Bristow, Allen P. *Police Supervision Readings.* Springfield, IL.: C.C. Thomas, 1971.

Bristow, Allen, ed. *Readings in Police Supervision.* Los Angeles: Los Angeles State College, 1963.

Brunton, Robert L. "Supervision: A Major Problem for Police Departments." *Police.* 5:1 (September-October, 1960), 14-18.

Burby, Raymond J. *Communicating with People: The Supervisor's Introduction to Verbal Communication and Decisionmaking.* Reading, MA.: Addison Wesley, 1970.

Clift, Raymond E. "Communication—The Key to Good Supervision." *Police.* 11:1 (September-October, 1957), 7-9.

Cooper, Alfred M. *How to Supervise People.* 4th ed. N.Y.: McGraw Hill, 1958.

D'Aprix, Roger M. "How to Get the Most from the People You Supervise." *Management Review* (June, 1974).

Donovan, Anthony F. *Management of Supervisors.* London: Macmillan, 1971.

Ecker, Paul et al. *Handbook for Supervisors.* 2nd ed. Englewood Cliffs, N.J.: Prentice Hall, 1970.

Eckles, Robert W. et al. *Essentials of Management for First Line Supervision.* N.Y.: Wiley, 1974.

Famularo, Joseph J. *Supervisors in Action: Developing Your Skills in Managing People.* N.Y.: McGraw Hill, 1961.

Ficker, Victor B. *Effective Supervision.* New ed. Columbus, OH.: Merrill, 1975.

Gocke, B.W. and G.T. Payton. *Police Sargeant's Manual.* Los Angeles, CA.: Legal Book, 1972.
Preparations and techniques for passing promotional examinations, basic police organization and management and techniques of police supervision.

Haimann, Theo and Raymond Hilgert. *Supervision: Concepts and Practices of Management.* Cincinnati, OH.: Southwestern, 1972.

Hankey, Richard O. "Preparing for Supervision." *Police.* 6:5 (May-June, 1962), 22-25.

Hannaford, Earle S. *Supervisors Guide to Human Relations.* Chicago: National Safety Council, 1967.

Hansen, David A. "The Skull Session: Coordination and Communication Among Police Supervisors." *Police.* 15:6 (July-August, 1971), 73-74.

Harding, L. Bud. "The Newly Appointed Supervisor." *Law and Order.* 15:12 (December, 1967), 28-29.

Harrison, Kenneth R. "Policy Becomes ACTION with the First Line Supervisor." *Police Chief.* XLI:2 (February, 1974).

Hezel, Carl. *The Supervisor's Basic Management Guide: An A-Z Manual on Supervisory Effectiveness.* N.Y.: McGraw-Hill, 1965.

Iannone, N.F. *Supervision of Police Personnel.* Englewood Cliffs, N.J.: Prentice Hall, 1975.

Kelly, J.A. *Police Reference Notebook, Section 2—Supervision.* Gaithersburg, MD.: IACP, 1971.
Classroom manual surveying principles of supervision as applied to police personnel.

King, Glen D. *First Line Supervisor's Manual.* Springfield, IL.: C.C. Thomas, 1961.

Kovezynski, James. "Looking Up at Supervision." *Law and Order.* 20:8 (August, 1972), 20-21, 26.

Lateiner, Alfred R. *Modern Techniques of Supervision.* N.Y.: Lateiner, 1965.

LeGrande, J.L. "Commentary of Police Supervision." *Police.* 13:4 (March-April, 1969), 50-57.

Lomax, Joe B. "Eight Remedies for the Supervisor's Headache." *Law and Order.* 23:5 (May, 1975), 36, 38-41.

Molden, Jack B. "Induction of New Employees." *Police Chief.* 38:12 (December, 1971), 39-40, 42.

Morgan, James E. *Principles of Administrative and Supervisory Management.* Englewood Cliffs, N.J.: Prentice Hall, 1973.

Osterloh, William J. *Police Supervisory Practice.* N.Y.: Wiley, 1974.

Pfiffner, John M. *The Supervision of Personnel.* Englewood Cliffs, N.J.: Prentice Hall, 1958.

Plunkett, W. Richard. *Supervision: The Direction of People at Work.* Dubuque, IA.: William C. Brown, 1975.

"Police Traffic Supervision." *Police Chief.* 33:7 (July, 1966).

Reeves, Elton T. *So You Want to Be a Supervisor!* N.Y.: AMA, 1971.

Rudkin, Donald and Fred D. Veal, Jr. *Principles of Supervision.* N.Y.: Petrocelli, 1973.

Sergiovanni, T. and R. Starratt. *Emerging Patterns of Supervision: Human Prospectives.* N.Y.: McGraw Hill, 1971.

Sirota, D. "Pragmatic Approach to People Problems." *Harvard Business Review.* 51 (January, 1973), 120-128.

Special Problems Supervisors Must Handle. N.Y.: AMA, 1968.

Supervisor and his Squad—A Guide to Understanding and Motivating Policemen. Evanston, IL.: Traffic Institute Northwestern University.
Supervisory skills inherent in effective counseling and motivation of police.

Thurley, Keith and Hans Wirdenius. *Supervision: A Reappraisal.* N.Y.: Crane Russak, 1973.

Truell, George F. "Ten Steps to Effective Supervisions." *Supervisory Management* (October, 1973).

Uhles, Ernest N. *How to Become an Effective Supervisor: A Survival Manual for the Man in the Middle.* Hicksville, N.Y.: Exposition, 1971.

Vanderbosch, C.G. *Traffic Supervision.* Gaithersburg, MD.: IACP, 1969.

VanDersal, William R. *The Successful Supervisor.* N.Y.: Harper & Row, 1968.

Whisenand, Paul M. *Police Supervision: Theory and Practice.* Englewood Cliffs, N.J.: Prentice Hall, 1971.

Wilson, Howard. *Supervisory Skills.* Irvine, CA.: Administrative Research Associates, 1973.

MANAGEMENT FUNCTIONS

ALLOCATION OF RESOURCES

Bloch, P.B. *Equality of Distribution of Police Services—A Case Study of Washington, D.C.* Washington: NCJRS (Microfiche) 1974.

Bristow, Allen P. *Effective Police Manpower Utilization.* Springfield, IL.: C.C. Thomas, 1969.

Brostron, Curtis. "Computerized Resource Allocation in St. Louis." *Police Chief.* XXV:11 (November, 1968), 47-52.

Chiaramonte, R.M. "Do You Need Ten More Men?" *Police Chief.* XXXIII:2 (February, 1966), 12-16.

Ferguson, Fred. "Each Municipality Should Assess Its Law Enforcement Needs." *Journal of California Law Enforcement* (July, 1967), 1-7.

Goldstein, H. "Guidelines for Effective Use of Police Manpower." *Public Management.* 45 (October, 1963), 218-222.

Gylys, Julius A. "Economics of Scale in Provision of Metropolitan Police Services." *Police.* 15:6 (July-August, 1971), 79-82.

Kapsch, S. *Minnesota Police Organization and Community Resource Allocations.* Washington: NCJRS, 1970.

Kenney, John P. et al. "Field Patrolmen Workload in California." *Journal of California Law Enforcement* (January, 1970), 124-131.

Lane, Jean R. "Maui County Police Department Time Expenditure Analysis." *Police.* 4:6, (July-August, 1960), 18-22.

McTewan, T. *Allocation of Patrol Manpower Resources in the St. Louis Police Department—Experiment V 1.* Springfield, VA.: NTIS, 1968.

Martin, J.P. *Application of Modern Techniques of Resource Allocation in the Field of Crime Problems.* Washington: NCJRS (Microfiche) 1973.
Two separate essays one of which deals with the economic implications of resource allocation and the other with the sociological factors and effects.

Nixon, J.W. "Computer-Based Resource Allocation Important Tool for Norfolk Police." *Law and Order.* 18:10 (October, 1970), 90-92, 94, 108.

Pini, Geno J., Randall Cohen and Michael E. O'Neill. "POSSE: The Blending of Technology and Human Resources." *Police Chief.* XLII:10 (October, 1975), 18, 20-21, 271.

Shumate, Robert P. and Richard F. Crowther. "Quantitative Methods for Optimizing the Allocation of Police Resources." *Journal of Criminal Law, Criminology and Police Science.* 57:2 (June, 1966), 197-206.

St. Louis Metropolitan Police Department. *Allocation of Patrol Manpower Resources in the St. Louis Police Department: An Experiment V 2.* Springfield, VA.: NTIS, 1966.

St. Louis Metropolitan Police Department. *Allocation of Patrol Manpower Resources in the St. Louis Police Department: Supplementary Report.* Springfield, VA.: NTIS, 1969.

International Association of Chiefs of Police. *System to Provide Facts for Assignment, Deployment and Analysis.* Gaithersburg, MD.: IACP, 1969.
Computerized system developed by the Dorset and Bournemouth Constabulary (England) to use manpower more efficiently.

Roberts, Paul A. et al. *Manpower Planning for the Public Service.* Chicago: International Personnel Management, 1971.

Taylor, Charles R. and A.M. Andrews. "An Aid in Patrol Force Distribution." *Law and Order.* 14:2 (February, 1966), 58-61.

BUDGETING

Budgeting—General

Burkhead, Jessie. *Governmental Budgeting.* N.Y.: Wiley, 1956.

Chase, Samuel B., Jr., ed. *Problems in Public Expenditure Analysis.* Washington: Brookings Institution, 1968.

Dalton Hugh. *Principles of Public Finance.* 4th ed. East Orange, N.J.: Kellog, 1954.

Ferretti, Fred. *The Year the Big Apple Went Bust.* N.Y.: Putnam, 1976.

Golembiewski, Robert T. and Jack Rabin. eds. *Public Budgeting and Finance: Readings in Theory and Practice.* 2nd ed. Itasca, IL.: Peacock, 1975.

Haveman, Robert and Julius Margolis. *Public Expenditures and Policy Analysis.* Chicago: Markhan, 1970.

International Association of Chiefs of Police. *Fiscal Management.* Gaithersburg, MD.: IACP, 1968

Jacobs, Jane. *The Economy of Cities.* N.Y.: Random, 1970.

Jones, Reginald L. and H. George Trentin. *Budgeting: Key to Planning and Control.* N.Y.: AMA, 1971.

Kaufman, Charles N. "The Budget Process: Dollarizing Law Enforcement Planning." *FBI Law Enforcement Bulletin.* 38:9 (September, 1969).

Lee, R. *Public Budgeting Systems.* Baltimore: University Park, 1973.

Martin, J.W. *Crime Control: A Challenge to State Budgeting: NASBO (National Association of State Budget Officers) Institute on Crime Control, University of Kentucky, June, 1969.* Lexington, KY.: Council of State Governments, 1970.

Collection of papers presented at a 1969 conference on the causes and effects of crime and the financial management of efforts to control it.

Meltsner, Arnold J. *Politics of City Revenue.* Berkeley: University of California Press, 1971.

Moak, Lennox L. and Kathryn W. Killin. *Manual of Techniques for the Preparation, Consideration, Adoption and Administration of Operating Budgets.* Chicago: Municipal Finance Officers Association, 1963.

Mosher, Frederick C. *Program Budgeting: Theory and Practice with Particular Reference to the United States Department of the Army.* Chicago: Public Administration Service, 1959.

Newman, Herbert E. *Introduction to American Public Finance.* N.Y.: Wiley, 1968.

Novick, David. *Program Budgeting: Program Analysis and the Federal Budget.* Cambridge: Harvard University Press, 1966.

Onderko, Kenneth P. and James T. McBride. "The Police Finance Officer." *Law and Order.* 22:5 (May, 1974), 6-7.

Scott, Claudia. *Forecasting Local Government Spending.* Washington: Urban Institute, 1972.

Schultz, W. and C. Harris. *American Public Finance.* 8th ed. Englewood Cliffs, N.J.: Prentice Hall, 1965.

Stanley, David L. "An Approach to Departmental Budgeting." *Journal of California Law Enforcement* (January, 1975), 106-110.

Steiss, Allan W. *Public Budgeting and Management.* Lexington, MA.: Lexington, 1972.

Sweeny, Allen and John N. Wisner, Jr. *Budgeting Fundamentals for Nonfinancial Executives.* N.Y.: AMA, 1976.

Taylor, Strevell G. "Budgeting Forms a Vital Part of Police Operations." *FBI Law Enforcement Bulletin.* 25:11 (November, 1956), 22-24.

Wildavsky, Aaron. *The Politics of the Budgetary Process.* Boston: Little, Brown, 1964.

Planning, Programming, Budgeting (PPB)

Dolan, John F. "The PPB Concept." *Police Chief.* XXXV:7 (July, 1968), 28-31.

General Services Administration Office of Finance. *Implementing PPB (Planning, Programming, Budgeting) in State, City and County—A Report on the 5-5-5 Project.* Washington: George Washington University, 1969.

George Washington University. *Program Planning for State, County, City.* Washington: George Washington University, 1967.

Applications of planning-programming-budgeting system (PPB) concepts to state and local government activities.

Hennessy, J.J. "The Management of Crime: PPB's and Police Management." *Police Chief.* XXIX:7 (July, 1972), 62-67.

Horey, Harold. *Planning, Programming, Budgeting—Approach to Government Decision Making.* N.Y.: Praeger, 1968.

Hoover, Larry T. "Planning-Programming-Budgeting Systems: Problems of Implementation for Police Management." *Journal of Police Science and Administration.* 2:1 (March, 1974), 82-93.

Leahy, Frank J., Jr. "Planning-Programming-Budgeting System." *Police Chief.* XXV:7 (July, 1968), 16-27.

Lyden, Freemont and Ernest Miller. *Planning, Programming, Budgeting: A Systems Approach to Management.* Chicago: Markham, 1968.

McGivney, Joseph and Robert Hedges. *Introduction to PPB's: Planning, Programming, Budgeting Systems.* Columbus, OH.: Merrill, 1972.

Martin, John A. "Staffing and Manpower Analysis in Support of Planning, Programming and Budgeting." *Police.* 14:1 (September-October, 1969), 70-73.

O'Brien, John T. "Planning, Programming, Budgeting in the Police Department of the City of New York." *Police.* 15:5 (May-June, 1971), 51-54.

O'Neill, Michael E. "A Program Planning Budget System: An Impetus for Change in a Police Organization." *Police.* 16:1 (September, 1971), 50-51.

Pence, Gary. "PPB's: A Pilot City Project." *Police Chief.* XXXVII:7 (July, 1971), 52-57.

Shoup, Donald C. *Program Budgeting for Urban Police Service.* N.Y.: Praeger, 1971.

Tenzer, A.J. and J.B. Benton. *Applying the Concepts of Program Budgeting to the New York City Police Department*. Santa Monica, CA.: Rand, 1969.

CHANGE

Argyris, Chris. *Organization and Innovation*. Homewood, IL.: Irwin, 1965.

Baade, Fritz. *Race to the Year 2000: Our Future—A Paradise or the Suicide of Mankind?* Garden City, N.Y.: Doubleday, 1962.

Bennis, Warren G., Kenneth D. Benne and Robert Chin. *The Planning of Change: Reading in the Applied Behavioral Sciences*. 2nd ed. N.Y.: Holt, Rinehart and Winston, 1969.

Brown, Gary E. "A Transition in Blue." *Police Chief*. XLII:7 (July, 1975), 18, 79, 81.

Cahn, Edgar S. and Berry A. Passetts. eds. *Citizen Participation: Effecting Community Change*. N.Y.: Praeger, 1971.

"Change Through Training." *FBI Law Enforcement Bulletin*. 39:7 (July, 1970), 2-4, 25.

Christiansen, R. *Futuristic Community Development: Crime Impact—East Central Florida, 1974-1984*. Cambridge, MA.: Arthur D. Little, 1973.

Cizanckas, Victor. "A Profile of Tomorrow's Police Officer and His Organization." *Police Chief*. XLII:6 (June, 1975), 16-18, 86.

Coates, Joseph F. "The Future of Crime in the United States from Now to the Year 2000." *Police Sciences*. (1972), 27-45.

Coch, L. and J.R.P. French, Jr. "Overcoming Resistance to Change."''' *Human Relations*. 1:4 (1948), 512-532.

Coster, C.M. "Law Enforcement in the Mainstream of Change." *National Sheriff*. 24:5 (1972), 10-28.

D'Apprix, Roger M. *In Search of a Corporate Soul*. N.Y.: AMA, 2976.

Dix, Robert H. *Columbia: The Political Dimensions of Change*. New Haven CT.: Yale University Press, 1967.

Doig, J.W. "The Police in a Democratic Society: Police Problems, Proposals and Strategies for Change." *Public Administration Review* (September-October, 1968).

Dompka, Robert J. "Officer—Rock that Boat." *Law and Order*. 17:12 (December, 1969), 17-21.

Drew, Bernard. "Can the Police Service Manage Change?" *Police Review. (GB)* (January 2, 1976).

Duncan, Robert B. "Organizational Climate and Climate for Change in Three Police Departments." *Urban Affairs Quarterly*. 8:2 (December, 1972), 215-245.

Elliott, J.F. *New Police: A Description of a Possible Form of What the Municipal Police Will Evolve Into, Why They Must Change, and How This Evolution May Be Accomplished*. Springfield, IL.: C.C. Thomas 1973.
Description of a plan to radically alter the police function from a 'service' orientation to a crime prevention orientation.

Fabun, Don. *The Dynamics of Change*. Englewood Cliffs, N.J.: Prentice Hall, 1967.

Felkenes, George T. "Police Planning: A Stimulus for Needed Organizational Change." *Police*. 16:10 (June, 1972), 24-27.

Grossman, Lee. *The Change Agent*. N.Y.: AMA, 1974.

Guest, Robert H. *Organizational Change: The Effects of Successful Leadership*. Homewood, IL.: Dorsey, 1962.

Hannah, John A. "In Support of Orderly Change." *Police*. 14:5 (May-June, 1970), 42-43.

Hoffer, Eric. *Ordeal of Change*. N.Y.: Harper & Row, 1967.

Ingleburger, Robert M., John E. Angell and Gary Pense. *Changing Urban Police: Practitioners View*. Washington: LEAA, 1973.

Jenkins, H.T. "Police Must Accept Change More Rapidly Than Other Community Groups." *Police Chief* (June, 1963), 18-24.

Katsampes, Paul. "Participation in Policing." *Police Chief*. XLI:12 (December, 1974), 60-65.

Kaufman, Herbert. *The Limits of Organizational Change*. University, AL.: University of Alabama Press, 1971.

Kelley, Clarence M. "Receptiveness to Change." *Police Chief*. XL:23 (December, 1973), 32-34.

King, Albert S. "Expectation Effects in Organizational Change." *Administrative Science Quarterly* (June, 1973).

Kreps, G.A. "Change in Crisis: Relevant Organizations Police Departments and Civil Disturbances." *American Behavior Scientist*. 16:3 (1973), 356-367.

Kreuzer, Otto. "People in Change." *Police Chief*. XXLV:5 (May, 1967), 11-14.

Lippitt, Gordon L. *Organizational Renewal*. N.Y.: Appleton Century Crofts, 1969.

Maass, William. "Making Organizations Adaptive to Change." *Innovation*. 30 (1972).

Meyer, John C., Jr. "Policing the Future." *Police Chief*. XXXVIII:7 (July, 1971), 14-17.

Milakovich, M.E. *Change in Law Enforcement Agencies in Response to Federal Criminal Justice Legislation*. Washington: NCJRS, 1971.

Nonet, Phillepe. *Administrative Justice: Advocacy and Change in a Government Agency*. N.Y.: Russell Sage, 1969.

Powell, Clifford R. "Law Enforcement: Its Place in the Future." *Police Chief*. XLI:11 (November, 1974), 67-72.

Ronken, Harriet O. and Paul R. Lawrence. *Administering Changes: A Case Study of Human Relations in a Factory*. Westport, CT.: Greenwood, [1952] 1972.

Sheehan, Robert. "A Commitment to Change." *Journal of Criminal Law, Criminology and Police Science*. 60:3 (September, 1969). 381-386.

Sherman, Clayton V. and Mark B. Silber. "You Can Make Changes That Stick." *Supervisory Management* (December, 1973).

Skibbins, Gerald L. *Organizational Evolution: A Program for Managing Radicial Change.* N.Y.: AMA, 1974.

Sourisseau, Leslie S. "The Diffusion of Innovations." *Police Chief.* XXXIX:8 (August, 1972), 20-26.

Spicer, Edward H. *Human Problems in Technological Change.* N.Y.: Wiley, 1967.

Spreen, Johannes F. "Tomorrow's Police—Protectors or Pursuers?" Police. 16:4 (December, 1971), 21-25.

Stanfield, R.L. *American Federalism: Into the Third Century: Its Agenda.* Washington: NCJRS (Microfiche) 1974.

Recommendations to revitalize local government, build stronger states, achieve balanced growth and housing opportunity and streamline and humanize the administration of justice.

Toch, H. *Agents of Change: A Study in Police Reform.* N.Y.: Wiley, 1975.

A police training program designed to test the premise that change can be perpetuated and passed on by using a participatory model in which the targets of change are converted into the agents of change.

Toch, H. "Change Through Participation (and vice versa)." *Journal of Research in Crime and Delinquency (1970).*

Toffler, Alvin. "Coping with Future Shock." Playboy (March, 1970).

Tushman, Michael. *Organizational Change: An Exploratory Study and Case History.* Ithaca, N.Y.: New York State School of Industrial and Labor Relations, Cornell University, 1974.

University of Maryland Institute of Criminal Justice and Criminology. *Change Process in Criminal Justice.* Washington: GPO, 1972.

Process of criminal justice change with emphasis on the interaction between operating agency heads and officials and groups attempting to act as agents of change.

University of Maryland Institute of Criminal Justice and Criminology. *Innovation in Law Enforcement.* Springfield, VA.: NTIS, 1972.

Vastola, Anthony. "Police Innovations: Issues and Answers." *Police Chief.* XLII:12 (December, 1975), 38-40.

Watson, Nelson A. "The Perception of Change in Contemporary Society." *Police Chief.* 37:4 (April, 1970), 60-67.

"Who Changes in a Changing World?" *Police Chief.* 39:8. (August, 1972).

Wilkins, L.T. *Crime and Crime Prevention Measures of 1990.* Washington: NCJRS (Microfiche) 1974.

Contains predictions about criminal activities in relation to the technological developments within and without the criminal justice system.

Wilkins, Leslie T. "Crime in the World of 1990." *Futures* (September, 1970), 203-214.

Williams, H.W. *Change Agent in the Criminal Justice System: A Selection of Papers from the Proceedings of the Orientation Program for Community Based Law Enforcement Science Advisors, March 11, 22, 1974, McLean, Virginia.* Washington: NCJRS (Microfiche) 1974.

Program sponsored by the national institute of law enforcement and criminal justice (NILECJ) to instruct private consultant specialists how to bring about changes and improvements in the criminal justice system.

Wilson, Godfrey and Monica Wilson. *Analysis of Social Change.* N.Y.: Cambridge University Press, 1968.

Zurchers, James C. and Robert A. Bush. "Bridging the Implementation Gap." *Police Chief.* XLI:5 (May, 1974), 20-23.

CONFERENCE LEADERSHIP

Auger, B.Y. *How to Run Better Business Meetings.* N.Y.: AMA, 1973.

Brilhart, John K. *Effective Group Discussion.* 2nd ed. Dubuque, IA.: William C. Brown, 1974.

Copeman, G. and M. Wade. "Are Board Meetings Inefficient?" *Business Management* (November, 1967).

Miller, Ernest. *Conference Leadership.* Rev. ed. N.Y.: AMA, 1972.

Tilson, John Q. *How to Conduct a Meeting.* Dobbs Ferry, N.Y.: Oceana, 1950.

CONSULTANTS

Flammang, Chris J. "Technical Assistance for Police Executives." *Police Chief.* XXXIX:6 (June, 1972), 26-41.

Governors' Mutual Assistance Program. *Sources of Information on Criminal Justice: A Preliminary Reference for Planners and Researchers.* Washington: National Governor's Conference, 1972.

List of sources of technical advice and hard data now in existence.

Hasler, G. "The Security Consultant—A Summary of the Essential Qualities of the Independent Expert." *Security Gazette.* 17:9 (1975), 305.

Martin, John A. "Selection and Use of Outside Consultants: Suggested Guidelines for the Law Enforcement Executive." *Police.* 16:11 (July, 1972), 38-40.

Porter, Jack D. "The Pro Police Approach." *Police Chief.* XXXV:4 (April, 1968), 14-19.

Schmidt, Donald J. "Waterbury Takes on the Business Community." *Police Chief.* XLI:6 (June, 1974), 38-40.

Use of management and other skills from the community by police departments.

Shaw, William. "Technical Assistance Can Be Obtained from Public Spirited Citizens." *Law and Order.* 16:1 (January, 1968), 28-34.

Method by which police departments can obtain free technical assistance from a private sector.

CONTROL

Control—General

Gourley, G. Douglas. "Encouraging Compliance with Policies." *Police.* 5:2. (November-December, 1960) 53-56.

Gregory, J.L. "Performance Control." *Police Chief.* (October, 1970).

Hudson, James R. "Organizational Aspects of Internal and External Review of the Police." *Journal of Criminal Law, Criminology and Police Science.* 63:3. (1972) 427-433.

Landis, Eugene A., Jr. "Cruiser Meters for Accountability and Control." *Police.* 9:4. (March-April, 1965) 20-21.

Ramstrom, Dick. *The Efficiency of Control Strategies.* Stockholm: Almquist and Wiksell, 1967.

Schrotel, Stanley R. "Supervising the Use of Police Authority." *Police.* 11:2. (November-December, 1957) 15-17.

Stone, Donald. "The Control and the Discipline of Police Forces." *The Annals.* (November, 1929) 63-73.

Discipline

Anderson, R.E. "Are Our Large City Police Departments Being Neutralized?" *FBI Law Enforcement Bulletin* (August, 1968), 9-11.
Deals not only with concept of lack of discipline within the department, but also with concept of too much discipline put on department from outside, therefore lessening police authority.

Avins, Alfred. *Penalties for Misconduct on the Job.* Dobbs Ferry, N.Y.: Oceana, 1972.

Black, James M. *Positive Discipline.* N.Y.: AMA, 1970.

Blalock, Joyce. "Managing for Effective Discipline: Legal Issues in Discipline." *Police Chief* (June, 1976).

Dempsey, Robert R. "Police Disciplinary Systems." *Police Chief.* XXXIX:5 (May, 1972), 52-56.

"Discipline as a Supervisory Responsibility." *FBI Law Enforcement Bulletin* (June, 1970), 22-26.
Discipline used both as training and punishment.

Gourley, G. Douglas. "Police Discipline." *Journal of Criminal Law and Police Science.* 41 (1950), 91-92.

Gregory, J.L. "Performance Control" *Police Chief* (October, 1970).

Handling Problems of Discipline. N.Y.: AMA, 1967.

Hillgren, James S. and L.W. Spradlin. "A Positive Disciplinary System for the Dallas Police." *Police Chief.* XLII:7 (July, 1975), 65-67.

Huberman, John. "Discipline Without Punishment." *Harvard Business Review* (July-August, 1964), 62-68.

Kaufman, Charles N. "The Danger From Within: Organization Stagnation." *FBI Law Enforcement Bulletin* (February, 1973), 3-6.
The dangers of allowing a law enforcement agency to stagnate. Although article does not deal with discipline exclusively, lack of discipline is part of the cycle of stagnation.

Kenney, John P. *Police Management Planning.* Springfield, IL.: C.C. Thomas, 1959.
Discusses how discipline affects all members of a department and how a department can establish a positive approach to discipline.

Knochuizen, Ralph. *Question of Police Discipline in Chicago: An Analysis of the Proposed Office of Professional Standards.* Evanston, IL.: Chicago Law Enforcement Study Group, 1974.

Koontz, Harold and Cyril O'Donnell. *Principles of Management: An Analysis of Managerial Functions.* 4th ed. N.Y.: McGraw Hill, 1968, 585-588.

Leonard, Tony. "Discipline Is About Thinking, Not Shouting." *Police Review (GB),* (January 2, 1976), 14.

MacFarline, Robert I. "Managing for Effective Discipline: Increasing Officer Confidence in Discipline." *Police Chief* (May, 1976).

Melnicoe, William B. *Elements of Police Supervision.* Beverly Hills: Glencoe, 1969, 77-95.

Morgan, James E. *Principles of Administrative and Supervisory Management.* Englewood Cliffs, N.J.: Prentice Hall, 1973.
Discusses the disciplinary action process.

Pedersen, Bjorn. "Managing for Effective Discipline: Direction and Control Through Written Directions." *Police Chief* (April, 1976).

Prout, Robert S. "A Classification of Internal Disciplinary Actions by State Police and Highway Patrols." *Police Chief* (November, 1973), 52-53.

Rutledge, William. "Police Discipline." *Journal of Criminal Law and Criminology* (1950).

Southwestern Law Enforcement Institute. *Police Management.* Springfield, IL.: C.C. Thomas, 1962.
Indicates how healthy discipline is created and maintained in a police department, the necessity of its continuance for successful administration, and the influence of adequate periodic performance appraisals on its continuance.

Stessin, Lawrence. *Employee Discipline.* Washington: Bureau of National Affairs, 1960.

"The Supervisor and Morale." *FBI Law Enforcement Bulletin* (November, 1970), 13-15.

Terry, George R. *Principles of Management.* Homewood, IL.: Richard D. Irwin, 1968.

Wolf, Thomas A. "Police Discipline." *Traffic Digest and Review.* 8 (February, 1960), 5-8, 32-33.

Inspections

Andrews, A.M. "Let's Stand Inspection." *Law and Order.* 12:4 (April, 1964), 50, 52-53.

Campbell, G.K. and J. Daly. *Implementation of a Staff Inspection System in the Massachusetts State Police.* Washington: NCJRS, 1971.

Disser, L.R. and Roland M. Kissinger. "Inspection: A Management Tool." *Police Chief.* XLII:8 (August, 1975), 12-13.

Hoover, J.E. "Timely Inspection of Essential Value in Law Enforcement." *RCMP Gazette.* 24:9 (September, 1962).

"Inspections: An Executive Tool for Improvement." *FBI Law Enforcement Bulletin.* 26:5 (May, 1957), 17-20.

Los Angeles Police Department. *Task Force Inspection Guide.* Los Angeles: LAPD, 1970.

Skousen, W. Cleon. "The Revival of Rigid Inspections." *Law and Order*. 12:10 (October, 1964), 38-41.

Smith, Joseph L. "Police Inspection and Complaint Reception Procedures." FBI Law Enforcement Bulletin. 43:2 (February, 1974), 12-15.

Smith, R. Dean. "Inspection and Control." *Police Chief* (July, 1964).

"Timely Inspections of Essential Value in Law Enforcement." *FBI Law Enforcement Bulletin* (May, 1962).

Trull, Edna. *The Administration of Regulatory Inspectional Services in American Cities*. N.Y.: Municipal Administration Service, 1932.

"Using Inspections to Improve Your Police Operations." *FBI Law Enforcement Bulletin* (June, 1959).

Wren, Pauline, "The Police Inspectorate." *Police Review (GB)*, 79 (May 14, 1971).

Manuals

"An Effective Police Manual." *FBI Law Enforcement Bulletin*. 38:3 (March, 1969), 15-18.

Boyle, H.H. Jr. and L.J. Ferolite. *Illinois Law Enforcement Manual*. Beaver Dam, WI.: Masterprint, 1973.

Callister, R.W. et al. "An Effective Police Manual." *FBI Law Enforcement Bulletin*. 38:3 (March, 1969).

Keller, E. John. "Policy Manuals: Rules and Regulations—How Important?" *Law and Order*. 22:3 (March, 1974), 24-31.

King, Everett M. *Sheriff's Manual*. Washington: National Sheriff's Association, 1960.

MacDonald, Lloyd D. "Preparing a New Police Policy Manual: The Cambridge Experience." *Police Chief* (April, 1974), 68-73.
Policy manual was developed with the active participation of representative groups.

Oregon State Police. *Oregon State Police Administrative Handbook*. Chicago: American Bar Association, 1970.

Rook, Roger. *Handbook for Peace Officers*. Oregon City, OR.: Roger Rook, 1974.

Scottsdale Police Department. *Model Police Manual*. Washington: NCJRS, n/d.

Rules and Regulations

Ayres, Loren. "Standards of Police Conduct and Performance." *Law and Order*. 12:4 (April, 1964), 56-58, 60,62.

Caplan, G.M. "The Case for Rulemaking by Law Enforcement Agencies." *Law and Contemporary Problems*. 36:4 (1971), 500-514.

Chicago Police Department Legal Unit. *Drafting and Enforcing Police Rules of Conduct*. Chicago: Chicago Police Department, 1970.

Christian, Robert H. "Manual of Rules and Regulations for Small Police Departments." *Police*. 5:6 (July-August, 1961), 77-79; (September-October, 1961), 41-43; (November-December, 1961), 47-48.

International Association of Chiefs of Police. *Model Rules and Regulations: Manual of Rules*. Gaithersburg, MD.: IACP, 1967.

Pomrenke, Norman E. *Law Enforcement Manual: Rules and Regulations*. Gaithersburg, MD.: IACP, 1967.

Trambukis, Leo P. "A Police Regulations Manual—Its Prepation and Purpose." *FBI Law Enforcement Bulletin*. 35:12 (December, 1966), 2-6.

Wadman, Robert. *Rules and Regulations for State and Local Law Enforcement Agencies*. Springfield, IL.: C.C. Thomas, 1975.

DECENTRALIZATION

Ehrle, Raymond A. "Management Decentralization Antidote to Bureaucratic Ill." *Personnel Journal*. 49 (May, 1970), 396-397.

MacCullough, A.V. "In Defense of Decentralization." *Advanced Management* (July, 1960).

DECISION MAKING

Axelrod, Robert. *The Structure of Decision*. Princeton, N.J.: Princeton University Press, 1976.

Alexis, Marcus and C. Wilson. *Organizational Decision Making*. Englewood Cliffs, N.J.: Prentice Hall, 1967.

Brinkers, Henry S., ed. *Decision Making: Creativity, Judgement and Systems*. Columbus, OH.: Ohio State University Press, 1972.

Bristow, Allen P. and E.C. Gabard. *Decision-Making in Police Administration*. Springfield, IL.: C.C. Thomas, 1961.

Brown, Rex V. et al. *Decision Analysis: An Overview*. N.Y.: Holt Rinehart and Winston, 1974.

Brown, Rex V. et al. *Decision Analysis for the Manager*. N.Y.: Holt Rinehart and Winston, 1974.

Brown, Robert Goodell. *Management Decisions for Productive Operations*. Hinsdale, IL.: Dryden, 1971.

Cooper, Joseph D. *The Act of Decision Making*. Garden City, N.Y.: Doubleday, 1961.

Davis, Morris and Marvin Weinbaum. *Metropolitan Decision Processes: An Analysis of Case Studies*. Chicago, IL.: Rand McNally, 1969.

DeArmond, Frederick. *Executive Thinking and Action*. Chicago: Wolfe, 1952.

DeBono, Edward. *Lateral Thinking for Management*. N.Y.: AMA, 1971.

Dibrell, George. "Decision Making at the Constituent Level." *Police Chief* (April, 1974), 59.

Fair, Ernest W. "Check-List for Easier Decision Making." *Law and Order*. 12:10 (October, 1964) 64-65.

Gouran, Dennis S. *Discussion: The Process of Group Making*. N.Y.: Harper & Row, 1974.

Grosman, Brian A. *Police Command—Decisions and Discretion.* Toronto: Macmillan, 1975.

Johnson, Rossall J. *Executive Decisions.* 2nd ed. Cincinnati, OH.: Southwestern, 1970.

Harrison, E. Frank. *The Managerial Decision Making Process.* Boston: Houghton Mifflin, 1975.

Havighurst, Clark C. ed. *Administrative Discretion: Problems of Decision Making by Government Agencies.* Dobbs Ferry, N.Y.: Oceana, 1973.

Lynch, Thomas C. "Guidelines to Aid Police in Making Constant Daily Decisions." *Journal of California Law Enforcement* (January, 1967), 169-175.

McAllister, John A. "Decision Making and Policy." *Police.* 16:11 (July, 1972), 46-53.

Miller, Gordon. *Decision Making: A Look at the Process.* N.Y.: AMA, 1974.

Moore, P.G. *Case Studies in Decision Analysis.* N.Y.: Penguin, 1976.

Moore, P.G. and H. Thomas. *The Anatomy of Decisions.* N.Y.: Penguin, 1976.

Participative Decision Making. N.Y.: AMA, 1974.

Pettigrew, Andrew W. *Politics of Organizational Decision Making.* N.Y.: Barnes and Noble, 1973.

Schlaifer, Robert. *Analysis of Decisions Under Uncertainty.* N.Y.: McGraw Hill, 1969.

Sullivan, D.C. and L.J. Siegel. "How Police Use Information to Make Decision: An Application of Decision Games." *Crime Delinquency.* 18:3 (1972), 253-262.

Tainiter, Melvin. *The Art and Science of Decision Making.* Syosset, N.Y.: Timetable, 1971.

White, D. *Decision Methodology.* N.Y.: Wiley, 1975.

White, D. *Decision Theory.* Chicago: Aldine, 1970.

Young, Stanley. *Management: A Decision-Making Approach.* Belmont, CA.: Dickenson, 1968.

DELEGATION

Gardner, Neely D. *The Art of Delegating.* Garden City, N.Y.: Doubleday, 1965.

Heintze, R.A. "Delegation: Help or Hindrance?" *Management Methods* (November, 1959).

Laird, Donald A. *The Techniques of Delegating: How to Get Things Done Through Others.* N.Y.: McGraw Hill, 1957.

Mason, J.G. "How to Build Your Delegating Skills." *Supervision* (April, 1965).

McConkey, Dale D. *No-Nonsense Delegation.* N.Y.: AMA, 1974.

Practicing the Art of Delegation. N.Y.: AMA, 1968.

Scott, D.H. "Plan and Delegate, That's How to Make More Time." *Sales Management* (September 4, 1959).

Scott, Rose H. "You Owe It to Yourself to Delegate." *Administrative Management* (December, 1972).

EXECUTIVE TIME MANAGEMENT

Brown, G. "Finding Time to Manage." *Management Review* (September, 1973).

Burger, C. "How to Find Enough Time." *Nations Business* (September, 1974).

Chapralis, S. "How Are You Wasting Your Time?" *Supervisory Management* (November, 1971).

Choate, R.K. "You Can Make the Time You Need." *Office Executive* (December, 1960).

Collicoat, S. "Shorter Hours for Top Executives." *Management Review* (April, 1973).

Crawford, J. "I've Got Time: Have You? An Executive's Time Management." *Sales Management* (March 6, 1964).

Danielson, L.E. "Organize Your Time to Get More Done." *Supervisory Management* (July, 1963).

Fergason, G. "Have Your Time and Use It Too." *Best's Insurance News* (1967).

Gibbons, C.C. "Time: You Can Make a Friend of a Foe." *Supervisory Management* (March, 1972).

Green, T.B. "Procrastination Isn't All Bad." *Supervisory Management* (March, 1972).

Heywood, J.D. "Manage Your Time by Managing Your Activities." *Supervisory Management* (May, 1974).

"How Managers Manage Their Time." *Industry Week* (November 22, 1971).

"How to Get Rid of a Bulging Brief Case: By Effective Time Planning." *Business Management* (January, 1964).

Jackson, J.H. and R.L. Hayen. "Rationing the Scarcest Resource: A Manager's Time." *Personnel Journal* (October, 1974).

Jackson, J.H. and L.L. Steinmetz. "Time Saving Techniques." *Supervisory Management* (June, 1972).

Josephs, R. "Control Your Personal Time Better to Get More Better Work Done." *American Business* (February, 1960).

Josephs, R. "Stop Wasting Your Time, Mr. Executive." *Management Methods* (April, 1959).

Kelly, A. "Making the Best Use of Your Time." *International Management* (July, 1973).

Kerfoot, G. "Worrisome World of the Procrastinator: Managing Your Time at the Office." *Office* (May, 1965).

Levinson, R.E. "Executive Escape Hatch—Or How to Avoid Detail." *Management Review* (August, 1973).

Long, L.M. "Lost Time: A Leak in the Dike." *Supervision* (October, 1962).

MacKenzie, R.A. "Toward a Personalized Time Management Strategy." *Management Review* (February, 1974).

"Make Your Time More Productive." *Nations Business* (April, 1963).

Manna, J.R. "Got a Minute, Chief? Executive Time Saving." *Office* (August, 1964).

Margiloff, I.B. "Making Every Minute Count." *Administrative Management* (January, 1972).

Mason, J. "How to Kill Time Productively." *Business Management* (March, 1964).

May, J.W. "How to Use Managerial Time." *Office* 1969.

Meyer, P.J. "Extra-Hour." *Best's Insurance News* (October, 1965).

"Minute Saved Is Production Earned: Thompson Ramo Woolridge Program for Full Day's Work." *Steel* (February 22, 1960).

Morrow, W.V. "Can You Be More Efficient." *Industry Week* (March 12, 1973).

Omken, W. and D.L. Wass. "Management Time: Who's Got the Monkey." *Harvard Business Review* (November, 1974).

Perkin, I.R. "Five Ways to Manage Your Office Time." *Administrative Management* (September, 1966).

Reid, P.C. "Be a Time Miser: How One Supervisor Learned How to Make More Productive Use of His Time." *Supervisory Management* (January, 1965).

Rice, P.L. "Making Minutes Count (Executives)." *Business Horizons* (December, 1973).

Schindall, H. "How to Add Hours to Your Day." *Administrative Management* (February, 1965).

"Teaching Managers to Do More in Less Time." *Business Week* (March 3, 1975).

"Thirty-Seven Ways You Can Save Time." *Business Management* (April, 1964).

Trickett, J.M. "More Effective Use of Time." *Supervisory Management* (November, 1962).

Uris, A. "Easing the Pressure of Time: Advice for Executives." *Administrative Management* (June, 1964).

Webster, E. "How to Make the Best Use of Time." *International Management* (September, 1971).

Webster, E. "You Can Automate Your Routine Tasks." *Supervisory Management* (December, 1964).

FEEDBACK

Dyer, William G. "Encouraging Feedback." *Management Review* (September, 1974).

Kaufman, Herbert. *Administrative Feedback: Monitoring Subordinates Behavior.* Washington: Brookings, 1973.

Keefe, William Ford. *Listen, Management: Creative Listening for Better Managing.* N.Y.: McGraw Hill, 1971.
A good manager is a good listener, according to the author. The author outlines the communication chain that should exist between employer and employee.

Keller, E. John. "The Attitude Survey: A Useful Tool." *Law and Order.* 22:10 (October, 1974).

Kreins, Edward S. "Employee Participation: New Concepts for Feedback and Input to Management." *Police Chief.* XXXIX:11 (November, 1972), 36-38.
Police Department surveyed employees as to attitudes toward what was good and bad, right or wrong about department.

Shaw, William. "Result of Technology Survey." *Law and Order.* 15:9 (September, 1967), 70-74.
Survey to determine police needs and attitudes toward technological equipment.

GRIEVANCE HANDLING

Baer, Walter, W. *Grievance Handling.* N.Y.: AMA, 1970.

Cochran, Murray O. "Guidelines for a Grievance Committee. *Police Chief.* 37:11 (November, 1970), 54-55.
Internal machinery for the handling of personnel problems.

How to Handle Grievances. N.Y.: AMA, 1975.

Swope, G.S. *Dissent: The Dynamic of Democracy.* N.Y.: AMA, 1972.

Von Mol, L.J. *Effective Procedures for Handling Employee Grievances.* Chicago: Civil Service Assembly, 1953.

INTERNAL COMMUNICATIONS

Albrecht, Karl G. "Five Ways to Short-Circuit Your Communications." *Supervisory Management* (June, 1974), 2-7.

Anastasi, Thomas E. *Communicating for Results.* Menlo Park, CA.: Cummings, 1972.

Athanassiades, John C. "Communication Distortion." *Police Chief.* XXXIX:5 (May, 1972), 50-51.

Bassett, Glenn A. *The New Fare of Communication.* N.Y.: AMA, 1968.

Bassett, Glenn A. "What Is Communication and How Can I Do It Better?" *Management Review* (February, 1974), 25-32.

Brock, Luther A. *How to Communicate by Letter and Memo.* N.Y.: McGraw Hill, 1974.

Bromage, Mary C. "Bridging the Corporate Communications Gap." *Advanced Management Journal.* 41 (Winter, 1976).

Bromage, Mary C. "The Management of Communications." *Advanced Management Journal.* 38:2 (April, 1973).

Brown, David S. "Barriers to Successful Communication." *Management Review* (January, 1976).

Campbell, James H. *Dimensions in Communication, Readings.* Belmont, CA.: Wadsworth, 1965.

Carter, Robert M. *Communication in Organizations.* Detroit: Gale, 1972.

Chappell, R.T. and W.L. Read. *A Textbook of Business Communications.* 2nd ed. London: MacDonald and Evans, 1969.

Chiarmonte, Robert M. "Eliminating the Rank-Barrier in Personal Communications." *Law and Order.* 22:6 (June, 1974), 50-51.

Chiarmonte, Robert M. "Let the Man on the Road Know. . .Someone Cares." *Police Chief* (April, 1974), 37.

Coffin, Royce A. *The Communicator.* N.Y.: AMA, 1975.

Communicating Effectively. N.Y.: AMA, 1975.

Communicating with Subordinates. N.Y.: AMA, 1974.

Communications: Downward and Upward. N.Y.: National Retail Merchants, 1967.

Concepts of Communication: Interpersonal, Intrapersonal and Mathematics. N.Y.: Wiley, 1971.

Collett, Merrill, et al. *Streamlining Personnel Communications.* Chicago: Public Personnel Association, 1969.

Connelly, J. *A Manager's Guide to Speaking and Listening.* N.Y.: AMA, 1967.

DeMare, George. *Communicating for Leadership: A Guide for Executives.* N.Y.: Ronald, 1968.

DeVito, Joseph A. *Communication: Concepts and Processes.* Englewood Cliffs, N.J.: Prentice Hall, 1971.

Effective Communication on the Job. N.Y.: AMA, 1963.

Farace, Richard V. and Donald McDonald. "New Directions in the Study of Organizational Communication." *Personnel Psychology.* (Spring, 1974) 1-19.

Ferguson, Charles W. *Say It With Words.* Lincoln, NB.: University of Nebraska Press, 1959.

Foltz, Roy G. *Management by Communication.* Philadelphia: Chilton, 1973.

Gray, John W. *Communication and Leadership.* Reston, VA.: National Association of Principals, 1973.

Haney, William V. *Communication Patterns and Incidents.* Homewood, IL.: Irwin, 1960.

Herriot, Peter. *Language and Teaching.* London: Methven, 1971.

Hovland, Carl Iver. *Communication and Persuasion.* New Haven, CT.: Yale University Press, 1953.

Interpersonal Communication in the Modern Organization. Englewood Cliffs, N.J.: Prentice Hall, 1961.

Keefe, William. *Listen: Management.* N.Y.: McGraw Hill, 1971.

Keffe, William. *Open Minds.* N.Y.: AMA, 1975.

Kenney, John P. "Internal Police Communications." *Journal of Criminal Law, Criminology and Police Science.* 46:4 (November-December, 1955), 547-553.

McDonough, Adrian M. *Information Economics and Management Systems.* N.Y.: McGraw Hill, 1963.

McGlasson, James C. "Formal Directives Management: Its Application to Law Enforcement." *Police Chief.* XXXIX:7. (July, 1972) 42-45.

Martin, Howard Hastings. *Speech Communication: Analysis and Readings.* Boston: Allyn and Bacon, 1968.

Marting, E., R.E. Finley and W. Ward. *Effective Communication on the Job.* N.Y.: AMA, 1963.

Maude, Barry. *Practical Communication for Managers.* N.Y.: Longman, 1974.

Maya, Richard J. "Communication and Conflict in Organizations." *Human Resource Management.* 13 (Winter, 1974).

Menning, Jack H. and C.W. Wilkinson. *Communicating Through Letters and Reports.* 5th ed. Homewood, IL.: Irwin, 1972.

Montgomery, Donald E. "How to Get Your Message Across." *Supervisory Management* (February, 1975).

More, Harry W., Jr. "Administrative Communications Models." *Police.* 10:1 (September-October, 1965), 33-35.

Morgan, John S. *Getting Across to Employees: A Guide to Effective Communications on the Job.* N.Y.: McGraw Hill, 1964.

Phillips, David C. *Oral Communications in Business.* N.Y.: McGraw Hill, 1955.

Purdue Research Foundation. *Communication Within the Organization: An Interpretive Review of Theory and Research.* N.Y.: Harper & Row, 1976.

Redfield, Charles E. *Communication in Management.* Chicago: University of Chicago, 1958.

Rice, Joseph A. "Communication Barriers: Individual Quirks and Corporate Personalities." *Supervisory Management* (April, 1976).

Shurter, Robert LeFevre. *Written Communication in Business.* N.Y.: McGraw Hill, 1957.

Sigband, Norman B. *Communications for Management.* Glenview, IL.: Scott Foresman, 1969.

Silber, Mark B. "Manager Communications: Organization Lifeline." *Defense Management Journal* (January, 1973), 29-32.

Sinclair, Susan. "Transactional Analysis or What Do You Mean, My Report Was Late?" *Supervisory Management* (October, 1972), 2-11.

Smith, J.N. "Operation Speakeasy: An Experiment in Communication." *Management Review* (March, 1973).

Stull, James B. "The Benefits of Open Communication." *Supervisory Management* (July, 1975).

Sussman, Lyle. "Communication: What Are Your Assumptions?" *Supervisory Management* (January, 1976).

Treece, Malra. "Cut the Cost of Communications." *Supervisory Management* (February, 1976).

The Use of Communication Tools. N.Y.: AMA, 1967.

Vardaman, George T. and Patricia B. Vardaman. *Communications in Modern Organizations.* N.Y.: Wiley, 1973.

Wiksell, Wesley. *Do They Understand You?* N.Y.: Macmillan, 1960.

Writing Better Letters, Reports and Memos. N.Y.: AMA, 1975.

LEADERSHIP

Amacom's Magazine. *Leadership on the Job.* N.Y. AMA, 1966.

Andrews, R.A. *Leadership and the Police Supervisor.* Evanston, IL.: Traffic Institute Northwestern University, 1971.

Argyris, Chris. *Executive Leadership.* Hamden, CT.: Archon, 1967.

Axelrod, Nathan. *Executive Leadership.* Indiannapolis: Bobbs, 1969.

Bartol, Kathryn and Max Wortman. "Male Versus Female Leaders." *Personnel Psychology* (Winter, 1975).

Basil, Douglas Constantine. *Leadership Skills for Executive Action.* N.Y.: AMA, 1971.

Bell, Wendell, Richard Hill and Charles Wright. *Public Leadership.* San Francisco: Chandler, 1961.

Bennis, Warren. *The Unconscious Conspiracy: Why Leaders Can't Lead.* N.Y.: AMA, 1976.

Beer, Michael. *Leadership, Employee Needs and Motivation.* Columbus, OH.: Ohio State University, 1966.

Blanchard, Kenneth and Paul Hersey. "So You Want to Know Your Leadership Style?" *Training and Development Journal* (February, 1974).

Brown, Gary. "Assuming Command of a Small Police Department." *Police Chief.* XLIII:1 (January, 1976), 14, 70.

Buchanan, Paul C. *The Leader and Individual Motivation.* N.Y.: Association, 1962.

Carlisle, Howard. *Situational Management: A Contingency Approach to Leadership.* N.Y.: Amacom, 1973.

Chapman, Samuel G. "Developing Personnel Leadership." *Police Chief.* XXXIII:3 (March, 1966), 24-35.

Clarke, Bruce. *Guidelines for the Leader and the Commander.* Harrisburg, PA.: Stackpole, 1963.

Cribbin, James. *Effective Managerial Leadership.* N.Y.: AMA, 1972.

Crutchfield, Carroll. "Familiarity Breeds Respect." *Law and Order.* 13:6 (June, 1965), 50-53.

Department of the Army. *Military Leadership.* Washington: GPO, 1961.

Ellis, Albert. *Executive Leadership: A Rational Approach.* Secaucus, N.J.: Citadel, 1972.

Fiedler, Fred Edward. *Leadership and Effective Management.* Glenview, IL.: Scott Foresman, 1974.

Fiedler, Fred E. *A Theory of Leadership Effectiveness.* N.Y.: McGraw Hill, 1967.

Folley, Vern L. "Leadership in Law Enforcement." *Law and Order.* 18:11 (November, 1970), 46, 48, 90.

Goble, Frank G. *Excellence in Leadership.* N.Y.: AMA, 1972.

Gouldner, Alvin Ward. *Studies in Leadership.* N.Y.: Russell and Russell, 1965.

Grosman, Brian A. *Police Command: Decisions and Discretion.* Toronto: Macmillan, 1975.

Hays, Samuel H. and William A. Thomas. *Taking Command.* Harrisburg, PA.: Stackpole, 1967.

Hendricks, James F. "Moral Responsibility and Training for Leadership." *Police.* 16:1 (September, 1971), 66-67.

Killian, Ray A. *Managers Must Lead!* N.Y.: AMA, 1966.

Klos, Louis A. "Measure Your Leadership with the Managerial Grid." *Supervisory Management* (April, 1974).

McClellan, George B. "Observations on Police Leadership." *Journal of Criminal Law, Criminology and Police Science.* 57:3 (September, 1966), 354-355.

McGregor, Douglas. *Leadership and Motivation.* Cambridge, MA.: MIT Press, 1966.

Meares, Ainslie. *How to Be a Boss: A Practicing Psychiatrist on the Managing of Men.* N.Y.: Coward McCann and Goeghagen, 1971.

More, Harry W., Jr. "Police: Community Leadership." *Journal of California Law Enforcement* (October, 1969), 73-78.

Parker, Willard Eagleson et. al. *Front-Line Leadership.* N.Y.: McGraw Hill, 1969.

Passett, Barry A. *Leadership Development for Public Service.* Houston, TX.: Gulf, 1971.

Pell, Arthur R. "Better Results Through Better Leadership." *Police.* 13:5 (May-June, 1969), 15-18.

Pell, A.R. *Police Leadership.* Springfield, IL.: C.C. Thomas, 1967.
This is a description of some aspects of leadership psychology as they apply to the professionalization of police.

Peoples, Edward E. "Measuring the Qualities of Police Leadership." *Police Chief.* XLI:5 (May, 1974), 30-31.

Pursley, Robert D. "Leadership and Community Identification Attitudes Among Two Categories of Police Chief: An Exploratory Inquiry." *Journal of Police Science and Administration.* 2:4 (December, 1974), 414-422.

Roskill, Stephen Wentworth. *The Art of Leadership.* London: Collins, 1964.

Rytten, Jack Edward. "Principles of Effective Leadership." *Police.* 4:5 (May-June, 1960), 70-73.

Saul, John R. "A Bowl of Jello." *Law and Order.* 14:9 (September, 1966).

Savord, George H. "Organizing for Team Leadership." *Journal of California Law Enforcement* (July, 1973), 22-26.

Schaller, Lyle E. *Change Agent: The Strategy of Innovative Leadership.* Nashville, TN.: Abingdon, 1972.

Scott, Clifford L. *Leadership for the Police Supervisor.* Springfield, IL.: C.C. Thomas, 1960.

Skousen, W. Cleon. "Field Commanders: Key to Efficient Patrol." *Law and Order.* 20-11 (November, 1972), 8-13.

Spencer, Gilmour and Keith Jewell. "Police Leadership: A Research Study." *Police Chief* (March, 1963), 40-45.

Stead, Phillip J. "The Humanism of Command." *Police Chief.* XLI:1 (January, 1974), 26-28.

Steinmetz, Lawrence. "Understanding: The Natural Born Leader That's in You." *Administrative Management* (October, 1974).

Stogdill, Ralph M. *Handbook of Leadership: A Survey of Theory and Research.* N.Y.: Free Press, 1974.

Suarez, Eugene F. "Developing Leadership Potential." *Police Chief.* XXV:7 (July, 1968), 48-49.

Sullivan, Robert E. "Qualities of Leadership." *Police.* 7:3 (January-February, 1963), 30-33.

Tead, Ordway. *The Art of Leadership.* N.Y.: McGraw Hill, 1935.

Towler, Juby E. "Introduction to the Art of Leadership." *Police.* 6:6 (July-August, 1962), 70-78.

U.S. Department of the Navy. *United States Navy Leadership Manual.* Washington: GPO, 1962.

Woolery, Todd W. "Police Leadership." *Police Chief.* XXXLV:5 (May, 1967), 24-25.

Zaleznik, Abraham. *Human Dilemmas of Leadership.* N.Y.: Harper & Row, 1966.

MORALE

Arnwine, Henry B. "Development of Morale in the Police Department." *Police* (July-August, 1963); (September-October, 1963).

Baehr, Melany E. and Richard Renck. "The Definition and Measurement of Employee Morale." *Administrative Science Quarterly.* 3 (1958), 157-184.

Bagley, Gerald L. "Play Ball—The Value of a Sports Program. *Police* (January-February, 1964).

Blum, Richard H. and William J. Osterloh. "Keeping Policemen on the Job. Some Recommendations Arising from a Study of Men and Morale." *Police.* X:10 (May-June, 1966), 28-32.

Coon, Thomas F. "Police Morale." *Police* (July-August, 1967).

Dyas, Robert D. "The Mental Miasma—A Police Personnel Problem." *Police.* 3:6 (July-August, 1959), 65-69 (September-October, 1959), 35-38.

Giese, W.J., H.W. Ruter. "An Objective Analysis of Morale." *Journal of Applied Psychology.* 33 (1949).

Gocke, B.W. "Morale in a Police Department." *Journal of Criminal Law and Criminology.* 36 (September, 1945).

Post, Richard D. "Morale Consideration in a Police Environment." *Police.* 14:3 (January-February, 1970), 65-73.

Roethlisberger, F.J. *Management and Morale.* Cambridge, MA.: Harvard University Press, 1946.

"The Supervisor and Morale." *FBI Law Enforcement Bulletin* (November, 1970), 13-15, 30.

Survey Research Center. *Effective Morale.* Ann Arbor: University of Michigan Press, 1950.

Tripamer, Alfred L. "Building Morale." *Law and Order.* 19:2 (February, 1971), 22.

Woods, Walter A. "Employee Attitudes and Their Relation to Morale." *Journal of Applied Psychology.* XXVIII (1944).

Worthy, James C. "Organization and Structure and Employee Morale." *Management of Human Resources.* N.Y.: McGraw Hill, 1962.

MOTIVATION

Atkinson, J.W. and J.O. Raynor. *Motivation and Achievement.* N.Y.: Halstead, 1974.

Bartoshuk, A.K. *Motivation.* Dubuque, IA.: William C. Brown, 1966.

Bindra, Dalbir and James Stewart, eds. *Motivation.* rev. ed. Baltimore: Penguin, 1972.

Bolles, Robert C. *Theory of Motivation.* 2nd ed. N.Y.: Harper & Row, 1975.

Brown, James S. *Motivation of Behavior.* N.Y.: McGraw Hill, 1961.

Buck, Ross W. *Human Motivation and Emotion.* N.Y.: Wiley, 1976.

Cofer, Charles N. and M.H. Appley. *Motivation: Theory and Research.* N.Y.: Wiley, 1964.

Dowling, William F. *How Managers Motivate: The Imperatives of Supervision.* N.Y.: McGraw Hill, 1971.

Dichter, Ernest. *Motivating Human Behavior.* N.Y.: McGraw Hill, 1971.

Ferguson, E.D. *Motivation: An Experimental Approach.* N.Y.: Holt Rinehart and Winston, 1976.

Ford, Robert N. *Motivation Through the Work Itself.* N.Y.: AMA, 1969.

Gellerman, Saul W. *Management by Motivation.* N.Y.: AMA, 1968.

Gellerman, Saul W. *Motivation and Productivity.* N.Y.: AMA, 1963.

Heckhausen, Heinz. *Anatomy of Achievement Motivation.* Washington: Academic, 1967.

Herzberg, F., B. Mausner and B. Snyderman. *The Motivation to Work.* 2nd ed. N.Y.: Wiley, 1959.

Killian, Ray A. *Human Resources Management: An Roi Approach.* N.Y.: AMA, 1976.

Levinson, Harry. "Assinine Attitudes Towards Motivation." *Harvard Business Review* (January-February, 1973).

McClelland, David C. et al. *The Achievement Motive.* N.Y.: Irvington, 1976.

Macarov, David. *Incentives to Work.* San Francisco; Jossey Bass, 1970.

Mali, Paul. "A Practical Scheme that Motivates People." *Administrative Management* (March, 1973).

Mang, Norbert V. "The Evolution of Labor Utilization." *Police Chief.* XLI:11 (November, 1974), 30-32.

Maslow, A. *Motivation and Personality.* N.Y.: Harper & Row, 1954.

Maslow, A.H. "A Theory of Human Motivation." *Psychological Review.* 50 (July, 1943), 370-396.

Motivation and Job Performance. N.Y.: AMA, 1968.

Motivation: Key to Good Management. N.Y.: AMA, 1974.

Murrell, Hywel. *Motivation at Work.* London: Methuen, 1976.

Myers, M.S. "Who Are Your Motivated Workers." *Harvard Business Review.* 42 (1964), 73-88.

Schroeter, Louis C. *Organizational Plan.* N.Y.: AMA, 1970.

Teedan, Richard and B.D. Smith. *Motivation.* N.Y.: McGraw Hill, 1967.

Tierney, Ernest T. "Change: A Great Motivator." *S A M Advanced Management Journal* (October, 1973).

Valle, Fred P. *Motivation: Theories and Issues.* Belmont, CA.: Brooks Cole, 1975.

Viteles, Morris S. *Motivation and Morale in Industry.* N.Y.: Norton, 1953.

Vroom, Victor H. *Work and Motivation.* N.Y.: Wiley, 1964.

Weger, John J. *Motivating Supervisors.* N.Y.: AMA, 1971.

Wilson, Harold. *Motivation, Morale and What Men Want from their Jobs.* Irvine, CA.: Administrative Research, 1969.

Wilson, M.R. *Motivate with a Mule or Recognition.* Washington: NCJRS (Microfiche) 1974.

POLICY

Appleby, Paul H. *Policy and Administration.* University, AL.: University of Alabama Press, 1975.

Barres, Anthony. "A Rational Road for a Sensible Police Policy." *Police Chief.* XXXVI:6 (June, 1969), 36-41.

Gass, S.I. et al. *Evaluation of Policy-Related Research: Reviews and Critical Discussion of Policy-Related Research in the Field of Police Protection: Final Report.* Washington: NCJRS (Microfiche) 1974.

Lerner, Daniel and Harold D. Lasswell, eds. *Policy Sciences.* Stanford, CA.: Stanford University Press, 1971.

Lewin, Arie Y. and Melvin F. Shakum, eds. *Policy Science: Methodologies and Cases.* Elmsford, N.Y.: Pergamon, 1975.

Lindblom, Charles E. *Policy-Making Process.* Englewood Cliffs, N.J.: Prentice Hall.

Lynch, Thomas D. *Policy Analysis in Public Policy Making.* Lexington, MA.: Lexington, 1975.

McNichols, Thomas. *Policy Making and Executive Action.* 4th ed. N.Y.: McGraw Hill, 1972.

Peak, G.W. "Policy-Making and Organized Responsibilities of the Top Executive." *Michigan Business Review* (November, 1971).

Remington, Frank J. and Herman Goldstein. "Law Enforcement Policy: The Police Role in Its Formulation and Development." *Journal of California Law Enforcement* (October, 1967), 90-108.

Richardson, J.J. *Policy Making Process.* Atlantic Highlands, N.Y.: Humanities, 1969.

Ripley, Randall B. and Grace A. Franklin. *Policy Making in the Federal Executive Branch.* N.Y.: Free Press, 1975.

Smith, George A., Jr. et al. *Policy Formulation and Administration: A Case Book of Top Management Problems in Business.* 6th ed. Homewood, IL.: Irwin, 1972.

Watson, Nelson A. "Probing Police Policy." *Police.* 9:4 (March-April, 1965), 78-81.

PRODUCTIVITY

Chapman, J.I. and S. Sonenblum. *Police Service Production Function: A Measure of Police Output and Its Relationship to Police Inputs.* Berkeley, CA.: Institute of Government and Public Affairs, 1972.

The various stages of statistical analysis needed to evaluate an agency's performance are applied to the police service in the city of Los Angeles.

Comrie, M.D. and E. Kings. "Urban Workloads." *Police Research Bulletin.* 23 (1974), 32-38.

Dart, Richard, Val Lubans and Ralph Showalter. *Plan to Increase Police Productivity: A Report on the Reorganization of the East Hartford Police Department.* Bethesda, MD.: Social Development, 1974.

Gylys, Julius A. "Application of a Production Function to Police Patrol Activity." *Police Chief.* XLI:7 (July, 1974), 70-71.

Hirsch, Gary B. and Lucins J. Riccio. "Measuring and Improving the Productivity of Police Patrol." *Journal of Police Science and Administration.* 2:2 (June, 1974), 169-184.

Holzer, Marc. "Police Productivity: A Conceptual Framework for Measurement and Improvement." *Journal of Police Science and Administration.* 1:4 (December, 1973), 459-467.

Lind, R.C. and J.P. Lipsky. "The Measurement of Police Output: Conceptual Issues and Alternatives Approaches." *Law Contemporary Problems.* 36:4 (1971), 566-588.

Morgan, J.P. and R. Scott Fosler. "Police Productivity." *Police Chief.* XLI:7 (July, 1974), 28-30.

National Commission on Productivity. *Improving Police Productivity: More for Your Law Enforcement Dollar—A Brief for Elected Officials.* Washington: NCJRS n/d.

National Commission on Productivity. *Opportunities for Improving Productivity in Police Service.* Washington: NCJRS (Microfiche) 1973.

Ostrom, Elinor and William H. Baugh. *Community Organization and the Provision of Police Services.* Beverly Hills, CA.: Sage, 1973.

Measurement of police output in 3 Indiana Communities. Results showed a consistent pattern of better services by the smaller police departments.

Ostrom, E. "On the Meaning and Measurement of Output and Efficiency in the Provision of Urban Police Services. *Journal of Criminal Justice.* 1:2 (1973).

Parks, R.B. *Complementary Measures of Police Performance.* Washington: NCJRS (Microfiche) 1974.

Discusses a variety of indicators and operational measures for the output of neighborhood police agencies.

Parks, R.B. *Measurement of Performance in the Public Sector: A Case Study of the Indiannapolis Police Department.* Washington: NCJRS (Microfiche) 1971.

QUALITY CONTROL

Alprin, Geoffrey M. "District of Columbia's Case Review Section Studies the 'No Paper' Phenomenon." *Police Chief.* XL:4 (April, 1793), 36-41.

Case review of court cases by Washington, D.C. Police revealed 25% were not acted upon.

Block, Richard L. "Police Action as Reported by Victims of Crime." *Police.* 15:2 (November-December, 1970), 43-49.

Cizanckas, Victor I. "Police Patrol for Black Americans." *Police Chief.* XXXVII:2 (February, 1970), 26-29.

Public opinion survey obtaining feed-back on police operations. Excellent example.

DeChance, Robert E. "Quality Control in Law Enforcement." *Law and Order.* 18:7 (July, 1970), 60-61.

Use of quality control forms by field supervisors. Sgts interview randomly selected citizens to ascertain the quality of service received from the department.

Diamond, Harry. "Quality Control in Police Work." *Police Chief.* XXXV (February, 1968), 40-44.

Furstenberg, F.F., Jr. and C.F. Wellford. "Calling the Police: The Evaluation of Police Service." *Law Society Review.* 7:3 (1973), 393-406.

Advocates periodic citizen surveys in order to evaluate quality of police service.

Gregory, J.L. "Performance Control." *Police Chief.* 37:9 (October, 1970), 22, 252-255.

Toch, Hans. "Quality Control in Police Work." *Police.* 16:1 (September, 1971), 42-44.

PART VIII
POLICE PERSONNEL MANAGEMENT

POLICE PERSONNEL FUNCTIONS

PERSONNEL—GENERAL

Appel, Stephen W. "Need Some Additional Manpower?" *Police Chief*. XXXIX:12 (December, 1972), 12-16.
Study advocates thorough investigation and documentation to prove the need for more manpower.

Argyris, Chris. *Integrating the Individual and the Organization*. N.Y.: John Wiley, 1964.

Beach, Dale S. *Personnel, The Management of People at Work*. 2nd ed. N.Y.: Macmillan, 1970.

Blum, Richard S. and William J. Osterich. "Keeping Policemen on the Job: Some Recommendations Arising from a Study of Men and Morale." *Police* (May-June, 1966), 28-32.
Provides a summary of a random survey of California police agencies probing why police enter and leave the profession, with recommendations to help the exodus.

Bopp, William J. *Police Personnel Administration: The Management of Human Resources*. Boston: Holbrook, 1974.

California Commission on Peace Officer Standards and Training. *Law Enforcement Personnel Records Management—A Center for Police Management Study*. Washington: NCJRS (Microfiche), 1974.

Cayer, N. Joseph. *Public Personnel Administration in the United States*. N.Y.: St. Martin, 1975.

Chruden, Herbert J. and Arthur W. Sherman. *Personnel Management*. 4th ed. Cincinnati: South Western, 1972.

Civil Service Assembly of the United States and Canada. *Placement and Probation in the Public Service*. Chicago: Civil Service Assembly of the United States and Canada, 1946.

Crane, Donald P. *Personnel Management: A Situational Approach*. Belmont, CA.: Wadsworth, 1974.

Desatnick, Robert L. *Innovative Human Resource Management*. N.Y.: AMA, 1972.

Eisenberg, T., D.A. Kent, and C.R Wall. *Police Personnel Practices in State and Local Governments*. Washington: Police Foundation, 1973.

Epstein, S. *Applied Behavioral Research in Police Personnel Problems*. Washington: NCJRS (Microfiche), 1971.

Famularo, Joseph, ed. *Handbook of Modern Personnel Administration*. N.Y.: McGraw-Hill, 1972.

Feaker, Fred. "A Treatise on Internal Relations." *Law and Order*. 12:6 (May, 1964), 64-65.

Flippo, Edwin B. *Principles of Personnel Management*. N.Y.: McGraw-Hill, 1966.

Frederickson, H. George et al. *Public Personnel Administration: Threshold or Cross Road?* Chicago: International Personnel Management, 1970.

Fremont Police Department. *Manpower Analysis Study of the Fremont (CA.) Police Department*. Washington: NCJRS (Microfiche), 1972.

French, Wendell L. *Personnel Management Process: Human Resource Administration*. N.Y.: Houghton Mifflin, 1974.

Garmire, Bernard L. "Appointment of Outside Police Chiefs." *Public Management*. 42 (August, 1960), 170-175.

Greenlaw, Paul S. and Robert D. Smith. *Personnel Management: A Management Science Approach*. N.Y.: Intext, 1970.

Guidelines for Drafting a Public Personnel Administration Law. Chicago: International Personnel Management, 1973.

Hamner, W. Clay and Frank L. Schmidt. *Contemporary Personnel*. Chicago: St. Clair, 1974.

Hewitt, William H. *New Directions in Police Personnel Administration*. Lexington, MA.: Lexington, 1976.

Hipskind, V.K. "Police Personnel Accident Reports and Records." *Police* (March-April, 1965).

Jucius, Michael J. *Personnel Management*. 8th ed. Homewood, IL.: Irwin, 1975.

Killian, Ray A. *The Working Woman: A Male Manager's View*. N.Y.: AMA, 1971.

Kroeger, Lewis J. et al. *Public Personnel Administration Progress and Prospects*. Chicago: International Personnel Management, 1968.

Larsen, George, Jr. "Police Personnel Turnover." *Traffic Digest and Review*. 7 (November, 1959), 13-16.

Law Enforcement Personnel Records Management—A Center for Police Management Study. Sacramento: California Office of Recruitment, 1974.

Lopez, Feliex M. *Personnel Interviewing*. N.Y.: McGraw, 1975.

Luksus, Edmund G. "Comparative Ratio Analysis as a Tool for Estimating Personnel Requirements." *Journal of California Law Enforcement* (October, 1973), 71-79.

McFarland, Dalton E. *Personnel Management: Theory, Practice*. N.Y.: Macmillan, 1968.

Marting, Elizabeth, ed. *AMA Book of Employment Forms*. N.Y.: AMA, 1967.

Matthews, Lempi. *Tips Worth Tapping: A Collection of More Than 100 Suggestions for Improving Personnel Practices.* Chicago: Public Personnel Association, 1960.

Presents over 100 tips for handling more efficiently, and with greater imagination, all aspects of a personnel program. Ideas presented are drawn from actual practice.

Mead, F.J. "Personnel Department of the Royal Canadian Mounted Police." *Police College Magazine* (Autumn, 1954), 254-260.

Megginson, Leon C. *Personnel: A Behavioral Approach to Administration.* Rev. ed. Homewood, IL.: Dow Jones-Irwin, 1972.

Meriam, Lewis. *Public Personnel Problems, from the Standpoint of the Operating Officer.* Washington: Brookings Institution.

Nigro, Felix A. *Personnel Administration, Public Administration: Readings and Documents.* N.Y.: Rinehart, 1951.

Nigro, Felix A. *Public Personnel Administration,* N.Y.: Holt, 1959.

Odiorne, George S. *Personnel Administration by Objectives.* Homewood, IL.: Dow Jones-Irwin, 1971.

Paulson, S. Lawrence. "Orientation Programs for the Police Family." *Police Chief.* XLI:3 (March, 1974), 63-64.

Piggott, S. *Personnel Administration* N.Y.: McGraw, 1973.

Pigors, Paul J.W. and Charles A. Myers. *Personnel Administration: A Point of View and Method.* 6th ed. N.Y.: McGraw-Hill, 1969.

Plippo, E.B. *Principles of Personnel Management.* N.Y. McGraw, 1971.

Powell, Norman J. *Personnel Administration in Government.* Englewood Cliffs, N.J.: Prentice Hall, 1956.

"Punched Cards Locate Special Police Skills." *American City* (October, 1957).

Reddin, Thomas. "Are You Oriented to Hold Them?" *Police Chief.* XXXLLL:3 (March, 1966), 12-14.

Reining, Henry, Jr. *Cases of Public Personnel Administration.* Dubuque, IA.: William C. Brown, 1949.

Savord, George H. "How Many Men." *Police.* 6:6 (July-August, 1962), 66-69.

Scheer, Wilbert E. *Personnel Director's Handbook.* Chicago: Dartnell, 1970.

Scott, Walter D. et al. *Personnel Management.* 6th ed. N.Y.: McGraw, 1961.

Shafritz, Jay M. *Public Personnel Management: The Heritage of Civil Service Reform.* N.Y.: Praeger, 1975.

Shaw, William. "Keep Your Gadgets—Just Give Me More Men." *Law and Order.* 14:12 (December, 1966), 44-63.

Sikula, Andrew F. *Personnel Administration and Human Resources Management.* N.Y.: Wiley, 1975.

Stahl, O. Glenn. *The Personnel Job of Government Managers.* Chicago: Public Personnel Association, 1971.

Stahl, O. Glenn. *Public Personnel Administration.* N.Y.: Harper & Row, 1971.

Stahl, O. Glenn and Richard A. Stanfenberger. *Police Personnel Administration.* Washington: Police Foundation, 1974.

Toomey, William C. "Analysis of Comparative Personnel Problems in Police Administration." *Police.* 15:6 (July-August, 1971), 26-32.

Waite, William W. *Personnel Administration.* Totowa, N.J.: Littlefield, 1964.

Whisenand, P.M. and R.E. Hoffman. *Chicago Police Department—An Evaluation of Personnel Practices.* Washington: NCJRS, 1972.

Wilson, O.W. "Problems in Police Personnel Administration." *Journal of Criminal Law, Criminology and Police Science.* 43 (March-April, 1953), 840-847.

Wright, Grace H. *Public Sector Employment Selection: A Manual for the Personnel Generalist.* Chicago: International Personnel Management, 1974.

Yaney, Joseph P. *Personnel Management: Reaching Organizational and Human Goals.* Columbus, OH.: Merrill, 1975.

Zabka, John R. *Personnel Management and Human Relations.* Indianapolis, IN.: Bobbs, 1971.

AFFIRMATIVE ACTION

Affirmative Action Plan for N.E.A. West Haven, CT.: National Education Association, 1975.

BNA Editorial Staff, eds. *Equal Employment Opportunity Act of 1972.* Washington: Bureau of National Affairs, 1973.

Beetbower, Dale T. "Equal Employment Opportunity vs. Police Professionalism." *Police Chief.* XLII:5. (May, 1975) 65-66.

Blumrosen, Alfred W. *Black Employment and the Law.* New Brunswick, N.J.: Rutgers University Press, 1971.

Boyer, Jacque K. and Edward Griggs. *Equal Employment Opportunity Program Development Manual.* Washington: U.S. Department of Justice, Office of Civil Rights Compliance, 1974.

EEO — Avoiding Compliance Headaches. N.Y.: AMA, 1975.

Fighting Discrimination in Employment and Occupation: A Worker's Education Manual. Washington: International Labor Office, 1975.

Glazer, Nathan. *Affirmative Discrimination: Ethnic Inequality and Public Policy.* N.Y.: Basic, 1976.

Probes the essentially negative impact affirmative action has had on social justice in America.

Guion, Robert. "Employment Tests and Discriminatory Hiring." *Industrial Relations* (February, 1966).

Jongeward, Dorothy and Dru Scott. *Affirmative Action for Women: A Practical Guide.* Reading, MA.: Addison & Wesley, 1973.

Kent, Deborah Ann. *Discrimination in the Use of Written Tests in Employee Selection.* Gaithersburg, MD: IACP, September, 1972.

Kirkpatrick, James J. et al. *Testing and Fair Employment:*

Fairness and Validity of Personnel Tests for Different Ethnic Groups. N.Y.: New York University Press, 1968.

McLean, Herbert E. and Ann Kerr. "The New Careers Program." *Law and Order.* 17:10 (October, 1969), 102-106.
Program to obtain Eskimos for Alaska State Police.

Mansfield, W.E. *Affirmative Action Proposal.* Chicago: International Personnel Management, 1974.

Margolis, R.J. *Who Will Wear the Badge?* Washington: GPO, 1971.
An examination of barriers to minority recruitment by police and fire departments in the United States.

Miles, Thomas C. "Could You Afford to Lose Your LEAA Support?" *Police Chief.* XXXIX:11 (November, 1972), 76.

Morgan, John S. *White Collar Blacks: A Breakthrough?* N.Y.: AMA, 1970.

Norgren, Paul H. and Samuel E. Hill. *Toward Fair Employment.* N.Y.: Columbia University Press, 1964.

Pitt, Paul J. "EEOC and the Grantee." *Police Chief.* XL:2 (February, 1973), 26-31.

"Quick Guide to Leading Cases on Police Employment." *Law and Order.* 22:9 (September, 1974), 88-89.
Examines policeman's rights under law.

Staff of Humanic Designs Division of Information Sciences, Inc. *How to Eliminate Discriminatory Practices: A Guide to EEO Compliance.* N.Y.: AMA, 1975.

Suich, J.J. "Height Standards in Police Employment and the Question of Sex Discrimination: The Availability of Two Defenses for a Neutral Employment Policy Found Discriminatory Under Title VII." *Southern California Law Review.* 47:2 (1974), 585-640.

U.S. Commission on Civil Rights. *For All People, By All People. Report on Equal Opportunity in State and Local Government Employment.* Washington: GPO, 1969.

Vanagunas, Stanley. "Police Entry Testing and Minority Employment." *Police Chief.* XXXIX:4 (April, 1972), 62-64.

Wallace, Phyllis A. *Equal Employment Opportunity and the A.T. & T. Case.* Cambridge, MA.: MIT Press, 1975.

Williams, Samuel L. "Law Enforcement and Affirmative Action." *Police Chief.* XLII:2 (February, 1975), 72-73.

AWARDS

Blanks, W. Winfield. "To Protect and to Serve." *Police.* 13:2 (November-December, 1968), 90-92.
Medal of Valor Awards, L A P D.

Chiaraminte, R.M. "Personnel Management: Personnel Recognition." *Police Chief.* XXXLV:5 (May, 1967), 26-27.

"Citation for Bravery." *Law and Order.* 7 (May, 1959).

Gourley, G. Douglas. "Recognition and Status for Rank and File Policemen." *Journal of Criminal Law and Criminology.* 40:1 (May-June, 1949), 75-84.

BACKGROUND INVESTIGATION

"Access to Police Records by U.S. Civil Service Commission." *Police Chief.* XLII:3 (March, 1976).

Bouza, Anthony V. "The Policeman's Character Investigation: Lowered Standards or Changing Times?" *Journal of Criminal Law, Criminology and Police Science.* 63:1 (1972).

Garner, Gerald W. "Prerequisites and Training for Contemporary Police." *Law and Order* (March, 1976), 38-53.

Goldstein, Leo S. *Perspectives on Law Enforcement: Characteristics of Police Applicants.* Princeton, N.J.: Educational Testing Service, 1971.

Gugas, Chris. "Better Policemen Through Better Screening." *Police.* 6:6 (July-August, 1962), 54-58.

Hooke, James R. and Herbert H. Krauss. "Personality Characteristics of Successful Police Sergeant Candidates." *Journal of Criminal Law, Criminology, and Police Science.* 62:1 (1971), 104-106.

Inglin, R.D. "Applicant Screening in the Los Angeles Police Department." *Polygraph.* 3:2 (1974), 177-1S8.

La Barbera, Salvador. "The Development of Character Screening Procedures in the Selection of New York City Policemen." *Police Management Review* (October, 1963), 13-19 (November, 1963), 17-25.

Lee, Edward L. "Conducting the Background Investigation of Police Applicants." *Police Chief.* XXXIX:6 (June, 1972), 50, 56.

Levy, Ruth J. *Investigation of a Method for Identification of the High-Risk Police Applicant.* Berkeley, CA.: Institute for Local Self-Government, 1970.

Levy, Ruth J. "Predicting Police Failures." *Journal of Criminal Law, Criminology and Police Science.* 58:2 (1967), 265-266.

McAllister, John A. "Character Investigation of Police Candidates." *FBI Law Enforcement Bulletin.* 35:4 (April, 1966), 17-19.

McConnell, William A. *A Relationship of Personal History to Success as a Police Patrolman.* Unpub. Master's thesis. Colorado State University, January 1967.

Matarazzo, Joseph D. et al. "Characteristics of Successful Policemen and Firemen Applicants." *Journal of Applied Psychology.* 48:5 (1964), 123-133.

Stene, Jack. "Police Applicant Screening." *FBI Law Enforcement Bulletin.* 36:8 (August, 1967), 9-11.

BIORHYTHM

Anderson, R.K. "Man's Timing Mechanism." *ASSE Journal* (February, 1973).

Jones, Robert and Lyle Knowles. "Police Accidents and the Ups and Downs of Life Cycles." *Police Chief.* XLII:10 (October, 1975), 58-61.

Knowles, Lyle and Robert Jones. "Police Altercations and the Ups and Downs of Life Cycles." *Police Chief.* XLI:11 (November, 1974), 51-54.

Lewis, M. "Biorhythm: How to Cope With Your Ups and Downs." *Family Circle* (June, 1971).

MacKenzie, J. "How Bio Rhythms Affect Your Life." *Science Digest* (August, 1973), 18-22.

CAREER DEVELOPMENT

Brandstatter, A.F. "A Career Concept for Police." *Journal of Criminal Law, Criminology and Police Science.* 61:3 (September, 1970), 438-445.

Career Development for Law Enforcement. Washington: NCJRS, 1973.

Ford, Else M. *Leadership Responsibilities for the Development of Employees.* Unpub. Master's thesis. Indiana University, 1952.

Hinrichs, John R. *High-Talent Personnel.* N.Y.: AMA, 1966.

Hunter, K.E. "Career Development for the Police Service." *Police.* [Eng.] (July, 1975), 20-22.

Kozoll, Charles E. *Staff Development in Organizations: A Cost Evaluation for Managers and Trainers.* Reading, MA.: Addision-Wesley, 1974.

Leonard, V.A. *The Police of the 20th Century.* Brooklyn, N.Y.: Foundation, 1964.

Los Angeles County Sheriff's Department. *Career Development for Law Enforcement.* Springfield, VA.: NTIS, 1973.

Lubans, Valdis and Richard F. Dart. *Career Ladder Study for the Portsmouth (VA.) Police Department.* Hartford, CT.: Social Development, 1976.

McKain, Robert J., Jr. *Realize Your Potential.* N.Y.: AMA, 1975.

Misner, Gordon E. *The Development of "New Careerist" Positions in the Richmond Police Department.* Walnut Creek, CA.: Contra Costa Council of Community Services, 1967.

Misner, Gordon E. "Mobility and the Establishment of a Career System in Police Personnel Administration." *Journal of Criminal Law, Criminology and Police Science.* 54:4 (December, 1963), 529-539.

Pitchess, Peter J. "Career Development for Professional Law Enforcement." *Police.* 15:1 (September-October, 1970), 5-10.

Sheppard, D.I. and A.S. Glickman. *Guidelines for Examining and Constructing Police Career Path Programs.* Springfield, VA.: NTIS, 1971.

Sheppard, D.I. and A.S. Glickman. *Method for Constructing Career Paths to Meet Requirements of Tomorrow's Police.* Springfield, VA.: NTIS, 1971.

Thompson, Vance. *Rookie Cop's Guidebook: How to Make a Success of Your Police Department Career.* Hicksville, N.Y.: Exposition, 1970.

Whisenand, P.M. *Police Career Development.* Springfield, VA.: NTIS, 1973.

CIVIL SERVICE

Bendix, Reinhard. *Higher Civil Servants in American Society.* Westport, CT.: Greenwood, 1974 (repr. of 1949 ed.).

Carpenter, William. *The Unfinished Business of Civil Service Reform.* Port Washington, N.Y.: Kennikat, 1973.

Foulke, William D. *Fighting the Spoilsman: Reminiscenses of the Civil Service Reform Movement.* N.Y.: Arno, 1974 (repr.).

Hoogerboom, Eri. *Outlawing the Spoils: A History of the Civil Service Reform Movement, 1865-1883.* Urbana: University of Illinois Press, 1968.

Mainzer, L.C. *Political Bureaucracy: The American Public Service.* Glenview, IL.: Scott Foresman, 1973.

Robson, William A. ed. *The Civil Service in Britain and France.* Westport, CT.: Greenwood, 1975 (repr. of 1956 ed.).

Smith, Darrell H. *The United States Civil Service Commission: Its History, Activities and Organization.* N.Y.: AMS (repr. of 1928 ed.).

Tribe, David. *The Rise of the Mediocracy.* Baltimore: Graylock, 1976.

COMPENSATION

Berg, J. Gary. *Managing Compensation.* N.Y.: AMA, 1976.

Crawford, William. "Police Salaries—A Critical View." *Law and Order.* 11:9 (September, 1963).

Danielson, William F. *Police Compensation.* Washington: IACP, 1967.

Eastman, George D. "Seattle Policemen Paid Less Than Laborers." *American City.* 4:83 (April, 1950).

Kaufman, Charles N. "Wage and Salary Administration." *Police Chief.* XXXVII:6 (June, 1970), 54-56.

Krause, Robert D. *The Pros and Cons of Longevity Pay Plans.* Chicago: Public Personnel Association, 1959.

Larson, Walter J. "Prices Pinch Policeman's Pocketbook." *Police Chief.* XXVII:9 (September, 1970).
Description of the escalator clause in police wage contracts simply means wages are tied to the Consumer Price Index. Offers a list of places to write for information about CPI.

Mawhinney, Robert L. "State Police and Patrol Compensation." *State Government.* 26 (January, 1953).

McBeath, Gordon and D.U. Rands. *Salary Administration.* 2nd ed. N.Y.: Beekman, 1975.

Moonman, Jane. *Effectiveness of Fringe Benefits in Industry.* N.Y.: Beekman, 1973.

Patterson, Peter. *Employers' Guide to Equal Pay.* Washington: International Publications Service, 1972.

Pay Rates in the Public Service: Survey of 62 Common Job Classes in a Selected Group of U.S. and Canadian Governmental Jurisdictions. Chicago: International Personnel Management, 1975.

Personnel Policies in Municipal Police Departments. Washington: International City Management Association, 1972.
Survey data on urban police manpower needs, salary levels, benefits, retirement and disability practices, labor negotiations and aircraft utilization.

"Police Management." *FBI Law Enforcement Bulletin.* 36:11 (November, 1966), 17-19.
Critical analysis of compensation and fringe benefits.

"Police Salaries Have Lagged in St. Louis." *American City.* 5 (May, 1949).
St. Louis police are underpaid in relation to other cities.

Salary Schedule Supplements for Extra Duties. West Haven, CT.: National Education Association, 1972.

Salary Trends for Police Patrolmen, Firefighters, and Refuse Collectors. Washington: International City Management Association, 1972.
Statistical tables presenting past and predicted changes in the median salaries of firefighters and police patrolmen by size of city.

U.S. Bureau of Labor Statistics. *Salary Trends: Firemen and Policemen, 1924-1964.* Washington: GRP, April, 1965.

U.S. Law Enforcement Assistance Administration. *Expenditure and Employment Data for the Criminal Justice System, 1968-69.* U.S. Bureau of the Census. Washington: GPO, December, 1970.

CONDITIONS OF SERVICE

Bancroft, Raymond L. "Municipal Law Enforcements 1966." *Nations Cities* (February, 1966).

Danielson, William F. *Should Police and Firemen Get the Same Salary?* Chicago: Public Personnel Association, 1964.

Fraternal Order of Police. *A Survey of . . . Salaries and Working Conditions of the Police Departments in the United States.* Cincinnati: Fraternal Order of Police, Annual.

Hopkins, E.J. *A Study and Survey of Municipal Police Departments in the State of New Jersey.* Trenton, N.J.: Law Enforcement Council, 1958.

I.A.C.P. *Comparative Data Report: State and Provincial Police.* Washington: I.A.C.P., Periodically.
Gives data on training, operation, administration and personnel.

Kansas City Police Department. *Survey of Municipal Police Departments.* Kansas City, MO.: KCPD, Annual.
Salaries, fringe benefits, working conditions, etc. for major U.S. Police Departments.

HEIGHT REQUIREMENTS

Dempsey, C.A. *Study of Police Height Requirements.* Washington: NCJRS, 1974.

Gunderson, E.K. "Body Size, Self-Evaluation, and Military Effectiveness." *Journal of Personality and Social Psychology* (1965), 902-906.

Hoobler, Raymond and J.A. McQueeney. "A Question of Height." *Police Chief* (November, 1973), 42-48.

Portland (OR.) Bureau of Police. *Analysis of Assaulted and Non-Assaulted Officers by Height, Weight, Tenure and Assignment.* Portland, OR.: Portland (OR.) Bureau of Police, 1973.
In this analysis of factors affecting safe exercise of police duties, height is found to be a major factor in the number of times an officer was assaulted.

Talbert, Terry L. "Study of the Police Officer Height Requirement." *Public Personnel Management* (March-April, 1974), 103-110.

INCENTIVES

Chiaramonte, Robert M. "The Blue Max." *Police Chief.* XL:4 (April, 1973), 24-25.
A special incentive recognition program by Ohio State Highway Patrol. Created to find stolen cars.

Greiner, J.M. and H.P. Hatry. *Managing Human Resources in Local Government—A Survey of Employee Incentives.* Washington: NCJRS (Microfiche), 1973.

Jewell, Donald O. and George E. Manners. *Dynamic Incentive Systems.* Atlanta, GA.: Georgia State University Business, 1976.

Satyanarayana, J. *Incentives in Productivity in Public Enterprises.* Thompson, CT.: Interculture, 1975.

Von Kass, H.K. *Making Wage Incentives Work.* N.Y.: AMA, 1971.

JOB ANALYSIS

Berwitz, C.J. *The Job Analysis Approach to Affirmative Action.* N.Y.: Wiley, 1975.

Job Evaluation. Washington: International Labor Office, 1972.

McGowan, H.E. and G.M. Riley. *Job Analysis of the Position of Uniformed Police Officer.* Washington: NCJRS (Microfiche), 1975.

Mundel, Marvin E. *Motion and Time Study: Principles and Practice.* 4th ed. Englewood Cliffs, N.J.: Prentice Hall, 1970.

Patchen, Martin. *Participation, Achievement and Envolvement on the Job.* Englewood Cliffs, N.J.: Prentice Hall, 1969.

JOB DESCRIPTIONS

Berenson, Conrad. *Job Descriptions: How to Write and Use Them.* Swarthmore, PA.: Arthur Croft, 1968.

Bowey, Angela. *Job and Pay Comparisons.* Washington: International Publications Service, 1974.

Cooper, Robert. *Job Motivation and Job Design.* Washington: International Publications Service, 1975.

Linenberger, O. James. "The Police Chief from Another Perspective—A Notable Job Description." *Police Chief.* XXXIX:6 (June, 1972), 22-24.

Speck, Dale H. "Los Angeles Has a Plan for the Police Profession." *Journal of California Law Enforcement.* V (January, 1971), 106-111.

JOB SATISFACTION

Allen, G.R. "Sources of Job Satisfaction and Dissatisfaction." *Banking.* 60 (December, 1967).

Argyle, Michael. *The Social Psychology of Work.* Baltimore: Penguin, 1972.

Armstrong, Thomas B. "Job Content and Context Factors Related to Satisfaction for Different Occupational Levels." *Journal of Applied Psychology.* 55 (February, 1971), 57-65.

Beer, Michael. "Organizational Size and Job Satisfaction." *Academy of Management Journal.* 7 (March, 1964), 34-44.

Blai, Boris, Jr. "A Job Satisfaction Predictor." *Personnel Journal.* 42 (October, 1963) 453-456.

Dunnette, Marvin D., John P. Campbell and Milton D. Hakel. "Factors Contributing to Job Satisfaction and Job Dissatisfaction in Six Occupational Groups." *Organizational Behavior and Human Performance.* 2 (May, 1967), 143-174.

Ewen, Robert B. "Some Determinants of Job Satisfaction: A Study of the Generality of Herzberg's Theory." *Journal of Applied Psychology.* 48 (June, 1964), 161-163.

Glasgow, E.H. et al. "Arrest Performance Among Patrolmen in Relation to Job Satisfaction and Personal Variables." *Police Chief.* XL:4 (April, 1973), 28-34.

Greenblatt, Alan. "Maximizing Productivity Through Job Enrichment." *Personnel* (March-April, 1973), 31-40.

Handyside, John D. "Satisfactions and Aspirations." *Occupational Psychology.* 35 (October, 1961), 213-244.

Hulin, Charles L. "A Linear Model of Job Satisfaction." *Journal of Applied Psychology.* 49 (June, 1965), 209-216.

Hulin, Charles L. "Sex Differences in Job Satisfaction." *Journal of Applied Psychology.* 48 (February, 1964), 88-92.

Ivancevich, J.M. and J.H. Donnelly. "Job Satisfaction Research: A Management Guide for Practitioners." *Personnel Journal.* 47 (March, 1968), 172-177.

Job Enrichment. N.Y.: AMA, 1974.

Kahn, R.L. "Productivity and Job Satisfaction." *Personnel Psychology.* 13:3 (1960), 275-278.

Katzell, Ramond A., Richard S. Barrett and Treadway, C. Parker. "Job Satisfaction, Job Performance and Situational Characteristics." *Journal of Applied Psychology.* 45 (April, 1961), 65-72.

King-Taylor, L. *Not for Bread Alone: An Appreciation of Job Enrichment.* N.Y.: Beekman, 1973.

Lahiri, Dilip K. and Sujesh Srivastva. "Determinants of Job Satisfaction in Middle-Management Personnel." *Journal of Applied Psychology.* 51 (June, 1967), 254-265.

Lawler, Edward E. and Lyxan Porter. "The Effect of Performance on Job Satisfaction." *Industrial Relations.* 7:11 1967 20-27.

Morse Fafcy. *Satisfactions in the White-Collar Job.* Ann Anbor: Institute for Social Research, University of Michigan, 1953.

Morse, Nancy and Robert S. Weiss. "The Function and Meaning of Work and the Job" *American Sociological Review* 20 (1955), 191-198.

Myers, M. Scott. *Every Employee a Manager: More Meaningful Work Through Job Enrichment.* N.Y.: McGraw-Hill, 1970.

Patchen, M. "Absence and Employee Feelings About Fair Treatment." *Personnel Psychology.* 13:3 (1960), 349-360.

Porter, Lyman W. "Job Attitudes in Management: Perceived Deficiencies in Need Fulfillment as a Function of Job Level." *Journal of Applied Psychology.* 46 (December, 1962), 375-384.

Porter, Lyman W. and Vance F. Mitchell. "Comparative Study of Need Satisfactions in Military and Business Hierarchies." *Journal of Applied Psychology.* 51 (April, 1967), 139-144.

Reiss, A.J., Jr. *Career Orientations, Job Satisfaction and the Assessment of Law Enforcement Problems by Police Officers.* Washington: GPO, 1967.

Ross, I.C. and A. Zander. "Need Satisfactions and Employee Turnover." *Personnel Psychology.* 10:3 (1957), 327-328.

Slocum, John W., Jr. and Michael J. Misshauk. "Job Satisfaction and Productivity." *Personnel Administration.* 33 (March-April, 1970), 52-58.

Slocum, John W.R. and Paul M. Topichak. "A Cross Cultural Study of Need Satisfaction and Importance for Operative Employees." *Personnel Psychology.* 24 (Autumn, 1971), 435-445.

Slocum, John W.R. and Paul M. Topichak. "Do Cultural Differences Affect Job Satisfaction?" *Journal of Applied Psychology.* 56 (April, 1972), 177-178.

Troxell, J.P. "Elements in Job Satisfaction." *Personnel.* 31 (1954).

Wernimont, Paul F. "Intrinsic and Extrinsic Factors in Job Satisfaction." *Journal of Applied Psychology.* 50 (February, 1966), 41-50.

Yorks, Lyle. *A Radical Approach to Job Enrichment.* N.Y.: AMA, 1976.

LABOR RELATIONS

Labor Relations—General

Advisory Commission on Intergovernmental Relations. *Labor-Management Policies for State and Local Government—A Commission Report.* Washington: GPO, 1969.

Anderson, Arvid. "Labor Relations to the Public Service." *Wisconsin Law Review* (July, 1961), 601-635.

Anderson, Arvid and Hugh D. Jascourt. *Trends in Public Sector Labor Relations: An Information and Reference Guide for the Future.* Chicago: International Personnel Management, 1975.

Bowers, Mollie H. *Labor Relations in the Public Safety Services.* Chicago: International Personnel Management, n/d.

Bowers, M.H. "Police Administrators and the Labor Relations Process." *Police Chief.* 42:1 (1975), 52-59.

Guidelines and Papers from the National Symposium on Police Labor Relations, June 9-12, 1974. Gaithersburg, MD.: International Association of Chiefs of Police, 1974.

Roberts, Harold S. *Labor-Management Relations in the Public Service.* Honolulu: University Press of Hawaii, 1970.

Collective Bargaining and Arbitration

Anderson, Howard J., ed. *Role of the Neutral in Public Employee Disputes.* Washington: Bureau of National Affairs, 1972.

Aussieker, M.W. *Police Collective Bargaining.* Chicago: Public Personnel Association, 1969.

Baer, Walter E. *Labor Arbitration Guide.* Homewood, IL.: Dow Jones-Irwin, 1974.

Burpo, John H. "Improving Police Agency and Employee Performance Through Collective Bargaining." *Police Chief.* XLI:2 (February, 1974), 36-38.

Colosi, Thomas R. and Steven B. Rynecki. *Federal Legislation for Public Sector Collective Bargaining.* Chicago: American Arbitration Association and International Personnel Management Association, 1975.

Cook, Alice. "Public Employee Bargaining in New York City." *Industrial Relations.* 9:3 (May, 1970).

Devyer, F.T. *Arbitration: Its Differences and Draw-backs.* Beaverton, OR.: International School Book Service, 1964.

Edwards, H.T. "The Emerging Duty to Bargain in the Public Sector." *Michigan Law Review.* 71:5 (1973), 885-934.

Fueille, Peter. *Final Offer Arbitration.* Chicago: International Personnel Management, 1975.

Gould, William. "Public Employment: Mediation, Fact Finding and Arbitration." *American Bar Association Journal.* (September, 1969).

Hallem, T.A. et al. "Project Collective Bargaining and Politics in Public Employment." *UCLA Law Review.* 19:6 (1972), 887-1051.

Heisel, W.D. and J.D. Hallihan. *Questions and Answers on Public Employee Negotiations.* Chicago: Public Personnel Association, 1967.

Levi, M.A. *Conflict and Collusion—Police Collective Bargaining.* Washington: NCJRS (Microfiche), 1974.

An examination of the recent evolution of police collective bargaining in the cities of New York, Detroit, and Atlanta through the political, social, and behavioral context in which police labor negotiations take place.

McKelvey, Jean T. "Factfinding in Public Employment Disputes: Promise or Illusion?" *Industrial and Labor Relations Review* (July, 1966).

Maddox, Charles W. *Collective Bargaining in Law Enforcement.* Springfield, IL.: C.C. Thomas, 1975.

Moloney, N.C. "How the State's New Labor Negotiation Legislation Will Affect the Police Labor Scene." *Washington Law Enforcement Journal.* 4:2 (1974), 14-15, 57, 59.

More, Harry W., Jr. "The Era of Police Collective Bargaining." *Law and Order.* 17:6 (June, 1969), 103.

Moskow, Michael H. et al. *Collective Bargaining in Public Employment.* N.Y.: Random, 1970.

Neel, Steven M. "Collective Bargaining: A Problem for the Civil Service System." *Police Chief.* 38:4 (April, 1971), 72-77.

Olmos, Ralph A. "A New Approach to Collective Bargaining for Police Unions." *Police Chief.* XLI:2 (February, 1974), 28-30.

Olmos, Ralph and Thomas Savage. "Some Problems in Preparing and Conducting Contract Negotiations." *Law and Order.* 23:2 (February, 1975), 58-59.

Prasow, Paul and Edward Peters. *Labor Arbitration and Collective Bargaining.* N.Y.: McGraw, 1970.

Shaw, L.C. and T. Clark, Jr. "The Practical Differences Between Public and Private Sector Collective Bargaining." *UCLA Law Review.* 19:6 (1972), 867-886.

Trotta, Maurice. *Arbitration of Labor Management Disputes: A Reference Guide.* N.Y.: American Management, 1974.

Warner, Kenneth O. and Mary L. Hennessy. *Public Management at the Bargaining Table.* Chicago: Public Personnel Association, 1967.

Wehringer, Cameron K. *Arbitration: Precepts and Principles.* Dobbs Ferry, N.Y.: Oceana, 1969.

Welsh, Lawrence. "Pay Negotiations in the Police Service." *Police Journal.* [Eng.] (April-June, 1972), 161-164.

Winckoski, Bernard G. "The Name of the Game: Collective Bargaining." *Police Chief.* XXXVI:12 (December, 1969), 36-39.

Wurf, Jerry. "The Case Against Compulsory Arbitration." *The Public Employee.* XXXI:3 (March, 1966).

Police Membership in Teamsters

Dobbs, Farrell. *Teamster Politics.* N.Y.: Monad, 1975.

Dobbs, Farrell. *Teamster Power.* new ed. N.Y.: Monad, 1973.

"Now Policemen Are Joining Teamsters." *U.S. News and World Report* (January 16, 1967), 86.

"Teamsters 'Harness Policemen.'" *Texas Lawman.* 35 (March, 1967), 6-7.

Police Strikes

Anderson, Arvid. "Strikes and Impasse Resolution in Public Employment." *Michigan Law Review* (March, 1969).

"Another Headache for Cities: Strikes by Public Workers." *U.S. News and World Report* (August 1, 1966), 78-79.

Bilik, Al. "Toward Public Sector Equality, Extending the Strike Privilege." *Labor Law Journal* (August, 1969), 522-545.

Bopp, William J. "The Boston Police Strike of 1919." *Police.* 16:11 (July, 1972), 54-58.

Burpo, H.J. "The Legal and Management Aspects of Police Strikes." *Public Safety Labor Reporter* (November, 1968).

Burton, John and Charles Krider. "The Role and Consequences of Strikes by Public Employees." *Yale Law Journal* (January, 1970).

"Chicago Without Police? Really?" *Chicago Police Star.* 8 (August, 1967).

"City Without Cops." *Police World.* 14 (Winter, 1969).
Montreal police strike.

Clark, Gerald. "What Happens When the Police Strike." *The New York Times Magazine* (November 16, 1969), 45, 176-196.

"Cop-Out in New York." *Newsweek.* 77 (January 25, 1971).

Harvey, Paul. "Policeman Must Not Strike." *FBI Law Enforcement Bulletin.* 36:1 (January, 1967), 11-12.

Lev, Edward R. "Strikes by Government Employees: Problems and Solutions." *Journal of the American Bar Association* (August, 1971), 771-777.

Lyons, Richard L. "The Boston Police Strike of 1919." *The New England Quarterly.* 20:2 (June, 1947), 147-168.

Nevling, Floyd M. "The Police Pay Problem: A Solution." *Law and Order.* 17:10 (October, 1969), 18-23.

"New York: The Cops Return." *Newsweek.* 77 (February 1, 1971).

Nichols, John F. "Management and Legal Aspects of Police Strikes." *Police Chief.* XXXIX:12 (December, 1972), 38-43.

Reynolds, Gerald W. and Anthony Judge. *The Night the Police Went on Strike.* London: Weidenfield, 1968.

Russell, Francis. *City in Terror: 1919—The Boston Police Strike.* N.Y.: Viking, 1975.

Russell, Francis. "The Strike That Made A President." *American Heritage.* 14:6 (October, 1963).
The 1919 police strike in Boston and the politics involved in this crisis situation.

Saso, Carmen D. *Coping with Public Employee Strikes.* Chicago: Public Personnel Association, 1970.

Sheehan, Robert. "Lest We Forget." *Police.* 4:2 (November-December, 1959), 8-14.
The 1919 Boston police strike.

Wardwoll, William. "Strike." *Police.* [Eng.] (November, 1969).
A two-page article on the 1969 Montreal police strike.

White, Sheila. "Work Stoppages of Government Employees." *Monthly Labor Review.* 92:12 (December, 1969), 30.

Police Unions

Bopp, William J., ed. *The Police Rebellion: A Quest for Blue Power.* Springfield, IL.: C.C. Thomas, 1971.

Bowers, Mollie H. "The Dilemma of Impasse Procedures in the Public Safety Services." *Police Chief.* XLI:2 (February, 1974), 32-34.

Bowron, Fletcher. "Police Unions." *U.S. Municipal News.* 13 (April 1, 1946).

Brostron, Curtis. "Police Employee Organizations." *Police Chief.* XXXVI:12 (December, 1969), 6-9.

Burpo, John H. *The Police Labor Movement, Problems and Perspectives.* Springfield, IL.: C.C. Thomas, 1971.

Coon, Thomas F. "The Police Uniform Should Not be a Unionsuit." *Police.* 6:6 (July-August, 1962), 62.

"Cops and Unions, Jackson, Mississippi." *Newsweek.* 24 (July 3, 1944).

"Court Decides Against Police Union." *Public Management.* 3 (March, 1946), 89-90.

Dahlstrom, Donald L. "Police Unionism: An Administrator's Alternative." *Police.* 15:4 (March-April, 1971), 45-46.

Denman, Robert E. "Unionization of Police." *Police Chief.* XXXVL:12 (December, 1969), 44-50.

Gifford, James P. "Professionalizing Police Labor Relations: The New York City Police Department's Response to Unionization." *Journal of Police Science and Administration.* 2:1 (March, 1974), 94-106.

Halphern, Stephen C. "Do Police Unions Have Any Effect on Police Department Operations?" *Police Chief.* XLI:2 (February, 1974).

Halphern, Stephen C. *Police-Association and Department Leaders: The Politics of Cooperation.* Farnborough: D.C. Heath, 1974.

Halphern, S.C. "Police Employee Organizations and Accountability Procedures in Three Cities: Some Reflections on Police Policy-Making." *Law Society Review.* 8:4 (1974), 561-582.

Heustis, Carl E. "Police Unions." *Journal of Criminal Law, Criminology and Police Science.* 48:6 (March-April, 1958), 643-646.

Hollady, Roy E. "Police Unions—Programs of Negation." *Police.* 6:2 (November-December, 1961), 63-69.

Hutchinson, Kay B. and Hervey A. Juris. "The Legal Status of Municipal Police Employee Organizations." *Industrial and Labor Relations Review* (April, 1970).

Igleburger, Robert M. and John E. Angell. "Dealing With Police Unions." *Police Chief.* XXXVII:5 (May, 1971), 50-55.

Juris, Hervey A. "The Implications of Police Unionism." *Law and Society Review* (November, 1971), 231-245.

Juris, Hervey A. and Peter Feuille. *Impact of Police Unions—A Summary Statement.* Washington: NCJRS, 1974.

Juris, Hervey and Peter Feuille. *Police Unionism.* Lexington, MA.: Lexington Books, 1973.

Juris, Hervey A. and Kay B. Hutchison. "The Legal Status of Municipal Police Employee Organizations." *Industrial and Labor Relations Review* (April, 1970), 352-363.

Kelsey, John. "Association Becomes Trade Union for 140,000 Police." *Current Municipal Problems.* 12:2 (1970), 184-185.

Kooken, D.L. and L.D. Ayres. "Police Unions and the Public Safety." *Annals.* 291 (January, 1954), 152-158.

Kronholm, William C. "Blue Power: The Threat of the Militant Policeman." *Journal of Criminal Law, Criminology and Police Science* (June, 1972), 294-299.

Levi, M.A. *And the Beat Goes On—Patrolmen's Unionism in New York City.* Washington: NCJRS (Microfiche), 1974).
A history of the Patrolmen's Benevolent Association's (PBA) transformation from a strong line organization to a de facto union.

Levine, Marvin J. *Public Manager's Guide to Union Representation.* Chicago: International Personnel Management, 1975.

Loewenberg, J. "Labor Relations for Policemen and Firefighters." *Monthly Labor Review* (May, 1968).

More, Harry W., Jr. "A Law Enforcement Association as a Pressure Group." *Police* (May-June, 1967).

Murray, E.P. "Should the Police Unionize?" *Nation.* 188 (June, 1959), 530-533.

Olmos, Ralph A. "Some Effects of Police Unionism on Discipline." *Police Chief* (April, 1974), 24, 25, 26, 28.

"P.B.A.'s Role in Police Union." *The Chief* November 12, 1969.

"Police Employee Organizations." *Police Chief.* XXXVI:12 (December, 1969), 51-55.

"Police Restricted as to Union Membership." *National Municipal Review* (May, 1946), 250-251.

"Police Unions are a Threat to Needed Discipline." *Saturday Evening Post.* 234:10 (June 3, 1961).

"Police Unions in 28 Cities, Officials of Four Cities Prohibit Unions." *Public Management.* 5 (May, 1944), 139-141.

Pomerleau, Donald D. "The Eleventh Hour!" *Police Chief.* XXXVI:12 (December, 1969), 40-42.

Ruchelman, L. *Who Rules the Police.* N.Y.: New York University Press, 1973.
Impact of police political activism on urban political environments, with particular emphasis from the perspective of civil accountability and control.

Schweppe, Emma. *The Firemen's and Patrolmen's Union in the City of New York.* N.Y.: King's Crown, 1948.

Showalter, Ralph and Richard F. Dart. *Potentials for Police Union Management Relations in American Towns—A Guide for Police Administrators and Police Union Leaders.* Hartford, CT.: Social Development Corporation, 1976.

Smith, Joseph D. "Police Unions: An Historical Perspective of Causes and Organizations." *Police Chief.* XLII:11 (November, 1975), 24-28.

Smith, Russell A. "State and Labor Advisory Reports on Public Employment Labor Legislation: A Comparative Analysis." *Michigan Law Review* (March, 1969), 891-918.

"Three Cities Oppose Police Affiliation with Labor Unions." *Public Management.* 4 (April, 1946), 112-114.

"A Union of Policemen?" *American Labor* (September, 1969), 53-59.

Walsh, Robert E. *Sorry, No Government Today, Unions vs. City Hall.* Boston: Beacon, 1970.

Wahlen, Howard. "Police Representation: Good or Bad?" *Law and Order.* 18:12 (December, 1970), 40-41.

Wellington, Harry and Ralph Winter. *The Unions and the Cities.* Washington: Brookings Institution, 1971.

LATERAL ENTRY

Advisory Commission on Intergovernmental Relations (ACIR). *Transferability of Public Employee Retirement Credits Among Units of Government, A Commission Report.* Washington: GPO, 1963.

Calvert, G.N. *Portable Police Pensions—Improving Inter-Agency Transfers.* Washington: GPO, 1971.
Survey of existing pension systems and suggestions for funding and operation of alternate portable pension plans.

Fine, Glen E. and Richard A. Baratta. *Lateral Entry for California Law Enforcement.* Sacramento: The Commission on Peace Officers Standards and Training, 1969.

Hewitt, William H. "Police Personnel Administration: Lateral Entry." *Police.* 15:3 (January-February, 1971), 13-19; (March-April, 1971), 33-44; (May-June, 1971), 55-64.

Marin, Glenn A. "Lateral Transfer in the Police Service." *Police Chief.* XXXV:11 (November, 1968), 26-30.

Scott, James C. *An Analysis of Lateral Entry as a Means of Obtaining Municipal Police Supervisors and Administrators in the United States.* Pullman: Washington State University, 1965.

Smith, Leroy A. "Lateral Entry: An Inside Job." *Police Chief.* 38:8 (August, 1971), 52-55.

Tafoya, William L. "Lateral Entry: A Management Perspective." *Police Chief* (April, 1974), 60-62.

Wolk, Sam N. *Lateral Entry into the Public Service.* Washington: U.S. Civil Service Commission, 1966.

MANAGEMENT DEVELOPMENT

Aaron, Thomas J. "The Capable Police Executive: Key to Dynamic Police Administration." *Police.* 10:1 (September-October, 1964), 50-51.

Albrook, R.C. "How to Spot Executives Early." *Fortune.* 78:2 (July, 1968), 106-111.

Appley, Lawrence A. *Formula for Success.* N.Y. AMA, 1974.

Basile, Joseph. *The Cultural Development of Managers, Executives and Professionals.* Baltimore: Helicon, 1968.

Bowen, Charles P. "Let's Put Realism into Management Development." *Harvard Business Review* (July-August, 1973).

Cady, Edwin Laird. *Developing Executive Capacity.* Englewood Cliffs, N.J.: Prentice Hall, 1958.

Capune, W.G. "Police Management Development: An Assessment." *International Criminal Police Review.* 28 (1973), 293-297.

Desatnick, Robert L. *A Concise Guide to Management Development.* N.Y.: AMA, 1970.

"Five Corporate Directors Tell What They Look for in a Chief Executive." *Business Management* (May, 1966).

Hanneman, W.C. and T.W. Harrell. "Changing Characteristics of Corporate Presidents." *Personnel* (September, 1964).

Lopez, Felix M. *The Making of a Manager.* N.Y.: AMA, 1970.

Markwell, D.S. and T.J. Roberts. *Organization of Management Development Programmes.* N.Y.: Beekman, 1969.

Newman, Charles L. and Barbara R. Price. "Police Executive Development: An Educational Program at the Pennsylvania State University." *Police Chief* (April, 1974), 74-77.

Roberts, Albert R. "An Overview of Staff Development and Training in Law Enforcement." *Public Personnel Review.* 31 (July, 1970), 166-168.

Silber, Mark S. and Sherman V. Clayton. *Managerial Performance and Promotability.* N.Y.: AMA, 1974.

Taylor, Charles R. "Executive Development for Police (in Illinois)." *FBI Law Enforcement Bulletin.* 39:8 (August, 1970), 16, 18, 20.

Torrington, Derek P. and David F. Sutton. *Handbook of Management Development.* N.Y.: Beekman, 1973.

Uris, Auren. *Developing Your Executive Skills.* N.Y.: McGraw-Hill, 1955.

Wilson, Robert C. "Spotting Managerial Ability." *Personnel.* 48 (May-June, 1971), 60-65.

York, Orrell A. "Executive Development for Police (in New York)." *FBI Law Enforcement Bulletin.* 39:8 (August, 1970), 17, 19.

MOONLIGHTING

Leahy, Raymond A. "Right of Municipality to Prohibit Outside Employment by Police Officers." *New Jersey Municipality.* 33 (February, 1956), 27-28.

Mitchell, Ewan. "Is Moonlighting Legal?" *Security and Protection* (May, 1975), 19-21, 22.

Outwood, M. "Moonlighting and the Police Service." *Police Review.* 83 (1975), 680-681, 695.

Perrella, Vera C. "Moonlighters: Their Motivations and Characteristics." *Monthly Labor Review.* 93 (August, 1970), 57-64.

PENSIONS

Altes, Murray. "Pensions vs. Inflation." *Police Chief.* XXXIII:9 (September, 1966), 15-17.

Burns, Evelyn. *Social Security and Public Policy.* N.Y.: McGraw-Hill, 1956.

Calvert, G.N. *Portable Police Pensions—Improving Interagency Transfers.* Washington: GPO, 1971.

Ferber, Charles S. "Social Security and the Police Officer." *Law and Order.* 16:10 (October, 1968), 104-105.

Kaplan, Robert S. *Financial Crisis in the Social Security System.* Washington: American Enterprise, 1976.

Melown, J.J. and E.T. Allen. *Pension Planning.* rev. ed. Homewood, IL.: Down Jones-Irwin, 1972.

Meyers, Robert J. *Social Security.* Homewood, IL.: Irwin, 1975.

Raphael, Marios. *Pensions and Public Servants.* Atlantic Highlands, N.J.: Humanities, 1964.

Rhodes, Gerald. *Public Sector Pensions.* Toronto: University of Toronto Press, 1965.

Rubin, H. *Pensions and Employee Mobility in the Public Service.* Millwood, N.Y.: Kraus, 1965 (repr.).

Sciacca, Carl. *How to Get the Most Out of Your Social Security and Monthly Benefits.* Hicksville, N.Y.: Exposition, 1974.

Shore, Warren. *Social Security: The Fraud in Your Future.* N.Y.: Macmillan, 1975.

Shreve, Charles H. "Social Security for Peace Officers." *San Francisco Police and Peace Officer Journal.* 23 (1961).

PROBATIONARY PERIOD

Blumer, Alice and Earl Housenfluck. "Evaluating Recruit Performance: Putting It All Together During Basic Training." *Police Chief.* XLI:3 (March, 1974), 69-73.

LaVallee, Albert. *A Consideration of the Police Probationary Period as Part of the Selection Procedure."* Unpub. Master's thesis. University of Southern California, 1954.

Mulholland, F.A. *New Mexico—Study of Police Agency Retention of Police Academy Graduates—Summary.* Washington: NCJRS (Microfiche), 1974.

Murray, James M. "Reviewing Probationary Officers." *Police Chief.* XXXVII:6 (June, 1971), 42-43.

Tubbs, Billie R. "The Probationary Period as a Means of Raising Professional Standards." *Journal of California Law Enforcement* (January, 1968), 158-163.

PROMOTIONS

Durrer, William L. "Who Is Promotable?" *Police Chief.* XXXVII:6 (June, 1970), 30-36.

Epstein, S. and R.S. Laymon. *Guidelines for Police Performance Appraisal, Promotion and Placement Procedures.* Springfield, VA.: NTIS, 1973.

Harrison, Leonard. "How to Take a Test—And Get Promoted." *Law and Order.* 14:2 (February, 1966), 8-9, 42-43, 46.

Kelly, Michael J. *Police Chief Selection—A Handbook for*

Local Government. Washington: Police Foundation, 1976.

Kohlan, Richard G. "Police Promotional Procedure in Fifteen Jurisdictions." *Public Personnel Management*. 2:1 (June-July, 1973).

Koverman, Robert B. "Promotions: A Small Department Responds to the Problem of Career Advancement." *Police Chief*. XLII:12 (December, 1975), 16, 72.

Martin, Desmond D. and William J. Hearney. "Can We Strengthen the Police Promotional System: A Challenge to Modern Police Administration." *Police Chief*. XLI:5 (May, 1974), 38-40.

"Police Management, Recruiting Methods." *FBI Law Enforcement Bulletin*. 35:12 (December, 1966), 11-13.

"Police Management, Selection Procedures." *FBI Law Enforcement Bulletin*. 36:1 (January, 1967), 25-28.

Sands, Edith. *How to Select Executive Personnel*. N.Y.: Reinhold, 1963.

VanKirk, Marvin L. "Selection of Sargeants." *FBI Law Enforcement Bulletin* (March, 1975), 12-15.

Walker, James W. "Who Really are the Promotables?" *Personnel Journal*. 49 (February, 1970), 123-127.

RATING SYSTEMS

Balch, David E. "Performance Rating Systems—Suggestions for the Police." *Journal of Police Science and Administration*. 2:1 (March, 1974), 40-49.

Barrett, Richard S. *Performance Rating*. Chicago: Science Research Associates, 1966.

Beck, George N. "Municipal Police Performance Rating." *Journal of Criminal Law, Criminology, and Police Science*. 51 (January-February, 1961), 567.

Beveridge, W.E. *Interview in Staff Apprisal*. N.Y.: International Publications Service, 1975.

Boyd, J.E. "Assessing a Policeman's Performance." *Canadian Police Chief*. 64:1 (1975), 8-10.

Cherry, Robert. "Performance Review: A Note on Failure." *Personnel Journal*. 49 (May, 1970), 398-403.

Clarke, Victor J. and Hrand Saxenian. "Objectivity in Performance Evaluation." *Police*. 10:2 (November-December, 1965), 33-36.

Dudycha, George J. "Rating and Testing Policemen." *Police*. 1:1. (September-October, 1956), 37-49.

Epstein, Sidney and Richard S. Laymon. *Guidelines for Police Performance Appraisal, Promotion and Placement Procedures*. Washington: NCJRS, 1973.

International Association of Chiefs of Police. *Guide to Performance Evaluation and Promotional Potential Rating*. Gaithersburg, MD.: IACP, n/d.

Kellogg, Marion S. *What to Do About Performance Appraisal*. Rev. ed. N.Y.: AMA, 1975.

Knowles, Lyle and Joseph C. DeLadurantey. "Performance Evaluation." *Journal of Police Science and Administration*. 2:1 (March, 1974), 28-33.

Kuykendall, Jack L. and Orville M. Butts. "Appraisal of Employee Performance." *Journal of California Law Enforcement* (October, 1973), 98-106.

Landy, F.J. *Police Personnel Appraisal—A Report on Phase 1*. Springfield, VA.: NTIS, 1973.
Determination of existing state of performance appraisal and the development of patrolman job performance evaluation scales.

Olson, B.T. *Designing a Police Performance Evaluation Form—An Experiment in Organizational Involvement*. N.Y.: College Notes and Texts, 1969.

Prince, L.N.W. "There's a Loss of Faith in Staff Appraisal Schemes." *Police Review*. [Eng.] (June 11), 1976. 752-753.

Randell, G.A. *Staff Appraisal*. N.Y.: International Publications Service, 1975.

Robinson, David. "Issues in Job Performance Evaluation." *Police*. 15:3 (January-February, 1971), 41-46.

Valentine, Raymond F. "Appraisal Interviewing: Flexibility is the Key." *Supervisory Management* (November, 1965).

Walsh, Jude T. "Performance Ratings for Police Supervisors." *Police Chief* (April, 1974), 51-53.

Whisler, T.L. and S.F. Harper. *Performance Appraisal: Research and Practice*. N.Y.: Holt, Rinehart and Winston, 1962.

Wraith, Ronald. *Appraisal for Staff Development: A Public Sector Study*. Dublin: Royal Institute of Public Administration, 1975.

RECRUITMENT

Boyd, Ellsworth. "Recruiting Program and $50 Award." *Law and Order*. 14:2 (February, 1966), 66-67, 76.

Carroll, Joseph T. "Recruiting and Training of Police Personnel." *FBI Law Enforcement Bulletin* (December, 1964).

Coon, Thomas F. "Police Residence Requirements—A Calm Review." *Police*. 16:11 (July, 1972), 30-31.

Coss, Frank. *Recruitment Advertising*. N.Y.: AMA, 1968.

Davis, Ritchie T. "Mobile Recruitment Facility." *FBI Law Enforcement Bulletin* (March, 1976), 26-28.
Utilization of a bus for recruitment services in the Michigan State Police.

Dillman, Everett G. "Analyzing Police Recruitment and Retention Problems." *Police*. 8:5 (May-June, 1964), 22-26.

Goodin, Carl V. "Effective Staffing." *Police Chief*. XL:2 (February, 1973), 24-25.

Halladay, Everett F. "Let the Recruits Recruit." *Law and Order*. 17:10 (October, 1969), 113-114.

Hamilton, Lander C. and Donald Bimstein. "Attracting College Graduates to Police Departments." *Police Chief*. XXXIX:8 (August, 1972), 40-43.

Hawk, Roger H. *The Recruitment Function*. N.Y.: AMA, 1967.

Huddleston, Bert. "Streamlined Recruitment." *Law and Order.* 16:4 (April, 1968), 73-74.

Kelly, J.A.F. and R.C. Barnum. "Operation: Police Manpower." *Police Chief.* XXXVI:7 (July, 1969), 45-52.
Activities of Department of Defense Training Program to provide trained police recruits from military personnel.

Lawder, Lee E. "From One War into Another." *Law and Order.* 18:6 (June, 1970), 46-48, 50.

"Municipal Employee Residency Requirements and Equal Protection." *Yale Law Journal.* 84:8 (1975), 1684-1704.

Oliver, William E. "Join Us! A Recruiting Program That Works." *Police Chief.* 37:9 (October, 1970), 32, 34-35.

Perry, Jack. "A New Concept in Police Recruiting." *Police Chief.* XXXVI:6 (June, 1969), 42.

Petrie, Harry P. and Sid Panush. "Making a Good Recruiting Program Better." *Public Personnel Review* (July, 1958).

"Police Management Standards for Recruitment." *FBI Law Enforcement Bulletin.* 35:10 (October, 1966), 15-19.

Race, Joseph H. "A Recruitment Aid." *Law and Order.* 17:12 (December, 1969), 107-108.

Shepard, George H. "Are We Aiming Too Low in Recruiting?" *Police Chief.* 34:1 (January, 1967), 20, 22-26.

Skinner, Leonard E. "Recruitin the College Man." *Police Chief.* 34:2 (February, 1967), 38-46.

Wechter, Harry L. "Case History: Problem—Solution." *Law and Order.* 15:3 (March, 1967), 70-73.

Wright, L. *Me . . . A Cop—The Evaluation Report of a Law Enforcement Recruitment Project.* Washington: NCJRS (Microfiche), 1974.

RETIREMENT

Aaron, Thomas J. "Your Own Security Contracting Business: Retirement or Second Career Opportunity." *Law and Order.* 18:12 (December, 1970), 56, 58-64.

Bleakney, Thomas. *Retirement Systems for Public Employees.* Homewood, IL.: Irwin, 1972.

Bucklay, Joseph C. *Retirement Handbook.* 4th ed. N.Y.: Harper & Row, 1971.

Clark, Bruce C. "The Retirement Talent Drain." *Army.* 20 (August, 1970), 34-37.

Cooley, Leland F. and Lee M. Cooley. *How to Avoid the Retirement Track.* N.Y.: Nash, 1972.

Corlett, Shelby. *Retirement Is What You Make It.* Anderson, IN.: Warner, 1973.

Jackson, James F., III. "A Word About Retirement Programs." *Law and Order.* 16:2 (February, 1968), 16-18.

Margolius, Sidney. *Your Personal Guide to Successful Retirement.* N.Y.: Random House, 1969.

Merrell, Donald L. "Peace Officers' Expectations of Retirement Programs." *Journal of California Law Enforcement* (July, 1973), 40-45.

Munnich, J.M. *Adjustment to Retirement.* Beaverton, OR.: International School Book Service, 1970.

"Police Retirement at Sixty Years of Age." *Police News.* 49 (July, 1970), 2-3, 5-6.

Sunshine, John. *How to Enjoy Your Retirement.* N.Y.: AMA, 1974.

SELECTION

Arther, Richard O. "Why Does Police Work Attract So Many Failures?" *Law and Order.* 12:9 (September, 1964), 62-69.

Barth, Ray. "In His Father's Footsteps." *Law and Order.* 17:6 (June, 1969).
Father and son in police work.

Beyer, William C. and Helen C. Toerring. "The Policeman's Hire." *Annals* (November, 1929), 135-146.

Birtcher, B.L. *Guide for Recruitment and Selection of Police Personnel.* Washington: NCJRS (Microfiche), 1972.

Blum, R.H. *Police Selection.* Springfield, IL.: C.C. Thomas, 1964.

Blum, Richard H., William L. Goggin, and Earl Whitmore. "A Study of Deputy Sheriff Selection Procedures." *Police.* 6:2 (November-December, 1961), 59-62.

Blum, Richard H. et al. "A Further Study of Deputy Sheriff Selection Procedures." *Police.* 6:4 (March-April, 1962), 77-79.

Carter, D.M. "Officer Selection in the British Army." *Police Journal.* [Eng.] (April-June, 1973), 182-186.

Champagne, Anthony M. and Beatriz Champagne. "An Analysis of an Alternative to the Present Method of Police Selection: Conscription of Police in Argentina." *Police* (March, 1972).

Chiaramonte, Robert M. "Applicant Screening." *Police Chief.* XLI:7 (July, 1974), 49-50.

Chicago Police Department. *Psychological Assessment of Patrolman Qualifications in Relation to Field Performance.* Springfield, VA.: NTIS, 1968.
Research to develop effective procedures and establish general standards for patrolman selection.

Cohen, B. *Prior Arrest Record and Police Performance—Testimony Before the City of New York Commission on Human Rights.* N.Y.: Rand, 1972.
A previous arrest history for a petty crime has virtually no bearing on the later job performance of nearly 2,000 police officers appointed in New York in 1957.

Colavelli, Nick J. and Saul M. Siegel. "A Method of Police Personnel Selection." *Journal of Criminal Law, Criminology and Police Science.* 55:2. 1964, 287-289.

Coppock, Robert W. and Barbara B. Coppock. *How to Recruit and Select Policemen and Firemen.* Chicago: Public Personnel Association, 1958.

Donovan, J.J. *Recruitment and Selection in the Public Service.* Chicago: Public Personnel Association, 1968.

Dubois, P.H. and R. Watson Tabs. "Selection of Patrolmen." *Applied Psychology*. 34:2 (April, 1950), 90-95.

Dunnette, Marvin D. and Stephan J. Motowidlo. *Police Selection and Career Assessment*. Washington: LEAA (November, 1976).

Ferinden, William E., Jr. "Psychological Criteria in the Selection of Police Candidates." *Police*. 13:5 (May-June, 1969), 33-34.

Fox, Harry G. "Nineteen." *Police Chief*. 38:2 (February, 1971), 30, 32.
Philadelphia's lowering of entrance age to 19 years.

Frost, Thomas M. "Selection Methods for Police Recruits." *Journal of Criminal Law, Criminology and Police Science*. 46:1 (May-June, 1955), 135-145.

Gamol, Anne Marie, Norbert S. Slowiskowski, and Chet Doyle. "Detective Selection Gets a New Twist in Chicago." *Public Personnel Review*. 26:1 (1965), 40-43.

Gugas, Chris. "A Scientifically Accurate Method of Personnel Screening." *Police* (November-December, 1961).

Heckman, R.W. and R.W. Groner. *Development of Psychiatric Standards for Police Selection*. Springfield, VA: NTIS, 1972.
Research program aimed at assessing personality characteristics relevant to job performance and determining nationally applicable personality standards.

Houghton, R.A. "Los Angeles Overhauls Its Police Recruitment and Its Basic Training Program." *Police Chief* (August, 1968).

International Association of Chiefs of Police. *Police Personnel Selection Survey*. Washington: IACP, 1971.
Collection of data relating to cities over 50,000.

International Association of Chiefs of Police. *Survey of Selection Methods*. Washington: IACP, 1962.

Kennedy, Stephen P. "New York City Police Stiffen Requirements." *Police*. 5:3 (January-February, 1961), 70.

Kent, Deborah Ann and Terry Eisenberg. "The Selection and Promotion of the Police Officers: A Selected Review of Recent Literature." *Police Chief* (February, 1972).

Kreins, E.S. and E.E. Shev. "Psychiatric Techniques in the Selection and Training of a Police Officer." *Police Chief* (April, 1968).

Lawder, Lee E. and Ernie Alder. "Career Camp Experiment." *Law and Order*. 18:12 (December, 1970), 92-94.

McAllister, John A. "Don't Sacrifice Quality for Quantity." *FBI Law Enforcement Bulletin*. 39:1 (January, 1970), 17-19.

McCreedy, Kenneth R. "Selection Practices and the Police Role." *Police Chief*. XLI:7 (July, 1974), 41-43.

Marsh, Stewart. "Validation of the Selection of Deputy Sheriffs." *Public Personnel Review*. 23 (January, 1962), 41-44.

Martin, Desmond D., William J. Kearney, and George D. Holdefer. "The Decision to Hire: A Comparison of Selection Tools." *Business Perspectives*. 7:3 (Spring, 1971), 11-15.

Matarazzo, Joseph D. et al. "Characteristics of Successful Policemen and Firemen Applicants." *Journal of Applied Psychology*. 48 (April, 1964), 123-133.

Mills, Robert B. "Use of Diagnostic Small Groups in Police Recruit Selection and Training." *Journal of Criminal Law, Criminology and Police Science*. 60:2 (June, 1969), 238-241.

Narrol, Harvey G. and Eugene G. Levitt. "Formal Assessment Procedure in Police Selection." *Psychological Reports*. 12:3 (1963), 691-694.

Newman, J.M. and G.E. Irving. *Hearing and Vision Standards for Public Safety Personnel*. Washington: NCJRS (Microfiche), 1974.

New York Municipal Police Training Council. *New York—Height, Weight and Physical Fitness Standards for Police Officer Candidates, 1974*. rev. ed. Washington: NCJRS (Microfiche), 1974.

The OSS Assessment Staff. *Assessment of Men*. N.Y.: Rinehart, 1948.

Pell, Arthur R. *Recruiting and Selecting Personnel*. N.Y.: Regents, 1969.

Rutherford, James W. "Recruitment Is More Than a Classified Ad." *Law and Order*. 14:3 (March, 1966), 10, 12-14, 16.

Schultz, Don. "Who Are We Putting on Our Streets?" *Law and Order* (February, 1970), 82-84.

Seberhagan, Lance W. et al. *Legal Aspects of Personnel Selection in the Public Service*. Chicago: International Personnel Management, 1973.

Shepard, G.H. "Are We Aiming Too Low in Recruiting?" *Police Chief* (January, 1967).

Skinner, Leonard E. "Recruiting the College Man." *Police Chief* (February, 1967).

Spencer, Gilmore and Robert Nichols. "A Study of Chicago Police Recruits: Validation of Selection Procedures." *Police Chief*. XXXVII:6 (June, 1971), 50-55.

Sterling, James W. "The College Level Entry Requirement: A Real or Imagined Cure-All." *Police Chief*. XLI:8 (August, 1974), 28, 30-31.

Talney, Ronald G. "Police Personnel Procurement." *Police* (March-April, 1968).

Teske, Raymond, Jr. "Contact Lenses: Potential Solution to the Shortage of Qualified Applicants for Positions as Law Enforcement Personnel." *Police*. 15:3 (January-February, 1971), 30-33.

Teske, Raymond, Jr. and Bardin H. Nelson. "Selected Requirements for Law Enforcement Personnel." *Police*. 16:11 (July, 1972), 32-35.

Thweatt, William H. "Improving Police Selection on a Shoestring Budget." *Police Chief*. XXXIX:11 (November, 1972), 60-63.

Wilson, James Q. "What Makes a Better Policeman." *Atlantic.* 223 (March, 1969).

Wyrick, M.E. "Where the Cops Come From." *Police Chief.* 33:10 (1965).

Yoder, Norman. *The Selection and Training of Public Safety Personnel in American Municipalities.* Unpub. Doctoral dissertation. Ohio State University, 1942.

TESTING

Testing—General

Adkins, Dorothy C. *Construction and Analysis of Achievement Tests.* Washington: GPO, 1947.

Presents basic concepts and methods in the development and analysis of achievement tests. Covers test planning, test construction, basic statistical tools, and analysis of test results.

Bimstein, Donald. "Standardized Testing for Police Personnel." *Police Chief.* XXXVI:2 (February, 1969), 44-47.

Brannon, Bernard C. "A Proposed Uniform Law Enforcement Examination Act." *Police.* 4:2 (November-December, 1959), 71-73.

Burton, Alan. "Testing Candidates for Police Dispatcher." *Police Chief* (April, 1974), 63-65.

Byham, William C. and Morton E. Spitzer. *The Law and Personnel Testing.* N.Y.: AMA, 1971.

Eisenberg, Terry and Roger W. Reinke. "The Use of Written Examinations in Selecting Police Officers: Coping With the Dilemma." *Police Chief.* XL:3 (March, 1973), 24-28.

Furcon, J. *Some Questions and Answers About Police Officer Selection Testing.* Chicago: Industrial Relations Center, 1972.

Major results and practical implications of two projects aimed at the identification and validation of more effective written tests for police officer selection.

Gallati, Robert R.J. "Police Personnel Testing Experience of the New York City Police Department." *Police.* 4:5 (May-June, 1960), 76-77; (July-August, 1960), 23-25.

Goldstein, Leo S. "Characteristics of Police Applicants." *Police Chief.* XXXIX:5 (May, 1972), 58-60.

Grady, Bernard E. "IQ Test: The New Castle County Experience." *Police Chief.* XL:2 (February, 1973), 66-67.

Lawshe, Charles H. and M.J. Balma. *Principles of Personnel Testing.* 2d ed. N.Y.: McGraw, 1966.

Marx, G. T. *Application of Some Alternative Measures—Validation of the 1972 Massachusetts Police Selection Exam—Working Paper.* Washington: NCJRS (Microfiche), 1974.

This report discusses the development of a new police selection exam and a proposed method of validating this exam to see that it actually measures job-related abilities.

Monroe, Clark J. "Testing Procedures for the Selection of Personnel." *FBI Law Enforcement Bulletin.* 27:7 (July, 1958), 20-21, inside back cover.

Neumann, Gail et al. "Job-Related Tests and Police Selection Procedures." *Police Chief.* XLI:2 (February, 1974), 43-45, 66.

Newman, James M. et al. *Investigation of a Method for Identification of the High-Risk Police Applicant: An Analysis and Interpretation Based on Available Data.* Berkeley, CA.: Institute for Local Self Government, 1971.

Office of Strategic Services. *Assessment of Men.* N.Y.: Rinehart, 1948.

Parker, L. Craig, and Marvin C. Roth. "The Relationships Between Self-Disclosure, Personality and a Dimension of Job Performance of Policemen." *Journal of Police Science and Administration.* 1:3 (September, 1973), 282-286.

Pollack, Norman C. "Use of Written Tests for Police Officer Selection." *Public Personnel Review.* 25 (April, 1964), 124-128.

Tiemann, H.A., Jr. *Patrol Selection Research—Final Report.* Washington: NCJRS (Microfiche), 1972.

Watson, P. "How to Find a Good Bomb Expert; Methods of British Army Psychiatrists." *Psychology Today* (August, 1974).

Wood, Dorothy. *Test Construction: Development and Interpretation of Achievement Test.* Columbus, OH.: Merrill, 1960.

Assessment Centers

Albrecht, P.A. "Validation of a Multiple Assessment Procedure for Managerial Personnel." *Journal of Applied Psychology.* 43 (1964), 351-359.

Assessment Centers. N.Y.: AMA, 1974.

Bray, D.W. "The Assessment Center Method of Appraising Management Potential''' in J.W. Blood (ed.) *The Personal Job in a Changing World.* N.Y.: AMA, 1964.

Bray, D.W. and D.L. Grant. "The Assessment Center in the Measurement of Potential for Business Management." *Psychological Monographs.* 80 (1966).

Bray, D.W. and J.L. Moses. "Personnel Selection." *Annual Review of Psychology.* 23 (1972), 545-576.

Byham, W.C. "The Assessment Center as an Aid in Management Development." *Training and Development Journal* (December, 1971).

Byham, W.C. "Assessment Center for Spotting Future Managers." *Harvard Business Review.* 48:4 (1970), 150-160 plus appendix.

Byham, W.C. and G.C. Thornton, III. "Assessment Centers: New Aid in Management Selection." *Studies in Personnel Psychology.* 2:2 (1970), 21-35.

Byham, W.C. and R. Pentecost. "The Assessment Center: Identifying Tomorrow's Managers." *Personnel Magazine* (September-October, 1970).

Cambell, R.J. and D.W. Bray. "Assessment Centers: An Aid in Management Selection." *Personnel Administration.* 30:2 (1967), 6-13.

DiCostanzo, F. and T. Andretta. "The Supervisory Assessment Center in the Internal Revenue Service." *Training and Development Journal* (1970), 12-15.

D'Arcy, Paul F. "In New York City Assessment Center

Program Helps Test Managerial Competence." *Police Chief.* XLI:12 (December, 1974), 52-53, 74.

Driggs, Don and Paul M. Whisenand. "Assessment Centers: Situational Evaluation." *Journal of California Law Enforcement.* 10:4 (April, 1976), 131-135.

"Eeny, Meeny, Miney—Supervisor?" *Industry Week* (November 16, 1970), 28-32.

Finkle, R.D. and W.S. Jones. *Assessing Corporate Talent: A Key to Managerial Manpower Planning.* N.Y.: Wiley, 1970.

Flanagan, S.C. "Some Considerations in the Development of Situational Tests." *Personnel Psychology.* 7 (1954), 461-464.

Ghiselli, E.E. "Managerial Talent." *American Psychologist.* 8 (1963), 631-642.

Grant, D.L. and D.W. Bray. "Contributions of the Interview to Assessment of Management Potential." *Journal of Applied Psychology.* 53 (1969), 24-34.

Grant, D.W., W. Katkovsky, and D.W. Bray. "Contributions of Projective Techniques to Assessment of Management Potential." *Journal of Applied Psychology.* 51 (1967), 226-232.

Greenwood, J.M. and W.J. McNamara. "Leadership Styles of Structure and Consideration and Managerial Success." *Personnel Psychology.* 21 (1968), 85-98.

Guion, R.M. *Personnel Testing.* N.Y.: McGraw-Hill, 1965.

Guyton, T. "The Identification of Executive Potential." *Personnel Journal.* 48:11 (1969), 866-872.

Harris, H. *The Group Approach to Leadership Testing.* London: Kegan Paul, 1959.

Hopkins, H.F. "The Assessment Center in Police Selection." *Texas Police Journal* 22:11 (1974), 1-5, 20-21.

Jaffee, C.L. "A Tri-dimensional Approach to Management Selection." *Personnel.* 46 (1967), 453-455.

Jaffee, C.L., J. Bender, and D. Calvert. "The Assessment Center Technique: A Validation Study." *Management of Personnel Quarterly* (Fall, 1970), 9-14.

Korman, A.K. "The Prediction of Managerial Performance." *Personnel* (March-April, 1969).

Krout, A.I. and G.S. Scott. "Validity of an Operational Management Assessment Program." *Journal of Applied Psychology.* 56:2 (April, 1972), 124-129.

McConnell, J.H. "The Assessment Center: A Flexible Program for Supervisors." *Personnel* (September-October, 1971).

McConnell, J.H. "The Assessment Center in the Smaller Company." *Personnel* (March-April, 1969).

McFarlan, F. *The Management Game.* N.Y.: Macmillan, 1970.

Morris, B.S. "Officer Selection in the British Army, 1942-1945." *Occupational Psychology.* 23 (1949), 219-234.

Moses, J.L. "Assessment Center Performance and Management Progress." *Studies in Personnel Psychology.* 4 (1972), 7-12.

OSS. *Assessment of Men: Selection of Personnel for the Office of Strategic Services.* N.Y.: Johnson Reprint Corp., [1969].

Prine, E.D. "Assessments of Higher Level Personnel: An Analysis of Interviewers' Predictions of Job Performance." *Personnel Psychology.* 15 (1962), 319-344.

Sadoka, J.M. "Factor Analysis of OSS Situation Tests." *Journal of Abnormal and Social Psychology.* 47 (1962), 843-852.

Stern, G.G., M.I. Stein, and B.S. Bloom. *Methods in Personality Assessment.* Glencoe: Free Press, 1956.

Taft, R. "Multiple Methods of Personality Assessment." *Psychological Bulletin.* 56 (1959), 333-352.

Wollowick, H.B. and W.J. MacNamara. "Relationship of the Components of an Assessment Center to Management Success." *Journal of Applied Psychology.* 53 (1969), 348-352.

Oral Boards

Berger, Bernard and Solomon Hoberman. "Notes on the Use of Group Oral Tests." *Public Personnel Review* (July, 1955), 143-147.

Fear, Richard A. *The Evaluation Interview.* 2nd ed. N.Y.: McGraw-Hill, 1973.

The Oral Interview. San Francisco: Davis Coaching School, 1959.

"Oral Tests." *Association for Professional Law Enforcement Quarterly Journal.* 5:2 (July-September, 1959); (October-December, 1963). Entire issues devoted to oral boards.

"Preparation for Oral Tests." *Police Administration and Review.* 13 (October, 1958) (entire issue).

Physical Agility

Goldstein, L.S. *Physical Activities Survey of Police Officers in New Jersey—Final Report.* Washington: NCJRS, 1973.

Graves, John F. "Physical Condition Tests for Smaller Communities." *Public Personnel Review.* 21 (April, 1960), 133-136.

McGhee, L. Gary. "Job-Related Pre-Employment Physical Agility Tests." *Police Chief.* XLIII:1 (January, 1976), 42-43.

Osborn, Gary D. "Validating Physical Agility Tests." *Police Chief.* XLIII:1 (January, 1976), 43-45.

Wilkie, Richard C. "Job Related Physical Test for Patrol Officers." *Police Chief.* XLI:5 (May, 1974), 42-44, 47.

Wilkie, R.C. *King County (WA.)—Department of Public Safety—Job Related Physical Agility Test—Draft.* Washington: NCJRS (Microfiche), 1973.

Woods, Marcella D. "The University of Washington Police Officer Physical Efficiency Battery." *Police Chief.* XLIII:2 (February, 1976), 59-60, 65.

Promotional

Elsenberg, Terry and Roger Reinke. "The Weighting of

Scores in Promotional Exams: A Little-Known Problem." *Police Chief.* XXXIX:6 (June, 1972), 45-49.

Horstman, Preston. "Leaderless Group Discussion as an Assessment Tool for Supervisory and Command Promotions." *Journal of Police Science and Administration.* 2:1 (March, 1974), 34-37.

King, Richard A. and Cornelius J. O'Kane. "The Total Examination Environment: A Successful Police Promotional Experience." *FBI Law Enforcement Bulletin* (May, 1976), 2-8.

Meyer, Herbert H. and Greydon M. Worbois. "The Use of Tests in the Selection of Supervisors." *Police.* 2:5 (May-June, 1958), 57-60.

Psychological Testing

Anastasi, Anne. *Psychological Testing.* N.Y.: Macmillan, 1968.

Baehr, Melany et al. *Psychological Assessment of Patrolman Qualification in Relation to Field Performance.* Washington: GPO, 1969.

Cronbach, L.J. *Essentials of Psychological Testing.* 3rd ed. N.Y.: Harper & Row, 1970.

Due, Floyd O. "Screening Police Applicants." *Police Chief.* XLII:2 (February, 1975), 73-74.

Furcon, E.C. and R.G. Froemel. *Longitudinal Study of Psychological Test Predictors and Assessments of Patrolman Field Performance.* Springfield, VA.: NTIS, 1971.

Good, Patricia K. and John Brantner. *Practical Guide to the MMPI.* Minneapolis: University of Minnesota Press, 1974.

Gottesman, Jay. *Personality Patterns of Urban Police Applicants as Measured by the MMPI.* Hoboken, N.J.: Laboratory of Psychological Studies, 1969.

Gottesman, Jay. *The Utility of the MMPI in Assessing the Personality Patterns of Urban Police Applicants.* Hoboken, N.J.: Laboratory of Psychological Studies. Stevens Institute of Technology, 1975.

Gottlieb, M.C. and C.F. Baker. "Predicting Police Officer Effectiveness." *Journal of Forensic Psychology.* 6 (December, 1974), 35-46.

Hathaway, S.R.A. "A Coding System for MMPI Profile Classification." *Journal of Consulting Psychology.* 11 (1947), 334-337.

Heckman, R.W. and R.W. Groner. *Development of Psychiatric Standards for Police Selection.* Springfield, VA.: NTIS, 1972.

Holt, Robert R. *Assessing Personality.* N.Y.: Harcourt Brace Jovanovich, 1971.

Kates, Solis L. "Responses, Strong Blank Scales, and Job Satisfaction Among Policemen." *Journal of Applied Psychology.* XXXIV (1950), 249-254.

Levy, Ruth J. "Predicting Police Failures." *Journal of Criminal Law, Criminology and Police Science.* 58:2 (June, 1967), 265-276.

Murphy, J.J. "Current Practices in the Use of Psychological Testing by Police Agencies." *Journal of Criminal Law, Criminology and Police Science.* 63:4 (1972), 570-576.

Narrol, Harvey G. and Eugene E. Levitt. "Formal Assessment Procedures in Police Selection." *Psychological Reports.* 12 (1963), 691-694.

Oglesby, Thomas W. "The Use of Emotional Screening in the Selection of Police Applicants." *Police.* 2:3 (January-February, 1958), 49-53.

Oglesby, T.W. "Psychiatric Testing for Police Candidates." *Public Management.* 40:23 (January, 1958).

Rhead, Clifton et al. "The Psychological Assessment of Police Candidates." *American Journal of Psychiatry.* 24 (1968), 1575-1580.

Thurstone, Lewis L. "The Intelligence of Policemen." *Journal of Personnel Research.* I (1922).

U.S. Law Enforcement Assistance Administration. *Psychological Assessment of Patrolman Qualifications in Relation to Police Performance.* Washington: GPO, 1968.

Situational

Chenoweth, James H. "Situational Tests—A New Attempt at Assessing Police Candidates." *Journal of Criminal Law.* 52 (July-August, 1961), 232-238.

Mills, Robert B., Robert J. Devitt, and Sandra Tonkin. "Situational Tests in Metropolitan Police Recruit Selection." *Journal of Criminal Law, Criminology and Police Science.* 57:1 (March, 1966), 99-106.

WORKLOAD

O'Neill, Michael and Carlton Bloom. *A Comparative Study of the Field Patrolman's Workload in Selected Police Departments of California Cities as Compared with the Long Beach Police Department.* Unpub. Master's thesis. California State University, Long Beach, January, 1971.

Webster, John A. "Police Task and Time Study." *Journal of Criminal Law, Criminology and Police Science.* 61:1 (March, 1970), 94-100.

Study shows that police spend more than 50% of their time with non-criminal activities and less than 3% with crimes against persons.

POLICE PERSONNEL BY RACE, SEX, AGE, LEGAL AND RESERVE STATUS

MINORITIES IN LAW ENFORCEMENT

Alex, Nicholas. *Black In Blue.* N.Y.: Appleton-Century-Crofts, 1969.
Study of Black police in N.Y. City. Discusses in detail unique problems faced by Black police officers.

Armbrister, Trevor. "The Lonely Struggle of the Black Cop." *Reader's Digest* (March, 1971), 123-127.

Banks, Lucy J. "Kansas City Top Cop." *Ebony* (October, 1970), 35.
One of few Negro police chiefs in America.

Bannon, J.D. and G.M. Wilt. "Black Policemen—A Study of Self-Images." *Journal of Police Science and Administration.* 1:1 (January, 1973), 21-29.

Banton, Michael. *The Policeman in the Community.* N.Y.: Basic, 1964.
This classic study briefly mentions to problems of Black policemen. Banton indicates Black policemen are "more correct" regarding the acceptance of gratuities than their White counterparts. See pp. 57, 66, 116, 173-175.

"The Black Cop: A Man Caught in the Middle." *Newsweek.* 78 (August 16, 1971), 19-20.

Calame, Dyron E. "Man in the Middle—Negro Cop Takes Abuse from White Colleagues, Scornful Black Militants." *The Wall Street Journal* (September 4, 1968).

Chapman, Samuel G. "Wanted: Dedicated Blacks for Police Jobs." *Christian Science Monitor* (August 16, 1969), 11.
City police forces across the United States are trying to recruit Blacks. Competition with industry is intense; a poor police image in the Black community is a hindrance. But slowly Black percentages are growing.

Cohen, B. "Minority Retention in the New York City Police Department. A Pilot Study." *Criminology.* 11:3 (1973), 287-306.

Gazell, James A. "Attitudes of Non-White Police Personnel Toward Retention." *Police Law Quarterly.* 3:3 (April, 1974), 12-21.
Blacks and Chicanos stay on job because of personal satisfaction, not economic benefit.

Gazell, James A. "Police Recruitment: How Black and Brown Personnel View It." *Police Law Quarterly.* 2:4 (1973), 19-29.

Grand, Robert J., Richard W. Milne, and Kenneth J. White. "Minority Recruiting: The Tucson Police Experience." *Journal of Police Science and Administration.* 3:2 (June, 1975), 197-202.

Hall, Richard. "We Get It from Both Sides: The Dilemma of the Black Cop." *Life* (September 18, 1970).

Harrison, Paul. "Black Police." *New Society* (October 30, 1975), 269-270.

Hunt, I.C. and B. Cohen. *Minority Recruiting in the New York City Police Department.* N.Y.: Rand, 1971.
An attempt to learn the reasons for difficulties in minority recruiting and explore the effectiveness of current programs.

Johnson, Charles S. "Negro Police in Southern Cities." *Public Management* (1944), 70-80.

Kephart, William M. "The Integration of Negroes into the Urban Police Force." *Journal of Criminal Law, Criminology and Police Science.* 45 (September-October, 1954), 325-334.

Kephart, Charles S. *Racial Factors and Urban Law Enforcement.* Philadelphia: University of Pennsylvania Press, 1957.
A study of the interaction between Negro and White police personnel, between Negro policemen and Negro offenders, and White policemen and Negro offenders of Philadelphia.

Kimbrough, Jess. *Defender of the Angels; A Black Policeman in Old Los Angeles.* N.Y.: Macmillan, 1969.

King, Wayne. "The Drive to Get Negroes on the Police Force—And Why It's Not Easy." *Detroit Scope Magazine* (June 29, 1968).

Kronholm, William C. "Blue Power: The Threat of the Militant Policeman." *Journal of Criminal Law, Criminology and Police Science.* 63:2 (1972), 294-299.

Lawyer, David N. "The Dilemma of the Black Badge." *Police Chief.* XXXV:11 (November, 1968), 22-25.

Link, Terry. "Black and White and Blue." *San Francisco Magazine.* 12 (June, 1970), 16-19.

Margolis, Richard J. *Who Will Wear the Badge? A Report of the United States Commission on Civil Rights.* Washington: GPO, 1970.

"More Cities Hire Negro Policemen." *Police Journal (N.Y.)* 32 (July-August, 1947).

Narayan, Rudy. "Britain: The Case for West Indians in the Metropolitan Police." *Race Today* (June, 1972), 201-202.

Poinsett, Alex. "The Dilemma of the Black Policeman." *Ebony.* 126 (May, 1971), 123-131.

Rolph, C.M. "Colored Police?" *New Statesman.* 68 (November 20, 1964), 781-782.

Rudwick, Elliott M. "Negro Police Employment in the Urban South." *Journal of Negro Education.* 30 (March, 1961), 102-108.

Rudwick, Elliott M. "The Negro Policeman in the South." *Journal of Criminal Law, Criminology and Police Science.* 51:2 (March-April, 1961).

Rudwick, Elliott M. "Police Work and the Negro." *Journal of Criminal Law, Criminology and Police Science* (March-April, 1960), 596-599.

Rudwick, Elliott M. "The Southern Negro Policeman and the

White Offender." *Journal of Negro Education.* 30 (Fall, 1961), 426-431.

Rudwick, Elliott M. "The Unequal Badge." *Journal of Criminal Law, Criminology and Police Science* (July-August, 1960).

Rudwick, Elliott M. *The Unequal Badge: Negro Police in the South.* Atlanta: Southern Regional Council, 1962.

Sax, Richard M. "Why It Hurts to Black and Blue." *Issues in Criminology.* 4:1 (Fall, 1968), 1-11.

Scott, J.F. *Study of Role Conflicts Among Policemen.* Ann Arbor, MI.: University Microfilms, 1968.
Study which assesses the influence of racial identity on the occurrence of conflicts in the official behavior of Negro policemen.

Social Development Corporation. *New Careers: Police Community Relations.* Bethesda, MD.: Social Development Corporation, n/d.
Background and suggestions for recruiting minority group members to serve as community-police liaison officers.

Teahan, J.E. "A Longitudinal Study of Attitude Shifts Among Black and White Police Officers." *Journal of Social Issues.* 31:1 (1975), 47-56.

Teahan, J.E. "Role Playing and Group Experience to Facilitate Attitude and Value Changes Among Black and White Police Officers." *Journal of Social Issues.* 31:1 (1975), 35-45.

"Urban League Is Recruiting More Minorities for Employment in Criminal Justice Agencies." *Carolina Law.* 22:6 (1972), 89-90.

Van Blaricon, D.P. "Recruitment and Retention of Minority Race Persons as Police Officers." *Police Chief* (September, 1976), 60-64.

Williams, W.S. *Attitudes of Black and White Policemen Toward the Opposite Race.* Ann Arbor, MI.: University Microfilms, 1970.
Examination of relationships between contacts and of the attitudes of Black church members, Black police, White church members and White police toward the opposite race.

Williams, Edward D. *The First Black Captain.* NY: Vantage, 1975.

POLICEWOMEN

Books

Abrecht, Mary E. and Barbara L. Stern. *The Making of a Woman Cop.* N.Y.: Morrow, 1976.

Allen, Mary S. *Lady in Blue.* London: Paul, 1936.

Allen, Mary S. and J.H. Heyneman. *The Pioneer Policewomen.* London: Chatto and Windres, 1925.

Anderson, Mary. *Women in Law Enforcement.* Portland, OR.: Metropolitan, 1973.

Bloch, P.B. and D. Anderson. *Policewomen on Patrol: Final Report.* Washington: Police Foundation, 1974.

Bloch, P., D. Anderson, and P. Gervais. *Police Women on Patrol.* 3 vols. Washington: The Urban Institute, 1973.

Cirile, Marie. *Detective Marie Cirile: Memoirs.* Garden City, N.Y.: Doubleday, 1975.

Condor, Stella. *Woman on the Beat: The True Story of a Policewoman.* London: Hale, 1960.

Cramer, James. *Uniforms of the World's Police.* Springfield, IL.: C.C. Thomas, 1968.
Some descriptions of policewoman uniforms.

Cramer, James. *The World's Police.* London: Cassell, 1964.
Contains some limited information about policewomen.

Ewing, Elizabeth. *Women in Uniform Through the Centuries.* London: Batsford, 1975.

Fleming, Alice. *New on the Beat: Women Power in the Police Force.* N.Y.: Coward, 1976.

Gourley, G. Douglas. *Patrol Administration.* 2nd ed. Springfield, IL.: C.C. Thomas, 1974.
Briefly covers policewomen activities.

Hamilton, Mary E. *The Policewoman, Her Services and Ideals.* N.Y.: Stokes, 1924.

Harvey, S. *London Policewomen.* London: Angus and Robertson, 1958.

Higgins, Lois L. *Policewoman's Manual.* Springfield, IL.: C.C. Thomas, 1961.

Hilton, Jennifer. *Gentle Arm of the Law: Life as a Policewoman.* Ealing: Transworld, 1973.

Horne, Peter. *Women in Law Enforcement.* N.Y.: McGraw-Hill, 1975.

Hutzel, Eleanore L. *The Policewoman's Handbook.* N.Y.: Columbia University Press, 1933.

Kelly, Vince. *Rugged Angel: The Amazing Career of Policewoman Lillian Armfield.* Sydney: Angus and Robertson, 1961.

King, Irene and Caryl Thurman. *She's a Cop, Isn't She?* N.Y.: Dial, 1975.

Knoohuizen, Ralph and Richard Gutman. *Women in Police Work in Chicago* Chicago: Chicago Law Enforcement Study Group, 1974.

Lock, Joan. *Lady Policewoman.* London: M. Joseph, 1968.

Management Information Service Report. *Policewomen.* Washington: International City Management Association, September, 1973.

Metropolitan Police. *Conditions of Entry and Terms of Service as Woman Police Officer.* London: Metropolitan Police, 1937.

Milton, Catherine and Laura Crites. *Women in Law Enforcement.* Washington: Management Information Service International City Management Association, September 1973.

Milton, Catherine Higgs et al. *Women in Policing: A Manual.* Washington: Police Foundation, 1975.

Muro, Dianne P. *Woman on Patrol.* Valley Forge, PA.: Judson, 1976.

Owings, Chloe. *Women Police: A Study of the Development and Status of the Women Police Movement.* Montclair, N.J.: Patterson Smith, 1969 [1925]).

Palelog, S. *Women Police of Poland (1925-1939).* London: Association for Moral and Social Hygiene, 1957.

Police Foundation. *A Symposium About Women in Policing.* Washington: Police Foundation. May 28-30, 1977.

Rudman, Jack. *Policewomen.* N.Y.: National Learning Corporation, 1969.

Stanley, Clifford R. *The Purpose of a Lifetime: A Profile of Barbara Mary Denis De Vitre, O.B.E., 1905-1960.* Chichester: Barry Rose, 1972.
Britain's first woman assistant inspector of constabulary.

Tancred, Edith. *Women Police.* London: National Council of Women of Great Britain, 1951.

Uhnak, Dorothy. *Policewoman.* N.Y.: Simon & Schuster, 1964.

U.S. Department of Justice, Law Enforcement Assistance Administration. *Policewomen.* Washington: LEAA, November, 1974.

U.S. Department of Justice, Law Enforcement Assistance Administration. *Study Affirms Policewoman's Work.* Washington: GPO, 1974.

Washington, Brenda E. *Deployment of Female Police Officers in the United States.* Gaithersburg, MD.: IACP, 1974.

Wyles, Lilian. *A Woman at Scotland Yard: Reflections on the Struggles and Achievements of Thirty Years in the Metropolitan Police.* London: Faber & Faber, 1952.

Periodicals

Aaron, Thomas J. "Policemen and Metermaids." *Police* (May-June, 1956).

Albro, Agness. "Women Police Commissioner Gives Account of Important Work Done by Los Angeles Policewomen." *Pacific Coast International Law Enforcement News.* 14 (1947).

Anable, David. "Women in Blue Tackle Paperwork, Muggers." *Christian Science Monitor* (February 4, 1974), 1, 10.

Andrew H. "The 'New' Military Police." *Military Police Law Enforcement Journal.* 1:5 (1975), 18-19.

Armat, Virginia. "Policewomen in Action." *Saturday Evening Post.* 247 (July, 1975).

Armat, Virginia. "Policemen on Patrol." *Reader's Digest* (July, 1975).

Barlow, V.M. "Policewoman—An Asset to Law Enforcement." *Australian Police Journal* (October, 1975), 293-295.

Bauer, Douglas. "A Night in the Life of a Lady Cop." *Today's Health* (September, 1975).

Becke, Shirley. "The First Half-Century." *Police Journal.* [Eng.] (November, 1969), 42, 478-482.

Becke, S.C. "Law Enforcement: The Feminine Angle." *International Journal of Offender Therapy and Comparative Criminology.* [Eng.] 17:2 (1973), 196-201.

Becke, S. "Metropolitan Uni-Sex." *Police Journal.* 46 (1973), 274-279.
Describes equality for women police in the London Metropolitan Police Force. Also, outlines promotional opportunities for women.

Becke, Shirley. "Training of Women Police as Specialists." *Police Journal.* [Eng.] (April, 1963), 167-170.

"Berlin Policewomen." *Life.* 24 (April 12, 1948).

Berry, Vareece. "Pasadena's (Texas) Policewomen Protect School Crossings." *Law and Order* (December, 1955).

Bloch, Peter B. "Reply to Questions Raised in Re: 'Policewomen on Patrol.' " *Police Chief.* XLII:7 (July, 1975), 22-23.

Borgenicht, Miriam. "Welcome Policewomen." *Parent's Magazine.* 20 (November, 1945).

Bouza, Anthony V. "Women in Policing." *FBI Law Enforcement Bulletin* (September, 1975), 2-7.

Boyd, Margaret M. "The Role of the Policewoman." *Police Yearbook.* Washington: IACP, 1953.

Brown, Edythe. "The Policewoman." *Police Journal.* 22 (June, 1936), 20-21.

Buwolda, I.W. "Policewoman—Yesterday, Today, and Tomorrow." *Journal of Social Hygiene.* 31 (May, 1945), 290-293.

Calvert, C. "What It's Like to be a Woman Cop." *Mademoiselle* (September, 1973).

Carson, Norma B. "Policewomen Are an Important Factor in Law Enforcement." *FBI Law Enforcement Bulletin* (October, 1953).

Chapman, Samuel G. and Robert L. Fienberg. "Waco, Texas: The City with Five Friendly Faces." *Police* (March-April, 1961).

Chasen, W. "New York's Finest Female Division." *New York Times Magazine* (November, 20, 1955).

Clifford, Alice E. "The Policewoman in Family Problems." *Police Yearbook.* Washington: IACP, 1959.

Connolly, V. "Job for a Lady: Detroit's Women Police Tackle the Girl-Delinquency Problem." *Collier's.* 113 (June 10, 1944). 18-19.

Conrad, Rex D. and John Gloriosi. "Policewomen: Agency Adjustment Through a Group Approach." *Police Chief* (April, 1975).

Crites, Laura. "Women in Law Enforcement." *Management Information Service* (September, 1973).

Davenport, John C. "Policewomen Serve with Success in Law Enforcement." *FBI Law Enforcement Bulletin.* 27:8 (August, 1958), 3-6, 23.

Davis, J.C. "Woman's Work in a Police Department." *Policewomen's International Bulletin.* 5:9 (June, 1929).

De Courey, Anne. "The Female Arm of the Law." *SARP* (May, 1972), 5-7.

Detzer, K. "Detroit Lady Cops." *American Mercury.* 54 (March, 1942), 345-351.

Dilucchio, J.Q. "In Miami: Female Officers on the Department." *Police Chief.* 42:4 (1975), 56-57.

Dixon, Lonny. "The Unusual Role of Women Officers in Homicide Work." *FBI Law Enforcement Bulletin.* 32:2 (February, 1963), 18-19.

Dunlavey, Mary A. "The Women Police—Here to Stay?" *Law and Order.* 23:4 (April, 1975), 78-79.

Edmiston, Susan. "Policewomen: How Well Are They Doing in a 'Man's Job'?" *Ladies Home Journal* (April, 1975).

Elmes, Frank. "Policing's Own Major Barbara." *Police Review*. [Eng.] (January 19, 1973).

Fagerstrom, Dorothy. "A Cooperative Attitude." *Law and Order*. 15:9 (September, 1967), 13-14, 96.

Fagerstrom, Dorothy. "Deputy Commissioner Gertrude Schimmel." *Law and Order*. 22:11 (November, 1974), 90-91.

Fagerstrom, Dorothy. "Designed for the Women in Blue." *Law and Order* (August, 1958), 6, 8, 60-61.

Fagerstrom, Dorothy. "Make the Most of Every Opportunity." *Law and Order* (November, 1960).

Fagerstrom, Dorothy. "Policewomen's Viewpoint on Behavioral Problems." *Law and Order*. 17:12 (December, 1969), 88-95.

Fagerstrom, Dorothy. "Practical Handbag for Policewomen." *Law and Order* (February, 1964).

Fagerstrom, Dorothy. "Wider Horizons for Policewomen." *Law and Order*. 18:9 (September, 1970), 81-83.

Field, Annita. "Women in Police Work." *International Police Chronicle*. 7 (March-April, 1959), 29-36.

"First Nisei Woman Deputy." *California Peace Officer*. 7 (November-December, 1956).

"First State Policewomen in Connecticut; WASPS in Virginia." *Police Chief*. XL:5 (May, 1973), 63.

Fischberg, C. "Copping In: A Chilly Welcome for Women in Blue." *MS* (May, 1975).

Folley, Vern L. "Police Officer of the Issue." *Police*. 14:5 (May-June, 1970), 14-15.

Folley, Vern L. "Police Officer of the Issue." *Police*. 15:2 (November-December, 1970), 10-11.

Folley, Vern L. "Police Officer of the Issue." *Police*. 15:4 (March-April, 1971), 47, 48.

Folley, Vern L. "Police Officer of the Issue." *Police*. 15:6 (July-August, 1971), 66.

Folley, Vern L. "Police Officer of the Issue." *Police*. 16:4 (December, 1971), 64-65.

Foster, Reginald. "Women in Security." *Security and Protection* (March, 1975), 4-6.

Fremayne, Penelope. "Policewomen in Cypress." *Police College Magazine* (Spring, 1959), 333-334.

Garmire, Bernard L. "Female Officers in the Department." *FBI Law Enforcement Bulletin*. 43:6 (June, 1974), 11-13.

Gibbons, Thomas J. "Policewomen Undercover." *Law and Order* (September, 1956), 4, 9, 18-19.

Granville, W. "Policewomen in 1979." *Police College Magazine* (Autumn, 1969), 23-24.

Gray, George. "Obituary: Miss Dorothy Peto: The Guiding Light of Women Police." *Job*. (March 8, 1974).

Gray, Naomi Swett. "Women Car Checkers Prove Their Worth." *Police Chief* (December, 1960).

Halsey, Ashley, Jr. "Lady Cops of the Dope Squad. Philadelphia." *Saturday Evening Post*. 229 (March 30, 1957), 36-37.

Hawkins, W.V. "Patrol Women: Yes or No?" *Current Municipal Problems* (Fall, 1973), 148-149.

Higgins, Lois L. "Bombay and a Lovely Policewoman." *Law and Order*. 12 (July, 1964).

Higgins, Lois L. "A Career in Law Enforcement for Women." *Police*. 6:5 (May-June, 1962), 46-49.

Higgins, Lois. "Golden Anniversary of Women in Police Service." *Law and Order*. 8:8 (August, 1960).

Higgins, Lois. "Historical Background of Policewomen's Service." *Journal of Criminal Law, Criminology and Police Science*. 41:6 (1951), 822-833.

Higgins, Lois. "More About Women in Law Enforcement." *Law and Order* (September, 1962).

Higgins, Lois. "The Policewoman." *Police*. 3:2 (November-December, 1958), 66-69.

Higgins, Lois. "The Policewoman." *Law and Order* (November, 1958), 4.

Higgins, Lois. "Women in Law Enforcement." *Law and Order*. 10:8 (August, 1962).

Higgins, Lois. "Women Police Service." *Journal of Criminal Law, Criminology and police Science*. 41 (1950), 101-106.

Hilton, Jennifer. "Women in the Police Service." *Police Journal*. [Eng.] (April, 1976), 93-103.

Hindman, R.E. "A Survey Related to the Use of Female Law Enforcement Officers." *Police Chief*. 42:4 (1975), 58-59.

Survey of Ventura County Sheriff's Deputies shows that there is a low acceptance for female deputies in areas considered to be hazardous.

Horne, Peter. "Policewomen and International Women's Year." *Law and Order* (October, 1975), 66-70.

Horne, Peter F. "The Role of Women and the Police Reserves." *Law Enforcement* (September-October, 1973).

Horne, P.P. "The Role of Women in Law Enforcement. *Police Chief*. 40 (1973), 60-63.

Howard, J.I. "The Outlook for Women in Police Work." *Pennsylvania Chiefs of Police Association Bulletin* (Spring, 1952), 8-11.

Hutzel, Eleonore L. "The Policewoman." *Annals* (November, 1929), 104-114.

Hutzel, E.L. "Policewoman's Role in Social Protection." *Journal of Social Hygiene*. 30 (December, 1944), 538-544.

"It's Farewell to Mrs. Becke." *Job* (April 19, 1974).

Jenkins, Roy. "Catch Your Recruits Younger and Give the Women a Chance." *Police*. [Eng.] (August, 1974).

Kelley, Geraldine A. "Policewomen Play Important Role in Philadelphia, Pennsylvania." *FBI Law Enforcement Bulletin*. 26:10 (1957), 3-7.

Kempton, M. "All We Want for Christmas Is Our Jobs Back." *MS.* (December, 1975), 69-72.

Keyes, Edward. "Meet . . . A Policewoman!" *Cosmopolitan* (November, 1971).

Kruckenberg, J. "Women in Policing: Reflections of a Changing Community." *Police Law Quarterly.* 4:1 (1974), 23-33; 4:2 (1975), 27-35.

Lamber, J.C. and V.I. Streib. "Women Executives, Managers and Professionals in the Indiana Criminal Justice System." *Indiana Law Review.* 8:2 (1974), 297-372.

Leevey, J. Ray. "The Role of the Police Matron." *Journal of Criminal Law, Criminology and Police Science.* 39 (1949).

"Legacy of a Lady." (Lillian May Armfield, Australia's first Policewoman). *New South Wales Police News* (November, 1971).

"Lieutenant is a Lady; Marilyn Olson of Chicago Police Force." *Good Housekeeping.* 145 (July, 1957).

Loon, Ho Geok. "History of the Women Police in the Singapore Police Force." *Singapore Police Journal* (January, 1974), 48-52.

Lyon, Thomas. "The Trooper Was a Lady." *Law and Order* (May, 1973), 70-71, 81.

McCombs, H. "Lady Constable: Sis Dickerson Polices a Tough Texas County." *Life.* 19 (September 7, 1945), 19-20.

Manley, Charles S. "Metermaids are Here to Stay." *Nation Cities.* 3 (November, 1965).

Melchionne, Theresa M. "Changing Role of Policewomen." *Police Journal.* [Eng.]. 47:4 (October-December, 1974), 340-358.

Melchionne, Theresa M. "Current Status and Problems of Women Police." *Journal of Criminal Law, Criminology and Police Science.* 58:2 (June, 1967), 257-260.

Melchionne, Theresa. "The Policewoman." *Police Chief.* 33 (December, 1966), 12, 52.

Melchionne, Theresa M. "Role of Policewoman in the Investigative Function." *The Police Yearbook.* Washington: IACP, 1960. 166-170.

Melchionne, Theresa M. "The Role of the Policewoman in Working with Youth—The Bridge Between." *Law and Order* (July, 1961).

Mishkin, Barry D. "Female Police in New York City." *SARP* (April, 1975), 12-13.

"More Cities Employ Policewomen." *American City.* 63 (February, 1948).

"More Cities Hire Policewomen." *American City* (March, 1950).

Morgan, Ted. "Policewomen in Washington Share the Beat with Skeptical Men." *Law Enforcement.* 5 (March, 1975), 12-14.

Mormon, R.R. et al. "Multiple Relationship Between Age, Education, Police Experience and TAV Variables Correlated to Job Rating on 101 Female Deputy Sheriffs." *Police* (February, 1972).

Morton, H.R. "Fresno Downtown Traffic Controlled by Ten Uniformed Women Officers." *Western City.* 32 (May, 1956), 36-37.

"My Daughter the Policewoman." *Ebony.* 20 (October, 1965), 82-84.

"No Longer Men or Women—Just Police Officers." *U.S. News and World Report* (August 19, 1974).

Ogbuaku, G.O. "Ladies on the Force in Nigeria." *National Women.* 35 (November, 1956).

Olson, Marilynn G. "Women in Police Work." *Police Yearbook.* Washington: IACP, 1957.

"One of Frankfurt's New Women Traffic Wardens." *Illustrated London News.* 238 (March 11, 1961).

"Operatic Beat, Policewomen on Duty at San Francisco Opera." *Newsweek.* 58 (September 18, 1961).

Owens, James M. "Policewoman in the Line." *Police.* 3:1 (September-October, 1958), 21-22.

Perlstein, Gary R. "Certain Characteristics of Policewomen." *Police* (January, 1972).

Perlstein, Gary R. "Female Police: The Need for Research." *Police.* 15:1 (September-October, 1970), 62-63.

Perlstein, G.R. "Policewomen and Policemen: A Comparative Look." *Police Chief.* XXXIX:3 (March, 1972), 72-74, 83.

Phillips, Wayne. "Detective Story, Female Department." *New York Times Magazine* (February 28, 1960).

Pigeon, Helen D. "Policewomen in the United States." *Journal of Criminal Law and Criminology.* XVIII (1926-27).

Pires, A.S. "Word with a Brazilian Policewoman: Hilda Macedo." *America.* (July, 1957), 9, 26-27.

Pogrebin, L.C. "Working Women: Law Enforcement Officers." *Ladies Home Journal* (September, 1973).

"Policewoman's Lot: Aspects of Her Training at Mill Meece." *Illustrated London News.* 223:531 (October 3, 1953).

Powers, William F. "State Police Women in Mass." *Law and Order* (March, 1968).

Price, Barbara R. "Study of Leadership Strength of Female Police Executives." *Journal of Police Science and Administration.* 2:2 (June, 1974), 219-226.

Purcell, Philip. "Use of Policewomen is Valuable Asset to Law Enforcement." *FBI Law Enforcement Bulletin* (May, 1960).

Reed, Joseph F. "Professional Policewomen." *FBI Law Enforcement Bulletin.* 17 (May, 1948).

Reynolds, Gail. "A Police Woman on Patrol." *Journal of California Law Enforcement.* 9:2 (October, 1974), 69-70.

Rink, S.E. "Arresting Females, the Policewomen's Story." *Law and Order* (November, 1953).

Robinson, K. "Promising Career Opportunities for

Women." *Saturday Evening Post.* 246 (November, 1974).

Salzbrenner, Dorothy. "Military Policewomen." *Law and Order.* 11:2 (February, 1963).

Sandler, Georgette and Ellen Mintz. "Policemen, Policewomen and the Masculine Ethic." *New York State Psychological Association* (April, 1973).

Sandrock, Tom. "Britain's 'Girls in Blue'." *Indian Police Journal* (October, 1970).

"Sargent Audrey Fletcher: Policewoman of the Year." *California Peace Officer.* 8 (May-June, 1958).

Schmidt, Shauna. "Career Opportunities for Women in San Francisco Bay Area Police and Sheriff's Departments." *Journal of California Law Enforcement.* 8:4 (April, 1974), 191-193.

Scott, Harold. "Policewomen in Great Britain." *International Criminal Police Review* (May, 1953).

Sherman, Lewis J. "Evaluation of Policewomen on Patrol in a Suburban Police Department." *Journal of Police Science and Administration* (1975), 334-338.

Sherman, Lewis J. "A Psychological View of Women in Policing." *Journal of Police Science and Administration.* 1:4 (December, 1973), 383-394.

Shpritzer, Felicia. "A Case for the Promotion of Policewomen in the City of New York." *Police.* 5:6 (July-August, 1961), 57-60.

Skousen, W. Cleon. "Unisex or Just Sex?" *Law and Order.* 23 (September, 1975).

Snow, Margaret. "Woman's Role in Crime Control." *Police Yearbook.* Washington: IACP, 1956.

Sonder, Frederic, Jr. "Crime Busters in Skirts." *Reader's Digest* (November, 1957).

"South Bend's Auxiliary Policewomen." *American City.* 63 (March, 1948).

Stevenson, Gloria. "The Force of Change: New Opportunities for Women in Police Work." *Occupational Outlook Quarterly* (Winter, 1972).

Street, N.T. "The Role of Women in Law Enforcement." *National Police Journal.* 8:1 (1973), 12-15.

Sumner, Francis. "Lady Is a Cop." *Look.* 20 (March 6, 1956), 48-53.

Sweeney, Francis. "The Policewoman and Crime." *Police Chief* (January, 1959).

Talney, Ronald G. "Women in Law Enforcement: An Expanded Role." *Police.* 14:2 (November-December, 1969), 49-51.

Tanored, Edith. "Women Police Abroad." *Police Journal.* [Eng.] (1931), 75-187.

Tarry, Frederick T. "Women Constables." *Police Journal.* [Eng.] (1944), 48-53.

Tenny, Evabel. "Women's Work in Law Enforcement." *Journal of Criminal Law, Criminology and Police Science.* XLIV (July-August, 1953), 239-246.

Tenny, Fred. "The Qualifications Required for Policewomen and the Development of Tests for Measuring Such Qualifications." *Policewomen's International Bulletin.* 4:3 (August, 1928), 5-6.

"Tide of Change Brings New Opportunities: Policewomen's Role Compared with the Past." *Patrol* (June, 1975).

Tremayne, Penelope. "Policewomen in Cyprus." *Police College Magazine* (Spring, 1959), 333-335.

Vollmer, August. "Meet the Lady Cop." *Survey.* LXIII (March, 1930), 101-106.

Walrod, Truman. "Careers for Women in Law Enforcement." *National Sheriff* (May-June, 1968).

Walsh, Jude T. "Policewomen on Patrol." *Police Chief.* XLII:7 (July, 1975), 20-22.
Criticism of *Police Women on Patrol—Final Report* by Peter B. Bloch and Deborah Anderson.

Washington, B.E. "The Officer Is a Lady." *Traffic Safety.* 74:9 (1974), 22-25, 36.

Weldy, William O. "Women in Policing: A Positive Step Toward Increased Police Enthusiasm." *Police Chief.* XLIII:1 (January, 1976), 46-47.

Wells, Alice S. "Policewoman Badge Number One." *Law and Order.* 9 (January, 1961), 75-76.

Wilson, Jerry V. "Committee on Women in Police Service Report." *Police Yearbook.* Washington: IACP, 1975.

"Women Police in Cities." *Public Management.* 24 (August, 1942).

"Women Police in Italy." *International Criminal Police Review* (June-July, 1960), 62-64.

Wren, Pauline. "Auxiliary Girl Cadets in Leeds." *Police Journal.* [Eng.]. 38 (1965), 570-572.

Unpublished Materials

Biddle, Ralph W., Jr. *Special Problems in Training of Policewomen.* Quantico, VA.: FBI NA Research Paper, 90th Session (August, 1972).

Ejde, Karen. *The Logical Utilization of Female Police Officers.* Quantico, VA.: FBI NA Research Paper, 94th Session (August, 1973).

Ford, Eileen M. *The Policewoman: Her Changing Role in Law Enforcement.* Quantico, VA.: FBI NA Research Paper, 93rd Session (June, 1973).

Harris, Patricia F. *Policewomen: The Historical Evolution of Her Role in the U.S.* Unpub. Master's thesis. Michigan State University, 1967.

Hehn, Alice M. *The Role of Women in Police Work.* Quantico, VA.: FBI NA Research Paper, 92nd Session (March, 1973).

Klapak, John R. *The Role of Women in Police Work.* Quantico, VA.: FBI NA Research Paper, 92nd Session (March, 1973).

O'Neill, Patricia. *Policewomen: A View of Self-Images.* Quantico, VA.: FBI NA Research Paper, 93rd Session (June, 1973).

Perlstein, Gary R. *An Exploratory Analysis of Certain Characteristics of Policewomen.* Unpub. Doctoral dissertation. Florida State University, 1971.

Shepherd, Roosevelt E. *A Study of the Utilization of*

Policewomen in Large United States Departments. Unpub. Master's thesis. Michigan State University, 1971.

CADETS

Bagley, Gerald L. "A Police Cadet Program for the City of Whittier." *Police.* 10:1 (September-October, 1965), 65-69; (November-December, 1965), 68-72.

Bornhoffer, Frank and Paul R. Flaugher. "Police Cadet System Works at Cincinnati." *FBI Law Enforcement Bulletin* (August, 1956).

Cauthen, W.R. "Columbia Cadet Corps Highly Successful." *Carolina Law.* 24:2 (1974), 66-70.

Cauthen, William R. "Police Cadet Corps." *FBI Law Enforcement Bulletin.* 43:2 (February, 1974), 22-25.

Chapple, Norman L. *Police Cadet Trainings: Selected British Programs.* Kent, OH.: Kent State University, 1971.

Cromwell, P.F., Jr. "Training—Education—Understanding Bridge the Gap." *Police Chief.* XXXIX:3 (March, 1972), 54-56.

Erie County Technical Institute. *College Education for Police Cadets.* Buffalo, N.Y.: Erie County Technical Institute, 1967.

Flaugher, Paul. "The Police Cadet." *Journal of Criminal Law, Criminology and Police Science.* 47:4 (November-December, 1956), 500-507.

Germain, Fred. "Teen Police Learn and Lend a Hand." *Law and Order.* 22:5 (May, 1974), 40-42.

Huck, K.H. "Police Cadets: A Valuable Resource." *Police Chief.* XXXV:7 (July, 1968).

Kane, Joseph C. "Youth in Police Service." *Police Chief.* XL:2 (February, 1973), 16, 65.

Looney, Francis B. "Nassau County's Police Cadets." *Police Chief.* XXXV:2 (February, 1968).

Nemetz, W.C. "How Trained Assistants Increase Effective Police Power." *Police Chief.* XL:1 (January, 1973), 20, 64.

O'Reiley, Patrick. "San Diego Establishes Police Cadet Program." *Police.* 5:2 (November-December, 1960), 6-9.

Osterburg, James W. and Hillard J. Trubitt. "Recommendations Based Upon a Study of Police Cadet Programs in the United States." *Journal of Criminal Law, Criminology and Police Science.* 61:3 (September, 1970), 459-462.

Osterburg, James W., Hillard J. Trubitt, and Richard A. Myren. "Cadet Programs: An Innovative Change?" *Journal of Criminal Law, Criminology and Police Science* 58:1 (March, 1967), 112-118.

Pilot, Joan. "Two Is a Good Beginning." *Law and Order.* 16:5 (May, 1968), 108-111.

"Police Cadets in Victoria, Australia." *International Criminal Police Review* (March, 1976), 79-80.

Savord, George H. "The Police Cadet Program." *Journal of California Law Enforcement* (October, 1973), 80-84.

Seares, Robert S. "The Police Cadet." *Annals of the American Academy of Political and Social Science.* XXXIX (January, 1954), 107-112.

Sorenson, Clyde A. "Police Cadet Program Provides Useful Recruitment Tool." *Minnesota Muncipalities.* 47 (October, 1962), 286-288.

Tocchio, O.J. "It's Time to Develop a New Caliber of Policeman." *Police.* 14:3 (January-February, 1970), 14-19.

Vandertill, Gordon E. "Police Cadet Programs in Michigan." *Michigan Municipal Review.* XL (June, 1967), 142-143.

Veich, Anthony M. "Recruitment and the Police Cadet Program." *Law and Order.* 14:2 (February, 1966), 14-16, 18, 61.

Weizenecker, Raynor. "Have You Considered a Teenage Cadet Program?" *FBI Law Enforcement Bulletin* (November, 1970), 16-19.

CIVILIAN

Chamberlain, Charles S. "The Role of Civilian Personnel in Law Enforcement." *Law and Order.* 20:8 (August, 1972), 52-56.

"Civilians in Traffic." *Law Enforcement Executive.* 5 (October, 1970), 3-6.

Clark, Jasper S. "Los Angeles Recruit Civilian Traffic Director." *Traffic Digest Review.* 17 (January, 1969), 14-16.

Magruder, Clarice. "The Police Executive Secretary." *Police.* 7:3 (January-February, 1963), 20-21.

Schwartz, Alfred I. et al. *Employing Civilians for Police Work.* Washington: The Urban Institute, 1975.

COMMUNITY SERVICE OFFICERS

Booz-Allen and Hamilton Inc. *Community Service Officer—Cluster Evaluation—Final Report.* Washington: NCJRS (Microfiche), 1974.

Erikson, James M. "Community Service Officer." *Police Chief.* XL:6 (June, 1973), 40-46.

Laughlin, Ralph W. "Experiment With Low-Key Enforcement Now S.O.P." *Police Chief.* XLI:6 (June, 1974), 22-24.
Use of community service officers in resort area.

"Police Community Services Officers: The Atlanta Ordinance." *Police Chief.* XXXV:5 (May, 1968).

RESERVES

Reserves—General

ABT Associates, Inc. *Log Angeles County—Sheriff's Department—Reserve Deputy Sheriff Program—Exemplary Project Validation Report.* Washington: NCJRS (Microfiche), 1975.

"Auxiliary." *New Yorker.* (December 18, 1971), 28-30.

Bradley, Vincent. "Pacific Grove's Auxiliary Police Marine Unit." *Police Chief.* 30:8 (August, 1963).

Buckley, Ernest L. "Fort Worth's Ready Reserve." *Law and Order.* 14:11 (November, 1966), 32-39.

Buckley, Robert. "California Law Experiment Reserve Program." *Journal of California Law Enforcement* (April, 1969), 223-225.

"Citizen Reserve Living up to Expectations." *Police Journal.* St. Louis. 19 (November, 1966), 6-7.

Coddington, T.G. *Survey of Reserve Law Enforcement in Arizona—Research Practicum, December 1974.* Washington: NCJRS, 1974.

Culverhouse, E.A. "The Law Student-Policeman." *FBI Law Enforcement Bulletin.* 39:5 (May, 1970), 10-13.
Resort city, Virginia Beach, Virginia, recruits law students for extra summer help.

Dubin, Morton. "The New York City Auxiliary Police." *Law and Order.* 21:8 (August, 1973), 95-97.

Elmes, Frank. "Police Reserves." *Police Review.* [Eng.] 83 (January 17, 1975), 75.

Flynn, P.J. "Berwick's Volunteer Police." *American City.* 74 (April, 1959).

Harvison, C.W. "The R.C.M.P. Reserve." *R.C.M.P. Quarterly.* 12 (April, 1947), 287-291.

Holmgren, R. Bruce. "Police Reserves?" *Police.* 5:3 (January-February, 1961), 14-17; 5:4 (March-April, 1961), 32-34.

Jessup, Jacob A. "A Study of the Use of Police Reserves or Auxiliaries." *Police.* 4:3 (January-February, 1960), 26-29.

Job, Glenn T. "Sheriff's Mounted Posse Increases Police Strength." *FBI Law Enforcement Bulletin.* 27:2 (February, 1958), 18-20.

Johnston, Walter L. "The Undeveloped Muscle." *Law and Order.* 18:12 (December, 1970), 68, 70.

Jordan, Truett. "Police Auxiliary Group Highlights Youth Program." *FBI Law Enforcement Bulletin.* 26:7 (July, 1957), 20-22.

King, E.M. *Auxiliary Police Unit.* Springfield, IL.: C.C. Thomas, 1960.

Kinley, N.J. "Reserve Police Corps." *Police Chief.* XXXV:4 (April, 1968), 52-54.

Lamb, R. "Emergency Auxiliary Units." *FBI Law Enforcement Bulletin.* 43:5 (1974), 11-12.
Describes activities of Sheriff's Disaster Search and Rescue Unit of the Las Vegas, Nev. metropolitan police section composed of police reserves.

Laughlin, Ralph W. "On the Beach: Low-Key Law Enforcement." *Police Chief.* XXXIX:3 (March, 1972), 22-23.

Lucas, H.E. "Police Reserve Lends Valuable Aid: Hays, Kansas." *American City.* 78 (February, 1963).

Mallery, John W. "Reserve Police Survey." *Law and Order.* 19:3 (March, 1971), 52, 54-55, 72-73.
Survey of departments utilizing reserve police. Statistics on working conditions, duties and numbers.

Manning, Frank W. "Help When You Need It." *FBI Law Enforcement Journal.* 35:9 (September, 1966), 14-18.

National Police Law Enforcement Institute. *The 1965 Study of the Use of Reserve Police: Basic Organization, Basic Training.* Venice, FL.: National Police Law Enforcement Institute, 1965.
Detailed information on selection training and other data on reserve police.

"Ohio Legion Aids Highway Patrol." *FBI Law Enforcement Bulletin.* 35:8 (August, 1966), 17-23.

Russell, Norman H. "One Way to Develop a Department's Resources." *Police Chief.* XLI:11 (November, 1974), 66-67.

Shidel, Terrence J. and Donald F. Komara. "Orientation and Training Programs for Auxiliary Police." *Police Chief.* XLI:11 (November, 1974), 55-59.

Skousen, W. Cleon. "Does a Police Reserve Really Pay Off?" *Law and Order.* 21:3 (March, 1973), 8, 10-12, 14-15.

Southward, Grant B. "Summer Manpower Recruitment." *Law and Order.* 15:5 (May, 1967), 60-62.
Use of law students as summer reserve police officers.

Stavely, Steven H. "The Professional Police Reserve Officer." *Police Chief.* XLII:9 (September, 1975), 35-37.

Swanson, C.R., Jr. "Police Minimum Standards and Auxiliary Officers." *Police Chief.* 38:8 (August, 1971), 60-63.

Tyler, Roy A. "Law Students as Patrolmen—A Successful Virginia Beach Experiment." *Police.* 14:1 (September-October, 1969), 53-55.

Unsinger, P.C. *Personnel Practices of Reserve/Auxiliary Law Enforcement Programs.* Springfield, VA.: NTIS, 1973.

U.S. Department of Defense, Office of Civil Defense. *Basic Auxiliary Police.* Washington: GRP, 1961.

Van Cleve, W. "Community Liaison Patrol." *FBI Law Enforcement Bulletin.* 43:6 (1974), 26-27.

Zeis, Harold S. "Organization and Functions of an Emergency Reserve." *FBI Law Enforcement Bulletin* (August, 1956).

Explorer Scouts

Bayer, S.C. "Youth and Law Enforcement." *Law and Order.* 16:10 (October, 1968), 90-91.

Bettfreund, John W. "An Examination of Normalcy." *FBI Law Enforcement Bulletin.* 38:12 (December, 1969), 14-16, 21.

Folsom, A.O., Jr. "Youths Form State-Wide Law Enforcement Organization." *Law and Order.* 19:12 (December, 1971), 120-121, 128.

Myers, George K. "Boy Scouts Announce New Exploring Program." *Police.* 3:2 (November-December, 1958), 40-41.

Neal, Ray K. "Law Enforcement Explorer Posts." *Police Chief.* XXXVI:3 (March, 1969).

Pitchess, Peter J. "Exploring Law Enforcement." *Journal of California Law Enforcement* (April, 1975), 156-158.

Renyhart, John. "Law Enforcement Explorers Get Involved." *Police Chief.* XLII:12 (December, 1975), 54, 74.

"Youths Form Statewide Law Enforcement Organization." *FBI Law Enforcement Bulletin.* 41:1 (January, 1972), 14-15.

Junior Police

Bomberger, A.E. "Sheridan Youth Police Reserves." *Law and Order.* 18:8 (August, 1970), 96-97.

Youthful reserves, ages 14½ to 21, perform non-criminal police duties and involve themselves in service projects. Vandalism has dropped 72% and minors in possession has dropped 81%.

Britton, Robert. "A Network for Crime Prevention." *Law and Order.* 15:9 (September, 1967), 88-89.

Jr. Deputy program sponsored by National Association of Sheriffs.

Bush, Stan G. "Youth to the Rescue." *Law and Order.* 15:1 (January, 1967), 50-53.

Activities of youth rescue unit, Littleton, Colorado.

Costa, Rudy. "TOPS Aid Police Community Relations." *Law and Order.* 17:10 (October, 1969), 98-101.

TOPS or Teens on Patrol program, low-income youngsters, fourteen to eighteen used to patrol and report non-criminal situations.

Cotron, Robert J. "Chests Out for Law Enforcement!" *FBI Law Enforcement Bulletin.* 37:7 (July, 1963), 2-6.

Downey, Isabelle T. "Eau Galle Junior Police League." *Law and Order.* 18:6 (June, 1970), 58-59.

Organization of youngsters 10 to 16 years of age.

Knopf, Terry. *Youth Patrols: An Experiment in Community Participation.* Waltham, MA.: Brandeis University, 1969.

Lombard, William. "Keeping the Inner City Cool." *Law and Order.* 16:5 (May, 1968), 113-119.

TOP, Teens on Patrol, patrol in Rochester, N.Y. Excellent paper on this program.

"Respect for Law Begins at an Early Age." *FBI Law Enforcement Bulletin.* 38:3 (March, 1969), 12-13.

Jr. Deputy Sheriff League of Collier County Florida. Has a membership of nearly 1,000 boys.

Yount, Kathy. "Kirkwood Police Junior Aide Program." *Police.* 15:6 (July-August, 1971), 33-35.

VOLUNTEERS

Barr, H. *Volunteers in Prison After-Care.* London: George Allen & Unwin, 1971.

Three-year pilot project based in London concerned with citizens involvement and liaison between a statutory and voluntary organization.

Blubaum, Paul E. "Maricopa County Sheriff's Department Volunteer Program." *Police Chief.* XLIII:2 (February, 1976), 34-36.

Unique volunteer program using the elderly and disabled. Volunteers answer 'phones, man switchboards, handle records, serve as Chaplains and many other activites.

Burgoon, Janet, and Joan Winter. *Operating Manual for a Volunteer Talent Pool.* Winnetka, IL.: Winnetka Volunteer Talent Pool, 1968.

Cohen, Nathaniel. *The Citizen Volunteer: His Responsibility, Role and Opportunity in Modern Society.* N.Y.: Harper & Row, 1962.

Freund, Janet. *A Guide for Coordinators of Volunteers and Volunteer Services in Schools.* Winnetka, IL.: Winnetka Public Schools, 1966.

Jamer, T. Margaret. *School Volunteers.* N.Y.: Public Education Association, 1961.

Janowitz, Gayle. *Helping Hands: Volunteer Work in Education.* Chicago: University of Chicago Press, 1965.

Law Enforcement Assistance Administration. *Volunteers in Law Enforcement Programs, Staff Study.* Washington: NCJRS, 1972.

Review of citizen participation projects which donated manpower to police, court, corrections, and probation activities.

Naylor, Harriet H. *Volunteers Today: Finding, Training, and Working With Them.* N.Y.: Association Press, 1967.

Olesen, A.J. *Volunteers as Family Counselors.* N.Y.: Home Advisory and Service Council, 1972.

Process by which volunteers are interviewed, assessed, selected, and trained for family counseling in a New York City service agency.

Oliver, J.P. "Paraprofessionals: The Precinct Receptionist Program." *Police Chief.* 40:1 (1973), 40-41.

Pell, Arthur L. *Recruiting, Training and Motivating Volunteer Workers.* N.Y.: Pilot Books, 1972.

Schindler-Rainman, Eva and Ronald Lippit. *The Volunteer Community; Creative Use of Human Resources.* Ann Arbor, MI.: Institute for Social Research, University of Michigan, 1971.

Stenzel, Anne K. and Helen M. Feeney. *Volunteer Training and Development: A Manual for Community Groups.* N.Y.: Seabury, 1968.

Turner, Kenneth A. "A New Approach to Juvenile Probation." *Law and Order.* 17:9 (September, 1969), 94-97.

Use of citizens as probation officers, known as the Auxiliary Probation Service.

Unkovic, Charles M. and Jean Reiman Davis. "You Can Fight Crime!" *Police.* 16:4 (December, 1971), 56-58.

Use of volunteers with released offenders.

Weinbrug, I.C. *Volunteers Help Youth.* Washington: GPO, 1971.

PART IX
POLICE EDUCATION AND TRAINING

POLICE EDUCATION

EDUCATION

Acheson, David C. "Tapping our Resources." *Police Chief.* 34:2 (February, 1967), 33-35.

Barber, John C. "University of California Police Program." *FBI Law Enforcement Bulletin.* 43:11 (November, 1974).

Bard, Bernard. "Should Cops Go to College?" *The Lion* (May, 1973).

Berg, Ivar. *Education and Jobs: The Great Training Robbery.* N.Y.: Praeger, 1970.

Beto, G.J. and R. Marsh. "Problems in the Development of an Undergraduate Criminal Justice Curriculum." *Federal Probation* (December, 1974).

Bopp, William J. "A Dying Art?" *Police Chief.* XXXVII:4 (April, 1970), 42-47.

Boye, Robert F. "Making Law Enforcement Education Relevant to Police Needs." *Law and Order.* 19:2 (February, 1971), 20-21.

Brandstatter, A.F. "Education Serves Police, Youth and Community." *Police Chief.* 33:8 (August, 1966), 12-14.
Briefly describes the police administration programs at Michigan State University.

Brandstatter, A.F. *History of Police Education in the United States.* Washington: Police Science Degree Programs: A Conference Report, June 8-9, 1967.

Brown, Lee P. "Police and Higher Education: The Challenge of the Times." *Criminology.* 12:1 (May, 1974), 114-124.

Brown, Lee P. "An Unforeseen Problem Resulting from College Educated Policemen." *Police.* 10:3 (January-February, 1966), 72-73.

Bryan, Robert S. "The Chief Speaks Out." *Police.* 13:2 (November-December, 1968), 56-57.

Bugenske, Joseph E. "We Are Doing the Job." *Law and Order.* 14:8 (August, 1966), 82-83.

Burrow, W.W. "College Education and the Police Officer of Tomorrow." *Texas Police Journal.* 22:1, 1-3, 21.

Carter, Robert M. and E.K. Nelson. "The Law Enforcement Education Program—One University's Experience." *Journal of Police Science and Administration.* 1:4 (December, 1973), 491-494.

Chambelin, Neil C. "The Need to Develop Guidance Services in Criminal Justice Education." *Police Chief.* XLII:8 (August, 1975), 42-45.

Clark, D.E. and Samuel G. Chapman. *Forward Step—Educational Background for Police.* Springfield, IL.: C.C. Thomas, 1966.

Constantine, Thomas A. "Higher Education for Police—Some Operational Difficulties." *Police Chief.* XXXIX:6 (June, 1972), 18-20.

Cook, Fred J. "John Jay: College for Cops." *Nation.* 211 (November 30, 1970), 555-558.

Cross, Wilbur. *The Weekend Education Source Book.* N.Y.: Harpers Magazine.
Describes weekend colleges, seminars, short courses. Lists costs, accommodations, credits, degrees, facilities, and subjects taught at over 300 centers.

Cusack, W.E. and Donald Apai. "Law Enforcement Education in New Jersey." *Police Chief.* XXXVII:8 (August, 1970), 56-58.

Day, Frank D. "Administration of Criminal Justice: An Educational Design in Higher Education." *Journal of Criminal Law, Criminology and Police Science.* 56:4 (December, 1965), 540-544.

Deppe, Donald A. "A Decade of Service to Law Enforcement Personnel." *Police.* 4:6 (July-August, 1960), 68-71.

Erickson, James M. and Matthew J. Neary. "Criminal Justice Education: Is It Criminal?" *Police Chief.* XLII:8 (August, 1975), 38-40.

Fagerstrom, Dorothy. "Education by Degrees." *Law and Order.* 16:2 (February, 1968), 13-15, 80.
Survey to determine educational needs and trends.

Finkel, William P. "Job Wanted: Educated Policeman." *Law and Order.* 18:12 (December, 1970), 119-125.

Folley, Vern L. "Incipiency of Police Education in Pennsylvania." *Police* (March-April, 1966).

Folley, Vern L. "The Sphere of Police Education." *Law and Order.* 15:2 (February, 1967), 16-24, 78.

Freeman, Richard B. *The Over-Educated American.* N.Y.: Academic, 1976.

Gambino, Fred, Jr. "Higher Education for Police, Pros and Cons." *Law and Order.* 21:2 (February, 1973), 58-66.

Gardiner, Jerome D. "A Re-Examination of Police Preparatory Education." *Law and Order.* 23:3 (March, 1975), 30, 32-33, 53.

Geary, David P. "College Educated Cops—Three Years Later." *Police Chief.* XXXVII:8 (August, 1970), 59-62.

Giddings, Larry A. "Criminal Justice Curriculum: A New Approach to Criminal Justice Administration." *Police Chief.* XXXVII: (February, 1970), 44-45.

Gould, Edward W. "Does a Policeman Need to Have a College Degree to Be a Professional?" *Law and Order.* 21:2 (February, 1973), 68-69.

Gross, Solomon. "Higher Education and Police: Is There a Need for a Closer Look?" *Journal of Police Science and Administration.* 1:4 (December, 1973), 477-483.

Newitt, William H. "The Objectives of a Formal Police Education." *Police.* 9:2 (November-December, 1964), 25-27.

Hoffman, Jonathan. "Can Colleges Make Better Cops?" *College Management* (November, 1972).

Hoover, Larry T. *Police Educational Characteristics and Curricula.* Washington: NCJRS, 1975.

Howland, John T. "The Boston Police Baccalaureate Program." *FBI Law Enforcement Bulletin.* 38:4 (April, 1969), 2-5, 20.

International Association of Chiefs of Police. *Law Enforcement Education Directory.* Washington: IACP, Annual.

Jagiello, R.J. "College Education for the Patrolman—Necessity or Irrelevance?" *Journal of Criminal Law, Criminology and Police Science* (1971).

Jagiello, Robert. "A 'Minus' in Police Legal Education." *Police Chief.* XXXVI:2 (February, 1969), 20-24.

Keller, E. John. "A Municipal Police College." *Law and Order.* 13:2 (February, 1965), 6-9, 42.

Kessler, Francis R. "An Academic Approach to Police Service." *FBI Law Enforcement Bulletin.* 36:5 (May, 1967), 9-11.

Kuchel, G.L. "The Development of a University Police Science Program." *Law and Order.* 14:12 (December, 1966,) 86-87, 95.

Kuldau, Von D. "Criminal Justice Education: Myths or Reality?" *Police Chief.* XLII:8 (August, 1975), 18-19.

Kuldau, Von D. "Education: Punishment or Reward?" *Police Chief.* XLI:8 (August, 1974), 25-26.

Kuykendall, Jack L. "Toward an Integrated-Professional Model of Administration of Justice Education." *Journal of California Law Enforcement* (January, 1976), 103-109.

Kuykendall, Jack L. and Armand P. Hernandez. "A Curriculum Development Model: Quality Control Programming in Justice Education." *Police Chief.* XLII:8 (August, 1975), 20-25.

Kuykendall, Jack and Armand P. Hernandez. "A University's Administration of Justice Program (An Organizational Analysis at San Diego State University)." *Journal of Police Science and Administration.* 2:3 (September, 1974), 297-307.

Lankes, George A. "How Should We Educate the Police?" *Journal of Criminal Law, Criminology and Police Science.* 61 (December, 1970).

Lankes, George A. "A Profile of the Police Science Student." *Police Chief.* 38:4 (April, 1971), 60-64.

Survey shows that police science students compare favorably with students with other majors. Also describes admission requirements for police science students.

Lateef, A. Bari. "A Proposed Curriculum in Forensic Science." *Canadian Society of Forensic Science Journal.* 7:1 (March, 1974), 26-36.

Lejins, Peter P. *Introducing a Law Enforcement Curriculum at a State University.* A report of the National Institute of Law Enforcement and Criminal Justice. Washington: GPO, 1970.

Looney, Francis B. "College Education for Police." *Law and Order.* 17:10 (October, 1969), 40-41.

Loughrey, Leo C. and Herbert C. Friese, Jr. "Curriculum Development for a Police Science Program." *Journal of Criminal Law, Criminology and Police Science.* 60:2 (June, 1969), 265-271.

Mark, Jack A. "You Too Can Be 'El Exigente'—The Demanding One." *Police Chief.* XLII:8 (August, 1975), 50-53.

Maryland Governor's Commission. *Report on Maryland Criminal Justice Higher Education Programs.* Cockeysville, MD.: Maryland Governor's Commission, 1974.

Mathias, William J. "A Criminal Justice Curriculum for an Urban Society." *Police Chief.* XXXVI:8 (August, 1969), 16-18.

Meehan, James B. "Police Participation in the College Training of Police." *Police.* 8:4 (March-April, 1964), 24-27.

Melichar, Dudley W. and I. Gayle Shuman. "A Criminal Justice Curriculum Development Model." *Police Chief.* XLI:8 (August, 1974), 32, 34.

Michael, Geraldine. "Social Science Education for Police Officers." *Police Chief.* XXXVIII:6 (June, 1971), 56-61.

Mirich, John J. and Eugene Voris. "Police Science Education in the United States: A National Need." *Journal of Criminal Law, Criminology and Police Science.* 56:4 (December, 1965), 545-54.

Moloney, Neil W. "Seattle's Satellite Campus." *Police Chief.* (September, 1973), 40-41.

Moore, Merlyn D. "The Field and Academia: A Message." *Police Chief.* XLII:8 (August, 1975), 66-69.

Morgan, James P., Jr. "Responsibilities of Universities to the Criminal Justice System." *Police.* 15:2 (November-December, 1970), 50-54.

Morgan, J.P., Jr., and A. Lee McGehee. "Criminal Justice Degree Development in Georgia." *Police.* 15:3 (January-February, 1971), 71-74.

Moynahan, J.M. "A Social Science Approach to the Education of Law Enforcement Personnel." *Police.* 14:1 (September-October, 1969), 71-74.

Myren, Richard A. "Academia and the Criminal Justice System: Development of a Role." *Police Chief.* 33:8 (August, 1966), 20, 22, 24, 26.

Advocates development rather than continuous haphazard growth.

Myren, Richard A. "Core Curriculum for Undergraduate Academic Police Training." *Journal of Criminal Law, Criminology and Police Science.* 49:5 (January-February 1959), 507-509.

Nelson, Jack. "Police Degrees: School Exploits Law, Order Issue." *Police Chief.* XXXVI:6 (June, 1969), 8-16.

O'Reilly, James T. "Bridging the Gap: Law Enforcement and Legal Education." *Police Chief* (November, 1973), 54-57.

O'Rourke, William J. "Should All Policemen Be College Trained?" *Police Chief.* 38:12 (December, 1971), 36-38.

Overson, H. Wayne. "Police and Radical Politics: Are College Cops Being Prepared to Deal with Revolution?" *Law and Order.* 20:3, (March, 1972), 79-83.

Pantaleoni, C.A. "Law Enforcement Academia: Crossroad or Concern?" *Police Chief.* 38:8 (September, 1970), 42-47.

Patrick, H.W. "Salt Lake City Police Department: Career Education in Law Enforcement." *Police Chief.* XLII:7 (July, 1975), 56-57.

Perlstein, Gary R. and Bernard C. Brannon. "Coordination in Criminal Justice Education." *Police.* 15:4 (March-April, 1971), 19-20.

Pettit, Ronald E. "The Need for Continuing Education." *Law and Order.* 18:2 (February, 1970), 26-30.

Peva, James R. "Send an Officer to Law School." *Police Chief.* 38:4 (April, 1971), 58-59.

Prout, Robert. "Criminal Justice Internships: Exposure or Attainment?" *Police Chief.* XLII:8 (August, 1975), 36-37.

Rotella, S.G. and R.E. McCann. "Law Enforcement Education in Chicago." *Police Chief.* XXXVII:8 (August, 1970), 52-55.

Sandman, Henry J. "Partners for an Improved Community: Police and the University." *Police Chief.* XL:4 (April, 1973), 42-44.

Schroeder, Oliver, Jr. "Police Education: A University Aids the Smaller Departments." *Police.* 4:2 (November-December, 1959), 15-18.

Shaw, William. "Keep Your College Graduates—Just Give Me Dedicated Men!" *Law and Order.* 17:4 (April, 1969), 34-41.

Sheehan, Robert. "Internship: A New Concept in Police Education." *Police Chief.* 33:8 (August, 1966), 34, 36, 38, 68.

Shenkman, Frederick A. "The Role of Criminal Justice Education in the Modern University." *Police Chief.* XLI:7 (July, 1974), 67-69.

"Special Notice: Degree Mills." *Police Chief.* XXXV:9 (September, 1968).

Sterling, James W. "The College Level Entry Requirement: A Real or Imagined Cure-All?" *Police Chief* (August, 1974).

Stinchcomb, James B. "The Student Internship in Law Enforcement Curricula." *Police.* 7:2 (November-December, 1962), 34-35.

Tamm, Quinn. "After College—What?" *The Police Chief* (February, 1965).

Tenney, Charles. *Higher Education Programs in Law Enforcement and Criminal Justice.* Washington: GPO, 1971.

Tracy, Charles A. "Law Enforcement Baccalaureate Education in Southern Oregon." *Police.* 15:6 (July-August, 1971), 39-43.

University of Montreal. *Montreal University—International Centre for Comparative Criminology—Annual Report, 1972-1973.* Washington: NCJRS (Microfiche), 1973.

Unsinger, Peter C. "Everything You Wanted to Know About the External Degree But Were Afraid to Ask." *Police Chief.* XL:2 (February, 1973), 64-65.

Wachtel, Julius. "The Need for Change in Police Science Curricula." *Police Chief.* XXXIX:11 (November, 1972), 64-66.

Whisenand, Paul M. "The Upgrading of Educational Requirements for California Police Officers." *Journal of California Law Enforcement* (October, 1967), 80-86.

Whisenand, Paul M. "The Upgrading of Educational Requirements for Police: Unplanned for Personnel Problems." *Police Chief.* 33:8 (August, 1966), 39-40, 42, 43.

Discusses problems relating to the recruitment and retention of college graduates.

Whitehouse, Jack E. "The United States Police Academy: A Proposal." *Journal of California Law Enforcement.* IV (March, 1970), 115-119.

This article advances a proposal for a national police academy patterned after the military service academies. What this type of education would mean to the police service and the objectives of the proposal are discussed. The discipline of students, possibilities for a library, advantages and road blocks are also discussed.

TWO-YEAR COLLEGES

Allen, Ralph W. "Community College: A Policeman's Best Friend." *Pennsylvania Law Enforcement Journal.* 26 (December, 1969), 12-13, 23, 25.

Brantley, Wilbur R. "The Island Hopping Criminal Justice Professor." *Police.* 13:4 (March-April, 1969), 63-67.

Burrow, W.W. "Texas Core Curriculum in Law Enforcement." *Police Chief.* XXXIX:9. (September, 1972) 48-49.

Caldwell, D.P. "Community Cooperation." *Police Chief.* 33:7. (July, 1966) 48-50.

Crockett, Thomas S. and James D. Stinchcomb. *Guidelines for Law Enforcement Education Programs in Community and Junior Colleges.* Washington: American Association of Junior Colleges, 1968.

Guynn, Arnold L. and Moses A. Leon. "There's a New Look at Law Enforcement at Pima College." *Police Chief.* (November, 1973) 61-62.

Logan, John F. "Law Enforcement Education and the Community College." *Police Chief.* XLII:8 (August, 1975), 26-30.

McAllister, John. " 'Revving Up' Rural Personnel." *Police Chief.* XXXVII:5 (May, 1970), 52-54.

McArthur, Jack. "The Development of California's Standardized Two Year College Police Curriculum." *Journal of Criminal Law, Criminology and Police Science.* 57:3 (September, 1965), 360-364.

Negley, James C. "Pre-Service Training in California Junior Colleges." *Police.* 7:3 (January-February, 1963), 22-25.

Prout, Robert S. "An Analysis of Associate Degree Programs in Law Enforcement." *Journal of Criminal Law, Criminology and Police Science* (December, 1972).

Rossi, Steve S. "A Community Involvement Program for Police Students." *Police.* 16:11 (July, 1972), 59-64.

Stinchcomb, James D. "The Community College and Its Impact." *Police Chief.* 33:8 (August, 1966), 28, 30, 32, 73.

Vaupel, Carl F. "Analysis of Two-Year Police Science Programs." *Police.* 13:6 (July-August, 1969), 18-25.

Yankee, William J. *A Description and Evaluation of the Associate Degree Law Enforcement Curricula in the Public Community and Junior Colleges of Michigan.* Unpub. Doctoral dissertation. Michigan State University, 1970.

ACCREDITATION

Ashburn, Franklin Glendon. "Time to Test the Rhetoric." *Police Chief.* XLII:8 (August, 1975), 46-48.

Miller, Jerry N. "Characteristics of Specialized Accreditation." *Police Chief.* XXXVII:8 (August, 1970), 32-33.

Misner, Gordon D. "Accreditation of Criminal Justice Education Programs." *Police Chief.* XLII:8 (August, 1975), 14-16, 78.

Patterson, Frank M. "College Credit for Trooper Training." *Police Chief.* 34:2 (February, 1967), 36-37.

Territo, Leonard. "College Credit for Law Enforcement Training Courses: Recent Trends and Future Projections." *Police Chief.* XLII:8 (August, 1975), 32-34, 78.

CORRESPONDENCE COURSES

Cooke, E. Dickerson. "A School at Home." *Law and Order.* 13:2 (February, 1965), 34-35.

Studdert, Stephen M. "Earn College Credit—At Home." *Law and Order.* 19:6 (June, 1971), 92, 94-95.

"University at Home." *Law and Order.* 14:2 (February, 1966).

EDUCATION AND TRAINING

Ashburn, Franklin G. "The Danger of Selective Bias in Law Enforcement Education and Training." *Police* (November-December, 1967).

"Basic Training of Police in Quebec." *Bulletin of the Canadian Criminology and Correction Association.* 2:3 (1973).
Community colleges will provide theoretical training and the Nicolet Police College will provide the practical training. Recruits will have 2.5 years of college plus 6 months at the police college when they enter the police force.

Cancilla, Robert C. "Higher Education and Training for Police Officers." *Journal of California Law Enforcement* (October, 1974), 61-68.

Cromwell, P.F., Jr. "Training—Education—Understanding Bridge the Gap." *Police Chief* (March, 1972).

Jones, Ralph H. et al. "What Is the Number One Problem in Education and Training?" *Police Chief* (August, 1970).

Kuykendall, Jack L. and Armand Hernandez. "Undergraduate Justice System Education and Training at San Jose State." *Journal of Criminal Justice* (1975).

Langhoff, Norman. "An Essay: Police Education and Training—A Foundation for Change." *Criminal Law Bulletin* (May, 1972).

O'Neill, Michael E. and Jerome E. Lance. "Education vs. Training: A Distinction." *Journal of California Law Enforcement* (April, 1970), 201-203.

Parker, William L. "Training and Education: A Big 'Plus' for the Nashville Police Department." *Police Chief.* XL:2 (February, 1973), 36-37.

Santarelli, Donald E. "Education for Concepts, Training for Skills." *Police Chief.* XLI:8 (August, 1974), 20, 76.

"What Is the Number One Problem in Education and Training?" *Police Chief.* XXXVII:8 (August, 1970), 16-17.

Wilson, Brooks W. "Education and Training: An Assessment of Where We Are and Where We Are Going." *Police Chief.* XLI:8 (August, 1974), 23-24, 71.

EDUCATIONAL INCENTIVE PAY

Allen, William A. "Premium Pay for the College Trained Officer." *Police Chief.* XXXV:8 (August, 1968), 70-73.

Bristow, Allen P. "Educational Recognition by California Law Enforcement." *Police* (July-August, 1967).

Bristow, Allen P. "Survey Indicates California Law Enforcement Stresses Education." *Journal of California Law Enforcement* (July, 1967), 19-22.
Survey of monetary incentives for college education.

Crockett, T.S. and John Moses. "Incentive Plans for Law Enforcement Education." *Police Chief.* XXXVI:8 (August, 1969), 28-52.

Hamann, A.D. "An Educational Oriented Incentive Pay Plan." *Police Chief.* XXXV:3 (March, 1968), 40-42.

Kane, Walter C. "Police Educational Incentive Pay Plans." *Law Enforcement Executive.* 5 (September, 1970) (entire issue).

"Police Educational Incentive Pay Plan." *Management Information Service Reports.* 2 (May, 1970), 4-11.

Stinchcomb, James D. "Higher Pay for Higher Education." *Police Chief.* XXXIV:8 (August, 1967), 40-43.

Webb, Donald G. "Police Administrators and the Personnel Incentive Policy." *Police Chief.* 38:4 (April, 1971), 66-67, 69-70.

SCHOLARSHIPS

Cusack, William E. "New Jersey Police Training Commission Scholarship Program." *Police.* 15:5 (May-June, 1971), 70-77.

Law Enforcement Assistance Administration. *Law Enforcement Education Program—Guideline Manual.* Washington: NCJRS (Microfiche), 1974.

Neuling, Floyd M. "College Can Be Free." *Law and Order.* 18:2 (February, 1970), 16-17, 94.
Discusses scholarships, financial help, G.I. bill, and others.

POLICE TRAINING

TRAINING—GENERAL

Aaron, Thomas J. "Considering a Training Program." *Law and Order,* 14:10 (October, 1966), pp. 14-15, 32.

Adams, Thomas F. *Training Officer's Handbook.* Springfield, IL: C.C. Thomas, 1964.

Asselt, K.A. Van. "Development of a Statewide Training Program." *Police Chief,* XXXLV:4 (April, 1967), pp. 55-56.

Auten, James H. "Determining Training Needs." *Police,* 15:1 (September-October, 1970), pp. 25-28.

Auten, James H. *Training in the Small Department.* Springfield, IL: C.C. Thomas, 1973.
Aspects of the training function ranging from the responsibilities of management personnel to the instructional role assumed by the individual

Auten, James H. "Training Within the Small Department." *Law and Order,* 18:2 (February, 1970), pp. 42, 44-45.

Ayoob, Massad F. "Explosives Training Course for Police." *Law and Order,* 21:2 (February, 1973), pp. 73-74.

Bigelow, Richard H. "Certification and Professionalization Through Police Training." *Law and Order,* 18:2 (February, 1970), pp. 46, 94.
Author advocates the certification of training officers.

Bimstein, Donald. "Improving Departmental Training Programs." *Police,* 15:5 (May-June, 1971), pp. 22-25.

Briscoll, James. "Shoplifting Seminar." *Law and Order,* 17:4 (April, 1969), pp. 86-90.

Buckley, John L. "Professional Training for Civil Defense." *Law and Order,* 11:8 (August, 1963), pp. 40-41, 49.

Burger, Kurt. *Mental Illness and Law Enforcement.* St. Louis, MO: Law Enforcement Center, Washington University, 1970.

Chapman, Charles C. "Training to Meet Unusual Occurrences." *Police* (May-June, 1962), pp. 50-51.

Clift, Raymond E. "Police Training." *The Annals of the American Academy of Political and Social Science,* CCXCI (January, 1954), pp. 113-118.

Coffman, Carl. "Police Training and Deterrence." *Law and Order* (March, 1976), pp. 59-61.

The Commission on Peace Officer Standards and Training. *Training Assessment and Planning.* Sacramento: California Office of Procurement, Publications Section, 1975.

Cox, David. "A Systems Model for Selection of Peace Officer Instructors." *Police Chief,* XLII:9 (September, 1975), pp. 26-28.

Culloo, Leo A. "New Jersey's Motorized Classrooms." *Police Chief,* XXXV:8 (August, 1968), pp. 45, 55-56.
Use of trailer as mobile classroom. Can accommodate thirty students along with a number of training aides.

Curtis, S.J. "The Psychology of Security Training." *Police,* 4:5 (May-June, 1960), pp. 47-50.

Davis, I.K. et al. *Organization of Training.* N.Y.: McGraw, 1973.

Daxe, Arnold. "Military Police Training." *Military Police Journal* (October, 1970), pp. 11-14.

Day, Frank D. "An Instructional Approach to Criminal Interrogation." *Police,* 2:5 (May-June, 1958), pp. 47-52.

Doyle, Edward and George D. Olivet. "An Invitation to Understanding: The Citizen and His Constitutional Rights." *Police Chief,* XXXIX:3 (March, 1972), pp. 18-20.

Doyle, Edward and George D. Olivet. "An Invitation to Understanding—Law Enforcement Integrity." *Police Chief,* XXXIX:5 (May, 1972), pp. 34-44.
Report of an anti-corruption workshop conducted by NYPD.

Drawbaugh, C.C. "Evaluating the Concept of Mobile Training." *Police Chief,* XXXV:8 (August, 1968), pp. 56-50.
Evaluation of trailer used as mobile classroom.

Edwards, K. Dean. "The Police Officer as Instructor." *Police Chief,* XLII:8 (August, 1975), pp. 60-63.

Engle, C. Donald. "Police Training in Non-Crime Related Functions." *Police Chief,* XLI:6 (June, 1974), pp. 61-65.

Fagerstrom, Dorothy. "Dedicated to Progress." *Law and Order,* 13:2 (February, 1965), pp. 22-24, 65.

"FBI Training Programs." *FBI Law Enforcement Bulletin,* 37:5 (May, 1968), pp. 7-11, 24.

Describes activities of the FBI National Academy and Field Training programs.

Felkenes, George T. "A Regional Training Approach." *Police Chief,* XLI:8 (August, 1974), pp. 38, 40-41.

Finkelman, Jay M. and Walter Reichman. "Police Training Strategies: A Contingency Model." *Journal of Police Science and Administration,* 2:4 (December, 1974), pp. 423-428.

Folley, Vern L. "College Based Police Training." *Law and Order,* 22:3 (March, 1974), pp. 32-34, 36, 37-38, 40.

Freeman, Sydney. "A Systems Approach to Law Enforcement Training." *Police Chief,* XXXV:8 (August, 1968), pp. 61-69.

Gammage, Allen Z. *Police Training in the United States.* Springfield, IL: C.C. Thomas, 1963.

Gardner, Martin R., Sr. "Cross Media Training: A Possible Solution to a Real Problem." *Law and Order,* 19:5 (May, 1971), pp. 84-85, 91, 93.
Description of the training of civilians in police work.

Gibson, Winston A. *An Educational Curriculum for Police Training.* Unpub. Doctoral dissertation. Michigan State University, 1972.

Glaser, Rollin O. and Calvin P. Otto. *The Management of Training.* Reading, MA: Addison-Wesley, 1970.

"A Good Officer is a Trained Officer." *FBI Law Enforcement Bulletin,* 36:5 (May, 1967), pp. 12-13.

Grant, Harvey D. "Delaware State Fire School." *Law and Order* (November, 1975), pp. 60-65.
The training of policemen at Delaware's State Fire School. Topics covered are rescue, first aid, water rescue operations.

Gruzanski, Charles V. "National Police Training Program Survey." *Police* (September and October, 1966).

Harrison, Leonard H. "Standardized Police Training in New Jersey." *Police Chief,* XLI:8 (August, 1974), pp. 44-45.

Heaphy, John. "Field Training." *Police Chief,* XXXVII:2 (February, 1970), pp. 41-43.
Transition training from academy to actual field operations.

Hess, Fred. "Police Training—Small Communities." *Journal of Criminal Law, Criminology and Police Science,* 49:1 (May-June, 1958), pp. 75-77.

Holding, D.H. *Principles of Training.* Elmsford, N.Y.: Pergamon, 1965.

Jameson, Samuel Haig. "Controversial Areas in 20th Century Policing: Quest for Quality Training in Police Work." *American Society of Criminology,* 1964, pp. 123-133.

Jameson, Samuel Haig. "Quest for Quality Training in Police Work." *Journal of Criminal Law, Criminology and Police Science,* 57:2 (June, 1966), pp. 210-215.

Jameson, Samuel Haig. "The Quest for Quality Training to Cope With Modern Police Problems." *Journal of California Law Enforcement* (January, 1967), pp. 150-155.

Kaplan, Alvin. "New York City Police Academy's Approach to Teaching Law to Police Recruits." *Police Chief,* XLII:8 (August, 1975), pp. 64-65.

Keefe, Mary L. and Henry T. O'Reilly. "Rape: Attitude Training for Police and Emergency Room Personnel." *Police Chief,* XLII:11 (November, 1975), pp. 36-37.

Kelly, D.B. "Operation Combine." *Law and Order,* 16:9 (September, 1968), pp. 66-67, 96.

Kennedy, D.B. *Applied Sociology for Police.* Springfield, IL: C.C. Thomas, 1972.
Designed specifically as a basic sociology text, this document presents an introduction to the field as it relates to the police officer.

Kimble, Joseph P. "Police Training Today and the Challenge for Tomorrow." *Police,* 9:1 (September-October, 1964), pp. 11-14.

Latchaw, A. James. "Assistance for State Police." *Law and Order,* 14:7 (July, 1966), pp. 42-43, 64.

Lawder, Lee E. "Maryland State Police Training Program." *Law and Order,* 19:3 (March, 1971).

Lawder, Lee E. "Mobile Training Unit for Kentucky Law Enforcement." *Law and Order,* 19:3 (March, 1971).

Law Enforcement Assistance Administration. *Police Training and Performance Study.* Washington, D.C.: GPO, September, 1970.

Lawless, Thomas and Jesse Peterman. "Auto Theft and the Uniformed Officer." *Police Chief,* XL:6 (June, 1973), pp. 58-62.

Lechat, Rene. "The Criminal Police Training Museum." *International Criminal Police Review* (May, 1962), pp. 154-164.

McGrath, James J. "Economy and Efficiency in Police Training." *Law and Order,* 13:10 (October, 1965), pp. 68-70, 73.

Martin, J.A. "Training in Louisiana." *Police Chief.* XXXI (February, 1964).

Matt, A. Robert. "The Most Important Man." *Police,* 4:3 (January-Fabruary, 1960), pp. 62-63.

Maxwell, M.A. "Portland Police Tactical Platoon Gets Army Training." *Police Chief,* XXX (May, 1963).

Mirich, John J. "The Qualified Policeman—The Backbone of Society." *Journal of Criminal Law, Criminology and Police Science* (September-October, 1959), p. 316.

More, Harry W., Jr. "Law Enforcement Training in Institutes of Higher Learning." *Police,* 5:3 (January-February, 1961), pp. 6-9.

Mount, Tom and A.J. Ikehara. *Practical Diving: A Complete Manual for Compressed Air Divers.* Carol Coral Gables, FL: University of Miami Press, 1975.

Moyer, Clifford A. "Developing a Criminal Justice Training Program." *FBI Law Enforcement Bulletin,* 40:11 (November, 1971), pp. 24-26.

Moynahan, J.M. "Training the Police Officer in a Liberal Arts College." *Police Chief* (November, 1973), pp. 58-60.

Muehleisen, Gene S. *Identifying and Meeting Training Needs.* Jacksonville, FL: National Conference on Law Enforcement Education, 1970.

Murphy, G.M. and O.R. Tyus. "The University Role in Police Training." *Police Chief,* XXIV:8 (August, 1967), pp. 44-47.

Nadler, Leonard. *Employee Training in Japan.* Los Angeles: Ed. and Training, 1965.

Nielson, Robert C. "Equal Time for Unequal History: Police Training in Black American History." *Police Chief,* XLI:8 (August, 1974), pp. 59-61.

Olson, Bruce. *Regional Law Enforcement Training.* Detroit, MI: Metropolitan Fund, 1968.

O'Neill, Michael E. and Frank R. Benaderet. "Training: A Conceptual Model for Organizational Development." *Police Chief,* XL:2 (February, 1973).

Oregon Board on Police Standards and Training. *Oregon—District Advanced Training for Police Officers—Project Report, July 1, 1971 to June 30, 1972.* Washington, DC: NCJRS (Microfiche), 1972.

Otto, Calvin P. *The Management of Training.* Reading, MA: Addison-Wesley, 1970.

Price, Barbara Raffel. "Police Personnel in Pennsylvania and the Development of Line Level Training Programs." *Police,* 15:4 (March-April, 1971), pp. 6-13.

Project Star (System and Training Analysis of Requirements)—Police Officer Training Program. Santa Cruz, CA: Davis, 1974.

Quinn, Patrick Kevin. "Training Through Practical Experience." *Law and Order,* 18:12 (December, 1970), pp. 54-55, 56.

Reese, Charles D. "Police Academy Training and Its Effects on Racial Prejudice." *Journal of Police Science and Administration,* 1:3 (September, 1973), pp. 257-26S.

Richey, Larry D. "The Question of Stress Training." *Police Chief,* XLI:5 (May, 1974), pp. 63-67.

Richman, G.C. "Training Requirements for Local Police." *New Jersey State League of Municipalities* (February, 1955), pp. 9-12.

Robbins, David W. "Training Program for Police in a Small Community." *FBI Law Enforcement Bulletin,* 27:4 (April, 1958), pp. 11-12.

Robinson, David D. "Characteristics of an Effective Police Training Program." *Police,* 14:3 (January-February, 1970), pp. 42-46.

Schnur, Alfred C. "Pre-Service Training." *Journal of Criminal Law, Criminology and Police Science,* 50:1 (May-June, 1959), pp. 27-33.

Stevenson, Jan A. "Training the Police Armorer." *Law and Order,* 17:3 (March, 1969), pp. 72-77.

Swedmark, Donald C. *Developing the Company Training Program: A Guide to Their Organization, Administration and Evaluation.* Santa Fe Springs, CA: Davlin, 1975.

Todd, Francis. *Teaching About Alcohol.* N.Y.: McGraw-Hill, 1973.

Tracey, William R. *Designing Training and Development Systems.* N.Y.: AMA, 1971.

Tracey, William R. *Managing Training and Development Systems.* N.Y.: AMA, 1974.

"Training for the Future." *FBI Law Enforcement Bulletin,* 43:3 (March, 1974).

Vincent, William. "A 'Minus' in Our Modern Police Training Programs." *Police Chief,* XXXVI:2 (February, 1969), pp. 26-27.

Wasby, Stephen L. "Police Training and Criminal Procedure." *Police Chief,* 39:10 (October, 1972), pp. 24, 28, 30-31.

Webb, Horace S. "The Police Professional: Consistent Training Plus Standardization." *Police Chief,* XXXIX:4 (April, 1972), pp. 76-77.

Wechter, Harry L. "Professional Training—Are We Doing the Job?" *Law and Order,* 14:4 (April, 1966), pp. 84, 93.

White, Charles W. "A Few Trained Men Can Revitalize a Police Force." *American City,* 66:19 (November, 1951).

Wilson, Howard. *Employee Training.* Irvine, CA: Administration Research, 1972.

Wright, B.L. *Law Enforcement Training Program—An Evaluation of Participant and Supervisory Attitudes.* Washington, D C: NCJRS (Microfiche), 1973.

Zachen, J. and M. Bard. "Effect of Conflict Management Training on Police Performance." *Journal of Applied Psychology,* 58:202 (1973).

Zlochower, Sol and James R. Rush. "Delivery: Deliverance—New Method of Delivering Training in Southern Illinois." *Police Chief,* XLI:8 (August, 1974), pp. 35-37.

ACADEMIES AND OTHER CENTERS FOR POLICE TRAINING

Adkins, E.H., Jr. "An Idea for a Foreign Police Academy." *Police,* 6:4 (March-April, 1962), pp. 62-65.

Allan, David L. "F.B.I. National Academy." *Guardian* (Spring, 1975), pp. 55-58.

Archer, Calbe J. "Leavenworth and the Military Police Officer." *Military Police Journal* (July, 1970), pp. 4-7.

Baddeley, Fred. "The National College of England and Wales." *Journal of Criminal Law, Criminology and Police Science,* 63:3 (1972), pp. 434-438.

Barnett, B.J. "Florida Highway Patrol Academy." *Law and Order,* 23:5 (May, 1975), pp. 28-30.

Bassett, James E., III. "Kentucky's State Police Academy." *State Government,* 35 (Winter, 1962), pp. 34-36.

Belicka, Leonard. "International Academy Is Unique Educational Facilities." *Military Police Journal* (September, 1965).

Blanks, William Winfield. "Citadel of Training." *Law and Order,* 13:2 (February, 1965), pp. 10-13, 40.

Bramshill Police College. *Bramshill Police College.* Rev. ed. Washington, DC: NCJRS (Microfiche), 1973.

Description of facilities and training programs at the college at Bramshill in Hampshire near London.

Chiaramonte, Robert M. "The New Ohio State Highway Patrol Academy." *Law and Order,* 14:9 (September, 1966), pp. 78-80.

Dales, Douglas S. "New York State Police Plan New Academy." *Law and Order,* 16:2 (February, 1968), pp. 82-83.

Frost, Thomas M. "Police Training Facilities and Training Personnel." *Journal of Criminal Law, Criminology and Police Science,* 47:4 (November-December, 1956), pp. 475-481.

Grey, George. " 'Bramshill' More than Just an Old House." *Job* (January 25, 1974), pp. 4-5.

Johnson, Alexis. "The Role of Police Forces in a Changing World." *U.S. Department of State Bulletin,* 65 (September 13, 1971), pp. 280-283.

Johnson, Jack. "Open for Business." *Law and Order,* 14:6 (June, 1966), pp. 60-61, 74.
Florida's Highway Patrol training academy at Tallahassee.

Kline, J.S. and R.S. Weaver. "Regional Police Academy for North Central Texas." *Police Chief,* XXXVI:5 (May, 1969), pp. 22-24.

Moffatt, R.G. "Introduction to the Canadian Police College." *Canadian Police Chief* (October, 1974), pp. 34, 56, 76.

"New Academy for New York State Police." *Police Chief,* XXXV:2 (February, 1968).

"New England State Police Staff College Opens." *Police Chief,* 33:6 (June, 1966).

Petterson, Sandy. "Monument to Training." *Law and Order,* 16:2 (February, 1968), pp. 8-11, 84.

Poland, Alan B. "The Delaware State Police Academy." *Law and Order,* 21:2 (February, 1973), pp. 24-28, 67.

"The Police Academy." *Spring 3100,* 36 (January, 1965), pp. 11-28.

Rayfield, William D. "Police Training Center." *FBI Law Enforcement Bulletin,* 37:5 (May, 1968), pp. 15-16, 27.

Schkolnick, Herman. "Training New York's Finest." *Law and Order,* 23:3 (March, 1975), pp. 34-36.

Scottish Police College. *Scottish Police College.* Washington, DC: NCJRS, 1972.

Skillen, Charles R. "Versatile Instruction." *FBI Law Enforcement Bulletin,* 41:12 (December, 1972), pp. 21-24.
Activities of the Montana Law Enforcement Academy, Bozeman, Montana.

Sloane, Charles F. "State Academies for Police." *Journal of Criminal Law, Criminology and Police Science,* 45:6 (March/April, 1955), pp. 729-735.

Stead, P.J. "Police College, Bramshill." *International Criminal Police Review* (August-September, 1970), pp. 207-212.

Stone, Robert J. "The Making of a Trooper." *Law and Order,* 14:1 (January, 1966), pp. 44-46.
Training program for New Jersey State Troopers.

Sweeney, Faye B. "The Practical Patrolman School." *Law and Order,* 14:10 (October, 1966), pp. 8-9, 78.

Taylor, William. "Bramshill and Sandhurst: Training for Leadership Compared." *Police College Magazine* (Autumn, 1970), pp. 7-12.

Whitehouse, Jack E. "The United States Police Academy: A Proposal." *Police* (November-December, 1966).

Williams, Mason. "A Giant Step Forward in Police Training Schools." *Law and Order,* 20:9 (September, 1972), pp. 98-102.

AMBUSH AND SNIPER

Busch, Ted N. "Countersniper Ranges." *Law and Order,* 20:5 (May, 1972), pp. 46-50.

Storm, Bill. "Special Ambush Squad Training." *Law and Order,* 12:6 (June, 1964), pp. 74-75, 77.
Stake-out training for Philadelphia Police Department.

U.S. Army Department. *Sniper Training and Employment.* Washington, DC: GPO, 1969.

ARREST

Neithercutt, M.G. *Arrest Decisions as Preludes to? An Evaluation of Policy Related Research.* Vol. 1: *Administrative Summary and Training Script.* Washington, DC: NCJRS (Microfiche), 1974.
Two-part volume which provides a synopsis of the "adapt?" project and contains a police training script designed for use by police departments in staff training.

Neithercutt, M.G. *Arrest Decisions as Preludes to? An Evaluation of Policy Related Research.* Vol. 2: *Study Design, Findings, and Policy Implications.* Washington, DC: NCJRS (Microfiche), 1974.
Part two of a three-volume final report on the "adapt?" project, which describes the study, including background information, and gives an overview of methodology and a narrative report of findings.

Neithercutt, M.G. *Arrest Decisions as Preludes to? An Evaluation of Policy Related Research.* Vol. 3: *Technical Appendix.* Washington, D.C.: NCJRS (Microfiche), 1974.
Final volume of a three-volume report on the "adapt?" project, which discusses study design, presents detailed study findings, and makes specific observations about methodological concerns of the study.

AVIATION

Franey, W.H. "An Academy for Police and Public Safety Aviation." *Police Chief,* XXXVII:6 (June, 1971), pp. 16-18.

"IACP Helicopter School." *Police Chief* (February, 1971).

CITIZEN TRAINING PROGRAMS

Adults

Bauer, Willie. "Beaumont, Texas Fights the Weed." *Law and Order,* 18:11 (November, 1970), pp. 14-19.

Brody, Leon. *Highway Safety and Driver Education.* N.Y.: Prentice-Hall, 1954.

Camp, William F. "Firearms Instruction for Civilians by Police Officers." *Law and Order,* 12:8 (August, 1964), pp. 64, 66.

Clifton, Reid. "Florida Highway Patrol Holds Defensive Driving Courses." *Law and Order,* 19:10 (October, 1971), pp. 38-39.

Donaldson, D.T. "Ships at Sea Traffic Safety Program." *FBI Law Enforcement Bulletin,* 39:5 (May, 1970), pp. 2-6, 28-30.

Driessen, Gerald. "The Fallacy of the 'Untrained Driver.' " *Police* (September-October, 1969), pp. 46-49.

Fisher, James H. "The Pistol Packing Posse." *Law and Order,* 14:12 (December, 1966), pp. 38-53.
Police firearms training program for housewives.

Fox, Harry G. "Improving the Quiet Driver." *Law and Order,* 17:6 (June, 1969), pp. 18-24.
Police training course for deaf and hard-of-hearing drivers.

Fox, Harry G. "Silent—But Skilled." *Police Chief,* XXXV:11 (November, 1968), pp. 32-33.
Police driver training program for the deaf.

Hamilton, Lander C. and Bernard R. Kaplan. "Police and Schools." *Police Chief,* XXXLV:3 (March, 1967), pp. 54-57.
Training of school teachers by police about police functions.

Imhoff, Chris. "Improving Community Relations by Providing the National Safety Council's Defensive Driving Course." *Police Chief* (December, 1972).

Kadlowec, Bill and Marshall Swanson. "Educating the Drinking Driver." *Law and Order,* 24:6 (June, 1976), pp. 38-40.

Landstreet, Barent F. and Daniel W. Kriss. "Fairfax, Virginia, Alcohol Safety Action Program." *Police Chief,* XLI:5 (May, 1974), pp. 26-27.

Larson, John C. "On Rehabilitating Chronic Traffic Offenders." *Journal of Criminal Law, Criminology and Police Science,* 47:1 (May/June, 1956), pp. 46-50.

Rudge, Tom. "Road-E-O For Drinks." *Law and Order,* 15:8 (August, 1967), pp. 12-15, 83.
Accident prevention demonstration volunteers were given various amounts of alcohol and then they attempted to drive a tricky course. Tests clearly showed to a large crowd that driving skills were impaired.

Tebbs, Charles B. "It Could Happen in Your Town." *Law and Order,* 13:12 (December, 1965), pp. 34, 36, 60.
Police training of female citizens in self protection.

Tobias, Jerry. "Drug Clinic." *Police Chief,* XXXVII:5 (May, 1970).

Truett, John T. "Driver's Improvement School." *Law and Order,* 15:3 (March, 1967), pp. 36-37, 52.
Police education program directed to citizens with poor or bad driving records.

Juveniles

Baird, Ron. "Teaching Youngsters Traffic Safety." *Law and Order,* 12:6 (June, 1964), pp. 78-79.

Brey, William. "Friendly Town." *FBI Law Enforcement Bulletin* (April, 1972), pp. 16-20.

Cox, Edward F. "A Conscientious Student Traffic Safety Program." *FBI Law Enforcement Bulletin,* 36:5 (May, 1967), pp. 2-5.

Gardiner, Martin R., Sr. "Teaching Pedestrians Safety in Elementary Grades." *Law and Order,* 19:6 (June, 1971), pp. 50, 52, 54.

Hagman, Lawrence C. "A Traffic Safety Program for Kindergarten Children." *Law and Order,* 18:10 (October, 1970), pp. 28-31.

Kane, Thomas E. "Bicycle Safety Alert." *Law and Order* (December, 1974), pp. 22-25.

Lawder, Lee E. "Mike, the Talking Bike." *Law and Order,* 17:3 (March, 1969), pp. 42-43.

Lawder, Lee E. "Teaching Safety Through Magic." *Law and Order,* 16:10 (October, 1968), pp. 61-64.

Loftus, Michael Thomas. "The Talking Traffic Light." *FBI Law Enforcement Bulletin,* 36:1 (January, 1967), pp. 13-16.

Muhlhahn, William. "Two Decades and Three Thousand Youngsters." *Law and Order,* 13:9 (September, 1965), pp. 20-21.
Police program to teach markmanship to youngsters.

Nyhus, V.D. "Kids and Skids." *Police Chief,* XXXVII:6 (June, 1970), p. 18.

Skousen, W. Cleon. "A Traffic Safety Program for High Schools." *Law and Order,* 16:6 (June, 1968), pp. 10-14.

Steinline, Robert D. "Safety Town: A Community Effort." *Law and Order,* 20:3 (March, 1972), pp. 90-92.

Tobin, Thomas W. "Children on Bicycles." *Law and Order,* 12:6 (June, 1964), pp. 29-30.

Walsh, D.E. "Don't All Bicycles Talk?" *Police Chief,* XLII:6 (June, 1975).
Bicycle safety training program in Richland, Washington.

CIVIL DISORDER

Adderly, David L. "Civil Disturbance Refresher." *Military Police Law Enforcement Journal,* 2:1 (Spring, 1975).

Crockett, T.S. "Riot Control Agents: Planning Chemical Agent Training." *Police Chief,* XXXVI:9 (September, 1969), pp. 63-76.

Dragnich, Alix. "Crowd Control Training in Nassau County." *Law and Order,* 20:5 (May, 1972), pp. 24-29, 35.

Gardner, Martin R. "Civil Disturbance Training Program." *Law and Order,* 17:12 (December, 1969), pp. 104-106.

Hansen, David A. "Students Are Invited to Riot at City Hall." *Police Chief,* XLI:5 (May, 1974), pp. 54-56.

Havlick, Robert J. "All Types of Cities Are in Need of Police Training for Crowd and Riot Control." *Journal of California Law Enforcement* (October, 1966), pp. 109-116.

Kelly, D.B. "Operation Combine." *Police Chief,* XXXV:6 (June, 1968), pp. 42-44.

Ogle, Alice. "San Francisco's Peacemakers; Special Training for Police Pays Off in Smooth Handling on Civil Rights Disorders." *America,* (September 5, 1964), pp. 232-233.

Shillow, Robert. *The Training of Police Officers to Control Civil Rights Demonstrators.* N.Y.: Harper and Row, 1965.

Tebbs, Charles. "A Visit to a Tear Gas Demonstration." *Law and Order,* 13:10 (October, 1965), pp. 74-76, 90.

Turner, Carl C. "Planning and Training for Civil Disturbances." *Police Chief,* XXXV:5 (May, 1968), pp. 22-28.

U.S. Department of the Air Force. Headquarters. U.S. Air Force. *Civil Disturbance and Riot Control Training—Instructor Guide.* Washington, DC: GPO, 1970.

Programmed instructions include manual of arms, squad formations, use of gas or smoke, combat exercise, and key to questionnaire.

Williams, Mason. "The Smith and Wesson Weaponry Academy Chemical Agents and Non-Lethal Weapons." *Law and Order,* 19:2 (February, 1971), pp. 50-55.

COMMUNITY RELATIONS

Caldwell, Harry D. "The Challenge of Police-Community Relations Training, Part I." *FBI Law Enforcement Bulletin,* 43:8 (August, 1974); 43:9 (September, 1974.

Cizon, F.A. and W. Smith. *Some Guidelines for Successful Police-Community Relations Training Programs.* Springfield, VA: NTIS, 1970.

Techniques for planning, promoting, and implementing programs drawn from the experience of three urban experimental projects.

DePuy, Blanche. "A Case of Cultural Rub: The Spanish Inheritance and John Law." *Police,* 10:2 (November-December, 1965), pp. 15-17.

Advice on dealing successfully and humanely with individuals of Spanish heritage.

Flint, R.T. *Initiating Community Awareness Among Policemen: Community Awareness Training in the Minneapolis Police Academy.* Detroit: Midwestern Psychological Association, May, 1971.

Hogan, Ed. "Police and Urban Violence." *Journal of California Law Enforcement,* 8:4 (April, 1974), pp. 167-176.

Howard, John P. "Integrating Public Relations Training for Police Officers." *Police,* 7:1 (September-October, 1962), pp. 57-58.

Hughes, J.J. "Training Police Recruits for Service in the Urban Ghetto, A Social Worker's Approach." *Crime and Deliquency,* 18:2 (1972), pp. 176-183.

Kdehne, F.W. *Albuquerque Police Department, Race and Cultural Relations Training—Evaluation Report.* Springfield, VA: NTIS, 1972.

Kirwan, William E. "P-CR-Interdepartmental Traffic Science Training." *Police Chief,* 38:3 (March, 1971), pp. 34-35.

Manella, F.L. "Traveling Workshops in Police-Community Relations." *Police Chief,* XXXVII:9 (September, 1970), pp. 36-37.

Pfister, G. "Outcomes of Laboratory Training for Police Officers." *Journal of Sociological Issues,* 31:1 (1975), pp. 115-121.

Sata, L.S. "Laboratory Training for Police Officers." *Journal of Sociological Issues,* 31:1 (1975), pp. 107-114.

Schultz, A.A. "P-CR-Regional Training for Professional Proficiency." *Police Chief,* 38:3 (March, 1971), pp. 50-51.

Stotland, E. and W. Guppy. "Community Relations Training in the Seattle Police Academy." *Journal of Social Issues,* 31:1 (1975), pp. 139-144.

Tielsch, George P. "Community Resource Field Training for Police Recruits." *Police Chief,* XXXIX:11 (November, 1972), pp. 30-31.

West, Michelek. "California Policemen Go Back to School." *Law and Order,* 19:9 (September, 1971), pp. 33, 66.

CRIMINALISTICS

Bonamarte, M.F. and Andrew H. Principe. "Training a Task Force of Evidence Technicians." *Police Chief,* XXXVII:6 (June, 1970), pp. 48-53.

Dey, Luther M. "Seminars on Law Enforcement Photography." *FBI Law Enforcement Bulletin,* 37:12 (December, 1968), pp. 6-9.

Fernez, Frederick. "Evidence Technicians: Innovation in Training, Photographic, and Field Operation Techniques." *Law and Order,* 21:7 (July, 1973), pp. 66-71.

Fisher, Robert. "School for Scientific Law Enforcement Stresses Photography to Document Evidence." *Law and Order,* 20:4 (April, 1972), pp. 55-58.

Payton, George T. "Training Patrolmen to Dust for Latent Prints." *Police,* 8:4 (March-April, 1964), pp. 41-45.

CRISIS INTERVENTION

Barocas, Harvey and Myron L. Katz. "Dayton's Pilot Training Program in Crisis Intervention." *Police Chief,* XXXVIII:7 (July, 1971), pp. 20-26.

Driscoll, James, Robert Meyer, and Charles Schanic. "Training Police in Family Crisis Intervention." *Journal of Applied Behavioral Sciences,* 9:1 (1973), pp. 62-82.

Flint, Robert T. "Crisis Intervention Training." *FBI Law Enforcement Bulletin,* 43:8 (August, 1974), pp. 6-9, 21.

Glaser, E.M. *A Program to Train Police Officers to Intervene in Family Disturbances.* Final Report for LEAA Human Interaction Research Institute. Los Angeles: (April, 1970).

Herzog, F. et al. *Crisis Intervention Training—An Experimental Evaluation Program in Immediate Action*

Decision Making. Washington, DC: NCJRS (Microfiche), 1974.

Hinton, J. *Dying.* Baltimore: Penguin, 1967.

Katz, Myron. "Family Crisis Training: Upgrading the Police While Building a Bridge to the Minority Community." *Journal of Police Science and Administration,* 1:1 (March, 1973), pp. 30-35.

Marin County Criminal Justice Planning Agency. *Marin County (CA) Violence Prevention and Family Intervention Project—Project Number 1488—First Year Evaluation Report, September 30, 1974.* Washington, DC: NCJRS (Microfiche), 1974.

Murphy, Robert B. et al. "Training Patrolmen to Become Crisis Intervention Specialists." *Police Chief,* XLII:12 (December, 1975), pp. 44-45.

Phelps, Lourn G. et al. "Training an Entire Patrol Division in Domestic Crisis Intervention." *Police Chief,* XXXVIII:7 (July, 1971), pp. 18-19.

Reitz, W.E. "Evaluation of Police Family Crisis Training and Consultation." *Canadian Police Chief,* 63:3 (1974), pp. 29-32.

Rolde, E.J. et al. "A Law Enforcement Training Program in a Mental Health Center Catchment Area." *American Journal of Psychiatry,* 130:9 (1973), pp. 1002-1005.

Schonborn, Karl. *To Keep the Peace—Crisis Management in Law Enforcement.* N.Y.: National Conference of Christians and Jews, 1976.

Schreiber, F. Barry and John Andrews. "Crisis Intervention Training for Police Using Civilian Instructors: A Practical Model." *Police Chief* XLII:10 (October, 1975), pp. 254-258.

Schwartz, Jeffry A. "Domestic Crisis Intervention: Evolution of a Police Training Program." *Crime Prevention Review,* 2:4 (July, 1975), pp. 9-16.

Spitzner, Joseph H. and Donald H. McGee. "Family Crisis Intervention Training, Diversion, and the Prevention of Crime." *Police Chief,* XLII:10 (October, 1975), pp. 252-253.

DANGEROUS SITUATIONS

Bozza, Charles and Tim Holbrook. "Officer Survival." *Police Chief,* XXXIX:9 (September, 1972), pp. 32-35.

Buck, Walter E. " 'Hands-On' Training." *Police Chief,* XL:6 (June, 1973), pp. 48-50.
Program to train policemen to handle drunk and other unruly offenders.

Culley, J.A. "Defusing Human Bombs—Hostage Negotiations." *FBI Law Enforcement Bulletin,* 43:10 (1974), pp. 10-14.
Describes training program for 68 detectives with the NYPD to handle hostage negotiations. Author recommends only trained officers be allowed to negotiate.

Megerson, John S. "A Stitch in Time . . ." *Law and Order,* 22:9 (September, 1974), pp. 6, 9-12, 14, 16.
Describes situational training for dangerous situations.

Roth, Jordan and Robert Downey. *Officer Survival—Arrest and Control.* Santa Cruz, CA: Davis, 1976.

Swan, Richard A. " 'Special Threat Situation' Team Training." *Military Police Law Enforcement Journal* (Spring Quarter), 1974.

Vandall, Frank J. *Police Training for Tough Calls—Discretionary Situations.* Atlanta, GA: Center for Research in Social Change, 1976.

Weyant, James M. "Tactical Training Exercise: Barricaded Felony Suspect." *Law and Order,* 18:6 (June, 1970), pp. 92-95.

DISASTER

Diamond, Harry, ed. "Training to Meet Unusual Occurrences." *Police,* 6:5 (May-June, 1962), pp. 50-51.

Sampson, William C. "Mock Disaster Training Program." *FBI Law Enforcement Bulletin,* 41:1 (January, 1972), pp. 16-20, 31.

Stoeffel, Skip. *Disaster-Survival Education Lesson Plans.* Tacoma, WA: Survival Education Association, 1974.

Wood, Alan C. "England's Police Mobile Training Column." *Law and Order,* 15:9 (September, 1967), pp. 42-43.
Police disaster preparedness program.

DRIVING

Ayoob, Massad F. "Skid Control Training for Police." *Law and Order,* 22:11 (November, 1974), pp. 28, 30, 33, 42.

Babb, Harry N. "Emergency Vehicle Operations Clinic." *Police Chief,* XXXIX:8 (August, 1972), pp. 32-33.

Bachofner, Will E. "Fast but Safe Driving." *FBI Law Enforcement Bulletin* (June, 1966).

Bohardt, Paul H. and Richard J. Magaldi. "The Battered Car Syndrome: An Improved Approach to Driver Safety and Education." *Police Chief* (November, 1969), pp. 20-21, 36-38.

Book of Safe Driving. Philadelphia: Lippincott, 1962.

Caldwell, Bernard R. "Teaching Troopers Pursuit Driver Training." *Police Chief* (May, 1959).

Clifton, Reid. "Florida Highway Patrol Holds Defensive Driving Courses." *Law and Order* (October, 1971).

Fales, E.D. "New Facts About Skidding That May Save Your Life." *FBI Law Enforcement Bulletin* (May, 1965).

Fernstrom, Eric G. and Robert V. Ragsac. *Hazardous Driving Obstacle Course.* Santa Cruz, CA: Davis, 1975.

Floherty, John Joseph. *Youth at the Wheel: A Reference Book On Safe Driving.* Philadelphia: Lippincott, 1937.

Ford, Ruth E. *Your Driving Eye.* Indianapolis: Bobbs-Merrill, 1962.

Franzmeier, Steve. "Troopers Learn Vehicle and Personal Limitations in Pursuit Course." *Traffic Digest and Review,* 11 (August, 1963), pp. 8-11.

Halsey, Maxsell Nichol. *Skillful Driving: How to Master the 200 Most Crucial Situations of Modern Traffic.* Garden City, N.Y.: Doubleday, 1959.

"Hazardous Driving Obstacle Course: Santa Clara City/County Officers Learn Defensive Driving." *Police Chief* (October, 1973).

Houck, Russell and Larry McClanahan. "Aid to Police Driving." *Law and Order* (November, 1975), pp. 54-57.
Training for high-speed driving for police officers.

Hoyt, Walter A., Jr. "Let's Provide Updated Training for Emergency Service Personnel." *Traffic Digest and Review* (October, 1967).

"Hydroplaning." *Driver* (February, 1974).

Jones, Edward White. "Expert Training Required for Police Pursuit Driving." *FBI Law Enforcement Bulletin* (September, 1960).

Joy, A.F. "Police Driver Training Program Pays Off." *Law and Order,* 11 (November, 1968), pp. 33-36.

Kearney, Paul William. *How to Drive Better and Avoid Accidents.* N.Y.: Crowell, 1963.

Kearney, Paul William. *I Drive the Turnpikes and Survive.* N.Y.: Ballantine, 1956.

Lauer, A.R. "Driver Refresher Course for Firemen, Police and Public Transportation Drivers." *Police,* 5:2 (November-December, 1960).

McCleverty, John J. "Police Driver Training." *FBI Law Enforcement Bulletin,* 39:5 (May, 1970), pp. 16-21.

McDonald, R.M., D.K. Sheley, and J.B. Stinchcomb. *Virginia Emergency Vehicle Operator's Curriculum Guide.* Richmond, VA: Publications Office, Virginia Highway Safety Division, 1975.

Mahurin, Walker M. "Advanced Behind-the-Wheel Driver Training for Law Enforcement." *Police Chief,* XLII:11 (November, 1975), pp. 40-41.

Matias, George. "Special Training in Winter Driving Given Iowa Police." *FBI Law Enforcement Bulletin* (January, 1963).

Matthews, Jim. "LAPD Driver Training." *Road Test,* 6 (June, 1970), pp. 30-33.

Peters, George A. "Academy of Defensive Driving." *Law and Order,* 21:12 (December, 1973), pp. 62-64.
Twenty-four hour course 80% of which is behind the wheel.

Pudinski, Walter. "Driver Performance Study." *FBI Law Enforcement ulletin* (January, 1974).

"Safety Recommendations to Reduce Fog Accidents." *Police Chief* (June, 1973).

Shelton, Thomas B. "Skidpan Training." *FBI Law Enforcement Bulletin,* 38:10 (October, 1969), pp. 10-11.

Sportsmanlike Driving. Washington, DC: American Automobile Association, 1947.

U.S. National Highway Safety Bureau. *Basic Training Program for Emergency Medical Technician—Ambulance: Concepts and Recommendations.* Washington, DC: GPO, 1970.

U.S. National Highway Safety Bureau. *Basic Training Program for Emergency Medical Technician—Ambulance: Instructor's Lesson Plan.* Washington, DC: GPO, 1970.

DRUNK DRIVING

Carnahan, J.E. *DWI (Driving While Intoxicated) Law Enforcement Training Project—Course Guide.* Washington, DC: NCJRS (Microfiche), 1974.

Carnahan, J.E. and C.L. Drevenskracht. *DWI (Driving While Intoxicated) Law Enforcement Training Project—Evaluation Aids Packet and Media Log.* Washington, DC: NCJRS (Microfiche), 1974.

Carnahan, J.E. et al. *DWI (Driving While Intoxicated) Law Enforcement Training Project—Student Manual.* Washington, DC: NCJRS (Microfiche), 1974.

Chiaramonte, R.M. "Special Training Offered Ohio Law Enforcement Officers in Use of Breath Testing Devices." *Police Chief,* XXXVI:1 (January, 1969), pp. 18-19.

Kusaila, Joseph. "The New York D.W.I. Seminars." *Law and Order,* 13:6 (June, 1965), pp. 16-18, 46.

ENGLISH

Allen, Harold Allen. *Readings in Applied English Linguistics.* N.Y.: Appleton-Century-Crofts, 1964.

Austin, J.L. *How to Do Things with Words.* Cambridge, MA: Harvard University Press, 1962.

Balch, Donald and Kenneth G. Neville. *Something About Sentences: A Practical Grammar.* N.Y.: Macmillan, 1969.

Berelson, Bernard. *Content Analysis in Communication.* Glencoe, IL: Free Press, 1952.
Berelson explains the various forms and uses of content analysis. "In the classic sentence 'who says what to whom, how, with what effect' communication content is the what."

Cherry, Colin. *On Human Communication.* Cambridge, MA: MIT, 1957.

Flammang, Chris J. "A Summary of the Spelling Competence of Students in Four Basic Police Training Classes." *Police,* 16:11 (July, 1972), pp. 25-29.

Gowen, James A. *English Review Manual.* N.Y.: McGraw-Hill, 1970.

Harney, Malachi L. "Watch Your Semantics." *Police,* 4:6 (July-August, 1960), pp. 40-42.

Lewis, Norman. *Thirty Days to Better English.* Garden City, N.Y.: Doubleday, 1965.

Past, Ray. *Language as a Lively Art.* Dubuque, IA: W.C. Brown, 1970.
An attempt to make the study of language exciting. The author explores some of the basic meanings of the use of language.

Smith, Patrick D. and Robert C. Jones. *Police English.* Springfield, IL: C.C. Thomas, 1969.

Stratton, Clarence. *Guide to Correct English.* N.Y.: McGraw-Hill, 1949.
A guide to the technical points in our writing. The author explores the uses of different parts of speech.

FIREARMS

Agosta, Roy. *Manual of Basic Police Firearms Instructions and Safe Handling Practices.* Springfield, IL: C.C. Thomas, 1974.

"Are Your Men Sick of Your Target Range?" *Police Chief,* XLII:5 (May, 1975), pp. 48-50.

Bors, Louis E. "Innovations in Night Combat Shooting with the Black Lamp." *Law and Order,* 17:11 (November, 1969), pp. 57, 64.

"Bouncing Bullets." *FBI Law Enforcement Bulletin,* 38:10 (October, 1969), pp. 2-5.
The technique of ground ricohet shooting.

Briggs, Frank. *You Can Be an Expert Rifleman.* N.Y.: Grossett and Dunlap, 1963.

Bullum, Bill and Frank T. Hanenkrat. *Position Rifle Shooting.* Chicago: Follett, 1975.

Busch, Ted. "Streamlined Outdoor Firearm Training." *Law and Order,* 14:5 (May, 1966), pp. 54-58.

Camp, Walter F. "Introducing the New Man to the Firing Range." *Law and Order,* 13:12 (December, 1965).

Camp, William F. "Advantages of Combat Shooting." *Law and Order,* 17:12 (December, 1969), pp. 64-66.

Carson, Dale. "Need a Firearms Range?—Build It!" *FBI Law Enforcement Bulletin,* 39:10 (October, 1965), pp. 6, 7.

Cheshire, L.L. "The 'How to' of Hip Shooting." *Police,* 4:4 (March-April, 1960), pp. 33-35.

Cross, Albert C. "The Problems of Marksmanship Training in the Smaller Police Department." *Police,* 5:2 (November-December, 1960), pp. 33-36.

De Long, Thomas A. "Newton Square (PA) P.D. Firearms Training." *Law and Order,* 22:7 (July, 1974), pp. 50-53.

"The Exertion Course." *FBI Law Enforcement Bulletin,* 44:1 (1975), pp. 14-15.
The introduction of physical stress into firearms training at the FBI Academy. This is an advanced course for those who have been trained in target and combat shooting.

"Firearms Training Pays Dividend." *FBI Law Enforcement Bulletin,* 27:2 (February, 1958).

Fox, Bill. "Riot Gun Trap Shoot." *Law and Order,* 18:9 (September, 1970), pp. 14-17, 107.

"The French Sureté Nationale's Training Centre for Shooting" *Traffic Safety,* 64:4 (April, 1964), pp. 8-10.

Gibbs, Louis E. "A Little City with a Big Firearms Training Program." *Law and Order,* 15:2 (February, 1967), pp. 40-44.

Greening, John A. "A Simplified Firearms Familiarization and Combat Training Course." *Law and Order* (October, 1975), pp. 61-62.

Hess, John J. "Checklists for Firearms Instructors." *Law and Order,* 13:4 (April, 1965), pp. 30, 32-33.

Hess, John J. "Comprehensive Firearms Training." *Law and Order,* 13:1 (January, 1965), pp. 53-55.

Hicks, Lee J. "Point Gun, Pull Trigger." *Police Chief,* XLII:5 (May, 1975), pp. 52-55.

Ireland, Robert A. "Six O'Clock or Center Hold." *Police,* 2:6 (July-August, 1958), pp. 25-27.

Katsanis, Eugene R. "The Bancroft Quick-Draw Program." *Law and Order,* 20:4 (April, 1972), pp. 94-96, 98-100.

Keller, E. John. "Train for Actual Combat Conditions." *Law and Order,* 11:8 (August, 1963), pp. 54-57, 63.

Keller, E. John. "Where Do We Go from Here?" *Law and Order,* 13:7 (July, 1969), pp. 52-59.

Klein, Charles H. "Instinct Combat Shooting." *Law and Order,* 19:10 (October, 1971), pp. 14-19.

Land, E.J. (Jim) and Valvert L. Fox. "The Police Rifleman, a Neglected Capability." *Law and Order,* 21:10 (October, 1973), pp. 68-70.

Lawder, Lee E. "It's a Push-Button World." *Law and Order,* 13:6 (June, 1965).
Automated pistol range.

Lawder, Lee E. "Shooting by Instinct." *Law and Order,* 17:8 (August, 1969).

Lease, Richard J. "Future Developments in Combat Training." *Police,* 7:2 (November-December, 1962), pp. 55-68.

Lease, Richard J. "Police Combat Skills and Related Skills as Living Assurance." *Police,* 9:1 (September-October, 1964), pp. 80-87.

Lease, Richard J. "Preparing for Combat Readiness." *Police,* 7:4 (March-April, 1963), pp. 33-36.

Loux, William F. "A Police Firearms Range." *Law and Order,* 15:12 (December, 1967), pp. 70-74.

Loux, William F. "Rhode Island Law Enforcement Officer's Firearms Qualifications." *Law and Order,* 8:10 (October, 1970), pp. 44-48.

Luellen, Elwood T. "Intensive Firearms Drill: Your Best Weapon!" *Police,* 9:4 (March-April, 1965), pp. 62-63.

Luellen, Elwood T. "Trigger Control." *Police,* 10:4 (March-April, 1966), pp. 60-61.

MacAloon, F.G. "Combat Match." *Law and Order,* 17:5 (May, 1969), pp. 48-50.

McGlone, Terry. "The Kaukanna Range—Almost the Real Thing." *Law and Order,* 18:10 (October, 1970), pp. 38, 40.

Marcher, S. "Training Pays Off." *The American Rifleman,* 102 (December, 1954), pp. 17-19, 76.

Matt, A. Robert. "Police Firearms Training Program." *Police,* 4:3 (January-February, 1960), pp. 72-73.

"Mobile Firing Range." *FBI Law Enforcement Bulletin,* 41:12 (December, 1972).

Moyer, Frank A. and Robert J. Scroggie. *Special Forces Combat Firing Techniques.* Boulder, CO: Paladin, 1971.

National Rifle Association. *NRA Police Firearms Instructor Manual.* Washington, DC: National Rifle Association, 1968.

Nichols, Robert M. *The Secrets of Double Action Shooting.* N.Y.: Putnam, 1950.

Phalan, Reed T. "Double-Action—With Accuracy." *Law and Order,* 16:10 (October, 1968), pp. 84-88, 94.

Prehl, Jack. "Straight from the Shoulder." *Law and Order,* 13:7 (July, 1965), pp. 48-50; 12:9 (September, 1964), pp. 29-30.

Roberts, Duke. "Flexible Target Systems for Combat Training." *Law and Order,* 13:9 (September, 1969), pp. 30-34.

Ross, Robert. "Matt—The Matchmaker." *Law and Order,* 17:8 (August, 1969), pp. 102-106.

Rummel, Bartlett. "Police Firearms Training: An Inquiry Into the Governmental Duty to Provide Adequate Training." *National Rifleman,* (August, 1963).

Sadowski, Fred. "Firearms Training." *Law and Order,* 20:10 (October, 1972).

Santiago, Julio A. "Night Survival for Police Officers." *Law and Order,* 21:10 (October, 1973), pp. 52-53.
Night time fire arms training.

Saul, John R. "The NCPC: A Night Combat Pistol Course. Part 1." *Law and Order,* 14:10 (October, 1966), pp. 22-30; 14:11 (November, 1966), pp. 50-55.
Night combat pistol training.

Skillen, Charles. "Professional Training for the Automatic Pistol." *Law and Order,* 23:3 (March, 1975), pp. 46-49.

Smith, Charles L. "Auto-Pistol Combat Course." *Law and Order,* 22:10 (October, 1974), pp. 26-27, 30, 33.

Stanbury, Percy and G.L. Carlisle. *Shot Gun Marksmanship.* N.Y.: Barnes, 1963.

Stevenson, Jan A. "Combat Competition—Is It Worth It?" *Law and Order,* 17:4 (April, 1969), pp. 96-99; 17:5 (May, 1969), pp. 82-88.

Stevenson, Jan A. "Combat Practice at Home." *Law and Order,* 17:10 (October, 1969), pp. 52-58, 116.
Use of plastic training ammunition and pellet guns.

Stevenson, Jan A. "Police Firearms Training—Full Speed Ahead in the Wrong Direction." *Law and Order,* 16:10 (October, 1968), pp. 18-30.

"Techniques and Training Aids with Handguns." *FBI Law Enforcement Bulletin,* 25:10 (October, 1956), pp. 16-20.

"Training Courses in Double Action Police Shooting." *FBI Law Enforcement Bulletin,* 27:2 (February, 1958), pp. 12-16.

U.S. Department of the Treasury. *Firearms Identification for Law Enforcement Officers.* Washington, DC: GPO, 1970.
Visual aide and description of weapons classified as firearms.

Van Horn, William P. and David J. Duffey. "Unique Shotgun Training Developed in Garden Grove." *Police Chief,* XLII:5 (May, 1975), pp. 55-56.

"The Weapons Industry at a Glance." *Law and Order* (October, 1975), pp. 34-35.

Weston, P.B. *Combat Shooting for Police.* Springfield, IL: C.C. Thomas, 1970.
Police combat shooting manual focusing on use of hand guns when confronting an armed opponent.

Weston, Paul B. "Double Action Shooting." *Police,* 3:3 (January-February, 1959), pp. 58-59.

Weston, Paul B. "Training for Combat Effectiveness." *Police,* 3:4 (March-April, 1959), pp. 56-58.

Weston, Paul B. "Trigger Control Through Sighting and Aiming." *Police,* 6:3 (January-February, 1962), pp. 66-68.

Williams, Mason. "Bar Dot Sighting System." *Law and Order,* 19:12 (December, 1971), pp. 38-39, 49.

Williams, Mason. "The Good Guys and the Bad Guys." *Law and Order* 22:7 (July, 1974), pp. 54-59.

Williams, Mason. "The Heene Report, Part IV, Training Personnel and Pistol Maintenance." *Law and Order,* 19:1 (January, 1971), pp. 50-52, 54, 56, 58.

Williams, Mason. "Is This the Police Academy of the Future?" *Law and Order,* 18:8 (August, 1970), pp. 48, 50-51.
The Smith-Wesson Law Enforcement Academy. Courses cover all types of weaponry including tear gas and non-lethal weapons.

Williams, Mason. "The Miller Combat Matches." *Law and Order,* (October, 1975), pp. 30-32, 70.

Williams, Mason. "The Smith and Wesson Weaponry Academy, Part I, Firearms." *Law and Order,* 19:1 (January, 1971), pp. 62-69.

Williams, Mason. "The West Point Rifle and Pistol Indoor Range." *Law and Order,* 19:9 (September, 1971), pp. 52-56.

Young, Truman. "Survey of Shooting/Reloading Programs in Police Departments." *Law and Order* (February, 1966).

FIRST AID

Adams, Michael F. "Call for an Oxygen Unit." *Law and Order,* 15:9 (September, 1967), pp. 76-78.

Chaiken, Jan M., Edward J. Ignall, and Warren E. Walker. *Training Course in Deployment of Emergency Services—Instructors' Manual.* Santa Monica, CA: Rand, 1975.

Committee on Cardiopulmonary Resuscitation of the American Heart Association. *Cardiopulmonary Resuscitation—A Manual for Instructors.* N.Y.: Heart Association, 1967.

Hill, J. "Emergency Care Training for Kansas Highway Patrol." *Law and Order,* 19:12 (December, 1971), pp. 82-84, 86, 88.

Holbert, Harry W. "Maryland State Police Training Includes First Aid Refresher Course." *Law and Order,* 18:1 (January, 1970), pp. 46-47.

"Oklahoma City School for Handling Emergency Victims." *Traffic Digest and Review,* 3:11 (November, 1955).

Raymond, Thomas T. "Realistic Emergency Medical Training for the Police Professional." *Police Chief,* XL:4 (April, 1973), pp. 26-27.

U.S. Department of Transportation. National Highway Traffic Safety Administration. *Emergency Medical Services—Crash Injury Management for Traffic Law Enforcement Officers—Course Guide.* Washington, DC: NCJRS (Microfiche), 1973.

U.S. Department of Transportation. National Highway Traffic Safety Administration. *Emergency Medical Services—Crash Injury Management for Traffic Law Enforcement Officers—Instructor's Lesson Plans.* Washington, DC: NCJRS (Microfiche), 1973.

HUMAN RELATIONS

Boer, Byron L. and Bruce C. McIver. "Human Relations Training: Laboratories and Team Policing." *Journal of Police Science and Administration,* 1:2 (June, 1973), pp. 162-167.

Grange, Joseph. "Understanding Conflict: Experience and Behavior." *Police Chief,* XLI:7 (July, 1974), pp. 36-37, 78.

Huseman, Richard C. "Interpersonal Communication Training for Police: An Evaluation." *Journal Police Science and Administration,* 1:3 (September, 1973), pp. 355-361.

Huseman, Richard C. "Video-Tape Role Playing." *Law and Order,* 20:10 (October, 1972), pp. 74, 76-78.
Inter-personal communication training for police.

McManus, George. "Human Relations Training for Police." *Journal of Criminal Law, Criminology and Police Science,* 46:1 (May-June, 1959), pp. 105-111.

Manella, Frank L. "Humanism in Police Training." *Police Chief,* 38:2 (February, 1971), pp. 26-2S.
Contains a 4-point credo for police humanism.

Newman, L.E. and J.L. Steinberg. "Consultation with Police on Human Relations Training." *American Journal of Psychiatry,* 126:10 (April, 1970), pp. 65-73.

Russell, H.E. and A. Beigel. *Understanding Human Behavior for Effective Police Work.* N.Y.: Basic, 1976.

Siegel, Arthur I., Philip J. Federman, and Douglas G. Schultz. *Professional Police-Human Relations Training.* Springfield, IL: C.C. Thomas, 1963.

Sikes, M.P. and S.E. Cleveland. "Human Relations Training for Police and Community." *American Psychologist,* 24:8 (August, 1969), pp. 766-769.

IN-SERVICE

Auten, James H. "The Supervisor's Role and In-Service Training." *Law and Order,* 21:2 (February, 1973), pp. 34, 36-41.

Berg, Harold. "Training on Patrol: A TOP Program." *Police Chief,* XLI:11 (November, 1974).

Donaldson, Clyde. "Slide/Sound Training Programs Developed by California Highway Patrol." *Law and Order,* 20:9 (September, 1972), pp. 56-57.

Jones, Ralph H. "Statewide Inservice Training for Police Officers." *FBI Law Enforcement Bulletin,* 40:11 (November, 1971), pp. 16-20, 29.

Lunnen, Larry E. "A Continuous In-Service Training Program for a Small Department." *Law and Order,* 16:9 (September, 1968), pp. 98-103.

Matt, A. Robert. "Officer Continuation Training." *Police,* 5:1 (September-October, 1960), pp. 6-9.

Michigan State University. *Training Bulletins for Planning and Research Units in Medium-Sized Police Departments.* Springfield, VA: NTIS, 1968.
Planning practices and activities to improve operations for medium-sized police departments (75-200 full-time employees) are enumerated.

Rogers, Howard L. "Determining Police Training Needs: In-Service." *Police,* 6:4 (March-April, 1962), pp. 55-61.

INVESTIGATION

Brantley, Wilbur R. "Team Teaching in Criminal Investigation." *Police,* 13:5 (May-June, 1969), pp. 52-54.

Carick, Noel. "The Detective School of Melbourne, Australia." *Law and Order,* 13:12 (December, 1965), pp. 80-81.

Cronin, John D. "Institutes for the Training of Coroners' Investigators." *Police,* 13:1 (September-October, 1968), pp. 44-45.

Miller, S.I. "Model Detective Training Program." *International Criminal Police Review,* 28 (October, 1974), pp. 210-219.

Siemon, J.M. and C.C. Black. "A New Approach to Interservice Training." *FBI Law Enforcement Bulletin,* 42:11 (1973), pp. 11-15.
Training school for investigators. Forty-one topics in the curriculum are described.

"Training in Enforcement Law and Criminal Investigation for Treasury Agents." *Police,* 9:4 (March-April, 1965), pp. 94-97.

U.S. Congress. Committee on Government Operations. *Unmet Training Needs of the Federal Investigator and the Consolidated Federal Law Enforcement Training Center—Thirtieth Report.* Washington, DC: GPO, 1970.
Report resulting from a study of the functions, responsibilities, and training requirements of Federal investigative personnel.

JUVENILE DELINQUENCY

Dessler, Francis R. "A Delinquency Control Institute for the Working Police Officer." *Law and Order,* 17:9 (September, 1969), pp. 110-113.

Fagerstrom, Dorothy. "New York City Police Department's First D.C.I." *Law and Order,* 13:12 (December, 1965), pp. 22-25.
Delinquency Control Institute.

Manella, Frank L. "A Program to Cope with Youth Violence in Schools." *Law and Order,* 18:9 (September, 1970), pp. 24, 26-27.

Watson, Nelson and Robert Walker. *Training Police for Work with Juveniles.* Washington, DC: IACP, 1965.

LETTERING

Benson, John H. and A.G. Carey. *Elements of Lettering.* 2nd ed. N.Y.: McGraw, 1950.

Biegeleisen, J.I. *ABC of Lettering.* Rev. ed. N.Y.: Harper and Row, 1971.

Mitchell, Frederic. *Practical Lettering and Lay Out.* 2nd ed. Chester Springs, PA: Dufour, 1960.

Wright, Harry B. *Lettering.* 3rd ed. N.Y.: Pitman, 1962.

MANAGEMENT

Buren, R. Michael. "A Police Management Training Program: Efficient Use of Man and Money?" *Journal of Police Science and Administration,* 1:3 (September, 1973), pp. 294-302.

Carlin, Vincent A. "Police Executive Development Course." *Police,* 5 (January-February, 1961), pp. 62-65.

Day, Frank D. "Police Administrative Training." *Journal of Criminal Law, Criminology and Police Science,* 47:2 (July/August, 1956), pp. 253-255.

Fitzsimons, Patrick. "The N.Y.P.D./AMA Connection." *Law and Order,* 23:5 (May, 1975), pp. 61, 86-87.

Galvin, R.T. *Chief Police Executives, Training Program—Final Report on Management Phases.* Washington, DC: NCJRS (Microfiche), 1968.
Experimental training program designed to train police chiefs to better cope with their administrative responsibility and to develop materials on the most useful methods of instruction.

Hartenstein, Annette A. "A Cooperative Approach to Police Management Training." *Journal of Police Science and Administration,* 1:4 (December, 1973), pp. 433-439.

Kelley, Douglas. "A Progressive Law Enforcement Education Program." *FBI Law Enforcement Bulletin,* 38:10 (October, 1969), pp. 12-17.

Lawder, Lee E. "Four State Police Agencies Begin Management Training." *Law and Order,* 20:6 (June, 1972), p. 105.

McNair, Alex. "Senior Command Course [Bramshill]." *Guardian* (Glasgow) (Winter, 1974), pp. 50-51.

Maier, Norman et al. *Role-Play Technique: A Handbook for Management and Leadership Practice.* San Diego, CA: University Associates, 1975.

Peck, John E. and Manohar D. Nasta. "Simulating the Operation of an Urban Police Department." *Police Chief,* XLII:10 (October, 1975), pp. 66, 68, 70.

Rose, William P. "Executive Conferences: A Device for Executive Development and Training." *Police Chief,* XLI:11 (November, 1974), pp. 26-27.

Walker, Robert N. "A Training Program for Development of the Command-Level Ranks." *Police Chief,* XXXV:7 (July, 1968), pp. 50-52.

Wilson, Howard. *Effective Conference and Discussion Techniques for Training.* Irvine, CA: Admin. Res., 1969.

Zeira, Joram. "Training the Top-Management Team for Planned Change." *Training and Development Journal* (June, 1974).

MAP READING

Jennings, J.H. *Elementary Map Interpretation.* New Rochelle, N.Y.: Cambridge University Press, 1960.

Kjellstrom, Bjorn. *Be Expert with Map and Compass: The Orienteering Handbook.* Rev. ed. Totowa, N.J.: Scribner, 1976.

MOTORCYCLE OPERATION

California Highway Patrol. *Motorcycle Training Manual.* Rev. ed. Sacramento: CHP, 1957.

Home Office. *Motorcycle Road Craft: The Police Motorcyclists Manual.* London: HMSO, 1965.

Mahurin, Walker. "Motorcycle Training Program." *Law and Order,* 23:4 (April, 1975).

Northwestern University Traffic Institute. *Motorcycle Operation—A Manual for Riders.* Evanston, IL: Traffic Institute, Northwestern University, 1964.

Traffic Institute Staff. *Police Motorcycle Instructors' Manual for Training Motorcycle Riders.* Evanston, IL: Traffic Institute, 1974.

MOUNTAINEERING

Blackshaw, Alan. *Mountaineering.* Baltimore, MD: Penguin, 1965.

Bridge, Raymond. *Climbing: A Guide to Mountaineering.* N.Y.: Scribner, 1975.

Casewit, Curtis W. *The Mountaineering Handbook.* Philadelphia: Lippincott, 1968.

Roscoe, D.T. *Mountaineering: A Manual for Teachers and Instructors.* Levittown, N.Y.: Transatlantic, 1976.

NARCOTICS

Bludworth, E. *Three Hundred Most Abused Drugs—A Pictorial Handbook of Interest to Law Enforcement Officers and Others.* Rev. ed. Tampa, FL: Trend House, 1973.
Color photographs and ingredients of the most commonly abused amphetamines, barbiturates, tranquilizers, and opiates.

"BNDD Plans Conference with Law Enforcement Officials Across the Nation." *Police Chief,* XXXVII:2 (February, 1970).

Garza, Manuel R. "United Nations Narcotics Training Program." *Police Chief,* XLII:5 (May, 1975), pp. 38-39.

Kasper, Eugene L. "Drug Abuse Recognition for Recruit Policemen." *Law and Order,* 18:8 (August, 1970), pp. 100-104.

Miller, Gary J. "Narcotic Enforcement Officers Training Program." *Police,* 15:5 (May-June, 1971), pp. 33-38.

OBSERVATION AND MEMORY

Allmers, Herbert. "Experiment in Observation." *Law and Order,* 13:12 (December, 1965), pp. 102-103.

Basinger, Louis F. *The Techniques of Observation and Learning Retention: A Handbook for the Policeman and the Lawyer.* Springfield, IL: C.C. Thomas, 1973.

Kellett, Michael. *How to Improve Your Memory and Concentration.* N.Y.: Simon and Schuster, 1975.

Lawder, Lee E. "Notes on Training in Observation and Memory." *Law and Order,* 15:2 (February, 1967), pp. 52-53.

Pantaleoni, C. Alex. "Seeing More While Looking Less." *FBI Law Enforcement Bulletin,* 36:7 (July, 1967), pp. 9-11.

Redmount, Robert S. "The Psychological Basis of Evidence Practices: Memory." *Journal of Criminal Law, Criminology and Police Science,* 50:3 (September / October, 1959), pp. 249-264.

Soule, Rolland L. "Flash Recognition Training in Law Enforcement Work." *Journal of Criminal Law, Criminology and Police Science.* 49:6 (March-April, 1959), pp. 590-660.
Visual recognition and identification training.

ORGANIZED CRIME CONTROL

Bohardt, Paul H. and Howard M. Rasmussen. "The Selection and Training of Organized Crime Investigators." *Police Chief,* 38:9 (September, 1971), pp. 34-45.

Dunman, William H. "Organized Crime Training: The Institute Approach." *Police Chief,* XLII:8 (February, 1975), pp. 54-56.

Peat, Marwick, Mitchell and Company. *Organized Crime Law Enforcement Training Conference—Instructor's Guide.* Washington, DC: NCJRS (Microfiche), 1972.

U.S. Department of Justice. Law Enforcement Assistance Administration. *Training for Organized Crime Control.* Washington, DC: GPO, March, 1971.

PERSONNEL EXCHANGE PROGRAMS

Adams, Gerald B. "Law Enforcement Interdepartment Educational Exchange Program." *Police Chief,* XL:4 (April, 1o73), pp. 22-23.

Baer, William J. *Police Personnel Exchange Programs—The Bay Area Experience.* Washington, DC: Communications Department, Police Foundation, 1976.

Boyett, J.H. *Exchange of Personnel Among Attorney Generals' Offices.* Washington, DC: NCJRS (Microfiche), 1975.

Clzanckas, Victor et al. "Increased Regional Cooperation in Policing: The Bay Area Middle Management Exchange." *Police Chief,* XLII:11 (November, 1975), pp. 22, 66.

"Exchange Experiment in California." *Police Chief,* XXXLV:3 (March, 1967), pp. 50-51.

Holston, Bill. "The 'McCloud Plan' Works for Cottage Grove." *Police Chief,* XLI:8 (August, 1974).

McCormack, Robert J. "Middle Management Exchange." *Police Chief,* XL:1 (January, 1973), pp. 42-44.

PHYSICAL FITNESS

Physical Fitness—General

Bagley, Gerald L. "Play Ball—The Value of a Sports Program." *Police,* 8:3 (January-February, 1964), pp. 78-79.

Bendor, Jay A., Harold M. Kaplan, and Alex J. Johnson. "The Problems of Physical Conditioning in Police Work." *Police Chief,* XXX:7 (August, 1963), pp. 7-8.

Cathey, Richard E. "Why Weight?" *FBI Law Enforcement Bulletin,* 40:10 (October, 1971), pp. 13-15.

Federal Bureau of Investigation. *Physical Fitness for Law Enforcement Officers.* Washington, DC: GPO, 1972.

Guaring, John. "The Importance of Physical Fitness." *Law and Order,* 18:4 (April, 1970), pp. 60, 62, 64.

Jensen, Clayne and A. Garth Fisher. *Scientific Basis of Athletic Conditioning.* Philadelphia: Lea and Febiger, 1972.

Johnson, Harry J. *Keeping Fit in Your Executive Job.* N.Y.: AMA, 1962.

Kaminski, Jack J., Jr. "Police Physical Fitness: A Personal Matter." *Police Chief,* XLII:9 (September, 1975), pp. 39-40.

Lawder, Lee E. "Florida Highway Patrolmen Keep Physically Fit." *Law and Order,* 20:7 (July, 1972), pp. 44, 53.

Lindell, James W. "Year-Round Police Fitness Training." *Police Chief,* XLII:9 (September, 1975), pp. 38, 64.

Peebler, J.R. "How Fit Are You?" *Police,* 6:3 (January-February, 1962), pp. 69-72.

Pohndorf, Richard H. and Richard E. Cathey. "Fitness Changes During a 14-Week Basic Law Enforcement Training Program." *FBI Law Enforcement Bulletin,* (January, 1975), pp. 20-24.

"Run For Your Life." *FBI Law Enforcement Bulletin,* 36:10 (October, 1967), pp. 2-6.

Shanahan, Michael G. "A Factor for Survival: Police Officer Physical Efficiency." *Police Chief,* XLIII:2 (February, 1976), pp. 58-60.

Spackman, Robert R. and William F. Vincent. *Physical Fitness in Law Enforcement: A Guide to More Efficient Service.* Cardondale: Southern Illinois University Press, 1969.

Thalassites, Leo. "Physical Fitness Ideal." *FBI Law Enforcement Bulletin,* 43:1 (January, 1974).

Weingarten, Gilad. "Research in Physical Fitness." *Law and Order,* 18:11 (November, 1970), pp. 50-53.

Police Olympics

Kenzie, Cliff. "California Police Olympics Off to a Flying Start." *Law and Order,* 16:1 (January, 1968), pp. 76-78.

Turtletaub, Stanley. "The National Police Olympics." *FBI Law Enforcement Bulletin,* 39:6 (June, 1970), pp. 7-10.

POLYGRAPH

"An Academy of Polygraph ('Lie Detector') Examiners." *Journal of Criminal Law, Criminology and Police Science,* 45:3 (September/October, 1954), pp. 359-362.

Watts, Dell R. "Education of Police Personnel to the Use of the Polygraph." *Police,* 1:1 (September-October, 1956), pp. 23-28.

PSYCHOLOGY

Caughley, J.G. "Correctional Psychology for Law Enforcement Officers." *Journal of Criminal Law, Criminology and Police Science,* 49:2 (July/August, 1958), pp. 184-188.

Dudycha, George. *Psychology for Law Enforcement Officers.* Springfield, IL: C.C. Thomas, 1971.

Green, Edward J. *Psychology for Law Enforcement.* N.Y.: Wiley, 1976.

Hanna, E.M. "Police Training Includes Psychological Development." *Public Management,* 39 (September, 1957).

Hardy, R.E. *Applied Psychology in Law Enforcement and Corrections.* Springfield, IL: C.C. Thomas, 1973.

Kennedy, D.B. and B. Kennedy. *Applied Psychology for Police.* Springfield, IL: C.C. Thomas, 1972.

Meerloo, Joost A.M. "Mental First Aid." *Police,* 3:1 (September-October, 1958), pp. 63-65.

Reiser, Martin. *Practical Psychology for Police Officers.* Springfield, IL: C.C. Thomas, 1973.

Wicks, R.J. *Applied Psychology for Law Enforcement and Correction Officers.* N.Y.: McGraw-Hill, 1974.
Theoretical and practical tenents of basic and abnormal psychology applied to law enforcement and corrections, including techniques of interviews and interrogation.

Wicks, Robert J. "Presenting Psychological Concepts to Police and Corrections Officers." *Police Chief,* XLI:11 (November, 1974).

RECRUIT

Chapple, Norman L. *Police Cadet Training: Selected British Programmes.* Kent, OH: Kent State University, 1972.

Crockett, T.S. and J.A. Kelly. *Police Reference Notebook—Instructors' Guide.* Gaithersburg, MD: IACP, 1971.

Earle, Howard H. *Police Recruit Training.* Springfield, IL: C.C. Thomas, 1973.

Edwards, Don. "Police Trainee Program." *Journal of California Law Enforcement,* (July, 1974), pp. 31-37.

Ehrlich, Henry. "Wanted: Good Policeman." *Look* 26 (July 3, 1962), pp. 18-21.

Houghton, R.A. "Los Angeles Overhauls Its Police Recruitment and Its Basic Training Program." *Police Chief,* XXXV:8 (August, 1968), pp. 34-44.

Jones, Donald T. "Advice to a Rookie." *Law and Order,* 17:6 (June, 1969), pp. 116-121.

O'Brien, S. "The Making of a London Policeman." *International Journal of Offender Therapy, and Contemporary Criminology,* 16:3 (1972), pp. 272-277.
A recruit training program which stresses people situations and events.

Rogers, Howard L. "Are You Planning a Police Recruit Training Program?" *Police,* 6:3 (January-February, 1962), pp. 46-48.

Taylor, Charles R. and John R. Kleberg. "A Decade of Police Training in Illinois: A Basic Police Training Course Evaluation." *Police,* 13:4 (March-April, 1969(, pp. 28-34.

Wechter, Harry L. "Case History: Problem-Solution." *Law and Order,* 15:5 (May, 1967), pp. 54-58, 77.

Wright, Thomas B. "Making of a Mountie." *Law and Order,* 15:5 (May, 1967), pp. 64-69.
Recruit training for RCMP.

York, Orrell A. "New York Statewide Training Program for Municipal Police." *State Government,* 35 (Winter, 1962), pp. 30-33.

RESERVE

Knowles, Lyle and Richard Propster. "Regional Training for Reserve Police Officers." *Journal of California Law Enforcement,* (January, 1976), pp. 96-99.

Michigan Office of Civil Defense. *Training Manual for Auxiliary Police.* Lansing: Office of Civil Defense, 1954.

Pitchess, Peter J. "Training for Reserve Deputies." *National Sheriff,* (March-April, 1968).

Sill, A.W. "Sets Up Intensive Training for Police Reserves (West Covina, Calif.)." *Public Management,* 42 (May, 1960).

ROLL CALL

Barber, William E. *A Study to Determine the Nature and Scope of Police Roll Call Training in Cities with 25,000 to 100,000 Population in the United States.* Unpub. Doctoral Dissertation. Michigan State University, 1973.

Burnetti, George J. "Roll Call Training." *Police Chief,* XXXIV:8 (August, 1967), pp. 28-33.

Dilworth, Donald C. "Richmond's Key for Roll Call Training." *Police Chief,* XXXIX:11 (November, 1972), pp. 40-45.

Higginbotham, Charles E. "Roll-Call Training: A Worldwide Technique." *Police Chief,* XLII:5 (May, 1975), pp. 28-29.

McDaniel, William E. "Another Form of Roll-Call Training." *Law and Order,* 18:2 (February, 1970), pp. 22-24.

Miller, Gary J. and Marc Bradshaw. "Roll Call Training: A Program for In-Service Training." *Police Chief,* XLI:8 (August, 1974), pp. 48-50.

Price, Clifford S. "Roll Call Training: Stop Gap or Necessity." *Police Chief,* XLI:8 (August, 1974), pp. 46-47.

Shearer, W.T. "Roll Call Training: We Can Do Better." *Journal of California Law Enforcement,* 9:2 (1974), pp. 82-85.

SAFETY

Gardner, James E. *Safety Training for the Supervisor.* Reading, MA: Addison-Wesley, 1969.

Hipskind, V.K. "Training the Police Officer to Be a Safe Worker." *Police,* 9:2 (November-December, 1964), pp. 71-77.

Howe, Walter J. "Do YOU Really Know Guns?" *Police,* 1:4 (March-April, 1957), pp. 44-46.

SELF DEFENSE

Kubota, Takaynki and Paul F. McCaul. *Baton Techniques and Training.* Springfield, IL: C.C. Thomas, 1972.

Maertz, Richard C. *Wrestling Teaching Guide.* N.Y.: Barnes, 1973.

Sparks, Raymond D. *Wrestling Illustrated: An Instructional Guide.* N.Y.: Ronald, 1960.

SENSITIVITY

Bimstein, Donald. "Sensitivity Training and the Police." *Police,* 14:5 (May-June, 1970), pp. 75-79.

Levanthal, Jerome I. "Subtle Sensitivity Training." *Police Chief,* 37:9 (October, 1970).

Meyer, Schuyler M., III and Charles S. Topham. "Sensitivity Training/Rap Sessions for Police and Pupils." *Police Chief,* 38:9 (September, 1971), pp. 63-65.

Porpotage, Frank M., II. "Sensitivity Training." *Police Chief,* 39:10 (October, 1972), pp. 60-61, 286-287.

Schultz, Donald O. "Police Sensitivity Training." *Law and Order,* 18:11 (November, 1970), pp. 44-45.

Singer, Henry A. "The Cop as Social Scientist." *Police Chief,* XXXVII:4 (April, 1970), pp. 52-58.

Skousen, W. Cleon. "Sensitivity Training—A Word of Caution." *Law and Order,* 15:11 (November, 1967), pp. 10-12, 70.

Wegener, William F. "Defusing Offensive Rhetoric." *Law and Order,* 20:6 (June, 1972), pp. 102-103.

Zacker, J. "Understanding One's Clients: An Attempt to Improve Sensitivity and Morale in Police Recruits." *Psychological Reports,* 31:3 (1972), pp. 999-1008.

SPANISH

Bomse, Marguerite D. and Julian H. Alfaro. *Practical Spanish for School Personnel, Fireman, Policeman and Community Agencies.* Elmsford, N.Y.: Pergamon, 1974.

Dobrian, Walter A. *Conversational Spanish.* N.Y.: Dodd, 1966.

Garcia, Mariano. *Spanish for Law Enforcement Officers.* Silver Springs, MD: Institute of Modern Languages, 1972.

Hayden, Philip A. and John J. Moreno. *Practical Spanish for Public Safety Personnel.* Santa Cruz, CA: Davis, 1970.

Kercheville, Francis M. *Practical Spoken Spanish.* Albuquerque: University of New Mexico Press, 1969.

Larson, Donald M. and William A. Smalley. *Becoming Bilingual: A Guide to Language Learning.* Pasadena, CA: William Carey Library, 1974.

Pei, Mario. *How to Learn Languages and What Languages to Learn.* N.Y.: Harper and Row, 1966.

SUPERVISORY

Bristow, Allen P. "Training in the Evaluation of Police Personnel." *Police,* 5:2 (November-December, 1960), pp. 17-20.

Esbeck, Edward S. and George Halverson. "Stress and Tension—Team Building for the Professional Police Officer." *Journal of Police Science and Administration,* 1:2 (June, 1973), pp. 153-161.
Training program for recognizing and interpreting the effects of stress.

McCarthy, James J. "New Concept in Supervisory Officer Training." *Journal of California Law Enforcement,* (April, 1970), pp. 175-178.

Reisner, Martin. "Training Police Sergeants in Early Warning Signs of Emotional Upset." *Mental Hygiene Magazine,* (July, 1971).

Statewide Police Command and Supervisory Training, Three Demonstration Projects—New Jersey, North Carolina, Arkansas. Springfield, VA: NTIS, 1968.
Final project reports of demonstration training efforts to expand in-service professional education opportunities for police personnel.

Stone, David M. and Frank D. Presto, III. "The P.O.P.E.S. Program." *Law and Order,* (March, 1976), pp. 74-77.

Sunnyvale Department of Public Safety. *Supervisory Techniques.* Santa Cruz, CA: Davis, 1969.

Course outline and lesson plans designed to assist instructors of a course dealing with the principles of police supervision.

Wicker, Irving B., Jr. "Training Law Enforcement Officers to Rate." *Police,* 16:10 (June, 1972), pp. 46-49.

TRAFFIC

Caldwell, Bernard R. "Northwestern University Pioneers Traffic Training and Research." *Police,* 5:1 (September-October, 1960), pp. 27-30.

Godfrey, Anne M. "Police Officers Learn by Doing in Traffic Institute Program." *Law and Order,* 20:9 (September, 1972), pp. 76-78.

Hale, A. and J.W. Hamilton. *Police Traffic Services Basic Training Program.* Vol. 1. *Course Guide.* Washington, DC: GPO, 1972.

Aid for the training administrator in planning and conducting the basic training program for police traffic services.

Hale, A. and J.W. Hamilton. *Police Traffic Services Basic Training Program.* Vol. 2. *Instructor's Lesson Plans.* Washington, DC: GPO, 1972.

Lesson plans constituting the classroom and field training phases of the basic training program for police traffic services.

Hale, A. and J.W. Hamilton. *Police Traffic Services Basic Training Program.* Vol. 3. *Student Study Guide.* Washington, DC: GPO, 1972.

Basic student's reference text, containing a summary of information presented in the lesson plans, as well as graphic exhibits also referenced in the lesson plans.

Road Abuses. Evanston, IL: Northwestern University Traffic Institute, 1961.

Training manual describing procedures in regulating actions which can contribute to hazardous road conditions.

WRITING

Brown, Bruce. *Thought, Thesis, Theme: An Introduction to Rhetoric.* Belmont, CA: Dickenson, 1969.

Effective writing is the focus of this work. Brown discusses prewriting, writing and rewriting.

Campbell, James H., ed. *Dimensions in Communication.* Belmont, CA: Wadsworth, 1965.

Patterson, F.M. "A Writing Course for Law Enforcement Officers." *Police Chief,* 38:8 (August, 1971), pp. 42-43.

Pence, Raymond Woodburg. *A Manual of the Mechanics of Writing.* N.Y.: Macmillan, 1921.

TEACHING TECHNIQUES

TEACHING TECHNIQUES

Adams, Thomas F. *Training Officers' Handbook.* Springfield, IL.: C.C. Thomas, 1964.

Clark, D. Cecil. *Using Instructional Objectives in Teaching.* Glenview, IL.: Scott Foresman, 1972.

Costello, Lawrence and George N. Gordon. *Teach With Television.* N.Y.: Hastings House, 1961.

Fakler, John. "TV Role-Playing for Training." *Law and Order,* 18:2 (February, 1970), pp. 32-34, 36, 38.

Gilbert, James N. "From the Street to the Classroom." *Police Chief,* XLI:8 (August, 1974), pp. 26-27.

Haley, Keith N. "Responsibilities of the University Law Enforcement Teacher." *Police,* 16:9 (May, 1972), pp. 48-55.

Harrison, Leonard H. *How To Teach Police Subjects, Theory, and Practice.* Springfield, IL.: C.C. Thomas, 1964.

How To Improve Training Skills. N.Y.: Preston, 1975.

James, Ian. "Use of the Business Game in Police Training." *Police Review (GB),* 25 (October, 1974), p. 1372.

Kaplan, Alvin. "New York City Police Academy's Approach to Teaching Law to Police Recruits." *Police Chief,* XLLL:8 (August, 1975), pp. 64-65.

Klotter, John C. *Techniques for Police Instructors.* Springfield, IL.: C.C. Thomas, 1963.

Knowles, Lyle. "Teaching Cops." *Police Chief,* 38:2 (February, 1971).

Lovin, Bill C. and Emery Reber Casstevens. *Coaching, Learning and Action.* N.Y.: AMA, 1971.

Lyng, John F.X. "Eleven Keys to Successful Teaching." *Law and Order,* 15:8 (August, 1967), pp. 72-73.

Matt, A. Robert. "PTO-Communicate!" *Police,* 5:4 (March-April, 1961), pp. 23-27.

Myren, Richard A. "Teaching Law to Law Enforcers." *Police,* 3:6 (July-August, 1959), pp. 48-50; 4:1 (September-October, 1959), pp. 32-34.

Newport, Al. "Oklahoma's 'Living Textbook' Program." *Law and Order* (December, 1974), pp. 50-51, 53.

Compiling textbooks from magazines, newspapers, periodicals, etc.

O'Neill, M.E. and K.R. Martensen. *Criminal Justice Group*

Training—A Facilitator's Handbook. La Jolla, CA.: University Associates, 1975.

Popham, W. James. *Instructional Objectives.* Chicago: Rand McNally, 1969.

Pratt, W.N. "Preparing a Course You're Called Upon to Teach." *Supervisory Management,* 15 (April, 1970), pp. 13-16.

Quane, Roger. "Individualized Instruction." *Police Chief,* XL:6 (June, 1973), pp. 70-62.

Rausch, Edwin. "Games for Training." *Law and Order,* 18:2 (February, 1970), pp. 40, 94.

Soule, Rolland L. "Role Playing—A New Police Training Tool." *Police,* 4:4 (March-April, 1960), pp. 19-22.

Stoker, Mack. "The Permissive Approach in Teaching." *Police,* 4:2 (November-December, 1959), pp. 74-77.

AUDIO-VISUAL AIDS

Abrams, Nick. *Audio-Visual Resource Guide.* 9th ed. Cincinnati: Friendship, 1972.

Allen, Paul C. "Police-Made Slide Shows Enhance Pleasanton Traffic Safety Program." *Law and Order,* 20:10 (October, 1972), pp. 60-63.

Bohan, Robert C. "TV Drama Helps Train Police Officers." *Police Chief,* XXXLV:4 (April, 1967).

Brown, James S. *A.V. Instructional Manual.* 3rd ed. N.Y.: McGraw, 1973.

Crowhurst, Norman H. *Audio Systems Hand-Book.* Blue Ridge Summit, PA.: Tab, 1969.

Dorset, Lloyd G. *Audio-Visual Teaching Machines.* Englewood Cliffs, N.J.: Educational Technology, 1971.

Gammage, Allen Z. "Sound Recordings as Police Training Aids." *Police,* 6:5 (May-June, 1962), pp. 35-38; 6:6 (July-August, 1962), pp. 15-18.

Gammage, Allen Z. "The Third Dimension in Police Training." *Police,* 6:4 (March-April, 1962), pp. 52-54.
Visual aids, mock-ups, models etc.

Gardner, Martin R. "Police Vehicle Instruction-Information Aid." *Law and Order,* 16:12 (December, 1968), pp. 40-42, 113.
Use of program cassette tapes as training aids.

Gardner, Martin R., Sr. "Some Uses of Media in Law Enforcement Training Programs of the Future." *Law and Order,* 19:2 (February, 1971), pp. 38, 30-37.

Goetz, Rachel. *Visual Aids for the Public Service.* Chicago: Public Administration Service, 1954.

Heubener, Theodore. *Audio-Visual Techniques in Teaching Foreign Languages.* Rev. ed., N.Y.: New York University Press, 1967.

Minor, E.D. *Simplified Techniques for Preparing Visual Instructional Materials.* N.Y.: McGraw-Hill, 1962.

Nelson, Leslie W. *Instructional Aids—How to Make and Use Them.* Dubuque, IA.: William C. Brown, 1970.

Parsons, Robert L. "Helping the Regions Help Themselves." *Law and Order,* 18:9 (September, 1970), pp. 42, 44.

Reefsvold, Margaret Irene. *Guides to Newer Educational Media—Films, Filmstrips, Phonorecords, Radio, Slides, Television.* Chicago: American Library Association, 1961.

Rigg, R.P. *Audiovisual Aid and Techniques in Managerial and Supervisorial Training.* N.Y.: Olympic Media Information, 1972.

Schmid, Calvin F. *Handbook of Graphic Presentation.* N.Y.: Ronald, 1954.

Sharkitt, Robert L. "Training and Investigative Uses of Audiovisual Equipment." *Police Chief* (November, 1973), pp. 63-64.

"Television Production by Police." *FBI Law Enforcement Bulletin,* 38:9 (September, 1969).

"Visual Aids: An Important Part of Your Safety Program." *Security World,* 7 (February, 1970).

Wittich, Walter A. and Charles F. Schuller. *Audio Visual Materials: Their Nature and Use.* N.Y.: Harper, 1953.

FILMS

Ader, M. *Film Manual of Poverty Law and Related Social Issues.* Chicago: Northwestern University School of Law, 1972.

Air Force Film Directory (AFM 95-2). Washington: D.C.: GPO [n.d.].
In two volumes. Vol. 2 contains films cleared for public use.

Allen, Irving Lewis. *An Annotated and Classified List of 16 mm Films on Urban Studies: New Towns, Urban Proglems, City and Regional Planning.* Monticello, IL: Council of Planning Librarians, 1975.

Bristow, Allen P. *Police Film Guide.* Walteria, CA.: Police Research, 1968.

Carter, Clarence R. "A Police Film Library." *FBI Law Enforcement Bulletin,* 40:10 (November, 1971), pp. 7-9, 29.

Dillon, Clinton O. "Training Films Test Police Firearms Use." *Law and Order,* 20:7 (July, 1972), pp. 38-43.

Drug Abuse Films. 2nd ed. Washington, D.C.: National Coordinating Council on Drug Education [n.d.].
Summaries and evaluations of current audiovisual materials on narcotics.

Fagerstrom, Dorothy. "Directory of Public Relations Films." *Law and Order,* 13:3 (March, 1965), pp. 50-52, 57.

Fagerstrom, Dorothy. "Directory of Training Films." *Law and Order,* 13:2 (February, 1965), pp. 58-64.

Harrison, Leonard H. "Use of the Training Film." *Police,* 7:6 (July-August, 1963), pp. 75-77.

Incledon, George. "Film Exchange Program." *Law and Order,* 23:3 (March, 1975).

International Association of Chiefs of Police. *Police Film Catalog.* Washington, D.C.: IACP, 1971.

Lawder, Lee E. "Police Training Films by Professionals." *Law and Order,* 16:4 (April, 1968), pp. 52-53.
Making police training films.

Liacher, James L., ed. *Feature Films on 8 mm and 16 mm: A Directory of Feature Films Available for Rental, Sale and Lease in the United States.* 4th ed. N.Y.: Bowker, 1974.
More than 15,000 commercial documentary and experimental films are listed.

National Safety Council. *National Directory of Safety Films.* Chicago: National Safety Council [published irregularly].

Owens, Richard G. "Central Jersey Police Film Library." *Law and Order,* 22:4 (April, 1974), pp. 74-76.

Schildecker, Charles B. "Film: What Should It Accomplish in Your Training Program." *FBI Law Enforcement Bulletin,* 42:9 (September, 1973), pp. 29-31.

Seltz-Petrash, Ann. *A.A.A.S. Science Film Catalog.* N.Y.: Bowker, 1975.
Guide to 5,600 films relating to pure, applied and social sciences.

PROGRAMMED INSTRUCTION

Brightman, R.W. *Computer Assisted Instruction Program for Police Training.* Washington, D.C.: GPO, 1971.
Computer assisted instruction training in search and seizure, rules of evidence, and evaluation of the effectiveness of the computer assisted learning system.

Butler, Franklin C. "Programmed Instruction and Instructional System." *Training Directors Journal,* 18 (August, 1964).

Lang, Phil, ed. *Programmed Instruction.* Chicago: University of Chicago Press, 1967.

McCauley, R. Paul, D.T. Shanahan, and R. Cosenza. "Computer-Assisted Instruction and the Police Administration Curriculum: An Experiment." *Police Chief,* XLII:10 (October, 1975), pp. 44, 46-47.

Mathias, W.J. "Potential of Programmed Instruction." *Police Chief,* XXXIV:8 (August, 1967), pp. 53-54.

Mathias, W.J. "Programmed Instruction." *Police Chief,* 33:8 (August, 1966), pp. 44-46.

Minnesota Governor's Commission on Crime Prevention and Control. *Minnesota—CADAVRS (Computer Assisted Dial Access Video Retrieval Systems)—Project Evaluation.* Washington, D.C.: NCJRS (Microfiche), 1974.

O'Day, Edward F. et al. *Programmed Instruction: Techniques and Trends.* Englewood Cliffs, N.J.: Prentice Hall, 1971.

Ofeish, Gabriel D. *Programmed Instruction.* N.Y.: AMA, 1965.

Programmed Instruction—Introduction. Montgomery: Alabama Rehabilitation Research Foundation, 1968.

Silvern, Leonard C. *Program Instruction and Computer Assisted Instruction.* Los Angeles: Education and Training, 1967.

Spiech, John A. "An Introduction to Programmed Instruction." *Journal of Criminal Law, Criminology and Police Science,* 58:2 (June, 1967), pp. 279-283.

PART X
POLICE–COMMUNITY RELATIONS

POLICE-COMMUNITY RELATIONS

COMMUNITY RELATIONS

Books

Angell, John et al. *A National Survey of Police and Community Relations, Prepared for the President's Commission on Law Enforcement and Administration of Justice, Field Surveys V.* Washington, D.C.: GPO, 1967.

Banton, Michael. *Police-Community Relations.* London: Collins, 1973.

Bopp, William J. *Police-Community Relationships.* Springfield, IL.: C.C. Thomas, 1972.

Brown, John and G. Howes. *Police and the Community.* Indianapolis: Heath, 1975.

Cohen, Sylvan H. *Police-Community Problems: Essays on Malice in Blunderland.* N.Y.: MSS Information, 1975.

Cromwell, P.F. and G. Keefer. *Police-Community Relations.* St. Paul, MN.: West, 1973.
Collection of articles emphasizing the interaction between the policeman's conception of his role and his effect on society.

Earle, H.H. *Police-Community Relations—Crisis in Our Time.* Springfield, IL.: C.C. Thomas, 1972.

Eisenberg, Terry et al. *Police-Community Action: A Program for Change in Police-Community Behavior Patterns.* N.Y.: Praeger, 1973.

Epstein, Charlotte. *Intergroup Relations for Police Officers.* Baltimore: Williams and Wilkins, 1962.

Fink, J. and L.G. Sealy. *Community and the Police—Conflict or Cooperation.* N.Y.: Wiley, 1974.

Gardner, Michael. *Improving Police-Community Relations.* Washington, D.C.: NCJRS, 1973.

Geary, D.P. *Community Relations and the Administration of Justice.* N.Y.: Wiley, 1975.

Hale, Charles D. *Police Community Relations.* N.Y.: Delmar, 1974.

Holcomb, R.L. *Police and the Public.* Springfield, IL.: C.C. Thomas, 1971.
Common-sense measures for the police to cultivate the good will of the public.

Hollingsworth, Dan. *Rocks in the Roadway: A Treatise on Police-Public Relations.* Chicago: Stromberg-Allen, 1954.

Klyman, F.I. and F.B. Hannon. *Police Roles in a Changing Community—A Community Relations Planning Guide for Law Enforcement Agencies.* Wichita, KN.: Wichita State University, 1973.
Series of 29 articles investigating police-community relations, including both general discussion and personal experiences.

Lohman, Joseph D. and Gordon E. Misner. *The Police and the Community: The Dynamics of Their Relationship in a Changing Society—Volumes 1 and 2, Field Surveys IV.* Washington, D.C.: GPO, 1967.

National Survey of Police and Community Relations. Washington, D.C.: GPO, 1967.

Newark Human Rights Division. *Newark (NJ)—Police Community Relations Program.* Washington, D.C.: NCJRS (Microfiche) [n.d.].

Niederhoffer, A., and A.B. Smith. *New Directions in Police-Community Relations.* Corte Madera, CA.: Rinehart, 1974.

Norris, Donald F. *Police Community Relations,* Lexington, MA.: Lexington, 1973.

Portune, R. *Changing Adolescent Attitudes Toward Police.* Cincinnati: W.H. Anderson, 1971.

Platt, Robert M., ed. *Concept of Police-Community Relations.* Kennedale, TX.: Criminal Justice Press, 1973.

Platt, Robert M., ed. *Improving the Police Image.* (Police-Community Relations Series, vol. 1), Kennedale, TX: Criminal Justice Press, 1974.

Radelet, L.A. *Police and the Community—Studies.* Beverly Hills, CA.: Glencoe, 1973.

Reiss, A.J. *Police and the Public.* New Haven, CT.: Yale University Press, 1971.

Siegel, Arthur and R.C. Baker. *Police Human Relations Training.* Wayne, PA.: Applied Psychological Services, 1960.

Steadman, Robert F., ed. *The Police and the Community.* Baltimore: John Hopkins University Press, 1972.

Strecher, Victor. *The Environment of Law Enforcement: A Community Relations Guide.* Englewood Cliffs, N.J.: Prentice Hall, 1971.

Wasserman, Robert, Michael Paul Gardner, and Alan S. Cohen. *Improving Police/Community Relations.* Washington, LEAA, 1973.

Whisenand, Paul M. *Police Community Relations: A Reader.* Pacific Palisades, CA.: Goodyear, 1973.

Williams, Marden E. *The Portsmouth Police Story: Successful Blueprint for Police-Community Relations.* Jericho, N.Y.: Exposition, 1973.

Periodicals

Allman, James. "Establishing a Police-Community Relations Office." *Police Chief,* 32 (March, 1965), pp. 11-12, 14.

Almond, William D. and David J. Pontarelli. "A Colorado First." *Police Chief,* XLII:9 (September, 1975), pp. 44-45.

Anderson, Richard R. "Omaha's Communications Net Sparks 3.5 Million Police H.Q." *Law and Order,* 19:1 (January, 1971), pp. 22-26.

Anderton, Jean and Fred Ferguson. "Police-Community Relations Coffee Klatch Program." *Police,* 13:5 (May-June, 1969), pp. 19-22.

Arm, Walter. "Police-Public Relations: The Climate of Law and Order." *Public Relations Journal,* 22 (January, 1966), pp. 8-10.

Ahsenhust, Paul H. "Police and the Public Attitude." *Police,* 3:1 (September-October, 1958), pp. 30-33.

Baddeley, Fred. "British Police-Community Involvement." *Police* (May, 1972), pp. 24-29.

Baker, J. Wilson. "An Organization with a Heart." *FBI Law Enforcement Bulletin,* 39:2 (February, 1970), pp. 19-21.

Boys Ranch sponsored by Alabama Sheriff's Association.

Bayly, H.P. "Chesapeake's Police-Community Relations Effort." *Law and Order,* 21:3 (March, 1973), pp. 42-43.

Becker, Harold K. "Is It Too Late for Police-Community Relations?" *Police,* 15:6 (July-August, 1971), pp. 13-15.

Bell, Robert L. et al. "Small Group Dialogue and Discussion: An Approach to Police-Community Relations." *Journal of Criminal Law, Criminology and Police Science,* 60:2 (June, 1969), pp. 242-246.

Bishop, L.K. "Building Cooperation Between the Citizen and the Policeman." *Chieftan,* IV (Spring, 1957), pp. 13-14.

Bissonette, Raymond. "Citizen Observation of Police Work: Experiments in Learning." *Police Chief,* XLII:3 (March, 1976), pp. 44-45.

Bivens, Ernest H. "Kentucky State Police Trooper Island Project." *Law and Order,* 18:5 (May, 1970), pp. 78-82.

Summer camp for underprivileged boys conducted by state police.

Blagg, Clifford D. "Improved Community Relations Via Attitude Qualification." *Police,* 15:3 (January-February, 1971), pp. 47-49.

Boone, H.V. "Police and Community Relations: Police Role in Labor-Management Disputes." *Police,* 10:1 (September-October, 1965), pp. 52-57.

Bowers, Ron. "A Total PCR Effort." *Police Chief,* XL:3 (March, 1973), pp. 48-51.

Boye, R.F. "Educational TV as a Tool of Police Administration." *Police Chief,* XXXV:3 (March, 1968), pp. 24-34.

Brant, Billy G. "Profiled in Sound." *Law and Order,* 21:3 (March, 1973), pp. 56-59.

Radio programs which interview Kansas Highway Patrolmen in the field.

Brexler, Otto. "Training Parodies." *Law and Order,* 17:3 (March, 1969).

Brown, Lee P. "Dynamic Police-Community Relations at Work." *Police Chief,* XXXV:4 (April, 1968), pp. 44-50.

Brown, Lee P. "P-CR. Typology." *Police Chief,* 38:3 (March, 1971), pp. 16, 18-21.

Outlines four types of community-relations programs.

Brown, William P. "The Police and Community Conflict." *Police,* 8:5 (May-June, 1964), pp. 51-59.

Byrne, Edward C. "Toward Police Professionalism: Making Friends for Lawful Behavior." *Law and Order,* 18:8 (August, 1970), pp. 108-110.

Cable, Kenneth M. "P-CR. The Chief and the Community." *Police Chief,* 38 (March, 1971), pp. 24, 26-27.

Cahil, Thomas J. "Special Unit Revives Police-Community Relations." *American City* (June, 1965).

Casper, Joseph J. "Effectiveness of Any Police Organization Is Related to Public Opinion." *Journal of California Law Enforcement* (July, 1966), pp. 20-23.

Chalkley, Mason T. "Make It and Report It." *Law and Order* (March, 1972), pp. 44-47, 63.

Police establishment of their own radio program.

Cherry, Dick. "Modern AV Communications Helps Boulder Police Fight Drug Program with Information." *Law and Order,* 20:1 (January, 1972), pp. 44-47.

Clark, Ben. "Law Enforcement Needs Citizen Cooperation in Combating Community Problems." *Police* (January-February, 1966).

Clark, Donald E. "The Role of the Individual Officer in Building Public Support for Law Enforcement." *Police,* 8:6 (July-August, 1964), pp. 77-78.

Cohen, Sylvan H. "The Police-Community Relations: At This Point in Time." *Police Chief,* XLI:3 (March, 1974), pp. 40-42.

Coon, Thomas F. "The Friendly Cop." *Police,* VII:3 (January-February, 1963), pp. 58-59.

Cormack, J.A. "A Plan of Action in Police Community Relations." *Police Chief,* XXXIV:9 (September, 1967), pp. 50-51.

Costa, Rudy. "Summer Police-Youth Program." *Law and Order,* 21:12 (December, 1973), pp. 52-53.

The employment of young people within the Norwalk, Conn. Police Department. Department cooperates with poverty agency.

Couch, D. "Mobile City Government, a New Concept." *Texas Police Journal,* 22:8 1974, pp. 10-12, 20-21.

Coy, John T. "A Personal Look at the Police and the Community." *Police Chief,* XLI:3 (March, 1974), pp. 57-59.

Crowe, Henry P. "Police-Community Relations." *FBI Law Enforcement Bulletin,* 33:5 (May, 1964), pp. 15-18.

Cullen, John F. "Singing Boston Cops." *Law and Order,* 19:7 (July, 1971), pp. 88-89.

Cullis, Harry. "From Street Beat to Down Beat." *Police Chief,* XLI:3 (March, 1974), pp. 34-36, 38.

David, Jack et al. "Police Community Relations: A Process Not a Product." *Police Chief,* XLII:3 (March, 1976), pp. 16-18.

Davids, Fredrick E. "Policing by Permission." *Police Chief,* XXXV:12 (December, 1968), pp. 56-57.

Davis, Edgar. "A Method of Approach to the Tasks of a Human Relations Officer." *Police,* 15:3 (January-February, 1971), pp. 61-64.

Dieterle, Paul. "New Hampshire State Police 'Contacts' Avert Hampton Riots." *Law and Order,* 13:11 (November, 1965), pp. 56, 58-59, 62.
New Hampshire State Police activities at beach resort area.

Donald J.R. "Eliminating the Language Barrier." *Police Chief,* XXXVII:6 (June, 1971).

Donio, M.J. "Crime, Fear, Urban Retreat and the Problems of Law Enforcement." *Enforcement Journal,* 13:3 (1974), pp. 8-9, 24.
Because of technological advance police have become remote from public. Recommends closer contact with public.

Duncan, Bill. "Community Relations—California Style." *Law and Order,* 17:3 (March, 1969), pp. 10-13, 48.

Duncan, Bill. "Talk-Ins with Young People." *Law and Order,* 16:2 (February, 1968), pp. 22-25.

Eagan, John G. "Pilot 100." *Police Chief,* XXXIX:3 (March, 1972), pp. 42-43.

Earle, Howard H. "An Analysis of Recommendations on Police-Community Relation." *Journal of California Law Enforcement* (July, 1967), pp. 32-34.

Earle, Howard H. "Police Community Relations: The Role of the First-Line Peace Officer." *Police,* 14:1 (September-October, 1969), pp. 23-28.

Edwards, Jim. "Communications Systems Keynote Efficiency at Sayveville Police Department." *Law and Order,* 19:1 (January, 1971), pp. 20-21.

Eliason, Kevin D. "Citizen on Patrol." *Law and Order,* 18:11 (November, 1970), pp. 32-33.

Epstein, David G. "Police Community Relations: Another View." *Law and Order,* 23:3 (March, 1975), pp. 25-29.

"Explosive Words and Phrases." *FBI Law Enforcement Bulletin,* 39:1 (January, 1970), pp. 7-11.

Fagerstrom, Dorothy. "Law Enforcement Day in Norwich, Conn." *Law and Order,* 15:3 (March, 1967), pp. 30-32.

Feledick, Winifred Mertens. "Personal Touch." *Law and Order,* 11:5 (May, 1963).

Fink, Joseph. "Police in a Community—Improving a Deteriorated Image." *Journal of Criminal Law, Criminology and Police Science,* 59:4 (December, 1968).

Foley, Charles P. "Police/Community Program Uses Talking Slides." *Police Chief,* XXXIX:3 (March, 1972), pp. 44-48.
Public information program stressing crime prevention.

Formby, William A. and Vergil L. Williams. "P.A.S.T.—The Tuscaloosa Police-Action Service Team." *Police Chief,* XLI:6 (June, 1974), pp. 42-43.

Foster, Bill. "P-CR. Rhymes Against Crime." *Police Chief,* 38:3 (March, 1971), pp. 52-53.
Police program for grades 1-3 in Dallas, Texas.

Fox, Harry G. "Community Relations: A Something for Nothing Proposition." *Police Chief,* XXXVI:9 (September, 1969), pp. 14-18.

Fox, Harry G. "C.R.O.P.—Community Relations Orientation of Police." *Police Chief,* XXXV:6 (June, 1968), pp. 22-26.

Fox, Harry G. "Gang Youth and Police: Live In." *Police Chief,* 37:9 (October, 1970), pp. 26, 233-235.

Fox, Harry G. "Light Your Candle." *Police Chief,* XXXV:8 (August, 1968), pp. 32-33.

Fox, Harry G. "Mini-Town Meetings." *Police Chief,* XXXVII:4 (April, 1970), pp. 20-24.

Fox, Harry G. "Operation Handshake." *Police Chief,* XXXVI:1 (January, 1969), pp. 20-22.

Fox, Harry G. "Up the Down Escalator of Police Community Relations." *Police Chief,* XXXVII:6 (June, 1971), pp. 28-31.

Fox, William M. "A Measure of the Effectiveness of Case Method in Teaching Human Relations." *Personnel Administration,* 26:4 (1963), pp. 53-57.

Freeman, Nolen W. "The Years of Question." *Law and Order,* 17:3 (March, 1969), pp. 14, 48.

Geluix, J. "The Police and the Public." *Current Municipal Problems.* XV:3 (Winter, 1974), pp. 273-278.

Gentel, W.T. "P-CR. Implementing Change through Personnel Participation." *Police Chief,* 38:3 (March, 1971), pp. 36, 38-41.

Gerlach, Luther P. "Focus: Center Power." *FBI Law Enforcement Bulletin,* 37:5 (May, 1968), pp. 12-13.

Goldstein, Herman. "Police Response to Urban Crisis." *Public Administration Review,* XXVIII:5 (September/October, 1968).

Gonzales, Manuel. "You're on the Air." *FBI Law Enforcement Bulletin,* 38:3 (March, 1969), pp. 9-10.

Gould, Alfred C. "Comments from a Small Department." *Law and Order,* 16:8 (June, 1968).

Gourley, Dudley D. "The Need for Marketing in the Police Field." *Police Chief,* XLI:7 (July, 1974).

Granato, Russell. "The PCR Officer: A Dilemma." *Police Chief,* XXXVI:1 (January, 1969).

Gray, B.M., II. "Police Reports to the Community." *Police Chief,* XLI:3 (March, 1974), pp. 54-56.

Green, R.P. "Good Guy Citations." *Police,* 16:1 (September, 1971), pp. 33-34.

Gross, Solomon. "P-CR. Campus Confrontation—Northwestern Style." *Police Chief,* 38:3 (March, 1971), p. 42.
Student-police organized rap sessions.

Haagensen, Kenneth W. "Are We Really Getting through to People?" *FBI Law Enforcement Bulletin,* 38:2 (February, 1969), pp. 8-10, 25.

Hammond, Barry. "External Influences on Police-Community Relations." *Police Chief,* XLI:3 (March, 1974), pp. 60-62.

Haney, Matthew T. "Pulpit Patrol." *Law and Order,* 18:7 (July, 1970).
Ride-along program for community clergymen.

Hardesty, Thomas J. "Ads for a New Image." *Police Chief,* 38:2 (February, 1971).

Harvis, T.O. "Your Image." *Law and Order,* 21:3 (March, 1973), pp. 20-21, 62.

Hart, Edward J. "Good Police Radio . . . Today." *Law and Order,* 19:1 (January, 1971), pp. 42-44, 46.

Hernandez, Armand P. "An Open Letter." *Police Chief,* XLI:3 (March, 1974), pp. 51-53.

Hill, Margaret. "Selling C.R. by T.V. and Other Media." *Police Chief,* XLII:6 (June, 1975), pp. 50-52.

Hill, Raymond M. "The Novato Police Department and Police-Community Relations." *Police,* 14:3 (January-February, 1970), pp. 33-41.

Hill, Raymond M. "Police-Community Relations." *Journal of California Law Enforcement* (July, 1969), pp. 17-22.

Hogan, Edward J. and James Fagin. "Integrating the Policeman into the Community." *Police Chief,* XLI:12 (December, 1974), pp. 54-56.

Holladay, Everett F. "Footbridges for Law Enforcement." *Law and Order,* 19:1 (January, 1971), p. 18.

Imhoff, Chris. "Improving Community Relations by Providing the National Safety Council's Defensive Driving Course." *Police Chief,* XXXIX:12 (December, 1972), pp. 48-53.

Jenkins, Herbert T. "Atlanta (GA) Is Meeting a Challenge." *Law and Order,* 14:3 (March, 1966), pp. 68, 70-72.

Johnson, Thomas A. "Police Community Relations: Attitudes and Defense Mechanisms." *Issues in Criminology,* 1:4 (Fall, 1968), pp. 69-75.

Kenn, H.L. "Take Another Look." *Law and Order,* 18:5 (May, 1970), pp. 64-65.

Kimble, Joseph P. "Kids and Cops and Stuff Like That." *Police Chief,* XXXV:8 (August, 1968), pp. 20-24.

Kimbrough, Richard B. and Donald J. Grubb. "Community College Tells C.J. 'Like It Is' to Rural High Schools." *Police Chief,* XLII:6 (June, 1975), pp. 54-56.
Jr. college instructors explaining criminal justice in high schools.

Klyman, Fred I. "The Police-Community Relations Survey: A Quantitative Inventory of Services and Work Units." *Journal of Police Science and Administration,* 2:1 (March, 1974), pp. 77-81.

Klyman, F. "A Survey of Police-Community Relations." *Police Law Quarterly,* 3:1 (1973), pp. 13-27.

Kreps, G.A. and J.M. Weller. "The Police-Community Relations Movement Conciliatory Responses to Violence." *American Behavioral Scientist,* 16:3 (1973), pp. 402-412.

Laizure, C.J. "Making Youth Aware of Their Police Department." *Law and Order,* 14:5 (May, 1966), pp. 26-28.

"Lexington Police Department States Hot Wheels Rally." *Law and Order,* 18:6 (June, 1970), pp. 96-97.

McGarry, Doyle. "An Invitation to Understanding." *Police Chief,* XXXVII:6 (June, 1971), pp. 20-27.

McKamy, Kent. "A New Tool for Community Relations." *Law and Order,* 20:3 (March, 1972), pp. 34, 36-38, 40.

Manella, Frank L. "The Three Worlds of Youth." *Police Chief,* XXXIX:9 (September, 1972), pp. 53-54.

Melchionne, Theresa. "Community Relations: Dynamic Police-Community Dialogues." *Law and Order,* 16:9 (September, 1968).

Meldelsohn, Robert A. "Police-Community Relations: A Need in Search of Public Support." *American Behavioral Scientist,* 13:5 (May/June, 1970); 13:6 (July/August, 1970).

Michael, Gaston F. "Operation Reassurance." *Law and Order,* 22:6 (June, 1974), pp. 84-86.
Police program whereby shut-ins, the elderly and others in need are contacted by police on a regular basis to make sure everything is alright.

Morris, Earl F. "The Police and the Community: A Lawyer's View." *FBI Law Enforcement Bulletin,* 37:5 (May, 1968), pp. 3-5, 23.

Morton, Ted. "What Can I Do? How Can I Help?" *Police Chief,* XXXIX:7 (July, 1972), pp. 36-37.

Nelson, John R. "Fort Wayne's Answer to Youth In-Activity." *Law and Order,* 18:2 (February, 1970), pp. 96-98.

Olson, Bruce T. "Public Preferences for Police/Community Relations Programs." *Police Chief,* XXXIX:9 (September, 1972), pp. 64-67.

Palo, Jack W. "For Sale: Small Town Police Department." *Police Chief,* XXXIX:9 (September, 1972).

Pantaleoni, Mrs. G., Jr. "Policemen a Child's Best Friend." *Police Chief,* 31 (September, 1964).

Parker, W.H. "The Police Role in Community Relations." *Journal of Criminal Law, Criminology and Police Science,* 47:3 (September/October, 1956), pp. 368-379.

Partree, Cecil A. "Recipe for Respect: The Policeman's Role." *FBI Law Enforcement Bulletin,* 41:12 (December, 1972), pp. 12-14, 28.

Peck, Leo G. "Developing a Precinct or District Committee." *Police Chief,* 32:2 (March, 1965), pp. 24-27.

Peters, Bernard. "That People May Know." *Police Chief,* XXXLV:3 (March, 1967), pp. 28-32.

Peters, Emil E. "Law Students Police Action Program." *FBI Law Enforcement Bulletin,* 38:11 (November, 1969), pp. 16-17.
Ride-along program for law students.

Pierce, Chester M. "Psychiattic Aspects of Police-Community Relations." *Mental Hygiene,* 46:1 (1962).

Pitchess, Peter J. "Adopt a Deputy." *Law and Order,* 17:3 (March, 1969), pp. 68-71.

Pitchess, Peter J. "Los Angeles County Adopt-A-Deputy Program." *Police Chief,* XXXV:11 (November, 1968), pp. 36-37.

Pogue, Emmett. "Community Relations: A Changing Role in Law Enforcement." *Law and Order,* 20:3 (March, 1972), pp. 16-18, 20-21.

Police Chief, 37:3 (March, 1971).
Contains 13 articles on police-community relations.

"Police Plus Public Involvement Equals Community Understanding." *Police Chief,* XXXIX:3 (March, 1972), pp. 58-61.

Polizzi, Charles S. "Youth Program Reduces Delinquency." *Law and Order,* 14:5 (May, 1966), pp. 14-18, 68.
Activities of Milford, Conn. police-sponsored drum and bugle corps.

Radelet, L.A. "Police-Community Relations." *Social Order* (1960), pp. 219-225.

Radelet, Louis A. "Police-Community Relations: At This Point in Time." *Police Chief,* XLI:3 (March, 1974), pp. 24-25, 28-32.

Rankin, Theodore L. "P-CR. Fact or Farce." *Police Chief,* 38:3 (March, 1971), pp. 62-64.

Ratzlaff, David E. "Cry for a Candle." *Law and Order,* 14:5 (May, 1966), pp. 12-13.

Raymond, Harold R. "A One-Man Community Relations Program for a Small Department." *Police Chief,* XLII:3 (March, 1976), pp. 42-43.

Reasons, C.E. and B.A. Wirth. "Police-Community Relations Units: A National Survey." *Journal of Social Issues,* 31:1 (1975), pp. 27-34.

Reiser, Martin and J. Leonard Steinberg. "A Human Relations Handbook for Police Officers: To Protect and Serve: An Information Guide for Police Officers to Increase Effectiveness in the Community." *Police* (August, 1972).

Roberts, Michael A. "A Community Relations Program for a Small Department." *Police Chief,* XLI:3 (March, 1974), pp. 49-50.

Rouzer, Vaul E. "Essay Program—A New Approach to Youth Problem." *FBI Law Enforcement Bulletin,* 27:4 (April, 1958), pp. 17-19.

Salamone, Russell J. "Seminar for Juveniles." *Law and Order,* 13:2 (February, 1965), pp. 68-70.

"A Saturday with the Police in Stockton, California." *Police Chief,* XXXV:6 (June, 1968).

Savord, George H. "Selling Law Enforcement to Your Public." *Police,* 13:6 (July-August, 1969), pp. 6-11.

Schott, Jacob W. "The Policeman and His Public." *FBI Law Enforcement Bulletin,* 38:2 (February, 1969), pp. 17-19.

Schultz, Donald O. "Make Your C-R Man a Civilian." *Police Chief,* XXXVII:9 (September, 1970).

Seay, Howard W. "Police-Community Relations." *Law and Order,* 19:4 (April, 1971), pp. 56, 58, 60, 62, 64, 66, 68.

"Send a Child to Camp . . . Says the Jos. Schlitz Brewing Co." *Police Chief,* 37:9 (October, 1970), pp. 24, 246-247.

Shalin, Neil. "The Creation of a Police Community Relations Program." *Law and Order,* 19:3 (March, 1971), pp. 28, 30-32.

Shepard, George H. "The Juvenile Specialist in Community Relations." *Police Chief,* XXXVII:1 (January, 1970), pp. 33-37.

Sides, Eugene. "Police and Community Relations." *Law and Order,* 19:3 (March, 1971), pp. 14, 16, 18, 20-21.

Smith, Paul M. "Trooper Island." *FBI Law Enforcement Bulletin,* 38:11 (November, 1969), pp. 12-15.
Summer camp for underprivileged boys sponsored by Kentucky state police.

"Special Event and Open House Checklist." *Police Chief,* XXXLV:3 (March, 1967), pp. 40-47.

"Special Unit Revives Police-Community Relations, San Francisco." *American City* (1965).

Stockstill, Mike. "The Rap Session." *Law and Order,* 20:4 (April, 1972), pp. 15-16, 18.

Tabashneck, Bruce. "Cop-In and Ride-Along." *Police Chief,* 38:8 (August, 1971), pp. 72-73.

Thibodeaux, Donald J. "Camp Win-a-Friend." *FBI Law Enforcement Bulletin* (October, 1975), pp. 19-23.

Thibodeaux, Donald J. "Conservation of Youth." *Police Chief,* XL:6 (June, 1973), pp. 68-69.
Boys camps sponsored by Louisiana state police.

"This Cop Is Not for Sale." *Law and Order* (December, 1974).
Description of poster.

Tielsch, George P. "Communications with the Public." *Police Chief,* XLI:3 (March, 1974), pp. 20, 23.

Tooley, F. Jane. "The Omaha Police-Community Relations Camp." *Police Chief,* 39:10 (October, 1972), pp. 62-63, 288-289.

Trabucco, Edmund A. and Dana A. Skiff. "Police-Community Relations as a Function of Credibility." *Police Chief,* XLI:3 (March, 1974), pp. 44, 46, 48, 85.

Tucker, Justus M. "Police Community Relations." *Texas Police Journal* (April, 1967).

van der Walt, Piet J. "Police and Public." *Police,* 14:5 (May-June, 1970), pp. 28-31.

Walsh, D.E. "Contacts!" *Police Chief,* XXXIX:6 (June, 1972).

Watson, Nelson A. "The Fringes of Police-Community Relations." *Police Chief,* 33:8 (August, 1966), pp. 8-9, 64-68.

Wilson, Robert and Robert Stammerjohn. "Bridging the Gaps." *Police Chief,* XXXVII:5 (May, 1970), pp. 34-37.

Witt, Walter C., Jr. "Sell Your Police Department." *Law and Order,* 13:12 (December, 1965), pp. 26-27.

Wright, Edward. "Checking the CQ—Courtesy Quotient." *Police Chief,* XXXVI:3 (March, 1969), pp. 40-41.

Wrightington, Donald. "The Uniformed Officer and the Juvenile." *Law and Order,* 16:9 (September, 1968), pp. 84-88.

Wynn, Ed R. "Building Interprofessional Cooperation between Police and Community Agencies." *Police,* 9:5 (May-June, 1965).

Yearwood, Homero. "Police Community Relations." *Issues in Criminology,* 1:4 (Fall, 1968), pp. 45-57.

York, Orrell and William G. McMahon. "Only Through Professional Behavior." *Police Chief* (November, 1969), pp. 24-25, 40.

"Your Friend the Policeman." *FBI Law Enforcement Bulletin,* 36 (August, 1967), pp. 12-13.
Children's booklet describing activities of Richman, CA P.D.

Zadeh, Stella. "L.A.P.D.: Bridging the Community Gap?" *California Sun Magazine* (July, 1971), pp. 16-24.

Zeitz, Leonard. "A New Approach toward Resolving the Police Dilemma." *Police,* 15:1 (September-October, 1970), pp. 58-61.

Pamphlets and Unpublished Materials

ABT Associates, Inc. *Dayton—Police Department-Neighborhood Assistance Officer Program—Exemplary Project Validation Report.* Washington, D.C.: NCJRS (Microfiche), 1975.

Allen, Robert F. and Saul Pilnick. *Conflict Resolution: Team Building for Police and Ghetto Residents.* Union, N.J.: Scientific Resources, 1968, (Mimeographed).

Baltimore Police Department. *Baltimore Police Department-Community Relations.* Washington, D.C.: NCJRS (Microfiche).
A summary of existing police-community relations programs, including citizen involvement programs, college-oriented programs, the officer friendly project, crime prevention programs, and special community activities.

Edwards, George. *The Police on the Urban Frontier.* N.Y.: Institute of Human Relations, 1968.

Hart, Robert Peter. *History and Evaluation of the St. Louis Committees for Better Community-Police Relations: May 1955 to March 1957.* Unpub. Master's Thesis, St. Louis University, 1957.

Littman, Sol. *The Policeman Looks at Himself.* N.Y.: Anti-Defamation League of B'nai B'rith, 1967.

National Conference of Christians and Jews. *Crisis in Law Enforcement.* N.Y.: National Conference of Christians and Jews [n.d.].
Program designed to improve police-community relations, assist in police education, and develop community responsibility.

Surratt, James E. *A Survey and Analysis of Special Police Services in Large Public School Districts of the United States.* Unpub. Doctoral Dissertation, Duke University, 1974.

Wiemer, R.E. and F. Reyes, Jr. *Dade County (FL)—Safe Streets Unit Project—Grant 73-DF-04-0004—Final Report.* Washington, D.C.: NCJRS (Microfiche), 1974.

PUBLIC RELATIONS

Alden, Reginald J. "Police Public Relations." *Law and Order,* 14:10 (October, 1966), pp. 16-21.

Ashenhust, Paul N. "Police Public Relations." *Police,* 2:4 (March-April, 1958), pp. 7-12.

Ashenhust, Paul H. "Steps toward Good Public Relations." *Police,* 3:2 (November-December, 1958), pp. 53-54.

Ayoob, Massad F. "Effective Public Relations for the Small Department." *Law and Order* (March, 1976), pp. 26-32.

"Better Public Relations Urged for Law Enforcement." *FBI Law Enforcement Bulletin,* 35:1 (January, 1966), pp. 8-12.

Canfield, B.R. and H.F. Moore. *Public Relations: Principles, Cases and Problems.* 6th ed. Homewood, IL.: Irwin, 1973.

Center, Allen H. *Public Relations Practices: Case Studies.* Englewood Cliffs, N.J.: Prentice Hall, 1975.

Chamberlain, Charles S. "Public Relations in the Small Department." *Law and Order* (September, 1968).

Clark, Ben. "Public Relations Scores High in Riverside County Sheriff's Department." *Police,* 10:2 (November-December, 1965), pp. 75-77.

Coon, Thomas F. "How Are Your Public Relations?" *Police,* 5:4 (March-April, 1961), pp. 76-77.

Crisford, John N. *Public Relations Advances.* Boston, MA.: Cahners, 1973.

Crittenden, Bradford M. "California Highway Patrol and Public Relations." *Law and Order,* 14:11 (November, 1966), pp. 14-22.

Crook, Clayton. "Twelve Month Public Relations Program." *Law and Order,* 17:9 (September, 1969), pp. 80-85, 88.

Cutlip, Scott M. and Allen H. Center. *Effective Public Relations.* 4th ed. Englewood Cliffs, N.J.: Prentice Hall, 1968.

Dow, John P. "A P.R. Program Aimed at Businessmen." *Law and Order,* 14:12 (December, 1966).

Dunlap, Floyd C. "A Low-Budget Public Relations Program for a Small Department." *Police Chief,* XL:3 (March, 1973), pp. 38-39.

Euston, M.A. "Promoting Good Public Relations." *Law and Order,* 15:3 (March, 1967), pp. 8-11, 52.

Fagerstrom, Dorothy. "Personal Public Relations." *Law and Order,* 17:3 (March, 1969), pp. 24-34.

Fitzgerald, Stephen E. *Communicating Ideas to the Public.* N.Y.: Funk and Wagnalls, 1950.

International City Management Organization. *Public Relations in Local Government,* Washington, D.C.: International City Managers, 1975.

Johnson, Jack W. "Good Public Relations Is Good Business." *FBI Law Enforcement Bulletin,* 39:7 (July, 1970), pp. 5-7, 31.

Klein, Charles H. "Street Level PR." *Law and Order,* 22:9 (September, 1974), pp. 64-65.

LaCouture, Ron. "The Police, the Press and Public Relations." *Police,* 6:1 (September-October, 1961), pp. 44-46.

Lawder, Lee E. "The Importance of GOOD Public Relations." *Law and Order,* 16:12 (December, 1968), pp. 116-117, 119.

Lawder, Lee E. "A Ready-Made Public Relations Tool." *Law and Order,* 13:3 (March, 1965), pp. 8-9, 46.

Lewis, Geoffrey A. *Public Relations for Local Government.* Boston, MA.: Cahners, 1973.

Lloyd, Herbert. *Public Relations.* 2nd ed. N.Y.: International Publications Service, 1974.

McClung, T.E. "Courtesies and Services Promote Public Relations." *FBI Law Enforcement Bulletin,* 27:1 (January, 1958), pp. 22-24.

Marshal, Saul H. *Public Relations Basics for Community Organizations.* 5th rev. ed. Hollywood, CA.: Creative, 1975.

Mawrence, Mel. "Chronology of a Day in Police Public Relations." *Law and Order,* 15:3 (March, 1967), pp. 12-21.

Moore, Charles E. "Public Relations: Public Responsibility." *Police Chief,* XXXLV:3 (March, 1967), pp. 12-27.

Morris, Charles F. "Open House—The Gateway to Improved Public Relations." *Police,* 1:5 (May-June, 1957), pp. 20-21.

Nolte, Lawrence W. *Fundamentals of Public Relations: Professional Guidelines, Concepts, and Integrations.* Elmsford, N.Y.: Pergamon, 1974.

"Police-Public Relations Programs." *Police Chief,* 33:5 (May, 1966), p. 18.

Scheidt, James. "A Public Relations Program for the Small Department." *Law and Order,* 17:8 (August, 1969).

Steinberg, Charles S. *The Creation of Consent: Public Relations and Practice.* N.Y.: Hastings House, 1975.
Analysis of how information campaigns influence public opinion.

Stoutt, Tony. "A PR Program Designed for 6 to 12 Year Olds." *Law and Order,* 23:3 (March, 1975), pp. 42-45.

"The True Measure of Police/Public Relations." *Police Chief,* XL:3 (March, 1973).

Van Dyke, L.B. "Name Tags—An Aid in Public Relations." *Law and Order,* 12 (March, 1964).

Vaupel, Carl F., Jr. "Improving Police Effectiveness and Police Relations." *Police,* 15:1 (September-October, 1970), pp. 19-20.

Whalen, Howard. "P.R. Program for the Small Police Department." *Law and Order,* 15:3 (March, 1967).

Wheeler, Pan Dodd. "Police Public Relations: The Public of the Police Unit." *Police,* 1:4 (March-April, 1957), pp. 7-11.

Wrightington, Donald. "Public Relations for a Small Department." *Law and Order,* 16:6 (June, 1968), pp. 76-79.

ANTI-POLICE SENTIMENT

Blanks, W. Winfield. "Officer Needs Help." *Police Chief,* 38:2 (February, 1971), pp. 48-49.
Discusses anti-police sentiment.

Falk, Gerhard J. "The Public's Prejudice Against the Police." *American Bar Association Journal,* 50 (1964).

LeGrande, J.L. "A Re-Examination of the Public Prejudice Against the Police." *American Bar Association Journal,* 51 (1965).

Lohman, Joseph D. "Current Decline in Respect for Law and Order." *Federal Probation* (December, 1967).

McKetta, Frank. "Police: 'Whipping Boy' for Social Ills as Symbols of Authority." *Pennsylvania Chiefs of Police Association Bulletin* (Fall, 1969).

McKinnon, Harold R. "Hidden Power Behind the Law." *Police Chief,* 30 (March, 1963), pp. 10-12.

McRuer, J.C. "Current Decline in Respect for Law and Order—Is There a Remedy?" *Legal Aid Brief Case,* 25 (October, 1966), pp. 4-8.

Odell, Brian Neal. "America's New Anti-Police Sentiment." *Police Chief,* XL:3 (March, 1973), pp. 52-55.

"The Policeman and His Public." *America* (November 25, 1961).

CITIZEN CONTACTS

Black, Donald J. and Albert J. Reiss, Jr. "Patterns of Behavior in Police and Citizen Transactions." *Studies of Crime and Law Enforcement in Major Metropolitan Areas: Field Surveys III, II, Section I. Report to the President's Commission of Law Enforcement and Administration of Justice.* Washington, D.C.: GPO, 1966.

Brecher, Edward and Ruth. "Don't Take the Police for Granted." *Parents,* 39: (March, 1964), pp. 56-57.

Coates, Robert B. and Alden D. Miller. "Patrolmen and Addicts. A Study of Police Perception and Police-Citizen Interaction." *Journal of Police Science and Administration,* 2:3 (September, 1974), pp. 308-321.

Garrett, W. *Policeman and His Delinquent—Critical Factors in Police-Juvenile Encounters.* Ann Arbor, MI.: University Microfilms, 1972.
Extent to which police expect boys to be involved in delinquent behavior, based on their social class membership and their demeanor.

George, B.J., Jr. "Police Practices and the Citizen." *Police,* (March-April, 1966).

Hartjen, Clayton J. "Police-Citizen Encounters: Social Order in Interpersonal Interaction." *Criminology,* 10:1 (May, 1972), pp. 61-84.

Katz, Michael. "Violence and Civility in a Suburban Milieu." *Journal of Police Science and Administration,* 2:3 (September, 1974), pp. 239-249.

LaFave, Wayne. "Street Encounters and the Constitution: *Terry, Sibron, Peters,* and Beyond." *Michigan Law Review,* 67 (1968).

Lipsky, Michael. *Law and Order: Police Encounters.* Chicago: Aldine, 1970.

Lohman, Joseph and Gordon Misner. *The Police and the Community: The Dynamics of Their Relationship in a Changing Society: Field Survey IV. Report for the President's Commission on Law Enforcement and Administration of Justice.* Washington, D.C.: GPO, 1966.

Lundman, R.J. and J.C. Fox. *Drunkenness in Police-Citizen Encounters.* Washington, D.C.: NCJRS (Microfiche). [n.d.].

Piliavin, Irving and Scott Briar. "Police Encounters with Juveniles." *American Journal of Sociology,* 70 (September, 1964).

Snibbe, Richard H. "Police Visability—Positive or Negative?" *Police* (July-August, 1968).

Thompson, Jim. "Police Controls over Citizen Use of the Public Streets." *Journal of Criminal Law, Criminology and Police Science,* 49:6 (March-April, 1959), pp. 562-569.

Watson, Nelson A. *Improving the Officer-Citizen Contact.* Washington, D.C.: IACP, 1969.

CITIZEN SUPPORT OF POLICE

Arens, Richard and Harold D. Lasswell. *In Defense of Public Order,* N.Y.: Columbia University Press, 1961.

Arm, Walter. "The Case for the Police." *Police Chief,* XXVIII:4 (April, 1961).

Ball, John. "Police Administrator and the Crime Writer." *Police Chief,* XLII:5 (May, 1975), pp. 62-64.

Bennett, T. Lawrence. "Historical Analysis of the Issues: Pending Legislation." *Police Chief,* XLIII:1 (January, 1976), pp. 19, 68-69.
Death benefits for police.

Bishop, L.K. "Building Cooperation between the Citizen and the Policeman." *Chieftan,* 4 (Spring, 1957), pp. 13-14.

Burden, Ordway P. "Hundred Clubs Nationwide." *FBI Law Enforcement Bulletin,* 43:9 (September, 1974), pp. 8-10.

Carrington, Frank. "AELE: Citizens in Support of Law Enforcement." *Traffic Digest and Review,* 19 (March, 1971), pp. 6-8.

Clark, D. "Police under Pressure." *Catholic World* (January, 1966), pp. 228-232.

Dettleff, John S. "The Police-Clergy Team Concept." *Law and Order,* 17:9 (September, 1969), pp. 8, 104.
Program where clergymen ride with patrol officers on a regular basis.

Durk, David B. "Support Your Local Police." *Atlantic,* 223:3 (March, 1969), pp. 103-104.

Flanagan, William J. "This Minority . . . Is the Police." *Law and Order,* 14:9 (September, 1966), pp. 8-11, 50.

Friend, Jerry L. "On Target—Police Community Cooperation Builds Range." *FBI Law Enforcement Bulletin,* 42:1 (January, 1973), pp. 25-31.

Gould, Charles L. "A Minority That Is Indispensable." *FBI Law Enforcement Bulletin,* 40:11 (November, 1971).

Gelb, Richard. "How Business Can Help Law Enforcement." *Police Chief,* XXXV:3 (March, 1968), pp. 36-37.

Grothaus, Stanley R. "Kiwanis Police Support." *Police Chief,* XXXIII:2 (February, 1966), pp. 18-20.

Handlin, Oscar. "Community Organization as a Solution to Police-Community Problems." *Police Chief,* XXXII:3 (March, 1965), pp. 16-22.

Hollingsworth, D. *Citizen Support for the Police.* Evanston, IL.: Traffic Institute, Northwestern University, 1972.
Motivation of citizen support groups includes convincing the public of the value of police, recognizing citizens' needs, and improving police performance.

Hollingsworth, Dan. "What Can Support of Citizens Do for Police." *Traffic Digest and Review* (1963).

Hutcheson, John D., Jr. *Organized Citizen Participation in Urban Areas.* Atlanta, GA.: Emory University, 1964.

Kirk, Clif. "I Salute You." *Police Chief,* XLI:5 (May, 1974).

Kuchel, G.L. "The Public: A Part of the Problem." *Police Chief* (November, 1969), pp. 32-33.

Lumbard, Edward J. "The Citizen's Role in Law Enforcement." *Journal of Criminal Law- Criminology and Police Science,* 56:1 (March, 1965), pp. 67-72.

Malkin, Sy. "What Are the 100 Clubs?" *Law and Order,* 23:4 (April, 1975)l pp. 56-57.

Marshaling Citizen Power Against Crime. Washington, D.C.: Chamber of Commerce of the U.S., 1970.
Helps the interested citizen understand what he can do, either individually or through organizations. to help improve police, courts and corrections.

Marx, Gary T. and Dane Archer. "Citizen Involvement in the Law Enforcement Process." *American Behavioral Scientist* (September, 1971).

Minanovich, Clement S. "Programming for Citizen Participation in Police Action Programs." *Police Chief,* 32:3 (March, 1965), pp. 27-31.

Moore, Gerald W. "I'm Ashamed of Having Been So Indifferent." *FBI Law Enforcement Bulletin,* 36:9 (September, 1967), p. 13.

Oldham, C.C. "Citizen Studies of Law Enforcement Programs: A Help or a Hindrance?" *Police Chief,* XXXLV:6 (June, 1967), pp. 26-32.

Ordway, P. Burden. "Hundred Clubs Testify to Need for Federal Legislation." *Police Chief,* XLIII:1 (January, 1976), pp. 18, 66, 67.

Patrick, J. Milton. "Let's Stand Up for America." *FBI Law Enforcement Bulletin,* 39:5 (May, 1970), pp. 7-9, 30.

Powers, William F. "A Timeless Reminder." *Law and Order,* 15:8 (August, 1967), pp. 34-41.

"Public Support of Law Enforcement." *FBI Law Enforcement Bulletin,* 34:11 (November, 1965).

"Respect for the Police." *America,* 93 (April 16, 1955).

Ruby, D.W. "Civic Organization Can Help Police." *Police Chief,* 31 (July, 1964).

Skousen, W. Cleon. "Citizens Committees Organized Support Local Police." *Law and Order,* 14:9 (September, 1966), pp. 14-17, 94.

Ustjanauskas, Anthony. "Hundred Club: The Club with a Heart." *Police Chief,* 37:9 (October, 1970), pp. 40, 42.

Whitehouse, Jack E. "Citizens' Complaints and Commendations." *Law and Order,* 15:12 (December, 1967), pp. 82-85.

HUMAN RELATIONS

Dean, J.P. and Alex Rosen. *A Manual of Intergroup Relations.* Chicago: University of Chicago Press, 1955.

Fagerstrom, Dorothy. "Knowledge—The Policeman's Weapon for Human Rights." *Law and Order,* 15:2 (February, 1967), pp. 6, 70.

Gregory, G. Howard. "A Practical Guide to Human Relations." *Law and Order,* 21:9 (September, 1973), pp. 52-54, 56, 58, 82; 21:10 (October, 1973), pp. 54-59; 21:11 (November, 1973), pp. 30-33.

Ichheiser, Gustav. *Appearance and Realities: Misunderstanding in Human Relations.* San Francisco, CA.: Jossey-Bass, 1970.

Kenney, John P. "Police and Human Relations in Management." *Journal of Criminal Law, Criminology and Police Science* 45:2 (July/August, 1954), pp. 222-228.

Nobel, J.D. "The Intergroup Worker." *Police Chief,* XXXLV:6 (June, 1967), pp. 44-47.

Reeves, Elton T. *How to Get Along With Almost Everybody.* N.Y.: AMA, 1973.

Rustomji, M.K. *Getting Along Better With People: One Hundred and Twenty Eight Proven Ways.* Thompson, CT.: Interculture, 1975.

Sides, Eugene. "Police Human Relations—A Bridge over Troubled Waters." *Law and Order,* 19:7 (July, 1971), pp. 32-35.

Watson, N.A. *Issues in Human Relations.* Gaithersburg, MD.: IACP, 1973.

Ziecher, Irving B. "Human Relations and the Police." *Law and Order* (April, 1956).

POLICE CRITICS

Ahern, James F. *Police in Trouble: Our Frightening Crisis in Law Enforcement.* N.Y.: Hawthorn, 1972.

Beckman, Erik. "Law Enforcement: An Invitation to Join the 20th Century." *Police,* 16:4 (December, 1971), pp. 42-43.

Brooks, Thomas R. "Why 7 out of 10 Cops Will Use the Third Degree." *FACT* (November-December, 1965).
Totally unobjective sensationalist paper using material and statistics out of context.

"The Cops." *Nation* (April 21, 1969).

FOCUS/MIDWEST, 6 [n.d.].
Entire issue devoted to analysis of police departments in Illinois and Missouri. Apparently published in conjunction with St. Louis ACLU.

Garrison, Omar V. *Spy Government: The Emerging Police State in America.* N.Y.: Lyle Stuart, 1967.
Text with bibliography.

Hahn, H. "A Profile of Urban Police." *Law and Contemporary Problems,* 36:4 (1971), pp. 449-466.
Critical account of urban police.

Harris, Richard. *Justice, The Crisis of Law, Order, and Freedom in America.* N.Y.: Dutton, 1970.

Jacobs, Paul. "The Los Angeles Police: A Critique." *Atlantic,* 95 (December, 1966).

"Kicking the Coppers." *Newsweek,* 62 (December 30, 1963).

Kimble, Joseph P. "Why Isn't Anyone Listening?" *Law and Order,* 14:9 (September, 1966).

Kuh, Richard H. "The 'Rest of Us' in the 'Policing the Police' Controversy." *Journal of Criminal Law, Criminology and Police Science,* 57:3 (September, 1966), pp. 244-250.

Law Enforcement: The Matter of Redress. Los Angeles: ACLU, 1969.

Leavy, James. "Self-Defense against the Police." *McGill Law Journal* (November, 1973), pp. 413-328.

Leinwand, G. *Police—An Exploration of the Controversy Surrounding the Role of the Men in Blue in American Cities.* N.Y.: Pocket Books, 1972.
Collection of readings on the effectiveness of the law enforcement system, from the points of view of the police and their critics.

Misner, Gordon E. "Enforcement: Illusion of Security." *Nation,* 208 (1969).

Newton, H.P. "A Citizen's Peace Force." *Crime and Social Justice* (1974), pp. 36-39.
Another of the reoccurring writers who advocate abolishing the police and forming some form of "citizens' militia."

Packer, Herbert L. "The Courts, the Police and the Rest of Us." *Journal of Criminal Law, Criminology and Police Science.* 57:3 (September. 1966), pp. 238-243.

Rexroth, Kenneth. "The Fuzz." *Playboy* (July, 1967).

Rolph, C.H. "American Policeman." *New Statesman* (August 1, 1969).

Rolph, C.H. "Police Violence." *New Statesman* (July, 1963), pp. 66-102.

Rubin, Sol. "Police Must Live Within the Law." *Police Chief,* 33:5 (May, 1966), pp. 9, 11.

Turner, William W. *The Police Establishment.* N.Y.: Putnam's, 1968.

Walker, Daniel. "The Chicago Police Riot." *Life* (December 6, 1968), pp. 34-39.

Zeichner, Irving B. "Generations of Policemen." *Law and Order,* 15:9 (September, 1967), pp. 6-7.

PUBLIC SPEAKING

Baicker, Isaac J. *Speak Expertly in Four Weeks.* N.Y.: Exposition, 1955.

Bryant, Donald C. and Karl R. Wallace. *Fundamentals of Public Speaking,* 4th ed. Englewood Cliffs, N.J.: Prentice Hall, 1969.

Brown, LeRoy C. *How to Make a Good Speech.* N.Y.: F. Fell, 1964.

Bureau of Narcotics and Dangerous Drugs. *Public Speaking on Drug Abuse Prevention—A Handbook for the Law Enforcement Officer.* Washington, D.C.: GPO, 1970.

Flesch, Rudolf. *Say What You Mean.* N.Y.: Harper and Row, 1972.

Forley, Maurice. *Public Speaking Without Pain.* N.Y.: McKay, 1965.

Friedman, Edward L. *The Speaker's Handy Reference.* N.Y.: Harper and Row, 1967.

Garrett, Howard George. *How to Hold an Audience; The Key to Successful Public Speaking.* N.Y.: Citadel, 1957.

Holm, James Noble. *Productive Speaking for Business and the Profession.* Boston: Allyn and Bacon, 1967.

Howell, William Smiley. *Presentational Speaking for Business and the Profession.* N.Y.: Harper and Row, 1971.

Karr, Harrison M. *Now You're Talking!* 2nd ed. Danville, IL.: Interstate, 1968.

King, Everett M. *The Officer Speaks in Public.* Springfield, IL.: C.C. Thomas, 1958.

Kruger, Arthur N. *Effective Speaking: A Complete Course.* Cincinnati: Van Nostrand Rinehold, 1970.

Loyd, Glen. "Win That Audience." *Police,* 15:3 (January-February, 1971), pp. 77-78.

Marx, Jerry. *Officer, Tell Your Story.* Springfield, IL.: C.C. Thomas, 1967.

O'Reilly, Bob. "Police Department's Speakers Bureau." *Law and Order,* 13:3 (March, 1965), pp. 18-21.

Stedman, William. *Guide to Public Speaking.* Englewood Cliffs, N.J.: Prentice Hall, 1971.

Strother, Edward S. and Allen W. Huckleberry. *Effective Speaker.* N.Y.: Houghton Mifflin, 1968.

Truby, J. David. "When You Are Asked to Speak." *Law and Order,* 19:6 (June, 1971), pp. 86-90.

White, Eugene E. *Practical Public Speaking.* N.Y. MacMillan, 1964.

Willingham, Ronald L. *How to Speak So People Will Listen.* Waco, TX.: World, 1968.

MINORITIES IN THE COMMUNITY

INTEGRATION

Calhoun, L.S. *Desegregation Works: A Primer for Parents and Teachers.* Evanston, IL.: Integrated Education Associates, 1968.

Handlin, Oscar. "The Goal of Integration." In: Talcott Parsons and Kenneth B. Clark, eds. *The Negro American.* Boston: Houghton Mifflin, 1966.

Hill, Herbet. *Citizen's Guide to Desegregation.* Westport, CT.: Negro University Press, 1955.

Kluger, Richard. *Simple Justice: The History of Brown v. Board of Education and Black America's Struggle for Equality.* N.Y.: Knopf, 1976.

Knapp, Robert B. *Social Integration in Urban Communities.* N.Y.: Teachers College, 1960.

Morris, Willie. *Yazoo: Integration in a Deep-Southern Town.* N.Y.: Harper, 1971.

Pelason, J.W. *Fifty-Eight Lonely Men: Southern Federal Judges and School Desegregation.* Urbana: University of Illinois Press, 1971.

JUSTICE AND MINORITIES

Allen, F.A. *Crimes of Politics—Political Dimensions of Criminal Justice.* Cambridge, MA.: Harvard University Press, 1973.

Argues against criminalizing activity that opposes political and social goals of particular power groups when such goals are not an essential part of the constitutional consensus for political and social order.

Allison, Junius L. "Poverty and the Administration of Justice in the Criminal Courts." *Journal of Criminal Law, Criminology and Police Science,* 55:2 (June, 1964), pp. 241-245.

A. Philip Randolph Institute, New York. *Reluctant Guardians—A Survey of the Enforcement of Federal Civil Rights Laws.* Springfield, VA.: NTIS, 1969.

Based on assumption that poor people are usually denied their civil rights in employment, education, and other areas.

Hindelang, Michael J. "Equality Under the Law." *Journal of Criminal Law, Criminology and Police Science,* 60:3 (September, 1969), pp. 306-313.

Long, Elton. *American Minorities: The Justice Issue.* Englewood Cliffs, N.J.: Prentice-Hall, 1975.

Overby, Albert W., Jr. *Discrimination Against Minority Groups in the Administration of Justice.* Consultant Paper, President's Commission on Law Enforcement and the Administration of Justice, Washington, D.C.: GPO, 1967.

Reasons, C.E. and J.L. Kuykendall. *Race, Crime and Justice.* Pacific Palisades, CA.: Goodyear, 1972.

Race, crime and justice probes deeply into the criminal justice system for minority groups and recommends important policy changes.

Sanerville, Bill. "Double Standards in Law Enforcement with Regard to Minority Status." *Issues in Criminology,* 4:1 (Fall, 1968), pp. 35-43.

U.S. Congress, Committee on Civil Rights. *Mexican-Americans and the Administration of Justice in the South-West.* Washington, D.C.: GPO, 1970.

MINORITY GROUP RELATIONS

Adams, Thomas F. "Police-Minority Group Relations." *Police,* 7:6 (July-August, 1963), pp. 35-37.

Allen, Robert F. and Saul Pilnick. *Conflict Resolution: Team Building for Police and Ghetto Residents.* Union, N.J.: Scientific Resources, 1968 (mimeo).

Banton, Michael P. *Race Relations.* N.Y.: Basic, 1967.

Barton, Milton L., ed. *Minorities in a Changing World.* N.Y.: Knopf, 1967.

Bayley, D.H. and H. Mendelsohn. *Minorities and the Police: Confrontation in America.* N.Y.: Free Press, 1969.

Berleman, W.C. "Police and Minority Groups. The Improvement of Community Relations." *Crime and Delinquency,* 18:2 (1972), pp. 160-167.

Berry, Brewton. *Race and Ethnic Relations.* 3rd ed. Boston: Houghton Mifflin, 1965.

Black, Harold and Marvin J. Labes. "An Analogy to Police-Criminal Interaction." *American Journal of Orthopsychiatry,* 37 (July, 1967).

Blalock, Hubert M., Jr. *Toward a Theory of Minority-Group Relations.* N.Y.: Wiley, 1967.

Brown, Gordon. *Law Administration and Negro-White Relations in Philadelphia.* Philadelphia: Bureau of Municipal Research, 1947.

California Attorney General's Advisory Commission On Community-Police Relations. *The Police in the California Community.* San Francisco: Office of The Attorney General of California, 1973.

Cizanckas, Victor I. and Carlton W. Purviance. "Changing Attitude of Black Youths." *Police Chief* (March, 1973).

Cross, Granville S. "The Negro, Prejudice, and the Police." *Journal of Criminal Law, Criminology and Police Science,* 55:3 (September, 1964), pp. 405-411.

Cross, Stan and Edward Renner. "An Interaction Analysis of Police-Black Relations." *Journal of Police Science and Administration,* 2:1 (March, 1974), pp. 54-61.

De Puy, Blanche. "A Case of Cultural Rub: The Spanish Inheritance and John Law." *Police* (November, 1965).

Edwards, George. *The Police on the Urban Frontier,* N.Y.: American Jewish Committee, 1968.

Gordon, Mitchell. "Police Brutality: Tension Won't Ease Unless Enforcement Agencies Help to Dispel Hostility of Negroes." *Wall Street Journal,* 166: 1965.

Green, Constance. *The Secret City: A History of Race Relations in the Nation's Capital.* Princeton: Princeton University Press, 1967.

Hale, E.C. "Police, Minorities and Mobs." *New South* (September, 1961), pp. 6-9, 12.

Hammer, Richard. "Report from a Spanish Harlem 'Fortress'." in Bernard E. Segal, ed. *Racial and Ethnic Relations,* N.Y.: Crowell, (1966), pp. 324-330.

Kephart, W.M. *Racial Factors and Urban Law Enforcement.* Philadelphia: University of Pennsylvania Press, 1957.

Kimble, Joseph P. "A Policeman Looks at Race Relations." *Police,* 7:4 (March-April, 1963), pp. 79-81.

Kuykendall, Jack L. "Police and Minority Groups: Toward a Theory of Negative Contacts." *Police,* 15:1 (September-October, 1970), pp. 47-55.

Lahey, Edwin A. "Cops Unsung Heroes in Racial Tragedy." *Journal of Criminal Law, Criminology and Police Science,* 56:2 (June, 1965).

Lambert, John R. *Crime, Police, and Race Relations: A Study in Birmingham.* N.Y.: Oxford University Press, 1970.

Lehman, Paul. "A Comment on the Police and the Kerner Report." *Issues in Criminology,* 1:4 (Fall, 1968), pp. 61-65.

Lohman, Joseph D. *The Police and Minority Groups.* Chicago: Chicago Park Police, 1947.

McEntire, Davis and Robert B. Powers. *A Guide to Race Relations for Police Officers.* Sacramento: Department of Justice, 1946.

Mack, Raymond W. *Prejudice and Race Relations.* Chicago: Quadrangle, 1970.

Manella, Frank L. "Group Differences as They Affect the Police." *Police Chief,* XLI:6 (June, 1974), pp. 51-52.

Martin, A. "The Police and the Black Community." *Police Law Quarterly,* 3:4 (1974), pp. 22-36.

Mason, Philip. *Race Relations.* N.Y.: Oxford University Press, 1970.

Prinslow, R.J. "Positive Approach to Minority Problems." *Law and Order,* 20:7 (July, 1972), pp. 66-72.

"Race and Law Enforcement: A Guide to Modern Police Practices." *New South* (February, 1952), pp. 1-20.

Shaffer, Helen B. "Negroes and the Police." *Editorial Research Reports* (September 21, 1964), pp. 683-699.

Stecher, Victor. *When Subcultures Meet: Police Negro Relations.* London: Academic Press, 1967.

Toch, Hans. "Cops and Blacks: Warring Minorities." *Nation,* 208:491 (1969).

U.S. Commission on Civil Rights, Mississippi Advisory Committee. *Administration of Justice in Mississippi. A Report.* Washington, D.C.: GPO, 1963.

Weckler, Joseph E. and Theodore E. Hall. *Police and Minority Groups.* Chicago: Chicago Park District Press, 1944.

Wilson, P.R. "Police-Ethnic Relations in Australia." *New Community,* 3:3 (1974), pp. 220-226.

POLICE IN THE GHETTO

Allen, Robert F., Saul Pilnick, and Stanley Silverzweig. "Conflict Resolution—Team Building for Police and Ghetto Residents." *Journal of Criminal Law, Criminology and Police Science,* 70:2 (June, 1969), pp. 251-255.

Anderson, R.E. "The Ghetto Is too Important to Be Abandoned to the Police After Dark." *Police Chief,* XXXVI:4 (April, 1969), pp. 16-18.

Armbrister, Trevor. "Law and Order—White Cop in the Black Ghetto: How Far Do You Go? Where Do You Draw the Line?" *Saturday Evening Post* (November 16, 1968).

Byrn, R.M. "Urban Law Enforcement: A Plea from the Ghetto." *Criminal Law Bulletin,* 5 (1969), pp. 125-136.

Chase, L.Q. "West Indians and the Police: Some Observations." *New Community,* 3:3 (1974), pp. 205-210.

Gross, S. "The Police of the Twenty-Third Precinct and the East Harlem Community." *Journal of Social Issues,* 31:1 (1975), pp. 145-161.

Judge, A. "The Police and the Colored Communities: A Police View." *New Community,* 3:3 (1974), pp. 199-204.

Kempton, Murray. "How Cops Behave in Harlem." *New Republic* (August 22, 1964).

Kilbane, Marjory and Patricia Claire. *Police, Courts, and the Ghetto.* new ed. West Haven, CT.: Pendulum Press, 1969.

Kimble, Joseph P. " 'Black Power' in a White Machine Furnishes Many Law Enforcement Problems." *Journal of California Law Enforcement* (January, 1968), pp. 132-137.

Levy. Burton. "Cops in the Ghetto: A Problem of the Police System." *American Behavioral Scientist* (March-April, 1968), pp. 31-34.

Mathias, William J. "P-CR. Perceptions of Police Relationships with Ghetto Citizens." *Police Chief,* 38:3 (March, 1971), pp. 44-49.

Mathias, William J. "Perceptions of Police Relationships with Ghetto Citizens." *Police Chief,* 38:4 (April, 1971), pp. 78-85.

Osofsky, Gilbert. "The Enduring Ghetto." *Journal of American History,* 55 (1968), pp. 243-255.

Ostrom, E. and G.P. Whitaker. *Community Control and Governmental Responsiveness—The Case of Police in Black Neighborhoods.* Washington, D.C.: NCJRS (Microfiche).

Study which compares the caliber of police services in five small and large scale governments in the Chicago metropolitan area.

Schulz, D.A. "Some Aspects of the Policeman's Role as It Impinges Upon Family Life in a Negro Ghetto." *Sociological Focus,* 2 (1969), pp. 63-72.

Skolnick, Jerome H. *The Police and the Urban Ghetto.* Chicago: American Bar Foundation, 1968.

Turner, V. Simpson. "Police Work in the Ghetto." *Law and Order,* 16:9 (September, 1968), pp. 80-82.

Walker, Tom. *Fort Apache: Life and Death in New York City's Most Violent Precinct.* N.Y.: Crowell, 1976.

Wallach, I.A. *Police Function in a Negro Community.* Vol. 1. *Summary and Conclusions.* Springfield, VA.: NTIS, 1970.

Police function and its implementation in the urban Negro community.

Wallach, I.A. *Police Function in a Negro Community.* Vol. 2. Springfield, VA.: NTIS, 1970.

An empirical study of the police function and its implementation in the urban Negro community.

Whittemore, L.H. "A Hard Con and His Patient Partner on a Menacing Beat." *Life* (June 20, 1969).

Wilson, J.Q. "The Police in the Ghetto." in R.F. Steadman, ed. *The Police and the Community,* Baltimore: Johns Hopkins University Press, 1972.

Wintersmith, R.I. *Police and the Black Community.* Lexington, MA.: Lexington, 1974.

RACISM

Allport, Gordon W. *ABC's of Scapegoating.* Cambridge, MA.: Harvard University Press, 1965.

Allport, Gordon W. *The Nature of Prejudice.* Boston: Beacon, 1954.

Anti-Semitism. St. Lawrence, MA.: Two Continents, 1975.

Bettelheim, Bruno and Morris Janowitz. *Dynamics of Prejudice.* N.Y.: Harper and Row, 1950.

Bettelheim, Bruno and Morris Janowitz. *Social Charge and Prejudice.* N.Y.: Free Press, 1964.

Baldwin, James. "The White Man's Guilt." *Ebony,* 20 (August, 1965), pp. 47-48.

Caplovitz, David and Candace Rogers. *Swastika, 1960—The Epidemic of Anti-Sematic Vandalism in America.* N.Y.: Anti-Defamation League, 1961.

Cook, James G. *The Segregationists.* N.Y.: Appleton-Century-Crofts, 1962.

Cox, O.C. "Race Prejudice and Intolerance—A Distinction." *Social Forces,* 24:2 (December, 1945).

Daniels, Roger. *Politics of Prejudice: The Anti-Japanese Movement in California and the Struggle for Japanese Exclusion.* Paterson, N.J.: Atheneum, 1968.

Fagerstrom, Dorothy. "Prejudice—Man's Blind Spot." *Law and Order,* 14:9 (September, 1966), pp. 18-23, 42.

Feldstein, Stanley, ed. *Poisoned Tongue: A Documentary History of American Racism and Prejudice.* Caldwell, N.J.: Morrow, 1972.

Glock, Charles and Ellen Siegelman. *Prejudice U.S.A.* N.Y.: Praeger, 1969.

Grier, William H. and Price M. Cobbs. *Black Rage.* N.Y.: Basic, 1968.

Hentoff, Nat, ed. *Black Anti-Semitism and Jewish Racism.* N.Y.: Schocken, 1970.

Himelhoch, Jerome. "Is There a Bigot Personality?" *Commentary,* 3 (March, 1949).

Jones, J. *Prejudice and Racism.* Reading, MA.: Addison-Wesley, 1972.

King, Martin Luther. *Where Do We Go from Here: Chaos or Community?* N.Y.: Harper, 1967.

King, Martin Luther. *Why We Can't Wait.* N.Y.: Harper, 1964.

Lapiders, Frederick R. and David Burrows, eds. *Racism: A Case Book.* N.Y.: Crowell, 1971.

Lightfoot, Claude M. *Racism and Human Survival: The Lessons of Nazi Germany for Today's World.* N.Y.: International Publications, 1972.

Mack, Raymond W. *Prejudice in Race Relations.* N.Y.: Watts, 1970.

Montagu, A. *Man's Most Dangerous Myth; The Fallacy of Race.* N.Y.: Columbia University Press, 1945.

Monte, Anita and Gerald Leinwand, eds. *Racism.* N.Y.: Pocket Books, 1972.

Myers, G.A. *History of Bigotry in the United States.* N.Y.: Random House, 1943.

Myrdal, Gunnar. *An American Dilemma: The Negro Problem and Modern Democracy.* N.Y.: Harper and Row, 1962.

Newly, I.A. *Jim Crow's Defense; Anti-Negro Thought in America.* Baton Rouge: Louisiana State University Press, 1965.

Parkes, James. *Anti-Semitism.* Chicago: Quadrangle, 1964.

Reese, Charles D. "Police Academy Training and Its Effects on Racial Prejudice." *Journal of Police Science and Administration,* 1:3 (September, 1973), pp. 257-268.

Rose, Arnold M., ed. *Race Prejudice and Discrimination: Readings in Intergroup Relations in the United States.* N.Y.: Knopf, 1951.

Rose, Peter J. *The Subject Is Race.* N.Y.: Oxford University Press, 1968.

Saenger, Gerhart. *The Social Psychology of Prejudice.* N.Y.: Harper, 1954.

Schulke, Flip, ed. *Martin Luther King, Jr.* N.Y.: Norton, 1976.

Selznick, Gertrude J. *The Tenacity of Prejudice: Anti-Semitism in Contemporary America.* N.Y.: Harper and Row, 1969.

Silberman, Charles. *Crisis in Black and White.* N.Y.: Random House, 1964.

Smith, L.E. *Killers of the Dream.* rev. ed. N.Y.: Norton, 1961.

U.S. Commission on Civil Rights. *Racism in America and How to Combat It.* Washington, D.C.: GPO, 1970.

Van den Berghe, Pierre L. *Race and Racism: A Comparative Perspective.* N.Y.: Wiley, 1967.

Westin, A.F. and B. Mahoney. *Trial of Martin Luther King.* N.Y.: Crowell, 1974.

Zeichner, Irving B. "The Swastika Writhes Again." *Law and Order,* (May, 1960).

SEGREGATION

Abrams, Charles. *Forbidden Neighbors: A Study of Prejudice in Housing.* N.Y.: Harper, 1955.

Canty, Donald. *A Single Society: Alternatives to Urban Apartheid.* N.Y.: Praeger, 1969.

Grossack, Martin M., ed. *Mental Health and Segregation.* N.Y.: Springer, 1963.

LaGuma, Alex, ed. *Apartheid: A Collection of Writings on South African Racism.* N.Y.: International Publishing Co., 1971.

Pomeroy, William J. *Apartheid Axis: United States and South Africa.* N.Y.: International, 1971.

Safa, Helen Icken. "The Case for Negro Separatism: The Crisis of Identity in the Black Community." *Urban Affairs Quarterly,* 4:1 (September, 1968), pp. 45-64.

Weinstein, Allen and Frank Otto Gatell, eds. *The Segregation Era 1863-1954: A Modern Reader.* N.Y.: Oxford University Press, 1970.

Wilson, Allen. *Consequences of Segregation.* San Francisco: Bond and Fraser, 1969.

Yuan, D.Y. "Voluntary Segregation: A Study of New York Chinatown." In: Milton L. Barron, ed. *Minorities in a Changing World.* N.Y.: Knopf, (1967), pp. 263-276.

SLAVERY

Abel, Annie H. *Slave Holding Indian.* 3 Vols. Saint Clair Shores, MI.: Scholarly Press (repr. of 1919-1925 ed.).

Brown, Richard Q. *Slavery in American Society.* Indianapolis: Heath, 1969.

Carroll, Joseph C. *Slave Insurrections in the United States, 1800-1865.* Westport, CT.: Negro University Press (repr. 1938 ed.).

Duff, J.B. and L.A. Greene. *Slavery: Its Origin and Its Legacy.* Northbrook, IL.: AHM, 1975.

Ebony (September, 1963).

Special issue in commemoration of the 100th anniversary of the Emancipation Proclamation.

Elkins, Stanley M. *Slavery: A Problem in American Institutional and Intellectual Life.* Chicago: University of Chicago Press, 1959.

Filler, Louis. *Slavery in the United States of America.* Cincinnati: Van Nostrant Reinhold, 1972.

Hollander, Barney. *Slavery in America: Its Legal History.* London: Bowes, 1962.

Klein, H.S. *Slavery in the Americas.* N.Y.: Watts, 1972.

Langdon-Davies, John. *Slave Trade and Its Abolition.* N.Y.: Grossman, 1965.

Liston, Robert A. *Slavery in America.* Vol. 1. *The History of Slavery, 1619-1865.* N.Y.: McGraw, 1970.

Mannix, Daniel P. and Malcolm Cowley. *Black Cargoes, A History of the Atlantic Slave Trade.* N.Y.: Viking, 1962.

Mullin, Gerald, ed. *American Negro Slavery: A Documentary History.* N.Y.: Harper and Row, 1975.

Phillips, Ulrich Bonnell. *American Negro Slavery.* Gloucester, MA.: Peter Smith, 1959.

Ransford, Oliver. *Slave Trade: The Story of Transatlantic Slavery.* Levittown, N.Y.: Transatlantic, 1972.

Slave Narratives: A Folk History of Slavery in the U.S. From Interviews with Former Slaves. 17 vols. Saint Clair Shores, MI.: Scholarly Press, 1941.

Slave Trade. 95 vols. Totowa, N.J.: Irish Academy Press, 1971.

Smith, Abbott E. *Colonists in Bondage: White Servitude and Convict Labor in America, 1607-1776.* Chapel Hill: University of North Carolina Press, 1947.

Thomas, John L., ed. *Slavery Attacked: The Abolitionist Crusade.* Englewood Cliffs, N.J.: Prentice-Hall, 1964.

Wish, Harvey, ed. *Slavery in the South.* N.Y.: Farrar, Straus and Giroux, 1964.

Winks, Robin, ed. *Slavery: A Comparative Perspective.* N.Y.: New York University Press, 1972.

MINORITIES IN AMERICA

Minority Groups—General

Arnold, David O. *The Sociology of Subcultures.* Berkeley, CA.: Glendessary Press, 1970.

Barron, Milton L., ed. *Minorities in a Changing World.* N.Y.: Knopf, 1967.

Burrows, Edwin G. *Hawaiian Americans: An Account of the Mingling of Japanese, Chinese, Polynesian, and American Culture.* New Haven: Yale University Press, 1947.

Chyz, Yaraslav and R. Lewis. "Agencies Organized by Nationality Groups in the United States." *Annals, American Academy of Political and Social Science.* 262 (March, 1949), pp. 148-158.

Cornwell, Elmer E. "Bosses, Machines, and Ethnic Groups." *Annals of the American Academy of Political and Social Science.* (May, 1954), pp. 22-39.

The Emerging Minorities in America: A Resource Guide for Teachers. Santa Barbara, CA.: American Bibliographical Center, CLIO Press, 1972.

Francis. E.K. "The Nature of the Ethnic Group." *American Journal of Sociology,* 52:5 (March, 1947), pp. 393-400.

Gittler, Joseph B. *Understanding Minority Groups.* N.Y.: Wiley, 1956.

Glenn, Max E. *Appalachia in Transition.* St. Louis: Bethany, 1970.

Gordon, Milton M. "The Concept of the Subculture and its Application." *Social Forces,* 26:1 (October, 1947), pp. 40-42.

Kramer, Judith R. *The American Minority Community.* N.Y.: Crowell, 1970.

Lieberson, Stanley. *Ethnic Patterns in American Cities.* N.Y.: Glencoe, 1963.

McDonagh, Edward C. *Ethnic Relations in the United States.* N.Y.: Appleton-Century-Crofts, 1953.

Mack, Raymond W. and Troy S. Duster. *Patterns of Minority Relations.* N.Y.: Anit-Defamation League of B'nai B'rith, 1964.

Miller, S.M. and Frank Riessman. "The Workingclass Subculture: A New View." *Social Problems,* (1951).

Porteus, S.D. "Ethnic Group Differences." *Mankind Quarterly,* (January, 1961).

Rademaker, John A. *These Are Americans.* Palo Alto, CA.: Pacific, 1951.

Wagley, Charles and Marvin Harris. *Minorities in the New World.* N.Y.: Columbia University Press, 1958.

Yinger, J. Milton. "Contraculture and Subculture." *American Sociological Review,* 25 (October, 1960), pp. 625-635.

American Indians

Binis, Hamilton. "Indian Uprising for Civil Rights." *Ebony,* 22 (February, 1967).

Cohen, Warren H. and Philip J. Mause. "The Indian: The Forgotten American." *Harvard Law Review,* 81 (June, 1968).

Dennis, H.C. *The American Indian 1492-1970: A Chronology and Fact Book.* Dobbs Ferry, N.Y.: Oceana, 1971.

Hagan, William I. *American Indians.* Chicago: University of Chicago Press, 1961.

Hertzberg, Hazel W. *The Search for an American Indian Identity: Modern Pan Indian Movements.* Syracuse, N.Y.: Syracuse University Press, 1971.

McNickie, D'Arcy. *The Indian Tribes of the United States.* N.Y.: Oxford University Press, 1962.

Sorkin, Alan L. *American Indians and Federal Aid.* Washington, D.C.: Brookings, 1971.

Taylor, T.W. *States and Their Indian Citizens.* Washington, D.C.: GPO, 1972.
History of the development and the current relationships between tribal, state, and federal government activities.

Arabs

Arab Americans and Almanac. rev. ed. Los Angeles: News Circle, 1976.

Aswad, Barbara C. *Arabic Speaking Communities in American Cities.* N.Y.: Center for Migration Studies, 1974.

Hagopian, Elaine C. and Ann Paden, eds. *The Arab-Americans; Studies in Assimilation.* Wilmette, IL.: Median University Press International, 1969.

Chinese

Barth, Gunther Paul. *Bitter Strength, A History of the Chinese in the U.S., 1850-1870.* Cambridge, MA.: Harvard University Press, 1964.

Fan, Ting C. *Chinese Residents in Chicago.* San Francisco: R and E Research Associates, 1974.

Lee, Rose Hum. *The Chinese in the United States of America.* Hong Kong: Hong Kong University Press, 1960.

Lyman, Stanford. *Chinese Americans.* N.Y.: Random, 1974.

Cubans

Fagen, Richard R. et al. *Cubans in Exile.* Stanford, CA.: Stanford University Press, 1968.

Thomas, John P. "Cuban Refugees in the United States." *International Migration Review,* 1 (Spring, 1967), pp. 46-57.

Wenk, Michael G. "Adjustment and Assimilation: The Cuban Refugee Experience." *International Migration Review,* 3 (Fall, 1968), pp. 38-49.

Danes

Christman, Noel J. *Ethnic Influence on Urban Groups: The Danish Americans.* San Francisco: R and E Research Associates, 1975 (repr. of 1966 ed.).

Nelson, Nina. *Denmark.* N.Y.: Hastings, 1974.

Filipinos

Burma, John H. "The Background of the Current for Filipino-Americans." *Social Forces,* 30 (October, 1951), pp. 42-48.

Kim, Hyung-Chan and Mejiac Cuison. *The Filipinos in America.* Dobbs Ferry, N.Y.: Oceana, 1976.

Mariano, Honorante. *The Filipino Immigrants in the U.S.* San Francisco: R and E Research Associates, 1972.

French

Fosdick, L.J. *The French Blood in America.* Baltimore: Genealogical, 1973 (repr. of 1906).

McDermott, John F., ed. *Frenchmen and French Ways in the Mississippi Valley.* Urbana: University of Illinois Press, 1969.

Pula, James S. *The French in America.* Dobbs Ferry, N.Y.: Oceana, 1975.

Germans

Furer, Howard B. *The Germans in America 1607-1970.* Dobbs Ferry, N.Y.: Oceana, 1973.

O'Connor, Richard. *The German-Americans.* Waltham, MA.: Little, 1968.

Rippley, La Verne. *The German-Americans.* Boston: Twayne, 1976.

Greeks

Burgess, Thomas. *Greeks in America.* San Francisco: R and E Research Associates, 1970 (repr. of 1913 ed.).

Saloutos, Theodore. *The Greeks in the United States.* Cambridge: Harvard University Press, 1964.

Vlachos, E.C. *Assimilation of Greeks in the United States.* NY.: International, 1969.

Gypsies

Clark, Marie W. "Vanishing Vagabonds: The American Gypsies." *Texas Quarterly,* 10 (Summer, 1967), pp. 204-210.

Clebert, Jean-Paul. *The Gypsies.* Baltimore: Penguin, 1963.

Dawson, Robert. "Offenses Committed by Gypsies in the West Riding of Yorkshire." *Gypsy Lore Society Journal* (July-October, 1970), pp. 120-126.

Gropper, Renac. *Gypsies in the City: Cultural Patterns and Survival.* Princeton, N.Y.: Darwin, 1975.

Kenrick, Donald and Grattan Puxon. *The Destiny of Europe's Gypsies.* N.Y.: Basic, 1972.

Leland, Charles Godfrey. *Gypsy Sorcery and Fortune-Telling.* N.Y.: Dover, 1971.

Rehfisch, Farnham, ed. *Gypsies, Tinkers and Other Travelers.* London: Academic Press, 1975.

Suttlerland, Anne. *Gypsies: The Hidden Americans.* N.Y.: Free Press, 1975.

Webb, Godfrey E. *Gypsies, The Secret People.* Westport, CT.: Greenwood, 1974 (repr. of 1960 ed.).

Yoors, Jan. *The Gypsies.* N.Y.: Simon and Schuster, 1967.

Irish

Duff, John B. *Irish in the United States.* Belmont, CA.: Wadsworth, 1971.

Griffin, William D. *The Irish in America.* Dobbs Ferry, N.Y.: Oceana, 1973.

Potter, George W. *To the Golden Door: The Story of the Irish in Ireland and America.* Boston: Little, Brown, 1960.

Shannon, William V. *American Irish.* rev. ed. N.Y.: Macmillan, 1966.

Italians

Amfithealtrof, Erik. *The Children of Columbus: An Informal History of the Italians in the New World.* Boston: Little, Brown, 1973.

LoGatton, A.F. *The Italians in America.* Dobbs Ferry, N.Y.: Oceana, 1972.

Lopreato, Joseph. *Italian Americans.* N.Y.: Random, 1970.

Rolle, Andrew F. *The American Italians.* Belmont, CA.: Wadsworth, 1972.

Whyte, William F. *Street Corner Society.* Chicago: University of Chicago Press, 1955.

Japanese

Arkoff, Abe. "Need Patterns in Two Generations of Japanese-Americans in Hawaii." *Journal of Social Psychology,* 50 (1959), pp. 75-79.

Hosokawa, Bill. *Nisei; The Quiet American.* N.Y.: Morrow, 1969.

Iga, Mamoru. "The Japanese Social Structure and the Source of Mental Strain of Japanese Immigrants in the U.S." *Social Forces,* 35:3 (March, 1951), pp. 271-278.

Kitano, Harry H.L. *Japanese Americans: The Evolution of a Subculture.* Englewood Cliffs, N.J.: Prentice-Hall, 1969.

Leathers, Noel L. *The Japanese in America.* Minneapolis: Lerner, 1967.

Petersen, W. "Family Structure and Social Mobility Among Japanese Americans." *Abstracts. American Sociological Association* (1967), pp. 119-120.

Smith, Bradford. *Americans from Japan.* Philadelphia: Lippincott, 1948.

Jews

Fein, I.M. *Making of an American Jewish Community.* Philadelphia: Jewish Publications Society of America, 1971.

Gordon, Albert I. *Jews in Suburbia.* Westport, CT.: Greenwood, 1973.

Learsi, Rufus. *The Jew in America: A History.* rev. ed. N.Y.: Ktav, 1972.

Sanders, Ronald. *The Down Town Jews: Portraits of an Immigrant Generation.* N.Y.: Harper and Row, 1969.

Sklare, Marshall. *American Jews.* N.Y.: Random, 1971.

Wirth, Louis. *Ghetto.* Chicago: University of Chicago Press, 1956.

Mexican-Americans

Burma, John H., ed. *Mexican-Americans in the United States.* Scranton, PA.: Canfield, 1970.

Burma, John H. *The Spanish-Speaking Groups in the United States.* Durham, N.C.: Duke University Press, 1954.

Garcia, Richard A. *The Chicanos in America: Chronology and Fact Book.* Dobbs Ferry, N.Y.: Oceana, 1976.

Griffith, Beatrice. *American Me.* Boston: Houghton Mifflin, 1948.
Mexican-Americans in Los Angeles.

Lewis, O. *The Children of Sanchez: Autobiography of a Mexican Family.* N.Y.: Random, 1961.

Lewis, O. *Five Families: Mexican Case Studies in the Culture of Poverty.* N.Y.: Basic, 1959.

Meier, Matt S. *The Chicanos: A History of Mexican-Americans.* N.Y.: Hill and Wang, 1972.

Moore, Joan W. *Mexican-Americans.* 2nd ed. Englewood Cliffs, N.J.: Prentice-Hall, 1976.

Moquin, Wayne. *A Documentary History of the Mexican Americans.* N.Y.: Praeger, 1971.

Nava, Julian. *Viva La Raza: Readings on Mexican-Americans.* N.Y.: D. Van Nostrand, 1973.

Paredes, Americo. "Texas' Third Man: The Texas-Mexican." *Race,* 4 (May, 1963), pp. 49-58.

Penolosa, Fernado. "The Changing Mexican-American in Southern California." *Sociological Social Research,* 51 (July, 1967), pp. 405-417.

Servin, Manuel P. *Mexican-Americans.* 2nd. ed. Riverside, N.J.: Glencoe, 1974.

Steiner, Stan. *La Raza, the Mexican Americans.* N.Y.: Harper, 1970.

Negroes

Adoff, Arnold. *Black on Black.* N.Y.: Macmillan, 1968.
Commentaries by Negro Americans. Highly recommended.

Black Americans: A Study Guide and Source Book. San Francisco: R and E Research Associates, 1975.

Butcher, M.J. *The Negro in American Culture.* 2nd ed. N.Y.: Knopf, 1972.

Davis, John P., ed. *The American Negro Reference Book.* Englewood Cliffs, N.J.: Prentice-Hall, 1965.

Goldstein, Rhoda L., ed. *Black Life and Culture in the United States.* N.Y.: Crowell, 1971.

Hughes, Langston. *Fight for Freedom: The Story of the NAACP.* N.Y.: Norton, 1962.

Myrdal, Gunnar. *American Dilemma.* Rev. ed. N.Y.: Harper and Row, 1962.

Robinson, Armstead L. et al. *Black Studies in the University: A Symposium.* New Haven, CT.: Yale University Press, 1969.

Polish

Thomas, W.I. and Florian Znaniecki. *The Polish Peasant in Europe and the United States.* 2 vols. N.Y. Dover, 1958.

Young, Marjorie. *Journeys to Glory.* N.Y.: Harper and Row, 1976.

Puerto Ricans

Berle, Beatrice Bishop. *Eight Puerto Rican Families in Sickness and in Health.* N.Y.: Columbia University Press, 1958.

Fitzpatrick, Joseph P. *Puerto Rican Americans: The Meaning of Migration to the Mainland.* Englewood Cliffs, N.J.: Prentice-Hall, 1971.

Padilla, Elena. *Up From Puerto Rico.* N.Y.: Columbia University Press, 1958.

Senior, Charlence. *The Puerto Ricans: Strangers Then Neighbors.* Chicago: Quadrangle, 1965.

Scandinavians

Babcock, K.C. *Scandinavian Element in the United States.* N.Y.: Arno, 1969 (repr. of 1914 ed.).

Evjen, John O. *Scandinavian Immigrants in New York.* Baltimore: Genealogical, 1972 (repr. of 1916 ed.).

Fonkalsrud, A.O. *The Scandinavian American.* San Francisco: R and E Research Associates. [n.d.].

Wetterman, August. *The History and Review of the Scandinavian Society of San Francisco.* San Francisco: R and E Research Associates, 1970.

WASP

Anderson, Charles H. *White Protestant Americans: From National Origins to Religious Group.* Englewood Cliffs, N.J.: Prentice-Hall, 1970.

Binzen, Peter. *Whitetown, U.S.A.* N.Y.: Random, 1970.

Killian, Lewis M. *White Southerners.* N.Y.: Random, 1970.

Krickus, Richard. "The White Ethnics: Who Are They and Where Are They Going?" *City* (May-June, 1971), pp. 23-33.

Religions in America

Baeck, Leo. *Essence of Judaism.* N.Y.: Schocken, 1961.

Blau, Joseph L. ed. "Reform Judaism: A Historical Perspective." N.Y.: Ktav, 1961.

Brauer, Jerald C. *Protestantism in America: A Narrative History.* Rev. ed. Philadelphia: Westminister, 1972.

Ellis, John T. *American Catholicism*. Chicago: University of Chicago Press, 1969.

Feinsilver, A. *Aspects of Jewish Belief*. N.Y.: Ktav, 1973.

Ferm, Vergilus. *The American Church of the Protestant Heritage*. Westport, CT: Greenwood, 1972.

Hosteler, John A. *Amish Society*. Baltimore: Johns Hopkins University Press, 1970.

Hudson, W.S. *American Protestantism*. Chicago: University of Chicago Press, 1961.

Liu, William T. and Nathaniel J. Pallone. *Catholics U.S.A.: Perspectives on Social Change*. N.Y.: Wiley, 1970.

Nelson, E. Eugene and L. Fevold. *The Lutheran Church Among Norwegian Americans: A History of the Evangelical Lutheran Church*. 2 vols. Minneapolis: Augsburg, 1960.

O'Dea, Thomas F. *The Mormons*. Chicago: University of Chicago Press, 1957.

Rosten, Leo, ed. *Religions of America*. N.Y.: Simon Schuster, 1975.
Describes the beliefs, attitudes, church practices, and memberships of America's 20 leading denominations.

Shields, Currin. *Democracy and Catholicism in America*. N.Y. McGraw-Hill, 1958.

PART XI
POLICE EQUIPMENT

POLICE EQUIPMENT

EQUIPMENT—GENERAL

Ahern, John J. "Air Cushion Restraint Systems." *Police Chief,* XLI:7 (July, 1974), pp. 34-45.
Description of air bags.

Beeman, Joseph. "Photoresistor Photographic Slave Units." *Journal of Criminal Law, Criminology and Police Science,* 49:5 (January-February, 1959), pp. 510-512.
Device which, when activated by the light from a camera light, will fire a flash unit some distance away without connecting electric cords.

Blumstein, Alfred. "Science and Technology for Law Enforcement." *Police Chief,* XXXVI:12 (December, 1969), pp. 56-61.

Bowren, Patricia. "Measuring Wheel Aids Accident Investigation." *Law and Order,* 12:6 (June, 1964).
Describes the rolatape traffic model 200 measuring wheel.

Brumgardt, John R. "Riot Control Equipment." *Military Police Journal* (January, 1972).

Buckley, John L. "How to Select the Proper Security and Equipment Surveillance Systems." *Law and Order,* 12:5 (May, 1964), pp. 37-38.

Christian, W.J. and P.M. Dubivsky. "Basic Information on Fire Detection Devices." *Security World* (March, 1974).

Coughlin, John A. "Visible Memory Aid." *Law and Order,* 12:7 (July, 1964), pp. 14-15.
Patrol car status board.

Crockett, T.S. and J.P. Kruse. "Riot Control Agents—Part III. Protective Masks." *Police Chief,* XXXVI:3 (March, 1969), pp. 46-50.

Cunningham, J.E. *Security Electronics.* Indianapolis: H.W. Sams, 1970.
Narrative and pictorial description of the principles of operation of various electronic security devices.

DeBrocky, William. "Consolidation of Service Bomb Squad." *Law and Order,* 23:6 (June, 1975), pp. 75-80.

Dobbyn, Ronald C. *Selection Guide to Hearing Protectors for Use on Firing Ranges—Law Enforcement Standards Program.* Washington, D.C.: GPO, 1976.

Duffy, William. "The Whys, Whens and Hows of Tear Gas Masks." *Law and Order,* 16:5 (May, 1968), pp. 50-53.

"Equipment Loans to Police from Department of Defense." *Police Chief,* XXXIX:4 (March, 1972).
Explanation as to how to obtain equipment from Department of Defense.

Fagerstrom, Dorothy. "Practical Handbag for Policewomen." *Law and Order,* 12:2 (February, 1964).

Gould, J.A. "Binoculars." *Police Research Bulletin* (Autumn, 1973).

Gould, J.A. "Monoculars." *Police Research Bulletin* (Spring, 1974).

Grabowski, M.S. "Equipment Needed by the Scientific Crime Scene Investigator." *Fingerprint and Identification Magazine,* 37 (December, 1955), pp. 16-20.

Haslund, A. "Use of Wire-Recorder in Criminal Investigation." *International Criminal Police Review,* 79 (June-July, 1954), pp. 168-170.

Hlavinka, Paul. "Beating the Lack of Money Problem." *Law and Order,* 17:1 (January, 1969), pp. 71-76.
Small department using many home made devices to save money.

Kendall, Richard C. "Police Department Rescue Equipment." *Law and Order* (November, 1975).

King, H.E. *Assessment of Technology Applicable to Body-Mounted Antennas.* Washington, D.C.: NCJRS, 1973.
A discussion of electrically small antennas, antenna types, body effects on the antenna, and factors in system design.

Lawder, Lee E. "A Modern Shield for Law Enforcement." *Law and Order,* 14:8 (August, 1966), pp. 14-16.
Use of clear plastic shields for protection during disorders.

Maher, George. "Disguised Blessing." *Police Chief,* XLI:7 (July, 1974), pp. 22-26.
Discription of a bomb disposal trailer.

Martello, Francis L. "Before the Last Resort." *Police,* 5:3 (January-February, 1961), pp. 22-23.
Use of physical restraint devices.

Martin, Robert W. "Transparent Bullet-Resisting Glazing Materials Separating Fact from Fiction." *Police,* 16:10 (June, 1972), pp. 28-32.
Analysis of bullet proof glass and other bullet resisting transparent materials.

Matt, A. Robert. "Hydraulics to the Rescue." *Law and Order,* 13:12 (December, 1965), pp. 92-93.

Minton, Warren B. "Laser Beam Traps Jersey Speeders." *Law and Order,* 19:6 (June, 1971), pp. 84-85.
Description of the Accu-Rate, a low power laser control computer system for the measurement of speed.

Moore, R.T. *Barrier Penetration Tests.* Washington, D.C.: NCJRS, (Microfiche), 1974.
Description and results of tests to determine the resistance of various structural barrier panels and wire-mesh security fences to forcible penetration.

Mosburg, Margo. "Despensaflare: A Faster Way of Placing Flares." *Law and Order,* 14:9 (September, 1966), pp. 68-69.
Description of an emergency flare carrying case.

National Institute for Law Enforcement and Criminal Justice. *Hearing Protectors for Use on Firing Ranges—Law Enforcement Standards Program.* Washington, D.C.: GPO, 1973.

National Institute of Law Enforcement and Criminal Justice. *Portable Ballistic Shields—Law Enforcement Standards Program.* Washington, D.C.: NCJRS, 1973.

Ott, Harry R., Jr. "Astro Telescope Used to Study Crime." *Law and Order,* 23:7 (July, 1975), pp. 38, 40, 42.

Overvold, Lowell D. "Laser Beam Fingerprint Transmission." *Law and Order,* 23:7 (July, 1975), pp. 50-54.
Describes the laser fax system.

"Palm Printer." *FBI Law Enforcement Bulletin,* 30:5 (May, 1970).

Patrick, L.M. "A Safe and Acceptable Restraint." *Law and Order,* 16:7 (July, 1968), pp. 53, 69.
Use of vehicle shoulder harness which locks with any abrupt stopping action, then releases.

Penn, Charles D. "Electrical Protection for the Electronic Police Force." *Police Chief,* XLII:10 (October, 1975), pp. 48-49.

Pilot, Joan. "Instant Replay for the Traffic Violator." *Law and Order,* 17:6 (June, 1969), pp. 38-41.
Use of portable video tape by New Hampshire State Police.

Sapp, Butch. "Rescue." *Law and Order* (February, 1976), pp. 54-55.
Describes hydraulic metal cutter and rescue van with other rescue devices.

Senoren, Cleto B. "Police Combat Power." *Police,* 16:4 (December, 1971), pp. 2-4.

Serdahely, Franz. "Powerful Flashlight Beam for Patrol Use." *Law and Order* (October, 1975), pp. 20-21.
Describes SL20 flashlight manufactured by Streamlight Inc. Reported to be 5 times as powerful as an ordinary flashlight.

Shaw, William. "Emergency Power Plants." *Law and Order,* 12:6, pp. 36-39.
Recommends installation in every P.D. Describes process of the need, the unit and operation and control.

Shaw, William. "Facsimile Status Report." *Law and Order* 16:12 (December, 1968), pp. 56-59, 114.
The mechanical transmission of photographs, fingerprint cards, handwriting samples, etc.

Shaw, William. "Put Relays to Work for Your Department." *Law and Order,* 16:9 (September, 1968), pp. 46-50.
Description of the use of electronic relays.

Shaw, William. "Riot Control Technology: 1971 Update." *Law and Order,* 19:6 (June, 1971), pp. 15-16, 18-23.

Smythe, Hayes. "Warning: School Crossing." *Law and Order,* 15:2 (February, 1967), pp. 12-14, 35.
Use of tall warning devices at school crossings. Five flags are placed on high standing pole.

"Surveillance Equipment—Its Functions and Uses." *Security World,* 12:2 (1975), pp. 15-16, 43, 47; 12:5 (1975), pp. 28-30.

Sweeney, Faye B. "New Fingerprint Device for Small Departments." *Law and Order,* 16:7 (July, 1968), pp. 43-44.
Fingerprint stand specifications and other details included.

Taub, Harold. "The Quick Make." *Law and Order,* 13:7 (July, 1965).
Use of facsimile transmissions called Policefax used to transmit fingerprints internally within Police Department. Checking time reduced from 6 hours to less than 1 hour.

"Temporary Restraining Devices." *FBI Law Enforcement Bulletin,* 37:8 (August, 1968), pp. 14-17.
Describes several types of restraining devices for hands and feet.

Valera, Milton. "Light Overcomes Darkness." *Law and Order,* 16:11 (November, 1968), pp. 68-72.
The nightsun SX-16 helicopter spotlight.

Valera, Milton. "Portable Xenon Searchlight." *Law and Order,* 18:7 (July, 1970), pp. 100-101.

Wolverton, B.C. and S.N. Merrill. *Skin Irritant Decontaminant (SID).* Springfield, VA.: NTIS, 1968.
Non-toxic solution developed to relieve skin irritation caused by riot control agents.

Wynn, E.R. "The Third Rider in Greensboro Patrol Cars." *Law and Order,* 21:8 (August, 1973), pp. 92-93.
Describes the Argo tachograph—a device that provides a written record of what each patrol car is doing at all times.

ARMOR

"Body Armor Roundup." *Law and Order* (December, 1975), pp. 58-62.

"Bullet Stopping Wear." *Law and Order,* 23:8 (August, 1975), pp. 98-100.

Cohen, William A. "Survival Through Body Armor." *Police Chief,* XLI:10 (October, 1975), pp. 268-270.

Collins, Whit. "Evaluating Fabric Body Armor for Police." *Law and Order* (January, 1976), pp. 20, 23, 26, 27, 30-33.

Copp, William C. "Coming On Strong." *Law and Order,* 23:5 (May, 1975).

Hare, G.B. and P.H. Klaus. *LEAA (Law Enforcement Assistance Administration) Police Equipment Survey of 1972.* Vol. 6. *Body Armor and Confiscated Weapons—Law Enforcement Standards Programs.* Washington, D.C.: NCJRS (Microfiche), 1974.

Hunt, H.H. "A Survey of Personal Armor." *Law and Order,* 17:1 (January, 1969), pp. 40-45.

Kennel, R.P. and L.G. King. *Equipment Systems Improvement Program—Protective Armor Development Program—Final Report.* Vol. 2. *Technical Discussion.* Washington, D.C.: NCJRS (Microfiche), 1974.

National Institute of Law Enforcement and Criminal Justice. *Ballistic Resistance of Police Body Armor—Law Enforcement Standards Programs.* Washington, D.C.: GPO, 1972.

Strangle, J.W. et al. "Survey of Personnel Armor." *Law and Order,* (January, 1969).

Williams, Mason. "Body Armor and Its Application to Police Work." *Law and Order* 19:7 (July, 1971), pp. 72-75.

Williams, Mason. "An Evaluation of Bullet Proof Vests for Police." *Law and Order,* 21:10 (Ocrober, 1973), pp. 42-47.

Williams, Mason. "The Five!" *Law and Order* (December, 1975), pp. 56-68.

AUTOMOTIVE

Ackerman, David W. "Control Box for Switches." *Law and Order,* 15:2 (February, 1967), pp. 54-57.
Centralized control box for patrol vehicles emergency device switches.

Cook, Charles K. "A New Concept in Emergency Equipment Control." *Law and Order,* 13:10 (October, 1965), pp. 60, 62.
Control unit in police vehicles for siren, red lights, brakelights, etc.

Hooper, L.C. "High Output Alternators used by Providence P.D." *Law and Order,* 17:11 (November, 1969), pp. 86-87.

Katella, Wes. "Mobile Communicator." *Law and Order,* 21:12 (December, 1973), pp. 54-55.
Describes a digital reader board mounted on top of patrol vehicle. Unit is capable of flashing different messages to motorists such as "accident," "merge left" etc.

McHenry, Dick. "Auto Stabilizer—An Aid to Safer Driving." *Police,* 15:1 (September-October, 1970), pp. 56-57.

"Mini Arrow Board Does Maxi Traffic Routing." *Law and Order,* 19:1 (November, 1971).
Electronic board mounted on top of patrol car. Directs traffic with flashing arrow.

Miller, William C. "Whipping the Whiplash Problem." *Law and Order,* 13:11 (November, 1965), pp. 34-36, 38.
The use of headrests in police vehicles.

"Panic Stops—Test Tires for Stopping Ability." *Police,* 3:3 (January-February, 1959), pp. 26-27.

"Plastics Help Save Lives of Pennsylvania Policemen." *Law and Order,* 18:9 (September, 1970).
Describes a rollbar which incorporates the use of a plastic shield between front and rear.

Rhoades, John W. "Switch Confusion Eliminated." *Law and Order,* 16:12 (December, 1968), pp. 52-53.
Use of switch box in police vehicles to control emergency equipment.

Stephenson, Mark A. "A New Switching System for Emergency Vehicles." *Law and Order,* 15:11 (November, 1967), pp. 8-9.

Stratton, James E. "The Alternator—Solution for Heavy Drain on the Electrical System." *Law and Order,* 11:11 (November, 1963), pp. 44-46.

"A Word About Brakes." *Law and Order,* 14:11 (November, 1966), pp. 42-43.

BADGES

"Badge of Honor: The Police Shield." *Spring 3100,* 29 (March, 1958), pp. 4-7, 44.

"Badges Trace Back to 1350." *Police Journal (St. Louis),* 19 (November, 1966).

Donahue, Vincent J. "Air Police Badge." *Police Chief,* 25 (November, 1958).

Ferland, Joseph R. "Origin of Sheriff's Star Remains a Mystery." *National Sheriff,* 17 (March-April, 1965).

Hill, Cecil E. "Badges with History." *Police Chief,* 25 (April, 1958).
Illustrated article on historic Texas badges.

"History of Badge Symbolizes the Law in 'Old Dominion'." *FBI Law Enforcement Bulletin,* 29 (May, 1960), pp. 18-21.

"History of Police Badge." *South Dakota Peace Officer,* 40 (November-December, 1970).

Hopfer, Westley M. "From Badges to Collector's Items." *Police,* 9:4 (March-April, 1965), pp. 60-61.

Miller, Steve. "A Badge for All Reasons." *Journal of California Law Enforcement,* 9:2 (October, 1974).

"Our Badges." *Police World (GB),* 4 (July-August, 1959).

BATTERIES

Gasparotti, J.J. *Battery Power Supplies for Police Electronics—Equipment Systems Improvement Program Report.* Washington, D.C.: NCJRS, 1973.
Review of battery types presently used to power portable police radio transceivers and those newly developed types which seem suitable for such use.

Law Enforcement Standards Laboratory. *Batteries for Personal/Portable Receivers.* Washington, D.C.: NCJRS, 1975.

Scott, W.W., Jr. *Batteries Used with Law Enforcement Communications Equipment—Chargers and Charging Techniques—Law Enforcement Standards Program.* Washington, D.C.: GPO, 1973.
Basic charge characteristics of sealed nickel-cadmium and sealed lead-acid batteries and cells, many of which are used in law enforcement communications equipment.

U.S. Department of Commerce, National Bureau of Standards. Law Enforcement Standards Laboratory. *Batteries for Personal/Portable Transceivers—Law Enforcement Standards Program.* Washington, D.C.: NCJRS (Microfiche), 1975.
Performance requirements and test methods for batteries used in personal/portable transceivers by law enforcement agencies.

BLAZERS

Cizanckas, Victor. "Experiments in Police Uniforms: An Internal Report." *Police Chief,* XXXVII:4 (April, 1970), pp. 28-29.

Clark, Ben. "A New Look in Law Enforcement." *Police,* 14:1 (September-October, 1969), pp. 18-22.

Clement, Richard C. "A New Uniform Concept for Peace Officers." *Law and Order,* 17:8 (August, 1969), pp. 76-78.

Geary, David P. "Police Fad or Future?" *Police Chief,* XXXVI:4 (April, 1969), pp. 8-9.

Heller, Nathan K. "Guidelines for Purchasing Career Apparel." *Law and Order,* 19:5 (May, 1971), pp. 58-60, 62-64.

Matz, James L. "Our Blue Blazer Program." *Law and Order,* 18:11 (November, 1970), pp. 20, 22.

Tenzel, James H. and Victor Cizanckas. "The Uniform Experiment." *Journal of Police Science and Administration,* 1:4 (December, 1973), pp. 421-424.

Wiley, Ronald E. and C.D. Cochran. "Blazers: A National Survey of Police Attitudes." *Police Chief,* XXXIX:7 (July, 1972), pp. 68-70.

Wiley, R.E. and C.D. Cochran. *Responses to the Police Uniform—A Study of the Effect of the Civilian Blazer in Police Work.* Springfield, VA.: NTIS, 1971.

The relationship between physical appearance of police officers and emotional responses of persons coming in contact with the officers was studied.

Zurcher, C. James, Alan J. Garcia, and Ellen Curtis. "Testing the Blazer Concept in Palo Alto, California." *Police Chief,* XLIII:1 (January, 1976), pp. 28-29.

CAMERAS

Albright, James M. "Low-Cost Surveillance Cameras Used in Spokane Police to Cut Crime." *Law and Order,* 20:9 (September, 1972), pp. 104, 106-110.

Describes use of Kodak cartridge cameras in stake-outs.

Hamlin, George L. and Charles G. Grover. *Selections and Application Guide to Fixed Surveillance Cameras—Law Enforcement Standards Program.* Washington, D.C.: NCJRS, 1974.

Lydle, Chris. "Small Cameras for Big Results." *Law and Order,* 15:9 (September, 1967), pp. 90-94.

Patterson, Pat. "Economy Police 'Mug' Camera." *Law and Order,* 18:7 (July, 1970), pp. 50-51.

Schernhorst, John N. "The Stereometric Detail." *Police,* 10:3 (January-February, 1966), pp. 6-13.

Use of the stereometric camera for accident and crime scene recording.

C.B. RADIOS

Germain, Fred. "Civilian Use of Police Monitors: Boon or Bombshell." *Law and Order,* 18:11 (November, 1970), pp. 96-97, 99.

Shaw, William. "The Class D Citizen Band Revisited." *Law and Order,* 12:10 (October, 1964), pp. 84-85, 88.

Shaw, William. "A Judge Authorizes the Jamming of the 27MHz Citizen's Band." *Law and Order* (December, 1975), pp. 22-27.

CLOSED CIRCUIT T.V.

Burke, Martin. "From Crime to Court." *Law and Order,* 18:2 (February, 1970), pp. 68-70, 72.

Closed Circuit T.V. for South Carolina law enforcement training.

"Cell Block Monitored on Television." *FBI Law Enforcement Bulletin,* 33:5 (May, 1964).

"Cutting Administrative Expenses with Closed Circuit T.V." *Business Week* (January 30, 1971).

Goodwin, Larry G. and Thomas Koehring. *Closed Circuit Television Production Techniques.* Indianapolis: Howard W. Sams, 1970.

Hansen, David A. and John J. Kolbmann. "Can You Use Television in Your Department?" *FBI Law Enforcement Bulletin,* 39:3 (March, 1970), pp. 3-6, 21.

Hansen, D.A. and J.J. Kolbmann. *Closed Circuit Television for Police.* Springfield, IL.: C.C. Thomas, 1970.

Equipment, personnel, television, and video tape uses.

Kamen, Ira. "Coded TV—A New PD Weapon." *Police,* 7:1 (September-October, 1962), pp. 17-20.

Use of closed circuit T.V. for line ups.

Lamb, Ralph. "Television—A Boom to Jail Operations." *FBI Law Enforcement Bulletin,* 33:5 (May, 1964), pp. 10-14.

Maccalden, M.S. et al. *Feasibility Study of Closed Circuit Television of Traffic Surveillance.* Washington, D.C.: NCJRS (Microfiche), 1973.

Mahoney, Bill. "Protecting Life of Property with T.V." *Law and Order,* 12:5 (May, 1964), pp. 30-32.

T.V. monitoring of public areas, beach, public streets, amusement areas.

May, Frank. "Wide Awake Eye of Beverly Hills." *Law and Order,* 14:1 (January, 1966), pp. 22-23.

Closed circuit T.V. in city jail.

Shaw, William. "Cable T.V.—Does It Have Law Enforcement Possibilities?" *Law and Order,* 18:9 (September, 1970), pp. 28, 30-33.

Shaw, William. "3D Television—A Potential Law Enforcement Tool." *Law and Order,* 19:3 (March, 1971), pp. 38, 40-43, 46.

Strom, J.P. "Closed Circuit Television for Inservice Police-Training." *FBI Law Enforcement Bulletin,* 38:6 (June, 1969), pp. 11-18, 22-24.

Stormes, John M. *Television Communications Systems for Business and Industry.* N.Y.: Wiley, 1970.

Szereto, S. *Closed Circuit Television Surveillance Truck.* Washington, D.C.: NCJRS, 1969.

Closed circuit television and video tape equipment to assist police with stakeouts in high crime areas, security during visits of dignitaries, and riot control.

Thomas, William O. "T.V. by Laser Beam Transmission. Police Aid in Combating Crime." *FBI Law Enforcement Bulletin* (February, 1974), pp. 6-11.

Wand, Hal. "It Can't Happen Here." *Law and Order,* 16:1 (January, 1968), pp. 22-23.

Closed circuit system used throughout police building.

Wortman, Leon. *Closed-Circuit Television Handbook*. 3d. ed. Indianapolis: Sams, 1974.

Younger, Evelle J. "Cooperative Closed-Circuit TV Training." *Police Chief,* XXXV:9 (September, 1968).

COPIERS

Bilitz, Walter. "Document Copier Aids Police." *Law and Order,* 22:2 (February, 1974), pp. 48, 50.

DiCroce, Anthony. "Versatile Copying Equipment Reduces Paperwork Backlog." *Law and Order,* 22:7 (July, 1974), pp. 66-69.

Schoen, Arthur. "Prompt Prisoner Processing Equipment." *Law and Order,* 14:8 (August, 1966), pp. 10-12, 41.
Use of electrostatic coping machine for reproducing booking records, fingerprints, etc.

CRIME SCENE KITS

Keltz, James. "A Small Department Solves the Crime Scene Problem." *Law and Order,* 18:4 (April, 1970), pp. 44-46.
Utilization of a portable crime scene kit. Can be carried in the back of a station wagon.

Muller, Howard L. "Supplemental Equipment of the Investigator." *Law and Order,* 20:9 (September, 1972).
Suggestions for crime scene investigations kit for detectives rather than lab unit.

Musial, Joseph. "Miami Mobile Crime Labs." *Law and Order,* 23:7 (July, 1975), pp. 46-68.
Equipment is carried in various kits and suitcases. Special vehicle not needed.

Osther, R.D. "A Scientific Scene of Crime Kit." *Police Journal,* 36:5 (May, 1963), pp. 222-225.

Starkey, Norris J. "You Can Make Your Own Major Crime Kit." *Law and Order,* 12:7 (July, 1964), pp. 16-17.

Vandiver, James B. "Improve Your Crime Scene Kit." *Law and Order,* 20:8 (August, 1972), pp. 108-114; 20:9 (September, 1972), pp. 30-31, 68, 70.

EDGED WEAPONS

Angolia, John R. *Edged Weaponry of the Third Reich.* Washington, D.C.: Quaker, 1974.

Atwood, James P. *Daggers and Edged Weapons of Hitler's Germany.* Alhambra, CA.: Bordon. [n.d.]

Hawley, W.M. *Introduction to Japanese Swords.* Hollywood, CA.: Hawley, 1973.

Hughes, B.R. and Jack Lewis. *Gun Digest Books of Knives.* Chicago: Follet, 1973.

Peterson, Harold L. *American Knives.* N.Y.: Scribner, 1958.

Woods, Jim. *Guns and Ammo Guide Book to Knives and Edged Weapons.* Los Angeles: Petersen, 1974.

EMERGENCY WARNING DEVICES

Jones, F.E. and T.L. Quindry. *Summary Report on Emergency Vehicle Sirens—Law Enforcement Standards Program.* Washington, D.C.: NCJRS, 1974.

Paulson, Lawrence. "Blue Lights: Status of and Present Use." *Police Chief* (November, 1973), pp. 20-24-25.

Pierce, E.T. and M.A. McPherson. *Emergency Vehicle Warning Devices—Interim Review of State-of-the-Art Relative to Performance Standards—Law Enforcement Standards Program.* Springfield, VA.: NTIS, 1971.
Progress report on Law Enforcement Assistance Administration sponsored research program being done by National Bureau of Standards to develop performance standards for vehicle emergency warning lights and sirens.

U.S. Department of Justice. Law Enforcement Assistance Administration. *Emergency Vehicle Warning Devices.* Washington, D.C.: GPO, (May, 1972).

FACILITIES

Archer, Russell D. "A Modern Police Building for a Small Department." *FBI Law Enforcement Bulletin,* 26:10 (October, 1957), pp. 12-15.

Booz, Philip E. "Keeping Pace With Community Growth." *FBI Law Enforcement Bulletin,* 38:6 (June, 1969), pp. 9-11, 20.

Breier, Harold A. "A New Police Building for Milwaukee." *FBI Law Enforcement Bulletin,* 40:10 (October, 1971), pp. 16-19, 31.

Ciarrusso, Joseph I. "Modern Administration Building Facilitates Police Operation." *FBI Law Enforcement Bulletin,* 39:1 (January, 1970), pp. 12-16.

"Community Police Building." *Connecticut Architect* (January-February, 1967).

Crane, Edward. "Building for Tomorrow." *Police Chief,* XXXVII:6 (June, 1970), pp. 57-63.

Driver, Robert W. "Municipal Justice Building, Orlando, Florida." *Police Chief,* XLI:1 (January, 1974), pp. 40-41.

Dunn, James C. "Modern Police Facilities for Rome, N.Y." *FBI Law Enforcement Bulletin,* 33:4 (April, 1964), pp. 12-15.

Flaherty, John F. "New Building Houses Police and Fire Department." *FBI Law Enforcement Bulletin,* 26:4 (April, 1957), pp. 12-20.

Foster, Lelan A. "Better Service Through Modern Facilities." *FBI Law Enforcement Bulletin,* 35:9 (September, 1966), pp. 19-20.

Garmire, Bernard L. "A Future Model for the Miami Police Department." *Police Chief,* 38:11 (November, 1970), pp. 24, 26-27.

Hackl, D.J. "Law Enforcement Facilities Must Work for People." *Law and Order,* 20:9 (1972), pp. 34-36, 38-42, 44.

"Houston's New Police Building." *American City,* 69 (July, 1954).

Jacobs, Walter. "Planning for the Year 2000." *Law and Order,* 24:6 (June, 1976), pp. 62-64.

Larson, R.C. and K.A. Stevenson. *On Insensitivities in Urban Redistricting and Facility Location.* Springfield, VA.: NTIS, 1971.

Linke, Jack. "Modern Facilities for Culver City Police." *Law and Order,* 16:12 (December, 1968), pp. 107-113.

Linke, Jack. "New Police Facilities in Englewood Cliffs, N.J." *Law and Order* (January, 1976), pp. 34-36.

Linke, Jack. "Police Architect Marion J. Varner's Success: Town of Dover Law Enforcement Center, Toms River, New Jersey." *Police Chief,* XLI:1 (January, 1974), pp. 42-44.

McGowan, James F. "Criminal Justice Unit, Broward County Community College, Fort Lauderdale, Florida." *Police Chief,* XLL:1 (January, 1974), p. 46.

Madson, Elmer A. "New Green Bay Police Facility." *FBI Law Enforcement Bulletin* (April, 1970), pp. 10-12.

Martin, Charles J. "Police Professionalism—An Appropriate Building." *Journal California Law Enforcement,* 9:1 (July, 1974), pp. 20-23.

Mitchell, Joseph. "Building on a Budget." *Police Chief,* XXXVII:6 (June, 1970), p. 38.

"Municipal Court and Police Building, Shaker Heights, Ohio." *Police Chief,* XLI:1 (January, 1974), p. 47.

Morgan, Thomas B. "A New Outlook with New Facilities." *FBI Law Enforcement Bulletin,* 36:5 (May, 1967), pp. 6-8.

Mueller, Eugene L. "Award-Winning Police Facility." *FBI Law Enforcement Bulletin,* 36:12 (December, 1967), pp. 12-13, 25.

Musick, James. "Build for the Future." *FBI Law Enforcement Bulletin,* 38:4 (April, 1969), pp. 6-8, 23.

"One Police Plaza, New York City 10038." *Police Chief,* XLI:1 (January, 1974), pp. 36-37.

"Other Buildings." *Police Chief,* XLI:1 (January, 1974).

Paschal, Caraker. "Notes: Relation of Architecture to Correctional and Rehabilitative Facilities." *Police Chief,* XLI:1 (January, 1974).

Pavillard, Dan. "New Home for Tucson (Arizona) Police." *Police Chief,* 37:11 (November, 1970), pp. 20-22.

"Police Department, Baltimore, Maryland." *Police Chief,* XLI:1 (January, 1974).

Police Facilities, Planning and Design. Washington, D.C.: IACP, [n.d.]

"Police Headquarters in Modern Design." *FBI Law Enforcement Bulletin,* 28:4 (April, 1959), pp. 17-18.

Salerno, James J. "New Headquarters Building Aid Police Work." *FBI Law Enforcement Bulletin,* 27:2 (February, 1958), pp. 9-11.

Skirvin, Weldon Jean and Robert S. Smith. "A Design Programming Process for Criminal Justice Training Facilities." *Police Chief,* XLI:1 (January, 1974), pp. 58-63.

Sommers, William A. "Franklin's Police Build Their Own Building." *Police,* 7:3 (January-February, 1963), pp. 16-19.

Varner, Marion J. "A Policeman Is Not an Architect." *Police Chief,* 37:11 (November 1970), pp. 28-30, 32-34.

Varrelman, David A. "Thoughts on Police Building Design." *Police Chief,* 37:11 (November, 1970), pp. 14-15, 18.

Vogel, Joshua A. *Police Stations: Planning and Specification.* Seattle: Bureau of Government Research and Services, University of Washington, 1954.

Ward, A. Leroy. "Before and After in Neptune, New Jersey." *Police Chief,* XLI:1 (January, 1974), pp. 48-49.

Webb, Giles H. "Modern Facilities Aid Police Training Programs." *FBI Law Enforcement Bulletin,* 38:3 (March, 1969), pp. 2-5.

Wise, Leon M. "Engineering Psychology Applied to Police Facilities." *Law and Order* (January, 1976), pp. 38-42.

Wright, J.M. "Progress in Richmond (VA)." *Law and Order,* 13:3 (March, 1965), pp. 74-44, 82.

FIREARMS

Firearms—General

Applegate, Rex. "The Shape of the Future." *Law and Order,* 14:7 (July, 1966), pp. 28-33, 39.
Describes teargas, darts, hypodermic syringe projectile, hollow charge bazooka, high explosive projectile, dye marker darts and others.

Arms and Armor Annual. Northfield, IL.: Digest, 1973.

Baker, A.J. *Russian Infantry Weapons of World War Two.* N.Y.: Arco, 1971.

Blackmore, Howard L. *Guns and Rifles of the World.* N.Y.: Viking, 1965.

Bristow, Allen P. "Prospectus—Police Armament Research Project." *Police,* 7:1 (September-October, 1962), pp. 78-80.

Brown, Marshall J. "New Sight Improves Accuracy." *Law and Order,* 14:12 (December, 1966), pp. 36-37.
Use of rifle gun sight for shotguns and rifles.

Buxtons Guide: Foreign Firearms. Greennwich, CT.: J.S. Herold, 1963.

Chappel, Charles E. *Gun Collectors Handbook of Values. 1975-1976 Values.* 11th rev. ed. Washington, D.C.: Howard, 1975.

Fox, Valvert Lucius. "Special Weapons for Special Assignments." *Law and Order,* 19:10 (October, 1971), pp. 62-65.

German Infantry Weapons. Forest Grove, OR.: Normount, 1966.

"Guns." *Guns* (August, 1957).

Hess, John J. "Sidearms Belong at the Right." *Law and Order,* 12:7 (July, 1964), pp. 50, 52.

International Association of Chiefs of Police. *Police Weapons Center—Final Report.* Gaithersburg, MD.: IACP, 1971.

Contains four sections in two unnumbered volumes. Data collected and analyzed by the International Association of Chiefs of Police police weapons center on firearms, chemical weapons, batons, explosive disposal, and protective equipment for police use.

"J.C. Higgins Firearms." *Bulletin of the Bureau of Criminal Investigation,* 22:3 (1957), pp. 8-11.

Kjellgren, G.L.M. "The Practical Range of Small Arms." *The American Rifleman,* 118:3 (March, 1970), pp. 40-44.

Krcma, V. *Identification and Registration of Firearms.* Springfield, IL.: C.C. Thomas, 1971.
An illustrated book on the identification of firearms and the location of the identifying numbers.

MacFaggen, George. "Firearms Clean-up Simplified." *Law and Order,* 17:5 (May, 1969), pp. 73-78.

McLean, Donald B. *F A L Auto-Rifles.* Wickenburg, AZ.: Normount, 1969.

Martello, Francis L. "Before the Last Resort." *Police,* 5:4 (March-April, 1961), pp. 44-46.

Murtz, H.A. *Gun Digest Book of Exoloded Firearms Drawings.* Chicago: Follett, 1974.

Nonte, George C., Jr. *Pistolsmithing.* Harrisburg, PA.: Stackpole, 1975.

O'Connor, Jack. *Complete Book of Rifles and Shotguns.* N.Y.: Harper, 1961.

Perkins, Walter E. "Evaluation of Enforcer Combat Grips." *Law and Order,* 14:8 (August, 1966), pp. 76-78.

Prehle, Jack. "Straight from the Shoulder." *Law and Order,* 13:3 (March, 1965), pp. 34, 36-37.

Published Ordinances, Firearms. Washington, D.C.: GPO, 1973.
Covers state laws local ordinances and federal laws on regulations pertaining to firearms ammunition and the importation of firearms.

"A Question of Guns." *Newsweek* (June 24, 1968).

Rensselaer, S. Van. *American Firearms.* Watkins Glen, N.Y.: Century House, 1976.

Roberts, Duke. *An Introduction to Modern Police Firearms.* Beverly Hills, CA.: Glencoe, 1969.

Romig, Clarence H. "What Gun Would You Recommend." *Law and Order,* 19:4 (April, 1971), pp. 74, 78.

Schroeder, Joseph J., Jr. *Gun Collectors Digest.* Chicago: Follett, 1973.

"Sidearms Belong—Where?" *Law and Order,* 12:5 (May, 1964), pp. 50-52.
Pro and con argument about right hand and cross draw techniques.

Smith, W.H. and J.E. Smith. *Small Arms of the World—A Basic Manual of Small Arms.* 10th ed. Harrisburg, PA.: Stackpole, 1973.
Illustrated, detailed, and extensive country-by-country survey of the pistols, rifles, carbines, and machine guns manufactured and in use throughout the world.

Steinwedel, Louis W. *Gun Collectors Fact Book.* N.Y.: Arco, 1975.

Stevenson, Jan. "A Voice in Disagreement." *Law and Order,* 14:5 (May, 1966), pp. 46-53.
Author urges the use of firearms being carried on the right hip.

Stoner 63 Weapon's System. Boulder, CO.: Paladin, 1968.

Tanner, Hans, ed. *Guns of the World.* Los Angeles: Petersen, 1972.

Wessel, Thomas E. "How Pneumatic Arms Work." *American Rifleman* (August, 1962).

Ammunition

Applegate, Rex. "Federal Evaluation of Police Handgun Ammunition." *Law and Order,* 23:9 (September, 1975), pp. 58, 60-61, 68.

Applegate, Rex. "The Federal Performance Rating of Commercially Available Police Handgun Ammunition." *Law and Order* (January, 1976), pp. 2, 6, 9.

Applegate, Rex. "Results: Federal Evaluation of Police Handgun Ammunition." *Law and Order* (December, 1975), pp. 19-21.

Ayoob, Massad F. "Inexpensive Ammunition." *Law and Order* (February, 1976).

Barnes, Frank C. *Cartridges of the World.* Chicago: Follett, 1972.

Bearse, Ray. *Center Fire American Rifle Cartridges, 1892-1963.* South Brunswick, N.J.: A.S. Barnes, 1966.

Cirillo, Jim. "Is Current Police Ammunition Adequate." *Law and Order,* 17:10 (October, 1969), pp. 16-17.

Davis, Edward M. "Considerations on Hollow-point Ammunition." *Police Chief,* XLII:9 (September, 1975), pp. 22-23, 63.

DiMaio, Vincent J.M. "A Comparison of the Wounding Effects of Commercially Available Handgun Ammunition Suitable for Police Use." *FBI Law Enforcement Bulletin,* 43:12 (December, 1974), pp. 3-8.

DiMaio, Vincent J.M., J. Allan Jones, and Charles S. Petty. "Ammunition for Police: A Comparison of the Wounding Effects of Commercially Available Cartridges." *Journal of Police Science and Administration,* 1:3 (September, 1973), pp. 269-273.

Dobbyn, R.C., W.J. Bruchey, Jr., and L.D. Shubin. *An Evaluation of Police Handgun Ammunition: Summary Report.* Washington, D.C.: LEAA, (October, 1975).

"Dumdum Debate; Police Use of Hollow-Point Dumdum Bullets." *Newsweek* (September 9, 1974).

Hand Loaders Digest. Chicago: Gun Digest, 1962.

Hanson, Robert L. "Challenged Reply." *Police Chief,* XLII:9 (September, 1975), pp. 24-25.

Heidtke, John J. "Handgun Cartridge Tests." *FBI Law Enforcement Bulletin,* 36:2 (February, 1967), pp. 2-8.

Jackson, Tim. "Safety Blank Ammunition." *Law and Order,* 23:2 (February, 1975).

National Rifle Association. *Illustrated Reloading Handbook.* Washington, D.C.: National Rifle, 1961.

Nonte, George C., Jr. "Hot Loads in Light Guns." *Law and Order* (October, 1970), pp. 34-36, 72, 74, 76-77.

Nonte, George C., Jr. *Modern Handloading.* N.Y.: Winchester, 1972.

Owen, Irvin K. "What About Dumdums?" *FBI Law Enforcement Bulletin* (April, 1975), pp. 3-6.

Parsons, Kevin. "Safety Slug. The Name of the Game Is 'Shock'." *Law and Order,* 22:10 (October, 1974), pp. 8, 10, 44.

Sloan, Clyde. "Dud May Cost a Life—Yours." *Law and Order,* 12:9 (September, 1964), pp. 24, 26, 28.

Townsend, Whelan. *Why Not Load Your Own: Basic Handloading for Everyone.* 4th ed. Washington, D.C.: Combat Forces Press, 1957.

Turcus, Daniel. "KTW .30 cal. Carbine Round." *Law and Order,* 17:10 (October, 1969), pp. 101-107.

Ulery, Joseph A. "The Hollow-point and Law Enforcement." *Police Chief,* XLII:10 (October, 1975), pp. 26, 28-29, 271.

Waters, Ken. "Most Extensive Tests Ever on .38 Special Police Loads, Precision Reloading." *Shooting Times* (May, 1964), pp. 46-49, 62.

Williams, Mason. "K.T.W. Ammunition." *Law and Order,* 21:9 (September, 1973), pp. 84-86, 88, 90, 92.

Williams, Mason. "Laboratory and Field Test: Hume Cartridge Carrier, Wesson .357 Revolver, Super Vel Ammunition." *Law and Order,* 18:6 (June, 1970), pp. 70-74, 76, 81.

Williams, Mason. "Police Cartridge Velocities and Variations." *Law and Order,* 21:11 (November, 1973), pp. 78-81; 21:12 (December, 1973), pp. 40-41, 66.

Williams, Mason. "Quad Custom Ammo." *Law and Order* (October, 1975), pp. 64-65.
Multi-projectiles contained in a single cartridge. Can be used with .38, .357 magnum and .45 weapons.

Williams, Mason. "Slugs and Buckshot Loadings." *Law and Order,* 20:9 (September, 1972), pp. 52-55.

Williams, Mason [illegible]3-D Police Ammunition, Caliber .38 Special." *La*[illegible]*er,* 20:1 (January, 1972), pp. 48-53.

Woods, Jim. *Guns and Ammo Complete Guide to Black Power.* Los Angeles: Petersen, 1974.

Young, Truman. "Survey on Shooting/Reloading Programs in Police Departments." *Law and Order,* 14:2 (February, 1966), pp. 50, 52.

Handguns

Ayoob, Massad F. "Ruger's Stainless Steel Security-Six Revolver." *Law and Order,* 22:8 (1974), pp. 86-90.

Bady, Donald B. *Colt Automatic Pistols.* Rev. ed. Alhambra, CA.: Borden, 1973.

Blair, Claude. *Pistols of the World.* N.Y.: Viking, 1969.

Boothroyd, Geoffrey. *The Handgun.* N.Y.: Crown, 1970.

Ennis, H.P. "Does Your Handgun Do What It's Supposed to Do?" *Police Chief,* XXXIV:9 (September, 1967), pp. 40-42.

Foux, William F. "Two or Four Plus." *Law and Order,* 13:10 (October, 1965), pp. 78, 80.

Grennell, Dean A. *Handgun Digest.* Chicago: Follett, 1972.

Grennell, Dean A. *Law Enforcement Handgun Digest.* Chicago: Follett, 1972.

Hatcher, Julian S. *Pistols and Revolvers and Their Use.* Marshalton, DE.: Small Arms Technical, 1927.

Hatcher, Julian S. "Smith and Wesson Model 41 Target Pistol." *The American Rifleman* (January, 1958).

Hoffschmidt, E.J. *Know Your Walther P.38 Pistols.* Stanford, CT.: Blacksmith, 1975.

Hoffschmidt, E.J. "Newhausen Pistol." *American Rifleman,* 103:2 (February, 1955), pp. 48-49.

Hoff, I.V. *Military Pistols and Revolvers: The Handguns of the Two World Wars.* N.Y.: Arco, 1970.

Josserand, Michel and Jan Stevenson. *Pistols, Revolvers and Ammunition.* N.Y.: Crown, 1972.

Kroma, V. and L. Olsen. "Indicators in Automatic Pistols." *The American Rifleman,* 112:8 (August, 1964), pp. 48-50.

Larson, E. Dixon. *Colt Tips.* Union City, TN.: Pioneer, 1972.

Lawder, Lee E. "Revolver Reloaders." *Law and Order,* 12:2 (February, 1964).

Nonte, George C. *Pistol and Revolver Guide.* South Hackensack, N.J.: Stoeger, 1975.

Parsons, Kevin. "A 'Super' Combination for Law Enforcement." *Law and Order* (October, 1975), pp. 10-13.
Describes several automatic pistols.

Perkins, Walter E. "S and W Chief's Model 60, Stainless Steel Version." *Law and Order,* 14:1 (January, 1966), pp. 34, 36-37.

Roth, S. *Thirty-Eight Caliber Weapon Effectiveness—Equipment Systems Improvement Program Report.* Washington, D.C.: NCJRS, 1973.

Sherry, Edward P. "A Time for Change? Do We Dare Not?" *Law and Order,* 20:10 (October, 1972), pp. 52-54, 56.
Pros and cons of automatics versus revolvers.

Smith, W.H.B. *Book of Pistols and Revolvers.* Harrisburg, PA.: Stackpole, 1969.

Steindler, R.A. "A New Concept in Police Pistols." *Law and Order,* 21:10 (October, 1973), pp. 71-74.

Steindler, R.A. ".22 LR Auto-Loading Pistol." *Law and Order,* 21:10 (October, 1973), pp. 48-50.

Stevenson, Jan A. "The Case for .41." *Law and Order,* 13:1 (January, 1965), pp. 48-50, 52, 58.

Stevenson, Jan A. "Charter Arms' Undercover .38." *Law and Order,* 14:10 (October, 1966), pp. 44-57, 74.

Stevenson, Jan A. "Colt's Diamondback." *Law and Order,* 15:8 (August, 1967), pp. 74-78.

Stevenson, Jan A. "Four Guns in One (And They All Shoot Well)." *Law and Order,* 16:4 (April, 1968), pp. 80-88.
The Hecler and Koch semi-auto pistol which fires .22 LR, .25 ACP, .32 and 380.

Stevenson, Jan A. "New from Chapter—Another Inch of Barrel and a Superb Set of Stocks." *Law and Order,* 16:1 (January, 1968), pp. 54-58, 73.

Stevenson, Jan A. "Walther's TPH, New Salvation for Ultra Concealment." *Law and Order,* 16:10 (October, 1968), pp. 42-46.

Triggs, J.M. "Whitney .22 Automatic Pistol." *The American Rifleman,* 112:8 (August, 1964), pp. 56-57.

Wallack, Bob. "The Smith and Wesson .41." *Law and Order,* 12:9 (September, 1964), pp. 22-23.

Wallack, Bob. "Two or Four." *Law and Order,* 13:12 (December, 1965), pp. 70, 72.
Discusses revolver barrel length.

Weston, Paul B. "The .357 Magnum." *Police,* 3:6 (July-August, 1959), pp. 26-28.

Williams, Mason. "Adoption of the S and W 9 m/m Pistol by the Illinois State Police." *Law and Order,* 19:3 (March, 1971), pp. 44-46.

Williams, Mason. "After Six, Then What?" *Law and Order,* 22:6 (June, 1974), pp. 62-65, 75.
Discussion on revolver loading.

Williams, Mason. "The American Firearms Mark 4 .25 Caliber Pistol." *Law and Order,* 19:4 (April, 1971), pp. 76-78.

Williams, Mason. "The Astra .357 Magnum Revolver." *Law and Order,* 21:3 (March, 1973), pp. 60-61.

Williams, Mason. "The Behlert Bobcat Browning Pistol." *Law and Order,* 21:8 (August, 1973), pp. 85-85, 88-89.

Williams, Mason. "The Charter Arms 44 Special Revolver." *Law and Order,* 22:4 (April, 1974), pp. 29-31, 42.

Williams, Mason. "The Colt Combat Commander." *Law and Order,* 19:10 (October, 1971), pp. 46-48, 67.

Williams, Mason. "Colt's Detective Special." *Law and Order,* 20:10 (October, 1972), pp. 24-25.

Williams, Mason. "The Colt 38 Super for Police Work." *Law and Order,* 18:5 (May, 1970), pp. 60-63.

Williams, Mason. "The Colt 2″ Barrel .357 Magnum Lawman Revolver." *Law and Order,* 20:3 (March, 1972), pp. 66-68.

Williams, Mason. "The Dan Wesson Police Revolver." *Law and Order,* 18:7 (July, 1970), pp. 70-72, 74, 76.

Williams, Mason. "The D.B. Wesson Police Revolver." *Law and Order,* 20:8 (August, 1972), pp. 104-106.

Williams, Mason. "The Heene Report, Part I, .38 Special versus .45 ACP." *Law and Order,* 18:10 (October, 1970).

Williams, Mason. "The Mag-Naport Principles as Applied to Handguns for Law Enforcement." *Law and Order,* 20:12 (December, 1972), pp. 54-57.
Gas venting for handguns at end of barrel.

Williams, Mason. "The Mauser 1970 Model HSc Pistol." *Law and Order,* 18:4 (April, 1970), pp. 38-41.

Williams, Mason. "The New Weather PPKIS." *Law and Order,* 18:2 (February, 1970), pp. 74-79.

Williams, Mason. "The Police Bulldog 38 Special." *Law and Order,* 24:6 (June, 1976), pp. 50-54.

Williams, Mason. "The Ruger Police Model Security Six Revolver." *Law and Order,* 19:6 (June, 1971), pp. 78-83.

Williams, Mason. "The Seecamp Model 1911 Double Action Modification." *Law and Order,* 21:10 (October, 1973), pp. 76-79.

Williams, Mason. "The Six Second Revolver Reloader." *Law and Order,* 22:2 (February, 1974), pp. 70-72.

Williams, Mason. "The Starlight 9 mm for Police Work." *Law and Order,* 19:11 (November, 1971), pp. 72-75.

Williams, Mason. "The .22 or the .25 for Law Enforcement." *Law and Order,* 18:9 (September, 1970), pp. 120-122, 124.

Machine Guns

Johnson, Thomas M. "The AK47." *Army* (June, 1970), pp. 40-45.

McLean, Donald B., ed. *UZI Submachine Gun.* Wickenburg, AZ.: Normount, 1969.

Miller, Burt. "The Most Versatile Police Arm." *Law and Order,* 19:10 (October, 1971), pp. 42-44, 65-67.
Description of armalite line of rifles and machine guns.

Nelson, T.V. and H.B. Lockhoven. *The World's Submachine Guns.* Alexandria, VA.: T.B.N. Enterprizes, 1962.

Steele, David E. "A Modern Machine Pistol for Police and Military." *Law and Order,* 19:5 (May, 1971), pp. 26-27, 33-35.
Describes the Ingram M-11, Israeli UZI, the Czech VZOR Model 61, and other small machine guns.

Stevenson, Jan A. "Smith and Wesson's M76." *Law and Order,* 16:6 (June, 1968), pp. 48-54.

Weston, Paul B. "Greater Fire-Power for Police." *Police,* 3:5 (May-June, 1959), pp. 48-49.
The armalite AR-15 rifle in point 222 magnum calibre.

Non-Lethal Weapons

Allison, B. "Bean-Bag Bullets and Nausea Darts, Plus Other Non-Lethal Weapons." *Science Digest* (May, 1975).

"Anti-riot Sprays: Are They Safe, or Hazardous?" *U.S. News and World Report* (June 2, 1969).

Coates, S.F. *Nonlethal Weapons for Use by U.S. Law Enforcement Officers.* Springfield, VA.: NTIS, 1967.

Degarmo, J.W., Jr. "The Future of Non-lethal Weapons in Law Enforcement." *Police,* 16:12 (1972), pp. 50-51.

"Disabling Without Killing." *Time* (May 5, 1967).

"Flashlight or Dangerous Weapon?" *FBI Law Enforcement Bulletin* (March, 1976), pp. 8-9.
Describes stun-gun which is an alleged non-lethal weapon. Gun has been used in robberies in Florida, California, and Ohio.

Gardner, S. "Can New Non-Lethal Weapons Control Riots?" *Popular Science* (December, 1967).

Mainhardt, Robert. "The Stun Gun, a Non-Lethal Weapon." *Law and Order,* 18:10 (October, 1970), pp. 86-88.

"Newest Anti-riot Weapon: Bullets of Wood." *U.S. News and World Report* (July 20, 1970).

"New Non-Lethal Weapons." *Life* (November 24, 1967).

Reddin, Thomas J. "Non-Lethal Weapons—Curse or Cure?" *Police Chief,* XXXIV:12 (December, 1967), pp. 60-63.

Roy, David. "Police Work with Industry to Create Non-Lethal Weapons." *Law and Order,* 19:4 (April, 1971), pp. 24-26, 34-36.

Security Planning Corporation. *Non-Lethal Weapons for Law Enforcement, Research Needs and Priorities.* Springfield, VA.: NTIS, 1972.

"A Study on Non-Lethal Weapons for Law Enforcement." *Canadian Police Chief,* 62:1 (1973), pp. 34-35.

U.S. Department of Commerce, National Technical Information Service. *Gradient and Less Lethal Devices in Control of Urban Violence.* Springfield, VA.: NTIS, 1973.

"Wanted: Police Weapons That Do Not Kill." *Reader's Digest* (February, 1968).

"Weapons That Don't Kill." *Newsweek* (October 18, 1971).

Rifles

"Aircraft Survival Rifle." *Royal Canadian Mounted Police Gazette* (June, 1973).

Greenwood, Colin. "Police Rifle." *Police Review,* 83 (October 17, 1975), pp. 1304-1305.

O'Connor, Jack. *Rifle Book* 2nd, rev. ed. Westminister, MD.: Knopf, 1964.

Prehle, Jack. "More About the MI Carbine." *Law and Order,* 11:11 (November, 1963), pp. 59-60.

Smith, W.H.R. *The Book of Rifles Completely Revised and Updated.* Harrisburg, PA.: Stackpole, 1963.

Stecle, David E. "A New Countersniper System." *Law and Order,* 19:10 (October, 1971), pp. 52-56.
A description of the Remington 7.62 mm rifle w/scope.

Williams, Mason. "The M-I 30 Caliber Carbine for Police Work." *Law and Order,* 20:6 (June, 1972), pp. 66-67, 70-71, 108.

Williams, Mason. "The Rifle in Police Work." *Law and Order,* 22:10 (October, 1974), pp. 78-85, 88, 91; 22:11 (November, 1974), pp. 22, 24-26; 22:12 (December, 1974), pp. 37-40, 54; 23:2 (February, 1975), pp. 50-51.

Williams, Mason. "The .308 vs. the .223 For Police Work." *Law and Order,* 21:4 (April, 1973), pp. 98-101, 107.

Williams, Mason. "The U.S. Rifle M-1-A." *Law and Order,* 21:2 (February, 1973), pp. 70-72.

Shotguns

Ayoob, Massad F. "The Double Barrel Shotgun in Police Work." *Law and Order,* 23:4 (April, 1975), pp. 74-77; 23:5 (May, 1975), pp. 44, 46-47, 50.

Butler, David F. *American Shot-Gun.* N.Y.: Winchester, 1073.

Williams, Mason. "The 12 Gauge Shotgun. Part I: Reloading." *Law and Order,* 20:5 (May, 1972), pp. 68-69, 72, 74-75.

Prehle, Jack. "A New Riot Shotgun." *Law and Order,* 13:12 (December, 1965), pp. 64, 66-68.

Robinson, Roger H. *The Police Shotgun Manual.* Springfield, IL.: C.C. Thomas, 1973.

Swearengen, Thomas F. "Assessing the New Remington Shotgun." *Law and Order,* 18:1 (January, 1970), pp. 62-71.

Swearengen, Thomas F. "The Definder, MKI." *Law and Order,* 18:10 (October, 1970), pp. 54-58.
A multi-barrel shotgun.

Swearengen, Thomas F. "Evaluation of the Model 10 Combat Shotgun." *Law and Order,* 17:4 (April, 1969), pp. 60-68.

Swearengen, Thomas F. "Model 10 Series B Police Shotgun." *Law and Order,* 20:5 (May, 1972), pp. 54-61, 75.

Silencers

Bixler, O.C. et al. *Analytical and Experimental Studies of Weapon Muffling.* Los Angeles: Ling-Temco-Vought, (August, 1967).

DeMulle, David. "Silencers For Small Arms." *Ordinance* (March-April, 1969), pp. 512-514.

Fulton, C. *Silent Weapon System Cartridge Design and Development (Phase I-Design).* Philadelphia: Frankford Arsenal, (November, 1962).

Gustafson, G.A. *Tests of Silencer for .45 Caliber M3 and M1928 A1 Submachine Guns.* Aberdeen Proving Ground, MD.: U.S. Army, (March 12, 1944).

Harrison, E.H. *NRA Firearms and Ammunition Fact Book: Silencers.* Washington, D.C.: National Rifle Association, 1964.

Hobart, F.W.A. "Silencers." *Gun Review* (May, 1970); (June, 1970); (July, 1970).

McLean, Donald B. *Firearms Silencers.* Forrest Grove, OR.: Normount, 1968.

Shaw, William. "Some Brief Notes on Silencers for Small Arms." *Law and Order,* 21:12 (December, 1973), pp. 14, 16-18.

Skochko, Leonard and Harry A. Greveris. *Silencers.* Philadelphia: Frankford Arsenal, (August, 1967).

Small Caliber Weapons Silencing Devices. Washington, D.C.: Department of Defense, July, 1964.

Sterett, Larry S. "Silencers." *Gun Digest* (1964), pp. 135-138.

Thomas, Donald G. *U.S. Silencer Patents.* Boulder, CO.: Paladin, 1973.

Truby, J. David. *Silencers, Snipers, and Assassins: An Overview of Whispering Death.* Boulder, CO.: Paladin, 1972.

Truby, J.D. "Whispering Death: Silencers." *Shooting Times* (August, 1970).

Zip-Guns and Modifications

Koffler, Bruce Barak. "Zip Guns and Crude Conversions—Identifying Characteristics and Problems." *Journal of Criminal Law, Criminology and Police Science,* 61:1 (March, 1970), pp. 115-125.

McCarthy, John J. "Beware—A Dangerous Weapon." Law and Order, 17:10 (October, 1969), pp. 39-40.
Weapon fires a point 22 caliber tear gas cartridge. It does not

appear to be a weapon. It is the size of an ordinary spark plug and in a way resembles one.

Minnery, J. *Improvised Modified Firearms,* vol. 1. Boulder, CO.: Paladin Press, 1975.

Smith, Leslie L. "Zip Guns." *Police,* 7:3 (January-February, 1963), pp. 10-12.

"Unusual Firearms Cigarette Lighter Gun." *Bulletin of Bureau of Criminal Investigation* (1957).

"Zip-Gun." *FBI Law Enforcement Bulletin* (November, 1966).

FIRST AID

American College of Surgeons, Committee on Trauma. "Essential Equipment for Ambulances." *Bulletin, American College of Surgeons* (May 1970).

Bastrup, Harold A. "The Squad First Aid Kit." *Law and Order,* 17:9 (September, 1969), pp. 106-108.

"Proper Equipment for an Emergency Ambulance." *Police,* 1:1 (September-October, 1956), pp. 21-22.

Van Voorhis, M.D. "The Portable Resuscitator." *Law and Order,* 14:12 (December, 1966), pp. S4-85.

Young, Carl B., Jr. "First Aid Equipment for the Emergency Ambulance." *Police,* 3:6 (July-August, 1959), pp. 21-23.

HANDCUFFS

Ayoob, Massad. "The Ins and Outs of Handcuffs." *Law and Order,* 21:10 (October, 1973), pp. 26-31.

Farrell, Michael J. "Handcuffs." *Police,* 10:4 (March-April, 1966), pp. 69-73.

Describes many types of handcuffs, contemporary and from the past.

Loux, William F. "A Word About Handcuffs." *Law and Order,* 14:10 (October, 1966), pp. 76-78.

Negley, James C. "Handcuffed . . . Will You Bet Your Life?" *Law and Order,* 17:9 (September, 1969), pp. 90-92, 113.

Westfall, M. *Metallic Handcuffs—Law Enforcement Standards Program.* Washington, D.C.: NCJRS (Microfiche), 1974.

HELMETS

Alexander, Harold. "Police Helmetry." *Law and Order,* 22:11 (November, 1974), pp. 86-88.

Calvano, Nicholas J. *Ballistic Helmets—Law Enforcement Standards Program.* Washington, D.C.: NCJRS, 1975.

Calvano, Nicholas J. *Crash Helmets—Law Enforcement Standards Program.* Washington, D.C.: NCJRS, 1975.

Calvano, Nicholas J. *Riot Helmets—Law Enforcement Standards Program.* Washington, D.C.: NCJRS, 1974.

"Crash Helmets for Police Motorcycle Drivers." *FBI Law Enforcement Bulletin.* 25:11 (November, 1956).

Florence, David W. "Helmets in the Line of Duty." *Police,* 13:2 (November-December, 1968), pp. 48-50.

Patrick, L.M. "Don't Lose Your Head." *Law and Order,* 13:5 (May, 1965), pp. 66-69.

"Report on Flammability of Plastics Used for Riot Helmets." *Police Chief* (March, 1969).

Wargovich, M.J. and M.L. Lonky. *Evaluation of an All-Purpose Communication/Protective Helmet—Final Report.* Springfield, VA.: NTIS, 1973.

The communication/protective helmet system consisted of a helmet with face shield and transducer/receiver, a neck protector, a radio, and a gas mask, to be used by police.

HOLSTERS

DeDonato, Emil. "Leather Craftsmen." *Law and Order,* 22:4 (April, 1974), pp. 56-57.

Fox, Valvert Lucius. "Holsters for the Special Weapons Arsenal." *Law and Order,* 20:10 (October, 1972), pp. 46-48, 50.

Greenwood, Colin. "Where's Your Horse, Cowboy? The Selection of Police Holsters." *Police Review (GB),* (July 23, 1976), pp. 928-930.

Ruehl, George. "Holsters for Law Enforcement Officers." *Law and Order,* 19:6 (June, 1971), pp. 96-98.

Sharp, Victor R. "Holsters That We Live With." *Law and Order,* 18:12 (December, 1970), pp. 108-110, 112, 114, 116, 118.

Stevenson, Jan A. "Bucheimer's Hank Sloan Holster." *Law and Order,* 16:2 (February, 1968), pp. 48-61.

Stevenson, Jan A. "Coathanger Holster: Fastest Thing in the Closet." *Law and Order,* 15:2 (February, 1967), pp. 62-67, 73.

Stevenson, Jan A. "Seventrees Holsters, Ltd . . . New Name in Custom Concealment." *Law and Order,* 16:7 (July, 1968), pp. 76-79.

Weston, Paul B. "Hide-Out Holster Builder." *Police,* 4:1 (September-October, 1959), pp. 39-42.

Williams, Mason. "Cain Combat Holsters." *Law and Order,* 20:11 (November, 1972), pp. 88-90.

Williams, Mason. "George Aurit, Saddlemaker." *Law and Order,* 23:7 (July, 1975).

METAL DETECTORS

Law Enforcement Standards Laboratory. *Tests of Hand-Held Metal Weapons Detectors—Law Enforcement Standards Program.* Washington: D.C.: GPO, 1976.

National Institute of Law Enforcement and Criminal Justice. *Walk-Through Metal Detectors for Use in Weapons Detection—Law Enforcement Standards Program.* Washington, D.C.: NCJRS, 1974.

Performance requirements and test methods for devices which indicate the presence of metal carried on a person passing through a specific space.

U.S. Department of Commerce, National Bureau of Standards. *Hand-Held Metal Detectors for Use in Weapons Detection—Law Enforcement Standards Program.* Washington, D.C.: NCJRS (Microfiche), 1974.

NIGHT VISION DEVICES

Quinn, W.F. *Evaluation of Night-Vision Equipment for Law Enforcement Applications.* Washington, D.C.: NCJRS, 1970.

Richmond, Joseph C. *Active Night Vision Devices—Law Enforcement Standards Program.* Washington, D.C. NCJRS, 1975.

Richmond, Joseph C. *Passive, First Generation Night Vision Devices—Law Enforcement Standards Program.* Washington, D.C.: NCJRS, 1975.

"Seeing by Starlight and Invisible Light." *Design News* (July 7, 1975); (July 21, 1975).

Shaw, William. "Startron MK 303A—Passive Night Vision System." *Law and Order,* 19:12 (December, 1971), pp. 110-111.

RADAR

Berry, Fred. "Speed Control: Is Radar Still the Best Route?" *Law and Order,* 19:2 (February, 1971), pp. 56-58, 60-62.

Cable, Kenneth M. "Warning: Speed Checked by Radar." *Law and Order* (September, 1970).

Linton, Robert. "A Primer for Radar and Radar Testimony." *Law and Order,* 16:6 (June, 1968).

UNIFORMS

Bickman, Leonard. "Social Roles and Uniforms: Clothes Make the Person." *Psychology Today* (April, 1974).

Blanks, William W. "Tarnished Badge or Bright Shield." *Police Chief,* XL:12 (December, 1973).

Burke, Gary M. "Utility Riot Suit." *Law and Order,* 19:12 (December, 1971), pp. 104, 106-108.

Carper, R.S. *Detailed Operational Requirements for Protective Garments for Law Enforcement Agencies—Equipment Systems Improvement Program Report.* Washington, D.C.: NCJRS, 1973.

Carper, R.S. *Detailed Requirements Analysis for Protective Garments—Equipment Systems Improvement Program Report.* Washington, D.C.: NCJRS, 1973.

Copp, William C. "Uniforms First With Bergen County Chiefs." *Law and Order,* 22:8 (August, 1974), pp. 84, 95-96.

Copp, William C. "Wool Won't Burn—Only Smolder." *Law and Order,* 22:10 (October, 1974), pp. 89-90.

Dragnich, Alix. "A New Committee Keeps Pace with Changing Uniforms." *Law and Order,* 20:8 (August, 1972), pp. 97-98.

Dragnich, Alix. "Take Pride in Your Uniform." *Law and Order,* 21:8 (August, 1973), pp. 66-68, 89.

"Emergency Uniforms for Los Angeles County." *Police Chief,* XXXVI:4 (April, 1969).

Hutchens, H.V. "High Visibility Garments." *Police Research Bulletin* (Summer, 1975), pp. 3-32.

Lovejoy, Mike. "Flammability and Police Uniforms." *Law and Order,* 23:8 (August, 1975).

Pitchess, Peter J. "Los Angeles County Sheriff's Department Uniforms." *Journal of California Law Enforcement* (April, 1969).

Reynolds, James P. "The Good Image." *Law and Order,* 14:8 (August, 1966).

Russell, Luther D. "Emergency Uniforms." *Law and Order,* 17:12 (December, 1969), pp. 70-71.

Shaw, Lew. "The Role of Clothing in the Criminal Justice System." *Journal of Police Science and Administration,* 1:4 (December, 1973), pp. 414-420.

Speck, Dale H. "Modernizing Our Uniforms." *Police Chief,* 38:8 (August, 1971), pp. 22, 25.

Wolfe, Howard A. "Uniforms: An Integral Part of Police Work." *Law and Order,* 23:8 (August, 1975).

Wolfe, Howard A. "Uniforms: Tradition and Innovation." *Law and Order,* 22:8 (August, 1974), pp. 16, 18-19.

Woodruff, Waid S. "LAPD Takes on a New Look." *Law and Order,* 17:8 (August, 1969), pp. 46-54.

VASCAR

Council, F.M. "Retesting of Vascar Operations The Effect of a One Year Period of Use." *Traffic Digest and Review,* 18 (June-July, 1970), pp. 10-13.

Davis, Jim. "Vascar—A 5-Year Evaluation Report." *Law and Order,* 19:9 (September, 1971), pp. 36, 38, 40, 42, 44-45.

"How Vascar Works." *Law Officers,* 3 (Winter, 1971).

Konkle, Robert K. "Indiana State Police Use Vascar for Testing Speed." *Law and Order,* 19:11 (November, 1971), pp. 60-63, 71.
Electronic computer used to actually judge speed. Used in at least 39 states.

VEHICLES

Vehicles—General

Campbell, Charles and Jan Hoffman. "Yes, Robin, There Is a Batmobile." *Law and Order,* 24:6 (June, 1976), pp. 78-79, 86.
Vehicle used to test and process drunk drivers by Metropolitan Police Department (Nashville).

Carpenter, R.M. "Motor Scooters Prove Valuable in New York Pilot Program." *Law and Order,* 16:6 (June, 1968), pp. 58-62.

Conley, R.W. "Jet Drive Patrol Boats." *Law and Order* (November, 1975), pp. 72-73.

Dean, Maurice F. and M.A. Euston. "The Snowmobile: The Tool of Modern Law Enforcement." *FBI Law Enforcement Bulletin,* 37:4 (April, 1968), pp. 2-6.

Heyen, Harry C. "Does Your City Need a Mobile Field Headquarters." *FBI Law Enforcement Bulletin,* 36:8 (August, 1967), pp. 17-21.
Description of a mobile self contained field headquarters unit. Vehicle is a 4-wheel drive Dodge with a 175 in. wheel base. The body is 14′ by 7′ wide and 6′ by 2″ high.

"Hovercraft For Police and Rescue." *STS Newsletter,* 13:5 (June, 1971).

Motorcycle Magazine Editor. *Motorcycle Buyers Guide 1976.* 5th ed. Los Angeles: Petersen, 1975.

Murphy, Jack. "Motorized Meter Maids." *Law and Order,* 14:6 (June, 1966), pp. 10-11, 15.

"18-Horsepower Vehicle Tested in Kansas City." *Law and Order,* 22:11 (November, 1974), pp. 98-99.
Use of Cushman three-wheel vehicles in traffic enforcement.

"1971 Mobile Patrol Roundup." *Law and Order,* 18:11 (November, 1970), pp. 54, 56, 58, 60, 62, 64, 70, 72, 74-76.

Neuling, Floyd M. "Park Police Shift to Low Gear." *Law and Order,* 18:11 (November, 1970), pp. 34-36, 42.
Use of 4-wheel drive vehicles for patrol in rural areas.

"Rescue Vehicles Come in Many Sizes." *Law and Order* (November, 1975).

Silvarman, Allen. "Building and Use of a Mobile Surveillance Unit." *Law and Order,* 13:4 (April, 1965), pp. 76-78.

"Special Automobiles for Transporting Prisoners." *FBI Law Enforcement Bulletin,* 27:1 (January, 1958).

Armored

"Armored Ambulance for NYPD." *Police Chief* (April, 1973).

Craney, Edward J. "Crowd Control Vehicles." *Law and Order,* 10:11 (November, 1962).

Rayfield, W.D. "The Thompson Tank." *Law and Order,* 12:7 (July, 1964).

Savage, Harry M. "Riots Spawn Manufacture of Peace Van." *Police,* 15:2 (November-December, 1970), pp. 67-68.

Settelmaire, Robert. "Unique Rescue Vehicle Has Special Electrical Needs." *Law and Order,* 18:2 (February, 1970), pp. 80-81.
Description of rubber tracked-R-2 multipurpose rescue vehicle-has quarter inch armor plate and can carry 15 fully equipped men.

Shaw, William. "A Design Concept for a Riot Control Vehicle." *Law and Order,* 16:2 (February, 1968), pp. 26-28.

Foreign Vehicles

Gray, Thomas K. "The Hmmmmmmmmm Police Patrol Car". *Police Chief* (November, 1973), pp. 14-15.
Use of Mazda Patrol Vehicles.

Lydle, Chris. "Imported Police Vehicles." *Law and Order,* 16:12 (December, 1968), pp. 64-71.

Meyers, Ina. "Police Beetles." *Law and Order,* 16:6 (June, 1968), pp. 32-34.

"Police Experiment with Compact Cars." *Western City,* 36 (May, 1960).

Mobile Crime Units

Cotron, Robert J. "Our Mobile Crime Unit." *Law and Order,* 14:2 (February, 1966), pp. 75.

Ferrari, Marlo J. "Camden Police Mobile Crime Unit." *Police,* 7:2 (November-December, 1962), pp. 72-73.
Mobile Crime Unit in a Chevrolet Van.

"New Design in Mobile Crime Unit." *FBI Law Enforcement Bulletin,* 26:6 (June, 1957), pp. 22.

Nowak, Edward G., Jr. "Rhode Island State Police Operates Lab on Wheels." *Law and Order,* 19:7 (July, 1971), pp. 48-51, 55.
Utilizes a large walk-in international van.

Samen, Charles C. "Mini-Lab on Wheels." *FBI Law Enforcement Bulletin,* 38:5 (May, 1969), pp. 12-15, 23.

Patrol Cars

Bunten, E. and P. Klaus. *LEAA Police Department Survey of 1972,* vol. 7. *Patrol Cars-Law Enforcement Standards Program.* Washington, D.C.: NCJRS (Microfiche), 1974.

Byrne, Edward C. "Outfitting a Patrol Car." *Law and Order,* 19:11 (November, 1971), pp. 32-34, 36.

Dockendorff, Robert L. "Suggestions for the Design of a Multifunction Patrol Vehicle." *Police,* 14:1 (September-October, 1969), pp. 7-9.

Dodson, Warren. "A Public Safety Cruiser." *FBI Law Enforcement Bulletin,* 36:7 (July, 1967), pp. 13-16.
Station wagon cruisers equipped for handling emergency services.

Fagerstrom, Dorothy. "Facts and Figures on Mobile Patrol." *Law and Order,* 16:11 (November, 1968), pp. 65-66, 82.

Furr, Richard P., William O. Dwyer, and John L. Fletcher. "Patrol Car Selection: A Systems-Analysis Approach." *Police,* 16:10 (June, 1972), pp. 55-57.

Hindes, Don. "Looking for Trouble." *Law and Order,* 15:9 (September, 1967), pp. 80, 81.
Use of station wagons as patrol vehicles equipped with stretchers, oxygen, resusitator, and other first aid equipment.

Los Angeles County Sheriff's Department. *Los Angeles County-Sheriff's Department—Vehicle Testing and Evaluation Program—Report Number 2—1973-74 Vehicle Test Results.* Washington, D.C.: NCJRS (Microfiche), 1974.

Ludwig, H.G. *Study of the Police Patrol Vehicle.* Springfield, VA.: NTIS, 1970.
The relation of the patrol vehicle to the department, procurement of better vehicles and policies for use, operation, and replacement.

Massey, R.G. *Police Patrol Car—State of the Art—Law Enforcement Standards Program.* Washington, D.C.: NCJRS, 1975.

Mulcahy, L.J. "The Case for the Unmarked Police Car." *Police Chief,* 29:7 (July, 1962), pp. 12-14.

Munroe, Allen E. *Uniform Police Vehicle Specifications.* N.Y.: National Association of Fleet Administration, Inc., 1975.

Piercy, William Donald. "The Police Patrol Car." *Journal of Criminal Law, Criminology and Police Science,* 45:6 (March-April, 1955), pp. 748-759.

Swartz, Merrill and Jim Berger. "The Police Car of Tomorrow." *Law and Order,* 19:11 (November, 1971), pp. 24-27.

Wynne, G. Ray. "Tomorrow's Police Car." *Police Chief,* XXXVI:1 (January, 1969).

X-RAY

Mercer, W.R. "Nondestructive Testing Techniques and Methods for Security and Police Work." *Canadian Police Chief,* 62:4 (1973), pp. 30-31.

Smith, Charles. "X-Ray Standards for Law Enforcement." *Police Chief,* XXXIX:5 (May, 1972).
National Bureau of Standards analysis of X-Ray systems for police use.

Staiger, Jerome W. and Ralph O. Wollan. "Radiation Protection Precautions in X-Ray Evaluation of Suspicious Packages." *Police,* 16:4 (December, 1971), pp. 7-12.
Use of X-Ray equipment and examining suspected bombs.

X-Ray Systems for Bomb Disarmament. Washington, D.C.: LEAA, 1976.

PART XII
LAW ENFORCEMENT—ISSUES AND PROBLEMS

ISSUES AND PROBLEMS IN LAW ENFORCEMENT

POLICE—GENERAL

Ahern, James F. "How We Handcuff Our Police." *Redbook* (April, 1971).

Banton, Michael. *The Policeman in the Community.* N.Y.: Basic, 1964.

Becker, Sidney. *Law Enforcement Inc.* N.Y.: Manor, 1975.

Berkley, George E. *The Democratic Policeman.* Boston: Beacon, 1969.

Bordua, David J. *The Police: Six Sociological Essays.* N.Y.: Wiley, 1967.

A series of articles dealing with police problems, the innovations in practice and organizations to meet the changing urban society, and the complex problems of reducing the police role to its proper scope.

Brown, John and Graham House. *Police in the Community.* Lexington, MA.: Lexington Books, 1975.

Caldwell, A.B. "The Police and the Citizen—Individual Rights vs. Common Security." *Police,* 7:2 (November-December, 1962), pp. 77-81.

Cooper, Lynn et al. *Iron Fist and the Velvet Glove: An Analysis of the U.S. Police.* Berkeley, CA.: Center for Research on Criminal Justice, 1975.

Corman, James C. "Law Enforcement in the Administration of Justice." *William and Mary Law Review,* 10:3 (1969), pp. 579-585.

Curran, James, T., ed. *Police and Law Enforcemnent—1972.* N.Y.: AMS, 1974.

Curran, James T. and Richard H. Ward. *Police and Law Enforcement, 1973-1974.* vol. 2. N.Y.: AMS, 1975.

Day, Edward J. "Society and Law Enforcement." *Security World* (October, 1966).

Devlin, Patrick Arthur. "The Police in a Changing Society." *Journal of Criminal Law, Criminology and Police Science,* 57:2 (June, 1966), pp. 123-129.

Ferguson, John P. "Answers to Criticism." *Police Yearbook,* Washington, D.C.: IACP, 1963.

"Freedom of the Streets." *Police Chief,* XLII:11 (November, 1975).

Friedlander, C.P. and E. Mitchell. *Police—Servants or Masters?* London: Hart-Davis Educational, 1974.

Gallati, Robert R.J. "Scapegoats No More." *Police* (September, 1971).

Ganz, Alan S. et al. *The Cities and the Police.* Chicago: University of Chicago Press, 1968.

Gustin, A.C. "A Police Officer Reacts." *Journal of Social Issues,* 31:1 (1975), pp. 211-215.

Hahn, Harlan, ed. *Police in Urban Society.* London: Sage, 1970.

Jacob, Herbert. *Urban Justice: Law and Order in American Cities.* Englewood Cliffs, N.J.: Prentice Hall, 1973.

Jayewardene, C.H.S. *Police and the Changing Society: Problems, Issues and Solutions.* Ottawa: Department of Criminology, University of Ottawa, 1973.

Killinger, George G. and Paul F. Cromwell, Jr. *Issues in Law Enforcement.* Rockleigh, N.J.: Holbrook, 1975.

Kinton, Jack F., ed. *American Police in the 70's.* Naperville, American Society, 1975.

Knights, P.D. "Police in a Changing Society." *The Police Journal (GB),* (December, 1966).

Lucas, F.E. " 'Legend of Lenient Justice'." *National Sheriff,* 25:4 (1973).

McDowell, Charles P. *Police in the Community.* Cincinnati: Anderson, 1975.

McFadden, James P. "Who Will Protect the Police?" *National Review* (April 5, 1966).

Martin, J.P. and Gail Wilson. *The Police: A Study in Manpower.* London: Heineman, 1969.

Mirich, John J. "The Qualified Policeman—The Backbone of Society." *Journal of Criminal Law, Criminology and Police Science,* 50:3 (September/October, 1959), pp. 315-317.

National Institute of Law Enforcement and Criminal Justice. *Conferences on Critical Topics in Law Enforcement.* Washington, D.C.: NTIS, 1969.

This report documents the major results of two conferences on critical topics in law enforcement.

Niederhoffer, Arthur and Abraham S. Blumberg, eds. *The Ambivalent Force: Perspectives on the Police.* Waltham, Ginn, 1970.

Patrick, Clarence H. *The Police, Crime, and Society.* Springfield, IL.: C.C. Thomas, 1972.

"The Police and the Rest of Us." *Atlantic* (March, 1969) (entire issue).

President's Commission on Law Enforcement and the Administration of Justice. *Task Force Report: The Police.* Washington, D.C.: GPO, 1967.

Shoham, Shlomo. "The Two Sides of the Barricade." *Police,* 9:2 (November-December, 1964), pp. 28-35.

Skolnick, Jerome H. and Thomas C. Gray. *Police in America.* Waltham, MA.: Little, 1975.

Steadman, Robert F., ed. *The Police and the Community.* Baltimore, MD.: Johns Hopkins University Press, 1972.

Summers, Marvin and Thomas Barth. *Law and Order in a Democratic Society.* Columbus, OH.: Merrill, 1970.

Viano, Emilio C. and Jeffrey H. Reiman eds. *Police in Society.* Lexington, MA.: Lexington, 1975.

Vollmer, August. *The Police and Modern Society.* Berkeley: University of California Press, 1936.

Waters, J.R. and S.A. McGrath. *Introduction to Law Enforcement.* Columbus, OH.: Merrill, 1974.

Wilson, James Q. "The Police and Their Problems: A Theory." *Public Policy,* XII (1963), pp. 189-216.

Wilson, Jerry. *Police Report: A View of Law Enforcement.* Waltham, MA.: Little, 1975.

Wright, G.R. and J. Marlo. *Police Officer and Criminal Justice.* N.Y.: McGraw-Hill, 1970.

AMERICAN EXTREMIST GROUPS

Extremism—General

"Busting RAM: Plot to Assassinate Moderate Negro Leaders." *Time* (June 30, 1967).

Munson, Don. "America's Brown Beret Revolution." *Saga* (August, 1968).

Overstreet, Harry and Bonaro Overstreet. *The Strange Tactics of Extremism.* N.Y.: Norton, 1964.

"Prisons—A Target of Revolutionaries." *FBI Law Enforcement Bulletin,* 43:9 (September, 1974).

Sackett, Russell. "Plotting a War on Whitey." *Life* (June 10, 1966).
Discusses RAM, Black extremists which advocates using violence to gain power and killing all police officers.

Schultz, D.O. and S.K. Scott. *The Subversive.* Springfield, IL.: C.C. Thomas, 1973.
Description of SDS, Black Panthers, Black Muslims, Communist parties, Weathermen, White Panthers and others.

Steverson, D.L. "The Revolutionary Arsonist." *Fire Arson Investigator,* 24:1 (1973), pp. 27-36.
Discusses various extremists groups, SDS, Black Panthers, etc. and the tactics and incendiary and explosive devices used.

Anarchism

Carter, April. *Political Theory of Anarchism.* N.Y.: Harper and Row, 1971.

Guerin, Daniel. *Anarchism: From Theory to Practice.* N.Y.: Monthly Review, 1970.

Forman, James. *Anarchism.* N.Y.: Dell, 1976.

Hoffman, Robert L., ed. *Anarchism.* N.Y.: Lieber-Atherton, 1970.

Joll, James. *Anarchists.* N.Y.: Grosset and Dunlap, 1966.

Lee, Vernon. *Gospels of Anarchy.* N.Y.: Gordon, 1976.

Marx, Karl et al. *Anarchism.* N.Y.: Beekman, 1973.

Runkle, Gerald. *Anarchism.* N.Y.: Dell, 1972.

Black Muslims

Barnette, Aubrey. "The Black Muslims Are a Fraud." *Saturday Evening Post* (February 27, 1965), pp. 23-29.

"Black Muslim." *Life,* 54 (May 31, 1963).

"Black Muslims' Cry Grows Louder: 'The White Devils' Day Is Almost Over'." *Life* 54: (May 3, 1963), pp. 22-33, 78-79.

Brown, Lee P. "Black Muslims and the Police." *Journal of Criminal Law, Criminology and Police Science.* 56:1 (March, 1965), pp. 119-126.

Drzazga, John. "Muslim Terrorists." *Law and Order,* 11:5 (May, 1963), pp. 38-41, 56-57.

Essien-Udom, E.U. *Black Nationalism: A Search for an Identity in America.* Chicago: University of Chicago Press, 1962.

Hentoff, Nat. "Elijah in the Wilderness." *Reporter,* 23:2 (August 4, 1960), pp. 37-40.

Lincoln, C. Eric. *The Black Muslims in America.* Boston: Beacon, 1961.

Lincoln, C. Eric. "Black Muslims." *Police Chief,* 30 (June, 1963), pp. 13-14, 16.

Lomax, Louis. *When the Word Is Given . . .* Cleveland: World, 1963.

"Malcolm X." *Playboy,* 10:5 (May, 1963), pp. 53-54.

"Nation of Islam." *Oakland Police Department Training Bulletin,* 10:10 [n.d.].

Shack, William A. "Black Muslims: A Nativistic Religious Movement among Negro Americans." *Race* (1961).

Sherrill, Robert. "We Want Georgia, So. Carolina, Louisiana, Mississippi, and Alabama—Right Now . . . We Also Want 400 Billion Dollars Back Pay." *Esquire* (January, 1969), p. 71.

Black Panthers

Anderson, J. "Panther: Black Men in Extremes." *Dissent,* 17:2 (1970), pp. 120-123.

Anthony, Earl. *Picking Up the Gun: A Report on the Black Panthers.* N.Y.: Dial, 1970.

Baruch, Ruth-Marion and Pirkle Jones. *The Vanguard: A Photographic Essay on the Black Panthers.* Boston: Beacon, 1970.

"The Case of Clark Squire: Computer Programmer, Black Panther, Prisoner; Interim Report." *Computers and Automation,* 20 (February, 1971), pp. 36-41.

Chevigny, Paul. *Cops and Rebels.* N.Y.: Irvington, 1972.

Epstein, Edward J. "The Panthers and the Police: A Pattern of Genocide?" *New Yorker,* 46 (February 13, 1971).

Foner, Philip S., ed. *Black Panthers Speak.* N.Y.: Lippincott, 1970.

Freed, Donald. *Agony in New Haven: The Trial of Bobby Seale, Erica Huggins and the Black Panther Party.* N.Y.: Simon and Schuster, 1973.

Heath, G.L., ed. *The Black Panther Leaders Speak.* Metuchen, N.J.: Scarecrow, 1976.

Heath, G.L. *Off the Pigs! The History and Literature of the Black Panther Party.* Metuchen, N.J.: Scarecrow, 1976.

Kempton, Murray. *The Briar Patch.* N.Y.: Dutton, 1973.

Major, Reginald. *A Panther Is a Black Cat.* N.Y.: Morrow, 1971.

Marine, Gene. *The Black Panthers.* N.Y. New American Library, 1969.

Moore, Gilbert. *A Special Rage.* N.Y.: Harper, 1971.

Rogers, R. "Black Guns on Campus: Black Panthers and the U.S." *Nation* (May 5, 1969), pp. 55-560.

Sachs, Patricia, ed. *The Black Panthers.* N.Y.: Universal, 1969.

Schanche, Don A. *Panther Paradox: A Liberal's Dilemma.* N.Y.: McKay, 1970.

Seale, Bobby. *Seize the Time; The Story of the Black Panther Party and Huey P. Newton.* N.Y.: Random House, 1970.

Stern, Sol. "The Call of the Black Panthers." *The New York Times Magazine* (August 6, 1967).

Sutton, John. *Black Panther Banner.* N.Y.: William-Frederick, 1973.

U.S. Committee on Internal Security. *The Black Panther Party, Its Origins and Developments.* Washington, D.C.: GPO, 1970.

U.S. Congress: Committee on Internal Security. *Gun Barrel Politics: The Black Panther Party, 1966-1971; Report.* Washington, D.C.: GPO, 1971.

Zimroth, P.L. *Perversions of Justice—The Prosecution and Acquittal of the Panther.* Vol. 21. N.Y.: Viking, 1974.

Communism

Aubry, Arthur S., Jr. "Law Enforcement and Communism." *Police,* 6:6 (July-August, 1962), pp. 30-32.

Colegrove, Kenneth. *Democracy Versus Communism.* N.Y.: Van Nostrand, 1957.

Curtis, Michael, ed. *Marxism.* Chicago: Aldine, 1970.

Dallin, Alexander and George W. Breslauer. *Political Terror in Communist System.* Stanford, CA.: Stanford University Press, 1970.

Decter, Moshe, ed. *Profile of Communism: A Fact By Fact Primer.* rev. ed. N.Y.: Macmillan, 1961.

Draskovich, Slobodan. *Will America Surrender?* Old Greenwich, CT.: Devin Adair, 1972.

Gordin, Abby. *Communism Unmasked.* N.Y.: Gordon, 1976.

Gripp, Richard C. *Political System of Communism.* N.Y.: Dodd, 1973.

Hammond, Thomas T. and Robert Farrell, eds. *Anatomy of Communist Take Overs.* New Haven, CT.: Yale University Press, 1975.

Howe, Irving and Lewis Coser. *American Communist Party: A Critical History.* N.Y.: Da Capo, 1974.

Hyde, Douglas. *Communism Today.* Notre Dame, IN.: University of Notre Dame, 1973.

International Commission of Jurists. *The Hungarian Situation and the Rule of Law.* The Hague: International Commission of Jurists, 1957.

Meyer, F.S. "Communist Party and the New Left." *National Review* (February 27, 1968).

O'Neal, James and G.A. Werner. *American Communism: A Critical Analysis of Its Origins, Development and Programs.* rev. ed. Westport, CT.: Greenwood, 1972.

Overstreet, Harry A. and Bonard Overstreet. *Iron Curtain.* N.Y.: Norton, 1963.

Ozinga, James R. *Communism—A Tarnished Promise.* Columbus, OH.: Merrill, 1975.

Schwartz, Harry, ed. *The Many Faces of Communism.* N.Y.: Berkeley, 1962.

Shanon, David A. *Decline of American Communism: A History of the Communist Party in the United States Since 1945.* Chatham, N.D.: Chatham Book Seller, 1971 (repr. of 1969 ed.).

Skousen, W. Cleon. *The Communist Attack on U.S. Police.* Salt Lake City: Ensign, 1966.

Skousen, W. Cleon. "Communists Declare War on U.S. Police." *Law and Order,* 14:1 (January, 1966) through (May, 1966) (5 parts).

U.S. Committee on Internal Security. *The Theory and Practice of Communism in 1970.* Washington, D.C.: GPO, 1970.

Far Right

Bell, Daniel. *The Racial Right.* Garden City, N.Y.: Doubleday, 1963.

Foster, Arnold and Benjamin R. Epstein. *Danger on the Right.* N.Y.: Random House, 1964.

Lipset, Seymour Martin. *The Politics of Unreason—Right-Wing Extremism in America, 1790-1970.* N.Y.: Harper and Row, 1970.

Prager, Arthur. "Here Comes the Hate Groups." *Nation Cities,* 2 (November, 1964), pp. 22-24.
Description of anti-Communist movements.

Facism

Basch, Ernst. *The Fascist: His State and His Mind.* N.Y.: AMS (repr. of 1937 ed.).

Bell, Leland V. *In Hitler's Shadow: The Anatomy of American Nazism.* Port Washington, N.Y.: Kennikat, 1973.

Forman, James. *Fascism.* N.Y.: Dell, 1976.

"George L. Rockwell, U.S. Nazi." *Fact,* 15 (October, 1963), pp. 271-280.

Greene, N., ed. *Fascism: An Anthology.* Northbrook, IL.: AHM, 1968.

Hale, Ovon J. *Captive Press in the Third Reich.* Princeton: Princeton University Press, 1964.

Hamilton, Alastair. *Appeal of Fascism.* N.Y.: Avon, 1973.

Hayes, Paul. *Fascism.* N.Y.: Free Press, 1973.

Herzstein, Robert E. *Adolph Hitler and the German Trauma, 1913-1945. An Interpretation of the Nazi Phenomenon.* N.Y.: Putnam, 1974.

Nolte, Ernst. *Three Faces of Fascism.* N.Y.: New America Library, 1969.

Poulantzas, Nicos. *Fascism and Dictatorship: International and the Problem of Fascism.* N.Y.: Humanities, 1975.

Reich, Wilhelm. *Mass Psychology of Fascism.* N.Y.: Simon and Schuster, 1974.

Schuddekopf, Otto-Ernst. *Fascism.* N.Y. Praeger, 1973.

Weinrich, Max. *Hitler's Professors.* N.Y. Yivo Institute, 1946.

Ku Klux Klan

Alexander, Charles C. *The Ku Klux Klan in the Southwest.* Lexington, KY.: University Press of Kentucky, 1965.

Chalmers, David M. *Hooded Americanism: The First Century of the Ku Klux Klan, 1865-1965.* Garden City, N.Y.: Doubleday, 1965.

Damer, Eyre. *When the Ku Klux Rode.* Westport, CT.: Negro University Press (repr. of 1912 ed.).

Frost, Stanley. *Challenge of the Klan.* N.Y.: AMS (repr. of 1924 ed.).

Horn, Stanley F. *Invisible Empire: The Story of the Ku Klux Klan, 1866-1971.* Brooklyn, N.Y.: Haskill, 1969 (repr. of 1939 ed.).

Huie, William B. *Three Lives for Mississippi.* N.Y. Trident, 1965.

Jackson, Kenneth T. *Ku Klux Klan in the City, 1915-1930.* N.Y.: Oxford University Press, 1967.

"The Ku Klux Klans—1965." *Fact,* 16 (May, 1965), pp. 321-336.

Lester, J.C. and D.L. Wilson. *Ku Klux Klan.* N.Y.: Da Capo, 1973 (repr. of 1905 ed.).

Lowe, David. *Ku Klux Klan: The Invisible Empire.* N.Y.: Norton, 1967.

McLlhany, William H. *Klandestine.* New Rochelle, N.Y.: Arlington House, 1975.

Randel, William P. *The Ku Klux Klan: A Century of Infamy.* Philadelphia: Chilton, 1965.

Trelease, Allen W. *White Terror: The Ku Klux Klan Conspiracy and Southern Reconstruction.* London: Secker and Warburg, 1972.

Tyler, Charles W. *K.K.K.* Plainview, N.Y.: Books for Libraries (repr. of 1902 ed.).

U.S. House of Representatives. Committee on Un-American Activities. *The Present-Day Ku Klux Klan Movement.* Washington, D.C. GPO, 1967.

Minute Men

Albares, Richard P. *Nativist Paramilitarism in the United States: The Minuteman Organization.* Chicago: University of Chicago, 1968.

Jones, J. Harry. *The Minutemen.* N.Y. Doubleday, 1968.

Office of the Attorney General, State of California. *Para Military Organizations in California.* Sacramento: Office of the Attorney General, 1965.

New Left

Abel, L. "Seven Heroes of the New Left." *New York Times* (May 5, 1968), pp. 30-31.

Boeme, Lillian R. *Carte Blanche for Chaos.* New Rochelle, N.Y.: Arlington House, 1970.

Boorstin, D.J. "New Barbarians; Radicalism in the United States." *Esquire* (October, 1968), pp. 155-162.

Bouscaren, Anthony and Danial Lyons. *Left of Liberal.* N.Y.: Twin Circle, 1969.

"Chicago's Aftermath: The Radical Strategy." *Business Week* (September 7, 1968).

Ciandi, J. "New Left: Why Violence?" *Saturday Review* (January 23, 1971).

"Goal of the New Left; Down with Everything." *U.S. News and World Report* (January 20, 1969), pp. 56-57.

Gorkin, L. "Here Is the Latest Radical Plan, Interview." *Look* (November 17, 1970).

Howe, Irving, ed. *Beyond the New Left.* N.Y.: McCalls, 1970.

Howe, I. "Political Terrorism: Hysteria on the Left." *New York Times Magazine* (April 12, 1970), pp. 25-27.

Jacobs, Paul and Saul Landau. *The New Radicals: A Report with Documents.* N.Y.: Random House, 1966.

Luce, Philip Abbot. *The New Left.* N.Y.: McKay, 1966.

Rosenthal, C.F. *American Student Left, An Historical Essay.* Washington, D.C. NCJRS. [n.d.].
Course and character of the American student leftist movement during the twentieth century.

Stolz, Matthew F. *Politics of the New Left.* Beverly Hills, CA.: Glencoe, 1971.

Teodori, Massimo. *The New Left: A Documentary History.* Indianapolis, IN.: Bobbs-Merrill, 1969.

U.S. Senate Committee on the Judiciary. *Extent of Subversion in the "New Left": Hearings Before 91st Congress, 2nd Session.* Washington, D.C.: GPO, 1970.

SDS

Adelson, Allan. *SDS.* N.Y.: Scribners, 1972.

Daniels, S. "The Weathermen." *Government and Opposition,* 9:1 (1974), pp. 430-459.

Jacobs, Harold, ed. *Weatherman.* San Francisco: Ramparts Press, 1970.

Kifner, John. "A Spectator's Guide to the Trouble Makers." *Esquire* (February, 1969).

SLA

Boulton, David. *Making of Tania Hearst.* London: New English Library, 1975.

Pearsall, R.B., ed. *Symbionese Liberation Army—Documents and Communications.* Amsterdam: Rodopi N V Keizergracht, 1974.

APATHY

Brown, David L. "Apathy—It Can Kill You." *Law and Order,* 13:5 (May, 1965).

Day, Frank D. "Community Indifference and the Growth of Crime." *Police,* 10:3 (January-February, 1966), pp. 25-30.

Miller, J. Guy. "Whose Side Are We On?" *Police,* 8:5 (May-June, 1964).

Strull, Gene. "Partners in Crime." *Police Chief,* XXXV:6 (June, 1968), pp. 28-32.

ASSOCIATIONS

Associations—General

Berney, Don. *Law and Order Politics: A History of Role Analysis of Police Officer Organizations.* Unpub. Doctoral Dissertation, University of Washington, 1971.

Capune, W. Garrett. "U.S. Police Associations." *Criminologist,* (Apring, 1971).

Childers, F.B. "Southern California Training Officers' Association Story." *Law and Order,* 13:10 (October, 1965), pp. 56, 58.

Coon, Thomas F. "The Meeting of Investigators." *Police,* 10:1 (September-October, 1965), pp. 84-85.
Information about the Society of Professional Investigators.

Cuadra, C.A. and H.H. Isaacs. *Information Center for Law Enforcement.* Springfield, VA.: NTIS, 1964.

"Directory of Law Enforcement Organization." *Police Chief,* 32 (February, 1965), pp. 42-44.

Gifford, J.P. *The Political Relations of Patrolmen's Benevolent Association in New York City.* Unpub. Doctoral Dissertation, Columbia University, 1970.

Halpern, Stephen. *Police—Association and Department Leaders.* Lexington, MA.: Lexington Books, 1974.

Meyer, John C., Jr. "Rank and File Perceptions of Police Employee Association Functions." *Police* (January, 1972).

Musick, James A. "Peace Officers' Association Raises Police Standards." *FBI Law Enforcement Bulletin,* 27:4 (April, 1958), pp. 3-5, 22.

Palmer, Garth M. "Policemen's Club Benefits Officers and Agency." *FBI Law Enforcement Bulletin,* 26:8 (August, 1957), pp. 20-21.

Survey of Police Employee Organizations. Washington, D.C.: IACP, 1969.

Snyder, W.J. "The Association for Professional Law Enforcement." *Journal of Criminal Law, Criminology and Police Science* (1956-1957), pp. 601-604.

Spiro, D.W. "A High Yield, Low Risk Investment for Police Associations." *Law Officer,* 8:2 (1975), pp. 20-22.
Recommends police associations pool their capital for investment purposes.

Whitehouse, Jack E. "A Forward Look for Police Associations." *Law and Order,* 11:9 (September, 1963), pp. 8-9, 11, 13, 24.

IACP

Boyd, Brian S. "The Founding of the IACP—1893." *Police Chief,* XXXVII:5 (May, 1971), pp. 16-18.

Darwick, Norman. "IACP's Police Management Division: Proficient and Versatile." *Police Chief,* XLII:5 (May, 1975), pp. 44-46.

Garza, Manuel R. "IACP's Advisory Committee on International Policy." *Police Chief,* XLII:5 (May, 1975).

Hypes, Diane. "IACP Research Division: New Approaches to Crime Prevention." *Police Chief,* XLII:5 (May, 1975), pp. 40-42.

"IACP—Its History and Its Purpose." *Police Chief,* XXXII:10 (October, 1965).

Stone, Donald C. and Arnold Miles. "A Debt Acknowledged." *Police Chief,* XL:5 (May, 1973), pp. 30-31.

Thompson, John. "History of IACP: Progress and Delays Mark the Years 1930-1960." *Police Chief,* XL:5 (May, 1973), pp. 24-29.

ATTITUDES

Police Attitudes

Bernitt, Richard O. *A Study of the Attitudes Held by Police and Fire Chiefs and City Managers Toward the Integration of Police and Fire Services.* Unpub. Master's Thesis, Michigan State University, 1962.

Bolinger, Harry E. "Police Officers' Views on Collective Bargaining and Use of Sanctions." *Police Chief,* XLI:2 (February, 1974), pp. 39-42.

Bouma, Donald H. "Police Perceptions of Youth Hostility." *Law and Order,* 18:9 (September, 1970), pp. 46, 48, 50-51.

Bouma, Donald H. and Marie Vogel. "Police Riots and the Inner City." *Law and Order,* 16:5 (May, 1968), pp. 39-40.
Police attitudes towards riots, rioters and related subjects.

Chang, Dae H., Donald L. Blazicek and William Winter. "Jurisdictional Problems on Lake Michigan: A Special Reference to Police Perception and Attitude." *Police,* 16:4 (December, 1971), pp. 13-17.

Dynes, Russell R., E.R. Quaramtelli and James L. Ross. "Police Perspectives and Behavior in a Campus Disturbance." *Journal of Police Science and Administration,* 2:3 (September, 1974), pp. 344-351.

Goldhaber, Gerald M., Donna Fossum and Sally Black. "Police-Student Attitudes and Attitude Perceptions of Each Other." *Law and Order,* 20:4 (April, 1972), pp. 101-106.

Crawford, Thomas J. "Police Overperception of Ghetto Hostility." *Journal of Police Science and Administration,* 1:2 (June, 1973), pp. 168-174.

Groves, W.E. and Peter Rossi. "Police Perceptions of a Hostile Ghetto." *American Behavioral Scientist,* 13:5 (May-June, 1970); 13:6 (July-August, 1970).

Guller, Irving B. "Higher Education and Policemen: Attitudinal Differences between Freshmen and Senior Police College Students." *Journal of Criminal Law, Criminology and Police Science* (September, 1972), pp. 400-401.

Hahn, Harian. "Ghetto Assessments of Police Protection and Authority." *Law and Society Review,* 6:2 (November, 1971), pp. 183-194.

Huseman, R.C. and S.H. McCurley. "Police Attitudes toward Communication with Public." *Police Chief,* XXXIX:12 (December, 1972), pp. 68-73.

Kelly, Joseph A. and Thomas W. O'Rourke. "An Apprisal of the Attitudes of Police Officers toward the Concept of

Police-Community Relations." *Journal of Police Science and Administration,* 1:2 (June, 1973), pp. 224-231.

"The Law Enforcement Officer Speaks Out." *FBI Law Enforcement Bulletin* (April 1, 1970), pp. 16-22.
Police attitudes towards a wide variety of topics relating to police working conditions.

Lefkowitz, J. *Job Attitudes of Police.* Springfield, VA.: NTIS, 1971.
Assessment and relation of job attitudes of the 425 sworn patrolmen and command personnel of the Dayton police department to their personal history data.

Lentz, William P. "Police and Reference Group Attitudes Toward Delinquency Control." *Police,* 15:4 (March-April, 1971), pp. 27-28.

Lentz, William P. "Police Attitudes toward Delinquency Control." *Law and Order,* 17:6 (June, 1969), pp. 42-44.

Love, Harold D. "Attitudes and Knowledge of Non-Police and Policemen toward Law and Law Enforcement." *Police,* 16:1 (September, 1971), pp. 9-10.

Meyer, John C., Jr. "Both Sides Now." *Police Chief,* XXXIX:4 (April, 1972), pp. 68-75.
Police attitudes toward national union. Majority of those surveyed are opposed to a national union for police.

Meyer, John C., Jr. "Police Attitudes and Performance Appraisal: The Forest and Some Trees." *Journal of Police Science and Administration,* 1:2 (June, 1973), pp. 201-208.

Meyer, J.C., Jr. "Rank and File Perceptions of Police Employee Association Functions." *Police,* 16:5 (1972), pp. 47-52.

Oh, John C.H. "Police in a Midwestern Community." *Police,* 14:3 (January-February, 1970), pp. 53-58.
Police attitudes toward the courts and court decisions, violence, capital punishment and the role and status perceptions of police officers.

Olson, Bruce T. "Police Opinions of Work: An Exploratory Study." *Police Chief,* XXXVIII:7 (July, 1971), pp. 28-38.

Opinion Research Corporation. *Police-Community Relations: A Survey Among New York City Patrolmen.* Princeton, N.J.: Opinion Research, 1968.

Rafky, David M. "Police Race Attitudes and Labeling." *Journal of Police Science and Administration,* 1:1 (March, 1973), pp. 65-86.

Rafky, David M. et al. "Are Cops Prejudiced?" *Police Chief,* XL:3 (March, 1973), pp. 60-62.
Racial attitudes of police comparable with Americans in general.

Schafer, William J., III. "An Old Conditioned Reflex." *Police,* 13:4 (March-April, 1969), pp. 76-80.

Silverman, Harold. "Police Attitudes towards Community Relations Training." *Police Chief,* XXXV:6 (June, 1968), pp. 57-59.

Smith, Alexander B., Bernard Locke, and William F. Walker. "Authoritarianism in College and Non-College Oriented Police." *Journal of Criminal Law, Criminology and Police Science,* 58:1 (March, 1967), pp. 128-132.

Smith, D.C. and E. Ostrom. *Effects of Training and Education on Police Attitudes and Performance—A Preliminary Analysis.* Washington, D.C.: NCJRS (Microfiche), 1974.
Study illustrated that higher levels of education did not affect attitudes toward work, community and other factors.

Verinis, J.S. and Virgil Walker. "The Policeman and His Sensitivity to Crime." *Police Chief,* XXXVI:6 (June, 1969), pp. 32-34.

Wacker, John R. and Lyle Knowles. "Victimless Crimes: Perception and Attitudes of Television Writers, High School Teachers, and Police Officers." *Police Chief,* XLII:11 (November, 1975), pp. 38-39.

Watson, Nelson A. and James A. Sterling. *Police and Their Opinions.* Washington, D.C.: IACP, 1969.
Exhaustive survey on police attitudes on numerous aspects of law enforcement, crime, and criminal justice. Excellent study.

Wilson, James Q. "Police Morale, Reform, and Citizen Respect. The Chicago Case." in David J. Bordua, ed. *The Police.* N.Y.: Wiley, 1967.

Wilson, W.C. "Law Enforcement Officers' Perceptions of Pornography as a Social Issue." *Journal of Sociological Issues,* 29:3 (1973), pp. 41-52.

Citizen Attitudes

Abelson, H. "Public Attitudes and Experience with Erotic Materials." *Technical Reports of the Commission on Obscenity and Pornography,* vol. 4. Washington, D.C.: GPO, (1970), pp. 1-38.

Aberbach, Joel D. and Jack L. Walker. "Political Trust and Racial Ideology." *American Political Science Review,* 64 (December, 1970), pp. 1199-1219.
Blacks are generally lower on the political trust index than are whites. Some related items were examined and include personal experiences of police mistreatment.

"After the Riots: A Survey." *Newsweek* (August 21, 1967), pp. 18-19.

Allman, James J. "The Public Attitude toward Police." *Police Chief,* 30 (1963).

Almond, Gariel A. and Sidney Verba. *The Civic Culture.* Princeton: Princeton University Press, 1963.
An international study concerned with how people feel about their country and political affairs. Five countries were examined, U.S., Great Britain, Germany, Italy and Mexico. Among many other questions, the respondent was asked to imagine himself in minor trouble with the police and express his expectations in terms of being treated equally and considerately by the police. In all countries except Mexico, the police were viewed with as much or more favor than the general governmental authorities.

Amo, Michael E. and John R. Bittner. "College Student Attitudes toward Marijuana." *College Student Survey,* 4:2 (Fall, 1970), pp. 52-54.

Ball, John C. "Delinquent and Non-Delinquent Attitudes toward the Prevalence of Stealing." *Journal of Criminal Law, Criminology and Police Science,* 48:3 (September-October, 1957), pp. 259-274.

Bayley, David H. and Harold Mendelsohn. *Minorities and the Police: Confrontation in America.* N.Y.: Free Press, 1969.

Bearwood, R. "The New Negro Mood." Fortune Magazine, 77:1 (January, 1968), pp. 146-152.

Most respondents were more optimistic about employment, housing and general conditions. Majority endorsed aggressive nonviolent tactics, 69% expressed a desire for better police protection.

Berg, Dorothy F. *A Study of Citizens' Reaction to Crime in the District of Columbia and Adjacent Suburbs.* Washington, D.C.: Office of Crime Analysis Government of the District of Columbia, 1972.

Biderman, Albert D. "Surveys of Population Samples for Estimating Crime Incidence." *The Annals of the American Academy of Political and Social Science,* 374 (November, 1967), pp. 16-33.

This study found victimization to be far more common than suggested, by national or local statistics.

Biderman, Albert D. et al. *Report on a Pilot Study in the District of Columbia on Victimization and Attitudes Toward Law Enforcement.* Washington, D.C.: GPO, 1967.

Biderman, Albert D. et al. *Salient Findings on Crime and Attitudes Toward Law Enforcement in the District of Columbia.* Washington, D.C.: Bureau of Social Science Research, 1966.

Findings: 1) self-report of crime victimization greatly exceed police reports of crime; 2) safety is of major concern-advocated means of coping are better police protection, stricter law enforcement and more severe penalties; 3) in general, attitudes toward police are favorable; however, there is some dissent, due to disenchantment with the legal system; 4) in direct contacts with the police, people are usually satisfied, criticisms center mainly on lack of thoroughness or effectiveness. Also, there is the feeling that Negro citizens receive poorer treatment than Whites.

"Black and White: A Major Survey of U.S. Racial Attitudes Today." *Newsweek* (August 22, 1966).

Block, Richard L. "Fear of Crime and Fear of the Police." *Social Problems,* 19:1 (Summer, 1971), pp. 91-101.

Block, Richard L. *Police Action, Support for the Police and the Support for Civil Liberties.* Paper read at the American Sociological Association, Washington, D.C.: August, 1970.

Victims (both black and white) are more likely to support increases in the protection of civil liberties and less likely to support increased police power than non-victims. Police action has little effect on victim's support for police or protection of civil liberties. Since victimization appears to indicate failure of police protection (and thus caused a decrease in support), Block recommends strengthening of police efforts in the area of crime prevention.

Block, Richard L. "Support for Civil Liberties and Support for the Police." *American Behavioral Scientist,* 13:5-6 (May-August, 1970), pp. 781-796.

Boggs, Sarah L. "Formal and Informal Crime Control: An Exploratory Study of Urban, Suburban and Rural Orientations." *Sociological Quarterly,* 12 (Summer, 1971), pp. 319-327.

Central city residents, especially blacks, feel that violent crime is likely to happen. Rural and suburban residents rely more heavily on informal control than people in the central city. Formal controls are more important to urban population. Black central city residents feel more dependent on, but are less satisfied with, the kind of formal police protection they receive.

Bouma, D.H. *Kids and Cops—A Study in Mutual Hostility.* Grand Rapids: William B. Eerdmans, 1969.

Study of police-youth relations conducted among junior high age youth and police in three Michigan cities—Grand Rapids, Kalamazoo, and Muskegon Heights.

Bowen, John J. "A Driver Looks at Traffic Enforcement. *Journal of Criminal Law, Criminology and Police Science,* 57:2 (June, 1966), pp. 218-220.

Brink, William and Louis Harris. *Black and White.* N.Y.: Simon and Schuster, 1966.

Burbrink, R.D. *Analysis of Citizen Evaluations of the Bloomington (IN) Police Department—The Relationship Between Young People and the Police.* Washington, D.C.: NCJRS, (Microfiche).

Analysis revealed a disproportionately low estimation of police by those under age 30, and it is reasoned that a predominantly negative interaction with police and the wish for more permissive law enforcement are the causes.

Butler, Edgar W. et al. *Community Service Unit: First Report and Preliminary Evaluation.* Winston-Salem, N.C.: Winston-Salem Police Department, July, 1967.

Campbell, Angus. *White Attitudes Toward Black People.* Ann Arbor: University of Michigan, 1971.

Campbell, Angus and Howard Schuman. *Racial Attitudes in Fifteen American Cities.* Ann Arbor: Survey Research Center, Institute for Social Research, University of Michigan, 1970.

Cantril, A.H. and Charles W. Roll, Jr. *Hopes and Fears of the American People.* N.Y.: Universe, 1971.

A survey of public attitudes toward law and order, drugs, racial problems, national unrest and others.

Carte, Gene E. "Changes in Public Attitudes toward the Police: A Comparison of 1938 and 1971 Surveys." *Journal of Police Science and Administration,* 1:2 (June, 1973), pp. 182-200.

Casey, Edmund Joseph. *Citizen Attitudes Toward the Police and Law Enforcement.* Unpub. Doctoral Dissertation, St. Louis University, 1966.

Center for the Study of Crime, Delinquency and Corrections. *Police-Community Relations in Granite City Illinois.* Carbondale: Center for the Study of Crime, Delinquency and Corrections, Southern Illinois University, December, 1970.

Survey sample of 540 adults and 149 youths. 84% of the adults and 76% of the youths felt they do a "good job" in enforcing the law; 76% of the adults and 78% of the young people felt that police provide adequate protection for the community; and 42% of the adults were favorable toward their children entering a law enforcement career, 26% of the youths sampled expressed an interest in law enforcement as a career.

Cizanckas, Victor I. "Police Patrol for Black Americans." *Police Chief* (February, 1970).

A survey report of opinions expressed by a cross-section of Black Americans in Menlo Park Calif. The police needs and aspirations of Black Americans are very similar to those of White Americans.

Cizanckas, Victor I. and Carlton W. Purviance. "Changing Attitudes of Black Youths." *Police Chief,* XL:3 (March, 1973), pp. 42-45.

Clark, John P. and Eugene P. Wenniger. "The Attitudes of Juveniles toward the Legal Institution." *Journal of Criminal Law, Criminology and Police Science,* 55:4, pp. 482-489.

Coe, Rodney M. and Austin B. Duke. "Public Attitudes toward the Police." *Police,* 8:x (September-October, 1963), pp. 73-75.

Cohen, Nathan, ed. *The Los Angeles Riots: A Socio-Psychological Study.* N.Y.: Praeger, 1970.

Conklin, John E. *Public Reactions to Crime: A Survey of Two Communities.* Unpub. Doctoral Dissertation, Harvard University, 1969.

Conrad, J.P. *Crime and Its Correction—An International Survey of Attitudes and Practices.* Berkeley: University of California Press, 1969.

A survey of attitudes and various correctional methods used in treatment of offenders.

Conway, M. Margaret. *Public Opinion on Crime and Law Enforcement in the United States.* Washington, D.C.: Bureau of Social Science Research, June, 1971.

Coombs, Clyde H. "Thurstone's Measurement of Social Values Revisited Forty Years Later." *Journal of Personality and Social Psychology,* 6:1 (1967), pp. 5-91.

Longitudinal study (1927-1967) dealing with citizen attitude toward the seriousness of crime. Some of the findings include: 1) there was more homogeneity of attitudes toward the seriousness of crime 40 years ago than today; 2) offenses against the person are now judged relatively more serious and sex offenses relatively less so; and 3) offenses against property, with the exception of arson, are judged less serious relative to the others than they were 40 years ago. Some sex differences are noted.

Crosby, Robert and David Snyder. *Crime Victimization in the Black Community: Results of the Black Buyer Survey.* Bethesda, MD.: Resource Management Corporation, October, 1969.

Crosby, Robert and David Snyder. *Crime Victimization in the Black Community: Results of the Black Buyer II Survey.* Bethesda, MD.: Resource Management Corporation, February, 1970.

Derbyshire, Robert L. "Children's Perceptions of the Police: A Comparative Study of Attitudes and Attitude Change." *Journal of Criminal Law, Criminology and Police Science,* 59:2 (June, 1968), pp. 183-190.

Doleschal, Eugene. "Hidden Crime." *Crime Delinquency Literature,* 2:5 (October, 1970), pp. 546-568.

Dow, Thomas E., Jr. "The Role of Identification in Conditioning Public Attitude toward the Offender." *Journal of Criminal Law, Criminology and Police Science,* 58:1 (March, 1967), pp. 75-79.

Ennis, Philip H. *Victimization in the U.S.: A Report of a National Crime Survey:* Prepared for the President's Commission on Law Enforcement and the Administration of Justice. Field Surveys, II. Washington, D.C.: GPO, 1967.

Erskine, H. "The Polls: Recent Opinions of Racial Problems." *Public Opinion Quarterly,* 32 (Winter, 1968-1969), pp. 696-703.

Feagin, Joe R. "Home-Defense and the Police: Black and White Perspectives." *American Behavioral Scientist,* 13:5-6 (May-August, 1970), pp. 797-814.

Based on data from this study the author concludes that a majority of black and white Americans had to be prepared to defend their own against crime and violence, and that such protection could not be left to the police. Also noted was a growing tendency toward black and whites to arm themselves.

Funkhouser, G. Ray and David Popoff. "Your Thoughts on Crime and Punishment." *Psychology Today,* 3:6 (November, 1969), pp. 53-58.

Furstenberg, Frank F., Jr. "Public Reaction to Crime in the Streets." *American Scholar,* 40:4 (August, 1971), pp. 601-610.

Gallup, George. "Gallup Poll Shows Confidence of United States Public in Police Service." *Journal of California Law Enforcement* (January, 1968), pp. 130-131.

Gallup Incorporated. "The Public: A Hard Line." *Newsweek* (March 8, 1971).

This public opinion survey results indicate a widespread feeling that the system has deteriorated seriously over the past five years. Seventy-five percent of the respondents felt that the system's most serious failure is that criminals receive insufficient punishment; most were willing to grant the police board new power to facilitate a tougher system of justice. Factors most often selected as causes of crime were drug addiction and lack of parental discipline.

Gamson, William A. and James McEvoy. "Police Violence and Its Public Support." *Annals,* 391 (September, 1970), pp. 97-110.

Gardiner, John A. "Public Attitudes toward Gambling and Corruption." *Annals,* 374 (November, 1967), pp. 123-134.

Gardiner, John A. and David N. Olson. "Wincanton: The Politics of Corruption." *Task Force Report: Organized Crime,* Washington, D.C.: GPO, 1967.

Appendix B, pp. 61-79.

Gibbons, Don C. "Crime and Punishment: A Study in Social Attitudes." *Social Forces,* 47:4 (June, 1969), pp. 391-397.

Gibbons, Don C., Peter G. Garabedian, and Joseph Jones. *Opinions on Crime Problem, Due Process, and Related Matters—San Francisco and Portland.* Portland: Portland State University, [n.d.] (mimeo).

Gitchoff, G.T. "Police Response to Juvenile Hostility in Suburbia." *Police Chief* (January, 1971).

Glaeseman, Paul et al. *Black Attitudes Toward the Police: Ambivalence and Inconsistency.* Paper presented at the 21st annual meeting of the Society for the Study of Social Problems, Denver, Colorado: August, 1971.

Goldner, N.S. and R. Koenig. "White Middle-Class Attitudes toward an Urban Policeman's Union. A Survey of a Problem in Community-Police Relations." *Crime Delinquency,* 18:2 (1972), pp. 168-175.

Citizens highly critical of union activity.

Goode, Erich. "Multiple Drug Use among Marijuana

Smokers." *Social Problems,* 17:1 (Summery, 1969), pp. 48-64.

Study showed that among marijuana users, the use of drugs, other than marijuana, was more characteristic than it was exceptional. 68% had taken at least one other drug at least once.

Gourley, G.D. "Workshop on 'Law Enforcement, Public Schools' Reveals New Student Attitudes." *Journal of California Law Enforcement* (April, 1968), pp. 198-200.

Hahn, Harlan. "Cops and Rioters: Ghetto Perceptions of Social Conflict and Control." *American Behavioral Scientist,* 12:5-6 (May-August, 1970), pp. 761-779.

Hahn, Harlan. "Riot-Precipitating Police Practices: Attitudes in Urban Ghettos." *Phyon,* (Second Quarter, 1970), pp. 183-193.

Hahn, Harlan and Joe R. Feagin. "Philosophy of Law and Urban Violence." *Soundings,* LII:1 (Spring, 1969), pp. 110-117.

Data indicate that most residents have little respect for the legal system. Only 8 percent believed that the law was fair to all people; less than 5 percent thought that laws are equally enforced. Eighty-three percent felt that there was discrimination in police treatment of local people; the same proportion did not believe that policemen and local judges were totally honest.

Hampton, Peter J. "Student Attitudes towards Law and Order." *Law and Order,* 18:9 (September, 1970), pp. 34-37.

Harold Lewis Malt Associates. *An Analysis of Public Safety as Related to the Incidence of Crime in Parks and Recreation Areas in Central Cities.* Washington, D.C.: HUD, March, 1972.

Study showed that crime in parks was almost nonexistent, in an 11-city survey of police and park officials. However, citizens believed crime was widespread in parks and avoided using them.

Hartley, Eugene, Max Rosenbaum, and Alvin Snadowsky. "Crime as Seen by Psychotherapists." *Police,* 12:1 (September-October, 1967), pp. 77-80.

Hindelang, Michael J. "Public Opinion Regarding Crime, Criminal Justice, and Delinquency." *Journal of Research in Crime and Delinquency* (1973).

Hirsch, Herbert and Donohew Lewis. "A Note on Negro-White Differences in Attitudes toward the Supreme Court." *Social Science Quarterly,* 49:3 (December, 1968), pp. 557-563.

Blacks perceive the Supreme Court positively, and white view it negatively.

Hulin, Charles L. and Brendan A. Maher. "Changes in Attitudes toward Law Concomitant with Imprisonment." *Journal of Criminal Law, Criminology and Police Science,* 50:3 (September/October, 1959), pp. 245-248.

Institute for Community Studies. *Evaluation of the Community Action Program of Kansas City, Missouri.* 2 vols. Kansas City: Institute for Community Studies, November, 1969.

Institute for Local Self-Government. *Criminal Victimization in Maricopa County.* Berkeley: Institute for Local Self-Government, June, 1969.

Compared citizens reporting of Part I and Part II crimes. In this sample almost two thirds had never been victimized. 79% of Part I crimes were reported to police and only 43% of Part II crimes were reported to police.

Institute of Governmental Affairs. *Factors Contributing to the Police Image and Police-Community Relations in Four Wisconsin Cities.* Madison: Institute of Governmental Affairs: University of Wisconsin University Extension, 1967.

Iowa Urban Community Research Center. *A Guide to Surveys in the Data Bank of the Iowa Urban Community Research Center.* Iowa City: University of Iowa, [n.d.].

Davenport residents' opinion were solicited regarding present services of the area, including police protection and court services, the quality of educational resources, recreation, shopping, etc. Respondents were also questioned about the needs of the city and their perception of the extent of selected problems including narcotic addiction, youth gangs, gambling, vandalism, organized crime and disrespect for laws.

Jacob, Herbert. "Black and White Perceptions of Justice in the City." *Law and Society Review,* 6:1 (August, 1971), pp. 69-89.

Jacob, Herbert. *Questionnaire: Citizen Reaction to Public Officials.* Madison: Survey Research Laboratory, University of Wisconsin, 1969.

Jacob, Herbert. *Questionnaire: Study of Citizen Attitudes—Milwaukee.* Madison: Survey Research Laboratory, University of Wisconsin, 1969.

Joint Commission on Correctional Manpower and Training. *Public Looks at Crime and Corrections.* College Park, MD.: American Correctional Association. [n.d.].

Survey of public attitudes toward corrections, contact with ex-offenders and corrections as a career.

Justice, Blair. *Violence in the City.* Fort Worth: Texas Christian University, 1969.

Kaminskaya, V.I. and I.B. Michajlovskaya. *Public Opinion About Criminal Justice.* Paper presented to the Working Committee of Sociology of Law 7th World Congress of Sociology, Varna: Bulgaria, September, 1970.

Kay, Barbara A. "Can You Change This Image?" *Police,* 10:2 (November-December, 1965), pp. 30-32.

Attitudes of male and female felony offenders toward the police and legal institutions.

Kinsey, Barry A. "The Police and Public Opinion." *Police,* 4:2 (November-December, 1959), pp. 78-80.

Kuchel, G.L. and A.P. Pattavina. "Juveniles Look at Their Police." *Police,* 13:4 (March-April, 1969), pp. 13-17.

Kuchel, G.L. and A.P. Pattavina. "Polling the Public." *Police Chief,* XXXVI:3 (March, 1969), pp. 27-35.

Survey to determine citizen attitude about the Omaha Police Department.

Levy, Sheldon G. "The Psychology of Political Activity." *Annals,* 391 (September, 1970), pp. 83-96.

Losciuto, L. et al. "Methodological Reports on a Study of Public Attitudes toward and Experience with Erotic Materials." *Technical Reports of the Commission on Obscenity and Pornography.* vol. 4, Washington, D.C.: GPO (1970), pp. 139-256.

Louis, Harris and Associates. *The Public Looks at Crime and Corrections.* Washington, D.C.: Joint Commission on Correctional Manpower and Training, February, 1968.

Love, Harold D. "Attitudes and Knowledge of the Public Concerning Drug Abuse." *Police,* 15:3 (January-February, 1971), pp. 39-40.

McCaghy, C.H. *Nature and Correlates of Criticism of Police.* Washington, D.C.: NCJRS, (Microfiche) [n.d.].

McCaghy, Charles H., Irving L. Allen, and David J. Colfax. "Public Attitudes toward City Police in a Middle-Sized Northern City." *Journal of the American Society of Criminology,* 6 (May 1, 1968).

Hartford, Connecticut residents were generally very satisfied with their police; non-whites were more critical of the police than whites; and the primary source of dissatisfaction among the respondents was a perceived inability or unwillingness of the police to act as law enforcers.

McClain, J. Dudley. "How the New College-Age Voters in Texas View the Right of Policemen to Unionize and Strike." *Police Chief,* XXXIV:11 (November, 1972), pp. 67-79.

McIntyre, Hennie. "Public Attitudes toward Crime and Law Enforcement." *Annals,* 374 (November, 1967), pp. 34-46.

Mathias, W.J. *Citizen Perceptions Toward Law Enforcement in the Model Neighborhood Area of Atlanta, Georgia.* Unpub. Doctoral Dissertation. University of Georgia, Athens: 1969.

Mathias, W.J. "The Ghetto Resident's View of Police Procedure and Their Constitutionality." *Police Chief,* XXXVII:5 (May, 1971), pp. 64-67.

Mathias, W.J. "Perceptions of Crime by Model Neighborhood Residents in Atlanta, Georgia." *Police,* 15:6 (July-August, 1971), pp. 60-65.

Mathias, William J. "Perceptions of Police Relationships with Ghetto Citizens." *Police Chief* (April, 1971).

Maxwell, N. "Passing Judgment: How Little Town Reacts When Banker is Accused of Taking $4.7 Million." *The Wall Street Journal* (August, 1972).

Mendelsohn, Harold and Irving Crespi. *Polls, Television and the New Politics.* Scranton, PA.: Chandler, 1970.

Moynahan, J.M. "Perceptions of Police Legal Powers." *Police Law Quarterly,* 2:4 (1973), pp. 5-8.

Comparison of the attitudes of firemen, students, teachers, probation and parole officers and jail inmates. General criticism of legal restrictions, lack of police power and lack of authority to make searches.

Murphy, Walter F. and Joseph Tanenhaus. "Public Opinion and Supreme Court: The Goldwater Campaign." *Public Opinion Quarterly,* XXXII:1 (Spring, 1968), pp. 31-50.

Mylonas, Anatassios D. and Walter D. Reckless. "Prisoners' Attitudes toward Law Legal Institutions." *Journal of Criminal Law, Criminology and Police Science,* 54:4 (December, 1963), pp. 479-4S4.

Neyhart, Amos E. "Driver Attitudes." *Police,* 4:2 (November-December, 1959), pp. 31-34.

O'Mahony, Francis. "Why Hate Cops?" *American Mercury,* 88 (June, 1959), pp. 112-116.

Ostrom, Elinor and Gordon Whitaker. *Does Local Community Control of Police Make a Difference? Some Preliminary Findings.* Prepared for presentation at the Western Political Science Association meeting. Albuquerque, N.M.: April 8-10, 1971.

Portune, R. *An Analysis of the Attitudes of Junior High School Pupils Toward Police Officers.* Cincinnati: University of Cincinnati, 1965.

Portune, R. *Pupil Attitude Toward Police in the Cincinnati Public Schools.* Cincinnati: University of Cincinnati, 1970.

"Public Poll Gives Strong Support to FBI." *FBI Law Enforcement Bulletin,* 35:10 (October, 1966), p. 14.

Reiss, Albert J. and Donald J. Black. *Studies in Crime and Law Enforcement in Major Metropolitan Areas.* vols. 1 and 2. Washington, D.C.: GPO, 1967.

This report includes four studies: 1) measurement of the nature and the amount of crime; 2) public perceptions and recollections about crime, law enforcement, and criminal justice; 3) patterns of behavior in police and citizen transactions; 4) career orientations, job satisfaction, and the assessment of law enforcement problems by police officers.

Rektor, B. "Citizens' Consensus." *Police,* 16:4 (December, 1971), pp. 54-55.

Citizen-edited survey about quality of police service.

Richardson, Richard J. et al. *Perspectives on the Legal Justice System, Public Attitudes and Criminal Victimization.* Chapel Hill: Institute for Research in Social Science, Manning Hall, University of North Carolina, 1972.

Robinson, J.P. "Public Reaction to Political Protest: Chicago, 1968." *Public Opinion Quarterly,* 34 (Spring, 1970), pp. 1-9.

Rogers, B.D. and C.M. Lipsey. *Metropolitan Reform—Citizen Evaluations of Performances in Nashville—Davidson County, Tennessee.* Washington, D.C.: NCJTS, (Microfiche) [n.d.].

Roll, Charles W., Jr. and Albert H. Cantril. *Polls: Their Use and Misuse in Politics.* N.Y.: Basic, 1972.

Schneph, V. *Study of Political Socialization in a Subculture, Negro Children's Knowledge of and Attitudes Toward the Police, Law and Freedom.* Ann Arbor, MI.: University Microfilms, 1966.

Attempt to ascertain to what extent children acquired a commitment to or were socialized to accept the legal aspects of the political system.

Shaw, M. and W. Williamson. "Public Attitudes to the Police." *Criminologist,* 7 (1972), pp. 18-23.

Simon, R.J. and W. Shackelford. "The Defense of Insanity: A Survey of Legal and Psychiatric Opinion." *Public Opinion Quarterly,* 29 (Fall, 1965), pp. 411-430.

Small Business Administration. *Crime Against Small Business.* A Report transmitted to the Select Committee on Small Business, United States Senate. Washington, D.C. GPO, April 3, 1969.

Smigel, Erwin O. "Public Attitudes toward 'Chiseling' with Respect to Unemployment Compensation." *American Sociological Review,* 18 (January, 1953), pp. 59-67.

Smith, P.E. and R.O. Hawkins. "Victimization, Types of Citizen-Police Contacts, and Attitudes towards the Police." *Law and Society Review,* 8:1 (1973), pp. 135-152.

Toro-Calder, Jaime, Cefering Cedeno, and Walter C. Reckless. "A Comparative Study of Puerto Rican Attitudes toward the Legal System Dealing with Crime." *Journal of Criminal Law, Criminology and Police Science,* 59:4 (December, 1968), pp. 535-541.

Trubowitz, Julius. *Changing the Racial Attitudes of Children: The Effects of an Activity Group Program in New York City Schools.* N.Y.: Praeger, 1969.

Turner, Anthony G. "The San Jose Methods Test of Known Crime Victims." *Statistical Division Technical Series—Report, No. 1.* Washington, D.C.: LEAA (July, 1971).

Udell, Jon G. and Robert S. Smith. "Attitudes and the Usage of Other Drugs among Users and Nonusers of Marijuana in High School Population." *Wisconsin Project Reports* 4: (October, 1969).

Udell, Jon G. and Robert S. Smith. "Attitudes, Usage and Availability of Drugs among Wisconsin High School Students." *Wisconsin Project Reports,* 4:1 (July, 1969).

University of Cincinnati. *Key City Police—Juvenile Attitude Project.* Washington, D.C.: NCJRS, 1969.

Veysey, Laurence R. *Law and Resistance: American Attitudes Toward Authority.* N.Y.: Harper and Row, 1970.

Watt, Norman and Brendan A. Maher. "Prisoners' Attitudes toward Home and the Judicial System." *Journal of Criminal Law, Criminology and Police Science,* 49:4 (November-December, 1958), pp. 327-330.

Wattenberg, William W. "Changing Attitudes toward Authority." *Police,* 7:3 (January-February, 1963), pp. 34-37.

"What's Bothering Americans: A Nationwide Survey." *U.S. News and World Report* (October, 1970), pp. 32-36.

Wheeler, Michael. *Lies, Damn Lies, and Statistics.* N.Y.: Liveright, 1976.
Exposure of opinion poll-taking in the U.S.

White, David Manning and Lewis D. Barnett. "College Students' Attitudes on Pornography." *Technical Reports on the Commission of Obscenity and Pornography,* vol. 1. Washington, D.C.: GPO (1970), pp. 181-184.

Wilcox, Allen and Leonard Weinberg. *Nevada Public Opinion Survey.* Reno: Bureau of Governmental Research, University of Nevada, 1968.
Issues of the day that were of concern to the respondents were attitudes toward the Supreme Court, solution to the crime problem, student demonstration, permissible law breaking and wire tapping by police.

Wirths, Claudine Gibson. "The Development of Attitudes toward Law Enforcement." *Police,* 3 (November/December, 1958), pp. 50-52.

Yankelovich, Daniel. "What They Believe." *Fortune* (January, 1969).

Zeitz, Leonard. "Survey of Negro Attitudes to Law." *Rutgers Law Review,* XIX (1965).

BOUNTIES

Barrett, James E. "Bank Robbery Reward Program—Stimulating Public Interest and Assistance!" *FBI Law Enforcement Bulletin* (December, 1975), pp. 9-12.

"Bounties Offered for Tips Leading to Convictions of Heroin Pushers." *National Observer* (September 27, 1971).

Phillips, James R. "Should Law Enforcement Be Excluded from 'Bounty' Provisions?" *Police Chief,* XL:1 (January, 1973), pp. 51-59.

CIVIL LIABILITIES OF POLICE

Alberta, Mark E. and Keith M. Werban. "Federal Cause of Action Against a Municipality for Fourth Amendment Violations by Its Agents." *George Washington Law Review* (April, 1974), pp. 850-868.

Blalock, Joyce. *Civil Liability of Law Enforcement Officers.* Springfield, IL.: C.C. Thomas, 1974.
Discussion of civil liability of policemen, supervisors, and others in the criminal justice system—jailers, guards, wardens, national guardsmen, and private police.

Blalock, Joyce. "Civil Liability of Officers." *FBI Law Enforcement Bulletin,* 41:2 (February, 1972), pp. 6-8, 29-30.

Chodos, Hillel. "Pleading Problems in Police Malpractice Cases." *Law in Transition,* 11 (1965).

Dakin, Carol F. "Municipal Immunity in Police Torts." *Cleveland—Marshall Law Review,* 14 (1965).

"Defense of Police Officers at Municipal Expense." *Public Management,* 31 (September, 1949).

Foote, Caleb. "Tort Remedies for Police Violations of Individual Rights." *Minnesota Law Review,* 39 (1955).

Ford, William D. "A Legislative Proposal." *Police Chief,* XXXIX:12 (December, 1972), pp. 66-67.
Cohgressman advocates the use of federal funds to indemnify law enforcement officers for the cost of defending frivolous civil actions.

Ichord, Richard H. "A Legislative Proposal: Preventing the Frivolous Civil Rights Lawsuit against Police." *Police Chief,* XXXIX:7 (July, 1972), pp. 34-35.

Knoohuizen, Ralph, Thomas R. Meites, and Deborah Palmer, eds. *Legal Materials on Police Misconduct and Civil Damage Actions in Federal Courts.* Evanston, IL.: Chicago Law Enforcement Study Group, 1972.

Lanning, Jay D. "Liability of Private Person Assisting Police Officers." *Police,* 15:2 (November-December, 1970), pp. 35-37.

"Liability of the Police Administrator for Property Damage During Riots." *Police Chief* (February, 1970).

May, Michael and Lewis R. Titus, Jr. "Sovereign Immunity and Law Suits against Peace Officers." *Journal of California Law Enforcement,* 10:4 (April, 1976), pp. 127-130.

"Measuring Damages for Violations of Individuals' Constitutional Rights." *Valparaiso University Law Review,* 8:2 (1974), pp. 357-373.

"1963 Today." *FBI Law Enforcement Bulletin* (October, 1968), pp. 19-22.

"Police Chief Not Liable for Damages During Riot in Pampano Beach." *Police Chief* (May, 1970).

Rich, B.A. *Sovereign, Immunity—The Liability of Government and Its Officials.* Washington, D.C.: NCJRS, 1975.

Schmidt, Wayne W. *Survey of Police Misconduct Litigation, 1967-1971.* Evanston, IL.: Americans for Effective Law Enforcement, Inc., 1974.

Sheehan, Thomas M. "Municipal Liability for Excessive Use of Force by the Police." *Police* (May-June, 1967).

Sulnick, Robert H. *Civil Litigation and the Police: A Method of Communication.* Springfield, IL.: C.C. Thomas, 1976.

"Tort Remedies for Police Violations of Individual Rights." *Minnesota Law Review,* 39 (April, 1955), pp. 493-516.

Turchin, Marc E. and David J. Lee. "Civil Liability of Police Officers." *Journal of California Law Enforcement,* 9:3 (January, 1975), pp. 121-125.

Wahlen, Howard. "Defending Police against Lawsuits." *Police Chief,* 29:4 (April, 1962).

Walters, Douglas M. "Civil Liability for Improper Police Training." *Police Chief,* XXXVIII:11 (November, 1971), pp. 28-36.

CIVIL RIGHTS

Civil Rights—General

Abernathy, M. Glenn. *Civil Liberties Under the Constitution.* N.Y.: Dodd, Mead, 1968.

Allen, R.C. *Legal Rights of the Disabled and Disadvantaged.* Washington, D.C.: GPO, [n.d.].

Aron, Raymond. *An Essay on Freedom.* N.Y.: World, 1970.

Asch, Sidney H. *Police Authority and the Rights of the Individual.* N.Y.: Arco, 1967.

Barker, Lucius Jefferson. *Freedoms, Courts, Politics: Studies in Civil Liberties.* Englewood Cliffs, N.J.: Prentice Hall, 1965.

Beddard, Ralph. *Human Rights and Europe: A Study of the Machinery of Human Rights: Protection of the Council of Europe.* London: Sweet and Maxwell, 1973.

Berger, Morroe. *Equality by Statute—The Revolution in Civil Rights.* Garden City, N.Y.: Doubleday, [n.d.].

Bowes, Stuart. *The Police and Civil Liberties.* London: Lawrence and Weshart, 1966.

Burke, Joan Martin. *Civil Rights.* 2nd ed. N.Y.: Bowker, 1974.

Caldwell, Arthur B. "The Police and the Citizen—Individual Rights vs. Common Security." *Police,* 7:2 (November-December, 1962), pp. 77-81.

Capaldi, Nicholas, ed. *Clear and Present Danger: The Free Speech Controversy.* N.Y.: Pegasus, 1970.

Carr, Robert K. *Federal Protection of Civil Rights: Quest for a Sword.* Ithaca, N.Y.: Cornell University Press, 1947.

Chafee, Zechariah. *Freedom of Speech.* N.Y.: Harcourt, 1920.

Chapple, Norman L. "Freedom of Assembly—Constitutional Right or Lynch Law?" *Journal of Criminal Law, Criminology and Police Science,* 55:3 (September, 1964), pp. 425-433.

"Civil Liberties and Police Power." *Commonwealth* (April 3, 1964).

Clark, Donald E. "Minority Group Rights and the Police." *Police Chief,* 32 (March, 1965), pp. 43-45.

Clowers, Norman L. "Prejudice and Discrimination in Law Enforcement." *Police,* 8:2 (November-December, 1963), pp. 50-54 (January-February, 1964).

Conway, Edward J. "Equality Before the Law." *Interracial Review* (August, 1954), pp. 132-135.

Convitz, Milton R. *Fundamental Liberties of a Free People: Religion, Speech, Press, Assembly.* Ithaca, N.Y.: Cornell University Press, 1957.

Cook, J.G. *Constitutional Rights of the Accused—Pre-Trial Rights (With 1974 Supplement).* Rochester, N.Y.: Lawyers Co-Operative Publishing, 1972.
Survey of the development of federal constitutional protections for persons accused of crimes and of the current dimensions of these protections.

Cray, Ed. "The Police and Civil Rights." *Frontier,* 13:8 (1962).

Creamer, J. Shane. *A Citizen's Guide to Legal Rights.* N.Y.: Holt, Rinehart and Winston, 1971.

Cross, Granville J. "The Negro, Prejudice, and the Police." *Journal of Criminal Law, Criminology and Police Science* (September, 1964).

Cushman, Robert E. *Civil Liberties in the United States.* Ithaca, N.Y.: Cornell University Press, 1956.

Davidson, Mattew. "The Negro and the Police: Facing a Vital Problem." *Negro Digest* (April, 1965).

Duchacek, Ivo D. *Rights and Liberties in the World Today.* Santa Barbara, CA.: Clio, 1973.
Comparative analysis of bills of rights around the world.

Edwards, George E. "Order and Civil Liberties: A Complex Role for the Police." *Michigan Law Review,* 64 (1965).

Emerson, Thomas I. and David Haber. *Political and Civil Rights in the United States.* 2 vols. Buffalo, N.Y.: Dennis, 1959.

Ennis, Bruce and Loren Siegel. *The Rights of Mental Patients.* N.Y.: Dutton, 1973.

Ennis, Edward J. "Police Protections of Civil Rights—An Opportunity and a Challenge." *Police* (July-August, 1965), pp. 80-82.

Equal Employment Opportunity Commission, 7th Annual Report. Washington, D.C.: GPO, 1973.

Fellman, David. *Constitutional Right of Association.* Chicago: University of Chicago Press, 1963.

Fellman, David. *The Defendant's Rights Today.* Madison: University of Wisconsin Press, 1976.

Fellman, David. *The Defendant's Rights Under English Law.* Madison: University of Wisconsin Press, 1966.

Fraenkel, Osmond Kessler. *The Rights We Have.* N.Y.: Crowell, 1974.

Friedman, Leon, ed. *Southern Justice.* N.Y.: Random House, 1965.

Gay, Peter B. and Richard H. Prunier. *The Policeman and the Accused.* Cambridge, MA.: University of Cambridge Press, 1966.

Gelhorn, Walter. *American Rights: The Constitution in Action.* N.Y.: Macmillan, 1960.

Gelhorn, Walter. *Individual Freedom and Governmental Restraints.* Baton Rouge: Louisiana State University Press, 1956.

Gillers, Stephen. *Getting Justice: The Rights of People.* N.Y.: Basic, 1971.

Gross, Zenith and Alan Reitman. *Police Power and Citizen's Rights.* N.Y.: ACLU, 1967.

Gubler, B.H. *Constitutional Analysis of the Criminal Jurisdiction and Procedural Guarantees of the American Indian.* Washington, D.C.: NCJRS (Microfiche), 1963.

A legal examination of cases that bear on constitutional guarantees and jurisdictional disputes concerning the American Indian with references to historical precedents.

Herman, Lawrence. *Right to Counsel in Misdemeanor Court.* Columbus: Ohio State University Press, 1974.

Hill, Alfred. "The Bill of Rights and the Supervisory Power." *Columbia Law Review,* 69 (1969), pp. 181-215.

King, Donald B., ed. *Legal Aspects of the Civil Rights Movement.* Detroit, MI.: Wayne State University Press, 1965.

Kluchesky, Joseph T. *Police Action in Minority Problems.* N.Y.: Freedom House, 1946.

Konvitz, Milton R. *Expanding Liberties: Freedom's Gains in Postwar America.* N.Y.: Viking, 1966.

Lazarus, Arthur, Jr. "An Indian Bill of Rights." *North Dakota Law Review,* 45:3 (Spring, 1969), pp. 337-352.

Leeke, William D. "Some Aspects of the Effects of Inmate Suits on Correctional Systems." *FBI Law Enforcement Bulletin,* 43:7 (July, 1974), pp. 10-15.

Lindman, Frank T. and Donald M. McIntire. *The Mentally Disabled and the Law; The Report on the Rights of the Mentally Ill.* Chicago: University of Chicago Press, [n.d.].

Long, H.A. "The Dilemma: Crime and Constitutional Rights." *Police Chief,* 32:6 (June, 1965).

McCord, John. *With All Deliberate Speed: Civil Rights Theory and Reality.* Urbana: University of Illinois Press, 1969.

Maddison, J.C. "Civil Liberties and the Police." *Australian Journal of Forensic Science* (June, 1974), pp. 254-260.

Marnell, William H. *The First Amendment: The History of Religious Freedom in America.* Garden City, N.Y.: Doubleday, 1964.

Mayers, Lewis. *Shall We Amend the Fifth Amendment?* N.Y.: Harper, 1959.

Maylan, Charles E., Jr. *Right of the People to be Secure—An Examination of the Fourth Amendment.* Houston, TX.: National College of District Attorneys, College of Law, 1976.

Metager, Walter P. et al. *Dimensions of Academic Freedom.* Urbana: University of Illinois Press, 1968.

Newman, Edwin. *Civil Liberty and Civil Rights.* Dobbs Ferry, N.Y.: Oceana, 1964.

Newman, Edwin. *Police, The Law and Personal Freedom.* Dobbs Ferry, N.Y.: Oceana, 1964.

O'Neil, Robert M. *Free Speech: Responsible Communications Under Law.* 2nd ed. Indianapolis, IN.: Bobbs, 1972.

Palmer, J.W. *Constitutional Rights of Prisoners.* Cincinnati: Anderson, 1973.

Guide and reference manual for those actively involved in the correctional process, to familiarize them with the law and recent cases on prisoner rights.

Parker, W.H. "The Police Role in Civil Rights." *Los Angeles Bar Bulletin* (January, 1965).

Pious, Richard M. *Civil Rights and Liberties in the 1970's.* N.Y.: Random, 1973.

Powell, Lewis F. "Civil Liberties Repression: Fact or Fiction?" *FBI Law Enforcement Bulletin,* 40:10 (October, 1971), pp. 9-12.

Purcell, Philip. "Civil Rights." *Police,* 10:3 (January-February, 1966), pp. 92-93.

"Racial Violence and Civil Rights Law Enforcement." *University of Chicago Law Review* (Summer, 19510, pp. 769-783.

Reder, M.W. "Citizen Rights and the Cost of Law Enforcement." *Journal of Legal Studies,* 3:2 (1974), pp. 435-455.

"Rights of the Accused." *FBI Law Enforcement Bulletin,* 35:9 (September, 1966), pp. 21-25.

"Rights of the Accused—Their True Basis." *Phillipine Law Journal,* 31 (February, 1956).

"The Right to a Public Trial vs. the Protection of Public Morals." *Journal of Criminal Law, Criminology and Police Science,* 45:4 (November/December, 1954), pp. 449-456.

Rodgers, Jack W. "Civil Liberties and Law Enforcement." *Police,* 5:6 (July-August, 1961), pp. 10-14; (September-October, 1961), pp. 45-51.

Rosengart, Oliver and Gail Weinheimer. *Rights of Suspects.* N.Y.: Avon, 1974.

Rudovsky, D. *Rights of Prisoners—The Basic ACLU (American Civil Liberties Union) Guide to a Prisoner's Rights.* N.Y.: Avon, 1973.

Designed for use by the prison inmate and other non-specialists, this book sets forth prisoner's rights and suggests how they can be protected.

Schroeder, Oliver, Jr. "New Procedures of Scientific Investigation and the Accused's Rights." *Journal of Criminal Law, Criminology and Police Science,* 49:3 (September-October, 1958), pp. 265-275.

Schroeder, Theodore A. *Constitutional Free Speech Defined and Defended.* N.Y.: Da Capo, 1919. (Repr.)

Schulz, Leonard F. "Gault Decision and the Police." *Police,* 13:1 (September-October, 1968), pp. 46-48.

Stemm, Paul G. "The Role of Common Law Concepts in Modern Criminal Jurisprudence (A Symposium): II. Infamy and the Officer Holder." *Journal of Criminal Law, Criminology and Police Science,* 49:3 (September-October, 1958), pp. 250-255.
Discusses whether a person who has been convicted of various crimes is fit to hold public office.

Sterling, Dorothy. *Tear Down the Walls: A History of the American Civil Rights Movement.* N.Y.: Doubleday, 1968.

Storey, Robert G. *Our Unalienable Rights.* Springfield, IL.: C.C. Thomas, 1965.

Tetu, P.R. *Within the Law—A Handbook on Civil Liberties for the Law Enforcement Officer.* South Berlin, MA.: Research, 1972.
Constitutional background of civil liberties problem is illustrated by Supreme Court decisions on relationship of rights of citizens and police powers of states.

U.S. Commission on Civil Rights. *Law Enforcement: A Report on Equal Protection in the South.* Washington, D.C.: GPO, 1965.

U.S. Commission on Civil Rights. *Mexican Americans and the Administration of Justice in the Southwest.* Washington, D.C.: GPO, 1965.

Van Dyke, Vernon. *Human Rights, The United States and World Community.* N.Y.: Oxford University Press, 1970.

Williamson, E.G. and John L. Cowan. *The American Students' Freedom of Expression: A Research Appraisal.* Minneapolis: University of Minnesota Press, 1966.

Williamson, J.L. "The Right to Counsel at Pretrial Photographic Identification." *FBI Law Enforcement Bulletin,* 41:6 (1972), pp. 25-29.

Wolk, Allan. *Presidency and Black Civil Rights: Eisenhower to Nixon.* Cranbury, N.J.: Fairleigh Dickenson, 1971.

Zander, M. "Informing the Suspect of His Rights in a Police Station." *Law Society's Gazette,* 69 (1972).

Zarr, Melvin. *The Bill of Rights and the Police.* Dobbs Ferry, N.Y.: Oceana, 1970.

Zeichner, Irving B. "The Police Image." *Law and Order,* 11:8 (August, 1963), pp. 12-13.
Civil rights of arrested persons.

Privacy

Breckenridge, Adam. *The Right to Privacy.* Lincoln: University of Nebraska, 1970.

Brenton, Myron. *The Privacy Invaders.* N.Y.: Coward-McCann, 1964.

Brown, Robert M. *The Electronic Invasion.* N.Y.: John F. Rider, [n.d.].

Brucker, Herbert. *Freedom of Information.* N.Y.: MacMillan, 1949.

The Computer and Invasion of Privacy. N.Y.: Arno, 1967.

"Computer Data Bank—Privacy Controversy Revisited: An Analysis and Administrative Proposal." *Catholic University Law Review* (Spring, 1973).

"The Constitutional Right of Privacy: An Examination." *Northwestern University Review,* 69:2 (1974), pp. 263-301.

Davis, D.L. et al., eds. *Surveillance, Dataveillance and Personal Freedoms. Use and Abuse of Information Technology.* Fair Lawn, N.J.: R.E. Burdick, 1973.

DeBalogh, Frank G. "Public Administrators and 'The Privacy Thing': A Time to Speak Out." *Public Administration Review* (September/October, 1972), pp. 526-530.

Dixon, R.G. et al. *Right of Privacy: A Symposium.* N.Y.: Da Capo, 1971.

Ernst, Morris L. and Alan W. Schwartz. *The Right to Be Let Alone.* N.Y.: Macmillan, 1962.

Gotlieb, A.E. "Computers and Privacy." *Journal of Canadian Bar Association,* (October, 1971).

Great Britain Committee on Privacy. *Report of the Committee on Privacy Presented to Parliament by the Security of State for the Home Dept, The Lord High Chancellor and the Sec. of State for Scotland by Command of Her Majesty, July 1962.* London: HMSO, 1972.

Gross, Hyman. *Privacy, Its Legal Protection.* Dobbs Ferry, N.Y.: Oceana, 1964.

Henderson, Robert P. "Controlling the Computer's Threat to Privacy." *Michigan Business Review* (November, 1971), pp. 9-14.

Kerbec, Matthew. *Legally Available U.S. Government Information as a Result of the Public Information Act.* Arlington, VA.: Output Systems, 1970.

Long, Edward V. *The Intruders: The Invasion of Privacy by Government and Industry.* N.Y.: Praeger, 1967.

Massachusetts Governor's Commission on Privacy and Personal Data. *Massachusetts—Governor's Commission on Privacy and Personal Data—Report of the Director, November 1974.* Washington, D.C.: NCJRS (Microfiche), 1974.

Mayer, M.F. *Rights of Privacy.* N.Y.: Law-Arts, 1972.
The response of American courts to cases of an individual's right to privacy.

Meldman, J.A. "Centralized Information Systems and the Legal Right to Privacy." *Marquette Law Review* (Winter, 1972).

Messick, Hank. *Secret File.* N.Y.: Putnam, 1969.

Metz, D.W. "A Special Vigilance." *FBI Law Enforcement Bulletin,* 44:3 (1975), pp. 7-11.
Description of the federal privacy committee which reviews the need for privacy protections by agencies of the federal government.

Miller, A.R. "Computer Data Banks and Individual Privacy: An Overview." *Columbia Human Rights Law Review* (Winter, 1972).

Miller, A.R. "Personal Privacy in the Computer Age: The Challenge of a New Technology in an Information-

Oriented Society." *Michigan Law Review* (April, 1969).

Miller, Richard. "Computers and the Law of Privacy." *Datamation* (September, 1968), pp. 49-55.

Packard, Vance. *The Naked Society*. N.Y. MacKay, 1964.

Pipe, G.R. "Privacy: Establishing Restrictions on Government Inquiry." *American University Law Review* (June, 1969).

Police Foundation. *Model Rules—Release of Arrest and Conviction Records—Project on Law Enforcement Policy and Rulemaking—Approved Draft. (Rev.) June, 1974.* Tempe: Arizona State University, 1974.

Prisendorf, Anthony. "The Computer vs. the Bill of Rights." *Nation* (October 31, 1966).

Privacy—The Control of Personal Information. Columbus, OH.: Xeros Education, 1971.

Prosser, William L. "Privacy." *California Law Review,* 48 (1960).

Raines, John C. *Attack on Privacy.* Valley Forge, PA.: Judson, 1974.

Rehnquist, W.H. "Is an Expanded Right of Privacy Consistent with Fair and Effective Law Enforcement? Or: Privacy, You've Come a Long Way, Baby." *Kansas Law Review,* 23:1 (1974), pp. 1-22.

"Rights to Privacy and Police Effectiveness." *Police Chief,* XL:P6 (June, 1974).

Rosenberg, Jerry M. *The Death of Privacy.* N.Y.: Random House, 1969.

Rule, J.B. *Private Lives and Public Surveillance—Social Control in the Computer Age.* N.Y.: Schocken, 1974.

Scalletta, Phillip J. "The Computer as a Threat to Individual Privacy." *Data Management* (January, 1971).

Shaw, William. "Invasion of Privacy." *Law and Order,* 15:5 (May, 1967), pp. 12-13, 46.

Sills, Arthur J. "Automated Data Processing and the Issue of Privacy." *State Government* (Spring, 1967), pp. 92-101.

Sills, Arthur J. "The Police Blotter and the Public's Right to Know." *FBI Law Enforcement Bulletin,* 38:6 (June, 1969), pp. 6-8.

U.S. Congress. Senate Subcommittee on Constitutional Rights. *Criminal Justice Data Banks, 1974—Hearings Before the Senate Subcommittee on Constitutional Rights on S. 2542, S. 2810, S. 2963 and S. 2964, March 5-7, 12, 14, 1974.* 2 vols. Washington, D.C.: NCJRS (Microfiche), 1974.

U.S. Congress. Senate Subcommittee on Constitutional Rights. *Federal Data Banks and Constitutional Rights—A Study of Data Systems on Individuals Maintained by Agencies of the United States Government—Summary and Conclusions.* Washington, D.C.: NCJRS (Microfiche), 1974.

U.S. Department of Health, Education and Welfare. *Records, Computers and the Rights of Citizens.* Washington, D.C.: GPO, 1973.
Report on the potential harmful consequences of using an automated personal data system and proposed safeguards against such abuses.

U.S. Senate Ad Hoc Subcommittee on Privacy and Information Systems. *Privacy: The Collection, Use, and Computerization of Personal Data.* Washington, D.C.: GPO, 1974.

Westin, Alan F. *Privacy and Freedom.* N.Y.: Atheneum, 1970.

Weston, Allen F. and Michael A. Baker. *Data Banks in a Free Society.* N.Y.: Quadrangle, 1974.

COMMUNITY CONTROL

Altshuler, Alan A. *Community Control: The Black Demand for Participation in Large American Cities.* Indianapolis, IN.: Bobbs-Merrill, 1970.

Hallman, Howard. *Neighborhood Control of Public Programs.* N.Y.: Praeger, 1970.

Kotler, Milton. *Neighborhood Government, The Local Foundations of Political Life.* Indianapolis, IN.: Bobbs-Merrill, 1969.

CONSOLIDATION

Advisory Committees. *Report of Advisory Committees for the Consolidation of the City of Richmond and Henrico County.* Richmond, VA.: Advisory Committees, July 1, 1961.

Bilek, Arthur J. "Regionalize We Must." *Police,* 15:6 (July-August, 1971), pp. 2-3.

Bollens, John C. *Special District Governments in the United States.* Berkeley: University of California, 1957.

Booth, David A. *Metropolitics: The Nashville Consolidation.* East Lansing, MI.: Institute for Community Development, Michigan State University, 1963.

Boydston, Horace E. "The Santa Clara Valley Intelligence Unit." *Police Chief* (November, 1973), pp. 26-31.

Burgess, James V. "Consolidation in Georgia: Columbus and Muscogee County Merge Governments January 1." *Nations Cities* (December, 1970).

Carson, Dale. "Consolidation: The Jacksonville Experience." *Police Chief,* XXXVI:3 (March, 1969), pp. 44-45.

Carson, Dale G. and Donald K. Brown. "Law Enforcement Consolidation for Greater Efficiency." *FBI Law Enforcement Bulletin,* 39:10 (October, 1970), pp. 11-15.

City/County Consolidation Steering Committee. Final Report. Sacramento: City/County Consolidation Steering Committee, June, 1971.

Coon, Thomas F. "Pros and Cons of Consolidation." *Law and Order,* 17:5 (May, 1969), pp. 42-47.

"Consolidation Charter Proposed for Charleston." *National Civic Review,* 61:5 (May, 1972).

Cresap, McCormick, and Paget Inc. *Improving Police Service in Suburban Cook County.* 2 vols. Chicago: Cresap, McCormick, and Paget, Inc., 1971.

Doran, R.A. *Feasibility Study of Regionalized Police Service for the Barrington (IL) Area.* Washington, D.C.: NCJRS (Microfiche), 1974.

Dowd, D.D., Jr. "The Stark County MEG Unit—A Response to Fragmented Law Enforcement." *FBI Law Enforcement Bulletin,* 41:9 (1972), pp. 13-15.
Area-wide undercover operation in Ohio.

Dzikiewicz, Eugene. "Atlanta Metropol: A Regional Approach to Police Problems." *Traffic Digest and Review,* 17 (October, 1969), pp. 14-15.

Eastman Middleton Associates. *Consolidation of Police Services—The Snohomish County Experience—Plans for Improvement.* Springfield, VA.: NTIS, 1971.
Objective, implementation plans and scheduling, and cost considerations for consolidating police services, as proposed after a study of existing services.

Eastman Middleton Associates. *Consolidation of Police Services—The Snohomish County Experience—A Status Report and Key Recommendations.* Springfield, VA.: NTIS, 1971.
Evaluation of existing police services within the county, analysis of need for services, and recommendations for improving services by consolidation and coordination.

Elmes, Frank. "Amalgamation." *Police Review (GB),* 74 (December, 1966).

Erie County, New York Citizens Committee on Intermunicipal Affairs. *Consolidation of Police Services in Erie County New York.* Buffalo: Citizens Committee on Intermunicipal Agencies, July 12, 1968.

Erie County, New York Legislature Document. *A Report on Central Police Services for the Police Departments of Erie County.* Buffalo: NY Legislature, December 19, 1969.

Fabbri, John. "Coordination of Police Resources Will Pay Big Dividends." *Journal of California Law Enforcement* (July, 1967), pp. 14-18.

Fillebrown, T. Scott. "The Nashville Story." *National Civic Review,* LVIII:5 (May, 1969), pp. 197-200, 210.

Flaugher, P.R. "The Cincinnati/Hamilton County Regional Crime Information Center: Operation, Security, Ethics." *Police Chief,* 40:10 (1973), pp. 24-27.

Garza, Manuel R. *Multi-Agency Narcotics Unit Manual.* Washington, D.C.: LEAA, August, 1976.

Governmental Research Institute. *County, City, Consolidation.* Lincoln, NB.: Governmental Research Institute, 1972.

Hamilton, Randy. *ABAG Appraised: A Quinquenial Review of Voluntary Regional Cooperative Action Through the Association of Bay Area Governments.* Berkeley, CA.: Institute for Local Self-Government, 1965.

Hanson, Ivan. *Evaluating Enabling Laws for Special Districts: A Case Study in Oklahoma.* Washington, D.C.: Economic Research Service, U.S. Department of Agriculture, May, 1966.

Hawkins, Brett W. *Nashville Metro: The Politics of City-County Consolidation.* Nashville, TN: Vanderbilt University Press, 1966.

Hedges, Skipper R. "M-Squad (Metropolitan Major Case Squad)." *Law and Order,* 17:4 (April, 1969), pp. 100-107.

House, Edward T. and Joseph Y. DeCuyper. "Clay County, Missouri, Investigative Squad Coordinates Law Enforcement Effort." *Police Chief* (November, 1973), pp. 32-34.

International Association of Chiefs of Police. *A Survey of Police Services in Metropolitan Dade County, Florida.* Washington, D.C.: IACP, 1963.

Kreutzer, Walter E. "New Directions for U.S. Law Enforcement." *Police Chief,* 39:10 (October, 1972), pp. 34-37.

Lankes, George A. "Central Services for Police." *Journal of Police Science and Administration,* 2:1 (March, 1974), pp. 66-76.

Lawson, Bruce G. *Merger and Consolidation of Local Government Units in the State of Oregon.* Eugene: University of Oregon, 1969.

McCann, S. Anthony. *County-Wide Law Enforcement: A Report on a Survey of Central Police Services in 97 Urban Counties.* Washington, D.C.: National Association of Counties Research Foundation, 1975.

Mailey, Hugo V. "Merged Police Departments." *Traffic Digest and Review,* 19: (March, 1971).

Makielski, S.J., Jr. *City-County Consolidation: A Guide for Virginians.* Charlottesville: Institute of Government of Virginia, 1969.

Martin, Richard. *Consolidation: Jacksonville—Duval Dynamics of Urban Political Reform.* Jacksonville, FL.: Convention, 1968.

Massachusetts Legislative Research Council. *Voluntary Municipal Merger Procedures.* Boston: Massachusetts Legislative Research Council, 1970.

"Metro Police Proves Effective in Nashville." *Metropolitan Area Problems News and Digest,* VI:5 (September/October, 1963).

Miller, James N. "Metro-Toronto's Answer to Urban Sprawl." *Reader's Digest,* (August, 1967).

Morris, G.M. et al. *Evaluation of the Northern York County (PA) Regional Police Department.* Washington, D.C.: NCJRS (Microfiche), 1974.

"New Role for County Police?" *Public Management,* 50: (January, 1968).

Norrgard, David L. *Regional Law Enforcement—A Study of Intergovernmental Cooperation and Coordination.* Chicago: Public Administration Service, 1969.
Advantages of intergovernmental programs and arrangements in the area of local law enforcement and the means for implementing such programs.

Ostrom, E. and R.B. Parks. *Suburban Police Departments—Too Many and Too Small.* Beverly Hills, CA.: Sage, 1973.
Examination of four hypotheses derived from arguments for the consolidation of police within metropolitan area and consequent elimination of most suburban police forces.

Ostrom, Elinor, Robert B. Parks, and Gordon P. Whitaker. "Do We Really Want to Consolidate Urban Police Forces? A Reappraisal of Some Old Questions." *Public Administration Review,* XXXIII:5 (September-October, 1973), pp. 423-432.

Parsonson, R.T. "The Regional Trend in Law Enforcement." *Police Chief,* 38:8 (August, 1971), pp. 26-28.

Pasquan, A.L. "Current Status of Enabling Legislation for Intergovernmental Police Service Agreements or Consolidation." *Police,* 16:8 (1972), pp. 8-16.

Ploscowe, Morris. "Consolidation of Law Enforcement Units." *Case and Comment.* 58 (January/February, 1953), pp. 10-14.

Pock, Max A. "Are Metropolitan Police Districts Legally Feasible?" *Journal of Public Law,* 12: 1963.

Pock, Max A. *Consolidating Police Functions in Metropolitan Areas.* Ann Arbor: Legislative Research Center, University of Michigan, 1962.

Post, Richard S. "Regional Service Centers." *Law and Order,* 18:11 (November, 1970), pp. 91-95.

Public Administration Service, Chicago. *Coordination and Consolidation of Police Service.* Washington, D.C.: NCJRS, 1966.
Analysis of the problems of local police administration and potential of coordination or consolidation of services as an aid to repression of crime.

"Regionalization of Police Services." *Police Chief,* 38:8 (August, 1971).

Richmond Regional Planning Commission. *Local Component Law Enforcement Plan for the Richmond Metropolitan Region.* Springfield, VA.: NTIS, 1969.

Riepe, William. "Consolidation Coming—Beware!" *Law and Order,* 18:10 (October, 1970), pp. 24-26.

Schmandt, Henry J. and William H. Standing. *The Milwaukee Metropolitan Study Commission.* Bloomington: Indiana University Press, 1965.

Schmandt, Henry J., Paul G. Steinbieker, and George P. Wendell. *Metropolitan Reform in St. Louis: A Case Study.* N.Y.: Holt, Rinehart and Winston, 1961.

Skoler, D.L. and J.M. Hetler. *Criminal Administration and the Local Government Crisis—The Challenge of Consolidation.* Washington, D.C.: NCJRS, 1969.
Importance of consolidation is discussed in light of increasing demands upon criminal justice functions and the growing fiscal crises of local governments.

Smith, Bruce. *A Regional Police Plan for Cincinnati and Its Environs.* N.Y.: Institute of Public Administration, 1932.

Smith, T. Owen. "Atlanta Metropol." *FBI Law Enforcement Bulletin,* 36:3 (March, 1967), pp. 10-13.

Sofen, Edward. *The Miami Metropolitan Experiment.* Garden City, N.Y.: Doubleday, 1966.

Steinberg, Carl W. "Regionalism in the Criminal Justice System: What Role for the County?" *American County,* 36 (May, 1971), pp. 47-49.

Steiner, Gilbert Y. *Metropolitan Government and the Real World: The Case of Chicago.* Chicago: Center for Research in Urban Government, Loyola University, 1966.

"Texas County Consolidates Law Enforcement Functions." *National Civic Review,* XLI:1 (January, 1972), pp. 34-35.

Washington State Research Council. *City-County Consolidation: A Study of Its Possibilities for Walla-Walla, Washington.* Olympia: Research Council, January, 1967.

Wesenberg, B.B. "One Police Department for Two Cities." *American City,* 75 (February, 1960).

Williams, Albert L. "A Regional Approach to Drug Abuse." *Police Chief,* XXXIX:4 (April, 1972), pp. 26-29.
Regional drug enforcement unit in Santa Clara County, California.

Winters, John M. *Interstate Metropolitan Areas.* Ann Arbor: University of Michigan Law School Legislative Research Center, 1962.

Yancey, T. "The Yuma City-County Narcotics Task Force." *FBI Law Enforcement Bulletin,* 44:5 (1975), pp. 11-13.
Consolidation of the narcotics squads of the city and county of Yuma. Unit contains 10 agents and a small airplane.

CONTRACT LAW ENFORCEMENT

Booz-Allen and Hamilton, Inc. *California Contract Cities Association—Determination of Law Enforcement Contractual Costs.* Washington, D.C.: NCJRS (Microfiche), 1971.
A study to delineate the statutory responsibilities of the office of sheriff, identify the functions performed and their cost, together with a formula to be used in charging for contracted services.

"Contract Police Service, RCMP." *Police Chief,* 31 (June, 1964).

Earle, Howard H. "Contract Law Enforcement." *Police,* 6:1 (September-October, 1961), pp. 11-14.

Fennell, D.A. and C. Thurn. *Contract Policing—An Attitudinal Study of North Dakota Government and Law Enforcement Officials.* Washington, D.C.: NCJRS, (Microfiche), [n.d.].
This study assessed city and county officials' attitudes toward contract policing in order to determine the feasibility of establishing such a system in the state.

Misner, Gordon E. "The Police Service Contract in California: Instrument of Functional Integration." *Journal of Criminal Law,* 52 (November-December, 1961), pp. 445-452.

CO-OPERATION

Advisory Commission on Intergovernmental Relations. *State-Local Relations in the Criminal Justice System—A Commission Report.* Springfield, VA.: NTIS, 1971.

Boatner, Haydon L. "Civil-Military Police Partnership." *Police,* 3:2 (November-December, 1958), pp. 38-39.

Bridge, Patricia Ann. "Communication Barriers within the Criminal Justice System." *Police Chief,* XXXIX:4 (April, 1972), pp. 30-33.

Brostron, Curtis. "Liaison between Police and Industrial Security Officers." *Police,* 8:6 (July-August, 1964), pp. 60-62.

Buckley, John L. "Law Enforcement and Industrial Security Interface . . . a Model of Successful Relationship."

Law and Order, 12:7 (July, 1964), pp. 46, 48, 66-67; 12:8 (August, 1964), pp. 54-58.

Buckley, John L. "The Value of Security Contacts to Law Enforcement." *Law and Order,* 12:1 (January, 1964), pp. 60-62.

Council of Europe Librarie Berger-Levrault. *Legal Cooperation in Europe.* N.Y.: Manhattan, 1972.

Council of Europe Librarie Berger-Levrault. *Explanatory Report on the European Convention on the International Validity of Criminal Judgments.* N.Y.: Manhattan, 1970.

Devore, L.L. "Police/Probation Reciprocal Training." *California Youth Authority Quarterly,* 25:2 (1972), pp. 36-39.

Drivon, Lawrence. "Co-Operation between Peace Officers, Prosecutors and the Public." *Journal of California Law Enforcement* (July, 1966), pp. 35-38.

Erickson, R.J. et al. *Criminal Justice Seminar Report on Interagency Communication Problems.* Washington, D.C: NCJRS, (Microfiche) [n.d.].

Feledick, Winifred Martens. "The Personal Touch." *Law and Order,* 11:5 (May, 1963), pp. 64-65.

Fox, Harry G. and Clovinda Margolis. "Rap and Rapport: Police and Mental Health Pros." *Police Chief,* 38:12 (December, 1971), pp. 46-48.

Interdepartmental Council to Coordinate All Federal Juvenile Delinquency Programs. *Interdepartmental Council to Coordinate Federal Juvenile Delinquency Programs, Report.* Springfield, VA.: NTIS, 1973.

Johnson, Charles C. "Cooperation between Police and Prosecutor." *FBI Law Enforcement Bulletin,* 26:9 (September, 1957), pp. 19-21.

Keller, E. John. "Prosecution of Employees—Industry/Law Enforcement Cooperation." *Law and Order,* 22:11 (November, 1974), pp. 109, 116.

Kelly, James P. "Schools v. Cops." *Police Chief,* 38:4 (April, 1971), pp. 40-41.
Recommends closer cooperation between school and police personnel.

Kowalewski, Victor A. "Police and Social Service Agencies: Breaking the Barrier." *Police Chief,* XLII:10 (October, 1975), pp. 259-262.

Kuykendall, Jack and James V. Gould. "Cooperative Police Services: A Study Design." *Police,* 16:9 (May, 1972), pp. 40-47.

Laroche, B., J.J. Sigal, and M. Grayston. "Collaboration between a Police Force and the Psychiatric Service of a General Hospital: A Study of Outcome." *Canadian Journal of Criminology and Corrections,* 16:2 (1974), pp. 162-172.

McLaughlin, Glen H. "Traveling Thieves: The Problem and Some Techniques in Dealing with It." *Police,* 6:4 (March-April, 1962), pp. 28-30.

Moynahan, J.M. "Theory and Practice in Law Enforcement." *Police Chief,* 38:12 (December, 1971), pp. 44-45.

Muir, A.A. "Some Modest Proposals for Promoting Co-Operation between Different Police Forces." *Police College Magazine* (Spring, 1958), pp. 149-143.

Murphy, P.V. "Cooperation in the Criminal Justice System." *Crime and Delinquency,* 18:1 (January, 1972), pp. 42-48.

Parker, W.L., Jr. "The Accessibility of Police Officers to Defense Counsel." *Police Chief,* XXXVII:5 (May, 1971), pp. 40-44.

Penner, G. Lewis. "An Experiment in Police and Social Agency Cooperation." *Annals of American Academy of Police and Social Science,* 322 (1959).

Post, Richard S. "P-CR. Relations with Private Police Services." *Police Chief,* 38:3 (March, 1971), pp. 54-56.

Ramsey, Lloyd B. "Military and Police Cooperation." *Police Yearbook,* Gaithersburg, MD.: IACP, June, 1972.

Reisman, Leonard E. "Relating the Police Community to the Academic Community." *Police Chief,* 33:8 (August, 1966), pp. 16, 18.

Ruiz, P., W. Vasquez, and K. Vasquez. "The Mobile Unit: A New Approach in Mental Health." *Community Mental Health Journal,* 9:1 (1973), pp. 18-24.
Psychiatric care provided to poor by hospital mobile units. Author cites poor relations with police and unit is not available 24 hours a day.

Shawyer, Carl D. "Inter-Agency Relations." *Law and Order,* 13:9 (September, 1965), pp. 54-66.

Sims, A.C.P. and R.L. Symonds. "Psychiatric Referrals from the Police." *British Journal of Psychiatry* (1975), pp. 171-178.

Smith, Dwight C., Jr. "Cooperative Action in Organized Crime Control." *Journal of Criminal Law, Criminology and Police Science,* 59:4 (December, 1968), pp. 491-498.

Studdart, Stephen H. "Idaho State Police Teams with U.S. Air Force—The M-A-S-T Program." *Law and Order,* 20:11 (November, 1972), pp. 60-61.
Air Force assistance to victims of traffic and other accidents.

Thomson, D. and H. Treger. "Police-Social Work Cooperation with the Overburden of the Juvenile Court." *Police Law Quarterly,* 3:1 (1973), pp. 28-39.

Tocchio, O.J. "Procedural Problems Inhibiting Effective County and Community-Wide Resolution of Battered Child Problems." *Police,* 14:5 (May-June, 1970), pp. 16-21.

U.S. Advisory Commission on Intergovernmental Relations. *State/Local Relations in the Criminal Justice System: A Commission Report.* Washington, D.C.: GPO, 1971.

Williams, Gerald O. "Cooperation on the Border." *FBI Law Enforcement Bulletin* (October, 1968), pp. 12-17.
Cooperation between Alaska troopers and R.C.M.P.

DETENTION

American Civil Liberties Union. *Secret Detention by the Chicago Police.* N.Y.: Glencoe, 1959.

Bases, N.C. and W.F. McDonald. *Preventive Detention in the District of Columbia—The First Ten Months.* Washington, D.C.: Georgetown Institute of Criminal Law, 1972.

Background of the statute, study of the cases involved, some aspects of the operations, and conclusions emerging from the ten months' experience.

Beaver, C.W. *Emergency Detention Manual—Temporary Detention of Civil Disturbance Violators Prior to Court Action.* Washington, D.C.: U.S. Bureau of Prisons, 1969.

Carson, Dale G. "Emergency Mass Detention." *Police,* 8:6 (July-August, 1964), pp. 74-75.

"Detention, Arrest and Salt Lake City Police Practice." *Utah Law Review,* 9 (1965).

King, Dan. "Some Reflections on Investigative Detention." *Law and Order,* 12:9 (September, 1964), pp. 81-82.

La Fave, Wayne. "Detention for Investigation by the Police: An Analysis of Current Practices." *Washington University Law Quarterly* (1962), pp. 331-399.

"The Law of Arrest: Constitutionality of Detention and Frisk Acts." *Northwestern University Law Review,* 59 (1964).

Miller, J.D. "Investigative Detention." *FBI Law Enforcement Bulletin,* 43:11 (1974), pp. 10-15; 32:12 (1974), pp. 23-27; 44:1, pp. 25-29.

Munro, C.R. "Police Powers without Miranda: The Legality of Police Detention." *New Law Journal,* 125 (1975), pp. 137-138.

Laws governing the police detention of suspects in Great Britain.

Preventive Detention. N.Y.: ACLU, 1971.

American Civil Liberties Union arguments against preventive detention, focusing on the infringement of constitutional rights.

"Preventive Detention before Trial." *Harvard Law Review* (May, 1966).

Preventive Detention: An Empirical Analysis. Chicago: American Bar Foundation, 1971.

Rutkowski, A.C. "Detention of Juveniles." *Carolina Law,* 24:6 (1974), pp. 24-25.

U.S. Congress Senate Committee on the Judiciary. *Preventive Detention—Hearings Before the Subcommittee on Constitutional Rights.* Washington, D.C.: GPO, 1970.

Verbatim transcript of Senate hearings on proposed 1969 bail reform act with an extensive compilation of materials relating to bail and pretrial release.

University of Chicago Law School. *Criminal Justice in Extremis—Administration of Justice During the April 1968 Chicago Disorder.* Chicago: American Bar Foundation, 1969.

Wald, M.S. "May Day Revisited." *Criminal Law Bulletin,* 10:5 (1974), pp. 377-435' 516-543.

Mass detention of 13,000 demonstrators in April/May 1971 by Washington, D.C. Analysis of entire process.

Wayne, Gerald. "The Case for Investigative Detention." *Law and Order,* 12:1 (January, 1964), pp. 28-29, 59.

Wilkins, Leslie T. "Persistent Offenders and Preventative Detention." *Journal of Criminal Law, Criminology and Police Science,* 57:3 (September, 1966), pp. 312-317.

DIPLOMATIC IMMUNITY

Bloomfield, Louis M. and Gerald F. Fitzgerald. *Crime Against Internationally Protected Persons: Prevention and Punishment. An Analysis of the UN Convention.* N.Y.: Praeger, 1975.

Cahier, Philippe and Luke T. Lee. *Vienna Conventions on Diplomatic and Consular Immunities.* N.Y.: Carnegie-Endow, 1968.

Lammers, John C. "Diplomatic Immunity." *Law and Order,* 12:9 (September, 1964), pp. 38, 40.

O'Brien, John T. *International Functions of the Police Department in the City of New York.* Unpub. Doctoral Dissertation, New York University, 1967.

Saulsbury, Donn D. "Procedures for Checking Status of Persons Claiming Diplomatic Immunity." *Journal of California Law Enforcement* (January, 1967), pp. 165-168.

U.S. Department of State. *Foreign Consular Offices in the United States.* Washington, D.C.: GPO, [n.d.].

State-by-state listing of foreign consular offices. Department of State Publication No. 7846.

ENERGY PROBLEMS

Aerospace Corporation. *Methods for Reducing Police Car Fuel Consumption—Equipment Systems Improvement Program.* vol. 1. Washington, D.C.: NCJRS, 1974.

Disser, L.R. "Fuel Conservation." *Law and Order,* 22:11 (November, 1974), pp. 54, 56, 69.

Eliot, W.A. and J.J. Gasparotti. *Notes Concerning the Impact of the Energy Crisis on the Criminal Justice System Equipment Systems Improvement Program Report.* Washington, D.C.: NCJRS, 1973.

John, Harvey N., Jr. and Dwight E. Pitman. "Take 15: Gasoline Shortage and Police Patrol." *Police Chief* (April, 1974).

Leighton, R. *Economics of Energy—Alternative Strategies for Conserving A Dwindling Regional Resource.* Washington, D.C.: NCJRS, (Microfiche) 1974.

Miller, H.L. "From Gasoline to LPG." *Law and Order,* 17:1 (January, 1969).

Changing police engines to use liquid petroleum gas.

Tuthill, S.J. *Action Taken by the Midwestern States in Response to Fuel Shortages, 1972-1973.* Washington, D.C.: NCJRS, (Microfiche) 1973.

Fourteen Governors summarize their experience, their executive activity, legislation, and plans for meeting the projected crisis of the 1973-1974 heating season.

U.S. Department of Commerce, National Bureau of Standards. *Eleven Ways to Reduce Energy Consumption and Increase Comfort in Household Cooling.* Washington, D.C.: GPO, 1974.

ENTRAPMENT

Entrapment—General

Caton, J.E. "The Entrapment Defense in Kansas: Subjectivity versus an Objective Standard." *Washburn Law Journal,* 12:1 (1972), pp. 64-76.

Cowen, Richard A. "The Entrapment Doctrine in the Federal Courts, and Some State Court Comparisons." *Journal of Criminal Law, Criminology and Police Science,* 49:5 (January-February, 1959), pp. 447-463.

Gleeson, Tom. "Police Entrapment—A Defence for the Future." *Police Review (GB),* (January 2, 1976).

Hardy, B.A. "The Traps of Entrapment." *American Journal of Criminal Law,* 3:2 (1975), pp. 165-204.

Heydon, J.D. "Problems of Entrapment." *Cambridge Law Journal,* 32:2 (November, 1973), pp. 268-286.

Miller, J.D. "The Entrapment Defense." *FBI Law Enforcement Bulletin,* 42:2 (1973), pp. 22-27; 42:3 (March, 1973), pp. 18-23.

Sneiderman, B.M. "A Judicial Test for Entrapment: The Glimmerings of a Candian Policy on Police-Instigated Crime." *Criminal Law Quarterly,* 16:1 (1973), pp. 81-111.

Tiffany, L.P. and D.M. McIntire. *Detection of Crime—Stopping and Questioning, Search and Seizure, Encouragement and Entrapment.* Boston: Little Brown, 1967.

"The Viability of the Entrapment Defense in the Constitutional Context." *Iowa Law Review,* 59:3 (1974), pp. 655-670.

Williams, John B. "Entrapment—A Legal Limitation on Police Techniques." *Journal of Criminal Law, Criminology and Police Science,* 48:3 (September-October, 1957), pp. 343-348.

Agents Provocateurs

Gordon, F.A. "The Agent Provocateur." *Police,* 10:3 (January-February, 1966), pp. 5253.

Khan, A.N. "Agent Provocateur."*Police Review (GB),* (April 30, 1076), pp. 536-538.

Marx, G.T. "Thoughts on a Neglected Category of Social Movement Participation: The Agent Provocateur and the Informant." *American Journal of Sociology,* 80:2 (1974), pp. 402-442.

Stickland, C. "Agents Provocateurs." *Police Review (GB),* 82: (1974), pp. 523-525.

ETHICS

Ethics—General

Anderson, Ralph E. "Police Integrity: Accent on the Positive." *Police Chief,* XL:12 (December, 1973), pp. 38-42.

"The Athenian Oath." *Police Chief,* XL:2 (February, 1973.

Ball, John H. "The Development of a Code of Police Practice: Some Perspectives and Problems." *Police Chief,* XLI:1 (January, 1974), pp. 20-23.

Barclay, William. *Ethics in a Permissive Society.* N.Y.: Harper and Row, 1972.

Batten, Joseph T. "Our Race for Inner Space." *Police Chief,* 34:2 (February, 1967), pp. 16, 18, 20, 22, 24, 26, 28, 30-32.
Essay on the state of police art.

Bristow, Allen P. "A Matter of Professional Ethics." *Police,* 5:1 (September-October, 1960), pp. 59-60.

Cooper, H.S. "The Role of Police Integrity." *Police Yearbook,* Washington, D.C.: IACP, 1962.

Davis, E.M. "Professional Police Principles." *Federal Probation,* 35:1 (1975), pp. 29-34.

Deutsch, A. "Plight of the Honest Cop." *Colliers,* 132 (September 18, 1953), pp. 23-27.

Douglas, Paul H. *Ethics in Government.* Westport, CT.: Greenwood, 1972. (repr. of 1952 ed.).

"Ethics in the Public Service." *Public Personnel Review.* 23 (October, 1962), pp. 281-283.

Hansen, David A. *Police Ethics.* Springfield, IL.: C.C. Thomas, 1973.

Hollingsworth, C.A. "Law Enforcement Requires Code of Personal Conduct." *FBI Law Enforcement Bulletin,* 26:11 (November, 1957), pp. 25-26.

"International Code of Ethical Standards for Police Drafted." *Police Chief,* XLII:5 (May, 1975), pp. 46-47.

James, Jesse R. "A Code of Ethics for Auxiliary Police." *Law and Order* (May, 1959).

Jones, William Thomas. *Approaches to Ethics, Representative Selections from Classical Times to the Present.* N.Y.: MCGraw-Hill, 1962.

Keller, E. John. "Ethics in the Security Industry." *Law and Order,* 21:4 (April, 1973).

Kooken, Don L. *Ethics in Police Service.* Springfield, IL.: C.C. Thomas, 1957.

"Law Enforcement Code of Ethics." *California Peace Officer,* 7 (January-February, 1957), pp. 8-9.

MacIver, Robert M. "The Social Significance of Professional Ethics." *The Annals of the American Academy of Political and Social Sciences,* CCXCVII (January, 1955), pp. 118-24.

McLaurin, S.H. "Ethics in Professional Conduct." *Texas Police Journal,* 23:2 (1975), pp. 6-9.

Melden, A.I., ed. *Ethical Theories: A Book of Readings with Revisions,* 2nd ed. Englewood Cliffs, N.J.: Prentice Hall, 1967.

Mullick, B.N. "Police Ethics." *Police Journal (GB),* 47:1 (1963), pp. 4-6.

Payton, George T. "Ethics and Professional Law Enforcement." *Police Chief,* 33:6 (June, 1966), pp. 24-26, 28-30, 32-41.

Ross, Jewell L. "History of the Law Enforcement Code of Ethics." *Police Chief,* XLI:8 (August, 1974), pp. 68-70.

Sokol, Ronald P. *Law Abiding Policeman.* rev. 2nd ed. Charlottesville, VA.: Michie, 1970.

Stover, Glenn. "A Policeman's Prayer." *Law and Order,* 15:8 (August, 1967).

Swinson, James D. "Integrity in Law Enforcement." *FBI Law Enforcement Bulletin* (May, 1965), pp. 17-19.

Weirman, Charles L. "Cops Should Get Tickets Too!" *Police Chief,* XXXIX:7 (July, 1972), pp. 45-55.

Wood, Raymond D. "Military Policeman's Code of Ethics." *Military Police,* 10 (November, 1959), pp. 9-11.

Gratuities

Bale, James F. "Brother, Can You Spare a Dime?" *FBI Law Enforcement Bulletin,* 36:9 (September, 1967), pp. 7-8.

Pileggi, Nicholas. "The Long Palm of the Law." *Esquire* (April, 1967).

Sollenberger, David R. "Controlling Gifts Acceptance." *Personnel Administration* (July-August, 1963), pp. 39-45, 64.

Whitehouse, Jack E. "The Policeman's First Commandment: Thou Shalt Not Be a Moocher." *Law and Order,* 14:5 (May, 1966), pp. 69-74.

EXCLUSIONARY RULE

Abbott, Thomas P. et al. *Law and Tactics in Exclusionary Hearings.* Washington, D.C. Coiner, 1969.

Beade, H.W. "Illegally Obtained Evidence in Criminal and Civil Cases: A Comparative Study of a Classic Mismatch." *Texas Law Review,* 51:7 (1973), pp. 1325-1362; 52:4 (1974), pp. 621-702.

Burpo, John H. "The Exclusionary Rule—Answer for an Organized Society?" *Police,* 15:1 (September-October, 1970), pp. 14-18.

Canon, B.C. "Is the Exclusion Rule in Failing Health? Some New Data and a Plea against a Precipitous Conclusion." *Kentucky Law Journal,* 62:3 (1973-1974), pp. 681-730.

Cox, William J. "The Decline of the Exclusionary Rule: An Alternative to Injustice." *Southwestern University Law Revie* (Spring, 1972).

Finzen, B.A. "The Exclusionary Rule in Search and Seizure: Examination and Prognosis." *University of Kansas Law Review,* 20:4 (1972), pp. 768-790.

George, James, Jr. *Constitutional Limitations on Evidence in Criminal Cases.* N.Y.: Practicing Law Institute, 1969.

McGarr, Frank J. "The Exclusionary Rule: An Ill-Conceived and Ineffective Remedy." *Journal of Criminal Law, Criminology and Police Science,* 52 (1961).

"On the Limitations of Empirical Evaluations of the Exclusionary Rule: A Critique of the Spiotto Research and United States V. Calandra." *Northwest University Law Review,* 69:5 (1974), pp. 740-798.

Spiotto, J.E. "Search and Seizure: An Empirical Study of the Exclusionary Rule and Its Alternatives." *Journal of Legal Studies,* 2:1 (1973), pp. 243-278.

Spiotto, James E. "The Search and Seizure Problem—Two Approaches: The Candian Tort Remedy and the U.S. Exclusionary Rule." *Journal of Police Science and Administration,* 1:1 (March, 1973), pp. 36-49.

EXTERNAL CONTROL OF POLICE

Aaron, Thomas J. "The Dilemma of Judicial Review." *Police* (March-April, 1965).

Alberta, M.E. and K.M. Werhan. "A Federal Cause of Action against a Municipality for Fourth Amendment Violations by Its Agents." *George Washington Law Review,* 42:4 (1974), pp. 850-868.

Beisel, A.R. *Control Over Illegal Enforcement of the Criminal Law: Role of The Supreme Court.* Boston: Boston University Press, 1955.

Breitel, C.D. "Controls in Criminal Law Enforcement." *University of Chicago Law Review,* 27:3 (1960), pp. 427-435.

Buller, Arthur. "Legal Remedies against Corrupt Law Enforcement Officers." *Journal of Criminal Law, Criminology and Police Science,* 48:4 (November-December, 1957).

Burger, Warren E. "Who Will Watch the Watchman?" *American University Law Review* (1964), pp. 1-23.

Corcoran, Charles W. "Federal Court Remedies against State and Local Police Abuses." *Journal of Criminal Law and Criminology,* 39:4 (March-April, 1948-1949), pp. 490-498.

Davis, K.C. "An Approach to Legal Control of the Police." *Texas Law Review,* 52:4 (1974), pp. 703-725.
Author recommends police should be controlled by exclusionary rule, tort liability and judically supervised police rule-making.

Gassman, Benjamin. "The Effect of Recent United States Supreme Court Decisions on Law Enforcement." *Bar Bulletin,* 22:5 (1964-1965), pp. 210-219.

Goldstein, Herman. "Administrative Problems in Controlling the Exercise of Police Authority." *Journal of Criminal Law, Criminology and Police Science,* 58 (June, 1967), pp. 160-172.
Describes some of the complex problems encountered in exerting control over police conduct. Cites several forms of police misconduct, factors inherent in nature of police functions that complicate review and control of police actions.

Inbau, Fred. "The Courts Have No Right to Police the Police. This Is an Executive Not a Judicial Function." *Journal of Criminal Law, Criminology and Police Science,* 52, (1961), pp. 209-212.

"Judicial Review of Police Methods in Law Enforcement." *Texas Law Review* (April, 1966), pp. 939-964.

Kamisar, Yale. "Public Safety vs. Individual Liberties: Some Facts and Theories." *Journal of Criminal Law, Criminology and Police Science,* 53:2 (June-August, 1962).

Kamisar, Yale. "Some Reflections on Criticizing the Courts and Policing the Police." *Journal of Criminal Law, Criminology and Police Science,* 53:4 (December, 1962).

Kamisar, Yale. "When the Cops Were Not 'Handcuffed', " in Niederhoffer and Blumberg, *The Ambivalent Force: Perspectives on the Police.* Waltham, MA.: Ginn, 1970.

La Fave, Wayne R. "Improving Police Performance through the Exclusionary Rule: Current Police and Local Court Practices, Part 1." *Missouri Law Review,* 30:3 (1965), pp. 391-458.

La Fave, Wayne R. "Improving Police Performance through the Exclusionary Rule: Defining the Norms and Training the Police, Part 2." *Missouri Law Review,* 30:4 (1965), pp. 566-610.

La Fave, Wayne R. and Frank J. Remington. "Controlling the Police—The Judge's Role in Making and Reviewing Law Enforcement Decisions." *Michigan Law Review,* 63:6 (1965).

Linden, A.M. "Tort Law As Ombudsman." *Canadian Bar Review,* 51:1 (1973), pp. 155-168.
Civil law as a method to control police involved in wrongful conduct.

McGarr, Frank J. "The Exclusionary Rule: An Ill-Conceived and Ineffective Remedy." *Journal of Criminal Law, Criminology and Police Science,* 52:3 (September-October, 1961).

Packer, H.L. "The Courts, the Police, and the Rest of Us." *Journal of Criminal Law, Criminology and Police Science,* 57:3 (1966), pp. 328-243.

Packer, Herbert L. "Policing the Police: Nine Men Are Not Enough." *New Republic,* 153 (1965).

Packer, Herbert L. "Who Can Police the Police?" *New York Review* (September 8, 1966).

Paulsen, Monrad G. "The Exclusionary Rule and Misconduct by the Police." in Claude R. Sowle *Police Power and Individual Freedom,* Chicago: Aldine, 1962.

"Policing the Police." *Economist,* 207 (May 18, 1963).
Everybody wants an efficient police force; everybody fears the powers that a strong force might acquire.

Riley, David P. "Should Communities Control Their Police?" *Civil Rights Digest,* 2:4 (Fall, 1969).

Ruchelman, Leonard. *Who Rules the Police?* Washington Square, N.Y.: New York University Press, 1973.

Skousen, W. Cleon. "Is Massive Federal Aid to Local Police Dangerous?" *Law and Order,* 17:4 (April, 1969), pp. 10-14.

Wells, W.T. "Public Control and the Police." *Political Quarterly,* 30 (April, 1959), pp. 141-148.
Indicates lack of control of police agencies outside metropolitan police districts.

Wilson, J.V. and G.M. Alprin. "Controlling Police Conduct: Alternatives to the Exclusionary Rule." *Law Contemporary Problems,* 36:4 (1972), pp. 488-499.

EXTRADITION

Council of Europe. *Legal Aspects of Extradition Among European States.* N.Y.: Manhattan, 1970.

Council of Europe, Strasbourg. *Explanatory Report on the European Convention on Extradition.* N.Y.: Manhattan, 1969.
General observations on the proceedings of the committee which drafted the multilateral convention, comments on the individual articles, and a text of the convention.

Council of State Governments. *The Handbook on Interstate Crime Control.* Chicago: Council of State Governments, 1966.

European Committee on Crime Problems. *Legal Aspects of Extradition Among European States.* N.Y.: Manhattan, 1970.
The texts of three reports by international law experts on problems raised by the implementation and application of the European convention on extradition.

Murphy, John J. *Arrest By Computer: Controversy Over Bail and Extradition.* Lexington, MA.: Lexington, 1975.

Sullivan, Francis C. "What about Extradition?" *Police,* 5:1 (September-October, 1960), pp. 50-51.

FIREARMS USE POLICY

Beatty, Thomas P. "Side Arm." *Law and Order,* 19:10 (October, 1971), pp. 58, 60, 68-70.
Shooting policy and advice on the safe handling of firearms.

Bjelejac, J.M. *Madison (WI)—Recommended Policy Guidelines for the Use of Deadly Force.* Washington, D.C.: NCJRS, (Microfiche) 1972.

Chapman, Samuel G. "Police Policy on the Use of Firearms." *Police Chief,* XXXLV:7 (July, 1967), pp. 16-33.

Chapman, Samuel G. and Thompson S. Crockett. "Gunsight Dilemma: Police Firearms Policy." *Police,* 7:4 (March-April, 1963), pp. 20-25.

Dragnich, Alix. "To Shoot or Not to Shoot—Split Second Decision." *Law and Order,* 21:4, pp. 90-95.

Gilligan, P.M. "Police Policy Formulation on Firearms: Some Considerations." *Police Chief,* XXXVII:5 (May, 1971), pp. 61-64.

"A Model Firearms Use Policy." *Police Chief,* XXXLV:7 (July, 1967), pp. 33-37.

Phalan, Reed T. "You're Under Arrest! Halt or I'll . . . (Do What?)." *Law and Order,* 16:9 (September, 1968), pp. 70-78.

Watson, Nelson A. "A Big Question: What Is Your Policy on the Use of Firearms?" *Police Chief,* XXXLV:7 (July, 1967), pp. 12-13.

Wilson, Jerry V. "Deadly Force." *Police Chief,* XXXIX:12 (December, 1972), pp. 44-46.
Guidelines for the use of deadly force.

FIRE/POLICE INTEGRATION

Ayres, Loren D. "Integration of Police and Fire Services." *Journal of Criminal Law, Criminology and Police Science,* 47:4 (November-December, 1956), pp. 490-496.

Baum, Bernard A. and Robert H. Goodin. "The Effective De-Specialization of Jobs: A Case Study." *Public Personnel Review,* 29 (October, 1968), pp. 222-226.

"Boulder, Colo.: City to Combine Police, Fire Functions." *Public Management,* 50 (October, 1968).

Bruce, Howard I. *P.F.I., A Survey: Police-Fire Integration in the United States and Canada.* Cleveland: Bureau of Governmental Research, October, 1961.

"Can We Trust Togetherness? Police-Fire Integration, Pushed by Some Municipalities May Impair Effectiveness of Both Forces." *Journal of American Insurance,* 39 (November, 1963).

Dornfeld, Steven R. "Suburban Fire-Police Integration a Must." *American City,* 85 (February, 1970).

Holstrom, John D. "Fire-Police Integration—Current Trends." *Police* (March-April, 1959).

James, Charles S. "The Integration of Fire and Police Services." *Public Management* (February, 1954).

James, Charles S. *Police and Fire Integration in a Small City.* Chicago: Public Administration Service, 1955.

James, Charles S. *Police and Fire Integration in the Smaller Cities.* Chicago: Public Administration Services, 1955.

Leonards, Glensford. *Report on the Integration of the Police and Fire Services in the City of Oak Park, Michigan.* Oak Park, MI.: (September 20, 1954).

More, H.W., Jr. *New Era of Public Safety.* Springfield, IL.: C.C. Thomas, 1970.
Basic processes involved in providing for public safety by combining police-fire services.

Report No. 1 of the Special Committee Re Unification of the Police and Fire Departments in the Metropolitan Area. For Consideration by the Council of the Municipality of Metropolitan Toronto on November 1, 1955. Toronto: September 29, 1955.

FIRE/POLICE PAY PARITY

Berrodin, Eugene F. "Should Police and Firemen Get the Same Salary?" *Public Management,* 47 (January, 1965), pp. 3-9.

Buck, William D. "Fire Fighters' and Police Salaries." *Public Management* (August, 1965).

Danielson, William F. *Breaking the Traditional Custom of Paying Identical Salaries to Policemen and Firemen: A Case Study.* Berkeley, CA.: Personnel Department, 1964.

Danielson, William F. *Police Compensation.* Washington, D.C.: IACP, 1967.

Danielson, William F. *Should Policemen and Firemen Get the Same Salary?* Chicago: Public Personnel Association, [n.d.].

Danielson, William F. "The Trend to Separate Police and Firemen's Salaries." *Western Magazine* (December, 1964), pp. 20-22.

Grant, Robert J. and Paul Saenz. "The Police/Fire Parity Issue." *Police Chief,* XXXV:11 (September, 1968), pp. 53-59.

McCutcheon, James T. "Should Police and Fire Salaries Be Equal?" *Tax Digest,* 42:4 (1964), pp. 111-113, 133-136.

Sackley, Arthur. "Trends in Salaries of Firemen and Policemen." *Monthly Labor Review,* 88 (February, 1965), pp. 159-163.

IMMUNITY

Jenks, Clarence Wilfred. *International Immunities.* London: Stevens, 1961.

Singer, Alan D. "State Grants of Immunity—The Problems of Interstate Prosecution Prevention." *Journal of Criminal Law, Criminology and Police Science,* 58:2 (June, 1967), pp. 218-223.

JURISDICTION

Council of Europe Librarie Berger-Levrault. *European Convention on the Transfer of Proceedings on Criminal Matters.* N.Y.: Manhattan, 1972.
International agreement which allows one country to prosecute under its own law persons suspected of having committed a crime in another country.

Rice, Paul J. "Court Martial Jurisdiction—The Service Connection Standard in Confusion." *Journal of Criminal Law, Criminology and Police Science,* 61:3 (September, 1970), pp. 339-351.

Shubber, S. *Jurisdiction Over Crimes on Board Aircraft.* The Hague: Martinus Nijhoff, 1973.

JUSTICE

Bergler, Edmund and A.M. Meerloo Joost. *Justice and Injustice.* N.Y.: Grune and Stratton, 1963.

Blumberg, Abraham S., ed. *The Scales of Justice.* New Brunswick, N.J.: Transaction, 1973.

Delvecchio, Giorgio. *Justice: An Historical and Philosophical Essay.* N.Y.: Philosophical Library, 1953.

Harris, Richard. *Justice.* N.Y.: Dutton, 1970.

Jackson, Paul. *Natural Justice.* London: Sweet and Maxwell, 1973.

"Justice on Trial, a Special Report." *Newsweek* (March 8, 1971).

Kamisar, Yale, Fred E. Inbau, and Thurman Arnold. *Criminal Justice in Our Time.* Charlottesville: University of Virginia Press, 1965.

Karlen, Delmar. *Anglo-American Criminal Justice.* N.Y.: Oxford University Press, 1967.

Logan, A.B. *Justice in Jeopardy—Strategy to Revitalize the American Dream.* Springfield, IL.: C.C. Thomas, 1973.

MacKenzie, John P. *The Appearance of Justice.* N.Y.: Scribner, 1974.

Mendelsohn, Robert I. *The Politics of Local Justice.* Boston: Little Brown, 1970.

Waelder, Robert. "The Concept of Justice and the Quest for an Absolutely Just Society." *Journal of Criminal Law, Criminology and Police Science,* 57:1 (March, 1966), pp. 1-6.

MUTUAL AID

Baines, J.M. *Mutual Aid Planning—A Manual Designed to Assist in the Development of Law Enforcement Mutual Aid Systems.* Washington, D.C.: NCJRS, 1973.

Results of a nationwide study of the exchange of personnel, services, and/or equipment between law enforcement agencies during times of emergency.

Boomer, John R. "Collective Violence and the California Highway Patrol." *Law and Order,* 20:5 (May, 1972), pp. 76-78, 80-82.

California Disaster Office. *Law Enforcement Mutual Aid Plan.* Sacramento: Disaster Office, 1967.

Council of Europe Librarie Berger-Levrault. *European Convention on Mutual Assistance in Criminal Matters.* N.Y.: Manhattan, 1971.

Jennings, Donald. "A Practical Mutual Aid System." *Washington Police Journal* (December, 1969).

Johnson, George S. and Robert R. Stack. "Intergovernmental Law Enforcement Agreements." *Police Chief,* 39:1 (January, 1972), pp. 32, 34-35.

Kranig, Wayne A. "Mutual Aid—A Practical, Workable, Tested Solution to Today's Law Enforcement Dilemma." *Police* (May-June, 1968).

Kranig, Wayne A. "Mutual Aid Provides a Practical Solution to a Law Enforcement Problem." *Journal of California Law Enforcement* (April, 1968), pp. 208-210.

Kranig, Wayne. "Mutual Aid to Prepare for Disasters." *Police Chief,* XXXVI:5 (May, 1969), pp. 12-17.

Kranig, Wayne and K.L. Yudowitch. "Mutual Aid in Law Enforcement." *Police Chief,* XXXVII:6 (June, 1970), pp. 64-68.

NATIONAL POLICE FORCE

"Next: A National Police Force?" *U.S. News and World Report* (December 7), p. 164.

Topping, C.W. "Can a National Police Force Serve a Municipality Effectively?" *Police,* 7:2 (November-December, 1962), pp. 6-10.

OMBUDSMEN

Aaron, Richard I. "Utah Ombusdman: The American Proposals." *Utah Law Review* (March, 1967), pp. 32-93.

Abraham, Henry. "A People's Watchdog against Abuse of Power." *Public Administration Review,* 20 (1960), pp. 152, 157.

Abrahamson, Max W. "The Grievance Man: In Ireland?" *Administration (Ireland),* 8:3 (1960), pp. 238-242.

Aikman, C.C. "The New Zealand Ombusdman." *Canadian Bar Review,* 42 (September, 1964), pp. 399-432.

Anderson, Stanley V. *Canadian Ombudsman Proposals.* Berkeley: Institute of Governmental Studies, University of California, 1966.

Anderson, Stanley V. "Connecticut Ombudsman?" *Case and Comment,* LXX (March/April, 1965), pp. 1-9.

Anderson, Stanley V., ed. *Ombudsman for American Government?* Englewood Cliffs, N.J.: Prentice-Hall, 1968.

Anderson, Stanley V. "The Ombudsman: Public Defender against Maladministration." *Public Affairs Report,* 6 (April, 1965), pp. 1-4.

Anderson, Stanley V. "The Scandinavian Ombudsman." *American-Scandinavian Review,* 52 (December, 1964), pp. 403-409.

Andren, Nils. "The Swedish Office of Ombudsman." *Municipal Review,* 33 (1962), pp. 820-821.

Andren, Nils. "The Swedish Ombudsman." *Ango-Swedish Review* (May, 1962), pp. 97-103.

Archibald, Kathleen and Ben Bagdikian. *Televised Ombudsman.* N.Y.: Rand, 1968.

Arnold, Richard S. "An Ombudsman for Arkansas." *Arkansas Law Review,* (1967), pp. 327-335.

Ascher, Charles S. "The Grievance Man or Ombudsmania." *Public Administration Review* (June, 1967), pp. 174-178.

Benchley, Nathaniel. "Ombudsman." *New Yorker,* 43 (July 1, 1967), pp. 33-35.

Bexeluis, A. "The Swedish Ombudsman." *University of Toronto Law Journal,* 17 (1967), pp. 170-176.

Bingham, T.C. "Ombudsman: The Dayton Model." *University of Cincinnati Law Review,* 41 (1972).

Caiden, Gerald and Nimrod Raphaeli. "The Ombudsman Debate in Israeli Politics." *Parliamentary Affairs,* 21 (September, 1968), pp. 201-215.

Capozzola, John M. "An American Ombudsman—Problems and Prospects." *Western Political Quarterly,* 21: (June, 1968), pp. 289-301.

A survey and analysis of the Ombudsman Officer in Scandanavia, its assets and liabilities, and feasibility and suggested criteria for its adoption to the United States.

Chapman, Bruce. "The Ombudsman." *Public Administration,* XXXVIII (Winter, 1960), pp. 303-310.

Christensen, Bent. "The Danish Ombudsman." *University of Pennsylvania Law Review* (September/October, 1969), pp. 25-31.

D'Alemberte, Talbot. "The Ombudsman, a Grievance Man for Citizens." *University of Florida Law Review* (Spring, 1966).

Davis, Kenneth Culp. "Ombudsmen in America: Officers to Criticize Administrative Actions." *University of Pennsylvania Law Review* (June, 1961).

"Enforcing Environmental Policy: The Environmental Ombudsman." *Cornell Law Review,* 56 (May, 1971).

Farley, M.C. "An American Ombudsman: Due Process in the Administrative State." *Administrative Law Review,* 16 (Summer, 1964), pp. 212-221.

Fitzharris, Timothy L. *The Desirability of a Correctional Ombudsman.* Berkeley: Institute of Governmental Studies, University of California, 1973.

Gellhorn, Walter. *Ombudsman and Others: Citizens' Protectors in Nine Countries.* Cambridge, MA.: Harvard University Press, 1966.

Gellhorn, Walter. "The Ombudsman's Relevance to American Municipal Affairs." *American Bar Association Journal,* 54 (February, 1968), pp. 134-140.

Gordon, Robert M., Sr. "The Ombudsman Proposal." *Law and Order,* 15:5 (May, 1967).

Gwyn, W.B. *Barriers to Establishing Urban Ombudsmen—The Case of Newark.* Berkeley: University of California, Berkeley Institute of Government Studies, 1974.

A monograph which details the efforts to establish an ombudsman in Newark, outlines the reasons for the failure of this effort, and provides information that could improve chances of establishing ombudsmen elsewhere.

"Handling the People's Grievances: Ombudsman." *Christian Century,* 82 (October 27, 1965), pp. 1310-1311.

Hartke, V. "Ombudsman: Mediator between the Citizen and His Government." *California West Law Review,* 10:2 (1974), pp. 325-358.

Havel, James T. "The Ombudsman." *Your Government,* 23 (January 15, 1968), pp. 1-3.

Hirsch, J. "The Genesis of the Israel Public Complaints Commissioner." *Public Administration,* 13 (1972), pp. 119-128.

Hollands, John H. "Ombudsmen in Buffalo." *Legal and Briefcase,* 26:5 (1968), pp. 224-230.

Ikeda, W.H. "Ombudsman in Hawaii! The Basic Premises." *Hawaii Bar Journal,* 7 (April, 1970).

"Is an Ombudsman Essential to Protect Rights of Aggrieved Citizens?" *Journal of California Law Enforcement* (July, 1967), pp. 7-13.

Jagerskiold, Stig. "The Swedish Ombudsman." *University of Pennsylvania Law Review* (June, 1961).

Johnson, J.C. "Why an Ombudsman?" *Australian Police Journal* (April, 1975), pp. 118-124.

Kass, Benny. *Ombudsman: A Proposal for Demonstration in Washington, D.C.* Washington, D.C.: Center for Metropolitan Studies, 1968.

King, David C. "What This Country Needs Is a Good Ombudsman." *Kiwanis Magazine* (April, 1967), pp. 23-24, 53-54.

Klesment, Johannes. *The Ombudsman and Related Systems of Governmental Supervision in Scandinavian and Other Countries.* Washington, D.C.: Library of Congress, European Law Division, 1961.

McClellan, G.B. "Role of the Ombudsman." *University of Miami Law Review,* 23 (Spring, 1969).

Mitchell, J.D.B. "The Ombudsman Fallacy." *Public Law* (1962).

Nader, Ralph. "An Ombudsman for the U.S.?" *Christian Science Monitor* (April 1, 1963).

Olson, B.T. *Ombudsman on the West Coast—An Analysis and Evaluation of the Watchdog Function of the California Grand Jury.* Michigan: Community Development, 1968.

Author considers the four major grand jury functions to be good government advocate, social commentator, community referee, and health and safety inspector.

"The Ombudsman." *Your Government* (January 15, 1968), pp. 1-3.

"Ombudsman at Work." *Economist,* 203 (June, 1962).

Poole, K.P. "Organizing the Ombudsman." *Local Government Chronicle* (November, 1969), pp. 2074-2076.

Reuss, Henry S. "An American Ombudsman?" *Public Management,* 49 (October, 1967), pp. 265-267.

Rowat, Donald C., ed. *The Ombudsman: Citizen's Defender.* Toronto: University of Toronto Press, 1965.

Rowat, Donald C. *The Ombudsman Plan: Essays on the Worldwide Spread of an Idea.* Toronto: McClellan and Stewart, 1973.

Sanders, Marion K. "Sweden's Remedy for Police Brutality." *Harpers,* 229 (November, 1962).

"Savannah's Ombudsman." *American City,* 83 (June, 1968).

Sawer, Geoffrey. *Ombudsman.* New Rochelle, N.Y.: Cambridge Press, 1964.

Sharpley, George. "Ombudsman: A Representative Democracy's Finest Hour." *Police Chief,* XXXVI:1 (January, 1969), pp. 12-17.

Stacy, Frank A. *The British Ombudsman.* Oxford: Clarendon, 1971.

Tibbles, Lance. "The Ombudsman." *Newsweek,* 71 (January 8, 1968).

Utley, T.E. *Occasion for Ombudsman.* London: Johnson, 1961.

Vieg, John A. *Progress Versus Utopia: The Use of Plans, Examples, Complaints and Standards of Improving Public Administration.* N.Y.: Asia, 1963.

Walton, Leland M. "Ombudsman Experiment in Seattle, Washington." *Western City,* 49 (June, 1973), pp. 9-10.

Whisenand, P.M. and G.T. Felkenes. "An Ombudsman for Police." *Police Chief,* XXXIV:11 (November, 1967), pp. 18-27.

POLICE AND POLITICS

The Police and Politics

Allen, Francis A. *Crimes of Politics: Political Dimensions of Criminal Justice.* Cambridge: Harvard University Press, 1974.

Bent, Alan Edward. *The Politics of Law Enforcement: Conflict and Power in Urban Communities.* Lexington, MA.: Lexington, 1974.

"Birch Policemen." *Commonwealth,* 81 (December 18, 1964).

"Conspiracy on the Right: John Birch Society Members." *New Republic,* 153 (November 28, 1964), pp. 3-4.

Farbell, Arthur M. "Political Intrusions in Police Service." *Police Yearbook,* Washington, D.C.: IACP, 1958.

Furstenberg, Mark H. "Police and Politics." *Police Chief,* XXXV:8 (August, 1968), pp. 12-18.

Gibson, Frank K. "The Police and Politics." *Police Chief,* XLII:5 (May, 1975), pp. 68-69.

Gunther, Max. "Cops in Politics—A Threat to Democracy." *True* (February, 1970).

Hamann, Albert D. and Rebecca Becker. "The Police and Partisan Politics in Middle-Sized Communities." *Police* (July-August, 1970).

Hoffman, Paul. "Police Birchites: The Blue Backlash." *Nation* (December 7, 1964).

Holliday, Roy E. "The Police Administrator: A Politician?" *Journal of Criminal Law, Criminology and Police Science,* 53: (December, 1962), pp. 526-527.

Madgwick, P.J. *American City Politics.* Boston: Routledge and Kegan, 1970.

Ruchelman, L. *Police Politics—A Comparative Study of Three Cities.* Cambridge, MA.: Ballinger, 1974.
Investigation and comparison of important issues of police policy in New York, Philadelphia, and Chicago for the period covering 1966 to 1969.

Tolchin, Susan J. *Police Policy Area as a Subsystem of New York City olchin,/ Politics.* Unpub. Doctoral Dissertation, New York University, 1968.

Viteritti, Joseph P. *Police, Politics and Pluralism in New York City: A Comparative Study.* Los Angeles: Sage, 1973.

City Politics—General

Banfield, Edward C. *Big City Politics: A Comparative Guide to the Political Systems of Nine American Cities.* N.Y.: Random, 1965.

Banfield, Edward. *Political Influence.* N.Y.: Free Press, 1961.

Banfield, Edward C. and James Q. Wilson. *City Politics.* Cambridge: Harvard University Press, 1963.

Boyarski, Bill and Nancy Boyarski. *Backroom Politics.* Los Angeles: J.F. Tarcher, 1974.

Dahl, Robert A. *Who Governs? Democracy and Power in an American City.* New Haven, CT.: Yale University Press, 1961.
Excellent analysis and research framework; thorough presentations of all aspects of power, politics; a major analysis and contribution to the field of power politics and local government.

Skolnick, Jerome H. "Guerrilla Politics in California." *New Society,* 16 (October, 1975), pp. 136-137.

POLICE AUTHORITY

Asch, Sidney H. *Police Authority and the Rights of the Individual.* N.Y.: Arco, 1971.

Donnelly, Richard C. "Police Authority and Practices." *Annals* (January, 1962).

Goldstein, Herman. "Administrative Problems in Controlling the Exercise of Police Authority." *Journal of Criminal Law, Criminology and Police Science,* 58:2 (June, 1967), pp. 160-172.

Haugh, John J. "The Scope of the Legal Responsibility and Authority of the Police Department." *Police,* 13:1 (September-October, 1968), pp. 72-81.

Wilson, O.W. "Police Authority in a Free Society." *Journal of Criminal Law, Criminology and Police Science,* 54:2 (June, 1963), pp. 175-180.

POLICE DISCRETION

Aaron, Thomas J. *The Control of Police Discretion: The Danish Experience.* Springfield, IL.: C.C. Thomas, 1966.

Abernathy, M. Glenn. "Police Discretion and Equal Protection." *South Carolina Law Quarterly,* 14: (1962).

Adler, Martin D. "The Application of Discretion in Enforcement of the Law in Mental Health Situations." *Police,* 9:2 (November-December, 1964), pp. 48-53.

Archuleta, A.O. "Police Discretion v. Plea Bargaining." *Police Chief* (April, 1974).
There are negligible similarities between plea bargaining and police discretion to constitute any kind of parallel.

Banton, Michael P. "Police Discretion." *New Society,* (1963).

Barrett, Edward. "Police Practices and the Law—From Arrest to Release or Charge." *California Law Review,* 50:11 (1962).

Bassett, Joel. "Discretionary Power and Procedural Rights in the Granting and Revoking of Probation." *Journal of Criminal Law, Criminology and Police Science,* 60:4 (December, 1969), pp. 479-502.

Bittner, Egon. "Police Discretion in Emergency Apprehension of Mentally Ill Persons." *Social Problems* (Winter, 1967), pp. 278-292

Black, Donald J. "Production of Crime Rates." *American Sociological Review* (1970), pp. 733-748.

Block, Richard L. "Police Action as Reported by Victims of Crime." *Police* (November-December, 1970).
Examines police discretion. National survey.

Bozza, Charles M. "Motivations Guiding Policemen in the Arrest Process." *Journal of Police Science and Administration,* 1:4 (December, 1973), pp. 468-476.

Buckner, H.T. *Police—The Culture of a Social Control Agency.* Ann Arbor, MI.: University Microfilms, 1967.
Decisions involving police discretion are explained as the result of interaction between three different levels of social control—morality, custom, and law.

Clissit, H.F.C. "The Exercise of Discretion in the Enforcement of Law." *Police Journal,* 42:12 (1969), pp. 564-571.
An award-winning essay delineating the dilemma between police discretion and the need to have laws obeyed. Offers the philosophical and practical implications of the exercise of police discretion.

Crisafi, Frank J. and Fred A. Wileman. *Guidelines for Discretion.* Madison: Institute of Government Affairs, University of Wisconsin, 1971.
Twelve models for local law enforcement agencies.

Davis, Kenneth Culp. *Discretionary Justice; A Preliminary Inquiry.* Baton Rouge: Louisiana State University Press, 1969.

Fisk, James G. *Police Officer's Exercise of Discretion in the Decision to Arrest: Relationship to Organizational Goals and Societal Values.* Los Angeles: University of California at Los Angeles, Institute of Government and Public Affairs, 1974.

Goldstein, Herman. "Administrative Problems in Controlling the Exercise of Police Authority." *Journal of Criminal Law, Criminology and Police Science,* 58 (1967).

Goldstein, Herman. "Police Discretion: The Ideal versus the Real." *Public Administration Review* (September, 1963), pp. 140-148.

Goldstein, Joseph. "Police Discretion Not to Invoke the Criminal Process: Low Visibility Decisions in the Administration of Law." *Yale Law Journal,* LXIX (1960), pp. 543-594.

Greenberg, Reuben M. "Police Discretion v. Discriminatory Law Enforcement." *Police Chief,* XLI:7 (July, 1974).

Grosman, B.A. "The Discretionary Enforcement of Law." *Chitty's Law Journal,* 21:2 (1973), pp. 46-52.

La Fave, Wayne. *Arrest.* Boston: Little Brown, 1965.

La Fave, Wayne R. "The Police and Nonenforcement of the Law." *Wisconsin Law Review* (1962).

McBride, James T. "Do We Need Computerized Justice?" *Police Chief,* XLII:10 (October, 1975), pp. 54-55.

Meyer, John C., Jr. "The Reactive and Proactive Models of Information Search and Utilization by Police: Search for an Alternative." *Journal of Police Science and Administration,* 1:3 (September, 1973), pp. 311-318.

Osborough, Nial. "Police Discretion Not to Prosecute Students: A British Problem." *Journal of Criminal Law, Criminology and Police Science,* 56:2 (June, 1965), pp. 241-245.

Pepinsky, H.E. *Police Decisions to Report Offenses.* Ann Arbor, MI.: University Microfilms, 1972.
Study of police discretionary actions when responding to citizen calls for assistance or reports of crime.

Petersen, D.M. *Police, Discretion and the Decision to Arrest.* Ann Arbor, MI.: University Microfilms, 1968.
Examination of the factors and influences which affect the uniformed policeman's decision to arrest.

"Police Discretion." *Iowa Law Review* (April, 1973), pp. 893-973.

"Police Discretion and the Judgement That a Crime Has Been Committed—Rape in Philadelphia." *University of Pennsylvania Law Review,* 117 (1968).

Reiss, Albert J. "Discretionary Justice in the United States." *International Journal of Criminology and Penology* (February, 1974), pp. 181-205.

Schiller, Stephen A. "More Light on a Low Visibility Function: The Selective Enforcement of Laws." *Police Law Quarterly* (Summer, 1972), pp. 6-11; (Autumn, 1972), pp. 20-32; (Winter, 1973), pp. 17-20; (Spring, 1973), pp. 35-44.

Schmidt, Wayne W. "A Proposal for a Statewide Law Enforcement Administrative Law Council." *Journal of Science and Administration,* 2:3 (September, 1974), pp. 330-338.
Advocates legalizing discretionary and other aspects of the police function.

Wileman, Fred A., ed. *Guidelines for Discretion.* Madison: Institute of Governmental Affairs, University of Wisconsin, January, 1970.
Five models for local law enforcement agencies.

Zurcher, James C. and Betsy S. Cohen. "Officer Discretion Limits and Guidelines." *Police Chief* (June, 1976).

POLICE FUNCTION

American Bar Association Project on Standards for Criminal Justice. *Standards Relating to the Urban Police Function.* N.Y.: American Bar Association, 1972.

Berkley, George. "How the Police Work." *New Republic* (August 2, 1969).

Butler, Alan J. *The Law Enforcement Process.* N.Y.: Alfred, 1976.

Center for the Study of Democratic Institutions. *The Police: An Interview with William H. Parker.* Santa Barbara, CA.: Center for the Study of Democratic Institutions, 1962.

Charlotte USAC Project. *Charlotte—Integrated Municipal Information System Project—The Police Function Concept.* Springfield, VA.: NTIS, 1973.
A systems analysis approach to a conceptualization of the city's police function.

Clift, Raymond E. *Police and Public Safety.* Cincinnati: W.H. Anderson, 1963.

Cullinane, M.J. "The Police Patrol Officer: The Backbone of Law Enforcement." *Police Chief* (September, 1973), pp. 37-39.

Diamond, Harry. "Police Service: A Look at Obligations." *Police,* 6:1 (September-October, 1961), pp. 30-35.

Dumpleton, John. *Law and Order: The Story of the Police.* Chester Springs, PA.: Dufour Editions, 1968.

"Fifteen Recommendations for Improving the Police Function." *Police Chief,* XXXVII:6 (June, 1971), pp. 64-76.

Goldstein, Herman. *Policing A Free Society.* Cambridge, MA.: Ballinger, 1977.

Hahn, Harlan, ed. *Police in Urban Society.* Beverly Hills, CA.: Sage, 1971.

Jameson, Samuel H. "Law Enforcement in a Free Society." *Law and Order,* 17:8 (August, 1969), pp. 94-99.

Kennard, John P. De B. "Some Reflections on Law Enforcement." *Law and Order,* 14:11 (November, 1966), pp. 24-26, 82.

Miller, Frank. *The Police Function.* Mineola, N.Y.: Foundation, 1971.

Misner, Gordon E. "The Urban Police Mission." *Issues in Criminology,* 3:1 (Summer, 1967), pp. 35-46.

Pfiffner, John M. *The Function of the Police in a Democratic Society.* Los Angeles: School of Public Administration, University of Southern California, 1967.

Reiss, Albert J., Jr. *The Policing of Everyday Life, Our Police Standards and Conduct, Toward a Civil Society.* New Haven, CT.: Yale University Press, 1969.

Schwartz, L.B. and S.R. Goldstein. *Law Enforcement Handbook for Police.* St. Paul, MN.: West, 1970.

Thomas, J.L. "The Scarecrow Function of the Police." *Police Journal,* XIX (1946).

POLICE HUMOR

Irwin, Bud. *A Policeman's Lot.* South Brunswick, N.J.: Barnes, 1968.

Pulling, Christopher. *Mr. Punch in the Police.* London: Butterworths, 1964.

POLICE IMAGE

Bolldworth, Jimmy E. "Image of a Law Enforcement Officer in the Community." *National Sheriff* (February/March, 1972).

Brooks, William D. and W. Frederick Gustav. "Police Image: An Exploratory Study." *Journal of Communication,* 20:4 (December, 1970), pp. 370-374.

di Grazia, Robert J. "The Police Image and Public Support." *Police Chief,* XXXLV:3 (March, 1967), pp. 52-53.

Hughes, L.E. "The Police Image." *Kansas Law Enforcement Journal* (March-April, 1965).

Janowitz, Morris and Deil Wright. "The Prestige of Public Employment: 1929 and 1954." *Public Administration Review* (Winter, 1956), pp. 15-22.

Mailick, Sidney. "Public Service Prestige: Problem and Paradox." *Public Personnel Review,* 10 (July, 1949), pp. 155-162.

Murphy, Michael J. "Improving the Law Enforcement Image." *Journal of Criminal Law, Criminology and Police Science,* 56:1 (March, 1965), pp. 105-108.

National League of Cities. "Survey Shows Police Personnel Shortages, Salary and 'Image' Problems." *Journal of California Law Enforcement* (October, 1966), pp. 76-89.

THE POLICE IN WARTIME

Barfuss, G.H. "Civilian Defense Auxiliaries in St. Paul—Recruitment and Training." *Minnesota Municipalities,* 27 (April, 1942), pp. 136-137.

Cato, E. Raymond. "California Highway Patrol Is Operating on War Basis.' *California Highway Patrolman,* 5 (February, 1942), pp. 6-7, 52.

"Crime in London in 1940." *FBI Law Enforcement Bulletin,* 11 (January, 1942), pp. 45-46.

Duties of the Police in the Event of Invasion. [Confidential] Southampton: Southampton Constabulary (March, 1942).

Gabrielson, W.A. "Honolulu. Police Radio Was Boon to Public." *American City,* 58 (March, 1943).

Game, P. "Britain's Police in War." *Journal of Criminal Law, Criminology and Police Science,* 35 (July, 1944), pp. 121-127.

Gwynn-Brown, Arthur. *F.S.P.: An N.C.O.'s Description of His and Others' First Six Months of War, January 1st-June 1st, 1940.* [Field Security Personnel] London: Chatto and Windus, 1942.

International Association of Chiefs of Police. *Selective Service and Other Wartime Personnel Problems.* Washington, D.C.: IACP, October, 1942.

Landstreet, Barent F. "Police Problems in War-Caused Emergency." *Police Yearbook,* Washington, D.C.: IACP, 1961.

Larsen, R. "Maui Police and the War." *Journal of Criminal Law and Criminology,* 33 (January, 1943), pp. 410-415.

"Lessons of the Cities." *Police Journal (GB),* 14 (July-September, 1941), pp. 292-304.

"Plans for Civil Defense." *Spring 3100,* 12 (July, 1941), pp. 4-8.

Police Review. *ABC for Special Constables and Police War Reserves.* 4th ed. London: Police Review Publishing, 1942.

Reay, W.T. "Metropolitan Special Constabulary: The War Force—The Reserve." *Police Journal (GB),* (1928), pp. 317-334.

Reith, Charles. *Police Principals and the Problem of War.* London: Oxford University Press, 1940.

Rogers, E.F. "Air Raid Protection for Police Officers." *Police Journal (GB),* 13 (January-March, 1940), pp. 66-72.

"Selective Service Director Clarifies Status of Police Personnel in Selective Draft." *Police Chiefs Newsletter,* 7 (December, 1940).

Turner, C. "Police Duty at Air-Raid Incidents." *Police Journal (GB),* 14 (January-March, 1941), pp. 35-49.

"Wartime and Emergency Duties of Police." *FBI Law Enforcement Bulletin,* 11 (January, 1942), pp. 3-28.

White, W.H. "New Patrolman Trained for Wartime Duty." *California Highway Patrolman,* 5 (February, 1942), pp. 24-25, 64.

Wilson, Frank J. *War Activities of the Secret Service.* N.Y.: IACP, 1942.

POLICE MALPRACTICE

Police Malpractice—General

American Civil Liberties Union. *Police Malpractice in Watts Riot.* Los Angeles: American Civil Liberties Union, 1965.

American Civil Liberties Union. *Secret Detention by the Chicago Police.* Glencoe, IL.: Free Press, 1959.

American Civil Liberties Union of Southern California. *Law Enforcement: The Matter of Redress.* Los Angeles: Institute of Modern Legal Thought, 1969.

Analysis of ACLU-sponsored police malpractice centers located in minority communities.

Broadway, Fred M. "Police Misconduct: Positive Alternatives." *Journal of Police Science and Administration,* 2:2 (June, 1974), pp. 210-218.

Chevigny, Paul. "Abuses of Police Power." *Atlantic* (March, 1969).

Chevigny, Paul. *Cops and Rebels: A Study in Provocation.* N.Y.: Pantheon, 1972.

Chevigny, Paul. *Police Power: Police Abuse in New York City.* N.Y.: Pantheon, 1969.

Cogshall, Fred J. "Are We Buying the Trojan Horse? Need for Police Respect of Constitutional Rights." *Journal of Criminal Law and Criminology,* 40:2 (July-August, 1949).

"Doctor Strange Cop." *Newsweek* (November 29, 1971).

Garrison, Omar V. *Spy Government: The Emerging Police State in America.* N.Y.: Lyle Stewart, 1962.

Ingersoll, John E. "The Police Scandal Syndrome." *Police Chief,* 30:5 (August, 1963), pp. 10-49.

"Observing Police Misconduct." *Science News* (May 29, 1971), pp. 367-368.

Playboy Panel. "Crisis in Law Enforcement." *Playboy* (March, 1966).

Rexroth, Kenneth. "The Fuzz." *Playboy* (July, 1967)m

Samuels, Gertrude. "I Don't Think the Cop Is My Friend." *New York Times Magazine* (August 7, 1966).

Police Brutality

Beyle, Herman C. and Spencer D. Parratt. "Approval and Disapproval of Specific Third Degree Practices." *Journal of Criminal Law and Criminology,* 28 (November-December, 1937), pp. 526-550.

Beyle, Herman C. and Spencer D. Parratt. "Measuring the Severity of the Third Degree." *Journal of Criminal Law and Criminology,* 24 (1933-1934), pp. 485-503.

Bowers, Robert J. "Nature of the Problem of Police Brutality." *Cleveland—Marshall Law Review,* 14:3 (1965), pp. 601-609.

Brooks, Thomas R. "Necessary Force—Or Police Brutality?" *New York Times Magazine* (December 5, 1965).

Byrd, R.C. "Police Brutality or Public Brutality?" *Police Chief* (February, 1966).

"Contagion of Violence." *New Statesman,* 58 (July 25, 1959).

Cray, Ed. *The Big Blue Line.* N.Y.: Coward-McCann, 1967.

Feder, B. *Policeman and the Citizen—The Politics of Law and Order.* N.Y.: American Book, 1973.

Booklet discussing police brutality, misconduct, abuse of authority, legal limitations, and the disturbance at the 1968 Democratic National Convention in Chicago.

Gorden, Mitchell. "Police 'Brutality': Tension Won't Ease Unless Enforcement Agencies Help to Dispel Hostility of Negroes." *Wall Street Journal,* 116 (1965).

Hale, E.C. "The True Victims of Police Brutality Are the Police Themselves." *Police Chief,* 30 (June, 1963), pp. 30-32.

Hopkins, E.J. *Our Lawless Police.* N.Y.: (Doubleday, 1951).

Inbau, Fred E. "Behind Those 'Police Brutality' Charges." *Reader's Digest* (July, 1966).

Kauper, P.G. "Judicial Examination of the Accused—A Remedy for the Third Degree." *Michigan Law Review,* 73:1 (1974), pp. 39-70.

Lavine, Emmanuel. *The Third Degree.* N.Y.: Vanguard, 1930.

Nugent, Francis. "Police Brutality." *Police Chief,* 31 (March-April, 1964).

Parker, William H. "Police Chief Talks of Police Brutality." *U.S. News and World Report,* 57 (August 10, 1964), pp. 33-36.

"The Police and Civil Rights." *Frontier,* 13:5 (May, 1962).

"Police Brutality—Fact or Fiction?" *U.S. News and World Report* (September 6, 1965), pp. 37-40.

"Preliminary Examinations and the 'Third Degree'." *Baylor Law Review,* 2 (Winter, 1950), pp. 131-158.

Raab, Selwyn. *Justice in the Back Room.* Cleveland, OH.: World, 1967.

Reiss, A.J. "Police Brutality—Answers to Key Questions." *Transaction,* (July-August, 1968).

Shaw, Eleanor F. "Police Brutality???" *Police* (March-April, 1968).

"Third Degree—Its Historical Background, the Present Law and Recommendations." *Kentucky Law Journal,* 43 (Spring, 1955).

Wilson, O.W. "Police Brutality." *Police Chief,* 30 (November, 1963).

Police Corruption

Astor, Gerald. *The New York Cops: An Informal History.* N.Y.: Scribner's, 1971.

Outlines various police scandals.

"Bad Connection." *Newsweek* (November 29, 1971).

Bahn, Charles. "Psychology of Police Corruption: Socialization of the Corrupt." *Police Journal (GB),* 48:1 (January, 1975), pp. 30-36.

Barker, Thomas and Julian Roebuck. *Empirical Typology of Police Corruption: A Study in Organizational Deviance.* Springfield, IL.: C.C. Thomas, 1973.

Beigel, H. "The Investigation and Prosecution of Police Corruption." *Journal of Criminal Law and Criminology,* 65:2 (1974), pp. 135-156.

Brannon, W.T. *The Crooked Cops.* Evanston, IL.: Regency, 1962.

"The Burglar Who Taught Cops How to Be Robbers." *Life* (February 1, 1960), pp. 20-21.

Cook, Fred J. "Corrupt Society." *Nation,* 196 (June, 1963), pp. 472-474.

Describes the Denver Police Department and how police officers were committing burglaries.

"Corruption: An Archetype or an Anachronism?" *Police Chief,* XLI:12 (December, 1974).

Coster, C.M. "Misbehavior Must Not Be Tolerated." *National Sheriff,* 25:5 (1973), pp. 6-7, 30, 32.

Dempsey, Lawrence J. "The Knapp Commission and You." *Police Chief,* XXXIX:11 (November, 1972), pp. 20-29; XL:1 (January, 1973), pp. 22-36.

Deutsch, Albert. *The Trouble with Cops.* N.Y.: Crown, 1954.

Droge, Edward F., Jr. *Patrolman: A Cop's Story.* N.Y.: New American Library, 1973.

Foster, G.P. *Police Administration and the Control of Police Criminality—A Case Study Approach.* Ann Arbor, MI.: University Microfilms, 1966.
Presentation and analysis of Denver's 1961 confrontation with police corruption and criminal activity by police officers.

Fox, Harry G. "The Reputation of an Honest Man." *Law and Order,* 22:6 (June, 1974), pp. 66, 68-69.

Gilbert, Ivy L. *A Case Study of Police Scandal: An Investigation into Illegitimate Norms of a Legitimate Enforcement Agency.* Unpub. Master's Thesis, University of Texas, El Paso, June, 1965.

Goldstein, Herman. *Police Corruption: A Perspective on Its Nature and Control.* Washington, D.C.: Police Foundation, 1975.

"Infection from Above; Criminals on the Police Force." *Nation,* 193 (October 21, 1961).

Ingersoll, John E. "The Police Scandal Syndrome, Conditions Leading to an Apparent Breakdown in Police Service." *Crime and Delinquency* (1964).

Keller, E. John. "Let's Cover It Up." *Law and Order* (November, 1975), pp. 71-83.

Kelly, W.H. "When the Police Are Corrupt." *Canadian Police Chief,* 63:1 (1974), pp. 21-22.

Knapp Commission Report on Police Corruption. N.Y.: Braziller, 1973.
Findings of the commission appointed to determine the incidence, prevalence, and causes of police corruption in New York City.

Maas, Peter. *Serpico.* N.Y.: Viking, 1973.
Experiences of NYPD patrolmen. Discusses major and minor aspects of police corruption.

McNamara, J.D. "The Impact of Bureaucratic Dysfunctions on Attempts to Prevent Police Corruption." *Police Journal,* 48:1 (1975), pp. 37-44.

Methvin, Eugene H. "How Organized Crime Corrupts Our Law Enforcers." *Reader's Digest* (January, 1972), pp. 85-89.

Misner, Gordon E. "Organization and Social Setting of Police Corruption." *Police Journal,* 48:1 (January, 1975), pp. 45-51.

Mockridge, Norton and Robert Prall. *The Big Fix.* N.Y.: Holt, 1954.

Muller, Jack and Paul Neimark. *I, Pig, Or How the World's Most Famous Cop, Me, Is Fighting City Hall.* N.Y.: Morrow, 1971.

Murphy, Patrick V. "Police Corruption." *Police Chief,* XL:12 (December, 1973), pp. 36-37, 72.

Murtagh, John M. "Gambling and Police Corruption." *Atlantic* (November, 1960).

NCCD Law Enforcement Council. "Official Corruption. A Position Statement." *Crime and Delinquency,* 20:1 (1974), pp. 15-19.

"New York's Rotten Apples." *Newsweek,* 78 (July 12, 1971).

Parsons, James C. "A Candid Analysis of Police Corruption." *Police Chief,* XL:3 (March, 1973), pp. 20-22, 67.

Peterson, V.W. "Chicago Police Scandals." *Atlantic,* 206 (1960), pp. 58-64.

Peterson, Virgil W. "Issues and Problems in Metropolitan Area Police Services." *Journal of Criminal Law, Criminology and Police Science,* 48:2 (July/August, 1957), pp. 127-148.

"Police Corruption: Psychological and Organizational Factors." *Police Journal* (January, 1975).

Price, Barbara R. "Police Corruption: An Analysis." *Criminology* (August, 1972), pp. 161-176.

Reid, Ed. *The Shame of New York.* London: Gollancz, 1954.

"Report of Committee on Lawless Enforcement of Law." *Science and Scientific Crime Detection,* 1:6 (1964).

Report on Police Corruption and the Quality of Law Enforcement in Philadelphia, Pennsylvania. Philadelphia: Pennsylvania Crime Commission, 1974.

Rolph, C.H. "American Policeman." *New Statesman,* 58 (August 1, 1959), pp. 127-128.

Shecter, L. and W. Phillips. *On the Pad—The Underworld and Its Corrupt Police, Confessions of a Cop on the Take.* N.Y.: Putnam, 1973.

Sherman, Lawrence W., ed. *Police Corruption: A Sociological Prospective.* Garden City, N.Y.: Doubleday, 1974.

Smith, Ralph Lee. "Cops as Robbers." *Police,* 9 (May-June, 1965).

Smith, Ralph L. "The Problem of the Problem." *The Nation,* 208 (1969).

Smith, Ralph Lee. *The Tarnished Badge.* N.Y.: Crowell, 1964.

Smith, Sandy. "You Can't Expect Police on the Take to Take Orders." *Life* (December 6, 1968).

Smith, William H.T. "Deceit in Uniform." *Police Chief* (September, 1973), pp. 20-21.
Corruption and "code of silence" in a police department.

Souryal, Safwat A. "Stages of Police Corruption." *Police Chief,* XLII:2 (February, 1975), pp. 63-65.

Stead, Philip John. "Some Notes on Police Corruption: The English Experience." *Police Journal (GB),* (January, 1975), pp. 24-29.

Stern, Mort. "What Makes A Policeman Go Wrong, by a Former Denver Police Officer as Told to Mort Stern." *Journal of Criminal Law, Criminology and Police Science,* 59:2 (June, 1968), pp. 97-101.

Stoddard, Ellwyn R. "The Informal 'Code' of Police Deviancy: A Group Approach to 'Blue-Coat Crime'." *Journal of Criminal Law, Criminology and Police Science,* 59:2 (June, 1968), pp. 201-213.

Stoker, Charles F. *Thicker 'n Thieves.* Santa Monica, CA.: Sidereal, 1951.
Police corruption in Los Angeles prior to Willam H. Parker becoming chief.

"Taking Dirty Money." *Time,* 98 (September 13, 1971).

Ward, Richard H. "Police Corruption: An Overview." *Police Journal (GB),* (January, 1975), pp. 52-54.

Werner, M.R. "That Was New York." *The New Yorker,* 31 (November 19, 1955).

Whaley, Bobbie G. "I Was a Burglar with a Badge." *Saturday Evening Post,* 235 (February 10, 1962), pp. 86-89.
Confessions of a Denver policeman who committed 43 burglaries.

Wilson, James Q. "The Police and Their Problems: A Theory on Why Misconduct Occurs Chiefly in Big-City Departments." *Public Policy,* Yearbook of the Graduate School of Public Administration. Cambridge, MA.: Harvard University, 1963.

Wittles, David G. "Why Cops Turn Crooked." *Saturday Evening Post,* 221 (April 23, 1949), pp. 26-27.

POLICEMAN'S RIGHTS

Belli, Melvin. "Thoughts on Peace Officer's Compensation for Injuries via the Court System." *Journal of California Law Enforcement* (April, 1975), pp. 143-144.
Describes two court cases for duty-related injuries.

Blunt, Robert C. "The Battered Policeman: A Law Enforcement Officer Sues for Assault and Battery." *FBI Law Enforcement Bulletin,* 43:9 (September, 1974), pp. 26-31.

Blunt, Robert C. "A Law Enforcement Officer Sues for Defamation." *FBI Law Enforcement Bulletin,* 43:2 (February, 1974).

Burpo, John H. "The Policeman's Bill of Rights." *Police Chief,* XXXIX:9 (September, 1972), pp. 18-26.
Proposals examining policemen's rights.

Lloyd, Bob. "A Policeman Has Civil Rights, Too." *Law and Order,* 12:7 (July, 1964).
Advocates prosecuting those who file false police reports.

"Prohibiting Political Activity." *Police Chief* (July, 1972).
Ohio police captain brought suit against City of Toledo alleging that certain rules of the Toledo Police Department violated his First Amendment freedoms.

Sherrow, Dale Ellsworth. "Dismissal of Police Officers for Exercising Privilege against Self-Incrimination." *Journal of Criminal Law and Criminology,* 38:6 (March-April, 1947-1948), pp. 613-619.

Tamm, Q. "Crimes against the Police." *Carolina Law,* 22:6 (1972), pp. 96-101.

POLICE MEMORIALS

Davis, E.M. "The Police Memorial—A City Remembers." *Police Chief,* XXXIX:8 (August, 1972), pp. 18-19.

"Hall of Fame Honors Police Dead." *American City,* 80 (January, 1965).

Kelley, Dayton. "Ranger Hall of Fame." *FBI Law Enforcement Bulletin* (May, 1976), pp. 16-23.

Marx, Jerry. "Oklahoma Dedicates Peace Officer Memorial." *FBI Law Enforcement Bulletin,* 38:8 (August, 1969), pp. 7-11.

"National Peace Officers' Memorial Day." *Police Chief,* XL:5 (May, 1973).

POLICE PATRON SAINT

"Prayer to Saint Michael, Patron Saint of Police Officers." *On Guard* (October, 1958).

POLICE POWER

Leigh, L.H. *Police Powers in England and Wales.* London: Butterworths, 1975.

Leigh, Leonard H. "Prolegomenon to a Study of Police Powers in England and Wales." *Notre Dame Lawyer* (1973), pp. 861-880.

Sargent, Tom. "Police Powers: A General View." *Criminal Law Review* (November, 1966), pp. 583-593.

Stotland, E. "Police Power and Community Power: A Final Editorial Comment." *Journal of Social Issues,* 31:1 (1975), pp. 217-218.

POLICE PRACTICE

Ayes, Loren. "Standards of Police Conduct and Performance." *Law and Order,* 12 (April, 1964).

Donnelly, Richard C. "Police Authority and Practices." *The Annals of the American Academy of Political and Social Science,* 339 (January, 1962), pp. 90-110.

George, B.J. "Police Practices and the Citizen." *Police,* 10:4 (March-April, 1966).

Manning, B. *Enforcing the Criminal Law.* Washington, D.C.: NCJRS, (Microfiche) 1975.

Stinchcombe, Arthur L. "Institutions of Privacy in the Determination of Police Administration Practice." *American Journal of Sociology,* 69:2 (1963).

Southern Regional Council. "Police Practice in Alabama." *New South* (1964).

Watson, N.A. "Developing Guidelines for Police Practices." *Police Chief,* 31 (September, 1964).

Weistart, J.C. *Police Practices.* Dobbs Ferry, N.Y.: Oceana, 1972.
Anthology focusing on controversial issues concerning the practices and policies of law enforcement agencies.

POLICE REFORM

Advisory Commission on Intergovernmental Relations. *For A More Perfect Union—Police Reform.* Washington, D.C.: GPO, 1971.
Suggestions for State legislation to improve the police function, with sample drafts of acts, explanations of their purpose, and definitions.

Ahern, J.F. "Let's Recognize That the Patrolman Is the Department." *Police Digest* (1972), pp. 6-9.
The patrolman today exists for the sake of superior and corrupt politicians. Offers suggestions for reform.

Carte, Gene E. and Elaine A. Carte. *Police Reform in the United States: The Era of August Vollmer, 1905-1932.* Berkeley: University of California Press, 1975.

Detzer, Karl. "Crime Ridden Chicago Cleans House." *Reader's Digest* (September, 1962).

Kenney, John P. "A Master Plan for Reorganization of the Police Department, City, and County of Denver." *Police,* 7:4 (March-April, 1963), pp. 66-69.

Leposky, George. "Chicago's Police Reforms." *Crime and Detection,* 1 (November, 1966), pp. 94-106.

Saunders, Charles B., Jr. *Upgrading the American Police: Education and Training for Better Law Enforcement.* Washington, D.C.: Brookings Institution, 1970.

Sherman, Lawrence W. "The Sociology and Social Reform of the American Police: 1950-1973." *Journal of Police Science and Administration,* 2:3 (September, 1974), pp. 255-262.

Welch, H. Oliver and Charles Cory. "A Mandate for State Planning: Upgrading Law Enforcement." *Police Chief,* XXXVII:2 (February, 1970), pp. 30-36.

POLICE REVIEW BOARDS

Abbot, D.W. and E.T. Rogowsky. *Police, Politics and Race: The New York City Referendum on Civilian Review.* N.Y.: American Jewish Committee, [n.d.].

Abraham, H.J. "People's Watchdog against Abuse of Power." *Public Administration Review* (1960), pp. 152-157.

American Civil Liberties Union. *Police Power and Citizens Rights: The Case for an Independent Police Review Board.* N.Y.: American Civil Liberties Union, [n.d.].

Ark, Jacob. "Court Voids Powers of Police Review Boards." *Law and Order,* 14 (March, 1966), pp. 38, 40, 45, 53.

Arm, Walter. "Civilians Shouldn't Judge Cops." *Saturday Evening Post,* 239 (May 7, 1966), pp. 12-14.

Barton, Peter G. "Civilian Review Boards and the Handling of Complaints against the Police." *University of Toronto Law Journal,* 20 (Winter, 1970), pp. 448-469.

Beral, Harold and Marcus Sisk. "Administration of Complaints by Civilians against Police." *Harvard Law Review,* 77 (January, 1964).

Black, Algernon. *The People and the Police.* N.Y.: McGraw-Hill, 1968.
Charts, tables. The Civilian Complaint Review Board of the New York City Police Department as viewed by its former chairman, with analysis of its methods of operation. Strength and weakness.

Bray, Robert J., Jr. "Philadelphia's Police Advisory Board—A New Concept in Community Relations." *Villanova Law Review,* VII (1962).

Broderick, Vincent L. "An Open Letter on Police Review Board." *Police,* 10 (May-June, 1966).
To Mayor John Lindsay of N.Y.C. from Police Commissioner Broderick. Broderick attacks Lindsay's "Law Enforcement Task Force" and calls his civilian review board an "administrative travesty and unfair to the public."

Brooks, Thomas R. " 'No!' Says the P.B.A.: 25,000 Police against the Review Board." *New York Times Magazine* (October 16, 1966), pp. 36-37, 124, 126, 128-129, 131-133.

Brown, Lee P. "Police Review Boards: An Historical and Critical Analysis." *Police,* 10:6 (July-August, 1966), pp. 19-20.

Burger, Warren E. "Who Will Watch the Watchman?" *Texas Police Journal* (March, 1966), pp. 1-6.

"Civilian Review of the Police." *Life,* 61 (October, 21, 1966).

Clark, Robert S. *The Monitoring of Police Agencies: An Inquiry into the Place of Monitoring Information.* Unpub. Doctoral Dissertation, New York University, 1970.
Discusses and analyzes the operation of police review boards.

Coxe, Spencer. "Police Advisory Board: The Philadelphia Story." *Connecticut Bar Journal* (1961), pp. 138-142.

Elam, Jerry. "Wake Up." *Police,* 5:6 (July-August, 1961), pp. 54-56.

Ennis, Edward J. "Police Protections of Civil Rights—An Opportunity and a Challenge." *Police* (July-August, 1965), pp. 80-82.

Gellhorn, Walter. "Police Review Boards: Hoax or Hope?" *Columbia University Forum,* IX (Summer, 1966), pp. 5-10.

Grant, Melvin James. *An Evaluation of the New York City Police Department's Civilian Complaint Review Board in the Field of Civil Rights.* Unpub. Master's Thesis, City University of New York, 1962.

Hewitt, William H. "New York City's Civilian Complaint Review Board Struggle: Its History, Analysis and Some Notes." *Police* (May-June, 1967), (July-August, 1967), (September-October, 1967).

Hewitt, William H. "An Open Letter on Police Review Boards." *Police* (May-June, 1966).

Hudson, James R. "Police Review Boards and Police Accountability." *Law and Contemporary Problems,* 36 (Autumn, 1971), pp. 515-538.

Keller, E.J. "Friend or Foe—A Penetrating Study of the Civilian Police Review Board." *Law and Order,* 13:10 (October, 1965), pp. 85-88.

Locke, Hubert G. "Police Brutality and Civilian Review Boards: A Second Look." *Journal on Urban Law,* 44 (Summer, 1967), pp. 625-633.

McDermott, Thomas F. "Death of a Review Board." *Police,* 12:1 (September-October, 1967).

Marossi, Ruth and Gerald Krefetz. "Philadelphia Policing the Police." *Reporter* (July 19, 1962), pp. 39-40.

Marshall, G. "The Police Policed." *New Society,* 23 (1973).
Home Office in Great Britain is establishing a civilian element into their complaints against police procedures.

Melnicoe, W.B. "Police Review Boards." *Journal of Lambda Alpha Epsilon,* 29 (October, 1966).

Moore, Norman H. "Police Review Boards." *Minnesota Police Journal,* 34 (January-February, 1962).

Murdy, Ralph G. "Civilian Review Boards in Review." *FBI Law Enforcement Bulletin,* 35:7 (July, 1966), pp. 14-18.

Murdy, Ralph G. "Is There a Board in Your Future?" *Police Chief,* 32:6 (June, 1965).

Naegle, Timothy D. "Civilian Complaints against the Police in Los Angeles." *Issues in Criminology,* 3:1 (1967), pp. 7-34.

National Capital Area Civil Liberties Union. *A Proposed Revision of the System for Processing Civilian Complaints Against Police Misconduct in the District of Columbia.* Washington, D.C.: National Capital Area Civil Liberties Union, (June, 1964), (mimeo).

Neier, Aryeh. "Civilian Review Boards—Another View." *Criminal Law Bulletin,* 2 (October, 1966), pp. 10-18.

Norris, Harold. "Constitutional Law Enforcement Is Effective Law Enforcement: Toward a Concept of Police in a Democracy and Citizens' Advisory Board." *University of Detroit Law Journal,* 43:2 (1965), pp. 203-204.

"Philadelphia's Police Advisory Board, a New Concept in Community Relations." *Villanova Law Review* (1962).

"Police Abuse and Civilian Review." *Civil Liberties,* 239 (September, 1966), pp. 4-5.

Police Advisory Board of the City of Philadelphia. *Annual Reports, 1959, 1960, 1961, 1962.* Philadelphia: Police Advisory Board, [n.d.].

"Police Review Boards: IACP Critique of the Study." *Police Chief* (February, 1964).

"Policing the Police." *Newsweek,* 67 (March 7, 1966), pp. 27-28.

"Policing the Police: Are Civilian Review Boards the Answer?" *Senior Scholastic,* 89 (October 21, 1966), pp. 7-8.

Russell K. "Police." *New Society,* 22 (1972), pp. 277-278.
Outlines pressures exerted on the Home Office to introduce an independent non-police element into the police complaints procedure.

Samuels, Gertrude. "Who Shall Judge a Policeman?" *New York Times Magazine* (August 2, 1964), pp. 8, 34, 46.

Skousen, W. Cleon. "What about a Citizen's Police Advisory Board?" *Law and Order,* 14:8 (August, 1966), pp. 90-91, 98.

Smith, Charles L., ed. *Police Review Boards.* Berkeley: Institute of Governmental Studies, University of California, 1965.

Trecker, Harleigh B. *Citizen Boards at Work—New Challenges to Effective Action.* N.Y.: Association Press, 1970.

"Who Polices the Police?" *Time,* 85 (April 30, 1965).

POLICE ROLE

Adams, T.F. *Law Enforcement—An Introduction to the Police Role in the Criminal Justice System.* 2nd ed. Englewood Cliffs, N.J.: Prentice-Hall, 1973.

Aldrich, Alexander. "The Police Role in the Social Investigation." *Legal Aid Review,* 57:3 (Fall, 1959), pp. 14-19.

Alletto, William C. "The Sheriff's Role in Law Enforcement." *Police,* 5:6 (July-August, 1961), pp. 48-50.

Anthony, J.F. "The Ambivalent Role of Police." *Police Digest* (Spring/Summer, 1973), pp. 14-16, 31.

Arm, Walter. *The Policeman; An Inside Look at His Role in a Modern Society.* N.Y.: Dutton, 1969.

Banton, Michael. "Definition of the Police Role." *New Community,* 3:3 (Summer, 1974), pp. 164-171.

Berkeley, George E. *The Democratic Policeman.* Boston: Beacon, 1969.

Brown, A.J. "The Changing Theories, Practices, and Role of the Police." *Police Chief,* XLII:3 (Marcy, 1976), pp. 20-24.

Brown, Dennis C. "Education and Training: Perspectives of the Police Role" *Police,* 16:1 (September, 1971) pp. 21-24.

Cain, Maureen E. *Society and the Policeman Role.* Boston: Routledge and Kegan, 1973.

Day, Frank D. "Criminal Law Enforcement and a Free Society." *Journal of Criminal Law, Criminology and Police Science,* 54:3 (September, 1963), pp. 360-365.

Doig, Jameson W. "The Police in a Democratic Society." *Public Administration Review,* 28:393 (1968).

Edwards, George. "Order and Civil Liberties: A Complex Role for the Police." *Michigan Law Review,* 64 (1965).

Eldefonso, E. *Youth Problems and Law Enforcement.* Englewood Cliffs, N.J.: Prentice-Hall, 1972.
Role of the police in relation to the overall problems of juvenile delinquency, the drug problem, and the operations of the juvenile court.

Esselstyn, T.C. "The Social Role of a County Sheriff." *Journal of Criminal Law, Criminology and Police Science* (July/August, 1953), pp. 177-184.

Fagerstrom, Dorothy. "Traffic Safety Conference Reports on the Police Role." *Law and Order,* 16:6 (June, 1968), pp. 8, 79.

Fleek, T.A. and T.J. Newman. "The Role of the Police in Modern Society." *Police,* 13:4 (March-April, 1969), pp. 21-27.

Gabor, I.R. and C. Low. "The Police Role in the Community." *Criminology,* 10:4 (1973), pp. 383-414.

Garmire, B.L. "The Police Role in an Urban Society." in R.F. Steadman, *The Police and the Community.* Baltimore: Johns Hopkins University Press, 1972.

Goode, William J. "A Theory of Role Strain." *American Sociological Review,* 25 (August, 1960), pp. 486-490.

Goldstein, Herman. "Police Response to Urban Crisis." *Public Administration Review* (September/October, 1968), pp. 417-423.
Offers a descriptive analysis of the current dual-faceted police function, and presents compelling reasons why in the current social context, the police service role must be refined to meet the new challenges. Also presents some methods to achieve that end.

Groth, Carl H. "Police and Society." *Police* (September-October, 1967).

Hall, Jerome. "Police and Law in a Democratic Society." *Indian Law Journal,* 28 (1953).

Higgins, George V. "Omnicompetence and Omnibus Crime Control: the Policeman as Specialist." *Journal of Criminal Law, Criminology and Police Science,* 60:1 (March, 1969), pp. 113-122.

Horan, Michael J., John M. Baines, and Sami G. Hajjar. "The Sheriff's Role in Law Enforcement: Dimensions of Change." *Police,* 16:1 (September, 1971), pp. 11-20.

Hotson, Robert C. "Examination of the Peace Officer and the Law Officer Concepts of the Urban Police Role." *Canadian Police Chief* (July, 1976), pp. 25-28, 44.

Humphrey, Dorothy P. "Why a Cop?" *Police Chief,* XXXVI:7 (July, 1969), pp. 38-39.

Johnson, Elmer H. "Interrelatedness of Law Enforcement Programs: A Fundamental Dimension." *Journal of Criminal Law, Criminology and Police Science,* 60:4 (December, 1969), pp. 509-516.

Johnson, Elmer H. "Police: An Analysis of Role Conflict." *Police* (January-February, 1970).

Kerr, John. "Role of Police in the Modern Community." *Australian Police Journal* (January, 1976), pp. 25-32.

Killinger, G.G. and P.F. Cromwell, Jr. *Issues in Law Enforcement.* Boston: Holbrook, 1975.

Kinton, Jack F., ed. *Police Roles in the 70's.* Aurora, IL.: Social Science and Sociological Resources, 1975.

Knight, R. "The Police Role in Our Permissive Society." *Police Journal,* 27:3 (1973), pp. 165-188.

Kobetz, R.W. *Police Role and Juvenile Delinquency.* Gaithersburg, MD.: IACP, 1971.
Policy guidelines, administrative and organizational concepts, and training suggestions for police-juvenile operations.

Kynell, Kermit S. "The Role of the Police in a Democratic State." *Police,* 3:3 (January-February, 1959), pp. 23-25.

Lawder, Lee E. "Notes on the Policeman." *Law and Order,* 21:9 (September, 1973), pp. 98-103.

McConahy, Malcolm W. "The Role of the Police in Mental Health." *Police* (January-February, 1962).

McDowell, Charles P. *Police in the Community.* Cincinnati, OH.: W.H. Anderson, 1975.

McEntire, Davis and Joseph E. Weckler. "The Role of the Police." *Annals of the American Academy of Political and Social Science,* 224 (1946), pp. 82-89.

Miller, Gary J. "The Future Role of the Police in the Treatment of Alcoholism." *Police* (January-February, 1969).

Mintz, Ellen and Georgette Bennett Sandler. "Instituting a Full Service Orientation to Policing." *Police Chief,* XLI:6 (June, 1974), pp. 44-50.

Misner, Gordon E. "The Urban Police Mission." *Issues in Criminology,* 3:1 (1967), pp. 35-46.

Ness, Elliot. "New Role of the Police." *Survey* (March, 1944).

Nightingale, John. "Role of Police Authorities." *Police (GB),* (July, 1975).

O'Connor, D. "The Modern Approach to the Police Function." *Australian, New Zealand Journal of Criminology,* 7:2 (1974), pp. 68-86.

O'Connor, George W. and Nelson A. Watson. *Juvenile Delinquency and Youth Crime, The Police Role: An Analysis of Philosophy, Policy, Opinion.* Washington, D.C.: IACP, 1965.

Parker, W.H. "The Police Service—A Key to Community Quality." *Journal of Criminal Law, Criminology and Police Science,* 55:2 (June, 1964), pp. 273-279.

Patrick, C.H. *Police, Crime and Society.* Springfield, IL.: C.C. Thomas, 1972.
An overview of the problem of crime and the role which the policeman plays in dealing with crime and other problems.

Peterson, D.M. "The Police Officer's Conception of Proper Police Work." *Police Journal (GB),* 47:2 (1974), pp. 173-177.

Preiss, Jack J. and Howard J. Ehrlich. *An Examination of Role Theory: Case of State Police.* Lincoln: University of Nebraska Press, 1966.

Remington, Frank. "The Role of the Police in a Democratic Society." *Journal of Criminal Law, Criminology and Police Science,* 56:3 (1965), pp. 361-365.

Roberg, Roy R. *The Changing Police Role.* San Jose, CA.: Justice Systems Development, 1975.

Rogovin, Charles H. "Improving Criminal Justice: The Police Role." *Police,* 15:2 (November-December, 1970), pp. 3-4.

Rosenbluh, Edward S. et al. "Is the Policeman Obsolete?" Police Chief, XXXIX:5 (May, 1972), pp. 68-69.

Sagalyn, Arnold. "Role of the Local Police." *Police Yearbook,* Washington, D.C.: IACP, 1963.

Scott, James F. *Study of Role Conflict Among Policemen.* Unpub. Doctoral Dissertation, Indiana University, 1968.

Selzman, Robert M. "The Police, the Public, Public Order and the Law." *Police Chief,* XXXVI:3 (March, 1969), pp. 36-39.

Slavin, James M. "The Police Department Role. What the Local Official Should Know About It." *New Jersey Municipalities* (June, 1964).

Terris, Bruce J. "The Role of the Police." *Annals,* 58 (November, 1967), pp. 58-69.

Viano, E.C. and J.H. Reiman, eds. *The Police in Society.* Farnborough (GB): D.C. Heath, 1975.

Walrod, Truman. *The Role of Sheriff: Past—Present—Future.* Washington, D.C.: National Sheriff's Association, 1975.

Ward, Richard D. "The Police Role: A Case of Diversity." *Journal of Criminal Law, Criminology and Police Science,* LXI (December, 1970), pp. 580-586.

Watson, N.A. *The Police and the Changing Community.* Washington, D.C.: IACP, 1965.

Young, P. "Police in Our Changing Society." *Candian Police Chief,* 62:4 (1973), pp. 21-22.

POLICE SONGS

Pulling, Christopher. "The Policeman in Song." *Police World,* 6 (Summer, 1961), pp. 4-8.

PROFESSIONALISM

Aaron, Thomas J. "Education and Professionalism in American Law Enforcement." *Police,* 10:2 (November-December, 1965), pp. 37-41.

Anderson, A. Stanley. "The Junior College and Police Professionalism." *Police,* 6:3 (January-February, 1962), pp. 14-15.

Anderson, R.E. "Paths to Professionalization." *Police Chief,* XXXVII:8 (August, 1970), pp. 48-51.

Ashenhust, Paul H. "The Goal: A Police Profession." *Journal of Criminal Law, Criminology and Police Science,* 49:6 (March-April, 1959), pp. 605-607.

Aubry, Arthur S., Jr. "Law Enforcement: Professional Status." *Police,* 8:3 (January-February, 1964), pp. 15-19.

Beckman, Erik. "Police Personnel: Toward Professional Relationships." *Journal of California Law Enforcement,* 8:4 (April, 1974), pp. 200-202.

Brereton, George H. "The Importance of Training and Education in the Professionalization of Law Enforcement." *Journal of Criminal Law, Criminology and Police Science* (May-June, 1961), pp. 111-121.

Brereton, George H. "Law Enforcement—A Profession." *Police,* 1:5 (May-June, 1957), pp. 12-19.

Burson, R.H. "Operation Bootstrap." *Police Chief,* XXXIV:11 (November, 1967), pp. 38-39.

Cain, Maureen. "Police Professionalism: Its Meaning and Consequences." *Anglo-American Law Review,* 1:2 (1972), pp. 217-231.

Cancilla, Robert C. "Professionals." *Police,* 16:11 (July, 1972), pp. 4-5.

Carr-Saunders, A.M. and P.A. Wilson. *The Professions.* N.Y.: Humanities, 1964.

Carte, Gene Edward. "August Vollmer and the Origins of Police Professionalism." *Journal of Police Science and Administration,* 1:3 (September, 1973), pp. 274-281.

Chackerian, R. and R.F. Barrett. "Police Professionalism and Citizen Evaluation." *Urban Affairs Quarterly,* 8:3 (March, 1973), pp. 345-349.

Charney, John A. "Professional vs Non-Professional." *Police,* 7:3 (January-February, 1963), pp. 38-39.

Derning, Don R. "The ABC's of Professionalism." *Police Chief,* XXXIX:7 (July, 1972), pp. 24-26.

Dompka, R.J. "A National Police Standards Act—The First Step toward Professionalism?" *Law and Order* (July, 1971), pp. 86-87.
Discussion on what is professionalism as it applies to police and what must be done for police to be recognized as professionals.

Etzioni, Amatai. *Semi-Professions and Their Organizations.* Glencoe, IL.: Free Press, 1969.

Gardner, Harold J. "The Emergence of a Profession." *Police,* 2:5 (May-June, 1958), pp. 44-46.

Goode, W.J. "Encroachment, Charlatanism, and the Emerging Profession." *American Sociological Review,* 25:6 (December, 1960).

Harvie, Robert A. "The Myth of Police Professionalism?" *Police,* 16:4 (December, 1971), pp. 59-61.

Hildebrand, James A. "The Detective Bureau—A Path to Professionalization in Metropolitan Police Departments." *Police,* 13:3 (January-February, 1969), pp. 41-47.

Hughes, E.C. *"Professions": The Professions in America.* Boston: Beacon, 1967.

Kalaidjian, William G. "What Makes the Occupation of Policeman a Profession." *Law and Order,* 13:5 (May, 1965), pp. 57-60.

Kelley, Clarence M. "Professional Status." *Law and Order,* 22:3 (March, 1974), pp. 10-13.

Kelling, George L. and Rogert B. Kliesmet. "Resistance to the Professionalization of the Police." *Police Chief,* XXXVII:5 (May, 1971), pp. 30-39.

Kennedy, Stephen P. "Law Enforcement as a Profession." *American City,* 71 (January, 1956), pp. 124-125.

Kenney, John P. "Police Service Growing in Professional Recognition." *Trojan in Government,* 7: (August, 1956), pp. 1-2.

Kreutzer, Walter E. "The Elusive Professionalization That Police Officers Seek." *Police Chief,* XXXV:8 (August, 1968), pp. 26-31.

LaCouture, Ron A. "One Answer to Professionalization." *Police,* 7:3 (January-February, 1963).

Lentin, Joseph R. "Police Professionalism: A Plan for the Future." *Law and Order,* 21:6 (May, 1973), pp. 46, 48-51.

Liu, Daniel S.C. "Professional Standards of the Police Service." *Police,* 5:3 (January-February, 1961), pp. 45-47.

Lutz, Carl F. "Overcoming Obstacles to Professionalism." *Police Chief,* XXXV:9 (September, 1968), pp. 42-52.

Martin, Charles J. "Police Professionalism—An Appropriate Building." *Journal of California Law Enforcement* (July, 1974), pp. 20-23.

Mirich, John J. and Eugene F. Voris. "Recognition of Local Law Enforcement as a Profession: The Time Has Surely Come!" *Police,* 9:4 (March-April, 1965), pp 42-43.

Moynahan, J.M. "Am I a Professional?" *Police Chief,* XXXVII:2 (February, 1970).

Muir, A.A. "A Profession?" *Criminologist,* 8 (1973), pp. 23-25.

"The Police Service As a Profession." *Police Review (GB),* 83 (1975), pp. 1176-1177.

Price, Carroll S. "Ethics and Professionalization in American Law Enforcement." *Police,* 7 (May-June, 1963), pp. 6-12.

Price, Carroll S. "Police Prestige—Hopeless?" *Police,* 6:1 (September-October, 1961), pp. 38-40.

Roddenbury, E.W. "Achieving Professionalism." *Journal of Criminal Law, Criminology and Police Science* (1953), pp. 111-115.

Rushing, Joe B. "Let's Go Professional." *Law and Order,* 13:4 (April, 1965), pp. 52-54, 56.

Skousen, W. Cleon. "The Police Profession." *Law and Order,* 23:9 (September, 1975), pp. 8, 10, 12, 14, 16.

Sloane, Charles R. "Police Professionalization." *Journal of Criminal Law, Criminology and Police Science,* 45:1 (May/June, 1954), pp. 77-79.

Smith, Harvey L. "Contingencies of Professional Differentiation." *American Journal of Sociology,* 62:4 (January, 1958).

Soderquist, L.D. "Upgrading the Service." *Police Chief,* XXXVI:8 (August, 1969), pp. 53-75.

Stefanic, Martin D. "Professionalization in Law Enforcement." *Police Chief,* XLI:7 (July, 1974), pp. 62-63.

Stinchcomb, James D. "It's Time for the Police to Take a Professional Stand." *Police Chief,* XXXVII:2 (February, 1970), pp. 37-40.

Vandiver, James V. "The Profits and Problems of Professionalism." *Military Police Journal,* 20 (September, 1970), pp. 9-12.

Vollmer, Howard M. and Donald L. Mills. *Professionalization.* Englewood Cliffs, N.J.: Prentice-Hall, 1966.

White, S.O. "A Perspective on Police Professionalism." *Law Society Review,* 7:1 (1972), pp. 61-85.

Wike, Leroy E. "IACP Strides Ahead toward Its Goal of Professionalization." *FBI Law Enforcement Bulletin* (October, 1960).

Wilson, Lyndon A.S., Jr. "Toward Police Professionalism." *Law and Order,* 19:4 (April, 1971), pp. 92-96.

Wilson, Lyndon A.S., Jr. "Toward Police Professionalism: An Alternative to Repression." *Police,* 16:6 (July-August, 1971), pp. 36-38.

Zendzian, Craig A. "Top Cop: A Study in Police Professionalism." *Police Chief,* 39:2 (February, 1972).

SEARCH AND SEIZURE

Abramowitz, N.S. "Searches Incident to Arrest: The Expanding Exception to the Warrant Requirement." *Georgetown Law Journal,* 63:1 (1974), pp. 223-240.

Ames, C.C. "Automobile License Checks and the Fourth Amendment." *Virginia Law Review,* 60:4 (1974), pp. 666-696.

"Area Search Warrant in Border Zones: *Almeida-Sanchez* and *Camara.*" *Yale Law Journal,* 84:2 (1974), pp. 355-372.

Bartholomew, Paul C. "The Constitution and the Citizen." *Police,* 10:4 (March-April, 1966), pp. 32-37.

Berner, B.G. "Search and Seizure: Status and Methodology." *Valparaiso University Law Review,* 8:3 (1974), pp. 471-583.

Boutwell, J. Paul. "Bullet Removal Surgery." *FBI Law Enforcement Bulletin* (March, 1976), pp. 10-14.
Legal aspects of the seizure of bullets for evidence.

Burke, J.J. "Searches by Private Persons." *FBI Law Enforcement Bulletin,* 41:10 (1972), pp. 22-26.

Cohen, S. "A Criminologist Looks at Search and Seizure." *Police Law Quarterly,* 2:2 (1973), pp. 5-8.

Cook, V.L. "Third-Party Consent Searches: An Alternative Analysis." *University of Chicago Law Review,* 41:1 (1973), pp. 121-145.

"Cops vs. the Courts: Standards of Police Search and Seizure." *Time* (August 28, 1964).

Creamer, J.S. *Law of Arrest, Search, and Seizure.* 2nd ed. Philadelphia: Saunders, 1975.

Fisher, Edward C. *Search and Seizure.* Evanston, IL.: Traffic Institute, Northwestern University, 1970.

Fortier, R.F. "The Police as Good Samaritan: Constitutional Dimensions of the Emergency Exception to Search and Seizure Doctrine." *Police Law Quarterly,* 3:3 (1974), pp. 22-37.

Gerla, H.S. "Search of a Motor Vehicle Incident to a Traffic Arrest: The Outlook After *Robinson* and *Gustafson.*" *Ohio State Law Journal,* 36:1 (1975), pp. 97-113.

Grant, R.P., Jr. "Standing to Contest Illegal Searches and Seizures." *Mississippi Law Journal,* 46:1 (1975), pp. 147-168.

Griswold, Erwin N. *Search and Seizure: A Dilemma of the Supreme Court.* Lincoln: University of Nebraska Press, 1975.

Israel, J.H. "Legislative Regulation of Searches and Seizures: The Michigan Proposals." *Michigan Law Review,* 74:2 (1974), pp. 222-316.

Kynell, Kermit S. "Search and Seizure: A Reply." *Police,* 5:5 (May-June, 1961), p. 31.

Landynski, Jacob W. *Search and Seizure and the Supreme Court: A Study in Constitutional Interpretation.* Baltimore: Johns Hopkins University Press, 1966.

Levinson, D.R. "Search Incident to Arrest for Minor Traffic Violations." *American Criminal Law Review,* 11:3 (1973), pp. 801-816.

McLaughlin, Donald J. "The Protective Sweep." *FBI Law Enforcement Bulletin,* 43:8 (August, 1974), pp. 25-30.

McLaughlin, Donald J. "Search Incident to Arrest—Constructive Possession." *FBI Law Enforcement Bulletin,* 40:12 (December, 1971), pp. 21-24.

Markle, Arnold. *Law of Arrest and Search and Seizure: State's Attorney's Guide for the Prosecution and/or the Law Enforcement Officer.* Springfield, IL.: C.C. Thomas, 1974.

Marks, T.C., Jr. "*United States v. Robinson* and *Gustafson v. Florida:* Extending the Boundaries in Search and Seizure." *Detroit College Law Review,* 2 (1975), pp. 211-227.

Martin, E.C. "Recent Developments. Criminal Procedure—Warrantless Search of the Person Incident to a Lawful Arrest." *Tennessee Law Review,* 41:5 (1974), pp. 932-943.

Miles, J.G., Jr. and J.B. Wefing. "The Automobile Search and the Fourth Amendment: A Troubled Relationship." *Seton Hall Law Review,* 4:1 (1972), pp. 105-144.

"Model Rules for Law Enforcement: Warrantless Searches of Persons and Places—With Commentary." *Criminal Law Bulletin,* 9:8 (1973), pp. 645-683.

Rifas, R.A. "A Law Enforcement Officer's Outline: Plain View Seizure of Evidence." *Police Law Quarterly,* 3:1 (1973), pp. 40-54.

Ringel, William E. *Searches and Seizures, Arrests and Confessions.* N.Y.: Boardman, 1972.

Santana, M.R. "*Almeida-Sanchez* and Its Progeny: The Developing Border-Zone Search Law." *Arizona Law Review,* 17:1 (1975), pp. 214-249.

Search and Seizure. Binghamton, N.Y.: Gould (annual loose leaf).

"Search and Seizure: A New Horizon." *Contemporary Drug Problems,* 3:1 (1974), pp. 21-44.
Dessenting opinions of Justices Marshal, Douglas, and Brennan in *U.S. vs. Robinson.*

"Search of Motor Vehicles." *FBI Law Enforcement Bulletin,* 36:3 (March, 1967), through 36:11 (November, 1967).

"Search of Premises by Consent." *FBI Law Enforcement Bulletin.* 37:2 (February, 1968), through 37:5 (May, 1968).

"Search of the Person." *FBI Law Enforcement Bulletin,* 35:1 (January, 1966), through 35:4 (April, 1976).

Soulsby, Hugh G. *The Right of Search and the Slave Trade in Anglo-American Relations, 1814-1862.* Baltimore: Johns Hopkins University Press, 1935.

Varon, Joseph A. *Searches, Seizures and Immunities.* 2 vols. rev. ed. Indianapolis, IN.: Bobbs, 1974.

Waples, G.L. "From Bags to Body Cavities: The Law of Border Search." *Columbia Law Review,* 74:1 (1974), pp. 53-87.
Searches by U.S. custom service.

"Warrantless Automobile Searches: The Meaning of *Chambers v. Maroney.*" *Journal of American Trial Lawyers Association,* 34 (1972), pp. 174-201.

"Warrantless Search Incident and Arrest: New Standards for Delayed Searches, *United States v. Edwards.*" *University of Colorado Law Review,* 46:4 (1975), pp. 587-608.

Wefing, J.B. and J.G. Miles, Jr. "Consent Searches and the Fourth Amendment: Voluntariness and Third Party Problems." *Seton Hall Law Review,* 5:2 (1974), pp. 211-283.

Zeichner, Irving B. "The Law Refresher." *Law and Order,* 16:9 (September, 1968).

SOCIAL CONTROL

Akers, Ronald L. and Richard Hawkins. *Law and Control in Society.* Englewood Cliffs, N.J.: Prentice Hall, 1975.

Ardrey, Robert. *Social Contract: A Personal Inquiry into the Evolutionary Source of Order and Disorder.* Paterson, N.J.: Atheneum, 1970.

Arens, Richard and Harold D. Lasswell. *In Defense of Public Order.* N.Y.: Columbia University Press, 1961.

Bernard, L.L. *Social Control.* N.Y.: Macmillan, 1939.

Cohen, Albert K. *Deviance and Control.* Englewood Cliffs, N.J.: Prentice Hall, 1966.

Cowger, C.D. and C.R. Atherton. "Social Control: A Rationale for Social Welfare." *Social Work,* 19:4 (1974), pp. 456-462.

Cumming, Elaine. *Systems of Social Regulation.* Chicago: Aldine, 1968.

Derbyshire, Robert L. "The Social Control Role of the Police in Changing Urban Communities." *Excerpta Criminologica,* 6 (1966).

Hadden, T. "Making People Good by Law." *New Society,* 13 (1969), pp. 79-81.

Hunt, William E. *Human Behavior and Its Control.* Cambridge, MA.: Schenkman, 1972.

Pound, Roscoe. *Social Control Through Law.* New Haven, CT.: Yale University Press, 1942.

Reubington, Earl. *Alcohol Problems and Social Control.* Columbus, OH.: Merrill, 1973.

Rock, P. *Making People Pay.* London: Routledge and Kegan Paul, 1973.
Analysis of the debt-collection process in England; debtors were imprisoned.

Rock, P. and M. Mcintosh. *Deviance and Social Control.* London: Tavistock, 1974.

Ross, Edward A. *Social Control: A Survey of the Foundation of Order.* N.Y.: Johnson, 1970. (repr. of 1901 ed.).

Roucek, Joseph S. *Social Control.* 2nd ed. Westport, CT.: Greenwood, 1956.

Sites, Paul. *Control: The Basis of Social Order.* Port Washington, N.Y.: Dunellen, 1973.

Scott, John P. and Sarah F. Scott. *Social Control and Social Change.* Chicago: University of Chicago Press, 1971.

Spiller, Robert, ed. *Social Control in a Free Society.* Westport, CT.: Greenwood, 1975. (repr. of 1960 ed.).

Turk, A.T. *Legal Sanctioning and Social Control.* Washington, D.C.: GPO, 1972.

Ulrich, Roger E. et al. *Control of Human Behavior.* 3 vols. Glenview, IL.: Scott Foresman, 1974.

Walker, N. and M. Argyle. "Does the Law Affect Moral Judgments?" *British Journal of Criminology,* 4 (1964), pp. 570-581.

Watkins, C. Ken. *Social Control.* N.Y. Longman, 1975.

Weinberg, Kirsons. *Deviant Behavior and Social Control.* Dubuque, IA.: W.C. Brown, 1974.

Young, Roland. *American Law and Politics: The Creation of Public Order.* N.Y.: Harper and Row, 1967.

SOCIAL SCIENCES IN LAW ENFORCEMENT

Bard, Morton. "Implications of Collaboration between Law Enforcement and the Social Sciences." *FBI Law Enforcement Bulletin,* 43:7 (July, 1974), pp. 20-25.

Bielinski, Brunon. "Importance to Psychiatrist of First on Scene Officer's Observation." *Police,* 6:5 (May-June, 1962), pp. 26-29.

Carpenter, Rod. "Psychology and Its Ever-Changing Ways." *Police Chief* (April, 1971).

Elkins, A.N. and G.O. Papenek. "Consultation with the Police: An Example of Community Psychiatry Practice." *American Journal of Psychiatry* (1966).

Kennedy, Stephen P. "The Police and the Social Sciences." *Police,* 4:5 (May-June, 1960).

Kreins, Edward S. "The Behavioral Scientist in Law Enforcement." *Police Chief,* XLI:2 (February, 1974), pp. 46-48.
Use of behavioral scientist in selection, training, psychiatric evaluation, etc.

Kreins, E.S. and E.E. Shev. "Psychiatric Techniques in the Selection and Training of a Police Officer." *Police Chief,* XXXV:4 (April, 1968), pp. 10-13.

Lundstedt, Sven. "Social Psychological Contribution to the Management of Law Enforcement Agencies." *Journal of Criminal Law, Criminology and Police Science,* 56 (September, 1965), pp. 375-381.

Mann, P.A. *Psychological Consultation with a Police Department—A Demonstration of Cooperative Training in Mental Health.* Springfield, IL.: C.C. Thomas, 1973.
Psychological consultation service provided to a Texas police department leads to new methods of providing mental health services to a community.

Peterson, M. "Guideline for Psychologists in Police Consultation." *International Mental Health Research Newsletter,* 16:4 (1974), pp. 5-7.
Some review of the literature.

Rankin, James. "Psychiatric Screening of Police Recruits." *Public Personnel Review* (July, 1959).

Shev, Edward E. and James Wright. "The Uses of Psychiatric Techniques in Selecting and Training Police Officers As Part of Their Regular Training." *Police,* 15:5 (May-June, 1971), pp. 13-16.

Steinberg, J.L. and D.W. McEvoy. *The Police and the Behavioral Sciences.* Springfield, IL.: C.C. Thomas, 1974.

SPECIALIZATION

Murphy, William A. "Specialization of Police Duty." *Police Chief,* 29 (October, 1962), pp. 18-22.
Explains specialization.

Webb, Kenneth W. et al. *National Evaluation Program, Phase I Summary Report: Specialized Patrol Projects.* Washington, D.C.: LEAA, 1975.

Wilson, James Q. *Thinking About Crime.* N.Y.: Basic, 1975.
Wilson concludes that specialized patrol operations may hold great promise but need more evaluation. See pp. 81-97.

STATE STANDARDS COMMISSIONS

Bradel, Don. "Statewide Quality Control for Law Enforcement Personnel." *Police Chief,* XLII:8 (August, 1975), pp. 41-42.

Brereton, George H. "California Studies Mandatory Minimum Police Personnel Standards." *Police,* 11:1 (September-October, 1957), pp. 25-28.

Catlin, D. and L.T. Hoover. "Role of Law Enforcement Training Commissions in the United States." *Journal of Criminal Justice,* 1:4 (1973), pp. 347-352.
Reviews activities of 39 state police training commissions.

Dompka, R.J. "A National Police Standards Act—The First Step toward Professionalism." *Law and Order,* 19:7 (1971), pp. 86-87, 90.

Greenfield, Joel. "California's Law Enforcement Education Standards—A Case for Review and Revision." *Journal of California Law Enforcement* (January, 1976), pp. 100-102.

Kassoff, Norman C. "State Laws on Police Training Standards." *Police Chief,* 33:8 (August, 1966), pp. 10-11.

Kline, Fred and Phil Hanna. "POST: A Program for Professionals." *Law and Order,* 22:3 (March, 1974), pp. 42, 50.

"Minimum State Standards: A Legislative Blueprint." *Police Chief,* 34:1 (January, 1967), pp. 36-38.

"A Review of State Minimum Standard Training Laws." *Police Chief,* XXXV:8 (August, 1968), pp. 76-83.

Wall, Charles R. and Leo A. Culloo. "State Standards for Law Enforcement Selection and Training." *Journal of Police Science and Administration,* 1:4 (December, 1973), pp. 425-532.

STYLES OF POLICING

Brodsky, Stanley L. "Models of Police Behavior." *Police,* 13:5 (May-June, 1969), pp. 27-2S.
Describes several models; soldier, inspector, clerk, and helping agent.

Chapman, Brian. *Police State.* N.Y.: Praeger, 1970.
Chapman describes two styles of policing: 1) "Artisanal" which sees the police function as being workmanlike, pragmatic and plodding; 2) and the "Romantic" which is a combination of the priest, the soldier and the artist. See pp. 95-105.

Kuykendall, Jack L. "Styles of Community Policing." *Criminology,* 12:2 (August, 1974), pp. 229-240.
Describes four different philosophies or styles of policing.

Ostrom, Elinor. *Community Organization and the Provision of Police Services.* Beverly Hills, CA.: Sage, 1973.

Whyte, William Foote. *Street Corner Society.* Chicago: University of Chicago Press, 1943.
Insightful account of police-neighborhood relations shows police to be too little concerned with individuals and too impersonal.

Wilson, James Q. *Varieties of Police Behavior.* Cambridge, MA.: Harvard University Press, 1968.

TENURE OF CHIEFS OF POLICE

Flanagan, William J. "What's Happening to Police Chiefs?" *Law and Order,* 12:10 (October, 1964), pp. 66-69.

Hathaway, Gregory O. "The Problem of Tenure." *Police Chief,* XXXIII:9 (September, 1966), pp. 18-19.

Lunden, Walter A. "The Mobility of Chiefs of Police." *Journal of Criminal Law, Criminology and Police Science,* 49:2 (July/August, 1958), pp. 178-183.

Skousen, W. Cleon. "We Change Chiefs Too Often." *Law and Order,* 14:10 (October, 1966), pp. 10-13, 34.

UNARMED POLICE

Greenwood, Colin. "Evil Choice." *Criminal Law Review* (January, 1975), pp. 4-11.
Arming British police.

Roberts, B.R. "Arms for the Police." *Police College Magazine,* 12:4 (1973), pp. 19-23.
Author states that use of firearms by the police in Great Britain will increase but there will be no universal arming of police.

USE OF DEADLY FORCE BY POLICE

"Brazilian Death Squads." *American Magazine,* 125:4 (August 21, 1971), pp. 80-81.

Bristow, Allen P. "Police Officer Shooting—A Tactical Evaluation." *Journal of Criminal Law, Criminology and Police Science,* 54:1 (March, 1963), pp. 93-95.

California Department of Justice, Bureau of Criminal Statistics. *Peace Officer Involved Homicides in California, 1971-1972.* Washington, D.C.: NCJRS, (Microfiche) 1974.

"Criminal Law—Right of Officer to Kill to Prevent Escape of Suspected Felon." *University of Pennsylvania Law Review,* 94 (April, 1946), pp. 327-330.

Harding, R.W. *The Police Killings in Australia.* Ringwood, Victoria: Penguin, 1970.

Harding, R.W. and R.P. Fahey. "Killings by Chicago Police, 1969-1970: An Empirical Study." *Southern California Review,* 46:2 (1973), pp. 284-315.
Describes 79 killings.

Hartung, Frank E. *Crime Law and Society.* Detroit: Wayne State University Press, 1965.
Hartung reports that the pattern for killing committed by police is that of a declining rate. See pp. 149-150.

Kobler, A.L. "Figures (and Perhaps Some Facts) on Police Killings of Civilians in the United States, 1965–1969." *Journal of Social Issues,* 31:1 (1975), pp. 185-191.

Kobler, A.L. "Police Homicide in a Democracy." *Journal of Social Issues,* 31:1 (1975), pp. 163-184.

"Killing Suspected Felon Fleeing to Escape Arrest." *Kentucky Law Journal,* 38 (May, 1950), pp. 609-617.

Knoohuizen, Ralph, Richard P. Fahey, and Deborah J. Palmer. *Police and Their Use of Fatal Force in Chicago.* Evanston, IL.: Chicago Law Enforcement Study Group, 1972.

Robin, Gerald D. "Justifiable Homicide by Police Officers." *Journal of Criminal Law, Criminology and Police Science,* 54:2 (June, 1963), pp. 225-231.

Robin, Gerald D. "Police Slayings of Criminals." *Police,* 8:6 (July-August, 1964), pp. 32-35.

"Shooting the Fugitive." *South African Law Journal,* 73 (May, 1956).

Special Reports: Mortality From Each Cause: United States 1952-1954. Washington, D.C.: National Office of Vital Statistics, 1956.
Lists justifiable homicides by police officers. Lumps civilian and military police in same category.

VIGILANTES

"American Citizen Crime Fighters." *Reader's Digest,* 96 (June, 1970), pp. 225-226.

Birney, Hoffman. *Vigilantes.* Philadelphia: Pennsylvania Publishing, 1929.

Brown, Richard Maxwell. "The American Vigilante Tradition." in *Violence in America: Historical and Comparative Perspectives. A Staff Report to the National Commission on the Causes and Prevention of Violence.* Washington, D.C.: GPO, June, 1969.

Brown, Richard Maxwell. "Legal and Behavioral Perspective on American Vigilantism." *Perspectives in American History,* V (1971), pp. 95-144.

Brown, Richard Maxwell. *The South Carolina Regulators.* Cambridge: Harvard University Press, 1963.

Brown, Richard M. *Strain of Violence: Historical Studies of American Violence and Vigilantism.* N.Y.: Oxford University Press, 1975.

"Chicago's Black Vigilantes: Anti-Drug Afro-American Group Attack Team." *Newsweek,* 78 (September 27, 1971).

Coblentz, Stanton A. *Villains and Vigilantes.* N.Y.: Yoseloff, 1936.

Cohen, F.G. "The Indian Patrol in Minneapolis: Social Control and Social Change in an Urban Context." *Law and Society Review,* 7:4 (1973), pp. 779-786.
Patrol organized to arrange for Indian drunks to be taken home and to watch police activities.

Dimsdale, Thomas J. *Vigilantes of Montana.* Norman: University of Oklahoma, 1953.

McConnell, William J. and Howard R. Driggs. *Frontier Law: A Story of Vigilante Days.* N.Y.: AMS (repr. of 1924 ed.).

Madison, Arnold. *Vigilantism in America.* N.Y.: Seabury, 1973.

Marx, Gary T. and Dane Archer. *Citizen Involvement in the Law Enforcement Process: The Case of Community Police Patrols.* Revisions of a paper presented at the annual meeting of the American Political Science Association, Los Angeles, 1970. (mimeo).

Marx, G.T. and D. Archer. *Urban Vigilante.* Washington, D.C.: NCJRS, 1973.
Study of 28 groups organized across the country in the 1960's by citizens concerned with policing their own neighborhoods.

Marx, G.T. and D. Archer. "The Urban Vigilante." *Psychology Today,* 6:8 (1973), pp. 45-50.
Describes citizen patrols and defense groups.

"More and More Vigilantes—Legal—and Illegal." *U.S. News and World Report,* 72 (February 4, 1974), pp. 40-42.

Moynahan, J.M. "Victims Who Look for Their Criminals." *Police Chief,* XXXIX:8 (August, 1972), pp. 34-39.

Nelson, H.A. "The Defenders: A Case Study of an Informal Police Organization." *Social Problems,* XV (1967-1968), pp. 127-147.

Nunis, Doice B. *San Francisco Vigilantes of 1856.* Glendale, CA.: A.H. Clark, 1971.

WIRETAPPING

American Bar Association. *Electronic Surveillance, Standards Relating to.* Chicago: American Bar Association, 1971.
American Bar Association standards and commentary on the electronic surveillance of communications.

Bagdikan, Ben H. "Big Brother Is Listening." *Saturday Evening Post* (June 6, 1964).

Brento, Myron. *Privacy Invader.* N.Y.: Coward-McCann, 1964.

Bullard, Garry R. "Wiretapping and the Supreme Court." *Journal of Criminal Law, Criminology and Police Science,* 49:4 (November-December, 1958), pp. 342-349.

Carley, N.M. "Electronic Advances Aid Snoopers." *Wall Street Journal* (April 9, 1963).

Carroll, John M. *Secrets of Electronic Espionage.* N.Y.: (Dutton, 1966).

Carroll, John M. *The Third Listener: Personnel Electronic Espionage.* N.Y.: Dutton, 1969.

"Constitutional Law—Electronic Surveillance by Bugged Agents Is Not a Search and Seizure within the Fourth Amendment—*United States vs. White* (United States Supreme Court, 1971)." *Albany Law Review,* 36:2 (Winter, 1972), pp. 451-458.

Coon, Thomas F. "To Tap or Not to Tap." *Law and Order,* 14:10 (October, 1966), pp. 86-90.

"Court and Electronic Surveillance—To Bug or Not to Bug—What Is the Exception?" *St. John's Law Review,* 47:1 (October, 1972), pp. 10-46.

Cranwell, J.L., Jr. "Judicial Fine-Tuning of Electronic Surveillance." *Seton Hall Law Review,* 6:2 (1975), pp. 225-267.

Cunningham, J.E. *Security Electronics.* Indianapolis, IN.: Howard W. Sams, 1970.

Dash, Samuel. *The Eavesdroppers.* New Brunswick, N.J.: Rutgers University Press, 1959.

Dash, Samuel. "The Moral Dilemma of Wire Tapping." *Coronet* (March, 1961).

Debrie, M.A. "The Use of Electronic Methods by the Police." *International Criminal Police Review,* 185 (February, 1965), pp. 42-51.

Donnelly, Richard C. "Electronic Eavesdropping." *Notre Dame Lawyer,* 38:6 (1963), pp. 667-689,

"Electronic Surveillance and Constitutional Rights: Some Recent Developments and Observations." *George Washington Law Review,* 33 (1964).

Fabian, F.M. and Harry W. More, Jr. "The Admissibility of Evidence Obtained by Wire Tapping." *Police,* 9:3 (January/February, 1965), pp. 30-34.

Fairfield, William S. and Charles Clift. *The Wire Tappers.* N.Y.: Fortnightly, 1955.

Fales, E.D., Jr. "Are They Listening in?" *Popular Science* (January, 1965).

Gallagher, E.J. and R.M. Hollis. "Federal Decisions on the Constitutionality of Electronic Surveillance Legislation." *American Criminal Law Review,* 11:3 (Spring, 1973), pp. 639-694.

Graham, Fred P. "Police Eavesdropping: Law Enforcement Revolution." *Criminal Law Bulletin,* 7 (June, 1971).

Kent, R.J. "Wiretapping: Morality and Legality." *Houston Law Review* (1965).

Landever, A.R. *Electronic Surveillance and the American Constitutional System.* Ann Arbor, MI.: University Microfilms, 1969.

Lapidus, E.J. *Eavesdropping on Trial.* Rochelle Park, N.J.: Hayden, 1974.

Lemond, A. *No Place to Hide.* N.Y.: St. Martin's, 1975.

Matthews, R.B. "Bugs and Taps—A Practical Look. Pointers to the Recognition and Detection of Surreptitious Listening Devices." *Security Gazette,* 15:8 (1973), pp. 274-275.

Merrigan, J.A. "Wiretapping in Domestic Security Cases." *Loyola Law Review,* 20:1 (1974), pp. 199-213.

Murphy, Walter F. *Wiretapping on Trial: A Case Study in the Judicial Process.* N.Y.: Random, 1965.

Neville, A.C. "Foiling the Electronic Eavesdroppers: A Survey of Available Countermeasures." *Security World,* 12:4 (1975), pp. 20-21, 101.

North, Steven. ". . .the Whole Truth—Tips on Taps." *Law and Order,* 22:10 (October, 1974), p. 86.

O'Neill, Joseph F. "TAC II—The Electronic Stakeout." *FBI Law Enforcement Bulletin,* 43:6 (June, 1974).

Orfield, L.B. "Wiretapping in Federal Criminal Cases." *Texas Law Review* (1964).

Pollock, David. *Methods of Electronic Audio Surveillance.* Springfield, IL.: C.C. Thomas, 1972.

Saxbe, W.B. "Electronic Surveillance." *Law Officer,* 7:4 (1974), pp. 26-31.

Saxbe, William B. "Wiretapping and Electronic Surveillance." *Police Chief,* XLII:2 (February, 1975), pp. 20-22.

Scott, Hugh. "Wiretapping and Organized Crime." *Harvard Law Journal,* 14:1 (1968), pp. 1-28.

Scoular, Robert F. "Wiretapping and Eavesdropping from Olmstead to Katz." *St. Louis University Law Journal,* 12 (1968), pp. 513-549.

Shattuck, J.H.F. "National Security Wire Taps." *Criminal Law Bulletin,* 11:1 (1975), pp. 7-28.

Shaw, William. "The Average Citizen's Fear of Electronic Eavesdropping." *Law and Order,* 23:9 (September, 1975), pp. 34, 36, 38, 40, 42.

Shaw, William. "The Legal Aspects of Radio Surveillance and Eavesdropping." *Law and Order,* 15:1 (January, 1967), pp. 34-38, 78.

Silvarman, Allen B.I. "Electronic Spy Devices." *Police,* 10:1 (September-October, 1965), pp. 6-10.

Silver, Edward S. "Wiretapping and Electronic Surveillance." *Journal of Criminal Law, Criminology and Police Science,* 55:1 (March, 1964), pp. 114-115.

Silver, Edward S. "The Wiretapping-Eavesdropping Problem: A Prosecutor's View." *Minnesota Law Review* (1960).

Spindel, Bernard B. *The Ominous Ear.* N.Y.: Award House, 1968.

Sullivan, Francis C. "Wire Tapping in England." *Police,* 5:2 (November-December, 1960), pp. 42-44.

Sullivan, Francis C. "Wire Taps." *Police,* 4:1 (September-October, 1959), pp. 51-53.

Wilson, O.W. "Wiretapping Is Not Unconstitutional, None of a Citizen's Rights Is Absolute." *Journal of California Law Enforcement* (July, 1966), pp. 6-11.

"Wiretapping, Eavesdropping and Your Right to Privacy." *Communications* (March, 1973), pp. 28, 30-41.

THE ENVIRONMENT OF POLICING

THE POLICE EXPERIENCE—GENERAL

Banton, Michael. "Social Integration and Police Authority." *Police Chief* (April, 1963), pp. 8-30.

Barnes, Margaret Anne. *Murder in Coweta County.* NY: Reader's Digest, 1976.
Describes social atmosphere of a county sheriff during a murder investigation.

Black, Harold and Marvin J. Labes. "Guerilla Warfare: An Analogy to Police-Criminal Interaction." *American Journal of Orthopsychiatry* (July, 1967).

Bourbon, Frank C. "Moral Aspects of Law Enforcement." *Police Chief,* 32:1 (January, 1965), pp. 35-37; 32:2 (February, 1965), pp. 32-35; 32:3 (March, 1965) pp. 47-51; 32:4 (April, 1965), p. 62; 32:5 (May, 1965), pp. 45-58; 32:6 (June, 1956), pp. 51-54.
Series consists of six sub-areas: integrity, courage, responsibility, sacrifice, prejudice and reputation.

Breckenridge, A.C. "Wanted: Uniform Law Enforcement." *Journal of Criminal Law, Criminology and Police Science,* 45:2 (July-August, 1954), pp. 170-175.

Casper, Joseph J. "The Highest Law." *Law and Order,* 16:12 (December, 1968), pp. 15-21.

Donaldson, Robert. "So You Want to Become a Policeman." *Law and Order,* 17:6 (June, 1969), p. 126.

Dubinsky, Steven and Leo Standora. *Decoy Cop.* NY: Ace, 1974.

Ellis, George. *A Man Named Jones.* NY: Signet, 1963.

Eszterhas, J. *Narc.* NY: Simon and Schuster, 1974.

Fisher, Dave. *The Incredible Scooter Cops.* Greenwich CT: Fawcett, 1974.

Geis, Gilbert. "The Social Atmosphere of Policing." *Police,* 9:1 (September/October, 1964), pp. 75-79.

Gelb, Barbara. *On the Track of Murder: Behind the Scenes with a Homicide Commando Squad.* NY: William Morrow, 1975.

Greenberg, Dave. *Play It to a Bust.* NY: Hawthorn, 1975.

Harvey, Paul. "What Are Policemen Made of?" *FBI Law Enforcement Bulletin,* 37:1 (January, 1968).

Hughes, Everett C. "Good People and Dirty Work." *Special Problems,* 10 (Summer, 1962), pp. 3-11.

Kirkham, George L. "From Professor to Patrolman: A Fresh Prospective on the Police." *Journal of Police Science and Administration,* 2:2 (June, 1974), pp. 127-137.

Kirkham, George L. "Professor's 'Street Lessons.'" *FBI Law Enforcement Bulletin* (March, 1974), pp. 14-22.

Kirkham, George L. *Signal Zero.* Philadelphia: Lippincott, 1976.

Kuykendall, Jack L. "Police Deviancy in the Enforcement Role: Situational Cooperation/Compliance-Response Hierarchy of Deviant and Non-Deviant Power Strategies." *Police,* 15:6 (July-August, 1971), pp. 44-51.

Lynch, Gerald W. "Cooperation and Competition among Police Officers." *Journal of Police Science and Administration,* 1:3 (September, 1973), pp. 319-335.

McAllister, Robert. *The Kind of Guy I Am.* NY: Popular Library, 1958.

MacNamara, Donald E. J. and Marc Riedel. *Police — Perspectives, Problems, Prospects.* NY: Praeger, 1974.

Mills, James. "The Detective." *Life* (December 3, 1956), pp. 90-123.

Mott, Paul E. et al. *Shift Work: A Social, Pychological and Physical Consequence.* Ann Arbor: University of Michigan Press, 1965.

Murphy, George A. "The Price of a Policeman's Life." *Police Chief* (September, 1972), p. 8.

Radano, Gene. *Stories Cops Only Tell Each Other.* NY: Stein and Day, 1974.

Radano, Gene. *Walking the Beat: A New York Policeman Tells What It's Like on His Side of the Law.* Mountain View CA.: World, 1968.

Reiss, A.J. and D.J. Black. *Studies in Crime and Law Enforcement in Major Metropolitan Areas.* vol. 2 Washington DC: GPO, 1967.
Motivational dynamics of police conduct and attitudes as related to the role of the citizen, and police perceptions of their occupation and organization.

Reynolds, Quentin. *Headquarters.* NY: Harper, 1955.

Robinson, Barry and Martin J. Dain. *On the Beat: Policemen at Work.* NY: Harcourt, Brace and World, 1968.

Rokeach, Milton, Martin G. Miller, and John A. Snyder. "The Value Gap between Police and Policed." *Journal of Social Issues,* 27:2 (1971), pp. 155-171.

Schmidt, Virginia. "A Highway Patrolman's Day." *California Highway Patrolman,* 35 (May, 1971).

Schott, Joseph L. *No Left Turns.* NY: Praeger, 1975.
Author is a 23-year veteran of the FBI who accurately describes life in the FBI under J. Edgar Hoover.

Schultz, Donald O. *Special Problems in Law Enforcement.* Springfield, IL: C.C. Thomas, 1971.

Schultz, Don. "Who Are We Putting on Our Streets?" *Law and Order,* 18:2 (February, 1970), pp. 82, 88.

Sepe, John and Louis Telano. *Cop Team.* NY: Pinnacle, 1975.

Skelly, John F. *Portrait of a Precinct.* Unpub. Master's Thesis, City University of New York, John Jay College of Criminal Justice, January, 1969.

Skolnick, Jerome H. *Justice Without Trial: Law Enforcement in a Democratic Society.* NY: Wiley, 1967.

Smith, W.H.T. and D.A. Sprecher. *The Police Leader Looks at Unrest Within the Department.* Falls Church, VA: Leaderships Resources, 1974.

Steiner, P. "Policeman's Lot Anecdotes." *New York Times Magazine* (September 29, 1957).

Strecher, Victor G. *The Environment of Law Enforcement.* Englewood Cliffs, NJ: Prentice Hall, 1971.

Toch, Hans. "A Note on Police 'Experience.'" *Police* (March-April' 1967).

Toma, David. *Toma.* NY: Dell, 1973.

Trubitt, Hillard J. "The Hand that Holds the Baton." *Journal of Criminal Law, Criminology and Police Science,* 58:3 (September, 1967), pp. 414-417.

Unger, Stanford J. *FBI.* Boston: Little Brown, 1975.

Vasile, Nick. *Sado Cop.* Chicago: Playboy, 1976.
Author is former Washington DC vice officer. Graphic, realistic description of police activities. Also describes political corruption.

Walker, T. Mike. *Voices from the Bottom of the World: A Policeman's Journal.* NY: Grove, 1969.

Wambaugh, Joseph. *The Blue Knight.* Boston: Little Brown, 1972.
Although novels, the Blue Knight, the Choir Boys and the New Centurions realistically describe the multiple aspects of the police experience.

Wambaugh, Joseph. *The Choir Boys.* NY: Delacorte, 1975.

Wambaugh, Joseph. *The New Centurions.* Boston: Little Brown, 1970.

Wainwright, Loudon. "A Tough Time to Be a Good Cop." *Life* (August 4, 1967).

Webster, James A. *The Realities of Police Work.* Dubuque IA: Kandall/Hunt, 1973.

Westley, William A. "Secrecy and the Police." *Social Forces,* 34:3 (1956).

"What Is a Policeman?" *FBI Law Enforcement Bulletin* (November, 1970), pp. 6-8, 26-28.

Whited, Charles. *Chiodo: Undercover Cop.* Chicago: Playboy, 1973.

Whitehead, Don. *Border Guard.* NY: Avon, 1963.

Whitehouse, Jack E. "A Preliminary Inquiry into the Occupational Disadvantages of Law Enforcement Officers." *Police,* 9 (May-June, 1965), pp. 30-35, 9 (July-August, 1965), pp. 35-40.

Whitman, Arthur. "What Makes a Good Cop?" *Parade* (September 14, 1969).

Whittemore, L.H. *Cop: A Closeup of Violence and Tragedy.* NY: Holt, Rinehart and Winston, 1969.

Whittemore, L.H. "A Hard Cop and His Patient Partner on a Menacing Beat." *Life* (June 30, 1969).

Whittemore, L.H. *The Super Cops.* NY: Bantam, 1973.

Williams, Robert H. *Vice Squad.* Crowell, 1973.

Wilson, James Q. "Generational and Ethnic Differences among Career Police Officers." *American Journal of Sociology,* LXIX: (March, 1964), pp. 522-528.

Wilson, James Q. "The Patrolman's Dilemma." *New Yorker* (September 9, 1968), pp. 16-25.

Wilson, James Q. *Varieties of Police Behavior: The Management of Law and Order in Eight Communities.* Cambridge: Harvard University Press, 1968.

Wilson, James Q. "What Makes a Better Policeman?" *The Atlantic* (March, 1969).

Wolfgang, Marvin E. "The Police and Their Problems." *Police,* 10:4 (March-April, 1966), pp. 50-56.
Discusses social isolation, alienation, solidarity, danger, violenke and other factors.

Woodruff, Waid S. "Cops in Conflict." *Law and Order,* 21:3 (March, 1973), pp. 66-68, 70, 72-76.
Excellent article on the police environment in the LAPD.

Youngblood, Rufus W. *20 Years in the Secret Service: My Life with Five Presidents.* NY: Simon and Schuster, 1973.

ACCULTURATION

Lee, J.F. *Attitudes and Attitude Change in Law Enforcement Officers.* Washington DC: NCJRS, (Microfiche) 1970.

McNamara, J.H. *Role Learning for Police Recruits — Some Problems in the Process of Preparation for the Uncertainties of Police Work.* Ann Arbor MI: University Microfilms, 1967.
Organizational and social psychological problems of preparing recruits for the uncertainties of police work in the New York City Police Department.

Sharp, Douglas J. *Attitude Change During Initial Police Training*. Birmingham: Aston University, 1972.

Shils, Edward A. and Morris Janowitz. "Cohesion and Disintegration in the Wehrmacht in World War II." *Public Opinion Quarterly,* 12 (Summer, 1948), pp. 280-315.

Discipline in combat is not maintained by formal sanction but by the norms of the small unit — peer expectations.

Sterling, J.W. *Changes in Role Concepts of Police Officers*. Gaithersburg MD: IACP, 1972.

Nature and extent of selected changes in role concepts as they occurred over a 21-month period for a group of 113 police recuits in four cities.

Teasley, C.E. and Leonard Wright. "The Effects of Training on Police Recruit Attitudes." *Journal of Police Science and Administration,* 1:2 (June, 1973), pp. 241-248.

Van Maanen, J. *Pledging the Police — A Study of Selected Aspects of Recruit Socialization in a Large, Urban Police Department*. Springfield VA: NTIS, 1972.

Examination of the process of becoming a policeman as experienced by four police recruit classes in a large urban department.

Vega, William. "The Liberal Policeman: A Contradiction in Terms?" *Issues in Criminology,* 14:1 (Fall, 1968), pp. 15-33.

Describes the acculturation process police recruits undergo, especially the change in political attitudes.

Webb, Donald G. and Gene F. Westergren. "The Detraining Syndrome." *Police Chief* (November, 1973), pp. 36-40.

ALCOHOLISM

Dunne, J.A. "Alcoholism among Police Officers." *Law Officer,* 7:1 (1974), pp. 32-34.

NYPD program to aid officers who are problem drinkers; 70% of the policemen treated stayed off the bottle and were still employed by the Department 4 years after returning to duty.

Dunne, J.A. "Counseling Alcoholic Employees in a Municipal Police Department." *Quarterly Journal for the Study of Alcoholism,* 34:2 (1973), pp. 423-434.

NYPD program. Counselors are recovered alcoholic policemen. 75% of those involved in the program were returned to duty.

Dishlacoff, Leon. "The Drinking Cop." *Police Chief,* XLIII:1 (January, 1976), pp. 32-39.

Follman, Joseph F., Jr. *Alcoholics and Business Problems, Costs, Solutions*. NY: AMA, 1976.

Helping the Alcoholic Employee. NY: AMA, 1974.

CYNICISM

Niederhoffer, Arthur. *Behind the Shield: The Police in Urban Society*. Garden City, NY: Doubleday, 1967.

Rafky, D.M. "Police Cynicism Reconsidered. An Application of Smallest Space Analysis." *Criminology,* 13:2 (1975), pp. 168-192.

Replicates Niederhoffer's work. This study shows that cynicism is not prevalent among police outside of NY city.

DIVORCE

Athearn, Forben. *How to Divorce Your Wife: The Man's Side of Divorce*. Garden City, NY: Doubleday, 1976.

Bass, H.L. and M.L. Rein. *Divorce or Marriage: A Legal Guide*. Englewood Cliffs, NJ: Prentice Hall, 1976.

Durner, James A. et al. "Divorce: Another Occupational Hazard." *Police Chief,* XLII:11 (November, 1975), pp. 48-53.

Franks, Maurice R. *How to Avoid Alimony*. NY: New American Library, 1976.

Lichtenberger, James P. *Divorce: A Study in Social Causation*. NY: Columbia University Press, 1969.

Metz, Charles V. *Divorce and Custody for Men: A Guide and Primer Designed Exclusively to Help Men Win Just Settlements*. Garden City, NY: Doubleday, 1968.

Olmsted, Gerald T. *Divorce and the Police Profession: Marriage Dissolution Among Deputy Sheriffs of Los Angeles County*. Unpub. Master's Thesis. California State Universtiy, Long Beach, 1973.

Rodell, John S. *How to Avoid Alimony*. NY: Pocket Books, 1970.

Weiss, Robert S. *Marital Separation*. NY: Basic, 1975.

EMOTIONAL/PSYCHOLOGICAL PROBLEMS

Blum, Richard H. "The Problems of Being a Police Officer." *Police* (November-December, 1960), (January-February, 1961).

Caprio, Frank S. and Frances S. Leighton. *How to Avoid a Nervous Breakdown*. NY: Hawthorn, 1969.

Lefkowitz, J. "Psychological Attributes of Policemen: A Review of Research and Opinion." *Journal of Social Issues,* 31:1 (1975), pp. 3-26.

Montefiore, Canon H. et al. *Death Anxiety: Normal and Pathological Aspects*. NY: MSS Information, 1973.

Parker, Rolland S. *Emotional Common Sense: How to Avoid Self Destructiveness*. NY: Harper and Row, 1973.

Rankin, James H. "Preventive Psychiatry in the Los Angeles Police Department." *Police,* 1:6 (July-August, 1957), pp. 24-29.

Reiser, Martin. "Mental Health in Police Work and Training." *Police Chief,* XLI:I (August, 1974), pp. 51-52.

Reiser, Martin. "Training Police Sergeants in Early Warning Signs of Emotional Upset." *Mental Hygiene Magazine* (July,)971).

Reiser, Martin et al. "An Early Warning Mental Health Program for Police Sergeants." *Police Chief,* XXXIX:6 (June, 1972), pp. 38-39.

Runkel, Peter R. *The Law Unto Themselves*. NY: Bantam, 1970.

Popular account of 11 psychiatric case studies of police officers.

Scarlet, Iain. "Police Paranoia." *Spectator* (October, 1975), p. 482.

Schlossberg, Harvey, and Lucy Freeman. *Psychologist With a Gun.* NY: Coward McCahn and Geoghegan, 1974.

Schoonmaker, Alan N. *Anxiety and the Executive.* NY: AMA, 1969.

Toch, Hans H. "Psychological Consequences of the Police Role." *Police,* 10:1 (September-October, 1956), pp. 22-25.

Wambaugh, Joseph. *The Onion Field.* NY: Delacorte, 1973.
Story of the mental deterioration of an officer who witnessed his partner's murder and was almost murdered himself.

Watson, Nelson A. *Emotional Stability.* Gaithersberg MD: IACP, 1969.

Watson, N.A. *Threats and Challenges (Issues in Human Relations).* Gaithersburg, MD: IACP, 1969.
Nature of threat situations arising from interpersonal relationships with particular attention to their manifestation in police work.

INCOME TAX PROBLEMS

Arkin, Joseph. "Tax Pointers for the Police Officer." *Law and Order,* 12:2 (February, 1964), pp. 16, 65.

Battersby, Mark E. "Tax Ruling Affects Policemen." *Law and Order,* 18:8 (August, 1970), pp. 106-107, 110.
Discusses tax exemption for meals and other expenses. IRS has ruled against the police in the case described here.

PHYSICAL PROBLEMS

Health Problems — General

Barnaby, J.T. *Fatigue.* NY: Crane Russak, 1973.

Barry, A.J., E.M. Bernauer, and P.A. Mole. "The Energies of Police Officers." *Police,* 7:5 (May-June, 1963), pp. 39-45.

Berman, Sam S. *Boston Police Diet and Weight Control Program.* NY: Frederick Fell, 1972.

Cerney, J.V. "Does 'Flatfoot' Always Mean 'Cop?'" *Police,* 7:2 (November-December, 1962), pp. 11-12.
Describes foot and leg problems among police.

Cerney, J.V. "Feet: Their Effect on Marksmanship." *Police,* 6:6 (July-August, 1962), pp. 38-39.
Problems of foot disorders in law enforcement.

Cerney, J.V. "Foot Disability — A Crime That Doesn't Pay." *Police,* 7:6 (July-August, 1963), pp. 78-79.

Cerney, J.V. "Poor Posture in Policemen Basic Problem in Arthritis." *Police,* 8:2 (November-December, 1963), pp. 37-39.

Cerney, J.V. "Trouble Afoot in Crime Detail." *Police,* 7:4 (March-April, 1963), pp. 18-19.

Chapman, A.J. and George J. Race. "Trauma and Cancer: A Survey of Recent Literature." *Journal of Forensic Sciences* (April, 1969).

Dwyer, William O. and Darwin L. Mormon. "Use of Contact Lenses in Law Enforcement." *Police,* 16:2 (October, 1971), pp. 16-17.

Dyne, N. "Chiropody and the Policeman." *Police College Magazine* (Spring, 1961), pp. 383-389.
Describes foot problems.

Englebardt, Stanley L. *How to Avoid Your Heart-Attack.* NY: Reader's Digest, 1974.

Hashimoto, K. et al. *Methodology in Human Fatigue Assessment.* NY: International Publications Service, 1971.

Pembrook, Linda. *How to Beat Fatigue.* Garden City, NY: Doubleday, 1975.

Rynearson, Edward H. "Obesity (The Overweight Problem)." *Police,* 1:1 (September-October, 1956), pp. 56-57.

Firing Range Health Hazards

Alpaugh, E.L. "Lead Concentrations in Indoor Firing Ranges." *National Safety News,* 77: (February, 1958).

Anania, T.L. et al. *Lead Exposure at an Indoor Firing Range.* Washington DC: NCJRS, (Microfiche) 1974.

Busch, Ted. "Shooting Range Ventilation." *Law and Order* (October, 1975), pp. 36-38, 71.
Ventilation important because of lead intoxification, lead poisoning and other harmful factors.

Gilligan, P.M. "Save Those Ears! The Need for Hearing Protection in Firearms Training." *Iowa Law Enforcement Journal,* 4:2 (1975), pp. 41-45, 61.

Harrison, Powell. "Health Control in Indoor Ranges." *Police* (September-October, 1966).

"Indoor Rifle Ranges (Small-Bore Weapons), Ventilations." *Design Manual, Training Facilities.* Washington DC: Department of Navy, (NAVFAC DM-27), (December, 1967).

"Lead Poisoning Is Caused Occasionally at Shooting Galleries." *Baltimore Health News,* 24: (June, 1947).

"Long Illness of Police Officers Leads to Discovery of Lead Exposure on Firing Range." *Industrial Health Monthly,* 11 (December, 1951).

Ross, C.R. et al. "Survey of Lead Hazard in Indoor Firing Ranges." *American Industrial Hygiene Association Journal,* 21 (June, 1960).

Stiefel, L. Hody. *Composition of the Exhaust Products of Military Weapons.* Philadelphia: Frankford Arsenal Report, March, 1970.

U.S. Department of the Navy. *Indoor Firing Ranges: Lead Hazard.* Washington DC: U.S. Department of the Navy, August, 1961.

POLICE PERSONALITY

Balch, R.W. "The Police Personality: Fact or Fiction." *Journal of Criminal Law, Criminology and Police Science,* 63:1 (1972), pp. 106-119.

Brenner, Arline R. and James M. Levin. "Off-Duty Policeman and Bystander 'Apathy.'" *Journal of Police Science and Administration,* 1:1 (March, 1973), pp. 61-64.
Study shows that off-duty policemen are more willing to help strangers with difficulty than students studying for the ministry.

Chocran, N. "Authority Orientations of Police Officers." *Journal of Applied Psychology,* 60:5 (1975), pp. 641-643.

Clowers, Norman L. "Prejudice and Discrimination in Law Enforcement." *Police,* 8:3 (January-February, 1964), pp. 42-45.

Cross, Arthur C. and Kenneth R. Hammond. "Social Differences between Successful and Unsuccessful State Highway Patrolmen." *Personnel Revue,* 12 (1951), pp. 159-161.

Cruse, D. and J. Rubin. *Determinants of Police Behavior.* Springfield VA: NTIS, 1972.

Discussion of a methodology for analyzing police behavior and examining the interrelationship of variables which affect police patrol performance.

Dodd, David J. "Police Mentality and Behavior." *Issues in Criminology,* 3:1 (1965), pp. 47-67.

Hilldebrand, James A. "A Detective Personality Profile." *Police Chief,* XXXLIII:1 (January, 1976), pp. 40-41.

Hogan, Robert. "Personality Characteristics of Highly Rated Policemen." *Personnel Psychology* (1971), pp. 679-686.

Knowles, Patrick and Rolf Peterson. "Measurement of Flexibility in State Police Officers." *Journal of Police Science and Administration,* 1:2 (June, 1973), pp. 219-223.

McNamara, John H. "Uncertainties in Police Work: The Relevance of Police Recruits' Backgrounds and Training." in David Bordua, ed., *The Police: Six Sociological Essays.* NY: Wiley, 1967.

Nowicki, Stephen, Jr. "A Study of the Personality Characteristics of Successful Policemen." *Police,* 10:3 (January-February, 1966), pp. 39-41.

Owens, Robert G. and Ronald M. Sindberg. "Personality Traits of Supervisors and Their Administrative Judgment." *Police Chief,* XL:5 (May, 1973), pp. 70-73.

Prytula, Robert et al. "The Personality and Characteristics of Police Officers and Their Attitudes toward Others." *Police Chief,* XXXIX:12 (December, 1972). p. 54.

Rubin, J. "Police Identity and the Police Role." in R.F. Steadman, *The Police and the Community.* Baltimore: Johns Hopkins University Press, 1972.

Author examines the interaction of stress, fatigue and per-·sonality of police behavior.

Skolnick, Jerome H. "A Sketch of the Policeman's Working Personality." in Arthur Niederhoffer and Abraham S. Blumberg, *The Ambivalent Force: Perspectives on the Police.* Waltham, MA: Ginn, 1970.

Tifft, Larry L. "The 'Cop Personaltiy' Reconsidered." *Journal of Police Science and Administration,* 2:3 (September, 1974), pp. 266-27S.

Trojanowicz, Robert C. *Comparison of the Behavioral Styles of Policemen and Social Workers.* Unpub. Doctoral Dissertation, Michigan State University, 1969.

Varsos, Milton, "The Police Profile." *Law and Order,* 18:11 (November, 1970), pp. 24-30, 45.

POLICE SUBCULTURE

Arnold, David. *The Sociology of Subcultures.* Berkeley, CA: Glendessary, 1970.

Buckner, Hubbard T. *Police: The Culture of Social Control Agency.* Unpub. Doctoral Dissertation, University of California, Berkeley, 1967.

Drummond, Douglas S. *Police Culture.* Beverly Hills, CA: Sage, 1976.

Fortier, Kenneth N. "The Police Culture — Its Effects on Sound Police-Community Relations." *Police Chief,* (February, 1972), pp. 33-35.

Goldsmith, Jack and Sharon S. Goldsmith eds. *Police Community: Dimensions of an Occupational Subculture.* Pacific Palisades, CA: Palisades, 1974.

Hale, Charles D. *The Isolated Police Community: An Occupational Analysis.* Unpub. Master's Thesis, California State University, Long Beach (June, 1972).

POLICE SUICIDES

Friedman, P. "Suicide among Police: A Study of 93 Suicides among New York City Policemen, 1934-1940." in E. Schneidman, ed., *Essays in Self Destruction.* NY: Science House, 1968.

Heiman, Michael F. "The Police Suicide." *Journal of Police Science and Administration,* 3:3 (September, 1975), pp. 267-273.

Heiman, Michael F. "Police Suicides Revisited." *Suicide,* 5:1 (Spring, 1975), pp. 5-20.

Lewis, Rodney W. "Toward an Understanding of Police Anomie." *Journal of Police Science and Administration,* 1:4 (December, 1973), pp. 484-490.

Discusses stress, danger-stress and suicide among police officers.

Nelson, Zane P. and Wilford Smith. "The Law Enforcement Profession: An Incident of High Suicide." *Omega,* 1:4 (1970), pp. 293-299.

Schlickit, M.A. "Suicide in the Naval Service." *American Journal of Psychiatry* (December, 1974), pp. 1328-1331.

POLICE WIDOWS

Chapman, Samuel G. "Your Widow Faces the Future." *Law and Order,* 13:5 (May, 1965), pp. 30-31, 34.

Danto, Bruce L. "A Study: Bereavement and the Widows of Slain Police Officers." *Police Chief,* XLI:2 (February, 1974), pp. 51-57.

Lynch, Charles D. "The Forgotten Responsibility." *Law and Order,* 18:1 (January, 1970), pp. 48-49.

Dade County public safety department program to aid the family of a slain officer. Program extends beyond an initial sympathy visit.

Marcovitz, E. "What Is the Meaning of Death to the Dying Person and His Survivors?" *Omega* (Spring, 1973), pp. 13-26.

Marris, P. *Widows and Their Families.* London: Routledge and Kegan Paul, 1958.

POLICE WIVES AND FAMILIES

Anderson, K.S. "Education of Police Officers' Children." *Police College Magazine,* 13:3, pp. 16-18.

Cancilla, Robert C. and Peter C. Unsinger. "The PHT Degree." *Police Chief,* XLII:2 (February, 1975), p. 75.

Drakeford, John W. *Games Husbands and Wives Play.* Nashville, TN: Broadman, 1971.

Fagerstrom, Dorothy. "An Open Letter to Police Wives." *Law and Order,* 19:5 (May, 1971), pp. 72-75.

James, Pat and Martha Nelson. "Police Family — A Wife's Eye View." *FBI Law Enforcement Bulletin* (November, 1975), pp. 12-15.

James, Pat and Martha Nelson. *Police Wife: How to Live With the Law and Like it.* Springfield, IL: C.C. Thomas, 1975.

Mergerson, John. "The Officer's Lady." *Police Chief* (October, 1973).

Megerson, John S. "The Officer's Lady: A Follow Up." *Police Chief* (January, 1976).

Mitchell, Sheila. "The Policeman's Wife — Urban and Rural." *Police Journal (GB),* 48:1 (January-March, 1975), pp. 79-88.

Survey of two Scottish police forces. Wives felt their lives were affected by police duty. Negative aspects of living in police housing and the social effects of being identified as a police wife.

Mitchell, Sheila. *Results of a Survey of Policemen's Wives in Scottish Forces.* Stirling (GB): Stirling University, Sociology Department. [n.d.]

Niederhoffer, Arthur and Elaine Niederhoffer. *Police Family.* Lexington, MA: Lexington, 1975.

Platt, R.M. "The Policeman and His Family, a Unique Social Entity." *Texas Police Journal,* 23:8 (1975), pp. 1-3.

Rafky, D. "My Husband the Cop." *Police Chief,* 41:8 (1974), pp. 62-65.

Survey reveals up to one quarter of police wives are dissatisfied with their husband's occupations.

Renne, Karen. "Correlates of Dissatisfaction in Marriage." *Journal of Marriage and the Family* (February, 1970).

Russell, Maud. *Detective's Wife.* NY: Speller, [n.d.]

Siedenberg, Robert. *Corporate Wives — Corporate Casualties.* NY: AMA, 1973.

Sheehy, Gail. "The Lonely Fear of a Policeman's Wife." *McCalls,* 98 (March, 1971).

Stratton, John. "The Law Enforcement Family: Programs for Spouses." *FBI Law Enforcement Bulletin* (March, 1976), pp. 16-22.

L.A. County Sheriff Department program designed to bring understanding to the police wife. Spouses attend lectures, tour facilities, ride-along-program, given advice on services available to department employees and spouses.

Stratton, John. "Pressures in Law Enforcement Marriages: Some Considerations." *Police Chief,* XLII:11 (November, 1975), pp. 44-47.

"Views from Down Under." *FBI Law Enforcement Bulletin* (March, 1976), p. 15.

Comments of an Australian police wife.

Vogel, Linda J. *Helping a Child Understand Death.* Phildelphia: Fortress, 1975.

Weber, Barbara E., ed. *Handbook for Law Enforcement Wives.* NY: Dell, 1974.

Weber, Barbara. "The Police Wife." *Police Chief,* XLIII:1 (January, 1976), pp. 48-49.

Wolf, Anna W. *Helping Your Child Understand Death.* NY: Child Study, 1972.

ROLE CONFLICT

Johnson, Elmer H. "Police: An Analysis of Role Conflict." *Police,* 14:3 (January-February, 1970), pp. 47-52.

McAlhone, Beryl. "Blurring in the Sex Roles in the Police." *Observer Review* (April, 1975), p. 24.

Manack, T.J. "Role Strain of the Small Town Policeman." *Dissertation* (1973).

Scott, J.F. *Study of Role Conflict Among Policemen.* Ann Arbor, MI: University Microfilms, 1968.

SOCIAL ISOLATION

Clark, John P. "Isolation of the Police: A Comparison of the British and American Situations." *Journal of Criminal Law, Criminology and Police Science* (September, 1965).

Dempsey, John C. *Isolation of the Police Officer.* Unpub. Master's Thesis, Colorado State University, 1967.

Packard, Vance. *A Nation of Strangers.* NY: David McKay, 1972.

Parker, L. Craig, Jr. "Self-Disclosing Behavior in Police Work." *Police Chief,* XXXVIII:7 (July, 1971), pp. 44-46.

Help for isolation and psychological problems.

Weines, Roberts. *Loneliness: The Experience of Emotional and Social Isolation.* Cambridge, MA: MIT Press, 1973.

STRESS

Cobb, S. and R. Rose. "Hypertension, Peptic Ulcer, and Diabetes in Air Controllers." *Journal of American Medical Association,* 4 (1973), pp. 487-492.

Delanoy, Michael. "Stress and the Law: Michael DeLanoy on the High Cost of Being a Policeman." *Guardian* (July 29, 1974).

Dohrenwend, Barbara S. and Bruce P. Dohrenwend. *Stressful Life Events: Their Nature and Effects.* NY: Wiley, 1974.

Elsenberg, Terry. "Labor-Management Relations and Psychological Stress: View from the Bottom." *Police Chief,* XLII:11 (November, 1975), pp. 54-58.

Gardner, Martin R. "Neuromuscular Relaxation as a

Methodological Approach to Stress Conditioning." *Police,* 15:4 (March-April, 1971), pp. 73-76.

Grinker, Roy R. and John P. Spiegel. *Men Under Stress.* Philadelphia: Blakiston, 1945.
Describes the stress of flying in combat.

Hayton, T.H. "Stress Syndrome and the Police Service." *Police Review (GB),* 82 (September 20, 1974), p. 1204.

Henderson, Robert W. "We All Have Our Limits." *Law and Order,* 22:11 (November, 1974).

Hillgren, J.S. and R.B. Bond. "Stress in Law Enforcement: Psycho-Physiological Correlates and Legal Implications." *Journal of Forensic Psychology,* 6 (December, 1974), pp. 25-34.

Janis, Irwing L. *Stress and Frustration.* NY: Harcourt Brace Jovanovich, 1971.

Kroes, William H. *Society's Victim — The Policeman — An Analysis of Job Stress in Policing.* Springfield, IL: C.C. Thomas, 1976.

Kroes, William H., Joseph J. Hurrell, Jr., and Bruce Margolis. "Job Stress in Police Administrators." *Journal of Police Science and Administration,* 2:4 (December, 1974), pp. 381-387.
Job stress caused by conflicting demands from superiors, subordinates and community. Job stress has a number of negative effects on the administrator's family, home and personal life.

Kroes, William, Bruce L. Margolis, and Joseph J. Hurrell, Jr. "Job Stress in Policemen." *Journal of Police Science and Administration,* 2:2 (June, 1974), pp. 145-155.

Kroes, William H. et al. *Job Stress in Policemen.* Washington DC: GPO, [n.d.]

Lamott, Kenneth. *Escape from Stress: Hope to Stop Killing Yourself.* NY: Putnam, 1974.

Levi, L. *Stress and Distress in Response to Psycho-Social Stimuli.* Elmsford, NY: Pergamon, 1972.

Levinson, Harry. *Executive Stress.* NY: Harper and Row, 1970.

McLean, A., ed. *Occupational Stress.* Springfield, IL: C.C. Thomas, 1974.

Margolis, B.L. and W.H. Kroes. "Occupational Stress and Strain." *Occupational Mental Health,* 2:4 (1974), pp. 4-6.

Reiser, Martin. "Some Organization Stresses on Policemen." *Journal of Police Science and Administration,* 2:2 (June, 1974), pp. 156-159.

Reiser, Martin. "Stress, Distress, and Adaptation in Police Work." *Police Chief,* XLIII:1 (January, 1976), pp. 24-27.

Sarason, I.G. and C.D. Spielberger, eds. *Stress and Anxiety.* NY: Halstead, 1975.

Selye, Hans. *Stress of Life.* rev. ed. NY: McGraw Hill, 1975.

Taylor, Robert. "Stress at Work." *New Society* (October 17, 1974), pp. 140-143.

VALUES

Chwast, Jacob. "Value Conflicts in Law Enforcement." *Crime and Delinquency,* 11:2 (April, 1965), pp. 151-161.
Describes and analyzes the cause and effect of police values and how they conflict with social values and inhibit professionalism.

Sikula, Andrew F. "The Values and Value Systems of Muncipal Policemen." *Police,* 16:9 (May, 1972), pp. 59-63.

Teeran, James J., Sr. and Bernard Dolnick. "The Values of the Police: A Reconsideration and Interpretation." *Journal of Police Science and Administration,* 1:3 (September, 1973), pp. 366-369.

VIOLENCE

Bruster, Bill. "Living with Violence." *Law and Order,* 20:10 (October, 1972), p. 85.

Male, Les. "Violence Is a Part of a Policeman's Daily Life." *Police (GB),* (May, 1976), pp. 14-15.

Westley, William A. *Violence and the Police.* Cambridge, MA: MIT Press, 1970.

PART XIII
COMPARATIVE POLICE ADMINISTRATION

ISSUES IN COMPARATIVE POLICE ADMINISTRATION

COMPARATIVE POLICE ADMINISTRATION — GENERAL

Alper, B.S. and J.F. Boren. *Crime: International Agenda, Concern and Action in the Prevention of Crime and Treatment of Offenders,* 1846-1972. Lexington, MA: Health Lexington, 1972.
History and survey of the variety of international, regional, official and nongovernmental organizations concerned with crime, their interests and proposals.

Berkley, George. *The Democratic Policeman.* Boston: Beacon, 1969.

Blaustein, A.P. *Manual on Foreign Legal Periodicals and Their Index.* Dobbs Ferry, NY: Oceana, 1962.

Blaustein, A.P. and G.H. Flantz. *Constitutions of the Countries of the World.* Dobbs Ferry, NY: Oceana.
Vols 1-10 available; approximately 12 constitutions per volume. Issued quarterly in loose-leaf form.

Brean, Herbert. "The Evil Domain of World Crime." *Life,* 48:88 (January 11, 1960).
Broad discussion of lawlessness throughout the world.

Byrnes, Asher and M. Konvitz. *Government Against the People.* NY: Dodd Mead, 1946.
The character and function of police forces in various countries; chiefly Russia, England, and the U.S.A.

Clifford, W. "Crime in World Perspective." *International Criminal Police Review,* (August-September, 1970), pp. 231-232.

Conrad, John P. *Crime and Its Correction. An International Survey of Attitudes and Practices.* Berkeley: University of California Press, 1970.

Coutts, J.A., ed. *The Accused: A Comparative Study.* London: Stevens, 1967.
Purpose of this study is to examine how the liberty of the individual is protected in the various codes of criminal procedure in several dozen countries of the world.

Cramer, James. "Uniforms of the World's Police." *Police,* 16:4 (December, 1971), pp. 66-67.

Cramer, James. *Uniforms of the World's Police with Brief Data on Organization, Systems, and Weapons.* Springfield, IL: C.C. Thomas, 1968.

Cramer, James. *The World's Police.* London: Cassell,
Outstanding review of the police agencies of the world. Has some information on almost every country.

Deb, R. "How to Deal with Interstate Criminals." *International Criminal Police Review* (March, 1960), pp. 76-86.

Dorey, M.A. and G.J. Swidler. *World Police Systems — A Factual Text, Part I.* Boston: Northeastern University, 1974.
Brief description of the structure and organization of the police and court systems in selected European, Asian, African, and North American countries.

"Fifth International Counterfeit Currency Conference." *International Criminal Police Review* (March, 1970), pp. 86-96.

Foreign Countries: The Police of Europe, Africa, and Asia. Heidelburg: U.S. Army, 1963.
Prepared by the Provost Marshall, U.S. Army, Europe, October 1, 1963. Articles originally published in *Police Chief* from 1959-1963 (USAREUR PAM 550-1).

Fraser, Gordon. *Modern Transportation and International Crime.* Springfield, IL: C.C. Thomas, 1970.

Gellhorn, Walter. *Ombudsmen and Others: Citizens' Protectors in Nine Countries.* Cambridge, MA: Harvard University Press, 1966.

General Secretariat, Interpol. "A Typical Counterfeiting Organization." *International Criminal Police Review,* 167 (April, 1963), pp. 123-124.

Graham, H.H. "International Prosecution." *International Criminal Police Review* (October, 1970).

Grant, Charles D. "Policing an International Festival." *FBI Law Enforcement Bulletin* (April, 1971).

Green, Timothy. *The Smugglers, An Investigation into the World of the Contemporary Smuggler.* NY: Walker, 1969.

Griffin, John I. "International Criminal Statistics." *Police* (September-October, 1958), pp. 58-60.

Heaton, D.H. "International Traffic in Stolen Gems." *RCMP Gazette,* 28:5 (1966).

Horrigan, Thomas J. "The International Assc. of Auto Theft Investigators: Its Organization." *Police Chief,* (November, 1966).

International Criminal Police Organization — INTERPOL. *Report on the International Symposium for Heads of Police Training Colleges.* Paris: INTERPOL, October, 1965.

"International Currency Counterfeiting." *International Criminal Police Review* (December, 1966), pp. 296-301.
Summary of counterfeiting activities throughout the world.

International Exchange of Information on Current Criminology Research Projects in Member States. Vol. 10, NY: Manhattan, 1970.

International Symposium for Research in Comparative Criminology. Quebec: University of Montreal, 1969.

Lowes, Peter D. *The Genesis of International Narcotics Control*. Geneva: Librairie Droz, 1966.

Morris, Charles V. "Worldwide Concern with Crime." *Federal Probation,* 24 (December, 1960), pp. 21-30.

Morrison, Gilbert. "International Frauds: Conspiracy to Defraud International Banks." *International Criminal Police Review* (October, 1969). pp. 211-213.

Mueller, G.O.W. and Edward M. Wise. *International Criminal Law*. South Hackensack, NJ: Rothman, 1966.

Nepote, Jean "Drug Addiction and Traffic." *International Criminal Police Review* (August-September, 1960), pp. 198-209.

Newman, Graeme R. *Comparative Deviance: Perception and Law in Six Cultures*. NY: Elsevier, 1976.

Ostler, R.D. "Criminal Investigation — Criminals Incorporated." *Police Journal (GB),* (April, 1965).
Three countries develop a "Ghost" squad to observe the actions of several suspects.

Peaslee, Amos J. *Constitutions of Nations*. 4 vols. NY: International Publications Service, 1974.

Poulantzas, Nicholas Michael. *The Right of Hot Pursuit in International Law*. Leiden: Sijthoff, 1969.

Reith, Charles. *The Blind Eye of History*. London: Faber and Faber, 1952.
Reith's thesis is that any society which does not enforce its own laws perishes. Gives a number of historical examples.

Rowat, Donald C., ed. *The Ombudsman: Citizen's Defender*. London: George Allen and Unwin, 1965.

Schleimer, H. "Album of Criminal Offenders." *International Criminal Police Review* (October, 1963), pp. 235-238.

Sellin, Thorsten. *Systems of Reporting Crimes Known to Police in Selected Foreign Countries*. Consultant Paper, President's Commission on Law Enforcement and Administration of Justice, Washington DC: GPO, 1967.

Shearer, I.A. *Extradition in International Law*. Dobbs Ferry, NY: Oceana, 1971.

Singer, K. *Crime Omnibus*. London: W.H. Allen, 1962.

Singer, K. *My Greatest Crime Story, by Police Chiefs of the World*. London: W.H. Allen, 1956.

Singer, K. *My Strangest Case, by Police Chiefs of the World*. London: W.H. Allen, 1957.

Soderman, Harry D. "Science and Criminal Investigation." *Annals* (November, 1929), pp. 237-248.

Sowle, Claude R., ed. *Police Power and Individual Freedom*. Chicago: Aldine, 1962.
Compares legal aspects of policing in the U.S. and seven foreign countries.

Stokes, Joseph M. "International Cooperation in Police Administration." *Police Yearbook,* Washington DC:, IACP, 1957.

Sullivan, Francis C. "The Police and Criminal Procedures in Foreign Countries." *Police,* 4:6 (July-August, 1960), pp. 26-27.

"Symposium on International Frauds." *International Criminal Police Review* (November, 1968), pp. 254-258.
Sponsored by INTERPOL. Topics covered were frauds in connection with air travel documents, travelers checks, gold traffic, bank frauds and smuggling.

Szabo, Denis. *Comparative Criminology — Significance and Tasks*. Montreal: University of Montreal, International Centre for Comparative Criminology, 1973.

Turkel, Siegfried. "Criminalistic Institutes and Laboratories." *Annals* (November, 1929), pp. 199-204.

Wighton, Charles. *Dope International*. London: Muller, 1960.

Wolfgang, Marvin E. "International Criminal Statistics: A Proposal." *Journal of Criminal Law, Criminology and Police Science,* 58:1 (March, 1967), pp. 65-69.

COLONIAL POLICE

Adam, J.H. Stanley. "British South African Police in Southern Rhodesia." *Police Journal (GB),* I (October, 1928), pp. 553-567.

Adam, W.P.C. "The Jamaica Constabulary." *Police Journal,* V (April, 1932), pp. 257-266.

Adams, W.C. "Constabulary of North Borneo." *Police Journal (GB),* 1 (April, 1929), pp. 310-315.

Bourne, K.M. "Shanghai Municipal Police: Chinese Uniform Branch." *Police Journal (GB),* 2 (January, 1929), pp. 26-36.

Bruce, C.D. "Shanghai: The International Settlement and Its Municipal Police Force." *Police Journal (GB),* 1 (January, 1928), pp. 128-138.

Clarke, W.T. "Natal Mounted Police." *Police Journal (GB),* IV (July, 1931), pp. 337-350.

Courtney, Roger. *Palestine Policeman: An Account of the Eighteen Dramatic Months in the Palestine Police Force During the Great Jew-Arab Troubles*. London: Herbert Jenkins, 1939.

Cox, Edmund C. *Police and Crime in India,* London: Stanley Paul, 1911.

Cumming, John. "The Police Services of the Empire." *United Empire,* XXI: 130.

Curray, J.C. *The Indian Police*. London: Faber and Faber, 1932.

Dowbiggin, Herbert. "Colonial Policing." *Police College Magazine* (Spring, 1960), pp. 144-147.

Foran, W. Robert. *The Kenya Police, 1887-1960*. London: Robert Hale, 1962.

Gillespie, W.H. *Gold Coast Police, 1844-1938*. Accra: Gold Coast, Government Printer, 1955.

"The Gold Coast Police." *Police Journal (GB),* 5 (January, 1932), pp. 94-100.

Graves, Brian. "Law Enforcement in Tropical Islands." *FBI Law Enforcement Bulletin* (January, 1972).

Griffiths, Percival. *To Guard My People: The History of the Indian Police*. London: Benn, 1971.

Gwynn, Charles W. *Imperial Policing*. London: Macmillan, 1934.

Harding, Colin. *Frontier Patrols: History of the British South Africa Police and Other Rhodesian Forces*. London: G. Bell, 1939.

Hearn, C.V. *Desert Assignment*. London: Hale, 1963.

Hearn, C.V. *Foreign Assignment*. London: Hale, 1961.

Heath, A.J. Kingsley, "Palestine Police Force under the Mandate." *Police Journal (GB)*, 1 (April, 1928), pp. 78-88.

Hole, H. Marshall. "Police Forces of Southern Rhodesia." *Police Journal (GB)*, (1930), pp. 435-446.

Holman, D. *Bwana Drum*. London: W.H. Allen, 1964.

Holt, H.P. *The Mounted Police of Natal*. London: Murray, 1913.

Hoorweg, A. "The Dutch East Indian Police." *Police Journal*, II (October, 1929), pp. 579-595.

Jeffrey, Charles. *The Colonial Police*. London: M. Parrish, 1952.

Maurogordato, A.S. "The Trinidad Constabulary." *Police Journal (GB)*, 5 (July, 1932), pp. 407-412.

Morton, G. *Just the Job (Some Experiences of a Colonial Policeman)*. London: Hodder and Stoughton, 1957.

Peters, E.W. and Hugh Barnes, eds. *Shanghai Policeman*. [n.p.]: Rich and Cowan, 1937.

Rountree, F.R.G. "Mauritius Police Force." *Police Journal (GB)*, III (January, 1930), pp. 50-62.

Sempill, C.I. "Making of an East African Policeman." *Police Journal (GB)*, (1928), pp. 669-681.

Stevens, H. Lynn. *Autobiography of a Border Policeman, Bechuanaland and Matabeleland*. London: Witherby, 1927.

Stevens, H. Lynn. "Bechuanaland Border Police in the Early 'Nineties.'" *Police Journal (GB)*, (1931), pp. 211-224.

Walne, J.W.W. "Policing North Borneo." *Police College Magazine* (Autumn, 1961), pp. 89, 90, 93, 94.

Wheeler, R. de-L. "Problems of Modern Colonial Policing." *Police College Magazine* (Spring, 1961), pp. 390-393.

Wilson, Arnold T. "The Iraq Police: A Notable Example of British Administrative Adaptability." *Police Journal*, 1 (January, 1928), pp. 31-38.

COMMON MARKET

Campbell, Allen R. *Common Market Law*. 2nd. ed. 3 vols. Dobbs Ferry, NY: Oceana, 1975.

Campbell, D. "British Police in the Common Market." *Police*, (GB), (October, 1971), pp. 28, 30.

Glazer, John and Pam Jones. "Meet Your Brothers-in-Law." *Job* (January 14, 1972), pp. 4-5.
Briefly describes the police forces in the common market.

Stephen, D. "Police, Europe and the Movement of People." *Police Journal*, 46:3 (1973), 242-249.
Consequences for Great Britain's involvement in the common market. Discusses the possibility of a multi-national police unit.

DEVELOPING NATIONS

Bayley, David. *Public Liberties in the New States*. Chicago: Rand McNally, 1964.

Ben-dor, G. "The Role of the Police in Political Development." *Police Journal (GB)*, 47:2 (1974), pp. 101-114.
Author states police are less likely to involve themselves in coups d' etat than the military. Outline of ways in which police can contribute to political development.

Clinard, M.B. and D.J. Abbott. *Crime in Developing Countries — A Comparative Perspective*. NY: Wiley, 1973.
Cross-cultural comparison that describes the nature and the causes of crime in developing countries with particular reference to Uganda.

Hoff, Rodger L. "The Role of Police Forces in Developing Nations." *Military Police Journal* (January, 1972), pp. 5-9.

Lunden, Walter A. "The Increase of Criminality in Underdeveloped Countries." *Police*, 6:5 (May-June, 1962), pp. 30-34.

Rizkalla, S. "Crime and Criminal Justice in the Developing Countries." *ACTA Criminology*, 7 (1974), pp. 169-191.

INTERNATIONAL POLICE FORCE

Bloomfield, Lincoln P. *International Military Forces: The Question of Peacekeeping in an Armed and Disarmed World*. Boston: Little, 1964.

Bowett, D.W. *United Nations Forces: A Legal Study*. NY: Praeger, 1964.

Collier, Barron. "International World Police." *Journal of Criminal Law and Criminology*, 23 (September-October, 1932), pp. 545-548.

Hocking, W.E. "Is a World Police Possible?" *Christian Century*, 61 (November 23, 1944), pp. 1347-1349.

Lefever, Ernest W. *Crisis in the Congo: A United Nations Force in Action*. Washington DC: Brookings, 1965.

Lukban, Joseph. "International Policing and Global Peace." *Police*, 9:4 (March-April, 1965), pp. 90-92.

Offutt, Milton. *The Protection of Citizens Abroad by the Armed Forces of the United States*. Baltimore: Johns Hopkins University Press, 1928.

INTERPOL

Bellour, J.C. "Counterfeit Currency Group at the I.C.P.O. INTERPOL General Secretariat." *International Criminal Police Review* (February, 1976), pp. 46-48.

Benhamou, E. "The Crook with Fifty Names." *International Criminal Police Review* (November, 1965), pp. 262-264.

Dressler, D. "The International Criminal Police Commission." *Police Journal (NY)*, 18 (August, 1931), pp. 7-9; (September, 1931), pp. 9-10, 23, (November, 1931), pp. 7, 24-25.

Elmes, Frank. "INTERPOL." *Police Review (GB),* (December 7, 1973).

Fooner, Michael. *INTERPOL.* Chicago: Henry Regnery, 1973.

Forrest, A.J. *INTERPOL.* London: Wingate, 1955.

Giannoules, Kenneth S. "INTERPOL: Myth or Fact." *Law Enforcement,* 25 (July-August, 1970), pp. 16-19.

Giannoules, Kenneth S. "INTERPOL: Your APB to the World." *Police Chief* (November, 1973), pp. 16-19.

Hasler, Terry. "INTERPOL: Where Does the Future Lie Now?" *Job* (September 21, 1973).

Houten, M.C. van. "International Co-Operation of Criminal Police: Its History and Aims." *Police Journal (GB),* (1930), pp. 482-497.

International Criminal Police Organization (INTERPOL). *Powers and Duties of the Police with Regard to Detention.* Saint Cloud, France: INTERPOL, 1965.

INTERPOL General Secretariat. "I.C.P.O. — INTERPOL." *International Criminal Police Review,* 28:267 (1973), 28:268 (1973).
Two complete issues of the review describe the history and achievements of INTERPOL on its 50th anniversary.

Lee, Peter G. *INTERPOL.* NY: Stein and Day, 1976.

Lukban, Joseph. "International Policing and Global Press." *Police,* 9:4 (March-April, 1965), pp. 90-91.

More, Harry W., Jr. "International Criminal Police Commission." *Police,* 13:5 (May-June, 1969), pp. 13-14.
Brief history of INTERPOL.

Nepote, Jean. "International Criminal Police Organization — INTERPOL." *Journal of California Law Enforcement* (July, 1970), pp. 18-21.

"Role of INTERPOL." *Police Review (GB),* (January 17, 1975), pp. 71-73.

Sagalyn, Arnold. "The Pursuit of International Criminals through INTERPOL." *Journal of Criminal Law, Criminology and Police Science* (June, 1966).

Sagalyn, Arnold. "The Role of INTERPOL." *Police Chief,* XXXII:12 (December, 1965), pp. 57-59.

Siragusa, Charles. "INTERPOL: The Enforcement Attack on International Crime." *International Criminal Police Review* (May, 1960), pp. 130-136.

Tullett, Tom. *Inside INTERPOL.* London: Frederick Muller, 1963.

SOCIAL CONTROL IN PRIMITIVE SOCIETY

Barkun, Michael. *Law Without Sanctions: Order in Primitive Societies and the World Community.* New Haven, CT: Yale University Press, 1968.

Diamond, A.S. *Primitive Law, Past and Present.* rev. 3rd. ed. NY: Barnes and Noble, 1971.

Hartland, E. Sydney. *Primitive Law.* Port Washington, NY: Kennikat, 1971. (repr. of 1924 ed.).

Hoebel, E.A. "Law — Ways of Primitive Eskimos." *Journal of Criminology and Criminal Law,* 31 (1940), pp. 663-683.

Hogbin, H. Ian. *Law and Order in Polynesia: A Study of Primitive Legal Institutions.* NY: Harcourt, 1934.

Mueller, Gerhard O.W. "Tort, Crime and the Primitive." *Journal of Criminal Law, Criminology and Police Science,* 46:3 (September-October, 1955), pp. 303-332.

SOCIAL CONTROL IN THE ANCIENT WORLD

Bonner, Robert J. and Gertrude E. Smith. *Administration of Justice from Homer to Aristotle,* 2 vols. Westport, CT: Greenwood, 1969. (repr. of 1938 ed.).

Buckland, William Warwick. *A Text-Book of Roman Law from Augustus to Justinian.* NY: Cambridge University Press, 1921.

Declareuil, J. *Rome, The Law-Giver.* NY: Knopf, 1926.

Freeman, Peter. *Justice in Plato's Republic.* NY: Philosophical Library, 1957.

Gilbert, Gustav. *The Constitutional Antiquities of Sparta and Athens.* Chicago: Argonaut, 1968. (repr. of 1895 ed.).

Jones, A.H. *Criminal Courts of the Roman Republic and Principat.* Totowa, NJ: Rowman, 1972.

Lawson, F.H. *Roman Law Reader.* Dobbs Ferry, NY: Oceana, 1969.

Lee, R.W. *Elements of Roman Law, with a Translation of the Institute of Justinian.* 3rd. ed. London: Sweet and Maxwell, 1952.

Mendelsohn, Samuel. *Criminal Jurisprudence of the Ancient Hebrews.* NY: Hermon, 1968.

Nicholas, Barry. *An Introduction to Roman Law.* Oxford: Clarendon Press, 1975. (repr. of 1962 ed.).

Parker, H.M.D. *Roman Legions.* Oxford: Clarendon Press, 1928.

Reynolds, P.K. Baille. "Police in Ancient Rome." *Police Journal (GB),* (1928), pp. 432-442.

Reynolds, P.K.B. *Vigils of Imperial Rome.* London: Oxford University Press, 1926.

Schulz, Fritz. *Principles of Roman Law.* NYNY: Oxford University Press, 1936.

Wolff, Hans J. *Roman Law: An Historical Introduction.* Norman: University of Oklahoma Press, 1964.

TOTALITARIANISM

Agger, Robert and Daniel Goldrich. *The Rulers and the Ruled.* NY: Wiley, 1964.

Arendt, Hannah. *The Origins of Totalitarianism.* new ed. NY: Harcourt Brace and World, 1966.

Becket, James. *Barbarism in Greece: A Young American Lawyer's Inquiry into the Use of Torture in Contemporary Greece, with Case Histories and Documents.* NY: Walker, 1970.

Buchheim, Hans. *Totalitarian Rule: Its Nature and Characteristics.* Middletown, CT. Wesleyan University Press, 1968.

Burch, Betty B., ed. *Dictatorship and Totalitarianism: Selected Readings.* Cincinnati, OH: Van Nostrand Rinehold, 1964.

Dallin, Alexander and George W. Breslauer. *Political Terror in Communist Systems.* Stanford, CA: Stanford University Press, 1970.

Friedrick, Carl J. *Totalitarianism.* NY: Grosset and Dunlap, 1964.

Germino, D.L. *The Italian Fascist Party in Power: A Study in Totalitarian Rule.* NY: Fertig, 1971.

Hallgarten, C. George W. *Devils or Saviors: A History of Dictatorship Since 1600 B.C.* NY: Humanities, 1960.

Ionescu, Ghita. *The Politics of the European Communist States.* London: Weidenfeld and Nicolson, 1968.

Lefever, Ernest W. *Spear and Scepter: Army, Police and Politics in Tropical Africa.* Washington DC: Brookings Institution, 1970.

McClosky, Herbert and John E. Turner. *The Soviet Dictatorship.* NY: McGraw-Hill.
The theory and practice of Soviet power and politics as they are today.

Moore, Barrington, Jr. *Social Origin of Dictatorship and Democracy.* Boston: Beacon, 1966.

Omari, T. Peter. *Kwame Nkrumah: The Anatomy of an African Dictatorship.* NY: Africana, 1970.

Payne, Stanley G. *Falange: A History of Spanish Fascism.* Stanford, CA: Stanford University Press, 1966.

Radel, J.L. *Roots of Totalitarian Government.* NY: Crane-Russak, 1975.

Schapiro, Leonard. *Totalitarianism.* NY: Praeger, 1972.

Skilling, H. Gordon. *Governments of Communist East Europe.* NY: Crowell, 1966.

Soyinka, Wole. *The Man Died.* NY: Harper and Row, 1972.
In part discusses police and prisons in Nigeria.

Szirmai, Z., ed. *Law in Eastern Europe.* vol. 3. *Federal Criminal Law of the Soviet Union,* NY: Humanities, 1958. (15 vols.).

Szirmai, Z., ed. *Law in Eastern Europe,* vol. 9. *Soviet Criminal Law,* NY: Humanities, 1958. (15 vols.).

Triska, Jan F., ed. *Constitutions of the Communist Party States.* Stanford, CA: Hoover Institute on War, Revolution and Peace, Stanford University, 1969.

Ulc, Otto. *Judge in a Communist State: A View from Within.* Athens: Ohio University Press, 1972.

Wiarda, Howard J. *Dictatorship and Development: The Methods of Control in Trujillo's Dominican Republic.* Gainesville: University Presses of Florida, 1968.

TOTALITARIAN POLICE

Aronson, Shlomo. *The Beginnings of the Gestapo System.* Edison, NJ: Transaction, 1969.

Bailey, Sidney D. "Police Socialism in Tsarist Russia." *Review of Politics,* 19 (October, 1957), pp. 462-471.

Barron, John. *KGB: The Secret Work of Soviet Secret Agents.* London: Hodder and Stoughton, 1974.

Beck, F. and W. Godin. *Russian Purge and the Extraction of Confession.* NY: Viking, 1950.

Benda, Harry J., James K. Krikura, and Koichi Kishi. *Japanese Military Administration in Indonesia: Selected Documents.* New Haven, CT: Yale University, 1965.

Bramstedt, E.K. *Dictatorship and Political Police: The Technique of Control Through Fear.* NY: Oxford University Press, 1945.
Description of political police in Germany, France and Italy.

Brissand, Andre. *Nazi Secret Service.* London: Badley Head, 1974.

Broszat, Martin et al. *Anatomy of the S.S. State.* London: Collins, 1968.

Burke, G.F. "The Gestapo." *Lancashire Constabulary Journal* (October, 1967).

Chapman, Brian. *Police State.* NY: Praeger, 1970.

Crankshaw, Edward. "Gestapo." *Nation,* 182 (May 26, 1956).

Crankshaw, Edward. *Gestapo: Instrument of Tyranny.* NY: Viking, 1957.

Deacon, Richard. *History of the Russian Secret Service.* London: Muller, 1972.

Delarve, Jacques. *The Gestapo: A History of Horror.* NY: Dell, 1964.

de Zaaijer, H.R. "Law Enforcement." *Annals,* 245 (May, 1946), pp. 9-18.
Describes impact of Nazi German occupation upon the courts and police of the Netherlands.

Goefer, Frederick. "The Nazi Penal System." *Journal of Criminal Law and Criminology,* 35:6 (March-April, 1945).

Goodman, Derick. *Villainy Unlimited. The Truth About the French Underground Today.* London: Elek Books, 1957.

Gruenberger, Richard. *Hitler's S.S.* NY: Delacorte, 1971.

Hemissart, Paul. *Wolves in the City: The Death of French Algeria.* Albans: Hart-Davis, 1971.

Hohne, Heinz. *Order of the Death Head: The Story of Hitler's S.S.* NY: Coward, 1970.

International Commission against Concentrationist Regimes. *Police-State Methods in the Soviet Union.* Boston: Beacon, 1953.

Kempner, Robert M.W. "The German National Registration System As a Means of Police Control over Population." *Journal of Criminal Law and Criminology,* 36:5 (1947).

Krausnick, Helmut and Martin Bronzat. *Anatomy of the S.S. State.* Albans: Paladin, 1970.

McKale, Donald M. *The Nazi Party Courts: Hitler's Management of Conflict in His Movement, 1921-1945.* Lawrence, KS: Regents, 1974.

Manvell, Roger. *S.S. and Gestapo: Rule by Terror.* NY: Ballantine Books, 1969.

Mikes, George. *Study in Infamy.* London: Duetsch, 1959.
Description of the Hungarian AVO.

Mollo, Andrew. *A Pictorial History of S.S., 1923-1945.* London: Macdonald and Janes, 1976.

Orlow, Dietrich. *The Nazis in the Balkans: A Case Study of Totalitarian Politics.* Pittsburgh: University of Pittsburgh Press, 1968.

Payne, Howard C. *The Police State of Louis Napoleon Bonaparte, 1851-1860.* Seattle: University of Washington Press, 1966.

Prato, C. "Le Deuxieme Gestapo." *Nation,* 152 (June 21, 1941), pp. 720-722.

Rosenberg, Hans. *Bureaucracy, Aristocracy: The Prussian Experience. 1660-1815.* Boston: Beacon, 1966.

Thompson, Craig. *The Police State.* NY: Sutton, 1950.

"Trying to Purge the Manchukuo Police from All Impurities." *China Weekly Review,* 67 (February 24, 1934).

Vassilyew, A.T. *Ochrana: The Russian Secret Police.* Philadelphia: J.B. Lippincott, 1930.

Walkin, Jacob. *The Rise of Democracy in Pre-Revolutionary Russia: Political and Social Institutions Under the Last Three Czars.* London: Thames and Hudson, 1963. See Chapter 3: "The Police State — Czarist Version."

Williams, Gerald O. "Political Police — Historical Origins and Development." *Police,* 9:4 (March-April, 1965) 9:5 (May-June, 1965).

Wolin, Simon and Robert M. Slusser, eds. *The Soviet Secret Police.* NY: Praeger, 1957.

AMERICAN POLICE HISTORY

General

Adams, Orville D. *Training for the Police Service.* Washington DC: GPO, 1938.

Allsop, Kenneth. *The Bootleggers and Their Era.* Garden City, NY: Doubleday, 1961.

American Municipal Association. *Municipal Training Schools for Police Officials Conducted by State Leagues of Municipalities.* Chicago: American Municipal Association, December, 1932.

Andrews, Rex R. "Modern Police Administration." *Municipality,* 36 (January, 1940).

Archer, John. "To All Young Police Officers: The Origins of Policing." *Canadian Police Chief,* 60 (July, 1971), pp. 13, 15-16, 19-20.

Bellman, A. "A Police Service Rating Scale." *Journal of Criminal Law and Criminology,* 26 (May, 1937), pp. 74-114.

Berque, Harry. "How States Train Police." *Police Journal (NY),* XXXI (August, 1935), pp. 18-20.

Bopp, William J. *A Short History of American Law Enforcement.* Springfield, IL: C.C. Thomas, 1972.

Campbell, C. Wellington. "History of Law Enforcement." *International Police Academy Review,* 5 (April, 1971), pp. 5-9, 16.

Carleton, William G. "Cultural Roots of American Law Enforcement." *Current History,* 52:311 (1967), pp. 1-7.

Clarke, Bruce C. "U.S. Law Enforcement." *Military Police Journal,* 10 (February, 1960).

Coates, Robert M. *The Outlaw Years: The History of the Land Pirates of the Natchez Trace.* Detroit, MI: Gale, 1974. (repr. of 1930 ed.).

"Comparative Costs of European and American Police." *Journal of Criminal Law and Criminology,* VII (1916-1917).

Corey, Herbert. *Farewell Mr. Gangster: America's War on Crime.* NY: D. Appleton-Century, 1936.

Daniels, Jonathan. *Devil's Backbone: The Story of the Natchez Trace.* NY: McGraw, 1962.

DeQuincey, Thomas. *On Murder Considered as One of the Fine Arts.* NY: Arnold, 1925.

Dequiros, C. Bernaldo. *Modern Theories of Criminality.* Boston: Little, 1911.

"A Development of American Police Patrol." *Virginia Trooper,* 17 (November, 1970), pp. 12-19.

Folgelson, Robert M., ed. *Administration of Justice in the United States.* NY: Arno, 1974. (repr. of 1910 ed.).

"Foreign and Domestic Police Systems." *Journal of Criminal Law and Criminology,* V (1914-1915).

Franck, Harry A. *Zone Policeman 88: A Close Range Study of the Panama Canal and Its Workers.* NY: Century, 1913.

Garofalo, Raffaele. *Criminology.* Boston: Little, 1914.

Hale, G.W. *Police and Prison Encyclopedia.* Boston: Richardson, 1894.

Hamilton, Lander C. "A Brief History of Police, Part III." *Police,* 13:2 (November-December, 1968), pp. 69-75.

Harrison, Richard. *The Story of the World's Police.* London: Phoenix House, 1954.

Hoogenboom, Ari. *Outlawing the Spoils — A History of the Civil Service Reform Movement, 1865-1883.* Urbana: University of Illinois Press, 1961.

Horan, James D. and Howard Swiggett. *The Pinkerton Story.* NY: Putnam's, 1951.

Hyde, W.C. "Training Oregon's Police." *Commonwealth Review,* XIX (July, 1937), pp. 202-208.

Jeffery, Clarence Ray. "Pioneers in Criminology: The Historical Development of Criminology." *Journal of Criminal Law, Criminology and Police Science,* 50:1 (May-June, 1959), pp. 3-19.

"Kansas Police School." *Kansas Government Journal.* XXIII (October, 1937), pp. 17-20.

Kimble, Joseph P. "Daydreams, Dogma, and Dinosaurs." *Police Chief,* XXXVI:4 (April, 1969), pp. 12-15.

Kirchner, F.J. *Index to the Police Forces of the British Empire, the U.S. America, and Foreign Countries, 1884.* London: Police Review Publishing, 1931.

Larson, John A. "Psychology in Criminal Investigation." *Annals* (November, 1929), pp. 258-268.

Latulipe, Francis X. "First Federal Training School." *Police and Peace Officer Journal,* XIII (December, 1935), p. 26.

Lester, W.H. Drane. *Crime In Eurpoe and the United States.* Peace Officer Association of California Proceedings, 19 (1937), pp. 19-19.

Scotland Yard, Russian police systems, Italian carabinieris, American police, Federal Bureau of Investigation, Bertillon systems; ballistics, scientific methods of crime investigation.

Levine, S.A. *Allan Pinkerton: America's First Private Eye.* NY: Dodd Mead, 1963.

McWatters, George S. *Detectives of Europe and America, or Life in the Secret Service: A Selection of Celebrated Cases, A Revelation of Struggles and Triumphs of Renowned Detectives.* Hartford: J.B. Burr, 1878.

MacQuarrie, T.W. "San Jose State College Police School." *Journal of Criminal Law and Criminology,* 26 (July, 1935), pp. 255-261.

Mason, Robert A. "A Brief History of Police Communications." *Police,* 3:4 (March-April, 1959), pp. 50-53.

"Minnesota Police Training School." *Minnesota Municipalities,* XXI (May, 1936), pp. 141-144.

Missouri Association for Criminal Justice. *The Missouri Crime Survey.* Montclair, NJ: Patterson Smith, 1968. (repr. of 1926 ed.).

"Missouri's Police School." *National Police Officer Journal,* 7:1 (January, 1936), pp. 1-2.

"Modern Methods of Police Training." *Toledo City Journal,* XIX (September, 1934), pp. 345-346.

"Montana Police Academy Organized in Great Falls." *Pacific Northwest Law Enforcement News,* IV (October, 1937), pp. 21-22.

Mosse, George L. *Police Forces in History.* Beverly Hills, CA: Sage, 1975.

Murrell, C.D. "1934 Police Training School." *Kansas Municipal Journal,* 20 (July, 1934).

Nash, Jay Robert. *Bloodletters and Badmen.* NY: M. Evens, 1973.

National Commission on Law Observance and Enforcement. *Wickersham Commission Reports.* 14 vols. Montclair, NJ: Patterson Smith, (repr. of 1931 ed.).

National Police Commission. *Official Proceedings of the National Police Convention.* NY: Arno, (repr. of 1871 ed.).

Nolting, O.F. "Important Considerations in the Selection of Patrolmen." *American City,* 40 (April, 1929), pp. 124-125.

Parry, James W. "Police Schools and Training." *Michigan Police Journal,* VI (August-September, 1936), pp. 14-16.

Phillipson, Coleman. *Three Criminal Law Reformers: Becarria, Bentham, Romilly.* London: Dent, 1923.

"Police Instruction: The Law of the Realm." *Toledo City Journal,* XVII (October, 1932), pp. 357-358.

"Police Motorcycles, 1905-1935." *National Police Officer,* 6:3 (December, 1936).

"Police Training School." *Journal of Criminal Law and Criminology,* XXV (July-August, 1934), pp. 338-339.

"Professionalizing Police Work." *Public Management,* XIV (March, 1934), pp. 99-100.

Purvis, Melvin H. *The Violent Years.* NY: Hillman, 1960.

Ragsdale, George T. "The Police Training School." *Annals* (November, 1929).

Reith, Charles. *The Blind Eye of History.* London: Faber and Faber, 1952.

Reticker, Ruth and Leon C. Marshall. *Expenditures of Public Money for the Adminstration of Justice in Ohio: 1930.* Baltimore: Johns Hopkins University Press, 1933.

Richardson, James F. *Urban Police in the United States: A Brief History.* Port Washington, NY: Kennikat, 1974.

Robinson, Louis N. *History and Organization of Criminal Statistics in the United States.* Montclair, NJ: Patterson Smith, 1969. (repr. of 1911 ed.).

Shalloo, Jeremiah P. "The Private Police of Pennsylvania." *Annals* (November, 1929), pp. 55062.

Skehan, J.J. *Modern Police Work. Brooklyn,* NY: R.V. Busuino, 1939.

Uniform Crime Reporting, A Complete Manual for Police. NY: J.J. Little, 1929.

U.S. National Commission on Law Observance and Enforcement. *Report of Prosecution.* Washington DC: GPO, 1931.

U.S. Works Progress Administration. *Division of Women's and Professional Projects. Definition of Police Beats.* WPA Technical Series Public Administration Circular No. 2. Washington DC: WPA, August 2S, 1937.

Vollmer, August. "Curriculum for Peace Officers." *Journal of Criminal Law and Criminology,* 25 (May-June, 1934), pp. 138-140.

Vollmer, August. *The Police Beat Proceedings.* IACP 40th Annual Convention, pp. 304-318.

Vollmer, August. *Police in Modern Society.* Washington DC: Consortium Press, 1969. (repr. of 1936 ed.).

Vollmer, August. "Police Progress in the Past Twenty-Five Years." *Journal of Criminal Law and Criminology,* 1933.

Vollmer, August. "The Prevention and Detection of Crime as Viewed by a Police Officer." *Annals* (May, 1926).

Vollmer, August. *Report on Police.* Washington DC: GPO, 1931.

One of Wickersham Commission reports.

Vollmer, August. "The School for Police as Planned at Berkeley." *Journal of the American Institute of Criminal Law and Criminology* (1916).

Wells, Alice Stebbins. "Reminiscences of a Police Woman." *Police Reporter,* 23 (September, 1929).

Whalen, Grover A. "A New York Police College." *Police Journal* (1930), pp. 342-358.

Williams, Jack Kenny. "Catching the Criminal in Nineteenth Century South Carolina." *Journal of Criminal Law, Criminology and Police Science.* 46:2 (July-August, 1955), pp. 264-271.

Wilson, O.W. "Controlling Police Investigations through a Follow-up System." *Public Management* (June, 1932).

Wilson, O.W. "1937 Kansas Police School." *Kansas Government Journal.* XXIII (December, 1937), pp. 22-23.

City Police

Bacon, Seldon D. *The Early Development of American Municipal Police.* Unpub. Doctoral Dissertation, Yale University, 1939.

Bond, Horatio. "The Threefold Task of Arson Squads," *American City.* 48 (December, 1933).

Borough, R. "Law and Order in Los Angeles." *The Nation* (July 6, 1927).

Brace, Charles Loring. *The Dangerous Classes of New York.* Montclair, NJ: Patterson Smith, 1967. (repr. of 1880 ed.).

"Brass Buttons, Blue Coats: History of the New York City Police Uniform." *Spring 3100,* 34 (April, 1963), pp. 10-15, 42.

Browne, William. *Stopping That Clubbing.* NY: Privately printed, 1887.

Bruce, James. *Tattling of a Retired Police Officer.* Everett, MA: [n.n.], 1927.

Bureau of Municipal Research. *Report on a Survey of Buffalo.* NY: Bureau of Municipal Research, 1915.
Chapter on the police department covered pp. 214-367.

Burns, R.V. "History of the New York Police Department." *Police Journal (NY),* 1S:6 (July, 1931), pp. 16-17, 21.

Business Methods of New York City's Police Department. NY: Bureau of Municipal Research, 1911.

Byrnes, Thomas. *1886 Professional Criminals of America.* NY: Random House, 1969.

Cahalane, Cornelius Francis. *The Policeman.* NY: Arno, 1970. (repr. of 1923 ed.).

Cantwell, Edward P. *A History of the Charleston Police Force from the Incorporation of the City, 1783 to 1908.* Charleston: Furlong, 1908.

Chicago Civil Service Commission. *Chicago Police Investigations: Three Reports.* NY: Arno, 1971. (repr. of 1898 ed.).

"The Chicago Police Department: Its History." *Annual Report.* Chicago: Police Department, 1955, pp. 6-13.

Citizen's Police Committee. *Chicago Police Problems.* Montclair, NJ: Patterson Smith, 1969 (repr. of 1931 ed.).

Control of Baltimore Police. Collected reports, NY: Arno, 1971 (repr. of 1860 ed.).

Costello, Augustine E. *History of the Police Department of Jersey City.* Jersey City, NJ: Police Relief Association, 1891.

Costello, Augustine E. *History of the Police Department of New Haven from the Period of the Old Watch in Colonial Days to the Present Time.* New Haven, CT: Relief Book Publishing, 1892.

Costello, Augustine. *Our Police Protectors: History of the New York Police from the Earliest Period to the Present Time.* Montclair, NJ: Patterson Smith, 1970 (repr. of 1885 ed.).

Crime Commission of Chicago. *A Study of the Administration of Criminal Justice with Respect to Auto Larceny and Related Cases from 1/2/34 to 3/31/34.* Chicago: Crime Commission of Chicago, April 31, 1934.

Crump, Irving and John W. Newton. *Our Police.* NY: Dodd, 1935.

Davis, James E. *Tactical Area Plan.* Los Angeles, CA: LAPD, 1937.

Detroit Police Department. *Story of the Detroit Police Dept., 1916-17. . . .* Detroit: Inland Press, 1917.

Duke, William C. *The Policeman; His Trials and His Dangers.* rev. ed. Atlanta, GA: Converse, 1911.

Dyson, Verne. *The Policeman and the City's Woes.* Kansas City, MO: Clandoin, 1909.

Fales, William E.S. *Brooklyn's Guardians: A Record of the Faithful and Heroic Men Who Preserve the Peace in the City of Homes.* Brooklyn: [n.n.], 1887.

Folsom, De Francias, ed. *Our Police: A History of the Baltimore Force from the First Watchman to the Latest Appointee.* Baltimore: Ehlers, 1888.

Fosdick, Raymond et al. *Criminal Justice in Cleveland.* Montclair, NJ: Patterson Smith, 1968 (repr. of 1922 ed.).

Garrett, Earle W. "Organization and Administration of a Police Department." *New York State Association of Chiefs of Police Proceedings.* 35 (1935), pp. 45-56.

Gault, Robert H. "On the Third Degree." *Journal of Criminal Law and Criminology,* 23 (September-October, 1932), pp. 370-371.

"The Good Old Days, a Brief Exploration into Police Conditions Existing in New York City 94 Years Ago." *Spring 3100,* 11 (August, 1940), pp. 16-17, 20-21.
Describes rules and regulations of 1846 for NYPD.

Grerne, Francis V. *The Police Department of the City of New York: A Statement of Acts . . . .* NY: City Club, 1903.

Grey, M.P.L. "History of the San Francisco Police Department." *Venture* (Autumn, 1971), pp. 56-59.

Hall, Theo E. "O.W. Wilson's Legacy to Wichita: 1928-1929." *Police Chief,* XLII:3 (March, 1976), p. 71.

"A Haphazard History of the Chicago Police Department, 1833 to About Now." *Chicago Police Star,* 7 (January, 1966), pp. 4-7.

Harring, Sidney L. and Lorraine M. McMullin. "Buffalo Police, 1872-1900 Labour Unrest, Political Power and Creation of the Police Institution." *Crime and Social Justice* (Fall-Winter, 1975), pp. 5-14.

Harrison, Leonard W. *Police Administration in Boston.* Cambridge: Harvard University Press, 1934.

Hichborn, Franklin. *The System.* Montclair, NJ: Patterson Smith, 1969. (repr. of 1915 ed.).

"History." *Spring 3100* (July-August, 1951, entire issue).

History of the Department of Police Service of Springfield, Mass., from 1636 to 1900: Historical and Biographical. Springfield, MA: Police Relief Association, 1900.

History of the New Orleans Police Department. New Orleans: Crockett, 1900.

History of the Police Department of Bridgeford, Conn., from the Days of the Old City Watch, to the Present System of Police Protection. Bridgeford: Relief Book Publishing, 1892.

History of the Police Department of Columbus, Ohio, from the Earliest Times to the Present with a Record of the Principle Crimes Committed. Columbus: Ohio Police Benevolent Association, 1908.

History of the Police Department of Newark. Newark: Relief Publishing, 1893.

Illinois Association for Criminal Justice. *The Illinois Crime Survey.* Montclair, NJ: Patterson Smith, 1968 (repr. of 1929 ed.).

Kaufman, A. *Superintendent Walling's Memoirs and Historic Supplement of the Denver Police.* [n.p.]: Caxton Book Concern, 1890.

Lewis, Alfred H. *Confessions of a Detective.* NY: Barnes, 1906.

McArthur, Jack. "Police Recruitment and Training, Yesterday and Today." *Law and Order.* 13:8 (August, 1965), pp. 74-81.
Berkeley P.D. history and contemporary activities.

McNutt, George W. *My Twenty-Three Years Experience as a Detective.* Kansas City: Empire, 1923.

Mann, Henry, ed. *History of Pittsburgh Police Force.* Pittsburgh, PA: [n.n.], 1889.

Miller, Frederic C. *History, Organization and Methods of the Police.* Unpub. Doctoral Dissertation, University of Minnesota, 1908.

Monkkonen, Erick H. *Dangerous Class: Crime and Poverty in Columbus, Ohio 1860-1885.* Cambridge, MA: Harvard University Press, 1975.

New Haven Police Mutual Aid Association. *History of the Department of Police Service of New Haven from 1639 to 1899.* New Haven: Police Mutual Aid Association, 1899.

"New Police of Philadelphia." *Journal of Prison Discipline.* 6 (April, 1851), pp. 85-88.

O'Connell, Dan. "Police Organization of Honolulu." *Police and Peace Officer Journal.* 11 (November, 1937), pp. 15-16.

Older, Fremont. *My Own Story.* NY: Macmillan, 1926.
Description of San Francisco P.D.

Paddock, William H. *History of the Police Service of Albany, from 1609 to 1902 . . .* Albany NY: Police Beneficiary Association, 1902.

Peck, William F. *History of the Police Dept. of Rochester, New York, from the Earliest Time to May 1, 1903 . . .* Rochester, NY: Police Benevolent Association, 1903.

"Pittsburgh's Police." *Survey,* 47 (1921), pp. 201-202.

"A Police Force Arresting Distress." *Survey,* 35 (1915).
Description of some of the work done by the New York Police Department.

Police in New York City: An Investigation. NY: Arno, (repr. of 1913 ed.).

"Police Reorganization in Chicago." *Journal of Criminal Law,* 3 (1912-1213), pp. 670-674.

Post, Melville D. *The Man Hunters . . .* NY: Sears, 1926.

Reed, Lear B. *Human Wolves, Seventeen Years of War on Crime, in Which Is Told . . . Dramatic Story of the Rebuilding of Kansas City's Police Department.* Kansas City, MO: Brown-White Lowell, 1941.

Report of the Special Commission on the New Haven Police Department. New Haven, CT: Police Department Commission, 1904.

Report on a Survey of the Department of Public Safety, Syracuse, NY. NY: Bureau of Municipal Research, 1914.

Report on a Survey of the Department of Safety of Denver, Colorado. NY: Bureau of Municipal Research, 1914.

Report on the Board of Police and Police Department. Baltimore: Joint Standing Committee on Police and Jail, 186.

Richardson, J.F. *Urban Police in the United States.* Port Washington, NY: Kennikat, 1974.

Rosenhouse, Leo. "Police Signals During the Gay Nineties." *Police Times.* 8:5 (January, 1971).

Russell, William F. "Prevention of Juvenile Crime: Unemployed Boys' Bureau Conducted by the Chicago Police Department." *Police Journal* (1931), pp. 60-67.

Savage, Edward H. *Police Records and Recollections. Or, Boston by Daylight and Gaslight for Two Hundred and Forty Years.* Montclair, NJ: Patterson Smith, 1970. (repr. of 1873 ed.).

Shaw, Alonzo B. *Trails in Shadow Land: Stories of a Detective.* Columbus, OH: Hann, 1910.

Smith, Bruce. *The Balitmore Police Survey.* NY: Institute of Public Administration, 1941.

Smith, Bruce. *Chicago Police Problems.* Chicago: University of Chicago Press, 1931.

Smith, Bruce. "Department of Public Safety of Camden, NJ," in *Report of Administrative Survey, City of Camden.* NY: Bureau of Municipal Research, 1923.

Smith, Bruce. *The New Rochelle Police Survey.* NY: Institute of Public Administration, 1941.

Spiller, Phillip N. *A Short History of the San Antonio Police Department.* Unpub. Master's Thesis, Trinity University, 1954.

Sprogle, Howard O. *The Philadelphia Police, Past and Present.* NY: Arno, (repr. of 1887 ed.).

Sullivan, J.M. "Police Gleanings." *Journal of Criminal Law and Criminology,* 3 (1912-1913), pp. 393-399.

Survey of the Police Department of Schenectady, NY. NY: Bureau of Municipal Research, 1918.

Turano, Anthony M. "The Brutalities of the Police." *American Mercury,* 32 (July, 1934), pp. 341-350.

"Turning Chicago's Police Crisis." *Survey,* 37 (1917), pp. 462-463.

Valentine, Lewis J. *Nightstick: The Autobiography of Lewis J. Valentine, Former Police Commissioner.* NY: Dial, 1947.

Walling, George W. *Recollections of a New York Chief of Police*. Montclair, NJ: Patterson Smith, 1970. (repr. of 1890 ed.).

Warner, Sam B. *Crime and Criminal Statistics in Boston*. NY: Arno, 1974. (repr.).

White, Leslie T. *Me, Detective*. NY: Harcourt Brace, 1936.

Whitehouse, Jack E. "Historical Perspectives on the Police Community Service Function." *Journal of Police Science and Administration*. 1:1 (1973), pp. 87-92.

Wilson, George D. "Chief Emil Harris — Second Chief of Los Angeles Police Department." *L.A. Police Beat*. 28 (May, 1972), pp. 9-10.

Wilson, George D. "From the Archives . . . History of the Los Angeles Police Department." *L.A. Police Beat*. 28 (April, 1972).

Wilson, George D. "From the Archives: The 1901 Annual Report." *L.A. Police Beat*. 28 (June, 1972).

Woods, Arthur. *Crime Prevention*. NY: Arno, (repr. of 1918 ed.).

Woods, Arthur. *Policemen and Public*. NY: Arno, (repr. of 1919 ed.).

Whitlock, Brand. *On the Enforcement of Law in Cities*. Montclair, NJ: Patterson Smith, 1969. (repr. of 1913 ed.).

Colonial America

Ames, Susie M., ed. *County Court Records of Accomack-Northhampton, Virginia; 1640-1645*. Baltimore, MD: Genea Log, 1972. (repr. of 1931 ed.).

Billas, George Athan, ed. *Law and Authority in Colonial America*. NY: Baree, 1965.

Bond, Carroll T. *The Court of Appeals of Maryland, A History*. Baltimore: Barton, 1928.

Chitwood, Oliver P. *Justice in Colonial Virginia*. NY: Da Capo, 1971. (repr. of 1905 ed.).

Goebel, Julius, Jr., and T. Raymond Naughton. *Law Enforcement in Colonial New York: A Study in Criminal Procedure (1664-1776)*. NY: Commonwealth, 1944.

McCaine, Paul M. *County Court in North Carolina Before 1750*. NY: AMS, 1970. (repr. of 1954 ed.).

Powers, Edwin. *Crime and Punishment in Early Massachusetts*. Boston: Beacon Press, 1966.

Rankin, Hugh F. *Criminal Trial Proceedings in the General Court of Colonial Virginia*. Charlottesville: University Press of Virginia, 1965.

Scott, Arthur P. *Criminal Law in Colonial Virginia*. Chicago: Chicago University Press, 1930.

Scott, Kenneth. *Counterfeiting in Colonial New York*. NY: American Numicmatic, 1953.

Scott, Kenneth. *Counterfeiting in Colonial Pennsylvania*. NY: American Numicmatic, 1955.

Sellin, Thorsten. "The Philadelphia Gibbet Iron." *Journal of Criminal Law, Criminology and Police Science*. 46:1 (May-June, 1955), pp. 11-25.
Description of iron body framework to display executed prisoners.

Semmes, Raphael. *Crime and Punishment in Early Maryland*. Montclair, NJ: Patterson Smith, 1970 (repr. of 1938 ed.).

Williams, Jack Kenny. *Vogues in Villany: Crime and Retribution in Antebellum South Carolina*. Columbia: University of South Carolina Press, 1959.

Federal Law Enforcement

Baker, Lafayette Charles. *History of the United States Secret Service*. Philadelphia: L.C. Baker, 1867.

Blatt, Heiman K. *Treasury Enforcement Agent*. NY: Arco, 1941.

Burnham, George P. *American Counterfeits*. Boston: A.W. Lowering, 1879.

Burnham, George P. *Memoirs of the United States Secret Service*. Boston: Lee, 1872.

Burnham, George P. *Three Years with Counterfeiters, Smugglers, and Boodle Carriers; with Accurate Portraits of Prominent Members of the Detective Force in the Secret Service*. Boston: J.P. Dale, 1879.

Foote, H.C. *Universal Counterfeiter and Bank Note Detection, at Sight*. NY: Oliver, 1851.

Foster, Thomas B. "The United States Secret Service." *Police and Peace Officers Journal* (December, 1932).

Germain, John J. "Federal Police — A Great Cooperation Bureau." *Police Journal (NY)*. 21 (December, 1934), pp. 5-6.

Germain, John J. "Federal Police — Hoover's Special Agents. Many Crimes Formerly Classed As Local Now Fall in Their Province." *Police Journal (NY)* 21 (October, 1934).

Heath, Laban. *Heath's Greatly Improved and Enlarged Infallible Government Counterfeit Detector, at Sight*. 2nd ed. Boston: L. Heath, 1866.

Heath, Laban. *Memoirs of the United States Secret Service*. Boston: L. Heath, 1872.

Holverstatt, Lyle J. *Preliminary Inventory of Records of United States Secret Service*. Washington DC: U.S. National Archives, 1949.

Langeluttig, Albert. *Department of Justice in the United States*. Dubuque, IA: William C. Brown, (repr. of 1927 ed.).

Moran, W.H. "Inside Stories of the Secret Service." *American Mercury*. August, 1937.

Preston, William, Jr. *Aliens and Dissenters: Federal Suppression of Radicals, 1903-1933*. NY: Harper and Row, [n.d.].

Roosevelt, Theodore. *Special Message (Relative to Secret Service) Communicated to the House of Representatives on January 4, 1909*. Washington DC: GPO, 1909.

Schmeckebier, Lawrence F. *Customs Service: Its History, Activities, and Organization*. NY: AMS Press, (repr. of 1924 ed.).

Seagle, William. "The American National Police." *Harper's* (November, 1934), pp. 751-761.

Senate Reports. 75th Congress. 1st Session. *Inquiry Pursuant to Resolution Authorizing Investigation of Secret Service.* Washington DC: GPO, 1909.

Smith, Darrell H. and Fred W. Powell. *Coast Guard: Its History, Activities and Organization.* NY: AMS, (repr. of 1929 ed.).

Tucker, R. "White House Shadows." *Colliers.* 93 (February 24, 1934).

U.S. Congress. Senate. *Draft of Clause of Appropriation for Suppressing Counterfeiting.* Executive Document No. 88, Washington DC: GPO, April 25, 1894.

U.S. Department of Interior. *Secret Service of the Department of Interior . . . In Response to Senate Resolution of April 29, 1912.* Washington DC: GPO, 1912.

U.S. House. *Extracts from Hearings Before the Subcommittee of the House Committee on Appropriations . . . Relative to Secret Service.* Washington DC: GPO, 1909.

U.S. Revised Statutes. *Counterfeiting and Other Crimes; A Digest for the Information of Operatives of the Secret Service Division, Treasury Department.* Washington DC: GPO, 1899.

Wilkie, Donald Weare. *American Secret Service Agent.* NY: F.A. Stokes, 1934.

Woodward, P.N. *Secret Service of the Post Office Department.* Swengel, PA: Reiner, 1976, (repr. of 1876 ed.).

Forensic and Technical Sciences

Beattie, R.H. "Sources of Statistics on Crime and Correction." *Journal of American Statistical Association.* (September, 1959).

"45 Years of Service to the Nation." *FBI Law Enforcement Bulletin.* 38:7 (July, 1969), pp. 12-16.

Gray, Robert M. "A History of the Utah State Bureau of Criminal Identification and Investigation." *Utah Historical Quarterly.* XXIV:2 (April, 1956), pp. 171-179.

Hunter, T.P. *History of the Bureau of Criminal Identification and Investigation.* Unpub. paper, Sacramento, Department of Justice, State of California. [n.d.].

Moenssens, A.A. "Origins of the FBI Identification Division." *Fingerprint Identification Magazine.* 56:1 (1974), pp. 10-17, 22.

Thompson, Fletcher D. "Golden Anniversary of FBI Identification Division." FBI Law Enforcement Bulletin. 43:7 (July, 1974), pp. 3-9.

Thorwald, Jurgen. *The Century of the Detective.* NY: Harcourt, 1965.
Detailed popular history of the development of forensic sciences. The history continues with *Crime and Science* below.

Tuttle, Harris B. "History of Photography in Law Enforcement." *Fingerprint and Identification.* 43 (October, 1961), pp. 3-28.

Wilson, O.W. "Wichita's Use of the Lie Detector." *American City.* (July, 1933).

Police Control of Slavery

Bacon, Selden D. *The Early Development of American Municipal Police.* Unpub. Doctoral Dissertation, Yale University, 1939.
See Chapter VIII Charleston which describes the relationship between local law enforcement and slavery.

Campbell, Stanley W. *Slave Catchers: Enforcement of the Fugitive Slave Law, 1850-1860.* Chapel Hill: University of North Carolina Press, 1970.

Henry, Howell M. *Police Control of the Slave in South Carolina.* Westport, CT: Negro University Press, (repr. of 1914 ed.).

Sheriffs

Emerson, F.W. "Los Angeles County Sheriff's Department." *Civic Affairs.* 5 (October, 1937), pp. 3-4.

Gwynne, Abraham E. *A Practical Treatise on the Law of Sheriff and Coroner, with Forms and References to the Statutes of Ohio, Indiana, and Kentucky.* Cincinnati: Derby, 1849.

Harlow, William S. *Duties of Sheriffs and Constables, Particularly Under the Practice in California and the Pacific States and Territories.* 3rd. rev. ed. San Francisco: Bancroft, 1907.

Heiges, R.E. *The Office of Sheriff in the Rural Counties of Ohio.* Unpub. Doctoral Dissertation, Columbia University, 1933.

Hopping, Richard C. *A Sheriff-Ranger in Chuckwagon Days.* NY: Pageant, 1952.

Jackson, William A. *The Office of Sheriff in Iowa.* Unpub. Doctoral Dissertation, University of Iowa, 1924.

Karraker, Cyrus H. *Seventeenth-Century Sheriff: A Comparative Study of the Sheriff in England and the Chesapeake Colonies, 1607-1689.* Plainview, NY: Books for Libraries, 1973, (repr. of 1930 ed.).

Lamb, Iven S., Jr. "The Sheriff in History — and in Florida." *Sheriff's Star.* 15 (July, 1971), pp. 1-2.

Murfree, William L. *A Treatise on the Law of Sheriffs and Other Ministerial Officers.* St. Louis: Thomas, 1884.

Smith, Borden D. *The Powers, Duties and Liabilities of Sheriffs, Coroners and Constables, with Notes of Judical Decisions, and Practical Forms, Adapted to all the States.* Albany, NY: Little, 1883.

Williams, Gorham D. *The Massachusetts Peace Officer, A Manual for Sheriffs, Constables, Police and Other Civil Officers.* Boston: Reed, 1891.

State Police

Groome, John C. *A Reply to "The American Cossack" Concerning the State Police and Strikes.* Harrisburg, PA: State Police Department, 1914.

Liu, Dan S.C. "Organization and History of Police Service in Hawaii." *FBI Law Enforcement Bulletin.* (September, 1957), pp. 3-6.

Mayo, Katherine. "Demobilization and the State Police." *North American Review.* 209 (1919), pp. 786-794.

Mayo, Katherine. *Justice to All: The History of the*

Pennsylvania State Police. NY: Houghton Mifflin, 1920.

Mayo, Katherine. *The Standard-Bearers: True Stories of the Heroes of Law and Order*. Boston: Houghton, 1918.

The New York State Police: The First Fifty Years, 1917-1967. Albany: New York State Police, 1967.

"1920-1959: California Association of California Highway Patrolmen Has Anniversary." *California Highway Patrolman*. 23:4 (June, 1959), (entire issue).

O'Brien, Daniel L. "Half-Century Mark for Illinois State Police." *Police Chief. 39:6* (June, 1972), pp. 62-72.

Pennsylvania State Federation of Labor. *American Cossack*. NY: Arno, 1971 (repr. of 1915 ed.).

Smith, Bruce. "Rural Justice in New York State." *Journal of Criminal Law*. 14 (1923-1924), pp. 284-289.

Smith, Bruce. "State Police: An American Experiment in Rural Protection." *Police Journal (GB)*, (1930), pp. 20-29.

Vollmer, A. and A. Parker. *Crime and the State Police*. Berkeley: University of California Press, 1935.

Texas Rangers

Aten, Ira. *Six and One Half Years in the Ranger Service: The Memoirs of Ira Aten, Sergeant, Company D, Texas Rangers*. Bandera, TX: Frontier Times, 1945.

Conger, Roger M. et al. *Rangers of Texas*. Waco, TX: Texian. [n.d.].

Douglas, Claude L. *The Gentlemen in White Hats: Dramatic Episodes in the History of the Texas Rangers*. Dallas: South-West, 1934.

Durham, George and Clyde Wantland. *Taming the Nueces Strip: The Story of McNelly's Rangers*. Austin: University of Texas Press, 1962.

Frost, H. Gordon and John H. Jenkins. *I'm Frank Hammer: The Life of a Texas Peace Officer*. Austin, TX: Jenkins, 1968.

Gillett, James B. *Six Years with the Texas Rangers*. [n.p.]: Peter Wolff, 1943.

Hopper, W.L. *Famous Texas Land Marks*. Dallas: Arrow, 1966.
Covers many western outlaws and a number of Texas Rangers.

House, Edward M. *Riding for Texas: The True Adventures of Captain Bill McDonald of the Texas Rangers*. NY: John Day, 1936.

Jennings, Napoleon A. *A Texas Ranger*. Austin, TX: Steck, 1959, (repr. of 1899 ed.).

Keating, Bern. *Illustrated History of the Texas Rangers*. Chicago: Rand, 1975.

Kilgore, D.E. *A Ranger Legacy*. Austin, TX: Madrona, 1973.

Maltby, William J. *Captain Jeff; or, Frontier Life in Texas with the Texas Rangers; Some Unwritten History and Facts in the Thrilling Experiences of Frontier Life . . .* Colorado, TX: Whipkey, 1906.

Martin, Jack. *Border Boss: Captain John R. Hughes, Texas Ranger*. San Antonio, TX: Naylor, 1942.

Pike, James. *Scout and Ranger*. NY: DaCapo, 1972, (repr. of 1932 ed.).

Preece, Harold. *Lone Star Man: Ira Aten, Last of the Old Texas Rangers*. NY: Hastings House, 1960.

Stephens, Robert W. *Texas Ranger Indian War Pensions*. Quanah, TX: Nortex, 1976.

Sterling, William W. *Trails and Trials of a Texas Ranger*. Norman: University of Oklahoma Press, 1969.

Webb, Walter P. *Texas Rangers*. (new ed.) Austin: University of Texas Press, 1965.

The West

Arnold, Dave. "Pat Garrett's Hunt for Billy the Kid." *Outpost*. (September, 1975), pp. 9-11.

Cook, D.J. *Hands Up: Or Twenty Years of Detective Life in the Mountains and on the Plains*. Norman: University of Oklahoma Press, 1971.

DeNevi, Don. *Western Train Robberies*. Millbrae, CA: Celestial Arts, 1976.

Drago, Harry S. *Great Range Wars: Violence on the Grasslands*. NY: Dodd, 1970.

Drago, Harry S. *Legend Makers: Tales of the Old-Time Peace Officers and Desperadoes of the Frontier*. NY: Dodd, 1975.

Drago, Harry S. *Road Agent and Train Robbers*. NY: Dodd, 1973.

Fulton, Maurice G. *History of the Lincoln County War*. Tucson: University of Arizona Press, 1968.

Gard, Wayne. *The Chisholm Trail*. Norman: University of Oklahoma Press, 1954.

Gard, Wayne. "The Fence Cutters." *Southwestern Historical Quarterly*. LI:1 (July, 1947).

Gard, Wayne. *Frontier Justice*. Norman: University of Oklahoma Press, 1949.

Gard, Wayne. *Rawhide Texas*. Norman: University of Oklahoma Press, 1965.

Gard, Wayne. *Sam Bass*. NY: Houghton Mifflin, 1936.

Hayes, Jess. *Sheriff Thompson's Day: Turbulence in the Arizona Territory*. Tucson: University of Arizona Press, 1968.

Hicks, Sam. "The Avenging Angels — The First in Their Field." *Police*. 4:4 (March-April, 1960), pp. 56-59.
Early law enforcement in Utah territory in the mid-1800s.

Jordan, Phillip D. *Frontier Law and Order: Ten Essays*. Lincoln: University of Nebraska Press, 1970.

Keleher, William A. *Violence in Lincoln County*. Albuquerque: University of New Mexico Press, 1970.

McCarty, John L. *Maverick Town: The Story of Old Tascosa*. Norman: University of Oklahoma Press, 1946.

MacLeod, William C. "Police and Punishment among Native Americans of the Plains." *Journal of Criminal Law and Criminology*. 28 (July-August, 1937), pp. 181-201.

Miller, Joseph. *The Arizona Rangers*. NY: Hastings House, 1972.

Miller, Nyle H. and Joseph W. Snell. *Great Gunfighters of the Kansas Cow Towns, 1867-1886.* Lincoln: University of Nebraska Press, 1967.

Ogle, Ralph H. *Federal Control of the Western Apaches, 1848-1886.* (rev. ed.), Albuquerque: University of New Mexico Press, 1970.

Raine, William MacLeod. *Famous Sheriffs and Western Outlaws.* Garden City, NY: Doubleday, 1929.

Raine, William MacLeod. *Forty Five Calibre Law: The Way of Life of the Frontier Peace Officer.* Evanston, IL: Row Peterson, 1941.

Raine, William MacLeod. *Guns of the Frontier: The Story of How Law Came to the West.* Boston: Houghton Mifflin, 1940.

Shirely, Glenn. *Law West of Forth Smith: A History of Frontier Justice in the Indian Territory, 1834-1896.* Lincoln: University of Nebraska Press, 1969.

Siringo, Charles A. *A Cowboy Detective: A True Story of Twenty Two Years With a World Famous Detective Agnecy.* NY: Ogilvie, 1912.

Tilghman, Zoe. *Marshall of the Last Frontier.* Glendale, CA: A.H. Clark, 1964.

THE POLICE OF GREAT BRITAIN

GENERAL

Blom-Cooper, L.J. "An Ombudsman in Britain?" *Public Law.* (1960), pp. 145-151.

Vexler, R. *England: A Chronology and Fact Book.* Dobbs Ferry, NY: Oceana, 1973.

CRIME

Borrell, Clive and Brian Cashinella. *Crime in Britain Today.* Boston: Routledge and Kegan, 1975.

Crime and Punishment. 6 pts., 63 vols., Totowa, NJ: Irish Academy Press, 1971.

Gibson, Evelyn. *Robbery in London.* London: Macmillan, 1961.

Hay, Douglas. *Albion's Fatal Tree: Crime and Society in Eighteenth Century England.* London: Allen Lane, 1975.

Home Office. *Criminal Statistics, England and Wales, 1975: Statistics Relating to Crime and Criminal Proceedings for the Year 1975.* London: HMSO, 1976, (annual).

Jeffrey, Clarence Ray. "The Development of Crime in Early English Society." *Journal of Criminal Law, Criminology and Police Science.* 47:6 (March-April, 1957), pp. 647-666.

Keeton, George W. and George Schwarzenberger. *Jeremy Bentham and the Law, a Symposium.* London: Stevens, 1948.

Lunden, Walter A. "Murders, Infanticides and Criminal Justice in England and Wales, 1925 to 1955." *Police.* 4:4 (March-April, 1960), pp. 74-77.

McClintock, Frederick H. and N. Howard Avison. *Crime in England and Wales.* London: Heinemann, 1968.

Pike, Luke Owen. *A History of Crime in England.* 2 vols., Montclair, NJ: Patterson Smith, 1968. (repr. of 1873-1876 ed.).

Plint, Thomas. *Crime in England: Its Relation, Character and Extent as Developed from 1801-1848.* NY: Arno, 1974. (repr.).

Samuels, G. "Crime Wave in Law-Abiding England." *New York Times Magazine.* (May 13, 1962).

Tobias, John J. "Social History of Crime." *Police Journal (GB),* (November, 1963), pp. 548-551.

Walker, Niguel. *Crime and Punishment in Britain. An Analysis of the Penal System in Theory, Law and Practice.* Edinburgh: Edinburgh University Press, 1965.

CRIMINAL LAW

Bellamy, J.G. *Law of Treason in England in the Later Middle Ages.* NY: Cambridge University Press, 1970.

Bryan, J.W. *Development of the English Law of Conspiracy.* NY: DaCapo, 1970.

Chenery, John T. *An Introduction to the Law and Practice of Betting and Bookmaking.* London: Sweet and Maxwell, 1961.

"A Comparative Study of Criminal Law Administration in the United States and Great Britain." *Journal of Criminal Law, Criminology and Police Science.* 50:1 (May-June, 1959), pp. 59-68.

Curtis, E.E. et al. *Law of the United Kingdom and Ireland — Library of Congress Classification Class D, Subclass KD.* Washington DC: NCJRS, (Microfiche), 1973.

Devlin, Patrick. *The Criminal Prosecution in England.* New Haven, CT: Yale University Press, 1961.

Evans, J.M. *Immigration Law.* London: Sweet and Maxwell, 1976.

Fitzgerald, Patrick J. *Criminal Law and Punishment.* Wxford: Clarendon, 1962.

Geldart, William. *Elements of English Law.* (8th ed.), NY: Oxford University Press, 1957.

A History of the Criminal Law of England. London: Macmillan, 1883.

Hughes, Graham. "The English Homicide Act of 1957." *Journal of Criminal Law, Criminology and Police Science.* 49:6 (March-April, 1959), pp. 521-532.

Jackson, R.M. *Machinery of Justice in England.* (6th ed.), NY: Cambridge University Press, 1972.

Leigh, L.H. *Criminal Liability of Corporations in English Law.* Atlantic Highlands, NJ: Humanities, 1969.

Moriarty, Cecil C.H. *Police Law: An Arrangement of Law and Regulations for the Use of Police Officers.* London: Butterworth, 1976.

Muir, A. "The Rules of the Game." *Criminal Law Review.* (June, 1973), pp. 341-343.
Rules of evidence.

O'Donnell, Bernard. *The Old Bailey and Its Trials.* NY: Macmillan, 1951.

Periman, M. and N. Morris. *Law and Crime: Essays in Honor of Sir John Barry.* NY: Gordon, 1972.

Radzinowicz, Leon. *A History of English Criminal Law.* (3 vols.) NY: Barnes and Noble, 1968.

Shoolbred, C.F. *The Administration of Criminal Justice in England and Wales.* Elmsford, NY: Pergamon, 1966.

Smith, John C. *The Law of Theft.* (3rd ed.), London: Butterworth, 1977.

Zander, M. "Are Too Many Professional Criminals Avoiding Conviction? A Study in Britain's Two Busiest Courts." *Modern Law Review.* 37:1 (1974), pp. 28-61.
Study shows that the overwhelming majority of defendants are convicted.

POLICE HISTORY

Police History — General

Adam, H.L. *The Police Encyclopedia.* (8 vols.), London: Waverley, 1920, 1925.

A Handy Guide to the Police Forces at Home and Overseas, Including the Railway and Dock Police, the Women Police, the Colonial Police and the Prison Service. (17th ed.), London: Police Review Publishing, 1934.

Anderson, John. "The Police." *Public Administration.* (1929), pp. 192-202.

Ashley, Brian. *Law and Order.* London: Batsford, 1967.

Ashley, Joe. "The Detectives: Joe Ashley's Short History of the Metropolitan Police." *Police World.* 16 (Spring, 1971), pp. 45-46, 50.

Barker, Herbert. "The Police and Their Functions." *Police Journal (GB),* 5 (July, 1932), pp. 378-386.

Benjamin, Harold. "Internal Police Administration of England." *Police Journal (GB),* (1931), pp. 598-622.

Bent, J. *Criminal Life: Reminiscences of Forty-Two Years as a Police Officer.* Manchester: J. Heywood, 1900.

Boyle, A. *Trenchard.* London: Collins, 1962.

Browne, Douglas G. *The Rise of Scotland Yard: A History of the Metropolitan Police.* London: Harrip, 1956.

Caminada, J. *Twenty-Five Years of Detective Life.* (2 vols.), Manchester: Heywood, 1901.

Campbell, George A. *Our Police Force.* London: Oxford University Press, 1943.

Cavanagh, T.A. *Scotland Yard, Past and Present.* London: Chatto and Windus, 1893.

Chapman, Samuel G. and Eric T. St. Johnston. *The Police Heritage in England and America: A Developmental Survey.* East Lansing: Institute for Community Development and Services, Continuing Education Service, Michigan State University, 1962.

Childs, W. *Episodes and Reflections: Being Some Records from Life of Major-General Sir Wyndham Childs.* London: Cassell, 1930.

Clark, E.F. *Truncheons.* London: H. Jenkins, 1935.

Clarkson, C.T. and J.H. Richardson. *Police.* London: Simpkin Marshall, 1889.

Clogger, T.J. "The Police." *Quarterly Review.* (January, 1967), pp. 80-90.

Cobb, Belton. *Critical Years at the Yard.* London: Faber and Faber, 1956.

Cobb, Belton. *The First Detectives.* London: Faber and Faber, 1957.

Cohen, Stanley. *Images of Deviance.* Harmondsworth: Penguin, 1971.

Conacher, J.B. "Peel and the Peelites, 1846-1850." *English Historical Review.* 73 (January, 1958), pp. 431-452.

Crawley, F.J. "The Technique of Investigation of the English Detective." *Annals.* (November, 1929), pp. 219-222.

Critchley, T.A. *The Conquest of Violence, Order and Liberty in Britain.* NY: Schocken, 1970.

Critchley, T.A. *A History of Police in England and Wales, 900-1966.* London: Constable, 1967.

Dalton, H. "The Thames Police." *Police Journal (GB),* 8 (January, 1935), pp. 90-103.

Deacon, Richard. *A History of the British Secret Service.* NY: Taplinger, 1970.

Dew, Walter. *I Caught Crippen: Memoirs of Ex-Chief Inspector Walter Dew.* London: Blackie, 1938.

Dilnot, George. *The Story of Scotland Yard.* London: G. Bles, 1926.

Dixon, A.L. "The English Police System." *Annals* (November, 1929), pp. 177-192.

Dumpleton, John. *Law and Oder: The Story of the Police.* (2nd ed.), London: Black, 1970.

Elmes, Frank. "A Chronology of Law Enforcement." *Police Review* (August 1, 1969), pp. 662-663.

Elmes, Frank. "Police in Modern Society." *Criminologist.* (February, 1970), pp. 29-35.

Fitzgerald, Percy. *Chronicles of Bow Street Police Office.* Montclair, NJ: Patterson Smith, 1972, (repr. of 1888 ed.).

Fleetwood, J.B. "Policing the Dockyards: A History of the Admiralty Constabulary." *Police Review (GB),* (October 1, 1971), pp. 1264-1265, 1276.

Ford, Richard. "Beneath Two Helmets: The History of Police Fire Brigades." *Police Review.* (1969), pp. 833, 836, 874, 875.

Glover, E.H. "The English Police: Its Origin and Development." *Police Chronicle,* (1934).

Glover, E.H. "London Metropolitan Police Now Have College." *Police Journal.* XXI (October, 1934), pp. 9-23.

Harrison, Richard. *Whitehall 1212: The Story of the Police of London.* London: Jarrolds, 1948.

Hart, Jenifer. *The British Police.* London: Allen and Unwin, 1951.

Hart, Jenifer. "The Reform of the Borough Police, 1835-1856." *English Historical Review.* 70 (July, 1955), pp. 411-427.

Howard, George. *Guardians of the Queen's Peace: The Development and Work of Britain's Police.* Feltham: Odhams, 1953.

Howe, Ronald. *Story of Scotland Yard: A History of the C.I.D. from the Earliest Times to the Present Day.* London: Arthur Barker, 1965.

Howgrave-Graham, H.M. *Light and Shade at Scotland Yard.* London: J. Murray, 1947.

Hudson, F. "The Story of Crime Prevention." *Canadian Police Chief.* 64:2 (1975), pp. 33, 35, 37-40.
Outlines the origin and development of crime prevention in England.

"In Praise of the London Police." *Saturday Review.* 155 (May 13, 1933).

Institute of Municipal Treasurers and Accountants and Society of County Treasurers. *Police Force Statistics.* London: IMTA, annual.

Janus (pseud). "Saunders Welch: First of the Modern Policemen." *Police College Magazine* (Spring, 1965), pp. 286-296.

Jones, W.R. "The Scope and Functions of Local and Central Control in Police Administration." *Police Journal (GB),* 5 (October, 1932), pp. 518-543.

Law, A. *Police Systems in Urban Districts.* Hertfordshire: King, 1919.

Lee, W.L. Melville. *A History of Police in England.* London: Methuen, 1901.

McGovan, J. *Hunted Down. Recollections of a City Detective.* London: John Menzies, 1884.

MacLaren, J. Anderson. "The Police Authorities of the United Kingdom: Their Constitution, Revenue and Responsibility at Law." *Juridical Review.* 10 (1910).

Maitland, Frederick W. *Justice and Police.* NY: Macmillan, 1885.

Martin, J.P. and Gail Wilson. *Police: A Study in Manpower: The Evolution of the Service in England and Wales, 1829-1965.* London: Heinemann, 1969.

Martienssen, Anthony. *Crime and the Police.* London: Secker and Warburg, 1951.

"Miss Deputy Commissioner Addition." *Survey* (July 15, 1931).

Morrish, Reginald. *The Police and Crime Detection To-day.* London: Oxford University Press, 1940.

Moser, Maurice and Charles F. Rideal. *Stories from Scotland Yard as Told by Inspector Moser.* London: George Routledge, 1890.

Moylan, John. *Scotland Yard and the Metropolitan Police.* (2nd ed.), NY: Putnam, 1934.

Muir, A.A. "Trenchard." *Police Journal.* (1962), pp. 230-233.

"New Policemen." *Spectator.* 150 (May 5, 1933).

Nightingale, J.C. "Police and the Theory of Government." *Police College Magazine* (March, 1952), pp. 127-130.

Nott-Bower, William. *Fifty-Two Years a Policeman.* London: E. Arnold, 1926.

Nunn, J.J. "Police Administration." *Police College Magazine* (Autumn, 1954), pp. 246-251.

Palmer, R.E. " 'Saunders Welch' — A Truly Great Policeman." *Essex and Southend-on-Sea Police Magazine* (Summer, 1969), pp. 61-67.

Parris, H. "The Home Office and the Provincial Police in England and Wales, 1856-1870." *Public Law.* (Autumn, 1961), pp. 230-255.

Pessell, J. "Our Police Forbears." *Police College Magazine.* (Autumn, 1954), pp. 265-269.

"Police and the Unemployed." *New Statesman and Nation.* 4 (November 5, 1932).

"Problems of Social Reform." *Saturday Review.* 153 (May 14, 1932).

Pringle, Patrick. *Hue and Cry: The Birth of the British Police.* London: Museum Press, 1955.

Pringle, P. *The Thief Takers.* London: Museum Press, 1958.

Pulling, Christopher. *Mr. Punch and the Police.* London: Butterworth, 1964.
Collection of cartoons and texts from *Punch* starting in 1841.

Pulling, Christopher. *Police.* (2nd ed.) London: Hale, 1967.

Radzinowicz, Leon. *History of English Criminal Law and Its Administration from 1750. (Vol. 4) Grappling for Control.* London: Stevens, 1968.

Radzinowicz, Leon. *A History of English Criminal Law from 1750.* (3 vols.), NY: Macmillan, 1957.

Reith, Charles. *Blind Eye of History.* Montclair, NJ: Patterson Smith, 1974.

Reith, Charles. *The Police Idea: Its History and Evolution in England in the Eighteenth Century and After.* London: Oxford University Press, 1938.

Reith, Charles. *A Short History of the British Police.* London: Oxford University Press, 1948.

Reith, C. and R.H. Cecil. "Police Apologists: Review of Short History of British Police." *Spectator.* 181 (July 23, 1948).

Rumbelow, Donald. *I Spy Blue: The Police and Crime in the City of London.* London: Macmillan, 1971.

Russell, D. "Arm of the Law." *Saturday Review.* 162 (September 5, 1936).

Savill, Stanley. *The Police Service of England: Its Organization, Disposition and Government . . .* (New ed.) London: Police Publishing, 1923.

Scott, Harold. *Scotland Yard.* London: Duetsch, 1954.

Sharpe, F.D. *Sharpe of the Flying Squad.* London: John Long, 1938.

Sheffield University Institute of Education. *The Police and Crime in the Mid-Nineteenth Century: A Study from Sheffield Sources.* Sheffield: Sheffield University Institute of Education, 1958.

Smith, H. *From Constable to Commissioner: The Story of Sixty Years, Most of Them Mis-Spent.* Albans: Chatto and Windus, 1910.

Solmes, Alwyn. *English Policeman, 871-1935.* London: Allen and Uwin, 1935.

Spenceley, T.H. "Police Discipline One Hundred Years Ago." *Police Journal.* (April-June, 1935), (July-September, 1935).

Spencer, H. "In Days of Yore." *Constables County.* (Autumn, 1970), pp. 19-29.

Tobias, John J. *Against the Peace.* Aylesbury: Ginn, 1970.

Tobias, John J. *Crime and Industrial Society in the 19th Century.* London: Batsford, 1967.

Tobias, John J. *The Influence of Social, Economic and Administrative Change on Crime and Criminals in Selected Areas of England, 1815-75.* Unpub. Doctoral Dissertation, London University, 1965.

Tobias, John J. "Origins of the Police Role." *Criminologist* (May, 1969), pp. 106-112.

Tobias, John J. "Police and Public in the United Kingdom." *Journal of Contemporary History* (January-April, 1972), pp. 201-219.

Thompson, Basil. *My Experiences at Scotland Yard.* NY: Doubleday, Page. 1923.

Thomson, Basil. *The Story of Scotland Yard.* NY: Literary Guild, 1936.

Thurston, Gavin. *The Clerkenwell Riot: The Killing of Constable Culley.* London: Allen and Unwin, 1967.

Webster, David. "English Police System." *Police Journal (GB),* (1929), pp. 571-578.

Wensley, F.P. *Forty Years of Scotland Yard: The Record of a Lifetime's Service in the Criminal Investigation Department.* Garden City, NY: Doubleday, Doran, 1931.

Wren, Pauline. "The Police Inspectorate." *Police Review* (May 14, 1971), pp. 619-620.

Constables

" 'Agrestis' Last Parish Constable." *Police College Magazine.* (Autumn, 1958), pp. 249-252.

Bacon, Francis (1st Viscount St. Albans). *The Office of Constables, Origin and Use of Courts Leet Sheriff's Turn, etc. . . .* [n.p.]: [n.n.] 1608.

Bryant, A. "Village Constable in English History." *Illustrated London News.* 243 (December 7, 1963).

Chitty, J., Jr. *Summary of the Office and Duties of Constables.* (3rd ed.) London: Shaw, 1844.

Fielding, John. *A Short Treatise on the Office of Constable.* (new ed.), A Millar in the Strand, 1762.

Lambard, William. *The Duty and Office of High Constables of Hundreds, Petty Constables, Tythingmen, and Such Inferior Ministers of the Peace.* [n.p.]: [n.n.], 1677.

Marshall, Geoffrey. *Police and Government: The Status and Accountability of the English Constable.* London: Methuen, 1965.

M., D. "Watch, Ward and Constables." *Police Journal.* (1930), pp. 289-303.

Simpson, H.B. "The Office of Constable." *English Historical Review.* XL (October, 1895), pp. 625-641.

Welch, Saunders. *Observations on the Office of Constable, with Cautions for the More Safe Execution of That Duty.* A Millar in the Strand, 1754.

Winship, P.J. "The Legal Status of a Constable and Its Implications . . . ." *Police College Magazine* (Spring 1970), pp. 45-47.

Customs Service

Baker, Robert L. *English Customs Service, 1307-1343. A Study of Medieval Administration.* Philadelphia, PA: American Philos., 1961.

Hoon, Elizabeth E. *Organization of the English Customs, System 1696-1786.* Westport, CT: Greenwood, 1968. (repr. of 1938 ed.).

Force Histories

Anley, F.R. "The Derbyshire Constabulary." *Metropolitan Police College Journal.* (Spring, 1936), pp. 61-71.

Baines, G. *History of Brighton Police, 1838-1967.* Brighton: Brighton Constabulary, 1967.

Bale, Islwyn. *Through Seven Reigns: A History of the Newport Borough Police.* Newport: Newport Constabulary, 1960.

Banks, C. *History of the County Borough of Hastings Police, 1836-1967.* Hastings: Hastings Constabulary, 1967.

Birch, Kenneth. "The Days When the Pwllheli Borough Force Numbered One Policeman." *Police Review* (August 4, 1972).

Bristol Constabulary. *Bristol Police Centenary, 1836-1936.* Bristol: Bristol Constabulary, 1936.

Cartner, E. *Northumberland County Constabulary: 1857-1957.* Morpeth: Northumberland Constabulary, 1957.

Cookes, Anne. *The Southampton Police Force: 1836-1856.* Southampton: City of Southampton Corporation, 1972.

Cramer, James. *A History of the Police of Portsmouth: The Story of the Constables, Tithingmen, Watchmen and Other Peace Officers of the Portsmouth Area from c.1241 to 1967.* Portsmouth: Portsmouth City Council, 1967.

Darwin, Charles A. *Southport County Borough Police, 1870-1969.* Southport: Southport Constabulary, 1969.

Derby Constabulary. *History of Derby Borough Police.* Derby: Derby Constabulary, 1966.

Dorset Constabulary. *Dorset Constabulary, 1856-1956.* Dorchester: Dorset Constabulary, 1956.

Durham Constabulary. *Report on the Re-Organization of the Constabulary, 1945-1949.* Aycliffe: Durham Constabulary, 1950.

East Riding of Yorkshire Constabulary. *East Riding of Yorkshire Police: 1857-1957.* Beverley: East Riding of Yorkshire Constabulary, 1957.

"Essex Was the First: A Force History in Brief" *Police Review* (October 31, 1969).

Flintshire Constabulary. *Flintshire Constabulary Centenary, 1856-1956.* Holywell: Flintshire Constabulary, 1956.

Ford, R. *The History of the Bournemouth Police.* Bournemouth: Bournemouth Constabulary, 1963.

Gillespie, W.H. "An Old Force." *Police Journal.* (1954), pp. 306-317.
History of the Deal Police.

Gloucestershire Constabulary. *Birth of the Gloucestershire Constabulary.* Cheltenham: Gloucestershire Constabulary, 1967.

Goslin, R.J. *Duty Bound: A History of the Bolton Borough Police Force, 1939-1969.* Bolton: Bolton Borough Council, 1970.

Gray, George. "Retiring Police Chief Traces the London Transport Force's History." *Job* (February 22, 1974).

Grimsby Constabulary. *Guardians of the Peace, 1846-1955: Souvenir Brochure of the Grimsby Borough Police Exhibition, April, 1955.* Grimsby: Grimsby Constabulary, 1955.

Hailstone, Alfred G. *Buckinghamshire Constabulary Centenary: One Hundred Years of Law Enforcement in Buckinghamshire, An Historical Survey.* Aylesbury: Buckinghamshire Constabulary, 1957.

Heaney, D.E. "Reflections on the Passing of the Blackpool Borough Police Force." *Lancashire Constabulary Journal.* (Winter, 1969), pp. 148-151.

Hunt, Walter W. *To Guard My People: An Account of the Origin and History of the Swansea Police.* Morriston, Swansea: Jones, 1957.

Hutchings, P. *The History of the Cornwall Constabulary, 1857-1957.* Bodmin: Corwall Constabulary, 1958.

Hutchings, Walter J. *Out of the Blue: History of the Devon Constabulary.* Exeter: Devon Constabulary, 1956.

Indge, W. *A Short History of the Berkshire Constabulary, 1856-1956.* Sulhamstead: Bershire Constabulary, 1956.

James, R.W. *To the Best of Our Skill and Knowledge: A Short History of the Cheshire Constabulary, 1857-1957.* Chester: Cheshire Constabulary, 1957.

Jones, J. Owain. *The History of the Caernarvonshire Constabulary, 1856-1950.* Caernarvonshire Historical Society, 1963.

Kyrke, R.V. *History of the East Sussex Police, 1840-1967.* Lewes: Sussex Police Authority, 1970.

La Nauze, Charles D. "The Bathurst Inlet Patrol." *Police Journal (GB),* 5 (January, 1935), pp. 13-23.

Moriarty, C.C.H. *Birmingham City Police Centenary, Monday, 20th November, 1939: The Formation of the Force, and Its Present Organization.* Birmingham: Birmingham Constabulary, 1939.

North Riding of Yorkshire Constabulary. *The First Hundred Years of the North Riding of Yorkshire Constabulary.* Northallerton: North Riding of Yorkshire Constabulary, 1956.

Owen, Hugh. *The History of the Anglesey Constabulary.* Bangor: Antiquerian Society and Field Club, 1952.

Pearson, S.C. *Lincolnshire Constabulary, 1857-1957.* Lincoln: Lincolnshire Constabulary, 1957.

Richards, R.J. "Policing Burmingham: In the Beginning." *Forward.* (Autumn, 1972), pp. 37-40.

Rumbelow, Donald. *I Spy Blue: The Police and Crime in the City of London From Elizabeth I to Victoria.* London: Macmillan, 1971.

Smith, Gordon H. *The Law Enforcement Agencies in Bradford in the Early 19th Century.* Leeds University thesis, Department of Adult Education and Extra-Mural Studies, Advanced Criminology, 1956-1959.

Southampton Constabulary. *A History of Southampton City Police, 1836-1967.* Southampton: Southampton Constabulary, 1967.

Stanley, C.R. "A Tribute to the Rutland Constabulary, 1848-1951." *Tally-Ho!* (Summer, 1968).

Stark, John. "The Police of the City of London." *Police Journal.* IV (January, 1931); IV (April, 1931).

Taylor, Denis. *999 and All That: The Story of Oldham Borough Police Force, Formed on November 14, 1849, and Amalgamated to Form Part of a New Lancashire County Constabulary on April 1, 1969.* Oldham: Oldham Corporation, 1968.

Thomas, R.L. *The Kent Police Centenary.* Maidstone: Kent Constabulary Centenary Booklet Sub-Committee, 1957.

Thompson, S.P. *Maintaining the Queen's Peace: A Short History of the Birkenhead Borough Police.* Birkenhead: Birkenhead Constabulary, 1958.

Trubshaw, W. "The Lancashire Constabulary: 80 Years Ago and Today." *Police Journal.* (1928), pp. 487-498.

Waller, Stanley. *Cuffs and Handcuffs: The Story of Rochdale Police Through the Years 1252-1957.* Rochdale: Rochdale Watch Committee, 1957.

Watt, Ian A. *A History of the Hampshire Constabulary.* Winchester: Hampshire Constabulary, 1967.

Webster, W.H.A. "Port of London Authority Police." *Police Journal.* 3 (1930), pp. 244-253.

Wheeler, J.D. "Administration of Suffolk and the Police." *Justice of the Peace and Local Government Review* (July 15, 1967), pp. 438-439.

Wheeler, J.D. *The Constables of West Suffolk From 1836.* Bury St. Edmunds: West Suffolk Constabulary, 1967.

Wheeler, J.D. "The West Suffolk Constabulary: An Outline History." *Police Journal.* (1962), pp. 67-70.

Medieval

Beard, Charles A. *Office of the Justice of the Peace in England in Its Origin and Development.* NY: B. Franklin, 1962. (repr. of 1904 ed.).

Bellamy, John. *Crime and Public Order in England in the Later Middle Ages.* London: Routledge and K. Paul, 1972.

Brown, R. Stewart. *Sergeants of the Peace in Medieval England and Wales.* Manchester: Manchester University Press, 1936.

Cam, Helen. *Hundred and the Hundred Roles: An Outline of Local Government in Medieval England.* NY: B. Franklin, 1960. (repr. of 1930 ed.).

Goldstein, Jackson Kevin. "Crime and Punishment in Early England." *Justice of the Peace* (April 5, 1975).

Jenks, Edward. *Law and Politics in the Middle Ages with a Synoptic Table of Sources.* NY: Franklin, 1970.

Jewdwine, J.W. *Tort, Crime and Police in Medieval Britain, A Review of Some Early Law and Custom.* London: Williams and Norgate, 1917.

Lambard, William. *The Duties of Constables, Borsholders, Tithing-men, and Other Such Low Ministers of the Peace.* NY: W.J. Johnson, 1969. (repr. of 1583 ed.).

Riggs, Charles H. *Criminal Asylum in Anglo-Saxon Law.* Gainesville: University Press of Florida, 1963.

Sanders, Wiley B., ed. *Juvenile Offenders for a Thousand Years: Selected Readings From Anglo-Saxon Times to 1900.* Chapel Hill: Universtiy of North Carolina Press, 1970.

Solmes, Alwyn. *The English Policeman, 871-1935.* London: G. Allen and Unwin, 1935.

Stenton, Doris M. *After Runnymede: Magna Carta in the Middle Ages.* Charlottesville: Virginia University Press, 1965.

Stenton, Doris M. *English Justice Between the Norman Conquest and the Great Charter, 1066-1215.* London: Allen, 1965.

Ullman, Walter. *The Medieval Idea of Law as Represented by Lucas De Penna: A Study in Fourteenth-Century Legal Scholarship.* NY: Barnes, 1969. (repr. of 1946 ed.).

Middle Ages to 1829

Armitage, Gilbert. *The History of the Bow Street Runners, 1729-1829* London: Wishart, 1932.

Ashley, Maurice. *Magna Carta in the Seventeenth Century.* Charlottesville: Virginia University Press, 1965.

Blizard, William. *Desultory Reflections on Police, with an Essay on the Means of Preventing Crimes and Amending Criminals . . .* [n.p.]: C. Dilly, 1785.

Colquihoun, Patrick. *A Treatise on the Commerce and Police of the River Thames.* Montclair, NJ: Patterson Smith, 1969. (repr. of 1800 ed.).

Darvall, Frank A. *Popular Disturbances and Public Order in Regency England.* NY: Oxford University Press, 1934.

Dunne, Lawrence. "Bow Street and the Police." *Police College Magazine* (September, 1952), pp. 192-197.

Elton, Geoffrey R. *Policy and Police: The Enforcement of the Reformation in the Age of Cromwell.* Cambridge: Cambridge University Press, 1972.

Fielding, Henry. *Inquiry into the Causes of the Late Increase of Robberies.* NY: AMS, 1975. (repr. of 1751 ed.).

Fielding, John. *Abstract of Sir John Fielding's Plan of Police, 1761.* British Museum Additional Manuscripts, 38, 334, 1761.

Fielding, John. *Plan for Preventing Robberies Within Twenty Miles of London.* [n.p.]: A. Millar, 1755.

Jempson, K. "Fielding's Force." *Police College Magazine.* (Spring, 1961), pp. 353-362.

Johnson, D.J. "Sir John Fielding's Plan of the Police." *Police College Magazine.* (Spring, 1967), pp. 52-57.

Judges, A.V. *The Elizabethan Underworld: A Collection of Tudor and Early Stuart Tracts and Ballads Telling of the Lives and Misdoing of Vagabonds, Thieves, Rogues and Cozeners, and Giving Some Account of the Operation of the Criminal Law.* (2nd ed.), London: Routledge and K. Paul, 1964. (repr. of 1930 ed.).

Langbein, John H. *Prosecuting Crime in the Renaissance: England, Germany, France.* Cambridge: Harvard University Press, 1974.

Leslie, Melville R. *The Life and Work of John Fielding . . .* [n.p.]: Lincoln Williams, 1934.

Moylan, J.F. "Police Reform Before Peel: The Fieldings and the Bow Street Police." *Police Journal (GB),* (1929) pp. 150-164.

Price, F.D. *Wiginton Constables' Books, 1691-1836.* Chichester: Phillimore, 1972.

Pringle, Patrick. *Hue and Cry, the Story of Henry and John Fielding and Their Bow Street Runners.* NY: William Morrow, 1956.

Pringle, Patrick. *The Thief Takers.* London: Museum Press, 1958.

Metropolitan Police

Allen, G.H.B. *Brief Considerations on the Present State of the Police of the Metropolis: With a Few Suggestions Towards Its Improvement.* London: [n.n.], 1821.

Cobb, Belton. *The First Detectives and the Early Career of Richard Mayne, Commissioner of Police.* London: Faber and Faber, 1957.

Colquihoun, Patrick. *A Treatise on the Police of the Metropolis.* (7th ed.). Montclair, NJ: Patterson Smith, 1969. (repr. of 1806 ed.).

House of Commons, Select Committee Appointed to Inquire into the State of the Police of the Metropolis. *First and Second Reports, with Minutes of Evidence and Appendices, 1817.* Shannon: Irish University Press, 1968.

House of Commons, [Select] Committee on the State of the Police of the Metropolis. *Third Report from the Select Committee on the Police of the Metropolis, [1818], with an Additional Report [1822], Minutes of Evidence and Apendices.* Shannon: Irish University Press, 1968

Janus [pseud]. "Patrick Colquihoun." *Police College Magazine.* (Autumn, 1965), pp. 10-17.

Lyman, J.L. "The Metropolitan Police Act of 1829: An Analysis of Certain Events Influencing the Passage and Character of the Metropolitan Police Act in England." *Journal of Criminal Law, Criminology and Police Science.* 55:1 (March, 1964), pp. 141-154.

Mainwaring, George. *Observations on the Present State of the Police of the Metropolis.* London: John Murray, 1821.

Reith, Charles. *British Police and the Democratic Ideal.* London: Oxford University Press, 1943.

Reith, Charles. *A New Study of Police History.* London: Oliver and Boyd, 1956.

Reith, Charles. "Preventive Principle of Police." *Journal of Criminal Law and Criminology.* 34 (September, 1943), pp. 206-209.

Reports From Select Committees on the Police of the Metropolis, with Appendices and Extracts from the Evidence of Rev. Thomas Thirlwall. (Contents: Nightly Watch of the Metropolis, 1812; Police of the Metropolis, 1816; Police of the Metropolis, Extracts from Thirlwall's Evidence, 1817.) Shannon: Irish University Press, 1969.

Wade, John. *A Treatise on the Police and Crimes of the Metropolis.* Montclair, NJ: Patterson Smith, 1970. (repr. of 1829 ed.).

CONTEMPORARY BRITISH POLICE

Books

Adams, H. *Policemen and the Police Force.* Oxford: Blackwell, 1962.

Adamson, I. *The Great Detective, Reginald Spooner.* London: Muller, 1966.

Alderson, John C. and Philip J. Stead, eds. *Police We Deserve.* London: Wolfe, 1973.

Allen, C.K. *The Queen's Peace.* London: Stevens, 1953.

Barr, Robert. *The Scotland Yard Story.* London: Hodder and Stoughton, 1962.

Baughman, U.E. *Secret Service Chief.* London: Heinemann, 1963.

Beveridge, P. *Inside the C.I.D.* London: Evans, 1957.

Borissow, M. *Dark Blue for Courage.* Maidstone: Angley Book, 1966.

Bowes, Stuart. *Police and Civil Liberties.* London: Lawrence and Wishart, 1966.

Bowker, A.E. *A Lifetime with the Law.* London: W.H. Allen, 1961.

Browne, Douglas G. and E.V. Tullett. *The Scalpel of Scotlaland Yard: The Life of Sir Bernard Spilsbury.* NY: Dutton, 1952.

Burt, L. *Commander Burt of Scotland Yard.* London: Heinemann, 1959.

Campbell, J. *Police Horses.* Newton Abbot Devon: David and Charles, 1967.

Chapple, Norman L. *Police Cadet Training: Selected British Programs.* Kent, OH: Kent State University, 1971.

Cherrill, F.R. *Cherrill of the Yard.* London: Transworld, 1956.

Chillingworth, Jon. *Policeman.* Guildford, Surrey: Lutterworth Press, 1961.

Coatman, John. *Police.* London: Oxford University Press, 1959.

Critchley, T.A. *Conquest of Violence: Order and Liberty in Britain.* NY: Schocken, 1970.

Delano, Anthony. *Slip-Up: Fleet Street, Scotland Yard and the Great Train Robbery.* NY: Quadrangle, 1975.

Devlin, J. Daniel. *Police Procedure, Administration and Organization.* London: Butterworth, 1966.

Devlin, Patrick. *The Enforcement of Morals.* London: Oxford University, 1965.

Dumpleton, John. *Law and Order: The Story of the Police.* (2nd ed.), London: Black, 1970.

Fairlie, G. *The Reluctant Cop.* London: Hodder and Stoughton, 1958.

Fallon, Tom. *The River Police.* London: Frederick Muller, 1956.

Firmin, Stanley. *Scotland Yard: The Inside Story.* London: Hutchinson, 1948.

Fish, Donald. *"The Lawless Skies." The Fight Against International Air Crime.* NY: Putnam, 1962.

Fowler, Norman. *Police in the Seventies: An Occasional Paper.* London: Bow, 1970.

Gorer, Geoffrey. *Exploring English Character.* NY: Criterion, 1955.
See especially "Modification of National Character: The Psychological Role of the Police in England." pp. 305-312.

Gosling, J. *The Ghost Squad.* London: W.H. Allen, 1959.

Harrison, Richard. *The C.I.D. and the F.B.I. . . .* London: Frederick Muller, 1956.
Comparison of F.B.I. with C.I.D.

Hart, J.M. *The British Police.* London: George Allen and Unwin, 1951.

Harvey, S. *London Policeman.* London: Angus and Robertson, 1958.

Hearn, C.V. *A Duty to the Public.* London: Muller, 1965.

Hewitt, William H. *British Police Administration.* Springfield, IL: C.C. Thomas, 1965.

Howe, Ronald. *The Story of Scotland Yard.* NY: Horizon, 1965.

Jackett, Sam. *Heros of Scotland Yard.* London: Hale, 1965.

Jackson, R.M. *Enforcing the Law.* NY: Macmillan, 1967.

Judge, Anthony. *A Man Apart: The British Policeman and His Job.* London: A. Barker, 1972.

Laurie, Peter. *Scotland Yard — A Study of the Metropolitan Police.* NY: Holt Rinehart and Winston, 1970.

Lucas, N. *The C.I.D.* London: A Barker, 1967.

McKnight, G. *The Murder Squad.* London: W.H. Allen, 1967.

Marshall, Geoffrey. *Police and Government, the Status and Accountability of the English Constable.* London: Methuen, 1965.

Martin, J.P. and G. Wilson. *The Police — A Study in Manpower.* London: Heinemann, 1969.

Merrilees, William. *The Short Arm of the Law.* London: John Long, 1966.

Millen, E. *Specialist in Crime.* London: George G. Harrap, 1972.

Minto, George A. *The Thin Blue Line.* London: Hodder and Stoughton, 1965.

Onselen, L. *A Rhapsody in Blue.* Folkstone, Kent: Bailey and Swinfen, 1960.

Perry, Gordon A. *Police and the Police Service.* Poole, Dorset: Blandford, 1974.

Prendergast, W. *Calling All Z-Cars.* London: J. Long, 1966.

Purcell, William E. *British Police in a Changing Society.* Oxford: Mowbrays, 1974.

Quinain, Louis. *Country Beat: A Police Constable's Story.* London: Methuen, 1946.

Rolph, C.H. *The Police and the Public: An Inquiry.* London: Heinemann, 1962.

Scott, Harold Richard. *Scotland Yard.* London: Duetsch, 1954.

Seth, R. *The Specials.* London: Gollancz, 1961.

Sillitoe, P. *Cloak Without Dagger.* London: Cassell, 1955.

Whitaker, Ben. *The Police.* London: Eyre and Spottiswoode, 1964.

Whitbread, J.R. *The Railway Policeman.* London: Harrap, 1961.

Wilkinson, G. *Special Branch Officer.* Feltham: Odhams, 1956.

Williams, Guy. *Inside New Scotland Yard.* Sussex: Priory, 1976.

Wood, James Playsted. *Scotland Yard.* NY: Hawthorn, 1970.

Periodicals

Allen, P. "Police of England." *Journal of Criminal Law and Criminology.* 37 (January, 1947), pp. 434-438.

Baddeley, Fred. "British Police — Community Involvement." *Police.* 16:9 (May, 1972), pp. 24-29.

Baddeley, Fred. "British Police Juvenile Liaison Schemes." *Police Chief.* XXXVII:5 (May, 1971), pp. 68-70.

Bainbridge, John. "Profiles: Constable Peter Roland Sawyer." *New Yorker Magazine.* 47 (August 14, 1971).

Baston, W.C. "The London River Police." *International Criminal Police Review* (January, 1954), pp. 3-11.

"Bobbies in Trouble." *Time.* 82 (August 30, 1963).

Bower-Nott, John. "Organization and Function of New Scotland Yard." *FBI Law Enforcement Bulletin.* 26:11 (November, 1957), pp. 5-10, 27.

Brett, D.T. "The Police College Library." *Police Journal (GB),* 39:1 (1966).

"British Airports Authority Constabulary." *Police Review (GB),* 74: (1966).

"British Bobbies Feel Safer Unarmed." *Reader's Digest.* 75 (July, 1959).

"Case for Inquiry." *Provincial Police Economist.* 189:1068 (December 20, 1958).

Cecil, R.N. "Changing Police." *Spectator.* 180:729 (June 18, 1948).

Chapman, Samuel G. "Rural Police Patrol in England and Wales." *Journal of Criminal Law, Criminology and Police Science.* 45:4 (September-October, 1954), pp. 349-358.

Chapman, Samuel G. "Urban Police Patrol in England and Wales." *Journal of Criminal Law, Criminology and Police Science.* 45:3 (September-October, 1954), pp. 349-358.

"College for Constables." *Economist.* 195:321 (April 23, 1960).

"Constables and the Commons." *Economist.* 187:391 (May 3, 1958).

Crookston, Peter. "Look! The Rape Squad Girls." *Sunday Times* (March 18, 1973).

Devlin, Patrick A. "The Police in a Changing Society." *Police Journal (GB),*(1966).

Dowbiggin, H.L. "Nottingham City Police Operational Training Course." *Police Journal.* XXI (October-December, 1948).

Ellis, J.T. "The Birmingham (England) City Police Training Center." *Traffic Digest and Review.* XIII (May, 1965), pp. 10-14.

"Finest in the World?" *Times Literary Supplement.* 3159 (September 14, 1962). pp. 681-682.

Foot, D. "Case of Mandy Rice-Davies." *Spectator.* 211 (August 9, 1963), pp. 166-167.

Green, H. "A Police Command and Control System." *FBI Law Enforcement Bulletin* (May, 1971).

Gregory, Eric and Peter Turner. "Unit Beat Policing in England: A New System of Police Patrol." *Police Chief.* XXXV:7 (July, 1968), pp. 42047.

Harding, J.K. "Breakthrough?" *Police Review (GB),* (March 8, 1974), p. 285.

Harris, John S. "Central Inspection of Local Police Services in Britain." *Journal of Criminal Law, Criminology and Police Science.* 45:1 (May-June, 1954), pp. 85-95.

Harris, R.E. "New Police College Opened in Britain." *Journal of Criminal Law.* XL (July, 1949), pp. 217-222.

Harris, R.E. "The Police Federation in Britain." *Journal of Criminal Law and Criminology,* 36:2 (1945-46).

Hearn, Cyril V. "The Police Role in Our Modern Democracy." *Police World (GB),* (Autumn, 1970), pp. 7-10.

Hewitt, C.R. "New Deal for the Police." *New Statesman and Nation.* 35 (May 29, 1948).

Hewitt, William H. "The 1966 British Police Manpower, Equipment and Efficiency Report." *Law and Order.* 18:5 (May, 1970), pp. 30-33.

Howard, Toni. "Real Life Sherlock: The Sophisticated Ex-Barrister Who Runs Scotland Yard's 'C.I.D.' " *Saturday Evening Post.* 234: (October 28, 1961), pp. 101-103.

"How Britain's Police Won Public Approval." *American City.* 59:15 (March, 1944).

"How They Got the Spies." *Newsweek.* 57 (January 23, 1961).

Inglis, Brian. "September Sunday." *Spectator.* 207:376 (September 22, 1961).

Kennard, John P. de B. "An English Policeman in the United States." *FBI Law Enforcement Bulletin* (October, 1967).

"Kicking the Coppers." *Newsweek.* 62 (December 30, 1963).

Latham, C. "Enforcement of Fines." *Criminal Law Review* (September, 1973), pp. 552-559.

Levy, B.W. "Price of Freedom." *20th Century.* 170 (Spring, 1962), pp. 111-122.

Lucas, Brian K. "The Independence of Chief Constable." *Public Administration* (Spring, 1960), pp. 1-15.

Lunden, Walter A. "Men of New Scotland Yard." *Police.* 13:2 (November-December, 1968), pp. 6-16.

Macdonald, Keith. "Police State in Britain?" *New Society* (January 8, 1976), pp. 50-51.

Mark, Robert. "Understanding Our Role." *Job* (March 27, 1970).

Marshall, G. "Police Responsibility." *Public Administration* (Autumn, 1960), pp. 213-226.

Maugham, A.M. "Grisly Story of Scotland Yard." *Holiday.* 31 (June, 1962), pp. 72-73.

Millward, Mervyn. "Leaves from a Policeman's Notebook." *Blackwood's Magazine.* 294 (December, 1963), pp. 499-508.

Mitchell, Robert. "An American Policeman in England." *FBI Law Enforcement Bulletin.* 36:7 (July, 1967), pp. 2-6, 16.

"Mounted Service of the Royal Air Force Police." *Illustrated London News.* 238 (April 8, 1961).

"Mystery in Britain, the Five." *Life.* 50 (January 20, 1961), pp. 6-8.

"New Model Police." *Economist.* 203 (June 2, 1962), pp. 873-874.

Nightingale, J. "Police and Bains." *Local Government Chronicle* (May 11, 1973).

"Night Vision Equipment for Police Use." *Police Research Bulletin.* (1967).

"No Police for Police." *Economist.* 211 (May 2, 1964), pp. 465-466.

"Not a Happy Lot." *Economist.* 200 (September 9, 1961).

Nott-Bower, John. "Growth and Ideals of the British Police." *Police Yearbook.* Wasgington DC: IACP, 1960.

Nott-Bower, John. "Organization and Function of New Scotland Yard." *FBI Law Enforcement Bulletin* (November, 1957), pp. 5-10.

"Nottingham Police System Which Seals the City in 2 1/2 Minutes." *Illustrated London News.* 208 (February 9, 1946), pp. 140-141.

"On the Beat." *The Spectator.* 204 (February 5, 1960).

Penaat, Edward F. "The British Police System." *Police Chief.* 26 (March, 1959), pp. 4-18.

"Police and Public." *The Spectator.* 211 (August 16, 1963).

"Police Service in the United Kingdom." *International Criminal Police Review* (January, 1967), pp. 2-10.

"Police Strengths." *Police Review (GB),* (December, 1974).

"Policing the Police." *The Economist.* 207 (May 18, 1963).

"Police Violence." *New Statesman and Nation.* 66 (June 26, 1963).

Pritt, D.N. "Police and the Fascists." *New Statesman and Nation.* 34 (August 23, 1947).

Regan, D.E. "The Police Service: An Extreme Example of Central Control over Local Authority Staff." *Public Law.* (Spring, 1966), pp. 13-34.

"Reports on the Police." *New Statesman and Nation* (December 10, 1960).

Rolph, C.H. "Best in the World." *New Statesman and Nation.* 63 (June 8, 1962).

Rolph, C.H. "The Police Bill." *New Statesman and Nation.* 66 (November 22, 1963).

Rolph, C.H. "Police Violence." *New Statesman and Nation* (June 26, 1963), pp. 66-102.

Rolph, C.H. "Reports on the Police." *New Statesman and Nation.* 60 (December 10, 1960).

Shawcross, Hartley. "Police and Public in Great Britain." *American Bar Association Journal.* 51:3 (1965), pp. 225-228.

Sheehan, Thomas M. "The Judges' Rules: A Discipline for Testimony and Interrogation." *Police.* 10:1 (September-October, 1956), pp. 61-64.
Rules of practice in questioning criminal suspects in Great Britain.

Southworth, Louis. "The City of London Police Force." *Crime and Detection.* 1 (November, 1966), pp. 2S-36.

Stead, P.J. "The Police College, Bramshill." *International Criminal Police Review* (August-September, 1970), pp. 207-212.

St. Johnston, T.E. "The Judges' Rules and Police Interrogation in England Today." *Journal of Criminal Law, Criminology and Police Science.* 57:1 (March, 1966), pp. 85-92.

Tarry, F.T., One of Her Majesty's Inspectors of Constabulary. "Training for Police Duties." *Police Journal (GB),* XXXII (July-September, 1959).

"Temporary Police College at Ryton-on-Dunmore." *Illustrated London News.* 233 (August 16, 1959), pp. 260-261.

Toch, Hans H. and R. Schulte. "Readiness to Perceive

Violence as a Result of Police Training." *British Journal of Psychology*. 52:4 (1961).

Toll, Ian. "A Glimpse at the London Metropolitan Policeman." *Police News*. 49 (September, 1970), pp. 10-11, 14-15.

Traini, R. "Beating the Forger." *Security Gazette*. 15:10 (1973), pp. 367-368.
Describes police and airline security efforts to combat ticket forgeries and bank-note counterfeiting in Great Britain.

Turner, R.B.F. "Fraud Prevention and Airline Security." *International Criminal Police Review* (January, 1969), pp. 19-26.

Waldron, John. "Scotland Yard — A New Look." *FBI Law Enforcement Bulletin*. 39:2 (February, 1970), pp. 10-15, 22-23.

Wilson, O.W. "The British Police." *Journal of Criminal Law, Criminology and Police Science*. 40:5 (January-February, 1950), pp. 637-650.

"You'll Learn Yet." *New Statesman and Nation*. 62 (October 13, 1961).

Government Publications

Cheshire Constabulary. *Cheshire (England) — Police Authority — Chief Constable's Annual Report, 1973*. Washington DC: NCJRS, (Microfiche), 1973.

Great Britain Royal Commission on the Police. "The Survey of Relations between the Police and the Public Carried Out by the Government Social Survey." in *Great Britain Royal Commission on the Police, 1962. Final Report*. London: HMSO, pp. 102-105.

Her Majesty's Chief Inspector of Constabulary. *England — Her Majesty's Chief Inspector of Constabulary — Report, 1973*. Washington DC: NCJRS, (Microfiche), 1974.

Home Office. *Higher Training for the Police Service in England and Wales*. London: HMSO, 1947.

Home Office. *Police in Counties and Boroughs*. London: HMSO, 1960.

Home Office. *Police of the Metropolis*. London: HMSO, 1960.

Home Office. *Police Service in Britain*. London: HMSO, 1947.

Home Office. *Police Training in England and Wales*. London: HMSO, 1961.

Home Office. *The Recruitment of People with Higher Educational Qualifications into the Police Service*. London: HMSO, 1967.

Home Office. *Report of a Working Party on Police Cadets*. London: HMSO, 1965.

Home Office. *Report of the Committee of the Police Council on Higher Police Training*. London: HMSO, 1962.

Home Office. *Report of the Committee on Police Extraneous Duties*. London: HMSO, 1953.

Home Office. *Royal Commission on the Police. Final Report*. London: HMSO, 1962.

Home Office. *Royal Commisssion on the Police. Index to Minutes of Evidence and Appendices*. London: HMSO, 1963.

Home Office. *Royal Commission on the Police. Interim Report*. London: HMSO, 1960.

Home Office. *Royal Commission on the Police. Minutes of Evidence 1 to 27 and Appendices I to IV*. London: HMSO, 1960-62.

Home Office. *Second Report of the Committee of the Police Council on Higher Police Training*. London: HMSO, 1963.

Home Office. *Supplementary Report of the Police Council Committee on the Special Course at the College*. London: HMSO, 1963.

Home Office and Scottish Home Departnent. *Report of the Committee on Police Conditions of Service*. (pts I and II), London: HMSO, 1949.

Johnson, Thomas W. *Observations of the British Police System*. Sacramento: State Printing Office, 1971.

Kingston Upon Hull City Police. *Kingston Upon Hull (England) — Chief Constable — Annual Report, 1973*. Washington DC: NCJRS, (Microfiche), 1974.

Leeds City Police. *Leeds (England) — City Police — Annual Report, 1973*. Washington DC: NCJRS, (Microfiche), 1973.

Liverpool Office of the Chief Constable. *Liverpool and Bootle — Police Authority — Report of the Chief Constable, 1973*. Washington DC: NCJRS, (Microfiche), 1974.

London Police. *London — Commissioner of Police of the Metropolis — Report, 1973*. Washington DC: NCJRS, (Microfiche), 1974.

London Police. *London (England) — Police — Annual Report of the Commissioner, 1973*. Washington DC: NCJRS, (Microfiche), 1974.

POLICE OF THE WORLD

THE WORLD'S POLICE — GENERAL

Africa — General

Abidjan Institute of Criminology. *West African Conference in Comparative Criminology, 1st Abidjan, Ivory Coast, June 1972 — Needs and Perspectives in the Matter of Crime Prevention and the Treatment of Delinquents in West Africa.* Washington DC: NCJRS, 1972.

Allott, Anthony N. *Essays in African Law.* Westport, CT: Greenwood, 1975. (repr. of 1960 ed.).

Arcand, S. and Y. Brillon. "Comparative Criminology: Africa." *ACTA Criminology.* 6 (1973), pp. 199-217.

Asian-African Legal Consultative Committee. *Constitutions of African States.* 2 vols., Dobbs Ferry, NJ: Oceana, 1973.

Bohannon, Paul. *African Homicide and Suicide.* Princeton: Princeton University Press, 1960.

Clifford, William. *An Introduction to African Criminology.* NY: Oxford University Press, 1974.

Gledhill, Alan. *The Penal Codes of Northern Nigeria and the Sudan.* London: Sweet and Maxwell, 1963.

Gulliver, Phillip H. *Social Control in an African Society.* NY: New York University Press, 1963.

Hutchinson, Thomas W. et al., eds. *Africa and Law: Developing Legal Systems in African Commonwealth Nations.* Madison: University of Wisconsin Press, 1968.

Kuper, Hilda and Leo Kuper, eds. *African Law: Adaptation and Development.* Berkeley: University of California Press, 1965.

Lefever, Ernest W. *Spear and Scepter: Army Police and Politics in Tropical Africa.* Washington DC: Brookings Institution, 1970.

Mensah-Brown, A. Kodwo. *Introduction to Law in Contemporary Africa.* New Platz, NY: Conch Magazine, 1975.

Milner, Alan. *African Penal Systems.* NY: Praeger, 1969.

Salacuse, Jeswald. *Introduction to Law in French Speaking Africa: Africa South of the Sahara.* (vol. 1), Charlottesville, VA: Michie, 1969.

Salacuse, Jeswald. *Introduction to Law in French Speaking Africa.* (vol. 2), Charlottesville, VA: Michie, 1975.

Seidman, Robert B. "Administrative Law and Legitimacy in Anglophonic Africa: A Problem in the Reception of Foreign Law." *Law and Society Review* (November, 1970), pp. 161-204.

Tanner, Ralph E.S. *Three Studies in East African Criminology — Crime in East Africa.* Uppsala, Sweden: Scandinavian Institute of African Studies, 1970.

Tanner, Ralph E.S. *Witch Murders in Sukumaland.* Uppsala, Sweden: Scandinavian Institute of African Studies, 1964.

"Third African Regional Conference of the I.C.P.O. INTERPOL." *International Criminal Police Review* (August-September, 1969), pp. 178-185.

Asia — General

Asian-African Legal Consultative Committee Secretary ed. *Constitutions of Asian Countries.* NY: International Publications Service, 1968.

"First South East Asian Regional Conference on Drugs." *International Criminal Police Review* (April, 1960), pp. 98-100.

Mei, Ko-Wang. "University Police Training in the Orient." *Police.* 5:1 (September-October, 1960), pp. 65-67.

Report of United Nations Consultative Group on Narcotics Problems in Asia and the Far East. NY: United Nations, [n.d.].

Tenny, Frank S. "Law Enforcement in the Far East." *Police.* 8:1 (September-October, 1963), pp. 45-46.

United Nations Asia and Far East Institute for the Prevention of Crime and Treatment of Offenders. *Resource Material Series No. 2.* Tokyo, Japan: United Nations, 1971.
Available in Microfiche from NCJRS.

Europe — General

Abraham, Henry J. *The Judicial Process: An Introductory Analysis of the Courts of the United States, England, and France.* NY: Oxford University Press, 1962.

"Aspects of European Policing." *Police Journal (GB),* (April-June, 1973), pp. 178-181.

Becker, Harold K. *Police Systems of Europe.* Springfield, IL: C.C. Thomas, 1973.
Makes detailed comparison of Liverpool and Copenhagen Police Departments. Also examines the police of ten other European countries.

Berkley, George. "The European Police: Challenge and Change." Public Administration Review. XXVIII:5 (September-October, 1968), pp. 424-430.
Discussion of police education systems; training for senior positions; lateral entry; policewomen; and the use of firearms. Also discusses civilian control of the police and the use of review boards.

Bianchi, Herman, Mario Simondi, and Ian Taylor eds. *Deviance and Control in Europe. Papers from the European Group for the Study of Deviance and Social Control.* NY: Wiley, 1975.

Blum, Richard H. "Police Personnel Selection in Europe." *Police.* 5:4 (March-April, 1961), pp. 39-41, 71; 5:5 (May-June, 1961), pp. 32-34; 5:6 (July-August, 1961), pp. 72-74.

Bramshill Police College, 10th Senior Command Course. *Exercise Europa.* Hampshire, England: Branshill Police College, 1973.

Branshill Police College, 11th Senior Command Course. *A Study of Police Recruitment and Training in Europe.* Hampshire, England: Bramshill Police College, 1974.

Bramshill Police College, 11th Senior Command Course. *A Study of Police Order in Six EEC Countries.* Hampshire, England: Bramshill Police College, 1974.

Bramshill Police College, 12th Senior Command Course. *Exercise "Europa" — Crime in Europe.* Hampshire, England: Bramshill Police College, 1975.

Christiansen, Karl. *The Postwar Trend in Crime in Selected European Countries. Consultant Paper.* Washington DC: GPO, 1967.

Christiansen, Karl O., ed. *Scandinavian Studies in Criminology.* (vol. 1), South Hackensack, NJ: Rothman, 1965.

Christie, Nils, ed. *Scandinavian Studies in Criminology.* (vol. 3), Boston: Universitet, 1971.

Council of Europe. *Compensation for Victims of Crime.* Strasbourg, France: Council of Europe, 1975.
Available in Microfiche from NCJRS.

Council of Europe European Committee on Crime Problems. *Collected Studies in Criminological Research.* (vol. 11), *Violence in Society.* Strasbourg, France: Council of Europe, 1974.
Available in Microfiche from NCJRS.

Council of Europe European Committee on Crime Problems. *Penal Aspects of Drug Abuse.* Strasbourg, France: Council of Europe, 1974.
Available in Microfiche from NCJRS.

Council of Europe European Committee on Crime Problems. *Practical Organization of Measures for the Supervision and After-Care of Conditionally Sentenced or Conditionally Released Offenders.* Strasbourg, France: Council of Europe, 1970.

Council of Europe European Committee on Crime Problems. *Sentencing.* Strasbourg, France: Council of Europe, 1974.

Crime and Delinquency Research in Selected European Countries. Washington, DC: GPO, 1971.
Brief review of European research from 1963 to 1970, describing the current state of research and the topics upon which it is focused.

Esmein, Adhemar. *History of Continental Criminal Procedure with Special Reference to France.* South Hackensack, NJ: Rothman, 1969. (repr. of 1913 ed.).

European Convention on Mutual Assistance in Criminal Matters. NY: Manhattan, 1971.
Treaty adopted by the member states of the Council of Europe which assures cooperation in criminal prosecution and evidence procurement.

Explanatory Report on the European Convention on Extradition. NY: Manhattan, 1969.

Explanatory Report on the European Convention on the International Validity of Criminal Judgments. NY: Manhattan, 1970.

Explanatory Report on the European Convention on Mutual Assistance in Criminal Matters. NY: Manhattan, 1969.

Fosdick, Raymond B. *European Police Systems.* Montclair, NJ: Patterson Smith, 1969. (repr. of 1915 ed.).

Glueck, Sheldon. *Continental Police Practice in the Formative Years — A Report Made in 1926 to Colonel Arthur Woods, Then Police Commissioner of the City of New York.* Springfield, IL: C.C. Thomas, 1974.
Report on 12 European municipal police systems, especially in German-speaking countries, emphasizing the professionalism of their methods and personnel.

Goerner, Edward A., ed. *Constitutions of Europe.* Chicago: Regnery, 1966.

Gollomb, Joseph. *Scotland Yard.* London: Hutchinson, 1926.
Discusses police systems of London, Paris, Berlin, and Vienna.

Kutchinsky, Berl. "Law and Education: Some Aspects of Scandinavian Studies into the General Sense of Justice." *ACTA Sociologicac.* 10:1-2. (1966), pp. 21-41.

Marchal, A. "Cooperation of Civilian and Military Police in Belgian and Swiss Law." *Military Law and Law War Review.* 11:1 (1972), pp. 171-179.

Nepote, Jean. 'European Police Co-Operation in Criminal Matters." *International Criminal Police Review* (May, 1970), pp. 142-147.

Neumann, Robert G. *European and Comparative Government.* NY: McGraw-Hill, 1960.

Scacciavillano, M. "Arrests Made on Strength of Telex Message between Rome and Cologne." *International Criminal Police Review* (January, 1968), pp. 24-25.

Sheehan, Albert V. *Criminal Procedure in Scotland and France — A Comparative Study, with Particular Emphasis on the Role of the Public Prosecutor.* Edinburgh: Her Majesty's Stationery Office, 1975.

Statistics of Police Strengths in Europe. Paris: INTERPOL, 1975.

Tegel, Heinrich F. "New Problems for the Police within the European Art Business." *Journal of Criminal Law, Criminology and Police Science.* 53:1 (March-May, 1962).

Turner, Carl C. "School Safety Patrols of Europe." *The Police Chief.* 29:8 (August, 1962).

United Nations Social Defence Research Institute. *Criminological Research and Decision Making — Studies on the Influence of Criminological Research on Criminal Policy in the Netherlands and Finland.* Rome: United Nations Social Defence Research Institute, 1974.

U.S. Department of Health, Education, and Welfare National Institute of Mental Health. *Crime and Delinquency Research in Selected European Countries.* Washington DC: GPO, 1971.
Brief review of European research from 1963 to 1970, describing the current state of research and the topics upon which it is focused.

Viteles, Morris S. "Psychological Methods in the Selection of Policemen in Europe." *Annals* (November, 1929), pp. 160-165.

Middle East — General

Anderson, James and Norman Dalrymple. *Islamic Law in the Modern World.* NY: New York University Press, 1959.

Liebesny, Herbert J. *The Law of the Near and Middle East:*

Readings, Cases and Materials. Syracuse, NY: State University of New York Press, 1975.

U.S. Department of the Army. *Area Handbook: Peripheral States of Arabian Peninsula.* Washington, DC: GPO, 1971.

Pacific — General

Alkire, William H. *Lomatrek Atoll and Inter-Island Socioeconomic Ties.* Carbondale, IL: University of Illinois Press, 1965.

Epstein, A.L. *Contention and Dispute: Aspects of Law and Social Control in Melanisia.* Beaverton, OR: International School Book Service, 1974.

Hogbin, H. Ian. *Law and Order in Polynesia.* NY: Cooper Square, 1973.

Trust Territory of the Pacific Islands: 1969 Annual Report to the Secretary of the Interior. Washington, DC: GPO, 1970.

Western Hemisphere — General

Clagett, Helen L. *The Administration of Justice in Latin America.* NY: Oceana, 1952.

Greaves, W.E., ed. *Reports of Cases in the Court of Appeal Windward Islands 1866-1904.* Dobbs Ferry, NY: Oceana, 1963.

Lindquist, John A. *Philosophy and Practices of Policing on Five Republics.* Ann Arbor, MI: University Microfilms, 1971.

Sherwood, D.J. "Police Cooperation on the Niagara Frontier." *RCMP Gazette.* 29:2 (1967), pp. 20-22.

Siches, Luis R. et al. *Latin American Legal Philosophy.* NY: Johnson, 1948.

Williams, Gerald. "Cooperation on the Border." *FBI Law Enforcement Bulletin* (October, 1968).
Alaska-Canada police cooperative efforts.

Wolff, P.O. *Marijuana in Latin America — The Threat It Constitutes.* Washington, DC: Linacre, 1949.

AFGHANISTAN

Smith, Harvey Henry. *Area Handbook for Afghanistan.* Washington, DC: GPO, 1969.

ALBANIA

DeRenzy-Martin, E.C. "Albanian Gendarmerie." *Near East.* 44 (March 28, 1935).

ALGERIA

"Crime in Algeria." *International Criminal Police Review* (December, 1969), pp. 284-286.

ANDORRA

Cramer, James. "Police Forces of the World: Andorra." *Police Review (GB),* 67 (September 4, 1959).

ANTIGUA

Antigua Royal Police Force Office of the Chief of Police. *Antigua — Royal Police Force — Annual Report on the Organization and Administration, 1972.* Washington, DC: NCJRS, (Microfiche), 1973.
A summary of departmental activities including data on personnel, organization, training, criminal investigation, traffic and other police areas.

ARGENTINA

General

Fitzgibbon, R.H. *Argentina: A Chronology and Fact Book.* Dobbs Ferry, NY: Oceana, 1973.

U.S. Department of the Army. *Area Handbook: Argentina.* Washington, DC: GPO, 1969-1974.

Crime

DeFleur, Lois B. *Delinquency in Argentina.* Pullman: Washington State University Press, 1970.

Criminal Law

Amadeo, Santos Primo. *Argentine Constitutional Law: The Judicial Function in the Maintenance of the Federal System and the Preservation of Individual Rights.* NY: Columbia University Press, 1943.

Police History

Almandos, Luis Reyna. "National Registry of Identification in the Argentine Republic." *Journal of Criminal Law and Criminology.* XXIV (1933-34).

Police

Carrasco, Felix. "Discipline in the Argentine Federal Police." *International Criminal Police Review* (August-September, 1969), pp. 198-201.

Cramer, James. "Police Forces of the World: Argentina." *Police Review (GB),* 68 (January 15, 1960).

de Pascale, Vincent. "Prison Interlude." *Inter-American.* 4:12 (March, 1945).

Dorrego, J.H. "Fingerprinting Mummified Bodies." *International Criminal Police Review* (May, 1969), pp. 134-137.

Gonzales, Alberto J. "The Argentinian Federal Police." *International Criminal Police Review* (May, 1963), pp. 146-149.

Rodriguez, A.E. "The Federal Police Museum in Argentina." *International Criminal Police Review* (February, 1966), pp. 54-56.

"The Telecommunications Systems of the Argentine Federal Police." *International Criminal Police Review.* (August-September, 1963), pp. 194-201.

AUSTRALIA

General

Sawer, Geoffrey. *Ombudsmen.* Victoria, Australia: Melbourne University Press, 1964.
Outlines ombudsmen activities in Australia and New Zealand. Good short overview.

U.S. Department of the Army. *Area Handbook: Australia.* Washington, DC: GPO, 1974.

Crime

Australia Parliament. *Drug Trafficking and Drug Abuse, Report From the Senate Select Committee.* Canberra: Australia Government Publication Service, 1971.

Barber, R. "An Investigation into Rape and Attempted Rape Cases in Queensland." *Australian New Zealand Journal of Criminology,* 6:4 (1973), pp. 214-230.

Lunden, Walter A. "Crime Down Under: In Tasmania, 1934-56." *Police.* 4:3 (January-February, 1960), pp. 6-10.

O'Sullivan, M. *Cameos of Crime.* Sydney, Australia: Jackson and O'Sullivan, 1935.

Vinson, T. "Homicides and Serious Assaults in New South Wales." *Anglo-American Law Review.* 3:1 (1974), pp. 29-36.

Wilson, Paul R. and Jill W. Brown. *Crime and the Community.* St. Lucia, Queensland, Australia: University of Queensland Press, 1973.

Criminal Law

Barry, John Vincent and G.W. Paton. *An Introduction to the Criminal Law in Australia.* London: Macmillan, 1948.

Cowen, Z. *Federal Jurisdiction in Australia.* NY: Oxford University Press, 1959.

Police History

Abbott, E.S. *Everybody's Friend: The Inspiring Career of Kate Cooks, M.B.E.* Adelaide: Hassell, 1939.

"Australian Mounted Police on Camels." *Illustrated London News* (April 23, 1949), pp. 540-541.

Bateson, Henry. "The Birth and Early History of the New South Wales Police Force." *Police Journal (GB),* 7: (January, 1934), pp. 112-116.

Burrows, W. *Adventures of a Mounted Trooper in the Australian Constabulary.* London: Routledge, Warne and Routledge, 1859.

Castieau, J.B. *The Reminiscences of Detective-Inspector Christie.* Melbourne: Robertson, [n.d.].

Centenary History of the Queensland Police Force: 1864-1963. Brisbane: Queensland Police Force, 1964.

Downer, S. *Patrol Indefinite: The Northern Territory Police.* Sydney: Angus and Robertson, 1963.

Dressler, Hofret Oscar. "The Australian Police." *Police Journal (GB),* II (July, 1929), pp. 437-452.

Gibson, N. *Victorian Police Scandals Exposed.* Melbourne: [n.n.], 1933.

Graves, H.E. *Who Rides? Events in the Life of a West Australian Police Officer.* London: Lovat Dickison, 1937.

Hare, F.A. *Last of the Bushrangers: An Account of the Capture of the Kelly Gang.* London: Hurst and Blackett, 1892.

Haydon, A.L. *Trooper Police of Australia: A Record of Mounted Police Work in the Commonwealth from the Earliest Days of Settlement to the Present Time.* London: Andrew Melrose, 1911.

Hoban, L.E. *A Centenary History of the New South Wales Police Force, 1862-1962.* Sydney: Police Department Centenary Committee, 1962.

Idriess, Ion L. *Man Tracks with the Mounted Police in Australian Wilds.* (6th ed.), Sydney: Angus and Robertson, 1935.

Idriess, I.L. *Outlaws of the Leopolds.* Sydney: Angus and Robertson, 1952.

Idriess, I.L. *Over the Range: Sunshine and Shadow in the Kimberlays.* (8th ed.), Sydney: Angus and Robertson, 1945.

Joy, William and Tom Prior. *The Bushrangers.* London: Miller, 1971.

Kennedy, E.B. *The Black Police of Queensland: Remininiscences of Official Work and Personal Adventures in the Early Days of the Colony.* London: John Murray, 1902.

Le Lievre, Charles. *Memories of an Old Police Officer.* Adelaide: W.K. Thomas, 1925.

Mitchell, James. "New South Wales Police: A Retrospect." *Police Journal (GB),* 2 (July, 1929), pp. 477-484.

New South Wales. *Royal Commission on Allegations Against the Police in Connection with the Suppression of Illicit Betting.* Sydney: Government Printer, 1936.

O'Halloran, M. *Western Australian Police Manual: A Catechism of the Duties of Police Constables and Principles of Law Applicable Thereto . . . 1914.* Perth: Law Book Company of Western Australia, 1914.

Outline and History of the Victoria Police Force. (rev. ed.), Melbourne: Public Relations Division, Victoria Constabulary, 1967.

Paul, W. *Victorian Police Manual for the Use of Officers and Members of the Victorian Police Force.* Melbourne: Government Printer, 1924.

Queensland Police Department Centenary Celebrations Brochure Committee. *A Centenary History of the Queensland Police Force, 1864-1963.* Brisbane: Government Printer, 1964.

Richards, E. *The History of the Australian Capitol Territory Police Force.* A paper delivered to the Canberra and District Historical Society on June 2, 1959.

Sadler, J. *Recollections of a Victorian Police Officer.* Melbourne: George Robertson, 1913.

Schmaal, E.J. "When Policemen Were Firemen." *Australian Police Journal.* (April, 1976), pp. 99-108.

Skinner, L.E. *Police of the Pastorial Frontier: Native Police, 1845-1859.* Lawrence, MA: University of Queensland Press, 1976.

Police

Barlow, V.M. and Jay Topley. "The Queensland Police Academy — Its Educational Planning and Rationale." *Australian Police Journal.* 26:1 (January, 1972), pp. 24-35.

Canacott, G.W. "The Human Factor in Police Communications." *International Criminal Police Review* (August-September, 1968), pp. 194-196.

Carick, Noel. "The Detective School of Melbourne, Australia." *Law and Order.* 13:12 (December, 1965), pp. 80-81.

Chappell, Duncan. *The Police and the Public in Australia and New Zealand.* St. Lucia: University of Queensland Press, 1969.

Chappell, Duncan and Paul Wilson. "Australian Attitudes to the Police: A Pilot Study." *British Journal of Criminology.* 8:4 (October, 1968), pp. 424-431.

Chappell, Duncan and Paul R. Wilson. "Police in Australia." *Current Affairs Bulletin.* (Australia), 46:7 (August, 1970), pp. 99-111.

Cramer, James. "Police Forces of the World: Canberra." *Police Review (GB),* 66 (December 12, 1958).

Downer, Sidney. *Patrol Indefinite: The Northern Territory Police Force.* Sydney: Angus and Robertson, 1963.

Duncan, A.M. *Report on All Aspects of Crime Investigation by the Criminal Investigation Branch of the Tasmanian Police Department.* Hobart: Government Printer, 1955.

Fraser, Gordon. "Australian International Airline Security." *Police.* 8:1 (September-October, 1963), pp. 30-32.

Hall, Victor C. *Outback Policeman.* London: Hale, 1971.

"Inside Story of the New South Wales Police." *Police Review (GB),* (July 16, 1976), pp. 903-904.

Kelly, Vince. *The Bogeyman: The Exploits of Sergeant C.J. Chuck, Australia's Most Unpopular Cop.* Sydney: Angus and Robertson, 1956.

Kelley, Vince. *The Shadow: The Amazing Exploits of Frank Fahy.* Sidney: Angus an Robertson, 1955.

Maddison, J.C. "Civil Liberties and the Police." *Australian Journal of Forensic Science.* 6:4 (1974), pp. 254-260.

Maxwell, C.B. *The Cold Nose of the Law.* Sydney: Angus and Robertson, 1948.

Mendelsohn, Oscar. *Liars and Letters Anonymous.* Melbourne: Lansdowne Press, 1961.
Questioned documents and forgery cases.

Mishkin, Barry D. "Policing Down Under." *Garda Review* (April, 1976), pp. 12-13, 15.

New South Wales. *Police Department: Choosing a Career: Opportunities in the Police Force of New South Wales.* Sydney: Police Department, 1962.

O'Brian, G.M. *The Australian Police Forces.* NY: Oxford University Press, 1960.

Police Forces in Australia. Canberra: United Kingdom High Commissioner's Office, 1957.

Poole, D. *Questions Which Have Been Asked in the Examinations Over the Past Nine Years Together with the Answers: For Sergeants 3rd Class, Sergeants 1st Class and Inspectors.* (4th ed.), Sydney: Warringah Secretarial Service, 1960.

Rogers, J.H. "Officer Training in the Australian and New Zealand Forces." *Police Journal (GB),* 39:5 (1966).

South Australia. *Crown Solicitor: Report of the Matter of Edwin Ross Ives and Others; Criticism of the Police [By] J.R. Kearnan, Crown Solicitor.* Adelaide: Government Printer, 1963.

South Australia. *Parliament: Report on the Police Training Academy, Fort Largs.* Adelaide: Government Printer, 1964.

St. Johnston, Eric. *A Report on the Victoria Police Force Following an Inspection by Col. Sir Eric St. Johnston.* Melbourne: Government Printer, 1971.

Swanton, B. and P.R. Wilson. "Police Occupational Standing — Prestige and Benefits." *Australian New Zealand Journal of Criminology.* 7:2 (1974), pp. 95-98.

Unstead, R.J. and W.F. Henderson. *Police in Australia.* London: A. and C. Black, 1973.

Wilson, P.R. "Police-Ethnic Relations in Australia." *New Community.* 3:3 (1974), pp. 220-226.

Wilson, Paul R. and John S. Western. *The Policeman's Position Today and Tomorrow: An Examination of the Victoria Police Force.* St. Lucia: University of Queensland Press, 1972.

Wilson, Roy A. "Police Administration in Australia." *Police.* 15:5 (May-June, 1971), pp. 44-50.

AUSTRIA

Criminal Law

Grassberger, Roland and Helga Nowotny. *The Austrian Penal Code.* South Hackensack, NJ: Rothman, 1966.

Police History

Gleispach, W. "Twenty-Five Years of Criminology in Austria." *Journal of Criminal Law and Criminology.* XXIV (1933-1934).

Grassberger, Roland. "University Institute of the Criminologic Sciences and Criminalistics in Vienna." *Journal of Criminal Law and Criminology.* XXIII (1932-1933).

Police

"Celebrating the Sixtieth Birthday of Vienna's Police Dog Squad." *London News.* 240 (February 24, 1962).

Cramer, James. "Police Forces of the World: Vienna." *Police Review (GB)* 66 (December 26, 1958).

Valant, Friedrich. "Training the Public in Road Safety." *International Criminal Police Review* (November, 1967), pp. 264-266.

BELGIUM

General

U.S. Department of the Army. *Area Handbook: Belgium.* Washington, DC: GPO, 1974.

Crime

Sohier, Jean. "Criminology and Anthropology." *International Criminal Police Review* (March, 1970), pp. 97-101.

Sohier, Jean. "A Rather Ordinary Crime: Shoplifting." *International Criminal Police Review* (June-July, 1969), pp. 161-166.

Police History

De Rechter, Gustave. "The School of Criminology and Scientific Police of Belgium." *Annals* (November, 1929), pp. 193-198.

Keffer, A. and F.E. Louwage. "The Belgian Police." *Police Journal.* I (July, 1928).

Police

Ashton, W.G. et al. *Policing Brussels.* Washington, DC: NCJRS, 1973.

Cornil, P. "Criminal Law and Road Traffic." *International Criminal Police Review* (February, 1968), pp. 30-35.

Cramer, James. "City Police of the World: Brussels." *Police Review (GB),* 66 (August 29, 1958).

Lechat, Rene. "The Criminal Police Training Museum." *International Criminal Police Review.* 58 (May, 1962), pp. 154-164.
Describes the police training museum used by the Belgian Police.

Louis, A. "Behind the Scenes." *International Criminal Police Review* (March, 1961), pp. 72-80; (April, 1961), pp. 105-110.
Vice activities in Belgium.

Louwage, F.E. "Belgium Police Official's Impressions from His Travels in the U.S.A." *Journal of Criminal Law, Criminology and Police Science.* 42 (1951-1952).

BELIZE (BRITISH HONDURAS)

Cramer, James. "Police Forces of the World: British Honduras." *Police Review (GB),* 66 (December 5, 1958).

BERMUDA

Police

Annual Report of the Bermuda Police Force. Submitted by the Commissioner of Police, annual.

Rose, Arthur. "Bermuda and Its Police." *Police College Magazine* (Spring, 1962), pp. 151-156.

Sedgwick, A.W. "The Criminal Code of Bermuda." *Bermuda Police Magazine* (Spring, 1966).

Sheehan, Thomas M. "Law Enforcement and Its Administration in Bermuda." *Police.* 10:3 (January-February, 1966), pp. 74-77.

BOLIVIA

General

U.S. Department of the Army. *Area Handbook: Bolivia.* Washington, DC: GPO, 1963.

Crime

Avalos Jibaja, Carlos. "Consultative Group on Coca Leaf Problems." *Bulletin of Narcotics.* 16:3 (1964).

"Bolivia Cocaine: Illicit Manufacture and Traffic." *International Criminal Police Review* (April, 1969), pp. 97-102.

Fernandez, Nicanor T. *Bolivian Coca — Marvelous Properties and Qualities of Coca. Opinions of Renowned Physicians and Naturalists.* La Paz, Bolivia: [n.n.], 1932.

BRAZIL

General

Fitzgibbon, R.H. *Brazil: A Chronology and Fact Book.* Dobbs Ferry, NY: Oceana, 1973.

U.S. Department of the Army. *Area Handbook: Brazil.* Washington, DC: GPO, 1964, 1971.

Crime

Bergman, E.W. *The Problems of Narcotic and Drug Addiction in Rio Grande Do Sul.* Report of State Bureau of Education and Prevention of the Problem of Addiction, 1965.

De Farias, Cordieiro. "Use of Maconha *(Cannabis sativa, L.)* in Brazil." *U.N. Bulletin on Narcotics.* 7:2 (May-August, 1955), pp. 5-19.

Police

David, J. and J. Amoroso Netto. "Chinese Who Disappeared in Brazil." *International Criminal Police Review* (November, 1959).

Lapagesse, E. "Explosive Compounds and Ballistic Powders for Use in Firearms." *International Criminal Police Review.* (May, 1970), pp. 158-165; (June-July, 1970), pp. 176-183.

Lapagesse, E. "The Police Officer: Selection and Professional Training." *International Criminal Police Review* (February, 1967), pp. 48-54.

Raposo Filho, Amerino. "A Major Reform of the Brazilian Police." *International Criminal Police Review* (August-September, 1966), pp. 186-196.

Souza, J.G. "Brazil, 'The Making of a Policeman': Santa Catarins School of Police." *International Police Academy Review.* 7 (July, 1971), pp. 1-4.

"Velazcos Gestapo." *Inter-American.* 5 (January, 1946), pp. 6-7.

BRITISH VIRGIN ISLANDS

Graves, Brian E. "Law Enforcement on Tropical Islands." *FBI Law Enforcement Bulletin.* 41:1 (January, 1972), pp. 3-6, 30.
The Royal Virgin Islands' Police Force.

BULGARIA

Dolaptchieff, N. "Criminal Law in Bulgaria." *Journal of Criminal Law and Criminology.* XXIII (1932-1933).

BURMA

General

U.S. Department of the Army. *Area Handbook for Burma.* Washington, DC: GPO, 1968.
Covers some aspects of law enforcement.

Crime

Mabileau, Jean. "Opium in the World: Reflections on a Mission in Burma." *International Criminal Police Review* (November, 1966), pp. 250-261.

Criminal Law

The Dangerous Drug Act and Rules Thereunder. Rangoon: Central Press, 1961.

The Opium Manual, Containing the Opium Act and the Rules and Directions Thereunder in Force in Burma. Rangoon: Central Press, 1964.

Police History

Young, J.W. "Burma Military Police." *Police Journal (GB),* 1 (July, 1928), pp. 374-391.

CAMEROON

"Chronicles of Africa: The Federal Police of the Cameroon." *Revue Moderne de la Police* (July-August, 1964), pp. 47-59.

CANADA

General

Hill, B. *Canada, a Chronology and Fact Book.* Dobbs Ferry, NY: Oceana, 1973.

Crime

The Canadian Corrections Association. *Indians and the Law. A Survey Prepared for the Hon. Arthur Laing, Department of Indian Affairs and Northern Development.* Ottawa: The Canadian Welfare Council, 1967.

Commission of Enquiry into the Administration of Justice on Criminal and Penal Matters in Quebec. *Crime, Justice and Society. (vol. 3). Crime in Quebec, Tome 2 — The Peaks of Quebec Criminality.* Washington, DC: NCJRS, (Microfiche) (n.d.].
Indicates the volume and nature of Canadian and Quebec crime and identifies and discusses the authors of crimes.

Commission of Enquiry into the Administration of Justice on Criminal and Penal Matters in Quebec. *Crime, Justice and Society. (vol. 3). Crime in Quebec, Tome 1 — Trends in Quebec Criminality.* Washington, DC: NCJRS, (Microfiche) [n.d.].
Analyzes fraudulent bankruptcy, armed robbery, and automobile thefts to discover weaknesses in legislation and criminal justice functioning relative to these crimes and offers recommendations.

Gromley, Shiela. *Drugs and the Canadian Scene.* Toronto: Pargurian Press, 1970.

McDonald, L. "Crime and Punishment in Canada: A Statistical Test of the 'Conventional Wisdom.'" *Canadian Review of Sociology and Anthropology.* 6 (November, 1969), pp. 212-236.

McGrath, W.T. *Crime and Its Treatment in Canada.* NY: Macmillan, 1971.
A collection of essays on the criminal justice system of Canada.

Normandeau, Andre. "The Measurement of Delinquency in Montreal." *Journal of Criminal Law, Criminology and Police Science.* 57:2 (June, 1966), pp. 172-177.

Seventy-Ninth Annual Report of Statistics of Criminal and Other Offences: For the Period January 1, 1954, to December 31, 1954. Canada: Canada Dominion Bureau of Statistics, 1956.

Silverman, Robert A. and James J. Teevon, eds. *Crime in Canadian Society.* Toronto: Butterworth, 1975.

Whitaker, Reginald. *Drugs and the Law, The Canadian Scene.* Toronto: Methuen, 1969.

Criminal Law

Law Reform Commission of Canada. *Law Reform Commission of Canada — Restitution and Compensation — Fines — Working Papers.* Ottawa: Information Canada, 1974.

Lefolii, Ken. "The Holy War to Destroy Bill 99." *Maclean's.* 77 (July 4, 1964), pp. 11-13.

Lyon, J. Noel and Ronald G. Atkey, eds. *Canadian Constitutional Law in a Modern Prospective.* Toronto: University of Toronto Press, 1970.

Police History

Artigue, J.D. *Six Years in the Canadian Northwest.* Toronto: Hunter, Rose, 1882.

Bruce, D. "Royal Canadian Mounted Police, 1873-1973." *Police World* (Autumn, 1973), pp. 10-13.

Cameron, W.B. *Blood Red the Sun.* Calgary, Alberta: Kenway, 1950.

Career in Scarlet with the Royal Canadian Mounted Police. Ottawa: RCMP, 1957.

"Century in Scarlet, 1873-1973." *Leader-Post* (May 22, 1973), Regina, Saskatchewan RCMP centennial edition.

Chambers, E.J. *The Royal North-West Mounted Police.* Montreal: Mortimer Press, 1906.

Conklin, J.J. "Forty-Four Years with Mounties: No Romance, Just Plain Hard Work." *State Trooper.* XI:5 (January, 1930).

Douthwaite, L. Charles. *Royal Canadian Mounted Police.* London: Blackie, 1939.

Fetherstonhaugh, R.C. *The Royal Canadian Mounted Police.* NY: Garden City Publishing, 1940.

Grierson, A.I. *The Mounties.* Toronto: Ryerson Press, 1947.

Hamilton, C.F. "Royal Canadian Mounted Police." *Police Journal (GB),* (October, 1928), pp. 641-656.

Harvison, C.W. *The Horsemen.* Toronto: Macmillan, 1967.

Higgitt, William L. "Serving Canada for 100 Years." *FBI Law Enforcement Bulletin*. 42:9 (September, 1973), pp. 2-7, 11.

Horrall, S.W. *Pictorial History of the Royal Canadian Mounted Police*. NY: McGraw-Hill, 1973.

Influence of the Royal Canadian Mounted Police in the Building of Canada. Ottawa: Royal Canadian Mounted Police, 1964.

Kemp, Vernon A.M. *Scarlet and Stetson: The Royal North-West Mounted Police on the Prairies*. Toronto: Ryerson Press, 1964.

Law and Order in Canadian Democracy: Crime and Police Work in Canada. (rev. ed.), Ottawa: RCMP, 1952.

Long, H.G. *Fort Macleod: The Story of the North-West Mounted Police*. Alberta: MacLeod Historical Association, 1958.

Longstreth, T. Morris. *The Scarlet Force: The Making of the Mounted Police*. Toronto: Macmillan, 1953.

Longstreth, T. Morris. *The Silent Force (R.C.M.P.)*. NY: Century, 1927.

Longstreth, T.M. "Some Geographical Difficulties of the R.C.M.P." *Police Journal (GB)*, (1929), pp. 37-50.

MacBeth, R.G. *Policing the Plains: Being the Real-Life Record of the Famous Royal North-West Mounted Police*. London: Hodder and Stoughton, 1921.

MacBrien, James. "A Brief History of Canada's 'Mounties'." *Police Journal (NY)*, 22:8 (October, 1936).

MacBrien, James. "The History and Work of the Royal Canadian Mounted Police." *International Association of Chiefs of Police Yearbook*. (1936/1937), pp. 20-31.

Murray, H.J. "Municipal Police in Canada." *Journal of Criminal Law, Criminology and Police Science*. 25 (November, 1934).

Ontario Constabulary — 60th Anniversary, 1909-1969. Ontario: Ontario Provincial Police, 1969.

Royal Canadian Mounted Police Centennial, 1873-1973. Ottawa: RCMP, 1973.

Sage, Walter N. "The North-West Mounted Police and British Columbia." *Pacific Historical Review*. XVIII:3 (August, 1949), pp. 345-361.

Steele, H. *Policing the Arctic*. Toronto: Ryerson Press, 1936.

"Story of the Royal Canadian Mounted Police." *Fingerprint Identification Magazine*. 55:2 (1973), pp. 10-14.

Turner, John Peter. *The Northwest Mounted Police, 1873-1893*. (2 vols.), Ottawa: Kings Printer, 1950.

Police

"An Awakening Shot?" *Newsweek*. 46:44 (December 26, 1955).

Canada Solicitor General. *Canada — Solicitor General — Annual Report, 1973-74*. Ottawa: Information Canada, 1975.

This annual report is concerned with the duties and accomplishments of the Secretariat, the Royal Canadian Mounted Police, the Canadian Penitentiary Service and the National Parole Board.

Cramer, James. "Police Forces of the World: Ottawa." *Police Review (GB)*, 67 (November 6, 1959).

Cramer, James. "Police Forces of the World: The Royal Canadian Mounted Police." *Police Review (GB)*, 66 (November 28, 1958).

"The Crime Problem in Canada: How the Mounties Handle It." *U.S. News and World Report*. 55 (July 29, 1963), pp. 66-68.

"Exit Under Fire." *Newsweek*. 46:44 (August 15, 1955).

Forrest, E.G. "There Are Strange Things Done — In the Midnight Sun." *RCMP Gazette*. 25:9 (September, 1963).

Gilbert, Jean-Paul. *The Montreal Police*. Unpub. Master's Thesis, University of Montreal, 1963.

Graham, H.H. "Ontario Provincial Police Activities." *Canadian Police Chief* (January, 1976), pp. 28-29.

Griffin, John I. "Canadian Police Statistics." *Police*. 3:2 (November-December, 1958), pp. 60-62.

Grube, G.M.A. "LeBel Report and Civil Liberties." *Canada Forum*. 23 (December, 1945), pp. 208-212.

"Headquarters' Scandal." *Newsweek*. 46:45 (July 11, 1955).

"Jump and Throttle." *Newsweek*. 58:57 (November 13, 1961).

Kelly, N. *The Men of the Mounted*. Toronto: J.M. Dent, 1949.

Kelly, William and Nora Kelly. *Policing in Canada*. Toronto: Macmillan of Canada, 1976.

Kemp, Vernon A.A. *Scarlet and Stetson: The Royal North-West Mounted Police on the Prairies*. Toronto: Ryerson, 1964.

Kemp, Vernon A.M. *Without Fear, Favor or Affection: Thirty-Five Years with the Royal Canadian Mounted Police*. NY: Longmans, Green, 1958.

Linkletter, J.A. "Mounties without Mounts." *Popular Mechanics* 117: (March, 1962), pp. 120-123.

McClellan, George B. "Royal Canadian Mounted Police." *The Police Yearbook*. Washington, DC: IACP, 1963.

McDonald, Margaret Josephine. *The Mounties: The Story of the Royal Canadian Mounted Police*. London: Oak Tree Press, 1967.

Manitoba Police Commission. *Manitoba — Police Commission — Annual Report, 2D. 1973*. Washington, DC: NCJRS, (Microfiche), 1974.

Mishkin, Barry D. "Redcoat Cops." *Garda Review* (May, 1976), pp. 21, 23, 31.

Nelson, Elmer K. "A New Approach to Graduate Training in Criminology at the University of British Columbia." *Journal of Criminal Law and Criminology*. 34:4 (November-December, 1953), pp. 433-437.

Neuberger, Richard Lewis. *Royal Canadian Mounted Police*. London: MacDonald (May, 1956).

"Ontario Police Act, 1947." *Canada Forum*. 27:28 (May, 1947).

Phillips, Alan. *The Living Legend. The Story of the RCMP*. Boston: Little, Brown, 1957.

Rethoret, H. *Fire Investigations.* Toronto: Recording and Statistical Corporation, 1945.

Rivett-Carnac, Charles. *Pursuit in the Wilderness.* Boston: Little, Brown, 1965.

Royal Canadian Mounted Police: Jurisdictional Organization. Ottawa: RCMP, 1954.

Royal Canadian Mounted Police. *Royal Canadian Mounted Police.* Ottawa: Edmond Cloutier, 1958.

Sheehan, Thomas M. "The Royal Canadian Mounted Police: An Administrative Outline." *Police.* 11:3 (1967).

Spettigue, D. *The Friendly Force.* Toronto: Longmans, Green, 1955.

Steele, Harwood. *RCMP: World Canadian Mounted Police.* NY: Grossman, 1968.

Stevenson, Edward H. "Training in the Royal Canadian Mounted Police." *Police Yearbook.* Washington, DC: IACP, 1962.

Task Force on Policing in Ontario. Ontario: Solicitor General, 1974.

Topping, C.W. "Can a National Police Force Serve a Municipality Effectively?" *Police.* 7 (November-December, 1962), pp. 6-10.
The policing by federal forces of the "wide-open spaces" and of selected municipalities in western Canada.

Van Norman, R.D. "Policing the Canadian North Land." *International Criminal Police Review* (October, 1961), pp. 232-238.

Willes, E.W. "Criminal Intelligence Service Canada." *Police Chief.* 38:9 (September, 1971), pp. 18-19.

Wright, Thomas B. "Making of a Mountie." *Law and Order* (May, 1967).

Young, Delbert A. *The Mounties.* Toronto: Hodder and Stroughton, 1968.

CHILE

Police

Cramer, James. "Police Forces of the World: Chile." *Police Review (GB),* 67 (September 18, 1959).

Fuentes, Carlos Rene. "Statistical Information." *International Criminal Police Review* (May, 1961), pp. 144-149.

CHINA — MAINLAND

General

Taire, Lucian. "The True Story of Red China." *U.S. News & World Report* (May, 1956).

Thomas, S.B. *Government and Administration in Communist China.* Westport, CT: Greenwood, 1974. (repr. of 1955 ed.).

U.S. Department of the Army. *Area Handbook: Communist China.* Washington, DC: GPO, 1967.

Waller, Derek J. *Government and Politics of Communist China.* Garden City, NY: Doubleday, 1971.

Criminal Law

Chen, Phillip. *Law and Justice: The Legal System in Communist China, 2400 B.C. to 1960 A.D.* Port Washington, NY: Dunellen, 1973.

Cohen, Jerome A., ed. *Criminal Process in the People's Republic of China, 1949-1963: An Introduction.* Cambridge: Harvard University Press, 1968.

Leng, Shao-Chuan. *Justice in Communist China: A Survey of the People's Judicial System of the Chinese Poeple's Republic.* Dobbs Ferry, NY: Oceana, 1967.

Police

Chu-Yi, Liu. "Chu Mao Tightened Their Rule by Slaughtering." *China in One Week.* (1953).

Deacon, Richard. *The Chinese Secret Service.* NY: Taplinger, 1974.
Author indicates that secret service methods are similar to police techniques.

"Outline of Chinese Communist Police System, Research of the Eight Reserve Police Officials Class, Taiwan Police Academy." *The Police and Peoples Gazette.* 12 (1953).

Watt, H.M. B. "Law and Order in People's Republic of China." *Justice of the Peace* (May 29, 1976), pp. 290-291.

Wei, Hen. *Courts and Police in Communist China.* Los Angeles: University of Southern California, 1952.

Wen, Bin Bin. "A Cross Section of How the Russian Secret Service Controlled the Chinese Police." *Democratic Line.* 12:12 (March, 1953).

Yee, Frank S.H. "Chinese Communist Police and Courts." *Journal of Criminal Law, Criminology and Police Science.* 48:1 (May-June, 1957), pp. 83-92.

CHINA (TAIWAN)

Crime

Kaser, David. *Book Pirating in Taiwan.* Philadelphia: University of Pennsylvania Press, 1969.

Criminal Law

Laws, Ordinances, Regulations and Rules Relating to the Judicial Administration of the Republic of China. NY: Pergamon, 1971.

Wang, Huai Ming. "Chinese and American Criminal Law: Some Comparisons." *Journal of Criminal Law, Criminology and Police Science.* 46:6 (March-April, 1956), pp. 796-832.

Police History

Chu, Kwang-shee. "The Chinese Central Police College." *Journal of Criminal Law and Criminology.* 36 (November-December, 1945), pp. 290-297.
Reviews extensively the central police college, its curriculum, facilities, and entrance requirements.

Gernet, Jacques. *Daily Life in China on the Eve of the Mongol Invasion, 1250-1276.* NY: Macmillan, 1962.
During the 13th century Hangchow had a highly developed police service. With over a million population the city was regularly patrolled. Groups of 5 soldiers were stationed 300 yards apart and they maintained the peace, kept the watch, enforced regulations and aided the fire service.

Liu, Wei-hsiang. *Police of Taiwan Under Japanese Occupation.* Taipei: Taiwan Provincial Police Administration, 1952.

"Trying to Purge the Manchukuo Police from all Impurities." *China Weekly Review.* 67 (February 24, 1934).

Yee, Frank S.H. "National Police Institute of China." *Journal of Criminal Law, Criminology.* 25 (January, 1935).

Police

Chen, Han-soon. *A Comparative Study of Police Systems of China and the United States.* Taipei: Police Friend's Journal, 1963.

Chu, Huan-shin. *Modern Police Work.* Taipei: Ta Pon Publisher, 1950.

Gee, Fa-hsian. *Theory and Practice of Using Police Weapons.* Taipei: Police Library, 1958.

Hus, Lee. *The Police Reconstruction in China.* Taipei: Police Library, 1955.

Hsu, Wei-shin. *Traffic Police.* Taipei: Police Library, 1960.

Hu, Fu-hsiang. *Police Dictionary.* Taipei: Police Library, 1951.

Huang, Kwan-wei. *Handbook of Police Service.* Taipei: Police Library, 1956.

Huang, K. J-T. *Questions and Answers on Taipei Police System of the Republic of China.* San Chung, Taiwan: Good Earth Press, 1973.
Organization, duties, and operations of the municipal police force and brief explanations of some of the laws and regulations they enforce.

Lee, Don-Ho. "Taiwan Police Progress." *Police Yearbook.* Washington, DC: IACP, 1956.

Leonard, V.A. "The Chinese Central Police College: A Unique Institution." *Police.* 16:11 (July, 1972), pp. 16-21.

Li, Chen-mao. *Problems Regarding Taiwan Police Personnel.* Taipei: Police Library, 1959.

Liang, Jun-lien. *Fire Police.* Taipei: Police Library, 1958.

Lo, Kivan. "Police in Free China." *Police Yearbook.* Washington, DC: IACP, 1956.

Mei, Ko-wang. *Police Work in War Areas.* Taipei: Ministry of Defense, 1959.

Mei, Ko-wang. *Tactics Used by Police Personnel.* Taipei: Ministry of Defense, 1959.

Mei, Ko-wang. "University Police Training in the Orient." *Police.* 5:1 (September-October, 1960), pp. 65-67.
Activities of Central Police College in Taipei.

Police Data of the Republic of China. Taipei: Ministry of Interior, 1960.

Sampson, Richard A., Jr. "The Police of the Republic of China." *Police Chief.* 28:9 (September, 1960).

Wang, Kou-pan. *Police Guide-Lines.* Taipei: Police Gazette, 1956.

Wang, Tai-Hsuing. "Police Progress in Free China." *Police Yearbook.* Washington, DC: IACP, 1957.

COLOMBIA

General

Weil, Thomas E. *Area Handbook for Colombia.* Washington, DC: GPO, 1970.

Crime

Kendall, S. "Street Kids of Bogota." *New Society.* 31 (1975), pp. 117-118.

Criminal Law

Columbia Penal Code. South Hackensack, NJ: Rothman, 1967.

Police History

Munoz, Humberto O. "National Police of Colombia, A Historical Probe." *International Police Academy Review.* 2 (April, 1968), pp. 1-3, 16.

Police

Londono-Cardonas, F.A. "Present State of the National Police of Colombia." *Revue Moderne de la Police* (May-June, 1965), pp. 27-35.

Vargas, Gonzalo Gil. "The Filing of Palm-Prints — An Experiment Undertaken in Colombia." *International Criminal Police Review* (January, 1963), pp. 2-5.

COSTA RICA

U.S. Department of the Army. *Area Handbooks: Costa Rica.* Washington, DC: GPO, 1970.

CUBA

General

Wilkerson, Loree. *Fidel Castro's Political Programs from Reformation to "Marxism-Leninism."* Gainesville: University of Florida Press, 1965.

Criminal Law

International Commission of Jurists. *Cuba and the Rule of Law.* Geneva: International Comnission of Justice, 1962.

Police History

Basuino, Rosalie. "An Informal Review of the Havana Police." *Police Journal (NY),* 23 (September, 1937), pp. 5-6.

Castellanos, Israel. "Evolution of Criminology in Cuba." *Journal of Criminal Law and Criminology.* XXIV (1933-1934).

Police

"Death in Mariano." *Time.* 50:42 (September 29, 1947).

"Miramar Seige." *Newsweek.* 30:45 (September 29, 1947).

"Venganza." *Inter-American.* 5:8 (September, 1946).

CYPRUS

General

U.S. Department of the Army. *Area Handbooks: Cyprus.* Washington, DC: GPO, 1971.

Police History

Gallagher, A.E. "The Development of the Police in Cyprus." *Police Journal.* 1 (July, 1928), pp. 470-474.

Police

Chosaland, Andre. "The Cyprus Police." *International Criminal Police Chronicle.* 16 (January-February, 1968).

Chosaland, Andre. "A Young Police Force: The Cyprus Police." *Revue Moderne de la Police* (January-February, 1968), pp. 33-37.

Cyprus Police Association. *Annual Report and Journal, 1970.* Falconwood, Kent: CPA, 1971.

Cyprus Police Association. *Annual Report and Journal, 1971.* Falconwood, Kent: CPA, 1972.

Harris, Ioannou. *Training of Senior Police Officers.* Cyprus: Cyprus Police Training School, 1973.

CZECHOSLOVAKIA

Cramer, James. "Police Forces of the World: Prague." *Police Review (GB),* 67 (February 27, 1959).

DENMARK

Crime

Jersild, Jens. "The Abuse of Narcotics in Denmark." *International Criminal Police Review* (May, 1968), pp. 124-129.

Kutchinsky, Berl. *An Analysis of the Recent Decrease in Registered Sexual Offenses in Denmark.* Copenhagen: Institute of Criminal Science, May 12, 1971.

Kutchinsky, Berl. "Sex Crimes and Pornography in Copenhagen: A Survey of Attitudes." in *Technical Reports of the Commission on Obscenity and Pornography.* (vol. 7), Washington, DC: GPO, 1970.

LeMaire, Louis. "Danish Experiences Regarding the Castration of Sexual Offenders." *Journal of Criminal Law, Criminology and Police Science.* 47:3 (September/October, 1956), pp. 294-310.

Wolf, P. "A Contribution to the Topology of Crime in Denmark." in K.O. Christiansen et al., eds. *Scandinavian Studies in Criminology.* (vol. 1), London: Tavistock, 1965.

Wolf, P. "Crime and Social Class in Denmark." *British Journal of Criminology.* 13 (July, 1962), pp. 5-17.

Criminal Law

The Danish Criminal Code. Copenhagen: G.E.C. Gad, 1958.

Police History

Mensen, V.H. "The Danish Police Forces." *Police Journal.* I (April, 1928), pp. 240-255.

Police

Aaron, Thomas J. *The Control of Police Discretion: The Danish Experience.* Springfield, IL: C.C. Thomas, 1966.

Becker, Harold K. "The Danish Police System." *Police.* 16:1 (September, 1971), pp. 52-55.

Cramer, James. "City Police of the World: Copenhagen." *Police Review (GB),* 66 (September 19, 1958).

The Organization of the Copenhagen Police. Copenhagen: Information Department of the Copenhagen Police, 1955.

Penaat, Edward F. "The Police of Denmark." *Police Chief.* 26 (September, 1959), pp. 4-8.

"Police Federation Study Tour: The Danish State Police." *Police (GB),* (August, 1970), pp. 28-29.

Rud, Poul. "Denmark's National Alarm System." *Security Gazette (GB), 9:1 (1967).*

"Spotlight on the Danes." Guardian (Winter, 1973), pp. 44-49.

"Two Aspects of International Fraud — Sweden and Denmark." *International Criminal Police Review* (March, 1969), pp. 71-77.

DOMINICAN REPUBLIC

U.S. Department of the Army. *Area Handbook: Dominican Republic.* Washington, DC: GPO, 1966.

ECUADOR

U.S. Department of the Army. *Area Handbook: Equador.* Washington, DC: GPO, 1966.

EGYPT

General

U.S. Department of the Army. *Area Handbook: Arab Republic (Egypt).* Washington, DC: GPO, 1964-1970.

Crime

D'Erlanger, Harry. *The Last Plague of Egypt.* London: L. Dickson and Thompson, 1936.

El-Saaty, H. *Juvenile Delinquency in Egypt.* Unpub. Doctoral Dissertation, University of London, 1946.

Goldsmith, Margaret Leland. *The Trail of Opium, the Eleventh Plague.* London: R. Hale, 1939.

Criminal Law

Brinton, Jasper Y. *Mixed Courts of Egypt.* New Haven, CT: Yale University Press, 1968. (repr. of 1930 ed.).

Ziadeh, Farhat J. *Lawyers, the Rule of Law and Liberalism in Modern Egypt.* Stanford, CA: Hoover Institute Press, 1968.

Police

Bunyard, Robert S. "Land of the Pharoah — 1975." *Tally-Ho* (Autumn, 1975), pp. 9-13.

Cramer, James. "Police Forces of the World: Cairo." *Police Review (GB),* 67 (May 22, 1959).

Halawa, El'Sadik F. "Higher Studies for Police in the United Arab Republic." *Indian Police Journal.* 12:1 (1965).

Halawa, El'Sadik. "The Ministry of Interior Police College." *International Criminal Police Review* (August-September, 1967), pp. 208-211.

Halawa, El'Sadik. "Public Relations and Police Work." *International Criminal Police Review* (April, 1967), pp. 121-123.

Hamdy, Abd El Aziz. "Developing Countries and the International Institute of Police Technology." *International Criminal Police Review* (April, 1966).

Hamdy, Abd El Aziz. "Fingerprinting and Police Science in Egypt." *International Criminal Police Review* (August-September, 1960), pp. 210-214.

Hamdy, Abd El Aziz. "An Interesting Case of Arson." *International Criminal Police Review* (August-September, 1970), pp. 223-230.

Seth, Ronald. *Russell Pasha.* London: Kimber, 1966.

Sheppard, J.M. "Egypt's Tourist Police." *Travel.* 103 (March, 1955), pp. 25-26.

ETHIOPIA

Criminal Law

Ewing, William H., ed. *Consolidated Laws of Ethiopia: An Un-Official Compilation of National Laws in Effect as of September 10, 1969.* (2 vols.), NY: International Publications Service, 1973.

Police

Mersha, Wedajo. "The Imperial Ethiopian Police." *International Police Academy Review.* 4 (October, 1970), pp. 1-4.

FIJI

General

Belshaw, Cyril S. *Under the Ivi Tree: Society of Economic Growth in World Fiji.* Berkeley: University of California Press, 1965.

Police

Cramer, James. "Police Forces of the World: Fiji." *Police Review (GB),* 67 (April 24, 1959).

FINLAND

General

Blom, Raimo. "Public Opinion about the Functioning of Social Institutions." *ACTA Sociologica.* 13:2 (1970), pp. 110-126.

Crime

Johnson, Elmer H. "Finland's Penal Colonies: The Forebearant Model and Community-Based Corrections." *Journal of Criminal Justice.* (1973), pp. 327-338.

Verkko, Veli. *Homicides and Suicides in Finland and Their Dependence on National Character.* Copenhagen: GEC, 1951.

Wuorinen, John G. "Finland's Prohibition Experiment." *The Annals* (September, 1932), pp. 216-226.

Criminal Law

Mekela, Klaus. "Public Sense of Justice and Judicial Practice." *ACTA Sociologica.* 10:1 (January, 1966), pp. 42-67.

Police

Cramer, James. "Police Forces of the World: Helsinki." *Police Review. (GB),* 67 (January 30, 1959).

"Finnish Central Criminal Police." *International Criminal Police Review* (May, 1966), pp. 138-145.

Jousimaa, Kyosti S. "The Police and the Schools — Finland." *Police Chief.* XXXII:11 (November, 1965), pp. 40-41.

Kanno, Eila. "Police Day in Finland." *FBI Law Enforcement Bulletin.* 36:6 (June, 1967), pp. 2-5.

Mishkin, Barry D. "Police of Finland." *Garda Review* (February, 1976), pp. 18-19.

Penaat, Edward F. "The Police of Finland." *Police Chief.* 26 (August, 1959).

Risku, Artturi M. "Traffic Problems in Finland." *Law and Order.* 8:9 (1960).

FRANCE

General

Ridley, F. and J. Blondell. *Public Administration in France.* NY: Barnes and Noble, 1965.

Contains treatments of the major activities of government-police, courts, economic planning, public works, education, welfare, etc.

Crime

Alfonsi, Phillipe. *Satan's Needle, a True Story of Drug Addiction and Cure.* NY: Morrow, 1972.

Batigne, Jacques. *Assignment in Marseilles: The Sensational Case Histories of a French Judge.* NY: Hart, 1974.

"Beatnicks in Paris." *International Criminal Police Review* (November, 1968), pp. 246-253.

Cheymol, J. et al. "The Problem of Cannabis (Marijuana or Hashish)." *International Criminal Police Review* (November, 1970), pp. 275-285.

Goodman, Derick. *Villainy Unlimited, the Truth About the French Underworld Today.* London: Eleck Books, 1957.

Nepote, Jean. "The Development of Crime in France." *International Criminal Police Review.* (April, 1960), pp. 101-107; (May, 1960), pp. 142-509.

Criminal Law

David, R. *French Law — Its Structure, Sources, and Methodology.* Baton Rouge: Louisiana State University Press, 1972.

David, R. and H. DeVries. *French Legal System.* Dobbs Ferry, NY: Oceana, 1958.

French Code of Criminal Procedure. South Hackensack, NJ: Rothman, 1964.

French Penal Code. South Hackensack, NJ: Rothman, 1960.

Ingleton, Roy D. "French Criminal Procedure." *Police Review (GB),* (November 16, 1976), pp. 1496-1498, 1500, 1503.

Police History

Bamford, Paul W. "Procurement of Oarsmen for the French Galleys, 1660-1748." *The American Historical Review.* 65 (October, 1959), pp. 31-48.

Canler, Louis. *Autobiography of a French Detective from 1818 to 1858: Most Curious Revelations of the French Detective Police System.* Stanton, CA: Arnold, 1976.

Cobb, Richard C. *Police and the People: French Popular Protest, 1789-1820.* NY: Oxford University Press, 1970.

"Course for Police in Paris." *Journal of Criminal Law and Criminology.* V (1914-1915).

De Polnay, P. *Napoleon's Police.* London: W.H. Allen, 1970.

Du Parco, Georges. *Secrets of the French Police.* London: Cassell, 1933.

Faralico, R. *The French Police from Within.* London: Cassell, 1933.

Galtier-Boissiere, Jean. *Mysteries of the French Secret Police.* London: Paul, 1938.

Gayet, Jean. "The Expert Examination of Handwriting in France in the 17th Century." *International Criminal Police Review* (June-July, 1963), pp. 165-176.

Guitet-Vauquelin, Pierre. "French Police: Its Evolution from Its Source to the Present Day." *Police Journal (GB),* (1928), pp. 605-620.

Hodgetts, E.A. Brayloy. *Vidocq: A Master of Crime.* [n.p.]: Sedwyn and Blount, 1928.

Morain, A. *The Underworld of Paris: Secrets of the Sureté.* London: Jarrolds, 1928.

Payne, Howard C. "A Day's Work of the Press Police During the Second Empire in France." *Police.* 1:3 (January-February, 1957), pp. 19-22.

Payne, Howard C. "An Early Concept of the Modern Police State in France." *Journal of Criminal Law, Criminology and Police Science.* 43:3 (September-October, 1952).

Payne, Howard C. "The French Commissaire of Police in the Mid-Nineteenth Century." *Police.* 5:1 (September-October, 1960), pp. 34-37; 5:2 (November-December, 1960), pp. 21-23.

Payne, H.C. "Theory and Practice of Police During the Second Empire in France." *Modern History* 30: (March, 1958), pp. 14-23.

Ploscowe, Morris. "Administration of Criminal Justice in France." *Journal of Criminal Law and Criminology.* XXIV (1933-1934).

Real, P.F. *Indiscretions of a Prefect Police: Anecdotes of Napoleon and the Bourbons from the Papers of Count Real.* London: Cassell, 1929.

Rhodes, H. *Alphonse Bertillon, Father of Scientific Detection.* London: Harrap, 1956.

Rude, George F. *Crowd in the French Revolution.* NY: Oxford University Press, 1959.

Stead, Philip John. *Vidocq.* London: Stables Press, 1953.

Vidocq, Eugene F. *Memoirs of Vidocq: Principle Agent of the French Police Until 1827.* (2 vols.), NY: Arno, 1976.

Williams, T.C. "Napoleon's Chief of Police." *Police College Magazine* (September, 1952), pp. 212-216.

Police

"Beat System of Paris." *International Criminal Police Review* (October, 1973), pp. 248-258.

Berenyi, Ivan. "The Changing Profile of the French Police." *Police Review (GB),* (October 24, 1969), pp. 1-2.

"Bodies in the Seine." *New Statesman.* 62 (November 3, 1960).

Borniche, Roger. *Flic Story.* Garden City, NY: Doubleday, 1975.

Chapman, Brian. "The Prefecture of Police." *Journal of Criminal Law and Criminology.* 44:4 (November-December, 1953), pp. 505-521.

"A Comparison with France." *Police Review (GB),* (November 24, 1961).

Cramer, James. "City Police of the World: Paris." *Police Review (GB),* 66 (August 1, 1959).

Cramer, James. "Police Forces of the World: Gendarmerie Nationale." *Police Review (GB),* 68 (April 15, 1960).

Cramer, James. "Police Forces of the World: Sureté Nationale." *Police Review (GB),* 67 (September 25, 1959); (October 2, 1959).

Deparden, Captain. "Traffic Duties of the French Gendarmerie." International Criminal Police Review (August-September, 1967), pp. 195-201.

Edmond-Smith, Joyce. "Police Forces in France." *New Community.* 3:3 (Summer, 1974), pp. 227-232.

"Flic Flac." *The Times Literary Supplement* (September 28, 1967).

"The French Sureté Nationale's Training Centre for Shooting." *International Criminal Police Review* (November, 1963), pp. 278-328.
Illustrated account of the weapons training course of the Sureté Nationale.

Grimaud, Maurice. "Traffic Problem in Paris." *International Criminal Police Review* (February, 1969), pp. 39-48.

Hartley, Anthony. "O Pays de Voltaire." *Spectator* (November 17, 1960).

Hawkins, H.J. "The C.R.S." *Police Journal (GB),* XLIV:2 (April-June, 1971), pp. 129-132.

Hawkins, H.J. "The Police Career in France." *Police Journal (GB), (May, 1970), pp. 214-221.*

Ingleton, Roy D. "The Police in France." Police Review (GB), (October 27, 1972); (November 3, 1972); (November 10, 1972).

Leon, George. "The Parisian and New York Police Forces." *Law and Order.* 23:9 (September, 1975), pp. 62-63.

"MP's in France." *Military Police Journal.* 11 (October, 1961), pp. 5-7.
Describes activities of French Police.

Nepote, Jean. "Science at the Service of the French Police." *International Criminal Police Review* (June-July, 1961), pp. 134-183.

"The 1968 Reform of the French Police." *International Criminal Police Review* (January, 1969), pp. 2-7.

"The Organization of French Police." *Public Administration.* 29 (Spring, 1951), pp. 67-75.

"The Police of Poitiers, France." *Military Police Journal.* 12 (March, 1963), pp. 20-22.

"The Police of Tours, France." *Military Police Journal.* 12 (May, 1963), pp. 17-18.

"Policing Rural Beats in Paris." *Police Journal* (October-December, 1958), pp. 278-280.

Prefecture de Police, Paris. "The Beat System in Paris." *International Criminal Police Review.* 28:271 (1973), pp. 248-258.

"Processing of Crime Records in the French Gendarmerie." *International Criminal Police Review* (October, 1970), pp. 238-244.

"Report on the Activities of the French Police Nationale 1969." *International Criminal Police Review* (May, 1970), pp. 166-168.

"Roughest City West of Suez." *Life.* 23 (September 8, 1947), pp. 103-107.

Stead, P.J. "The Police of France." *Medical-Legal Journal.* 33 (1965), pp. 3-11.

Stead, Philip John. *The Police of Paris.* London: Stables Press, 1957.
The nature and character of Paris Police organization. Contains bibliography of French language publications.

Yzerman, M. "French Police and Juvenile Delinquency." *International Criminal Police Review* (November, 1961), pp. 265-272.

GERMANY

General

Vexler, R. *Germany, A Chronology and Fact Book.* Dobbs Ferry, NY: Oceana, 1973.

Crime

Adlam, Gordon. "Juvenile Courts in the Federal Republic of Germany." *Criminal Law Review* (June, 1956).

Kaiser, Gunther and Thomas Wurtenburger, eds. *Criminological Research Trends in Western Germany. German Reports to the 6th International Congress on Criminology in Madrid, 1970.* New York: Springer-Verlag, 1972.

Lorenz, W. *Bank Robbery in the Federal Republic of Germany.* (vol. 2), Stuttgart, West Germany: Ferdinand Enke Verlag, 1972.
Analyses of the rationale, statutory basis, court practices, and reform proposals concerning the sentencing of offenders and the imposition of preventive imprisonment (sicherungsverwahrung) on recidivists.

Muller-Dietz, Heinz and Heike Jung. "The Reform of the Criminal Correction System in West Germany." *Canadian Journal of Criminology and Corrections.* 15:3 (July, 1973), pp. 274-280.

Schubert, D. *Bank Robbery in the Federal Republic of Germany.* (vol. 1), Stuttgart, West Germany: Ferdinand Enke Verlag, 1972.
Statistical description and analysis of the circumstances surrounding 297 bank robberies from 1964 to 1966 and of the social, psychological, and criminal records of the 360 offenders who were apprehended.

Criminal Law

Dreher, Edward. *The German Draft Penal Code — E.* 1962. South Hackensack, NJ: Rothman, 1966.

German Code of Criminal Procedure. South Hackensack, NJ: Rothman, 1965.

German Penal Code of 1871. South Hackensack, NJ: Rothman, 1961.

Herrmann, Joachim. "The Rule of Compulsory Prosecution and the Scope of Prosecutorial Discretion in Germany." *University of Chicago Law Review.* 41:3 (Spring, 1974), pp. 468-505.

Langbein, John H. "Controlling Prosecutorial Discretion in Germany." *University of Chicago Law Review.* 41:3 (Spring, 1974), pp. 439-467.

Mueller, G.O.W. *The German Code of Criminal Procedure.* London: Sweet and Maxwell, 1966(?).

Police History

Aschaffenburg, Gustav. *Crime and Its Repression.* Boston: Little, Brown, 1913.

Exner, Franz. "Development of the Administration of Criminal Justice in Germany." *Journal of Criminal Law and Criminology.* XXIV (1933-1934).

Gardner, Edith Rose. "Military Justice in the German Air Force During World War II." *Journal of Criminal Law, Criminology and Police Science.* 49:3 (September-October, 1958), pp. 195-217.

Heindl, Robert. "The Technique of Criminal Investigation in Germany." *Annals* November, 1929), pp. 223-236.

Kavanaugh, A.J. and O.W. Wilson. "Police Organization in Germany." *Public Management.* 15 (December, 1933), pp. 363-365.

Kempner, Robert M.W. "The German National Registration System as Means of Police Control of Population." *Journal of Criminal Law, Criminology and Police Science.* 36 (January, 1946), pp. 362-387.

Liang, Hsi-Huey. *The Berlin Police Force in the Weimar Republic.* Berkeley: University of California Press, 1970.
Citizen and criminal complaints were handled on basis of political affiliation of the complainant and the officer taking the complaint. Anything done to assist citizens had its basis in politics.

Michie, Allan A. "Policing Germany by Air." *Atlantic.* 174 (August, 1944), pp. 39-44.

Mirkine-Guetzeritch, B. "Decree Unifying the Police Forces." *The Political Quarterly.* 8:99 (January, 1937).
A review of the unification of the whole German police system.

Richardson, James F. "Berlin Police in the Weimar Republic: A Comparison with Police Forces in Cities of the United States." *Journal of Contemporary History* (January-April, 1972), pp. 261-275.

Riege, Paul. "Prussian Police." *Police Journal (GB),* 2 (July, 1929), pp. 225-246.

Schmidt, Franz. *A Hangman's Diary, Being the Journal of Master Franz Schmidt, Public Executioner of Nuremburg, 1573-1617.* Oxford: P. Allan, 1929.

Thomason, Frank J. "The Criminal Division of the Berlin Police Organization, 1877-1910." *Journal of Police Science and Administration.* 2:4 (December, 1974), pp. 429-443.

Wilson, O.W. "Police Training in Germany." *Police "13-13."* IX: 123 (July, 1934), pp. 3-6, 34-35.

Police

Adler, Johann A. "A Visit to the Bundeskriminalamt." *Police Chief.* 26 (March, 1959), pp. 12-21.

Bailey, B.E. "Heidelberg: The Police Story." *Military Police Journal.* 13 (August, 1963).

Becker, Heinrich. "The Infra-Red Microscope as an Aid to Police Investigations." *International Criminal Police Review* (March, 1963), pp. S4-88.

"Berlin Policewomen." *Life.* 24 (April 12, 1948).

"Berlin: Policing a Divided City." *Police (GB),* (October, 1971), pp. 16-17.

Carter, Alan F. "German Police and Their Publications." *Police Review (GB),* (September 5, 1975).

Cramer, James. "City Police of the World: Berlin." *Police Review (GB),* 66 (October 10, 1958).

Cramer, James. "Police Forces of the World: Hamburg." *Police Review (GB),* 68 (March 18, 1960).

Dullien, Richard. "To Stop a Thief." *FBI Law Enforcement Bulletin.* 33:5 (May, 1964), pp. 3-6, 22-23.
Efforts to stop car theft in West Germany.

Gainham, Sarah. "The Speigel Case." *The Spectator.* 209 (November 9, 1962), pp. 712-713.

"The German Police." *Police Chief.* 26 (April, 1959), pp. 4-6, 8.

Hawkins, Thomas F. "Germans Get Guns in U.S. Experiment." *U.S. News & World Report.* 24:66 (April 9, 1948).

Hill, C.B. "Stuttgart Police." *Military Police Journal.* 13 (November, 1963), pp. 16-17.

Hinz, Lieselotte. "Police and Sociology in West Germany." *Police Journal (GB),* XLVII:2 (April-June, 1974), pp. 161-172.

Howe, John J. "The Berlin Beat Abstract." *Journal of Criminal Law and Criminology.* 36 (January, 1946).

Jones, Sherbert B. "Customs Police of Germany." *Police Chief.* 29:9 (September, 1962).

Kienle, Otto. "Police of Baden-Wurttemberg." *Police Chief.* 29:1 (January, 1962).

Kosyra, Herbert. "The Man with the Heart of Stone." *International Criminal Police Review* (November, 1961), pp. 80-83.

Kroger, Wilhelm. "The Meeting of Two Police Ideas — Anglo-German Experiments in West Germany." *Journal of Criminal Law, Criminology and Police Science.* 51:2 (March-April, 1960-1961).

"Lie-Detector Tests and 'Freedom of the Will' in Germany." *Journal of Criminal Law, Criminology and Police Science.* 47:5 (January-February, 1957), pp. 570-579.

Littmann, Gerhard. "The Traffic Situation in Western Germany." *Police Yearbook.* Washington, DC: IACP, 1956.

"Lower Saxony." *Military Police Journal.* 13 (April, 1964), pp. 10-13.

Marder, Everett J. "The Police of Mannheim." *Military Police Journal.* 10 (August, 1961), pp. 18-20.

Melloh, James L. "The Police of Frankfurt am Main." *Military Police Journal.* 11 (February, 1962), pp. 16-19.

Melvin, C.T. and R.S. Griggs. *One Hundred Hours in Hamburg.* Washington, DC: NCJRS, (Microfiche), 1972.

Middendorff, Wolf. "Is There a Relationship between Traffic Offences and Common Crimes?" *International Criminal Police Review* (January, 1968), pp. 4-13.

Mylonas, Anastassios D. *Perception of Police Power: A Study in Four Cities.* New York: New York University School of Law Criminal Law Education and Research Center, 1973.
Comparative study of police in Cologne, Tel Aviv, Rome and New York.

"New Uniform of the West Berlin Police with Armpit Holster." *Illustrated London News.* 235 (November 14, 1959).

New York University School of Law Criminal Law Education and Research Center. *What Can a Police Officer Do? A Comparative Study: USA — German Federal Republic — Israel — Italy.* NY: New York University, School of Law, Criminal Law Education and Research Center, 1974.

"A Night with the Police." *Time.* 46 (December 31, 1945).

"One of Frankfurt's New Women Traffic Wardens." *Illustrated London News.* 238 (March 11, 1961).

"The Police of Bavaria." *Police Chief.* 30 (August, 1963), pp. 36-40.

Price, Clifford S. and Ronald J. Bostick. "IACP Goes to Germany." *Police Chief.* XXXIX:8 (August, 1972), pp. 53-55.

"Riding Their Motorbike." *Popular Science.* 167 (July, 1955).

Roberts, Ian. "Polizei." *Forward* (Autumn, 1972), pp. 6-9.

Schaefer, M. "International Frauds — Germany." *International Criminal Police Review* (April, 1969), pp. 91-98, (May, 1969), pp. 122-133.

Schulz, Georg. "The Criminal Investigation Bureau of Land, Lower Saxony." *Journal of Criminal Law, Criminology and Police Science.* 46:5 (January-February, 1956), pp. 722-725.

Schweppe, R. *FBI and BKA — The Federal Bureau of Investigation and the West German Federal Criminal Police Bureau (Bundeskriminalamt) — A Comparison of Organization and Competencies.* Stuttgart, West Germany: Ferdinand Enke Verlag, 1974.

Slocum, B. "Vigilantes in Homburgs." *Business Week.* 4:1 (July, 1953), pp. 60-64.

Todd, Tom. "Centralizing Criminal Records in West Germany." *Computer Weekly International* (April 18, 1974), pp. 10-11.

Turner, Carl C. "The Police of Bavaria." *Police Chief.* 30:8 (August, 1963), pp. 36-40.

"TV Camera Helps Control Traffic in Hamburg." *Police Review (GB),* 64 (May 25, 1956).

GERMANY — EAST

General

U.S. Department of the Army. *Area Handbook: East Germany.* Washington, DC: GPO, 1972.

Crime

Bucholz, Erich et al. *Socialist Criminology — Theoretical and Methodical Foundations.* Farnborough: D.C. Heath, 1974.

Police

Cramer, James. "Police Forces of the World: East Germany." *Police Review (GB),* 67 (July 24, 1959).

GIBRALTAR

Police

Bennett, David. "Police in Gibraltar." *Police World* (Summer, 1974), pp. 12-14.

Cramer, James. "Police Forces of the World: Gibraltar." *Police Review (GB),* 67 (November 13, 1959).

GHANA

Crime

Weinberg, S. Kirson. "Juvenile Delinquency in Ghana: A Comparative Analysis of Delinquents and Non-Delinquents." *Journal of Criminal Law, Criminology and Police Science.* 55:4 (December, 1964), pp. 471-481.

Criminal Law

Harvey, William B. *Law and Social Change in Ghana.* Princeton, NJ: Princeton University Press, 1966.

Police History

Gillespie, W.H. *Gold Coast Police, 1844-1938.* Accra, Gold Coast: Government Printer, 1955.

"Gold Coast Police." *Police Journal (GB),* 5 (January, 1932), pp. 94-100.

Police

Boyes, R.P. *Report on the Ghana Police Service.* Accra, Ghana: [n.n.], 1971.

Cramer, James. "City Police of the World: Accra (Ghana)." *Police Review.* 66 (October 3, 1958).

GREECE

Crime

Gardikas, C. "Some Characteristic Features of Crime." *International Criminal Police Review* (November, 1961), pp. 258-264.

Police

"The Affair Continues." *New Statesman and Nation.* 65 (June 7, 1963).

Cramer, James. "Police Forces of the World: Greece." *Police Review (GB),* 67 (August 14, 1959).

Garnelis, Nickolas. "The Greek Royal Gendarmery." *Police.* 13:1 (September-October, 1968), pp. 6-11.

GREENLAND

Greenland Criminal Code. South Hackensack, NJ: Rothman, 1970.

GUAM

Police

Anderson, Thomas H. "The Police of Guam." *Police Chief.* (January, 1970).
Organization and functions of Guam Police.

Guam: 1969 Annual Report to the Secretary of the Interior. Washington, DC: GPO, 1970.
Contains data on public safety and other general information on government services.

Guam LEAA Comprehensive State Plan — Abstract, 1971. Washington, DC: NCCD, 1971.
A digest of the 1971 law enforcement assistance administration comprehensive state plan has been compiled for Guam.

GUATEMALA

General

U.S. Department of the Army. *Area Handbook: Guatemala.* Washington, DC: GPO, 1970.

Police

Gonzalez Diaz, Oscar. "Development and Present Activities of the Police of Guatemala." *International Police Academy Review* (January, 1970), pp. 6-9.

GUERNSEY

Criminal Law

Marshall, Michael. *Criminal Law of the Bailiwick of Guernsey.* Dorchester: Friary Press, 1975.

Police

Le Cocq, Francois. "Police of Guernsey." *Police World* (Winter, 1964).

GUYANA

General

Despres, Leo. *Cultural Pluralism and Nationalist Politics in British Guiana.* Chicago: Rand McNally, 1967.

U.S. Department of the Army. *Area Handbook: Guyana.* Washington, DC: GPO, 1975.

Police History

Orrett, W. A. *History of the British Guiana Police.* Georgetown: Daily Chronicle, 1951.

White, A.D.M. "Bush Run in British Guiana." *Police Journal (GB),* (1929), pp. 211-217.

Police

Cramer, James. "Police Forces of the World: British Guiana." *Police Review (GB),* 67 (March 27, 1959).

HAITI

Lamarre, J.M. "Extradition Law in Haiti—Past and Present." *International Criminal Police Review,* (April, 1961), pp. 98-104. 98-104.

HONG KONG

General

Hong Kong's Border with China. Hong Kong: Government Information Service, Government Printer. [n.d.]

Crime

Hess, Albert G. *Chasing the Dragon.* Amsterdam: North Holland, 1964.

Hong Kong Government. *The Problem of Narcotic Drugs in Hong Kong.* Hong Kong: Government Press, 1959.

Whisson, Michael. "Sociological Aspects of the Illegal Use of Narcotics." In I.C. Jarvie, ed. *Hong Kong, A Society in Transition.* London: Routledge and Kegan, Paul, 1969.

Whisson, Michael G. *Under the Rug—the Drug Problem in Hong Kong.* [n.p.]: Council of Social Services, 1965.

Police

Andrew, Kenneth. *Hong Kong Detective.* London: John Long, 1962.

Commissioner of Police. *Annual Departmental Reports.* Hong Kong: Government Printer, annual.

David, J. "Hong Kong—Its Traffickers and Its Police." *International Criminal Police Review,* (May, 1960), 50-53.

Fletcher, Q. "Riot Control in Hong Kong." *FBI Law Enforcement Bulletin,* 38:12 (December, 1969), pp. 3-6, 20.

Hong Kong Police Force. *Policing Hong Kong.* Hong Kong: Police Force, 1968.

Hong Kong, Report of the Year. Hong Kong: Government Press, annual.

Kowloon Disturbances. 1966 Report of the Commission of Inquiry in Hong Kong. Hong Kong: Government Printer, 1967.

Livingstone, Irene C. "Royal Hong Kong Police." *Guardian (Glasgow),* (Winter, 1974), pp. 54-55.

Mangold, Tom. "Tigers and Flies—Tom Manigold on Police Corruption in Hong Kong." *Listener* (January 16, 1975), pp. 66-68.

Mishkin, Barry D. "Police of Hong Kong." *Garda Review* (March, 1976), pp. 23-24, 31.

Mishkin, Barry D. "Police of Hong Kong." *SARP* (March 1975), pp. 18-19.

"The Police Force of Hong Kong." *Far Eastern Economy Report,* 23 (July 4, 1957) pp. 23-26.

Speevak, Allan R. "The Royal Police of Hong Kong." *Police Chief,* 37:9 (October, 1970), pp. 16, 18, 21, 236-245.

HUNGARY

Criminal Law

Kalman, Lajos. *Lawyer in Communism. Boston, MA: Daughters of St. Paul, 1960.*

Police History

Dorning, Heinrich. "Hungarian State Police." *Police Journal (GB),* 2 (January, 1929), pp. 62-77.

Police

Ignotus, Paul. "The A.V.H.: Symbol of Terror." *Problems of Communism,* 6 (September-October, 1957), pp. 19-25.

Mikes, George. *A Study in Infamy.* London: Deutsch, 1959. The operations of the Hungarian Secret Police (AVO) based on secret documents issued by the Hungarian Ministry of the Interior.

Rektor, B. "Police Education in Hungary." *Police,* (April, 1972).

ICELAND

Crime

Hansen, J.P.H. and O. Bjarnason. "Homicide in Iceland 1946-1970." *Forensic Science,* 4:2 (1974) pp. 107-117.

Police

Cramer, James. "City Police of the World: Reykjavik." *Police Review (GB),* 66 (August 8, 1958).

INDIA

General

U.S. Department of the Army. *Area Handbook, India.* Washinon, DC: *GPO,* 1964, 1970, 1975.

Crime

Chandra, Sushil. *Sociology of Deviation and Defense in India.* NY: Paragon, 1967.

Chopra, R. and I. Chopra. "The Use of Cannabis Drugs in India." *U.N. Bulletin On Narcotics,* 9:1 (January-March, 1957).

Crime in India. New Delhi: Ministry of Home Affairs, Government of India, [n.d.]

Nag, Moni. "Beggar Problem in Calcutta and Its Solution." *The Indian Journal of Social Work,* 26:3 (1965), pp. 243-249.

Nayar, Balder R. *Violence and Crime in India.* Columbia, MO: South Asia Books, 1975.

Panigrahi, Lalita. *British Social Policy and Female Infanticide in India.* Mystic, CT: Verry, 1972.

Rao, L. Venugopal. *Facets of Crime in India.* Bombay: Allied, 1967.

Sangar, Satya P. *Crime and Punishment in Mughal, India.* Mystic, CT: Verry, 1967.

Saran, A.B. *Murder and Suicide Among the Munda and the Oraon (India).* Mystic, CT: Verry, 1974.

Sethna, Minocher Jehangirji. *Society and the Criminal, with Special Reference to the Problems of Crime and Its Prevention, Personality of the Criminal. . . .* [n.p.]: Leaders' Press, 1952.

Sheth, H. *Juvenile Delinquency in an Indian Setting.* Bombay: Popular Book Depot, 1961.

Snook, Russell A. "Facets of Crime in India." *Police Chief,* XXXV:4 (April, 1968).

Venugotala, Rao S. *Facets of Crime in India.* Bombay: Allied, 1962.

Criminal Law

Annual Survey of Indian Law. (vol. 1), New Delhi: Indian Law Institute, 1968.

Ghosh, S.K. *Law of Preventive Detention in India.* NY: International Publications Service, 1969.

Hingorani, R.C. *Indian Extradition Law.* NY: Asia, [n.d.]

Jain, M.P. *Indian Constitutional Law.* NY: International Publications Service, 1970.

Keith, Arthur Berriedale. *A Constitutional History of India,* 1600-1935. (2nd ed. rev.), NY: Barnes, 1969.

"Law in Other Lands: India." *Deuce,* (Spring, 1963), pp. 8-9.

Nigam, R.C. *Law of Crime in India.* (vol. 1), *Principles of Criminal Law,* NY: Asia, 1965.

Pylee, M.V. *Federal Courts in India.* NY: Paragon, 1966.

Sathe, S.P. *Administrative Law in India.* NY: International Publications Service, 1970.

U.S. Solicitor. *Handbook for Federal Indian Law.* NY: AMS, 1972 (repr. of GPO ed. 1942).

Police History

Blair, H. "Law and Order, the Great Betrayal, What Handing Over of the Indian Police Will Mean." *Saturday Review,* 156 (October 14, 1933), pp. 386-387.

Chatterjee, S.K. *History of Criminal Identification and Finger Print Bibliography.* Calcutta: P. Chatterjee, 1952.

Clarke, R. "Law and Order in the New India." *Asiatic Review,* 27 (July, 1931), pp. 407-422.

Cox, Edmund C. *My Thirty Years in India.* London: Mills and Boon, 1909.

Cox, E. *Police and Crime in India.* London: n/n, 1911.

Crossley, D. "Public Cooperation with the Police in South India." *Police Journal (GB),* 10 (January-March, 1937), pp. 87-93.

Curry, J.C. *The Indian Police.* London: Faber and Faber, 1932.

Edwardes, S.M. *The Bombay City Police, 1672-1860.* London: Oxford University Press, 1936.

Gayer, W.A. *Detection of Burglary in India.* Calcutta: Thacker Spinck, 1920.

Gouldsbury, C.E. *Life in the Indian Police.* (2nd ed.) London: Chapman and Hall, 1913.

Gourlay, W.R. *A Contribution to the History of the Police in Bengal.* Calcutta: Bengal Government Press, 1916.

History of Police Training College. (Basic Training Series). Moradabad, Uttar Pradesh: Police Training Centre, 1963.

History of the Andhra Pradesh Police, 1869-1961. Hyderabad: Deccan, 1961.

Hollins, S.T. *No Ten Commandments: Life in Indian Police.* London: Hutchinson, 1954.

Holt, H.P. *The Mounted Police of Natal.* London: [n.n.], 1913.

Indian Police Journal. *Indian Police Centenary, 1861-1961.* New Delhi: Statesman Press, 1961.

Kalia, Bankat Ram. *A History of the Development of the Police in the Punjab, 1849-1905.* [n.p.]: Punjab Government Record Office, 1929.

"Law and Order in India." *Near East,* 39 (April 30, 1931), pp. 498-499.

Majumdar, N. *Justice and Police in Bengal (1765-1793). A Study of the Nizamate in Decline.* Calcutta: Firms K.L. Mukhopadhyay, 1960.

Martineau, G.D. *Controller of Devils: A Life of John Paul Warburton, of the Punjab Police.* Dorset: Dorset, 1965.

Narayanaswamy, Sri K.G. *The History of the Madras Police.* Madras: Inspector General of Police, 1959.
Published on the hundredth anniversary of Madras Police. Covers history and detailed description of present organization.

Patra, A.C. *Administration of Justice Under the East India Company in Bengal Bihar and Orissa.* NY: Asia, [n.d.].

Peters, C.R. "Mounted Police in India: The United Provinces

M.P." *Police Journal (GB),* 4 (January, 1931), pp. 100-106.

Reid, R. "Assam Rifles in Peace and War; the Defense of India's Northeastern Frontier." *Blackwood's Magazine,* 261 (May, 1947), pp. 414-422.

Sahu, N.K. *History of Orissa Police.* Cuttack: Orissa Police Magazine, [n.d.]

Stead, C. "Future of the Police in India." *Great Britain and the East,* 47 (September 3, 1936), pp. 343-344.

Whalley, G.P. *The Control of Professional Crime.* Calcutta: Thacker, 1919.

Police

Bayley, David H. *Police and Political Development in India.* Princeton, NJ: Princeton University Press, 1969.

Bhusan, Sahais. "Separation of Law and Order and Investigation of Crimes." *Indian Police Journal,* 18:4 (1972), pp. 37-42.
Author states that investigative functions in India have been neglected on account of emphasis on the maintenance of law and order. Suggests specialization as improvement.

Chand, H. *The Powers of Police and Magistracy in India.* Allahabad: Law Publishing House, 1954.

Coatman, John. *Indian Police.* London: Indian Police Association, (UK), 1962.

Cramer, James. "Police Forces of the World: Delhi." *Police Review (GB),* 67 (June 19, 1959).

Deb, R. "How to Deal with Interstate Criminals." *International Criminal Police Review,* (March, 1960), pp. 76-86.

Deb, R. "Malpractices in Law Enforcement." *Indian Police Journal,* 19:3 (1973), pp. 42-47.

Deb, R. "Police and Juvenile Delinquency." *International Criminal Police Review,* (March, 1968), pp. 76-79.

Deb, R. *Principles of Criminology, Criminal Law and Investigation.* Calcutta: S.C. Sarkar, 1968.

Directory of Police Stations in India. New Delhi: Ministry of Home Affairs Intelligence Bureau, 1962.

Ghosh, Shri S.K. *Police and the Public.* Madhupatna: Orissa, 1964.

Griffiths, Percival. *To Guard My People: The History of the Indian Police.* London: Benn, 1971.

Gupta, A. "The Indian Police." *New Community,* 3:3 (1974) pp. 215-219.

Iyengar, N.K. "Detection of Death Due to Snake Bites." *International Criminal Police Review* (March, 1962), pp. 96-97.
Techniques used to reveal the presence of venoms in the blood of victims, 100 people die daily from snakebites in India.

Mehta, M.K. *The Identification of Handwriting and the Cross-Examination of Experts.* Bombay: N.M. Tripathi, 1961.

Mishra, B.B. "Postscript to the Pakur Case." *International Criminal Police Review* (May, 1960), pp. 177-181.

Mullick, B.N. *Civil Disturbances.* New Delhi: Government of India Press, 1966.

Nigam, S.R. *Scotland Yard and the Indian Police.* Allahabad: Kitab Mahal Private, 1963.

Police in India. New Delhi: Ministry of Information, Publication Division, 1958.

Puri, K.S. "Genuine but Forged." *International Criminal Police Review* (March, 1969), pp. 82-84.

Saha, S.R. "Calcutta City Police Administration: Some Problems." *Indian Police Journal,* 19:4 (1973) pp. 22-26.

Towards a New Police. Moradabad, Uttar Pradesh: Police Training College, 1964.

Triveda, J.P. "The City Police Administration." *Indian Police Journal,* 19:4 (1973), pp. 41-44.
Describes two types of administrative structure in India.

INDONESIA

General

U.S. Department of the Army. *Area Handbook: Indonesia.* Washington, DC: GPO, 1970-1975.

Police

Indonesia Constabulary. *Mission of the Indonesian National Police.* Djakarta: National Police Head Quarters, 1971.

Indonesian Police. *Glimpse on Activities of the Indonesian National Police.* Sidharto, Dunusubroto: Indonesian Police Information Service, 1976.

McQuady, Charles W. "Principals of the Indonesian Police." *Quarterly Journal of Association for Professional Law Enforcement,* 4 (October-December, 1958) pp. 27-28.

Mission of the Indonesian National Police. Djakarta: Indonesia Constabulary National Police Headquarters, 1971.

Soemarsono, Major. "Human Relations in the Indonesian Police." *Police Yearbook,* Washington, DC: IACP, 1956.

Wahjudi, R. "The Women Police in Djakarta." *International Criminal Police Review,* (May, 1966), pp. 135-137.

IRAN

General

Smith, Harvey Henry. *Area Handbook for Iran.* Washington, DC: GPO, 1971.

Police

Cramer, James. "Police Forces of the World: Tehran." *Police Review (GB),* 67 (April 10, 1959).

Ghorbani, Mustafa. "Transmission of Fingerprints—New Suggestion in the Field of Fingerprinting." *International Criminal Police Review* (October, 1962), pp. 255-258.
Discusses new method of fingerprint classification used by the Iranian Police.

Mazandi, Joseph A. and Edwin Mullee. "The Hunch That Saved Iran." *Reader's Digest,* 67 (September, 1955), pp. 57-60.
Rookie policeman inadvertently uncovered a communist plot to take over Iran.

Mobasser, Mohsen H. "National Police of Iran: A Successful Transition." *International Police Academy Review,* 2 (January, 1968), pp. 1-3, 12-15.

Nemati, M.R. *Police Training at the Police University of Iran.* Tehran: Police University, 1973.

IRAQ

General

U.S. Department of the Army. *Area Handbook: Iraq.* Washington, DC: GPO, 1971.

Police History

Wilson, A.T. "Iraq Police: A Notable Example of British Administration Adaptability." *Police Journal (GB),* (1928), pp. 31-38.

IRELAND

General

Griffin, W.D. *Ireland, A Chronology and Fact Book.* Dobbs Ferry, NY: Oceana, 1973.

Police History

Andrews, S.A. "The Royal Irish Constabulary." *Police Review (GB),* (January 18, 1963).

Breathnach, Seamus. *Irish Police from Earliest Times to the Present Day.* Dublin: Anvil, 1974.

Broeker, Galen. *Rural Disorder and Police Reform in Ireland, 1512-1836.* Toronto: University of Toronto Press, 1970.

Carroll, P. "Dublin's New Police of 1908." *Iris an Garda,* (1961), pp. 457-459.

Carroll, P. "Notes for a History of Police in Ireland." *Garda Review,* (January, 1971, through February, 1962).
Series of articles covering Irish policy history with a list of Irish references.

Curtis, R. *The History of the Royal Irish Constabulary.* Dublin: McGloeasher and Gil, 1871.

Evers, Francis A. "Way We Were." *Garda Review* (October, 1975), pp. 10-11.

Hood, W.J. and J.E. Sheperd. "A Short History of the Police in Ireland 1787-1922." *Ulstrview* (August, 1967, through February, 1969).

Inglis, Brian. *The Freedom of the Press in Ireland, 1784-1841.* London: Faber and Faber, 1954.

McCall-Smith, Alexander and Philip Magee. "Anglo-Irish Law Enforcement Report in Historical and Political Context." *Criminal Law Review* (April, 1975), pp. 200-213.

Manning, Maurice. "Window on the Past." *Garda Review* (April, 1976), pp. 16-17.

Martin, Patrick. "Making of a Police Force—1933." *Garda Review* (October, 1975), pp. 7-13.

O'Kelly, D.J. *Salute to the Garda, 1922-1958,* Dublin: Parkside Press, 1959.

Palmer, Stanley H. "Irish Police Experiment: The Beginnings of Modern Police in the British Isle, 1785-1795." *Police Science Quarterly,* 56:3, pp. 410-424.

Sheehan, P.A. "The Garda Siochana—Erin's Stout Civic Guard." *Police Journal (NY),* 21 (December, 1934), pp. 3-4.

Sullivan, Joseph Matthew. "Irish Police Gleanings." *Journal of Criminal Law and Criminology,* IV (1913-1914).

Police

Brady, Conor. "Noblest Profession." *Garda Review* (February, 1975), pp. 22-23.

Carroll, P. *Garda Siochana Guide.* Tralee: Kerryman, 1966.

Carroll, Patrick. "The Garda Siochana: The Irish Police Force." *FBI Law Enforcement Bulletin* (March, 1968).

Cooney, Patrick. "Garda and the Future." *Garda Review* (October, 1975), pp. 10-11.

Cosantoir, An. "Jubilee Year Tribute to Garda Siochana." *An Cosantoir: The Irish Defence Journal* (November, 1972), pp. 201-232.

Cramer, James. "Police Forces of the World: Garda Siochana." *Police Review (GB),* 67 (February 6, 1959).

Garda Siochana Directory. Kilmainham, Dublin: Garda Representative Body Police Headquarters, [n.d.].

Jackson, J.A. *The Irish Army and the Development of the Constabulary Concept.*
A paper presented to the Six World Congress of Sociology, 1966, (mimeo). Apparently the Army exists almost solely for the performance of constabulary duties.

Lydon, Sean. "Harriers—Another Look." *Garda Review* (March, 1976), pp. 13, 15.

McLean, A. "Training in Eire." *Police College Magazine* (Autumn, 1959), pp. 24-28, 31-32.

Martin, Patrick. "Back to the Streets." *Garda Review* (March, 1975), pp. 20-21, 23.
Report from the Leeside beat in Cork.

Martin, Patrick. "Man from Mayo. Famous Irish Policeman No. 8: Patrick Quinn." *Garda Review* (February, 1975), pp. 10-11.

Martin, Patrick. "Mark: The Making of a Policeman." *Garda Review* (March, 1975), pp. 19, 37.

Penaat, Edward F. "The Civil Guard Eirre: Garda Siochana." *Police Chief,* 26 (July, 1959), pp. 6-10.

Tobias, J.J. "The Policing of Ireland." *Criminologist* 5 (November, 1970), pp. 99-101.

ISLE OF MAN

Cramer, James. "Police Forces of the World: Isle of Man." *Police Review (GB),* 67 (May 8, 1959).

ISRAEL

General

Catarivas, David. *Israel.* London: Vista Books, 1959.

Littvinoff, B. *Israel, Chronology and Fact Book.* Dobbs Ferrrryy, NY: Oceana, 1973.

Crime

Reifen, D. "The Israel Youth Authority: Aspects of Detention and Release." *British Journal of Criminology,* 9:3 (1969), pp. 254-271.

Reifen, David. *The Juvenile Court in a Changing Society—Young Offenders in Israel.* Philadelphia: University of Pennsylvania Press, 1972.

Shoham, Shlomo. "Sentencing Policy of Criminal Courts in Israel." *Journal of Criminal Law, Criminology and PPPolice Science,* 50:4 (November-December, 1959), pp. 327-337.

Shoham, Shlomo, ed. *Israel Studies in Criminology.* (vol. 11), Jerusalem: Jerusalem Academic Press, 1973.

Shoham, Shlomo and Leon Shaskolsky. "An Analysis of Delinquents and Nondelinquents in Israel: A Cross Cultural Persspective." *Sociology and Social Research,* 53:3 (April, 1969), pp. 333-343.

Criminal Law

Abramowitz, Bernard. *Law of Israel.* Brooklyn, NY: Bennet, Rebecca [n.d.].

Israel: Criminal Procedure. South Hackensack, NJ: Rothman, 1967.

Muller, G.O.W. *The Israeli Criminal Procedure Law.* London: Sweet aaannedd Maxwell, 1967.

Rackman, Emanuel. *Israel's Emerging Constitution: 1948-51.* NY: Coluuummbia University Press, 1955.

Selected Judgments of the Supreme Court of Israel. (4 vols.), Dobbs Ferry, NY: Oceana, 1948-1960.

Tedeschi, G. *Studies in Israeli Law.* South Hackensack, NJ: Rothman, 1960.

Yadin, U. *The Israeli Criminal Procedure Law.* South Hackensack, NJ: Rothman, 1967.

Police History

"Guardians of the Palestinian Desert: Camel Corps: Photographs." *Asia and the Americas,* 46 (September, 1946).

Police

Ansley, N. "Israeli Police Polygraph School." *Polygraph* 2:2 (1973), pp. 146-157.

Caspi, Y. and Y. Gur. "The Student Safety Patrol. An Israeli Traffic Program." *FBI Law Enforcement Bulletin,* 42:5 (1973), pp. 18-21, 27.
College students working as traffic officers.

New York University School of Law Criminal Law Education and Research Center. *What Can a Police Do? A Comparative Study: U.S.A.—German Federal Republic—Israel—Italy.* New York: New York University, School of Law 1974.

Reifen, David. "New Ventures of Law Enforcement in Israel." *Journal of Criminal Law, Criminology and Police Science,* 58:1 (March, 1967) pp. 70-74.

Reifen, David. "Protection of Children Involved in Sexual Offenses: A New Method of Investigation in Israel." *Journal of Criminal Law, Criminology and Police Science,* 49:3 (September-October, 1958), pp. 222-229.

Rubenstein, Sidney S. "The Shield of David: Israel Police." *Police Chief* XXXVI:4 (April, 1969), pp. 40-52.

Schleimer, H. "Album of Criminal Offenders." *International Criminal Police Review* (October, 1973), pp. 235-238.
Describes files kept by the Israel police for 16 classes of criminals.

ITALY

General

Logatto, A.F. *Italy, Chronology and Fact Book.* Dobbs Ferry, NY: Oceana, 1973.

Criminal Law

Cappelletti, Mauro et al. *The Italian Legal System: An Introduction.* Stanford CA: Stanford University Press, 1967.

Fleetwood, J.B. "Criminal Procedure in Italy." *Police College Magazine,* (Autumn, 1955), pp. 24-36.

Police History

Dosi, Giuseppe. "The Royal Italian Carabineers." *Police Journal (NY),* 20 (January, 1934), pp. 3-4.

"Royal Carabineers of Italy." *Police Journal (GB),* (1928), pp. 48-61.

von Borisini, Victor. "School of Scientific Police in Rome." *Journal of Criminal Law and Criminology,* III (1912-1913).

Wolfgang, Marvin E. "Socio-Economic Factors Relating to Crime and Punishment in Renaissance Florence." *Journal of Criminal Law, Criminology and Police Science,* 47:3 (September-October, 1956), pp. 311-330.

Police

Andreotti, Francisco. "The Italian Police: Its Authority and Organization." *Police World,* 16 (Summer, 1970).

Berenyi, Ivan. "Italy's New-Style Police Network: Local Units with National Facilities." *Police (GB),* (May, 1972), pp. 14-15.

Corti, Ilio. "Computers in the Service of the Italian CID." *International Criminal Police Review* (April-May, 1966), pp. 126-134; (June-July, 1966), pp. 158-164.

Corti, Ilio. "Data Processing in the Italian Police." *International Criminal Police Review,* (June-July, 1964), pp. 158-167; (August-September, 1964), pp. 190-197.

Cramer, James. "Police Forces of the World: Rome." *Poliee Review (GB),* 66 (October 24, 1958).

Cramer, James. "Police Forces of the World: Italy." *Police Review (GB),* 67 (May 15, 1959).

Dunner, Gene. "The Police of Venice." *Police Chief,* 28:9 (September, 1961), pp. 18-19.

Ghisoni, P. "The Rome Municipal Police." *International Police Chronicle,* 7 (March-April, 1959), pp. 7-13.

Gomez y Paloma, Alvaro. "Application of Electronic

Systems to the Police Service in Italy." *Police,* 10:3 (January-February, 1966), pp. 42-48.

Hughes, Eileen. "Roman Police, How to Tell Them Apart." *Holiday,* 27 (April, 1960) pp. 115-118.

Italian Police: Functions, Organization, Operations. Rome: Ministry of the Interior, Department of Public Security, 1969.

McQuady, Charles W. "The Italian Carabinieri." *Quarterly Journal of Association Profession Law Enforcement,* 4 (October-December, 1958) pp. 22-23.

Mylonas, Anastassios D. *Perception of Police Power: A Study in Four Cities.* NY: New York University, School of Law, Criminal Law, Education and Research Center, 1973.
Comparative study of police in Cologne, Tel-Aviv, Rome and NY.

New York University, School of Law, Criminal Law Education and Research Center. *What Can a Police Officer Do? A Comparative Study: U.S.A.—German Federal Republic—Israel—Italy.* NY: New York University, School of Law. Criminal Education and Research Center, 1974.

Paceri, R. "The Italian Scientific Police Services Mobile Laboratory." *International Criminal Police Review* (March, 1965), pp. 73-76.

Paceri, Rocco. "A Triumph for Police Technique and Reasoning." *International Criminal Police Review* (August-September, 1969), pp. 190-192.

Scaparone, M. "Police Interrogation in Italy," *Criminal Law Review* (October, 1974), pp. 581-588.

Weber, Milton J. "MP's in Italy" *Military Police Journal,* 11 (November 1961), pp. 5-8.
Describes activities of Italian Police forces.

Zambonini, R. "Traffic Police in Italy: *International Criminal Police Review* (March, 1961), pp. 88-92.

JAMAICA

Police History

Adam, W.P.C. "Jamaica Constabulary." *Police Journal (GB),* 5 (April, 1932), pp. 257-266.

Jamaica Constabulary Force Centenary: November 28, 1867 to November 28, 1967. Kingston: Jamaica Constabulary, 1967.

Police

Cramer, James. "Police Forces of the World: Jamaica." *Police Review (GB),* 67 (January 9, 1959).

Moynahan, John. "The Police of Jamaica." *Police Chief,* 28:9 (September, 1961).

JAPAN

General

U.S. Department of the Army. *Area Handbook: Japan.* Washington, DC: GPO, 1961-1969.

Yefime. *Japan.* London: Vista Books, 1962.

Crime

Devilish Drug, Narcotic Photographic Document. Tokyo: Japan Ministry of Health and Welfare, 1963.

Doi, Toshiaki and Iwao Sugimoto. "Juvenile Recidivists. Property Offenders and Violent Offenders." *International Criminal Police Review* (January, 1967), pp. 24-28.

Hashimoto, Juzabaro, Sato Jasuko, and Tachibana Masaji. "Studies of High School Students Who Have Been Victims of Crimes—Several Analytical Investigations from the Viewpoint of Criminology." *Bulletin of the Criminological Research Department,* (1968), pp. 27-28.

Kumasaka, Y., R.J. Smith, and H. Aiba. "Crimes in New York and Tokyo: Sociocultural Perspectives." *Community Mental Health Journal,* 11:1 (1975), pp. 19-26.

Levy, Howard S. *Japanese Sex Crimes in Modern Times.* South Pasadena, CA: E. Langstaff, 1975.

Lunden, Walter A. "Juvenile Delinquency in Japan. Prewar and Postwar Years." *Journal of Criminal Law and Criminology,* 44 (November-December, 1953). pp. 428-432.

Miyazawa, Koichi. "Victimological Studies of Sexual Crimes in Japan." *Victimology,* 1 (Spring, 1976), pp. 107-129.

Takada, O. and K. Hara. *Japan—Summary of the White Paper on Crime,* 1971. Washington DC: NCJRS, (Microfiche) 1972.

Criminal Law

Abe, Haruo. "Criminal Justice in Japan." *American Bar Association Journal,* 47 (June, 1961), pp. 555-559.

Abe, Haruo. "Criminal Procedure in Japan." *Journal of Criminal Law, Criminology and Police Science,* 48:4 (November-December, 1957), pp. 359-368.

Abe, Haruo. "Self-Incrimination—Japan and the United States." *Journal of Criminal Law, Criminology and Police Science.* 46:5 (January-February, 1956), pp. 613-631.

Blakmore, Thomas L. *Criminal Code of Japan.* Rutland, VT: Tuttle, 1950.

Dando, S. *Japanese Criminal Procedure.* South Hackensack, NJ: Rothman, 1965.

Japan Ministry of Health and Welfare. *Narcotic Control Law, Awakening Drug Control Law, Cannabis Control Law, Opium Control Law.* Tokyo: Ministry of Health and Welfare, 1964.

Japan Ministry of Justice. *Prosecution and Disposition of Narcotic Offences.* Tokyo: Ministry of Justice, 1964.

Kakeuchi, Juhei and B.J. George, Jr., ed. *A Preparatory Draft for the Revised Penal Code of Japan.* South Hackensack, NJ: New York University School of Law, 1961.

Koshi, George M. *Japanese Legal Advisor: Crimes and Punishments.* Rutland, VT: Tuttle, 1970.

Maki, John M. *Court and Constitution in Japan: Selected*

Supreme Court Decisions, 1948-1960. Seattle: University of Washington Press, 1964.

Takamaji, Kengo et al. *Criminal Code of Japan.* Rutland, VT: Tuttle, 1955.

Police History

"Case of the Three Americans Arrested in Osaka." *China Western Review,* 72:2 (March, 1935).

"Japanese Police." *Journal of Criminal Law and Criminology,* VII (1916-1917).

Kaku, Sagataro. *Opium Policy in Japan.* Geneva: [n.n.], 1924.

"The Police of Japan." *Police Chief,* 30 (February, 1963), pp. 42-46.

History of the Japanese police force and police training. Other topics are: communication and equipment, scientific criminal investigation, police problems, and public and international relations.

Roth, Andrew. "Japan's Police Terror." *Nation,* 161 (September 15, 1945), pp. 250-251.

Wildes, Marry Emerson. "Japanese Police." *Journal of Criminal Law and Criminology, XIX* (1928-1929).

Police

Barnett, J. "The Japanese Traffic Police." *International Police Chronicle,* 62 (September-October, 1963), pp. 17-23.

Bayley, David H. *Forces of Order, Police Behavior in Japan and the United States.* Berkeley: University of California Press, 1976.

Chiba, Yujiro. "Revision of Police Duties Law." *Contemporary Japan,* 25 (March, 1959), pp. 621-634.

Clifford, William. *Crime Control in Japan.* Lexington, MA: D.C. Heath, 1976.

"Combating Crime in Japan" *International Criminal Police Review* (January, 1966), pp. 13-14.

Costello, William. "Cops and Robbers in Japan." *Nation,* 168 (January 22, 1949), pp. 96-97.

Cramer, James. "Police Forces of the World: Tokyo." *Police Review (GB),* 66 (December 19, 1958).

Criminal Police of Japan. Tokyo: National Poliee Agency, 1965.

Durin, Lucien. "The Japanese Police." *International Police Chronicle,* 14 (November-December, 1967), pp. 21-28.

Farrow, Frederick. "Police Work in Tokyo." *Police Review* (March, 1973), pp. 350-351.

"Guardians of the Safest City in the World [Tokyo]." *SARP* (June, 1972).

Hatano, Akira. "Things Which the Scene of Crime Tells." *International Criminal Police Review* (March, 1960), pp. 87-91.

Hayashi, K. "Destructive Operations against Gangster Organization." *International Criminal Police Review* (October, 1967), pp. 237-239.

Hidendori, Nakahara. "The Japanese Police." *Journal of Criminal Law, Criminology and Police Science,* 46 (November-December 1955), pp. 583-594.

Historical background, transition after World War II, reforms in 1954, and an outline of the present system of police in Japan.

"How World's Biggest City Keeps Crime Rate Low." *U.S. New & World Report,* 63 (October 9, 1967), pp. 75-76.

Imaizumi, Masataka. "Locating Buried Bodies." *FBI Law Enforcement Bulletin,* 43:8 (August, 1974), pp. 2-5.

Ishikawa, T. "Security Situation in Japan." *Guardian,* 1:1 (1972), pp. 29-34.

The Japanese Police. Tokyo: National Police Agency, 1965.

The Japanese Police System. Tokyo: National Police Agency, 1964.

Japan National Police Agency. *The Organizations for Control over Narcotics and the Laws and Regulations Concerning Narcotic Control.* Tokyo: National Police Agency, 1964.

"Jap Cops." *The New Yorker,* 22 (July 13, 1946) pp. 15-16.

Kawai, Hisato. "The Japanese Police." *Police Yearbook,* Washington DC: IACP 1956.

Miyoshi, Seiki. "Studies in Criminal Investigation." *International Criminal Police Review* (December, 1967), pp. 275-280.

Morris, I.I. "Policemen and Students in Japanese Politics." *Pacific Affairs,* 32 (March, 1959), pp. 5-17.

Nakahara, Hidenori. "The Japanese Police." *Journal of Criminal Law, Criminology and Police Science,* 46:4 (November-December, 1955), pp. 583-594.

"The Police of Japan."*Police Chief,* 30 (February, 1963), pp. 42-46.

Reynolds, Daniel G. "Japanese Police Go Democratic." *Police Chiefs Newsletter,* 14 (May, 1947).

Rinalducci, Ralph J. *The Japanese Police Establishment.* Springfield, IL: C.C. Thomas, 1974.

Schram, V. and B. Schram. "Report from Fuji." *Map Holiday,* 5:12 (February, 1949).

Shimasue, Tatsujiro. "The Maritime Safety Board (Coast Guard of Japan)." *Police Yearbook,* Washington, DC: IACP, 1958.

Sissons, D.C.S. "The Dispute over Japan's Police Law." *Pacific Affairs,* 32 (March, 1959), pp. 34-45.

Thornton, R.Y. "The Kidotai—Mobile Task Forces of Japan." *Police Chief,* XXXVIII:7 (July, 1971), pp. 65-73.

"Tokyo Motorcycle Cops Curb Speedsters in Photo Finish." *Spring 3100,* 29:11 (December, 1958).

"Traffic Control Tower in Tokyo" *Illustrated London News,* 241 (December 15, 1962).

Tsuchida, Kuniyasu. "Crime Combat Team." *FBI Law Enforcement Bulletin,* 39:9 (September, 1970), pp. 21-23.

Special investigation squad of the Tokyo Metropolitan Police.

Turner, Carl C. "Police of Japan." *Police Chief,* 30 (February, 1963).

Wildes, H.E. "The Postwar Japanese Police." *Journal of Criminal Law, Criminology and Police Science,* 43:5 (January/February, 1953), pp. 655-671.

Winant, T.T. "The Police of Tokyo." *Police Journal (GB),* 44 (April-June, 1971), pp. 167-172.

"Women Police in Japan." *International Criminal Police Review* (August-September, 1968) pp. 197-205.
Excellent article—covers history, recruitment, education, police women's allowances, responsibility and strength.

JERSEY

Police

Cramer, James. "Police Forces of the World: Island of Jersey." *Police Review (GB),* 68 (January 22, 1960).

Fenwick, R.G. *Report on the Inspection of the States of Jersey Police Force, June 15, 1971-July 2, 1971.* London: HMIC, Home Office, 1972.

Le Brocq, E.H. "Island of Jersey and Its Police System." *Police College Magazine* (Autumn, 1960), pp. 265-271.

"More About Jersey's Police." *Police Review* (September 8, 1972).

JORDAN

Police

Hoff, Rodger L. "Role of Police Forces in Developing Nations." *Military Police Journal* (January, 1972), pp. 5-9.

Lowe, Stuart. "The Royal Jordanian Police Force." *Warren* (Autumn, 1976), pp. 13-15.

KENYA

Criminal Law

Brown, Douglas. *Criminal Procedure in Uganda and Kenya.* London: Sweet and Maxwell, 1970.

Kennedy, D.C. *Digest and Guide to the Criminal Law of Kenya.* (2nd ed.) [n.p.]: East African Standard, 1954.

Kenya Law Reports. (vols. 1-29), 1897-1956. Dobbs Ferry NY: Oceana, 1967.

Laws of Kenya. (11 vols. and 4 supls.), Dobbs Ferry NY: Oceana, 1963-1968.

Trevelwan, E., ed. *Digest of the Decisions of the Supreme Court of Kenya in the Exercise of its Criminal Revisional Jurisdiction in the Years* 1899-1964. Dobbs Ferry, NY: Oceana, [n.d.]

Police History

Foran, W. Robert. *The Kenya Police* 1887-1960. London: Hale, 1962.

Sempill, C.I. "Criminal in Kenya Colony." *Police Journal (GB),* (1929), pp. 557-570.

Police

Castle, Barbara. "Justice in Kenya." *New Statesman and Nation,* 50 (December 17, 1955), pp. 821-822.

"The History, Organisation and Work of the Kenya (Railways and Harbours) Police." *Kenya Police Review* (September, 1974), pp. 4-6.

Kanyutu, J.N. "Relationship between Police and Public." *Kenya Police Review* (December, 1973), pp. 15-16.

Kasango, T.M. "Crime and Police in Urban Areas." *Kenya Police Review* (March, 1972), pp. 10, 12.

"The Kenya Police Dog Section." *International Criminal Police Review* (May, 1970), pp. 154-157.

"Why Colonel Young Resigned." *New Statesman and Nation,* 49:2 (January 1, 1955).

KOREA

General

U.S. Department of the Army. *Area Handbook: Korea.* Washington, DC: GPO, 1964.

Crime

Hahm, Pyong Choon and Byong Je Jon. "The Criminality of Abortion in Korea." *Journal of Criminal Law, Criminology and Police Science,* 56:1 (March, 1965), pp. 18-26.

Criminal Law

Korean Criminal Code. South Hackensack NJ: Rothman, 1960.

Ryu, Paul Kichyun. "The New Korean Criminal Code of October 3, 1953. An Analysis of Ideologies Embedded in It." *Journal of Criminal Law, Criminology and Police Science,* 48:3 (September-October, 1957), pp. 275-295.

Police

Forbes, Harry. "Korean Cops American Style." *Saturday Evening Post,* 219:6 (July 13, 1946).

Lee, Jong Kuck. "The Korean National Police." *International Police Academy Review,* 5 (April, 1971), pp. 12-16.

Metropolitan Police. Seoul: Korea Republic Police, [n.d.]

"National Police of Korea." *International Police Academy Review* (July, 1968), pp. 13-, 11.

"Speaking of Pictures." *Life,* 22 (June 24, 1947), pp. 20-22.

LAOS

Sirimat, Chanh. "The Lao National Police." *International Police Academy Review,* 4 (January, 1970), pp. 1-5.

LATVIA

Latvian Legation. "The Latvian Police: The Youngest European Police Force." *Police Journal (GB),* IV (April, 1931), pp. 232-241.

LEBANON

General

U.S. Department of the Army. *Area Handbook: Lebanon.* Washington, DC: GPO, 1969-1974.

Police

"The Green Plan." *International Criminal Police Review* (June-July, 1968), pp. 146-151.

Program to introduce health crops to replace cannabis in Lebanon.

Rizkallah, Elias. "The Police of Lebanon." *Police Chief,* 28:6 (June, 1961).

LESOTHO

Garner, Peter E. "Policing in Lesotho." *Police Journal (GB),* (January-March, 1971), pp. 41-47.

LIBERIA

Criminal Law

Konvitz, Milton R. *Liberian Law Reports.* (vol. 20), Ithaca, NY: Cornell University Press, 1975.

Liberia Supreme Court Report. (17 vols.), Ithaca, NY: Cornell University Press, 1959-1966.

Republic of Liberia. *Liberian Code of Laws Revised.* (vol. 1), Ithaca, NY: Cornell University Press, 1972.

Police

Minikon, Patrick. "The NBI—A Liberian Law Enforcement Agency." *FBI Law Enforcement Bulletin,* (June, 1966).

LIBYA

General

U.S. Department of the Army. *Area Handbook: Libya.* Washington, DC: GPO, 1969.

Police

Cramer, James. "Police Forces of the World: Tripolitania." *Police Review (GB),* 67 (April 3, 1959).

LIECHTENSTEIN

Cramer, James. "Police Forces of the World: Vaduz." *Poliee Review (GB),* 66 (November 7, 1958).

LUXEMBOURG

Cramer, James. "City Police of the World: Luxembourg." *Police Review (GB),* 66 (October 17, 1958).

MALAGASY

"Tananarive Police Laboratory." *International Criminal Police Review* (November, 1960), pp. 281-283.

MALAWI

Criminal Law

Laws of Malawi. (10 vols. and supls.), Dobbs Ferry, NY: Oceana, 1969-1970.

Milner, A., ed. *Malawi Law Reports, 1923-1962.* (6 vols.), Dobbs Ferry, NY: Oceana, 1968-1975.

Police History

Baker, C.A. "The Malawi Police Force—An Administrative History." *Police College Magazine,* 12:2, pp. 33-42.

Marlow, C. *A History of the Malawi Police Force.* Zomba: Malawi Constabulary, 1971.

MALAYA

General

U.S. Department of the Army. *Area Handbook for Malaysia.* Washington, DC: GPO, 1970.

Police History

Federation of Malaya and its Police, 1786-1952. Kuala Lumpur: Malaya Constabulary, 1953.

Moran, J.W.G. *The Camp Across the River: Further Recollections of an Officer in the Malayan Police Force.* London: Peter Davies, 1961.

Morrah, Patrick. *History of the Malayan Police.* Singapore: Tien Wah Press, 1968.

Also in *Journal of the Malayan Branch of the Royal Asiatic Society.* 36:2 (1968).

Pennefather-Evans, J.P. "Policing the Federated Malay States." *Police Journal (GB),* (1929), pp. 406-415.

Police

Adkins, E.H., Jr. "Malaya Controls Its Criminal Societies." *Police,* 7:2 (November-December, 1962), pp. 63-69.

Cramer, James. "Police Forces of the World: Malaya." *Police Review (GB),* 66 (November 14, 1958).

Suhara, John. "The Policeman of Today." *Royal Malaysia Police Magazine,* 35 (June, 1969).

MALTA

Cremona, J.J. *The Doctrine of Entrapment in Theft.* Valletta, Malta: Progress Press, 1960.

MAURITIUS

Rountree, F.R.G. "The Mauritius Police Force." *Police Journal (GB),* III (January, 1930), pp. 50-62.

MEXICO

General

U.S. Department of the Army. *Area Handbook: Mexico.* Washington, DC: GPO, 1975.

Crime

Hernandez, A. Frias. "Heroin Drug Traffickers." *International Criminal Police Review,* (January, 1960), pp. 10-18.

Discusses drug traffic between China and Mexico 1935-1939.

Jewell, Donald P. "Mexico's Tres Marias Penal Colony." *Journal of Criminal Law, Criminology and Police Science,* 48:4 (November-December, 1957), pp. 410-413.

Jud, G.D. "Tourism and Crime in Mexico." *Social Science Quarterly,* 56:2 (1975), pp. 324-330.
Author suggests crime increases because of the availability of victims and opportunity.

Criminal Law

Kerr, Robert J. *A Handbook of Mexican Law.* NY: Gordon, 1976.

Police History

MacLachlan, Colin M. *Criminal Justice in Eighteenth Century Mexico: A Study of the Tribunal of the Acordad.* Berkeley: University of California Press, 1975.

Mendoza, Salvador. "New Mexican System of Criminology." *Journal of Criminal Law and Criminology,* XXI (1930-1931).

Miranda, Teodoro G. "At Your Service; the Mexico City Police Department." *Pacific Coast International,* 4 (May, 1937), pp. 29-30.

Police

Barong-Lobato, Juan. "The Organization of the Police in Mexico." *International Criminal Police Review* (October, 1965), pp. 218-225.

"Mobile Laboratory for Federal District Police of Mexico City." *International Criminal Police Review* (June-July, 1966), pp. 178-180.

"New Methods in Old Mexico." *L.A. Police Beat,* 18 (July, 1963), pp. 12-13.
Activities of Mexico City Police Department.

Rector, D.B. "The Police of the City of Guadalajara." *Police,* 15:4 (March-April, 1971), pp. 77-80.

Reyes, Ed and Al Gayton. "International Cooperation in Law Enforcement." *California Peace Officer,* 7:4 (March-April. 1957).

Robbins, Charles W. "A New Outlook in Mexico Police Work." *Law and Order* (September, 1960), pp. 26-30.

Zubryn, Emil. "New Regulations for Mexico's Drivers." *Law and Order,* 8:7 (July, 1960).

MONACO

Cramer, James. "Police Forces of the World: Monaco." *Police Review (GB),* 66 (November 21, 1958).

MONGOLIA

Riasonovsky, V.A. *Fundamental Principles of Mongol Law.* Bloomington, IN: University Research Center, 1965.

NETHERLANDS

General

Smit, Pamela. *The Netherlands, Chronology and Fact Book.* Dobbs Ferry, NY: Oceana, 1973.

Crime

Adler, J.A. *A Dictionary of Criminal Science.* Amsterdam: Elsevier, 1961.

Timasheff, N.S. "The Dutch Prison System." *Journal of Criminal Law, Criminology and Police Science,* 48:6 (March-April, 1958), pp. 608-614.

Van De Waal, H., T. Wurtenberger, and W. Froentjes. *Aspects of Art Forgery.* The Hague: Martinus Nijhoff, 1962.

Police History

Bonger, W.A. "Development of the Penal Law in the Netherlands." *Journal of Criminal Law and Criminology,* XXIV (1933-1934).

Cohen, Leo A.A. "The Police Department of Amsterdam, Holland." *Police Journal (NY),* 20 (April, 2934), pp. 3-4; (May, 1934), pp. 6-7.

Police

Ashton, W.G. et al. *Report on Rotterdam Police.* Washington, DC: NCJRS, 1972.

Beaumont, D. "The Police in the Netherlands." *Constable's County* (Autumn, 1970).

Brink, F. "Parapsychology and Criminal Investigation." *International Criminal Police Review* (January, 1960), pp. 3-9.

Cramer, James. "City Police of the World: Amsterdam." *Police Review (GB),* 66 (August 22, 1958).

de Zaaijer, H.R. "Law Enforcement During German Occupation." *Annals,* 245 (May, 1946), pp. 9-18.

Huins, J.M.M. "Dutch Police." *Police College Magazine* (Autumn, 1969), pp. 36-37.

Jongboer, C.A. "The Netherlands Police." *Police Journal (GB),* 44:4 (October, 1971), pp. 312-317.

Kallenborn, J.W. "The Case of the Counterfeit Coupons." *International Criminal Police Review* (May, 1960), pp. 154-156.

McEwen, T. and R.C. Larson. "Patrol Planning in Rotterdam Police Department." *Journal of Criminal Justice,* 2:3 (1974), pp. 235-238.

McQuady, Charles W. "Behind the Scenes with an Active Security Department." *Quarterly Journal of Association for Professional Law Enforcement,* 4 (October-December, 1958), pp. 23-24.

Martens, J.M. "Police and Television in the Netherlands." *International Criminal Police Review* (April, 1959).

Meyjes, P. "Scientific Criminal Investigation Techniques under Dutch Law." *Journal of Criminal Law, Criminology and Police Science,* 51:6 (March-April, 1960-1961).

Mishkin, Barry D. "Going Dutch Police Style." *Garda Review* (September, 1976), pp. 23, 31.

"Netherlands Police." *International Criminal Police Review* (June-July, 1967), pp. 172-181.

Punch, Maurice. "Crime and the Free City—Amsterdam." *Garda Review* (December, 1974), pp. 4-7.

Punch, Maurice. "Neighborhood Bobbies, Rotterdam Style." *Police (GB),* (April, 1974), pp. 14-15.

Svensson, Arne and Otto Wendel. *Techniques of Crime Scene Investigation.* Amsterdam: Elsevier, 1966.

Templeton, Ian. "Netherlands Police." *Guardian* (Summer, 1975), pp. 61-63.

van Kaam, G.M. "The Assaying of Precious Metals and Controls or Hallmarks." *International Criminal Police Review* (April, 1970), pp. 122-129.

NETHERLANDS ANTILLES

Meyer, A. "Some Aspects of Prostitution as a Social Evil." *International Criminal Police Review* (January, 1961), pp. 22-25.

NEW GUINEA

Police History

Beaver, W.N. "Armed Constabulary of Papua and Its Possibilities." *Empire Magazine,* VIII:5 (1913).

Murray, I.H.P. "The Armed Constabulary of Papua (New Guinea)." *Police Journal (GB),* IV (October, 1931), pp. 571-582.

Police

Cramer, James. "Police Forces of the World: Papua and New Guinea." *Police Review (GB),* 67 (October 30, 1959).

Hayes, Maxwell R. "Police of Papua and New Guinea." *Police World,* 16 (Winter, 1971-1972), pp. 43-47.

Patsik, Tony. "Role of Police in New Guinea." *Australian Police Journal* (April, 1974), pp. 85-99.

Tufman, M.Z. "The Role of Police in Papua New Guinea." *Australian and New Zealand Journal of Criminology,* 7:2 (1974), pp. 87-94.

NEW ZEALAND

General

Powles, Guy. "The Citizen's Rights against the Modern State." *Public Administrative* (Australia), 23 (1964), pp. 42-68.
Author is New Zealand's ombudsman.

Crime

Drug Dependence and Drug Abuse in New Zealand. Wellington: New Zealand Board of Health, 1970.

O'Malley, Patrick. "Amplification of Maori Crimes: Cultural and Economic Barriers to Equal Justice in New Zealand." *Race* (July, 1973), pp. 47-57.

Schumacher, Mary. *Violent Offending—A Report on Recent Trends in Violent Offending and Some Characteristics of the Violent Offender.* Wellington: Justice Department, New Zealand, 1971.

Police

Caughley, J.G. and A.J.W. Taylor. "New Methods in the Promotion of Constables to Sergeants in the New Zealand Police Force." *Journal of Criminal Law, Criminology and Police Science,* 48:2 (July-August, 1957), pp. 207-212.

Chappell, Duncan. *The Police and the Public in Australia and New Zealand.* St. Lucia: University of Queensland Press, 1969.

Cramer, James. "Police Forces of the World: New Zealand." *Police Review (GB),* 67 (January 16, 1959).

New Zealand Department of Justice. *New Zealand—Department of Justice—Report for the Year Ended 31 March 1974.* Washington, DC: NCJRS, (Microfiche), 1974.

Orr, G.S. *Report on Administrative Justice in New Zealand.* Mystic, CT: Verry, 1964.

Rogers, J.H. "Officer Training in the Australian and New Zealand Forces." *Police Journal (GB),* 39:5 1966.

NICARAGUA

U.S. Department of the Army. *Area Handbook: Nicaragua.* Washington, DC: GPO, 1970.

NIGERIA

Criminal Law

Adefidiya, A. *Directory of Law Libraries in Nigeria.* Dobbs Ferry, NY: Oceana, 1970.

Elias, T.O. *Ground Work of Nigerian Law.* NY: Gordon, 1976.

Elias, T.O. *Nigerian Land Law and Custom.* NY: Gordon, 1976.

Gledhill, Alan. *The Penal Codes of Northern Nigeria and the Sudan.* London: Sweet and Maxwell, 1963.

Okonkwo, C.O. "Assaulting a Police Officer in the Execution of His Duty." *Nigerian Law Journal,* 7 (1973), pp. 1-12.

Police History

Geary, William N.M. *Nigeria Under British Rule.* NY: Barnes and Noble, 1965.

Shirley, W.R. *History of the Nigeria Police.* Lagos: Police Department, 1948.

Police

Bovell, Kerr. "Police of Nigeria." *Police Chief,* 29:10 (October, 1963).

Ezekiel-Hart, R.E. *Keepers of the Peace: Facts About the Nigeria Police Force.* Lagos: Police Department, 1962.

Ohonbamu, Obarogie. "Dilemma of Police Organization under a Federal System: The Nigerian Example." *Nigerian Law Journal,* 6 (1972), pp. 73-87.

Okonkwo, Cyprian O. *The Police and Public in Nigeria.* London: Sweet and Maxwell, 1966.

Soyinka, Wole. *The Man Died.* NY: Harper and Row, 1972.

Tamuno, Tek Ena. *The Police in Modern Nigeria, 1861-1965.* Ibadan, Nigeria: Ibadan University Press, 1965.

NORTH KOREA

Masao, Fukushima. *On the Socialist Constitution of the Democratic People's Republic of Korea.* Pyongyang: Foreign Languages, 1975.

NORTHERN IRELAND

General

Boyd, Andrew. *Holy War in Belfast: A History of the Troubles in Northern Ireland.* NY: Grove, 1972.

Police History

Brady, Conor. "R.U.C." Perspective from the Past." *Garda Review* (October, 1974), pp. 2-3.

Clark, H.W.S. *Guns in Ulster.* Belfast: Constabulary Gazette, 1967.
A history of the Ulster Special Constabulary in South Londonderry, 1920-1966.

Kennedy, Albert. "History and Organization of the Royal Ulster Constabulary." *Police Journal (GB),* (February, 1967); (March, 1967).

O'Neill, Frederick. "Presenting the Royal Ulster Constabulary." *Police Journal (NY),* 21 (March, 1935), pp. 9-10.

Police

Constabulary List and Directory, 34th Year. Belfast: Constabulary Gazette, 1972.

Cramer, James. "City Police of the World: Belfast." *Police Review (GB),* 66 (August 15, 1958).

Hezlet, Arthur. *The "B" Specials: A History of the Ulster Special Constabulary.* New Abbot, Devon: Tom Stacey, 1972.

Kennedy, Albert. "The Royal Ulster Constabulary." *Police Journal (GB),* 40 (February, 1967), pp. 53-67.

Morgan, W.H.D. "Forensic Science in Northern Ireland." *Police Journal (GB),* (January-March, 1959), pp. 46-52.

"The Royal Ulster Constabulary—A Brief Review of Its Constitution and Organization." *Police Review (GB),* (August 22, 1969).

Shaw, C.B. "Prosecution of Offenses in Northern Ireland." *Police Surgeon* (April, 1975), pp. 109-114.

Stanage, Basil. "Attractive and Acceptable Police Service for Ulster." *Police Review* (September 13, 1974), pp. 1172-1190.

"You Can't Win a Friend with a Gun: New Role and Leader for Northern Ireland Police." *Police Review (GB),* (October 17, 1969), pp. 909, 912, 913.

NORWAY

Crime

Pihlblad, C. Terence. "The Juvenile Offender in Norway." *Journal of Criminal Law, Criminology and Police Science,* 46:4 (November/December, 1955), pp. 500-511.

Criminal Law

Andenaes, Johannes. *The General Part of the Criminal Law of Norway.* South Hackensack, NJ: Rothman, 1965.

Haukaas, Kaare. *Norwegian Legal Publications in English, French and German.* Boston: Universitet, 1967.

Norwegian Penal Code. South Hackensack, NJ: Rothman, 1961.

Police

Cramer, James. "Police Forces of the World: Oslo." *Police Review (GB),* 67 (January 2, 1959).

Gjerde, Johan. "The Mystery of 'The Wednesday Grenade Man.'" *FBI Law Enforcement Bulletin* (January, 1968).

Hartman, Bernhard. "Police of Norway, 1957." *Police College Magazine* (Autumn, 1957), pp. 8-12, 15-18.

Muir, A.A. "Police in Norway." *Police Journal (GB),* 36 (September, 1963), pp. 424-427.

Rawlings, Frank. "The Norwegian Police." *Police Journal (GB),* 38 (February, 1965), pp. 55-57.

PAKISTAN

General

U.S. Department of the Army. *Area Handbook: Pakistan.* Washington, DC: GPO, 1971.

Crime

Afsarunddin, Mohammad. *Juvenile Delinquency in East Pakistan.* [n.p.].: University of Dacca, 1965.

Najmuddin, Dilshad. "The Kidnapping of Diplomatic Personnel." *Police Chief* (February, 1973).

Owen, John E. "Crime in Pakistan." *Journal of Criminal Law, Criminology and Police Science,* 50:6 (1959-1960).

Criminal Law

Fyzee, Asaf A. *Cases in the Muhammadan Law of India and Pakistan.* NY: Oxford University Press, 1965.

Police History

Razui, Nazir A. *Our Police Heritage: Saga of the Police Force of Pakistan and India.* Islamabad: Police Service of Pakistan, 1961.

Police

Cramer, James. "Police Forces of the World: SWAT." *Police Review (GB),* 67 (August, 1959).

Hasanat, Abul. "The CID in East Pakistan." *Journal of Criminal Law, Criminology and Police Science.* 48:4 (November-December, 1957), pp. 447-458.

PERU

General

U.S. Department of the Army. *Area Handbook: Peru.* Washington, DC: GPO, 1972.

Police History

"Police Training in Peru." *Journal of Criminal Law and Criminology,* 24 (March-April, 1934), pp. 1128-1129.

Police

Basauri, Carlos. "Forensic Odontology and Identification." *International Criminal Police Review* (February, 1961).

"An Interesting Police Exhibition in Peru." *International Criminal Police Review* (April, 1963), pp. 116-122.

PHILIPPINES

Crime

"The Philippines." *Time,* 89:22 (June 2, 1967), p. 24.
Describes the increase in crimes of all kinds, especially violence in the Philippines.

U.S. Treasury Department. *Traffic in Opium and Other Dangerous Drugs with Respect to the Philippine Islands, 1928-1936 and 1937-1940.* Philippines: Department of Public Instruction, [n.d.]

Zarco, Ricardo M. *A Sociological Study of the Illegal Narcotic Activity in the Philippines.* Unpub. Thesis, University of the Philippines, 1959.

Criminal Law

Gamboa, M.J. *Introduction to Philippine Law.* Dobbs Ferry, NY: Oceana, 1969.

Philippine Supreme Court Reports, Annotated: 1961-1975. (66 vols.), Dobbs Ferry, NY: Oceana, [n.d.].

Police

"Books for the Philippine Constabulary." *Police Chief,* 30 (October, 1963).

McQuady, Charles W. "Law Enforcement in Manila, P.I." *Quarterly Journal of Association for Professional Law Enforcement,* 4 (October-December, 1958), pp. 27-29.

"National Bureau of Investigation Drug Addiction Institute." *NBI Law Enforcement Monthly,* 3 (1965).

Tendero, Avelino and M. Ladd Thomas. *The Organization of the Manila Police Department.* Manila: Institute of Public Administration, University of Philippines, 1953.

Thomas, M. Ladd. "Philippine Police Systems." *Journal of Criminal Law, Criminology and Police Science,* 46:1 (May-June, 1955) pp. 116-121.

POLAND

General

Renkiewicz, F. *Poland, Chronology and Fact Book.* Dobbs Ferry, NY: Oceana, 1973.

Criminal Law

Jasinski, Jerzy. "Delinquent Generations in Poland." *The British Journal of Criminology,* 6:2 (1966).

"Lay Judges in the Polish Criminal Courts: A Legal and Empirical Description." *Case Western Reserve Journal of International Law,* 7:1980 (1975), pp. 198-209.

Penal Code of the Polish People's Republic. South Hackensack, NJ: Rothman, 1973.

Wagner, W.J., ed. *Polish Law Throughout the Ages.* Stanford,CA: Hoover Institute Press, 1970.

Police

Cramer, James. "Police Forces of the World: Warsaw." *Police Review (GB),* 67 (August 21, 1959).

Holyst, Brunon. "Factors Connected with Homicides and Their Importance in Investigations." *International Criminal Police Review* (March, 1969), pp. 78-81.

PUERTO RICO

Criminal Law

Beutel, Frederick K. *The Operation of the Bad Check Laws of Puerto Rico.* San Juan: University of Puerto Rico Press, [n.d.]

Reckless, Walter C., Jaime Toro-Calder, and Ceferina Cedeno. "A Comparative Study of Puerto Rican Attitudes toward the Legal System Dealing with Crime." *Journal of Criminal Law, Criminology and Police Science,* 59:4 (December, 1968), pp. 536-541.

Police

Cramer, James. "Police Forces of the World: Puerto Rico." *Police Review (GB),* 67 (September 11, 1959).

Puerto Rico LEAA Comprehensive State Plan—Abstract, 1971. Washington, DC: LEAA, 1971.

Roig, Salvador T. "Puerto Rico's Unique Position for Development of Police Programs for Central and South America." *Police Yearbook,* Washington, DC: IACP, 1959.

Velez, Pedro M., Jr. "Cher Chez La Femme." *International Criminal Police Review* (June-July, 1961), pp. 184-185.

RHODESIA

Police History

Blue and Old Gold. Cape Town: Howard B. Timmins, 1952.
Historical and other stories of the British South Africa Police.

Harding, Colin. *Frontier Patrols: History of the British South Africa Police and Other Rhodesian Forces.* London: G. Bell, 1938.

Hemans, H. *Log of a Native Commissioner.* Mystic, CT: Verry, 1971. (repr. of 1932 ed.).

Hole, H. Marshall. "The Police Forces of Southern Rhodesia." *Police Journal (GB)* III (July, 1930).

Loyd, Frank. *Rhodesian Patrol.* Ilfracombe Devon: A.H. Stockwell, 1965.

Police

"Police Demonstrating Bicycles Adapted for Patroling Rhodesian Railway Property." *Illustrated London News,* 235:178 (September 5, 1959).

"Presentation of Awards to Police Recruits Who Have Completed Training at the Northern Rhodesia Police Training School." *Illustrated London News,* 238:534 (April 1, 1961).

Turner, Carl C. "Police of Southern Rhodesia." *Police Chief,* 30 (April, 1963) pp. 40-44.

RUSSIA

General

"Biggest Lie of Them All." *Newsweek,* 55:44 (June 13, 1960).

Levine, Isaac D. "Why Soviet Takes Back Trotsky's Killer." *U.S. News & World Report,* 48 (May 23, 1960), pp. 85-86.

Schapiro, Leonard. *The Government and Politics of the Soviet Union.* NY: Random House, 1965.
Discusses local and state government, the framework of administration and the organs of control.

Werth, Alexander. "Russia, from Terror to Incentive." *Nation,* 190 (January 16, 1960), pp. 44-47.

Crime

Alexander, Edward. "Crime and Soviet Armenia." *Armenian Review,* 11 (November, 1958), pp. 3-12.

Beerman, R. "Study of the Soviet Criminal." *Soviet Studies,* 14:1 (July, 1962).

Berman, Nathan and E.W. Burgess. "The Development of Criminological Research in the Soviet Union." *American Sociological Review,* 2:2 (1937).

Brokhin, Uri. *Hustling on Gorky Street: Sex and Crime in Russia Today.* NY: Dial, 1975.

Connor, Walter D. *Deviance in Soviet Society—Crime, Delinquency, and Alcoholism.* NY: Columbia University Press, 1972.

Foltz, Charles. "Crime and Punishment in the Soviet Union Today." *U.S. News & World Report,* 56 (March 2, 1964), pp. 90-91.

Melinikova, E. "Delinquency Prevention in the Soviet Union." *International Journal of Offender Therapy,* 12:1 (1968), pp. 41-45.
The article asserts that all Soviet criminologists unanimously agree that the causes of juvenile delinquency are not inherent in the personality or constitutional or biological factors, but are sociologically conditioned. However, the social situation is not static and delinquency must be understood in the historical and changing context of society. Prevention is in raising living standards and re-educating, preventing recidivism and removing conditions conducive to crime.

Solomon, Peter H., Jr. *Soviet Criminology.* Unpub. Master's Thesis, Columbia University, 1967.

"Treatment of Addiction in the U.S.S.R." *International Criminal Police Review* (July, 1959).

"Whoever Steals Lives Better." *Reader's Digest* (August, 1976), pp. 126-127.

Criminal Law

Barry, Donald and Harold S. Berman. "The Soviet Legal Profession." *Harvard Law Review,* 82:1 (1968), pp. 1-41.

Berman, Harold J. *Justice in the USSR: An Interpretation of the Soviet Law.* Cambridge: Harvard University Press, 1963.

Berman, Harold J. *Soviet Criminal Law and Procedure—The RSFSR Codes.* (2nd ed.) Cambridge: Harvard University Press, 1972.

Berman, Harold J. and Miroslav Kerner. *Soviet Military Law and Administration.* Cambridge: Harvard University Press, 1955.

Chalidze, Valery. *To Defend These Rights: Human Rights and the Soviet Union.* London: Collins and Harvill, 1975.

Conquest, Robert, ed. *Justice and the Legal System in the U.S.S.R.* NY: Praeger, 1968.

Feifer, George. *Justice in Moscow.* NY: Simon and Schuster, 1964.

Feldbrugge, F.J. *Soviet Criminal Law: The General Part.* Leyden: A.W. Sythoff, 1964.

Feldbrugge, F.J. "Soviet Criminal Law—The Last Six Years." *Journal of Criminal Law, Criminology and Police Science,* 54:3 (September, 1963), pp. 249-266.

Grzybowski, Kazimierz. *Soviet Legal Institutions: Doctrines and Social Functions.* Ann Arbor: University of Michigan Press, 1962.

Gsovski, Vladimir and Kazimierz Grzybowski, eds. *Government and Law and Courts in the Soviet Union and Eastern Europe.* (2 vols.) NY: Praeger, 1959.

Hazard, John N. and Isaac Shapiro. *The Soviet Legal System.* Dobbs Ferry, NY: Oceana, 1962.

Hazard, John N. et al. *The Soviet Legal System.* (2nd ed.), Dobbs Ferry, NY: Oceana, 1969.

La Fave, Wayne R. *Law in the Soviet Society.* Urbana: University of Illinois Press, 1965.

Napolitano, T. "Outline of Modern Soviet Criminal Law." *International Commission Jurists Journal,* 6:1 (Summer, 1965).

Russel, Ralph. *Russia: Soviet Criminal Law and Procedure, The RSFSR Codes.* (2nd ed.) Cambridge MA: Harvard University Press, 1972.

Schlesinger, Rudolf. *Soviet Legal Theory: Its Social Background and Development.* London: Paul, 1945.

Terebilov, Vladimir. *Soviet Court: Guide to the Constitutional Principal of the Administration of Justice in the U.S.S.R..* Brooklyn Heights, NY: Beakman, 1975.

Tokes, Rudolph L., ed. *Dissent in the USSR: Politics, Ideologies and People.* Baltimore: Johns Hopkins University Press, 1975.

Translations on Soviet Law and Social Regulations. Washington, DC: Joint Publications Research Service, 1966.

Vyshinsky, Andrei Y. *The Law of the Soviet State.* NY: Macmillan, 1951.

Police History

Bailey, Sidney D. "Police Socialism in Tsarist Russia." *Review of Politics,* 19 (October, 1957), pp. 462-471.

Brunovsky, Vladimir. *The Methods of the OGPU, The Secret Police Organization of Soviet Russia.* NY: Harpers, 1931.

"The Cheka (1917-1921): Origin and Early Development of the Soviet Political Police." *Soviet Affairs,* (1956), pp. 1-23.

Deacon, Richard. *History of the Russian Secret Service.* London: Muller, 1972.

Gillin, John L. "Russia's Criminal Court and Penal System." *Journal of Criminal Law and Criminology,* XXIV (1933-1934).

Haensel, Vladimir. "Justified Murder in Russia." *Journal of Criminal Law and Criminology,* XXIII (1932-1933).

Koerber, Lenka Von. *Soviet Russia Fights Crime.* NY: Dutton, 1935.

Monas, S. *The Third Section: Police and Society in Russia Under Nicholas I.* London: Oxford University Press, 1961.

"Russian Secret Police." *Police Journal (GB),* (July, 1929), pp. 492-502.

Squire, Peter Stansfield. *The Third Department: The Establishment and Practices of the Political Police in the Russia of Nicholas I.* London: Cambridge University Press, 1968.

Vassilyew, A.T. *Ochrana: The Russian Secret Police.* Philadelphia: J.B. Lippincott, 1930.

Police

Amory, Robert, Jr. "Law Enforcement in Soviet Russia." *Police Yearbook,* Washington, DC: IACP, 1960.

Bakhanskaia, N. "New Legislation on the Volunteer Auxiliary Police." *Soviet Law and Government,* XIV:2 (Fall, 1975), pp. 3-11.

Beck, F. and W. Godin. *Russian Purge and the Extraction of Confession.* NY: Viking, 1950.

Berman, Harold J. *Justice in the U.S.S.R.: An Interpretation of Soviet Law.* (rev. ed.), Cambridge MA: Harvard University Press, 1963.

Bernaret, Elsa and Melville J. Ruggles. *Collective Leadership and the Political Police in the Soviet Union.* Santa Monica, CA: Rand, 1956.

"Brooklyn in Russia." *Newsweek,* 53:48 (April 27, 1959).
A city in Russia duplicates American life exactly to make agents more competent in spying.

Conquest, Robert. *Great Terror: Stalin's Purge of the Thirties.* NY: Macmillan, 1973.

Conquest, Robert. *Nation Killers: Soviet Deportation of Nationalities.* NY: Macmillan, 1971.

Conquest, Robert. *The Soviet Police System.* London: Bodley Head, 1968.

Cramer, James. "Police Forces of the World: Moscow." *Police Review (GB),* 67 (January 23, 1959).

Deriabin, P. and F. Gibney. "Kremlin Intrigue and Debauche." *Life,* 46 (March 30, 1959).

Deriabin, P. and F. Gibney. "Red Agent's Vivid Tale of Terror." *Life,* 46 (March 23, 1959).

Hammer, Darrell P. "Law Enforcement, Social Control and the Withering of the State: Recent Soviet Experience." *Soviet Studies,* 14 (April, 1963), pp. 379-397.

Hearn, C.V. *Russian Assignment: A Policeman Looks at Crime in the U.S.S.R.*. London: Hale, 1962.

Heilbrun, Otto. *The Soviet Secret Services.* NY: Praeger, 1956.

Hingley, Ronald. *Russian Secret Police: Muscovite, Imperial Russian and Soviet Political Security Operations, 1965-1970.* London: Hutchinson, 1970.

"If It's Spies You're Wondering about." *U.S. News & World Report,* 48 (June 27, 1960), pp. 70-73.
Report by State Department on Soviet spying. Number of spies were put at 300,000 of which 360 have been convicted.

"Iowa in the Ukraine." *Time,* 73 (April 27, 1959).

Meyer, Alfred G. *The Soviet Political System: An Interpretation.* NY: Random House, 1965.
Contains chapter on "control over the behavior of citizens."

Mikonov, N. "More Active Party Aid in Law Enforcement Urged." *Current Digest of Soviet Press,* 16 (June 3, 1964), pp. 17-19.

Moore, Barrington, Jr. *Terror and Progress—U.S.S.R.: Some Sources of Change and Stability in the Soviet Dictatorship.* NY: Harper and Row, 1966.

"Moscow: The Other Police." *New Statesman,* 66 (August 16, 1973).

Nosenko, Uri Ivanovich. "Under the Eye of the KGB—A Former Police Chief Looks Back." *Listener,* 22 (May, 1975).

O'Connor, Dennis M. "Soviet People's Guards: An Experiment with Civic Police." *New York University Law Review* (June, 1964).

Pospielovsky, Dimitry. *Russian Police Trade Unionism: Experiment or Provocation?* London: Weidenfeld and Nicolson, 1971.

"The Public Organizations of Moscow's Kuibyshev Borough in the Struggle against Violations of Soviet Law and the Rules of Socialist Society." *Current Digest of the Soviet Press,* 12 (December 14, 1960), pp. 10-12.

Romanov, A.I. *Nights Are Longest There: Smersh from the Inside.* London: Hutchinson, 1972.

Taylor, Pauline B. "The Role of the Investigator in Soviet Criminal Procedure." *Journal of International Commission of Jurists,* 7 (Summer, 1966), pp. 20-32.

Tikunov, V.S. "The Cheka as a Model of Human Law Enforcement." *Current Digest of Soviet Press,* 11 (August, 1959), pp. 8-13.

Volkov, Anatoly. "The Moscow Militia." *The Virginia Trooper,* 13:10 (1965), pp. 20-22.

SAMOA

Police

American Samoa LEAA Comprehensive State Plan—Abstract, 1971. Washington, DC: LEAA, 1971.
A digest of the 1971 law enforcement assistance administration comprehensive state plan has been compiled for American Samoa.

American Samoa: 1969 Annual Report to the Secretary of the Interior. Washington, DC: GPO, 1970.

Contains some data on public safety along with other government services.

Marsack, C.C. *Samoan Melody*. London: Robert Hale, 1961.
Includes details of tribal police.

Trussell, Tait. "Trouble in Paradise." *Nation's Business* (July, 1968), pp. 82-87.
This paper discusses how U.S. federal government involvement in Samoa has been a mixed blessing. Discusses a growing juvenile delinquency and crime problem.

SARAWAK

Cramer, James. "Police Forces of the World: Sarawak." *Police Review (GB),* 67 (March 29, 1959).

SAUDI ARABIA

U.S. Department of the Army. *Area Handbook: Saudi Arabia,* Washington, DC: GPO, 1971.

SCOTLAND

Crime

Arnott, Alison J.B. and Judith A. Duncan. *The Scottish Criminal.* Edinburgh: Edinburgh University, 1970.

Shields, J.V.M. and Judith A. Duncan. *The State of Crime in Scotland.* London: Tavistock, 1964.

Criminal Law

Gordon, Gerald H. *The Criminal Law of Scotland.* Edinburgh: W. Green, 1967.

Police History

Angus, J.W. *A Treatise on the Powers and Duties of Police Constables in Scotland.* Edinburgh: W. Green, 1922.

Germain, John J. "Glasgow and Its Police Force; City Which Pioneered for Social Betterment Has Little Crime Today." *Police Journal (NY),* 20 (August, 1934), pp. 6-8.

McLevy, James. *Casebook of a Victorian Detective.* Edinburgh: Canongate, 1975.

Rait, R.S. "Scottish Police in Early Times." *Police Journal (GB),* III (January, 1930), pp. 79-88.

Robertson, David. *A History of the High Constables of Edinburgh: With Notes on Watching, Warding and Other Subjects.* Edinburgh: Privately printed, 1924.

Ross, Roderick. "Edinburgh City Police." *Police Journal (GB),* III (October, 1930), pp. 498-508.

Ross, Donald A. "Scottish Police Administration in Town and Country." *Police Journal (GB),* III (July, 1930), pp. 412-424.

Steuart, James. "City Edinburgh Special Constabulary." *Police Journal (GB),* (1929), pp. 455-491.

Police

Banton, Michael. *The Policeman in the Community.* NY: Basic, 1964.
Comparison of Scottish and American police forces.

Glasgow Chief Constable. *Glasgow (Scotland)—Chief Constable—Report, 1973.* Washington, DC: NCJRS, (Nicrofiche), 1974.

Glasgow Police. *Glasgow (Scotland)—Police-Community Involvement—The Key to Crime Prevention, 1974.* Washington, DC: NCJRS, (Microfiche), 1974.

Grant, Douglas. *The Thin Blue Line: The Story of the City of Glasgow Police.* London: John Long, 1973.

Howlett, Hamilton. *Highland Constable: The Life and Times of Rob Roy MacGregor.* Edinburgh: William Blackwood, 1950.

Lunden, Walter A. "The Constabulary of Scotland." *Journal of Criminal Law, Criminology and Police Science,* 60:3 (September, 1969), pp. 402-407.

Mackenzie, Kenny. "First Decade of the Scottish Mountain Rescue Service." *Police Review (GB),* (September 5, 1975), pp. 112-113.

Mill, James. *The Scottish Police: An Outline of Their Powers and Duties.* Edinburgh: W. Green, 1944.

Scottish Information Office. *Tulliallan Castle, Scottish Police College.* Edinburgh: Howie and Seath, September, 1972.

Urquart, J. "Constitutional Position of the Police in Scotland." *Guardian* (Summer, 1974), pp. 19-20.

SIERRA LEONE

Miller, A., ed. *African Law Reports, Sierra Leone Series, 1950-1969.* (5 vols.) Dobbs Ferry, NY: Oceana, 1970-1972.

SINGAPORE

Police History

Ahmad, Hashim bin Haji. "History of the Singapore Police Force." *Singapore Police Magazine,* (1969).

Onraet, Rene. *Singapore: A Police Background.* [n.p.]: Dorothy Crisp, 1947.

Crime

Hill, H. "The Ganja (Cannabis) Problem in Singapore." *International Criminal Police Review* (October, 1968), pp. 210-220.

SOMALI

Criminal Law

Ganzglass, Martin R. *Penal Code of Somali Democratic Republic.* New Brunswick, NJ: Rutgers University Press, 1971.

Muhammad, Haji N. *Legal System of the Somali Democratic Republic.* Charlottesville, VA: Michie, 1972.

Police

Cramer, James. "Police Forces of the World: Somaliland." (British), *Police Review (GB),* 67 (June 5, 1959).

SOUTH AFRICA

Crime

Forman, Lionel. *South African Treason Trial.* London: Calder, 1957.

Freed, Louis F. *Crime in South Africa, An Integralist Approach.* Capetown: Juta, 1953.

Van der Walt, Piet J. "University Teaching of Criminology in the Republic of South Africa." *Journal of Criminal Law, Criminology and Police Science,* 52:2 (July-August, 1961).

Williamson, Robert C. "Crime in South Africa: Some Aspects of Causes and Treatment." *Journal of Criminal Law, Criminology and Police Science,* 48 (July-August, 1957), pp. 185-192.

Criminal Law

Brookes, Edgar Harry and J.B. Macaulay. *Civil Liberty in South Africa.* Cape Town: Oxford University Press, 1958.

Mathews, A.S. *Law, Order and Liberty in South Africa.* Berkeley: University of California, 1972.

May, Henry J. *South African Constitution.* Westport, CT: Greenwood, 1955.

Police History

Cooper, F.W. "Police Force of South Africa." *Police Journal (GB),* II (April, 1929), pp. 247-265.

Cooper, F.W. "Short History of the South African Police." *SARP* (May, 1972), through (April, 1973).

Gibbs, Peter. *The History of the British South Africa Police.* (vol. 1), *The First Line of Defense, 1899-1903.* Salisbury, Rhodesia: Kingston, 1972.

Gibbs, Peter. *History of the British South African Police.* (vol. 2) *The Right of the Line, 1903-1939.* Salisbury, Rhodesia: Kingston, 1974.

Godley, R.S. *Khaki and Blue: Thirty-Five Years' Service in South Africa.* [n.p.]: Lovat, Dickson and Thompson, 1935.

Hattersley, A.F. *The First South African Detectives.* Folkstone, Kent: Bailey and Swinfen, 1961.

Onselen, Lenno van. *A Rhapsody in Blue: A History of the South African Police.* Cape Town: Howard Timmins, 1960.

Outpost. XLIX:3 (March, 1971).
Sixtieth anniversary issue. *Outpost* is the magazine of the British South African Police.

Quirk, W.H. "Special Police Problems in the Union of South Africa." *Police Journal (GB),* (1928), pp. 284-290.

Police

Bloom, Harry. "The South African Police (Duties and Excesses in Handling Racial Incidents)." *Africa South,* 2 (October-December, 1957), pp. 8-20.

Blue and Gold: A Selection of Stories from "The Outpost," the Regimental Magazine of the British South Africa Police. Cape Town: Howard B. Timmins, 1953.

Boberg, Ulf. *Boberg Story.* Cape Town: Howard Timmins, 1957.
Autobiography of South Africa's famous C.I.D. Chief.

Cramer, James. "City Police of the World: Cape Town." *Police Review (GB),* 66 (September 12, 1958).

Coonje, R. "Social Work on Behalf of Personnel." *SARP,* 9:7 (1973), pp. 18-19.

Coonje, R. "South African Police Welfare Department." *SARP,* 8:10 (1972), pp. 7-8.

Joyner, William B. *Murder Squad.* Johannesburg: Keartland, 1968.

Mathews, Anthony S. *Law, Order and Liberty in South Africa.* Berkeley: University of California Press, 1972.

"Rubber-Lined Window Screen with an Aperture for a Gun Fitted to South African Police Car." *Illustrated London News,* 240:1042 (June 30, 1962).

Ruddick, I. "British South Africa Police." *British Transport Police Journal* (Winter, 1970).

Turner, Carl C. "The Police of the Republic of South Africa." *Police Chief,* 29:7 (July, 1962), pp. 16-20.

SPAIN

Criminal Law

Serramalera, Ricardo Ruiz. "Responsibilities of the Minor in Spanish Law." *International Criminal Police Review* (June-July, 1969), pp. 167-172.

Police History

Sanjurjo, Don Jose and Marquis Del Rif. "The Spanish Civil Guard." *Police Journal (GB),* IV (July, 1931), IV: (October, 1931).

Police

Gutierrez, Alfonso G. "The Body in a Fire Suicide." *International Criminal Police Review* (January, 1967), pp. 10-14.

Hinojosa, Viqueira. "Aspects of Motor Vehicle Theft in Spain." *International Criminal Police Review* (April, 1967), pp. 94-106.

"International Frauds—Spain." *International Criminal Police Review* (February, 1969), pp. 49-50.

Palmer, Trevor. "The Spanish Civil Guard." *Police World,* 16 (Spring, 1971), pp. 14-15.

SRI LANKA (CEYLON)

General

U.S. Department of the Army. *Area Handbook: Ceylon.* Washington, DC: GPO, 1971.

Crime

Ceylon Department of Census and Statistics. *Juvenile Probationers in Ceylon.* Ceylon: Government Press, 1957.

Delgoda, J.P. "Trends of Grave Crime in Ceylon—1940-1960." *British Journal of Criminology,* 5:4 (1965).

Wood, Arthur L. *Crime and Aggression in Changing Ceylon.* Philadelphia, PA: American Philos., 1961.

Wood, Arthur Lewis. "Crime and Aggression in Changing Ceylon: A Sociological Analysis of Homicide, Suicide, and Economic Crime." *Transactions of the Philosophical Society,* 51:8 (1961).

Criminal Law

Jennings, William Ivor. *The Constitution of Ceylon.* (2nd ed.), NY: Oxford University Press, 1951.

Police History

Dep, A.C. *A History of the Ceylon Police, Vol. II: 1866-1913.* Ceylon: Times of Ceylon, 1969.

Dowbiggin, H.L. "Ceylon Police and Its Development." *Police Journal (GB),* 1 (April, 1928), pp. 203-217.

Pippet, G.K. *History of the Ceylon Police, 1795-1870.* Ceylon: Times of Ceylon, 1938.

Police

Cramer, James. "Police Forces of the World: Ceylon." *Police Review (GB),* 67 (February 28, 1959).

Report of Commission of Inquiry into Joint Operation. By Units of Police, Army and Air Force for Detection of Ganja in Alutwewa . . . . Ceylon Sessional Papers, Colombo Government Publication Bureau, 1958.

Stourton, I.H.E.J. *Functions and Activities of the Ceylon Police and the Problems Connected Therewith.* Paper read by the Inspector-General of Police (at the) Seminar of the Political Science Association of Ceylon, February 11 1956.

SUDAN

Criminal Law

Faculty of Law University of Khartoum. *Sudan Law Reports, 1900-1940.* (2 vols.) Dobbs Ferry, NY: Oceana, 1969.

Police

Cramer, James. "Police Forces of the World: Khartoum, Sudan." *Police Review (GB),* 67 (February 13, 1959).

SURINAM

Cramer, James. "Police Forces of the World: Surinam." *Police Review (GB),* 67 (May 29, 1959).

SWEDEN

Crime

Aspelin, Erland et al. *Some Developments in Nordic Criminal Policy and Criminology.* Stockholm: Scandinavian Research Council for Criminology, 1975.
Available in Microfiche from NCJRS.

Bejerot, Nils. *Addiction and Society.* Springfield IL: C.C. Thomas, 1970.

Bejerot, Nils. "The Drug Problem in Sweden: The Social and Medical Point of View." *International Criminal Police Review* (May, 1970), pp. 148-153.

Buhena, Louis. *Deviant Behavior in Sweden.* Hicksville NY: Exposition, 1971.

Esbjornson, E. "The Drug Problem in Sweden." *International Criminal Police Review* (October, 1970), pp. 251-256.

Jornander, O. and C. Persson. "The Drug Problem in Sweden. *International Criminal Police Review* (November, 1969), pp. 235-241.

Nelson, Alvar. *Responses to Crime—An Introduction to Swedish Criminal Law and Administration.* Jerome L. Getz (tr), New York: New York University School of Law Criminal Law Education and Research Center, 1972.

Sweden National Council for Crime Prevention. *Swedish Studies on Juvenile Delinquency.* Stockholm: Sweden National Council for Crime Prevention, 1976.

Tee, Nechma. *Gambling in Sweden.* Totowa, NJ: Bedminster, 1964.

Criminal Law

Bruzelius, Anders and Ruth Bader Ginsburg. *Swedish Code of Judicial Procedure.* London: Sweet and Maxwell, 1968.

Nelson, A. *Responses to Crime—An Introduction to Swedish Criminal Law and Administration.* South Hackensack, NJ: Rothman, 1972.
Overview of the penal code, statistics for the different types of crime, and outlines of the national police, courts, and correctional systems.

Penal Code of Sweden. South Hackensack, NJ: Rothman, 1972.

Police History

Kinberg, Olof. "Criminal Policy in Sweden During the Last Fifty Years." *Journal of Criminal Law and Criminology,* XXIV (1933-1934).

"Training of Detectives in Sweden." *Journal of Criminal Law and Criminology,* XXII (1932-1933).

Police

"Against the Tide." *International Criminal Police Review* (August-September, 1966), pp. 210-212.

Becker, Harold K. and Einar O. Hjellemo. *Justice in Modern Sweden.* Springfield, IL: C.C. Thomas, 1976.

Cosmo, Carl Johan. "The Swedish Ticket and Automatic Data Processing." *International Criminal Police Review* (May, 1969), pp. 139-141.

Efraimsson, O. "Crime Prevention in the Newly Organized Swedish Police." *International Criminal Police Review,* 26:244 (1971), pp. 2-6.

Falkenstam, Curt. "1965 Reorganization in Sweden." *Police Chief,* 31 (February, 1964).

Falkenstam, Curt. "Opinions about Police in Sweden." *Police Chief* (September, 1973), pp. 34-36.

Frykholm, M.M. "Marking of Dentures in Sweden." *International Criminal Police Review* (November, 1970), pp. 287-290.

Hill, H.R. et al. *Sweden—Sophistication.* Washington, DC: NCJRS, 1973.

McQuady, Charles W. "Police Force in Sweden." *Quarterly Journal of Association for Professional Law Enforcement,* 4 (October-December, 1958), pp. 26-27.

Odin, Robert. "The Kungsten Murder." *International Criminal Police Review* (November, 1962), pp. 262-268.
The solution of a burglary and murder in Sweden.

"The Organization of the Swedish Police." *Police,* 8:5 (May-June, 1964), pp. 33-34.

Penaat, Edward F. "The Police of Sweden." *Police Chief,* 26 (October, 1959), pp. 10-14.

Persson, Carl. "Reorganization of Swedish Police." *FBI Law Enforcement Bulletin* (November, 1968), pp. 17-23.

Salzer, Michael E. "Police Training News: Swedish Police Training Stresses Education." *Police Chief* (August, 1967), pp. 48-49.

Sanders, Marion K. "Sweden's Remedy for 'Police Brutality.'" *Harper's,* 229 (1964), pp. 132-136.

Soderman, Harry. *Policeman's Lot.* NY: Funk and Wagnalls, 1956.
Autobiography of Harry Soderman: world renowned Swedish criminologist.

Sutton, Anthony J. "An Oxford Policeman in Stockholm." *Police Review (GB),* 71 (September 6, 1963).

Sweden National Police Board. *EDP (Electronic Data Processing) at the Swedish Police Board.* Washington, DC: NCJRS, (Microfiche), 1973.

Sweden National Police Board. *Swedish Police Organization.* Washington, DC: NCRJS, 1973.

"Sweden's New Police Organization." *International Criminal Police Review* (June-July, 1968), pp. 159-169.
Discusses consolidation.

"Swedish Police Training Stresses Education." *Police Chief,* XXXIV:8 (August, 1967), pp. 48-53.

"Two Aspects of International Fraud—Sweden and Denmark." *International Criminal Police Review* (March, 1969), pp. 71-77.

"What the Swedish People Think of Their Police." *International Criminal Police Review,* 28:278 (1974), pp. 132-133.

Young, Frank M. "Social Work of the Swedish Police: A Personal Study." *Police Review (GB),* (September 12, 1975), pp. 1149, 1151.

SWITZERLAND

Criminal Law

Berger, Roland. "Activities of the Geneva Criminal Court for Juveniles in 1959." *International Criminal Police Review* (August-September, 1960), pp. 215-217.

Police

Berger, Roland. "The Part of the Police in the Prevention and Treatment of Juvenile Delinquency." *International Criminal Police Review* (March, 1960), pp. 66-75.

Bischoff, P. "The Institute of Police Science at the University of Lausanne (Switzerland)." *Scientific Evidence and Scientific Crime Detection,* 1:5 (1964).

Boireau, J. "Mobile Police of the Swiss Cantons." *Canadian Police Chief,* 59 (April, 1970).

Cramer, James. "Police Forces of the World: Berne." *Police Review (GB),* 67 (May 1, 1959).

Ingleton, Roy D. "Police in the Vaud Canton of Switzerland." *Police Review (GB),* (January 16, 1976), pp. 81-82.

Loertscher, Walter. "Ideas on Crime Investigation." *International Criminal Police Review* (October, 1966), pp. 226-230.

Martens, J.M. "Police and Television in Switzerland." *International Criminal Police Review* (May, 1959).

Martin, E.P. "New Types of Adhesive Strips and Protection of Microscopic Evidence." *International Criminal Police Review* (August-September, 1966), pp. 200-204.

Mathyer, J. "The Lausanne Institute of Police Science and Criminology's First Half Century." *International Criminal Police Review* (May, 1959).

Mathyer, Jacques. "Training Senior Police Officers and Police Laboratory Personnel." *International Criminal Police Review* (June-July, 1969), pp. 152-158.

Wild, A. "Identification Equipment Used in Switzerland." *International Criminal Police Review* (February/March, 1967), pp. 72-77.

TANZANIA

Criminal Law

Martin, Robert. *Personal Freedom and the Law in Tanzania.* NY: Oxford University Press, 1974.

Police History

Tem, E.P. "Short History of the Tanganyika Police Force." *Tanzania Police Journal,* 2:1 (1966).

Police

Cannon, W.J. "The Lion-Men of Tanganyika." *Police Journal* (January-March, 1959).

Cramer, James. "Police Forces of the World: Tanganyika." *Police Review (GB),* 67 (March 6, 1959).

Cramer, James. "Police Forces of the World: Zanzibar." *Police Review (GB),* 67 (August 28, 1959).

Ferreia, J.X. "Tanzania Identification Bureau." *Tanzania Police Journal,* 2:1 (1966).

THAILAND

General

U.S. Department of the Army. *Area Handbook for Thailand.* Washington, DC: GPO, 1968.

Crime

Preliminary Socio-Economic Survey of Hill Tribes in Thailand, 1965-66. Bangkok: Thailand Central Bureau of Narcotics, 1965.

Tulalamba, Mora. "Crime Trends in Thailand." *International Criminal Police Review* (April, 1961), pp. 16-20.

United Nations. *Report of UN Survey Team on the Economics and Social Needs of the Opium Producing Areas in Thailand.* Bangkok and NY: United Nations, 1967.

United Nations Mission to Thailand. *Report of the United Nations Project Preparation Mission to Thailand in the Field of Narcotics Control, Oct.-Dec., 1970.* NY; United Nations, 1970.

Police History

Forty, C.H. "Sketch of Siam's Gendarmerie." *Police Journal (GB),* IV (July, 1931), pp. 425-437.

Police

A Collection of Facts Relating to Legal Measure, Prevention and Suppression of Narcotic Crime, Treatment for Drug Addicts. Thailand: Central Bureau of Narcotics, 1965.

"Control of Opium Sales in Thailand." *International Criminal Police Review* (April, 1959).

Mandukananda, Chamras. "The Police of Thailand." *Police Chief,* 28:6 (June, 1961), pp. 8-10, 44.

Sarmoupal, Tep. "Thailand's Front Line." *International Police Academy Review* 2 (October, 1968), pp. 1-3.

Tulalamba, Mora. "Thai Police Relations with Foreign Police Forces." *International Criminal Police Review* (January, 1960), pp. 19-21.

TONGA

Wylie, Campbell. *The Law of Tonga, Comprising All Laws, Acts and Ordinances in Force on the 1st Day of January 1967.* (rev. ed.) London: Sweet and Maxwell, 1967.

TRINIDAD

Police History

Mavrogordato, A.S. "Trinidad Constabulary." *Police Journal (GB),* 5 (July, 1932), pp. 407-412.

Trinidad and Tobago Commission of Inquiry. *Report into the Organization of the Police Force, October 1964.* Trinidad: Government Printer, 1965.

TUNISIA

Cramer, James. "Police Forces of the World" Tunis." *Police Review (GB),* 67 (June 26, 1959).

TURKEY

General

U.S. Department of the Army. *Area Handbook: Turkey.* Washington, DC: GPO, 1969.

Criminal Law

Glover, J.N. *Laws of the Turks and Caicos Islands.* (4 vols., rev. ed.) Dobbs Ferry, NY: Oceana, 1970-1975.

Mueller, G.O.W. *The Turkish Criminal Code.* London: Sweet and Maxwell, 1966.

Turkish Code of Criminal Procedure. South Hackensack, NJ: Rothman, 1962.

Turkish Criminal Code. South Hackensack, NJ: Rothman, 1965.

Police History

Swanson, Glen W. "The Ottoman Police." *Journal of Contemporary History* (January-April, 1972), pp. 243-260.

Police

"Bekcis, Hold Crime in Check." *Military Police Journal,* 13 (October, 1963).

Guven, Emin. "How to Identify Sharp Instruments." *International Criminal Police Review* (August-September, 1961), pp. 17-19.

Guven, E. "The Importance of Time and Place in Crime Investigation." *International Criminal Police Review* (April, 1967), pp. 118-120.

Hardman, Willard, Jr. "The Turkish Police." *Military Police Journal,* 19 (August, 1969), pp. 20-21.

Turkey, Ministry of the Interior. *Turkish Police in the 50th Anniversary of Republic.* Ankara: Ministry of the Interior, 1973.

UGANDA

Crime

Hassan, S.A.C. "Crime in Uganda." *International Criminal Police Review* (March, 1970), pp. 102-104.

Mushanga, Tibamanya. *Criminal Homicide in Uganda—A Sociological Study of Violent Deaths in Ankole, Kigezi and Toro Districts of Western Uganda.* Nairobi, Kenya: East African Literature Bureau, 1974.

Tanner, R.E.F. *Homicide in Uganda—1964.* Uppsala, Sweden: Scandinavian Institute of African Studies, 1964.

Criminal Law

Brown, Douglas. *Criminal Procedure in Uganda and Kenya.* NY: International Publications Service, 1965.

Burke, Fred G. *Local Government and Politics in Uganda.* Syracuse, NY: Syracuse University Press, 1964.

Police History

Harwich, C. *Red Dust: Memoirs of the Uganda Police, 1935-1955.* London: V. Stuart, 1961.

VENEZUELA

"Venezuela: Psychological Testing of Metropolitan Police (Caracas City Police) Recruits." *International Criminal Police Review,* 28:270 (1973), pp. 233-234.

VIETNAM

General

U.S. Department of the Army. *Area Handbook: South Vietnam.* Washington, DC: GPO, 1967.

Police

"News from Viet Nam." *Police Administration Division at Michigan State University,* 4 (October 10, 1958), pp. 6-13.

Porter, D.G. "Saigon's Secret Police." *Nation,* 210 (April 27, 1970), pp. 498-500.

VIRGIN ISLANDS (U.S.)

Virgin Islands LEAA Comprehensive State Plan—Abstract, 1971. Washington, DC: LEAA, 1971.

A digest of the 1971 law enforcement assistance administration comprehensive state plan has been compiled for the Virgin Islands.

YUGOSLAVIA

Hodzic, A. "Crime Prevention in Yugoslavia." *International Criminal Police Review* (March, 1961), pp. 66-71.

ZAMBIA

U.S. Department of the Army. *Area Handbook: Zambia.* Washington, DC: GPO, 1969.

ZAIRE (CONGO)

General

U.S. Department of the Army. *Area Handbook: People's Republic of Congo (Brazzaville).* Washington, DC: GPO, 1971.

Criminal Law

Crabb, John H. *Legal System of Congo—Kinshasa.* Charlottesville, VA: Michie, 1970.

Police

Hermas, H. "An Interesting Car Identification Case." *International Criminal Police Review* (August-September, 1960), pp. 194-197.

PART XIV
THE BARBARIANS—TERRORISM AND VIOLENCE

TERRORISM

TERRORISM

Books

Alexander, Yonah. *International Terrorism—National, Regional, and Global Perspectives.* NY: Praeger, 1976.

Ali, Tariz, ed. *The New Revolutionaries: A Handbook of the International Radical Left.* NY: Morrow, 1969.

Amneisty International. *Amnesty International Report on Torture.* NY: Farrar, Straus, and Giroux, 1975.

Angell, R.C. "The Sociology of Human Conflict." in E.B. McNeil, ed. *The Nature of Human Conflict.* Englewood Cliffs, NJ: Prentice-Hall, 1965, pp. 91-115.

Bassiouni, M.C., ed. *International Terrorism and Political Crimes.* Springfield, IL: C.C. Thomas, 1975.

Bell, J. Bowyer. *Transnational Terror.* Washington, DC: American Enterprise Institute for Public Policy Research, Hoover Institute,1975.

Bennett, R. *The Uses of Disorder.* NY: Random House, 1971.

Blackstock, P.W. *The Strategy of Subversion.* Chicago: Quadrangle, 1964.

Carlton, David, ed. *International Terrorism and World Security.* London: Croom Helm, 1975.

Clutterbuck, Richard. *Living with Terrorism.* London: Faber and Faber, 1975.

Crozier, Brian, ed. *Annual of Power and Conflict, 1975-76: A Survey of Political Violence and International Influence.* London: Institute for the Study of Conflict, 1976.

Crozier, B. *Study of Conflict.* London: Institute for the Study of Conflict, 1974.

Crozier, B., ed. *Ulster: Politics and Terrorism.* London: Institute for the Study of Conflict, 1973.

Dallin, Alexander and George W. Breslauer. *Political Terror in Communist Systems.* Stanford, CA: Stanford University Press, 1970.

Debray, Regis. *Revolution in the Revolution, Armed Struggle and Political Struggle in Latin America.* NY: MR Press, 1967.

Dinstein, Y. "Terrorism and the War of Liberation: An Israeli Perspective of the Arab-Israeli Conflict." in M.C. Bassiouni, ed. *International Terrorism and Political Crimes.* Springfield, IL: C.C. Thomas, 1975.

Dobson, Christopher. *Black September: Its Short, Violent History.* London: Hale, 1975.

Dobson, Christopher and Ronald Payne. *The Carlos Complex: A Pattern of Violence.* Dutton Green, Sevenoaks, Kent: Hodder and Stoughton, 1977.

Eisenberg, Dennis and Eli Landau. *Carlos: Terror International.* London: Corgi, 1976.

Federal Bureau of Investigation. *Domestic Terrorist Matters.* Washington, DC: NCJRS, (Microfiche), 1974.

Fisk, Robert. *Point of No Return: The Strike Which Broke the British in Ulster.* London: Deutsch, 1975.

Green, Gil. *Terrorism—Is It Revolutionary?* NY: New Outlook, 1970.

Gross, Feliks. *Violence in Politics: Terror and Political Assassination in Eastern Europe and Russia.* Atlantic Highlands, NJ: Humanities, 1973.

Grundy, Kenneth W. and Michael A. Weinstein. *Ideologies of Violence.* Columbus, OH: Merril, 1974.

Hale, H.W. *Terrorism in India: 1917-1936:* Columbus, MO: Southern Asia, 1974. (repr. of 1937 ed.).

Hampden-Turner C. *Radical Man: The Process of Psycho-Social Development.* Cambridge, MA: Schenkman, 1970.

Hyams, Edward. *Terrorists and Terrorism.* London: Dent, 1975.

Jenkins, B.M. *The Five Stages of Urban Guerrilla Warfare Challenge of the 1970's.* Santa Monica, CA: Rand, 1971.

Jenkins, B.M. *High Technology Terrorism and Surrogate War: The Impact of New Technology on Low Level Violence.* Santa Monica, CA: Rand, 1975.

Jenkins, B.M. *International Terrorism: A New Kind of Warfare.* Santa Monica, CA: Rand, 1974.

Jenkins, Brian. *International Terrorism: A New Mode of Conflict,* Los Angeles: Cresent, 1975.

Jenkins, B.M. *Terrorism Works—Sometimes.* Santa Monica, CA: Rand, April, 1974.

Jenkins B.M. and J. Johnson. *International Terrorism—A Chronology, 1968-1974.* Santa Monica, CA: Rand, 1975.

Kautsky, Karl. *Terrorism and Communism*. Westport, CT: Hyperion, 1973. (repr. 1920 ed.).

Kelley, C.M. *Terrorism—A Phenomenon of Sickness*. Clarmont, CA: Clarmont Men's College, 1974.

Lambrick, H.T., ed. *Terrorist*. Totowa, NJ: Rowman, 1972.

Leiden C. and K.M. Schmitt. *The Politics of Violence: Revolution in the Modern World*. Englewood Cliffs, NJ: Prentice-Hall, 1968.

Levytsky, Borys. *Stalinist Terror in the Thirties: Documentation from the Soviet Press*. Stanford, CA: Hoover Institute Press, 1972.

McKnight, Gerald. *Mind of the Terrorist*. London: Michael Joseph, 1974.

McKnight, Gerald. *Terrorist Mind: Why They Hijack, Kidnap, Bomb and Kill*. Indianapolis: Bobbs, 1975.

Mallin, Jay, ed. *Terror and Urban Guerrilas: A Study of Tactics and Documents*. Coral Gables, FL: University of Miami Press, 1972.

Mehden, F.R. Vonder. *Comparative Political Violence*. Englewood Cliffs, NJ: Prentice-Hall, 1973.

Merkl, Peter H. *Political Violence Under the Swastika: 581 Early Nazis*. Princeton, NJ: Princeton University Press, 1975.

Morf, G. *Terror in Quebec: Case Studies of the F.L.Q.* Toronto: Clark Irwin, 1970.

Moss, R. *Terrorism Versus Democracy*. London: Institute for the Study of Conflict, 1971.

Moss, R. and I. Hamilton. *The Spreading Irish Conflict*. London: Institute for the Study of Conflict, 1971.

Nieburg, H.L. *Political Violence: The Behavioural Process*. NY: St. Martins, 1961.

"Origins and Fundamental Causes of International Terrorism." in M.C. Bassiouni ed., *International Terrorism and Political Crimes,* Springfield, IL: C.C. Thomas, 1975, pp. 336-342.

Paine, Lauran. *Terrorists*. London: Hale, 1975.

Parry, Albert. *Terrorism—from Robespierre to Arafat*. NY: Vanguard, 1976.

Peachey, P. "Predicting Linkages Between Domestic Violence and International Aggression—Communal Sources of Anxiety." in J.D. Ben-Dak, ed. *The Future of Collective Violence—Societal and International Perspectives*. Lund, Sweden: Student Literature, 1974, pp. 37-33.

Pike, Douglas. *The Viet-Cong Strategy of Terror*. Saigon: United States Mission, 1970.

Popov, M.I. *The American Extreme Left: A Decade of Conflict*. London: Institute for Study of Conflict, 1972.

Powers, Thomas. *Diana: The Making of a Terrorist*. Boston: Houghton Mifflin, 1970.

Rapoport, D.C. *Assassination and Terrorism*. Toronto: CBC Learning Systems, 1971.

Salomone, F. "Terrorism and the Mass Media." in M.C. Bassiouni, ed., *International Terrorism and Political Crimes*. Springfield, IL: C.C. Thomas, 1975, pp. 43-46.

Smith, Colin. *Carlos: Portrait of a Terrorist*. London: Andre Deutsch, 1976.

Sobel, L.A. *Political Terrorism*. NY: Facts on File, 1975.

Stewart, J. and R.R. Reid. *The F.L.Q. Seven Years of Terrorism*. NY: Simon and Schuster, 1970.

Stolz, Matthew F. *Politics of the New Left*. Beverly Hills, CA: Glence, 1971.

Thomson, Blair. *Ethiopia: The Country That Cut Off Its Head: A Diary of the Revolution*. London: Robson, 1975.

Toman, J. "Terrorism and the Regulation of Armed Conflict." in M.C. Bassiouni, ed. *International Terrorism ad Political Crimes*. Springfield, IL: C.C. Thomas, 1975, pp. 133-154.

Trotsky, Leon D. *Terrorism and Communism: A Reply to Karl Kautsky*. Ann Arbor, MI: University of Michigan Press, 1961. (repr.)

Tunney, Thomas Joseph. *Throttled: The Defection of the German Anarchist Bomb Plotters*. Boston: Small, Maynard, 1919.

U.S. Department of Justice. *Domestic Tererrorist Matters*. Washington, DC: FBI, 1974.

Van Voris, William H. *Violence in Ulster: An Oral Documentary*. Amherst, MA: University of Massachusetts Press, 1975.

Walter, E.V. *Terror and Resistance: A Study of Political Violence*. NY: Oxford University Press, 1972.

Wilkinson, Paul. *Political Terrorism*. NY: Halstead, 1975.

Wilkinson, Paul. *Terrorism Versus Liberal Democracy: The Problems of Response*. London: Institute for the Study of Conflict, 1976.

Yglesias, Jose. *Chile's Days of Terror: Eyewitness Accounts of the Military Coup*. NY: Pathfinder, 1974.

Periodicals

"ABC's Grim T.V. First; Coverage of Terrorist Raid at Munich Olympics." *Newsweek* (September 18, 1972).

Abrahamsen, D. "Political Terror in the U.S.; What Next?" *U S News and World Report* (March 4, 1974).

Alves, M.M. "Brazil: What Terror Is Like." *Nation* (March 15, 1971).

"Ambush at the Gate of Tears; Tanker Attacked by Popular Front for the Liberation of Palestine." *Time* (June 28, 1971).

"Arabs; Open Approval (Munich Killings)." *Economist* (September 16, 1972).

"Arab Terrorism, Outraged World Seeks an Answer." *U.S. News & World Report* (September 18, 1972).

"As Violence Spreads U.S. Goes on Guard." *U.S. News & World Report* (November 2, 1970).

"Backdown in Bangkok; Black September Group Captures Israeli Embassy." *Time* (January 8, 1973).

Barron, S. "Soviet Plot to Destroy Mexico; Excerpt from KGB." *Reader's Digest* (November, 1971).

"Behind the Rise in Crime and Terror." *U.S. News and World Report* (November 13, 1972).

"Belfast Syndrome: Irish Violence Damages Psyches." *Science Digest* (September, 1973).

Bennett, R.K. "Brotherhood of the Bomb." *Reader's Digest* (December, 1970).

Bennett, R.K. "Terrorists Among Us: An Intelligence Report." *Readers Digest* (October, 1971).

Beristain, Antonio. "Terrorism and Aircraft Hijacking." *International Journal of Criminology and Penology* (November, 1974), pp. 347-389.

Bergquist, L. "French Canada's Strange Revolt; Role of F.L.Q. (Quebec Liberation Front). *Look* (December 3, 1963).

Bin, Cheng. "Hijacking and Sabotage." *New Society* (August 3, 1973), pp. 270-272.

"Blacker September; Reactions to Massacre in Khartoum." *Time* (March 19, 1973).

"Black September Assassins." *Newsweek* (March 19, 1973).

"Black September; Black Friday." *Economist* (March 10, 1973).

"Black September's Ruthless Few." *Time* (September 18, 1972).

"Bloodier Friday in the South; Dublin Bombing." *Time* (May 27, 1974).

"Blowing Up Bridges: Bombing of New York Offices." *Newsweek* (February 7, 1972).

"Bombers Cross the Irish Sea." *Economist* (February 26, 1972).

"Bombing Britain; More to Follow." *Economist* (April 13, 1974).

"Bombing Fallout: Tensions and Threats. New York City." *Business Week* (November 22, 1969).

"Bombs, Bullets and Fear, Ulster's Agony Flares Anew." *U.S. News & World Report* (April 22, 1974).

"Brutality with a Purpose; Political Weapon of the Viet Cong." *Time* (September 16, 1966).

Buckley, K. "On the Borderline; Thai-Malay Border Activities of Communist Terror Organization." *Newsweek* (January 19, 1970).

"Burn Yanqui Burn! Fire Bombs Aimed at Driving U.S. Owned Business Out of Puerto Rico." *Time* (June 28, 1968).

Callanan, E.F. "Terror in Venezuela." *Military Review,* 49:2 (1969), pp. 49-56.

Cantwell, R. "Shattered Face of Belfast Sport; Assassination of Bankmore Star Team Members." *Sports Illustrated* (November 12, 1973).

"Cease-Fire Strains; Fedayeen Attack on Shamir Kibbitz." *Time* (June 24, 1971).

Chesnoff, R. "Dangerous Border: Al Fatah." *Newsweek* (August 15, 1966).

Clutterbuck, Richard. "The Police and Urban Terrorism." *Police Journal (GB),* 48:3 (1975), pp. 204-215, 190.

Clutterbuck, Richard. "Terrorist Internationale." *Army Quarterly and Defense* (January, 1974), pp. 154-159.

"Compliments of the Season From the IRA." *Economist* (December 23, 1973).

Copeland, M. "Arabs and Terrorists." *National Review* (September 29, 1972).

"Crime and Punishment; Capture of Saudi Arabian Embassy in Paris by Feyadeen." *Time* (September, 1973).

"Croats in Australia; from Soccer to Bombs." *Economist* (September 23, 1972).

"Death by Plastic." *Newsweek* (February 5, 1962).

"Death in Distant Places; Sabotage of Swiss and Austrian Planes." *Time* (March 2, 1970).

"Dialectic of Bombs; Explosion in Jerusalems Mahaneh Yehunda Market." *Time* (November 29, 1968).

"Diplomacy by Terror: Is It Getting Out of Control." *U.S. News & World Report* (August 24, 1970).

Dugard, John. "International Terrorism: Problems of Definition." *International Affairs* (January, 1974), pp. 67-81.

"Dutch Terrorists; Held to Ransom." *Economist* (November 11, 1972).

"Enforcers; IRA Assault on Pregnant Women." *Newsweek* (April 24, 1972).

"Escalating Terror; West German Ambassador in Guatemala." *Newsweek* (April 13, 1970).

"Fallout from Khartoum." *Newsweek* (March 19, 1973).

"Fatal Error; Murder of a Bouchika by Israeli Killers." *Time* (August 6, 1973).

"Feeding the Wolf; Problems of the Palestinian Terrorist Groups." *Newsweek* (May 19, 1968).

Fellows, L. "Unknown War in the Sudan." *N.Y. Times Magazine* (September 22, 1968).

Femina, J.D. "Jodi and the Bomb." *Reader's Digest* (January, 1972).

"Fertile Soil for Terror." *Canada and World,* 36:12 (1970), pp. 16-19.

Finer, S.E. "On Terrorism." *New Society* (January 22, 1976), pp. 168-169.

Flieger, H. "Futility of Terror." *U.S. News & World Report* (March 19, 1973).

Forster, A. "Violence on the Fanatical Left and Right." *The Annals,* 364 (1966), pp. 141-148.

Fox, R.W. "Algeria, Israel and the Fatah." *Commonwealth* (May 8, 1970).

Franklin, David. "Strategy of Terrorism." *Foreign Affairs* (July, 1975). pp. 683-698.

Friendly, A. "Fedayeen." *Atlantic* (September, 1969).

"Fury Grows in Ulster." *Life* (November 12, 1971).

Gensler, M.D. "Cuba's Second Vietnam: Bolivia." *Yale Review* (March, 1971).

Geyer, G.A. "Blood of Guatemala." *Nation* (July 8, 1968).

Giniger, H. "Guatemala is a Battleground." *N.W. Times Magazine* (June 16, 1968).

Godin, G. "Notes on Terrorism." *Canadian Forum,* 51 (1971), pp. 26-67.

Goodheart, E. "Revolution and Social Change: On the Rhetoric of Violence." *Current,* 118 (1970), pp. 9-13.

Goulden, J.C. "Guatemala: Terror in Silence." *Nation* (March 22, 1971).

Grant, Z.B. "Commando Revolution: A Hundred Years War in the Middle East." *New Republic* (January 24, 1970).

Griffith, G.W. "Biological Warfare and the Urban Battleground." *Enforcement Journal,* 14:1 (1975), pp. 4-5.

Hall, R.A. "Violence and Its Effect on the Community." *Medical Legal Journal,* 43:3 (1975), pp. 89-100.
Terrorists tactics in Northern Ireland.

Hamilton, P. "A Cooperative Effort in Terrorism." *Security World,* 12:3 (1975).
Author states that terrorists are involved in a worldwide cooperative link-up in order to insure the availability and delivery of arms and explosives.

Hobsbawm, E.J. "Appraisal of Terrorism." *Canadian Dimension,* 9:1 (1972) pp. 11-14.

Horowitz, I.L. "Political Terrorism and State Power." *Journal of Political and Military Sociology,* 1:1 (1975), pp. 145-157.

"Horror and Death at the Olympics." *Time* (September 18, 1972).

"Horror Explodes in a Canadian Mailbox." *Life* (June 7, 1963).

"House on Fourth Street; Bomb Terrorists and Explosions, New York City." *Newsweek* (November 24, 1969).

"Houston: The Terrorists." *Newsweek* (May 3, 1971).

Howe, C. "Prevalence of Bombing." *Nation* (March 30, 1970).

Howe, I. "Political Terrorism: Hysteria on the Left." *New York Times Magazine* (April 12, 1970).

Hughes, E. "Brotherhood of Terror: Arab Terrorists Infiltrate Israel." *Time* (March 29, 1968).

Hughes, Edward. "Terror on Train 734." *Reader's Digest* (August, 1976), pp. 64-69.
South Moluccan seizure of a passenger train in Holland.

Hughes, Edward. "Yasser Arafat's Fight for the Palestinians." *Reader's Digest* (April, 1976), pp. 116-120.

Hutchinson, M.C. "The Concept of Revolutionary Terrorism." *Journal of Conflict Resolution,* 16:3 (1972), pp. 383-396.

"In the Shadow of the Gunmen." *Time* (January 10, 1972).

"Israel's Night of Carnage; Massacre at Tel Aviv's Lod International Airport." *True* (June 12, 1972).

"Israel; The Bombs Return." *Economist* (August 31, 1974).

"Is the Terror Tide Rising." *Senior Scholastic* (April 23, 1973).

"Italy; Bombs to the Right, Bombs to the Left." *Economist* (May 5, 1973).

Jack, H.A. "Terrorism: Another U.N. Failure." *America* (October 20, 1973).

"Japan's United Red Army." *Newsweek* (June 12, 1972).

Karber, P.A. "Urban Terrorism: Baseline Data and Conceptual Frame Work." *Social Science Quarterly,* 52:3 (1971), pp. 521-533.

Kearney, V.S. "Tiger Nasser Can't Rule; Palestinian Liberation Movement." *America* (February, 1970).

Keller, E. John. "Political Terrorism." *Law and Order,* 21:5 (May, 1973), pp. 25, 33.

Kelley, Clarence M. "Terrorism: A Phenomenom of Sickness." Res Publica-Claremont Men's College, 2:3 (1974).

"Killers of Khartoum." *Time* (March 12, 1973).

Law, J. "With the Arab of Commandos; No Peace for Israel: A Campaign of Terror." *U.S. News and World Report* (February 24, 1969).

"Lebanon: Along the Arafat Trail." *Time* (November 7, 1969).

Leber, J.R. "International Terrorism: Criminal or Political." *Towson State Journal of International Affairs,* 7:2 (1973).

Litt, J. and J. Kohl. "Guerrillas of Montevideo." *Nation* (February 28, 1972).

"Lydda Massacre; Murder by Proxy; Japanese Gunman Recruited by Popular Front for the Liberation of Palestine." *Newsweek* (June 12, 1972).

MacDonald, D. "Wind of Madness; Canada's Trial by Terror." *Reader's Digest* (March, 1972).

McGuire, E. Patrick. "Bomb Terrorism." *Law and Order,* 20:5 (May, 1972), pp. 62-66).

Mallin, J. "Terrorism as a Political Weapon." *Air University Review,* 22 (1971), pp. 45-52.

Martin, J. "Politics of Terror." *Partisan Review,* 38:1 (1971), pp. 95-103.

"Men Who Turned Canada Against Canada." *Economist* (October 24, 1970.

Meyer, A.H. "Foreign Terrorism Spreading to the U S?" *U.S. News & World Report* (July 16, 1973).

"Mideast: Blood and Hope; Maalot Massacre." *Newsweek* (July 8, 1974).

Moraes, D. "Indian Revolutionaries with a Chinese Accent: The Noxalities." *New York Times Magazine* (November 8, 1970).

"Morality of Terror." *Newsweek* (February 25, 1974).

"More Bonnie and Clyde; Bombings by Anachist Groups." *Time* (June 5, 1972).

Morente, F.L. "Terrorism." *Military Review,* 45:12 (1965), pp. 55-57.

Mosher, T.E. "Inside the Revolutionary Left." *Reader's Digest* (September, 1971).

Moss, R. "International Terrorism and Western Societies." *International Journal,* 28:3 (1973), pp. 418-430.

"Munich Killings." *Economist* (September 9, 1972).

"Murder. Tupamaros-Style." *Time* (August 24, 1970).

Neale, William D. "Terror; Oldest Weapon in Arsenal." *Army* (August, 1973). pp. 10-17.

"A New Wave in Terrorism." *Police Chief,* XLI:5 (May, 1974).

"Now, Bloody Tuesday; IRA Bombing of British Officers' Mess." *Time* (March 6, 1972).

"Nuclear Terrorism; Thinking the Thinkable." *Economist* (April 20, 1974).

"1971 Worst Year for Nationwide Bombings." *Police Officers Association of Michigan Law Enforcement Journal* (Spring, 1972).

"On the Other Side: Terror as a Policy; Viet Cong Terrorism." *Time* (December 5, 1969).

"Outrage Over the IRA." *Time* (June 5, 1972).

"Pattern of Terror; Latin America." *Time* (August 24, 1970).

"Pattern of Terror; Viet Cong-Style Terrorism in Phnom-Penh, Cambodia." *Time* (December 14, 1970).

Paust, J.J. "Terrorism and the International Law of War." *Military Law Review,* 64 (1974), pp. 1-36.

Peter, R. "Terrorists at Work; Report from Argentina." *National Review* (July 28, 1964).

"Plastic Bomb Terror Weapon: What Is It?" *U.S. News & World Report* (February 5, 1962).

Plastrik, S. "On Terrorism." *Dissent,* 21:2 (1974).

Porter, Cathy. "Five Women: The First to Be Terrorists." *New Society* (February 19, 1976), pp. 382-384.

Reed, D. "Fedayeen: Israel's Fanatic Foe." *Reader's Digest* (October, 1970).

Russell, Charles A. "Transnational Terrorism." *Air University Review* (January-February, 1976), pp. 26-35.

Schleimer, Joseph D. "Day They Blew up San Onofre: A Scenario for Sabotage at a Nuclear Power Plant." *Bulletin of the Atomic Scientists* (October, 1974). pp. 24-27.

Segre, D.V. and J.H. Adler. "The Ecology of Terrorism." *Encounter,* 40:2 (1973), pp. 17-24.

"Shadow of Death at Munich." *Life* (September 15, 1972).

"Shadow War; Murder of Y. Alon in Bethesda, Maryland." *Newsweek* (July 16, 1973).

Speck, Dale H. "A Growing Problem of Terrorism." *Journal of California Law Enforcement* (January, 1976), pp. 88-92.

"Story of the Bloodies Skyjacking; Terrorism in Rome Airport." *U.S. News & World Report* (December 31, 1973).

"Take Us Seriously; Murder of Diplomats in Khartoum." *Nation* (March 19, 1973).

Taylor, E. "Terrorists." *Horizon* (Summer, 1973).

Tereshchuk, David. "Bombing in Britian." *New Statesman* (January 9, 1976), pp. 32-33.

"Terror at the Tower; Explosion in the Tower of London." *Time* (July 29, 1974).

"Terror Bombing: Rising Techniques of Violence." *U.S. News & World Report* (March 23, 1970).

"Terror Fails to Stem Venezuela's Vote." *Life* (December 13, 1963).

"Terror in Johannesburg." *National Review* (August 25, 1964).

"Terror in Tel Aviv." *Newsweek* (September 16, 1968).

"Terrorism; Bluff Called." *Economist* (July 4, 1970).

"Terrorism: Desperate Deed." *Economist* (August 11, 1973).

"Terrorism in Tel Aviv." *Time* (September 13, 1968).

"Terrorism Is Developing into a Form of Total War." *U.S. News & World Report* (December 11, 1972).

"Terrorism: No Help from the U.N." *Economist* (December 23, 1972).

"Terrorism; Nowhere Is Safe." *Economist* (February 9, 1974).

"Terrorism Rampant." *Current,* (December, 1970).

"Terrorist." *Economist,* (October 24, 1970).

"Terrorist Acts Against United Nations Missions." *UN Monthly Chronicle* (November, 1971).

"Terrorist; And So It Goes On." *Economist* (February 9, 1974).

"Terrorist International." *Newsweek* (September 18, 1972).

"Terrorist's Goal: Sabotage Peace at All Cost." *U.S. News & World Report* (May 27, 1974).

"Terrorists Unpunished." *Economist* (February 2, 1974).

"Terrorists; Where Are They Now?" *Economist* (March 9, 1974).

"Terror to End Terror? Israeli Raid on Beirut." *Time* (April 23, 1973).

"Threat for Bicentennial Year—Terrorists Getting Ready." *U.S. News & World Report* (July 21, 1975), pp. 23-27.

"Trieste; Who Blew Up the Oil." *Economist* (August 12, 1972).

Tuckerman, A. "UN: New Look for 1972; Debate on Terrorism." *Nation* (October 2, 1972).

"Ulster; and Yet More Atrocity." *Economist* (August 26, 1972).

"Ulster: A Quiet Section Except for the Bullets and the Bombs." *Economist* (June 16, 1973).

"Ulster; Back to Bloody Sunday." *Economist* (August 25, 1972).

"Ulster: Bloody Dodge City." *Time* (November 22, 1971).

"Ulster: Death Comes in Small Parcels." *Economist* (December 11, 1971).

"Ulster; Russian Rockets." *Economist* (December 2, 1972).

"Ulster: The IRA Takes to the Air." *Economist* (July 27, 1974).

"Ulster, Torture and the Police." *New Statesman* (July 13, 1973), pp. 44-46.

"Unbreakable Bank: Attack on West Coast Branches of the Bank of America." *Newsweek* (November 9, 1970).

"U.S. Capitol Survives Bombing with Light Damage." *Engineering News* (March 11, 1971).

Van Dalen, H. "Terror as a Political Weapon." *Military Police Law Enforcement Journal,* 2:1 (Spring, 1975), pp. 21-26.

"Violence Has Economic Roots." *(Quebec) Business Week* (October 24, 1970).

"Violence: Worldwide Problem." *U.S. News & World Report* (September 28, 1970).

Walter, E.V. "Violence and the Process of Terror." *American Sociological Review,* 29:2 (1964), pp. 248-257.

"Week of the Bombs; Bombing in American Cities." *National Review* (March 10, 1970).

Weil, H.M. "Domestic and International Violence Forecasting Approach." *Futures,* 6:6 (1974), pp. 477-485).

Wharam, Alan. "Treason and the Terrorist." *New Law Journal* (April 29, 1976), pp. 428-429.

"What Can the IRA Now Hope to Achieve?" *Economist* (December 29, 1973).

White, C.A. "Terrorism: Idealism or Sickness." *Canada and World,* 39:4 (1974), pp. 14-15.

Wolf, J.B. "Black September: Militant Palestinianism." *Current History* (January, 1973).

Wolf, John B. "Terrorist Manipulation of the Democratic Process." *Police Journal (GB),* (April-June, 1975), pp. 102-112.

Woodcock, G. "Anarchism and Violence." *Canadian Forum,* 50 (1971).

"World Politics, New Style: Kidnapping, Hijacking, Bombing, Guerrilla Diplomacy." *U.S. News & World Report* (September 23, 1969).

Zahn, G.C. "Terrorism for Peace and Justice." *Commonwealth* (October 23, 1970).

Government Publications—Seminars

Jenkins, B.M. *International Terrorism: A New Kind of Warfare.* Santa Monica, CA: Arms Control and Foreign Policy Seminar, 1975.

United Nations General Assembly. *Ad Hoc Committee on International Terrorism Report.*NY: United Nations, [n.d.].

U.S. Congress. House Committee on Internal Security. *Terrorism: A Staff Study.* Washington, DC: GPO, 1974.

U.S. Congress. House Committee on International Security. *America's Maoists—The Revolutionary Union—The Venceremos Organization.* Washington, DC: GPO, 1972.

U.S. Congress. House Committee of International Security. *Revolutionary Activities Directed Toward the Administration of Penal or Correctional Systems.* (part 4), *Testimony of R.R. Norusis.* Hearings before the Committee on Internal Security 93rd Congress, 1st session. Washington, DC: GPO, 1973.

U.S. Congress. House Committee on International Security. *Terrorism,* part 1, Hearings before the Committee on Internal Security. Washington, DC: GPO, February-March, 1974.

U.S. Congress. House Committee on International Security, *Terrorism,* part 2, Hearing before the Committee on Internal Security. Washington, DC: GPO, May-June 1974.

U.S. Congress. House Committee on International Security, *Terrorism,* part 3. Washington, DC: GPO, June-July, 1974.

U.S. Congress. House Committee on International Security. *Terrorism,* part 4. Washington, DC: GPO, July-August, 1974.

U.S. Congress. House Committee on Internation Security. *Terrorism—A Staff Study.* Washington, DC: GPO, 1974.

U.S. Congress. Senate Commission on the Judiciary. *Terroristic Activity Inside the Weatherman Movement,* part 2. Washington, DC: GPO, October 18, 1974.

U.S. Congress. Senate Commission on the Judiciary. *Terroristic Activity, International Terrorism.* Washington, DC: GPO, May 14, 1975.

U.S. Congress. Senate Commission on the Judiciary. *Terroristic Activity Testimony of Dr. Frederick Schwarz,* part 3. Washington, DC: GPO, July 5, 1974.

University of Ottawa. Faculty of Law. *International Terriosm.* Proceedings of the Third Annual Meeting of the Canadian Council on Internal Law at the University of Ottawa (October 18-19, 1974).

Coup d'Etat

Andrews, William G. and Uri Ra'Ana. *Politics of the Coup-d'Etat; 5 Case Studies.* NY: Van Nostrand and Rhinehold, 1969.

First, Ruth. *The Barrel of a Gun: Political Power in Africa and the Coup d'etat.* Harmondsworth : Penguin, 1972.

Luttwak, Edward. *Coup d'Etat, a Practical Handbook.* NY: Knopf, 1969.

Marks, Stanley J. *Coup d'Etat.* Los Angeles: Bureau of International Affairs, [n.d.]

Oqeri, Eze II. *African Nationalism and Military Coups d'Etat.* New Paltz, NY: Couch Magazine, 1975.

Hostages

Acoca, M. "Hostages of a Mob of Miners." *Life* (January 3, 1964).

"Agonizing Choice: 1,000 White Civilians Held by Congo Rebels." *Newsweek* (November 30, 1964).

"Another Nasty Stunt; Kidnapping U.S. Colonel by Venezuela's F.A.L.N." *Time* (October 16, 1965).

"Arabs, Open Approval." (Munich Killings) *Economist* (September 16, 1972).

"At Dawson Field: Life as a Hostage." *Newsweek* (September 21, 1970).

"Backdown in Bangkok; Black September Group Captures Israeli Embassy." *Time* (January 8, 1973).

"Black September Black Friday." *Economist* (March 10, 1973).

"Blacker September; Reactions to Massacre in Khartoum." *Time* (March 19, 1973).

"Captives in the Hills." *Time* (December 20, 1963).

"Crime and Punishment; Capture of Saudi Arabian Embassy in Paris by Fedayeen." *Time* (September 17, 1973).

"Drama on the Desert; the Week of the Hostages." *Time* (September 21, 1970).

"Dutch Terrorists; Held to Ransom." *Economist* (November 11, 1972).

"Fallout from Khartoum." *Newsweek* (March 19, 1973).

"F.G. Carrasco's Escape Attempt from State Penitentiary in Huntsville, Texas." *Newsweek* (August 12, 1974).

"Four American Hostages Released by Bolivian Miners." *Department of State Bulletin* (January 6, 1965).

"Free at Last; American Hostages in Bolivia." *Time* (December 27, 1963).

"Germany: Shifting the Stable Door—Munich Killings." *Economist* (September 16, 1972).

"Helping Hostages; Kidnapping and Murder of K. VonSpreti in Guatemala." *Newsweek* (August 24, 1970).

"High Cost of Blackmail; Kidnapping and Death of Hostages at San Rafeal, California and Uraguay." *National Review* (August 25, 1970).

"Horror and Death at the Olympics." *Time* (September 18, 1972).

"The Hostage: A Game of Terror." *Newsweek* (February 25, 1974).

"Hostages." *Time* (December 27, 1963).

"In Arab Hands; Thirty-Eight U.S. Hostages." *U.S. News & World Report* (September 28, 1970).

"Killers of Khartoum." *Time* (March 12, 1973).

Knox, C. "Do As We Say; Kidnapping of U.S. Ambassador." *Time* (February 5, 1973).

Middendorff, W. *New Developments in the Taking of Hostages and Kidnapping—a Summary.* Washington, DC: NCJRS, 1975.

"Munich Killings." *Economist* (September 9, 1972).

"Take Us Seriously; Murder of Diplomats in Khartoum." *Nation* (March 19, 1973).

"Thais and the Terrorists: Black September Terrorists Seize Israeli Hostages." *Newsweek* (January 8, 1973).

"Tit for Tat; Exchange of Prisoners." *Newsweek* (October 27, 1969).

"Walking Out; Release of American Hostages: an Ethical Problem." *Newsweek* (December 30, 1963).

Letter Bombs

"And Now, Mail-a-Death; Letter Bombs Mailed to Israeli Diplomatic Officers." *Time* (October 2, 1972).

Campion, D.R. "Of Many Things; Letter Bombing." *America* (September 8, 1973) inside cover.

"Danger! Postman Coming." *National Review* (February 2, 1972).

Hughes, Mary Margaret. "Letter Bombs." *Security World* (March, 1973).

"Letter-Bombs; and Christmas Is Coming." *Economist* (November 18, 1972).

"Letter from Paris; Terrorist Practices." *New Yorker* (February 3, 1962).

"New Arab Terror: Murder by Mail." *Newsweek* (October 2, 1972).

"Terror Through the Mails." *Economist* (September 23, 1972).

"Troubles Spill Over; Letter Bomb Campaign." *Time* (September 10, 1973).

Terrorist Kidnappings

Adkins, E.H., Jr. "Protection of American Industrial Dignitaries and Facilities Overseas." *Security Management,* 18:3 (July, 1974), pp. 14, 16, 55.

Alves, M.M. "Kidnapped Diplomats: Greek Tragedy on Latin Stage." *Commonwealth* (June 26, 1970).

"Another Kidnap: J. Patterson, U.S. Vice Consul in Mexico." *Newsweek* (April 8, 1974).

"Argentine Kidnapping, Ultimate Cruelty." *Economist* (April 27, 1974).

"At Cross Purposes; Abduction of J.R. Cross by Quebec Separatists." *Newsweek* (October 9, 1970).

"Back in Action: Seizure of G.H.S. Jackson by Uruguay's Tupamaros." *Newsweek* (January 18, 1971).

Baumann, C.E. *The Diplomatic Kidnappings: a Revolutionary Tactic of Urban Terrorism.* Hague: Martinus Nijhoff, 1973.

"Crime Does Pay; Political Kidnappings." *Time* (April 23, 1973).

"Getting Tough; Kidnapping of 4 U.S. Airmen." *Newsweek* (March 15, 1971).

"Hanging Tough; Ransom Demands and Political Kidnappings." *Newsweek* (August 24, 1970).

"Helping Hostages; Kidnapping and Murder of K. Von Spreti in Guatemala." *Newsweek* (August 24, 1970).

"High Cost of Blackmail: Kidnappings and Death of Hostages at San Rafael, California and Uruguay." *National Review* (August 25, 1970).

Jenkins, B.M. *Terrorism and Kidnapping.* Santa Monica, CA: Rand, 1974.

"Kidnap Fever; Three Cases in Uruguay." *Newsweek* (August 17, 1970). (August 17, 1970).

"Kidnapping Diplomats, What's Back of Terrorist Tactics." *U.S. News & World Report* (April 20, 1970).

Knox, C. "Do As We Say; Kidnapping of a U.S. Ambassador." *Time* (February 5, 1973).

"Living in Fear; Executive Kidnapping." *Newsweek* (June 11, 1973).

Means, J. "Political Kidnappings and Terrorism." *North American Review,* 7:4 (1970), pp. 16-19.

"New Hazard of That Overseas Job; Kidnapping." *Business Week* (September 29, 1973).

"New Terror Tactic: Diplomatic Kidnapping in Latin America." *Time* (April 6, 1970).

O'Higgins, P. "Unlawful Seizure of Person by States." in M.C. Bassiouni, ed. *International Terrorism and Political Crimes*. Springfield, IL: C.C. Thomas, 1975, pp. 336-342.

O'Mara, R. "New Terrorism in Latin America; Snatching the Diplomats." *Nation* (May 4, 1970).

"Only Way (Montreal Kidnappings)." *Economist* (October 24, 1970).

"Parting Shots; Dangers of Being a Diplomat in Latin America." *Life* (June 26, 1970).

Peter, R. "It Was a Terrible Scene; Kidnappings and Deaths by Tupamaros in Uruguay." *National Review* (September 22, 1970).

"Price of Freedom; Kidnapping of T. Leonhardy, U.S. Consul General." *Time* (May 21, 1973).

U.S. Congress. House Committee on International Security, *Political Kidnappings, 1968-1973, A Staff Study*. Washington, DC: GPO, 1973.

"What to Do About Diplomat Snatching." *National Review* (April 21, 1970).

"What to Do When the Kidnapper Strikes." *Burroughs Clearing House* (July, 1972).

"Why Argentina Is Becoming Land of Vanishing American." *U.S. News & World Report* (March 11, 1974).

Wohlstetter, Roberta. "Kidnapping to Win Friends and Influence People." *Survey* (Autumn, 1974), pp. 1-40.

Terrorist Skyjacking

"Act of Patriotism; Hijacking of Olympic Airway's Plane by Arab Terrorist." *Time* (August 3, 1970).

"Airlines Versus Hijackers." *Newsweek* (October 26, 1970).

"Air Piracy Re-Erupts in Mideast with Hijacking of 747 to Yemen." *Aviation Week and Space Technology* (February 28, 1972).

"Airway War Escalates." *Business Week* (September 12, 1970).

Ajomo, M.A. "Hijacking or Unlawful Seizure of Aircraft." *Nigerian Law Journal*, 7 (1973), pp. 13-37.

"Arab Guerrillas Adopt Air Piracy as Tactic." *Aviation Week and Space Technology* (September 14, 1970).

Arey, James A. *Sky Pirates*. London: Allan, 1973.

"Battle of Flight 517; Skyjacking of Israeli Jet." *Time* (May 22, 1972).

"Brief and Bloody; Ethiopian Air Lines Flight 708." *Time* (December 18, 1972).

Buchanan, R. "Pictures on Board a Hijacked Plane." *Life* (June 19, 1970).

Buckley, W.F. "Skyjacker Problem." *National Review* (September 29, 1972).

Clutterbuck, Richard. "Air-Piracy—A Gleam of Hope for the World." *Army Quarterly* (July, 1974), pp. 402-408.

Clyne, Peter. *Anatomy of Skyjacking*. Levittown, NY: Translantic Arts, 1973.
Contains discussion of skyjacking trials near Zurich in 1969 and Tel Aviv in 1972, categorizes 6 types of skyjackers, and recommends establishment of international air code with a commission to police and adminster it.

"Death in Rome Aboard Flight 110." *Time* (December 31, 1973).

"El Al 707 Survives Cargo Hold Explosion and Other Air Incidents." *Aviation Week and Space Technology* (August 21, 1972).

"Exporting Violence: Bomb and Skyjack Plots by Arab Terrorist." *Time* (January 5, 1970).

"Flight to Nowhere; Skyjacked JAL 747." *Time* (August 6, 1973).

"Hijacking Indignation Increases." *Aviation Week and Space Technology* (June 19, 1972).

"Hijacking in the Skies: 48 Planes This Year; So Far." *U.S. News & World Report* (September 22, 1969).

Jenkins, L. "Hijack War; Palestinian Terrorists Hijack Four Airliners." *Newsweek* (September 21, 1970).

Jones, J.S. and S. Stone, "Skyjacked and Alive to Tell the Tale." *Newsweek* (July 17, 1972).

Khaled, L. "Chaos in the Sky; Palestinian Guerrillas Strike at the Big Jets." *Life* (September 18, 1970).

"Ordeal for the Innocent; Story of Hijacking Victims; Arab Hijackers." *U.S. News & World Report* (September 21, 1970).

"Political Violence: Aerial Piracy." *Strategic Survey* (1972), pp. 75-76.

"Real Life Thriller; Palestinian Guerrilla Hijacking." *Time* (March 6, 1972).

"Return of Black September; Skyjacker Secure Release of Arab Olympic Terrorists." *Time* (November 13, 1972).

Schultz, M. "Terror in Our Skies; Can We Stop It." *Popular Mechanics* (September, 1972).

"Skyjackers Strike Again; Palestinian Capture of Japan Airlines Plane." *Time* (July 30, 1973).

"Story of the Bloodiest Skyjacking; Terrorism in Rome Airport." *U.S. News & World Report* (December 31, 1973).

"Terror Attacks on Air Travel: What Can Be Done?" *U.S. News & World Report* (September 21, 1970).

Urban Guerrillas

"Almond-Blossom Battles; Israel Battles Palestinian Guerrillas in Lebanon." *Time* (March 13, 1972).

"Arab Guerrillas versus Arab Government." *Time* (June 22, 1970).

"Arab Guerrillas: Who Are They?" *Senior Scholastic* (September 28, 1970).

"Argentina: Chaos and Corpses." *Time* (July 9, 1973).

"Argentina; Peron's Enemies on the Left." *Economist* (May 5, 1973).

"Argentina; Two Killings." *Economist* (April 15, 1972).

Arias, M. "Bolivian Guerrilla Movement Comes to an End." *Christian Century* (January 6, 1971).

Armstrong, J.A. and K. DeWitt, eds. *Soviet Partisans in World War II.* Madison: University of Wisconsin Press, 1964.

Ascherson, Neal. "Urban Guerrillas of West Germany." *New Society* (April 10, 1975), pp. 66-68.

Asprey, Robert B. *Ware in the Shadows: The Guerrilla in History.* London: MacDonald and Jane's, 1975.

"Back to Guerrilla Warfare." *Time* (August 17, 1970).

Barrett, R.J. "Indicators of Insurgency." *Military Review,* 53:4 (1973), pp. 37-43.

Bejar, Hector. *Peru Nineteen Sixty Five: Notes on a Guerrilla Experience.* NY: Monthly Review, 1970.

Bell, J. Bowyer. *Myth of the Guerrilla.* NY: Knopf, 1971.

Bell, J.B. *Secret Army: A History of the IRA.* Cambridge, MA: MIT Press, 1972.

Beres, L.R. "Guerrillas, Terrorists and Polarity: New Structural Models of World Politics." *Western Political Quarterly,* 27:4 (1974), pp. 624-636.

"Black September Assassins." *Newsweek* (March 19, 1973).

Cabeal, Amilear. *Revolution in Guinea: Selected Texts.* NY: Monthly Review, 1972.

Caine, P.D. "Urban Guerrilla Warfare." *Military Review,* 50:2 (1970), pp. 73-78.

Bruce-Briggs, B. "Suburban Warfare." *Military Review,* 54:6 (1974), pp. 3-10.

Campbeu, Artur. *Guerrillas: The History and Analysis.* NY: Day, 1968.

Castro, E. "Crisis in Uruguay." *Christian Century* (September 13, 1972).

"Children of the Storm: The Arab Commandos." *Newsweek* (December 22, 1969).

"City as Battlefield; A Global Concern." *Time* (November 2, 1970).

Clutterbuck, R.L. *Protest and Urban Guerrilla.* London: Abeland-Schuman, Ltd., 1973.

Codo, E.M. "The Urban Guerrilla." *Military Review,* 51:8 (1971), pp. 3-10.

"Commandos: Peace Is Their Fear." *Newsweek* (September 21, 1970).

Craig, Alexander. "Urban Guerrilla in Argentina." *Canadian Defense Quarterly,* (Spring, 1975), pp. 19-27.

Craig, Alexander. "Urban Guerrillas in Latin America." *Survey,* 17:3 (1971), pp. 112-128.

Cross, J.E. *Conflict in the Shadows: The Nature and Politics of Guerrila War.* Garden City, NY: Doubleday, 1973.

Crozier, Brian. *The Rebels: A Study of Post-War Insurrections.* London: Chatto and Windus, 1960.

Cuthbert, S.J. *We Shall Fight in the Streets: Guide to Street Fighting."* Aldershot: Gale and Poldan, 1953.

Davidson, S. "Arafat: as Patient as a Camel; Interview." *Time* (July 16, 1973).

Deakin, T.J. *Legacy of Carlos Marighella.* Washington, DC: NCJRD, (Microfiche), 1974.
Overview of urban guerilla warfare organizations including tactics and philosophy.

Deakin, T.J. "The Legacy of Carlos Marighella." *FBI Law Enforcement Bulletin,* 43:10 (1974), pp. 19-25.

Defence, Ministry of, Library. *Bolivian Revolutionary Disturbances, 1967.* London: Ministry of Defence Library, 1970.

Dixon, C. Aubrey and Otto Heilbrum. *Communist Guerrilla Warfare.* NY: Praeger, 1955.

Dorsey, W.H. "Arab Commandos." *New Republic* (November 22, 1969).

Eckstein, H., ed. *Internal War: Problems and Approaches.* NY: Free Press, 1963.

Ellis, John. *Short History of Guerrilla Warfare.* Walton-on-Thames, (GB), Ian Allan, 1975.

ElRayyes, Riad and Dunia Nahas. *Guerrilla for Palestine.* London: Croom Helm, 1976.

"Elusive Guerrilla." *Time* (September 29, 1967).

Faleroni, A.D. "What is an Urban Guerrilla?" *Military Review,* 47:1 (1967), pp. 94-96.

Fainstein, N.I. and S.S. Fainstein. *Urban Political Movements: The Search for Power by Minority Groups in American Cities.* Englewood Cliffs, NJ; Prentice-Hall, 1974.

Fairbairn, Geoffrey. *Revolutionary Guerrilla Warfare: The Countryside Version.* Harmondsworth: Penquin, 1974.

Gellner, J. *Bayonets in the Streets—Urban Guerrilla at Home and Abroad.* Ontario, Canada: Collier-Macmillan, 1974.

Gerassi, M. "Uruguay's Urban Guerrillas." *New Left Review* (July-August), pp. 22-29.

Gerassi, M.N. "Uruguay's Urban Guerrillas; The Tupamaros." *Nation* (September 27, 1969).

Geyer, G.A. "Guatemala and the Guerrillas." *New Republic* (July 4, 1970).

Giap, Vo Nguyen. *Peoples War: Peoples Army; The Vietcong Insurrection Manual for Underdeveloped Countries.* NY: Praeger, 1962.

Gilio, M.E. *Tupamaro Guerrilla.* Translated by A. Edmondson, London: Saturday Review, 1972.

Gilio, M.E. *The Tupamaro Guerrillas: The Structure and Strategy of the Urban Guerrilla Movement.* London: Ballantine, 1973.

Goodsell, J.N. "Urban Guerrillas in Latin America." *Commentator,* 14:11 (1970), pp. 7-8.

"Great Escape: Tupamaros Jailbreak." *Newsweek* (September 20, 1971).

Greene, Thomas H. *Comparative Revolutionary Movements.* Englewood Cliffs, NJ: Prentice-Hall, 1974.

"Guerrilla Challenge." *Time* (August 2, 1968).

"Guerrilla Threat." *Newsweek* (August 17, 1970).

"Guerrilla Threat in the Middle East." *Time* (December 13, 1968).

"Guerrilla War in the U.S.A." *Scanlons Monthly* (January, 1971).

Guevara, Che. *On Guerrilla Warfare.* NY: Praeger, 1962.

Hamilton, Peter. "The Urban Guerrilla—A New Challenge for Security." *Canadian Police Chief,* 60 (October, 1971), pp. 30, 32-34, 36.

Harsch, J.C., M. Lener, and I.F. Stone. "Toward an Urban Guerrilla Movement." *Current* (May, 1970).

Harrigan, A. "Combat in Cities." *Military Review,* 46:5 (1966), pp. 26-30.

Hodges, D.C. *Philosophy of the Urban Guerrilla—The Revolutionary Writings of Abraham Gillen.* NY: Morrow, 1973.

Howard, A.J. "Urban Guerrilla Warfare in a Democratic Society." *Medicine, Science and the Law,* 12:4 (October, 1972), pp. 231-243.

Hyde, D. *The Roots of Guerrilla Warfare: A Background Book.* Chester Springs, PA: Dufour, 1968.

Jenkins, B.M. *Soldiers V. Gunmen: The Challenge of Urban Guerrilla Warfare.* Santa Monica, CA: Rand, 1974.

Jenkins, B.M. *An Urban Strategy for Guerrillas and Governments.* Santa Monica, CA: Rand, January, 1972.

Karnov, S. "This Is Our Enemy: Vietcong Guerrilla." *Saturday Evening Post* (August 22, 1964).

Kasurak, P. "Coping with Urban Guerrillas: Democracy's Dilemma." *Canadian Defense Quarterly,* 3:4 (1974), pp. 41-46.

Kohl, James and John Litt. *Urban Guerrilla Warfare in Latin America.* Cambridge, MA: MIT Press, 1974.

Lando, B. "Report: Latin America Guerrillas." *Atlantic* (December, 1967).

Laquer, Walter. "Origins of Guerrilla Doctrine." *Journal of Contempory History* (July, 1975), pp. 341-382.

Lawrence, D. "Terrorism and Guerrilla Warfare." *U.S. News & World Report* (October 9, 1972).

Leites, Nathan and Charles Wolf, Jr. *Rebellion and Authority: An Analytic Essay on Insurgent Conflicts.* Chicago: Markham, 1970.

Mack, A. "Non-Strategy of Urban Guerrilla Warfare." in J. Niezing, ed. *Urban Guerrilla—Studies on the Theory, Strategy, and Practice of Political Violence in Modern Societies.* Rotterdam: Rotterdam University Press, 1974. pp. 22-45.

Mallin, Jay, ed. *Strategy for Conquest: Communist Documents on Guerrilla Warfare.* Coral Gables, FL: University of Miami Press, 1970.

Mallin, Jay, ed. *Terror and Urban Guerrillas: A Study of the Tactics and Documents.* Coral Gables, FL: University of Miami Press, 1971.

Mao Tse-Tung. *Basic Tactics.* Translated by Stuart R. Schram, NY: Praeger, 1966.

Mao Tse-Tung. *On Guerrilla Warfare.* NY: Praeger, 1961.

Max, Alphonse. *Guerrillas in Latin America.* The Hague: Interdoc, 1971.

Mikache, Ferdnand Otto. *Secret Forces: The Technique of Underground Movements.* London: Faber and Faber, 1950.

Moss, Robert. *Urban Guerrillas in Latin America and Uruguay.* London: Institute for the Study of Conflict, 1970.

Moss, R. "Urban Guerrillas in Uruguay." *Problems of Communism,* 20:5 (1971), pp. 14-23.

Moss, R. *Urban Guerrillas: The New Face of Political Violence.* London: M. Temple Smith, 1972.

Moss, R. *Urban Guerrilla Warfare.* London: International Institute for Strategic Studies, 1971.

Moss, R. *The War for the Cities.* NY: Coward, 1972.

Nunez, C. *The Tupamaros: Urban Guerrillas of Uruguay.* NY: Times Change, 1970.

O'Ballance, Edgar. *Arab Guerrilla Power.* Handen, CT: Shoestring, 1974.

Oppenheimer, Martin. *The Urban Guerrilla.* Chicago: Quadrangle, 1969.

"Palestine Commandos: Who Wields the Power." *U.S. News & World Report* (September 21, 1970).

Papagos, Alexander. "Guerrilla Warfare." *Foreign Affairs* (January, 1952), pp. 215-230.

Paret, Peter and John W. Shy. *Guerrillas in the 1960's.* NY: Praeger, 1962.

Peterson, H.E. "Urban Guerrilla Warfare." *Military Review,* 52:3 (1972), pp. 82-89.

Petras, J. "Guerrilla Movements in Latin America." *New Politics,* 6 (1967), pp. 80-94.

Pomeroy, William J. *Guerrilla Warfare and Marxism.* NY: International, 1968.

Porzecanski, A.C. *Uruguay's Tupamaros: The Urban Guerrilla.* NY: Praeger, 1973.

Robinson, Donald, ed. *The Dirty Wars; Guerrilla Actions and Other Forms of Unconventional Warfare.* NY: Delacorte, 1968.

Sarkesian, Sam C., ed. *Revolutionary Guerrilla Warfare.* Chicago: Precedent, 1975.

Segal, R. "Dealing with Rising Guerrilla Warfare." *Current* (March, 1973).

Sully, Francis. *Age of the Guerrilla: The New Warfare.* NY: Parents Magazine, 1968.

"Tactic of Terror, Arab Commandos." *Nation* (March 3, 1969).

Teitler, G. "Urban Guerrilla as a Revolutionary Phenomenon and as a Recruiting Problem." in J. Niezing, ed. *Urban Guerrilla—Studies on the Theory, Strategy and Practice of Political Violence in Modern Societies.* Rotterdam: Rotterdam University Press, 1974. pp. 111-127.

Tellez, Antonio and Stuart Christie. *Sabate: Guerrilla Extraordinary.* London: Davis-Poynter, 1974.

"Terror in the Tuscaroras: Peggy Ann Bradnick Case." *Newsweek* (May 30, 1966).

"Terror on the Pond; Trial of Arab Terrorists." *Time* (December 5, 1969).

"Thais and the Terrorists: Black September Terrorists Seize Israeli Hostages." *Newsweek* (January 8, 1973).

Thayer, Charles W. *Guerrilla.* NY: Harper and Row, 1963.

"Those Urban Guerrillas." *Economist* (October 17, 1970).

Tinker, H. "Can Urban Guerrilla Warfare Succeed." *Current* (May, 1971).

Tinker, H. "The Future of Guerrilla Warfare: Can Urban Guerrilla Warfare Succeed?" *Current,* 129 (1971), pp. 52-57.

"Urban Guerrilla" *Economist,* June 5, 1971.

"Urban Guerrillas in Latin America." *Conflict Studies,* 8 (October, 1970), pp. 4-15.

U.S. Committee on Un-American Activities. *Guerrilla Warfare Advocates in the United States.* Washington, DC: GPO 1968.

U.S. Congress. Senate Commission on the Judiciary. *Terroristic Activity,* part 1, 93rd Congress, 2nd Session. Washington, DC: GPO, September 23, 1974.

U.S. Naval Institute. *Studies in Guerrilla Warfare.* Annapolis: U.S. Naval Institute, 1963.

"Visiting Team from Terror Tech; Indonesian Guerrilla Force." *Time* (September 4, 1964).

Wallace, J.N. "Why Arab Guerrillas Are Out of Control." *U.S. News & World Report* (September 21, 1970).

"What Castro Is Plotting: The Fight for a Hemisphere." *U.S. News & World Report* (October 9, 1967).

"What Israel Thinks of the Guerrillas." *U.S. News & World Report* (February 24, 1969).

"What 100 Castro-Type Guerrillas Can Do." *U.S. News & World Report* (June 26, 1967).

Wise, B. "New Vow Rouses the Arabs: Al Fatah." *Life* (December 20, 1968).

Wolf, J.B. "Palestinian Resistance Movement." *Current History* (January, 1971).

Wren, C.S. "Revolt of the Arab Refugees: We'll Meet in Tel Aviv." *Look* (May 13, 1969).

AMERICAN VIOLENCE

VIOLENCE

Abrahamsen, David. *Our Violent Society.* NY: Funk and Wagnalls, 1970.

"American Violence: Terror and Tragedy." *PTA* (September, 1968).

Arendt, Hannah. *On Violence.* NY: Harcourt Brace and World, 1969.

Bandura, Albert. *Aggression: A Social Learning Analysis.* Englewood Cliffs, NJ: Prentice-Hall, 1973.

Bard, Morton. "Iatrogenic Violence." *Police Chief* (January, 1971).

Bartimore, Roldo S. and Murray Gruber. "Cleveland: Recipe for Violence." *Nation* (June 26, 1967).

Ben-Dak, Joseph, ed. *Future on Collective Violence: Societal and International Prospectives.* NY: Humanities, 1975.

Berkowitz, L. and J. Macaulay. "The Contragion of Criminal Violence." *Sociometry,* 34 (June, 1971), pp. 238-260.

Bernstein, Saul, *Alternatives to Violence.* NY: Association Press, 1970.

Bienen, Henry. *Violence and Social Changes.* Chicago: University of Chicago Press, 1969.

Bienen, Henry. *Violence and Social Change: A Review of Current Literature.* Chicago: University of Chicago Press, 1969.

Bingham, J.B. and A.M. Bingham. *Violence and Democracy.* NY: World, 1970.

Blumenthal, M.D. "Predicting Attitudes Toward Violence." *Science* (June, 1972), pp. 1262-1303.

Boskin, Joseph. *Urban Racial Violence in the Twentieth Century.* Beverly Hills, CA: Glencoe, 1969.

Brown, Richard M., ed. *American Violence.* Englewood Cliffs, NJ: Prentice-Hall, 1970.

Caffi, Andrea. *A Critique of Violence.* Indianapolis: Bobbs Merrill, 1970.

Campbell, James S., Joseph R. Sahid, and David P. Stone. *Law and Order Reconsidered.* NY: Bantam, 1970.

Canada Solicitor General. *Commission of Inquiry into Certain Disturbances at Kingston Penitentiary, During April, 1971, Report of.* Ottawa: Information Canada, 1973.

An insurrection at a Canadian penitentiary is described and it, causes are ascertained in order to recommend more effective security measures to prevent further uprisings.

Coates, Joseph F. "Urban Violence: The Pattern of Disorder." *Annals* (January, 1973).

"Collective Violence." *Annals,* 391 (September, 1970). (entire issue.)

Critchley, T.A. *Conquest of Violence—Order and Liberty in Britain.* NY: Schocken, 1970.

Examination of the causes of violence at selected periods of English and Welsh history and measures taken by local and central authorities in response.

Crozier, B. *Annual of Power and Conflict, 1973-74. A Survey of Political Violence and International Influence.* London: Institute for the Study of Conflict, 1974.

Croizer, B. *Annual of Power and Conflict, 1975-75. A Survey of Political Violence and International Influence.* London: Institute for the Study of Conflict, 1975.

Curtis, L.A. *Criminal Violence—National Patterns and Behaviors,* Lexington, MA: Heath Lexington, 1974.

DeLigt, B. *Conquest of Violence* NY: Garland [n.d.].

DeMaris, Ovid. *America the Violent.* NY: Cowles, 1970.

Endleman, Shalom, ed. *Violence in the Street.* Chicago: Quadrangle, 1970.

Feagin, J.R. "Social Sources of Support for Violence and Nonviolence in a Negro Ghetto." *Social Problems,* (1968), pp. 432-441.

"Firearms and Violence in American Life." *Texas Police Journal,* 18 (March, 1970), pp. 9-13, (April, 1970), pp. 9-12, 21.

Fogelson, Robert M. "Violence and Grievances: Reflections on the 1960's Riots." *Journal of Social Issues,* 26:1 (Winter, 1970), pp. 141-163.

Fox, Vernon. *Violence Behind Bars.* NY: Vantage, 1956.

Geen, R.G. and L. Berkowitz. "Some Conditions Facilitating the Occurrence of Aggression After the Observation of Violence." *Journal of Personality,* 35 (December, 1967), pp. 666-676.

Gilula, Marshal F. and David N. Daniels. "Violence and Man's Struggle to Adapt." *Science,* 164 (April, 1969), pp. 396-405.

Goldaber, Irving. "Yet a New Kind of Violence." *Police Chief* (April, 1974).
Describes increasing violence among spectators at sporting events.

Goldin, Gurston D. "Violence: The Integration of Psychiatric and Sociological Concepts." *Notre Dame Lawyer,* 40:5 (1965), pp. 508-516.

Graham, H.D. and T.R. Gurr. *Violence in America—Historical and Comparative Perspectives,* Washington, DC: GPO, 1969.
Overview of violence in Europe and America, immigrant societies and the frontier tradition, the history of working class protest and violence.

Graham, H.D. and T.D. Gurr. "Violence in Perspective: An Essay Review." *Journal of Human Relations,* 2:4 (1972).

Graham, H.D. and S.P. Mahinka. *Violence—The Crisis of American Confidence.* Baltimore: Johns Hopkins University Press, 1971.
Twelve addresses from a symposium entitled 'The United States in the 1970's—Perspectives on Violence' examine the structural origins of social conflict.

Grimshaw, Allen. "Changing Patterns of Racial Violence in the U.S." Symposium, *Notre Dame Lawyer,* XL (1965).

Grimshaw, Allen D. "Police Agencies and the Prevention of Racial Violence." *Journal of Criminal Law, Criminology and Police Science,* 54:1 (1963).

Grimshaw, Allen Day. *Racial Violence in the U.S.* Chicago: Aldine, 1969.

Gunn, J. *Violence.* Praeger, 1973.
The natures and causes of violences in human society and a survey of its various forms.

Gunn, J. *Violence in Human Society.* Newton Abbot: David and Charles, 1973.

Harrington, J.A. "Violence: A Clinical Viewpoint." *British Medical Journal,* 1 (January 22, 1972), pp. 228-231.

Harris, Dale. *Violence in Contemporary American Society.* University Park: Pennsylvania State University Press, 1969.

Hartman, Katharine B. "An End to Violence." *Police,* 12:1 (September-October, 1967), pp. 94-96.

Hibbs, Douglas A., Jr. *Mass Political Violence: A Cross-National Causal Analysis.* NY: Wiley, 1973.

Hofsteader, Richard and Michael Wallace, eds. *American Violence: A Documentary History.* NY: Knopf, 1970.

Hollon, W. Eugene. *Frontier Violence.* NY: Oxford University Press, 1974.

Horowitz, R. and G. Schwartz. "Honor, Normative Ambiguity and Gang Violence." *American Sociological Review,* 39:2 (1974), pp. 238-251.

Huffman, Arthur V. "Violent Behavior-Possibilities of Prediction and Control." *Police,* 8:5 (May-June, 1964), pp. 13-16.

Hyde, D. "Violence and American Democracy." *Journal of Social Issues,* 26:1 (1970), pp. 59-77.

Jacobs, J. "Violence in the City Street: Excerpts from Death and Life of Great American Cities." *Harper's* (September, 1961).

Jenkins, George; "Urban Violence in Africa." *American Behavioral Scientist* (March-April), 1968.

Justice, Blair. *Effects of Racial Violence on Attitudes in the Negro Community.* Houston, TX: Rice University, 1968.

Justice, Blair. *Violence in the City.* Fort Worth: Texas Christian University Press, 1969.

Kirkman, James F., Sheldon Leirf, and William J. Crofty. *A Staff Report to the National Commission on the Causes and Prevention of Violence.* Washington, DC: GPO, 1969.

Knowlton, C.S. "Violence in New Mexico: A Sociological Perspective." *California Law Review,* 58:5 (1970).

Kroes, R. "Violence in America—Spontaneity and Strategy." in J. Niezing, ed. *Urban Guerrilla-Studies on the Theory, Strategy, and Practice of Political Violence in Modern Societies.* Rotterdam: Rotterdam University Press, 1974, pp. 81-93.

Larson, Otto N. *Violence and the Mass Media.* NY: Harper and Row, 1968.

"Lawlessness and Violence in America and Their Special Manifestations in Changing Negro-White Relationships." *Journal of Negro History,* 44:1 (January, 1959), pp. 52-72.

Lawrence, P. "Violence, How to Cure It." *U.S. News & World Report* (September 18, 1972).

McClintock, F.H. *Crimes of Violence.* London: Macmillan, 1963.

McCone, J.A. *Violence in the City: An End or a Beginning.* Los Angeles: Lucas Brothers, 1970.

McNeil, Elton. "Violence and Human Development." *Annals,* 364 (March, 1966).

Masotti, Louis H. and Jerome R. Corsi, eds. *Shoot-Out in Cleveland. Report to the National Commission on the Causes and Prevention Of Violence.* NY: Bantam, 1969.

Maybanks, E.F. "Police View of Violence and the Control of Violence." *Medicine, Science, and the Law* (October, 1972), pp. 262-265.

May, Rollo. *Power and Innocence: A Search for the Sources of Violence.* NY: Norton, 1972.

Moll, K.D. *Arson, Vandalism and Violence—Law Enforcement.* Washington, DC: NCJRS, 1972.
Study based on a comprehensive statistical data base of metropolitan fire department problems related to violence.

Montagu, Ashley, ed. *Man and Aggression.* NY: Oxford University Press, 1973.

Mulvihill, D.J. and M.M. Tumin. *Crimes of Violence.* (vol. 11), Washington, DC: GPO, 1969.
A search for the causes of violence and the means of prevention.

Mulvihill, D.J. and M.M. Tumin. *Crimes of Violence.* (vol. 12), Washington, DC: GPO, 1969.
A search for the causes of crimes and the means of prevention.

National Commission on the Causes and Prevention of Violence. *Crimes of Violence.* (vol. 13), Washington, DC: GPO, 1969.
A search for the causes of violence and the means of prevention.

Neiberg, H.L. "The Threat of Violence and Social Change." *American Political Science Review,* LVI (December, 1962), pp. 865-873.

Newton, George D. and Franklin E. Zimring. *Firearms and Violence in American Life: A Staff Report to the National Commission on the Causes and Prevention of Violence.* Washington, DC: GPO, 1969.

New York State Special Commission on Attica. *Attica—The Official Report of the New York State Special Commission on Attica.* NY: Bantam, 1972.
Investigation by a special governor's committee into the causes and handling of New York State's violent prison disorder.

Ng, Larry, ed. *Alternatives to Violence: A Stimulus to Dialogue.* NY: Time-Life, 1968.
Reviews basis of violence and some possible alternatives.

Owen, B.M. *Measuring Violence on Television—The Gerbner Index.* Springfield, VA: NTIS, 1972.

Parker, T.F. *Violence in the U.S.* (vol. 1), 1956-67. NY: Facts on File, 1974.

Parker, T.F. *Violence in the U.S.* (vol. 2), 1968-71. NY: Facts on File, 1974.

Parsons, M.B. "Violence and Code in Southern Justice." *Southern Atlantic Quarterly, 1961.*

Pasternack, Stefan A., ed. *Violence and Victims.* NY: Halsted, 1975.

Pelton, LeRoy H. *The Psychology of Non-Violence.* Elmsford, NY: Pergamou, 1975.

Pinkney, Alphonso. *American Way of Violence.* NY: Random, 1972.

Pokorny, Alex D. "Human Violence; A Comparison of Homicide, Aggravated Assault, Suicide, and Attempted Suicide." *Journal of Criminal Law, Criminology and Police Science.* 56:4 (December, 1965), pp. 488-497.

Rivera, Charles R. and Kenneth Switzer. *Violence.* Rochelle Park, NJ: Hayden, 1976.

Rosenthal, Alan. "Violence Is Predictable." *Today's Health,* (November, 1970).

Roucek, J.S. "The Sociology of Violence." *Journal of Human Relations,* V (Spring, 1957).

Schonborn, Karl L. *Dealing with Violence: The Challenge Faced by Police and Other Peacekeepers.* Springfield, IL: C.C. Thomas, 1975.

Short, J.F. and M.E. Wolfgang. *Collective Violence.* Chicago: Aldin, 1972.
Readings in theory and research on violence as a group phenomenon, with analysis of the forms, sources, and meanings of riot and rebellion.

Sorel, Georges. *Reflections on Violence.* NY: Collier, 1961.

Spiegel, John P. *The Tradition of Violence in Our Society.* Waltham, MA: Brandeis University Press, 1968.

Stark, R. and J. McEvoy. "Middle-Class Violence." *Psychology Today* (November, 1970).

Sugg, Carolyn, ed. *Violence.* Paramus, NJ: Paulist Newman, 1970.

Tamm, Quinn. "Violence in America." *Police Chief,* 38:1 (January, 1971), pp. 34-35, 41-44.

Taylor, Karl K. and Fred W. Soady, Jr. *Violence: An Element of American Life.* Rockleigh NJ: Holbrook, 1972.

"Terror in the Cities." *America* (March 2, 1963).

Toch, Hans. *Violent Men; An Inquiry into the Psychology of Violence.* Chicago: Aldine, 1969.

U.S. Congress. House Committee on Un-American Activities. *Guerrilla Warfare Advocates in the United States; A Report.* Washington, DC: GPO, 1968.

"The Violence." *Nation,* CCV:4 (August, 1967).

VonDerMehden, Fred R. *Comparative Political Violence.* Englewood Cliffs, NJ: Prentice-Hall, 1973.

Weisberg, B. "Racial Violence and Civil Rights Law Enforcement." *University of Chicago Law Review,* 18: (1951), pp. 769-783.

Wertham, Frederic. *The Show of Violence.* Garden City, NY: Doubleday, 1949.

West, D.J.P. Wiles and C. Stanwood. *Research on Violence.* Cambridge, England, University of Cambridge, Institute of Criminology, 1974.

Westley, William A. "Violence and the Police." *American Journal of Sociology,* 59 (July, 1953).

Widick, B.J. *Detroit: City of Race and Class Violence.* Chicago: Quadrangle, 1972.

Wolfgang, Marvin. *Patterns of Criminal Violence.* Philadelphia: University of Pennsylvania, 1958.

Wolfgang, Marvin E. "Violence, U.S.A." *Crime and Delinquency,* 14:4 (1968), pp. 289-305.

Wolfgang, M.E. and F. Ferracutt. *Subculture of Violence-Towards an Integrated Theory in Criminology.* NY: Barnes and Noble, 1967.

The sociological and clinical approach are seen as interdependent in the field of criminology through an in-depth analysis of violence, particularly homicide.

Yee, M.S. *Melancholy History of Soledad Prison—In Which a Utopian Scheme Turns Bedlam.* NY: Harper and Row, 1973.

Zevin, J. *Violence in America—What Is the Alternative.* Englewood Cliffs, NJ: Prentice-Hall, 1973.

A collection of articles which present an in-depth study of violence emphasizing its definition, causes, and effects and suggesting methods to combat it.

Zinberg, Norman E. and Gordan A. Gellman. "Violence: Biological Need and Social Control." *Social Forces,* 45:4 (June, 1967), pp. 533-541.

PART XV
THE CRIME PROBLEM

CRIMINOLOGY

CRIMINOLOGY

The Aldine Crime and Justice Annual, 1974. Chicago: Aldine, 1975.

Bersani, C.A. *Crime and Delinquency, A Reader.* N.Y.: Macmillan, 1970.

Collection of theoretical, empirical, and descriptive literature in criminology and in delinquency, prepared for an introductory college-level course.

Caldwell, Robert G. *Criminology.* (2nd. ed.) N.Y.: Ronald, 1965.

Chang, Dae H. *Criminology—A Cross Cultural Perspective.* (2 vols.) Durham, N.C.: Carolina Academic Press, 1976.

Council of Europe. *International Exchange of Information on Current Criminological Research Projects in Member States, 10.* N.Y.: Manhattan, 1970.

Council of Europe. *International Exchange of Information on Current Criminological Research Projects in Member States, 11.* N.Y.: Manhattan, 1971.

Council of Europe. *International Exchange of Information on Current Criminological Research Projects in Member States, 12.* N.Y.: Manhattan, 1972.

Criminology in America: The 20th Century. Aurora, IL.: Social Science and Social Research, 1975.

Denfeld, D. *Street-Wise Criminology.* Morristown, N.J.: General Learning Corporation, 1974.

First person accounts of different aspects of the criminal justice system which provide descriptions of behavior and support or refute existing theories.

Doleschal, Eugene. *Crime and Delinquency Research in Selected European Countries.* Washington, D.C.: GPO, 1971.

Drabek, Thomas E. and Sykes Gresham. *Law and the Lawless: A Reader in Criminology.* N.Y.: Random, 1969.

Dressler, D., ed. *Readings in Criminology and Penology.* N.Y.: Columbia University Press, 1964.

Compilation of articles for the student and worker in criminology, penology and juvenile delinquency.

Ferri, Enrico. *Criminal Sociology.* N.Y.: Appleton, 1915.

Foxe, A.N. *Advanced Studies in Criminology.* N.Y.: Tunbridge, 1972.

Papers on different criminological concerns taken from delivered addresses, published writings, and articles from journals on psychiatry, psychodynamics, and psychopathology.

Gibbons, D.C. *Society, Crime, and Criminal Careers: An Introduction to Criminology.* Englewood Cliffs, N.J.: Prentice-Hall, 1968.

Glaser, Daniel, ed. *Handbook of Criminology.* Chicago: Rand McNally, 1974.

Glueck, Sheldon and Eleanor Glueck. *Ventures in Criminology.* Cambridge: Harvard University Press, 1964.

Grapin, P. *Criminological Anthropology.* Paris, France: Presses Universitaires de France, 1973.

Grupp, Stanley E. *The Positive School of Criminology.* Pittsburgh: University of Pittsburgh Press, 1968.

Grygier, Tadeusz, ed. *Criminology and Intransition.* London: Tavistock, 1965.

Haskell, Martin R. and Lewis Yablonsky. *Criminology: Crime and Criminality.* Chicago: Rand McNally, 1975.

Henshel, Richard L. and Robert A. Silverman. *Perception in Criminology.* N.Y.: Columbia University Press, 1975.

Hood, Roger and Richard Sparks. *Key Issues in Criminology.* N.Y.: McGraw-Hill, 1970.

Kinton, Jack. *Criminology Tomorrow.* Aurora, IL.: Social Science and Social Research, 1974.

Knudten, R.D. *Crime in a Complex Society—An Introduction to Criminology.* Homewood, IL.: Dorsey Press, 1970.

A sociologically-oriented textbook dealing with the origins, manifestations and remedies for crime and delinquency.

Krisberg, Barry. *Crime and Privilege: Toward a New Criminology.* Englewood Cliffs, N.J.: Prentice-Hall, 1975.

Mannheim, H. *Comparative Criminology.* Boston: Houghton Mifflin, 1967.

A textbook of criminology covering research and methodology, factors and causes related to crime, and the sociology of crime.

Mannheim, Hermann, ed. *Pioneers in Criminology.* London: Stevens, 1960.

Quinney, Richard. *The Social Reality of Crime.* Boston: Little, Brown, 1970.

Attempts to reinterpret criminology to fit the times, describes how behavior patterns develop in relation to criminal definitions, and how criminal conceptions are formulated.

Quinney, Richard. *Criminology: Analysis and Critique of Crime in America.* Boston: Little, Brown, 1975.

Radzinowicz, L. and M. Wolfgang. *Criminal in Society.* N.Y.: Basic, 1971.
The nature of deviance, the proper scope of criminal law, the shape and trends of crime, the social disharmonies responsible for crime.

Reason, C.E. *Criminologist—Crime and the Criminal.* Pacific Palisades, CA.: Goodyear, 1974.

Reckless, Walter C. *American Criminology: New Directions.* N.Y.: Appleton-Century-Crofts, 1973.

Savitz, Leonard. *Dilemmas in Criminology.* N.Y.: McGraw-Hill, 1967.

Schaffer, Stephen. *Theories in Criminology: Past and Present Philosophies of the Crime Problem.* N.Y.: Random, 1969.

Short, J.F., Jr. *Modern Criminals.* (2nd ed.) N.Y.: Dutton, 1973.

Snodgrass, J. *American Criminological Tradition—Portraits of the Men and Idealogy in a Discipline.* Ann Arbor, MI.: University Microfilms, 1972.
Study of prominent researchers and theorists in crime and delinquency in the United States during the period 1915 to 1950.

Sutherland, E.H. and D.R. Cressey. *Criminology.* (8th ed.) Philadelphia: Lippincott, 1971.
A classic textbook on criminology geared to the needs of the student.

Sykes, G.M. and T.E. Drabek. *Law and the Lawless—A Reader in Criminology.* N.Y.: Random House, 1969.

Taft, D.R. and R.W. England. *Criminology.* (4th ed.) N.Y.: Macmillan, 1964.
This book follows the theoretical emphasis that crime in the United States is fundamentally an expression of the general culture.

Taylor, I. *New Criminology—For a Social Theory of Deviance.* London: Routledge and Kegan Paul, 1973.

Wolfgang, Marvin E. *Crime and Culture: Essays in Honor of Thorsten Sellin.* N.Y.: Wiley, 1968.

Wolfgang, Marvin E. "Criminology and the Criminologist." *Journal of Criminal Law, Criminology and Police Science,* 54:2 (June, 1963), pp. 155-162.

Wolfgang, Marvin E. et al. *Criminology Index: Research and Theory in Criminology in the United States 1945-1972.* (2 vols.) N.Y.: Elsevier, 1975.

Wolfgang, M.E. and L. Savitz. *Sociology of Crime and Delinquency.* N.Y.: Wiley, 1970.
Current sociological and empirical research and theory in criminology are the framework for the sixty-three articles of this book.

CHROMOSONAL ABNORMALITY (XYY SYNDROME)

Ashby, Eric. "Does XYY Mark the Crime Frontier." *Listener,* (October 16, 1975), pp. 495-496.

Marcus, Anthony M. "The XYY Syndrome: A Short Review, A Case Study and Investigatory Model." *Journal of Forensic Science,* 15 (April, 1970), pp. 154-172.

U.S. Department of Health, Education, and Welfare. National Institute of Mental Health, *XYY Chromosonal Abnormality, Report.* Washington, D.C.: GPO, 1970.

CLIMATE AND CRIME

Sells, S.B. and D.P. Will, Jr. *Accidents, Police Incidents and Weather: A Further Study of the City of Fort Worth, Texas 1968.* Fort Worth: Institute of Behavioral Research, Texas Christian University, 1971.

Will, D.P., Jr. and S.D. Sells. *Prediction of Police Incidents and Accidents by Meteorological Variables.* Fort Worth: Institute of Behavioral Research, Texas Christian University, 1969.

CRIME AND MENTAL ILLNESS

Crime and Mental Illness

Bergman, Rita E. *Sociopath: Selections in Anti-Social Behavior.* Hicksville, N.Y.: Exposition, 1968.

Berliner, Arthur K. "Some Aspects of Mental Abnormality in Relation to Crime." *Journal of Criminal Law, Criminology and Police Science,* 46:1 (May-June, 1955), pp. 67-72.

Bordua, David, ed. "Social Conflict and Schizophrenic Behavior in Young Adult Negro Males." *Psychiatry, XXIV* (November, 1961), pp. 337-346.

Brown, Bertram S. "Fantasy and Force: A Study of the Dynamics of the Mentally Retarded Offender." *Journal of Criminal Law, Criminology and Police Science,* 61:1 (March, 1970), pp. 71-77.

Clare, P.K. "Obstacles to the Treatment and Control of the Mentally Disturbed Offender: A Case Study." *Police,* 16:9 (May, 1972), pp. 30-37.

Cleckley, Harvey M. *The Mask of Sanity: An Attempt to Clarify Some Issues About the So-Called Psychopathic Personality.* (4th ed.) St. Louis: C.V. Mosby, 1964.

Cohen, Louis, H. *Murder, Madness and the Law.* Cleveland, OH.: World, 1953.

Ferentz, Edward J. "Mental Deficiency Related to Crime." *Journal of Criminal Law, Criminology and Police Science,* 45:3 (September-October, 1954), pp. 299-307.

Fingarette, H. *Meaning of Criminal Insanity.* Berkeley: University of California Press, 1972.

Greenwald, Robert. "Disposition of the Insane Defendent after 'Acquittal'—The Long Road from Commitment to Release." *Journal of Criminal Law, Criminology and Police Science,* 59:4 (December, 1968), pp. 583-594.

Guze, Samuel B. *Criminality and Psychiatric Disorders.* N.Y.: Oxford University Press, 1976.

Irvine, L.M. and T.B. Brelje. *Law, Psychiatry and the Mentally Disordered Offender.* (2 vols.) Springfield, IL.: C.C. Thomas, 1972.

Keldgord, Robert E. "Brain Damage and Delinquency—A Question and a Challenge." *Journal of California Law Enforcement* (October, 1969), pp. 53-58.

Morrow, William R. and Donald B. Peterson. "Follow-up of Discharged Psychiatric Offenders—'Not Guilty by Reason of Insanity' and 'Criminal Sexual Psychopaths'." *Journal of Criminal Law, Criminology and Police Science,* 57:1 (March, 1966), pp. 31-34.

Nice, Richard W. *Crime and Insanity.* N.Y.: Philosophical Library, 1958.

Partridge, Ralph. *Broadmoor: A History of Criminal Lunacy and its Problems.* London: Chatto, 1953.

Radzinowicz, Leon and S.W.E. Turner, eds. *Mental Abnormality and Crime.* London: MacMillan, 1949.

Rollin, H. *Mentally Abnormal Offender and the Law.* Elmsford, N.Y.: Pergamon, 1969.

Rosensweig, Saul. "Unconscious Self-Defense in an Uxoricide." *Journal of Criminal Law, Criminology and Police Science,* 46:6 (March-April, 1956), pp. 791-795.

Smart, Frances and Beatrice Brown. *Neurosis and Crime.* N.Y.: Barnes and Noble, 1970.

Sturm, Louella. *Mental Hospital Nightmare.* Hicksville, N.Y.: Exposition, 1973.

Thurrell, Richard J., S.L. Halleck, and A.F. Johnson. "Psychosis in Prison." *Journal of Criminal Law, Criminology and Police Science,* 56:3 (September, 1965), pp. 271-276.

Walker, N. *Crime and Insanity in England.* (vol. 1) *The Historical Perspective.* Edinburgh: University of Edinburgh Press, 1968.
Traditional legal problems of culpability of the offender, his fitness for trial, and the need for clemency, from pre-Norman through modern times.

Walker, N. and S. McCabe. *Crime and Insanity in England.* (vol. 2) *New Solutions and New Problems.* Chicago: Andine, 1973.
Treatment of the mentally disturbed criminal offender in prisons and hospitals.

Insanity Defense

Arens, Richard. *Insanity Defense.* N.Y.: Philosophical Library, 1974.

Bennett, D.E. "Insanity Defense—A Perplexing Problem of Criminal Justice." *Louisiana Law Review,* 16 (1956).

Clyde, Peter. *Guilty But Insane: Anglo-American Attitudes to Insanity and Criminal Guilt.* Sunbury-on-Thames (GB), Nelson, 1973.

Cohen, Louis H. *Murder, Madness and the Law.* Cleveland: World, 1952.

"Dissatisfaction with the Operation of the Durham Rule." *Notre Dame Lawyer,* 36 (1961).

Fingarette, H. *Meaning of Criminal Insanity.* Berkeley: University of California Press, 1972.
Problems and controversies connected with the interpretation and rationale of the insanity plea, and possible formats for a practicable insanity test.

Floch, Maurice. "The Concept of Temporary Insanity Viewed by a Criminologist." *Journal of Criminal Law, Criminology and Police Science,* 45:6 (March-April, 1955), pp. 685-689.

Goldstein, Abraham S. *The Insanity Defense.* New Haven, CT.: Yale University Press, 1967.

Goldstein, J. and J. Katz. "Abolish the 'Insanity Defense'—Why Not?" *Yale Law Journal,* 72 (1963).

Krash, A. "The Durham Rule and Judicial Administration of the Insanity Defense in the District of Columbia." *Yale Law Journal,* 70:6 (1961), pp. 905-906.

"Mental Disease and Criminal Responsibility: A Symposium. II." *The Catholic Lawyer,* 5:1 (Winter, 1959).
Prosecution problems and defense problems under the Durham Rule. Insanity as a defense in criminal law.

Royal Commission. *Report of the Royal Commission on Law of Insanity as a Defense in Criminal Cases.* Ottawa: Queen's Printer and Controller of Stationery, 1955.

Simon, Rita James. *The Jury and the Defense of Insanity.* Boston: Little, Brown, 1967.

Walker, Nigel. *Crime and Insanity in England: The Historical Perspective.* Edinburgh: Edinburgh University Press, 1968.

Weihofen, Henry. *Mental Disorder as a Criminal Defense.* Buffalo, N.Y.: Dennis, 1954.

Weintraub, Joseph. "Criminal Responsibility: Psychiatry Alone Cannot Determine It." *American Bar Association Journal,* 49 (1963).

White, W.A. *Insanity and the Criminal Law.* N.Y.: Macmillan, 1923.

Mental Competency

Allen, Richard C., Elyce Zenoff Ferster, and Henry Weihoffen. *Mental Impairment and Legal Incompetency.* Englewood Cliffs, N.J.: Prentice-Hall, 1968.

Bennett, David E. "Competency to Stand Trial: A Call for Reform." *Journal of Criminal Law, Criminology and Police Science.* 59:4 (December, 1968), pp. 569-582.

Gambino, R. *Concepts of Mental Disorder and Criminal Responsibility in Law.* Ann Arbor, MI.: University Microfilms, 1968.
Inquiry into the philosophies which support the various legal standards on criminal capacity, and a proposal for a new insanity test based on socioethical criteria.

Group for the Advancement of Psychiatry. *Misuse of Psychiatry in the Criminal Courts—Competency to Stand Trial.* N.Y.: Group for the Advancement of Psychiatry, 1974.

Harvard Medical School, Laboratory of Community Psychiatry. *Competency to Stand Trial and Mental Illness.* N.Y.: Aronson, 1975.

Leifer, R. "The Psychiatrist and Tests of Criminal Responsibility." *American Psychologist,* 19 (November, 1964), pp. 825-830.

Matthews, A. *Mental Disability and the Criminal Law—A Field Study.* Chicago: American Bar Foundation, 1970.

Silving, Helen. *Essays on Mental Incapacity and Criminal Conduct.* Springfield, IL.: C.C. Thomas, 1967.

U.S. Department of Health, Education, and Welfare, National Institute of Mental Health. *Competency to Stand Trial and Mental Illness.* Washington, D.C.: GPO, 1973.
Clarification of the applicable criteria—both legal and psychiatric—concerning an accused person's competency to stand trial.

Whitlock, F.A. *Criminal Responsibility and Mental Illness.* London: Butterworths, 1963.

Psychiatry and Criminal Law

Allen, Richard C. et al. *Readings in Law and Psychiatry.* (rev. ed.) Baltimore: Johns Hopkins University Press, 1975.

Biggs, John. *The Guilty Mind: Psychiatry and the Law of Homicide.* N.Y.: Harcourt, Brace, 1955.

Carpenter, Rod. "Psychology and Its Ever-Changing Ways." *Police Chief,* 38:4 (April, 1971), pp. 48, 53.
Outlines several psychological schools of thought.

Davidson, Henry A. "Psychiatrists in Administration of Criminal Justice." *Journal of Criminal Law, Criminology and Police Science,* 45:1 (May-June, 1954), pp. 12-20.

Dorcus, Roy M. and G. Wilson Shaffer. *Textbook of Abnormal Psychology.* Baltimore: Williams and Wilkins, 1950.

Ennis, B.J. *Prisoners of Psychiatry—Mental Patients, Psychiatrists, and the Law.* N.Y.: Harcourt Brace Jovanovich, 1972.
The author's opinion is that the legal rights of mentally disturbed persons are abrogated by present mental hygiene laws.

Feuss, Charles D., Jr. and Douglas Goldman. "The Function of a Psychiatrist in a Juvenile Court." *Police,* 8:4 (March-April, 1964), pp. 33-35.

George, B.J., Jr. *Effective Use of Psychiatric Evidence in Civil and Criminal Litigation.* N.Y.: Practicing Law Institute, 1974.

Glenn, Michael and Richard Kunnes. *Repression or Revolution? Therapy in the United States Today.* N.Y.: Harper and Row, 1973.

Glueck, Sheldon. *Law and Psychiatry: Cold War or Entente Cordiale.* Baltimore: Johns Hopkins University Press, 1962.

Guttmacher, Manfred S. *The Role of Psychiatry in Law.* Springfield, IL.: C.C. Thomas, 1968.

Guttmacher, Manfred S. and Henry Weihofen. *Psychiatry and the Law.* N.Y.: W.W. Norton, 1953.

Hakeem, M. "A Critique of the Psychiatric Approach to Crime and Correction." *Law and Contemporary Problems,* 23 (Autumn, 1958), pp. 650-682.

Halleck, Seymour L. *Psychiatry and the Dilemmas of Crime: A Study of Causes, Punishment, and Treatment.* N.Y.: Harper and Row, 1967.

Halleck, Seymour L. and Walter Bromberg. *Psychiatric Aspects of Criminology.* Springfield, IL.: C.C. Thomas, 1968.

"Heal Thyself: Suicides Among Psychiatrists." *Newsweek* (May 22, 1967).

Hock, Paul H. and Joseph Zubin. *Psychiatry and the Law.* N.Y.: Grune and Stratton, 1955.

Howard, Jan and Ansel M. Strauss, eds. *Humanizing Health Care.* N.Y.: Wiley, 1975.

Karpman, Ben. "On Reducing Tensions and Bridging Gaps Between Psychiatry and the Law." *Journal of Criminal Law, Criminology and Police Science.* 48:2 (July-August, 1957), pp. 164-174.

Katz, Jay, Joseph Goldstein, and Alan M. Dershowitz. *Psychoanalysis, Psychiatry and Law.* N.Y.: Macmillan, 1966.

Kiel, Frank W. "The Psychiatric Character of the Assailant as Determined by Autopsy Observations of the Victim." *Journal of Forensic Science,* 10:3 (July, 1965), pp. 267-270.

Kittrie, N.N. *Right to be Different—Deviance and Enforced Therapy.* Baltimore: Penguin, 1971.

MacDonald, John M. "Crime and Psychiatry." *Police,* 2:5 (May-June, 1958), pp. 30-32.

MacDonald, John M. *Psychiatry and the Criminal: A Guide to Psychiatric Examinations for the Criminal Courts.* Springfield, IL.: C.C. Thomas, 1969.

Marshall, James. *Law and Psychology in Conflict.* Indianapolis: Bobbs-Merrill, 1966.

Martindale, D. and E. Martindale. *Psychiatry and the Law—The Crusade Against Involuntary Hospitalization.* St. Paul, MN.: Windflower, 1973.

Meyers, Thomas J. "The Psychiatric Determination of Legal Intent." *Journal of Forensic Science,* 10:3 (July, 1965), pp. 347-365.

Meyers, Thomas J. "The Psychiatric Examination." *Journal of Criminal Law, Criminology and Police Science,* 54:4 (December, 1963), pp. 431-446.

Meyers, Thomas J. "Psychiatric Examination of the Sexual Psychopath." *Journal of Criminal Law, Criminology and Police Science,* 56:1 (March, 1965), pp. 27-31.

Morse, Howard Newcomb. "The Aberrational Man—A Tour de Force of Legal Psychiatry." *Journal of Forensic Sciences* (October, 1968).

Nordby, Vernon J. and Calvin S. Hall. *Guide to Psychologists and Their Concepts.* San Francisco: W.H. Freeman, 1974.

Overholser, Winfred. *The Psychiatrist and the Law.* N.Y.: Harcourt Brace Jovanovich, 1953.

Parlour, Richard R. and Richard A. Ibanez. "Psychiatric Contributions to the Processes of the Law." *Police,* 8:1 (September-October, 1963), pp. 12-17; 8:2 (November-December, 1963), pp. 58-62.

Polier, Justine Wise. *The Rule of Law and the Role of Psychiatry.* Baltimore: John Hopkins University Press, 1968.

Rappeport, Jonas R., ed. *The Clinical Evaluation of the Dangerousness of the Mentally Ill.* Springfield, IL.: C.C. Thomas, 1967.

Reinehe, Robert C. *Machine that Oils Itself: A Critical Look at the Mental Health Establishment.* Chicago: Nelson Hall, 1975.

Robitscher, Jonas. "Psychiatry and Changing Concepts of Criminal Responsibility." *Federal Probation* (September, 1967).

Robitscher, Jonas B. *Pursuit of Agreements: Psychiatry and the Law.* Philadelphia: Lippincott, 1966.

Salter, Andrew: *Case Against Psychoanalysis.* N.Y.: Harper and Row, 1972.

Sharp, Agnes A., ed. *A Dynamic Era of Court Psychiatry: 1914-1944.* Chicago: Chicago Psychiatric Institute of The Municipal Court of Chicago, 1944.

Suarez, John M. "A Critique of the Psychiatrists' Role as Expert Witness." *Journal of Forensic Science,* 12:2 (April, 1967), pp. 172-179.

Szasz, Thomas S. *Law, Liberty and Psychiatry.* N.Y.: Macmillan, 1963.

Szasz, Thomas S. *Psychiatric Justice.* N.Y.: Macmillan, 1965.

Szasz, Thomas S. "Psychiatry's 'Threat to Civil Liberties'." *National Review,* 1963.

Toch, Hans. *Legal and Criminal Psychology.* N.Y.: Holt, 1961.

Torrey, E. Fuller. *Death of Psychiatry.* Baltimore: Penguin, 1975.

Wesenin-Volpin, Alexander S. *Abuse of Psychiatry for Political Repression in the Soviet Union.* N.Y.: Arno, 1973.

Ziskin, Jay. *Coping with Psychiatric and Psychological Testimony.* Beverly Hill, CA.: Law and Psychology Press, 1970.

CRIME AND THE OCCULT

Leek, Sybil. *Driving Out the Devils: An Exorcists Case Book.* N.Y.: Putnam, 1975.

Masters, R.E. *Eros and Evil: The Sexual Psychopathology of Witchcraft.* Baltimore: Penguin, 1974.

Peacock, F. "Witchcraft and Its Effect on Crime in East Africa." *Police Journal,* (GB), (1929), pp. 121-131.

Tabori, Paul. *Crime and the Occult.* N.Y.: Taplinger, 1974.

CRIME AND THE PHASES OF THE MOON

Bauer, Stephan F. and Edward J. Hornick. "Lunar Effect on Mental Illness: The Relationship of Moon Phase to Psychiatric Emergencies." *American Journal of Psychiatry,* 125 (November 5, 1968), pp. 148-149.

Cottrell, John. "Moon Madness: Does It Really Exist?" *Science Digest* (October, 1969), pp. 24-29.

Lieber, Arnold L. and Carolyn R. Sherin. "Homicides and the Lunar Cycle: Toward a Theory of Lunar Influence and Human Emotional Disturbance." *American Journal of Psychiatry,* 129 (July, 1972), pp. 101-106.

Oliver, John F. "Moonlight and Nervous Disorders: A Historical Study." *American Journal of Psychiatry,* 99 (1943), pp. 579-584.

Osborn, Roger Dean. "The Moon and the Mental Hospital: An Investigation of One Area of Folklore." *Journal of Psychiatry and Mental Health Services* (March-April, 1968), pp. 88-93.

Pokorny, Alex D. "Moon Phases, Suicide and Homicide." *American Journal of Psychiatry,* 112 (July, 1964), pp. 66-67.

THE CRIMINAL

Classification of Offenders

Clinard, M.B. and R. Quinney, eds. *Criminal Behavior Systems: A Typology.* N.Y.: Holt, Rinehart and Winston, 1967.

Coe, Rodney M. and Albert J. Shafter. "Survey of Classification Systems in the United States." *Journal of Criminal Law, Criminology and Police Science,* 49:4 (November-December, 1958), pp. 316-320.

Eron, L.D., ed. *The Classification of Behavior Disorders.* Chicago. Aldine, 1966.

Ferdinand, Theodore N. *Typologies of Delinquency.* N.Y.: Random House, 1966.

Hurwitz, Jacob I. "Three Delinquent Types: A Multivariate Analysis." *Journal of Criminal Law, Criminology and Police Science,* 56:3 (September, 1965), pp. 328-334.

Morris, Albert. "The Comprehensive Classification of Adult Offenders." *Journal of Criminal Law, Criminology and Police Science.* 56:2 (June, 1965), pp. 197-202.

Roebuck, Julian B. *Criminal Typology—The Legalistic, Physical-Constitutional-Hereditary, Psychological-Psychiatric and Sociological Approaches.* Springfield, IL: C.C. Thomas, 1971.

Roebuck, Julian B. "A Criticism of Gibbons' and Garrity's Criminal Typology." *Journal of Criminal Law, Criminology and Police Science,* 54:4 (December, 1963), pp. 476-478.

Spencer, Carol. *A Typology of Violent Offenders.* Sacramento: Department of Corrections (September, 1966).

Criminal Behavior

"Aspects of Criminal Restraint on Acquisitive Conduct." *Columbia Law Review,* 38 (1938).

Baldwin, John and A.E. Buttoms. *Urban Criminal: A Study in Sheffield.* London: Tavistock, 1976.

Bromberg, W. *Crime and the Mind—An Outline of Psychiatric Criminology.* Westport, CT.: Greenwood, 1948.

An exposition of the emotional and intellectual attitudes of the criminal, together with the interplay of the individual offender with his society.

Clinard, M.B. and R. Quinney. *Criminal Behavior Systems—A Typology.* N.Y.: Holt, Rinehart and Winston, 1967.

A broad survey of recently accumulated knowledge concerning the various forms of criminal behavior.

Guenther, A.L. *Criminal Behavior and Social Systems—Contributions of American Sociology.* Chicago: Rand McNally, 1970.

Hammond, W.H. and Edna Chayen. *Persistent Criminals.* London: HMSO, 1963.

Jeffrey, C.R. "Criminal Behavior and Learning Theory." *Journal of Criminal Law, Criminology and Police Science,* 56:3 (September, 1965), pp. 294-300.

Jeffrey, Clarence Ray. "An Integrated Theory of Crime and Criminal Behavior." *Journal of Criminal Law, Criminology and Police Science,* 49:6 (March-April, 1959), pp. 533-552.

Laune, Ferris F. *Predicting Criminology,* Westport, CT.: Greenwood, 1974. (repr. of 1936 ed.)

Lipton, Dean. *The Faces of Crime and Genius: The Historical Impact of the Genius Criminal.* Cranbury, N.J.: A.S. Barnes, 1970.

National Institute of Law Enforcement and Criminal Justice. *Classification of Criminal Behavior.* Springfield, VA.: NTIS, 1973.

Four papers discussing the responsibilities and problems facing the criminal justice field in the establishment of a valid classification system.

Perdue, William C. "Criminosis Exhumed." *Corrective Psychiatry and Journal of Social Therapy,* 14:2 (1968), pp. 68-75.

Powell, Elwin H. "Crime as a Function of Anomie." *Journal of Criminal Law, Criminology and Police Science,* 57:2 (June, 1966), pp. 161-171.

Prins, Herschel. *Criminal Behavior: An Introduction to Its Causes and Treatment.* N.Y.: Beekman, 1974.

Schacter, Stanley. *Emotion, Obesity and Crime.* N.Y.: Academic, 1971.

Schuessler, Karl F. and Donald R. Cressey. "Personality Characteristics of Criminals." *American Journal of Sociology,* LV (March, 1950), pp. 476-484.

Short, James F., Jr. *Modern Criminals.* Edison, N.J.: Transaction, 1973.

Stebbins, Robert A. *Commitment to Deviance: The Non-professional Criminal in The Community.* Westport, CT.: Greenwood, 1971.

Toby, Jackson. "Social Disorganization and Stake in Conformity: Complementary Factors in the Predatory Behavior of Hoodlums." *Journal of Criminal Law, Criminology and Police Science,* 48:1 (May-June, 1957), pp. 12-17.

Turk, Austin T. "Prospects for Theories of Criminal Behavior." *Journal of Criminal Law, Criminology and Police Science,* 55:4 (December, 1964), pp. 454-461.

Vollmer, August. *The Criminal.* Brooklyn: Foundation, 1949.

Waldo, Gordon P. "The 'Criminality Level' of Incarcerated Murderers and Non-Murderers." *Journal of Criminal Law, Criminology and Police Science,* 61:1 (March, 1970), pp. 60-70.

Criminal Gangs

Asbury, Herbert. *The Barbary Coast: An Informal History of the San Francisco Underworld.* Garden City, N.Y.: Garden City, 1933.

Asbury, Herbert. *The French Quarter: An Informal History of the New Orleans Underworld.* Garden City, N.Y.: Garden City, 1938.

Asbury, Herbert. *The Gangs of New York: An Informal History of the New York Underworld.* Garden City, N.Y.: Garden City, 1928.

Asbury, Herbert. *Gem of the Prairie: An Informal History of the Chicago Underworld.* Garden City, N.Y.: Garden City, 1930.

Messick, Hank. *Gangs and Gangsters: The Illustrated History of Gangs From Jesse James to Murf The Surf.* N.Y.: Ballantine, 1974.

Criminal Tactics

Elliott, J.F. and Thomas J. Sardino. "The Time Required to Commit Crime." *Police,* 16:4 (December, 1971), pp. 26-29.

McParland, Thomas A. "Transistor Radios—The Criminal's Monitor for Police Dispatches." *Police,* 15:2 (November-December, 1970), pp. 32-34.

Plate, T. *Crime Pays—An Inside Look at Burglars, Car Thieves, Loan Sharks, Hit Men, Fences, and Other Professionals in Crime.* N.Y.: Simon and Schuster, 1975.

An expose' of criminal methods and the problems, economics, opportunities, difficulties, and the daily routine of crime as a profession.

Hells Angels

California Attorney General. *Hells Angels Motocycle Clubs.* Sacramento: Attorney General, 1965.

Reynolds, Frank. *Free Wheeling Frank, Secretary of the Angels.* N.Y.: Grove, 1967.

Thompson, Hunter. *Hells Angels: A Strange and Terrible Saga.* N.Y.: Random, 1967.

Offenders

Dyson, Frank. "The Repeat Offender." *Police Chief,* XL:6 (June, 1973), pp. 36-38.

Ellis, Albert. "A Study of 300 Sex Offenders." *International Journal of Sexology,* (1951), pp. 129-134.

Frishie, Louis V. "The Treated Sex Offender." *Federal Probation,* 12:2 (1958).

Health, E.D., Jr. "The Repeat Offender." *FBI Law Enforcement Bulletin,* 43:5 (May, 1974).

Martin, J.P. and D. Webster. *Social Consequences of Conviction.* London: Heinemann, 1971.

Longitudinal study of a group of men convicted in the Borough of Reading (England) in the course of one year.

Myers, S.G. *Analysis of the Chronic Offender Problem Within the Armed Forces.* Springfield, VA.: NTIS, 1965.

Review of theories and studies dealing with deviant behavior, focusing on personality factors, and methods for predicting and rehabilitating the chronic offender.

Plate, Thomas. *Crime Pays!* N.Y.: Simon and Schuster, 1975.

Describes professional criminals and why so few are caught and convicted.

Playfair, Giles and Derrick Sington. *The Offenders.* N.Y.: Simon and Schuster, 1957.

Roche, Philip Q. *The Criminal Mind.* N.Y.: Farrar, Straus and Cudahy, 1958.

Short, James F., Jr. *Law and Order: Modern Criminals.* (rev 2nd. ed.) Edison, N.J.: Transaction, 1973.

West, D.J. *Psychopathic Offenders.* Cambridge: Institute of Criminology, University of Cambridge, 1968.

CRIMINAL SOCIETIES AND TRIBES

Adkins, E.H., Jr. "Malaya Controls Its Criminal Societies." *Police,* 7 (November-December, 1962), pp. 63-69.

Bruce, George. *The Stranglers: The Cult of Thuggee and Its Overthrow in British India.* N.Y.: Harcourt, Brace and World, 1969.

Butt-Thompson, F.W. "Criminal Native Secret Societies of the West Coast of Africa." *Police Journal (GB),* (1931), pp. 263-272.

Chandler, David L. *Criminal Brotherhoods.* London: Constable, 1976.

Cheng, Ronald G.C. "A Study of the Fight Against Secret Societies." *Singapore Police Journal* (July, 1971), pp. 34-43.

Chesneaux, Jean. *Secret Societies in China: In the Nineteenth and Twentieth Century.* Ann Arbor, MI.: University of Michigan Press, 1972.

Daraul, Arkon. *Secret Societies: Yesterday and Today.* Atlantic Highlands, N.J.: Humanities, 1966.

Franzius, Enno. *History of the Order of Assassins.* N.Y.: Funk and Wagnalls, 1969.

Gayer, G.W. *Some Criminal Tribes in India.* Nagpur: Central Provinces Government Press, 1910.

Gunthorpe, E.J. *Notes on Criminal Tribes Residing in or Frequenting the Bombay Presidence, Berar and the Central Provinces.* Bombay: Times of India Press, 1882.

Heckethorn, Charles. *Secret Societies of all Ages and Countries.* (2 vols.) Secaucus, N.J.: University, 1965.

Hervey, Charles. *Some Records of Crime: Diary of an Officer of the Thuggee and Dacoitie Police 1866-1867.* (2 vols.) Maidenhead: Samson Low, 1892.

Kincaid, C.A. *The Outlaws of Kathiawar and Other Studies.* Bombay: Times of India Press, 1905.

MacKenzie, Norman, ed. *Secret Societies.* N.Y.: Holt, Rinehart and Winston, 1968.

Morgan, W.P. *Triad Societies in Hong Kong.* Hong Kong: Government Press, 1960.

Report on the Criminal Activities of Inter-State Gangs of Bawarieas. New Delhi: Ministry of Home Affairs, 1957.

Roper, William L. "Remember California's Bloody Tong Wars?" *California Highway Patrolman,* (March, 1958).

Sastri, E. Ramachandra. *History of the Criminal Tribes in the Madras Presidency.* Madras: Sri Rama Press, 1930.

Sleeman, James L. *Thug: A Million Murders.* Maidenhead, Berks: Samson Law, 1933.
Describes the suppression of thuggee by Sir W.H. Sleeman.

Tan, Jee Bah. "Secret Criminal Societies in Singapore." *FBI Law Enforcement Bulletin* (January, 1965), (February, 1965).

Webster, N.H. *Secret Societies and Subversive Movements.* Hollywood, CA.: Angriff Press, 1972.

Whalen, William J. *Handbook of Secret Organizations.* Milwaukee, WI.: Bruce, 1966.

Wilson, Colin. *Order of Assassins: The Psychology of Murder.* St. Albans (GB), Hart Davis, 1972.

DEVIANCE

Ball, D.W. "Privacy, Publicity, Deviance and Control." *Pacific Sociological Review,* 18:3 (1975), pp. 259-278.

Denisoff, R. Serge and Charles McCaghy, eds. *Deviance, Conflicts and Criminality.* Chicago: Rand, [n.d.].

Edgerton, R.B. *Deviant Behavior and Cultural Theory.* Reading, MA.: Addison Wesley, 1973.

Gibbons, Don C. and Joseph F. Jones. *The Study of Deviance: Perspectives and Problems.* Englewood Cliffs, N.J.: Prentice-Hall, 1975.

Gove, Walter, ed. *Labeling of Deviance.* N.Y.: Halsted, 1975.

Freedman, Jonathan and Anthony Doob. *Deviancy: The Psychology of Being Different.* N.Y.: Academic, 1968.

Jacobs, Jerry. *Deviance: Field Studies and Self Disclosures.* Palo Alto, CA.: Mayfield, 1974.

Palmer, Stuart. *Deviance and Conformity.* New Haven, CT.: College and University Press, 1970.

Rock, P. *Deviant Behavior.* London: Hutchinson, 1973.

Stebbins, Robert A. *Commitment to Deviance: The Non-professional Criminal in The Community.* Westport, CT.: Greenwood, 1971.

Vivona, C.M. *Meanings of Deviance.* N.Y.: MSS Information Corporation, 1973.

Weinberg, S.K. *Deviant Behavior and Social Control.* Dubuque, IA.: Brown, 1974.

Winslow, Robert W., ed. *Emergence of Deviant Minorities: Social Problems and Social Change.* Edison, N.J.: Transaction, 1972.

FAMOUS CASES AND ISSUES

Dillinger

Cromie, Robert and Joseph Pinkston. *Dillinger: A Short and Violent Life.* N.Y.: McGraw Hill, 1962.

Toland, John. *The Dillinger Days.* N.Y.: Random House, 1963.

Eichmann

American Jewish Committee. *The Eichmann Case in the American Press.* N.Y.: American Jewish Committee, 1962.

Arendt, Hannah. *Eichmann in Jerusalem: A Report of the Banality of Evil.* N.Y.: Viking, 1964.

"Eichmann Tells His Own Damning Story." *Life,* November 28, (December 5, 1960).

Green, L.C. "The Eichmann Case." *Modern Law Review,* (1960).

Harel, Isser. *The House on Garibaldi Street.* N.Y.: Viking, 1975.

Hausner, Gideon. "Eichmann and His Trial." *Saturday Evening Post* (November 3, 10, 17, 1962).

Hausner, Gideon. *Justice in Jerusalem.* N.Y.: Harper and Row, 1966.

Kittrie, Nicholas N. "A Post Mortem of the Eichmann Case—The Lessons for International Law." *Journal of Criminal Law, Criminology and Police Science,* 55:1 (March, 1964), pp. 16-28.

Paneth, Philip. *Eichmann: Technician of Death.* N.Y.: Speller, 1960.

Papadatos, Peter. *The Eichmann Trial.* London: Stevens, 1964.

Pearlman, Moshe. *Capture and Trial of Adolf Eichmann.* N.Y.: Simon and Schuster, 1963.

Robinson, Jacob. "Eichmann and the Question of Jurisdiction." *Commentary* (July, 1960).

Rogat, Yosal. *The Eichmann Trial and the Rule of Law.* Santa Barbara, CA.: Center for the study of Democratic Institutions, 1961.

Russell, Edward Frederick Langley. *The Record: The Trial of Adolf Eichmann for His Crimes Against the Jewish People and Against Humanity.* N.Y.: Knopf, 1963.

Silving, Helen. "In Re Eichmann: A Dilemma of Law and Morality." *American Journal of International Law,* (1961).

Taylor, Telford. "Large Questions in the Eichmann Case." *New York Times Magazine* (January 22, 1961).

Internment of Japanese-Americans in W.W. II

Arrington, Leonard J. *The Price of Prejudice: The Japanese-American Relocation Center in Utah During World War II.* Logan, UT.: Faculty Association, Utah State University, 1962.

Bloom, Leonard and Ruth Riemer. *Removal and Return: The Socioeconomic Effects of the War on Japanese-Americans.* Berkeley: University of California Press, 1949.

Bosworth, Allan R. *America's Concentration Camps.* N.Y.: Norton, 1967.

Daniels, Roper. *Decision to Relocate the Japanese Americans.* Philadelphia: Lippincott, 1975.

Daniels, Roger. *The Politics of Prejudice: The Anti-Japanese Movement in California, and the Struggle for Japanese Exclusion.* Berkeley: University of California Press, 1962.

Girdner, Audrie. *The Great Betrayal: The Evacuation of the Japanese-Americans During World War II.* N.Y.: Macmillan, 1969.

Grodzins, Morton. *Americans Betrayed: Politics and the Japanese Evacuation.* Chicago: Chicago University Press, 1949.

Kitagawa, Daisuke. *Issei and Nisei: The Internment Years.* N.Y.: Seabury, 1967.

Kutsuse, John I. and Leonard Brown. *Managed Casualty: The Japanese-American Family in World War II.* Berkeley: University of California Press, 1974.

McWilliams, Carey. *Prejudice: Japanese-Americans, Symbol of Racial Intolerance.* Boston: Little, Brown, 1944.

McWilliams, Carey. *What About Our Japanese Americans?* N.Y.: Public Affairs Committee, Pamphlet #41, 1944.

Myer, Dillon S. *Uprooted Americans: The Japanese-Americans and the War Relocation Authority During World War II.* Tucson: University of Arizona Press, 1971.

Spicer, Edward H. *Impounded People: Japanese-Americans in the Relocation Centers.* Tucson: University of Arizona Press, 1969.

TenBrock, Jacobus et al. *Prejudice, War, and the Constitution: Causes and Consequences of the Evacuation of the Japanese Americans in World War II.* Berkeley: University of California Press, 1954.

Thomas, Dorothy S. *The Salvage: Japanese American Evacuation and Resettlement.* Berkeley: University of California Press, 1952.

U.S. War Relocation Authority. *U.S. War Relocation Authority.* (11 vols.) N.Y.: AMS, 1946. (Repr. ed.)

Weelyn, Michi. *Years of Infamy: The Untold Story of America's Concentration Camps.* N.Y.: Morrow, 1976.

Palmer Red Raids

Feuerlicht, Roberta S. *America's Reign of Terror: World War I, Red Scare, and the Palmer Raids.* N.Y.: Random, 1971.

Jaffe, Julien F. *Crusade Against Radicalism: New York During the Red Scare, Nineteen Fourteen to Nineteen Twenty-Four.* Port Washington, N.Y.: Kennicat, 1972.

Murray, Robert K. *Red Scare.* N.Y.: McGraw-Hill, 1964.

Sacco-Vanzetti

Appel, Paul P. *Sacco-Vanzetti Case.* (6 vols., 2nd ed.) Mamaroneck, N.Y.: Appel, 1969.

Ehrmann, Herbert B. *The Case That Will Not Die: Commonwealth vs. Sacco and Vanzetti.* Boston: Little, Brown, 1969.

Frankfurter, Felix. *Case of Sacco and Vanzetti.* N.Y.: Grosset and Dunlap, 1962.

Lyons, Eugene. *Life and Death of Sacco and Vanzetti.* N.Y.: DeCapo, 1970. (repr. of 1927 ed.)

Montgomery, Robert H. *Sacco-Vanzetti: The Murder and Myth.* N.Y.: Devin-Adair, 1960.

Quesada, Fernando. *Sacco and Vanzetti.* N.Y.: Gordon, 1976.

Salem Witchcraft Trials

Boyer, Paul and Stephen Nissenbaumm. *Salem Possessed:*

The Social Origins of Witchcraft. Cambridge, MA.: Harvard University Press, 1974.

Drake, Samuel G. *Witchcraft Delusion in New England.* (3 vols.) N.Y.: B. Franklin, 1970. (repr. of 1866 ed.)

Gemmill, William N. *Salem Witchtrials: A Chapter of New England History.* Detroit: Gale, 1975. (repr. of 1924 ed.)

Hansen, Chadwick. *Witchcraft at Salem.* N.Y.: Braziller, 1969.

Neirns, Winfield S. *Witchcraft in Salem Village in 1692.* (5th ed.) N.Y.: B. Franklin, 1972. (repr. of 1916 ed.).

Records of Salem Witchcraft, Copied from the Original Documents. (2 vols.) N.Y.: DeCapo, 1969.

Upham, Charles W. *Salem Witchcraft.* (2 vols.) Williamstown, MA.: Cornerhouse, 1971. (repr. of 1867 ed.).

Scottsboro Boys

Bauer, Barbara and Robert Moss. *Judge Horton and the Scottsboro Boys.* N.Y.: Ballantine, 1976.

Carter, Dan T. *Scottsboro: A Tragedy of the American South.* N.Y.: Oxford University Press, 1971.

Patterson, Haywood and Earl Conrad. *Scottsboro Boy.* N.Y.: Macmillan, 1969.

FEAR OF CRIME

"Are You Personally Afraid of Crime? Readers Speak Out." *Life,* 72: (January 14, 1972), pp. 28-30.

Burnham, David. "Fear of Muggers Looms Large in Public Concern Over Crime." *New York Times,* (May 20, 1968).

Donio, Michael J. "Crime, Fear, Urban Retreat and the Problems of Law Enforcement." *Enforcement,* (July-September, 1974), pp. 8-9, 24.

Harris, Richard. *The Fear of Crime.* N.Y.: Praeger, 1968.

Herbert, Richard. "Is Everybody in Washington Scared?" *Washingtonian* (April, 1972).

Rosenthal, Jack. "The Cage of Fear in Cities Beset by Crime." *Life* (July 11, 1969).

FEMALE CRIME

Adler, Freda. *Sister in Crime.* N.Y.: McGraw-Hill, (1975).
Outlines the rise of female criminality.

Bishop, Cecil. *Women and Crime.* London: Chatto and Windus, 1931.

Brodsky, Annette, ed. *Female Offender.* London: Sage, 1975.

Gibbens, T.C.N. "Female Offenders." *British Journal of Hospital Medicine,* 6:3 (1971), pp. 279-282, 285-286.

"Modern Day Ma Barker." *FBI Law Enforcement Bulletin,* 34:11 (November, 1965), pp. 18-23.

Pollak, Otto. *The Criminality of Women.* Philadelphia: University of Pennsylvania Press, 1950.

Pratt, Paulette. "Why Women Turn to Crime." *Observer,* 8 (December, 1974), pp. 63, 64, 67, 68, 70.

Rosenblatt, E. and C. Greenland. "Female Crimes of Violence." *Canadian Journal of Criminology and Corrections,* 16:2 (1974).

Simon, Rita James. *Contemporary Women and Crime.* Washington, D.C.: GPO, 1975.

Slovenko, Ralph. "Are Women More Law-Abiding than Men?" *Police,* 8:6 (July-August, 1964), pp. 17-24.

Suval, Elizabeth M. and Robert C. Brisson. "Neither Beauty nor Beast: Female Criminal Homicide Offenders." *International Journal of Criminology and Penology,* (February, 1974), pp. 23-34.

Totman, Jane. "The Murderess." *Police,* 15:6 (July-August, 1971), pp. 16-22.

FIREARMS AND CRIME

"Firearms in Crime." *FBI Law Enforcement Bulletin,* 35:10 (October, 1966), pp. 22-24.

Greenwood, Colin. "Shotguns and Crime: Has the Government Cooked the Figures?" *Police (GB),* (January, 1974), pp. 12-14.

Hurley, John A. "Arming the Criminal." *Police,* 3:2 (November-December, 1958), pp. 7-8.

King, Daniel P. "Firearms and Crime." *Criminologist,* 8:28 (Spring, 1973), pp. 50-58.

"Massachusetts Adopts Mandatory Sentencing for Firearms Law Violators." *Police Chief,* XLII:5 (May, 1975), pp. 48-50.

Newton, G.D., Jr. and F.E. Zimring. *Firearms and Violence in American Life.* Washington, D.C.: GPO, 1969.

Shapiro, H. *Availability and Illegal Use of Handguns in New York State—Statement of Chairman Howard Shapiro on Behalf of the New York State Commission of Investigation at the Conclusion of the Public Hearing.* Washington, D.C.: NCJRS, (Microfiche), 1974.
Speech on how the easy availability of handguns affects crime rates and law enforcement.

Spiegler, Jeffrey H. and John J. Sweeney. *Gun Abuse in Ohio.* Cleveland, OH.: Governmental Research Institute, 1975.

LEGALIZED GAMBLING ISSUE

Adams, Harland B. *The Guide to Legal Gambling.* N.Y.: Citadel, 1966.

Computer Sciences Corporation. *Development of an Off-Track Betting System For The New York City Off-Track Corporation—Summary Description of Systems.* Washington, D.C.: NCJRS, (Microfiche), 1970.

Cook, V.G. *Gambling—A Source of State Revenue.* Lexington, KY.: Council of State Governments, 1973.
A review of legalized gambling activities, focusing on eight state lottery systems, off-track betting in New York City, and gambling in Nevada.

Eadington, W.R. *Economics of Gambling Behavior—A Qualitative Study of Nevada's Gambling Industry.* Reno: University of Nevada, 1973.

Eaton, Joseph W. "Gambling: Racket or Public Utility—A Science Brief for Legalized Numbers Games." *Police* (March-April, 1968), pp. 30-32.
This article discussed the concept of a legalized national lottery and its effect on society.

"Federalism and the Control of Radio and TV Lotteries." *Journal of Criminal Law, Criminology and Police Science,* 49:6 (March-April, 1959), pp. 579-582.

Gibbons, Thomas J. "Should Gambling Be Legalized?" *Saturday Evening Post* (January 3, 1959).

Lemmel, Maurice. *Gambling: Nevada Style.* Garden City, N.Y.: Doubleday, 1964.

Montana Board of Crime Control. *Montana—Gambling,* Washington, D.C.: NCJRS, (Microfiche), 1973.
Discusses the effects of legalized gambling.

New York Commission on Gambling. *New York—Commission on Gambling (Legalized Gambling—Report to the Governor and the Legislature).* Washington, D.C.: NCJRS, (Microfiche), 1973.

"Now, an Epidemic of Legalized Gambling." *US News & World Report* (July 23, 1973), pp. 22-26.

Peterson, Virgil. *Gambling, Should It Be Legalized?* Springfield, IL.: C.C. Thomas, 1951.
The author provides factual evidence that the existence of gambling in a community is detrimental to the best interests of all involved. Excellent.

U.S. Commission on the Review of the National Policy Toward Gambling. *The Stakes Are High.* Washington, D.C.: GPO, 1975.

Weinstein, D. and L. Deitch. *Impact of Legalized Gambling—The Socioeconomic Consequences of Lotteries and Off-Track Betting.* N.Y.: Praeger, 1974.

Wessel, Milton R. "Legalized Gambling: The Dreams and the Realities." *Nation,* 200 (January 18, 1965), pp. 46-48.

MINORITIES AND CRIME

Beach, Walter G. *Oriental Crime in California: A Study of Offenses Committed by Orientals in That State, 1900-1927.* Stanford, CA.: Stanford University Press, 1932.

Bonger, William A. *Race in Crime.* N.Y.: Columbia University Press, 1943.

Forslund, M.A. "A Comparison of Negro and White Crime Rates." *Journal of Criminal Law, Criminology, and Police Science,* 61 (June, 1970), pp. 214-217.

Forslund, Morris A. "Standardization of Negro Crime Rates for Negro-White Differences in Age and Status." *Rocky Mt. Journal of Sociology,* 1 (April, 1970), pp. 21-27.

Geis, Gilbert. "Statistics Concerning Race and Crime." *Crime and Delinquency,* 11 (April, 1965), pp. 142-150.

Graham, F.P. "Black Crime: The Lawless Image." *Harper's Magazine,* 241 (September, 1970), pp. 64-78.

Harvey, P. "Problems in Chinatown." *Human Events* (May 21, 1970).

Hayner, Norman S. "Variability in the Criminal Behavior of American Indians." *American Journal of Sociology,* 47 (January, 1942), pp. 602-613.

Hentiz, Hans Van. "The Criminality of the Negro." *Journal of Criminal Law and Criminology,* 30 (January-February, 1940), pp. 662-668.

Ianni, Francis A.J. *Black Mafia.* N.Y.: Simon and Schuster, 1974.

Ianni, Francis A.J. "New Mafia: Black, Hispanic and Italian Styles." *Society,* 11:3 (1974), pp. 26-39.

Johnson, G.B. "The Negro and Crime." In M.E. Wolfgang et. al., eds. *The Sociology of Crime and Delinquency,* (2nd ed.) N.Y.: Wiley, 1970.

Kitano, H.H.L. "Japanese-American Crime and Delinquency." *Journal of Psychology,* 66 (July, 1967), pp. 253-263.

Mihanovich, C.S. "Crimes Against the Person and Race." *Police Chief,* XXXLV:4 (April, 1967), pp. 42-44.

Peterson, J. "Thunder Out of Chinatown." *National Observer* (March 8, 1972), pp. 1-8.

Riffenburgh, Arthur S. "Cultural Influences and Crime Among Indian-Americans of the Southwest." *Federal Probation,* 28 (September, 1964), pp. 38-46.

Robins, L.N., P.A. West, and B.L. Herjanic. "Arrests and Delinquency in Two Generations: A Study of Black Urban Families and Their Children." *Journal of Child Psychology and Psychiatry,* 16:2 (1973), pp. 125-140.
Study indicated that parental arrest history was strong predictors of their offsprings' delinquency.

Rudwick, Elliot M. "Negro Crime and the Negro Press." *Police* (January-February, 1961).

Sollenberger. R.T. "Chinese-American Child Rearing Practices and Juvenile Delinquency." *Journal of Social Psychology,* 74 (February, 1968), pp. 13-23.

Spirer, Jess. *Negro Crime.* Baltimore: Johns Hopkins University Press, 1940.

Stephenson, R.M. and F.R. Scarpitti. "Negro-White Differentials and Delinquency." *Journal of Research in Crime and Delinquency,* 5 (July, 1968), pp. 122-133.

Tucker, Sterling. "The Ghetto, the Ghettoized, and Crime." *Federal Probation* (September, 1969).

Voss, Harwin L. "Ethnic Differentials in Delinquency in Honolulu." *Journal of Criminal Law, Criminology and Police Science,* 54:3 (September, 1963), pp. 322-327.

Wolfgang, M.E. "Race and Crime." In H.J. Sklare, ed. *Changing Concepts of Crime and Its Treatment.* London: Pergamon, [n.d.].

Wolfgang, Marvin E. and Bernard Cohen. *Crime and Race: Conceptions and Misconceptions.* N.Y.: Institute of Human Relations, 1970.

TATTOOS AND CRIME

Bendlage, G.A. "A Doctor Looks at Tattoos." *California Youth Authority Quarterly,* 19 (Spring, 1966), pp. 39-40.

Burchett, George. *Memoirs of a Tattooist.* N.Y.: Crown, 1958.

Butler, Joel R. "Diagnostic Significance of the Tattoo in Psychotic Homicide." *Corrective Psychiatry,* 14 (Summer, 1968), pp. 110-113.

Eckler, S. "Tattoo File Proves Its Utility in First Use." *Fingerprint and Identification Magazine,* 40:9 (March, 1959), pp. 18-19.

Elam, Jerry. "The Tattoo File." *Law and Order,* 8 (May, 1960), pp. 66-68.

Linch, Sam. "How Tattoos Help: Unique File of More than 90 Thousand Designs Often Leads Los Angeles Police to Decorated Criminals in a Hurry." *Popular Science,* 174 (April, 1959), pp. 104-107.

Mulhern, John J. "Value and Significance of Tattoos in Criminal Identification." *Military Police Journal,* 12 (November, 1962), pp. 9-20.

Post, Richard S. "The Relationship of Tattoos to Personality Disorders." *Journal of Criminal Law,* 59 (December, 1968), pp. 516-524.

VICTIMS

Arnold, P. *Lady Beware.* Garden City, N.Y.: Doubleday, 1974.

Aromaa, Kauko. "Victimization to Violence: A Gallup Survey." *International Journal of Criminology and Penology* (November, 1974), pp. 333-346.

Balus, Mary E. *Integrated Services for Victims of Crime: A County-Based Approach.* Washington, D.C.: National Association of Counties Research Foundation, 1975.

Bradley, Thomas. "The Forgotten Victim." *Crime Prevention Review* (October, 1975).

Carrington, Frank G. *The Victims.* New Rochelle, N.Y.: Arlington House, 1975.

Criminal Victimization in the United States, 1973. Washington, D.C.: NCJRS, 1976.

Crosby, Robert and David Snyder. *Crime Victimization in the Black Community.* Bethesda, MD.: Research Management, October, 1969.

Drapkin, I. and E. Viano. *Victimology.* Lexington, MA.: Heath Lexington, 1974.
Collection of theoretical and empirical works on the victim and his role, the criminal-victim relationship, crime motives, and the concept of provocative behavior.

Drazek, Stanley J. "The Cold Reality." *Police,* 15:1 (September-October, 1970), pp. 45-46.

Ennis, P.H. *Criminal Victimization in the United States—A Report of a National Survey.* Washington, D.C.: GPO, 1967.
Although nearly one-half of victim crimes go unreported, the surveyed crime approximated police statistics by category distribution.

Fattah, E.A. *Is the Victim Guilty—The Role of the Victim in Murder Incident to Robbery.* Montreal, Ontario: Presses de Universite de Montreal, 1971.

Geis, Gilbert. "Compensation for Crime Victims and the Police." *Police* (May-June, 1969).

Law Enforcement Assistance Administration. *The San Jose Methods Test of Known Crime Victims.* Washington, D.C.: GPO, 1972.

McDonald, John M. *Rape: Offenders and Their Victims.* Springfield, IL.: C.C. Thomas, 1974.

McDonald, William F., ed. *Criminal Justice and the Victim.* Beverly Hills, CA.: Sage, 1976.

Milliken, R.J. "The Sex Offender's Victim." *Federal Probation,* 14:3 (September, 1950), pp. 22-26.

National Advisory Commission on Criminal Justice Standards and Goals. *Victimization: Surveying Its History, Uses and Limitations. Report on the Criminal Justice System.* Washington, D.C.: GPO, 1973.

National Criminal Justice Information and Statistics Service. *Criminal Victimization in the United States—A Comparison of 1974 and 1975 Findings.* Washington, D.C.: NCJRS, 1977.

National Institute of Law Enforcement and Criminal Justice. *Criminal Victimization in the United States, January-July 1973—A National Crime Panel Survey Report.* (vol. 1), Washington, D.C.: NCJRS, 1974.

National Criminal Justice Information and Statistics Service. *Criminal Victimization in the U.S.: 1973 Advance Report,* (vol. I,) *May, 1975—A National Crime Panel Survey Report.* Washington, D.C.: NCJRS, (Microfiche), 1975.

National Criminal Justice Information and Statistics Service. *Criminal Victimization Surveys in 13 American Cities—Nation Crime Panel Surveys in Boston, Buffalo, Cincinnati, Houston, Miami, Milwaukee, Minneapolis, New Orleans, Oakland, Pittsburgh, San Diego, Etc.* Washington, D.C.: NCJRS, (Microfiche), 1975.

Putnam, Jerry D. and Denamae Fox. "A Program to Help the Victims of Crime." *Police Chief,* XLII; 3 (March, 1976), pp. 36-38.
Volunteer program in Aurora, Colorado Police Department. Works closely with women volunteers who provide care for the victims of crimes, especially assaults. Excellent program.

Ryan, W. *Blaming the Victim.* N.Y.: Pantheon, 1971.
Examines several economic and social situations in which the victims are blamed by society for their predicament.

Schafer, Stephen. *Victim and His Criminal—A Study in Functional Responsibility.* N.Y.: Random House, 1968.
Introduction to the study of criminal-victim relationships, with a history of victimology and the practice of victim compensation.

Schafer, William J., III. "How About a Constitution for the Victim." *Police,* 11:4 (March-April, 1967).

Schultz, Leroy G., ed. *Rape Victimology.* Springfield, IL.: C.C. Thomas, 1975.

Syvrud, G.A. *Victim of Robbery.* Ann Arbor, MI.: University Microfilms, 1967.
Inquiry into the role of the victim in the crime problem, the personal damage involved, and the victim's perception of his experience.

Thornberry, T.P. and E. Sagrin. *Images of Crime—Offenders and Victims.* N.Y.: Praeger, 1974.

U.S. Department of Commerce. Bureau of the Census. *Criminal Victimization Surveys in The Nation's Five Largest Cities—National Crime Panel Surveys of Chicago, Detroit, Los Angeles, New York, and Philadelphia.* Washington, D.C.: NCJRS, (Microfiche), 1975.

Weis, K. and S.S. Borges. "Victimology and Rape: The Case of the Legitimate Victim." *Issues in Criminology,* 8:2 (1973), pp. 71-115.

JUVENILE CRIME

JUVENILE CRIME

Juvenile Delinquency

Adams, Gary B., ed. *Juvenile Justice Management.* Springfield, IL.: C.C. Thomas, 1973.

Adkins, Ottie. "Discipline—The Answer to Juvenile Delinquency." *Law and Order* (December, 1975), pp. 36, 55.

American Orthopsychiatric Association. *Symposia on Child and Juvenile Delinquency.* Washington, D.C.: Psychodynamics, 1959.

Atlar, A.D. *Juvenile Delinquency.* N.Y.: International Publications, 1964.

Baker, Luann. "Give the Kid a Break." *Police Chief,* XLII:6 (June, 1975), pp. 64-65.

Balough, Joseph K. "Juvenile Delinquency Proneness." *Journal of Criminal Law, Criminology and Police Science,* 48:6 (March-April, 1958), pp. 615-618.

Barron, Milton L. *The Juvenile in Delinquent Society.* N.Y.: Knopf, 1954.

Baz, Edmund W. *Middle-Class Juvenile Delinquency.* N.Y.: Harper and Row, 1967.

Belson, William A. *Juvenile Theft: The Casual Factors.* N.Y.: Harper and Row, 1975.

Bernstein, S. *Alternatives to Violence—Alienated Youth and Riots, Race, and Poverty.* N.Y.: Associated Press, 1967.

Block, Herbert A. "Juvenile Delinquency: Myth or Threat." *Journal of Criminal Law, Criminology and Police Science,* 49:4 (November-December, 1958), pp. 303-309.

Bloch, Herbert Aaron. *Delinquency.* N.Y.: Random House, 1956.

Caldwell, Robert and James A. Black. *Juvenile Delinquency.* N.Y.: Ronald, 1971.

Cape, William H. "Juvenile Delinquency: Anguish, Fear and Hope." *Police Chief,* XXXIX:7 (July, 1972), pp. 56-61.

Cape, W.H. "Juvenile Delinquency: Challenge and Outlook." *Police Chief.* XXXLV 6 (June, 1967), pp. 34-37.

Cape, William H. "Juvenile Delinquency Revisited." *Police Chief,* XL:6 (June, 1973), pp. 64-67.

Carpenter, Mary. *Juvenile Delinquents: Their Condition and Treatment.* Montclair, N.J.: Patterson Smith, 1970.

Carr, L.J. *Delinquency Control.* (rev. ed.) N.Y.: Harper, 1950.

Cavan, Ruth Shonle, ed. *Readings in Juvenile Delinquency.* Philadelphia: Lippincott, 1964.

Cavan, R.S. and T.N. Ferdinand. *Juvenile Delinquency.* (3rd ed.) Philadelphia: Lippincott, 1975.

Chess, Abraham P. "Curfew for Juveniles?" *Police.* 4:5 (May-June, 1960), pp. 13-18, and, 4:6 (July-August, 1960), pp. 60-64.

Chwast, Jacob. "The Malevolent Transformation." *Journal of Criminal Law, Criminology and Police Science,* 54:1 (March, 1963), pp. 42-47.

Cicourel, Aaron V. *The Social Organization of Juvenile Justice.* N.Y.: Wiley, 1968.

Cloward, Richard A. and Lloyd B. Ohlin. *Delinquency and Opportunity: A Theory of Delinquent Gangs.* Glencoe, IL.: Free Press, 1960.

Cohen, Albert K. *Delinquent Boys: The Culture of the Gang.* Glencoe, IL.: Free Press, 1955.

Cronkhite, Clyde L. "Juvenile Crime Crisis: Cause and Remedy." *Police Chief,* XLI:12 (December, 1974), pp. 40, 42-45.

Cronkhite. Clyde L. "Juvenile Crime Crisis: What Can Be Done About It?" *Crime Prevention Review,* 2:3 (April, 1975), pp. 14-23.

Cronkhite, Clyde L. "Juvenile Crime." *Journal of California Law Enforcement* (October, 1974), pp. 51-59.

Donovan, Frank R. *Wild Kids.* Harrisburg, PA.: Stackpole, 1967.

Douglas, Jack D. *Youth in Turmoil.* Rockville, MD.: National Institute of Mental Health, Center for Studies of Crime and Delinquency, 1970.

Downes, David M. *The Delinquent Solution.* N.Y.: Free Press, 1966.

Eldefonso, Edward. *Law Enforcement and the Youthful Offender: Juvenile Procedures,* N.Y.: Wiley, 1967.

Empey, L.T. and S.G. Lubeck. *Explaining Delinquency.* Lexington, MA.: Heath, 1971.

Faust, F.L. and P.J. Brantingham. *Juvenile Justice Philosophy—Readings, Cases and Comments.* St. Paul, MN.: West, 1974.

Fine, Benjamin. *1,000,000 Delinquents.* Cleveland: World, 1955.

Forman, Robert E. "Delinquency Rates and Opportunities for Subculture Transmission." *Journal of Criminal Law, Criminology and Police Science,* 54:3 (September, 1963), pp. 317-321.

Forslund, M.A. and R.E. Meyers. "Delinquency Among Wind River Indian Reservation Youth." *Criminology,* 2:1 (1974), pp. 97-106.

Fyvel, T.R. *Troublemakers: Rebellious Youth in an Affluent Society.* N.Y.: Schocken, 1962.

Geis, Gilbert. *Juvenile Gangs.* Washington, D.C.: GPO, June, 1965.

Giallombardo, Rose. *Juvenile Delinquency: A Book of Readings.* N.Y.: Wiley, 1966.

Gibbons, Don C. *Delinquent Behavior.* Englewood Cliffs, N.J.: Prentice-Hall, 1970.

Gitchoff, G. Thomas. *Community Response to Racial Tension: An Exploratory Study of the Street-Gang Problem in Richmond, California.* Unpub. Master's Thesis, University of California, School of Criminology, Berkeley: September, 1966.

Glueck, Sheldon. *The Problem of Delinquency.* Boston: Houghton-Mifflin, 1959.

Glueck, Sheldon. *Unraveling Juvenile Delinquency.* N.Y.: Commonwealth Fund, 1950.

Goshen, Charles E. *Society and the Youthful Offender.* Springfield, IL.: C.C. Thomas, 1974.

Hagan, J.L. "The Labelling Perspective, the Delinquent, and the Police: A Review of the Literature." *Canadian Journal of Criminology and Corrections,* 14 (April, 1972), pp. 150-165.

Hahan, Paul H. *The Juvenile Offender and the Law.* Cincinnati: Anderson, 1971.

Hanna, John P. *Teenagers and the Law.* Boston: Ginn, 1967.

Hardy, Richard E. and John G. Cull. *Fundamentals of Juvenile Criminal Behavior and Drug Abuse.* Springfield, IL.: C.C. Thomas, 1975.

Harris, T.O. "Alternatives Available in Solving the Juvenile Problem." *Police Chief* (September, 1973), pp. 42-43.

Healy, William and Augusta F. Bronner. *Delinquents and Criminals: Their Making and Unmaking. Studies in Two American Cities.* N.Y.: Macmillan, 1926.

Hirschi, Travis. *Causes of Delinquency.* Berkeley: University of California Press, 1969.

Jaffe, Lester D. "Delinquency Proneness and Family Anomie." *Journal of Criminal Law, Criminology and Police Science,* 54:2 (June, 1963), pp. 146-153.

James, H. *Children in Trouble—A National Scandal.* Boston: Christian Science, 1969.
Case histories illustrating paths leading to delinquency, discussing institutions and reform schools, and examining the shortcomings of rehabilitation efforts.

Johnson, George S. "A Comprehensive Study on Rural Juvenile Delinquency." *Police,* 15:4 (March-April, 1971), pp. 58-62.

Johnson, Ronald A. "The Guilty Delinquent." *Police Chief* (September, 1973), pp. 16-18.

Jones, Howard. *Reluctant Rebels.* N.Y.: Association, 1960.

Juergensmeyer, John E. "Generation Gap—Why?" *Law and Order,* 17 (April, 1969), pp. 70-76.

"Juvenile Delinquency Report." *Canadian Police Chief* (January, 1976), pp. 6-8.

Kelley, Eugene R. "Comparative Incidents of Solitary and Group Delinquency Behavior." *Law and Order,* 19:4 (April, 1971), pp. 83-87.

Kenney, John P. and Dan G. Pursuit. *Police Work with Juveniles and the Administration of Juvenile Justice.* Springfield, IL.: C.C. Thomas, 1975.

Klare, Hugh J. and Rebecca Chaput de Saintonge. "Youth Culture and Delinquency." *Criminologist* (August, 1968).

Knudten, Richard D. and Stephen Schafer, eds. *Juvenile Delinquency: A Reader.* N.Y.: Random, 1970.

Kobetz, Richard W. *Police Role and Juvenile Delinquency.* Gaithersburg, MD.: IACP, 1971.

Kohn, George C. "Will Authority Hurt Children." *Law and Order* (December, 1974).

Korn, Richard R., ed. *Juvenile Delinquency.* N.Y.: Crowell, 1968.

Lalli, Michael. *Delinquency and City Life.* Washington, D.C.: LEAA, 1972.

Lander, Bernard. *Toward An Understanding of Juvenile Delinquency: A Study of 8,464 Cases of Juvenile Delinquency in Baltimore.* N.Y.: Columbia University Press, 1954.

Lanham, D. "Infant Malefactors." *Criminal Law Review* (June, 1973), pp. 327-328.
Children under 10 who are aware of their immunity and deliberately commit crimes.

Levin, M.N. and R. Sarri. *Juvenile Delinquency—A Study of Juvenile Codes in The U.S.* Ann Arbor, MI.: University of Michigan Press, 1974.

Loble, Lester H. and Max Wylie. *Delinquency Can Be Stopped.* N.Y.: McGraw-Hill, 1967.

Luden, Walter A. *War and Delinquency: An Analysis of Juvenile Delinquency in Thirteen Nations in World War I and World War II.* Ames, IA.: Art, 1963.

McGrath, J.H. *Comparative Study of Adolescent Drug Users, Assaulters and Auto Thieves.* Ann Arbor, MI.: University Microfilms.

Study of male juvenile delinquents, focusing on the drug user and drawing on psychological and sociological theories of the etiology of drug use.

MacIver, Robert Morrison. *The Prevention and Control of Delinquency.* N.Y.: Atherton, 1966.

MacNamara, Donald E.J. "Ten Premises Concerning Juvenile Delinquency." *Police,* 8:3 (January-February, 1964), pp. 71-74.

Manella, Frank L. "Exploding the Myths About Juvenile Delinquency." *Police Chief,* XLII:6 (June, 1975), pp. 61-63.

Marsh, Peter. "Careers for Boys: Nutters, Hooligans and Hardcases." *New Society,* 13 (May, 1976), pp. 346-348.

Martin, John M. and Joseph P. Fitzpatric. *Delinquent Behavior.* N.Y.: Random, 1965.

Matza, David. *Delinquency and Drift.* N.Y.: Wiley, 1964.

Mays, J.B. *Juvenile Delinquency, the Family and the Social Group—A Reader.* Harlow, Esses, England: Longman Group, 1972.

Monahan, Thomas P. "National Data on Police Dispositions of Juvenile Offenders." *Police,* 14:1 (September-October, 1969), pp. 36-45.

Neumeyer, Martin H. *Juvenile Delinquency in Modern Society.* (3rd ed.) Princeton, N.J.: Van Nostrand, 1961.

Oliver, I.T. " 'Mischievous Minors'." *Criminal Law Review* (July, 1974), pp. 419-423.

Handling of juveniles under 10 years old who are involved in antisocial behavior in Great Britain.

Parkhurst, Helen. *Undertoe: The Story of a Boy Named Tony.* N.Y.: Farrar Straus, 1959.

Platt, A.M. *Child Savers—The Invention of Delinquency.* Chicago: Chicago University Press, 1969.

An attempt to locate the social basis of humanitarian ideas and to reconcile the intentions of child savers with the institutions they helped to create.

President's Commission on Law Enforcement and Administration of Justice. *Task Force Report—Juvenile Delinquency and Youth Crime.* Washington, D.C.: GPO, 1967.

A socio-economic analysis of juvenile delinquency that is critical of society's approach to juvenile crime responds with recommendations and principles for change.

Quay, Herbert C. *Juvenile Delinquency: Research and Theory.* Cincinnati, OH.: Van Nostrand Rhinehold, 1965.

Reckless, Walter C. and Simon Dinitz. *Prevention of Juvenile Delinquency: An Experiment.* Columbus: Ohio State University Press, 1972.

Robbins, Lee N. and Shirley Y. Hill. "Assessing the Contributions of Family Structure, Class and Peer Groups to Juvenile Delinquency." *Journal of Criminal Law, Criminology and yolice Science,* 57:3 (September, 1966), pp. 325-334.

Rosenquist, C.M. and E.I. Megargee. *Delinquency in Three Cultures.* Austin: University of Texas Press, 1969.

Roucek, Joseph S. *Juvenile Delinquency.* N.Y.: Philosophical Library, 1958.

Rubin, Sol. *Crime and Juvenile Delinquency.* Dobbs Ferry, N.Y.: Oceana, 1958.

Sanders, Wiley B., ed. *Juvenile Offenders for a Thousand Years: Selected Readings from Anglo-Saxon Times to 1900.* Chapel Hill, NC.: University of North Carolina Press, 1970.

Schwiesow, Jim R. "What Makes Juveniles Delinquent?" *Law and Order,* 20:6 (June, 1972), pp. 72, 74-75, 96.

Seifert, Alan L. "Should Young Auto Thieves Go Unprosecuted?" *Police Chief* (April, 1974), pp. 54-55.

Sellin, T. and M. Wolfgang. *The Measurement of Delinquency.* N.Y.: Wiley, 1964.

Shanley, Fred J., D. Welty Lefever, Roger E. Rice. "The Aggressive Middle Class Delinquent." *Journal of Criminal Law, Criminology and Police Science,* 57:2 (June, 1966), pp. 145-152.

Shaw, C.R. and H.D. McKay. *Juvenile Delinquency and Urban Areas—A Study of Rates of Delinquency in Relation of Differential Characteristics of Local Communities in American Cities.* (rev. ed.) Chicago: University of Chicago Press, 1972.

Short, James F. and F. Ivan Nye. "Extent of Unrecorded Juvenile Delinquency: Tentative Conclusions." *Journal of Criminal Law, Criminology and Police Science,* 49:4 (November-December, 1958), pp. 296-302.

Snyder, Harry A. "Some Characteristics of the Delinquent." *Police,* 5:6 (July-August, 1961), pp. 51-53.

Solomon, Ben. "Curfews: Valuable or Worthless?" *Police,* 5:5 (May-June, 1961), pp. 51-54.

Spergel, Irving. *Racketville, Slumtown, Haulburg: An Exploratory Study of Delinquent Subcultures.* Chicago: University of Chicago Press, 1964.

Stulken, Edward H. "Misconceptions About Juvenile Delinquenty." *Journal of Criminal Law, Criminology and Police Science.* 46:6 (March/April, 1956), pp. 833-842.

Szurek, S.A. and I.N. Berlin, eds. *The Antisocial Child: His Family and His Community.* Palo Alto, CA.: Science and Behavior, 1969.

Tappan, Paul W. *Juvenile Delinquency.* N.Y.: McGraw-Hill, 1949.

Teele, James E., ed. *Juvenile Delinquency: A Reader.* N.Y.: Random, 1970.

Teeters, Negley K. and John Otto Reinemann. *The Challenge of Delinquency.* Englewood Cliffs, N.J.: Prentice-Hall, 1954.

Terry, R.M. "Discrimination in the Handling of Juvenile Offenders by Social-Control Agencies." *Journal of Research in Crime and Delinquency* 4 (July, 1967), pp. 218-230.

Thomas, Aquinas. "Profile of the Delinquent Boy." *Law and Order,* 13:11 (November, 1965), pp. 69-75.

Tobias, J.J. and F. Denomme. "The Affluent Suburban Delinquent." *Criminologist* 8:28 (1973), pp. 22-30.

Trojanowicz, Robert C. "Juvenile Delinquency and the Middle Class Parent." *Police* 15:5 (May-June, 1971), pp. 30-32.

Trojanowicz, Robert C. *Juvenile Delinquency: Concepts and Control.* Englewood Cliffs, N.J.: Prentice-Hall, 1973.

Tunley, Roul. *Kids, Crime and Chaos: A World Report on Juvenile Delinquency.* N.Y.: Harper, 1962.

Vaz, Edmund W. "Delinquency and the Youth Culture: Upper and Middle-Class Boys." *Journal of Criminal Law, Criminology and Police Science,* 60:1 (March, 1969), pp. 33-46.

Voss, H.L., ed. *Society, Delinquency and Delinquent Behavior.* Waltham, MA.: Little Brown, 1970.

Walker, Robert N. *Psychology of the Youthful Offender.* Springfield, IL.: C.C. Thomas, 1973.

West, D.J. *The Young Offender.* N.Y.: International Universities, 1967.

Wilson, J.Q. "The Police and the Delinquent in Two Cities." In S. Wheeler (ed.), *Controlling Delinquents.* N.Y.: Wiley, 1968.

Winslow, Robert W. *Juvenile Delinquency in a Free Society.* (2nd ed.) Encino, CA.: Dickenson, 1968.

Wise, Genevieve and Billy M. Jensen. "New Arrival in An Affluent Community—A Major Factor in Juvenile Delinquency." *Law and Order,* 20:8 (August, 1972), pp. 28, 30-32, 34-35.

Witmer, Helen L., ed. "Prevention of Juvenile Delinquency." *Annals,* (March, 1959).

Wright, Jack, Jr. and Ralph James, Jr. *A Behavioral Approach to Preventing Delinquency.* Springfield, IL.: C.C. Thomas, 1974.

"Youth Crime." *FBI Law Enforcement Bulletin,* 39:6 (June, 1970).

Juvenile Gangs

Bersahi, Carl A. *Crime and Delinquency.* London: Macmillan, 1970.

Bloch, Herbert and Arthur Neederhoffer. *The Gang: A Study in Adolescent Behavior.* N.Y.: Philosophical Library, 1958.

Cartwright, Desmond S. et al., eds. *Gang Delinquency.* Belmont, CA.: Brooks-Cole, 1975.

Cloward, R.A. and L.E. Ohlin. *Delinquency and Opportunity: A Theory of Delinquent Gangs.* N.Y.: Free Press, 1960.

Cohen, Albert Kircidel. *Delinquent Boys: The Culture of the Gang.* Glencoe, IL.: Free Press, 1955.

Collins, H. Craig. "Youth Gangs of the 70s: An Urban Plague." *Police Chief,* XLII:9 (September, 1975), pp. 50-54.

Hardman, Dale G. "Small Town Gangs." *Journal of Criminal Law, Criminology and Police Science,* 60:2 (June, 1969), pp. 173-181.

Haskings, James. *Street Gangs: Yesterday and Today.* N.Y.: Hastings House, 1974.

Keiser, R. Lincoln. *The Vice Lords: Warriors of The Streets.* N.Y.: Holt, Rinehart and Winston, 1969.

Klein, Malcolm W. *Juvenile Gangs in Context: Theory, Research, and Action.* Englewood Cliffs, N.J.: Prentice-Hall, 1967.

Krammer, Dale and Madeline Karr. *Teenage Gangs,* N.Y.: Holt, 1953.

Miller, Walter B. "Violent Crimes in City Gangs." *Annals,* 364 (March, 1966).
Theft is the most common offense of gangs.

Riccio, Vincent and Bill Slocum. *All The Way Down: The Violent World of Street Gangs.* N.Y.: Simon and Schuster, 1962.

Robin, Gerald D. "Gang Member Delinquency: Its Extent, Sequence and Typology." *Journal of Criminal Law, Criminology and Police Science.* 55:1 (March, 1964), pp. 59-69.

Short, James F., Jr. *Gang Delinquency and Delinquent Subcultures.* N.Y.: Harper and Row, 1968.

Teenage Gangs. N.Y.: New York Youth Board, 1957.

Thrasher, Frederic M. *The Gang: A Study of 1,313 Gangs in Chicago.* Chicago: University of Chicago Press, 1963.

Yablonsky, Lewis. *The Violent Gang.* N.Y.: Macmillan, 1962.
Classifies gangs into three types: delinquent gangs, violent gangs and social gangs.

Street Gang Work

Dumpson, James R. "An Approach to Antisocial Street Gangs." *Federal Probation,* 13 (1949).

Duran, Miguel. "What Makes a Difference in Working with Youth Gangs?" *Crime Prevention Review,* 2:4 (July, 1975), pp. 25-30.

Gandy, John M. "Preventive Work with Streetcorner Groups: Hyde Park Youth Project, Chicago." *Annals,* 332 (1959), p. 107.

Klein, M.W. *Street Gangs and Street Workers.* Englewood Cliffs, N.J.: Prentice-Hall, 1971.

Miller, Walter B. "Preventive Work with Streetcorner Groups: Boston Delinquency Project." *Annals,* 322 (1959).

Spergel, Irving. *Street Gang Work: Theory and Practice.* Reading, MA.: Addison-Wesley, 1966.

ORGANIZED CRIME

ORGANIZED CRIME

Books

Albini, Joseph L. *The American Mafia: Genesis of a Legend.* NY: Appleton-Century-Crofts, 1971.

Allen, Edward Joseph. *Merchants of Menace: The Mafia; A Study of Organized Crime.* Springfield, IL: C.C. Thomas, 1962.

Allen, Troy. *Gang Wars of the Twenties.* Chatsworth, CA: Barclay House, 1973.

Allsop, Kenneth. *The Bootleggers and Their Era.* Garden City, NY: Doubleday, 1961.

American Bar Association, Commission on Organized Crime. *Organized Crime and Law Enforcement.* 2 vols. NY: Crosby, 1952.

Anslinger, Harry J. and Will Oursler. *The Murderers: The Story of Narcotic Gangs.* NY: Farrar, Straus and Cudahy, 1961.

Aronson, Harvey. *The Killing of Joey Gallo.* NY: Putnam, 1973.

Asbury, Herbert. *The Barbary Coast—An Informal History of the San Francisco Underworld.* NY: Knopf, 1933.

Asbury, Herbert. *The Chicago Underworld.* NY: Knopf, 1940.

Asbury, Herbert. *The French Quarter—An Informal History of the New Orleans Underworld.* NY: Knopf, 1936.

Asbury, Herbert. *The Great Illusion.* Garden City, NY: Doubleday, 1950.

Asbury, Herbert. *Sucker's Progress.* NY: Dodd, Mead, 1938.

Bers, M. K. *Penetration of Legitimate Business by Organized Crime, an Analysis.* Springfield VA: NTIS, 1970.
Survey of legitimate business activities of selected members of organized criminal-groups in New York State and an analysis of their penetration into business.

Blok, Anton. *Mafia of a Sicilian Village, 1860-1960.* NY: Harper and Row, 1974.

Caughy, John W., ed. *Their Majesties, the Mob.* Chicago: University of Chicago Press, 1960.

Chafetz, Henry. *Play the Devil.* NY: Potter, 1960.

Chandler, David L. *Brothers in Blood: The Story of Criminal Brotherhoods.* NY: Dutton, 1975.

Chicago Crime Commission. *Spotlight on Organized Crime: The Chicago Syndicate.* Chicago: Chicago Crime Commission, 1967.

Clarke, Thurston and John J. Tigue. *Dirty Money: Swiss Banks, the Mafia, Money Laundering, and White Collar Crime.* NY: Simon and Schuster, 1975.

Clayton, Merle. *Union Station Massacre.* Indianapolis: Bobbs Merrill, 1975.

Commission on Law Enforcement and Administration of Justice. *Task Force Report: Organized Crime.* Washington DC: GPO, 1967.

Conklin, John E., ed. *The Crime Establishment: Organized Crime and American Society.* Englewood Cliffs, NJ: Prentice-Hall, 1973.

Cook, Fred J. *The Secret Rulers: Criminal Syndicates and How They Control the U.S. Underworld.* NY: Duell, Sloan and Pearce, 1966.

Cook, Fred J. *A Two Dollar Bet Means Murder.* NY: Dial, 1961.

Cooper, Courtney Ryley. *Ten Thousand Public Enemies.* Boston: Little, Brown 1935.

Cressey, Donald R. *Criminal Organization.* London: Heinemann, 1972.

Cressey, Donald R. "The Functions and Structure of Criminal Syndicates." In U.S. President's Commission on Law Enforcement and Administration of Justice, *Task Force Report: Organized Crime.* Washington, DC: GPO, 1967. Appendix, pp. 1-15.

Cressey, Donald R. *Theft of the Nation: The Structure and Operations of Organized Crime in America.* NY: Harper and Row, 1969.

DeFranco, E. J. *Anatomy of a Scam: A Case Study of a Planned Bankruptcy by Organized Crime.* Washington, DC: GPO, 1973.

DeLeeuw, Hendrik. *Underworld Story: The Rise of Organized Crime and Vice Rackets in the U.S.A..* London: Spearman, 1955.

Demaris, Ovid. *Captive City.* NY: Lyle Stuart, 1969.

Demaris, Ovid. *Lucky Luciano: The Mafioso and the Violent Thirties.* NY: Tower, 1972.

Dorman, Michael. *Payoff: The Role of Organized Crime in American Politics.* NY: McKay, 1972.

Drzazga, John. *Wheels of Fortune.* Springfield, IL: C.C. Thomas, 1963.

Feder, Sid. *The Luciano Story.* NY: McKay, 1954.

Fisher, David. *Hit #29.* Chicago: Playboy, 1974.

Fisher, David. *Killer: Autobiography of a Hit Man for the Mafia by Joey.* Chicago: Playboy, 1973.

Frasca, Dorn. *Vito Genovese: King of Crime.* (rev. ed.) NY: Avon, 1963.

Gaddis, Thomas E. *Killer: A Journal of Murder.* NY: Macmillan, 1970.

Gage, Nicholas. *Mafia! The Inside Story of Mafia in America and in Britain.* London: Talmy Franklin, 1973.

Gage, Nicholas. *The Mafia Is Not an Equal Opportunity Employer.* NY: McGraw-Hill, 1971.

Gage, Nicholas. *Mafia U.S.A..* Chicago: Playboy, 1972.

Gardiner, John A. *The Politics of Corruption: Organized Crime in an American City.* NY: Sage, 1970.

Gartner, Michael. *Crime and Business: What You Should Know About the Infiltration of Crime into Business and of Business into Crime.* Princeton, NJ: Dow Jones, 1971.

Goddard, Donald. *Joey,* NY: Harper and Row, 1974.

Halper, Albert, ed. *The Chicago Crime Book.* Cleveland, OH: World, 1967.

Hamilton, Charles. *Men of the Underworld: The Professional Criminals' Own Story.* NY: Macmillan, 1952.

Hammer, Richard. *Playboy's Illustrated History of Organized Crime.* Chicago: Playboy, 1975.

Herald, George W. and Edward D. Radin. *The Big Wheel.* NY: Morrow 1963.

Herman, Robert D. *Gambling.* NY: Harper and Row, 1967.

Hess, H. *Mafia and Mafiosi—The Structure of Power.* Lexington, MA: Lexington, 1973.

Hoffman, Paul and Ira Pecznick. *To Drop a Dime: The Mafia Hitman's Uncensored Story.* NY: Putnam, 1976.

Homer, F.D. *Guns and Garlic—Myths and Realities of Organized Crime.* West Lafayette, IN: Purdue University Press, 1974.

Ianni, Francis A.J. *Black Mafia.* NY: Simon and Schuster, 1974.

Ianni, F.A. *Ethnic Succession in Organized Crime—A Summary Report.* Washington, DC: GPO, 1973.

Ianni, Francis. *A Family Business: Kinship and Social Control in Organized Crime.* NY: Sage, 1972.

IIT Research Institute. *A Study of Organized Crime in Illinois.* Chicago: Chicago Crime Commission, 1971.
An extremely exhaustive study of the question, delving into the areas of public attitude concerning this problem, along with a discussion of the impact of the topic.

Katz, Leonard. *Uncle Frank.* NY: Drake, 1973.

Kefauver, Estes. *Crime in America.* Garden City, NY: Doubleday, 1951.

Kefauver, Estes. *The Kefauver Committee Report on Organized Crime.* NY: Didier, 1951.

Kennedy, William. *Legs.* NY: Warner, 1976.

King, Rufus. *Gambling and Organized Crime.* Washington, DC: Public Affairs, 1969.
Examination of illegal gambling and its interplay with organized crime and official corruption, with a review of gambling law enforcement since colonial times.

Knudten, Richard D. *The Christian Encounters Organized Crime.* St. Louis, MO: Concordia, 1972.

Kobler, John. *Ardent Spirits.* NY: Putnam's, 1973.

Kobler, John. *Capone,* NY: Putnam's, 1971.

Landesco, John. *Organized Crime in Chicago.* Chicago: University of Chicago Press, 1968.

Lasswell, H.D. and J.B. McKenna. *Impact of Organized Crime on an Inner City Community.* Springfield, VA: NTIS, 1972.

Lewis, Jerry D., ed. *Crusade Against Crime.* NY: Bernard Geis, 1961.

Lewis, Norman. *The Honored Society,* NY: Putnam's, 1964.

Lewis, Oscar. *Sage Brush Casinos.* Garden City, NY: Doubleday, 1953.

Lyle, John H. *The Dry and Lawless Years.* Englewood Cliffs NJ: Prentice-Hall, 1960.

Maas, Peter. *Valachi Papers.* NY: Putnam's, 1968.

Mack, J.A. and H.J. Kerner. *Crime Industry.* Farnborough, Haunts, England: Saxon House, 1975.
This study, originally presented as a report to the Council of Europe, discusses various aspects of European organized and professional crime, business-type and white-collar crime.

McClellan, John L. *Crime Without Punishment.* NY: Duell, Sloane and Pearce, 1962.

McConaughy, John. *From Cain to Capone: Racketeering Down the Ages.* NY: Brentano's, 1931.

McPhaul, Jack. *Johhny Torrio: First of the Gang Lords.* New Rochelle, NY: Arlington, 1970.

Martin, John B. *My Life in Crime.* NY: Harper and Row, 1952.

Martin, Raymond V. *Revolt in the Mafia.* NY: Duell, Sloan and Pearce, 1963.

Marx, Herbert J., ed. *Gambling in America.* NY: Wilson, 1952.

Messick, Hank. *Barboza.* NY: Dell, 1975.

Messick, Hank. *The Beauties and the Beasts: The Mob and Show Business.* NY: Mckay, 1973.

Messick, Hank. *Lansky.* NY: Putnam's, 1971.

Messick, Hank. *The Mobs and the Mafia: The Illustrated History of Organized Crime.* NY: Crowell, 1972.

Messick, Hank. *The Private Lives of Public Enemies.* NY: Wyden, 1973.

Messick, Hank. *Secret File.* NY: Putnam, 1969.

Messick, Hank. *Syndicate in the Sun.* NY: Macmillan, 1968.

Messick, Hank. *The Silent Syndicate.* NY: Macmillan, 1967.

Messick, Hank. *Syndicate Wife: The Story of Ann Drahmann Coppola.* NY: Macmillan, 1968.

Meyers, Sidney W. *The Great Las Vegas Fraud.* Chicago: Mayflower, 1958.

Mooney, Martin. *Crime Incorporated.* NY: Whittlesey, 1935.

Moore, Robin. *The French Connection.* Boston: Little, Brown, 1969.

Moscow, Alvin. *Merchants of Heroin.* NY: Dial, 1968.

Murray, George. *The Legacy of Al Capone.* NY: Putnam's, 1975.
Describes public corruption and the corrupt politicians and judges who rule Chicago.

Nash, Jay Robert. *Bloodletters and Badmen.* NY: Evans, 1973.

Nelli, Humbert S. *The Business of Crime. Italians and Syndicate Crime in the United States.* NY: Oxford University Press, 1976.

Olmstend, Charlotte. *Heads, I Win, Tails You Lose.* NY: Macmillan, 1962.

Pace, Denny and Jimmy Styles. *Organized Crime: Concepts and Control.* Englewood Cliffs NJ: Prentice-Hall, 1974.

Pantaleone, Michele. *The Mafia and Politics.* NY: Coward-McCann, 1966.

Peterson, Virgil W. *Barbarians in Our Midst—A History of Chicago Crime and Politics.* Boston: Little, Brown, 1952.
Historical view of corruption in Chicago. Peterson graphically illustrates that crime in Chicago did not start with Al Capone.

Poston, Richard W. *The Gang and the Establishment.* NY: Harper and Row, 1971.

Powell, Hickman. *Lucky Luciano: His Amazing Trial and Wild Witnesses.* Secaucus NJ: Citadel, 1975, (repr. of 1939 ed).

Prager, Ted and Larry Craft. *Hoodlums: New York.* NY: Retail Distributors, 1959.

Redstone, George. *The Conspiracy of Death.* NY: Bobbs-Merrill, 1965.

Reid, Ed. *The Anatomy of Organized Crime in America: The Grim Reapers.* NY: Bantam, 1970.

Reid, Ed. *The Green Felt Jungle.* NY: Triden, 1963.

Reid, Ed. *The Grim Reapers: The Anatomy of Organized Crime in America.* Chicago: Henry Regnery, 1962.

Reid, Ed. *Mafia.* (rev. ed.) NY: Signet, 1964.

Ross, Philip. *The Bribe.* NY: Harper and Row, 1976.

Rubner, Alex. *The Economics of Gambling.* NY: Macmillan, 1966.

Salerno, Ralph. *The Crime Confederation: Cosa Nostra and Allied Operations in Organized Crime.* Garden City, NY: Doubleday, 1969.

Sann, Paul. *Kill the Dutchman: The Story of Dutch Schultz.* New Rochelle, NY: Arlington House, 1971.

Schiavo, Giovanni. *The Truth about the Mafia and Organized Crime in America.* NY: Vigo, 1962.

Servadio, Gaia. *Mafioso: A History of the Mafia From Its Origins to the Present Day.* London: Secker and Warbug, 1976.

Siragusa, Charles. *The Trail of the Poppy: Behind the Mask of the Mafia.* Englewood Cliffs, NJ: Prentice-Hall, 1966.

Smith, Alson Jesse. *Syndicate City: The Chicago Crime Cartel and What to Do About It.* Chicago: Regnery, 1954.

Smith, D.C., Jr. *Mafia Mystique.* NY: Basic, 1975.

Sondem, Frederic. *The Mafia: Brotherhood of Evil.* NY: Farrar, Straus and Cudahy, 1959.

Stirling, Nora. *Your Money or Your Life.* Indianapolis: Bobbs Merrill, 1974.

Talese, Gay. *Honor Thy Father.* NY: World, 1971.

Teresa, Vincent and Thomas Renner. *My Life in the Mafia.* Garden City NY: Doubleday, 1973.

Touhy, Roger and Ray Brennan. *The Stolen Years.* Cleveland: Pennington, 1959.

Turner, Wallace. *Gambler's Money, The New Force in American Life.* Boston: Houghton-Mifflin, 1965.
A vividly documented expose of the spread of gangsters' methods and morals from "the Strip" in Las Vegas to Wall Street and beyond.

Tyler, Gus. *Organized Crime in America.* Ann Arbor: University of Michigan Press, 1962.
The author presents a collection of articles, some of which are directed toward the connection between organized crime and the various forms of gambling.

U.S. President's Commission on Law Enforcement and Administration of Justice. *Organized Crime—Annotations and Consultant's Papers.* Washington, DC: GPO, 1967.

Verra, Vincent L. *Death in the Family: The Mafia Way.* NY: Manor, 1976.

Volz, Joseph and Peter J. Bridge. *The Mafia Talks.* Greenwich, CT: Fawcett, 1969.

Warren, George. *Gang Wars of the Thirties.* Chatsworth, CA: Barclay, 1974.

Watsun, Frederick. *A Century of Gunmen: A Story of Lawlessness.* London: I. Nicholson and Watsun, 1931.

Williams, Roger M. *The Super Crooks.* Chicago: Playboy, 1973.

Wolf, George. *Frank Costello: Prime Minister of the Underworld.* NY: William Morrow, 1974.

Wyden, Peter. *The Hired Killers.* NY: Morrow, 1963.

Zeiger, Henry A. *The Jersey Mob.* NY: New American Library, 1976.

Zeiger, Henry A. *Sam the Plumber.* NY: Signet, 1970.

Periodicals

Adams, Thomas F. "Organized Crime in America." *Police,* 6:6 (July-August, 1962), pp. 11-14; 7:1 (September-October, 1962), pp. 37-38; 7:2 (November-December, 1962), pp. 21-24.

Adhern, J.F. "Organized Crime: The Invisible Source of Street Crime." *Police Digest,* 2:1 (1973), pp. 13-15.

Allen, Edward. "The Mafia: Mediator and 'Protector'." *Police,* 5:6 (July-August, 1961), pp. 18-25.

Allen, Edward J. "The Mafia—and Salvatore Carnevale." *Police,* 6:1 (September-October, 1961), pp. 26-29.

Allen, Edward J. "Merchants of Menace: The Mafia." *Police* 5:4 (March-April, 1961), pp. 6-12; 5:5 (May-June, 1961), pp. 72-76.

Anderson, Robert T. "From Mafia to Cosa Nostra." *American Journal of Sociology,* 71 (1965), pp. 302-310.

Bell, Daniel. "Crime as an American Way of Life." *Antioch Review,* 13:2 (1953), pp. 131-154.

Blakey, G. Robert. "Organized Crime in the United States." *Current History,* 52 (1967), pp. 327-333, 364.

Bloch, Herbert A. "The Gambling Business: An American Paradox." *Crime and Delinquency,* (October, 1962).

Brean, Herbert. "World Crime—A Series." *Life* (January 11, 18, 25, and February 1 1960).

"Bull Market in Thievery." *Forbes,* 102 (December 15, 1968), pp. 34, 37, 38.
The role of the Mafia in the stealing of securities.

"Cigarette Bootlegging: One of Organized Crime's Biggest 'Businesses'." *Police,* 15:2 (November-December 1970).

Cressey, Donald R. "Bet Taking, Cosa Nostra, and Negotiated Social Order." *Journal of Public Law,* 19 (1970), pp. 13-22.

Cressey, Donald R. "Organized Crime and Inner City Youth." *Crime and Delinquency,* 16 (1970), pp. 129-138.

Demison, G. "Big-Time Gambling's Menace to Pro Sports." *Readers Digest* (August, 1973), pp. 91-95.

Dickinson, W.B., Jr. "Interstate Crime Syndicates." *Editorial Research Report* (January 18, 1961), pp. 43-60.

Donfante, Jordan. "Mafia in Trouble on Its Home Grounds." *Life* (March 6, 1964).

Drzazga, John. "Gambling and the Law." *Journal of Criminal Law, Criminology and Police Science,* (November, 1951; May, 1952; September, 1952; January, 1953; January, February, 1954).

Edelhertz, H. "The Relationship Between White Collar Crime and Organized Criminal Activity." *Washington Law Enforcement Journal,* 4:3 (1974).

Eliasberg, Wladimir. "Corruption and Bribery." *Journal of Criminal Law, Criminology and Police Science* (September-October, 1951).

Fino, Paula."Bluenoses are Handing the Underworld 6 Billion a Year." *True* (May, 1961).
Illegal gambling and lotteries in U.S.

"Gambling." *Annals* (May, 1950).

Gibbons, Thomas. "Should Gambling Be Legalized." *Saturday Evening Post* (January 3, 1959).

Goettel, Gerard L. "Why the Crime Syndicate Can't Be Touched." *Harper's* (November, 1960).

Hagan, Charles B. "Wire Communications Utilities and Bookmaking." *Minnesota Law Review* (February, 1951).

Hills, Stuart. "Organized Crime and American Society." *Midwest Quarterly,* 9:2 (1968), pp. 171-182.

"The Illegal $2 Bet." *Parade* (November 9, 1961).

"It's Joe! They Got Joe!" *Newsweek,* 78 (July 12, 1971), pp. 30-32.

Johnson, Earl, Jr. "Organized Crime: Challenge to the American Legal System." *Journal of Criminal Law, Criminology and Police Science,* 54:2 (June, 1963), pp. 127-145.

Kelton, Harold W., Jr. and Charles M. Unkovic. "Characteristics of Organized Crime Groups." *Canadian Journals of Criminology and Corrections,* 13 (1971), pp. 68-78.

King, J. "Mobile Criminals and Organized Crime." *Police Journal,* 38:1 (January, 1965), pp. 17-27.

Maas, Peter. "Mafia: The Inside Story." *Saturday Evening Post* (August 10, 1963).

The Mafia Vs. America." *Time* (August 22, 1969).

Methvin, Eugene H. "How the Mafia Preys on the Poor." *Readers Digest* (September, 1970), pp. 49-55.

Methvin, Eugene H. "Mafia War on the A&P." *Readers Digest* (July, 1970), pp. 71-76.

"The Mob." *Life* (September, 1, 8, 15, 1967; August 30, 1968).

Moynihan, Daniel P. "The Private Government of Crime." *Reporter* (July 6, 1961).

Mulnix, D.B. "Organized Criminal Activities in Colorado." *Colorado Policemen,* 10:3 (1973), pp. 20-22, 29.

"New Ways Gangsters Muscle into Business." *Nation's Business* (August, 1965).

"Organized Crime." *Crime and Delinquency,* 8:4 (October, 1962).

"Organized Crime." *Police Chief,* XLII:2 (February, 1975).

"Organized Crime." *Police Chief,* XXXVII:11 (November, 1971).

"Organized Crime Robs All of Us." *Changing Times* (June, 1969).

Peterson, Virgil W. "Gambling—Should It Be Legalized?" *Journal of Criminal Law and Criminology,* XL (September-October, 1949).

Peterson, Virgil W. "Rackets in America." *Journal of Criminal Law, Criminology and Police Science,* 49:6 (March-April, 1959), pp. 583-489.

Pileggi, Nicholas. "The Lying, Thieving, Murdering, Upper-Middle-Class Respectable Crook." *Esquire* (January, 1966).

Roberts, Albert R. "Reflections on Gambling and Organized Crime." *Criminologica* 7:1 (1969), pp. 26-31.
Gambling is one of the major forms of organized crime in America. It is the principal source of income for organized criminal syndicates. The activities that flourish as a result of the syndicate's gambling profits are police corruption, narcotics, loan sharking, infiltration of legitimate business and labor racketeering.

Ruth, H.S. "Why Organized Crime Thrives." *Annals,* 374 (1967), pp. 113-122.

Salerno, Ralph F. "Banking and Organized Crime." *The Bankers Magazine,* 154 (Spring, 1971), pp. 59-63.

Salerno, Ralph F. "Organized Crime and Criminal Justice." *Federal Probation* 33 (1969), pp. 11-17.

Salerno, Ralph. "Organized Crime: An Unmet Challenge to Criminal Justice." *Crime and Delinquency,* 15:3 (1969), pp. 333-340.
Organized crime is defined as a self-perpetuating continuing criminal conspiracy designed for power and profit. It is estimated that its income is around six billion dollars untaxable and this from illegal gambling. The author says that the problems in the ghettos are directly linked to organized crime but crime in the ghettos is hidden because there are no victims who will complain. Only about 500 men are working on this problem. No state has yet passed any effective set of laws to control organized crime.

Selerno, Ralph. "Organized Crime's Growing Threat to American Business." *Business Management,* 35 (November, 1968), pp. 57-59.

Sellin, Thorsten. "Organized Crime as a Business Enterprise." *Annals,* 347 (1963), pp. 12-19.

Sheppard, Colin. "Mafia—A Sicillian Tradition." *Police Review (GB),* (January 3, 1975).

Silver, Edward S. "Organized Gambling and Law Enforcement." *Journal of Criminal Law, Criminology and Police Science,* 50:4 (November/December, 1959), pp. 397-404.

Smith, Dwight C. "Mafia: The Prototypical Alien Conspiracy." *Annals* (January, 1976), pp. 75-88.

Spahr, Charles E. "Comments on Organized Crime." *Police Chief,* XLII:2 (February, 1975).

"Statutory Trends Toward Legalization of Gambling." *Iowa Law Review* (May, 1940).

Surface, Bill. "Planned Bankruptcy: The Racket That Cheats Us All." *Readers Digest* (May, 1966).

Tamm, Quinn. "Organized Crime and Legitimate Businesses." *Police Chief,* XLII:2 (February, 1975), pp. 54-56.

Taylor, J.E. "Transmission of Racing Information by Wire in Missouri." *Missouri Law Review* (January, 1952).

Thornton, Robert V. "Organized Crime in the Field of Prostitution." *Journal of Criminal Law, Criminology and Police Science,* 46:6 (March-April, 1956), pp. 775-779.

"Underworld Moves in on Business." *U.S. News World Report* (May 5, 1969).

Velie, Lester. "The Underworld's Backdoor to Las Vegas." *Readers Digest* (November, 1974), pp. 207-214.

Velie, Lester. "Why Jimmy Hoffa Had to Die." *Readers Digest* (December, 1976), pp. 237-253, 257.

Walsh, Denny. "The Gorilla Cowed His Keepers." *Life,* 70 (June 25, 1971), pp. 42-52.

Wilson, Charles M. "Corruption, the Committee—and Senator McClellan." *Readers Digest* (June, 1959).

Zumbrun, Alvin J.T. "Organized Crime, Gambling, and Law Enforcement." *Police,* 8:4 (March-April, 1964), pp. 58-63.

Government Publications and Seminars

Allen, Edward J. *La Mafia and Omerta: Doctrine of the Underworld.* A paper presented to the 61st Annual Conference of the IACP at New Orleans, 1954.

Assembly Interim Committee on Judiciary, Report of Subcommittee on Rackets. *Organized Crime in California.* Sacramento: Assembly of State of California, 1957-59.

Maryland Crime Investigating Commission. *Gambling Devices within the United States.* Baltimore: Maryland Crime Investigation Commission, 1963.

Maryland Crime Investigating Commission. *The Gambling Rackets in Baltimore City.* Baltimore: Maryland Crime Investigating Commission, 1966.

New Jersey Law Enforcement Council. *Law Enforcement and Organized Gambling.* Newark: New Jersey Law Enforcement Council, 1956.

New York State Commission of Investigation. *Report: Racketeer Infiltration into Legitimate Business.* NY: New York State Commission of Investigation, 1970.

Pennsylvania Crime Commission, Office of the Attorney General, Department of Justice. *Report on Organized Crime.* Harrisburg: Pennsylvania Crime Commission, 1970.

U.S. Congress, House of Representatives, Select Committee on Crime. *Organized Crime in Sports.* Washington, DC: GPO, 1973.

U.S. Congress, House Select Committee on Crime. *Organized Criminal Influence in Horseracing, Report.* Washington, DC: GPO, 1973.

U.S. Congress, House Select Committee on Crime. *Organized Crime—Techniques for Converting Worthless Securities into Cash.* Washington, DC: GPO, 1972.

Focus on utilization of the completely worthless commercial paper of the Baptist Foundation by criminal elements all over the country to obtain hard cash.

U.S. Congress, Senate Committee on Government Operations. *Organized Crime—Securities—Thefts and Frauds (Second Series), Part I, Hearings.* Washington, DC: GPO, 1973.

Testimony and exhibits concerning the representation of stolen and counterfeit securities as legal transactions by organized criminal groups.

U.S. Senate, Committee on Government Operations. *Organized Crime—Stolen Securities.* Part IV. Washington, DC: GPO 1971.

Witnesses describe how hundreds of millions of dollars worth of securities have been stolen from the airports, the mails, and brokerage houses by organized crime.

U.S. Senate (McClellan Committee). *Gambling Report.* Washington, DC: GPO, 1962.

U.S. Senate. *Organized Crime and Illicit Traffic in Narcotics.* Part I. Washington, DC: GPO, 1963.

U.S. Senate, Select Committee on Small Business. *Crime Against Small Business: Report.* Washington, DC: GPO, 1969.

SPECIFIC CRIMES

CRIME—GENERAL

Alix, Ernest K. "The Functional Interdependence of Crime and Community Social Structure." *Journal of Criminal Law, Criminology and Police Science,* 60:3 (September, 1969), pp. 332-339.

Anthony, E. *Why Crime Persists.* Sussex, England: Barry Rose, 1973.

Beynon, E.D. "Crimes and Customs of the Hungarians in Detroit." *Journal of Criminal Law, Criminology, and Police Science,* 25 (January-February, 1935), pp. 755-774.

Bonger, Willem. *Criminality and Economic Conditions.* Bloomington: Indiana University Press, 1969.

Bossard, Andre. "Review of International Crime Trends." *International Criminal Police Review* (March, 1976), pp. 58-68.

Bray, William G. "Law and Order Versus Violence." *Police,* 9:4 (March-April, 1965).

Brown, William P. "Crimes of National Significance." *Journal of Criminal Law, Criminology and Police Science,* 55:4 (December, 1964), pp. 509-513.

Cavan, Ruth Shonle. "Underworld, Conventional and Ideological Crime." *Journal of Criminal Law, Criminology and Police Science,* 55:2 (June, 1964), pp. 235-240.

Cho, U.H. *Public Policy and Urban Crime.* Philadelphia: Ballinger, 1974.

Conrad, J.P. *Crime and Its Correction.* Berkeley: University of California Press, 1970.

"Crime: A $20,000,000,000 Annual Bill for Americans." *Senior Scholastic* (November, 1961).

"Crime Is a Worldwide Problem." *FBI Law Enforcement Bulletin,* 35:12 (December, 1966), pp. 7-10.

Dienstein, William. "Crime, the Criminal, and Society." *Police,* 14:1 (September-October, 1969), pp. 12-17.

Dinitz, Simon. *Critical Issues in the Study of Crime.* Boston: Little, Brown, 1968.

Evens, M.S. and M. Moore. *Lawbreakers—America's Number One Domestic Problem.* New Rochelle, NY: Arlington House, 1969.

Fordham, P. *Villains—Inside the London Underworld.* NY: Harper and Row, 1972.

Fraser, Gordon. *Modern Transportation and International Crime.* Springfield, IL: C.C. Thomas, 1970.

French, Stanley. *Crime Every Day.* Chichester: Barry Rose, 1976.

Galbo, Charles J. "Society, Crime, and the Criminal." *Police Chief,* XLII:3 (March, 1976).

Glaser, Daniel, ed. *Crime in the City.* NY: Harper and Row, 1970.

Hartung, Frank E. *Crime, Law and Society.* Detroit: Wayne State University Press, 1965.

Haskell, M.R. and L. Yablonsky. *Crime and Delinquency.* (20th ed.) Chicago: Rand McNally, 1974.
This textbook analyzes both the traditional problems of criminality and the new, complex problems raised by contemporary social, economic and political forces and events.

"Here's How Crime Problems Look to Enforcement Officials." *FBI Law Enforcement Bulletin,* 35:12 (December, 1966), pp. 16-29.

Jones, Howard. *Crime in a Changing Society.* Baltimore: Penguin, 1965.

Kampa, Leo. *The Enigma of Crime.* Philadelphia: Dorrance, 1972.

King, Daniel P. "Crime and the City." *Police,* 10:3 (January-February, 1966), pp. 65-67.

King, Daniel P. "Crime: A Perspective on the Problem." *Police,* 9:1 (September-October, 1964), pp. 96-98.

Klare, Hugh J. *Changing Concepts of Crime and Its Treatment.* London: Pergamon, 1966.

Letkemann, Peter. *Crime as Work.* Englewood Cliffs, NJ: Prentice-Hall, 1973.

Lunden, Walter A. "Crime and Affluence." *Police,* 14:3 (January-February, 1970), pp. 6-11.

Lunden, Walter A. "Unemployment and Crime." *Police,* 9:1 (September-October, 1964), pp. 6-10.

McClintok, F.H. *Crimes of Violence.* London: Macmillan, 1963.

McLennan, B.N. and J.S. Clark. *Crime in Urban Society.* NY: Dunellen, 1970.
Critical essays on the nature and extent of crime and the role of the courts and state and local governments in its control.

Maine, C.E. *The World's Strangest Crimes.* NY: Hart, 1967.

Mays, John Barron. *Crime and the Social Structure.* London: Faber and Faber, 1963.

Monte, K. *Crime in Mass Transportation Areas—An Overview.* Washington, DC: NCJRS, (Microfiche), 1973.
Examination of the crime problems within ANC generated by mass transit systems in New York City, Boston, Chicago, Cleveland, Toronto, and Philadelphia-New Jersey (the port authority transit corporation).

Moquin, Wayne and Charles Van Doren. *American Way of Crime: A Documentary History.* NY: Praeger, 1975.

Nettler, G. *Explaining Crime.* NY: McGraw-Hill, 1974.

O'Brien, John T. "Criminal Causation and Political Process." *Police,* 15:1 (September-October, 1970), pp. 29-33.

Peterson, Robert W., ed. *Crime and the American Response.* NY: Facts on File, 1973.

President's Commission on Law Enforcement and Administration of Justice. *Crime and Its Impact—An Assessment.* Washington DC: GPO, 1967.

Quinney, Richard. *The Social Reality of Crime.* Boston: Little, Brown, 1970.

Radzinowicz, Leon. *Ideology and Crime.* NY: Columbia University Press, 1966.

Reckless, Walter C. *The Crime Problem.* (4th ed.) NY: Appleton-Century-Crofts, 1967.

Reiss, A.J., Jr. *Studies in Crime and Law Enforcement in Major Metropolitan Areas.* (vol. 1), Washington, DC: GPO, 1967.
The measurement, classification and definition of crime, the effect of the crime problem on citizens as defined and experienced by them.

Reppetto, Thomas A. *Residential Crime.* Cambridge, MA: Ballinger, 1974.

Robin, G.D. *Employees as Offenders—A Sociological Analysis of Occupational Crime.* Ann Arbor, MI: University Microfilms, 1965.
Exploratory study of the dimensions of occupational crime of department store company employees.

Roughead, William. *Classic Crimes.* London: Cassell, 1951.

Rozell, Jack V. "What About Lawlessness." *Law and Order,* 16:9 (September, 1968), pp. 92-93.

Schur, E.M. *Our Criminal Society.* Englewood Cliffs, NJ: Prentice-Hall, 1969.

Small Business Administration. *Crime Against Small Business: A Report of the Small Business Administration.* Washington, DC: GPO, 1969.

Stephens, R.C. and R.D. Ellis. "Narcotics Addicts and Crime, Analysis of Recent Trends." *Criminology,* 12:4 (1975), pp. 474-488.
Study suggests that crimes against the person are becoming more prominent among addicts. Economic gain is the prime motive.

Symons, Julian. *A Pictorial History of Crime: 1840 to the Present.* NY: Crown, 1967.

Trasler, G. *The Explanation of Criminality.* London: Routledge and Kegan Paul, 1962.

Votey, H. and L. Phillips. *Economic Crimes: Their Generation, Deterrence and Control.* Springfield, VA: NTIS, 1969.

Watson, Nelson. "Police Philosophy: A Formula for Crime." *Police Chief,* XXIV:9 (September, 1967), pp. 10-16.

White, Bertha R. *Crimes and Penalties.* (2nd ed.) Dobbs Ferry, NY: Oceana [n.d].

Wiles, P. and W.G. Carson. *Crime and Delinquency in Britain—Sociological Readings.* London: Martin Robertson, 1971.
Readings devoted to the sociology of crime and delinquency and the methods of controlling them and the differences between these problems in Britain and the solutions that have been developed for them in America.

Wilkinson, F.T. and F. DeArmond. *The Realities of Crime and Punishment.* Springfield MO: Mycroft, 1972.

Wilson, James Q. "A Long Look at Crime." *FBI Law Enforcement Bulletin,* 44:2 (February, 1975), pp. 2-6.

Wilson, James Q. *Thinking about Crime.* NY: Basic, 1975.
Professor Wilson advises against expecting too much from our criminal justice system. Excellent.

Wolfgang, Marvin E. *Crime and Culture.* NY: Wiley, 1968.

ARSON

"Arson—How Great Is the Problem?" *Security Gazette,* 15:4 (1973).

Gardner, J. "Arson in Schools." *Security Gazette,* 17:2 (1975).

May, Robert E. "Arson: The Most Neglected Crime on Earth." *Police Chief,* XLI:7 (July, 1974), pp. 32-33.

Moll, K.D. *Arson, Vandalism and Violence—Law Enforcement.* Washington, DC: GPO, 1972.
Study based on a comprehensive statistical data base of metropolitan fire department problems related to violence.

"Sabotage through Fire." *FBI Law Enforcement Bulletin* (May, 1941).

Scott, L.G. "Arson, the Perfect Crime." *Washington Law Enforcement Journal,* 4:3 (1974), pp. 21-23.

Steinmetz, Richard C. "Arson in Times of War." *Police Journal,* 27 (March-April, 1941), pp. 3-4, 20-22.

Strom, M. "School Fires: Part of Our Overall Crime Problem." *Security World,* 11:3 (1974), pp. 20-23.

"Time to Get Tough with the Arsonist!" *Readers Digest* (November, 1976), pp. 245-250.

ASSASSINATIONS

Armbrister, T. "Death in Guatemala City." *Saturday Evening Post* (May 4, 1968).

Aronson, Harvey. *Killing of Joey Gallo.* NY: Putman's, 1973.

Belin, David. *November Twenty-Second, 1963: You Are the Jury.* NY: Quadrangle, 1963.

Belli, Melvin M. *Dallas Justice, The Real Story of Jack Ruby and His Trial.* NY: McKay, 1964.

Berkeley, Edmund C. "The Assassination of Senator Robert F. Kennedy." *Computers and Automation,* 19 (August, 1970), pp. 48-55.

Bishop, Jim. *The Day Kennedy Was Shot.* (2nd ed.) NY: Funk and Wagnals, 1968.

Bishop, Jim. *Day Lincoln Was Shot.* NY: Harper and Row, 1955.

Bonner, Judy. *Investigation of a Homicide: The Murder of John F. Kennedy.* Anderson, SC: Droke-Hallux, 1970.

Breitman, George and Herman Porter. *Assassination of Malcom X.* NY: Pathfinder, [n.d.].

Burgess, Alan B. *Seven Men at Daybreak.* Morley Yorkshire: Elmfield, 1973.
Assassination of Reinhard Heydrich.

Casto, Don. "Marijuana and the Assassins, and Etymological Investigations." *British Journal of Addiction,* 65 (November, 1970), pp. 219-225.

Crotty, William J., ed. *Assassinations and the Political Order.* NY: Harper and Row, 1971.

Donoghue, Mary A. *Mission: Assassination—The Politics of Murder.* Chatsworth CA: Major, 1975.

Donovan, Robert J. *The Assassins.* NY: Harper and Brothers, 1955.

Eddowes, Michael. *November 22: How They Assassinated Kennedy* St. Helier: Spearman, 1976.

Ellis, A. and J.M. Gullo. *Murder and Assassination.* Secaucus, NJ: Lyle Stuart, 1971.
Historical look at famous slayers, with a consideration of the causation and treatment of murder.

Fox, Syldan. *The Unanswered Questions About President Kennedy's Assassination.* (2nd ed.) Hauppauge, NY: University, 1975.

Frank, Gerold. *An American Death: The True Story of the Assassination of Dr. Martin Luther King, Jr. and the Greatest Manhunt of Our Time.* London: Hamilton, 1972.

Freed, Donald. *Killing of R.F.K.* NY: Dell, 1975.

Freedman, Lawrence Zelic. "Profile of an Assassin." *Police,* 10:4 (March-April, 1966), pp. 26-30.

"Getting Away with Murder." *Economist,* (November 4, 1972).

Ghosh, Tapan. *Gandhi Murder Trial.* NY: Asia, 1975.

Goldman, Peter. *Death and Life of Malcolm X.* NY: Harper and Row, 1973.

Grotty, William J., ed. *Assassinations and the Public Order.* NY: Harper and Row, 1972.

Hartogs, Renatus and Lucy Freedman. *The Two Assassins.* NY: Crowell, 1965.
Lee Harvey Oswald and Jack Ruby.

Hassel, Conrad V. "The Political Assassin." *Journal of Police Science and Administration,* 2:4 (December, 1974), pp. 399-403.

Heaps, Willard A. *Assassination: A Special Kind of Murder.* NY: Hawthorn, 1969.

Hearings Before the President's Commission of the Assassination of John F. Kennedy. Washington: GPO, 1964.

Horowitz, Irving M. *Assassination.* NY: Harper and Row, 1972.

Huie, William Bradford. *Three Lives for Mississippi.* NY: WCC, 1965.

Hurwood, Bernhardt J. "Society and the Assassin: A Background Book on Political Murder." NY: Parents' Magazine, 1970.

Jasz, Oscar and John D. Lawson. *Against the Tyrant: The Traditional Theory of Tyrannicide.* Glencoe, IL: Free Press, 1957.

Kapure, J.L. *Report of Commission of Inquiry into Conspiracy to Murder Mahatma Gandha.* (2 vols.) Columbia, MO: South Asia, 1970.

Khosla, Gopal. *Murder of the Mahatma and Other Cases from a Judge's Notebook.* Mystic, CT: Verry, 1963.

Kidner, John. *Enforcer: Reflections of a Professional Assassin.* Washington, DC: Acropolis, 1976.

Kirkham, J.F. *Assassination and Political Violence.* Washington, DC: GPO, 1969.
Social and political consequences of assassination and the environmental factors that encourage groups or individuals to attack political leaders are identified.

Kirkham, James F., Sehdon G. Levy, and William J. Crotty. *Assassination and Political Violence.* NY: Praeger, 1970.

Knight, Janet., ed. *Three Assassinations: The Deaths of John and Robert Kennedy and Martin Luther King.* NY: Facts on File, 1971.

Kurland, Gerald. *Assassination of President John F. Kennedy.* Charlotteville, NY: Sam Har, 1973.

Lawder, Lee E. "Reflections on a Disaster." *Law and Order,* 11:12 (December, 1963).
Assassination of John F. Kennedy.

Lomax, Louis. *To Kill a Black Man.* Los Angeles: Holloway, 1968. Assassination of Martin Luther King.

McConnell, Brian. *The History of Assassation.* Nashville: Aurora, 1970.

Manchester, William. *Death of a President.* NY: Harper and Row, 1967.

Morrow, Robert D. *Betrayal.* Chicago: Regency, 1976.
Assassination of John F. Kennedy.

Paine, Lauran. *Assassins.* London: Robert Hale, 1975.

Rapoport, D.C. *Assassination and Terrorism.* Toronto, Canada: CBC Learning Systems, 1971.

Rosenberg, Charles E. *The Trial of the Assassin Guiteau.* Chicago: University of Chicago Press, 1968.

Scott, Peter D. et al., eds. *The Assassination: Dallas and Beyond—A Guide To Cover Ups and Investigations.* NY: Random, 1976.

Skousen, W. Cleon. "Specter of the Political Assassin." *Law and Order,* 11:12 (December, 1963).

Szabo, P. "Assassination and Political Violence in Canada," in *Task Force Report on Assassination and Political Violence.* Washington, DC: GPO, 1969.

U.S. National Commission on Prevention of Violence. *Assassination and Political Violence.* Washington, DC: GPO, 1969.

U.S. Senate, Select Committee to Study Governmental Operations, Intelligence Activities. *Alleged Assassination Plots Involving Foreign Leaders.* Washington, DC: GPO, 1975.

"The Violent End of the Man Called Malcolm X." *Life,* 58 (March 5, 1965), pp. 26-31.

Warren Commission. *U.S. President's Commission on the Assassination of President Kennedy Hearings.* (26 vols.) Washington, DC: GPO, 1964.

"Wounded Soul: Assassination Attempt on Archbishop Makarios of Cyprus." *Time* (March 23, 1970).

ASSAULT

Pittman, David J. and William Handy. "Patterns in Criminal Aggravated Assault." *Journal of Criminal Law, Criminology and Police Science,* 55:4 (December, 1964), pp. 462-470.

Wenk, E.A. *Assaultive Youth—An Exploratory Study of the Assaultive Experience and Assaultive Potential of California Youth Authority Wards.* Springfield, VA: NTIS, 1972.
Study of youthful offenders to determine characteristics that seem to correlate with a proneness to commit violent acts when released under parole supervision.

AUTO THEFT

Berg, I.A. "A Comparative Study of Car Thieves." *Journal of Criminal Law, Criminology and Police Science,* 34 (1943), pp. 392-396.

Biles, David. *Car Stealing in Australia: Facts and Figures.* Canaberra: Australia Institute of Criminology, [n.d.].

"Car 'Cannibals' and Their Vices." *Journal of American Insurance,* 40 (March, 1964), pp. 18-21.

Hill, John L. "Motor Vehicle Theft Becomes a Major Crime Problem." *Texas Police Journal* (December, 1976).

Lunden, W.A. "Automobile Theft." *Iowa Sheriff,* 23 (1951).

"Motor Vehicle Thefts—A Uniform Crime Reporting Survey." *FBI Law Enforcement Bulletin* (August, 1975).

Savitz, Leonard D. "Automobile Thefts." *Journal of Criminal Law, Criminology and Police Science,* 50:2 (July-August, 1959), pp. 132-143.

Wedekind, Richard. "Automobile Theft, the Thirteen Million Dollar Parasite." *Journal of Criminal Law, Criminology and Police Science,* 48:3-4 (November-December, 1957), pp. 443-446.

BLACK MARKET

Clinard, Marshall Barron. *The Black Market: A Study of White Collar Crime.* NY: Rinehart, 1952.

Kaufman, Richard F. *War Profiteers.* Indianapolis, IN: Bobbs, 1971.

Lever, Harry. *Wartime Racketeers.* NY: Putnam's, 1945.

Redford, Emmette S. *Field Administration of Wartime Rationing.* Washington DC: GPO, 1947.

Rundell, Walter, Jr. *Black Market Money: The Collapse of U.S. Military Currency Control in World War II.* Baton Rouge: Louisiana State University Press, 1964.

Sandulescu, Jacques. *Hunger's Rogues: On the Black Market in Europe, 1948.* NY: Harcourt, Brace, Jovanovich 1974.

BURGLARY

Barnes, Robert Earl. *Are You Safe From Burglars?* Garden City, NY: Doubleday, 1971.

Black, Susan. "Burglary." *The New Yorker* (December 7, 14, 1963).

Bonger, William Adrain. *Criminality and Economic Conditions.* Boston: Little, Brown, 1916.
Burglary is committed by individuals whose principal or subsidiary occupation is theft and who, in general, do not consider it shameful.

"The Boom in Bank Robbery." *Fortune,* 61 (January, 1960), pp. 115-117.
Confronted by the all but impregnable bank vault, the safecrackers had more or less conceded their battle with bankers. Recent burglaries have occurred mainly in small, ill-protected banks.

"Burglars Prey on Small Banks." *FBI Law Enforcement Bulletin,* 34:10 (October, 1965), pp. 2-3.

"The Burglary Boom." *Newsweek,* 71 (January 29, 1968), pp. 73-74.
A new breed of housebreaker is operating in major U.S. cities who concentrates on easily hockable items.

Conklin, J.E. and E. Bittner "Burglary in a Suburb." *Criminology,* 11:2 (1973), pp. 206-232.

David, Pedro R., ed. *World of the Burglar: Five Criminal Lives.* Albuquerque: University of New Mexico Press, 1974.

Ferdinand, Theodore N. "The Criminal Patterns of Boston Since 1849." *American Journal of Sociology,* 73 (1967), pp. 84-99.
Analysis of arrest rates in Boston from 1849-1921. Burglary has shown a down tendency, although specific events have resulted in periodic upswings.

Gavzer, Jean. *A Thief's Journal.* NY: Grove, 1964.
Life story of a burglar.

Girard, Paul J. "Burglary Trends and Protection." *Journal of Criminal Law, Criminology and Police Science,* 50:5 (January/February, 1960), pp. 511-518.

Loth, David. "Are You Inviting Burglars?" *American Legion Magazine,* 87 (July, 1969), pp. 16-20.

Scarr, H.A. *Patterns of Burglary, Part 6—Related Technical Papers.* Springfield VA: NTIS, 1972.

Scarr, H.A. *Patterns of Burglary, Part 3—Tables and Figures.* Springfield VA: NTIS, 1972.

Scarr, H.A. *Patterns of Burglary, Part 5—Technical Appendices.* Springfield VA: NTIS, 1972.

Scarr, H.A. *Patterns of Burglary.* Washington DC: GPO, 1972.

Scarr, H.A. and J.L. Pinsky. *Patterns of Burglary, Part 1—An Intensive Study of the Crime in a Metropolitan Area.* Springfield VA: NTIS,1972.

Scarr, H.A. and D.S. Wyatt. *Patterns of Burglary, Part 4—Interview Schedules and Coding Manuals Used in the Victimization Study.* Springfield VA: NTIS, 1972.

"What Makes a Burglar." *Journal* (May-June, 1974), pp. 9-11.

COMPUTER CRIME

Adelson, Alan. "Embezzlement by Computer." *Security World* (September, 1968).

Allen, B.R. "Computer Fraud." *Financial Executive* (May, 1971).

Allen, Brandt. "Danger Ahead! Safeguard Your Computer." *Harvard Business Review* (November-December, 1968).

"Computer Criminals." *Journal of Criminal Law, Criminology and Police Science,* 60: (1969).

"Computers Breed New Type of Criminal." *Data Management* (August, 1972).

Dansiger, Sheldon J. "Embezzling Primer." *Computers and Automation* (1967).

"Embezzling by Computer." *Banker* (December, 1968).

Freed, R.N. "Computer Fraud—A Management Trap." *Business Horizons* (June, 1969).

Gelleman, Harvey S. "Using the Computer to Steal." *Computers and Automation* (April, 1971).

Kohn, Aaron M. "Computer Criminals." *Journal of Criminal Law, Criminology and Police Science,* 60:1 (March, 1969), pp. 1-2.

Leibholz, S.W. and L.D. Wilson. *Users' Guide to Computer Crime—Its Commission, Detection and Prevention.* Radnor PA: Chilton, 1974.

McKnight, Gerald. *Computer Crime: How a New Breed of Criminals Is Making Off With Millions.* NY: Walker, 1974.

McNail, John W. and Henry Zavislak. "Computer Chaos." *Police Chief,* XLI:7 (July, 1974), pp. 57-59.

Parker, Donn B., Susan Nycum, and S. Stepehn Oura. *Computer Abuse.* Springfield VA: NTIS, 1973.

Strother, Robert S. "Crime by Computer." *Reader's Digest* (April, 1976), pp. 143-148.

CONSPIRACY

Armstrong, John Simpson and Edward Shirley Trevor. *A Report of the Proceedings on an Indictment for a Conspiracy in the Case of the Queen V. Daniel O'Connell, John O'Connell.* Dublin: Hodges, 1844.

Clavir, Judy, ed. *The Conspiracy Trial.* Indianapolis: Bobbs-Merril, 1970.

"The Conspiracy Dilemma: Prosecution of Group Crime or Protection of Individual Defendants." *Harvard Law Review,* 62 (1948).

"Developments in the Law: Criminal Conspiracy." *Harvard Law Review,* 72 (1958-1959).

Epstein, Jason. *The Great Conspiracy Trial: An Essay on Law, Liberty and the Constitution.* NY: (Random House) 1970.

Flug, Phyllis and Michael J. Miller, eds. *Legal Concepts of Conspiracy: A Law Review Trilogy, 1922-1970.* NY: Arno, 1972.

COUNTERFEITING

Angell, Norman. *The Story of Money.* NY: F.A. Stokes, 1929.

Bloom, M.T. "Counterfeiting, A Growth Industry." *New York Times Magazine* (September 10, 1961).

Coudert, Louis L. *Security Printing.* NY: American Banknote, 1929.

"Counterfeit Bonds Are a Sign of Big Crime." *Business Week* (March 13, 1962).

Gide, Andre. *Counterfeiters.* NY: Random, 1973.

Kenner, Hugh. *Counterfeiters.* Garden City NY: Doubleday, 1973.

Landress, M.M. and Bruce Dobler. *I Made It Myself.* NY: Grosset and Dunlap, 1973.

Rekkas, Klearchos. *Counterfeiters.* Philadelphia: Dorrance, 1973.

Smith, Laurence. *Counterfeiting, Crime Against the People.* NY: W.W. Norton, 1944.

Surface, B. "Counterfeit Money Goes Mass Production." *Reader's Digest* (December, 1972).

Surface, B. "Making Money." *New York Times Magazine* (October 18, 1964).

Tocchio, O.J. "Counterfeiting: Another Merchant's Dilemma." *Police,* 8:2 (November-December, 1963). pp. 44-47.

"Wall Street Connection: V. Rizzo and a Stolen-and-Counterfeit-Securities Ring." *Newsweek* (July 23, 1972).

CRIMES AGAINST CHILDREN

Battered Child Syndrome

"The Abused, Battered, and Maltreated Child: A Review." *Trauma* (December, 1967), (entire issue).

Bakan, David. *Slaughter of the Innocents: A Study of the Battered Child Phenomenon.* San Francisco: Jossey-Bass, 1971.

Barnett, B. "Battered Babies." *Lancet,* 2 (September 12, 1970) pp. 567-568.

Barnett, B. "Violent Parents." *Lancet,* 2 (November 27, 1971), pp. 1208-1209.

Bell, Gwyneth. "Parents Who Abuse Their Children." *Canadian Psychiatric Association Journal,* 18:3 (June, 1973), pp. 223-228.

Bennie, E.H. and A.B. Sclare. "The Battered Child Syndrome." *American Journal of Psychiatry,* 125:7 (1969), pp. 975-979.

British Medical Journal. "Battered Babies." *British Medical Journal* (1969), pp. 667-668.

Brown, R.H. "The Battered Child Syndrome." *Journal of Forensic Science* (January, 1976), pp. 65-70.

Buist, N.R. "Violent Parents." *Lancet,* 1:36 (January 1, 1972).

Chase, Naomi. *A Child Is Being Beaten.* NY: Holt Rhinehart and Winston, 1975.

Criswell, Howard D., Jr. "Why Do They Beat Their Child? *Human Needs,* 1:9 (March 1973), pp. 5-7.

Davies, H. de la H. "Maltreated Children: Early Warning System and Follow-up Scheme." *Police Surgeon* (March, 1972), pp. 15-18.

Flynn, W.R. "Frontier Justice: A Contribution to the Theory of Child Battery." *American Journal of Psychiatry,* 127 (1970), pp. 375-379.

Fontana, Vincent J. "Physical Abuse of Children." *Pediatrics,* 45 (March, 1970), pp. 509-510.

Fontana, Vincent J. *Somewhere a Child Is Crying: Maltreatment and Prevention.* NY: Macmillan, 1973.

Gil, David G., ed. *Child Abuse and Violence.* NY: AMS, 1979.

Gil, David G. "Physical Abuse of Children." *Pediatrics,* 45 (March, 1970), pp. 510-511.

Gil, David G. "Violence Against Children." *Journal of Marriage and the Family,* 33:4 (1971), pp. 637-648.

Gil, David G. "Violence Against Children." *Pediatrics,* 49 (April, 1972).

Gil, David G. *Violence Against Children: Physical Child Abuse in the United States.* Cambridge, MA: Harvard University Press, 1970.

Goode, William J. "Force and Violence in the Family." *Journal of Marriage and the Family,* 33:4 (1971), pp. 624-636.

Gregg, G.S. and E. Elmer. "Infant Injuries: Accident or Abuse?" *Pediatrics,* 44 (September, 1969), pp. 434-439.

Havens, Leston L. "Youth Violence and the Nature of Family Life." *Psychiatric Annals,* 2:2 (1972), pp. 18-21, 23-25, 29.

Helfer, Ray E. and Henry Kempe. *The Battered Child.* Chicago: University of Chicago Press, 1968.

Jenkins, Richard L. et al. "Interrupting the Family Cycle of Violence." *Journal of the Iowa Medical Society,* 60:2 (1970), pp. 85-89.

Kempe, C. Henry et al. "The Battered-Child Syndrome." *Journal of American Medical Association,* 181 (1962), pp. 17-24.

Langshaw, W.C. "The Battered Child." *Australian Journal of Forensic Sciences,* 3:260 (1970).

Paulson, Morris J. and Phillip R. Blake. "The Physically Abused Child: A Focus on Prevention." *Child Welfare,* 48:2 (1969), pp. 86-95.

Raffalli, Henri Christian. "The Battered Child: An Overview of a Medical, Legal and Social Problem." *Crime and Delinquency,* 16:2 (1970), pp. 139-150.

Renvoize, J. *Children in Danger: The Causes and Prevention of Baby Battering.* London: Routledge and Kegan Paul, 1974.

Riley, Harris D. "The Battered Child Syndrome: General and Medical Aspects." *Southern Medical Journal,* 58:3 (1970), pp. 9-13.

Spinetta, J.J. et al. "The Child-Abusing Parent: A Psychological Review." *Psychological Bulletin,* 77 (April, 1972), pp. 296-304.

Stone, N.H. et al. "Child Abuse by Burning." *Surgical Clinics of North America,* 50 (December, 1970), pp. 1419-1424.

Van Stolk, H. *The Battered Child in Canada.* Toronto: McClelland and Stewart, 1972.

"Violent Parents." *Lancet,* 2 (November, 1971), pp. 1017-1018.

Wells, Coy L. "Investigating 'the Battered Child Syndrome'." *Military Police Journal,* 21:10 (June, 1972), pp. 21-24.

Zalba, Serapio R. "The Battered Child." *Transaction,* 8 (July/August, 1971), pp. 58-61.

Child Abuse

The Abused Child: Multidisciplinary Approach to Developmental Issues and Treatment. Cambridge, MA: Ballinger, 1976.

Alvy, K.T. "On Child Abuse: Values and Analytic Approaches." *Journal of Clinical Child Psychology,* 4:1 (1975), pp. 36-37.

Amiel, Shirley. "Child Abuse in Schools.'f2ZNorthwest Medicine, 71:11 (1972).

Bakan, D. *Slaughter of the Innocents.* San Francisco: Jossey-Bass, 1971.
Child abuse is traced from its ancient origins through its modern expression in hospital statistics.

Brem, Jacob. "Child Abuse Control Centers: A Project for the Academy?" *Pediatrics,* 45:5 (1970), pp. 894-895.

Danckwerth, Deward T. "Techniques of Child Abuse Investigation." *Police Chief,* XLII:3 (March, 1976), pp. 62-64.

Debenham, A.E. "Cruelty and Neglect." in A.E. Debenham (ed.), *Innocent Victims.* Sydney, Australia: Edward and Shaw, 1969, pp. 99-123.

DeCourcy, Peter. *A Silent Tragedy: Child Abuse in the Community.* Port Washington NY: Alfred, 1973.

De Frances, Vincent. "Child Abuse Is Common." *Gunsmoke Gazette* (November-December, 1971).

Densen-Gerber, Judianne. "Drug Addicted Parents and Child Abuse." *Contemporary Drug Problems,* II (1973), pp. 683-695.

Elmer, Elizabeth. *Children in Jeopardy: A Study of Abused Minors and Their Families.* Pittsburgh: University of Pittsburgh Press, 1967.

Fontana, Vincent J. "Factors Needed for Prevention of Child Abuse and Neglect." *Pediatrics,* 46:2 (1970), pp. 318-319.

Fontana, Vincent J. *The Maltreated Child: The Maltreatment Syndrome in Children.* Springfield, IL: C.C. Thomas, 1971.

Fraser, B.G. "A Pragmatic Alternative to Current Legislative Approaches to Child Abuse." *American Criminal Law Review,* 12:1 (1974), pp. 103-124.

Glazier, Alice E., ed. *Child Abuse: A Community Challenge.* Buffalo, NY: H. Stewart, 1971.

Heins, Marilyn. "Child Abuse—Analysis of a Current Epidemic." *Michigan Medicine,* 68:17 (1969), pp. 887-891.

Holter, Joan C. and Stanford B. Friedman. "Child Abuse: Early Case Finding in the Emergency Department." *Pediatrics,* 42 (July, 1968), pp. 128-138.

Knapp, Vrinda S. *Role of Juvenile Police in the Protection of*

Neglected and Abused Children. Unpub. Doctoral Dissertation, University of Southern California, 1961.

McKenna, J.J. "A Case Study of Child Abuse: A Former Prosecutor's View." *American Criminal Law Review,* 12:1 (1974), pp. 165-178.

Murdock, C.G. "The Abused Child and the School System." *American Journal of Public Health,* 60 (January, 1970), pp. 105-109.

Smith, Homer A. "The Legal Aspects of Child Abuse." *Southern Medical Bulletin,* 58:3 (1970), pp. 19-21.

Solomon, Theo et al. *The Mayor's Task Force on Child Abuse and Neglect*. NY: Center for Community Reseach, 1970.

Surdock, P.W., Jr. *Child Abuse and Neglect in Montana—Report, January 1, 1974 to June 30, 1974*. Washington, DC: NCJRS, (Microfiche), 1974.
Statistical report on the cases and/or families referred for abuse or neglect during this six-month period.

Swanson, L.D. "Role of the Police in the Protection of Children from Neglect and Abuse." *Federal Probation* (March, 1961), pp. 43-44.

CRIMES AGAINST THE ELDERLY

Bradley, Wayne W. "Case Corridor Safety for Seniors Project." *Police Chief,* XLIII:2 (February, 1976), pp. 43-45, 69.

Brown, Lee P. and Marlene A. Young. "Crime Prevention for Older Americans: Multnomah County's Victimization Study." *Police Chief,* XLIII:2 (February, 1976), pp. 38-42.

Cunningham, Carl L. "Crime and the Aging Victim." *MRI Quarterly,* (1973).

Ducovny, Amram. *The Billion Dollar Swindle: Frauds Against the Elderly*. NY: Fleet, 1969.

Forston, R. and J. Kitchens. *Criminal Victimization of the Aged—The Houston Model Neighborhood Area*. Washington, DC: NCJRS, 1974.

Godsmith, Jack. "Police and the Older Victim: Keys to a Changing Perspective." *Police Chief,* XLIII:2 (February, 1976), pp. 19-23.

Goldsmith, Jack and Noel E. Thomas. "Crimes Against the Elderly: A Continuing National Crisis." *Aging* (June-July, 1974).

Gross, Phillip J. "Law Enforcement and the Senior Citizen." *Police Chief,* XLIII:2 (February, 1976), pp. 24-27.

Leeds, Morton and Karen Evans. "Residential Crime: The Older Person as Victim." *Police Chief,* XLIII-(February, 1976), pp. 46-47, 69.

Midwest Research Institute. *Crimes Against Aging Americans—The Kansas City Study*. Kansas City MO: Midwest Research Institute, 1975.

Pope, Carl E. and William Feyerherm. "A Review of Recent Trends: The Effects of Crime on the Elderly." *Police Chief,* XLIII:2 (February, 1976), pp. 48-51.

Willis, Ron L. and Myra Miller. "Senior Citizen Crime Prevention Program." *Police Chief,* XLIII:2 (February, 1976), pp. 16-17.

Younger, Evelle J. "The California Experience: Prevention of Criminal Victimization of the Elderly." *Police Chief,* XLIII:2 (February, 1976), pp. 28-32.

FENCING

Chappell, D. and M. Walsh. " 'No Questions Asked': A Consideration of the Crime of Criminal Receiving." *Crime and Delinquency,* 20:2 (1974), pp. 157-168.

Hall, Jerome. "Theft, Law and Society." *American Bar Association Journal,* 54 (1968), pp. 960-967.

Klockars, Carl B. *The Professional Fence*. NY: Free Press, 1974.

Lyons, John F. "Lucrative Looting: Burglary, Holdup Loss Soars, Pushing Insurers into Red Ink, Rate Rise." *Wall Street Journal* (July 28, 1965).
Thieves are becoming increasingly aware of new markets for their loot. Better fences and professional methods are making crime pay.

McIntosh,, Mary. "Thieves and Fences: Markets and Power in Professional Crime." *British Journal of Criminology* (July, 1976), pp. 257-266.

O'Brien, John T. "Receiving Stolen Property." *Police,* 12:1 (September-October, 1967), pp. 67-70.

Roselius, T. and D. Benton. *Marketing Theory and the Fencing of Stolen Goods*. Springfield, VA: NTIS, 1971.

U.S. Congress Senate Select Committee on Small Business. *Analysis of Criminal Redistribution Systems and Their Economic Impact on Small Business*. Washington, DC: GPO, 1972.
Inquiry into the importance of fencing—the criminal redistribution of stolen goods—in the overall picture of crimes against property.

Walsh, Marilyn E. *The Fence: A New Look at the World of Property Theft*. Westport, CT: Greenwood, 1976.

Walsh, M. and D. Chappell. "Operational Parameters in the Stolen Property System." *Journal of Criminal Justice,* 2:2 (1974) pp. -13-129.

Yoder, Robert M. "The Best Friend a Thief Ever Had." *Saturday Evening Post,* 227 (December 25, 1954).
Biographical sketch of a fence.

FORGERY

Bloom, M.T. "Season of Good Will and Bad Checks." *New York Times Magazine* (December 18, 1960).

"Check Forgery." *Life* (September 6, 1943), pp. 47-48.

Hoffman, E.E. *Billion Dollar Check Racket*. NY: Vantage, 1962.

"How Big is the Bad Check Problem?" *Security World,* 11:7 (1974), pp. 30-36, 129-137.

Kwitny, Jonathan. *The Fountain Pen Conspiracy*. NY: Knopf, 1973.

Lymes, R. "Forgery for Fun and Profit." *Harper's* (February, 1968).

McGuire, E. Patrick. *The Forgers*. Bernardsville, NJ: Padric, 1969.

Wilson, Frank J. *Pirates with Pens*. NY: National Security, 1944.

HIJACKING

Surface, B. "Big Business of Hijacking." *Reader's Digest* (January, 1968).

Surface, B. "Easier than Robbing a Bank; Truck Robberies." *New York Times Magazine* (May 7, 1967).

HITCHHIKER CRIMES

California Highway Patrol. *California Crimes and Accidents Associated with Hitchhiking*. Washington, DC: NCJRS, (Microfiche), 1974.
Results of a study undertaken to determine the nature and seriousness of crimes involving hitchhikers, and the characteristics of hitchhikers and drivers involved in such crimes or accidents.

Porter, Frank L. "Hitchhiker Crimes Create Serious Police Problems." *FBI Law Enforcement Bulletin*, 25:10 (October, 1956), pp. 3-4.

HOMICIDE

Homicide—General

Abrahamsen, David. *The Murdering Mind*. NY: Harper and Row, 1973.

Adelson, Lester. *The Pathology of Homicide*. Springfield, IL: C.C. Thomas.

Barnes, Margaret. *Murder in Coweta County*. NY: Readers Digest, 1976.

Barnett, A. and D.J. Kleitman. *On Urban Homicide—A Statistical Analysis—Working Paper*. Washington, DC: NCJRS, (Microfiche), 1974.

Barnett, A and D.J. Kleitman. *On Urban Homicide—Working Paper*. Washington DC: NCJRS, (Microfiche), 1974.

Barnett, A., D.J. Kleitman, and R.C. Larson. "On Urban Homicide: A Statistical Analysis." *Journal of Criminal Justice*, 3:2 (1974), pp. 85-110.

Bensing, R.C. and J.R. Schroeder. *Homicide in an Urban Community*. Springfield, IL: C.C. Thomas, 1960.

Biggs, J., Jr. *The Guilty Mind: Psychiatry and the Law of Homicide*. Baltimore: Johns Hopkins University Press, 1955.

Bjerri, Andreas. *The Psychology of Murder: A Study in Criminal Psychology*. NY: Longmans, Green, 1927.

Blackburn, R. "Personality Types Among Abnormal Homicides." *British Journal of Criminology*, 11 (January, 1971), pp. 14-31.

Boudouris, James. "Classification of Homicides." *Criminology*, 11:4 (February, 1974), pp. 525-540.

Boudouris, James. *Trends in Homicide, Detroit: 1926-1968*. Unpub. Doctoral Dissertation, Wayne State University, 1970.

Brearly, Harrington Cooper. *Homicide in the United States*. Chapel Hill: University of North Carolina Press, 1932.

Brennan, K.S.W. "Child Murderers—An Analysis." *Criminologist*, 9:32 (1974), pp. 3-11.

Brittian, Robert P. "The Sadistic Murder." *Medical Science and the Law*, 10 (October, 1970), pp. 198-207.

Brophy, John. *The Meaning of Murder*. NY: Crowell, 1967.

Bullock, Henry Allen. "Urban Homicide in Theory and Fact." *Journal of Criminal Law, Criminology and Police Science*, 46:1 (January-February, 1955), pp. 565-575.

Camps, F.E. *Camps on Crime*. Newton Abbot: David and Charles Holdings, 1973.
The author reviews several famous British murders, pointing out the scientific approach to criminal investigation.

Cohen, Louis. *Murder, Madness and the Law*. NY: World, 1952.

Cole, K.E., Gary Fisher, and Shirley Cole. "Women Who Kill: A Socio-psychological study." *Archives of General Psychiatry*, 19 (July, 1968), pp. 1-8.

Collier, James. "Murder by Witchcraft." *Police College Magazine* (Autumn, 1962), pp. 356-359.

Criminal Justice Commission, Inc. *Criminal Homicides in Baltimore 1960-1964*. Baltimore: Criminal Justice Commission, 1967.

Cruvent, Bernard and Francis Waldrop. "The Murderer in the Mental Institution." *Annals*, 284 (November, 1952), pp. 42-43.

Damio, Ward. *Urge to Kill*. NY: Pinnacle, 1974.

Deford, Miriam A. *Murderers Sane and Mad: Case Histories in the Motivation and Rationale of Murder*. London: Abelard-Schuman, 1965.

Derleth, August. *Wisconsin Murders*. Sauk City WI: Arkham, 1968.

Dickson, Grierson. *Murder by Numbers*. London: Hale, 1958.

Doerner, William G. "Regional Analysis of Homicide Rate in the United States." *Criminology* (May, 1975), pp. 90-101.

Duncan, J.W. and G.M. Duncan. "Murder in the Family: A Study of Some Homicidal Adolescents." *American Journal of Psychiatry*, 127 (May, 1971), pp. 1498-1502.

DuRose, John. *Murder Was My Business*. London: W.H. Allen, 1971.

Gaddis, Thomas E. and James O. Long. *Killer—A Journal of Murder*. NY: Macmillan, 1970.

Gardiner, Muriel. *The Deadly Innocence: Portraits of Children Who Kill*. NY: Basic, 1976.

Gastil, R.D. "Homicide and a Regional Culture of Violence." *American Sociological Review*, 36 (June, 1971), pp. 412-427.

Gibson, E. and S. Klein. *Murder, 1957 to 1968—A Home Office Statistical Division Report on Murder in England and Wales. (With Annex by the Scottish Home and Health Department on Murder in Scotland)*. London: HMSO, 1969.

Gillin, John L. "The Wisconsin Murders." *Social Forces* (May, 1932).

Harlan, Howard. "Five Hundred Homicides." *Journal of Criminal Law and Criminology*. 40 (March-April, 1950), pp. 736-752.

Heymann, P.B. and W.H. Kenety. *Murder Trial of Wilbur Jackson—A Homicide in the Family*. St. Paul MN: West, 1975.

Higdon, Hal. *Crime of the Century: The Leopold and Loeb Case*. NY: Putnam, 1975.

Hollis, W. Slater. "On the Etiology of Criminal Homicides—The Alcohol Factor." *Journal of Police Science and Administration,* 2:1 (March, 1974), pp. 50-53.

Joey, with Dave Fisher. *Killer! Autobiography of a Hit Man for the Mafia*. Chicago: Playboy, 1973.

Keys, Edward. *The Michigan Murders*. NY: Readers Digest, 1976.

Kurland, A., J. Morganstern, and C.A. Sheets. "Comparative Study of Wife Murderers Admitted to a State Psychiatric Hospital." *Journal of Social Therapy,* 1 (1955), pp. 7-15.

Lalli, Michael and Stanley H. Turner. "Suicide and Homicide: A Comparative Analysis by Race and Occupational Levels." *Journal of Criminal Law, Criminology and Police Science,* 59:2 (June, 1968), pp. 191-200.

Lefkowitz, Bernard and Kenneth G. Gross. *The Victims: The Wylie-Hoffert Murder Case, and Its Strange Aftermath*. NY: Putnam, 1969.

Lester, David and Gene Lester. *Crime of Passion: The Murder and the Murderer*. Chicago: Nelson-Hall, 1975.

Lindsay, Philip. *The Mainspring of Murder*. London: John Long, 1958.

Los Angeles Police Department. *Gangland Killings, Los Angeles Area, 1900-1915*. Los Angeles: LAPD, 1952.

McDade, Thomas, *The Annals of Murder*. Norman: University of Oklahoma Press, 1961.

McDermaid, Gladys and Emil Winkler. "Psychiatric Studies of Homicide Cases." *Journal of Clinical Psychopathology,* XI:3 (July, 1950).

MacDonald, John M. *The Murderer and His Victim*. Springfield, IL: C.C. Thomas, 1961.

Martin, John B. *Why Did They Kill?* NY: Ballantine, 1953.

Meyer, A., B. Apfelberg, and C. Sugar. "Men Who Kill Women." *Journal of Clinical Psychopathology,* 7 (1946); 8 (1947).

Meyer, Gerald. *The Memphis Murders*. NY: Seabury, 1974.

Miner, John W. "The Phillips Case—A New Dimension in Murder." *Journal of Forensic Sciences,* 9:1 (January, 1964), pp. 1-10.

Moreland, Roy. *Law of Homicide*. Indianapolis IN: Bobbs-Merril, 1962.

Mowat, Ronald R. *Morbid Jealousy and Murder: A Psychiatric Study of Morbidly Jealous Murderers at Broadmoor*. London: Tavistock, 1966.

Neustatter, W. Lindesay. *The Mind of the Murderer*. NY: Philosophical Library, 1957.

Odin, Robert. "The Kungsten Murder." *International Criminal Police Review* (November, 1962), pp. 262-268.

Palmer, Stuart. "A Case Study of Fifty-one New England Murderers." *Police* 7:6 (July-August, 1963), pp. 65-67.

Palmer, Stuart. "Murder and Suicide in Forty Non-literate Societies." *Journal of Criminal Law, Criminology and Police Science,* 56:3 (September, 1965), pp. 320-324.

Palmer, Stuart H. *A Study of Murder*. NY: Crowell, 1960.

Penn, H.S. *Homicide in California*. Washington, DC: NCJRS, (Microfiche), 1974.

Perkins, Rollin M. "The Law of Homicide." *Journal of Criminal Law and Criminology,* 36 (March/April, 1946), pp. 412-427.

Podolsky, Edward. "Mind of the Murderer." *Journal of Criminal Law, Criminology and Police Science,* 45:1 (May/June, 1954), pp. 48-50.

Pokorny, Alex D. "A Comparison of Homicides in Two Cities." *Journal of Criminal Law, Criminology and Police Science,* 56:4 (December, 1965), pp. 479-487.

Polfrey, W.J.H. "The Wigans Murders." *Police Journal,* 36:6 (June, 1963), pp. 267.

Reinhardt, J.M. *Nothing Left But Murder*. Lincoln, NE: Johnson, 1970.

Reinhardt, James M. "The Sentimental Murderer: Why Does He Kill?" *Police,* 5:6 (July-August, 1961), pp. 75-76.

Reinhardt, James Melvin. *The Psychology of Strange Killers*. Springfield IL: C.C. Thomas, 1962.

Resnick, P.J. "Child Murder by Parents: A Psychiatric Review of Filicide." *American Journal of Psychiatry,* 126 (1969), pp. 325-334.

"Resume of Eleven Repeat Murders with Whom the Los Angeles Police Department Has Had Experience." *Association for Professional Law Enforcement Quarterly Journal,* 5 (January-March, 1960), pp. 16-20.

Reynolds, R. and E. Siegle. "A Study of Sado-Masochistic Marriage Partners. *Social Casework,* (December, 1959), pp. 545-551.

Schwartz, Emanuel K. "Child Murder Today (Playwrights and Psychologists View of Filicide in Life, Drama)." *Human Context,* 4:2 (1972), pp. 360-361.

Scott, P.D. "Parents Who Kill Their Children." *Medicine, Science, and the Law,* 13:2 (April, 1973), pp. 120-126.

Smith, George. "Murder of Infants by Parents in Situations of Stress." *Journal of Social Therapy,* 1:14 (First Quarter, 1960).

Sparrow, Gerald. *Murder Parade*. NY: Roy, 1967.

Stern, Edward. "The Medea Complex: The Mother's Homicidal Wishes to Her Child." *Journal of Mental Science,* 94 (April, 1948).

Tennyson, Jesse F. *Murder and Its Motives*. London: Harrop, 1952.

Thompson, Thomas. *Blood and Money*. NY: Doubleday, 1976.

Tuteur, Werner and Jacob Glotzer. "Further Observations on Murdering Mothers." *Journal of Forensic Sciences,* 11:3 (July, 1966), pp. 373-383.

Vass, Harwin L. and John R. Hepburn. "Patterns in Criminal Homicide in Chicago." *Journal of Criminal Law, Criminology and Police Science,* 59:4 (December, 1968), pp. 499-508.

Von Hentig, Hans. "Pre-murderous Kindness and Post-murder Grief." *Journal of Criminal Law, Criminology and Police Science,* 48:4 (November-December, 1957), pp. 369-377.

Wechsler, Herbert and Jerome Michael. *A Rationale of the Law of Homicide, 1949-1952.* London: Royal Commission on Capital Punishment, 1953.

West, Donald J. *Murder Followed by Suicide.* Cambridge, MA: Harvard University Press, 1965.

Weyden, Peter. *The Hired Killers.* NY: Morrow, 1963.

Willie, W.S. *Citizens Who Commit Murder.* St. Louis, MO: Warren H. Green, 1974.

Psychiatric case files and interview results for 200 murderers who were compared to deduce common factors and to gain insight into the mentality of murderers.

Wolfgang, M. "Husband-Wife Homicide." *Journal of Social Therapy,* 2 (1956), pp. 263-271.

Wolfgang, M. *Studies in Homicide.* NY: Harper and Row, 1967.

Twenty reports of research studies sociological, psychological, and psychiatric aspects of criminal and non-criminal (justifiable) homicide.

Wolfgang, Marvin E. "The Relationship of Alcohol and Criminal Homicide." *Quarterly Journal Studies of Alcohol,* 17 (Spring, 1956), pp. 411-425.

Wolfgang, "Victim Precipitated Criminal Homicide." *Journal of Criminal Law, Criminology and Police Science,* 48:1 (May/June, 1957), pp. 1-11.

Wright, Sewell Peaslee. *Chicago Murders.* NY: Duell, Sloan and Pearce, 1945.

Euthanasia

Downing, A.B. *Euthanasia and the Right to Death: The Case for Voluntary Euthanasia.* NY: Humanities, 1970.

Russell, O. Ruth. *Freedom to Die: Moral and Legal Aspects of Euthanasia.* NY: Behavioral, 1975.

Sanders, Joseph. "Euthanasia: None Dare Call It Murder." *Journal of Criminal Law, Criminology and Police Science,* 60:3 (September, 1969), pp. 351-359.

Mass Murderers

Allen, William. *Starkweather: The Story of a Mass Murderer.* NY: Houghton-Mifflin, 1976.

Armbrister, Trevor. *Act of Vegenance: The Yablonski Murders and Their Aftermath.* NY: Saturday Review, 1975.

Baer, Rosemary. *Reflections on the Manson Trial: Journal of a Pseudo-Juror.* Waco, TX: Word, 1972.

Capote, Truman. *In Cold Blood.* NY: Random, 1965.

Cheney, Margaret. *Massacre: The Calculated Killings of a Multiple Murderer.* NY: Walker, 1976.

Cooper, David E. *Manson Murders.* Morristown, NJ: General Learning, 1974.

Cray, E. *Burden of Proof—The Case of Juan Corona.* NY: Macmillan, 1973.

Detailed description of the trial of Juan Corona, the individual convicted of killing twenty-five migrant workers in California.

"Crime: Corona in Court." *Newsweek,* 77 (June 14, 1971).

Dicks, Henry V. *Licensed Mass Murders: A Socio-Psychological Study of Some S.S. Killers.* London: Heinemann, 1972.

Frank, Gerold. *The Boston Strangler.* NY: New America Library, 1966.

Freeman, Lucy. *Before I Kill More.* NY: Crown, 1955.

Gurwell, John K. *Mass Murder in Houston.* Houston: Cordovan, 1974.

Hanna, David. *Harvest of Horror: Mass Murder in Houston.* NY: Belmont-Tower, 1975.

Hume, A. Britton. *Death and the Mines: Rebellion and Murder in the U.M.W.* NY: Grossman, 1971.

Kinsey, Barry A. "A Study of Adverse Community Reaction to the Starkweather Case." *Police,* 4:4 (March-April, 1960), pp. 62-64.

Lewis, Arthur H. *Murder by Contract: The People Versus "Tough Tony" Boyle.* NY: Macmillan, 1975.

Moser, Don and Jerry Cohen. *The Pied Piper of Tucson.* NY: New American Library, 1967.

Olsen, Jack. *The Man With the Candy: The Story of the Houston Mass Murders.* NY: Simon and Schuster, 1974.

Reinhardt, James M. *The Murderous Trail of Charles Starkweather.* Springfield, IL: C.C. Thomas, 1960.

Schiller, Lawrence. *The Killing of Sharon Tate.* NY: New American Library, 1970.

William, Allen. *Starkweather.* Boston: Houghton-Mifflin, 1976.

KIDNAPPING

Dutch, Andrew K. *Histeria: Lindbergh Kidnap Case.* Ardmore, PA: Dorrance, 1975.

Goldblatt, Burt and Hank Messick. *Kidnapping: The Illustrated History From Its Origins to the Present.* NY: Dial, 1974.

Haring, J. Vreeland. *Hand of Hauptmann: The Handwriting Expert Tells the Story of the Lindbergh Case.* Montclair, NJ: Patterson Smith, 1937.

Lindbergh, Anne M. *Hour of Gold, Hour of Lead.* NY: New American Library, 1974.

Traini, R. "Kidnapping—A New Challenge to Security Thinking." *Security Gazette,* 16:6 (1974), pp. 229-230.

LIBEL

Dean, Joseph. *Hatred, Ridicule or Contempt: A Book of Libel Cases.* NY: Macmillan, 1954.

Phelps, Robert, *Libel: Rights, Risks, Responsibilities.* NY: Macmillan, 1966.

Lawhorne, C.D. *Defamation and Public Officials—The Evolving Law of Libel.* Carbondale: Southern Illinois University Press, 1971.

LYNCHING

Chadbourn, James H. *Lynching and the Law.* NY: Johnson, 1970. (repr. of 1933 ed.).

Cutler, James E. *Lynch Law: An Investigation into the History of Lynching in the United States.* Montclair, NJ: Patterson Smith, 1969. (repr. of 1905 ed.).

Ginzburg, Ralph. *100 Years of Lynching: The Shocking Record Behind Today's Black Militancy.* NY: Lancer, 1969.

National Association for the Advancement of Colored People. *Thirty Years of Lynching in the United States, 1889-1918.* NY: Crisis, 1919.

Raper, Arthur. *The Tragedy of Lynching.* NY: Dover, 1970. (repr. of 1933 ed.).

MUGGING

Hunt, Morton. *Mugging.* NY: Atheneum, 1972.

Shaw, Clifford. *The Jack-Roller.* Chicago: University of Chicago Press, 1930.

Willwerth, James. *Portrait of a Mugger.* NY: Evans, 1974.

NARCOTICS

Narcotics—General

The Alcohol-Narcotic Problem, A Handbook for Teachers. (5th ed.) Dallas: Texas Alcohol Narcotic Education, 1961.

American Drug Index. Philadelphia: Lippincott, Annual.

Anslinger, Harry J. and William F. Tompkins. *The Traffic in Narcotics.* NY: Funk and Wagnall, 1953.

Barber, Bernard. *Drugs and Society.* NY: Russell Sage Foundation, 1967.

Beacraft, Donald C. "Drug Education for Parents." *Law and Order,* 18:1 (January, 1970).

Berg, Dorothy F. *Illicit Use of Dangerous Drugs in the United States: A Compilation of Studies, Surveys, and Polls.* Washington, DC: GPO, 1970.

Blum, R.H. *Dream Seller, Perspectives on Drug Dealers.* Washington, DC: Joint Venture, 1972.

Brenner, J.H. et al. *Drugs and Youth—Medical, Psychiatric and Legal Facts.* NY: Liveright, 1970.

Chein, Isidor et al. *The Road to H: Narcotics, Delinquency and Social Policy.* NY: Basic, 1964.

Connelly, Bob. "Narcotics—Useage, Control Measures, and Inforcement." *Law Officer,* 2 (Winter, 1969), pp. 14-17.

Cuskey, Walter R. *Drug-Trip Abroad—American Drug—Refugees in Amsterdam and London.* Philadelphia: University of Pennsylvania Press, 1972.

Drug Enforcement Administration. *Drug Abuse and the Criminal Justice System—A Survey of New Approaches in Treatment and Rehabilitation.* Washington, DC: NCJRS, (Microfiche), 1974.

Epstein, S.S. and J. Lederberg. *Drug of Abuse—Their Genetic and Other Chronic Nonpsychiatric Hazards.* Cambridge, MA: MIT Press, 1971.

Faberow, Norman L. *The Cry for Help.* NY: McGraw-Hill, 1961.

Ferguson, Robert W. *Drug Abuse Control.* Boston, MA: Holbrook, 1975.

Finlator, John. *The Drugged Nation: A Narc's Story.* NY: Simon and Schuster, 1973.

Flagstaff Public Schools. *Narcotic and Drug Education—Grades K-12.* Washington, DC: GPO, 1971.

Francisco, J.T. "Drugs and Disease—A Pathologist's Viewpoint." *Journal of Forensic Sciences,* 10:4 (October, 1965), pp. 407-414.

Hafen, Brent. *Readings on Drug Use and Abuse.* Provo, UT: Brigham Young University Press, 1970.

Hardy, Richard E. and John G. Cull. *Drug Language and Lore.* Springfield, IL: C.C. Thomas, 1975.

Herron, Donald M. and L.F. Anderson. *Can We Survive Drugs?* Philadelphia: Chilton, 1973.

International Narcotics Control Board. *Report of the International Narcotics Control Board and Its Work in 1971.* NY: U.N., 1971.

King, Daniel P. "Some Comments on the Narcotics Problem in the United States." *Police* 10:1 (September-October, 1965), pp. 18-21.

King, Rufus. *The Drug Hang-Up: America's Fifty-Year Folly.* Springfield IL: C.C. Thomas, 1974.

Levine, Harvey R. *Legal Dimensions of Drug Abuse in the United States.* Springfield, IL: C.C. Thomas, 1974.

Levine, Samuel F. *Narcotics and Drug Abuse.* Cincinnati, OH: Anderson, 1971.

Ligi, Joseph. "America, A Drug Society." *Law and Order,* 18:12 (December, 1970), pp. 32-34.

Louria, Donald. *Nightmare Drugs.* NY: Pocket Books, [n.d.].

McLean, Gordon R. and Haskell Bowen. *High on the Campus.* Wheaton, IL: Tyndale House, 1971.

Milbauer, B. *Drug Abuse and Addiction—A Fact Book for Parents, Teen-Agers, and Young Adults.* NY: Crown, 1970.

Morgan, James P., Jr. "Don't Blame the Cops!" *Police Chief,* XXXIX: 7 (July, 1972), pp. 20-21.

Musto, D.F. *American Disease—Origins of Narcotic Control.* New Haven, CT: Yale University Press, 1973.
Struggle with narcotic addition from end of civil war to

present, with emphasis on years 1900-1940 when official attitudes crystallized into lasting policies.

"Narcotic Drugs." *International Criminal Police Review,* (December, 1966), pp. 290-296.

National Commission on Marijuana and Drug Abuse. *Drug Use in America—Problem in Perspective.* Washington, DC: GPO, 1973.

Nipper, J.D. "Narcotics and Juveniles." *Police Chief,* XXXLV: 6 (June, 1967), pp. 47-50.

Pomeroy, Wesley A. *Police Chiefs Discuss Drug Abuse.* Washington, DC: Drug Abuse, 1974.

President's Commission on Law Enforcement and Administration of Justice. *Task Force Report—Narcotics and Drug Abuse.* Washington, DC: GPO, [n.d.].
Recommendations for improving drug enforcement, i.e., finding the drugs and the people in the illicit traffic, and for improving research and education.

Resource Book for Drug Abuse Education. Washington, DC: GPO, 1971.

Roberts, C.F. and J. Ward. *Drug Abuse and Interpersonal Values.* Washington, DC: NCJRS, (Microfiche), 1974.

Seymour, Whitney. *Young Die Quietly: The Narcotics Problem in America.* NY: Morrow, 1972.

Siba, Foundation Study Group No. 12. *Curare and Curare-Like Agents.* Boston: Little, Brown, 1962.

Simmons, Luiz R.S. and Abdul A. Said *Drugs, Politics and Diplomacy: The International Connection.* Beverly Hills, CA: Sage, 1974.

Skousen, W. Cleon. "The Chief Takes a Hard Look at Drug Abuse." *Law and Order,* 17:3 (March, 1969), pp. 16-22, 84.

Stearn, Jess. *The Seekers.* Garden City NY: Doubleday, 1969.

Swidler, Gerald. *Handbook of Drug Interactions.* NY: Wiley, 1971.

Switzer, A.L. *Drug Abuse and Drug Treatment.* Washington, DC: NCJRS, (Microfiche), 1974.

Taylor, Norman. *Narcotics: Nature's Dangerous Gifts.* NY: Dell, 1963.

U.S. Congress. Senate. *Committee on Government Operations, Organized Crime and Illicit Traffic in Narcotics.* Washington, DC: GPO, 1965.

Wald, P. and P. Hutt. *Dealing with Drug Abuse—A Report to the Ford Foundation.* NY: Praeger, 1972.

Wiczai, Louis J. "Users Are Losers." *Law and Order,* 18:5 (May, 1970), pp. 24-25, 28.

Williams, John B., ed. *Narcotics.* Dubuque, IA: Brown, 1963.
Cites a study of the relationship between narcotics and crime, conducted by a Los Angeles policeman.

Wilner, Daniel M. and Gene G. Kassebaum, eds. *Narcotics.* NY: McGraw-Hill, 1965.

Zavrel, Robert and John B. McLaughlin. "The Drug Epidemic." *Police,* 16:9 (May, 1972), pp. 11-17.

Addiction

"Addicts Steal $2.6 Billion." *New York Times* (September 23, 1969).
According to a New York medical examiner, New York's heroin users may be stealing as much as $2.6 billion a year in property.

Alexander, Gary. "The Heroine Addict Can Be Cured." *Plain Truth Magazine,* 37 (February, 1972), pp. 18-20.

Aliano, George and Lyle Knowles. "The Addict as Non-Victim: Narcotics Crimes Versus Property Crimes." *Journal of California Law Enforcement* (1976), pp. 154-157.

Ball, John C. "Two Patterns of Narcotic Drug Addiction in the United States." *Journal of Criminal Law, Criminology and Police Science,* 56:2 (June, 1965), pp.203-211.

Ball, John C. and M.P. Lau. "The Chinese Narcotic Addict in the United States." *Social Forces* (September, 1966), pp. 68-72.

Barber, Bernard. *Drugs and Society.* NY: Sage, 1967.

Baridon, Philip C. *Addiction, Crime, and Social Policy.* Lexington, MA: Lexington, 1976.

Bill, Keith. *Shot to Hell.* Westwood, NJ: F.H. Rivell, 1967.

Brill, Leon and Louis Lieberman. *Authority and Addiction.* Boston: Little, Brown, 1969.
Study of 180 convictions involving narcotics. Thirty-five percent admitted to breaking and entering in order to support their habit.

Cushman, P., Jr. "Relationship Between Narcotic Addiction and Crime." *Federal Probation,* 38:3 (1974), pp. 38-43.
Survey illustrates that arrest rates rose rapidly and progressively after the start of addiction. Heroin users had much higher arrest rates than others.

Goldenberg, I.I. *Employment and Addiction—Perspectives on Existing Business and Treatment Practices.* Springfield, VA: NTIS, 1972.

Harns, Ernest, ed. *Drug Addiction in Youth.* NY: Pergamon, 1965.

Judson, Horace F. *Heroin Addiction in Britain.* London: Harcourt, Brace, Jovanovich, 1974.

Kolb, Lawrence. *Drug Addiction: A Medical Problem,* Springfield, IL: C.C. Thomas, 1962.

Lindesmith, Alfred R. *The Addict and the Law.* Bloomington: Indiana University Press, 1965.

Mauer, David W. and Victor H. Vogel. *Narcotics and Narcotic Addiction.* (3rd ed.) Springfield, IL: C.C. Thomas, 1967.

Meyers, Alan S., ed. *Social and Psychological Factors in Opiate Addiction.* NY: Bureau of Applied Social Research, 1952.
Review of relevant research. The evidence tends to support the view that addiction is the cause of violations of narcotic and other laws.

O'Brien, Kevin P. and Robert C. Sullivan. "The Addict Today—1970." *Police,* 14:5 (May-June, 1970), pp. 35-41.

O'Donnell, John A. and John C. Ball. *Narcotic Addiction.* NY: Harper and Row, 1966.

Preble, Edward and John J. Casey, Jr. "Taking Care of Business—The Heroin User's Life on the Street." *International Journal of the Addictions,* 4:1 (March, 1969), pp. 1-14.

Schur, Edwin M. *Narcotic Addiction in Britain and America—The Impact of Public Policy.* Bloomington: Indiana University Press, 1962.

U.S. Congress House Select Committee on Crime. *Narcotics Research, Rehabilitation, and Treatment, Part 2, Hearings.* Washington, DC: GPO, 1971.

Testimony on multiple aspects of the heroin addiction crisis in the United States; included kinds of research, treatment and rehabilitation which succeeded.

Yost, Orin R. *The Bane of Drug Addiction.* NY: Macmillan, 1954.

Amphetamines

Kalant, Oriana J. *The Amphetamines: Toxicity and Addiction.* Springfield, IL: C.C. Thomas, 1966.

Larrick, George P. "Misuse of Restricted Drugs—A Dangerous Problem." *Police,* 8:6 (July-August, 1964), pp. 10-12.

Skousen, W. Cleon. "Drug Abuse—The Amphetamines." *Law and Order,* 17:6 (June, 1969), pp. 10-14.

U.S. Congress, House Select Committee on Crime. *Amphetamines, Fourth Report by the Select Committee.* Washington, DC: GPO, 1971.

Cocaine

Bewley, Thomas. "Heroine and Cocaine Addictions." *Lancet,* (1965), pp. 800-810.

"Cocaine—Illicit Manufacture and Traffic." *International Criminal Police Review,* (1969), pp. 97-102.

Collier, H.O.J. "Supersensitivity and Dependence on Cocaine." *Nature* (1968), pp. 1327-1328.

Freud, S. "On Cocaine." *Physician's World* (March, 1974), pp. 49-54.

Edminister, S.A. et al. *The Cocaine Papers.* Vienna: Dunguin, 1963.

Emboden, William A., Jr. *Narcotic Plants.* NY: Macmillan, 1972.

Moser, Brian. *The Cocaine Eaters.* NY: Taplinger, 1967.

Woodly, R. *Dealer: A Portrait of a Cocaine Merchant.* NY: Holt, Rinehart and Winston, 1971.

Glue Sniffing

Mullings, Ernest B. "Airplane Glue." *Michigan's Health,* 54 (September-October, 1966), pp. 3-6.

Skousen, W. Cleon. "Drug Abuse: The Glue-Sniffers." *Law and Order,* 17:12 (December, 1969), pp. 22-30.

Sokol, Jacob. "A Sniff of Death." *FBI Law Enforcement Bulletin,* 39:10 (October, 1965).

Sterling, James Q. "A Comparative Examination of Two Modes of Intoxication—An Exploratory Study of Glue Sniffing." *Journal of Criminal Law, Criminology and Police Science,* 55:1 (March, 1964), pp. 94-99.

Hashish

Ciba, Foundation Study Group No. 12. *Hashish: Its Chemistry Pharmacology.* Boston: Little Brown, 1965.

Skousen, W. Cleon. "Drug Abuse: The Latest Fad—Hashish." *Law and Order,* 17:11 (November, 1969), pp. 10-14.

Heroin

Gould, Leroy et al. *Connections: Notes from the Heroin World.* New Haven, CT: Yale University Press, 1974.

Kunnes, Richard. *The American Heroin Empire: Power, Profits and Politics.* NY: Dodd, Mead, 1973.

Moscow, Alvin. "Merchants of Heroin." *Readers Digest* (August, 1968), and (September, 1968).

Rutherford, James W. and Alice A. Skvanz. "Who Needs Heroin?" *Law and Order,* 12:8 (August, 1964), pp. 15-18.

Skousen, W. Cleon. "Drug Abuse—The Story of Heroin." *Law and Order,* 17:10 (October, 1969), pp. 10-15, 97.

Wilner, Daniel M. et al. "Heroin Use and Street Gangs." *Journal of Criminal Law, Criminology and Police Science,* 48:4 (November-December, 1957) pp. 399-409.

Wilson, J.Q. et al. "The Problem of Heroin." *Public Interest,* 29 (Fall, 1972), pp. 3-28.

LSD

Alpert, Richard and Sidney Cohen. *LSD.* NY: New American Library, 1966.

Fagerstrom, Dorothy. "Prognosis Uncertain: A Commentary on LSD." *Law and Order,* 14:7 (July, 1966), pp. 44-46, 62.

Kerrigan, John F. "Some Observations on Psychedelic Drugs." *FBI Law Enforcement Bulletin,* 35:10 (October, 1966), pp. 2-6.

"LSD—What It Is, How It Affects the User, Where It Is Obtained, Its Legality." *Journal of California Law Enforcement* (July, 1966), pp. 24-27.

Schachter, Burt. "Psychedelic Drug Use by Adolescents." *Social Work,* 13:3 (July, 1968), pp. 33-39.

Skousen, W. Cleon. "Drug Abuse—The Instant Insanity Drugs." *Law and Order,* 17:8 (August, 1969), pp. 10-17, and 15:9 (September, 1967), pp. 83-87.

Marijuana

Alexander, Donald G. "Is Marijuana Really Dangerous?" *Nation's Cities* (December, 1969).

Cites the statistic that 75 percent of the burglaries in Albuquerque, New Nexico were committed by addicts or those who have been addicts.

Andrews, George and Simon Vinkenoog, eds. *The Book of Grass: An Anthology on Indian Hemp.* NY: Grove, 1967.

Ball, John C. "Marijuana Smoking and the Onset of Heroin Use." *British Journal of Criminology,* 7:4 (1967), pp. 408-413.

In 1962-1964 a follow-up study of former patients was undertaken. Of 242 ex-patients, 119 were interviewed. Findings revealed heroin use started in an unsupervised street setting while subjects were still teenagers. Opiate use was usually preceded by marijuana smoking with friends. In both cases of opiate and marijuana use the peer group was a dominant influence on the subjects.

Ball, John C., Carl D. Chambers, and Marion J. Hall. "The Association of Marijuana Smoking with Opiate Addiction in the United States." *Journal of Criminal Law, Criminology and Police Science,* 59:2 (June, 1968), pp. 171-182.

Bloomquist, E.R. *Marijuana—The Second Trip* (rev. ed.) Beverly Hills CA: Glencoe, 1971.

Giordano, Henry L. "Marijuana—A Calling Card to Narcotic Addiction." *FBI Law Enforcement Bulletin* (November, 1968), pp. 2-5, 16.

Grupp, S.E. et al. *Marijuana Muddle.* Lexington, MA: Health Lexington, 1973.

Hotis, Ronald W. "Marijuana—Facts and Opinions." *Law and Order,* 17:8 (August, 1969), pp. 84-88.

Hutton, Gary W. "Marijuana Cases: A Legal Problem." *Police Chief,* XLII:5 (May, 1975), pp. 58-59.

Johnson, B.D. *Marijuana Users and Drug Subcultures.* NY: Wiley, 1973.

Kamstra, Jerry. *Weed: Adventures of a Dope Smuggler.* NY: Harper and Row, 1974.

Kaplan, John. *Marijuana, the New Prohibition.* NY: World, 1970.

Keller, E. John. "The Effects of Marijuana Use in Industry." *Law and Order,* 23:4 (April, 1975), pp. 82-83.

Los Angeles Police Department. *Facts About Marijuana.* Los Angeles: LAPD 1963.

McNamara, John G. "Beware of the Marijuana Menace." *FBI Law Enforcement Bulletin,* 38:4 (April, 1969), pp. 9-11, 23.

McNorris, S.C. "What Price Euphoria? The Case Against Marijuana." *British Journal of Addiction,* 62 (March, 1967), pp. 203-208.

"The Marijuana Problem." *Newsweek* (July 24, 1967).

Munch, J.C. "Marijuana and Crime." *Bulletin on Narcotics,* 18:2 (April/June, 1966), pp. 15-22.

National Commission on Marijuana and Drug Abuse. *Marijuana—A Signal of Misunderstanding, First Report of the National Commission on Marijuana and Drug Abuse.* Washington, DC: GPO, 1972.

Russell, George K. *Marijuana Today.* NY: Myrin Institute, 1975.

Sabatino, Ludwig. "Marijuana—Background and Identification." *Law and Order,* 19:7 (July, 1971), pp. 18-20.

Skousen, W. Cleon. "Should Marijuana Be Legalized." *Law and Order,* 22:6 (June, 1974), pp. 8-10, 12-13.

Opium

Allen, Nathan. *Opium Trade as Carried on in India and China.* Boston, MA: Milford House, 1973. (repr. of 1853 ed.).

Beeching, Jack. *The Chinese Opium Wars.* NY: Harcourt Brace Jovonavich, 1975.

Chang, Hsin'pao. *Commissioner Lin and the Opium War.* Cambridge, MA: Harvard University Press, 1964.

Cunningham, Arthur. *Opium War, Recollections of Service in China.* Wilmington DE: Scholarly Resources, 1972.(repr. of 1845 ed.).

Fay, Peter Ward. *The Opium War, 1840-1842.* NY: Harcourt, Brace, Jovonavich, 1975.

Nelligen, A.R. *The Opium Question, with Special Reference to Persia.* London: Bale, 1927.

Opium: 1910-1941. (6 vols.) Wilmington, DE: Scholarly Resources, 1975.

Scott, James M. *The White Poppy: A History of Opium.* NY: Funk and Wagnalls, 1969.

Skousen, W. Cleon. "Drug Abuse—The Story of Opium." *Law and Order,* 17:9 (September, 1969), pp. 10-21.

Terry, Charles E. and Mildred Pellens. *The Opium Problem.* NY: Bureau of Social Hygiene, 1928.

Veeching, Jack. *Chinese Opium Wars.* NY: Harcourt Brace Javonovich, NY: 1976.

Walley, Arthur. *Opium Wars Through Chinese Eyes.* Chester Springs PA: Dufour, 1966.

Willoughby, Westel W. *Opium as an International Problem: The Geneva Conference.* NY: Arno, 1975. (repr. of 1925 ed.).

Peyote

Brown, Ted. "Peyote: Narcotic or Not?" *Police,* 6:1 (September-October, 1961), pp. 6-10.

Roseman, Bernard. *The Peyote Story.* Hollywood, CA: Wilshire, 1966.

OBSCENITY

Obscenity

Clor, Harry M. *Obscenity and Public Morality: Censorship in a Liberal Society.* Chicago: University of Chicago Press, 1969.

Dibble, Rex. "Obscenity: A State Quarantine to Protect Children." *USC Law Review* (Spring, 1966).

Eliasberg, W.G. "Art: Immoral or Immortal." *Journal of Criminal Law, Criminology and Police Science,* 45:3 (September/October, 1954), pp. 274-278.

Ernst, Morris L. and William Seagle. *To the Pure—A Study of Obscenity and the Censor.* NY: Viking, 1928.

Ford, John. *Criminal Obscenity: A Plea for Its Suppression.* NY: Revell, 1926.

Foster, Henry H., Jr. "The 'Comstock Load'—Obscenity and the Law." *Journal of Criminal Law, Criminology and Police Science,* 48:3 (September-October, 1957), pp. 245-258.

Mintz, John A. "Comment on Obscenity." *FBI Law Enforcement Bulletin,* 42:9 (September, 1973), pp. 21-23.

Rembar, Charles. *The End of Obscenity: The Trials of Lady Chatterley, Tropic of Cancer, and Fanny Hill.* NY: Random, 1968.

Censorship

Alpert, Hollis et al., eds. *Censorship: For and Against.* NY: Hart, 1971.

Clor, Harry M. *Obscenity and Public Morality: Censorship in a Liberal Society.* Chicago: University of Chicago Press, 1969.

Daily, Jay E. *Anatomy of Censorship.* NY: Marcel Dekker, 1973.

DeGrazia, Edward. *Censorship Landmarks.* NY: Bowker, 1969.

Ernst, Morris L. and Allen U. Schwartz. *Censorship:* NY: Macmillan, 1964.

McClellan, Grant S. *Censorship in the United States.* Bronx NY: Wilson, 1967.

Murphy, Terrence J. *Censorship: Government and Obscenity.* Baltimore: Helicon, 1963.

Nelson, Jack and Gene Roberts, Jr. *The Censors and the Schools.* Boston: Little, Brown, 1963.

Paul, James C.N. *Federal Censorship: Obscenity in the Mail.* NY: Free Press, 1961.

Thomas, Donald. *A Long Time Burning: The History of Literary Censorship in England.* NY: Praeger, 1969.

POLITICAL CRIME

Schafer, Stephen. *Political Criminal: The Problem of Morality and Crime.* NY; Macmillan, 1974.

Steiner, John M. "Power, Ideology and Political Crime." *International Journal of Criminology and Penology* (February, 1973), p. 5-14.

PORNOGRAPHY

Anchell, Melvin. "The Perverts Revolution." *Law and Order,* 18:8 (August, 1970), pp. 24, 26-28.
M.D. discusses why the young are not achieving sexual maturity.

Barrett, James K. "Inside the Mobs Smut Rackets." *Readers Digest* (November, 1973), pp. 128-132.

Clark, Oliver E. *A Critical Analysis of the President's Commission on Obscenity and Pornography.* Unpub. Master's Thesis, California State University, Long Beach, 1971.

Cochran, Murray O. "Pornography." *Police Chief,* XXXVII:4 (April, 1970) pp. 14-18.

Commission of Obscenity and Pornography. *Commission on Obscenity and Pornography—Report* Washington, DC: GPO, 1970.
Findings and recommendations of the advisory commission established by Congress to study the casual relation between pornography and antisocial behavior.

Commission on Obscenity and Pornography. *Commission on Obscenity and Pornography—Technical Report: Erotica and Antisocial Behavior.* (vol. 7) Washington, DC: GPO, 1971.
Empirical research papers which analyze the relationships between exposure to pornographic materials, deviant sexual behavior, and sex crimes.

Commission on Obscenity and Pornography. *Commission on Obscenity and Pornography—Technical Report: Erotica and Social Behavior.* (vol. 8) Springfield, VA: NTIS, 1971.
The results of several experiments which measured the effects of exposure to explicit sexual materials, on normal sexual activities, behavior, and attitudes.

Commission on Obscenity and Pornography. *Commission on Obscenity and Pornography—Technical Report: Legal Analysis.* (vol. 2) Washington, DC: GPO, 1971.
Analysis of Supreme Court decisions and state laws on obscenity and pornography and outline of the censorship laws of several foreign nations.

Commission on Obscenity and Pornography. *Commission on Obscenity and Pornography—Technical Report: The Market Place—Empirical Studies.* (vol. 4) Washington, DC: GPO, 1971.
Empirical studies of the marketplace for sexual materials with emphasis on retail outlets and their customers.

Commission on Obscenity and Pornography. *Commission of Obscenity and Pornography—Technical Report: The Market Place—The Industry.* (vol. 3) Washington, DC: GPO, 1971.
Description of the operation of the several industries that publish and distribute sexually oriented materials, and an estimate of the volume of this business.

Commission on Obscenity and Pornography. *Commission on Obscenity and Pornography—Technical Report: National Survey.* (vol. 6) Washington, DC: GPO, 1971.
Survey of Public attitudes toward and experience with erotic materials, including a detailed description of the methodological design of the study.

Commission on Obscenity and Pornography. *Commission on Obscenity and Pornography—Technical Report: Preliminary Studies.* (vol. 1) Washington, DC: GPO, 1971.
State of scientific knowledge on the effects of pornography and obscenity when the commission began its work.

Commission on Obscenity and Pornography. *Commission on Obscenity and Pornography—Technical Report: Societal Control Mechanisms.* (vol. 5) Washington, DC: GPO.
Society's responses to the presence of explicit sexual material, including industry self-regulation, citizen action groups, law enforcement, and sex education.

Drakeford, John W. and Jack Hamm. *Pornography: The Sexual Mirage.* Nashville, TN: Nelson, 1973.

Fagerstrom, Dorothy. "Pornography—A Moral Disease." *Law and Order,* 12:10 (October, 1964), pp. 8-16.

Gerber, Albert B. *Sex, Pornography and Justice.* NY: Stuart, 1965.

Goldstein, M.J., H.S. Kant, and J.J. Hartman. *Pornography and Sexual Deviance.* Berkeley: University of California Press, 1973.

Hewitt, Cecil R., ed. *Does Pornography Matter.* London: Routledge and K. Paul, 1961.

Holbrook, David, ed. *Case Against Pornography.* LaSalle, IL: Open Court, 1973.

Hyde, H.M. *A History of Pornography.* NY: Farrar, 1965.

Keating, Charles. *Pornography on Trial: A Brief Against Smut.* Washington, DC: Prospect House, 1974.

Kilpatrick, James J. *The Smut Peddlers.* Garden City, NY: Doubleday, 1960.

Kronhausen, Eberhard and Phyllis Kronhausen. *Pornography and the Law: The Psychology of Erotic Realism and Pornography.* NY: Ballantine, 1959.

Loth, David Goldsmith. *The Erotic in Literature: A Historical Survey of Pornography as Delightful as It Is Discreet.* NY: J. Messner, 1961.

Norwick, Kenneth. *Pornography: The Issues and the Law.* NY: Public Affairs Commission, 1972.

"The Porno Plague." *Readers Digest* (July, 1976), pp. 117-120.

"Pornography Goes Public." *Newsweek,* 76 (December 21, 1970).

Rist, Ray C., ed. *Pornography Controversy: Changing Moral Standards in American Life.* Edison, NJ: Transaction, 1974.

See, Carolyn. *Blue Money.* NY: McKay, 1974.

Smith, Alexander B. and Bernard Locke. "Pornography and Obscenity." *Police Chief,* XXXVIII:11 (November, 1971), pp. 61-65.

Stroller, Robert J. "Pornography and Perversion." *Archives of General Psychiatry,* 22:6 (1970), pp. 490-499.

Sunderland, Lane V. *Obscenity: The Court, the Congress, and the President's Commission.* Washington, DC: American Enterprise Institute for Public Policy Research, 1974.

Wilson, W. Cody. "Law Enforcement Officers' Perceptions of Pornography as a Social Issue." *Journal of Social Issues,* 29:3 (1973), pp. 41-51.

PROHIBITION

Merz, Charles *Dry Decade.* Seattle: University of Washington Press, 1970.

Waters, Harold. *Smugglers of Spirits: Prohibition and the Coast Guard.* NY: Hastings, [n.d.].

RAPE

Abel, Gene, Denis Madden, and Russel R. Christopher. *The Components of Rapists' Sexual Arousal.* Panel at the American Psychiatric Association Annual Meeting, May, 1975.

"Alleged Rape, An Invitational Symposium." *Journal Reproductive Medicine,* 12 (1974), pp. 133-152.

Amir, Menachem. "Forcible Rape." *Federal Probation,* 31 (March, 1967), pp. 51-58.
Analysis of 646 forcible rape cases in Philadelphia, Pa. 1958 and 1960.

Amir, Menachim. *Patterns in Forcible Rape.* Chicago: University of Chicago Press, 1971.

Astor, G. *Charge Is Rape.* Chicago, IL: Playboy, 1974.
Examines controversial questions, the history of laws relating to rape, myths, and facts, and characteristics of rapists.

Brodyaga, Lisa et al. *Rape and Its Victims: A Report for Citizens, Health Facilities, and Criminal Justice Agencies.* Washington, DC: LEAA, 1975.

Brownmiller, S. "Rashomon in Maryland: Giles-Johnson Rape Case." *Esquire* (May, 1968).

Brownmiller, Susan. *Against Our Will: Men, Women and Rape.* NY: Simon and Schuster, 1975.

Burgess, Ann W. and Linda L. Holmstrom. "Accountability: A Right of the Rape Victim." Paper read at the American Orthopsychiatric Association. San Francisco, CA: April 11, 1974.

Coote, Anna and Tess Gill. *Rape Controversy: The Law, the Myths, the Facts: Changes That Are Needed and What to Do if It Happens to You.* London: NCLC, 1975.

Cottell, Louis C. "Rape—The Ultimate Invasion of Privacy." *FBI Law Enforcement Bulletin,* 43:5 (May, 1974).

Cowley, S.C. and S. Gilbert. "Keeping Sex Sacred." *Newsweek* (January 26, 1976.)

Casida, June B. and Joseph Csida. *Rape: How to Avoid It and What to Do About It if You Can't.* Chatsworth, CA: Books for Better Living, 1974.

Goldberg, Jacob A. and Rosamund W. Goldberg. *Girls on the City Streets: A Study of 1400 Cases of Rape.* NY: Arno, 1974. (repr. of 1935 ed.).

Goldner, N.S. "Rape as a Heinous but Understudied Offense." *Journal of Criminal Law, Criminology and Police Science,* 63: (1972).

Greer, Germaine. "Seduction is a Four-Letter Word." *Playboy,* (September, 1974).

"Healthy Rise in Rape." *Newsweek* (July 31, 1972).

Hibbey, A. "Trial of a Rape Case: An Advocate's Analysis of Corroboration, Consent and Character." *American Criminal Law Review* (Winter, 1973).

Hoover, J.E. "Sex Books and Rape." *U.S. News and World Report.* March 11, 1968).

Horos, Carol V. *Rape: The Private Crime, A Social Horror.* NY: Tobey, 1974.

Koenig, R. "Rape: Most Rapidly Increasing Crime." *McCalls* (July, 1973).

Lear, M.W. "Q. If You Rape a Woman and Steal Her TV, What Can They Get You for in N.Y.? A. Stealing Her TV." *New York Times Magazine* (January 10, 1972).

"Least Punished Crime." *Newsweek* (December 18, 1972).

LeGrand, C.E. "Rape and Rape Laws: Sexism in Society and Law." *California Law Review,* 61:3 (1973), pp. 919-941.

Lippman, T.W. "Rape Case that Shook Maryland: Giles Case." *Reporter,* (March 7, 1968).

MacKellar, Jean. *Rape! The Bait and the Trap.* NY: Crown, 1975.

Mead, M. "Women and the New Pornography." *Redbook* (February, 1976).

Medea, Andrea and Kathleen Thompson. *Against Rape.* NY: Farrar, Straus and Giroux, 1974.

Meyer, M. "Rape: The Victim's Point of View." *Police Law Quarterly,* 3:3 (1974), pp. 38-44.

"Portrait of a Rapist." *Newsweek* (August 20, 1973).

Powers, R.T. *Gang Rapists and Their Victims.* Chatsworth CA: Barclay House, 1973.

"Reasonable Rape; Statutory Rape." *Time* (January 21, 1968).

Roucek, Joseph S. *Sexual Attraction and the Crime of Rape.* Charlotteville, NY: Sam Har, 1975.

Russell, Diana E.H. *Politics of Rape: The Victim's Perspective.* NY: Stein and Day, 1975.

Scacco, Anthony, Jr. *Rape in Prison.* Springfield, IL: C.C. Thomas, 1975.

Schiff, Arthur F. "A Statistical Evaluation of Rape." *Forensic Science,* 2:3 (August, 1973), pp. 339-349.

Schiff, Arthur Frederick. "Statistical Features of Rape." *Journal of Forensic Science,* 14:1 (January, 1969), pp. 102-110.

Schwendinger, J.R. and H. Schwendinger. "Rape Myths in Legal, Theoretical and Everyday Practice." *Crime and Social Justice,* (1974), pp. 18-26.

Sheppard, D.I. "Denver Will Launch Attack on Rape." *Law Officer,* 6:4 (1973).

Smith, Robert and James V. Giles. *American Rape: A True Account of the Giles-Johnson Case.* (new ed.) Washington DC: New Republic, 1975.

Storaska, F. *How to Say No to a Rapist and Survive.* NY: Random, 1975.

Tabori, Paul. *The Social History of Rape.* London: New English Library, 1971.

Viano, Emilio C. "Rape and the Law in the United States: An Historical and Sociological Analysis." *International Journal of Criminology and Penology* (November, 1974), pp. 317-328.

"Victim in a Forcible Rape Case: A Feminist View." *American Criminal Law Review* (Winter, 1973).

Wilson, Cassandra and Noreen Connell. *Rape: The First Source Book for Women.* NY: New American Library, 1974.

"Women Against Rape." *Time* (April 23, 1973).

Wood, P.L. "The Victim in a Forcible Rape Case: A Feminist View." *American Criminal Law Review,* 11:2 (1973), pp. 335-354.

ROBBERY

Andrews, J.A. "Robbery." *Criminal Law Review* (October, 1966), pp. 525-528.

"Are Banks Inviting Holdups?" *Journal of American Insurance,* 44: (September-October, 1968).

"Behind the Boom in Bank Robberies." *US News and World Report* (October,23 1967), pp. 65-66.

Bratter, Herbert. "Bank Holdups Are a Growing Problem." *Banking* (April, 1968), pp. 40-41, 109.

Camp, G.M. *Nothing to Lose—A Study of Bank Robbery in America.* Ann Arbor, MI: University Microfilms, 1968.
A study of why the number of bank robberies is increasing in the face of a very high capture rate and very severe sanctions.

Chaiken, Jan M., Michael Lawless, and Keith A. Stevenson. *Impact of Police Activity on Crime: Robberies on the New York City Subway System.* NY: Rand, 1974.

Conklin, J.E. *Robbery and the Criminal Justice System.* Philadelphia: Lippincott, 1972.

Dekelper, Irene. "Some Personal Views on Hold-ups." *International Criminal Police Review* (June-July, 1975), pp. 171-175.

Dunn, Christopher S. *The Patterns of Robbery Characteristics and their Occurrence Among Social Areas.* Washington, DC: NCJRS, 1976.

Einstadter, Werner Julius. *Armed Robbery: A Career Study in Perspective.* Unpub. Doctoral Dissertation, University of California, Berkeley, 1966.

Einstadter, Werner J. "The Social Organization of Armed Robbery." *Social Problems,* 17:1 (1969), pp. 74-83.

Foldessy, Edward. "Bank Robberies Jump to 7-a-Day Rate Despite New Detection Methods." *Wall Street Journal* (February 21, 1968).

Gibson, W.B. *The Fine Art of Robbery.* NY: Grosset and Dunlap, 1966.

Hauge,Elmer. "Bank Robbery in California: A 35-Year Comparison with Other States." *Journal of California Law Enforcement* (January, 1968), pp. 138-157.

McClintock, F.H. and E. Gibson. *Robbery in London.* London: Macmillan, 1961.

McDonald, Bill. "Crimes of Violence Against Banks." *Virginia Trooper,* 16 (August, 1968), pp. 5-9.

Normandeau, Andre. "Patterns in Robbery." *Criminologica* (November, 1968).

Normandeau, Andre. "Robbery in Philadelphia and London." *British Journal of Criminology,* 9:1 (1969), pp. 71-79.

Normandeau, Andre. *Trends and Patterns in Crime of Robbery.* Unpub. Doctoral Dissertation, University of Pennsylvania, 1968.

Ozenne, T. "The Economics of Bank Robbery." *Journal of Legal Studies,* 3:1 (1974), pp. 19-51.

Remsberg, Charles. "The Heisters Increase Their Haul." *New York Times Magazine* (January 16, 1966), pp. 61, 64, 66-67.

Sutton, Willie. *Where the Money Was.* NY: Viking, 1976.

SEX CRIMES

Sex Crimes—General

Allen, Clifford. *A Textbook of Psychosexual Disorders.* NY: Oxford University Press, 1969.

Assembly, State of California. *Preliminary Report of the Subcommittee on Sex Crimes.* Sacramento: State Assembly, 1949.

Barry, John. *Abnormal Side of Sex.* Chatsworth, CA: Brandon, 1974.

Bowling, R.W. "The Sex Offender and Law Enforcement." *Federal Probation,* 14 (September, 1950), pp. 11-16.

Bowman, Karl M. *Final Report on California Sexual Deviation Research.* Sacramento, CA: State Department of Mental Hygiene, 1954.

DeRiver, Joseph Paul. *Crime and the Sexual Psychopath.* Springfield, IL: C.C. Thomas, 1958.

Doshay, Lewis Jacob. *The Boy Sex Offender and His Later Career.* NY: Grune and Stratton, 1943.

Drzazga, John. *Sex Crimes.* Springfield, IL: C.C. Thomas, 1960.

Ellis, Albert and Ralph Brancale. *The Psychology of Sex Offenders.* Springfield, IL: C.C. Thomas, 1956.

Gebhard, P. *Sex Offenders: An Analysis of Types.* NY: Harper and Row, 1965.

Hampton, Wade T. *The Sexual Psychopath.* Los Angeles: Medco, 1965.

Karpman, Banjamin. *The Sexual Offender and His Offenses, Etiology, Pathology, Psychopathology, and Treatment.* NY: Julian, 1954.

Kobler, John. "The Sex Criminal, 'I Don't Know Why I Did It'." *Saturday Evening Post,* 240 (January 28, 1967).

Masters, R.E.L. *Forbidden Sexual Behavior and Morality: An Objective Re-Examination of Perverse Sex Practices in Different Cultures.* NY: Julian, 1963.

Masters, R.E.L. and Edward Lea. *Sex Crimes in History: Evolving Concepts of Sadism, Lust-Murder, and Necrophilia from Ancient to Modern Times.* NY: Julian, 1963.

Mohr, J.R., R.E. Turner, and M.B. Jerry. *Pedophilia and Exhibitionism.* Toronto: University of Toronto Press, 1964.

Moreland, Nigel. *An Outline of Sexual Criminology.* NY: Hart, 1967.

Oliver, Bernard J. *Sexual Deviation in American Society: A Social Psychological Study of Sexual Nonconformity.* New Haven, Ct: College and University Press, 1968.

Parker, Tony. *The Hidden World of Sex Offenders.* Indianapolis: Bobbs-Merrill, 1969.

Parker, Tony. *The Twisting Lane: Some Sex Offenders.* London: Hutchinson, 1969.

Ploscowe, Morris. *Sex and the Law.* Englewood Cliffs, NJ: Prentice-Hall, 1951.

Prall, Robert H. "Sex Crime Laws Fail." *Police,* 2:4 (March-April, 1958), pp. 32-33.

Reinhardt, James Melvin. *Sex Perversions and Sex Crimes.* Springfield, IL: C.C. Thomas, 1957.

Roeburt, John. *Sex-Life and the Criminal Law: A New Book.* NY: Belmont, 1963.

Rosen, Ismond, ed. *The Pathology and Treatment of Sexual Deviation.* NY: Oxford University Press, 1964.

Ruitenbeek, Hendrik Marinus. *The Psychotherapy of Perversions.* NY: Citadel, 1967.

Sagarin, Edward. *Odd Man In: Societies of Deviants in America.* NY: Quadrange, 1969.

Sagarin, Edward and Donald MacNamara, eds. *Problems of Sex Behavior.* NY: Crowell, 1968.

Shultz, Gladys Denny. *How Many More Victims? Society and the Sex Criminal.* Philadelphia: Lippincott, 1965.

Slater, Manning R. *Sex Offenders in Group Therapy.* LA: Sherbourne, 1964.

Slovenko, Ralph. *Sexual Behavior and the Law.* Springfield, IL: C.C. Thomas, 1965.

State Department of Mental Health. *Crucial Treatment and Control of Sexual Deviation.* Lansing, MI: State Department of Mental Health, 1951.

Storr, Anthony. *Sexual Deviation.* Baltimore: Penguin, 1964.

Child Molesters

Brennan, K.S. Walsh. "Child Molesters—An Analysis." *Criminologist,* 9:32 (1974), pp. 3-12.

McCaghy, Charles H. *Child Molesters: A Study of Their Careers and Deviance.* Unpub. Doctoral Dissertation, University of Wisconsin, 1966.

Tuteur, Werner. "Child Molesters and Men Who Expose Themselves—An Anthropological Approach." *Journal of Forensic Sciences,* 8:4 (October, 1963), pp. 515-525.

Incest

Berest, Joseph J. "Medico-Legal Aspects of Incest." *Journal of Sex Research* (August, 1968), pp. 195-205.
The author suggests that incest occurs at a much higher rate than indicated by available data. No theories to date fully explain all cases of incest today. The majority of cases involve father-daughter violation. In 75% of the cases the father was a psychopath, an alcoholic or both.

Hawkes, Daniel. *The Truth About Incest.* Edinburgh: Luxor Press, 1971.

Hughes, Graham. "The Crime of Incest." *Journal of Criminal Law, Criminology and Police Science,* 55:3 (September, 1964), pp. 322-331.

Kraemer, William. *Forbidden Love: The Normal and Abnormal Love of Children.* London: Sheldon Press, 1976.

Tormes, Yvonne M. *Child Victims of Incest.* Denver, CO: American Humane Association, Childrens' Division, 1969.

Virkkunen, M. "Incest Offenses and Alcoholism." *Medicine, Science, and the Law,* 14:2 (April, 1974), pp. 124-128.

Williams, J.E. Hale. "The Neglect of Incest: A Criminologist's View." *Medicine, Science, and the Law,* 14:1 (January, 1974) pp. 64-67.

Indecent Exposure

Cabinis, D. "Female Exhibitionism." *Journal of Legal Medicine,* 71:2 (1972), pp. 126-133.

Kinsella, Harry W. "Indecent Exposure: Punishable and Unpunishable." *Military Police Journal* (June, 1973), pp. 5-7.

Leigh, L.H. "Indecency and Obscenity: Indecent Exposure." *Criminal Law Review* (August, 1975), pp. 413-420.

MacDonald, John M. *Indecent Exposure.* Springfield, IL: C.C. Thomas, 1973.

Quist, Susan. *Indecent Exposure.* NY: Walker, 1974.

Rooth, Graham. "Indecent Exposure and Exhibitionism: A Psychiatric View." *Magistrate* (June, 1972), pp. 84-86.

Samuels, Alec. "Indecent Exposure." *Solicitors Journal* (April 16, 1976), pp. 260-261.

Transvestites

Feinbloom, Deborah H. *Transvestites and Transsexuals: Mixed Views.* NY: Delacorte, 1976.

Newton, Esther. *Mother Camp: Female Impersonators in America.* Englewood Cliffs, NJ: Prentice-Hall, 1972.

Prostitution

Benjamin, Harry and R.E.L. Masters. *Prostitution and Morality.* NY: Julian, 1964.

Bullough, Vern L. *The History of Prostitution,* New Hyde Park, NY: University Books, 1964.

Esselstyn, T.C. "Prostitution in the United States." *Annals,* 376 (1968).

Greenwald, Harold. *The Call Girl.* NY: Ballantine, 1958.

Greenwald, Harold. *The Elegant Prostitute: A Social and Psychoanalytic Study.* (rev. ed.) NY: Walker, 1970.

Hall, Susan. *Ladies of the Night.* NY: Trident, 1973.

Harris, Mervyn. *Dilly Boys: Male Prostitution in Piccadilly.* London: Croom Helm, 1973.

Henriques, Fernando. *Prostitution in Europe and the Americas.* NY: Citadel, 1965.

Khalaf, Samir. *Prostitution in a Changing Society: A Sociological Survey of Legal Prostitution in Beirut.* Beirut: Khayats, 1965.

Marlowe, Kenneth. *Mr. Madam: Confessions of a Male Madam.* Los Angeles: Sherbourne, 1964.

Murtagh, John and Sara Harris. *Cast the First Stone.* NY: McGraw-Hill, 1957.

"Prostitutes: The New Breed." *Newsweek,* 78 (July 12, 1971).

Stern, Jess. *Sisters of the Night.* NY: Popular Library, 1966.

Wells, John Warren. *Tricks of the Trade: A Hooker's Handbook of Sexual Techniques.* NY: New American Library, 1970.

Winick, Charles and Paul M. Kinsie. *The Lively Commerce: Prostitution in the United States.* NY: Quadrangle, 1971.

SHOPLIFTING

Alexander, Alfred and Val Moolman. *Stealing.* NY: Cornerstone Library, 1969.

Cameron, Mary Owen. *The Booster and the Snitch.* NY: Free Press, 1964.

"Cracking Down on Shoplifters." *Business Week* (November 1, 1952).

Fein, Sherman E. and Arthur M. Maskell. *Selected Cases on the Law of Shoplifting.* Springfield, IL: C.C. Thomas, 1975.

"Houston Finds a Cure for Shoplifting Spate." *Business Week* (June 6, 1953).

Lunden, Walter A. *Shoplifting Among College Students.* Ames: Iowa State University of Science and Technology, 1966.

Robin, Gerald D. "The American Customer: Shopper or Shoplifter?" *Police,* 8:3 (January-February, 1964), pp. 6-14.

Tobias, Jerry J. "Juvenile Shoplifting in an Affluent Suburban Community." *Law and Order,* 18:9 (September, 1970), pp. 76-80.

Tocchio, O.J. "Shoplifting—The Scourge of Mercantile Establishments." *Police,* 6:5 (May-June, 1962), pp. 8-15.

SKYJACKING

Agrawala, S.K. *Aircraft Hijacking and International Law.* Dobbs, Ferry NY: Oceana, 1973.

"Air Pirates: Castro Pulls Welcome Mat." *U.S. News & World Report* (December 4, 1972).

Amdur, N. "Pilot Said: There's an Armed Man Aboard—Eastern Airlines Flight to Washington, May 5." *Saturday Review* (June 10, 1972).

"Anatomy of a Skyjacker." *Time,* (December 5, 1969).

Armbrister, T. "Code 3100: Hijacker Aboard." *Readers Digest* (September, 1972).

Brown, J.G. "Pilot's Story of a Hijacking: Pandemonium in the Cockpit; Testimony before the House Interstate and Foreign Commerce Committee." *U.S. News & World Report* (February 24, 1969).

"Dilemma of the Airlines." *Newsweek* (March 9, 1970).

"Dreadful First for Aeroflot." *Time* (October 26, 1970).

Evans, A.E. "Report on Aircraft Hijacking in the United States: Law and Practice." *Criminal Law Bulletin,* 10:7 (1974), pp. 589-604.

"Flight to Trabzon; Hijacking Against Aeroflot." *Newsweek* (October 26, 1970).

"Fly Me to Pyongyang; Japan Airlines 727." *Newsweek* (April 13, 1970).

"The Futility of Aircraft Hijacking." *FBI Law Enforcement Bulletin,* 41:10 (October, 1972), pp. 16-17.

"Havana Top: Hassle Over Hijacking." *Senior Scholastic* (March 7, 1969).

"Hi Jack, Hi Fidel." *New Republic* (January 25, 1969).

"High and the Mighty: California to Rome Hijacking." *Newsweek* (November 10, 1969).

"Hijacking and Justice." *Commonwealth* (March 2, 1973).

Hubbard, D.G. *The Skyjacker: His Flights of Fantasy.* NY: Macmillan, 1971.

Lawrence, D. "Aerial Piracy: An International Crime." *U.S. News & World Report* (September 21, 1970).

McWhinney, Edward, ed. *Aerial Piracy and International Law.* Dobbs Ferry, NY: Oceana, 1971.

O'Donnel, John J. *Skyjacking: Problems and Potential Solutions.* Villanova, PA: Villanova University Press, 1973.

"Skyjackers Grow Bolder—But Most of Them Are Losers." *U.S. News & World Report* (April 24, 1972).

"Skyjacking: Constitutional Problems Raised by Anti-hijacking Systems." *Journal of Criminal Law, Criminology and Police Science,* 63:3 (1975), pp. 356-365.

Zeichner, Irving B. "Anti-Air Hijack Profile." *Law and Order* (October, 1972).

SMUGGLING

Dunn, John, ed. *Gold Smugglers.* New Rochelle, NY: Soccer, [n.d.].

Fraser, Duncan. *The Smugglers.* Montrose, Angus: Standard Press, 1971.

Green, Timothy. *The Smuggler: An Investigation into the World of the Contemporary Smuggler.* NY: Walker, 1969.

Kleiner, Richard. *Smugglers, Handbook.* NY: Drake, 1975.

Philipson, David. *Smuggling: History, 1700-1790.* Newton-Abbot, Devon: David and Charles, 1973.

Pringle, Patrick. *Smugglers.* NY: International Publications Service, 1965.

THEFT

Alexander, Alfred and Val Moolman. *Stealing.* NY: Cornerstone Library, 1968.

Frailing, Robert H. "Bicycle Theft—A Serious Crime." *FBI Law Enforcement Bulletin,* 43:6, pp. 7-10.

Gadwall, Graham. "Employee Perks—Tip of the Iceberg or Thin Edge of the Wedge? Protection of Company Assets from the Broader Viewpoint." *Security Gazette* (October, 1975), pp. 348-349.

Hancock, Nick. "Thefts from Construction Sites: Rip-offs That Get Written Off." *Canadian Police Chief* (July, 1976), pp. 6-8.

Horning, Donald N.M. *Blue Collar Theft: A Study of Pilfering By Industrial Workers.* Unpub. Doctoral Dissertation, Indiana University, 1963.

Kind, S.S., R.A. Outteridge, and E.A. Kilner. "Larceny of Poultry." *Police Journal,* 36:10 (October, 1963), pp. 481-485.

Lipman, M. *Stealing—How America's Employees Are Stealing Their Companies Blind.* NY: Harper and Row, 1973.
Expose of widespread theft of vast amount of merchandise from American companies by their employees.

Peabody, Robert R. "The New Thief on Campus." *Police Chief,* XLII:10 (October, 1975), pp. 246-247.
Study of bicycle theft on college campuses.

Reynolds, M.O. *Crime for Profit: Economics of Theft.* Ann Arbor, MI: University Microfilm, 1970.

TREASON

Beirne, Francis F. *Shout Treason: The Trial of Aaron Burr.* NY: Hastings, 1959.

Chambers, Whittaker. *Witness.* Chicago: Regnery, 1968.

Cooke, Alistair. *A Generation on Trial U.S.A. vs. Alger Hiss.* NY: Knopf, 1952.

Dreyer, P. *Future of Treason.* NY: Ballantine, 1973.
Autobiography of a South African expatriot, presumably guilty of treason in his own country.

Ducann, Charles G.L. *Famous Treason Trials.* NY: Walker, 1964.

Fineberg, S. Andhil. *The Rosenberg Case: Fact and Fiction.* Dobbs Ferry, NY: Oceana, 1953.

Forman, Lionel and E.S. (Solly) Sachs. *The South African Treason Trial.* NY: Monthly Review, 1958.

Grodzins, Morton. *The Loyal and the Disloyal: Social Boundaries of Patriotism and Treason.* Chicago: Chicago University Press, 1956.

Reuben, William A. *Frame-Up: Nixon vs. Alger Hiss.* NY: Stonehill, 1976.

Root, Jonathan. *The Betrayers: The Rosenberg Case: A Reappraisal of an American Crisis.* NY: Coward, 1963.

Sharp, Malcolm P. *Was Justice Done? The Rosenberg-Sobell Case.* NY: Monthly Review, 1956.

Smith, John C. *Alger Hiss.* NY: Holt, Rinehart and Winston, 1976.

West, Rebecca. *The New Meaning of Treason.* NY: Viking, 1964.

Zeligs, Meyer A. *Friendship and Fratricide.* NY: Viking, 1967.

VANDALISM

Clinard, Marshall B. and Andrew L. Wade. "Toward the Delineation of Vandalism as a Sub-type in Juvenile Delinquency." *Journal of Criminal Law, Criminology and Police Science,* 48:5 (January-February, 1958), pp. 493-499.

Goldmeier, H. "Vandalism: The Effects of Unmanageable Confrontations." *Adolescence,* 9:33 (1974), pp. 49-56.
Analyzes the vindictive vandal.

Grubbs, Frank L. "Vandalism to Rail Shipments of New Autos." *FBI Law Enforcement Bulletin,* 36:4 (April, 1967), pp. 2-6.

Kobetz, Richard W. "Juvenile Vandalism: The Billion Dollar Prank." *Police Chief,* XL:6 (June, 1973), pp. 32-35.

Lee, George E. "Vandalism and Neglect Still the Silent Voices." *Law and Order,* 12:6 (June, 1964), pp. 32-35.

Madison, Arnold. *Vandalism: The Not-So-Senseless Crime.* NY: Seabury, 1970.

Moll, K.D. *Arson, Vandalism and Violence—Law Enforcement Problems Affecting Fire Departments.* Washington, DC: GPO, 1972.
Study based on a comprehensive statistical data base of metropolitan fire department problems related to violence.

Sager, D. "Vandalism in Libraries: How Senseless Is It?" *Library Security Newsletter,* 1:1 (1975).

Sanders, M. and J.M. Welton. *Vandalism.* Springfield, VA: NTIS, 1972.
Review of current literature on vandalism, investigation into the nature of railroad vandalism, and recommendations for future research.

Schnell, John B. et al. *Vandalism and Passenger Security—A Study of Crime and Vandalism on Urban Mass Transit Systems in the United States and Canada: Final Report.* Springfield, VA: NTIS, 1973.

Shaw, William. "School Vandalism Problem." *Law and Order,* 20:5 (May, 1972), pp. 14, 16, 18-19, 34-35, and 20:6 (June, 1972), pp. 40-46.

Shaw, William. "Vandalism is Not Senseless." *Law and Order,* 21:2 (February, 1973), pp. 14-19.

Solomon, Ben. "The Anatomy of Vandalism." *Police,* 6:6 (July-August, 1962), pp. 26-29.

Vicino, F.L. and D. Peterson. *Mesa (AZ)—Public Schools—Vandalism and Theft Analysis, 1973-74.* Washington, DC: NCJRS, (Microfiche), 1974.

Wickam, Fred J. "Vandalism of Highway Traffic Signs." *FBI Law Enforcement Bulletin,* 36:4 (April, 1967), pp. 14-15.

Zimbardo, P.G. *Social-Psychological Analysis of Vandalism—Making Sense of Senseless Violence.* Springfield, VA: NTIS, 1970.
Economic discrimination encourages the anti-social behavior of vandalism but understanding the source of this alienation from property may lead to the remedy.

VICTIMLESS CRIMES

Barnett, W. *Sexual Freedom and the Constitution—An Inquiry into the Constitutionality of Repressive Sex Laws.* Albuquerque: New Mexico University Press, 1973.
Discussion of current constitutional arguments that are available to attack criminal laws on sex so as to exclude from their scope activities between consenting adults.

Davis, Edward M. "Victimless Crimes—The Case for Continued Enforcement." *Journal of Police Science and Administration,* 1:1 (March, 1973), pp. 11-20.

Geis, Gilbert. *Not the Law's Business—An Examination of Homosexuality, Abortion, Prostitution, Narcotics, and Gambling in the United States.* Washington, DC: GPO, 1972.
Discussion using material from an interdisciplinary range of literature, including law, psychology, sociology, and anthropology.

Geis, Gilbert. *Victimless Crimes.* NY: St. Martin, 1975.

Gitchoff, G. Thomas, Joseph Ellenbogen, and Elsie Ellenbogen. "Victimless Crimes: The Case Against Continued Enforcement." *Journal of Police Science and Administration,* 1:4 (December, 1973), pp. 401-408.

Kiester, E. *Crimes with No Victims—How Legislating Morality Defeats the Cause of Justice.* NY: Alliance for a Safer New York, 1972.
Survey of the social and economic costs to society of such victimless crimes as prostitution, homosexual activities and drunkenness.

Los Angeles Police Department. *Position Paper on Victimless Crimes.* Los Angeles: LAPD, March, 1972.

Los Angeles Police Department. *Victimless Crimes: A Research Project.* Los Angeles: LAPD, May, 1972.

Presidents Commission on Law Enforcement and Administration of Justice. *Task Force Report—Drunkenness.* Washington, DC; GPO, 1967.
Present methods of treating drunkenness offenders and an exploration of promising alternatives are re-examined.

Rooney, Elizabeth A. and Don C. Gibbons. "Social Reactions to 'Crimes Without Victims'." *Social Problems,* 13:4 (Spring, 1966), pp. 400-410.

San Francisco Committee on Crime. *San Francisco Committee on Crime—A Report on Non-Victim Crime in San Francisco—Part 3—Dangerous Drugs and Narcotics.* (11th rep.) Washington,DC: NCJRS, 1971.
This subject of drugs and narcotics is the most difficult to analyze and resolve of all those discussed in the report on non-victim crime.

San Francisco Committee on Crime. *San Francisco Committee on Crime—A Report on Non-Victim Crime in San Francisco—Part 2—Sexual Conduct, Gambling, Pornography.* (7th rep.) Washington, DC: NCJRS, 1971.
It is in matters of sex that criminal law has made its boldest efforts to legislate morals.

San Francisco Committee on Crime. *San Francisco—Non-Victim Crime Report—Part 1—Non-Victim Crime in San Francisco—Part 1—Basic Principles, Public Drunkenness.* Washington, DC: NCJRS, 1971.
The San Francisco Committee on Crime has the duty of reporting and making recommendations for a more effective and economical system of criminal law.

Sasser, Charles W. "Crime Without Victims." *Law and Order,* 23:6 (June, 1975), pp. 66-70.

Schur, E.M. *Crimes Without Victims—Deviant Behavior and Public Policy, Abortion, Homosexuality, Drug Addiction.* Englewood Cliffs, NJ: Prentice-Hall, 1965.
Sociological perspective on deviant behavior in relation to human needs, social values and institutions.

Schur, Edwin M. and Hugo A. Bedau. *Victimless Crimes: Two Sides of a Controversy.* Englewood Cliffs, NJ: Prentice-Hall, 1974.

Smith, A.B. and H. Pollack. "Crimes Without Victims." *Saturday Review* (December 4, 1971).

Westbrook, J.W. "Crimes Without Plaintiffs: The Challenging Concept of 'Victimless Crimes'." *Baylor Law Review,* 25:1 (1973), pp. 37-51.

WAR CRIMES

Appleman, John Alan. *Military Tribunals and International Crime.* Indianapolis: Bobbs-Merril, 1954.

Blum, Howard. *Wanted! The Search for Nazis in America.* NY: Quadrangle, 1976.

Creel, George. *War Criminals and Punishment.* NY: McBride, 1944.

Davidson, Eugene. *The Nuremberg Fallacy: Wars and War Crimes Since World War II.* NY: Macmillan, 1973.

Davidson, Eugene. *Trial of the Germans: An Account of the Twenty-Two Defendants Before the International Tribunal Nuremburg.* NY: Macmillan, 1972.

Dicks, Henry V. *Licensed Mass Murder: A Socio-Psychological Study of Some S.S. Killers.* NY: Basic, 1972.

Gilbert, G.M. *Nuremberg Diary.* NY: Farrar, 1947.

Glueck, Sheldon. *The Nuremberg Trial and Aggressive War.* NY: Knopf, 1946.

Harris, Whitney R. *Tyranny on Trial: The Evidence at Nuremberg.* Dallas, TX: Southern Methodist University Press, 1954.

Heydecker, Joe and Johannes Leeb. *The Nuremberg Trial.* Westport, CT: Greenwood, 1975. (repr. of 1962 ed.).

Horowitz, Irving L. *Genocide: State Power and Mass Murder.* Edison, NJ: Transaction, 1976.

Horwicz, Solis. *The Tokyo Trial.* NY: Carnegie, 1950.

Jackson, Robert H. *Nuremberg Case.* NY: Cooper Square, 1972. (repr. of 1947).

Kintner, Earl W., ed. *War Crimes Trials.* (vol. IV). *The Hadamar Trial.* London: Hodge, 1949.

Knoll, Erwin and Judith Neis McFadden, eds. *War Crimes and the American Conscience.* NY: Holt, 1970.

Minear, Richard H. *Victors' Justice: The Tokyo War Crimes Trial.* Princeton: Princeton University Press, 1971.

Reel, A. Frank. *Case of General Yamashita.* NY: Octagon, 1971.

Russell, Edward Frederick Langley. *The Knights of Bushido—A Short History of Japanese War Crimes.* London: Cassell, 1958.

Russell, Edward Frederick Langley. *The Scourge of the Swastika: A Short History of Nazi War Crimes.* London: Cassell, 1954.

Smith, Bradley F. *Reaching Judgement at Nuremberg.* NY: Basic, 1976.

Spaight, James M. *War Rights on Land.* London: Macmillan, 1911.

Stevens, E.H., ed. *Trial of Nikolaus Von Falkenhorst, Formerly Generalobert in the German Army.* Glasgow: Hodge, 1949.

Taft, D.R. "The Punishment of War Criminals." *American Sociological Review,* 11 (August, 1946), pp. 439-444.

Taylor, Telford. *Nuremberg Trials, War Crimes and International Law.* NY: Carnegie, 1949.

Trial of the Major War Criminals Before the International Military Tribunal. (42 vols.) NY: AMS, 1971. (repr. of 1949 ed.).

Woetzel, Robert K. *The Nuremberg Trials in International Law.* London: Stevens, 1960.

Zawodny, J.K. *Death in the Forest: The Story of the Katyn Forest Massacre.* Notre Dame, IN: University of Notre Dame Press, 1972.

WHITE COLLAR CRIME

Adams, Silas Walter. *The Legalized Crime of Banking.* Boston: Meador, 1958.

Aubert, Vilhelm. "White Collar Crime and Social Structure." *American Journal of Sociology,* LVIII (November, 1952), pp. 263-271.

"Bank Embezzlement Shows Big Increase Over Pre-War Years." *FBI Law Enforcement Bulletin* (April, 1952).

"Bank Fraud and Embezzlement." *FBI Law Enforcement Bulletin* (February, 1975).

Bennett, John C. *Outlaws in Swivel Chairs.* NY: Comet, 1958.

"Call for Diogenes; Billie Sol Estes Case." *Nation* (June 2, 1962).

Chamber of Commerce of the United States. *Handbook on White Collar Crime—Everyone's Problem, Everyone's Loss.* Washington, DC: Chamber of Commerce of the United States, 1974.

"Corporate Crime Wave." *Nation* (September 6, 1975), pp. 164-165.

Cort, D. "Embezzler." *Nation* (April 18, 1959).

Curtis, S.J. "Focus on the Future—A Look at Business Crime Today and Tomorrow." *Police,* 8:3 (January-February, 1964), pp. 20-24.

Dansinger, S.J. "Embezzling Primer." *Computers and Automation* (November, 1967).

Davids, Leo. "Penology and Corporate Crime." *Journal of Criminal Law, Criminology and Police Science,* 58:4 (December, 1967), pp. 524-531.

"Economic Crime: The Crippler." *FBI Law Enforcement Bulletin* (March, 1975).

Edelhertz, M. *Nature, Impact and Prosecution of White-Collar Crime.* Washington, DC: GPO, 1970.
Concern with street and organized crime has diverted public resources from white-collar crime which is viewed by being socially destructive and costly.

"Embezzlement—Motives, Methods and Precautions." *FBI Law Enforcement Bulletin,* 27:8 (August, 1958), pp. 15-18.

"Embezzlement Up: More Bank Employees Take More Money." *Business Week* (September 4, 1948).

"The Forty Thieves." *FBI Law Enforcement Bulletin,* 39:7 (July, 1970), pp. 16-19, 29-30.

Geis, Gilbert. "Toward a Delineation of White Collar Offenses." *Sociological Inquiry,* 32:171 (1962).

Geis, Gilbert., ed. *White-Collar Criminal: The Offender in Business and the Professions.* NY: Atherton, 1968.

Gibney, Frank. *The Operators.* NY: Harper, 1960.

"Growing Toll of Crimes Against Business." *U.S. News & World Report* (October 2, 1972).

Hartung, Frank E. "White Collar Offenses in the Wholesale Meat Industry in Detroit." *American Journal of Sociology,* LVI (July, 1950), pp. 25-35.

Hymoff, E. "Executive Rip-Off." *Harpers* (October, 1972).

Jaspan, N. *The Thief in the White Collar.* Philadelphia: Lippincott, 1960.

Kelley, Clarence M. "White-Collar Crime—A Serious Problem." *FBI Law Enforcement Bulletin* (September, 1974).

Kirk, J. "Wall Street Takes Stock of Stock Taking." *Banking* (January, 1970).

Laing, Philip P. "Hidden Crime, the Story of Embezzlement." *Police,* 4:1 (September-October, 1959), pp. 58-60.

Loughton, F. *Fraud and White-Collar Crime.* London: Elek, 1971.

McMenimen, H.N. *High Profitability—The Reward for Price-Fixing.* Washington DC: National Institute of Municipal Law Officers 1969.
Overcharge through conspirational activities and the span of years which the conspiracy has been in effect in New York City.

Nader, R. and M. Greer. "Crime in the Suites." *New Republic* (April 29, 1972).

National District Attorneys Association. *Economic Crime Project Newsletter, May-June-July 1974.* Washington, DC: NCJRS, (Microfiche), 1974.

Quinney, Earl R. "The Study of White Collar Crime: Toward a Reorientation in Theory and Practice." *Journal of Criminal Law, Criminology and Police Science.* 55:2 (June, 1964), pp. 208-214.

Randall, K.A. "Wheeler-Dealers and the Banking System" *Banking* (July, 1964).

Rice, R. *Business of Crime.* Westport, CT: Greenwood, 1956.
Account of five different twentieth century "business crimes"—criminal activities that have operated as businesses.

Robin, Gerald D. "White-Collar Crime and Employee Theft." *Crime and Delinquency* (July, 1974), pp. 251-262.

Schornack, J.J. "How the Embezzler Does His Thing." *Supervisory Management* (June, 1969).

"Scratching the Surface: Financial Dishonesty Among Government Employees." *Nation* (January 4, 1965).

"Scratchy Suit: R. Paul Weesner Accused of Embezzling $500,000." *Newsweek* (July 23, 1962).

Shrake, E. "Just a Simple Little Country Girl: Embezzling Funds Raised for Olympic Games." *Sports Illustrated* (April 15, 1968).

Sutherland, E.H. "Is White Collar Crime Crime?" *American Sociological Review* (April, 1945).

Sutherland, E.H. "White Collar Criminality." *American Sociological Review* (February, 1940).

Sutherland, Edwin H. *White Collar Crime.* NY: Holt, Rinehart and Winston, 1949.

"The Thief Inside." *Office,* 72 (August, 1970), pp. 12-15.

"Trusted Employees Can Be Worst Business Crooks." *Office* (October, 1967).

United States Department of Justice, Law Enforcement Assistance Administration. *The Nature, Impact and Prosecution of White-Collar Crime.* Washington, DC: GPO, 1970.

Votey, H.L. *Economic Crimes—Their Generation, Deterrence and Control.* Springfield, VA: NTIS, 1969.

Wade, M. and A. Leigh. "Embezzlement: An Expose of How the Executive Thief Operates and How He Gets Caught." *Business Management* (April, 1967).

"White Collar Thieves." *Credit and Financial Management* (October, 1968).

"Why Do Trusted Persons Commit Fraud?" *Journal of Accountancy* (November, 1951).

Ziegler, E.W. "Plus All You Can Steal: Larceny in Industry." *Nation* (September 12, 1959).

WIFE BEATING

"Battered Wives: Chiswick Woman's Aid." *Newsweek,* 82 (July 9, 1973).

"Battered Wives: How They're Fighting Back." *U.S. News & World Report,* 81 (September 20, 1976).

"Family Violence Study Purports Physical Force Is Commonplace." *Crime Control Digest,* 10:9 (March 1, 1976), pp. 3-4.

Francke, L.B. "Battered Women." *Newsweek,* 87 (February 2, 1976).

Jobling, M. "Battered Wives: A Survey." *Social Service Quarterly,* 47:4 (1974), pp. 142-146.

MacKenzie B. "Battered Women and the Law." *Police Review,* 83:4294 (1975).

Martin, Del. *Battered Wives.* San Francisco: Glide, 1976.

Pizzey, Erin. *Scream Quietly or the Neighbors Will Hear.* Harmondsworth: Penguin, 1974.

Scott, P.D. "Battered Wives." *British Journal of Psychiatry,* 125 (November, 1974), pp. 433-441.

PART XVI
ISSUES IN CRIMINAL JUSTICE

CRIMINAL JUSTICE—ISSUES AND PROBLEMS

CRIMINAL JUSTICE—GENERAL

Allen, F.A. *Borderland of Criminal Justice—Essays in Law and Criminology.* Chicago: University of Chicago Press, 1969.

The central problem of criminal justice remains essentially the political one of the relationship between the individual citizen and state.

American Friends Service Committee. *Struggle for Justice: A Report on Crime and Punishment in America.* N.Y.: Hill and Wang, 1971.

Becker, Harold K., George T. Felkenes, and Paul M. Whisenand. *New Dimensions in Criminal Justice.* Metuchen, N.J.: Scarecrow, 1968.

Blanchard, R.E. *Introduction to the Administration of Justice.* N.Y.: Wiley, 1975.

Blumberg, A.S. *Scales of Justice.* (2nd ed.) N.Y.: Dutton, 1973.

Collection of articles on different aspects of the United States system of justice, its problems, and inequalities.

Bratoon, Howard C. "Standards for the Administration of Criminal Justice." *Natural Resources Journal,* 10 (January, 1970), pp. 127-136.

Discusses history, development, objectives of American Bar Associations Project on Standards of Criminal Justice relating to police functions, pre-trial proceedings, criminal trials, prosecution and defense functions, sentencing and review.

Burger, Warren E. "Paradoxes in the Administration of Criminal Justice." *Journal of Criminal Law, Criminology and Police Science,* 58:4 (December, 1967), pp. 428-432.

Carter, Robert M. et al. "The Uncertain Future of Criminal Justice." *Police Chief,* XXXVII:5 (May, 1971), pp. 56-60.

Chambliss, William J. *Crime and the Legal Process.* N.Y.: McGraw-Hill, 1968.

"The Criminal Justice System." *Police Chief,* XLI:6 (June, 1974), pp. 56, 78.

Curran, James T., Austin Fowler, and Richard H. Ward, eds. *Police and Law Enforcement, 1972: An AMS Anthology.* N.Y.: AMS, 1973.

Eldefonso, Edward, Alan Coffey, and Richard C. Grace. *Principles of Law Enforcement.* N.Y.: Wiley, 1968.

Felkenes, George T. *Criminal Justice System—Its Functions and Personnel.* Englewood Cliffs, N.J.: Prentice-Hall, 1973.

Germann, A.C., F.D. Day, and R.R.J. Gallati. *Introduction to Law Enforcement and Criminal Justice.* Springfield, IL.: C.C. Thomas, 1972.

Ginsberg, M. "Rural Criminal Justice: An Overview." *American Journal of Criminal Law,* 3:1 (1974), pp. 35-51.

Goldman, Peter and Don Holt. "How Justice Works." *Newsweek,* LXXVII (March 8, 1971), pp. 20-46.

A young Chicago nergo is arrested for armed robbery. This article is the story of his trip through the criminal justice system and his subsequent imprisonment. The agencies and individuals involved with this man are also interviewed and studied thus giving a fairly accurate picture of what is happening to the justice system in a large metropolitan area.

Horgan, John J. *Criminal Justice.* N.Y.: McGraw-Hill, 1974.

Jackson, R.M. *Enforcing the Law.* (rev. ed.) Baltimore: Penguin, 1971.

Killinger, George G. and Paul F. Cromwell. *Issues in Law Enforcement.* Boston: Holbrook, 1975.

LeGrande, James L. *The Basic Process of Criminal Justice.* Beverly Hill, CA.: Glencoe, 1973.

Maryland University Institute of Criminal Justice and Criminology. *National Advisory Commission on Criminal Justice Standards and Goals—Progress Report—May, 1972.* Springfield, VA: NTIS, 1972.

Progress of the commission in developing national goals, performance standards, and priorities for reducing crime and delinquency.

Meyers, William, ed. *Justice in America.* N.Y.: Gordon and Breach, 1972.

Mills, James. *On the Edge.* Garden City, N.Y.: Doubleday, 1975.

Review of those caught up in an inadequate criminal justice system.

More, Harry W., Jr. and Richard Chang. *Contemporary Criminal Justice.* San Jose, CA.: Justice Systems Development, 1974.

Morris, N. *Aldine Crime and Justice Annual,* 1973. Chicago: Aldine, 1974.

Composed mainly of journal reprints, this reader contains what its editorial board considers to be the most important work on the subject of criminal justice from 1973.

Neubauer, David W. *Criminal Justice in Middle America.* Morristown, N.J.: General Learning, 1974.

Newman, D.J. *Introduction to Criminal Justice.* Philadelphia: Lippincott, 1975.

Perlman M. and N. Morris. *Law and Crime: Essays in Honor of Sir John Barry.* N.Y.: Gordon, 1972.

Pound, R. *Criminal Justice in America.* N.Y.: Da Capo, 1975.

Prassel, Frand R. *Introduction to American Criminal Justice.* N.Y.: Harper and Row, 1975.

President's Commission on Law Enforcement and Administration of Justice. *The Challenge of Crime in a Free Society.* Washington, D.C.: GPO, 1967.

Quinney, R. *Crime and Justice in Society.* Boston: Little Brown, 1969.

Remington, Frank J. et al. *Criminal Justice Administration.* Indianapolis: Bobbs-Merrill, 1968.

Rich, V. *Law and the Administration of Justice.* N.Y.: Wiley, 1975.

Riddle, Donald H. "The Emerging Field of Criminal Justice." *Police Chief,* XXXVII:8 (August, 1970), pp. 18-21.

Riesau, Victor D. "An Integrated Justice System." *Police Chief,* XXXVI:2 (February, 1969), pp. 48-54.

Schrag, C. *Crime and Justice—American Style.* Washington, D.C.: GPO, 1971.
A review of recent literature which surveys the state of the system of justice, identifies its major problems and assesses some of the more promising developments.

Schultz, Donald O. *Critical Issues in Criminal Justice.* Springfield, IL.: C.C. Thomas, 1975.

Silva, John W. *Introduction to Crime and Justice.* N.Y.: MSS Information, 1973.

Smith, A.B. *Crime and Justice in a Mass Society.* N.Y.: Holt, Rinehart and Winston, 1972.
Overview of the urban criminal justice system focusing on the development and evolution of the courts, the concepts of crime and criminal responsibility, and the functions of police, prosecution, and corrections.

Stuckey, Gilbert B. *Procedures in the Justice System.* Columbus, OH.: Merrill, 1976.

Swaton, J. Norman and Loren Morgan. *Administration of Justice: An Introduction.* N.Y.: Van Nostrand, 1975.

Trojanowicz, Robert C. and Samuel L. Dixon. *Criminal Justice and the Community.* Englewood Cliffs, N.J.: Prentice-Hall, 1974.

United Nations. Legislative and Administrative Series. *Social Defense—Prevention of Crime and Treatment of Offenders, Suppression of Traffic in Persons and of Exploitation of the Prostitution of Others.* N.Y.: Columbia University Press, March, 1953.

BAIL

American Bar Association. *Pretrial Release, Standards Relating to.* Chicago: American Bar Association, 1968.

"Bail—Ancient Practice Reexamined." *Yale Law Journal,* 70 (1961).

Clarke, S.H. *Evaluation of the Bail System in Charlotte-Mecklenbury, 1971-1972.* Springfield, VA.: NTIS, 1973.

Conklin, John E. and Dermot Meagher. "The Percentage Deposit Bail System: An Alternative to the Professional Bondsman." *Journal of Criminal Justice,* (1973), pp. 299-317.

De Haas, E. *Antiquities of Bail: Original and Historical Development in Criminal Cases to The Year 1275.* N.Y.: Columbia University Press, 1940.

Donelan, Charles A. "The Bondsman's Right to Arrest." *FBI Law Enforcement Bulletin,* 42:12 (December, 1972), pp. 25-28; 42:1 (January, 1973), pp. 9-13.

Freed, D.J. *Bail in the United States—1964.* Springfield, VA.: NITIS, 1964.
This report deals with the history of bail, the way it operates (1964) and the problem it creates.

Goldfarb, Ronald. *Ransom: A Critique of the American Bail System.* N.Y.: Harper and Row, 1965.

Hongisto, R.D. and C. Levine. "Workable Alternatives to the Present Bail System." *California State Bar Journal,* 47:6 (1972), pp. 577-581, 632-638.

Icf, Inc. *Evaluation of the 'Implementation of Bail Bond Project.'* Washington, D.C.: NCJRS, (Microfiche), 1973.

"Institution of Bail as Related to Indigent Defendants." *Louisiana Law Review,* 21 (1961).

Landis, Eugene A., Jr. "A Survey of Bail in the United States: Historical Development, Problems, Reforms, and Importance to the Police Profession." *Police,* (May-June, 1966).

McCarthy, David J., Jr. "Practical Results of Bail Reform." *Federal Probation,* (September, 1965).

Murphy, J.J. "Revision of State Bail Laws." *Ohio State Law Journal,* 32 (1971), pp. 451-486.

"Preliminary Examination Before Magistrates-Bailing of Accused" *Justice of the Peace,* (July 19, 1947), pp. 399-400.

Ryan, John V. "The Last Days of Bail." *Journal of Criminal Law, Criminology and Police Science,* 58:2 (December, 1967), pp. 542-550.

Skousen, W. Cleon. "The Newest Trend: Releasing Prisoners Without Bail." *Law and Order,* 13:12 (December, 1965), pp. 12-14, 16, 94.

Thomas, Wayne. *Bail Reform in America.* Berkeley: University of California Press, 1976.

Vera Institute of Justice. *National Conference on Bail and Criminal Justice. Proceedings of May 1964 and Interim Report April 1965.* Springfield, VA.: NTIS, [n.d.].

Walsh, David E. "Pre-Trial Release on Citation." *Police Chief,* XXXV:5 (May, 1968), pp. 56-57.

Wice, P.B. *Bail and Its Reform—A National Survey—Summary.* Washington, D.C.: GPO, 1973.
Empirical investigation of pretrial release in the United States, examing the traditional bail system and bail reform projects.

Wice, P.B. "Nonjudicial Actors." in P.B. Wice. *Freedom for Sale.* Lexington, MA.: D.C. Heath, 1974.

Wilson, Jerry V. "Bail Release Problems." *Journal of California Law Enforcement,* (January, 1970), pp. 132-137.

BEHAVIOR MODIFICATION

Barber, B. and S.J. Lally. *Research on Human Subjects—Problems of Social Control in Medical Experimentation.* N.Y.: Basic, 1973.

The expressed ethical standards on the use of human subjects in biomedical experimentation were compared to actual practices by researchers in this empirical study.

Hilts, Philip J. *Behavior Mod.* N.Y.: Harpers Magazine Press, 1975.

Jehu, Derek. *Behavior Modification in Social Work.* N.Y.: Wiley, 1972.

Kazdin. A.E. *Behavior Modification in Applied Settings.* Homewood, IL.: Dorsey, 1975.

Applications of operant principles, the implementation of behavior modification techniques, and measurement and evaluation of program effectiveness applied to such settings as hospitals, institutions, and schools.

Kennedy, Daniel B. and August Kerber. *Resocialization: An American Experiment.* N.Y.: Behavioral, 1973.

Koskoff, Yale D. *The Loser, Dark Side of the House.* N.Y.: Dial, 1968, pp. 165-205.

This section is a biography of Millard Wright a Pittsburg house burglar who underwent a lobotomy in hopes of curing his criminal tendencies. Having been released from prison about one and a half years after the lobotomy, Wright returned to his community and lead a normal life for about a year. He married and very quickly returned to crime of burglarizing for furs, jewelry and small appliances. He was arrested and returned to jail. During the night he committed suicide by cutting his wrists with his eye glasses. The surgeon who performed the lobotomy felt that Wright's brain was not changed but the lesions caused behavioral changes that were complex with regard to awareness, feelings, words and thoughts.

Martin, Reed. *Legal Challenges to Behavior Modifications: Trends in Schools, Corrections, and Mental Health.* Glen Rock, N.J.: Research, 1975.

Mikulas, William L. *Behavior Modification: An Overview.* N.Y.: Harper and Row, 1972.

Pizzat, F.J. *Behavior Modification in Residential Treatment for Children—Model of a Program.* N.Y.: Behavioral, 1973.

Implementing a program using the principles of operant conditioning with emotionally disturbed children.

Poteet, James A. *Behavior Modification.* Minneapolis: Burgess, 1973.

Sansweet, Stephen J. *The Punishment Cure.* N.Y.: Mason Charter, 1975.

Describes aversion therapy.

Schrag, Peter and Diane Divoky. *The Myth of the Hyperactive Child.* N.Y.: Pantheon, 1975.

Stumphauzer, Jerome S. *Behavior Therapy with Delinquents.* Springfield, IL.: C.C. Thomas, 1973.

Sundel, Martin and Sandra S. Sundel. *Behavior Modification in the Human Services: A Systematic Approach to Concepts and Applications.* N.Y.: Wiley, 1975.

U.S. Congress. House Subcommittee on Courts, Civil Liberties, and the Administration of Justice. *Behavior Modification Programs—Federal Bureau of Prisons—Hearing Before the House Subcommittee on Courts, Civil Liberties, and the Administration of Justice, February 27, 1974.* Washington, D.C.: NCJRS, (Microfiche), 1974.

Testimony and other materials concerning the extent to which behavior modification is being conducted and planned and the bureau's plans for the federal center for correctional research in Butner, North Carolina.

BRAINWASHING

Biderman, Albert D. *March to Calumny: The Story of America P.O.W.'s in the Korean War.* N.Y.: Macmillan, 1963.

Brown, James A.C. *Techniques of Persuasian: From Propaganda to Brainwashing.* Baltimore: Penguin, 1963.

Bryan, William H. *Legal Aspects of Hypnotism.* Springfield, IL.: C.C. Thomas, 1962.

Covers brainwashing. pp. 249-255.

Hunter, Edward. *Brainwashing: From Pavlov to Powers.* N.Y.: Bookmailer, 1960.

Lyng, John F.X. "Brainwashing and the Word Game." *Law and Order,* 18:9 (September, 1970), pp. 70, 72-73.

Meeloo, Joost A.M. *The Rape of the Mind: The Psychology of Thought Control, Menticide and Brainwashing.* Cleveland: World, 1956.

Schein, Edgar H. *Coercive Persuasion: A Social-Psychological Analysis of the "Brainwashing" of American Civilian Prisoners by the Chinese Communists.* N.Y.: Norton, 1961.

CAMERA IN THE COURTROOM

Geis, Gilbert and R.E.L. Talley. "Cameras in the Courtroom." *Journal of Criminal Law, Criminology and Police Science,* 47:5 (January-February, 1957), pp. 546-560.

Kingbury, N. and D. Corrigan. *Potential Uses of Court Related Video Recording.* Springfield, VA.: NTIS, 1972.

Survey on the availability and suitability of equipment, video recording experiments underway in local courts, and attitudinal and legal barriers to video applications.

Tuttle, Harris B. "Mock Trial Highlights Camera Use in Courts." *Police,* 4:5 (May-June, 1960), p. 74.

CAPITAL PUNISHMENT

American Bar Association, Section of Criminal Law. "Pros and Cons of Capital Punishment." *Proceedings,* (August 24-26, 1959), pp. 5-25.

American Law Institute and American Bar Association. Joint Committee on Continuing Legal Education. *The Problem of Punishing Homicide.* Philadelphia: American Law Institute, 1962.

Bacon, G. Richard, ed. "Capital Punishment." *Prison Journal,* 38 (October, 1958), pp. 34-74.

Bailey, William C. "Murder and Capital Punishment: Some Further Evidence." *American Journal of Orthopsychiatry,* (July, 1975).

Bailey, William C. "Use of the Death Penalty v. Outrage at Murder." *Crime and Delinquency,* (January, 1976).

Barzon, Jacques. "In Favor of Capital Punishment." *Crime and Delinquency,* 15:1 (January, 1969), pp. 21-42.

Bedau, Hugo Adam. *The Death Penalty in America.* (2nd ed.) Chicago: Aldine, 1967.

Bedau, Hugo Adam. "Deterrence and the Death Penalty: A Reconsideration." *The Journal of Criminal Law, Criminology and Police Science,* 61:4 (1970).

Bedau, Hugo Adam. "The Issue of Capital Punishment." *Current History,* 53 (1967), pp. 82-87, 116.

Bedau, Hugo A. "A Survey of the Debate on Capital Punishment in Canada, England and the United States, 1948-1958." *Prison Journal,* 38 (October, 1958), pp. 35-40.

Bedau, Hugo Adam and Chester M. Pierce. *Capital Punishment in the United States.* N.Y.: AMS, 1976.

Beman, Lamar T. *Selected Articles on Capital Punishment.* N.Y.: Wilson, 1925.

Black, Charles L., Jr. *Capital Punishment: The Inevitability of Caprice and Mistake.* N.Y.: Norton, 1974.

Block, Eugene B. *And May God Have Mercy . . . The Case Against Capital Punishment.* San Francisco: Fearon, 1962.

Bowers, W.J. *Executions in America.* Lexington, MA.: Heath Lexington, 1974.

"California Supreme Court Upholds Jury Discretion to Impose Death Penalty." *Journal of California Law Enforcement,* (January, 1969), pp. 142-150.

Calvert, E.R. *Capital Punishment in the Twentieth Century and The Death Penalty Enquiry.* Montclair, N.J.: Patterson Smith, 1973.

An argument against capital punishment in Great Britain on the grounds that it is immoral, unjust, and not a deterrent against crime.

Canada Minister of Justice. *Capital Punishment: Material Relating to Its Purpose and Value.* Ottawa: Queens Printer, 1965.

Cantwell, M.K. and J.F. Wallerstedt. *Capital Punishment, 1973.* Washington, D.C.: NCJRS, (Microfiche), 1975.

Information on prisoners under sentence of death during calendar year 1973, including age, sex, race, offense for which sentenced, duration of stay on death row, marital status, educational level, and legal status at arrest.

Capital Punishment. N.Y.: Department of Economic and Social Affairs, U.N. [nd].

"Capital Punishment." *The Prison Journal,* (October, 1958).

"Capital Punishment: The Case for and Against." *Police Chief,* 27 (June, 1960).

"Capital Punishment: It's Being Revived in Many States." *U.S. News & World Report,* 74 (March 4, 1974).

Capital Punishment 1973. Washington, D.C.: LEAA, 1975.

"Capital Punishment: Pros and Cons." *Association for Professional Law Enforcement Quarterly Journal,* (January-March, 1960), (entire issue).

"Chief Seeks Death for Police Slayers." *Crime Control Digest,* 9:2 (January 13, 1975).

Cohen, Bernard Lande. *Law Without Order: Capital Punishment and the Liberals.* New Rochelle, N.Y.: Arlington House, 1970.

Comment "In Defense of Capital Punishment." *Kentucky Law Journal,* 54 (1966).

Compton, Lynn D. "Capital Punishment." *Law Enforcement Legal Information Bulletin,* V (October-November, 1969), pp. 94-105.

Dann, Fobert. "The Deterrent Effect of Capital Punishment." *Bulletin,* (March, 1935).

"Death Penalty for Rape." *Nation,* (February 15, 1965).

"Death Penalty: A World Survey." *U.S. News & World Report,* 70 (May 31, 1971), pp. 38-40.

"Death Sentence for Manson Clan, But—." *U.S. News & World Report,* 70 (April 12, 1971).

Diamond, Bernard L. "Murder and the Death Penalty: A Case Report." *American Journal of Orthopsychiatry,* (July, 1975).

DiSalle, Michael Vincent. *The Power of Life or Death.* N.Y.: Random House, 1965.

Drzazga, John. "Capital Punishment." *Law and Order,* 9 (December, 1961), pp. 88-89.

Duff, Charles. *A Handbook on Hanging.* London: Richards and Sainsbury, 1928.

Duffy, Clinton T. and Al Hirsberg. *88 Men and 2 Women.* Garden City, N.Y.: Doubleday, 1962.

Dunlavey, Mary A. "Is Capital Punishment Worth Keeping." *Law and Order,* 20:6 (June, 1972), pp. 92, 94, 96.

Edwards, Stephen W. "The Death Penalty." *Journal of the California State Bar,* 25 (January-February, 1950), pp. 98-101.

Erskine, Hazel. "The Polls: Capital Punishment." *Public Opinion Quarterly,* 34:2 (Summer, 1970), pp. 290-307.

Eshelman, Byron and Frank Riley. *Death Row Chaplain.* Englewood Cliffs, N.J.: Prentice-Hall, 1962.

Flammang. C.J. "The Issue of Capital Punishment." *Law and Order,* 22:7 (July, 1974), pp. 28, 30, 32-34.

Florida Governor's Committee to Study Capital Punishment. *Florida Governor's Committee to Study Capital Punishment—Final Report.* Washington, D.C.: NCJRS, (Microfiche), 1972.

Folgelson, Robert M., ed. *Capital Punishment: 19th Century Arguments*. N.Y.: Arno, 1974.

Gold, Louis H. "A Psychiatric Review of Capital Punishment." *Journal of Forensic Science*, 6 (October, 1961), pp. 465-478.

Gowers, Ernest. *A Life for a Life? The Problem of Capital Punishment*. London: Chatto, 1956.

Gregg, G. "Death Penalty and Public Knowledge." *Psychology Today*, 10 (September, 1976), pp. 16-17.

Grenier, B. *Capital Punishment—New Material—1965-1972*. Ottawa: Information Canada, 1972.
Information on developments related to capital punishment that have taken place in Canada and other countries since June, 1965.

Hale, C.D. "The Death Penalty." *Iowa Law Enforcement*, 3:1 (1974), pp. 27-29.
Covers Gallup Polls conducted in 1953, 1960, and 1965. Author opposes death penalty.

Hale, Leslie. *Hanged in Error*. Harmondsworth: Penguin, 1961.

Hester, Reid K. and Ronald E. Smith. "Effects of a Mandatory Death Penalty on the Decisions of Simulated Jarors as a Function of Heinousness of the Crime." *Journal of Criminal Justice*, (1973), pp. 319-326.

Hochkammer, William O., Jr. "The Capital Punishment Controversy." *Journal of Criminal Law, Criminology and Police Science*, 60:3 (September, 1969), pp. 360-368.

Howard League for Penal Reform. *Murder and Capital Punishment in England and Wales*. Washington, D.C.: NCJRS, (Microfiche), 1974.

Joyce, James A. *Capital Punishment, A World View*. N.Y.: Grove, 1962.

Jayewardene, C.H.S. "Death Penalty and the Safety of Canadian Policemen." *Canadian Journal of Criminology and Corrections*, 15:4 (1973), pp. 356-366.

Kershaw, Alister. *A History of the Guillotine*. London: Calder, 1958.

Kingsley, Robert. "The Case Against Capital Punishment." *Los Angeles Bar Bulletin*, 32 (May, 1957), pp. 200-202.

Kinney, R. Rees. "In Defense of Capital Punishment." *Kentucky Law Journal*, 54 (Summer, 1966), pp. 742-756.

Koestler, Arthur. *Reflections on Hanging*. N.Y.: Macmillan, 1957.

Koestler, Arthur and C.H. Rolph. *Hanged by the Neck*. Harmondsworth: Penguin, 1961.

Laurence, John. *A History of Capital Punishment*. N.Y.: Citadel, 1960.

"Let's Put the Death Penalty in Proper Focus." *Police Chief*, XLI:1 (January, 1974).

Lockley, T. "Sentenced to Death: The Simcox Case." *Police Journal*, 37 (July, 1964).

Lunden, Walter A. "Death Penalty Delays." *Police*, 7:6 (July-August, 1963), pp. 18-22.

Lunden, Walter A. "The Death Penalty." *Police*, 5:5 (May-June, 1961), pp. 43-47; 5:6 (July-August, 1961), pp. 34-37.

McCafferty, James, ed. *Capital Punishment*. Chicago: Aldine, 1972.

McClellan, Grant S., ed. *Capital Punishment*. N.Y.: H.W. Wilson, 1961.

McMahon, Daniel F. "Capital Punishment." *Law Enforcement Bulletin*, (February, 1973).

MacNamara, Donald E.J. "A Survey of Recent Literature on Capital Punishment." *American Journal of Correction*, 24 (March-April, 1962), pp. 16-19.

Mark, Robert. "The High Cost of Hanging." *Police Journal* (GB), (October, 1965).

Meltsner, Michael. *Cruel and Unusual—The Supreme Court and Capital Punishment*. N.Y.: Random House, 1973.

Mironenko, Yuri P. "The Re-emergence of Death Penalty in the Soviet Union." *Soviet Affairs Analysis Service #28*, (1961-1962), pp. 1-5.

Moore, D. *Death Penalty—Legal Status Since Furman*. Washington, D.C.: NCJRS, (Microfiche), 1973.

Morris, Arval. "Thoughts on Capital Punishment." *Washington Law Review*, 35 (Autumn, 1960), pp. 335-361.

"Murder and the Penalty of Death." *Annals*, 184 (November, 1952).

National Criminal Justice Information and Statistics Service. *Capital Punishment, 1971-72, National Prisoner Statistics Bulletin Number SD-NPS-CP-1*. Washington, D.C.: NCJRS, (Microfiche), 1974.
Narrative and tabular presentation of the number of state prisoners under sentence of death categorized by age, sex, race, offence, and time spent on death row.

"National Prisoner Statistics." *Capital Punishment, 1975*. Washington, D.C.: LEAA (July, 1976).

Overholser, Winfred. *Report to the Royal Commission on Capital Punishment, 1949-1954*. London: HMSO, 1953.

Paine, Donald F. "Capital Punishment." *Tennessee Law Review*, 29 (Summer, 1969), pp. 534-551.

Patrick, Clarence H. "The Status of Capital Punishment: A World Perspective." *Journal of Criminal Law, Criminology and Police Science*, 56:4 (December, 1965), pp. 397-411.

Prettyman, Barrett; *Death and the Supreme Court*. N.Y.: Harcourt, Brace and World, 1961.

Reichert, William O. "Capital Punishment Reconsidered." *Kentucky Law Review*, 47 (Spring, 1959), pp. 397-419.

Reifsnyder, Richard. "Capital Crimes in the States." *Journal of Criminal Law, Criminology and Police Science*, 45:6 (March-April, 1955), pp. 690-693.

Roucek, Joseph Slabey. *Capital Punishment*. Charlottesville, N.Y.: Samhar, 1975.

Samuelson, Glenn W. "Why Was Capital Punishment Restored in Delaware?" *Journal of Criminal Law,*

Criminology and Police Science, 60:2 (June, 1969), pp. 148-151.

Savitz, Leonard D. "Capital Crimes as Defined in American Statutory Law." *Journal of Criminal Law, Criminology and Police Science,* 46:3 (September-October, 1955), pp. 353-363.

Savitz, Leonard D. "A Study in Capital Punishment." *Journal of Criminal Law, Criminology and Police Science,* 49:4 (November-December, 1958), pp. 338-341.

Schmidt, Franz. *A Hangman's Diary.* London: P. Allan, 1929.

Schwartz, Louis. *Memoranda: Punishment of Murder in Pennsylvania, Royal Commission on Capital Punishment, Memoranda and Replies to a Questionnaire Received from Foreign and Commonwealth Countries. Part II, United States of America.* London: HMSO, 1952.

Scott, George Ryley. *The History of Capital Punishment.* London: Torchstream, 1950.

Sellin, Thorsten, ed. *Capital Punishment.* N.Y.: Harper and Row, 1967.

Sellin, Thorsten. *The Death Penalty.* Philadelphia: American Law Institute, 1959.

Sellin, Thorsten. "Two Myths in the History of Capital Punishment." *Journal of Criminal Law, Criminology and Police Science,* 50:2 (July-August, 1959), pp. 114-117.

Shaw, William. "A Brief Report on the First Legal Electrocution." *Law and Order,* 22:8 (August, 1974), pp. 74, 76-79.

Solomon, George F. "Capital Punishment as Suicide and as Murder." *American Journal of Orthopsychiatry,* (July, 1975).

Springer, Charles E. "Against the Death Penalty." *Nevada State Bar Journal,* 25 (October, 1960), pp. 210-215.

Star, Jack. "The Bitter Battle over Capital Punishment." *Look,* 27 (May 7, 1963), pp. 23-29.

Teeters, Negley King. *Hang by Neck. The Legal Use of Scaffold and Noose, Gibbet, Stake, and Firing Squad from Colonial Times to the Present.* Springfield, IL.: C.C. Thomas, 1967.

Templewood, Viscount. *The Shadow of the Gallows.* London: Victor Gollancz, 1951.

Tucker, C.B. *Capital Punishment—A Study of Law and Social Structure.* Ann Arbor, MI.: University Microfilms, 1969.

Analysis of hypothesized relationships of occupational specialization and economic stratification to the use of capital punishment in the United States.

U.S. Committee on the Judiciary. *To Abolish the Death Penalty: Hearings . . . Before . . . 90th Congress, 2nd Session . . . March 20, 21, and July 2, 1968.* Washington, D.C.: GPO, 1970.

U.S. Congress. House Committee on the Judiciary. Subcommittee No. 3. *Capital Punishment Hearings.* Washington, D.C.: GPO, 1972.

Vendehaag, Ernest. "On Deterrence and the Death Penalty." *Journal of Criminal Law, Criminology and Police Science,* 60:2 (June, 1969), pp. 141-147.

Vedder, Clyde B. "The Case of Capital Punishment." *Police,* 6:1 (September-October, 1961), pp. 78-81.

Walker, Bill. *The Case of Barbara Graham.* N.Y.: Valentine, 1961.

West, Louis Jolyon. "Psychiatric Reflections on the Death Penalty." *American Journal of Orthopsychiatry,* (July, 1975).

Whittingham, Richard. *Martial Justice: The Last Mass Execution in the United States.* Chicago: Regnery, 1971.

Williams, Glanville. *Sanctity of Life and the Criminal Law.* N.Y.: Knopf, 1957.

COMPENSATING VICTIMS OF CRIMES

Cancilla, Robert C. "Compensating Victims of Crime." *Crime Prevention Review,* 2:4 (July, 1975), pp. 31-37.

Coon, Thomas F. "Public Defender and Victims Compensation Legislation, Their Part in the Criminal Justice System." *Police,* 16:4 (December, 1971), pp. 18-20.

"Criminal Injuries Compensation." *Police (GB),* (June, 1974), pp. 22-24.

Edelhertz, Herbert and Gilbert Geis. *Public Compensation to Victims of Crime.* N.Y.: Praeger, 1974.

Edwards, J.L.J. "Compensation to Victims of Crimes and Violence." *Federal Probation,* 30 (June, 1966), pp. 3-10.

Sets forth the theories, rationale, mechanics and comparisons of victim compensation plans in Britain, New Zealand, and the United States. Promotes personal reparation as a rehabilitative approach in the correctional process.

Geis, Gilbert. "Compensation for Crime Victims and the Police." *Police,* 13:5 (May-June, 1969), pp. 55-59.

Geis, Gilbert and Dorothy Zietz. "California's Program of Compensation in Crime Victims." *Legal Aid Briefcase,* 25 (December, 1966), pp. 66-69.

Harrison, D.H. "Compensation for Criminal Injuries." *Solicitors' Journal,* 110 (February, 1966), pp. 99-101.

Hudson, Joe and Burt Galaway. *Considering the Victim: Readings in Restitution and Victim Compensation.* Springfield, IL.: C.C. Thomas, 1975.

Mueller, Gerhard O.W. "Compensation for Victims of Crime:Thought Before Action." *Minnesota Law Review,* 50 (December, 1965), pp. 213-221.

New York Crime Victims Compensation Board. *New York Crime Victims Compensation Board. Annual Report, 7th, 1973.* Washington, D.C.: NCJRS, (Microfiche), 1974.

"Police Want Payment for Victims." *Police News,* 49 (November, 1970), pp. 2-3.

Schafer, Stephen. *Compensation and Restitution to Victims of Crime.* Montclair, N.J.: Patterson-Smith, 1970.

Shank, Willard. "Aid to Victims of Violent Crimes in California." *Southern California Law Review,* 43 (1970).

CRITICISM OF CRIMINAL JUSTICE SYSTEM

Ahern, James and Victor H. Bernstein. "How We Handcuff Our Police." *Environment,* (April-June, 1972), pp. 20-21.

Allen, Edward J. "Signs of the Times." *Police Chief,* XL:1 (January, 1973), pp. 44-47.

"American Justice at Work." *Current History,* (July, 1971), (entire issue).

Anderson, R.E. "Are Our Large City Police Departments Being 'Neutralized.'" *FBI Law Enforcement Bulletin,* 37:8 (August, 1968), pp. 9-11, 24-25.

Baker, Bruce R. "Integrating the Law with Street Tactics." *Journal of California Law Enforcement,* (April, 1970), pp. 171-174.
Describes difficulties in prosecuting rioters.

"Balance the Scales of Justice." *FBI Law Enforcement Bulletin,* 39:8 (August, 1970), pp. 6-8, 27.

Barth, A. "Why Handle Criminals with Kid Gloves." *Harper's,* (September, 1959).

Bazelon, David L. "The Concept of Responsibility." *Georgetown Law Journal,* 53:5 (1964).

Bell, John C., Jr. "Crime and Criminals." *FBI Law Enforcement Bulletin,* (January, 1969), pp. 2-4, 20.

Blumberg, Abraham S. *The Scales of Justice.* Edison, N.J.: Transaction, 1973.

Broderick, Vincent L. "The Supreme Court and the Police: A Police Viewpoint." *Journal of Criminal Law, Criminology and Police Science,* 57:3 (September, 1966), pp. 271-282.

Brown, Lawrence E. "Rough Road Ahead for the Police." *Law and Order,* 13:4 (April, 1965), pp. 80-83.

Bureau of National Affairs. *The Criminal Law Revolution and Its Aftermath.* Washington, D.C.: Bureau of National Affairs, 1974.

Callison, J.P. *Courts of Injustice.* Boston: Twayne, 1956.

Chamberlain, Brian. "We Catch Them Young—They Let Them Go!" *Police, (GB),* (May, 1976), pp. 11-14.

Chapman, Samuel G. "Functional Problems Facing Law Enforcement Stemming from Supreme Court Decisions." *Police,* (1966).

Clark, T.C. "The Courts, the Police and the Community." *Southern California Law Review,* 46:1 (1972), pp. 1-11.

Coon, Thomas F. "Let's Face Up to Law Enforcement Needs." *Police,* 10:2 (November-December,1965), pp. 82-84.

Cozaretta, V. "Relationship of Drug Traffickers and the Court." *Washington Law Enforcement Journal,* 4:4 (1974), pp. 16-17, 19, 37.
Critical examples of lenient sentences by judges for drug dealers.

D'Aifonso, John. *The Crime Gang.* San Diego: Viewpoint, 1969.
Conservative view of crime and courts.

Dalbey, Dwight J. "Alice in a Patrol Car." *FBI Law Enforcement Bulletin,* 35:7 (July, 1966), pp. 9-11.

Dalbey, Dwight J. " 'Alice' Would Have Questions Traveling in a Police Patrol Car." *Journal of California Law Enforcement,* (January, 1967), pp. 139-149.

Davids, Frederick E. "Policing by Permission." *Law and Order,* 18:5 (May, 1970), pp. 66, 68, 70.
Criticism of a lack of police authority.

DeWolf, L. Harold. *Crime and Justice in America—A Paradox of Conscience.* N.Y.: Harper and Row, 1975.

"Dissent from High Court Decision on Rights of Arrested Persons." *Journal of California Law Enforcement,* (October, 1960), pp. 100-106.

Doherty, James J. "Wolf! Wolf!—The Ramifications of Frivolous Appeals." *Journal of Criminal Law, Criminology and Police Science,* 59:1 (March, 1968), pp. 1-3.

Faulstich, William L. "Can Society Be Protected with Tools of Modern Law Enforcement?" *Journal of California Law Enforcement,* (January, 1967), pp. 181-184.

Ferguson, Robert J., Jr., C.B. Hanscom, and Bruce M. Goldstein. "Is Justice on Trial in America Today?" *Police,* 15:6 (July-August, 1971), pp. 54-59.

Forer, L.G. *No One Will Listen—How Our Legal System Brutalizes the Youthful Poor.* N.Y.: John Day, 1970.
The juvenile justice system is described in detail by a lawyer who was legal counsel to poor minority-group children in urban ghettos.

Fourt, Walter J. "Experience of the Ages Should Not Lightly Be Overruled by the Courts." *Journal of California Law Enforcement,* (July, 1966), pp. 1-5.

Gallati, Robert R.J. "Scapegoats No More." *Police,* 16:1 (September, 1971), pp. 2-3.

Gangi, W. ". . . and Set the Guilty Free." *Prosecutor,* 8:6 (1973), pp. 479-481.

Garber, Lyman A. *Of Men and Not of the Law. How the Courts Are Usurping the Political Function.* N.Y.: Devin Adair, 1966.

Garland, Norman M. "Collateral Attack on Juvenile Court Delinquency Decisions." *Journal of Criminal Law, Criminology and Police Science,* 57:2 (June, 1966), pp. 136-144.

George, B.J., Jr. "Police Practices and the Citizen." *Police,* 10:4 (March-April, 1966), pp. 38-42.

Giordano, Henry L. "Narcotic Law Enforcement and False Propaganda." *Police,* 10:4 (March-April, 1966), pp. 22-25.

Groth, Carl H. "Police and Society." *Police,* 12:1 (September-October, 1967), pp. 52-61.

Gutman, Daniel. "The Criminal Gets the Breaks." *Police Chief,* 32:2 (February, 1965), pp. 36-40.

"How Rest of World Handles Riots—Only U.S. Ties Hands of Police." *U.S. News and World Report,* (August 14, 1967).

Inbau, Fred E. "Democratic Restraints upon the Police." *Journal of Criminal Law, Criminology and Police Science,* 57:3 (September, 1966), pp. 265-270.

Jacob, Herbert. *The Potential for Reform of Criminal Justice.* Beverly Hills, CA.: Sage, 1974.

Jonsson, Erik. "Avalanche: The Cities and the Seventies." *FBI Law Enforcement Bulletin,* 38:3 (March, 1969), pp. 6-8, 21, 23.

"Judicial Law and the Police." *Police Chief,* XL:1 (January, 1973).

Katz, L. and L. Litwin. *Justice in the Crime—Pretrial Delay in Felony Cases.* Cleveland, OH.: Case Western Reserve University Press, 1972.

Excessive delay inherent in the present criminal justice system is shown by presenting the time lapses that exist between specific pretrial criminal procedures.

Kelley, Clarence M. "Realistic Assessments of Criminality Will . . . Stem the Growth of Crime." *FBI Law Enforcement Bulletin,* (April, 1975).

Kennedy, Robert F. "Crime in the Cities: Improving the Administration of Criminal Justice." *Journal of Criminal Law, Criminology and Police Science,* 58:2 (June, 1967), pp. 142-154.

Kimble, Joseph Paul. "Where Shall We Hide the Bodies?" *Police,* 16:11 (July, 1972), pp. 22-24.

Kirkwood, James. *American Grotesque; An Account of the Clay Shaw—Jim Garrison Affair in the City of New Orleans.* N.Y.: Simon, 1970.

Klein, Herbert R. *The Police: Damned if They Do—Damned if They Don't.* N.Y.: Crown, 1968.

This book is an account of a former New York City policeman's experiences of difficulties involved in the policeman's function of protecting the public, enforcing the law and maintaining law and order, while at the same time trying to avoid charges of police brutality. Insights are provided into police reactions of assaults on police, civil disorders, ban on wiretapping, the Miranda decision, civilian review boards and police corruption.

Latham, Frank B. *American Justice on Trial.* N.Y.: Watts, 1972.

Lefcourt, Robert. *Law Against the People: Essays to Demystify Law, Order and Courts.* N.Y.: Random, 1971.

Logan, A.B. *Justice in Jeopardy. Strategy to Revitalize the American Dream.* Springfield, IL.: C.C. Thomas, 1973.

Review of the basic problems of judicial administration and the criminal justice system along with a discussion of the recommendation of the judicial task force.

Lunden, Walter A. "How to Beat the Rap." *Police,* 2:5 (May-June, 1958), pp. 20-23.

Lunden, Walter A. "Inflation of Crime and Devaluation of Punishment." *Police,* 13:5 (May-June, 1969), pp. 23-26.

Mahan, Linda and Rita James Simon. "Quantifying Burdens of Proof." *Law and Society Review,* V (February, 1971), pp. 319-330.

Main, Jeremy. "Only Radical Reform Can Save the Courts." *Fortune,* LXXXII (August, 1970), pp. 111-114.

Mark, Robert. "Truth Not Guilt Is the Question That Matters." *Police (GB),* (September, 1975), pp. 16-17.

Mitford, J. *Kind and Usual Punishment—The Prison Business.* N.Y.: Knopf, 1973.

Moenssens, Andre A. "Public Clamor over Crime War." *Police,* 12:1 (September-October, 1967), pp. 16-19.

"1983 Today." *FBI Law Enforcement Bulletin,* 37:8 (August, 1968), pp. 2-4, 23-24.

"On Crime and Punishment." *Police Chief,* XLI:8 (August, 1974).

Osterburg, James W. "The Law—An Enforcement Tool." *Law and Order,* 14:2 (February, 1966), pp. 22-25.

Controls and limitations imposed on police by court decisions.

Osterburg, James W. and Richard A. Myrey. "How Long the Arm of Our Law?" *Police,* 9:3 (January-February, 1965), pp. 11-14.

Parker, William H. "If Police Fail, Anarchy Will Prevail . . . Freedom of Man Is at Stake." *Journal of California Law Enforcement,* (October, 1966), pp. 71-75.

Phalan, Reed T. "Station-House Interrogation and 'That Warren Court'." *Law and Order,* 15:5 (May, 1967), pp. 23-26, 50.

Phelan, J.R. "Innocent's Grim Ordeal." *Saturday Evening Post,* (February 2, 1963).

Phelps, Ferinez. "When Do Policemen Support the Courts?" *Police Chief,* XVI:9 (September, 1975), pp. 48-49.

Piggins, E.S. "Are We Handcuffing Law Enforcement?" *Vital Speeches,* (May 1, 1958).

"The Police Need Help." *Time,* (October 4, 1968).

Reddin, Thomas. "The Police and the Courts." *Los Angeles Bar Bulletin,* (October, 1967).

Ring, Peter Smith. "Will the Bar Help the Police?" *Police Chief,* XXXVI:7 (July, 1969), pp. 8-11.

Rowat, D.C. "We Need a New Defense Against So-Called Justice." *Maclean's* (January 7, 1961).

Rowley, James J. "Law Enforcement in the U.S. Is Facing Greatest Challenge in History." *Journal of California Law Enforcement,* (July, 1968), pp. 40-42.

Saxbe, W.B. "The Public Has Rights, Too!" *Law Officer,* 7:5 (1974), pp. 18-20.

Scheuer, James H. *To Walk the Streets Safely.* Garden City, N.Y.: Doubleday, 1969.

Schrotel, Stanley R. "Civil Rights for All." *Police,* 9:3 (January-February, 1965), pp. 21-23.

Scileppi, John F. "Is Society Shortchanged at the Bar of Justice?" *FBI Law Enforcement Bulletin,* 33:5 (May, 1964), pp. 7-9.

Scott, Edgar E. "The Mallory Decision and the Vanishing Rights of Crime Victims." *Police,* 4:5 (May-June, 1960), pp. 61-64; 4:6 (July-August, 1960), pp. 28-30.

Seymour, Whitney North, Jr. *Why Justice Fails.* N.Y.: Morrow, 1973.

Shawcross, Lord. "The Criminal Is Living in a Golden Age." *U.S. News & World Report* (November 1, 1965).

Silver, Isifore. *The Crime Control Establishment*. Englewood Cliffs, N.J.: Prentice-Hall, 1974.

Silverman, David W. "Protecting the Public from Ohio vs. Mapp." *American Bar Association Journal,* 51:3 (1965).

Sonder, F. "Take the Handcuffs Off Our Police." *Reader's Digest,* (September 1, 1964).

Tamm, Quinn. "Dangerous Dreams of Wishful Men." *Police,* 10:4 (March-April, 1966).

Tamm, Quinn. "Police Must Be More Free." *Police Chief,* 33:5 (May, 1966), pp. 8, 10.

Trebach, Arnold S. *The Rioting of Justice: Constitutional Rights and the Criminal Process*. New Brunswick, N.J.: Rutgers University Press, 1964.

Truby, J. David. "Let's Take the Handcuffs Off Our Police." *Police,* 15:1 (September-October, 1970), pp. 21-24.

U.S. Congress. House Select Committee on Crime. *Street Crime in America. Part 2, Corrections Approaches—Hearings Before the House Select Committee on Crime April 9-13, 16-19, May 1-3, 8-9, 1973*. Washington, D.C.: GPO, 1973.
Testimony and other materials concerning correctional reform and present methods of corrections.

U.S. Congress. House Select Committee on Crime. *Street Crime in America. Part 3, Prosecution and Court Innovations—Hearings Before the House Select Committee on Crime, April 9-13, 16-19, May 1-3, 8-9, 1973*. Washington, D.C.: GPO, 1973.
Testimony and other materials concerning the attempts by judges and attorneys to reform court and prosecution systems.

Van Allen, Edward J. *Our Handcuffed Police*. Mineola, N.Y.: Reportorial, 1968.

Vorenberg, James. "Is the Court Handcuffing the Cops?" *The New York Times Magazine* (May 11, 1969).

Waite, J.B. and K. Detzer. "Why Do Our Courts Protect Criminals?" *American Mercury,* (January, 1956).

Wilson, O.W. "Crime, the Courts, and the Police." *Journal of Criminal Law, Criminology and Police Science,* 57:3 (September, 1966), pp. 291-300.

Winters, John. "The Awareness of Crime and Youth Problems." *Law and Order,* 12:4 (April, 1964), pp. 64-67.

Younger, Evelle J. "The Appellate Syndrome." *Journal of California Law Enforcement,* (January, 1970), pp. 103-108.

Zinn, Fred L. "We Are in Trouble." *Police Chief,* XXXV:11 (November, 1968).

DETERRENCE

Ball, John C. "The Deterrence Concept in Criminology and Law." *Journal of Criminal Law, Criminology and Police Science,* 46:3 (September-October, 1955), pp. 347-354.

California Legislature Assembly. Committee on Criminal Procedure. *Deterrent Effects of Criminal Sanctions; Progress Report*. Sacramento: California Legislature, Committee on Criminal Procedure, 1968.

Fattah, E.A. *Study of the Deterrent Effect of Capital Punishment with Special Reference to the Canadian Situation*. Ottawa: Information Canada, 1972.
Capital punishment and homicide rates are analyzed, including changes in crimes of violence from 1962 to 1970.

Kobrin, Solomon et al. *Deterrent Effectiveness of Criminal Justice Sanction Strategies: Summary Report*. Washington, D.C.: LEAA, 1972.

Kobrin, S. and S.C. Lubeck. *Deterrent Effectiveness of Criminal Justice Sanction Strategies, Final Report*. Springfield, VA.: NTIS, 1972.

Lawrence, D.H. and L. Festinger. *Deterrents and Reinforcement the Psychology of Insufficient Reward*. Stanford, CA.: Stanford University Press, 1962.

Logan, C.H. "General Deterrent Effects of Imprisonment." *Social Forces* (September, 1972).

Riccio, L.J. "Direct Deterrence—An Analysis of the Effectiveness of Police Patrol and Other Crime Prevention Technologies." *Journal of Criminal Justice,* 2:3 (1974), pp. 207-217.

Thomas, C.W. and J.S. Williams. *Deterrence of Crime—A Reformulation of Chambliss' Typology of Deterrence*. Washington, D.C.: NCJRS, (Microfiche), 1974.

University of Maryland Institute of Criminal Justice and Criminology. *Deterrence of Crime In and Around Residences*. Washington, D.C.: GPO, 1972.

U.S. Center for Studies in Crime and Delinquency, National Institute of Mental Health. *Perspectives on Deterrence*. Washington, D.C.: GPO, 1971.

Zimring, F.E. and G.J. Hawkins. *Deterrence—The Legal Threat in Crime Control*. Chicago: University of Chicago Press, 1973.

DIVERSION

American Correctional Association. *Juvenile Diversion—A Perspective*. College Park MD.: American Correctional Association, 1972.

Annable, Peter F. "A Successful Experiment with Juveniles." *Police Chief,* XL:6 (June 6, 1973), pp. 52-54.

Bean, A.K. and F.R. Campbell. *Cluster Evaluation of Five Diversion Projects. Final Report, June 21, 1974*. Washington, D.C.: NCJRS, (Microfiche), 1974.
Measures the effectiveness of the projects in reducing the incidence and severity of delinquency among project clients.

Binder, Arnold, Robert P. Green, and Martha Newkirk. "University-Police Cooperative Approach to Juvenile Diversion: Evaluating Its Applicability and Effectiveness." *Journal of Criminal Justice,* (1973), pp. 255-258.

Brakel, S.J. and G.R. South. *Diversion from the Criminal Process in the Rural Community—Final Report of the American Bar Foundation Project on Rural Criminal Justice*. Chicago: American Bar Foundation, 1969.

Cain, Thomas J. "Youth Services: A Police Alternate to the Juvenile Justice System." *Law and Order,* 20:12

(December, 1972), pp. 30-32; 21:1 (January, 1973), pp. 20-23, 33.

California Department of Justice, Bureau of Criminal Statistics. *California Drug Diversion Program—An Initial Report.* Washington, D.C.: NCJRS, (Microfiche), 1973.
Description and report of a program whereby accused persons do not enter the court systems and are referred to community resources for treatment for 6-24 months.

California Taxpayers' Association. *Cluster Evaluation of Four Diversion Projects. Progress Report, January 28, 1974.* Washington, D.C.: NCJRS, (Microfiche), 1974.
Progress in the assessment of accomplishment of selected California Youth Services Bureau projects with the final proposed methodology and the evaluators, expectations concerning the comparability and relevancy of data.

Carter, G.W. et al. *Orange County (CA). Evaluation Progress Report of the Alternate Routes Project Following 19 Months of Development and Demonstration.* Washington, D.C.: NCJRS, (Microfiche), 1973.

Carter, Robert M. "The Diversion of Offenders." *Federal Probation* (December, 1972), pp. 31-36.

Charlotte (NC)—Relatives—A Comprehensive Description of the Environment. Washington, D.C.: NCJRS, (Microfiche), 1975.
Describes juvenile justice diversion project in Charlotte, North Carolina, which provides a legal and licensed temporary shelter for persons under 18 who have run away from home.

Citizen Dispute Settlement—The Night Prosecutor Program of Columbus, Ohio—A Relication Manual—An Exemplary Project. Washington, D.C.: NCJRS, 1974.

Cressey, D.R. and R.A. McDermott. *Diversion from the Juvenile Justice System.* Washington- D.C.: GPO, 1973.

Diversion from the Criminal Justice System. Rockville, MD.: National Institute of Mental Health, Center for Studies of Crime and Delinquency, (1971).

Dore, Maurice M. "Pre-Dispositional Options." *Police Law Quarterly* (April, 1975), pp. 5-12.

Field, M.H. and H.F. Field. "Marital Violence and the Criminal Process: Neither Justice nor Peace." *Social Service Review,* 47:2 (1973), pp. 221-240.

Gemignani, Robert J. "Youth Services Systems: Diverting Youth from the Juvenile Justice System." *Federal Probation* (December, 1972), pp. 48-53.

Grossman, Herbert. "Community Treatment of Adolescents." *Police,* 16:2 (October, 1971), pp. 48-51.

Harlow, E. and J.R. Wever. *Diversion from the Criminal Justice System.* Washington, D.C.: GPO, 1971.

Klapmuts, N. "Diversion from the Justice System." *Crime and Delinquency,* 6:1 (1974), pp. 108-131.

Lemert, Edwin M. *Instead of Court: Diversion in Juvenile Justice.* Rockville, MD.: National Institute of Mental Health, Center for Studies of Crime and Delinquency, 1971.

Marin County Criminal Justice Planning Agency. *Marin County (CA) Police Diversion Project. Evaluation of the 1st Project Year, September 1974.* Washington, D.C.: NCJRS, (Microfiche), 1974.

Maryland University, Institute of Criminal Justice and Criminology. *New Approaches to Diversion and Treatment of Juvenile Offenders.* Washington, D.C.: NCJRS, 1972.
Analysis of innovations in juvenile community-based corrections and in programs and proposals aimed at diverting the juvenile from the criminal justice system.

Mullen, Joan. *Dilemma of Diversion. Resources Materials on Adult Pretrial Intervention Programs.* Washington, D.C.: U.S. Department of Justice, LEAA, 1974.

Nimmer, R.T. *Alternatives to Prosecution—A Survey of the Practice of Diversion, draft 3.* Washington, D.C.: NCJRS, (Microfiche), 1973.
An intensive analysis of disposition patterns and rationale in two moderate-sized urban areas, exploring areas in which diversion commonly occurs and how crimes are handled in the absence of formal diversion programs.

Nimmer, R.T. *Diversion—The Search for Alternate Forms of Prosecution.* Chicago: American Bar Foundation, 1974.

Palmer, John W. "Pre-Arrest Diversion: Victim Confrontation." *Federal Probation* (September, 1974), pp. 12-18.

Parnsa, R. "Police Discretion and Diversion of Incidents of Intra-Family Violence." *Law of Contemporary Problems,* 36:4 (1971), pp. 539-565.

Peoples, Darlin. "Youth Development Services: An Alternative." *Law and Order* (December, 1975), pp. 12-14.

Perlman, H.S. *Legal Issues in Addict Diversion—A Layman's Guide.* Chicago: American Bar Association, 1974.

Richmand (CA) Police Department. *Diversion of Juvenile Offenders at the Richmond (CA) Police Department—Final Evaluation Report.* Washington, D.C.: NCJRS, (Microfiche), 1974.

Schregardus, Darell J. "Youth Diversion and the Myth of Parental Indifference." *Police Chief,* XLI:12 (December, 1974), pp. 48-51.

Sundeen, R.A., Jr. "Police Professionalization and Community Attachments and Diversion of Juveniles." *Criminology,* 11:4 (1974), pp. 570-580.

Tafoya, William L. "Project Intercept: Precursor to the Criminal Justice System." *Journal of California Law Enforcement,* 8:3 (January, 1974), pp. 147-152.

Tafoya, W.L. "Project Intercept: The Los Angeles Experience." *Journal of Criminal Justice,* 2:1 (1974), pp. 55-60.

University of Maryland, Institute of Criminal Justice and Criminology. *New Approaches to Diversion and Treatment of Juvenile Offenders.* Washington, D.C.: GPO, 1972.

U.S. Department of Health, Education, and Welfare. *Diverting Youth From the Correctional System.* Washington, D.C.: U.S. Department of Health, Education, and Welfare, 1971.

Weis, C.W. *Diversion of the Public Inebriate from the Criminal Justice System—Prescriptive Package.* Washington, D.C.: GPO, [nd].

DOSSIERS

"Constitutional Law—Civilian's Claim That Army's Data-Gathering System Makes a Chilling Effect on Their 1st Amendment Rights." *Villanova Law Review* (February, 1973).

Denault, H.J. and D. Parris. *Computerization of Government Files—What Impact on the Individual.* Chicago: American Bar Foundation, 1968.
Critical analysis of the need, the technology and the individual's interest involved in computerizing governmental record keeping.

McNamara, R.M., Jr. and J.R. Starr. "Confidentiality of Narcotic Addict Treatment Records: A Legal and Statistical Analysis." *Columbia Law Review,* 73:8 (1973), pp. 1579-1612.

"Secret Files, Legitimate Police Activity or Unconstitutional Restraint on Dissent?" *Georgetown Law Journal* (February, 1970), pp. 569-590.

U.S. Bureau of the Census. *Government Dossier: An Inventory of Government Information About Individuals.* N.Y.: Arno, 1968.

Wheeler, S. *On Record—Files and Dossiers in American Life.* N.Y.: Basic, 1969.
Description of the record keeping process through life, and the legal status of records.

GRAND JURIES

Clark, Leroy D. *Grand Jury: The Use and Abuse of Political Power.* N.Y.: Quadrangle, 1975.

Cobden, Lynn. "Grand Jury—Its Use and Misuse." *Crime and Delinquency* (April, 1976), pp. 149-164.

Edwards, G.J. *Grand Jury.* N.Y.: American, 1973.

Gelber, Seymour. "A Reappraisal of the Grand Jury Concept." *Journal of Criminal Law, Criminology and Police Science,* 60:1 (March, 1969), pp. 24-27.

Younger, Richard D. "The Grand Jury Under Attack." *Journal of Criminal Law, Criminology and Police Science,* 46:1 (May-June, 1955), pp. 25-49; 46:2 (July-August, 1955), pp. 214-225.

GUN CONTROL

Alviani, Joseph D. and William R. Drake. *Handgun Control—Issues and Alternatives.* Washington, D.C.: Handgun Control Project, U.S. Conference of Mayors, 1975.

Bakal, Carl. *No Right to Bear Arms.* N.Y.: Paper Back Library, 1968.

Bakal, Carl. *The Right to Bear Arms.* N.Y.: McGraw-Hill, 1966.

Compton, Lynn D. "California Peace Officers, D.A.'s, Adopt Gun Control Legislative Police." *Journal of California Law Enforcement* (January, 1966), pp. 123-127.

Defensor, H. Charles. *Gun Registration Now—Confiscation Later?* N.Y.: Vantage, 1970.

Glassen, Harold W. "Firearms Control: A Matter of Distinction." *Trial* (January-February, 1972).

Greenwood, Colin. *Firearms Control. A Study of Armed Crime and Firearms Control in England and Wales.* London: Routledge and Kegan Paul, 1972.
Discusses increase in the use of firearms by British criminals and firearm control laws.

"Gun Controls—How They Work in Other Countries." *U.S. News & World Report,* 66 (June 24, 1968), pp. 38-39.

Hansen, J.P.H. "Fatalities from Firearms in Denmark." *Forensic Science,* 4:3 (1974), pp. 239-245.
Firearms are carefully restricted in Denmark. A license is required except for shotguns and airguns. There are about 4 homicides a year using firearms.

Kukla, Robert J. *Gun Control.* Harrisburg, PA.: Stackpole, 1973.

Levi, E.H. "Control of Handguns." *Law Officer,* 8 (1975), pp. 15-18.

Roper, William L. "Cheap Guns for Killers." *The California Highway Patrolman* (December, 1967).

Serr, Harold A. "Gun Control Act Gets Results." *Police Chief,* XXXVII:1 (January, 1970), pp. 30-32.

Skousen, W. Cleon. "Gun Control or Political Control." *Law and Order,* 23:10 (October, 1975), pp. 22-27, 50.

Snyder, J.M. "Crime Rises under Rigid Gun Control." *American Rifleman,* (1969), pp. 54-55.
New Jersey's tough 1966 gun control law appears to have ushered in a period of skyrocketing crime. In 1965 New Jersey ranked 18 among the fifty states in total crimes committed. By 1968 it was ranked 10th in total crimes committed. In the total crime category the average rate for the most restrictive state was 59% greater than for the least restrictive states. Statistical information for the periods covered from the FBI.

Thornburgh, R.L. "Support the Police by Handgun Control." *American Bar Association Journal,* 59: (1973), pp. 404-406.

Treasury Department. *Published Ordinances—Firearms.* Washington, D.C.: GPO, 1971.
The Gun Control Act of 1968 and other ordinances define legal requirements for importers, manufacturers and dealers in firearms.

IMPEACHMENT

Bar Association of the City of New York. *Law of Presidential Impeachment.* N.Y.: Harper and Row, 1974.

Berger, Raoul. *Impeachment: The Constitutional Problems.* Cambridge, MA.: Harvard University Press, 1973.

McBride, H.E. *Impeach Justice Douglas: (vol. I) Subversion.* Hicksville, N.Y.: Exposition, 1971.

Marshall, P.J. *The Impeachment of Warren Hastings.* N.Y.: Oxford University Press, 1965.

JURY TRIALS

Bloomstein, Morris. *Verdict: The Jury System.* N.Y.: Dodd, Mead, 1968.

Broeder, D. "Plaintiff's Family Status as Affecting Jury Behavior." *Journal of Public Law,* 14 (1965), pp. 131-143.

Edenhofer, L.E. "Impartial Jury—Twentieth Century Dilemma: Some Solutions to the Conflict Between Free Press and Fair Trial." *Cornell Law Quarterly* (1966), pp. 306-327.

Galiher, R.W. "Crisis of the Jury System." *New York State Bar Journal,* 37 (1965), pp. 439-445.

Ganzer, M. "The Jury." *Brooklyn Barrister,* 10 (1959), pp. 152-157.

Gleisser, Marcus. *Juries and Justice.* So. Brunswick, N.J.: Barnes, 1968.

Guide to Juror Usage. Washington, D.C.: NCJRS, 1974.

Hara, M. "The Streamlined Jury System." *Southern California Law Review,* 36 (1962), pp. 89-108.

Icenogle, C.S. "Menace of the Hung Jury." *American Bar Association Journal* (1961), pp. 280-282.

Kalven, M. and M. Zeisel. *American Jury.* Chicago: Chicago University Press, (1971).

University of Chicago Law School jury study deals with the differing ways judge and jury decide the same case, emphasizing the jury decision making process.

Kaufman, I.R. "A Fair Jury—The Essence of Justice." *Judicature,* 51 (1967), pp. 88-92.

Landy, D. and E. Aronson. "The Influence of the Character of the Criminal and Victim on the Decisions of Simulated Jurors." *Journal of Experimental Social Psychology,* (1969), pp. 141-152.

McCabe, S. and R. Purves. *Jury at Work—A Study of a Series of Jury Trials in Which the Defendant Was Acquitted.* Oxford: Basil Blackwell, 1972.

McCart, Samuel W. *Trial By Jury.* N.Y.: Chilton, 1964.

A brief history and development of the jury system is followed by all aspects of what the juror will find in the courts. This progresses from selection rf jurors to the verdict and beyond to the appellate courts.

Mitchell, H. and D. Byrne. "The Defendant's Dilemma: Effect of Juror's Attitudes and Authoritarianism on Judicial Decisions." *Journal of Personality and Social Psychology,* 25: 1973.

Oglesby, D. "New Trends in Trial by Jury." *American Business Law Quarterly* (1967), pp. 191-202.

Pope, J. "Proper Function of Jurors." *Baylor Law Review,* 14 (1963), pp. 365-383.

Richards, R. "A New Look at Our Jury System." *Florida Bar Journal,* 41 (1967), pp. 92-100.

Ruppin, R. "One Lawyer's Dissent: American vs. English Arguments." *American Bar Association Journal,* 45 (1959), pp. 1257-1259.

Ryan, John V. "Less Than Unamimous Jury Verdicts in Criminal Trials." *Journal of Criminal Law, Criminology and Police Science,* 58:2 (June, 1967), pp. 211-217.

"Special Verdict—Majority Verdicts." *Washington Law Review,* 26 (1951), pp. 56-57.

Thompson, Jim. "A Handbook for Jurors in Criminal Cases." *Journal of Criminal Law, Criminology and Police Science,* 50:3 (September-October, 1959), pp. 285-290.

Vidmar, N. "Effects of Decision Alternatives on the Verdicts and Social Perceptions of Simulated Jurors." *Journal of Personality and Social Psychology,* 22 (1972), pp. 211-218.

Wolf, R.C. "Trial by Jury: A Sociological Analysis." *Wisconsin Law Review* (1966), pp. 820-830.

PLEA BARGAINING

Arcuri, Alan F. "Police Perceptions of Plea Bargaining: A Preliminary Inquiry." *Journal of Police Science and Administration,* 1:1 (March, 1973), pp. 93-101.

Bond, James E. *Plea Bargaining and Guilty Pleas.* N.Y.: Clark, Boardman, 1975.

Glenn, Gary F. "Does Crime Pay?" *Police Chief,* XLIII:1 (January, 1976), pp. 53-55.

Leaddy, Albert M. "Plea Bargaining—Trying to Get Out of the Trap." *Journal of California Law Enforcement* (January, 1976), pp. 85-87.

Newman, Edwin S. *Conviction: The Determination of Guilt or Innocence Without Trial.* Boston: Little, Brown, 1966.

PROSECUTION DISCRETION

Abrams, Norman. "Internal Policy: Guiding the Exercise of Prosecutorial Discretion." *UCLA Law Review,* 19:1 (October, 1971), pp. 1-58.

Castberg, A.D. *Prosecutorial Discretion—A Case Study.* Ann Arbor, MI.: University Microfilms, 1968.

A dissertation on the role of the prosecutor in the criminal justice system and the factors which affect his decision-making processes.

Cates, Aubrey M., Jr. "Can We Ignore Laws? Discretion Not to Prosecute." *Alabama Law Review,* 14:1 (Fall, 1961), pp. 1-10.

Grosman, Brian A. *The Prosecutor: An Inquiry into the Exercise of Discretion.* Toronto: University of Toronto Press, 1969.

Kadish, Mortimer R. and Sanford H. Kadish. "On Justice Rule Departures by Officials." *California Law Review,* 59:4 (June, 1971), pp. 905-960.

Kaplan, John. "The Prosecutorial Discretion—A Comment." *Northwestern Law Review,* 60:2 (May-June, 1965), pp. 174-193.

Lafave, Wayne R. "The Prosecutor's Discretion in the United States." *American Journal of Comparative Law,* 18:3 (1970), pp. 532-548.

McIntyre, D.M. and D. Lippman. *Prosecutors and Early Disposition of Felony Cases.* Chicago: American Bar Association, 1971.
Criteria for prosecutor's power to terminate felony cases at an early stage are seen as needed.

Miller, Frank W. *Prosecution: The Decision to Charge a Suspect with a Crime.* Boston: Little, Brown, 1969.

Mills, Richard. "The Prosecutor: Charging and Bargaining." *University of Illinois Law Forum* (Fall, 1966), pp. 511-522.

Newman, Donald J. "Pleading Guilty for Considerations: A Study of Bargain Justice." *Journal of criminal Law, Criminology and Police Science,* 46:6 (March-April, 1956), pp. 780-790.

"Prosecutorial Discretion in the Initiation of Criminal Complaints." *Southern California Law Review,* 42:3 (Spring, 1969), pp. 519-545.

Stein, L. "Prosecutorial Discretion in the Initiation of Criminal Complaints." *Southern California Law Review,* 42 (1968-1969), pp. 519-545.

PUNISHMENT

Andenase, J. "The General Preventive Effects of Punishment." *University of Pennsylvania Law Review,* 114 (May, 1966), pp. 949-983.

Andenase, Johannes. *Punishment and Deterrents.* Ann Arbor: University of Michigan Press, 1974.

Andenaes, Johannes. "Punishment and the Problem of General Prevention." *Journal of Criminal Law, Criminology and Police Science,* 43 (1952), pp. 176.

Andrews, William. *Old-Time Punishments.* London: Tabard, 1890. (repr.)

Appel, James B. and Neil J. Peterson. "What's Wrong with Punishment?" *Journal of Criminal Law, Criminology and Police Science,* 56:4 (December, 1965), pp. 450-453.

Barnes, Harry E. *The Story of Punishment.* Montclair, N.J.: Patterson Smith, 1972. (repr. of 1930 ed.)

Bazelon, David L. "The Imperative to Punish." *Atlantic* (July, 1960).

Becker, Gary S. "Crime and Punishment: An Economic Approach." *Journal of Political Economy,* 76 (March-April, 1968).

Boe, Erling E. and Russell M. Church, eds. *Punishment: Issues and Experiments.* N.Y.: Irvington, 1968.

Campbell, Byron A. and Russell M. Church, eds. *Punishment and Aversive Behavior.* Englewood Cliffs, N.J.: Prentice-Hall, 1974.

Church, R.M. "The Varied Effects of Punishment on Behavior." *Psychological Review,* 70 (September, 1963), pp. 369-402.

Council of Europe. *Effectiveness of Punishment and Other Measures of Treatment.* N.Y.: Manhattan, 1967.

Eglash, Albert. "Creative Restitution." *Journal of Criminal Law, Criminology and Police Science,* 48:6 (March-April, 1958), pp. 619-622.

Ezorsky, G. *Philosophical Perspectives on Punishment.* Albany: State University of New York Press, 1972.
Collection of philosophical writings on the concepts of punishment, the justification for punishment, the death penalty, strict liability, and punishment alternatives.

Gerber, Rudolph and Patrick McAnany, eds. *Contemporary Punishment: Views, Explanations and Justifications.* Notre Dame, IN.: University of Notre Dame, 1972.

Great Britain, Advisory Council on Treatment of Officers. *Corporal Punishment Report of the Advisory Council on the Treatment of Offenders.* London: HMSO, 1960.

Grupp, S.E. *Theories of Punishment.* Bloomington: Indiana University Press, 1971.
Collection of readings by leading philosophers and social scientists, discussing classical punishment theories—retributive, deterrent, rehabilitative, and integrative.

Harno, Albert J. "Crime and Punishment." *Journal of Criminal Law, Criminology and Police Science,* 46:1 (January-February, 1955), pp. 520-523.

Hart, Harold H. *Punishment: For and Against.* N.Y.: Hart, 1972.

Holz, W. and N.H. Azrin. "Interactions Between the Discriminative and Aversive Properties of Punishment." *Journal of Experimental Animal Behavior,* 5:2 (1962), pp. 229-234.

Honderich, T. *Punishment—The Supposed Justifications.* N.Y.: Harcourt Brace Jovanovich, 1970.
A clarification and assessment of classical and contemporary attempts to give moral justification for the practice of punishment.

Irwin, John and Donald R. Cressey. "Thieves, Convicts, and the Inmate Culture." *Social Problems,* 10 (Fall, 1962), pp. 142-155.
Imprisonment has little effect on the thief one way or another.

Isle of Man Constabulary. *Birching of Juveniles in the Isle of Man, 1960-1974.* Douglas: Isle of Man Constabulary, 1975.

Isle of Man Constabulary. *Corporal Punishment in the Isle of Man.* Douglas: Isle of Man Constabulary, [n.d.].

Jacob, Bruce R. "Reparation or Restitution by the Criminal Offender to His Victim: Applicability of an Ancient Concept in the Modern Correctional Process." *Journal of Criminal Law, Criminology and Police Science,* 61:2 (1970).

Knight, Douglas W. "Punishment Selection as a Function of Biographical Information." *Journal of Criminal Law, Criminology and Police Science,* 56:3 (September, 1965), pp. 325-327.

Lewis, C.S. "The Humanitarian Theory of Punishment." *Res Judicatae,* 6 (June, 1953), pp. 224-230.

Madden, Edward H. *Philosophical Perspectives on Punishment.* Springfield, IL.: C.C. Thomas, 1968.

Mattick, Hans V. "Some Latent Functions of Imprisonment." *Journal of Criminal Law, Criminology and Police Science,* 50:3 (September-October, 1959), pp. 237-244.

Mayer, A.J. "What Price Justice? States Face a Choice: Make Punishment Mild or Bolster Legal Aid." *Wall Street Journal,* 86 (June 26, 1972), pp. 1-14.

Meyer, Joel. "Reflections on Some Theories of Punishment." *Journal of Criminal Law, Criminology and Police Science,* 59:4 (December, 1968), pp. 595-599.

Middendorff, Wolf. *The Effectiveness of Punishment.* South Hackensack, N.J.: Fred B. Rothman, 1968.

Murphy, J.G. *Punishment and Rehabilitation.* Belmont CA.: Wadsworth, 1973.
Philosophical essays on punishment from multiple perspectives emphasizing its justification and alternatives, and problems of therapeutic rehabilitation.

Osborne, Harold W. "On Crime, Punishment and Deterrence." *Social Science Quarterly,* 49:1 (June, 1968), pp. 157-160.

Packer, H.L. *The Limits of the Criminal Sanction.* Stanford, CA.: Stanford University Press, 1968.

Pease, K. et al. *Community Service Orders—A Home Office Research Unit Report.* Palo Alto, CA.: Pendragon House, 1975.
Punishment involving community service instead of jail.

Reynolds, Steven E. and James M. Rock. "Justice in Punishment by Fines." *Journal of California Law Enforcement,* 10:4 (April, 1976), pp. 136-143.

Ross, H.L. and M. Blumenthal. "Sanctions for the Drinking Driver: An Experimental Study." *Journal of Legal Studies,* 3:1 (1973), pp. 53-61.

Rubin, Julius. "Crime and Punishment." *Corrective Psychiatry and Journal of Social Therapy,* 13:3 (1967), pp. 162-170.

Rusche, George and Otto Kirchheimer. *Punishment and Social Structure.* N.Y.: Russell and Russell, 1968.

Salem, R.G. and W.J. Bowers. "Severity of Formal Sanctions as a Deterrent to Deviate Behavior." *Law and Society Review,* 5 (August, 1970), pp. 21-40.

Schwartz, Barry. "The Effect in Philadelphia of Pennsylvania's Increased Penalties for Rape and Attempted Rape." *Journal of Criminal Law, Criminology and Police Science,* 59:4 (December, 1968), pp. 509-515.

Soloman, R.L. "Punishment." *American Psychologist,* 19 (April, 1964), pp. 239-253.

Toby, Jackson. "Is Punishment Necessary." *Journal of Criminal Law, Criminology and Police Science,* 55:3 (September, 1964), pp. 332-337.

Van Den Haag, Ernest. *Punishing Criminals: Concerning a Very Old and Painful Question.* N.Y.: Basic, 1975.

Westen, Derek A. "Fines, Imprisonment and the Poor: Thirty Dollars or Thirty Days." *California Law Review,* 57 (May, 1969).

RECIDIVISM

Arnold, William R. "A Functional Explanation of Recidivism." *Journal of Criminal Law, Criminology and Police Science,* 56:2 (June, 1965), pp. 212-220.

Bachman, Ralph. "Recidivism—A Threat to Law Enforcement." *Law and Order,* 15:9 (September, 1967), pp. 28-31.

Benford, M.D. "Major Violators Unit . . . Washington's New and Special Squad." *Law and Order,* 19:10 (October, 1971), pp. 28-31.
Police unit keeps track of major offenders and reports on their activities.

Black, Bertrum J. and Selma J. Glick. *Recidivism at the Hawthorne Cedar Knolls School.* N.Y.: Jewish Board of Guardians, [n.d.].

Cowden, James E. "Predicting Institutional Adjustment and Recidivism in Delinquent Boys." *Journal of Criminal Law, Criminology and Police Science,* 57:1 (March, 1966), pp. 39-44.

England, Ralph. "A Study of Post Probation Recidivism Among Federal Offenders." *Federal Probation,* 19 (1955).

Florida Division of Youth Services. *Florida. Division of Youth Services. Recidivism Study.* Washington, D.C.: NCJRS, (Microfiche), [n.d.].

Kennedy, D.B. and A. Kerber. *Resocialization—An American Experiment.* N.Y.: Behavioral, 1973.
Critique on socialization and resocialization processes, the failures of these processes, and the nature and extent of rehabilitation and recidivism.

Laulicht, Jerome. "Problems of Statistical Research: Recidivism and Its Correlates." *Journal of Criminal Law, Criminology and Police Science,* 54:2 (June, 1963), pp. 163-174.

MacLeod, Alastair W. *Recidivism. A Deficiency Disease.* Philadelphia: University of Penn Press, 1966.

Mandel, Nathan G. et al. "Recidivism Studied and Defined." *Journal of Criminal Law, Criminology and Police Science,* 56:1 (March, 1965), pp. 59-66.

Mandel, Nathan G. and Alfred J. Barron. "The MMPI and Criminal Recidivism." *Journal of Criminal Law, Criminology and Police Science,* 57:1 (March, 1966), pp. 35-38.

Metzner, Ralph and Gunther Weil. "Predicting Recidivism: Base-Rates for Massachusetts Correctional Institution Concord." *Journal of Criminal Law, Criminology and Police Science,* 54:3 (September, 1963), pp. 307-316.

O'Brien, John T. and Frederick J. Cavanagh. "A Study of Individual and Family Recidivism and a Police Response." *Journal of Police Science and Administration,* 2:3 (September, 1974), pp. 322-329.

Unkovic, Charles M. and William J. Ducsay. "An Application of Configurational Analysis to the Recidivism of Juvenile Delinquent Behavior." *Journal of Criminal Law, Criminology and Police Science,* 60:3 (September, 1969), pp. 340-344.

RESPONSIBILITY

American Law Institute. "Responsibility." *Journal of Criminal Law, Criminology and Police Science,* 46:4 (November-December, 1955), pp. 450-484.

Casselman, Chet. "Responsibility in Radio—TV News Coverage." *FBI Law Enforcement Bulletin,* (June, 1967), pp. 12-13.

Davis, P.E., ed. *Moral Duty and Legal Responsibility: A Philosophical—Legal Case Book.* N.Y.: Irvington, 1966.

Fearey, Robert A. "Concept of Responsibility." *Journal of Criminal Law, Criminology and Police Science.* 45:1 (May-June, 1954), pp. 21-28.

Gallogly, Edwards P. "The Law—Responsibility of Young and Old." *FBI Law Enforcement Bulletin,* 39:5 (May, 1970), pp. 22-25.

Hassel, C.B. "Criminal Law v. Criminology: A Question of Responsibility." *FBI Law Enforcement Bulletin,* 44:10 (1975), pp. 11-15.
The criminal law maintains man is responsible for his actions. Some criminologists believe that man has no real choice of actions and should not be held responsible.

Horosz, William. *Crisis of Responsibility: Man as the Source of Accountability.* Norman: University of Oklahoma Press, 1975.

Jacobs, Francis G. *Criminal Responsibility.* Highland, N.J.: Humanities, 1971.

Jeffery, C.R. *Criminal Responsibility and Mental Disease.* Springfield, IL.: C.C. Thomas, 1967.

Leibman, Morris I. "The Year of the Civil Delinquent." *FBI Law Enforcement Bulletin,* 36:2 (February, 1967), pp. 14-16, 27-28.

Mercier, Charles A. *Criminal Responsibility.* N.Y.: Physicians and Surgeons, 1926.

"Parents Responsible for Children's Crimes." *FBI Law Enforcement Bulletin,* 39:6 (June, 1970).

SENTENCING

American Bar Association. *Sentencing Alternatives and Procedures, Standards Relating To,* Chicago: American Bar Association, 1968.
American Bar Association's standards and commentary on sentencing alternatives available to the legislative and judicial process.

Blom-Cooper, Louis. "Sentencing: The Judges Have Too Much Power." *Police (GB),* (November, 1975), pp. 22-24.

Bullick, R. "Significance of the Racial Factor in the Length of Prison Sentences." *Journal of Criminal Law, Criminology and Police Science,* 52 (1961), pp. 411-415.

Carter, Robert M. and Leslie T. Wilkins. "Some Factors in Sentencing Policy." *Journal of Criminal Law, Criminology and Police Science,* 58:4 (December, 1967), pp. 503-514.

Clark, Donald E. "Community Service: A Realistic Alternative for Sentencing." *FBI Law Enforcement Bulletin* (March, 1976), pp. 3-7.

Dawson, Robert. *Sentencing: The Decision as to Type, Length, and Conditions of Sentence.* Boston: Little, Brown, 1969.

D'Esposito, Julian C., Jr. "Sentencing Disparity: Causes and Cures." *Journal of Criminal Law, Criminology and Police Science,* 60:2 (June, 1969), pp. 182-194.

Green, E. *Analysis of the Sentencing Practices of Criminal Court Judges in Philadelphia.* Ann Arbor, MI.: University of Microfilms, 1959.
The effects of legal, non-legal, and prosecutory criteria upon the penalties imposed by judges on convicted offenders, and the consistency in judge sentencing.

Green, Edward. "Inter-and Intra-Racial Crime Relative to Sentencing." *Journal of Criminal Law, Criminology and Police Science,* 55:3 (September, 1964), pp. 348-358.

Green, Edward. *Judicial Attitudes in Sentencing.* Westport, CT.: Greenwood, 1975. (repr. of 1961 ed.).

Hotis, John B. "A Law Enforcement Officer Looks at Sentencing." *FBI Law Enforcement Bulletin,* 41:8 (August, 1972), pp. 18-21.

Kelley, Clarence M. "A Lawman's Perspective of Sentencing." *FBI Law Enforcement Bulletin,* 43:7 (July, 1974), pp. 16-19.

Pope, Carl E. *Sentencing of California Felony Offenders.* Washington, D.C.: NCJRS 1975.

Rau, R. *Sentencing in the Federal District Courts.* Washington, D.C.: NCJRS, 1972.
Sentencing data from the 93 federal district courts for the years 1967-1970 on the extent of variation and its relationship to certain defendent characteristics.

Thomsen, Roszel C. "Sentencing the Dangerous Offender." *Federal Probation,* 32:1 (1968), pp. 3-4.
In determining what sentence is proper in a criminal case the basic principle should be that the function and purpose of criminal law is the protection of society. In sentencing dangerous offenders, the crime, the offender and the community should be considered. If the offender is dangerous a long sentence is considered to protect the community.

Walker, N. *Sentencing in a Rational Society.* N.Y.: Basic, 1971.
Reduction of prohibited conduct (reconviction) by a penal system which observes limits dictated by humanity and which deemphasizes consistency in sentencing.

SPEEDY TRIALS

American Bar Association. *Speedy Trials, Standards Relating to,* Chicago: American Bar Association, 1967.
Formulation of minimum standards on speedy trial in order to establish an official American Bar Association policy.

U.S. Congress Senate Committee on the Judiciary. *Speedy Trial-Hearing Before the Senate Subcommittee on Constitutional Rights on S. 754—A Bill to Give Effect to the Sixth Amendment Right to a Speedy Trial, April 17, 1973.* Washington, D.C.: GPO, 1973.
Testimony and other materials concerning speedy trial legislation.

WRONGFUL CONVICTIONS

Borchard, Edwin M. *Convicting the Innocent: Errors of Criminal Justice.* New Haven, CT.: Yale University Press, 1932.
Collection of 65 cases of erroneous convictions of innocent victims.

Brandon, Ruth and Christie Davies. *Wrongful Imprisonment: Mistaken Convictions and Their Consequence.* Hamden, CT.: Archon, 1973.

Gardner, Erle Stanley. "Miscarriages of Justice." *Police,* 2:6 (July-August, 1958), pp. 9-13.

Lassers, W.J. *Scapegoat Justice—Lloyd Miller and the Failure of the American Legal System.* Bloomington: Indiana University Press, 1973.

Story of Lloyd Miller's trial, conviction and subsequent exoneration of the rape-murder of an eight year old Illinois child.

Rodin, Edward D. *The Innocents.* N.Y.: Morrow, 1964.

LEGAL AND JUDICIAL ISSUES

COURTS

Courts—General

The American Assembly. *The Courts, the Public and the Law Explosion.* Englewood Cliffs, N.J.: Prentice-Hall, 1965.

Describes in a series of articles, the new burdens imposed on the courts and the legal order by technological changes and social tensions in contemporary society, serving to create a crisis in judicial administration.

American Judicature Society. *Courts of Limited Jusisdiction—A National Survey.* Washington, D.C.: GPO, 1975.

Baar, C. *Separate but Subservient: Court Budgeting in the American States.* Lexington, MA.: Lexington, 1975.

Callison, I.P. *Courts of Injustice.* N.Y.: Twayne, 1956.

Carr, Lowell J. "Most Courts Have to Be Substandard." *Federal Probation,* 13 (September, 1949), pp. 29-33.

"The Concept and Operation of a Central Violations Bureau." *Law and Order,* 13:1 (January, 1965), pp. 66-69.

Court handling of traffic violations.

Downie, Leonard Jr. *Justice Denied: The Case for Reform of the Courts.* N.Y.: Praeger, 1971.

Ellenbogen, Henry. "A Twentieth Century Approach to Judicial Administration." *FBI Law Enforcement Bulletin,* 35:5 (May, 1966), pp. 7-11.

Suggestions for court reform.

Frank, Gerome. *Courts on Trial: Myth and Reality on American Justice.* N.J.: Princeton, N.J.: Princeton University Press, 1949.

James, Howard. *Crisis in the Courts.* (rev. ed.) N.Y.: McKay, 1971.

Hughes, G. *Conscience of the Courts: Law and Morals in American Life.* Garden City, N.Y.: Doubleday, 1975.

Examines the roles of the courts in decisions regarding a long range of issues.

"Justice on Trial." *Newsweek,* (March 8, 1971), pp. 16-46.

Lineberry, William P., comp. *Justice in America: Law, Order, and the Courts.* N.Y.: Wilson, 1972.

Lum, H.T.F. "The Honolulu Family Court." *FBI Law Enforcement Bulletin,* 44:5 (1975), pp. 24-27.

Description of the development and jurisdiction of the family court in Hawaii. Includes philosophy and planning.

McGowan, Carl. *Organization of Judicial Power in the United States.* Evanston, IL.: Northwestern University Press, 1969.

Morrison, F.L. *Courts and the Political Process in England.* Beverly Hills, CA.: Sage, 1973.

A configurative and comparative description of the English Judicial System and its relationship to the Political System of the United Kingdom, with comparisons to the American Court System.

National Advisory Commission on Criminal Justice Standards and Goals. *Courts: Report of the National Advisory Commission on Criminal Justice Standards and Goals, 1973.* Washington, D.C.: GPO, 1973.

Proposals for the restricting and streamlining of the processing of criminal cases at state and local levels.

Opala, Marian P. "Judge-Controlled Nonautomated Felony Caseflow." *FBI Law Enforcement Bulletin* (January, 1975), pp. 30-31.

President's Commission on Law Enforcement and Administration of Justice. *Task Force Report: The Courts.* Washington, D.C.: GPO, 1967.

The report confines itself to those parts of the court system and the criminal process most in need of reform.

Radzinowics, L. and M. Wolfgang. *Criminal in the Arms of the Law.* N.Y.: Basic, 1971.

A collection of articles on the performance of police and the courts as they affect the offender.

Reed, J.H. *Application of Operations Research to Court Delay.* N.Y.: Praeger, 1973.

Statistical and modeling techniques applied to a computerized data bank of one year's criminal cases to assess alternative solutions to court delay.

Robertson, John A. *Rough Justice: Perspectives on Lower Criminal Courts.* Boston: Little, Brown, 1974.

Rodell, Fred. *Nine Men: A Political History of the Supreme Court from 1790 to 1955.* N.Y.: Random, 1955.

Salomon, Leon I., ed. *The Supreme Court.* N.Y.: Wilson, 1961.

"The Scandal of Court Congestion." *Time* (November 9, 1970), pp. 59, 61.

Schubert, G. *Judicial Policy Making: The Political Role of the Courts.* (rev. ed.) N.Y.: Scott, Foresman, 1974.

Seymour, W.N., Jr. *Why Justice Fails.* N.Y.: William Morrow, 1973.
Critique of American courts and justice emphasizing the prejudices and corrupting inluences of the men and institutions which compose the system.

Sheldon, Charles H. *American Judicial Process. Models and Approaches.* N.Y.: Dodd Mead, 1974.

Singleton, Donald. "The Mess in Our Criminal Courts." *American Legion,* 89 (October, 1970), pp. 24-29, 39-41.

U.S. Census Bureau. *National Survey of Court Organization.* Washington, D.C.: NCJRS, 1973.
State by state data on levels of jurisdiction, personnel, and cases handled.

Federal Courts

Becker, Theodore L. *The Impact of Supreme Court Decisions.* N.Y.: Oxford Universit6 Press, 1969.

Bickel, A.M. *Caseload of the Supreme Court and What, if Anything, to Do About It.* Washington, D.C.: American Enterprise Institute for Public Policy Research, 1973.

Bozell, L. Brent. *The Warren Revolution: Reflection on the Consensus Society.* New Rochelle, N.Y.: Arlington, 1966.

Cox, Archibald: *The Role of the Supreme Court in American Government.* N.Y.: Oxford University Press, 1976.

Fish, Peter G. *Politics of Federal Judicial Administration.* Princeton, N.J.: Princeton University Press, 1973.

Frankfurter, Felix. *Mr. Justice Holmes and the Supreme Court.* Cambridge, MA.: Harvard University Press, 1938.

Gillespie, Robert W. *Judicial Productivity and Court Delay: An Exploratory Analysis of the Federal District Courts.* Washington, D.C.: GPO, 1976.

Gordon, Rosalie M. *Nine Men Against America: The Supreme Court and Its Attack on American Liberties.* N.Y.: Devin, Adair, 1958.

Graham, Fred P. *The Self Inflicted Wound.* N.Y.: Macmillan, 1970.

Griffith, Kathryn. *Judge Learned Hand and the Role of the Federal Judiciary.* Norman: Oklahoma University Press, 1973.

Haddad, James B. "Retroactivity Should Be Rethought: A Call for the End of Linkletter Doctrine." *Journal of Criminal Law, Criminology and Police Science,* 60:4 (December, 1969), pp. 417-441.

Kurland, P.B. *Politics, the Constitution, and the Warren Court.* Chicago: Chicago University Press, 1970.
Evaluation of the Supreme Court under Earl Warren as an institution which becomes a political body that made national police.

Leonard, V.A. *Police, the Judiciary, and the Criminal.* Springfield, IL.: C.C. Thomas, 1969.
The impact of Supreme Court decisions from 1961 to 1969 on law enforcement agencies.

Levy, L.W. *Against the Law—The Nixon Court and Criminal Justice.* N.Y.: Harper and Row, 1974.
Explores criminal justice decisions since the Nixon appointees and judges them to have a prosecutorial bias.

Sayler, Richard H. et al., eds. *The Warren Court, a Critical Analysis.* N.Y.: Chelsea, 1969.

Spaniol, J.F. *United States Courts—Their Jurisdiction and Work.* Washington, D.C.: GPO, 1971.
Handbook describing the judicial branch of the Federal government, prepared by the committee on the Judiciary of the House of Representatives.

Juvenile Courts

Becemsterboer, Matthew J. "The Juvenile Courts: Benevolence in the Star Chamber." *Journal of Criminal Law, Criminology and Police Science,* 50:5 (January-February, 1970), pp. 464-476.

Carey, J.T., J. Goldfarb, and M.J. Rowe. *The Handling of Juveniles From Offense to Disposition.* Washington, D.C.: U.S. Department of Health, Education, and Welfare, [n.d.].

Cavenaugh, W.E. *Juvenile Courts, the Child and the Law.* Baltimore: Penguin, 1968.

Fox, Sanford J. *The Law of Juvenile Courts in a Nutshell.* St. Paul, MN.: West, 1971.

Herman, Stephen M. "Scope and Purposes of Juvenile Court Jurisdiction." *Journal of Criminal Law, Criminology and Police Science,* 48:6 (March-April, 1958), pp. 590-607.

Paulsen, M.G. and C.H. Whitebread. *Juvenile Law and Procedure—Juvenile Justice Textbook Series.* Reno, NV.: National Council of Juvenile Court Judges, 1974.

Rosenheim, Margaret K. *Justice for the Child—The Juvenile Court in Transition.* N.Y.: Free Press, 1962.

Criminal Appeals

"Cost of Appeal." *Montana Law Review,* 27 (1965), pp. 49-54.

Meador, D.J. *Criminal Appeals—English Practices and American Reform.* Charlottesville, VA.: University of Virginia Press, 1973.
The English system of criminal appeals is analyzed to identify successful procedures which present possibilities for adoption in American appellate courts.

World Court

Bustamante, Antonio D., ed. *The World Court.* N.Y.: Macmillan, 1925.

Fachiri, Alexander P. *The Permanent Court of International Justice: Its Constitution, Procedure and Work.* London: Oxford University Press, 1925.

Fleming, Denna Frank. *The United States and the World Court.* Garden City, N.Y.: Doubleday, 1945.

Hill, David Jayne. *The Problem of a World Court: The Story of an Unrealized American Idea.* N.Y.: Longmans, 1927.

Hudson, Manley O. *The Permanent Court of International Justice and the Question of American Participation.* Cambridge, MA.: Harvard University Press, 1925.

Jessup, Philip C. *The United States and the World Court.* Boston: World Peace Foundation, 1929.

Mueller, G.O.W. and E.M. Wise. *International Criminal Law.* S. Hackensack, N.J.: Fred B. Rothman, 1965.

CRIMINAL EVIDENCE

"Admissibility of Standard Writings." *FBI Law Enforcement Bulletin,* 35:5 (May, 1966), pp. 20-23.

Baade, Hans W. "Illegally Obtained Evidence in Criminal and Civil Cases: A Comparative Study of a Classic Mismatch II." *Texas Law Review* (April, 1974), pp. 621-702.

Conway, James V.P. *Evidential Documents.* Springfield, IL.: C.C. Thomas, 1959.

George, B.J., Jr. *Constitutional Limitations on Evidence in Criminal Cases.* N.Y.: Practicing Law Institute, 1973.

Heffron, Floyd Nichols. *Evidence for the Patrolman.* Springfield, IL.: C.C. Thomas, 1958.

Inbau, F.E. and N.E. Aspen. *Evidence Law for the Police.* Radnor, PA.: Chilton, 1972.
Major principles of evidence law including traditional, procedural and constitutional limitations on police presentations.

Klein, Irving J. *Law of Evidence for Police.* St. Paul, MN.: West, 1973.

Katsaris, K. *Evidence and Procedure in the Administration of Justice.* N.Y.: Wiley, 1975.

Klotter, John C. and Carl L. Meier. *Criminal Evidence for Police.* Cincinnati, OH.: Anderson, 1971.

Prince, Jerome. *Cases and Materials on Evidence.* Mineola, N.Y.: Foundation Press, 1972.

Redden, Kenneth R. and Stephen A. Saltzburg. *Federal Rules of Evidence Manual.* (new ed.) Charlottesville, VA.: Michie, 1975.

Rifas, R.A. *Legal Aspects of Video Tape and Motion Pictures in Law Enforcement.* Evanston, IL.: Northwestern University Traffic Institute, 1972.
Rules of admissibility and constitutional issues raised by use of video tape and motion pictures as evidence in criminal trials.

Rothstein, Paul F., ed. *Federal Rules of Evidence.* N.Y.: Boardman, 1973.

Stuckey, G.B. *Evidence for the Law Enforcement Officer.* (2nd ed.) N.Y.: McGraw-Hill, 1974.
Practical guide for the police officer and police-science student to the rules and regulations governing the collection, preservation, and presentation of evidence.

Underhill, H.C. *Criminal Evidence.* (3 vol., 5th ed.) Indianapolis: Bobbs, 1965. (with 1970 supplement)

Waltz, J.R. *Criminal Evidence,* Chicago: Nelson-Hall, 1975.
Plain language explanation of the principles and procedures of legal rules of evidence and applicable to criminal cases for nonlawyers, such as police who gather criminal evidence and serve as witness in court.

Wigmore, John H. *Evidence.* (10 vols., 3rd ed.) Waltham, MA.: Little, Brown, 1940. (with 1975 supplement)

CRIMINAL LAW

Barrett, Edward J. "Police and the Law. From Arrest to Release or Charge." *California Law Review,* 50:1 (1962).

Bassiouni, M. Cherif and Ved P. Nanda. *A Treatise on International Criminal Law.* Springfield, IL.: C.C. Thomas, 1973.

Belli, Melvin M. *The Law Revolution: Criminal Law.* Los Angeles, Sherbourne, 1968.

Bryan, James Wallace. *The Development of the English Law of Conspiracy.* Baltimore: Johns Hopkins University, 1909.

Chamelin, N.C. and K.R. Evans. *Criminal Law for Policeman.* Englewood Cliffs, N.J.: Prentice-Hall, 1976.
General legal principles and discussion of elements of various crimes.

Chamelin, Neil and Kenneth Evans. *Handbook of Criminal Law.* Englewood Cliffs, N.J.: Prentice-Hall, 1972.

Cohen, S. *Law Enforcement Guide to United States Supreme Court Decisions.* Springfield, IL.: C.C. Thomas, 1972.

Cooke, Charles W. "House Trailer—Vehicle or House?" *FBI Law Enforcement Bulletin,* 43:4 (April, 1974).

Curtis, Lynn A. *Criminal Laws.* Lexington, MA.: Lexington, 1974.

Curzon, L.B. *Criminal Law.* London: MacDonald and Evans, Ltd, 1973.

Day, Frank D. *Criminal Law in Society.* Springfield, IL.: C.C. Thomas, 1964.

Donnelly, Richard C., Joseph Goldstein and Richard D. Schwartz. *Criminal Law: Problems for Decision in the Promulgation, Invocation, and Administration of a Law of Crimes.* N.Y.: Free Press, 1962.

Editor of the Criminal Law Reporter. *The Criminal Law Revolution, 1960-1969.* Washington, D.C.: Bureau of National Affairs, 1969.

Felkenes, George T. *Criminal Law: Procedure and Cases.* Englewood Cliffs, N.J.: Prentice-Hall, 1975.

Felkenes, George T. "Right of Privacy and Police Surveillance by Aircraft." *Journal of Police Science and Administration,* 1:3 (September, 1973), pp. 345-348.

Frank, John. *American Law: The Case for Radical Reform.* N.Y.: Macmillan, 1973.

Freedman, Warren. *Society on Trial: Current Court Decisions and Social Change.* Springfield, IL.: C.C. Thomas, 1965.

Gammage, A.Z. and C.F. Memphill. *Basic Criminal Law.* N.Y.: McGraw-Hill, 1974.
Handbook on the substantive criminal law written especially for the present or prospective police officer.

Gill, D.R. *Law of Arrest, Search, and Investigation.* (rev. ed.) Chapel Hill, N.C.: University of North Carolina, Institute of Government, 1974.

Goldstein, Joseph. *Criminal Law: Theory and Process.* N.Y.: Free Press, 1974.

Gould, M. Ronald. "New York's Pending 'No Sock' Bill." *Law and Order,* 13:7 (July, 1965), pp. 22-23.
Bill to make it unlawful to resist an unlawful arrest.

Harvard Law Review Association. *Criminal Law: Essays on Criminal Law Selected from the Pages of The Harvard Law Review.* Cambridge, MA.: Harvard Law Review Association, 1972.

Honig, Richard M. "Criminal Law Systematized." *Journal of Criminal Law, Criminology and Police Science,* 54:3 (September, 1963), pp. 273-287.

Inbau, Fred E. and Marvin E. Asben. *Criminal Law for the Police.* Radnor, PA.: Chilton, 1969.

King, Daniel P. "Narcotics and the Nalline Tests: Legal Aspects." *Law and Order,* 12:6 (June, 1964), pp. 70-73.

Leonard, Donald S. "The Changing Face of Criminal Law." *Journal of Criminal Law, Criminology and Police Science,* 56:4 (December, 1965), pp. 517-522.

Levine, Howard. "Officer in Peril." *Police Chief,* XXXVII:9 (September, 1970).
Description of a bill which would make it a felony to place an officer in peril.

Loewy, A.H. *Criminal Law in a Nutshell.* St. Paul, MN.: West Publishing Company, 1975.

Medalie, Richard J. *Escobedo to Miranda.* Washington, D.C.: Lerner Law, 1966.

Milner, N.A. *Court and Local Law Enforcement—The Impact of Miranda.* Beverly Hills, CA.: Sage, 1971.
Study of changes in police procedures occurring in four Wisconsin cities-Green Bay, Kenosha, Racine, and Madison in the 14 months after the Miranda decision.

Moreland, Roy. *The Law of Homicide.* Indianapolis: Bobbs-Merril, 1952.

Mueller, Gerhard O.W. *Crime, Law and the Scholars: A History of Scholarship in American Criminal Law.* Seattle, WA.: University of Washington Press, 1969.

Mueller, G.O.W. and S.A. Teitler. *Comparative Criminal Law in the United States.* So. Hackensack, N.J.: Fred B. Rothman, 1970.

National Commission on Reform of Federal Criminal Laws. *National Commission on Reform of Federal Criminal Law.* (2 vol.) Washington, D.C.: GPO, 1970.

Poff, Richard H. "A Means to Improve Our Federal Criminal Laws." *FBI Law Enforcement Bulletin,* 36:3 (March, 1967), pp. 14-16.

Schafer, W.J. *Schafer's Cases—The Hard to Find Ones.* Springfield, IL.: C.C. Thomas, 1972.
Collections of brief summaries of criminal cases illustrating little known points of law.

Schaver, F.F. *The Law of Obscenity.* Washington, D.C.: Bureau of National Affairs, 1976.

Sholl, Reginald. "An Australian Lawyer Looks at Some Aspects of the Criminal Law in the U.S.A." *Police,* 12:1 (September-October, 1967), pp. 81-88.

Siegal, Barry. "Double Jeopardy and Due Process." *Journal of Criminal Law, Criminology and Police Science,* 59:2 (June, 1968), pp. 247-254.

Udell, G.G. *Crime Kidnapping and Prison Laws.* Washington, D.C.: GPO,1971.
Compendium of the texts of acts passed by congress relating to aspects of crime and corrections from 1902 to 1971 including the omnibus crime control acts.

U.S. Laws. *Public Law 91-452 Organized Crime Control Act of 1970.* Washington, D.C.: GPO, 1970.

U.S. Postal Service. *Mail Fraud Laws: Protecting Consumers, Investors, Businessmen, Patients, Students.* Washington, D.C.: GPO, 1971.

Wexler, D.B. *Law of Detainers.* Washington, D.C.: GPO, 1973.
Laws which hold prison inmates who face outstanding charges in other jurisdictions.

Willner, William Dean. "Knock or No Knock." *Enforcement Journal* (October-December, 1972).

Wootton, Barbara. *Crime and the Criminal Law: Reflections of a Magistrate and Social Scientist.* London: Stevens, 1963.

Young, Rudolph. *Criminal Law: Codes and Cases.* N.Y.: McGraw-Hill, 1972.

CRIMINAL PROCEDURE

Carlson, Ronald L. *Criminal Justice Procedure for Police.* Cincinnati: Anderson, 1970.

Epstein, David and David T. Austem. *Uniform Rules of Criminal Procedure: Comparison and Analysis.* Washington, D.C.: American Bar Association, 1975.

Faber, Stuart J. *Handbook of Criminal Procedure.* Hollywood, CA.: Good Life, 1975.

Ferdico, John N. *Criminal Procedure for the Law Enforcement Officer.* St. Paul, MN.: West, 1975.

George, B.M., Jr. *Constitutional Limitations on Evidence in Criminal Cases, 1973* (ed.) *With Supplemental Materials.* N.Y.: Practicing Law Institute, 1973.
Practical handbook presenting the current state of law in criminal procedure and admissibility of evidence based on recent Supreme Court decisions.

George, B. James, Jr. *Criminal Procedure Sourcebook, 1976.* (2 vol.) N.Y.: Practicing Law Institute, 1976.

Gourley, G. Douglas. "Criminal Procedure and Civil Rights." *Journal of Criminal Law, Criminology and Police Science,* 50:1 (May-June, 1959), pp. 71-76.

Graham, Kenneth and Leon Letwin. "The Preliminary Hearing in Los Angeles. Some Field Finding and Legal-Policy Observations." *UCLA Law Review,* 10:4 (March, 1971), 10:5 (May, 1971).

Herman, M.G., ed. *Federal Rules of Criminal Procedure.* N.Y.: Boardman, 1975.

Israel, Jerold H. and Wayne R. LaFave. *Criminal Procedure in a Nutshell—Constitutional Limitations.* (2nd ed.) St. Paul, MN.: West, 1975.

Rights of The Accused—Criminal Procedure and Public Security. Columbus, OH.: Xerox Education Center, 1971.
Case study of an average criminal prosecution from beginning to end, with emphasis on issued involved in arrest, trial, appeal, and constitutional law.

Traynor, Roger J. *The Riddle of Harmless Error.* Columbus: Ohio State University Press, 1970.
Chief Justice Traynor of the California Supreme Court discusses the harmless error as it effects court cases. What makes an error harmless as opposed to those errors that affect decisions. Many court cases dealing with the harmless error question are cited and discussed in the book.

Wright, R.G. and J.A. Marlo. *Police Officer and Criminal Justice.* N.Y.: McGraw-Hill, 1970.
Explanation of the criminal procedures used in a court system to acquaint police with the function and rationale for each step in criminal trials.

Zander, Michael. "Acquittal Rates and Not Guilty Pleas: What Do the Statistics Mean?" *Criminal Law Review,* (July, 1974), pp. 401-408.

MODEL PENAL CODE

Grad, Frank P. "The American Law Institute, Model Penal Code." *NPPA JOURNAL,* 4 (April, 1958), pp. 127-138.

Kuh, R.H. "Prosecutor Considers the Model Penal Code." *Columbia Law Review,* 63 (1963).

Missouri Committee to Draft a Modern Criminal Code. *Missouri: Proposed Criminal Code.* Washington, D.C.: NCJRS, (Microfiche), 1973.

National Council on Crime and Delinquency. *Model Rules of Court on Police Action From Arrest To Arraignment.* Washington, D.C.: National Council on Crime and Delinquency, 1969.

THE LAW—ISSUES AND PROBLEMS

Law—General

Abortion Laws: A Survey of Current World Legislation. Albany, N.Y.: World Health, 1970.

Akers, Ronald L. "Toward a Comparative Definition of Law." *Journal of Criminal Law, Criminology and Police Science,* 56:3 (September, 1965), pp. 301-306.

Baum, F.S. *Law of Self-Defense.* Dobbs Ferry, N.Y.: Oceana, 1970.

Cairns, Huntington. *Legal Philosophy From Plato to Hegel.* Baltimore: Johns Hopkins University Press, 1969.

Cranston, Alan. "California Makes First Use of Unique Good Samaritan Law." *Police* (September-October, 1966).

Dicey, A.V. *Lectures on the Relation Between Law and Public Opinion in England During the Nineteenth Century.* London: Macmillan, 1948.

Dorsey, Gray L. et al. *Law Reform: A Modern Perspective.* St. Louis: St. Louis University Press, 1968.

Friedland, Martin L. *Double Jeopardy.* Oxford: Clarendon, 1969.

Horwitz, Morton J. et al., eds. *American Law: The Formative Years.* (28 books) N.Y.: Arno, 1972.

McKee, Roger A. "P-CR—Legality of Forcible Haircuts." *Police Chief,* 38:3 (March, 1971), pp. 60-61.
Case law indicates that it is legal to force inmates to receive a haircut. Beards may not be cut in some cases on account of religious grounds.

Medalie, Richard J. *From Escobedo to Miranda: The Anatomy of a Supreme Court Decision.* Washington, D.C.: Lerner, 1966.

National Fire Codes. (16 vols.) Boston: National Fire Protection, 1976.

Post, Richard S. "Study of State's Requirements for Investigating." *Police Chief* (July, 1969).
Private investigations licensing requirements state by state study.

Rich, Vernon. *Law and the Administration of Justice.* N.Y.: Wiley, 1975.

Schafer, W.J. *Schafer's Cases—The Hard to Find Ones.* Springfield, IL.: C.C. Thomas, 1972.

Shaw, William. "The Legal Aspects of Radio Beacon Tracking Transmitters." *Law and Order,* 21:9 (September, 1973), pp. 32-34, 36, 38, 40, 94.

Wilson, Frank W. "The Law and the Urban Age." *FBI Law Enforcement Bulletin,* 39:2 (February, 1970), pp. 3-6, 16-17.

American Indian Laws

Cohen, Felix S. *Handbook of Federal Indian Law.* Washington, D.C.: GPO, 1941.

Law and the American Indian: Readings, Notes and Cases. Indianapolis: Bobbs-Merrill, 1973.

National American Indian Court Judges Association. *Criminal Court Procedures Manual—A Guide for American Indian Courts Judges.* Springfield, VA.: NTIS, 1971.
Guidelines in compliance with the Indian Civil Rights Act of 1968.

National American Indian Court Judges Association. *Criminal Court Procedures Manual—Research Document in Support of a Guide for American Indian Court Judges.* Springfield, VA.: NTIS, 1971.
Analysis of diverse systems of delivery of criminal justice by different Indian reservations ANC and impact the Indian Civil Rights Act may have on this diversity.

U.S. Solicitor for the Department of the Interior. *Federal Indian Law.* Dobbs Ferry, N.Y.: Oceana, 1966.

Waring, Antonio J., ed. *Laws of the Creek Nation.* Athens: University of Georgia Press, 1960.

Civil Disorder

Bassiouni, M.C. *Law of Dissent and Riots.* Springfield, IL.: C.C. Thomas, 1971.

Breckinridge, J.B. "Legislative Inadequacies and Needs." *Police Chief,* XXXVI:5 (May, 1969), pp. 48-53.

Treanor, G.F. *Riots and Municipalities.* Washington, D.C.: National Institute of Municipal Law Officers, 1967.
Report on the various aspects of municipal liability for damage caused by riots and mob action, and representative ordinances pertinent to riot control.

Civil Law

Administrative Law. Binghamton, N.Y.: Gould, 1976.

Allen, R.C. *Legal Rights of the Disabled and Disadvantaged.* Washington, D.C.: GPO, [n.d.]

Recommendations for legislative reform for the mentally and physically handicapped and the socially and economically disadvantaged.

Austin, R.H. "Why I'm for Buckle-up Laws." *Traffic Safety,* 74:5 (1974), pp. 11, 12-14, 36-38.

Bernard, H.Y. *Law of Death and Disposal of the Dead.* Dobbs Ferry, N.Y.: Oceana, 1966.

Chayet, Neil L. *Legal Implications of Emergency Care.* N.Y.: Appleton-Century-Croft, 1968.

Ginger, Ann Fagan, ed. *Human Rights Casefinder 1953-1969, The Warren Court.* Berkeley: Meiklejohn Civil Liberty, 1972.

Keller, Edward A. *The Case for Right-to-Work Laws: A Defense of Voluntary Unionism.* Chicago: Heritage Foundation, 1956.

Ranney, G. and E. Parker. *Landlord and Tenant.* Boston: Houghton Mifflin, 1970.

Illustrated civics textbook dealing with leases, evictions, and housing codes, as well as personal injury, and landlord and tenant rights and responsibilities.

Civil Service Law

Byham, W.C. and M.E. Spitzer. *Law and Personnel Testing.* N.Y.: AMA, 1971.

Farani, M. *Arbitration Laws.* N.Y.: International Publication Service, 1971.

Kaplan, H. Eliot. *The Law of Civil Service.* Albany, N.Y.: Matthew Bender, 1958.

The basic text on civil service law. Provides an authoritative judicial review of personnel reactions in government with brief exposition of the basic practices and procedures in administration of merit system laws.

Werne, Benjamin. *Law and Practice of Public Employment Labor Relations.* (3 vols.) Charlottesville, VA.: Michie,e974.

Common Law

Holmes, Oliver Wendell. *The Common Law.* Boston: Little, Brown, 1938.

Reinsch, Paul. *English Common Law in the Early American Colonies.* N.Y.: Gordon, 1976.

Constitutional Law

Aaron, Thomas J. "The Dilemma of Judicial Review." *Police,* 9:4 (March-April, 1965), pp. 35-36.

Eidelberg, Paul. *The Philosophy of the American Constitution: A Reinterpretation of the Intentions of the Founding Fathers.* N.Y.: Free Press, 1968.

Klotter, John C. and Jacqueline R. Kanovitz. *Constitutional Law For Police.* (2nd ed.) Cincinnati: W.H. Anderson, 1973.

Maddex, J.L., Jr. *Constitutional Law-Cases and Comments.* St. Paul, MN.: West, 1974.

This book is designed to assist the student of criminal justice and related fields in understanding the role of the supreme court in interpreting those provisions of the constitution which affect criminal justice.

Rogge, O. John. *The First and the Fifth: With Some Excursions into Others.* N.Y.: Nelson, 1960.

Tiffany, Lawrence P. "The Fourth Amendment and Police-Citizen Confrontations." *Journal of Criminal Law, Criminology and Police Science,* 60:4 (December, 1969), pp. 442-454.

Environmental Law

Baldwin, Malcolm F. and James K. Page, Jr. *Law and the Environment.* N.Y.: Walker, 1970.

Brecher, Joseph J. and Manuel E. Nestle. *Environmental Law Handbook.* Berkeley: California Continuing Education of the Bar, 1970.

Durning, Marvin B. *Legal Control of the Environment.* N.Y.: Practicing Law Institute, 1972.

Edelman, Sidney. *The Law of Air Pollution Control.* Wilton, CT.: Environmental Science Service, 1971.

Grad, Frank P. *Environmental Law: Sources and Problems.* N.Y.: Matthew Bender, 1971.

Greenwald, Alvin G. *Law of Noise Pollution.* Washington, D.C.: Bureau of National Affairs, May 1, 1970.

Landaw, Norman J. and Paul D. Rheingold. *The Environmental Law Handbook.* N.Y.: Ballantine, 1971.

Levi, Donald and Dale Colyer. "Legal Remedies for Pollution Abatement." *Science,* 175 (March 10, 1972), pp. 1085-1087.

Federal Law

Mortenson, Ernest R.s*Federal Tax Fraud Law.* Indianapolis: Bobbs, 1958. (with 1962 supplement)

O'Reilly, James T. "The Issues Now: Government Openness V. Law Enforcement Secrecy." *Police Chief,* XVII:2 (February, 1976), pp. 52-57.

Discusses the Freedom of Information Act as it relates to law enforcement.

Sokol, Ronald P. *Federal Habeas Corpus.* (2nd ed.) Charlottesville, VA.: Michie, 1969.

Sonnenreich, Michael R. *Handbook of Federal Narcotic and Dangerous Drug Laws.* Washington, D.C.: U.S. Bureau Narcotics and Dangerous Drugs, 1969.

United States Customs Law Digest. (5 vols.) Indianapolis: Bobbs, 1960. (with 1975 supplement)

Firearms Law

Braverman, Shelley. "The Federal Fire Arms Law." *Identification News,* 19:3 (December, 1960).

Fagerstrom, Dorothy. "The Police Officer's Guide to Pistol Regulations." *Law and Order,* 16:7 (July, 1968), pp. 90-97.

Guide for Police Officers regarding carrying firearms, exposed or concealed outside their own state. A state by state listing.

"Pistol Regulations in the 50 States. Better Check the Gun Laws in Each State First." *Law Officer,* 6:5 (1973), pp. 45-47.

Romig, Clarence H.A. "Federal and State Gun Laws Often Conflict." *Law and Order,* 19:10 (October, 1971), pp. 50-51.

Treasury Department. *Firearms—Published Ordinances.* Washington, D.C.: GPO, 1973.

State laws and local ordinances on the enforcement of the 1968 gun control act which refer to dealer licensing and business practices.

Your 1976 Guide to Firearms Regulation. Washington, D.C.: GPO, 1976.

International Law

Agrawala, S.K. *Aircraft Hijacking and International Law.* Dobbs Ferry, N.Y.: Oceana, 1973.

An analysis and evaluation of the provisions of several international conventions on hijacking, with an attempt to determine their efficacy as preventive and punitive measure.

Anand, Ram Prakash. *Studies in International Adjudication.* Dobbs Ferry, N.Y.: Oceana, 1969.

Mueller, Gerhard O. and E.M. Wise. *International Criminal Law.* S. Hackensack, N.J.: Rothman, 1965.

Pergler, Charles. *Judicial Interpretation of International Law in the United States.* N.Y.: Macmillan, 1928.

Poulantzas, N.M. *Right of Hot Pursuit in International Law.* Atlantic Highlands, N.J.: Humanities, 1969.

Sorensen, Max. *Manual of Public International Law.* N.Y.: St. Martin's, 1968.

Turack, Daniel C. *Passport in International Law.* Farnborough: Heath, 1972.

Juvenile Law

Fox, S.J. *Law of Juvenile Courts in a Nutshell.* St. Paul, MN.: West, 1971.

Resteiner, H.E. and L. Quinn. *Juvenile Law and Procedure.* Chicago: National District Attorneys Association, 1973.

Martial Law

Birkhimer, William E. *Military Government and Martial Law.* (2nd ed.) Kansas City: Franklin, 1904.

Rankin, Robert Stanley. *When Civil Law Fails: Martial Law and Its Legal Basis in the United States.* Durkham, N.C.: Duke University Press, 1939.

Military Law

Donelan, Charles A. "Civil Authority to Arrest Military Deserters." *FBI Law Enforcement Bulletin* (April, 1972), pp. 21-24.

Finch, Gaylord L. "Military Law and the Miranda Requirements." *Cleveland Marshall Law Review,* 17:3 (1968), pp. 537-551.

Ulmer, S. Disney. *Military Justice and the Right to Counsel.* Lexington: University Press of Kentucky, 1970.

U.S. Department of the Air Force. *Military Justice Guide.* Washington, D.C.: GPO, 1971.

Municipal Codes

Groll, R. and J. Zevin. *Law and the City.* Boston: Houghton Mifflin, 1970.

Rhyne, C.S. *Municipal Law.* Washington, D.C.: National Institute of Municipal Law Officers, 1957.

Treason

Chapin, Bradley. *American Law of Treason: Revolutionary and Early National Origins.* Seattle: University of Washington Press, 1964.

Hurst, James W. *Law of Treason in the United States: Collected Essays.* Westport, CT.: Greenwood, 1971.

Vehicle Code

National Committee on Uniform Traffic Laws and Ordinances. *Uniform Vehicle Code and Model Traffic Ordinance.* Charlottesville, VA.: Michie, 1968.

"New State Rankings for Uniform Vehicle Code." *Police Chief,* XLI:1 (January, 1974).

LEGAL PROFESSION

Legal Profession—General

Auerbactt, Gerald S. *Unequal Justice.* N.Y.: Oxford University Press, 1975.

Social history of the legal profession. Illustrates systematic exclusion of minorities.

Blankstein, Albert and Charles O. Potter. *The American Lawyer: A Summary of the Survey of the Legal Profession.* Chicago: Chicago University Press, 1954.

Bloom, Murray Teigh. *The Trouble with Lawyers.* N.Y.: Simon, 1968.

Carlin, Jerome. *Ethics and the Legal Profession.* N.Y.: Bureau of Applied Research, Columbia University, August, 1963.

Croust, Anton-Hermann. *The Rise of the Legal Profession in America.* (2 vols.) Norman: Oklahoma University Press, 1965.

Dorsen, Norman and Leon Friedman. *Disorder in the Court: Report of the Special Committee on Court Room Conduct of the Association of the Bar of the City of New York.* N.Y.: Pantheon, 1973.

Freeman, Morroe H. *Lawyer's Ethics in an Adversary System.* Indianapolis: Bobbs-Merrill, 1975.

Critical of trial lawyer tactics. Contains entire code of professional responsibility with annotations.

Goulden, Joseph C. *The Super Lawyers: The Small and Powerful World of the Great Washington Law Firms.* N.Y.: Weybright, 1972.

Green, Mark J. *The Other Government: The Unseen Power of Washington Lawyers.* N.Y.: Viking, 1975.

Hoffman, Paul. *"What the Hell Is Justice?" The Life and Trials of a Criminal Lawyer.* N.Y.: Simon, 1974.

Horsky, Charles A. *The Washington Lawyer.* Boston: Little, Brown, 1952.

Johnson, William J. *A Judicial Watergate: Discrimination in Licensing Lawyers and Other Facts.* Tempe, AZ.: W. Jacob Johnson, 1976.

Lumbard, J.E. "Better Lawyers for Our Criminal Courts." *Atlantic* (June, 1964).

Mayer, Martin. *The Lawyers.* N.Y.: Harper, 1967.

Mills, James. "I Have Nothing to Do with Justice." *Life,* 70 (March 12, 1971), pp. 57-59, 61-68.

Reichstein, Kenneth. "The Criminal Practitioner's Dilemma: What Should the Lawyer Do When His Client Intends to Testify Falsely?" *Journal of Criminal Law, Criminology and Police Science,* 61:1 (March, 1970), pp. 1-10.

Vanderwicken, Peter. "The Angry Young Lawyers." *Fortune* (September, 1971), pp. 74-77, 125-127.

Judges

Ashman, Charles R. *Finest Judges Money Can Buy and Other Forms of Judicial Pollution.* Farmingdale, N.Y.: Brown, 1975.

Boudin, Louis B. *Government by Judiciary.* (2 vols.) N.Y.: Godwin, 1932.

Braithwaite, W.T. *Who Judges the Judges.* Chicago: American Bar Foundation, 1971.
Retirement and removal procedures which are used in California, Illinois, Missouri, New Jersey and New York.

Brehm, B.L. *American Women Judges—A Survey of Their Backgrounds and Attitudes.* Washington, D.C.: NCJRS, (Microfiche), 1974.
Information on who our current women judges are, with emphasis on their career ladders, as well as their viewpoints on such current legal issues as the age of majority and factors important in sentencing.

Brownell, Herbegt. "Too Many Judges Are Political Hacks." *Saturday Evening Post* (April 16, 1964).

Chase, H.W. *Federal Judges—The Appointing Process.* Minneapolis: Minnesota University Press, 1972.
Interplay of personalities, institutions, and political consideration involved in the process of selecting federal judges.

Cohn, R.G. *To Judge wioh Justice—History and Politics of Illinois Judicial Reform.* Carbondale: Illinois University Press, 1973.
Analysis of the political, professional and personal influences which shaped the judicial article of the 1970 constitution of Illinois.

Desmond, Charles S. "Reflections of a State Reviewing Court Judge Upon the Supreme Courts Mandates in Criminal Cases." *Journal of Criminal Law, Criminology and Police Science,* 57:3 (September, 1966), pp. 301-304.

Gershenson, Alvin H. *The Bench Is Warped.* Beverly Hills, CA.: Book Company of America, 1964.

Goldberg, Louis P. *Lawless Judges.* N.Y.: DaCapo, 1970. (repr of 1935 ed.)

Henderson, S.A. *Canons of Judicial Ethics.* Washington, D.C.: NCJRS, (Microfiche), 1969.
Brief review of the history of the American Bar Association's canons of judicial ethics, along with a state listing of adopting jurisdictions, the canons adopted and the date of the state's action.

Hunter, John. *Judges and a Permissive Society.* Grand Rapids, MI.: Zondervan, 1975.

"Improving the Accountability of Judges." *Police Chief,* XL:12 (December, 1973), p. 8.

Jackson, Donald Dale. *Judges. (An Inside View of the Agonies and Excesses of an American Elite).* N.Y.: Atheneum, 1974.

Judicial Reform. Washington, D.C.: American Enterprise, 1971.

Newfield, J. *Cruel and Unusual Justice.* N.Y.: Holt, Rinehart and Winston, 1974.
Discusses incompetence of judges and brutality in New York State.

Peltason, Jack Walter. *Fifty-Eight Lonely Men: Southern Federal Judges and School Desegregation.* N.Y.: Harcourt, 1961.

Robin, Gerald D. "Judicial Resistance to Sentencing Accountability." *Crime and Delinquence* (July, 1975), pp. 201-212.

Schwartz, Herman. "Judges as Tyrants." *Criminal Law Bulletin,* VII (March, 1971), pp. 129-138.
This report describes the Chicago conspiracy trial and Judge Julius Hoffman's alleged tyrannical performance during the trial. In addition to Judge Hoffman, other judges and judges in general are discussed. Reasons for their tyrannical attitudes are studied.

Shetreet, S. *Judges on Trial.* N.Y.: North Holland, 1976.

Stein, D. *Judging the Judges—The Causes, Control and Cure of Judicial Jaundice.* Jericho, N.Y.: Exposition, 1974.

Wolfgang, Marvin E. "Murder, the Pardon Board, and Recommendations by Judges and District Attorneys." *Journal of Criminal Law, Criminology and Police Science,* 50:4 (November-December, 1959), pp. 338-346.

Prosecutors

American Bar Association. *Prosecution Function and the Defense Function, Standards Relating to,* Chicago: American Bar Association, 1971.
American Bar Association standards on the role and function of defense and prosecuting attorneys.

Aspen, Marvin E. "The Investigative Function of the Prosecuting Attorney." *Journal of Criminal Law, Criminology and Police Science,* 48:5 (January-February, 1955).

Boston University Law School. *Prosecution in the Juvenile Courts—Guidelines for the Future.* Washington, D.C.: NCJRS, 1973.
Guidelines and standards for an experimental prosecution program for the Boston Juvenile Court.

Carter, C.R. "A Way to Better Prosecution." *FBI Law Enforcement Bulletin,* 41:6 (1972), pp. 21-24.

Carter, L. *Limits of Order.* Lexington, MA.: Heath Lexington, 1974.

Danforth, Harold R. and James D. Horan. *The D.A.'s Man.* N.Y.: Crown, 1957.

Dughi, Louis J. "The Role of County and Prosecuting Attorneys with Respect to Alcoholism." *Journal of Criminal Law, Criminology and Police Science,* 49:4 (November-December, 1958), pp. 370-373.

Frank, Martin M. *Diary of a D.A.*. N.Y.: Holt, 1960.

Karton, Robert M. "Mob Violence and the Prosecuting Attorney." *Journal of Criminal Law, Criminology and Police Science,* 59:2 (June, 1968), pp. 167-170.

Keating, William J. *The Man Who Rocked the Boat.* N.Y.: Harper, 1956.

Kennedy, Stephen B. "Prosecutors and Police: Their Common Bond." *Journal of Criminal Law, Criminology and Police Science,* 49:4 (November-December, 1958), pp. 367-370.

Mills, James. *The Prosecutor.* N.Y.: Farrar, Straus, Giroux, 1969.

Moley, Raymond. *Politics and Criminal Prosecution.* N.Y.: Minton, 1929.

National Center for Prosecution Management. *A System for Manual Evaluation of Case Processing in the Prosecutor's Office.* Washington, D.C.: National Center for Prosecution Management, March, 1972.

Olender, Terrys T. *For the Prosecution, Miss Deputy D.A.* Philadelphia: Chilton, 1961.

Seymour, A. "Why Prosecutors Act Like Prosecutors." *Record of the New York City Bar Association,* 1956.

Wilcox, A.F. *Decision to Prosecute.* London: Butterworth, 1972.

Wright, D.B. "Duties of a Prosecutor." *Connecticut Bar Journal,* 33 (1959), pp. 293-296.

Public Defenders

Benner, L.A. and B.L. Neary. *Other Face of Justice—Report of the National Defenders Survey.* Chicago: National Legal Aid and Defenders Association, 1973.
Survey of indigent defense services provided by 3,110 counties.

Brownell, Emery A. *Legal Aid in the United States.* Rochester, N.Y.: Lawyers Co-op Publishing Company, 1951.

Callagy, Martin V. "Legal Aid in Criminal Case." *Journal of Criminal Law, Criminology and Police Science,* 42: (January-February, 1950), pp. 606-607.

Goldman, Mayer C. *The Public Defender.* N.Y.: G.P. Putman's, 1917.

Lytle, Clifford M. *Public Defender in Arizona.* Tucson: University of Arizona Press, 1969.

Maguire, John MacArthur. *The Lance of Justice: A Semi-Centennial History of the Legal Aid Society, 1876-1926.* Cambridge: Harvard University Press, 1928.

Mars, David. "Legal Aid, Public Defenders and Criminal Justice." *Police,* 1:3 (January-February, 1957), pp. 23-30.

Mars, David. "Public Defenders." *Journal of Criminal Law, Criminology and Police Science,* 46:2 (July-August, 1955), pp. 199-210.

Mishkin, Charles. "The Public Defender." *Journal of Criminal Law, Criminology and Police Science,* 23: (November, 1931).

Singer, Shelvin. *Public Defender Sourcebook.* N.Y.: Practicing Law Institute, 1976.

Smith, G.W. *Comparative Examination of the Public Defender and Private Attorneys in a Major California County.* Ann Arbor, MI.: University Microfilms. 1969.
Comparative study of the public defender and the private attorney as to the operations, the functions, and the effectiveness of each.

Smith, G.W. *Statistical Analysis of Public Defender Activities.* Springfield, VA.: NTIS, 1970.
Comparison of the disposition of cases handled by different types of defense attorneys.

Special Committee to Study Defender Systems. *Equal Justice for the Accused.* Garden City, N.Y.: Doubleday, 1959.

Statistics of Legal Aid and Defender Work in the United States and Canada, 1970. Chicago: National Legal Aid and Defender Association, 1970.
Statistical information on legal assistance and defender offices, including a detailed breakdown of civil and criminal cases handled and their disposition.

PART XVII
SOCIAL PROBLEMS

SOCIAL PROBLEMS

SOCIAL PROBLEMS—GENERAL

Alaska Science Conference, University of Alaska, 1969. *Change in Alaska: People, Petroleum, and Politics.* College: University of Alaska Press, 1970.

Bredemeier, Harry C. and Toby Jackson. *Social Problems in America.* N.Y.: Wiley, 1972.

Campbell, Angus and Phillip E. Converse. *The Human Meaning of Social Change.* N.Y.: Russell Sage Foundation, 1972.

Carter, Anne P. "The Economics of Technological Change." *Scientific American,* 214 (April, 1966), pp. 25-31.

Culbert, Michael. "Revolution: A Challenge to All." *Journal of California Law Enforcement* (July, 1969), pp. 1-7.

Culver, K. *Social Problems.* N.Y.: Holt, Rinehart and Winston, 1974.

Davis, F.J. *Social Problems.* N.Y.: Free Press, 1970.

Day, J. Edward. "The Problem of Morals." *Police Chief,* XXXIII:9 (September, 1966), pp. 20-25.

Demaris, Ovid. *Dirty Business: The Corporate, Political, Money, Power Game.* N.Y.: Avon, 1975.

Dorsen, Norman and Stephen Gillers. *None of Your Business: Government Secrecy in America.* Baltimore: Penguin, 1975.

Douglas, J. *Defining America's Social Problems.* Englewood Cliffs, N.J.: Prentice-Hall, 1974.

Dunlop, John T. *Automation and Technological Changes.* Englewood Cliffs, N.J.: Prentice-Hall, 1962.

Frank, Jerome D. "Galloping Technology: A New Social Disease." *Journal of Social Issues,* 22:4 (October, 1966), pp. 1-14.

Freeman, Howard E. and Norman Kurtz, eds. *America's Troubles.* Englewood Cliffs, N.J.: Prentice-Hall, 1973.

Friedman, Murray et al. *Overcoming Middle Class Rage.* Philadelphia: Westminster, 1971.

Gerlach, Luther P. and Virginia Hine. *Lifeway Leap: The Dynamics of Change in America.* Minneapolis: University of Minnesota Press, 1973.

Gilner, Robert. *American Society as a Social Problem.* N.Y.: Free Press, 1973.

Glazer, Nathan and Daniel Moynihan. *Beyond the Melting Pot.* Cambridge MA.: Harvard University Press, 1963.

Hapgood, David. *The Screwing of the Average Man.* N.Y.: Bantam, 1975.
Deals with consumer exploitation.

Hobsbawn, E. J. *Primitive Rebels: Studies in Archaic Forms of Social Movements in the 19th and 20th Centuries.* N.Y.: Praeger, 1959.

Hoelscher, H.E. "Technology and Social Change." *Science,* 166 (October, 1969), pp. 68-72.

Johnson, Elmer H. *Social Problems of Urban Man.* Homewood IL.: Dorsey, 1973.

Julian, Joseph. *Social Problems.* Englewood Cliffs, N.J.: Prentice-Hall, 1973.

Kane, John J. *Social Problems.* Englewood Cliffs, N.J.: Prentice-Hall, 1962.

Lamp, Ruth Deforest. *American Chamber of Horrors: The Truth About Food and Drugs.* N.Y.: Farrar, 1936.

Landis, Judson R. *Current Perspectives on Social Problems.* Belmont, CA.: Wadsworth, 1969.

Leinwand, Gerald. *The Traffic Jam: Problems of American Society.* N.Y.: Washington Square, 1969.

Lieberman, Jethro Koller. *How the Government Breaks the Law.* N.Y.: Stein and Day, 1972.

Lippencott, B.E. *Democracy's Dilemma: The Totalitarian Party in a Free Society.* N.Y.: Ronald, 1965.

Malikin, D. *Social Disability—Alcoholism, Drug Addiction, Crime and Social Disadvantage.* N.Y.: New York University Press, 1973.
Articles giving basic knowledge, research information and opinion about alcoholism, drug addiction, crime, and social disadvantage.

Merton, Robert and Robert A. Nesbit, eds. *Contemporary Social Problems.* (3rd ed.) N.Y.: Harcourt Brace, 1971.

Metcalf, Max. "The Loud Minority." *Law and Order,* 18:5 (May, 1970).

Morland, J.K. et al. *Social Problems.* N.Y.: Ronald, 1975.

Nader, Ralph. *Unsafe at Any Speed: The Designed-in Dangers of the American Automobile.* N.Y.: Grossman, 1965.

Odum, Howard W. *American Social Problems.* Plainview N.Y.: Books for Libraries, 1945.

Page, Joseph A. and Mary-Win O'Brien. *Bitter Wages: The Report on Disease and Injury on the Job.* N.Y.: Grossman, 1973.

Payne, Robert. *Corrupt Society.* N.Y.: Praeger, 1975.

Raab, Earl *Major Social Problems.* (3rd ed), N.Y.: Harper & Row, 1973.

Rivlin, Alice N. and P. Michael Timpane. *Ethical and Legal Issues of Social Experimentation.* Washington, D.C.: Brookings, 1975.

Scanzoni, John, ed. *Readings in Social Problems.* Boston: Allyn and Bacon, 1967.

Scarpitti, F. *Social Problems,* N.Y.: Holt, Rinehart and Winston, 1974.

Schmidt, Elizabeth. "The Curse of Affluency." *Law and Order,* 22:6 (June, 1974), pp. 56, 58, 60.

Sexton, Patricia. *The Feminized Male.* N.Y.: Random House, 1969.

Discusses the demoralizing and feminizing effects of women-dominated institutions during childhood and adolescence with a plea for real female liberation.

Sheehan, Thomas M. "Urbanism and Jane Jacobs: A Note for the Police." *Police,* 10:2 (November-December, 1965), pp. 27-29.

Smigel, Erwin O. *Handbook on the Study of Social Problems.* Chicago: Rand McNally, 1971.

Social Problems. Westminster, MD.: Communications Research Machines, 1975.

Social Problems. (3 pts., 9 vols.) Totowa, N.J.: Irish Academy Press, 1971.

Sutton, C.G. "Is Democratic Society Becoming Ungovernable?" *Police Review,* 79 (1971), pp. 397-400, 419.

Author anticipates many problems but believes democracies will survive.

Turner, James S. *The Chemical Feast: The Ralph Nader Study Group Report on Food Protection and the Food and Drug Administration.* N.Y.: Grossman, 1970.

Viano, E.C. and A.W. Cohn. *Social Problems and Criminal Justice.* Chicago: Nelson-Hall, 1975.

Weinberg, S.K. *Social Problems in Modern Urban Society.* (2nd ed.) Englewood Cliffs, N.J.: Prentice-Hall, 1970.

ABANDONED HOUSES

Akahoshi, George and Edna Gass *A Study of the Problems of Abandoned Housing and Recommendations for Action by the Federal Government and Localities.* Washington, D.C.: Linton, Mields and Coston, 1971.

Herbers, John. "Federal Housing Abandonment Blights Inner Cities." *New York Times,* (June 4, 1970).

"Housing Abandonment." *Architectural Forum* (April 1, 1971), pp. 42-45.

Ragsdale, Warner. "In the Inner Cities: Acres of Abandoned Buildings: Landlords are Now Fleeing the Inner City." *U.S. News & World Report* (January 26, 1970).

Sternlieb, George et al. "Crime in Abandoned Buildings." *Police Chief,* XLI:11 (November, 1974), pp. 40-42.

"The Wildfire of Abandonment: Entire Blocks are Rotting as Landlords Claim 'We Can't Make a Buck'." *Business Week* (April 4, 1970).

ABORTION

Bates, Jerome E. "The Abortion Mill: An Institutional Study." *Journal of Criminal Law, Criminology and Police Science,* 45:2 (July-August, 1954), pp. 157-169.

Bates, Jerome E. and Edward S. Zawadski. *Criminal Abortion: A Study in Medical Sociology.* Springfield, IL.: C.C. Thomas, 1964.

Beck, Mildred B. "The Destiny of the Unwanted Child: The Issue of Compulsory Pregnancy." In C. Reiterman (ed.) *Abortion and the Unwanted Child.* N.Y.: Springer, 1971, pp. 59-71.

Calderone, Mary Steichen. *Abortion in the United States.* N.Y.: P. Bittoeber, 1958.

Callahan, Daniel. "Abortion: A Summary of the Arguments." in *Aspects of Population Growth and the American Future Research Reports.* (vol. 6) Washington, D.C.: Government Printing Office, 1972.

Cimburg, G. "Studies of Criminal Abortion Cases in Ontario." *Journal of Forensic Sciences,* 12:2 (April, 1967), pp. 223-229.

Devereux, George. *A Study of Abortion in Primitive Societies: Environment and Cultural Behavior.* N.Y.: Julian, 1955.

"A Doctor Speaks Out for Abortion." *Pageant,* 13 (August, 1948).

Garnfield, David. *The Abortion Decision.* Garden City N.Y.: Doubleday, 1969.

Guttmacher, Alan F., ed. *The Case for Legalized Abortion.* Berkeley, CA.: Diablo, 1967.

Hall, Robert E., ed. *Abortion in a Changing World.* (2 vols.) N.Y.: Columbia University Press, 1970.

Hardin, Garrett. "We Need Abortion for the Children's Sake." in C. Reiterman, *Abortion and the Unwanted Child.* N.Y.: Springer, 1971, pp. 1-6.

Hardin, Garrett James. "Semantic Aspects of Abortion." *Review of General Semantics,* 24 (1967), pp. 263-281.

Hordern, A. *Legal Abortion: The English Experience.* Elmsford, N.Y.: Pergamon, 1971.

Horobin, G. W., ed. *Experience with Abortion.* New Rochelle, N.Y.: Cambridge University Press, 1973.

Lader, Lawrence. *Abortion.* Indianapolis: Bobbs-Merrill, 1966.

Leavy, Zad and Jerome M. Kummer. "Let's Talk About Abortions." *Police.* 5:6 (July-August, 1961), pp. 15-16.

Lowry, Thomas P. and Antha Lowry. "Abortion as a Preventive for Abused Children." *Psychiatric Opinion,* 8:3 (1971), pp. 19-25.

Mankekar, Kamia. *Abortion: A Social Dilemma.* Beaverton, OR.: International School Book Service, 1974.

Quennell, W.K. "Abortion." *RCMP Gazette,* 24:12 (December, 1962), pp. 307.

Reiterman, Carl. *Abortion and the Unwanted Child.* N.Y.: Springer, 1971.

Rosen, Harold, ed. *Therapeutic Abortion: Medical, Psychiatric, Legal Anthropological and Religious Considerations.* N.Y.: Julian, 1954.

Sarvis, Betty and Hyman Rodman. *Abortion Controversy.* (2nd ed.) N.Y.: Columbia University Press, 1974.

Schur, E.M. "Abortion and the Social System. *Social Problems,* 1955.

Stern, Loven G. "Abortion: Reform and the Law." *Journal of Criminal Law, Criminology and Police Science,* 59:1 (March, 1968), pp. 84-95.

Storer, Horatio R. and Franklin F. Heard. *Criminal Abortion.* N.Y.: Arno, 1974. (Repr.)

Walbert, David F. and Douglas Butler, eds. *Abortion, Society and the Law.* N.Y.: University Press Book Service, 1973.

Zielinski, Robert E. "Abortion." *Law and Order,* 15:8 (August, 1967), pp. 86-91, 93.

Ziff, Harvey L. "Recent Abortion Law Reforms (or Much Ado About Nothing)." *Journal of Criminal Law, Criminology and Police Science,* 60:1 (March, 1969) pp. 3-23.

AGGRESSION

Berkowitz, Leonard. *Aggression: A Social Psychological Analysis.* N.Y.: McGraw-Hill, 1962.

Berkowitz, Leonard. *Roots of Aggression, A Re-examination of the Frustration-Aggression Hypothesis.* Chicago: Atherton, 1969.

Dollard, J. et al. *Frustration and Aggression.* New Haven, CT.: Yale University Press, 1969.

Goldstein, Jeffrey H., ed. *Aggression and Crimes of Violence.* New York: Oxford University Press, 1975.

Henry, Andrew F. and James F. Short Jr. *Suicide and Homicide: Some Economics, Sociological and Psychological Aspects of Aggression.* Glencoe, IL.: Free Press, 1954.

Montagu, Ashley, ed. *Man and Agression.* N.Y.: Oxford University Press, 1968.

Montagu, Ashley *The Nature of Human Aggression.* N.Y.: Oxford University Press, 1976.
Montagu argues that aggression is learned and not inherited.

Scott, John Paul. *Aggression.* Chicago: University of Chicago Press, 1958.

Singer, J.L., ed. *The Control of Aggression and Violence: Cognitive and Physiological Factors.* N.Y.: Academic, 1971.

Storr, Anthony. *Human Aggression.* N.Y.: Atheneum, 1968.

ALIENATION

Benson, Dennis C. *The New Generation.* Atlanta, GA.: John Knox, 1968.

Brown, Michael. *The Politics and Anti-Politics of the Young.* N.Y.: Macmillan, 1969.

Dyson, J. W. *Political Alienation: A Study of Apathy, Discontent and Dissidency.* Unpub. Doctoral Dissertation, Indiana University, 1964.

Evanier, David and Stanley Silverzweig. *The Nonconformers: Articles of Dissent.* N.Y.: Ballantine, 1961.

Fortune. January, 1969.
Special issue on American youth.

Friedenberg, Edgar Z., ed. *Anti-American Generation.* New Brunswick, N.J.: Transaction, 1972.

Gordon, Suzanne. *Lonely in America.* N.Y.: Simon and Schuster, 1976.

Josephson, Eric and Mary Josephson. *Man Alone: Alienation in Modern Society.* N.Y.: Dell.

Lamb, Robert et al. *Political Alienation.* N.Y.: Saint Marten, 1975.

Maddox, John. *The Doomsday Syndrome: An Attack on Pessimism.* N.Y.: McGraw-Hill, 1972.

Meissner, William W. *Assault on Authority: Dialogue or Dilemma?* Mary Knoll, N.Y.: Orbis, 1971.

Packard, Vance. *A Nation of Strangers.* N.Y.: McKay, 1972.
Deals with high degree of population mobility. This leads to fragmentation and alienation.

Rude, Donald. *Alienation: Minority Groups.* N.Y.: Wiley, 1972.

Schwartz, David C. *Political Alienation and Political Behavior.* Chicago: Aldine, 1973.

Slater, Philip E. *The Pursuit of Loneliness: American Culture at the Breaking Point.* Boston: Beacon, 1970.

Urich, R. *Alienation: Individual or Social Problem.* Englewood Cliffs, N.J.: Prentice-Hall, 1970.

Von Mises, Ludwig. *Anti-Capitalistic Mentality.* South Holland, IL.: Libertarian, 1972.

Wein, Bibi. *The Runaway Generation: A Study in Depth of Our Alienated Children.* N.Y.: McKay, 1970.

BIRTH CONTROL

Chasteen, Edgar R. *The Case for Compulsory Birth Control.* Englewood Cliffs, N.J.: Prentice-Hall, 1972.

Crawford, Thomas J. "Beliefs About Birth Control: A Consistency Theory Analysis." *Representative Research in Social Psychology,* 4:1 (January, 1973), pp. 53-65.

Enke, Stephen. "Birth Control for Economic Development." *Science,* 164 (May 16, 1969), pp. 798-802.

Fryer, Peter. *The Birth Controllers.* London: Secker and Warburg, 1965.

Hardin, Garrett James. *Birth Control.* N.Y.: Pegasus, 1970.

Miles, Rufus E. Jr. "Ways of Stopping U.S. Population Growth." *University,* 46 (Fall, 1970), pp. 3-8, 33-36.

CORRUPTION IN SOCIETY

Political Bosses and Machines

Bean, Walton. *Boss Ruef's San Francisco: The Story of the Union Labor Party, Big Business, and the Graft Prosecution.* Berkeley: University of California Press, 1952.

Brownell, Blaine A. and Warren E. Stickle, eds. *Bosses and Reformers: Urban Politics in America, 1880-1920.* N.Y.: Houghton Mifflin, 1973.

Callow, Alexander B., ed. *City Bosses in America: An Interpretive Reader.* N.Y.: Oxford University Press, 1976.

Cook, Fred J. *American Political Bosses and Machines.* N.Y.: Watts, 1973.

Gosnell, Harold F. *Boss Platt and His New York Machine.* N.Y.: Russell, 1969. (Repr. of 1924 ed.)

Gottfried, Alex. *Boss Cermak of Chicago: A Study of Political Leadership.* Seattle, WA.: University of Washington Press, 1962.

Graham, Hugh D., ed. *Hewey Long.* Englewood Cliffs, N.J.: Prentice-Hall, 1970.

Halberstam, David. "Daley of Chicago." *Harper's* August, (1968).

Lynch, Dennis T. *Boss Tweed: The Study of a Grim Generation.* N.Y.: Arno, 1974.

McKean, Dayton D. *Boss: The Hague Machine in Action.* N.Y.: Russell, 1967. (Repr. of 1940 ed.)

Mandelbaum, Seymour. *Boss Tweed's New York.* N.Y.: Wiley, 1964.

Miller, Zane L. *Boss Cox's Cincinnati: Urban Politics in the Progressive Era.* N.Y.: Oxford University Press, 1968.

Milligan, Maurice M. *The Inside Story of the Pendergast Machine.* N.Y.: Scribner's, 1948.

Riordan, William L. *Plunkitt of Tammany Hall.* N.Y.: Dutton, 1963.

Salter, John T. *Boss Rule: Portraits in City Politics.* N.Y.: Arno, 1974.

Walsh, George. *Gentleman Jimmy Walker: Mayor of the Jazz Age.* N.Y.: Praeger, 1974.

Wendt, Lloyd and Herman Kogan. *Bosses in Lusty Chicago: The Story of Bath House John and Hinky Dink.* Bloomington: Indiana University Press, 1967.

Williams, T. Harry. *Hewey Long.* Westminster MD.: Knopf, 1969.

Zink, Harold. *City Bosses in the United States.* N.Y.: AMS, 1930 (repr.).

Political Corruption

Allen, Francis A. *Crimes of Politics: Political Dimensions of Criminal Justice.* Cambridge MA.: Harvard University Press, 1974.

Barnes, W.A. Jr. *Legislative Approaches to Campaign Finance, Open Meetings, and Conflict of Interest.* Raleigh N.C.: National Association of Attorneys General, 1974.

Boyd, James. *Above the Law. The Rise and Fall of Senator Thomas J. Dodd.* N.Y.: NAL, 1968.

Brooks, Robert C. *Corruption in American Politics and Life.* N.Y.: Arno, 1974 (repr.).

Burns, H. "Political Uses of the Law." *Howard Law Journal,* 17:4 (1973), pp. 760-774.

Author describes how politicians abuse the law against minorities. Repressive legislation, preventive detention, invasion of privacy, and other measures are covered.

Caddy, Douglas. *How They Rig Our Elections: The Coming Dictatorship of the Liberals and Big Labor.* New Rochelle, N.Y.: Arlington House, 1975.

Callow, Alexander. *The Tweed Ring.* N.Y.: Oxford University Press, 1965.

Crawford, Kenneth G. *Pressure Boys: The Inside Story of Lobbying in America.* N.Y.: Arno, 1974.

Dobyns, Fletcher. *The Underworld of American Politics.* N.Y.: Fletcher Dobyns, 1932.

Friedrich, Carl Joachin. *The Pathology of Politics: Violence, Betrayal, Corruption, Secrecy and Propaganda.* N.Y.: Harper and Row, 1972.

Goodman, Walter. *A Percentage of the Take.* N.Y.: Farrar, Straus, Giroux, 1971.

Heidenheimer, Arnold J. *Political Corruption.* N.Y.: Holt, Rinehart and Winston, 1970.

Joseph, Joan and Gerald Leinwand, eds. *Political Corruption: Prelude to Watergate.* N.Y.: Washington Square, 1974.

Schmidhauser, John et al. *Political Corruption.* Morristown, N.J.: General Learning, 1975.

Schultz, William and Eugene H. Methvin. "What You Can Do to Fight Corruption." *Readers Digest,* 104 (May, 1974), pp. 85-89.

Scott, James. *Comparative Political Corruption.* Englewood Cliffs, N.J.: Prentice-Hall, 1972.

Wise, David. *Politics of Lying: Government Deception, Secrecy and Power.* N.Y. Random, 1973.

Wyrick, S.T. *Legislation Concerning the Corruption of Public Officials.* Washington, D.C.: NCJRS, (Microfiche), 1974.

Union Corruption

Armbrister, Trevor. "Cleanup of a Corrupt Union." *Readers Digest* (May, 1973), pp. 105-109.

Boarman, Patrick M. *Union Monopolies and Antitrust Restraints,* Washington, D.C.: Labor Policy, 1963.

Bradley, Phillip D., ed. *The Public Stake in Union Power.* Charlottesville, VA: Virginia University Press, 1959.

Brown, Stuart. *A Man Named Tony: The True Story of the Yablonski Murders.* N.Y.: Norton, 1975.

Drucker, Peter F. *The Unseen Revolution: How Pension Fund Socialism Came to America.* N.Y.: Harper and Row, 1976.

There is more worker controlled capital in the U.S. than in many communist countries.

Finley, Joseph E. *Kingdom: The Rise and Fall of United Mine Workers.* N.Y.: Simon and Schuster, 1973.

Hoffa, James R. *Hoffa: The Real Story.* N.Y.: Stein and Day, 1975.

Hutchinson, John. "The Anatomy of Corruption in Trade Unions." *Industrial Relations,* 8 (February, 1969), pp. 135-150.

Johnson, Malcolm M. *Crime on the Labor Front.* N.Y.: McGraw-Hill, 1950.

Kennedy, Robert F. *The Enemy Within.* N.Y.: Harper, 1960.

Labor Racketeering: Activities Report. Washington, D.C.: GPO, 1967.

Mollenhoff, Clark R. *Tentacles of Power: The Story of Jimmy Hoffa*. Cleveland, OH.: World, 1965.

Petro, Sylvester. *Power Unlimited: The Corruption of Union Leadership. A Report on the McClellan Committee Hearings*. N.Y.: Ronald, 1959.

Rees, Albert. *The Economics of Trade Unions*. Chicago: University of Chicago Press, 1962.

"Rogues Around Hoffa—All with Police Records." *Readers Digest* (November, 1958).

Seidman, Harold. *Labor Czars: A History of Labor Racketeering*. N.Y.: Liveright, 1938.

Tomison, Maureen. *The English Sickness: The Rise of Trade Union Political Power*. Newton, Abbot, Devon: Tom Stacey, 1972.

U.S. Senate. *Labor Racketeering Activities Report*. Washington, D.C.: GPO, 1967.

Velie, Lester. "How the Teamsters Bankroll the Underworld." *Readers Digest* (September, 1974), pp. 105-109.

Velie, Lester. "How Unions Wield Political Power." *Readers Digest* (December, 1958).

Velie, Lester. "Is Jimmy Hoffa Caught in His Own Trap?" *Readers Digest* (December, 1958).

Velie, Lester. "The Mafia Tightens Its Grip on the Teamsters." *Readers Digest* (August, 1974), pp. 99-103.

Watergate

Boyan, A. Stephen Jr., ed. *Constitutional Aspects of Watergate: Documents and Materials*. (3 vols.) Dobbs Ferry, N.Y.: Oceana, 1975.

Breslin, Jimmy. *How the Good Guys Finally Won*. N.Y.: Viking, 1975.

Colson, Charles. *Born Again*. Des Plaines, IL.: Bantam, 1976.

Congressional Quarterly Staff. *Complete Watergate: Chronology of a Crisis*. Washington D.C.: Congressional Quarterly, 1975.

Dash, Samuel. *Chief Counsel*. N.Y.: Random, 1976.

Drew, Elizabeth. *Washington Journal: A Diary of the Events of 1973-1974*. N.Y.: Random, 1975.

Dean, John. *Blind Ambition*. N.Y.: Simon and Schuster, 1976.

Dean, Maureen and Hays Gorey. *MO—A Woman's View on Watergate*. N.Y.: Simon and Schuster, 1975.

Friedman, Leon, ed. *United States V. Nixon: The President Before the Supreme Court*. Ann Arbor, MI.: Bowker, 1974.

Halperm, Paul J., ed. *Why Watergate?* Pacific Palisades, CA.: Palisades, 1975.

Higgins, George V. *The Friends of Richard Nixon*. Boston: Little, Brown, 1975.

Horsley, R. Kent. *Highlights of the Watergate Tapes*. Salt Lake City, UT.: Hawkes, 1974.

Jaworski, Leon. *The Right and the Power*. Houston, TX.: Gulf, 1976.

Lukas, J.A. *Nightmare: The Underside of the Nixon Years*. N.Y.: Viking, 1976.

McCarthy, Mary. *Mask of State: Watergate Portraits—Including a Postscript on Pardons*. N.Y.: Harcourt Brace Jovanovich, 1975.

McCord, James W. Jr. *Piece of Tape. The Watergate Story, Fact and Fiction: Reference Handbook to the Watergate Cases*. Washington, D.C.: Washington Media, 1974.

Mankiewicz, Frank. *U.S. vs. Richard M. Nixon: The Final Crisis*. Westminster, MD.: Ballentine, 1975.

Mollenhoff, Clark R. *Game Plan for Disaster*. N.Y.: Norton, 1976.

Mollenhoff, Clark R. *The Man Who Pardoned Nixon*. N.Y.: St. Martin's, 1976.

Mosher, F.C. *Watergate*. N.Y.: Basic, 1974.

Myerson, Michael *Watergate: Crime in the Suites*. N.Y.: International, 1973.

New York Times Staff. *Impeachment of Richard M. Nixon, President of the United States: The Final Report of the Committee on the Judiciary, House of Representatives*. N.Y.: Viking, 1975.

The Presidential Transcripts. N.Y.: Dell, 1974.

Rather, Dan and Gary P. Gates. *The Palace Guard*. N.Y.: Warner, 1975.

Sussman, Barry. *The Great Cover-Up: Nixon and the Scandal of Watergate*. N.Y.: New American Library, 1974.

U.S. House of Representatives, Commission on the Judiciary. *Impeachment of Richard M. Nixon, President of the United States Report*. Washington, D.C.: GPO, 1974.

Watergate Hearings, Phase One. (9 vols.) Dallas, TX.: Leslie, 1973.

Watergate: The Waterloo of a President. Palm Springs, CA.: ETC, 1975.

White, Theodore. *Breach of Faith*. N.Y.: Dell, 1976.

CROWDING

Ardrey, Robert. *The Territorial Imperative*. N.Y.: Atheneum, 1966.

Bates, Marston. "Crowded People." *Natural History,* 77:8 (October, 1968), pp. 20-25.

Baxter, J.C. and B.F. Deanovich. "Anxiety Arousing Effects of Inappropriate Crowding." *Journal of Consulting and Clinical Psychology,* 35 (1970), pp. 174-178.

Beck, Robert J. and Rai Y. Okamoto. *Human Response to Patterns of Urban Density*. N.Y.: N.Y.C. Regional Planning Association, 1971.

Bell, Bernard I. *Crowd Culture*. Plainview, N.Y.: Books for Libraries, 1952.

Bell, R.W., C.E. Miller, and J.M. Ordy. "Effects of Population Density and Living Space Upon Neuroanatomy, Neurochemistry, and Behavior in the C57B1/10 Mouse." *Journal of Comparative Psychology,* 75 (1971), pp. 258-263.

Biderman, A.D., M. Lovria, and J. Bacchus. *Historical Incidents of Extreme Overcrowding.* Washington, D.C.: Bureau of Social Science Research, 1963.

Byrd, Caroline. *Crowding Syndrome: Learning to Live with Too Much and Too Many.* N.Y.: McKay, 1972.

Calhoun, John B. "Population Density and Social Pathology." *Scientific American,* 206:2 (February, 1962), pp. 139-146.

Carson, Daniel H. "Environmental Stress and the Urban Dweller." *Michigan Mental Health Research Bulletin,* 11:4 (Fall, 1968), pp. 5-12.

Carson, Daniel H. "Population Concentration and Human Stress." in B.P. Rourke (ed.) *Explorations in the Psychology of Stress and Anxiety.* Don Mills, Ontario: Longmans, 1969, pp. 24-42.

Carson, Daniel H. and B.L. Driver. *An Environmental Approach to Human Stress and Well-Being with Implications for Planning.* Ann Arbor, MI.: Mental Health Research Institute, University of Michigan, 1968.

Carson, Daniel H. and B.L. Driver "A Summary of an Ecological Approach to Environmental Stress." *American Behavioral Scientist,* 10:1 (1966), pp. 8-11.

Chermayeff, Serge and C. Alexander. *Community and Privacy: Toward a New Architecture of Humanism.* Garden City, N.Y.: Doubleday, 1963.

Christian, J.J. "Phenomena Associated with Population Density." *Proceedings of the National Academy of Sciences,* 47 (1961), pp. 428-449.

Cohen, Yehudi A. ed. *Man in Adaptation: The Biosocial Background.* Chicago: Aldine, 1968.

Colinvaux, Paul A., ed. *The Environment of Crowded Men.* N.Y.: MSS Educational Publishing, 1970.

Davies, D.E. "Physiological Effects of Continued Crowding." in A.H. Esser (ed.) *Behavior and Environment: The Use of Space by Animals and Men.* N.Y.: Plenum, 1971.

Esser, Aristide Henri "Experiences of Crowding: Illustration of a Paradigm for Man-Environment Relations." *Representative Research in Social Psychology,* 4:1 (January, 1973), pp. 207-217.

Flachsbart, P.G. "Urban Territorial Behavior." *Journal of the American Institute of Planners,* 35 (1969), pp. 412-416.

Freeman, Jonathan L. "Conceptualization of Crowding." in Sara Mills (ed.) *Population Distribution and Policy: The U.S. Commission on Population Growth and the American Future Research Reports.* (vol. 5), Washington, D.C.: GPO, 1972.

Freedman, Jonathan. *Crowding and Behavior.* San Francisco: W.H. Freeman, 1976.

Freedman, Jonathan L., S. Klevansky, and Paul R. Ehrlich. "The Effects of Crowding on Human Task Performance." *Journal of Applied Social Psychology,* 1 (1971), pp. 7-25.

Galle, O.R. et al. "Population Density and Pathology: What Are the Relations for Man?" *Science* (April, 1972), pp. 23-30.

Greenbie, Barrie B. "What Can We Learn from the Animals? Behavioral Biology and the Ecology of Cities." *Journal of the American Institute of Planners* (May, 1971).

Griffitt, W. and R. Vaitch. "Hot and Crowded: Influences of Population Density and Temperature on Interpersonal Affective Behavior." *Journal of Personality and Social Psychology,* 17 (1971), pp. 92-98.

Hutt, C. and M.J. Vaizey. "Differential Effects of Group Density on Social Behavior." *Nature,* 209 (1966), pp. 1371-1372.

Kutner, D. H. *Overcrowding: Human Responses to Density and Visual Exposure.* New Haven, CT.: Yale University Press, 1972.

Lantz, H.R. "Population Density and Psychiatric Diagnosis." *Sociology and Social Research,* 37 (1953), pp. 322-327.

Loo, Chalsa M. *Crowding and Behavior.* N.Y.: MSS Information, 1974.

Loo, Chalsa. "Important Issues in Researching the Effects of Crowding on Humans." *Representative Research in Social Psychology,* 4:1 (January, 1973), pp. 219-225.

Lyman, S.M. and M.B. Scott. "Territoriality: A Neglected Sociological Dimension." *Social Problems,* 15 (1967), pp. 236-249.

Olson, Mancur. "Rapid Growth as a Destabilizing Force." *Journal of Economic History,* 23 (December, 1963), pp. 529-552.

Schmitt, R.C. "Implications of Density in Hong Kong." *Journal of the American Institute of Planners,* 32 (1966), pp. 38-40.

Spector, P.E. "Population Density and Unemployment: The Effects on the Incidence of Violent Crime in the American City. *Criminology,* 12:4 (1975), pp. 399-401.
Strong relations between city size and violence. Area of the city also important factor.

Watts, R.E. "Influence of Population Density on Crime." *Journal of the American Statistical Association,* 26 (1931), pp. 11-21.

Zehner, Robert B. *Satisfaction with Neighborhoods: The Effects of Social Compatibility, Residential Density, and Site Planning.* Unpub. Doctoral Dissertation, University of Michigan, 1970.

DIVORCE

Krantzler, Mel. *Creative Divorce.* N.Y.: New American Library, 1975.

Mowrer, Ernest. *Family Disorganization: An Introduction to Sociological Analysis.* N.Y.: Arno, 1972.

Rosenblatt, Stanley *The Divorce Racket.* Los Angeles: Nash, 1969.

Sklar, Anna. *Runaway Wives.* N.Y.: Coward, 1975.

Stuart, Irving and Lawrence Abt. *Children of Separation and Divorce.* N.Y.: Grossman, 1972.

Torrents, J.N. *Abandoned Spouse.* Riverside, N.J.: Bruce, 1969.

ENVIRONMENT

Environment—General

Albertson, Peter and Margery Barnett, eds. *Managing the Planet.* Englewood Cliffs, N.J.: Prentice-Hall, 1972.

Aldous, Tony. *Battle for the Environment.* London: Fontana, 1972.

American Medical Association. *Proceedings of the Sixth Congress on Environmental Health.* Chicago: AMA, 1969.

Anderson, Walter, ed. *Politics and Environment: A Reader in Ecological Crisis.* Pacific Palisades, CA.: Goodyear, 1970.

Appleyard, Donald and Mark Lintell. "The Environmental Quality of City Streets: The Residents' Viewpoint." *Journal of the American Institute of Planners,* 38 (1972), pp. 84-101.

Baldauf, Richard J. "A Proposal for New Educational Programs to Meet the Environmental Crisis." *Nature Study,* 26:2 (1972), pp. 9-10.

Barkley, Paul W. and David W. Seckler. *Economic Growth and Environmental Decay: The Solution Becomes the Problem.* N.Y.: Harcourt Brace Jovanovich, 1972.

Barnett, John, ed. *Our Mistreated World: Case Histories of Man's Pillaging of Nature.* Homewood, IL: Dow Jones, 1966.

Bennett, John W. "Interaction of Culture and Environment in the Smaller Societies." *American Antrhopologist,* 46 (1944), pp. 461-478.

Blake, Peter. *God's Own Junkyard: The Planned Deterioration of America's Landscape.* N.Y.: Holt, Rinehart and Winston, 1964.

Boswell, Elizabeth M. *Federal Programs Related to Environment.* Washington, D.C.: Legislative Reference Service, U.S. Library of Congress, 1970.

Boughey, Arthus S. *Fundamental Ecology.* Scranton, PA.: Intext Educational, 1971.

Boughey, Arthur S. *Man and the Environment: An Introduction to Human Ecology and Evolution.* N.Y.: Macmillan, 1971.

Bredemeier, Harry C. and Judith Getis, eds. *Environments, People, and Inequalities: Some Current Problems.* N.Y.: Wiley, 1973.

Bresler, Jack Barry, ed. *Environments of Man.* Reading MA.: Addison-Wesley, 1968.

Bresler, Jack Barry ed. *Human Ecology: Collected Readings.* Reading, MA.: Addison-Wesley, 1966.

Bridgeland, William and Andrew J. Sofranko. *Community Structure and Citizen Mobilization: The Cases of Environmental Quality.* Urbana: Department of Agricultural Economics and Rural Sociology, University of Illinois, [n.d.].

Brown, Robert M., ed. *Man Versus Environment, the Dynamic Spectrum: Man, Health, and Environment.* Ann Arbor, MI.: National Sanitation Foundation, 1966.

Burch, William R. Jr. *Daydreams and Nightmares: A Sociological Essay on the American Environment.* N.Y.: Harper and Row, 1971.

Calder, Nigel *Eden Was No Garden: An Inquiry into the Environment of Man.* N.Y.: Holt, Rinehart and Winston, 1967.

Caldwell, Lynton Keith. "Human Environment." *Journal of Higher Education,* 37 (1966), pp. 149-155.

Chein, Isidor "The Environment as a Determinant of Behavior." *Journal of Social Psychology,* 39 (February, 1954), pp. 155-127.

Christy, Francis T. Jr. "Human Needs and Human Values for Environmental Resources." *Atlantic Naturalist,* 22:4 (October-December, 1967), pp. 209-216.

Cloud, Stanley W. and Ray March. "The Great Billboard Sellout." *Cry Calif,* 2:3 (Summer, 1967), pp. 35-39.

Cole, H.S.D. et al., eds. *Models of Doom: A Critique of the Limits of Growth.* N.Y.: Universe, 1973.

Commoner, Barry. *Environment.* N.Y.: Knopf, 1971.

Dee, Norbert and Howard Reiguam. "Comprehensive Environmental Analysis." *Battelle Research Outlook,* 4:2 (1972), pp. 25-28.

Dorfman, Robert and Nancy S. Dorfman, eds. *Economics of the Environment: Selected Readings.* N.Y.: W.W. Norton, 1972.

Fielding, G.J. *Locating Urban Freeways: Methods for Resolving Community Conflict, First Interim Report Submitted to the California Transportation Agency.* Irvine, CA.: University of California Press, 1969.

Finley, James R. and Janet K. Baker. "Social Elements in Environmental Planning." *Battelle Research Outlook,* 4:2 (1972), pp. 8-11.

Gilliam, Harold. *For Better or for Worse: The Ecology of an Urban Area.* San Francisco, CA.: Chronicle, 1972.

Johnson-Marshall, Percy. "The Urban Environment and the Motor Vehicle." *The International Journal of Environmental Studies,* 3:3 (July, 1972), pp. 167-171.

Jonsson, Erland. "Annoyance Reactions to External Environmental Factors in Different Sociological Groups." *ACTA Sociologica,* 7:4 (1963), pp. 229-263.

Lee, Douglas H.K. "Role of Attitude in Response to Environmental Stress." *Journal of Social Issues,* 22 (October, 1966), pp. 83-91.

Lowenthal, David. *Environmental Assessment: A Case Study of Boston.* N.Y.: American Geographical Society, 1972.

Lowenthal, David. *Environmental Assessment: A Case Study of Cambridge, Massachusetts.* N.Y.: American Geographical Society, 1972.

Lowenthal, David. *Environmental Assessment: A Case Study of Columbus, Ohio.* N.Y.: American Geographical Society, 1972.

Lowenthal, David. *Environmental Assessment: A Case Study of New York City.* N.Y.: American Geographical Society, 1972.

Marien, Gene. *America the Raped: The Engineering Mentality and the Devastation of a Continent.* N.Y.: Simon and Schuster, 1969.

Means, Richard L. "Ecology and the Contemporary Religious Conscience." *The Christian Century* (December 3, 1969), pp. 1546-1549.

Ogden, Samuel K. *America the Vanishing: Rural Life and the Price of Progress.* Brattleboro VT.: Greene, 1969.

Penchef, Ester, ed. *Four Horsemen: Pollution, Poverty, Famine, Violence.* San Francisco: Canfield, 1971.

Prindle, Richard A. "The Health Aspects of the Urban Environment." *Ekistics,* 25:151 (June, 1968), pp. 428-431.

Sagan, L.A. "Human Cost of Nuclear Power." *Science,* 177 (August 11, 1972), pp. 487-493.

Sims, John and Thomas Frederick Saarinen. "Coping with Environmental Threat: Great Plains Farmers and the Sudden Storm." *Annals of the Association of American Geographers,* 59 (1969), pp. 677-686.

Pollution—General

"America's Polluted Environment: Symposium." *Current History,* 59 (July, 1970), (entire issue).

Anderson, Paul K., ed. *Omega: Murder of the Ecosystem and Suicide of Man.* Dubuque, IA: William C. Brown, 1971.

Arkinson, George A. "Pollution, Protest, and Participation." *Ekistics,* 26 (November, 1968), pp. 430-431.

Auld, D.A.L., ed. *Economic Thinking and Pollution Problems.* Toronto: University of Toronto Press, 1972.

Boulding, Kenneth E. et al. *Economics of Pollution.* N.Y.: New York University Press, 1971.

Calder, Ritchie "Polluting the Environment." *Center Magazine,* 2:3 (May, 1969), pp. 7-12.

Carson, Rachel Louise. *Silent Spring.* Boston: Houghton Mifflin, 1962.

Davies, J. Clarence III. *The Politics of Pollution.* N.Y.: Pegasus, 1970.

Degler, Stanley E. and Sandra Bloom. *Federal Pollution Control Programs: Water, Air, and Solid Wastes.* Washington, D.C.: Bureau of National Affairs, 1971.

Graham, Frank Jr. *Since Silent Spring.* Boston: Houghton Mifflin, 1970.

Nader, Ralph. "The Profits in Pollution." *The Progressive,* 34:4 (April, 1970), pp. 19-22.

Rothman, Harry. *Murderous Providence: A Study of Pollution in Industrial Societies.* London: Hart-Davis, 1972.

Air Pollution

Auerback, Irwin L. and Kenneth Flieger. "The Importance of Public Education in Air Pollution Control." *Journal of the Air Pollution Control Association,* 17:2 (February, 1967), pp. 102-103.

Bates, David V. *A Citizen's Guide to Air Pollution.* Montreal: McGill-Queen's University Press, 1972.

Battan, Louis J. *The Unclean Sky.* Garden City, N.Y.: Doubleday, 1966.

Bower, Blair T. and W.R.D. Sewell. *Selecting Strategies for Air Quality Management.* Ottawa: Queen's Printer, 1970.

Downing, Paul B., ed. *Air Pollution and the Social Sciences: Formulating and Implementing Control Programs.* N.Y.: Praeger, 1971.

Engen, T. *Use of the Sense of Smell in Determining Environmental Quality.*
Paper presented at the American Association for the Advancement of Science Symposium: Indicators of Environmental Quality, Philadelphia, 1971.

Esposito, John C. *Vanishing Air: The Ralph Nader Study Group Report on Air Pollution.* N.Y.: Grossman, 1970.

Glasser, M., L. Greenburg, and F. Field. "Mortality and Morbidity During a Period of High Levels of Air Pollution." *Archives of Environmental Health,* 15 (1967), pp. 684-694.

Graham, Frank Jr. "The Infernal Smog Machine." *Audubon,* 70:5 (September-October, 1968), pp. 28-37.

Hickey, R.J. et al. "Relationship Between Air Pollution and Certain Chronic Disease Death Rates." *Archives of Environmental Health,* 15 (December, 1967), pp. 728-738.

Lave, Lester B. and Eugene P. Seskin. "Air Pollution and Human Health." *Science,* 169 (August 21, 1970), pp. 723-733.

Lewis, Howard R. *With Every Breath You Take: The Poisons of Air Pollution, How They Are Injuring Our Health and What We Must Do About Them.* N.Y.: Crown, 1965.

McDermott, Walsh. "Air Pollution and Public Health. *Scientific American,* 205 (October, 1961), pp. 49-57.

Rankin, Robert E. "Air Pollution Control and Public Apathy." *Journal of the Air Pollution Control Association,* 19:8 (August, 1969), pp. 565-569.

Rheingold, Paul. "Civil Cause of Action for Lung Damage Due to Pollution of Urban Atmosphere." *Brooklyn Law Review,* 33:1 (Fall, 1966), pp. 17-33.

Stern, Arthur C., ed. *Air Pollution.* (3 vols., 2nd ed.) N.Y.: Academic. 1968.

Wise, William. *Killer Smog: The World's Worst Air Pollution Disaster.* Chicago: Rand-McNally, 1968.

Environmental Control

"Air Pollution Control." *Law and Contemporary Problems,* 33:2 (Spring, 1968), (entire issue).

"Air Pollution Control: Cost vs. Benefits." *Science News,* 94 (November 16, 1968), pp. 503-505.

American Association of University Women. *A Resource Guide on Pollution Control.* Washington, D.C.: American Association of University Women, 1970.

Caldwell, Lynton Keith, ed. *Political Dynamics of Environmental Control.* Bloomington: Institute of Public Administration, Indiana University, 1967.

Clayton, K.M., ed. *Pollution Abatement.* North Pomfret, VT.: David and Charles, 1974.

Cooper, H.B. and A.F. Rossano. *Source Testing for Air Pollution Control.* N.Y.: McGraw-Hill, 1974.

Connor, Gregory J. and Robert A. Harvie. "The Role of the Police in Environmental Protection." *Police.* 16:10 (June, 1972), pp. 20-23.

Cornell Law Review, eds. "Symposium: Law and the Environment." *Cornell Law Review,* 55:5 (May, 1970), pp. 663-877 (entire issue).

Doyle, K.F. *Manpower for Pollution Control.* Washington D.C.: Bureau of National Affairs, January 8, 1971.

Eisenbud, Merril. "Environmental Protection in the City of New York." *Science,* 170 (November 13, 1970), pp. 706-712.

Fowler, E.D. and Dayanne Schurecht. *Environmental Control Research.* Chicago: U.S. Gypsum, 1969.

Freeman, Myrick. *The Economics of Pollution Control and Environment Quality.* N.Y.: General Learning, 1971.

Gillette, Robert "AEC's New Environmental Rules for Nuclear Plants May Open New Debate, Extend Delays, Raise Plant Cost." *Science,* 173 (September 17, 1971), pp. 1112-1113.

Hortsman, S.W., R.F. Wromble, and A.N. Heller. "Identification of Community Odor Problems by Use of an Observer Corps." *Journal of the Air Pollution Control Association,* 15:6 (June, 1965), pp. 261-264.

Leduc, Edgar C. et al. "Manpower Policies in Selected Air Pollution Control Agencies." *Journal of the Air Pollution Control Association,* 18:4 (April, 1968).

Megonnell, W.H. "Air Pollution Control: Its Impact Upon Municipalities, Industry, and the Individual." *Air Engineering,* 9:7 (July, 1967), pp. 12-14.

National Association of Counties Research Foundation. *Community Action Program for Water Pollution Control.* Washington, D.C.: National Association of Counties, 1967.

Nonhebel, Gordon, ed. *Processes for Air Pollution Control.* Cleveland, OH.: CRC, 1972.

Pfeiffer, B. and R.D. Gilbert. "Pollution Abatement Expenditures by the Electric Power Industry." *Public Utilities Fortnighty* 90:5 (August 31, 1972), pp. 21-28.

Rickson, Roy E. "Self-Interest and Pollution Control." *The Journal of Environmental Education.* 4:1 (Fall, 1972), pp. 43-48.

Sandman, Peter M. "Who Should Police Environmental Advertising?" *Columbia Journalism Review,* 10:5 (January-February, 1972), pp. 41-47.

Schachter, Esther R. *Enforcing Air Pollution Controls: Case Study of New York City.* N.Y.: Praeger, 1974.

Stolberg, A.L. "Noise Monitoring and the Law." *Law and Order,* (February, 1976), pp. 48-51.
Description of devices to measure noise levels.

Littering

Burgess, Robert L., Roger N. Clark, and John C. Hendee. "An Experimental Analysis of Anti-Litter Procedures." *Journal of Applied Behavior Analysis,* 4:2 (Summer, 1971), pp. 71-75.

Clark, Roger N., Robert L. Burgess, and John C. Hendee. "The Development of Anti-Litter Behavior in a Forest Campground." *Journal of Applied Behavior Analysis,* 5:1 (Spring, 1972), pp. 1-5.

Clark, Rober N., John C. Hendee, and Robert C. Burgess. "The Experimental Control of Littering." *Journal of Environmental Education,* 4:2 (Winter, 1972), pp. 22-29.

Public Opinion Surveys, Inc. *Who Litters and Why?* N.Y.: Keep America Beautiful (November, 1968).

Noise Pollution

Alexander, Walter. "Some Harmful Effects of Noise." *Canadian Medical Association Journal,* 99:1 (1968), pp. 27-31.

Anthrop, Donald F. "Environmental Noise Pollution: A New Threat to Sanity." *Bulletin of the Atomic Scientists,* 25:5 (May, 1969), pp. 11-16.

Anticaglia, J.R. and A. Cohen. "Extra-auditory Effects of Noise as a Health Hazard." *American Industrial Hygiene Association Journal,* 31 (1970), pp. 277-281.

Antonovsky, Aaron and Ilana Finkelstein. *A Social Science Approach to Noise Pollution.* Jerusalem: Israel Institute of Applied Social Research, 1972.

Baron, Robert Alex. "The Noise Receiver: The Citizen." *Sound and Vibration* (May, 1968), pp. 8-10.

Baron, Robert Alex. *The Tyranny of Noise.* N.Y.: St. Martin's, 1970.

Bateman, W.F. and Edward Ackerman. "Some Observations on Small-Town Noise." *Noise Control,* 1:6 (1955).

Bell, Alan. *Noise: An Occupational Hazard and Public Nuisance.* Geneva Switzerland: World Health Organization, 1968.

Beranek, Leo. "Noise." *Scientific American,* 215:6 (1966), pp. 66-76.

Berland, Theodore. *The Fight for Quiet.* Englewood Cliffs, N.J.: Prentice-Hall, 1970.

Bishop, D.C. *Predicting Community Response to Aircraft Noise, Part I.* Washington, D.C.: GPO, December, 1965.

Bolt, Beranek and Newman, Inc. *Noise Environment of Urban and Suburban Areas.* Washington, D.C.: GPO, 1967.

Borsky, Paul N. *Community Reactions to Air Force Noise, Parts 1 and 2.* Wright-Patterson Air Force Base, OH.: Wright Air Development Division, 1961.

Bragdon, Clifford R. *Noise Pollution: The Unquiet Crisis.* Philadelphia: University of Pennsylvania Press, 1970.

Branch, Melville C. Jr. "Outdoor Noise, Transportation, and City Planning." *Traffic Quarterly,* 25:2 (April. 1971), pp. 167-188.

Branch, Melville C. Jr. and R.D. Beland. *Outdoor Noise and the Metropolitan Environment.* Los Angeles: Department of City Planning, 1970.

Broadbent, D. "Effects of Noise on Behavior." in C.M. Harris, (ed.) *Handbook of Noise Control.* N.Y.: McGraw-Hill, 1957.

Burns, William. *Noise and Man.* Philadelphia: Lippincott, 1969.

Clark, Weldon. *Reaction to Aircraft Noise.* (T.R. 61-610). Arlington, VA.: U.S. Armed Services Technical Information Agency, 1961.

Cohen, A. et al. *Effects of Noise on Task Performance.* Cincinnati: Occupational Health Research and Training Facility, Division of Occupational Health, U.S. Public Health Service, 1966.

Glass, David C. and Jerome E. Singer. *Urban Stress: Experiments on Noise and Social Stressors.* N.Y.: Academic, 1972.

Griffiths, I.D. and F.J. Langdon. "Subjective Response to Road Traffic Noise." *Journal of Sound and Vibration,* 8 (1968), pp. 1-16.

Hildebrand, James L. *Noise Pollution and the Law.* N.Y.: William S. Hein, 1970.

Jonsson, Erland et al. "Annoyance Reactions to Traffic Noise." *Archives of Environmental Health,* 19:5 (1969), pp. 692-699.

Kryter, Karl D. *Effects of Noise on Man.* Washington, D.C.: Academic, 1970.

Kryter, Karl D. "Psychological Reactions to Aircraft Noise." *Science,* 151 (1966), pp. 1346-1355.

Kryter, Karl D. "Sonic Booms from Supersonic Transport." *Science,* 163 (1969), pp. 359-367.

Lynch, Charles J. "Noise Control." *International Science and Technology,* 52 (April, 1966) pp. 32-41.

McKennell, A.C. "Methodological Problems in a Survey of Aircraft Noise Annoyance." *Statistician,* 19 (1969), pp. 1-29.

"Noise Is Everybody's Problem." *California Highway Patrolman,* 34 (May, 1970), pp. 48-49.

Spater, George A. "Noise and the Law." *Michigan Law Review,* 63 (June, 1965).

Still, Henry. *In Quest of Quiet: Meeting the Menace of Noise Pollution: Call to Citizen Action.* Harrisburg, PA.: Stackpole, 1970.

Taylor, Rupert. *Noise.* Baltimore: Penguin, 1970.

Water Pollution

Alexander, Robert M. *Social Aspects of Environmental Pollution.* Corvallis, OR.: Water Resources Research Institute, Oregon State University, March, 1971.

Baxter, S.S. "Economic Considerations of Water Pollution Control." *Journal of the Water Pollution Control Foundation,* 37:10 (October, 1965), pp. 1363-1369.

Bishop, A. Bruce "An Approach to Evaluating Environmental, Social, and Economic Factors in Water Resources Planning." *Water Resources Bulletin,* 8 (August, 1972), pp. 724-734.

Clark, Colin. *The Economics of Irrigation.* Oxford: Pergamon, 1966.

Degler, Stanley E., ed. *Oil Pollution: Problems and Policies.* Washington, D.C.: BNA, 1969.

Marx, Wesley. *Oilspill.* San Francisco: Sierra Club, 1971.

HANDICAPPED

Lippman, Leopold. *Attitudes Toward the Handicapped: A Comparison Between Europe and the United States.* Springfield, IL.: C.C. Thomas, 1972.

Saunders, Franklin F. *Attitudes Toward Handicapped Persons: A Study of the Differential Effects of Fine Variables.* San Francisco: R. and E. Research, 1975.

TenBrock, Jacobus and Floyd W. Matson. *Hope Deferred: Public Welfare and The Blind.* Berkeley: University of California Press, 1959.

HOMOSEXUALITY

Cappon, Daniel. *Toward an Understanding of Homosexuality.* Englewood Cliffs, N.J.: Prentice-Hall, 1965.

Capprio, Frank S. *Female Homosexuality: A Psychodynamic Study of Lesbianism.* Secaucus, N.J.: Citadel, 1967.

"The Consenting Adult Homosexual and the Law." *University of Southern California Law Review,* 13 (1966), pp. 734-735.

Cory, Donald W. *The Lesbian in America.* Secaucus, N.J.: Citadel, 1964.

Fast, Julius and Hal Wells. *Bisexual Living.* New York: Pocket Books, 1975.

Gagnon, John H. "The Social Meaning of Prison Homosexuality." *Federal Probation,* 32 (1968), pp. 23-29.

Hoffman, Martin. *The Gay World: Male Homosexuality and the Social Creation of Evil.* N.Y.: Basic, 1968.

Humphreys, Laud. *Out of the Closets: The Sociology of Homosexual Liberation.* Englewood Cliffs N.J.: Prentice-Hall, 1972.

Hurwood, Bernhardt J. *The Bisexuals,* N.Y.: Fawcett World, 1974.

McIntosh, Mary. "The Homosexual Role." *Social Problems,* 16:2 (Fall, 1968).

Mitchel, Robert S. *The Homosexual and the Law.* N.Y.: Arco, 1969.

Plumer, Douglas. *Queer People.* Secaucus, N.J.: Citadel, 1965.

"A Psychosexual Deviation—The Homosexual." *Police,* 3:6 (July-August, 1959).

Rees, J.T. and H.V. Usill. *They Stand Apart: A Critical Survey of the Problems of Homosexuality.* N.Y.: Macmillan, 1955.

Skousen, W. Cleon. "U.S. Police in a Cultural Crisis, the Homosexual—Can He be Cured?" *Law and Order,* 19:12 (December, 1971), pp. 12-14-16-18-20.

Skousen, W. Cleon "U.S. Police in a Cultural Crisis—The Homosexual Epidemic." *Law and Order,* 19:9 (September, 1971), pp. 8-13.

Skousen, W. Cleon "U.S. Police in a Cultural Crisis, the Homosexual—How Much of a Security Risk?" *Law and Order,* 19:11 (November, 1971), pp. 8-13.

Skousen, W. Cleon "U.S. Police in a Cultural Crisis—What Causes Homosexuality?" *Law and Order.* 19:10 (October, 1971), pp. 8-13.

Stearn, Hess. *The Grapevine.* Garden City, N.Y.: Doubleday, 1964.

Vedder, Clyde B. and Patricia G. King. *Problems of Homosexuality in Corrections.* Springfield, IL.: C.C. Thomas, (1967), pp. 42-61.

West, Donald J. *Homosexuality.* Chicago: Aldine, 1968.

West, Donald H. *The Other Man: A Study of the Social, Legal and Clinical Aspects of Homosexuality.* N.Y.: Morrow, 1955.

Williams, Colin S. and Martin S. Weinberg. *Homosexuals and the Military: A Study of Less Than Honorable Discharge.* N.Y.: Harper, 1971.

HUMAN BEHAVIOR

Bates, Marston and W.R. Derrick Sewell, eds. "The Role of Weather in Human Behavior." *Human Dimensions of Weather Modification.* Chicago: University of Chicago Department of Geography, 1966.

McDonald, Hugh C. "Varying Human Behavior and the Times of the Day." *National Police Journal* (Winter, 1972).

Meerloo, Abraham M. *Patterns of Panic.* N.Y.: International Universities Press, 1950.

Russell, Harold E. and Allen Beigel. *Understanding Human Behavior for Effective Police Work.* N.Y.: Basic, 1975.

Stearns, Frederic. *Anger: Psychology, Physiology, Pathology.* Springfield, IL.: C.C. Thomas, 1972.

ILLEGITIMACY

Cobliner, W. Godfrey. "Teenage Out-of-Wedlock Pregnancy: A Phenomenon of Many Dimensions." *Bulletin of the New York Academy of Medicine,* 46:6 (1970), pp. 438-447.

Cutright, Phillip "Illegitimacy in the United States: 1920-1968." *Demographic and Social Aspects of Population Growth: The U.S. Commission on Population Growth and the American Future Research Reports.* (vol. 1) Washington, D.C.: GPO, 1972.

Davis, Kingsley. "Illegitimacy and the Social Structure." *American Journal of Sociology,* (1939).

Young, L.R. *Out of Wedlock: A Study of Problems of the Unmarried Mother and Her Child.* N.Y.: Mcgraw-Hill,,1963.

LEISURE

Chapin, F. Stuart Jr. "Free Time Activities and the Quality of Urban Life." *Journal of the American Institute of Planners,* 37:6 (1971), pp. 411-415.

Dumazedier, Joffre. *Toward a Society of Leisure.* N.Y.: Free Press, 1967.

MENTAL ILLNESS

Chu, Franklin and Sharland Trotter. *Madness Establishment: Ralph Nader's Study Group Report on the National Institute of Mental Health.* N.Y.: Grossman, 1974.

Fisher, Walter et al. *Power, Greed, and Stupidity in the Mental Health Racket* Philadelphia: Westminster, 1973.

Havemann, Ernest. "Alternatives to Analysis." *Playboy* (November, 1969).

Mercer, Jane R. *Labeling the Mentally Retarded.* Berkeley: University of California Press, 1973.

Scheff, Thomas J. *Labeling Madness.* Englewood Cliffs, N.J.: Prentice-Hall, 1975.

Szasz, Thomas S. "Commitment of the Mentally Ill: 'Treatment' or Social Restraint?" *Journal of Nervous and Mental Disease,* 125 (April-June, 1957).

Szasz, Thomas S. *Law, Liberty, and Psychiatry: An Inquiry into the Social Use of Mental Health Practices.* N.Y.: Macmillan, 1963.

Szasz, Thomas S., ed. *Manufacture of Madness: A Comparative Study of the Inquisition and the Mental Health Movement.* N.Y.: Harper and Row, 1970.

Szasz, Thomas S. *The Myth of Mental Illness: Foundations of a Theory of Personal Conduct.* N.Y.: Hoeber, 1961.

Zusman, J. and S. Shaffer. "Emergency Psychiatric Hospitalization via Court Order: A Critique." *American Journal of Psychiatry,* 130:12 (1973), pp. 1323-1326.

MORALITY

Hart, H.L.A. *Law, Liberty, and Morality.* Stanford, CA.: Stanford University Press, 1963.

Kalaidjian, William G. "Conduct: The Basic American Problem." *Law and Order,* 17:1 (January, 1969), pp. 58-61.

Stumpf, Samuel Enoch. *Morality and the Law.* Nashville, TN.: Vanderbilt University Press, 191966.

Whiteley, Charles H. and Winifred M. Whiteley. *The Permissive Morality.* London: Methuen, 1964.

Yankelovich, Daniel. *The New Morality: A Profile of American Youth in the Seventies.* N.Y.: McGraw-Hill.

NURSING HOMES

Falk, Ursula A. and Gerhard Falk. *The Nursing Home Dilemma.* San Francisco: R. and E. Research, 1976.

Gubrium, Jaber F. *Living and Dying at Murray Manor.* N.Y.: St Martin's, 1975.

Horn, Linda and Alma Griesel. *Nursing Homes: Citizens Action Guide.* Boston: Beacon, 1977.

Mendleson, Mary A. *Tender Loving Greed: How the Incredibly Lucrative Nursing Home "Industry" Is Exploiting America's Old People and Defrauding Us All.* N.Y.: Random House, 1975.

PERMISSIVE SOCIETY

Ibele, Oscar H. "Law Enforcement and the Permissive Society." *Police,* 10:1 (September-October, 1965), pp. 15-17.

Jacobsen, Chanoch, "Permissive Society and Its Victims: A Preliminary Statement." *International Journal of Criminology and Penology* (February, 1974), pp. 173-179.

Murphy, George Jr. "Why Can't Society Accept Inconveniences in Order to Stop Crime?" *Journal of California Law Enforcement* (April, 1968), pp. 211-212.

Nicholson, Lawrence. "The Children Are in Trouble." *Law and Order,* 20:3 (March, 1972), pp. 70-72.

Pitchess, Peter J. "A Permissive Society Has Engendered an Enormous Wave of Crime." *Journal of California Law Enforcement,* (July, 1968), pp. 37-39.

Purdy, E. Wildon. "The Enemy Within: Tolerance of Wrongdoing." *Law and Order,* 16:9 (September, 1968), pp. 64-96.

POPULATION

Agarwala, S.N. *Population.* Bombay, India: National Book Trust, 1972.

Austin, Arthur and John W. Brewer. "World Population Growth and Related Technical Problems." *Institute of Electrical and Electronics Engineers Spectrum,* 7:12 (December, 1964), pp. 43-54.

Back, D.W. and H.H. Winsborough. "Population Policy: Opinions and Actions of Government." *Public Opinion Quarterly,* 32 (Winter, 1968-69), pp. 634-645.

Bacon, Edmund N. "Urban Population Expansion and the Preservation of Nature." *Annals* (July, 1968).

Beale, Calvin L. "Natural Decrease of Population: The Current and Prospective Status of an Emergent American Phenomenon." *Demography,* 6 (May, 1969), pp. 91-99.

Beaujeu, Garnier J. *Geography of Population.* N.Y.: St. Martin's, 1966.

Borgstrom. G. *Too Many: A Study of the Earth's Biological Limitations.* N.Y.: Macmillan, 1969.

Brinkman, George L. "The Effects of Zero Population Growth on the Spatial Distribution of Economic Activity." *American Journal of Agricultural Economics,* 54:5 (December, 1972), pp. 964-971.

Brown, Harrison Scott and Edward Hutchings Jr., eds. *Are Our Descendents Doomed? Technological Change and Population Growth.* NN.Y.: Viking, 1972.

Callahan, Daniel, ed. *The American Population Debate.* Garden City, N.Y.: Doubleday, 1971.

Cautley, Patricia W. and Edgar F. Borgatta. "Population Growth: A Challenge to Psychologists." *Representative Research in Social Psychology,* 4:1 (January, 1973), pp. 5-21.

Clarke, John I. *Population Geography.* London: Pergamon, 1972.

Clinton, Richard L. and R. Kenneth Godwin. *Research in the Politics of Population.* Lexington, MA.: D.C. Heath, 1973.

Coke, James G. and Charles S. Leibman. "Political Values and Population Density Control." *Land Economics* (November, 1961).

Cook, Robert C. *Human Fertility: The Modern Dilemma.* London: Victor Gollancz, 1968.

Davis, Kingsley. "Population." *Scientific American,* 209 (September, 1963), pp. 62-71.

Day, Lincoln H. and Alice Taylor Day. *Too Many Americans.* Boston: Houghton Mifflin, 1964.

Demeny, Paul. "Welfare Considerations in U.S. Population Policy." in *Aspects of Population Growth Policy: The U.S. Commission on Population Growth and the American Future Research Reports.* (vol. 6), Washington, D.C.: GPO, 1972.

Doberenz, A.R. and N.B.G. Taylor, eds. *Population Growth,* Greenbay: College of Human Biology, University of Wisconsin, 1971.

Drury, Robert F. "Local Governments and Population Changes." in *Governance and Population: The U.S. Commission on Population Growth and the American Future Research Reports.* (vol. 4), Washington, D.C.: GPO, 1972.

Dumond, D.E. "Population Growth and Cultural Change." *Southwestern Journal of Anthropology,* 21 (1965), pp. 302-324.

Eckenrode, Robert T. "Behavioral Aspects of Pollution Control." *Consulting Engineer,* 32:3 (1969), pp. 168-173.

Ehrlich, Paul R. *The Population Bomb.* NY: Ballantine, 1968.

Elazar, Daniel J. "Population Growth and the Federal System." in *Governance and Population: The U.S. Commission on Population Growth and the American Future Research Reports.* (vol. 4). Washington, DC: GPO, 1972.

Farley, John U. "Population Control and the Private Sector." *Journal of Social Issues,* 23 (October, 1967), pp. 135-143.

Fawcett, James T., ed. *Psychological Perspectives on Population.* NY: Basic, 1973.

Fraser, Dean. *The People Problem.* Bloomington: Indiana University Press, 1971.

Frejka, Tomas. *The Future of Population Growth: Alternative Paths to Equilibrium.* NY: Wiley, 1973.

Frejka, Tomas. "Reflections on the Demographic Conditions Needed to Establish a U.S. Stationary Population Growth." *Population Studies,* 22 (November, 1968), pp. 379-397.

Fremlin, J.H. "How Many People Can the World Support." *New Scientist,* 24 (1964), pp. 285-287.

Glass, D.V. and Roger Revelle. *Population and Social Change.* NY: Crane-Russak, 1972.

Hauser, Phillip Morris. "Man and More Men: The Population Prospects." *Bulletin of the Atomic Scientists,* 20 (June, 1964), pp. 4-8.

Heilbroner, Robert L. "Growth and Survival." *Foreign Affairs,* 51 (October, 1972), pp. 139-153.

Howard, Walter E. "The Population Crisis Is Here Now." *Bioscience,* 19 (1969), pp. 779-784.

Johnson, Stanley. *Population Problem.* NY: Halstead, 1974.

Mamdani, Mahmood. *The Myth of Population Control: Family, Caste, and Class in an Indian Village.* NY: Monthly Review, 1972.

Mills, Edwin S. "Economic Aspects of City Sizes." in *Population Distribution and Policy: The U.S. Commission on Population Growth and the American Future Research Reports.* (vol. 5), Washington, DC: GPO, 1972.

Montgomery, Johnson C. "Population Explosion and United States Law." *Hastings Law Journal,* 22:3 (February, 1971), pp. 629-659.

Ng, Larry K. et al., eds. *Population Crisis: Implications and Plans for Action.* Bloomington: University of Indiana Press, 1965.

Parry, H.B., ed. *Population and Its Problems: A Plain Man's Guide.* NY: Oxford University Press, 1974.

Parsons, Jack. *Population Versus Liberty.* NY: Prometheus, 1973.

Petersen, William. *Population.* (3rd ed.). NY: Macmillan, 1974.

Pressut, R. *Population.* Baltimore: Penguin, 1971.

Reid, Sue T. and David L. Lyon. *Population Crisis: An Interdisciplinary Prospective.* Glenview IL: Scott Foresman, 1974.

Robinson, Warren C., ed. *Population and Development Planning.* Bridgeport CT: Key Book Service, 1975.

Shimm, Melvin G., ed. *Population Control.* Dobbs Ferry, NY: Oceana, 1961.

Steinberg, Ira S. *Population and Frustration.* Columbus: Ohio State University Press, 1974.

POVERTY

Aubert, Vilhelm, ed. *The Hidden Society.* Totowa, NJ: Bedminster, 1965.

Badikan, Ben H. *In the Midst of Plenty: The Poor in America.* Boston: Beacon, 1964.

Balogh, Thomas. *The Economics of Poverty.* NY: Macmillan, 1966.

Caploritiz, David. *Poor Pay More: Consumer Practices of Low Income Families.* NY: Free Press, 1967.

Caudill, Harry Monroe. *Night Comes to the Cumberlands: A Biography of a Depressed Area.* Boston: Little, Brown, 1963.

Clark, Kenneth B. *Dark Ghettos: Dilemma of Social Power.* NY: Harper, 1965.

Clements, F.W. "Geography of Hunger." *Australian Journal of Science,* 29 (January, 1967), pp. 206-213.

Cloward, Richard A. and Richard M. Elman. "Poverty, Injustice in the Welfare State." *The Nation* (February 28, and March 7, 1966).

Coles, Robert and Maria Piers. *Wages of Neglect.* Chicago: Quadrangle, 1969.

"Consumer Legislation and the Ghetto." *Journal of Urban Law,* 45 (1968), pp. 705-712.

"Cycle of Despair." *Life* (March 8, 1968).

Dumont, Rene and Rosier Bernard. *Hungry Future.* NY: Praeger, 1969.

Ferman, Louis A. et al., eds. *Poverty in America: A Book of Readings.* Ann Arbor: University of Michigan Press, 1966.

Glenn, Max E. *Appalachia in Transition.* St. Louis: Bethany, 1970.

Graham, James. *The Enemies of the Poor.* NY: Random House, 1970.

Greenblatt, M. et al., eds. *Poverty and Mental Health.* a Washington, DC: American Psychiatric Association, 1967.

Harrington, Michael. *The Other America: Poverty in the United States.* NY: Macmillan, 1963.

Hopcraft, Arthur. *Born to Hunger.* Boston: Houghton Mifflin, 1968.

Kriesberg, Louis. *Mothers in Poverty: A Study of Fatherless Families.* Chicago: Aldine, 1970.

Lewis, Oscar. "The Culture of Poverty." *Scientific American,* 214 (October, 1966), pp. 19-25.

McIver, R.M., ed. *The Assault on Poverty and the Role of the Individual.* NY: Harper and Row, 1965.

Meissner, Hannah H., ed. *Poverty in the Affluent Society.* NY: Harper and Row, 1966.

Paddock, William and Paul Paddock. *Famine, 1975. America's Decision: Who Will Survive?* Boston: Little, Brown, 1967.

Pillisuk, Mave and Phyllis Pillisuk, eds. *How the White Poor Live.* New Brunswick NJ: Transaction, 1971.

Rainwater, Lee. *Behind Ghetto Walls.* Chicago: Aldine, 1970.

Roach, Jack and Janet Roach, eds. *Poverty.* Baltimore: Penguin, 1972.

Roby, Pamela, ed. *The Poverty Establishment.* Englewood Cliffs, NJ: Prentice-Hall, 1974.

Rothman, David J., ed. *Poverty U.S.A., The Historical Record.* (44 vols.) NY: Arno, 1971 (repr.).

Schorr, Alvin L. *Poor Kids: A Report on Children in Poverty.* NY: Basic, 1966.

Seligman, Ben B. *Permanent Poverty: An American Syndrome.* NY: Quadrangle, 1968.

Street, David and John C. Legett. "Economic Deprivation and Extremism: A Study of Unemployed Negroes."

American Journal of Sociology, LXVII (July, 1961), pp. 53-57.

Theobald, Robert. *The Rich and the Poor: A Study of the Economics of Rising Expectations.* NY: New American Library, 1961.

Tussing, A. Dale. *Poverty in the Dual Economy.* NY: St. Martins, 1975.

Valentine, Charles. *Culture and Poverty.* Chicago: University of Chicago Press, 1968.

Wilbur, George L., ed. *Poverty: A New Prospective.* Lexington: University of Kentucky Press, 1975.

Wirth, L. *The Ghetto.* Chicago: University of Chicago Press, 1929.

Zucher, Lewis A. Jr. *Poverty Warriors: The Human Experience of Planned Social Intervention.* Austin: University of Texas Press, 1970.

SKID ROWS

Allsop, Kenneth. *Hard Travellin': The Hobo and His History.* NY: New American Library, 1970.

Bahr, H.M. "The Gradual Disappearance of Skid Row." *Social Problems,* 15 (Summer, 1967).

Bahr, Howard M. *Skid Row: An Introduction to Disaffiliation.* NY: Oxford University Press, 1973.

Bahr, H.M. and G.R. Garrett. "Women on Skid Row." *Quarterly Journal of Studies on Alcohol,* 34 (1973), pp. 1228-1245.

Bendiner, Elmer. *The Bowery Man.* NY: Thomas Nelson, 1961.

Bittner, Egon. "The Police on Skid-Row: A Study of Peace Keeping." *American Sociological Review,* 32 (1967).

Bogue, Donald J. *Skid Row in American Cities.* Chicago: Chicago University Press, 1963.
Blighted urban neighborhoods were discovered to contain several distinct groups of residents who must be dealt with separately in rehabilitation efforts.

Gammage, A.Z. *Alcoholism, Skid Row and the Police.* Springfield, IL: C.C. Thomas, 1972.
The purpose of this study was to analyze the problem of the public drunkenness offender on skid row and the manner in which this problem is being handled.

Garrett, G.R. and D.H. Volk. *Homeless Women in New York City.* NY: Columbia University Press, 1970.

Harris, Sara. *Skid Row U.S.A.* Garden City, NY: Doubleday, 1956.

Henry, Helga B. *Mission on Main Street.* Boston: W.A. Wilde, 1955.

"Law on Skid Row." *Chicago-Kent Law Review,* 38 (1961).

Wallace, Samuel E. *Skid Row as a Way of Life.* Totowa N.J.: Bedminster, 1959.

Wiseman, Jacqueline P. *Stations of the Lost—The Treatment of Skid Row Alcoholics.* Englewood Cliffs, N.J.: Prentice-Hall, 1970.

SLUMS

Brown, Claude. *Manchild in the Promised Land.* N.Y: New American Library, 1966.

Cayton, Horace and Drake St. Clair. *Black Metropolis: A Study of Negro Life in a Northern City.* (rev. ed., 2 vols.) N.Y.: Harper and Row, 1962.

Clinard, Marshall B. *Slums and Community Development—Experiments in Self-Help.* N.Y.: Free Press, 1966.

Contant, James B. *Slums and Suburbs.* N.Y.: New American Library, 1964.

Ferguson, Thomas and Mary G. Pettigrew. A Study of 388 Families Living in Old Slum Houses." *Glasgow Medical Journal,* 35 (1954), pp. 169-182.

Hunter, David R. *The Slums: Challenge and Response.* N.Y.: Free Press, 1964.

Meister, Richard J. *Black Ghetto: Promised Land or Colony.* Lexington, MA.: D.C. Health, 1972.

Minuchin, Salvador et al. *Families of the Slums: An Exploration of Their Structure and Treatment.* N.Y.: Basic, 1967.

Moore, William Jr. *The Vertical Ghetto: Everyday Life in an Urban Project.* N.Y.: Random House, 1968.

Osofsky, Gilbert. *Harlem: The Making of a Ghetto.* N.Y.: Harper and Row, 1966.

Rainwater, Lee. *Behind Ghetto Walls: Black Family Life in a Federal Slum.* Chicago: Aldine, 1970.

Riis, Jacob. *How the Other Half Lives: Studies Among the Tenements of New York.* N.Y.: Sagamore, 1957 (repr.).

Seeley, John R. "The Slum: Its Nature, Use and Users." *Journal of American Institute of Planners,* 25 (1959), pp. 7-14.

Sexton, Patricia. *Spanish Harlem: An Anatomy of Poverty.* N.Y.: Harper and Row, 1965.

Sternlieb, George. *The Tenement Landlord.* New Brunswick, N.J.: Urban Studies Center, Rutgers University Press, 1966.

Stokes, Charles. "A Theory of Slums." *Land Economics,* 48 (August, 1962).

Suttles, Gerald D. *The Social Order of the Slum.* Chicago: University of Chicago Press, 1970.

Wakefield, Dan. *Island in the City: The World of Spanish Harlem.* Boston: Houghton Mifflin, 1959.

SOCIAL CLASS

Cohen, Albert and Harold M. Hodges. "Characteristics of the Lower-Blue-Collar-Class." *Social Problems,* 10 (1963), pp. 303-334.

Cooper, Homer C. "Social Class Identification and Political Party Affiliation." *Psychological Reports,* 5 (June, 1959), pp. 337-340.

Hamilton, Richard F. "The Behavior and Values of Skilled Workers." in Arthur B. Shostak and William Gomberg (eds.) *Blue-Collar World.* Englewood Cliffs N.J.: Prentice-Hall, 1969.

Hunter, Floyd. *Community Power Structures.* N.Y.: Free Press, 1966.

Hyman, H.H. "The Value Systems of Different Classes." in R. Bendix and S. Lipset (eds.) *Class, Status, and Power.* N.Y.: Free Press, 1953.

Kohn, M.L. "Social Class and Parental Values." *American Journal of Sociology,* 64 (January, 1959), pp. 337-351.

Leggett, John C. *Class, Race and Labor: Working-Class Consciousness in Detroit.* N.Y.: Oxford University Press, 1968.

Lewis, Hylan. *Culture, Class and Poverty.* Washington, D.C.: Health and Welfare Council of the National Capital Area, 1967.

Mack, Raymond W. *Race, Class and Power.* N.Y.: American Book, 1963.

Miller, S.M. "The American Lower Class: A Typological Approach." *Social Research,* 31 (1964), pp. 1-22.

Miller, W.B. "Lower Class Culture as a Generating Milieu of Gang Delinquency." *Journal of Social Issues,* 14:3 (1958), pp. 5-19.

Montague, Joel B. Jr. *Class and Nationality.* New Haven, CT.: College and University Press, 1966.

North, Cecil C. "Class Structure, Class Consciousness, and Party Alignment." *American Sociological Review,* 2 (June, 1937), pp. 365-371.

Parsons, Talcott. "Social Classes and Class Conflict." *American Economic Review,* XXXIX (1949), pp. 16-20.

Pavenstedt, Eleanor, ed. *The Drifters: Children of Disorganized Lower Class Families.* Boston: Little, Brown, 1967.

Rainwater, Lee, Richard P. Coleman, and Gerald Handel. *Workingman's Wife: Her Personality, World and Life Style.* Dobbs Ferry, N.Y.: Oceana, 1959.

Westie, Frank R. and Margaret L. Westie. "The Social-Distance Pyramid: Relationship Between Caste and Class." *American Journal of Sociology,* 63 (September, 1957), pp. 190-196.

Whyte, William F. *Street Corner Society: The Social Structure of an Italian Slum.* (2nd ed.) Chicago: University of Chicago Press, 1955.

SOCIAL INDICATORS

Castle, Emery N. "Economics and the Quality of Life." *American Journal of Agricultural Economics,* 54 (December, 1972), pp. 723-735.

Corning, Peter A. *Can We Develop an Index for Quality of Life?* Paper presented at the Annual Meeting of the American Association for the Advancement of Science, Philadelphia: December, 1971.

Farber, Seymour M. "Quality of Living: Stress and Creativity." in F. Fraser Darling and John P. Milton (eds.) *Future Environments of North America.* Garden City N.Y.: Natural History Press, 1966. pp. 342-354.

Gastil, Raymond D. "Social Indicators and Quality of Life." *Public Administration Review,* 30 (November-December, 1970), pp. 596-601.

Gitter, A. George and S. Franklin. *Subjective Quality of Life: Indicators of Sixteen Aspects of Life.* Boston: Communication Research Center, 1971.

Krieger, Martin H. *Social Indicators for the Quality of Individual Life.* Berkeley: Institute of Urban and Regional Development, University of California, 1969.

Land, Kenneth C. *Social Indicator Models: An Overview.* N.Y.: Russell Sage, 1973.

Rettig, Salomon, and B. Pasamanick. "Changes in Moral Values Over Three Decades, 1929-1958." *Social Problems,* 6 (1959), pp.320-328.

Rettig, Salomon and Benjamin Pasamanick. "Changes in Moral Values as a Function of Adult Socialization." *Social Problems,* 7 (1959), pp. 117-125.

Sawchuk, R.N. and George A. Gitter. *Eight Subjective Indicators of Quality of Life.* Boston: Communication Research Center, Boston University, 1971.

Sheldon, Eleanor Harriet and Wilbert E. Moore. *Indicators of Social Change: Concepts and Measurements.* N.Y.: Russell Sage Foundation, 1968.

SUICIDE

Anderson, Dorothy B. and Leonore J. McLean, eds. *Identifying Suicide Potential.* N.Y.: Behavioral, 1971.

Beck, Aaron, Roy Beck and Maria Kovacs. "Classification of Suicidal Behavior." *American Journal of Psychiatry* (March, 1975), pp. 285-287.

Britt, Fulton E. *Felo-De-Se: A Treatise on the Recognition and Prevention of Suicidal Behavior.* N.Y.: Vantage, 1969.

Choron, Jacques. *Suicide.* N.Y.: Scribner, 1972.

Danto, Bruce L. "The Suicidal Inmate." *Police Chief,* 38:8 (August, 1971), pp. 56-59.

Durkheim, E. *Suicide: A Study in Sociology.* Glencoe, IL.: Free Press.

Farberow, N.L. and E.S. Schneidman. "Suicide and the Police Officer." *Police,* 2:6 (July-August, 1962), pp. 51-55.

Gibbs, Jack P. *Suicide.* N.Y.: Harper and Row, 1968.

Grollman, Earl A. *Suicide: Prevention, Intervention, Postvention.* Boston: Beacon Press, 1971.

Haughton, Anson "Suicide Prevention Programs in the United States: An Overview." *Bulletin of Suicidology* (July, 1968), pp. 25-29.

Hankoff, L.D. "When Is Suicide Preventable?" *American Journal of Psychiatry* (August, 1975), pp. 874-875.

Larson, Phil. "Suicide Prevention 'First Aid' Techniques." *Law and Order* (September, 1976).

Litman, Robert E. "Police Aspects of Suicide." *Police,* 10:3 (January-February, 1966), pp. 14-18.

MacDonald, John M. "Deliberate Death on the Highways." *Police* (March-April 1965).

McCulloch, J. Wallace and Alistair E. Philip. *Suicidal Behavior.* Elmsford, N.Y.: Pergamon, 1972.

Roberts, Albert R. "An Organizational Study of Suicide Prevention Agencies in the United States." *Police,* 14:5 (May-June, 1970), pp. 64-72.

Schneidman, Edwin S. and Norman L. Farberow. *Clues to Suicide.* N.Y.: McGraw-Hill, 1966.

Stengel, E. "Suicide and Social Isolation." *20th Century,* 173 (Summer, 1964), pp. 24-36.

"Suicidal Tendencies—Be Cautious." *FBI Law Enforcement Bulletin,* 26:2 (February, 1957), pp. 11-12.

"Suicide and Attempted Suicide." *Chicago Police Star,* 5 (March, 1964).

Tuckman, J. and W.F. Youngman. *Assessment of Suicide Risk in Attempted Suicide: Suicidal Behaviors.* Boston: Little, Brown, 1968.

Tuckman, J. and W.F. Youngman. "A Scale for Assessing Suicide Risk of Attempted Suicides." *Journal of Clinical Psychology,* 24 (1968), pp. 17-19.

Walrod, T.H. "Suicide Attempts—Who and Why." *National Sheriff,* 25:2 (1973), pp. 26, 30-31.

Zusman, J. and D. Davidson. *Organizing the Community to Prevent Suicide.* Springfield, IL.: C.C. Thomas, 1971.
Articles covering the matters of identifying the suicide problem, locating solutions, finding workers for prevention programs, and organizing prevention centers.

TERRITORY

Ardrey, Robert. *Territorial Imperative.* N.Y.: Dell, 1968.

Becker, F.D. and C. Mayo. "Delineating Personal Distance and Territoriality." *Environment and Behavior,* 3 (1971), pp. 375-381.

Howard, Eliot. *Territory in Birdlife.* Patterson, N.J.: Atheneum, 1964.

Lorenz, Konrad. *On Aggression.* N.Y.: Harcourt, 1966.

Los Angeles Police Department. *The Territorial Imperative, Decentralization Task Force Report, by the Office of Operations.* Los Angeles: LAPD, 1971.

Stokes, Allen W., ed. *Territory.* N.Y.: Halsted, 1974.

URBAN PROBLEMS

Adams, Robert M. *The Uruk Countryside: The Natural Setting of Urban Societies.* Chicago: University of Chicago Press, 1972.

Arango, Jorge. *The Urbanization of the Earth.* Boston: Beacon, 1971.

Banfield, Edward C. *The Unheavenly City.* Boston: Little, Brown, 1968.

Bellens, John and Henry Schmandt. *The Metropolis: Its People, Politics and Economic Life.* N.Y.: Harper and Row, 1970.

Blair, T.L. *International Urban Crisis.* N.Y.: Hill and Wang, 1974.

Chapin, F. Stuart Jr. *Urban Land Use Planning.* Urbana: University of Illinois Press, 1964.

Chermayeff, Serge and Alexander Tzonis. *Shape of Community: Realization of Human Potential.* Baltimore: Penguin, 1971.

Cook, J.A. "Gardens on Housing Estates: A Survey of User Attitudes and Behavior on Seven Layouts." *Town Planning Review,* 39 (1968), pp. 217-234.

Crawford, Clan. *Strategy and Tactics in Municipal Zoning.* Englewood Cliffs N.J.: Prentice-Hall, 1969.

Daedalus eds. "The Future Metropolis." *Daedalus,* 90:1 (Winter, 1961). (entire issue)

Daland, Robert T. *Comparative Urban Research: The Administration and Politics of Cities.* Beverly Hills, CA.: Sage, 1969.

Davies, J. Clarence III. *Neighborhood Groups and Urban Renewal.* N.Y.: Columbia University Press, 1966.

Davis, Kingsley. "Origin and Growth of Urbanization in the World." *American Journal of Sociology,* 60 (1955), pp. 429-437.

Duncan, Beverly, George Sabagh, and Maurice Van Arsdol Jr. "Pattern of City Growth." *American Journal of Sociology,* 67 (January, 1962), pp. 418-429.

Eckbo, Garrett. *Urban Landscape Design.* N.Y.: McGraw-Hill, 1964.

Edwards, Gordon. *Land, People and Policy: The Problems and Techniques of Assembling Land for the Urbanization of 100 Million New Americans.* West Trenton, N.J.: Chandler-Davis, 1969.

Faltermayar, Edward K. *Redoing America: A Nationwide Report on How We Can Make Our Cities and Suburbs Livable.* N.Y.: Harper and Row, 1968.

Flax, Michael J. *A Study in Comparative Urban Indicators: Conditions in 18 Large Metropolitan Areas.* Washington, DC: Urban Institute, 1972.

Forrester, Jay Wright. *Urban Dynamics.* Cambridge, MA.: MIT Press, 1970.

Fortune, eds. *The Exploding Metropolis.* Garden City, N.Y.: Doubleday, 1958.

Glazer, Nathan, ed. *Cities in Trouble.* Chicago: Quadrangle. 1970.

Greer, Scott. *Urban Renewal and American Cities: The Dilemma of Democratic Intervention.* Indianapolis: Bobbs Merrill, 1965.

Greer, Scott. "Urbanization Reconsidered: A Comparative Study of Local Areas in a Metropolis." *American Sociological Review,* 21: (1956), pp. 19-25.

Hauser, Phillip Morris and Leo F. Schnore, eds. *The Study of Urbanization.* N.Y.: Wiley, 1965.

Hoag, Edwin. *American Cities: Their Historical and Social Development.* Philadelphia: Lippincott, 1969.

Jacobs, Jane. *The Death and Life of Great American Cities.* N.Y.: Random House, 1961.

Keller, Suzanne. *The Urban Neighborhood.* N.Y.: Random House, 1968.

McKelvey, Blake. *The Urbanization of America, 1860-1915.* New Brunswick, N.J.: Rutgers University Press, 1963.

Murphy, Raymond E. *American City.* (2nd ed.) N.Y.: McGraw-Hill, 1974.

Rossi, Peter H. and Robert A. Dentler. *The Politics of Urban Renewal.* N.Y.: Free Press, 1961.

Schnore, Leo. *The Urban Scene.* N.Y.: Free Press, 1966.

Schnore, Leo and Harry Sharp. "The Changing Color of Our Big Cities." *Trans-Action,* 1964.

Weber, Michael and Anne Lloyd. *American City.* St. Paul, MN.: West, 1975.

Wood, Robert C. *Suburbia: Its People and Their Politics.* Boston: Houghton-Mifflin, 1959.

WELFARE

Cowger, C.D. and C.R. Atherton. "Social Control: A Rationale for Social Welfare." *Social Work,* 19:4 (1974) pp. 456-462.
Authors advocate deeper social worker involvement in social control.

Cull, John G. and Richard E. Hardy. *Big Welfare Mess.* Springfield, IL.: C.C. Thomas, 1973.

Elman, Richard M. *The Poorhouse State: The American Way of Life on Public Assistance.* N.Y.: Pantheon, 1966.

Foren, R. and R. Bailey. *Authority in Social Case Work.* Elmsford, N.Y.: Pergamon, 1968.

Galper, Jeffrey. *Politics of Social Services.* Englewood Cliffs, N.J.: Prentice-Hall, 1975.

Geismar, Ludwig L. *Preventive Intervention in Social Work.* Methuen, N.J.: Scarecrow, 1968.

Gell, Frank. *Black Badge: Confessions of a Case Worker.* N.Y.: Harper and Row, 1969.

Guggenbuhl-Craig, Adolph. *Power in the Helping Professions.* N.Y.: (Spring, 1971).

Handler, Joel F. *Coercive Social Worker: British Lessons for American Social Services.* Washington, D.C.: Academic, 1973.

Handler, Joel F. and Ellen Hollingsworth. *Deserving Poor: A Study of Welfare Administration.* Washington, D.C.: Academic, 1971.

Jones, Mervyn. *Life on the Dole.* London: Davis-Poynter, 1972.

May, Edgar *The Wasted Americans: Cost of Our Welfare Dilemma.* N.Y.: Harper and Row, 1964.

National Association of Social Workers. *Prevention in Social Work.* N.Y: National Association of Social Workers, 1974.

Sanders, Charles L. *Black Professionals: Perceptions of Institutional Racism in Health and Welfare Organizations.* Beaverton, OR.: International School Book Service, 1973.

Schneider, David Moses and Albert Deutsch. *The History of Public Welfare in New York State.* Chicago: University of Chicago Press, 1941.

Stanton, Esther. *Clients Come Last: Volunteers and Welfare Organizations.* Beverly Hills, CA: Sage, 1970.

Starr, Paul et al. *Discarded Army: The Nader Report on Vietnam Veterans and the Veteran's Administration.* N.Y.: Charter House, 1974.

Yelaja, Shankar A., ed. *Authority and Social Work: Concept and Use.* Toronto: Toronto University Press, 1971.

PART XVIII
MISCELLANEOUS

REFERENCE MATERIAL

DICTIONARIES

Abbreviations

Desola, Ralph. *Abbreviations Dictionary.* (rev. ed.), Des Moines, IA: Meridith, 1967.

Acronyms

Acronyms and Initialisms Dictionary, A Guide to Alphabetic Designations. Detroit: Gale Research, 1970.

Administration—Management

Banki, I.S. *Dictionary of Administration and Supervision.* Santa Cruz, CA: Davis, 1971.

French, Derek. *Dictionary of Management.* Washington, DC: International Publications, 1975.

Johannsen, Hano. *Management Glossary.* Harlow: Longmans, 1968.

Chemical

Bennett, Harry. *Concise Chemical and Technical Dictionary.* (2nd enlarged ed.), NY: Chemical, 1962.

Communications Hardware

Bones, R.A., ed. *Dictionary of Telecommunications.* NY: Philosophy Library, 1970.

Clason, W.E. *Dictionary of Television, Radar, and Antennas.* NY: American Elsevier, 1955.

Greene, F.W. *Technical Terms and Definitions Used with Law Enforcement Communications Equipment (Radio Antennas, Transmitters, and Receivers) — Law Enforcement Standards Program.* Washington, DC: GPO, 1973.

Terms related to land-mobile, portable, and base or fixed-station radio communications antennas, transmitters and receivers in the frequency of 25 to 960 MHZ.

Smith, Emerson. *Glossary of Communications.* Chicago: Telephony, 1971.

Computers

Chandor, Anthony, ed. *Dictionary of Computers.* Baltimore: Penguin, 1970.

Clason, W.E. *Dictionary of Computers Automatic Control and Data Processing.* (2nd ed.), NY: American Elsevier, 1971.

Rogers, Harold A. Jr. *Funk and Wagnalls Dictionary of Data Processing Terms.* NY: Funk and Wagnalls, 1970.

SEARCH Group, Inc. *Dictionary of Criminal Justice Data Terminology.* Washington, DC: NCJRS, 1976.

Trollhann, Lilian. *Dictionary of Data Processing.* NY: Elsevier, 1964.

U.S. Bureau of Budget. *Automatic Data Processing Glossary.* Washington, DC: GPO, 1962.

Criminal Slang

California Board of Corrections. *A Dictionary of Criminal Language.* Sacramento: California Board of Corrections, 1962.

Cromwell, Paul F. "Slang Usage in the Addict Subculture." *Crime and Delinquency.* 16 (January, 1970), pp. 75-78.

Golden, Hymen E., ed. *Dictionary of American Underworld Lingo.* NY: Twayne, 1950.

Hardy, R.E. and J.G. Cull. *Drug Language and Lore.* Springfield, IL: C.C. Thomas, 1975.

Landy, Eugene E. *The Underground Dictionary.* NY: Simon and Schuster, 1971.

Partridge, Eric. *Dictionary of Slang and Unconventional English.* NY: Macmillan, 1970.

Partridge, E. *Dictionary of the Underworld, British and American.* Santa Cruz, CA: Bonanza, 1968.

Schmidt, J.E. "Underworld English." *Police.* 4:2 (November-December, 1959).

Criminology

Adler, J.A. *Dictionary of Criminal Science.* NY: American Elsevier, 1960.

Nice, R.W. *Dictionary of Criminology.* NY: Philosophical Library, 1965.

Eleven hundred definitions containing terms dealing with the topics of criminology, penology, delinquency and anti-social behavior.

Drugs

Lingeman, Richard. *Drugs From A to Z: A Dictionary.* NY: McGraw-Hill, 1969.

Snowden, M. *Drug Terms.* Washington, DC: NCJRS, (Microfiche), [n.d.].

Environment

Gilpin, Alan. *Dictionary of Environmental Terms.* London: Routledge and Paul, 1976.

Firearms

Steindler, R.A. *Firearms Dictionary.* Harrisburg, PA: Stackpole, 1970.

Gambling

Salak, John. *Dictionary of Gambling*. NY: Philosophical Library, 1963.

A comprehensive dictionary covering all forms of gambling, from the terms used in the penny numbers games to those in the plush gambling casinos.

Gems

Copeland, Lawrence L. et al. *Diamond Dictionary*. Los Angeles: Gemological Institute of America, 1963.

Webster, Robert. *Gems: Their Sources, Descriptions and Identifications*. (2 vols.), London: Butterworth, 1962.

Law

Black, Henry Campbell. *Black's Law Dictionary, Definitions of Terms and Phrases of American and English Jurisprudence, Ancient and Modern*. (rev. 4th ed.), St. Paul, MN: West, 1968.

Dahl, Richard C. and John F. Whelan. *The Military Law Dictionary*. Dobbs Ferry, NY: Oceana, 1960.

Fricke, C.W. *Five Thousand Criminal Definitions — Terms and Phrases*. Los Angeles: Legal Book, 1968.

Words, phrases, and terms used in the administration of criminal law are defined.

Gifis, Steven H. *Law Dictionary*. Woodbury, N.Y.: Barron's Educational [n.d.].

Gilmer,W. Jr. *Cochran's Law Lexicon — Pronouncing Edition*. (5th ed.), Cincinnati, OH: Anderson, 1973.

Meaning and application of words, phrases, maxims, abbreviations and references to reports likely to be encountered by those associated with law.

Shapiro, Irving. *Dictionary of Legal Terms*. Binghamton, NY: Gould, 1969.

Radin, Max and Lawrence G. Greene. *Law Dictionary*. (rev. ed.), Dobbs Ferry, NY: Oceana, 1970.

Robb, L.A. *Dictionary of Legal Terms — Spanish-English and English-Spanish*. NY: Wiley, 1955.

Law Enforcement

Eastman, G.D. *Analysis of Words and Terms Relevant and Important to the Study and Teaching of Police Organization and Management in the American Municipal Police Service and Recommended Definitions*. Ann Arbor, MI: University Microfilms, 1965.

Clarification of terminology for more effective communication in personnel training and management.

Massey, R.G. and W.F. Druckenbrod. *Terms and Definitions for Police Patrol Cars — Law Enforcement Standards Program*. Washington, DC: NCJRS, 1974.

National Criminal Justice Reference Service. *Thesaurus and Indicators for Indexing Law Enforcement and Criminal Justice Information*. Washington, DC: NCJRS, 1973.

Ruffner, Frederick G. Jr. and Robert C. Thomas, eds. *Code Names Dictionary: A Guide to Code Names, Slang, Nick Names, Journalese and Similar Terms*. Detroit: Gale, 1963.

Medical

Anerican Medical Association. *Current Medical Terminology*. (3rd ed.), Chicago: American Medical Association, 1966.

Black's Medical Dictionary. (29th ed.), NY: Barnes and Noble, 1971.

Schmidt, Jacob E. *Police Medical Dictionary*. Springfield, IL: C.C. Thomas, 1968.

Medical-Legal

Bander, E.J. and J. Wallach. *Medical Legal Dictionary*. Dobbs Ferry, NY: Oceana, 1970.

Maloy, Bernard S. *The Simplified Medical Dictionary for Lawyers*. Mundelen, IL: Callaghan, 1960.

Paper

American Pulp and Paper Association. *The Dictionary of Paper*. Menasha, WI: George Banta, 1940.

Photography

Craeybeck, A.S. *Dictionary of Photography*. NY: American Elsevier, 1965.

Grover, C. *Photographic Terms and Definitions — Law Enforcement Standards Program*. Washington, DC: GPO, 1975.

Page, A. *Dictionary of Photographic Terms*. NY: Heineman, 1966.

Poisons

Mellan, Eleanor Ibert. *The Dictionary of Poisons*. NY: Philosophical Library, 1956.

Political Science

Khopkar, M.D. *Dictionary of Political Terminology*. Thompson, CT: Inter-Culture, 1970.

Laqueur, Walter. *Dictionary of Politics*. (rev. ed.), NY: Free Press, 1974.

Plano, Jack C. and M. Greenberg. *American Political Dictionary*. (3rd ed.), NY: Holt, Rinehart and Winston, 1972.

Psychiatry

American Psychiatric Association. *A Psychiatric Glossary, the Meaning of Words Most Frequently Used in Psychiatriy*. Washington, DC: American Psychiatric Association, 1958.

Hinsie, Leland Earl. *Psychiatric Dictionary*. (4th ed.), NY: Oxford University Press, 1970.

Social Sciences

Fairchild, H.P. *Dictionary of Sociology*. NY: Philosophical Library, 1944.

Hoult, T.F. *Dictionary of Modern Sociology*. Totowa, NJ: Littlefield, Adams, 1969.

Mitchell, Geoffrey Duncan. *A Dictionary of Sociology*. Chicago: Aldine, 1968.

Wedeck, H.E. *Dictionary of Gypsy Life and Lore*. NY: Philosophical Library, 1973.

Urban Affairs

Abrams, Charles and R. Kolodny. *The Language of Cities: A Glossary of Terms*. NY: Viking Press, 1971.

ENCYCLOPEDIAS

Criminology

Branham, Vernon C. and Samuel B. Kutash, eds. *Encyclopedia of Criminology*. NY: Philosophical Library, 1949.

Scott, Harold, ed. *The Concise Encyclopedia of Crime and Criminals*. NY: Hawthorn, 1961.

Drugs

White, William Jr. *Reference Encyclopedia of Drugs and Drug Abuse*. Philadelphia: North American, 1974.

Espionage

Seth, Ronald. *Encyclopedia of Espionage: From the Age of Jericho to the Age of James Bond*. Garden City, NY: Doubleday, 1974.

Firearms

Koller, Larry. *Arco Gunbook*. NY: Arco, 1962.

Mueller, Chester and John Olson. *Small Arms Lexicon and Concise Encyclopedia*. Hackensack, NJ: Stoeger Arms, 1968.

Peterson, Harold L., ed. *Encyclopedia of Firearms*. NY: Dutton, 1964.

Law Enforcement

Salottolo, A. Lawrence. *Modern Police Service Encyclopedia*. NY: Arco, 1970.

Management

Finch, Frank. *A Concise Encyclopedia of Management Techniques*. London: Heinemann, 1976.

Psychology

Eysenck, H.J., ed. *Encyclopedia of Psychology*. NY: Herder and Herder, 1972.

DIRECTORIES

Audio Visual

Criminal Justice Audio Visual Materials Directors. Washington, DC: NCJRS, 1974.

Aviation

Aerospace Industries Association of America, Inc. *Helicopter Operators — Commercial — Executive — Civil Government — And the Helicopter Flight Schools in the United States, Canada, and Puerto Rico — Directory, 1974*. Washington, DC: NCJRS, (Microfiche), 1974.

U.S. Department of Transportation Federal Aviation Administration. *Local Law Enforcement Organizations Participating in Aviation Security — Directory*. Washington, DC: NCJRS, (Microfiche), 1974.

Correctional Agencies

Directory of Correctional Institutions and Agencies — 1971 Edition. College Park, MD: ACA, 1971.

A directory of names, addresses, and telephone numbers of correctional institutions and agencies of the United States, Canada and Great Britain (1971).

Drugs

Directory of National Coordinating Council on Drug Abuse Education and Information, Inc. — 1971-1972. Washington, DC: NCCDE, [n.d.].

Location of resources and the identification of key people in a variety of drug oriented services and bureaus.

Student Association for Study of Hallucinogens. *Directory of Drug Information Groups*. Beloit, WI: Stash Press, 1970.

Watson, D. and S.B. Sells. *Directory of Narcotic Addiction Treatment Agencies in the United States, 1968-1969*. Washington, DC: GPO, 1970.

Programs and treatment approaches of federal, state, municipal, and private agencies.

Halfway Houses

International Halfway House Association. *International Halfway House Association Directory*. (4th ed.), Cincinnati: International Halfway House Association, 1972.

Interstate Agencies

Council of State Governments. *The Directory of Interstate Agencies*. Chicago: Council of State Governments, 1967.

Judges

National Council of Juvenile Court Judges. *Directory of Juvenile Court Judges*. Reno, NV: NCJCJ, 1972.

Names and addresses of individual judges organized in alphabetical listings by city, state, and judge surname and coded for attendance at annual training conferences.

Juvenile Delinquency

Directory of Federal Juvenile Delinquency and Related Youth Development Programs — A Handbook for Juvenile Delinquency Planners. Washington, DC: NCJRS, 1973.

Libraries

Krauzas, Anthony T. *Directory of Special Libraries and Information Centers*. (2nd ed.), Detroit: Gale, 1964-1966.

Mental Health

Selected Sources of Inexpensive Mental Health Materials — A Directory for Mental Health Educators. Washington, DC: GPO, 1972.

Annotated list of publishers of educational materials in mental health compiled to aid personnel conducting mental health education program.

Minorities

Directory: National Black Organizations. NY: AFRAM Associates, 1972.

Professional Societies

Walker, Loretta and Jane Somers. *Membership Directories of Professional Societies: A Check List*. Schenectady, NY: Union College Library, 1973.

Security Equipment

Securitech: The International Guide to Security Equipment, 1975. Tunbridge Wells: UNISAF, 1975.

Sheriffs

National Sheriff's Association. *Directory of Sheriffs of the United States*. Washington, DC: National Sheriff's Association, annual.
Available from National Sheriff's Association, Suite 209, 1250 Connecticut Ave. N.W., Washington 20036.

Underground Press

Glessing, Robert J. *The Underground Press in America*. Bloomington: Indiana University Press, 1970.

Universities and Colleges

"A Career in Law Enforcement." *Law and Order*. 8:7 (July, 1960), pp. 10, 12, 14, 16-18.
Directory of colleges, universities and schools.

Kobetz, Richard W. *Law Enforcement and Criminal Justice Education: Directory, 1975-1976*. Gaithersburg, MD: IACP, 1975.

PRIVATE POLICE INDUSTRY

INDUSTRIAL SECURITY — GENERAL

Becker, Theodore M. "Place of Private Police in Society: An Area of Research for the Social Sciences." *Social Problems*. 21:3 (1974), pp. 438-453.

Bray, S.E. and R. Hurley. *Freight Security Manual*. Los Angeles: Security World, 1970.
Guidelines for management security administrators and terminal managers of trucking firms in establishing and maintaining effective profit-saving security programs.

Brostron, Curtis. "The St. Louis Private Watchman Program." *Police*. 13:2 (November-December, 1968), pp. 27-28.

Buckley, John L. "A New Look at Industrial Security." *Law and Order*. 13:5 (May, 1956), through 13:7 (July, 1965).

Busby, Walter J. "Arson and the Security Officer." *Security World*. 8 (June, 1971), pp. 35, 37-39.

Carlton, S.A. "Surveying School Security and Costs." *Security World*, 11:2 (1974), pp. 26-27, 46.

Collins, William P. "Physical Security Planning." *Police Chief*. 37:9 (October, 1970), pp. 30, 248-251.

Davis, John R. "Internal Control." *Police*. 6:2 (November-December, 1961), pp. 17-18.

"Ex-police in Security." *Security Gazette*. 15:12 (1973).

Green, Gion and Raymond C. Farber. *Introduction to Security*. Los Angeles: Security World, 1975.

Hamilton, Peter. "The Police and the Security Industry. I. The Decline of Public Interest to Law and Order." *Police Journal*. 41 (1968), pp. 261-267.
Today the public protects their property less than ever. Many of our buildings offer easy targets to the illegal intruder.

Hamilton, Peter. "The Police and the Security Industry. II. The Rise of the Security Industry and Its Role in Crime Prevention." *Police Journal*. 41 (1968), pp. 297-303.
There are two parties to every theft — the thief and the owner. The affluent society needs a new concept of the responsibility of ownership.

Healy, Richard J. and Timothy J. Walsh. *Industrial Security Management: A Cost-Effective Approach*. NY: AMA, 1971.

Hemphill, C.F. *Security for Business and Industry*. Homewood, IL: Dow-Jones-Irwin, 1971.
Methods for reducing business losses due to theft, vandalism, fire, burglary, embezzlement, and other problems.

Hemphill, Charles F. and Thomas Hemphill. *The Secure Company*. Homewood, IL: Dow-Jones-Irwin, 1975.

Kakalik, James S. and Sorrel Wildhorn. *Current Regulation of Private Police: Regulatory Agency Experience and Views*. Washington, DC: LEAA, 1971.
Licensing and regulation of the industry in every state and several cities is described. This report also includes extensive data on regulatory agency experience, complaints, disciplinary actions taken, and the views of 42 agencies on needed changes in regulation.

Kakalik, James S. and Sorrel Wildhorn. *The Law and Private Police*. Washington, DC: LEAA, 1971.
This report discusses the law as it relates to the private police industry. It includes a general discussion of the sources of legal limitations upon private police activities and personnel and sources of legal powers, and an examination of specific legal problems raised by those activities and by the relationships between the users and providers of private security services. The legal doctrines governing particular security activities are evaluated and recommendations for improvement are offered.

Kakalik, James S. and Sorrel Wildhorn. *The Private Police Industry: Its Nature and Extent*. (vol. II). Washington, DC: LEAA, 1971.
This descriptive report covers the nature, size, growth and operation of the industry and its personnel. It also describes the results of a survey of private security employees.

Kakalik, James S. and Sorrel Wildhorn. *Special-Purpose Public Police*. Washington, DC: LEAA, 1971.
Descriptive information is presented on certain types of public forces not having general law-enforcement responsibilities. These include reserve police, special-purpose federal forces, special local law enforcement agencies, and campus police. These data provide a useful context for analyzing the role of private police.

Keller, E. John. "Contract Guard Services: To Be or Not to Be." *Law and Order*. 20:5 (May, 1972), pp. 98-99, and 20:6 (June, 1972), pp. 106-107.

Keller, E. John. "Industrial Security Surveys." *Law and Order.* 20:4 (April, 1972).

Kingsbury, A.A. *Introduction to Security and Crime Prevention Surveys.* Springfield, IL: C.C. Thomas, 1973.

Landes, W.M. and R.A. Posner. "The Private Enforcement of Law." *Journal of Legal Studies.* 4:1 (1975), pp. 1-46.

Lipson, Milton. *On Guard: The Business of Private Security.* NY: Quadrangle, 1975.
U.S. Private industry spends 4 billion a year on private protection and loses 50 billion in thefts and fraud.

Mart, Victor C. "Private Police." *Police Journal.* 48:2 (April-June, 1975), pp. 122-132.

Mart, Victor C. "Private Police Forces and the Growth of Commercial Security Organizations." *Police (GB),* (April, 1975), pp. 20-22.

Momboisse, Raymond M. *Industrial Security for Strikes, Riots and Disasters.* Springfield, IL: C.C. Thomas, 1968.

Oliver, E. and J. Wilson. *Practical Security in Commerce and Industry.* (2nd ed.), NY: Halstead, 1973.

Peel, J.D. *Fundamentals of Training for Security Officers — A Comprehensive Guide to What You Should Be, Know and Do to Have a Successful Career as a Private Patrolman or Security Officer.* Springfield, IL: C.C. Thomas, 1970.

Peel, John Donald. *The Training, Licensing, and Guidance of Private Security Officers.* Springfield, IL: C.C. Thomas, 1973.

Post, R.S. and A.A. Kingsbury. *Security Administration — An Introduction.* (2nd ed.), Springfield, IL: C.C. Thomas, 1973.
History and philosophy of security, legal basis for governmental and proprietary security, organizational concepts, and security procedures and techniques.

"Private Police Forces: Legal Powers and Limitations." *University of Chicago Law Review.* (1969), pp. 560-565.

Private Security Advisory Council. *Regulations of Private Security Services, Including a Model Private Security Licensing and Regulatory Statute.* Washington, DC: AMR Society for Industrial Security, 1976.

Sohn, David. "Drug Screening in Industry." *Law and Order.* 19:11 (November, 1971), pp. 84-87.

Strobl, Walter M. *Security: Theft Prevention, Security Development, Fire Protection, Emergency and Disaster Planning and Guard Organization.* NY: Industrial, 1973.

"Tightening Up on Plant Security." *Chemical Week* (January 13, 1971).

Traini, R. "Cutting Container Thefts." *Security Gazette.* 15:11 (1973), pp. 407-408.

U.S. Department of Transportation, Office of the Secretary of Transportation. *Guidelines for the Physical Security of Cargo.* Washington, DC: GPO, 1972.

Wathen, J.W. *Security Subjects — An Officer's Guide to Plant Protection.* Springfield, IL: C.C. Thomas, 1972.
Basic training manual on all aspects of industrial security for use by guards, supervisors, and private industries.

Wels, Byron. *Fire and Theft Security System.* Blue Ridge Summit, PA: Tab, 1971.

Woodruff, Ronald S. *Industrial Security Techniques.* Columbus, OH: Merrill, 1974.

Wright, K.G. *Cost-Effective Security.* NY: McGraw-Hill, 1972.
Businessmen's guidebook for providing cost-effective security for industrial facilities, cargo, and property.

INDUSTRIAL ESPIONAGE

Barlay, Stephan. *Double Cross: Encounters with Industrial Spies.* London: Hamilton, 1973.

Bergier, Jacques. *Secret Armies: The Growth of Corporate and Industrial Espionage.* Indianapolis: Bobbs, 1976.

"Business Spies Still Busy." *International Management* (June, 1969).

"Corporate Spies." *Time* (March 26, 1965).

Greene, Richard M. Jr., ed. *Business Intelligence and Espionage.* Homewood, IL: Dow-Jones-Irwin, 1966.

Hamilton, Peter. *Espionage and Subversion in an Industrial Society: An Examination and Philosophy of Defense for Management.* London: Hutchinson, 1967.

Hoyt, Douglas. "The Computer as a Target for the Industrial Spy." *Assets Protection* (Spring, 1975).

Keller, E. John. "The Secrets and Tricks of the Quietest Craft." *Law and Order.* 20:3 (March, 1972).

Shaw, William. "A Primer on Industrial Espionage." *Law and Order.* 17:8 (August, 1969) through 17:10 (October, 1969.

Walsh, Timothy J. *Protecting Your Business Against Espionage.* NY: AMA, 1973.

PRIVATE INVESTIGATION

Ackroyp, James J. *The Investigator: A Practical Guide to Private Detection.* Levittown, NY: Transatlantic, 1975.

Armes, Jay J. *Jay J. Armes, Investigator: The World's Most Successful Private Eye.* NY: Macmillan, 1976.

Goldfadder, Ed. *Tracer! The Search for Missing Persons.* Los Angeles: Nash, 1970.

Liebers, Arthur. *Investigators Handbook: A Complete Instruction Manual and Guide to Opportunities in the Vast Field of Commercial and Civil Investigation.* NY: Arco, 1972.

Otash, Fred. *Investigation Hollywood: Memoirs of Hollywood's Top Private Detectives.* Chicago: Regnery, 1976.

Post, Richard S. "A Study of State Requirements for Investigation." *Police Chief.* XXXVI:7 (July, 1969), pp. 31-32.
State by state licensing and other requirements for private police and investigators.

RAILROAD POLICE

Coon, Thomas F. "The Railroad Police." *The Bulletin of the Society of Professional Investigators* (January, 1965), pp. 14-17.

Coon, Thomas F. "The Railroad Police, the World's Largest Privately Supported Police System." *Police.* 9:2 (November-December, 1964), pp. 91-93.

Cusick, Robert J. "Railroad Security." *Law and Order.* 17:9 (September, 1962), pp. 101-102, 105.

Dewhurst, H.S. "Departmental Organization of the Railroad Police." *Police.* 1:1 (September-October, 1956), pp. 29-33, 36.

Dewhurst, H.S. *The Railroad Police.* Springfield, IL: C.C. Thomas, 1955.

Farley, William F. "Functions of the Railroad Police." *Journal of Criminal Law, Criminology and Police Science.* 42 (1951-52).

Foster, Reginald. " 'Nuts and Bolts' of Railway Security." *Security and Protection* (May, 1975), pp. 4-6.

Hartdorn, A.W. *Economic Benefits of Improved Security at a Railroad Piggyback Yard — Final Report.* Washington, CD: NCJRS, (Microfiche), 1947.

Reynolds, Williams F. "Airborne Assistance for Railroad Crime." *FBI Law Enforcement Bulletin.* 43:5 (August, 1974), pp. 16-21.

SPECIAL PURPOSE SECURITY UNITS

Burns Security Institute. *National Survey on Library Security.* Washington, DC: NCJRS, (Microfiche), 1973.

Colling, Russell L. *Hospital Security — Complete Protection for Health Care Facilities.* Culver City, CA: Security World, 1976.

Colling, Russell L. "Hospital Security Problems." *Police.* 6:5 (May-June, 1962), pp. 69-71.

Creekmore, E.L. "How Big Cities Train for School Security: A Nationwide Survey." *Security World.* 11:2 (1974), pp. 28-29, 46.

Fleming, George. "Security Police at Picatinny Arsenal." *Law and Order.* 12:9 (September, 1964).
Civilian security force policing a military base.

Flynn, Charles P. "Harness Racing Integrity." *Police Chief.* 37:9 (October, 1970), pp. 38-39.

Garden, A. Newell. "The Vertical Town Police." *Law and Order.* 14:9 (September, 1966), pp. 70-72.
Security for high-rise apartment buildings.

Grealy, J.I. "Safety and Security in the School Environment." *Security World.* 11:2 (1974), pp. 16-17, 42.

Keck, Caroline et al., eds. *A Primer on Museum Security.* Cooperstown, PA: New York State Historical Association, 1966.

Keller, E. John. "Food Market Security." *Law and Order.* 23:3 (March, 1975), pp. 71, 75.

Keller, E. John. "Hotel Security: How the Chief of Police Can Help." *Law and Order.* 20:8 (August, 1972), pp. 61-63.

Lawrence, N.L. "Bank Security — What Is Enough?" *FBI Law Enforcement Bulletin.* 42:11 (1973), pp. 2-7.

Miraval, Anthony J. "High Rise Security." *Security Management* (May, 1973).

Pakalik, Michael J. "Security and Protection in a Museum." *Police.* 3:1 (September-October, 1958), pp. 26-29.

San Luis, E. *Office and Office Building Security.* Los Angeles: Security World, 1973.

Traini, R. "Beating the Forger." *Security Gazette.* 15:10 (1973), pp. 367-368.
Describes police and airline security efforts to combat ticket forgeries and banknote counterfeiting in Great Britain.

MISCELLANEOUS ISSUES

AMERICAN CIVIL LIBERTIES UNION

Johnson, Donald Oscar. *The Challenge to American Freedom: World War I and the Rise of the American Civil Liberties Union.* Lexington: University of Kentucky Press, 1963.

Lamont, Carliss. *Trial of Elizabeth Gurley Flynn by the American Civil Liberties Union.* NY: Horizon, 1969.

Markmahn, Charles Lam. *The Noblest Cry: A History of the American Civil Liberties Union.* NY: St. Martin's, 1965.
Largely emotional account of history of ACLU.

BIOGRAPHY

Everett, Charles Warren. *The Education of Jeremy Bentham.* NY: Columbia University Press, 1931.

Gazell, James A. "O.W. Wilson's Essential Legacy for Police Administrators." *Journal of Police Science and Administration.* 2:4 (December, 1974), pp. 365-375.

"Hans Von Hentig, Eighty Years Old." *Journal of Criminal Law, Criminology and Police Science.* 58:4 (December, 1967).

Jennings, Dean. "Portrait of a Police Chief: Tough, Controversial Bill Parker of Los Angeles Has One of the Most Challenging Law Enforcement Problems in the U.S." *Saturday Evening Post.* 232 (May 7, 1960).

Lannarelli, Alfred. *From Cop to Priest.* Union City, CA: Precision Photo-Form, 1973.

Maestro, M. *Cesare Beccaria and the Origins of Penal Reform.* Philadelphia: Temple University Press, 1973.
Biography of Beccaria, Italian author of "On Crimes and Punishment" (1764) and major contributor to medieval criminal law reform.

Mitgang, Herbert. *The Man Who Rode the Tiger: The Life and Times of Judge Samuel Seabury.* Philadelphia: Lippincott, 1963.

"Orlando Winfield Wilson, Superintendent of Police, Chicago, Illinois." *APCO Bulletin.* 31 (September, 1965).

Parker, Alfred E. *Crime Fighter: August Vollmer.* NY: Macmillan, 1961.

"William H. Parker, in Memoriam." *L.A. Police Beat* (September, 1966, entire issue).

Wyden, Peter. "He Makes Cops Come Clean." *Saturday Evening Post.* 234 (August 12, 1961).

ADDENDUM

Some important studies not included in the main body of this work.
Author/titles are included in Index.

Bard, Morton and Joseph Zacker: *The Police and Interpersonal Conflict: Third-Party Intervention Approaches.* Washington: Police Foundation, 1976.

Bell, James and John Trutko: *Monitoring Criminal Investigations: The Rochester System.* Washington: Police Foundation, n.d.

Bloch, Peter B. and James Bell: *Managing Investigations: The Rochester System.* Washington: Police Foundation, 1976.

Boydstun, John E.: *San Diego Field Interrogation: Final Report.* Washington: Police Foundation, 1976.

Boydstun, John E. and Michael E. Sherry: *San Diego Community Profile: Final Report.* Washington: Police Foundation, 1975.

Boydstun, John E., Michael E. Sherry and Nicholas P. Moelter: *Patrol Staffing in San Diego: One or Two Officer Units.* Washington: Police Foundation, 1977.

Brill, Steven. Joan L. Wolfle, Program Officer: *Firearm Abuse: A Research and Policy Report.* Washington: Police Foundation, 1977.

Cascio, Wayne F.: *Police Personnel Management Information Systems: The Dallas and Dade County Experiences.* Washington: Police Foundation, 1977.

Eliff, John T.: *The Reform of FBI Intelligence Operations.* Princeton, New Jersey: Princeton University Press, 1979.

Fogelson, Robert M.: *Big-City Police.* Cambridge, Massachusetts: Harvard University Press, 1977.

Heaphy, John F., ed. *Police Practices: The General Administrative Survey.* Washington: Police Foundation, 1978.

Landy, Frank J.: *Performance Appraisal in Police Departments.* Washington: Police Foundation, 1977.

Marshall, Clifford: *Time Series Analysis of Reported Crime: A Methodological Study.* Washington: Police Foundation, 1978.

Milton, Catherine H., Jeanne Wahl Halleck, James Lardner and Gary L. Abrecht: *Police Use of Deadly Force.* Washington: Police Foundation, 1977.

Murphy, Patrick V., and Thomas Plate: *Commissioner: A View from the Top of American Policing.* New York: Simon and Schuster, 1977.

Pate, Tony, Robert A. Bowers and Ron Parks: *Three Approaches to Criminal Apprehension in Kansas City: An Evaluation Report.* Washington: Police Foundation, 1976.

Pate, Tony, Jack W. McCullough, Robert A. Bowers and Amy Ferrara: *Kansas City Peer Review Panel: An Evaluation Report.* Washington: Police Foundation, 1976.

Reinke, Roger: *Selection through Assessment Centers: A Tool for Police Departments.* Washington: Police Foundation, 1977.

Schwartz, Alfred I. and Sumner N. Clarren: *The Cincinnati Team Policing Experiment. Summary Report.* Washington: Police Foundation, 1977. *Technical Report.* Washington: Police Foundation, 1978.

Sherman, Lawrence W. and the National Advisory Commission on Higher Education for Police Officers: *The Quality of Police Education.* San Francisco: Jossey-Bass Inc., Publishers, 1978.

Stahl, O. Glenn and Richard A. Staufenberger, eds.: *Police Personnel Administration.* Washington: Police Foundation, 1976.

Tuchfarber, Alfred J. and William R. Klecka: *Random Digit Dialing: Lowering the Cost of Victimization Surveys.* Washington: Police Foundation, 1976.

White, Thomas H. and Peter B. Bloch: *Police Officer Height and Selected Aspects of Performance.* Published with the International Association of Chiefs of Police. Washington: Police Foundation, 1975.

Wilt, G. Marie, James Bannon, Ronald Breedlove, John W. Kennish, Donald M. Sandker and Robert K. Sawtell, Foreword by James Q. Wilson: *Domestic Violence and the Police Studies in Detroit and Kansas City.* Washington: Police Foundation, 1977.

Wolfe, Joan L. and John F. Heaphy, eds.: *Readings on Productivity in Policing.* Washington: Police Foundation, 1975.

Wycoff, Mary Ann and George L. Kelling: *The Dallas Experience.* Volume I: *Organizational Reform.* Volume II: *Human Resources Development.* Washington: Police Foundation, 1978.

INDEX